HISTORICA'S
WOMEN

1000 YEARS OF WOMEN IN HISTORY

Chief Consultant Dr Katherine Aaslestad

MILLENNIUM HOUSE

FOR MARGARET OLDS (1950–2007), A WOMAN
OF GREAT STRENGTH AND CHARACTER WHO
CONTRIBUTED GREATLY TO THE AUSTRALIAN
PUBLISHING INDUSTRY

Published in 2007 by Millennium House Pty Ltd
52 Bolwarra Rd, Elanora Heights, NSW, 2101, Australia
Ph: 612 9970 6850
Fax: 612 9913 3500
Email: rightsmanager@millenniumhouse.com.au
Website: www.millenniumhouse.com.au

ISBN: 978-1-921209-08-6

Authors
Millennium House would be happy to receive submissions
from authors. Please send brief submissions to
editor@millenniumhouse.com.au

Photographers and Illustrators
Millennium House would be happy to consider submissions from
photographers or illustrators. Please send submissions to
editor@millenniumhouse.com.au

Printed in China

Photo credits appear on page 575

Cover pictures

Front (l to r): Marie Curie; Mother Teresa; Germaine Greer; Queen
Victoria; Condoleezza Rice; Venus Williams; Princess Diana

Back (l to r): Coco Chanel; Yoko Ono; Pocahontas; Marilyn Monroe;
Margaret Thatcher; Marie Antoinette; Barbra Streisand

Preliminary page pictures

Page 1: Mother Teresa at her mission in Calcutta, India

Pages 2–3: Svetlana Savitskaya, Russian cosmonaut; Margaret Mead,
American anthropologist; Joan of Arc, French heroine; Amelia
Earhart, American aviator; Elizabeth I, English queen; Babe
Didrikson, American athlete

Page 5: A woman carries waste plastic containers through a street
in Calcutta, India

Page 10: *Allegorical portrait of Catherine the Great, Empress
of Russia*, by Johann Baptist Edler von Lampi, 1792–1793

Pages 12–13: Emmeline Pankhurst (front left) leads a suffragette
parade through London, 1911

Section opening pictures

Pages 20–21: *Cleopatra on the Terraces of Philae,* by Frederick Arthur
Bridgman, 1896

Pages 30–31: Princess Diana with landmine victims at Neves
Bendinha Orthopaedic Workshop in Luanda, Angola

Publisher	Margaret Olds
Managing editor	Janet Parker
Project manager	Kate Etherington
Chief consultant	Katherine Aaslestad
Consultant	Dale Spender
Contributors	Bronwyn Allen, Andrew Baker, Ingrid Banwell, Loretta Barnard, Louise Buchanan, Ivan Coates, Julia Collingwood, Thomas J. Craughwell, Bridget Dougherty, Neal Drinnan, Emma Driver, Carol Fallows, Terence FitzSimons, James Inglis, Kate McAllan, Alice Mills, Carla Molino, Amanda Peacock, Sarah Pickette, Lesley Pople, Charles A. Riley, Simon Roberts, Diane Robinson, Pamela Robson, Lisa Rumiel, Dale Spender, Barry Stone, Mike Thompson, Nikki Thompson, Marion Tyree
Editors	Maggie Aldhamland, Loretta Barnard, Monica Berton, Belinda Castles, Helen Cooney, Chris Edwards, Denise Imwold, James Inglis, Heather Jackson, Carol Jacobson, John Mapps, Susan Page, Jessica Perini, Anne Savage, Marie-Louise Taylor
Researchers	Loretta Barnard, Louise Buchanan, Neal Drinnan, Heather Jackson, Sarah Minns, Cathy O'Shannassy, Merry Pearson, Jan Watson
Picture research	Louise Buchanan, Steven Cork, Catherine Etteridge, Philippa Hutson, Denise Imwold, Rebecca Jarvis, Damien Kelly, Oliver Laing, Melody Lord, Heather McNamara, Teri Martin, Sarah Minns, Raffaella Morini, James Mulraine, Kay Parker, Wasila Richards, Lara Smith, Julie Stanton, Louise Ward, Liam Wilcox, Glen Wilson
Original design concept	Stan Lamond
Cover design	Bob Mitchell
Index	Tricia Waters
Typesetting	Dee Rogers
Production	Bernard Roberts
Production assistants	Wasila Richards, Liam Wilcox
Foreign rights	Kanagasabai Suppiah

Consultants

CHIEF CONSULTANT

Katherine Barbara Aaslestad is Associate Professor of History and a Woodburn Professor at West Virginia University, USA. She specializes in modern Germany, political culture, and military and gender history. She received her undergraduate education at Mary Washington College in Fredericksburg, Virginia, and her MA and PhD from the University of Illinois at Champaign-Urbana. She is the author of *Place and Politics: Local Identity, Civic Culture, and German Nationalism in North Germany during the Revolutionary Era* (Leiden: Brill Press, 2005). She has co-edited special issues on war and gender in *Central European History* and *European History Quarterly*. She has published articles on republican political culture in the Hanseatic cities, gender and consumption, and the Napoleonic Wars in northern Europe as book chapters in *Patriotism, Cosmopolitanism, and National Culture: Public Culture in Hamburg, 1700-1933* (Rodopi, 2003), *Gender in Transition* (Michigan, 2006), and *Napoleon and the Empire* (Palgrave, 2008). Dr Aaslestad has also won prestigious teaching awards from West Virginia University. She is currently working on two projects—transitions from war to stability following the Napoleonic Wars, and the relationship between urban education and citizenship formation in Hamburg, Berlin, and Munich from 1815 to 1933. She lives in West Virginia with her husband and three children.

CONSULTANT

Dale Spender has been an author, a feminist, and an educator for most of her life. She started her career as a high school teacher, went on to become a university lecturer at James Cook University in Queensland, Australia, and received her PhD from the University of London. She has lectured at many universities around the world, including MIT and Cambridge. She has written and edited more than thirty books that were concerned with the way knowledge was made, and how and why some people and events got left out of the record. Many of these books became university texts. She is also interested in the impact that the internet has had on society, politics, and knowledge making, and developed a "pick'n'play" data base (PoP IP) that covers hundreds of topics from free trade to piracy, and from women inventors to plagiarism. Dale is an educational consultant on digital literacy and internet culture, and provides professional skills that focus on the art of teaching with the new technologies. She writes on these topics for newspapers and other popular publications. She is also a founding member of the Second Chance Programme in Australia which raises money for homeless women.

Left: *The Chess Game*, by Sofonisba Anguissola, 1555

Contributors

Bronwyn Allen is a professional writer based in Sydney, Australia. She began her career as a journalist with News Limited and went on to write primarily for Australia's biggest selling newspaper, the *Sunday Telegraph*. She then worked in corporate communications for a national real estate franchise network before moving into a media relations and publicity role with one of Sydney's most prominent real estate businesses. Bronwyn is also a freelance copywriter and editor.

Andrew Baker is a senior teacher of PD/H/PE at Ku-ring-gai Creative Arts High School. He graduated from Wollongong University with a Bachelor Degree in Applied Science (Human Movement) and was awarded a Diploma in Education from the University of NSW. He has recently completed a Graduate Certificate in Writing through the University of Technology Sydney. Andrew lives on Sydney's northern beaches with his partner Ann and enjoys a capella singing and surfing. He is planning a European trip in 2008 to research his first novel.

Ingrid Banwell is a New Zealand-born writer and artist living in Sydney, Australia. She has traveled widely and is a graduate of the United Nations International School in New York. She has a master's degree with first class honors in painting and her work is held in public and private collections around the world. Ingrid has lived in New York, Mexico City, London, and Vienna and has worked in corporate communications, public relations, and market research for non profit, government, and commercial organizations. She has written press releases, annual reports, newsletters, business plans, and company profiles, as well as writing short stories. She has written and illustrated three children's picture books, and is currently working on her first novel.

Loretta Barnard is a freelance writer and editor who has worked in the publishing industry for over 25 years. She holds a Master of Arts in English Literature from the University of New South Wales, Australia, and gives occasional seminars on the writing process. She has been involved in a wide range of publications in a huge variety of fields, including biography, archeology, architecture, law, science, business, botany, and film, and she was one of the contributors to *Historica* (for Millennium House). Loretta is currently editing and annotating the writings of legendary Australian jazz drummer, Len Barnard. Her interests include music, theater, and literature.

Louise Buchanan has worked in book publishing and multimedia design and production for a number of years. She has worked on publications in various fields including arts and entertainment, anatomy, geology, astronomy, and gardening. She has a first class honors degree in Fine Arts from the University of New South Wales, Australia, and lives in Sydney, Australia.

Ivan Coates is currently working at the University of Sydney in Australia as an instructor in American historical and cultural studies, with a particular focus on American film and African-American history. He is working on research projects relating to African-Americans in New York City in the nineteenth and early twentieth centuries, and to Cold War films. He has also worked on various travel publications. Ivan would like to thank his wife for assisting him with advice, moral support, logistical support, intellectual stimulation, and encouragement in days that seem to become ever-busier, while maintaining her own full-time career.

Julia Collingwood has a BA in History and has worked in the Australian publishing industry as an editor and commissioning editor for thirty years. She co-authored two books, *Free and Low Cost Sydney* (Choice Books, 1999) and *The Sydney Opera House* (New Holland, 2000), and is currently writing an adventure story for 10- to 12-year-old children.

Thomas J. Craughwell is the author of more than a dozen books, most recently *Stealing Lincoln's Body* (Harvard University Press, 2007), and *Saints Behaving Badly* (Doubleday, 2006). He has written articles on history, religion, politics, and popular culture for the *Wall Street Journal,* the *American Spectator, U.S. News & World Report, Emmy* magazine, *Inside the Vatican,* and the national Catholic news weekly *Our Sunday Visitor.* He has served as a contributing writer to several Time-Life Books series; and he wrote History Book Club's first television commercial. Tom has appeared as a guest on CNN, the BBC, Discovery Channel, and over 100 radio programs. He lives in Connecticut, USA.

Bridget Dougherty is a writer and poet living on the south coast of New South Wales, Australia. She has written for numerous publications in Australia, the USA, the UK, and Indonesia, including the *Australian Financial Review,* and *Lloyd's List.* She has also worked as an editor and contributor on a number of books. Bridget is currently working on her first novel and is studying for her doctorate at the University of Wollongong. Her thesis explores what love means in contemporary Australian culture. She writes poetry in her spare time.

Neal Drinnan has worked in publishing and journalism for more than twenty years. He is an award-winning novelist, experienced travel writer, and has written on a wide range of historical and contemporary issues surrounding politics and gender. He was a contributing writer to *Historica* (2006), and is currently working on his sixth novel.

Emma Driver is a freelance book editor, writer, and musician and lives in Sydney, Australia. She has edited a range of Australian non-fiction and educational titles, and written sections of books including *The Other Half: Extraordinary Women and Life, Love and Famous Partners* (New Holland, 2006). Emma is the alter-ego of anti-fancypants food crusader Mandy Flombay, author of the cookbook *The Unknown Chef: As Not Seen on TV* (New Holland, 2006). Emma is also a singer, songwriter, and musician and performs regularly on the Sydney music scene.

Carol Fallows is a Sydney-based freelance author and editor. She established Australia's first parenting magazine in the 1980s which eventually lead to writing two best-selling parenting books, *Having a Baby* (Doubleday, 2005), and *The Australian Baby & Child Care Handbook* (Penguin, 1998). In addition Carol has written a number of other parenting publications for leading publishers. Carol has also edited magazines on health, nutrition, and gardening. Carol's historical books include *Love & War—Stories of War Brides from the Great War to Vietnam* (Bantam, 2002), which was the culmination of two years' research, and *War in the Black and White Memories* series. Carol writes extensively for both print and websites.

Terence FitzSimons has a background in teaching and writing, and holds a doctorate in the field of social history. His area of special interest is the Victorian era and in particular the gold rush period in Victoria, Australia. He has written journal articles on various aspects of life on the diggings. An avid collector of British and Irish folk songs and music, he is also an enthusiastic performer on the hurdy-gurdy.

James Inglis is an Australian writer and editor based in Melbourne. He specializes in reviews, interviews, and opinion pieces, and has been published in various Australian national and state newspapers and periodicals. His interests include adult learning, workplace training, design and presentation, and analysis of language, particularly where it is abused to conceal ulterior motives.

Kate McAllan has a BA Honors degree from Sydney University. She majored in Archeology and also studied Anthropology and Medieval History. She then worked as a research assistant at the Australian National University in the Department of Prehistory and Anthropology. After having a family, she sold books and worked as an editor in children's publishing. Now she is a freelance editor, researcher, and writer.

Alice Mills is Associate Professor of Literature and Children's Literature at the University of Ballarat, in Victoria, Australia. She was chief consultant for *Mythology* (Hachette Livre Australia, 2005), and her areas of research interest include fantasy, children's literature, and Jungian and psychoanalytic theory. Among her passions are opera, traveling, and Jung.

Carla Molino has a BA and a Diploma of Education from the University of Sydney, Australia, and a Graduate Diploma in Communication Management from the University of Technology, Sydney, as well as a Diploma in Editing from Macleay College. She is the author of several educational readers, and her first popular fiction novel, *Man Hunt*, written under the pseudonym Cathleen Ross, hit number one on the Virgin Publishing bestsellers' list. Her latest novel is being considered by several major publishers.

Amanda Peacock is a museum educator at the Art Gallery of New South Wales in Sydney, Australia. Her published works include *Murrimal: An Education Kit for the Aboriginal Collection* (Wollongong City Gallery, Australia), *Colonial Works* Education Kit (Wollongong City Gallery), and education material for the *Artbank: 25 Years* Education Kit (Australian Government publication), *Self Portrait: Renaissance to Contemporary* (Art Gallery of New South Wales), and *Giacometti: Sculptures, Prints and Drawings from the Maeght Foundation* (Art Gallery of New South Wales).

Sarah Pickette is a journalist and editor based in Sydney, Australia. She currently works for the in-flight Qantas magazine, *The Australian Way*, and has been on staff at the Australian *House & Garden*, the "Sunday Life" color supplement of Sydney's *Sun-Herald*, and Ansett and Air New Zealand's in-flight magazines, to name just a few.

Lesley Pople grew up in Sydney, Australia, and worked in the computer industry for many years. Seeking a change of direction, she enrolled as a mature-aged student at Macquarie University, where she won three university prizes, including the awards for first and second year English, before graduating with a first class honors degree in English Literature in 1995. Since then, Lesley has largely worked as a research writer in the publishing industry. In her spare time, she combines her interests in creative writing, visual communication, and current affairs to co-create topical artists' books for exhibitions at galleries and institutions around Australia.

Charles A. Riley II, PhD, is a cultural historian, arts journalist and author of twenty books, including *The Jazz Age in France* (Harry H. Abrams, 2004) and *Aristocracy and the Modern Imagination* (University Press of New England, 2002). He is a professor at the City University of New York and director of the International Center for Corporate Accountability.

Simon Roberts lives in Hobart, Tasmania, Australia. He worked as an air traffic controller in Melbourne and

Brisbane before resigning to study law. He currently works with the counter-terrorism unit of Tasmania Police and occasionally contributes to books on subjects such as mythology and history. Simon has traveled widely throughout Asia, Europe, and the Middle East; he has an interest in tracing the impact of historical events in shaping geopolitics in the early twenty-first century.

Diane Robinson has written on a plethora of subjects for various newspapers and magazines, and for internationally published books including *Natural Disasters* in 2006 and *Geologica* in 2007 (both for Millennium House). Writing for *Historica's Women* has allowed her to enter the fascinating world of swashbuckling pirates, cross-dressing actresses, remarkably brave feminists, and shy novelists. Diane lives in Sydney, Australia.

Pamela Robson is a writer of non-fiction books and feature stories based in Brisbane, Australia. A former journalist in the UK and Australia—she was with *The Australian* for 10 years—she has worked on a broad range of subjects but has a special interest in history, health, and pet care. Previous publications include the Optimum™ *Pet Care Guide* (2007), *The Food and Wine Atlas of Australia* (Fairfax Books, 2007), and *The Bush* (Random House, 2007). She is presently working on a quirky book about Australian place names.

Lisa Rumiel, a doctoral candidate in history at York University in Toronto, Canada, is in the final stages of writing her thesis on the role of doctors and scientists in the anti-nuclear movement in the United States. Her research interests include science, medicine, gender, expertise, and activism. She has taught American history, and the history of health and medicine in North America.

Barry Stone, a graduate of the Australian College of Journalism, is a freelance travel writer, and a regular

contributor to some of Australia's major newspapers, including Sydney's *Sun-Herald*, Brisbane's *Sunday Mail*, and the *Canberra Times*. Over the years, his travel pieces have often focused on those pioneering individuals who have been vital in opening previously inaccessible areas to tourism, as well as highlighting the history and growth of a region's built environment. This emphasis on history illustrates his belief that an understanding of the past, and the insights gained from it into the lives of those who have gone before us, enable the traveler to appreciate fully a destination, and therefore to have an enriched travel experience.

Mike Thompson holds a first class honors degree in History and is an academic tutor for the Department of History at the University of Sydney in Australia where he is also working on a PhD in American History. He has lectured, written, and researched in the fields of politics and history. His work on religion and foreign policy has been published by the American academic journal, *American Quarterly*. His interests lie at the intersection of religious, intellectual, and cultural history, aided in part by his earlier education in Classical Greek. His specialization is in thinkers responding to war, peace, and world crisis in the twentieth century. When he is not thinking about thinkers, New Zealand-born Mike enjoys watching his national team battle it out on the rugby field.

Nikki Thompson has an extensive background in English literature, holding a master's degree in Creative Writing. She was awarded the Fred Rush Convocation Prize 2006 for creative writing as a contribution to Australian literature. Nikki also holds an honors degree in English Literature and has taught at both the Australian Catholic University in Canberra and the University of Sydney. Some years ago, Nikki moved away from studying literature to writing it. Her children's fiction has been shortlisted in writing competitions, including that of the Children's Book Council of Australia (New South Wales). Nikki also enjoys working hands on with children and books in a primary school library in Sydney.

Marion Tyree completed a BA in medieval English literature at Macquarie University, Sydney, Australia, in 1991, followed by a Diploma in Book Editing and Publishing at Macleay College. Pursuing her love of gardening, Marion studied horticulture and has a Diploma of Landscape Design. She has contributed to a variety of publications. These include gardening magazines, several garden books including *Flora* and *Trees and Shrubs,* as well as *Horse Dreams: The Meaning of Horses in Women's Lives* (Spinifex Press, 2004). Marion edits and writes for *Landscape Outlook*, a landscape design journal. She has attended a number of fiction writing workshops and would like to spend more time on writing short stories or that "novel"! In her spare time she enjoys gardening, long walks, reading, bridge, and travel.

Page 8 (opposite): Nicostrata, fabled inventor of written language, from a manuscript by Antoine du Four, c. 1505.
Page 9 (above): Persian woman writing, from a late sixteenth-century fresco in the Palace of Chihil Sutun, Isfahan, Iran.

Foreword

History helps to define our world. When we realise what human beings have done in the past we have choices about what we can do in the present. This is why so many countries hold their history to be so important. It doesn't just remind them of the achievements of the past, but inspires them to do challenging things in the future.

History is equally important for women. Unfortunately, however, women have made few appearances in their own right in the history books—which are pretty much a record of men's achievements. This is not because women have not made history—as *Historica's Women* makes abundantly clear, it is because for most of history, women have not been the record keepers.

Women have lived in the shadow of men: they have often been denied education, occupation, and a political role. The great educational philosopher Jean-Jacques Rousseau decreed that men should be educated for the world, and women should be educated to please men. Such attitudes made it difficult for women to participate in public life, or to write and promote accounts of their triumphs and failures.

Despite all the restrictions, countless women have nonetheless "weaved their way round" the obstacles, and their record stands here as an important testimony. If it has seemed that no woman has ever done certain things before, then many may doubt that is possible for women to do such things today. But if it is the case that women have done amazing things—and against the odds—but that their achievements have been left out of the record, then women, as well as men, have a better understanding of women's full potential. And women of the past can, today, become inspirational.

This is why *Historica's Women* makes such a significant contribution. It not only helps to right the record by placing so many women in history but, by presenting such a remarkable array of women and their range of experience, it illuminates the human condition. Once women in history can stand alongside men, the picture looks very different.

Dale Spender

Contents

Women in History

Opposite page, top

Far from being overshadowed by her husband Ferdinand's sovereignty, Queen Isabella ruled Spain in partnership with him. She also pleaded for the just treatment of Native Americans in Spain's recently acquired colonies.

Above

Ex-slave, abolitionist, and activist Sojourner Truth challenged discrimination against her people and her sex. In 1864 she met with Abraham Lincoln to campaign against race-based segregation on city streetcars.

Right

The *Declaration of the Rights of Man*, put forward in 1789 by the National Assembly, failed to recognize, as Olympe de Gouges pointed out, half the population of France.

"Men, are you capable of being just? It is a woman who poses the question; you will not deprive her of that right at least? Tell me, what gives you sovereign empire to oppress my sex?" This was Olympe de Gouges's provocative response to the 1789 French *Declaration of the Rights of Man* that proclaimed equality before the law for all Frenchmen. She pointed out that this document omitted half the population of France. Unfortunately, de Gouges's remarkable 1791 *Declaration of the Rights of Women* gained women neither revolutionary citizenship nor political rights, and sadly it contributed to her death by guillotine in November 1793. The spirit of her criticism, which targeted hypocritical revolutionary leaders who drew on universal language and ideals while they ignored half the population, lives on in the pages of *Historica's Women*. This volume brilliantly reports on the lives of thousands of women—from queens to seamstresses—who have been largely overlooked in the historical record.

Like those eager eighteenth-century revolutionaries who accorded citizenship to men alone, historians for centuries wrote history with little regard for the female half of humanity. Those few women who found their way into the mainstream historical record were either from the ruling elite or directly associated with dramatic political change. Although women wrote their own historical accounts for hundreds of years, only in the 1960s and 1970s did women's history emerge as an area of formal study. Originally part of a feminist project

to make women visible in male-centered historical narratives, these histories led to a fundamental re-evaluation of the history itself. In fact, historians now address women's experiences in a much more complex fashion than they did forty years ago, and investigate the lives of peasants, working mothers, thieves, servants, nuns, widows, prostitutes, athletes, entertainers, and reformers, as well as the political, economic, and intellectual elites. As *Historica's Women* makes abundantly clear, in the case of women's history, there is much more to learn!

Secondary school and university curricula still treat women's history as peripheral to formal education. Textbooks often add a section or a few paragraphs about women at the end of chapters, and address women as one of many "minority" groups whose lives existed outside the main historical narrative and whose contributions to politics, the economy, and spiritual and intellectual life were negligible. Other texts present women primarily as "victims" and highlight the laws and customs that limited and denigrated them. Even in our time, the history of famous men in many ways remains universalized as the "normal" history of human society. In contrast, *Historica's Women* displays the rich range of experiences of women past in an artistic, informative, and entertaining presentation.

By focusing on women over the course of a thousand years, *Historica's Women* presents history in an exciting new format. Organized within a clear chronological framework that highlights key historical developments, this book integrates women directly into the historical narrative. Readers recognize at a glance the relationship between women's experiences and major events of the period. Lively text combined with powerful images strike the reader's imagination and arouse curiosity to read on. *Historica's Women* breaks down the restrictive traditional frameworks of national or regional histories: British, Asian, Russian, Latin American, Medieval, early modern, colonial, and so on. Rather, the book reaches widely—highlighting the interconnections between women across national borders, across continents, and across time. For example, Olympe de Gouges's call for women's equality in 1791 has echoes in former slave and abolitionist Sojourner Truth's "Ain't I a Woman?" speech in Akron, Ohio, in 1854; in Pandita Ramabai's public criticism of Indian patriarchy and traditional practices harmful to women in the 1880s; in activist Vida Goldstein's candidacy for parliament in early twentieth-century Australia; and in Japan's first literary journal for women, Hiratsuka Raicho's *Seito* in 1911.

Within these pages you will also find women who achieved prominence in their lifetime—Joan of Arc, Eleanor of Aquitaine, Isabella of Castile, Pocahontas, Florence

nuclear program in the 1970s, and long-serving British prime minister Margaret Thatcher radically recast the UK economy with deregulation and privatization during the 1980s. Since ancient Egypt women have occasionally served as prominent political leaders, but women's equal participation in the political process as voters and candidates is very new and remains a significant achievement of the nineteenth and twentieth century's equal rights movement. Until women gained a political voice with the vote (New Zealand introduced the world's first universal and equal suffrage in 1893 and Finland elected the first women—all 19 of them—to parliament in 1907) half the world's population were second-class citizens.

Historica's Women highlights women in a variety of leadership roles in humanitarian endeavors, where they played a central role in religion and reform movements. For example, Clare of Assisi founded and led the Order of Poor Ladies (or Poor Clares) in 1212 at the convent of San Damiano in Italy and claimed the privilege of poverty, prayer,

Nightingale, Josephine Baker, and Eleanor Roosevelt. Quick overviews of their lives and times explain why these women gained recognition. Queens like Margaret of Denmark, Elizabeth I of England, and African Nzinga of Ndonga and Matamba used a combination of warfare and diplomacy to expand political influence, as well as secure their states against invaders. The emergence of the Kalmar Union with Norway and Sweden in 1397 negotiated by Margaret, the defeat of the Spanish Armada in 1588 under Elizabeth's reign, and the successful resistance to Portuguese intrusion into her lands by Nzinga until her death in 1663 indicate the authority and autonomy that women possessed as rulers and leaders. Even such queens as Liliuokalani of Hawaii, who failed to secure her kingdom's autonomy from outside influences, left a lasting legacy as an articulate critic of American imperialism and was a much-loved leader who improved the living conditions of her people. Other queens left significant cultural legacies. Goharsad of the fifteenth-century Timurid Dynasty spread Persian language and culture across an empire extending from the Tigris to China, attracting artists, architects, and philosophers to her court in Herat.

In more recent times, political institutions redefined the scope of women's political influence. For example, Frances Perkins, Indira Gandhi, and Margaret Thatcher are twentieth-century leaders appointed and elected to offices where they left lasting if controversial legacies. Perkins, the 40th US Secretary of Labor and the first female cabinet member, played a key role in New Deal legislation. Indira Gandhi, the first female prime minister of India, accelerated her country's

Right
The Silent Spring, biologist
Rachel Carson's exposé on
the ecological effects of
the insecticide DDT, was
pivotal in the birth of the
environmental movement.

and works of mercy as had St Francis. Ann Lee, illiterate daughter of a blacksmith, left England for North America in 1774 and became the charismatic leader or "Mother in Christ" of the United Society of Believers in Christ's Second Appearing, best known for their utopian Shaker communities. Irish-born Amy Carmichael, one of the first Western missionaries to adopt Indian dress, departed for Asia as a missionary in 1883 and founded the Dohnavur Fellowship, a sanctuary for prostitutes and children. Other women addressed social problems through civic philanthropy. Amalie Sieveking and Charlotte Paulson established women's associations to assist victims of cholera and poverty in early nineteenth-century Hamburg. In the late nineteenth century, the writings of Helen Hunt Jackson, Ida Wells-Barnett, and Peruvian novelist Clorinda Matto de Turner dramatized the exploitation of indigenous Americans and the lynching of African-Americans. In 1912 Juliette Low founded the American Girl Guides, later known as Girl Scouts, to provide girls of all backgrounds with the opportunity to explore nature and learn self-reliance and resourcefulness.

Readers will notice that the women in *Historica's Women* were not merely passive observers; rather they were active participants in the central events of their times. For a variety of motives, countless women participated in warfare and combat. In 1541 Spanish-born Dona Inés De Suárez galvanized and led Spanish soldiers in the defence of Santiago against indigenous Indians. A continent away, Amina of Zaria, royal princess and accomplished warrior, led military campaigns over 34 years to extend the borders of Zaria (part of contemporary Nigeria) and secure its significance as the crossroad of the Saharan trade routes. Irish-born Kit Cavanaugh, disguised as a man, fought under the Duke of Marlborough against the French. When she died thirty-three years later in 1739, she was buried with full military honors in St Margaret's churchyard in Westminster. Across the Atlantic, Queen Alliquippa, leader of the Mingo Seneca tribe, allied with the British in the French and Indian Wars, contributing to the British military success. In 1813 Anna Lühring and Eleonore Prochaska donned male attire, joined the Prussian Lützow Free Corps, and fought against Napoleon's *Grande Armée*, as did artillery officer Agustina Zaragoza

in Spain. During the World War II, Soviet partisan Zoya Kosmodemyan-skaya, captured and executed by the German army in 1941, became the first female Hero of the Soviet Union in 1942. That same year the United States established the Women's Army Auxiliary Corps. These examples and countless others demonstrate that women fought and died like their male counterparts, though they are often forgotten today.

Historica's Women also highlights women who profoundly influenced their societies with powerful insights. Following an extended stay in the Ottoman Empire in 1717, Lady Mary Wortley Montagu introduced the Oriental practice of smallpox inoculation or "ingrafting," as she called it, to English physicians and high society at a time when the pox killed one in four. Over two hundred and fifty years later, naturalist and scientist Rachel Carson warned the public about the dangerous impact of extensive synthetic chemical pesticide use on the natural world in her book *Silent Spring,*

Above
Juliette Low, founder of
the Girl Scout movement
in the USA, helped to
develop resourcefulness,
confidence, and citizenship
in girls from a range of
different backgrounds.

Right
More than 150,000 women
served in the Women's
Army Corps (WAC) during
World War II, contributing
critical resources and
support to the war effort.

teachers in Europe, North America, and India in the Montessori curriculum and methods. From science to pedagogy, women introduced new ways of looking at the world and society that endure to this day.

Left
Dr Maria Montessori's child-centered educational theory recognized the rights of the child, and postulated that children's thought patterns differed from those of adults.

The subject of education for women has been passionately debated since the Middle Ages. Too much knowledge could "unsex" a woman, cause her to forget her traditional roles of wife and mother, and ultimately disrupt social

Below
American novelist Louisa May Alcott's novel *Little Women* was based on her childhood experiences with her three sisters.

and in 1963 testified before the US Congress, calling for new policies to protect human health and the environment. Drawing on her observations as Italy's first female doctor, Maria Montessori viewed many of the problems of special-needs children as educational rather than medical. In response, she developed a child-centered educational theory, the "Montessori Method," and in 1907 established preschools for workers' children in Rome. She trained thousands of

balance. Cultural notions of male supremacy and female inferiority, both intellectual and physical, also severely limited women's roles in society. Yet many examples reveal that lack of education combined with low social expectations—rather than lack of ability—limited women's intellectual development. For example, child prodigy Elena Cornaro Piscopia, proficient in language, mathematics, and music, studied theology and received a doctorate of philosophy in 1678 from the University of Padua, where she taught mathematics until her death. Despite her achievements, the University of Padua did not graduate another female doctorate of philosophy until the late twentieth century. Not surprisingly, many women were self-educated, as were Mary Wollstonecraft, Elizabeth Barret Browning, Louisa May Alcott, and Charlotte Perkins Gilman. They, like others, dedicated themselves to girls' education. Seamstress Sarah Schnirer opened the first library and school for Jewish girls in 1918 in Krakow, Poland. In the United States, Moravian, Wheaton, and Mt Holyoke Colleges were among the first to admit women; Oberlin College was the first co-educational institution in 1837. Although Cambridge University in England admitted women in the 1860s, they lacked equality with male students until 1947. The United States government passed *Title IX* in 1972 to help end gender-based discrimination in federally funded educational programs. Literacy and education empowered women—Iranian 2003 Nobel Peace Prize winner Shirin Ebadi said that women's words are "the most powerful tool we have to protect ourselves."

Below
Iranian lawyer and children's rights campaigner Shirin Ebadi was the first Muslim woman to win the Nobel Peace Prize.

Women's creativity and resourcefulness also appears in a range of written and visual works. Mother of fourteen and religious pilgrim Margery Kempe dictated the first known female autobiography in 1436. Marie Guyant, the first French nun to found an Ursuline convent school in New France (Quebec) in 1642, learned the language of the indigenous Indians and wrote Algonquin and Iroquois dictionaries and hundreds of letters documenting everyday life in colonial Canada. Along with their proficiency in writing novels and letters, women in the 1700s also developed journals and

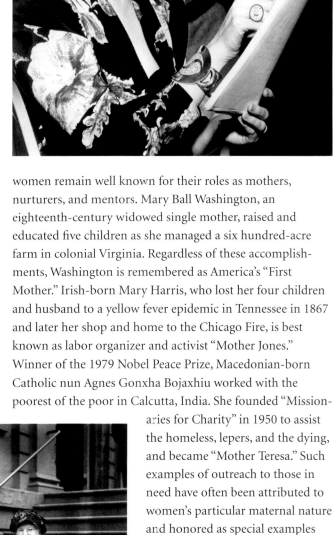

papers specifically for women, for example Eliza Haywood's *Female Spectator* (1744). Less highbrow than her nineteenth-century predecessors Jane Austen, the Bronte sisters, and Elizabeth Gaskill, Agatha Christie developed her own style of mystery writing and introduced a formidable female character, Miss Jane Marple, in 1930. During the Yuan Dynasty (1279–1368), Guan Daosheng emerged as a famous calligrapher, painter, and poet. She inscribed poems on her paintings which expressed devotion to her family. The famous French painter Berthe Morisot exhibited with her friends the Impressionists, but unlike her male counterparts, she focused on women, children, and domestic life, along with landscapes. German painter, sculptor, and printmaker Käthe Kollwitz recorded painful images of poverty, hunger, and war, and was the first woman admitted to the Prussian Academy of Art in 1919. In her war memorial *The Parents*, designed for a military cemetery in Flanders, she expressed a mother's painful loss of a son in World War I. After 1933 the National Socialist government classified her works as "degenerate" and forbade her from exhibiting.

Let's be honest, we cannot talk about women's lives without considering men too. Women and men have lived, loved, and fought together through the ages. There are numerous examples of famous couples whose personal and professional lives depended on each other: 1903 Physics Nobel Prize winners Marie (Maria) Sklodowska and Pierre Curie; American vaudeville, radio, and early television entertainers Gracie Allen and George Burns; Argentine first lady Eva Perón and her husband President Juan Domingo Perón, champions of the "*descamisados*." Of course, many relationships faltered: Catherine II and Peter III of Russia, Frida Kahlo and Diego Rivera, and Prince Charles and Lady Diana. Marriage and relationships altered over the course of time. Rarely based on bonds of love until modern times, marriage was more often an economic arrangement, political or diplomatic tool, or source of domestic labor and reproduction. Individual choice for marriage partners was often ignored in the face of family interests. Always in flux, shaped by gender-based hierarchies as well as fluid social definitions of feminine and masculine roles, marriage has transformed to reflect corresponding social standards and values. In fact, women's history has generated new ways of thinking about the nature of femininity and masculinity and the social and cultural environments that shape them.

Family status determined most women's lives. Of course, many

women remain well known for their roles as mothers, nurturers, and mentors. Mary Ball Washington, an eighteenth-century widowed single mother, raised and educated five children as she managed a six hundred-acre farm in colonial Virginia. Regardless of these accomplishments, Washington is remembered as America's "First Mother." Irish-born Mary Harris, who lost her four children and husband to a yellow fever epidemic in Tennessee in 1867 and later her shop and home to the Chicago Fire, is best known as labor organizer and activist "Mother Jones." Winner of the 1979 Nobel Peace Prize, Macedonian-born Catholic nun Agnes Gonxha Bojaxhiu worked with the poorest of the poor in Calcutta, India. She founded "Missionaries for Charity" in 1950 to assist the homeless, lepers, and the dying, and became "Mother Teresa." Such examples of outreach to those in need have often been attributed to women's particular maternal nature and honored as special examples of "women's work."

If some women clearly had a great capacity to nurture and care for their family and others, some did not. In South Africa's Pretoria Central prison, Daisey de Melker was executed in 1932 for poisoning two husbands with strychnine and her son with arsenic. Nurse Eleonore Baur joined the National Socialist Beerhall March in 1923 and later supervised SS medical experiments at Dachau concentration camp in 1944. Notorious sadist and serial

Above

Considered one of English literature's most influential novelists, Jane Austen's consummate language skills and insightful social commentary have continued to inspire modern culture.

Above right

The internationally successful American comedic couple Gracie Allen and George Burns remained performing partners and life partners until Gracie's death in 1964.

Right

Irish-born Mary Harris, known as "Mother Jones," was a prominent union organizer, educator, and community activist in the USA from the 1870s until she died in 1930.

killer Countess Erzsébet Báthory allegedly killed hundreds of young girls and bathed in their blood in order to retain youth and beauty. Her trial in 1611 revealed the torture and murder of between 40 and 650 girls and young women. Believing she saved thousands of lives, Charlotte Corday murdered Jean-Paul Marat as he bathed, and was sent to the guillotine four days later for her crime. Clearly, women can be praised for humanitarian deeds as well as condemned for heinous crimes.

Thinking about women in terms of their bodies or biology has shaped cultural ideas about reproduction, gender identity, and sexuality throughout history. The sexual and reproductive capacities of women were never considered purely private affairs. The status of women as mothers emerged as an increasingly public concern, especially in times of demographic transition. Sexual double standards and women's reproductive rights remain highly contested issues even now. If women suffer as pawns in patriarchal power plays, they also contribute differing visions of women's responsibilities regarding sexuality and reproduction. In 1930 Helena Lowenfeld Wright, a former medical missionary to China, founded the National Birth Control Council in England to provide married women with birth control to mitigate poverty. Bolshevik revolutionary Alexandra Kollontai assisted in writing new Soviet legislation that legalized divorce, birth control, and abortion and decriminalized prostitution and illegitimacy. As Commissar of Social Welfare, she supported education, free maternity and health care, childcare, collective kitchens, and job training for women, and in 1919 organized the Department for Women, the *Zhenotdel*, to facilitate women's full involvement in social, economic, and political life and meet the practical needs of children and pregnant women. But her radical vision was short-lived as the *Zhenotdel* folded in 1930. Four years later, the new National Socialist government in Germany appointed Gertrud Scholtz-Klink as National Women's Leader and leader of the *Deutsches Frauenwerk*, and she urged "valuable" German women to bear more children for the Fatherland. At the same time, Kato Shidzue popularized the birth control movement in Japan until her arrest in 1937. In the course of three decades, rival visions of women's autonomy and duty toward reproduction overlapped and competed with each other in private and public life.

Historica's Women implicitly raises the long-standing "women's questions," or *querelles des femmes*: what are the places and roles of women in society? Women and men have debated these questions in caves, homes, parliaments, churches, universities, medical offices, coffeeshops, and bars. This volume points out that the answers have been numerous—there is not just one place for women, but many. *Historica's Women* presents women in all their colorful complexity and dynamism. It affirms women's diversity and the importance of their contributions to the historical record.

Above
Alexandra Kollontai, a Bolshevik revolutionary and feminist, established the Department for Women, thus influencing the practical, social, and economic needs of Soviet women and children.

Left
Charlotte Corday, the assassin of French revolutionary Jean-Paul Marat, as depicted in the painting by Paul Jacques Aimé Baudry (1860).

From Prehistory
to the Year 999

"Lucy," early
human ancestor

Where Are All the Women?

Archeological evidence sheds much more light on men's lives than those of women. Why? The first fossil of an anatomically modern human—found in Africa—is 130,000 years old, and it is simply not possible to recreate the lives of ancient women in as much detail because so much of their material world was perishable. Unlike weapons and bone—the preserve of male hunters—textiles, food, and baskets, did not survive the ages. As a result, the historical record emphasizes the importance of the male hunter, and largely ignores the influential roles that women played in early cultures. The problem is compounded by the fact that the (invariably) men who wrote these early histories viewed women as subordinate, and therefore unimportant to the historical record. We need only look to the popular historical signposts for confirmation of this. The Stone Age, the Bronze Age, and the Iron Age all refer to man-made tools, and provide few clues about the many technological innovations devised by women—many of which were equally integral to the success of early societies. One may say that "String Revolution" is just as apt a description as "Stone Age" because of the simultaneous emergence of women's needle crafts, and the use of string to make important tools like baskets, fishing nets, animal snares, and baby transporters.

"[A WIFE'S] EYE IS THE EYE OF THE STORM."

PTAH-HOTEP,
C. 2450 BCE,
EGYPTIAN
PHILOSOPHER

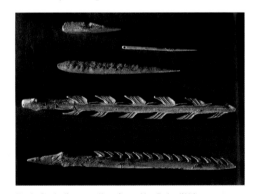

Tools, including needles, from the Paleolithic era.

An archeologist examines 3 million-year-old footprints.

Over the past forty years, the roles of women in prehistoric times have been seriously researched and reassessed. Many were spurred into action by the feminist movement of the 1960s and 1970s, perhaps in search of some evidence of a "golden age" when women ruled over men, or at least occupied positions of relative equality.

This research into the roles of women before the second millennium provides important clues for understanding the current roles of women in society, and how they have changed and continue to change. Women were not just caregivers in prehistoric times—even if this was perhaps their most consistent contribution to the development of civilization. Women have also made crucial and significant economic, technological, artistic, intellectual, political, religious, and spiritual contributions.

The Role of Women in Evolution

According to Charles Darwin's theory of natural selection, the pressures on men to hunt for food, find mates, and protect their community from outside aggression led to their greater physical strength. "Man the Hunter" was forced to stand upright on two feet so that he could find his prey among the high savannah grasses.

Man further ensured his success as a hunter by devising stone weapons for the kill and for hunting cooperatively with other men. Meanwhile, women tended to the needs of children and performed less physical chores as they waited for their mates to return with food for the community.

But the story is much more complex than this. There is evidence that big game hunting did not begin until 100,000 years ago, and before this hominids foraged for small animals and gathered edible plant foods. This was especially likely during the Lower Paleolithic Period (2,500,000–200,000 years ago) in eastern Africa, where the climate and environment ensured a constant supply of food. The tasks required for gathering and foraging were easily performed by both women

This female figure from Malta dates from 3400 BCE.

K e y   E v e n t s

Worldwide, 64 million years ago: Dinosaurs become extinct after approximately 146 million years.

Africa, 3.6 million years ago: Early hominids live in East Africa.

Rift Valley, Africa, 2.4 million years ago: Homo habilis ("handy man") evolves, and uses primitive tools.

Africa, 1.9 million years ago: Homo erectus ("upright man") evolves.

Africa, 1.8 million years ago: Homo erectus migrates north from Africa to the Middle East and beyond.

Europe and western Asia, 230,000–150,000 years ago: Homo neanderthalensis (Neanderthal man) arises.

East Africa, 135,000 BCE: Homo sapiens ("wise man") emerges.

Worldwide, 115,000 BCE: The last glaciations of the Ice Age begin.

Africa, 100,000 BCE: Homo sapiens migrates out of Africa.

Middle East, 90,000 BCE: Modern humans reach the Middle East.

Australia, 52,000–40,000 BCE: Aborigines reach Australia.

Europe, 40,000 BCE: Humans reach Europe.

Europe, 35,000 BCE: Feminine "Venus" figurines and fertility dolls play an key role in pagan rituals.

Europe, 28,000 BCE: Homo neanderthalensis becomes extinct.

Worldwide, 20,000–10,000 BCE: Women live shorter lives than men. Traditions develop around menstruation, puberty, and incest.

Worldwide, 12,000–9000 BCE: Ice thawing starts, melting polar ice caps and glaciers, which creates rising seas and increases flow to rivers like the Nile, Tigris, Euphrates, Ganges, and Yangtze.

Middle East, 10,000 BCE: In the Fertile Crescent, wild cereal grasses are harvested and wild sheep are farmed.

Worldwide, 8000 BCE: Melting of ice creates continents and fertile river valleys. Farming starts.

Middle East, 8000–6000 BCE: Wheat and barley farming begins in the Fertile Crescent.

Middle East, 7000 BCE: Goddess shrines are erected in Jericho. Rudimentary farming begins in southeastern Europe.

China, 6500 BCE: Rice farming begins in the Yangtze valley.

Turkey, 6000 BCE: Forty shrines to the Goddess occupy over 30 acres (12 ha) in Çatalhöyük.

Egypt, 6000 BCE: The Nile River floods, delivering fresh silt on an annual basis. People begin farming wheat, barley, sheep, and goats.

Middle East, 6000 BCE: Cattle are domesticated.

India, 6000 BCE: Farming begins in India.

China, 5800 BCE: Millet farming begins.

Europe, 5400 BCE: Farming begins in central and northern Europe.

and men, suggesting that the sexual division of labor (except in the area of childrearing) was not as pronounced as earlier scholars claimed. Many scholars say that it was not until the Upper Paleolithic period (40,000 years ago), when humans moved out of Africa and north to Europe and beyond, that the sexual division of labor was established. The rationale for having men travel outside of temporary settlements to hunt for large game—while women stayed closer to home—was that the burden of carrying young children precluded women from full participation in the long treks required during these excursions. These early hunter-gatherer societies were also very small and the danger of death while hunting big game very real, so these communities sought to protect women of child-bearing age.

However, there is no reason to believe that, once this division of labor was in place, women became totally passive actors. The dangers and difficulty of big game hunting suggest that these societies must have continued to rely on foraging and plant foods for survival. Because men were regularly engaged in hunting, foraging largely became the domain of women and children, and it is more than likely that the first technological innovations occurred in this area. In order to free their hands for digging and foraging, women invented a number of tools for carrying children and food. These were usually fashioned out of animal skins. Other important tools allowed female gatherers to dig up edible roots.

Two of the key features of our evolution toward becoming *homo sapiens* were our increased hairlessness, and our ability to stand upright on two feet. The example of our closest relative, the primate, is very instructive here. Primate offspring cling unassisted to the mother's chest hair while she negotiates her way through the wild, hands free for transportation, carrying, and procuring food. But the hairless hominid mother needed to use her arms to carry an infant, providing a great evolutionary incentive toward bipedalism. This was surely as important as the ability to see above tall grasses to find prey.

Women played a dominant role in social development in early societies—they maintained a constant presence at the camps, and were responsible for raising and teaching children— the same children who would grow up to participate in the hunter-gatherer economy and continue the process of evolution.

Venus of Lespugue.

Woman the Gatherer

During the Stone Age women spent their days tending to children and gathering wild plant food close to base camp. A wealth of evidence from the Uralic speakers of northern Eurasia between 10,000 and 4000 BCE provides a very good illustration of this. These ancient languages reveal that women took cradles, baskets, and pails into the fields to collect wild berries and seeds, eggs, mushrooms, and other useful items such as moss for bedding and cushions. They fashioned tools using the bark from birch, willow, and linden trees.

Some scholars have suggested that, since small animals and plants were more stable sources of food than large wild animals, it was most probably the

women who dictated when and whether to move to a new settlement.

The earliest evidence of rope (a braided cord) is dated at about 15,000 BCE. However, archeological evidence suggests that this technology developed at least 5,000 to 15,000 years earlier. The Gravettian cultures of central and eastern Europe, which spread south and west through France and Spain, lasted from 26,000 to 20,000 BCE, and archeologists have unearthed needles and beads that were entombed with women's remains. Sometimes the beads were lined up in neat rows, suggesting that they were sewn onto a garment, probably made from animal skins. Likewise, a "Venus" figurine discovered in Lespugue in southern France, and dated to 20,000 BCE, was adorned in a skirt with an intricately carved weave pattern and frayed fiber threads at the bottom.

Inanna or Ishtar

In Stone Age times, women cared for the children and tended the animals.

Key Events

Middle East, 4300 BCE: The Fertile Crescent nurtures Mesopotamia's first cities and civilizations.
Middle East, 4000 BCE: The goddess cult of Inanna or Ishtar takes hold.
Middle East, 4000 BCE: Sumerians settle at the site of Babylon. Legend has it that the goddess Tiamet created the universe.
Middle East, 3700 BCE: High priests run the temples and city-states of Mesopotamia. The people of Uruk, Sumeria, develop the first use of writing, with cuneiform script.

Middle East, 3700-3400 BCE: The first cities in Mesopotamia. Irrigation canals are used in farming and cattle.
China, 3500 BCE: Both sexes wear nail varnish. In Egypt henna decorates women's hands, nails, and feet.
Egypt, 3400-3200 BCE: Egyptians base their religion on totemic symbols of nature and sun god Ra.
Middle East, 3400-3200 BCE: Bronze is used in manufacturing.
Egypt, 3165-3100 BCE: King Menes rules and unites upper and lower Egypt, setting the precedent of god-king and founding the first dynasty.

Sumer, 3000-2000 BCE: Women draw water from the village well, manage their dowries, make business transactions, possess slaves, and have equal rights over children. They may be executed if adulterous, divorced if barren, or drowned for refusing men's conjugal rights.
China, 2700 BCE: Empress Se Ling-chi begins cultivating silk worms.
Babylonia, 2500 BCE: While trial marriage is allowed, a woman accused of adultery can be forced to swim across the Euphrates to prove her innocence.

Egypt, 2450 BCE: This advice is offered to husbands in *The Maxims of Ptah-Hotep:* "Love thy wife at home as is fitting. Fill her belly, clothe her back...she is a profitable field for her lord so do not contend with her at law and keep her from gaining control."
South America, 3000 BCE: Alpacas and llamas are domesticated.
Egypt, 2800-2600 BCE: Egyptians invent the first calendar of 365 days.
Egypt, 2700 BCE: Egyptians build the first pyramid tombs; papyrus is used for writing.

Egypt, 2700 BCE: The first female doctor to have her name recorded is Merit Ptah. Her name is engraved in a tomb in the Valley of Kings.
Americas, 2700 BCE: Meso-Americans are growing maize.
China, 2640 BCE: Lei-tzu, the wife of Chinese Emperor Huang Ti, discovers how to weave silk while unraveling a silkworm's cocoon.
Egypt, 2600 BCE: Egyptian priests expand religion to create a total belief system confirming divine kingship and royal authority. Women are employed as temple dancers.

Hatshepsut

Woman the Hunter?

While it is true that most Stone Age women adhered to the sexual division of labor that was being defined and refined by evolution, there is contemporary evidence suggesting that there may have been exceptions to the rule. Proponents of this thesis generally refer to modern examples of hunter-gatherer groups. For example, in the Philippines, the women of the Agta Negritos tribe occupy positions of relative equality with their male counterparts, playing a large role in hunting medium-sized game. Female big game hunters in Chipewyan communities of northern Saskatchewan, Canada, also indicate that the same role-sharing could well have applied in prehistoric times in similar environments.

"WHAT IS BEAUTIFUL IS GOOD; AND WHO IS GOOD WILL SOON BE BEAUTIFUL."

SAPPHO
(610–580 BCE),
GREEK POET

The Goddess Tradition in Prehistory

The earliest known artifact to depict a woman is the "Venus of Willendorf," named for the area of Austria where she was discovered in 1908. It is a 4.4-inch (11-cm) high limestone figurine of a woman with prominent breasts, belly, and vulva and with a face completely hidden by a crown of braids. She appears to be either pregnant, or more likely, what we would call morbidly obese. She is dated somewhere between 24,000 and 22,000 BCE and scholars believe that she was probably an icon used in goddess worship rituals. Similar figurines have been discovered all over Europe, from western France all the way to Russia, dating from 25,000 BCE (Stone Age) to 2000 BCE (Bronze Age). Over 60 figurines have been found from the

Venus of Willendorf.

Paleolithic period, all of which share similar characteristics to the Willendorf Venus.

We do not know whether these figurines are positive proof of goddess worship; particularly because both male and female figurines exist, as well as statues of animals and androgynous beings. But they have been found in a wide diversity of locations throughout the region, suggesting that they may have served a variety of cultural purposes. The earliest figures appeared in homesteads, while many of the later ones were located in shrines or graves. An argument against the existence of goddess worship during the Stone Age and the Bronze Age is that these societies lacked complex social, political, legal, and religious institutions, as existed in ancient Greece and Rome. Rather, evidence suggests that these early societies believed in spirits and forces in nature, many of which were given feminine attributes. Anatolia (modern Turkey) is the only place where there is strong evidence of goddess worship and this is based on later evidence of fertility cults. Goddess figurines from 6250 to 5400 BCE were also found here, both in and around several shrines.

The Original Mini Skirt

Aspects of these figurines show that ancient societies had different ideas about health, modesty, and beauty than we do in the modern world. Most figures are either completely naked or adorned in very short skirts which do little to cover the

Anatolian mother goddess from the sanctuary of Çatalhöyük.

genitalia. A disinterred young woman's remains in Egtved, Denmark was wearing a "Venusian" skirt, constructed of cording which fell just above the knees. The cords did very little to protect her modesty because the weighting of the cords ensured that the skirt swished freely back and forth as she walked. Similar garments have been found on female skeletons, many even shorter, and some without even a panel to cover the vulva. Scholars examining this evidence have concluded that the heavy emphasis on naked breasts, stomachs, and vulvas reinforces the cultural importance of respecting fertility in these societies. The fact that the "Venuses" tended to be fat is seen as further evidence—weightier women were more likely to be fertile and were much better equipped to breastfeed infants. This would have been especially valuable in forager communities when they experienced food shortages. This homage to voluptuousness is worthy of note to those modern observers who associate health, beauty, and well-being with thinness.

Key Events

Egypt, 2600-2500 BCE: The pyramid for pharaoh Khufu is completed at Giza. The Sphinx of Giza is built.
India, 2500 BCE: Hinduism begins.
Assyria, 2300 BCE: Princess, poet, and high priestess Enheduanna is the first known writer whose work has survived.
Mexico, 2300 BCE: Maize farming begins in Mexico and farming villages start to flourish. Pottery is first used in central America.
China, 2200 BCE: Chinese legend has it that painting as an art form is discovered by Lei, sister of the emperor.

Egypt, 2000 BCE: Egyptian women, long established as dancers and performers, now also run a wide variety of businesses, and often own land.
Mesopotamia, 2150 BCE: Babylon is flourishing on the lower Euphrates as the world's first library opens.
Britain, 2000 BCE: Stonehenge is built, showing the astronomical knowledge of the people of Wessex.
Peru, 2000 BCE: Peruvians are farming extensively.
Russia, 2000 BCE: People on the steppes domesticate the horse.

China, 1900 BCE: Bronze is used extensively for many creative and technological inventions.
Egypt, 1806-1802 BCE: Sobekneferu, last ruler of the Twelfth Dynasty, is the first female pharaoh of Egypt.
Babylon, 1730 BCE: The women of Babylon's temples occupy roles as priestesses and prostitutes of the goddess Ishtar.
China, 1700-1600 BCE: China's Shang dynasty is founded by King Tang, creating political stability.

Greece, 1650 BCE: Mycenaean civilization begins in Greece.
China, 1600 BCE: Pictographic writing begins in China.
Egypt, 1500 BCE: Women are permitted to study at the Heliopolis medical school.
China, 1500 BCE: Shamans in China are predominantly female. They are believed to be able to bring rain, and their power is supposedly shared with kings who mate with them.
Egypt, 1470 BCE: Queen Hatshepsut trades with east Africa.

China, 1400 BCE: Chinese bury dead royals with human sacrifices. They also build walled cities, use writing, and have wheeled vehicles.
Egypt, 1360 BCE: Nefertiti rules Egypt with husband Akhenaton.
Egypt, 1300-1250 BCE: The queen who became known as "God's wife," Queen Nefertari, shares the rule over Egypt with her husband King Ahmose. After his death, rules with her son. She is the only Egyptian queen to be deified in her lifetime.

Matriarchy: Myth or Reality?

Some have pointed to Venus figurines as evidence that matriarchy (the exercise of control, dominance, and power by women over men) existed during the Stone Age. Although we know that patriarchy was entrenched by the time the first written records were produced in the fourth millennium BCE in Egypt and the near East, there has been much speculation about whether matriarchal societies existed during the Paleolithic eras. On their own, the "Venus" statues are not proof—imagine drawing the same conclusion about our own society based on popular imagery of the Virgin Mary. There is evidence of matrilineal and matrifocal societies during the Paleolithic period, but no concrete proof of matriarchy. More convincing evidence of matriarchy is found in Minoan Crete during the Bronze Age, where many wall drawings depict women engaging in such public and physical pursuits as fighting and bull-jumping. However, most of these depictions are found in palaces, so these were probably portrayals of elite women. It is not possible to draw the same conclusions about lower class women, who occupied very different social positions in Crete. While pure matriarchies may not have existed, there nonetheless seems to have been more gender equality during the Paleolithic period. Although there was some gender division of labor, the value placed on the work of both sexes seems to have been equal and women apparently made quite a significant contribution to decision-making in these societies. It was not until much later—with the introduction of private property and warfare—that the subordination of women began to advance rapidly.

Women's lives altered radically after the Paleolithic era. Once the ice began to melt and the great herds of animals migrated north, southern European peoples began to settle the land. This process began around 10,000 years ago and is designated as the dawn of the Neolithic Era (New Stone Age). Archeological digs in Turkey, Syria, and Israel reveal that people settled these regions first, and only much later began farming the land and raising domestic animals. These early settlements were horticultural, and women became responsible for tending "kitchen-gardens." Thus, instead of gathering and foraging, women now began to play the role of small farmers—while also tending children and making cloth. Women also began to have more children—whereas reproduction rates were previously constrained by what women could carry, and what the community could afford to eat, these developing societies needed more people. Farming small plots of land was labor-intensive and children were welcome assistants. Likewise, farming yielded more food, so societies could afford to feed more children. The threat of infectious diseases in these new societies was also greater, so having more children offset higher mortality rates. Men's primary role in early Neolithic settlements was still hunting, so they were often away from home.

Helen of Troy

This procession of women, part of a Minoan fresco, was found at Knossos in Crete.

Minoan female idol.

Key Events

Middle East, 1250 BCE: Moses leads the Israelites out of Egypt toward the Promised Land.
Egypt, 1250 BCE: The Abu Simbel temple is built by pharaoh Ramses II.
Americas, 1220 BCE: Mayans settle the Yucatan peninsula.
Middle East, 1200 BCE: The Trojan War takes place, sparked by the abduction of Spartan queen, Helen of Troy, by Paris.
China, 1200 BCE: Fu Hao, a Chinese woman warrior, undertakes major military campaigns and expeditions.

Middle East, 1150 BCE: Deborah, the prophet and heroine of Hebrew scriptures leads Israel to victory over invading Canaanites.
Middle East, 1000 BCE: People are using iron weapons and tools.
Americas, 1000 BCE: South Americans cultivate maize.
Middle East, 1000-961 BCE: King David defeats Philistines and makes Jerusalem a political and religious center uniting Jewish tribes.
Middle East, 850 BCE: Prophets Elijah and Elisha promote the Jewish faith.

Greece, and Middle East 800 BCE: Greeks colonize Mediterranean and Black Sea to establish their empire. Biblical Old Testament narratives are being written.
Greece, 776 BCE: The first Olympic games are held.
Greece, 750 BCE: Homer writes *The Iliad* and *The Odyssey*.
Greece, 600 BCE: Theano, a philosopher, mathematician, and doctor, lived in this century. Believed to be the daughter of Pythagoras, she continued his school after his death.

Greece, 610-580 BCE: Sappho, the most famous early Greek poet, lives on the isle of Lesbos where she wrote her poem *Hymn to Aphrodite*, detailing her quest to seduce a young girl. Sappho is considered the "mother" of modern lesbianism.
Jerusalem, 586 BCE: Many women still worship the goddess Ishtar.
China, 604-531 BCE: The life and teachings of Lao-tzu give birth to Taoism in China.
Northern India/Nepal, 563-483 BCE: Siddhartha Gautama (Buddha) lives and teaches "the middle way."

India, 500 BCE: Buddha's aunt Mahaprajapati asks that Buddha establish nunneries where women may lead an ascetic life of prayer, free of everyday duties.
China, 551-479 BCE: Confucius teaches his philosophy.
Middle East, 539-521 BCE: Persia conquers Babylon, Egypt, and Rome.
Rome, 509 BCE: The Roman republic is founded.
Greece, 509-400 BCE: Greeks introduce the first limited democracy.

Aspasia

This harvest scene from the tomb of Sennedjem, Egypt, shows women participating in farming activities.

"ALL STRANGE AND TERRIBLE EVENTS ARE WELCOME; BUT COMFORTS WE DESPISE."

CLEOPATRA
(68–30 BCE),
EGYPTIAN QUEEN

Women as Innovators and Artisans

Women's work, and the invention of the loom during this period allowed them to make much larger pieces of fabric. It is reasonable to conclude that this was exclusively the result of innovation by women because in early depictions of weavers, women are always doing the work. Archeologists have recovered evidence of two distinct types of loom. One originated in Jarmo, Iraq, and spread south and southeast through Mesopotamia and the Levant and down into Egypt, all the way to India. The other originated in Hungary and spread to northern and western Europe. There is also widespread evidence that women weavers were extremely skilled at their trade. Many pieces of cloth recovered in archeological digs were not the utilitarian pieces of cloth one might expect to find in subsistence cultures. For example, a piece of linen discovered in Irgenhausen, Switzerland

(3000 BCE) contained a mix of triangle, checkerboard, and stripe patterns and at least three different fabric colors. Indeed, complex weaving patterns have been common throughout central Europe since about 5000 BCE. Pottery-making is another craft undertaken by women of this period. As with weaving and small-scale farming, pottery tools could be made at home with children. Much of the artwork adorning vases, bowls, and jugs during this period depicted fertility symbols, indicating that this was women's work.

Following the invention of the wheel during the Bronze Age, women's roles changed again. Large domestic animals plowed much larger plots of farm land, so men had less need to travel long distances to hunt. This change in farming practice

made it less practical for women to perform agricultural work because it was no longer possible for them to tend all the crops while fulfilling essential domestic functions. During this period, cities began to replace small settlements and metal-trading brought men increasingly into these new environments. The declining overlap in men's and women's roles led to a hardening of ideas about the differences between the sexes. The increasingly rigid sex roles of men and women were especially reinforced by the advent of warfare. As populations grew across Europe, men set off in search of new lands to exploit. During these quests they came upon different cultures, and large-scale territorial competitiveness was born. By the time of the first written accounts, it is clear that the relatively egalitarian nature of Stone Age and Bronze Age societies had already been replaced by patriarchy. It is constructive to look at ancient Greek, Roman, Celtic, Hebrew, and Germanic cultures to illustrate this.

Women in Pre-Christian Societies

Pre-Christian societies used the written word to subjugate women. Greek ideas about women were adopted by the Romans, who later spread them across continental Europe. Indeed, Roman laws and customs were influential long after the fall of the Roman Empire in the fifth century CE. Likewise, the diaspora of Hebrew peoples throughout the Mediterranean world greatly influenced the cultures surrounding them, particularly through the successful spreading of the message in the sacred text, the Torah (Old

Female divinity goddess from Angkor Wat, Cambodia.

Key Events

Testament). The Celtic and Germanic peoples, who took over after the fall of the Romans, modeled their laws and customs on these earlier examples, thus perpetuating the idea that women were inferior. Nevertheless, there are examples within all these ancient cultures that show that many women managed to transcend their prescribed social roles. Some refused to conform to the limited roles assigned to them by men, and provided an inspiring example for women of the second millennium who tried to break free.

In the fourth century BCE, Aristotle wrote: "The male is by nature superior, and the female inferior; and the one rules

A Pictish woman displaying her decorated body.

and the other is ruled." Roman censuses across the Empire through the second and fourth centuries CE indicate that these societies comprised far more men than women. In Roman Egypt there were 100 women for every 105 men; in Spain the ratio was 100 to 126; in Africa and Italy the ratio was 100 to 140, and in Rome proper the ratio was 100 to 131. Many women left their baby girls in public places, hoping that someone would take them in, but obviously many died. Many of the survivors were taken in by brothel owners and raised to be prostitutes.

The approved roles of women in these early cultures were limited to daughter, wife, mother, or widow. The Romans enforced this by precluding women from government positions. Hebrews forbade women from studying religious texts. Celtic and Germanic peoples excluded women from warfare—the most honorable of contemporary social activities. In all these cultures virginity was highly valued and women were not permitted legal control of self or property, except under exceptional circumstances. Authority over women passed from father to husband and this was enforced through both law and custom. Girls were often married off after their first menstruation, in arrangements that were as much economic transactions between men as a union between a woman and a man. It was during this era that modern ideas of conventional beauty emerged. Greek, Roman, Celtic, and Germanic writings and art promote the ideal of the fair haired, fair skinned, red lipped, curvaceous—yet slender—beauty.

The Birth of the "Double Standard"

Societies responded to marital infidelity in different ways—usually inequitable—depending on which partner transgressed. Hebrew law called for adulterous

wives to be killed, along with the man who dared to dally with her. Celtic and Germanic law permitted the killing of adulterous women, while husbands were able to recover her dowry value from the offending man. In all European (and most other) societies adultery by men was tolerated, even expected—as long as they avoided married women. The Greek lecturer Demosthenes (fourth century BCE) suggested that men had a specific use for each class of women. He wrote: "We (male citizens of Athens) have courtesans for the sake of pleasure, concubines for the daily care of the body, and wives to breed legitimate children and be a trustworthy guard of possessions indoors."

Women who did not fit the ideal of the obedient daughter or chaste wife were, paradoxically, both scorned and desired— even by the same men who fulfilled their desires for pleasure and pampering in the manner laid out by Demosthenes. Women who used sex to gain power were especially reviled—the Romans popularly referred to Cleopatra VII as *regina meretrix* ("prostitute queen") because she had sex with both Caesar and Mark Antony. Sexual congress between slave women and their masters was widespread. This practice was also common in Celtic and Germanic societies, and polygamy was widespread. In ancient Greece and Rome—among other places—prostitution was institutionalized and men commonly attended brothels.

Boadicea

A Roman woman with her maids.

Diana of Ephesus

The Power of Women

The Greeks referred to the female trinity Lotho (Spinner), Lachesis (Disposer of the Lots), and Atropos (Inflexible) as the three rulers of human fate. The Romans worshipped the female goddess Fortune, who is represented at many Roman shrines and temples.

In Greek, Roman, Celtic, and Germanic cultures, the earth was perceived as female, and various personifications of Mother Earth were worshipped to ensure human, animal, and plant fertility. The common denominator is that goddesses were associated with volatile and unpredictable natural forces. Many remnants of this early goddess worship still exist and are popular tourist attractions. The Temple of Artemis (Diana) at Ephesus—a goddess well-known throughout the Mediterranean world—was one of the seven wonders of the ancient world. Likewise, the Venus de Milo statue in Paris's Louvre gallery is actually an ancient Greek depiction of Aphrodite, the goddess of Love and the personification of ancient beauty. Moreover, both Greek and Roman society employed powerful priestesses who were thought to have great supernatural and religious powers. It was not until the first century CE that such women were disempowered by the Romans.

The Amazons, a tribe of female warriors, feature in mythology but it is unclear whether they actually existed. They are often mentioned in Greek literature, particularly Homer's *Iliad*. It is widely believed that they came to Athens around 1200 BCE; Greek historian Herodotus supposed that they came from Asia. Women's tombs containing female skeletons buried with jewels, weapons, and armor have been unearthed east of the Don River. Women are also depicted atop the Parthenon and the Acropolis.

Likewise, there are several examples of warrior women in the Old Testament, including the widow Judith, who killed Holofernes, an enemy general. The story tells that she pretended she was going to have sexual relations with him, but instead, grabbed his sword from a mount on the wall and cut off his head. She had her maid carry the severed head back to her people in a bag, and was celebrated as the savior of her people. Similar tales are told in Germanic and Celtic legends—even though women were generally prohibited from participating in warfare.

Cleopatra VII (69–30 BCE), the last queen of independent Egypt, is perhaps the most renowned of female rulers. While the historical record

> "LIFE IS AN ENFOLDMENT, AND THE FURTHER WE TRAVEL, THE MORE TRUTH WE WILL COMPREHEND."
>
> HYPATIA
> (C. 370–415 CE),
> MATHEMATICIAN
> AND PHILOSOPHER

A limestone relief of Cleopatra VII wearing the crown of Hathor.

and popular literature generally focus on her beauty and sexual prowess, this emphasis trivializes the fact that she successfully ruled her people for twenty years, staving off numerous incursions by the Romans. She was 17 when she ascended the throne, and during her period as ruler, had a child with Julius Caesar, and—after Caesar's murder—twins with Mark Antony.

While literacy and education were unattainable luxuries for almost all women during this time, some used their intelligence or family connections to secure leadership roles, especially during times of transition. Epitaphs of female doctors from first century CE Rome show that they often came from families with backgrounds in the scientific and medical arts. Likewise, the eight known female painters

The Amazon cavalry, from a fourth century BCE vase.

of this period are most often described as the wives or daughters of great painters. Hypatia (370–415 CE) was a professor of math and philosophy in Alexandria, following in her father's footsteps. She was renowned for inventing several scientific instruments, but was nonetheless burned to death by a mob, along with all of her written works.

Perhaps the most well-known early female writer was the Greek poet, Sappho (630 BCE), who came from the island of Lesbos. She was known in her time as a poetic genius and Plato once referred to her as the "Tenth Muse." She was married and had a child, but her most intimate love poems were addressed to both women and men.

Christianity and Women

In its infancy, Christianity was actually quite liberating for women—compared with their traditional prescribed

St Margaret of Antioch.

roles in European societies. The basis for the relative equality of the sexes in the early church was rooted in the teachings and actions of Jesus Christ, who taught that anyone who followed his teachings and example could earn a place in heaven, irrespective of gender or social position. Indeed, women occupied a central role in his ministry, and—as the New Testament declares—apart from John, only women stood by him during his persecution and crucifixion. Women prepared his body for burial and Jesus appeared only to Mary Magdalene after his resurrection.

Long after Jesus's death, women continued to occupy a prominent position in the church—but often as persecuted martyrs of the Roman Empire. Between

the death of Jesus and the fourth century CE, as Christianity became the favored religion in Europe, over 100,000 people were killed by the Romans. Among their number, St Catherine, St Margaret, and St Barbara were honored for the brutal means by which they met their end. Others, like St Agnes, St Davia, and St Anastasia, were venerated for leaving lives of affluence and privilege to work in the service of the church. Still others played a prominent role as Christian missionaries. According to legend, while Mary Magdalene was shipwrecked in the south of France, she converted many of the local people. Likewise, Ireland converted to Christianity as a result of the efforts of St Brigid (450–523 CE) and St Patrick.

By the eighth century CE the earliest religious orders were established. Many women lived in nunneries and devoted their lives to Christ and to charitable works and community service—under the watchful eye of male ecclesiastic bosses.

The story of Adam and Eve regained currency as an indicator of supposed female inferiority—as it was to the ancients. Church leaders emphasized the unclean nature of childbirth and menstruation, and the role of women as the chattels of men. And even though Jesus treated women as equals, church leaders pointed to the teachings of Paul and other New Testament writers who proclaimed women's inferiority.

As we have seen, women's roles from prehistory to the year 999 were constantly in flux. They were defined and redefined

based on various factors, such as child-care and economic needs, technological innovations, settlement patterns, warfare, religion, and constantly changing ideas about the proper roles for women in society.

Despite the sustained and concerted efforts of many men to "put women in their place and keep them there," women have continued to make very important and significant contributions to society and culture, not only as wives, daughters, and mothers, but also as technological innovators, great minds, spiritual leaders, healers, leaders, artists, philosophers, writers, and even as armed warriors.

Empress Irene of Byzantium

Mary Magdalene with the risen Jesus Christ.

From the Year
1000 to Today

Murasaki Shikibu

Two Empresses for Japan

Japan, c. 1000: The daughter of statesman and powerbroker Fujiwara Michinaga has been installed at court as the second empress of Emperor Ichijo. Twelve-year-old Shoshi has been named emperor's consort. This is a big blow for Empress Teishi, who has lost much support since the death of her father. Political intrigue at court has always been rife and Fujiwara Michinaga was quick to consolidate his position. He has convinced the emperor that it is both right and fitting to have two empresses, and in doing so he has fulfilled his ambitions of controlling the political scene in Japan.

The two empresses have established rival salons. Empress Teishi, considered by those who know her as a kind and gentle woman, has a retinue of devoted ladies-in-waiting, one of whom is the poet Sei Shonagon. Empress Shoshi also has a loyal group of female companions, among them Murasaki Shikibu, recently praised for her wonderful story of life, love, and adventure *Genji monogatari (The Tale of Genji),* and the poets Akazome Emon and Izumi Shikibu.

Sei Shonagan and Murasaki Shikibu are also literary and social rivals.

> "THOUGH THE BODY MOVES, THE SOUL MAY STAY BEHIND."
>
> MURASAKI SHIKIBU (973–1025), JAPANESE AUTHOR

> "BETTER TO BE AN OLD MAN'S DARLING THAN A YOUNG MAN'S SLAVE."
>
> ENGLISH PROVERB, ANONYMOUS

Women at court spend much of their time writing poetry, painting scenes from nature, and playing music. They also enjoy taking trips into the countryside. Although their lives seem idyllic, the emperor's consorts know that their good fortune—or otherwise—lies in the hands of the powerful men who have the emperor's ear.

Life at Court Revealed in *Pillow Book*

Japan, c. 1000: Sei Shonagon, a lady-in-waiting to the Empress Teishi for about ten years, has written a witty personal account of life in the Japanese court, which provides fascinating glimpses into how the other half lives.

Makura no soshi (Pillow Book) is a collection of observations and thoughts about such topics as the vanity of some women, the many comforts enjoyed by royal pets, the work that courtiers do, and who is having love affairs with who. She suggests ways to alleviate boredom and writes gossip, poetry, complaints, and lists. There are some 320 anecdotes, all wonderfully told, in this amusing informative collection.

The book has set tongues wagging because her descriptions are not always flattering, but many are enjoying the descriptions of court life in this period.

New Literary Salon to Open

Cordoba, Spain, 1031: With the death of her father, the Caliph of Cordoba, the gifted

Illustration from *The Tale of Genji*, written by court attendant Murasaki Shikibu.

This young Chinese girl is binding her feet so that they will fit into beautiful, tiny, lotus-shaped shoes.

poet Walladah bint al-Mustakfi has inherited a substantial fortune—enough to allow her to live the independent life she has always craved.

Already known for her verse and her erudition, Walladah is eager to establish her own literary salon, where she will host evenings of poetry and music with the literary and artistic elite of this Andalusian region of Spain.

Cordoba is known for its tolerance, its intellectual tradition, and its multifaceted culture, so Walladah's decision not to wear the veil and never to marry is not being frowned on as it might be in other, stricter Muslim societies. Her wealth and her strong streak of individualism may not be the norm among Muslim women, but Walladah is taking advantage of both.

It is rumored that the 30-year-old poet has taken a number of lovers, both men

North America, 1000: Leif Eriksson reputedly discovers North America.

China, c. 1000: The custom of binding young girls' feet to keep them artificially small becomes more common in the imperial court.

Europe, c. 1000: The epic tale of *Beowulf* is written down; it originated some centuries earlier.

Japan, c. 1000: Rival empresses Teishi/Sadako and Soshi/Akiko establish separate literary salons.

Japan, c. 1000: Sei Shonagon writes *Makura no soshi (Pillow Book)*, a series of essays and anecdotes of her life at court.

Japan, c. 1000: Murasaki Shikibu writes the world's first novel, *Genji monogatari (The Tale of Genji)*.

Gandersheim, Saxony (Germany), c. 1002: Hrosvitha, Benedictine nun, playwright, and poet, dies, aged about 65.

Peshawar, India, 1004: Mahmud of Ghazna defeats the armies of a Hindu confederacy. He annexes the Punjab and introduces Islam there.

Jerusalem, 1009: Caliph al-Hakim sacks the Church of the Holy Sepulcher and the tomb believed to be Christ's is hacked down to bedrock.

Hanoi, Vietnam, 1009: Ly Cong Uan founds the Ly Dynasty, and establishes Vietnam as an independent state.

England, October 18, 1016: Canute's Danish forces defeat the English army under Edmund Ironside at the Battle of Ashingdon, and Canute becomes king of England.

Java, Indonesia, 1016: Airlangga becomes the founding ruler of the Kingdom of Mataram, greatest of the medieval Southeast Asian island empires.

Orleans, France, 1022: The death by burning of male and female heretics is recorded.

Cordoba, Spain, 1031: Islamic poet Walladah bint al-Mustakfi uses an inheritance from her father to establish her own salon.

Norway, 1035: There is an uprising against the regent of Norway, Aelgifu, the Saxon noblewoman and mistress of Canute of Denmark. She had been appointed regent by Canute in 1030.

Constantinople, Byzantium, 1050: Empress Zoe, joint ruler of the Byzantine Empire, dies, aged about 72.

Germany, October, 1056: Agnes of Poitou, the widow of Emperor Henry III, becomes ruler of the Holy Roman Empire as regent for her son.

and women, among them the well-respected poet Ibn Zaydun.

She is also gaining a reputation for her choice of clothing, particularly her robes with elaborate embroidery on the sleeves. The sleeve of one robe is said to be embroidered with her own words, "I am fit for high positions, by God, and go on my way with pride." Well educated and very liberated, Walladah has the financial and intellectual freedom to become one of the most talented poets of her time.

Canute's Wife and Son Out!

Norway, 1035: King Magnus, who has been in exile since Canute declared himself king of Norway, has made a triumphant return to the capital city, following the uprising against Canute's hand-picked deputies—his son, Sweyn, and Sweyn's mother, Aelgifu, who jointly ruled Norway since 1028.

Canute became king of England in 1016, and had been king of Denmark since his brother Harald's death in 1019. In 1028, Canute expelled King Olaf II of Norway, saying that his claim to the throne was spurious, and he proclaimed himself king of Norway. This bold move thus consolidated his stranglehold on the region. But the practical difficulties associated with governing three kingdoms led to Canute appointing his son, Harthacanute, as the ruler of Denmark, while in Norway he installed his son, Sweyn, who, along with his mother, Aelgifu of Northampton, has been ruling the country with a very stern hand.

Aelgifu—described either as Canute's wife or mistress—is a powerful regent,

The mosque in Cordoba, a city renowned for its tolerance.

and her heavy-handed ways have not been popular among either landowners or the ordinary folk.

Aelgifu and Sweyn implemented a harsh system of taxation, and did not do anything to actively promote the economic well-being of the nation. By all accounts, the Saxon mother and son partnership has been quite greedy and manipulative.

The growing ill-will toward Aelgifu and Sweyn came to a head when the Norwegian nobility heard the news of Canute's death in England in November. Surging into action, the nobles have banded together and risen up to oppose

> **time out**
>
> In 1015, St Adelaide of Bellich, abbess of the Convent of Villich, dies. She introduced the rule of St Benedict into the convent and also took the unusual step of insisting that her nuns learn to read and write Latin.

the despised foreign king and regent, driving them out of Norway.

The recall of Magnus, the son of the ousted King Olaf, from his long exile in order to rule over Norway is good news for the country.

It is rumored that Aelgifu will return to England where she will live with her other son by Canute, Harald Harefoot.

Death of Empress Zoe

Constantinople, Byzantium, 1050: Empress Zoe Porphyrogenita has died, aged about 72. Joint ruler of the Byzantine Empire since the death of her father, Constantine VIII, in November 1028, Zoe has left the empire in the hands of her third husband, Constantine IX Monomachus, and her beloved sister Theodora.

When Zoe took the throne in 1028, she was already 50 years old and had not been married. But she agreed to marry Romanus III Argyrus upon her father's death, and they ruled the empire together. When Romanus died in 1034, in what many consider to be suspicious circumstances, Zoe married again, and she and Michael IV the Paphlagonian ruled together until Michael's death in 1041. For a short period, Michael V Calaphates ruled jointly with Empress Zoe, but his ill-advised plan to send her to a convent and claim sole power backfired when the populace banished him and brought Zoe back to Constantinople to reign jointly with her sister Theodora.

In June 1042, Zoe married her third husband, Constantine IX Monomachos, but she continued to rule the empire with Theodora. Intellectual life in the Byzantine court flourished under their guidance, although there were always rumors of scandal and political intrigue.

Zoe was often criticized for putting her own interests before those of the people, but as one of the last representatives of the Macedonian dynasty, the people had a great affection for her.

Empress Zoe of Byzantium

Japan, c. 1065: Lady Sarashina (real name unknown), author of *Sarashina nikki* (*Sarashina Diaries*) dies, aged about 50.

Europe, April, 1066: A comet is observed over Europe. It is also seen in Egypt, the Middle East, China, and Japan.

Hastings, England, October 14, 1066: The English forces of King Harold II are defeated by the Normans led by William of Normandy. Harold falls in battle.

London, England, December 25, 1066: William the Conqueror is crowned king of England.

Yemen, 1067: Queen Arwa takes control of the kingdom when her husband's ill health leaves him unable to rule.

Germany, 1068: The regency of the Holy Roman Empire is taken from Empress Agnes (Agnes of Poitou).

Westminster, England, 1076: The Council of Westminster decrees that a priestly blessing is required before a man gives his female relative in marriage.

England, 1077: The tapestry reputedly commissioned by Queen Matilda, commemorating the Battle of Hastings, is completed.

Durazzo, Albania, October 1081: Sikelgaita plays a significant role in the Norman invasion of Byzantium led by her husband, Robert Guiscard, commanding part of the Norman army in battle.

Warwickshire, England, c. 1086: Lady Godiva/Godgifu, patron of the arts and philanthropist, dies.

Melfi, Italy, 1089: Pope Urban II decrees that married priests may be imprisoned and their wives enslaved.

Canossa, Italy, 1092: Papal ally Matilda of Tuscany leads her forces to victory over Henry IV of Germany.

Edinburgh, Scotland, November 16, 1093: Margaret, Queen of Scotland and religious reformer, dies, aged about 48.

Clermont, France, 1095: Pope Urban II appeals to the Christian princes to wrest control of the Holy Land from the grip of the Turks.

Mainz, Germany, May 27, 1096: Members of the First Crusade led by Count Emico attack the Jews of the city, who had taken refuge together. The Jewish women kill each other and their children rather than fall to the Christians.

Jerusalem, July 15, 1099: The Crusaders seize Jerusalem from the control of the Fatimids of Egypt. Thousands of Muslims, Jews, and Orthodox Christians, men, women, and children alike, are slaughtered.

Queen Matilda
of England

Agnes Becomes Regent

Germany, October 1056: With the death of Henry III, the Holy Roman Emperor, early this month, his widow, Agnes of Poitou, has taken on the role of regent for her six-year-old son, Henry IV, to whom his father's allies have pledged allegiance.

The Pope, Victor II, who was named in the late king's will as a guardian of young Henry, is also expected to be a valuable adviser to Agnes in her role as regent. Agnes is, however, known to be close to the controversial Bishop of Augsburg, upon whom she relies for support and guidance, and already many are criticizing Agnes for her lack of judgment in placing her trust in him.

Agnes, daughter of William of Aquitaine, married Henry III in November 1043, and bore him five children, of whom Henry IV is the fourth child and first son. She has little political experience, and although she is attempting to make peace with her husband's detractors, many feel that she is unequal to the important task of being regent. Already she is talking about assigning various territories away from the empire, and this will seriously affect the young king's power base, already weakened in part by Henry III's ecclesiastical policies.

Battle of Hastings in Stitches

England, 1077: The Battle of Hastings in 1066—a decisive battle for King William—has been painstakingly recreated

Agnes of Poitou and Henry III, with Christ in majesty.

in a massive embroidery that has taken some years to complete. Queen Matilda, his devoted wife and consort, is rumored to have decided upon an embroidery to commemorate her husband's victory, but others attribute the commission to William's brother, Bishop Odo.

The elongated embroidery is 230 ft (70 m) long, yet just 20 in (50 cm) deep, and depicts the significant events of the Norman conquest of England. Among the representations are William the Conqueror himself and his worthy adversary, the former king, Harold Godwinson, as well as Edward the Confessor.

The English and Norman forces are easily distinguishable—the men of the English forces are shown with mustaches, while the invading Norman soldiers are depicted with the backs of their heads shaved. One disturbing panel of the tapestry shows a man with his eye pierced by an arrow—many believe this to be the unfortunate King Harold.

Another panel portrays the dramatic appearance of a mysterious shooting star in the night sky.

This amazing embroidery also depicts regular soldiers making their preparations for war. Various panels show men collecting wood and food for the journey, the ships setting out from the shores of Normandy, and troops riding through the countryside. The care and attention to detail is impeccable—even down to the adornment on the shields of the soldiers.

One count has the number of people depicted on the tapestry as more than 620.

Queen Matilda of Canossa supported Pope Gregory VII, defeating Henry IV of Germany in battle at Canossa.

It is believed that this magnificent work will be housed in the cathedral at Bayeux in France.

Warrior Wife Wins War

Durazzo, Albania, October 1081: Born in Salerno, Sikelgaita, the warrior wife of Robert Guiscard, has led a battalion of soldiers in the fight to gain control of Byzantium. Robert's strategy to marry his daughter into the Byzantine ruling family failed, and when his plan to extend Norman influence into Byzantium failed too, he invaded.

Sikelgaita and Robert were married in 1058, and she has been his adviser ever since, reportedly never leaving his side, even accompanying him to battle, dressed in her own armor. By all accounts, she is an accomplished swordswoman, and well equipped to lead Robert's men into battle. Although wounded in the fracas, Sikelgaita led her men decisively, and when Robert's reinforcements arrived, victory was certain. Whether Robert Guiscard successfully takes over Byzantium remains to be seen.

The Bare Facts about Lady Godiva

Warwickshire, England, c. 1086: Lady Godgifu, or Lady Godiva, as she is more commonly known across Warwickshire, has died. A well-known philanthropist and a deeply religious woman, Lady Godiva was the widow of Leofric, Earl of Mercia. She was a landowner and a benefactor to the church, and she and her husband founded a Benedictine monastery in Coventry in 1043. The couple were committed to improving educational standards, and also made substantial donations to other abbeys.

But it will be her famous ride in 1057 for which Godiva will be best remembered. At that time, in a daring rebuke to her husband's authority, she rode naked through the streets of Coventry, a protest against his severe system of taxation.

She had pleaded with Leofric to reduce the taxation burden on his tenants. This led to his questioning her commitment, saying that if she rode naked through the streets of Coventry, then he would reduce the levies. He never thought that she would go through with it, but she boldly accepted the challenge.

There are conflicting reports of the ride itself, one version suggesting that Lady Godiva requested that everyone stay indoors to protect her from prying eyes. The other version is that she rode through the marketplace, guarded by two knights, and that she used her long unbound hair to cover her nakedness. Whatever the

Lady Godiva's famous ride will long be remembered.

truth of the story, her actions bore positive results and Leofric agreed to reduce the high levies that he had imposed on his tenants. Godiva was truly a woman of the people.

Saintly Margaret Dies

Edinburgh, Scotland, November 16, 1093: Queen Margaret, whose husband, King Malcolm III, and son, Edward, died only days ago in battle against the English at Alnwick, has herself died, aged 48.

Malcolm of Canmore and Queen Margaret of Dunfermline.

Although she had been in ill health, many firmly believe that grief over these deaths was the cause of her own death.

Saxon-born Margaret, a granddaughter of Edmund Ironside, was educated in Hungary. She came to Scotland after the Norman conquest of England. Given safe harbor with King Malcolm, she married him in 1070 and bore eight children, six of them sons. Margaret was a much-loved monarch, known for her devotion to the church, and for her countless good deeds.

During her time as queen, Margaret supported hospitals, schools, and orphanages. She was a regular visitor to the sick and elderly. She built churches and abbeys, as well as the royal mausoleum at Dunfermline Abbey. She invited Benedictine monks into Scotland. Pilgrims have had cause to be grateful for her establishment of a ferry service and hostelry for those who visit the shrine of St Andrew, Scotland's patron saint.

Queen Margaret also devoted herself to reforming some of the practices of the church in Scotland, and she wanted to create much stronger bonds with Rome. She promoted the Sabbath as a day of rest, which immediately endeared her to the people. She insisted on the Lenten fast, actively promoted Easter communion, and made Latin the official language of the Mass, replacing the different local dialects previously in use across the land.

Margaret was refined and cultured and brought many positive changes to the royal court. She freely offered advice on etiquette and ceremonial matters, and also promoted trade and commerce between Scotland and Europe.

It is difficult to estimate the extent of Margaret's influence. She did not restrict her activities to religious matters, and, distressed by the seemingly constant bloodshed between Scotland and England, she also worked hard at bringing about true reconciliation between the two great countries.

Margaret of Scotland will be laid to rest in Dunfermline Abbey beside her husband.

Women Kill Their Children

Mainz, Germany, May 27, 1096: On what will surely be remembered as a black day for Jews, Crusaders have massacred thousands of innocent people in a ruthless rampage. The horror has been compounded by the actions of the Jewish people of Mainz, particularly the women. Wives and mothers have vowed never to surrender their faith or their lives to the Christian attackers, and they have slit the throats of their sons and daughters, their husbands and brothers, and then themselves, rather than live under heartless

Queen Margaret of Scotland

Marauding Crusaders on their way to the Holy Land are slaughtering Jews as they go.

Christian domination. Witnesses have reported that babies are being suckled at their mothers' breasts and then being sacrificed for God.

This crusade, sanctioned by Pope Urban II, is being led by Count Emico of Flonheim, who claimed he would convert Jews to Christianity; however, his anti-Semitism and his cruel streak have meant that he prefers to slaughter rather than to save souls. In other areas, Crusaders have forced Jews to renounce their faith and agree to be baptized, but many are choosing a martyr's death instead.

Not all Christians harbor anti-Jewish feeling and many are viewing the current events with shock. The archbishop of Mainz is reported to have protected some hundreds of Jews in the cathedral, but in spite of his help thousands have lost their lives in the Crusaders' quest. It is difficult to obtain accurate figures, but the city's Jewish population is greatly depleted.

Matilda of Boulogne

Widows Can Marry Again

England, 1100: In one of his first acts as king, Henry has signed the Charter of Liberties, which grants a number of rights not previously available. Of particular interest to women is the provision that widows, either with or without children, are permitted to keep their dowries, and are free to marry again if they so choose. They are also allowed to be guardians of any land left by their husbands.

Another section of the new Charter of Liberties guarantees the independence of the Church.

Henry I's Charter of Liberties allows widows to remarry.

"The earth which sustains humanity must not be injured. It must not be destroyed!"

HILDEGARDE OF BINGEN (1098–1178), BENEDICTINE NUN AND VISIONARY

Henry became king earlier this year following the death of his brother, William II. The Charter of Liberties, which makes the king theoretically subject to the rule of law, is understood to be in response to demands from the nobility, who are seeking a more centralized approach to government.

New Texts Focus on Women's Health

Salerno, Italy, 1100: Three new texts, their subject the ailments and conditions suffered by women, have been released. They are believed to have been written by Trotula of Ruggiero, a professor of medicine at Salerno and a woman much admired for her innovative approaches to traditional problems. She is said to have written the works in order to teach male physicians about female anatomy.

Her major work is *Passionibus Mulierum Curandorum*, which covers menstruation, conception, pregnancy, and childbirth, including discussion of breech births and cesarean sections. She advocates the use of herbal opiates to alleviate the pains of childbirth, a controversial notion among the medical fraternity. In this work, Trotula also describes the most effective ways of repairing the tears that many women experience during the process of childbirth.

Trotula has become an important figure in the educational community in Salerno, which has been accepting female students and teachers for some time. She is known both locally and abroad as a wise and sensitive healer, and her work on pre- and post-natal care is being taught in other institutions. Her students are instructed to put the comfort of their patients first—she recommends herbal baths and plenty of rest, arguing that this speeds the healing process.

Although the authorship of some of the material is in doubt, it is clear that the detailed discussion of women's health issues breaks new ground.

Last Judgment for Ava

Melk, Austria, February 1127: Ava of Melk, the poet often referred to as Frau Ava, has died, aged about 66. Not much is known about her life, beyond the facts that she lived as a recluse, and that she had two sons, Hartmann and Heinrich, who probably led monastic lives. She refers to herself as "the mother of two sons" in her last poem. But Ava will be remembered for her religious poetry, and because she was the first woman known to write in the German language.

Ava's five great poems all have spiritual subjects; her inspiration for her poetry appears to result from *lectio divina* (divine reading). The imagery she employs comes from both the scriptures and from German religious tradition. Her familiarity with the gospels and the liturgy has provided her with a wealth of material with which to embellish her verse.

Her first poem was *Johannes (John the Baptist)*, followed by *Leben Jesu (Life of Jesus)*, which praises the Savior's work in saving human souls. *The Seven Gifts of the Holy Spirit* lists wisdom, understanding, counsel, fortitude, knowledge, piety, and fear of God as essential characteristics for leading a good life. Ava's last two poems are *Antichrist* and *The Last Judgment*, which describe the end of the world, and the final judgment of the good and the evil.

time out

The Toltec queen Xochitl fell in battle in 1116 while leading an army of women. She is credited with discovering a fermentation process for the agave plant and producing the alcoholic beverage, pulque (tequila).

Matilda Loses Crown

England, November 1141: After months of imprisonment, Stephen again wears the

Matilda rejected Stephen's wife's pleas for his release.

Bernard of Clairvaux's visions inspired many to join the Crusades.

English crown. It has been a tumultuous few years—Matilda, the daughter and heir of the late King Henry, has a legitimate claim to be queen, and has been trying to remove Stephen from the throne for some years.

Before Henry died in 1135, he had secured Matilda's right to the succession when the barons pledged allegiance to her. However, when the time arrived, Stephen of Blois, Henry's nephew, seized the throne for himself, thus sparking the civil war between the cousins. Matilda, who has been married twice—first to Henry V, the Holy Roman Emperor, and next to Geoffrey of Anjou—based herself and her forces at the castle of her half-brother, Robert of Gloucester, and has the support of a large group of barons.

In February this year, Matilda's forces captured Stephen at the Battle of Lincoln and had him incarcerated. Having finally gained the upper hand, Matilda swept into London and took control of the country. However, she had not reckoned with the Londoners, disenchanted with

her arrogance, who refused to crown her as their queen.

Capitalizing on this setback, Matilda of Boulogne, Stephen's wife, gathered together a large contingent to oust Matilda from her base in Winchester. Matilda managed to escape, but while leading the rearguard, Robert was taken prisoner. This month, Matilda was forced to exchange Stephen for Robert, and now Stephen has returned triumphant to the throne of England.

The Visions of Hildegarde

Bingen, Germany, c. 1151: Abbess Hildegarde, the Benedictine nun, visionary, theologian, and composer, has completed her monumental work *Scivias (Know the Way)*, which she began in 1142.

Scivias is a detailed account of some 26 visions that Hildegarde has experienced, some of which are said to explain the meaning of certain religious texts. Hildegarde, who has been receiving divine visions since childhood, was anxious to have official sanction from the Church to write her work. Some of her writings were submitted to church officials in Mainz and after careful scrutiny, they were found to be valid, so permission to continue writing down accounts of her visions was granted.

Since then, Hildegarde of Bingen has been attracting a wide audience of people keen to hear her wise words and her guiding messages. So respected is she that even bishops and kings are said to seek her advice on both spiritual and worldly matters. She is sometimes called the "Sybil of the Rhine."

Hildegarde's other great passion is music. She has composed many hymns

and plays, often in plainchant, which utilizes just a single line of vocal melody.

Hildegarde, who was born in 1098, entered the convent at the age of 15 and became superior of the abbey at Disibodenberg upon the death of her mentor and teacher, Jutta the anchorite. In about 1147, she and a group of her nuns left for Rupertsberg near Bingen to found a new convent, where Hildegarde continued to write down her visions and tend to her many duties as abbess.

Scivias contains prophetic visions and cautions about sinful living. The work is divided into three main parts, the first book describing six of her visions, the second describing seven visions, and the third book explaining 13 visions. It is not an easy work to read, but scholars and theologians will find it an invaluable addition to the literature.

Hildegarde of Binger

Hildegarde's writing does not interfere with her duties as abbess.

Sri Lanka, c. 1156: Sugala Devi is captured when her army of rebellion is defeated by King Parakramabahu.
Constantinople, Byzantium, 1161: Manuel I Comnenus marries Maria of Antioch.
Schonau, Germany, c. 1161: Benedictine nun Elisabeth of Schonau records her visions with the help of her brother, who makes them widely known.
Nogent-sur-Seine, France, May, 1164: Héloise, abbess, and former lover of Peter Abelard, dies, aged about 62.

Rouen, France, September 10, 1169: Princess Matilda, one-time ruler of England, dies, aged about 68.
Canterbury, England, December 29, 1170: Archbishop Thomas Becket is murdered in Canterbury Cathedral.
England, c. 1170: French poet Marie de France writes rhyming fables and plays for the royal court.
Khandahar, Afghanistan, 1173: Mohammad Ghori becomes the Sultan of Afghanistan and plans the conquest of India.

Barking, England, c. 1176: Clemence of Barking writes *Vie de Sainte Catherine*, adapting an earlier Latin biography of Catherine of Alexandria, in Anglo-Norman verse.
Bingen, Germany, 1179: Hildegarde of Bingen, visionary, writer, and composer, dies, aged about 81.
Acre, Middle East, c. 1184: Agnes of Courtenay, adviser to Baldwin IV of Jerusalem and Queen Sibylla of Jerusalem, dies, aged about 50.
Hattin, Middle East, July 1187: The Battle of Hattin is a resounding victory for Saladin's forces.

Japan, 1188: Shikishi Naishinno, imperial princess, priestess, and poet, has some of her work published in *Senzaishu*.
Europe, May 1189: The Third Crusade begins.
London, England, July 1189: Eleanor of Aquitaine becomes regent for her son, Richard, while he fights in the Third Crusade.
Hohenbourg, Alsace, c. 1190: Abbess Herrad von Landsberg completes the major part of the *Hortus Deliciarum (Garden of Delights)*.

Worms, Germany, 1196: Eleazar of Worms writes an elegy describing the virtues of his wife, who was murdered in her home along with her daughters.
Meaux, France, March 1198: Marie of Champagne, proponent of courtly love, dies, aged about 53.
India, 1100s: Akka Mahadevi, Bhakti poet, dies, aged about 20.
Iraq, 1100s: Safiyya al-Baghdadiyya, poet, writes of the relationships between men and women.

Eleanor of Aquitaine

Rebellious Princess Defeated

Sri Lanka, c. 1156: Rebel princess Sugala Devi has been captured by the forces of King Parakramabahu and escorted out of Rahuna. The king, who has reigned since 1153, has brought a large measure of economic prosperity to the country, and he has long been insisting that all the regions of Lanka accord him sole leadership. But Sugala, mother of Manahbarana, has consistently refused to accept the king's over-riding authority.

In addition, since the death of her son, she has held possession of some sacred relics, among them the Tooth Relic of the Buddha, and Parakramabahu wanted that relic in the capital, Polunnaruwa.

Rahuna's defiant princess gathered together a force of rebel soldiers, and led her army in a long-running battle against the most powerful man in the country. Unfortunately she was no match for the royal forces. Many of her men have been executed, but Sugala Devi herself has been spared. Some reports suggest she has been taken to the king's palace, others say she has been sent to Pulattinagara.

Whether her actions are considered heroic or simply foolhardy, it is certain that Princess Sugala Devi's feisty rebellion will become an important story in Sri Lankan history.

> *"RICHES AND POWER ARE BUT GIFTS OF BLIND FATE, WHEREAS GOODNESS IS THE RESULT OF ONE'S OWN MERITS."*
>
> HÉLOISE (1101–1162)
> FRENCH ABBESS
> AND SCHOLAR

Reclining Buddha from the palace of King Parakramabahu in Sri Lanka.

Death of a Legend

Nogent-sur-Seine, France, May 1164: Héloise, abbess of the Oratory of the Paraclete, has died, aged around 62. A nun since the age of about 18, Héloise's intellect quickly led to her appointment as a prioress, responsible for the education of the nuns. In about 1129, she moved to the Paraclete and soon became abbess. Her erudition and leadership skills were highly regarded in France, and she was instrumental in establishing a number of other priories.

Héloise is also known for her controversial relationship with one of the greatest philosophers of our times, Peter Abelard, whom she met while still a girl of 17. Her guardian and uncle, Canon Fulbert, had arranged for his niece to have the best possible education, and word of her intelligence soon reached Abelard's ears. He became her private tutor, and soon after, her lover. When Héloise discovered she was pregnant, Abelard, some 20 years her senior, asked for her hand in marriage. But Héloise rejected the idea, pointing out that because married men are not permitted to be teachers, she did not wish to deprive others of his vast knowledge. However, to protect her good name, she did marry Abelard in secret, following the birth of their son. After this, Héloise immediately went into a convent.

Unfortunately, Fulbert found out about the marriage and became so enraged that he arranged for Abelard to be castrated, which led to Abelard entering monastic life. Abelard died in 1142, aged about 63, and is buried at the Paraclete.

What interests scholars and students is the correspondence between Héloise and Abelard, exchanged while both served God in their respective religious houses. In their letters, they discuss a range of philosophical and theological issues. It would seem that these two brilliant thinkers had a true marriage of minds—and a tragic love affair. Héloise is also to be laid to rest at the Paraclete.

King Baldwin's Mother Dies

Acre, Middle East, c. 1184: Agnes of Courtenay, the mother of King Baldwin IV of Jerusalem and Sibylla of Jerusalem, has died, aged about 50. Since Baldwin IV took the throne in 1174 at the age of 13, Agnes has acted as one of his closest and most trusted advisers.

Daughter of Joscelin II of Edessa, Agnes was born about 1136. She married Amalric, count of Jaffa and Ascalon, and heir to King Baldwin III, in 1157. Agnes's fortunes changed, however, when Baldwin III died in 1162 and the high court of Jerusalem named Amalric as king, on condition that he have his marriage to Agnes annulled on the grounds that they were distantly related. The court, however, recognized the succession rights of her children. In 1170, Agnes married Reginald of Sidon.

Maria of Antioch and Manuel I Comnenus.

When Amalric died in 1174 and Baldwin IV came to power, Agnes of Courtenay returned to court to work for her son, who soon came to trust her judgment. It is said that Agnes advised her son to marry his widowed sister off to Guy de Lusignan, who was briefly regent last year. Sadly, the intelligent Baldwin suffers from leprosy and is not expected to live much longer. Because he has no male heirs, the king has been trying to select a successor, his five-year-old nephew being one of the candidates.

Agnes had been in poor health recently and she died peacefully at her home.

Eleanor Leads Kingdom for Richard

London, England, July 1189: With the death of Henry II, his son Richard has ascended the throne, but as Richard is eager to set off for the Third Crusade, responsibility for the kingdom has been placed in the hands of his mother, Eleanor of Aquitaine. Eleanor is intelligent, powerful, and capable, and will be certain to look after Richard's interests in his absence.

Eleanor is no stranger to power. She inherited Aquitaine and Poitiers when her father died in 1137, and she married her first husband, Louis VII of France, when she was 15. The marriage produced two daughters. Inspired by the writings of Bernard of Clairvaux, she went with Louis on the Second Crusade, taking a group of women with her. But her marriage to Louis, already shaky, did not last and it was dissolved in 1152.

A few months later, Eleanor married Henry Plantagenet, count of Anjou, who in 1154 inherited the throne of England and became Henry II. She had gone from being queen of France to being queen of England. Eleanor bore Henry five sons

Eleanor of Aquitaine and her daughter-in-law Isabelle are led into captivity after rebelling against Henry II.

Héloise

and three daughters. That marriage was also unhappy—Henry is known to have been regularly unfaithful.

Eleanor returned to Aquitaine in 1168 to attend to her interests there, among them music and literature, interests she inherited from her grandfather William IX of Aquitaine, who was well known as a troubadour and soldier.

By 1172, Eleanor was back in England, and a year later she devised a plan to rid herself of her husband, even pitting his sons, Henry, Richard, Geoffrey, and John against him. When they fled to France to avoid retribution, Eleanor attempted to follow them, but was imprisoned by Henry for some 15 years. She was only released recently.

Because her oldest son Henry is dead, Richard is the new king, and has ordered

Herrad's "Garden of Delights"

Hohenbourg, Alsace, c. 1190: Herrad von Landsberg, abbess of the convent at St Odile, has finally completed her *Hortus Deliciarum (Garden of Delights)*, a massive illustrated encyclopedia she has been working on since about 1165. Its scope is impressive—it covers biblical and theological material, as well as all the known sciences. It describes the history of the world from its creation and explains the meaning of the scriptures. Herrad is a champion of culture and education, and she wants the book to be used primarily as a teaching text for nuns.

Written in Latin, *Hortus Deliciarum* also includes occasional German explanations of words and phrases to aid in comprehension. The work contains about 340 beautifully presented illustrations, some symbolic of various philosophical concepts, some historical depictions, some representations of biblical stories, all of which complement the text. There is a self-portrait of the abbess and a portrayal of the sisters at the convent. The manuscript also contains a number of religious songs and poems complete with musical notation.

Herrad, who was born at Landsberg in Alsace around 1130, entered the convent while still in her teens, and was made abbess in 1167. Well educated and with finely honed artistic skills, Herrad brings a wealth

that while he is away at the Crusades his mother's word should be taken as law.

of knowledge to this amazing compendium. She is a respected teacher and illuminator, and *Hortus Deliciarum* will serve students well for years to come.

Patron of Poets and Courtly Love Is Dead

Meaux, France, March 1198: Marie of Champagne, who spent much of her life promoting ideals of love and chivalry, has died, aged 53. She was the daughter of Louis VII of France and his first wife, Eleanor of Aquitaine.

Marie was married to Henry I of Champagne in 1164, and upon his death in 1181 she assumed the role of regent for her son, Henry II.

However, it is as a supporter and sponsor of literature that Marie will be best remembered. She encouraged such gifted writers as Chrétien de Troyes, as well as Andreas Capellanus, who wrote *De amore (On Love)*, which described the ideals of courtly love. The admirable notion of courtly love places woman at the very core of morality and as such, it is an inspiration for noblemen both in battle and in their personal lives.

A page from the *Hortus Deliciarum* by Herrad von Landsberg.

Marie of Champagne supported the ideal of courtly love.

Death of a Matriarch

Eleanor of Aquitaine

Fontrevault, France, April 1, 1204: One of the most influential women of her time, Eleanor of Aquitaine has died, at the age of about 82, at the Abbey of Fontrevault in Aquitaine. She outlived her two husbands and most of her children.

Born in 1122, Eleanor inherited the vast estates of Aquitaine and Poitiers at the age of 15. The same year, she married Louis VII, becoming Queen of France. During their marriage, they had two daughters, and Eleanor accompanied her husband on the Crusades. The marriage was annulled in 1152, and Aquitaine's estates were returned to her control.

She soon married Henry d'Anjou, 10 years her junior, and in 1154, he was crowned Henry II of England. Of her eight children with Henry, two were kings—Richard the "Lionheart," and John. Friction between Eleanor and her husband Henry culminated in her imprisonment in 1173 for inciting her sons against their father. After some

> *"[POVERTY]
> HAS MADE
> YOU POOR IN
> THINGS BUT
> EXALTED YOU
> IN VIRTUE."*
>
> CLARE OF ASSISI
> (c. 1193–1253),
> TO HER NUNS

15 years in prison, and following Henry's death, Eleanor took charge of England while Richard went on the Crusades. In 1192, when Richard was held to ransom by the Holy Roman Emperor, Henry IV, Eleanor raised the money for his release, a task that took almost two years. And, although she prevented John from taking the throne while Richard was alive, she supported him during his own reign.

Eleanor was a great patron of music and the arts, and her court was widely renowned for its erudition. Along with her first-born daughter, Marie of France, she promoted the concept of courtly love. An extremely capable politician, Eleanor carried this skill with her into old age, often arranging marriages and other alliances for the benefit of England. Her children and grandchildren were scattered over much of Europe. Several daughters made prestigious matches: Joan to William II of Sicily; Eleanor to Alfonso VIII of Castile; and Matilda to Henry of Saxony. Her granddaughter, Blanche, married the King of France.

Eleanor of Aquitaine will be buried near Henry II and their son Richard at the Abbey of Fontrevault.

Isabella of Angoulême married King John of England in 1200, when she was 12 years old.

Eleanor and Louis were blessed by Pope Eugene before setting off on the Second Crusade.

Marriage by Treaty

Norham, England, 1209: Peace was made between Scotland and England when the Treaty of Norham was signed this year by William the Lion of Scotland and England's King John.

Relations between the two monarchs have been strained since John took the English throne in 1199, and refused, as had his predecessors, to cede Northumbria to Scotland. At the time, William arranged an attack on the English forces, but at the last minute he decided to cancel his invasion plans.

A shaky peace has largely been in place since then, but tensions between the kings have been mounting steadily. Earlier this year, John gathered an army together and marched to Norham, near Berwick-on-Tweed in the north of England, where he demanded that William the Lion pay him £10,000 in order to stop a possible war.

He also demanded that William hand over his daughters, Margaret and Isabella, so that John's trusted advisers can arrange politically advantageous marriages for them. Of course, the political advantage is all for John, and many are commenting that this is a brilliant move on John's part, depriving William, as it does, of the right to marry his two daughters for his own political and strategic benefit. King John is expected to marry Margaret and Isabella to favored English nobles.

Belgium, 1200: The Beguine movement grows in numbers as more women join these autonomous, self-supporting religious communities on a permanent or temporary basis, and devote themselves to prayer and good works.

Middle East, 1202–04: The Fourth Crusade is undertaken.

Fontrevault, France, April 1, 1204: Eleanor of Aquitaine, a powerful and influential political figure, dies, aged about 82.

Japan, 1205: *Shinkokinshu*, an anthology of some 2,000 poems, is compiled. It includes about 50 poems by Shikishi Naishinno, who died four years earlier.

Basiani, Georgia, May 1204: Queen Tamara leads the Georgian forces to victory over invading Turkmen troops at the Battle of Basiani.

Japan, 1205: Hojo Masako, widow of the first Minamoto shogun, acts to protect the rights of her 11-year-old son by deposing her father as regent, in a complicated battle for political influence.

Delhi, India, 1206: Qutb-ud-din Aybak founds the Sultanate of Delhi, establishing Islamic rule across northern India.

Karakorum, Mongolia, 1206: Temüjin takes the title Genghis Khan and becomes the supreme ruler of all the Mongol tribes.

Norham, England, 1209: The Treaty of Norham brings peace between England and Scotland.

England, c. 1210: Daniel of Beccles writes *The Book of the Civilised Man*, a book of manners for men. Despite his poor opinion of women, he upholds the value of marriage.

Sri Lanka, 1211: Queen Lilavati begins her third period as ruler, having been deposed twice before.

Assisi, Italy, 1212: Clare of Assisi is inspired by Francis of Assisi to establish the Poor Clares.

Spain, July 16, 1212: The Christians' victory at the battle of Las Navas de Tolosa marks the beginning of the end of the Almohad grip on Spain.

Georgia, January 1213: Queen Tamara of Georgia dies, aged about 53. She is remembered as a great ruler who extended her country's territory widely.

France, July 27, 1214: Holy Roman Emperor Otto IV is defeated at Bouvines and Philip II of France emerges victorious.

Runnymede, England, June 15, 1215: King John signs the Magna Carta which limits the power of the King. Among its clauses are ones that outline the rights of widows and underage heirs.

Third Time Lucky for Lilavati?

Sri Lanka, 1211: Queen Lilavati, the consort of King Parakramabahu, who reigned for 33 years until his death in 1186, is back on the throne for the third time. Lilavati was reinstated by General Parakrama who deposed the usurper, Lokissara. The last decade in Sri Lanka has been very volatile, and the country has seen a succession of leaders since Lilavati's first reign from 1197 until 1200, generally regarded as a period of stability. But Lilavati was deposed by Sahassamalla, who was followed by three other rulers, although she took the throne again in 1209. In 1210, Lokissara, from southern India, defeated Lankan forces at Polonnaruwa and dethroned the Queen for the second time.

Some are saying that this is the last chance for the Sinhalese people of Sri Lanka to assert their dominance. Already the Queen is being advised to be wary of Parakrama Pandya, who is reported to aspire to the kingship.

A Female Franciscan Order

Assisi, Italy, 1212: At the convent of San Damiano, Clare of Assisi has, with the assistance of her friend and mentor, Francis of Assisi, founded a new order of religious women. Called the Order of Poor Ladies, Clare and her sisters in God have vowed to live simply and in poverty, relying entirely on charity, trusting that God will provide for them.

Clare, who was born on July 16, 1194, is the daughter of the Count of Sasso-Rosso, and many expected her to marry well. But two years ago, Clare heard the preaching of Francis, and was moved to follow his example. Always a devout and spiritual girl, the catalyst for her denial of earthly pleasures happened on Palm Sunday this year, when the bishop himself placed a palm into Clare's hands. Interpreting this as a sign, Clare secretly left her home and her comfortable life and went to see Francis. She cut her hair, donned a coarse tunic and promised to live her life according to the gospels.

Francis took Clare and her two companions to the Benedictine convent, where they were soon joined by Clare's sister, Agnes. They are expected to be based at San Damiano. Clare's humble manner and her reliance on the goodwill of others have prompted the local people to refer to members of the new order as the Poor Clares.

> ### time out
> When Christina the Astonishing died in 1224 in Belgium some regarded her as a saint, others as a madwoman. She is reported to have rolled in fire without suffering harm, and claimed to smell sin on people.

Georgia loses Tamara

Georgia, January 1213: The "King of Kings and Queen of Queens," Queen Tamara, has died, aged about 53. Tamara will be remembered as one of Georgia's greatest rulers, presiding over a period of territorial supremacy. During her reign, she brought neighboring Seljuk lands under her control, and Georgian territory now stretches from Azerbaijan to the northern Caucasus.

Born in 1156, Tamara was the daughter of King George III, who in 1178 designated her his heir. This turned out to be an inspired choice. Tamara displayed her political talents early in her reign, when, employing her negotiation skills, she quelled internal unrest. In 1191, her first husband, Yuri Bobolybski, from whom she was divorced in 1187, attempted a coup against her and her second husband, David Soslani, only to be thwarted. Tamara's reign was marked by battles against Georgia's Muslim neighbors. In 1204, at the famous battle of Basiani, Tamara led the army herself, defeating Turkmen forces, and rejected Islam as a way of life for her people.

A devout Christian, she built a number of churches and monasteries throughout the country, and at other revered Christian places, such as in the Holy Land. Her death brings to an end a genuine golden age for Georgia. Her son, George IV, is expected to take the throne.

Clare of Assisi

Clare of Assisi has established the Second Order of Franciscans, the Poor Clares.

Newark, England, October 9, 1216: King John dies, aged about 49. He is succeeded by his son, Henry III.
Middle East, 1217-21: The Fifth Crusade is undertaken.
Mantes, France, July 14, 1223: King Philip II dies, aged 67. He is succeeded by his son, Louis VIII.
Kamakura, Japan, August 16, 1225: Hojo Masako, powerful political figure, dies, aged about 69.
France, November 8, 1226: The death of Louis VIII makes his wife, Blanche of Castile, co-regent of France.

Central Asia, August 18, 1227: After building an extensive empire, warrior and leader Genghis Khan dies, leaving control of his vast realm to his son, Ogedei.
Middle East, 1228-29: In response to Jerusalem falling into the hands of the Muslims once more in 1224, the Sixth Crusade is undertaken.
L'Epau, France, December 23, 1230: Berengaria of Navarre, widow of King Richard of England, dies, aged about 67. She is the only queen of England not to visit the country during her reign.

Perugia, Italy, May 27, 1235: Elizabeth of Hungary, known for her religious devotion and charitable works, is canonized by Pope Gregory IX. Legend has it that as she was distributing bread to the poor, the bread was transformed into roses.
Mali, West Africa, 1235: Sundiata Keita emerges victorious from the Battle of Kirina, and establishes the Mali Empire.

Delhi, India, 1236: Razia is proclaimed Sultana of Delhi, taking up the throne again in response to public demand.
Russia, 1237: The Mongol forces, under the leadership of Batu Khan, invade Russia.
Liegnitz, Poland, April 5, 1241: The Mongol army overcomes the combined forces of the Polish army and the Teutonic knights.

Mongolia, 1241: After the death of Mongol leader Ogedei Khan, his wife, Toregene, becomes ruler, as regent.
Venice, Italy, 1242: Grand Doge Giacomo Tiepolo regulates the financial status of wives with reference to dowries and rights of widows in *Il Statuto Veneto*.

Berengaria of Navarre

Widows Free to Marry–or Not!

Runnymede, England, June 15, 1215: King John has today signed the Magna Carta, a new legal code that recognizes certain rights and freedoms for the people. The barons have long been unhappy with the King's arbitrary actions regarding the raising of revenue, and with what they see as a misuse of royal power. Knowing how much he relies on their support, especially for his military campaigns, they banded together to pressure John into agreeing to radical changes, including allowing the autonomy of the Church.

Of particular interest to women is the rather radical change of attitude toward widows. Until now, widows have been regarded as the King's "property"—he could confiscate their lands and he could compel them to remarry for his own political or monetary gain.

The new law clearly states that, "At her husband's death, a widow may have her marriage portion and inheritance at once and without trouble." It also states that, "No widow shall be compelled to marry, so long as she wishes to remain without a husband." Although there are some conditions attached to this, it is seen as a breakthrough for widows, who, until now, have been treated as chattels of the King.

In addition, underage heirs are now permitted to keep their inheritance without being fined. A guardian is only permitted to spend amounts that are "reasonable" for the land's upkeep until the heir comes of age.

> "WOMAN IS THE CONFUSION OF MAN."
>
> VINCENT OF BEAUVAIS, (c. 1190–1264), FRENCH ENCYCLOPEDIST

Nun-Shogun Dies

Kamakura, Japan, August 16, 1225: Powerful political figure Hojo Masako has died, aged about 69. She was born in 1156 or 1157. In 1179, Masako married Minamoto no Yoritomo, who became Japan's first shogun. Although at that time Yoritomo had been blacklisted by the influential Taira clan, Masako convinced her father that she should be permitted to marry him. Theirs was a successful partnership, and Yoritomo soon took over as ruler of Japan, with his capital in Kamakura. Masako was his most trusted adviser and many credit her as the true power behind the throne.

Following his death in 1199, her oldest son, Yoriie, became shogun, and she became a Buddhist nun, although she never entered a nunnery and always maintained her interest in politics. In 1204, after Yoriie's assassination, Masako's second son, Sanetomo, was named shogun. As has been the case in Japan for some time, the real power is in the hands of the regent, in this case, Masako's father, Hojo Tokimasa.

Tokimasa was supposedly involved in an attempt on Sanetomo's life in 1205, and Masako is known to have worked behind the scenes to have her father deposed and her brother, Yoshitoki, installed as the regent. Masako continued to wield considerable political influence, even after Sanetomo's death in 1219, when the shogunate was threatened by other forces seeking political dominance. Her death brings to an end the era of the "nun–shogun."

Hojo Masako's husband, Minamoto no Yoritomo became shogun of Japan.

Blanche is Regent of France

France, November 8, 1226: France has a new King, Louis IX, who has today succeeded to the throne following the death of his father, Louis VIII. But as the 11-year-old monarch is underage, his mother,

Blanche of Castile and her son, Louis IX, are popular with the Parisians.

Blanche of Castile, will be acting as regent until he reaches adulthood. She is also recognized as the legal guardian for her other children.

Louis VIII recognized his wife's considerable talents, and named her their son's regent well before his death. Blanche, daughter of King Alfonso VIII of Castile, and granddaughter of England's King Henry II, is a capable administrator. Some at court have been heard to have reservations about the fact that she is a woman and that she was born in Spain, but many others are confident that she will guide France through the regency period with skill and political confidence.

Blanche clearly understands the importance of her role, and she is moving for a speedy coronation for her young son, probably later this month. This will consolidate her position at court and prevent others from taking away Louis IX's right to reign. There are rumors that a group of nobles is already planning to challenge the new King, so her actions are timely. Blanche not only has her son's best interests at heart, but also the interests of the whole nation. She promises to be a strong and effective regent.

Death of Berengaria

L'Epau, France, December 23, 1230: The only Queen of England never to have set foot on English soil has died, aged about 67. Berengaria of Navarre, the widow of King Richard I, the "Lionheart," has been living quietly in France for many years. She died at the monastery in L'Epau.

The tomb of Berengaria lies in the Cistercian Abbey she founded at L'Epau.

Richard's mother, Eleanor of Aquitaine, chose Berengaria, the daughter of Sancho VI of Navarre, to be Richard's wife. She knew that Berengaria's generous dowry would help Richard to continue his campaigns of the Third Crusade. In 1191, Eleanor and her daughter, Joan, accompanied Berengaria to the Holy Land where Richard was fighting in the Crusades. Their ship was wrecked off Cyprus and the women were captured by the island's ruler, Isaac Comnenus. Richard quickly came to their rescue, taking control of Cyprus, and soon after, in May 1191, Richard and Berengaria were married on the island. They spent some time together in Palestine before Richard, on his return journey to Europe, was captured and imprisoned. Berengaria then went to France, where she helped to raise money for her husband's release. Although he was freed in 1194, when his mother, Eleanor, paid the ransom, Berengaria did not join her husband in England. The couple had no children, and rumors circulated that the late King may have had homosexual tendencies.

After Richard's death in 1199, Berengaria's English properties were taken by the new king, John, and Berengaria had little to live on. As much as she requested some kind of pension from the English monarch, her pleas were in vain. It was not until John's son, Henry III, took the throne, that some lands were returned to her. In her final years, Berengaria is said to have found solace in religion.

A New Saint in the Firmament

Perugia, Italy, May 27, 1235: In a moving formal ceremony today, Pope Gregory IX has canonized Elizabeth of Hungary, who died in 1231 at the young age of 24. The

devout Elizabeth was the daughter of King Andrew III of Hungary. From an early age she displayed great compassion for the sick and needy, even going so far as to fund the building of a hospital where she personally nursed ill and elderly people. She also went out every day, delivering bread and water to the destitute and hungry.

Elizabeth married Louis of Thuringia in 1221, when she was 14 and he was 21. By all accounts, it was a happy marriage, Louis firmly supporting her charitable works. She was devoted to her work in the community, and even gave away costly gowns and shoes. It is said that once when Louis asked to see what food his wife was taking to the poor, she removed the cover to find that the bread had been changed into roses, a sign, many believe, of God's pleasure in her work. When Louis died of a fever in 1227, Elizabeth sold all her possessions, leaving enough, however, to support her three small children, and distributed the money to those in need. She was widely considered to be gentle, caring, and selfless.

Known to have admired the teachings of Francis of Assisi, Elizabeth also founded a Franciscan monastery in Eisenach and helped establish a hospital at Marburg, where again, she personally tended to the needs of the sick. Her confessor was the strict Conrad of Marburg, who promoted self-mortification and asceticism.

After her untimely death, miracles of healing were said to have occurred at her grave, and steps were taken to have Elizabeth canonized. The pope ordered a close examination of these miracles and agreed that they had

indeed occurred, and from today, she will be known as St Elizabeth of Hungary.

Statute Guarantees Women's Financial Rights

Venice, Italy, 1242: The Grand Doge of Venice, Giacomo Tiepolo, has enacted a new law, *Il Statuto Veneto*, which formalizes and regulates the financial status of wives and widows, especially in regard to dowries.

The statute specifies that men must account to their wives for how they use their dowries, and that the capital must remain in the control of the wife, for her to spend as she wishes. Widows are also permitted to keep their dowries. Unfaithful wives, on the other hand, have no legal recourse and must surrender any dowries to the wronged husband.

Children, whether they are under age or have reached their majority, are also provided for in the statute. An interesting clause in the new law is that in the event of a married couple entering the religious orders, their property is to be divided equally between them.

Elizabeth of Hungary

Elizabeth of Hungary has been canonized by Pope Gregory IX.

Blanche of Castile

End of the Blanche Era

Paris, France, November 26, 1252: A truly remarkable woman has died today in Paris. Blanche of Castile, mother of Louis IX, was 64 years old. She had impressive antecedents: she was the daughter of Alfonso VIII of Castile and Eleanor Plantagenet of England, granddaughter of England's Henry II, and the niece of England's John I. When Blanche reached the age of 12, her grandmother, Eleanor of Aquitaine, saw special qualities in the girl, and arranged for her to be married to King Louis VIII of France.

Blanche will be remembered for acting as the regent for her son from 1226 to 1234, during which time she broke up a rebellious confederation of barons and repelled attacks from England, even going so far as to lead troops into battle herself. Although born in Spain, she was committed to France, and it is a hallmark of her reign that she worked for French unification almost since the time she arrived here as a young bride.

A strong and independent-minded woman, Blanche supported her husband in his unsuccessful 1216 bid to take the English throne. She was later involved with various battles against Henry III of England, and many acknowledge that she was not only courageous, but had a keen intellect and a great deal of political nous.

Blanche had another stint at the regency when Louis IX went to the Crusades in 1247, and it is clear that she stayed the King's most trusted adviser until her death today.

Mother of Mongolian Empire Dies

China, 1252: Sorghaghtani Beki, possibly the most enlightened woman the Mongolian empire has ever seen, has died. It is because of her that the people are confident the empire will continue to grow. Almost single-handedly she has ensured that khans should be direct descendants of the great Genghis Khan, who was Sorghaghtani's father-in-law. She was married to Tolui, Genghis Khan's youngest son. She has now essentially guaranteed that the empire will be left in the hands of her four sons: Mongke, Kublai, Hulagu, and Ariq Boke.

By using her superior intellectual and administrative skills, coupled with sheer determination, Sorghaghtani managed to have her son Mongke elected khan just last year. Since the death in 1227

> "*YOUR LIFE MAY BE, EVEN WHEN YOUR TONGUE IS SILENT, A CLEAR MIRROR.*"
>
> ANGELA OF FOLIGNO (1248–1309), ITALIAN MYSTIC

Both Francis and Clare of Assisi devoted their lives to God's work.

time out

In 1296 Agnes de Hagemon fell into a tub of hot yeasty mush used for brewing beer and was scalded to death. The beer gained value from this macabre brewing method and was sold at a considerably higher price than usual.

of Genghis Khan, there has been some uncertainty as to the line of succession. Genghis was succeeded by his son Ogadei, who was succeeded in 1241 by his son Guyuk. After Guyuk's death in 1248, family politics came into play, as many did not care for Guyuk's wife acting as regent for her young sons. This is when Sorghaghtani's influence came into its own, and she convinced Mongol leaders to keep the succession within the family, something that Guyuk's widow was unable to guarantee.

Sorghaghtani has long groomed her sons for leadership. She made sure they were educated and could speak a number of languages, skills needed for effective rulership. She is said to be especially fond of her second son, Kublai, although Sorghaghtani taught all four sons diplomacy, good horsemanship, and how to handle weapons. Sorghaghtani herself was a trailblazer. She managed her agricultural lands efficiently, treating the peasants well, thus obtaining their loyalty. Although she was a Nestorian Christian, she promoted tolerance of Buddhism, Taoism, Confucianism, and Islam, knowing that the empire would one day contain all these religious groups. An astute political observer and player, it now seems probable that the line of Tolui will expand and empower the Mongol Empire.

Margaret's Regency Comes to an End

Denmark, 1264: Eric V, who has been king of Denmark since the death of his father in 1259, has now assumed sole rulership of the kingdom. For the last five years, his mother, Margaret of Sambiria, has been regent for him. A highly competent regent, Margaret worked hard to achieve the throne for her son. When Christopher I died, the law of agnatic succession

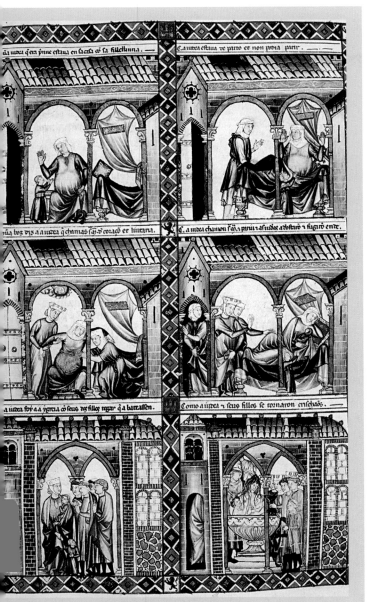

Scenes of private life–pregnancy, childbirth, and baptism.

Clare of Assisi

In 1262, she and Eric were imprisoned by a group of noblemen who wanted Abel on the throne. Albert, the Duke of Brunswick, helped to free them.

This contretemps prompted Margaret in 1262 to seek permission from Pope Urban IV to allow women to inherit the Danish throne. This would mean that in the event that Eric has no children, one of his two sisters would become queen. Although she is commended for her strength of character, and for her wise guidance during the regency period, it is now time for the young King to take the reins of government.

A Patroness for Silesia

Rome, Italy, March 26, 1267: Pope Clement IV has today canonized Hedwig of Andechs, Bavaria, and named her patroness of Silesia. Hedwig, who died in October 1243, was married to Henry of Silesia and together the couple performed many good deeds. They had six children, and then made a vow of chastity, which was, by all reports, strictly adhered to.

Wishing to spread German culture and language throughout Silesia, as well as give thanks to God, Hedwig and Henry established a number of monasteries over the years, among them the Cistercian convent at Trebnitz.

dictated that his brother, and former king, Abel of Denmark, should inherit the throne. Unfortunately, some ugly rumors circulated about Abel, among them that he arranged the death of his older brother Eric IV. Christopher's son Eric V was deemed to be the appropriate choice for new monarch. But Margaret's regency was marked by much political intrigue.

This is where Hedwig retired after Henry's death in 1238, having donated her fortune to the church. There she spent her days caring for the sick and engaging in other charitable works.

Divine Visions Revealed

Helfta, Saxony, Germany, c. 1270: The Cistercian nun and mystic, Mechtild of Magdeburg, has recently completed the seventh volume of her divine visions. Mechtild, who was born around 1210, began receiving visions from about the age of 12, and at 20 she became a Beguine, leading a life of prayer and devotion. Once under the spiritual guidance of the Dominicans, her visions intensified, and she was ordered to write an account of them. From 1250 until 1264, Mechtild worked diligently to record the visions she had received. That period, interrupted by occasional ill health and verbal attacks from skeptics, produced six volumes known as *Flowing Light of the Divinity*, and now a seventh volume has been added.

Mechtild writes with passion and clarity, and notably in German–rather than Latin. In fact, many consider that she is the first German woman to write about spiritual matters in her native language. Her depictions of Purgatory and Hell are vivid, Hell being described as having three levels: the lowest level contains fallen Christians, the middle level contains Jews, and the highest level contains unbelievers and pagans. She also reveals that Heaven sits on top of Purgatory and Hell, and that God imbues each of our souls with a little of his heavenly goodness.

Mechtild has only recently arrived at the convent at Helfta, having lived earlier at Magdeburg. She was encouraged to make the move because of the controversy generated by her writings. At Helfta she has an understanding and tolerant abbess to guide her.

Helfta, Saxony, Germany, c. 1285: Mechtild of Magdeburg dies, aged about 75. A Cistercian nun, she recorded her visions between 1250 and 1270.
Paris, France, 1285: Building work on Notre Dame is completed.
Cairo, Egypt, 1288: Ibn al-Nafis, renowned physician, dies, aged about 75. He was the first to document the workings of the pulmonary circulation of the body, gas exchange in the lungs, and the structure of the lungs.

Scotland, 1288: Though disputed as folklore, it is said that a law is passed, by order of Queen Margaret, allowing ladies to propose in a leap year, and that any man declining such a proposal could be fined.
Orkney Islands, September, 1290: Margaret, Maid of Norway and considered by many the rightful queen of Scotland, dies, aged 7.
Amesbury, England, June 26, 1291: Eleanor of Provence, queen consort of England's Henry III, dies, aged about 68.

Acre, Middle East, 1291: The Christian-held city of Acre falls to the Mamelukes, who had risen to power in Egypt in 1250.
England, 1291-94: King Edward I builds the "Eleanor Crosses," in memory of his wife Eleanor of Castile, who died in November 1290.
Poletains, France, 1294: Marguerite d'Oingt, prioress of the Carthusian sisters at Poletains, completes her *Speculum (Mirror)*, another work on meditations.

Florence, Italy, 1294: Beatrice Portinari, who died aged about 24, is immortalised by Dante Aligheri's first work, *La Vita Nuova (The New Life)*.
Kamakura, Japan, c. 1295: New rules restrict the right of women to inherit and own property.
Stirling Bridge, Scotland, September 11, 1297: William Wallace is victorious over English forces.
Monaco, 1297: The Grimaldi dynasty is established in Monaco.

Rome, Italy, 1298: Pope Boniface VIII issues a papal bull that enforces the strict enclosure of all nuns, regardless of the order. Prior to this, some nuns were active in the community.
India, c. 1298: Indian poet Janabai is born to a lower-caste Hindu family. Her poems focus on her devotion to the Hindu gods.
Turkey, c. 1299: Osman I establishes the Ottoman Empire.

Eleanor of Provence

Death of Bohemian Holy Woman

Prague, Bohemia, March 6, 1282: Agnes of Bohemia, known throughout the land as the woman who gave up marriage to a king for God, has died, aged about 77. Agnes was born around 1205, the daughter of King Ottocar of Bohemia and Constance of Hungary. She received her early education at the Cistercian monastery at Trebnitz and embraced God's word with a particular fervor. Her father betrothed her to Frederick II, Emperor of Germany and Holy Roman Emperor, but as the wedding day approached, Agnes felt certain that her destiny was not as a royal wife, but as a sister in God's service.

Frederick is reported to have been furious that the marriage was called off, but he quickly accepted and supported Agnes's decision, realizing that she had a higher calling. Soon after, Agnes began her good works. She arranged to have a Franciscan monastery, a Poor Clare convent (Saint Saviour), and a hospital built. She even organized for the Knights Hospitallers to run the hospital. During this time, she began a correspondence with Clare of Assisi, and when, in about 1236, Agnes decided to become a Poor Clare nun, Clare herself sent five sisters to Prague to help open the new cloister and settle Agnes into convent life.

Agnes led a life of piety, her good works a shining example to others. She tended to the poor and the sick. Pope Gregory IX appointed her abbess of the convent, although this was not a position she sought. She was also granted some divine visions, and is even said to have foretold the military victory of her brother Wenceslas against Austria.

Agnes inspired both men and women, and it is said that many other privileged women, wishing to emulate her, became Poor Clares, also devoting themselves to serving God and the community.

King's Mother Passes Away

Amesbury, England, June 26, 1291: Eleanor of Provence, queen consort of Henry III, died today, aged about 68. Daughter of Ramon Berenguer, Count of Provence, and Beatrice of Savoy, Eleanor came to England in January 1236 to marry Henry, and bore him five children, including the current king, Edward I.

She was an intelligent and forthright woman and was able to exert some influence on her husband. This, coupled with the fact that her attendants included quite a number of her French relatives, led to some disharmony in the kingdom, and in the 1260s, some of the barons, led by Simon de Montfort, staged a rebellion against Henry III.

Although the barons did object to Eleanor's authority with the King, their other major argument was against what they saw as the King's opposition to law reform. When the rebels assumed power in 1264, Eleanor went to France where she rallied English troops, hoping to lead them against de Montfort's forces. Unfortunately, her fleet was wrecked before it reached the English shores. Yet the rebellion was finally crushed in 1254, and Eleanor returned to England at last.

After Henry's death in 1272, many observers expected Eleanor to return to her homeland, but she remained in England, and helped to care for her grandchildren. She spent her final years in a convent at Amesbury, where she died peacefully today.

Twelve Crosses for Eleanor

England, 1294: This year King Edward I has completed the erection of 12 memorial crosses dedicated to his beloved wife Eleanor of Castile, who died of a fever in November 1290. When the Queen died in Harby, near Lincoln, the grieving King ordered that her remains be brought to Westminster Abbey in London. The solemn procession took almost two weeks, and there were 12 stops along the way. It is at each of these resting points that Edward ordered a cross to be built in Eleanor's honor. They are at Lincoln, Grantham, Stamford, Geddington, Northampton, Stony Stratford, Woburn, Dunstable, St Albans, Waltham, Cheapside, and Charing. Edward hopes that passers-by will stop at the crosses to pray for the soul of the dead Queen.

Eleanor, daughter of Ferdinand III of Castile, married Edward in 1254 when she was just 13 years old. Although, like most unions between royalty, it was a marriage of political convenience, they were devoted to one another. Not wishing to be apart from her husband, Eleanor even accompanied him on some of his military campaigns, including one to the Crusades. It was while they were in the Holy Land in 1272 that Henry III died, and Edward became king of England. The couple was separated in 1264–65 during the baronial rebellion against Henry III, when Eleanor was sent, for safety reasons, to France.

Edward and Eleanor had 16 children together; sadly, 10 died before their mother. Their son Edward is now heir to the throne, but the King is known to be concerned about the succession in the event of his son's death. It has been four years since Eleanor's death, and now royal watchers are wondering whether Edward will take another bride in order to ensure another male heir.

Whatever his marital intentions, the "Eleanor Crosses" are a very real testament to the love Edward had for his beloved wife of 36 years.

Mirror to the Soul

Poletains, France, 1294: Marguerite d'Oingt, prioress of the Carthusian sisters at Poletains, has finally completed her *Speculum (Mirror)*, another literary

> "FROM SUFFERING I HAVE LEARNED THIS: THAT WHOEVER IS SORE WOUNDED BY LOVE WILL NEVER BE MADE WHOLE UNLESS SHE EMBRACE THE VERY SAME LOVE WHICH WOUNDED HER."
>
> MECHTILD OF MAGDEBURG (1210–1285), GERMAN MYSTIC

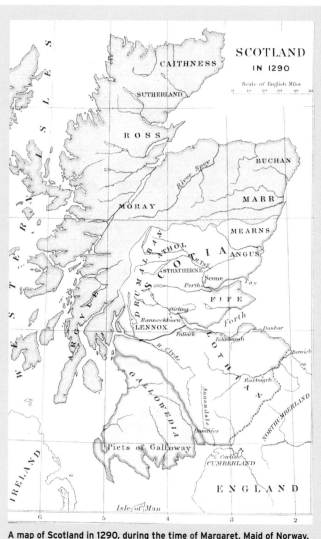

A map of Scotland in 1290, during the time of Margaret, Maid of Norway.

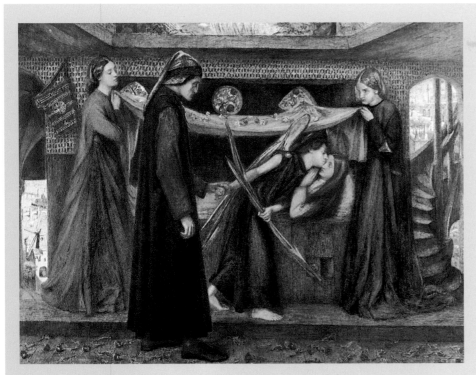

Dante's dream of the death of Beatrice Portinari, who is said to be the inspiration for his *La Vita Nuova*.

Eleanor of Castile

know that she aroused the talent of a promising wordsmith. The opening sonnet of *La Vita Nuova* tells the dream Dante had of her that inspired him to write this groundbreaking work.

Nuns Forced Indoors

Rome, Italy, 1298: In a surprise move, Pope Boniface VIII has issued a papal bull that enforces the strict enclosure of all nuns. The *Periculoso*, as the decree is called, categorically states that all nuns shall remain cloistered in their monasteries, regardless of their order or their rank in the convent hierarchy. Prior to this, nuns enjoyed the freedom to go into the community fulfilling their ministrations to the sick, needy, and impoverished. The *Periculoso* now forbids such activities. The one exception is when a sister has contracted an infectious illness: in this case, she can be removed in order not to spread disease.

Some commentators are saying that Pope Boniface feels threatened by the influence exerted by religious women, but the official line is that the decree was drawn up to ensure that nuns were kept safe from physical harm.

work with meditations as its subject. Marguerite has been a member of the Carthusian house for many years, becoming its prioress in about 1288. Carthusian sisters, like their male counterparts in the monasteries, live lives marked by austerity and devotion.

Some six years ago, Marguerite d'Oingt wrote her *Pagina Meditationum (Page of Meditations)*, the first of her works on the topic. Marguerite is a mystic and sees meditation as a crucial part of a person's intimate communion with God. She uses simple, direct, yet very poetic language, aiming to teach readers to get to the essence of how to meditate and thus achieve a holy state. The *Pagina Meditationum* was written in Latin, but the *Speculum* is composed in the local vernacular, Franco–Provencal. This is because Marguerite wants her words to be as accessible to as many people as possible. She has been working on the *Speculum* for a few years, and it promises to become her best known opus; already, many other men and women of religion are reading her message and disseminating it among the wider community.

Not a great deal is known about Marguerite's ancestry. Some say she was born into a wealthy family in Lyon, but as she has so wholeheartedly embraced the spiritual life, the truth about her origins is likely to remain a mystery.

Beatrice Gets a New Life

Florence, Italy, 1294: Young Italian poet Dante Alighieri has just published a work called *La Vita Nuova (The New Life)*. Already being acclaimed as a

literary tour de force, it is also notable for its immortalization of the beautiful Beatrice Portinari, who tragically died four years ago. Dante first met Beatrice when they were children and the poet was immediately entranced by her grace and beauty.

Written in both verse and prose, Dante follows many of the conventions of courtly love—where the lover acts only with respect and where a physical union between lovers is impossible. His moving descriptions of his platonic, yet genuine romantic love for Beatrice are bound to resonate with readers, more so considering that the work is written in Italian, rather than the more traditional Latin. He refers to Beatrice as his salvation, and it is clear that their reportedly "slight" acquaintance has had little bearing on his innermost feelings. He has elevated her to the status of creative force in his life and work.

Little is known of Beatrice herself, other than her marriage in 1287 to the Florentine banker Simon de Bardi. It is, however, enough to

Nuns at prayer, from a thirteenth-century French manuscript.

Margaret of Carinthia

Concubine to Nun: Story Published

Japan, 1307: Lady Nijo has published a fascinating account of her life, first at the Japanese imperial court and later as a Buddhist nun.

She started writing the *Towazugatari (Confessions of Lady Nijo)* three years ago, following the death of the retired emperor Go-Fakakusa. Structurally, the book is loosely modeled on the Heian classic, *The Tale of Genji*, in that it is part court journal and part travel journal, interspersed with stories throughout.

The first three books of the *Towazugatari* discuss Lady Nijo's time at court. She was given by her father to Go-Fukakusa as a concubine when she was 14. In 1272, at the age of about 15, she gave birth to a child, but he did not survive for long. What followed was a difficult time—Nijo's father died and there was deep political rivalry between Go-Fukakusa and his brother, Kameyama. Nijo was anxious to protect her position at court. Her book tells of her bringing other women to Go-Fukakusa's bed, and of her own affairs, one with the emperor's brother.

In 1283, Nijo's affairs and her alleged defiance of strict tradition resulted in her expulsion from court. Feeling a lack of purpose, she adopted the habit of a Buddhist nun and traveled around Japan on various pilgrimages. Her time as a nun is covered in the last two books of her autobiography, which describe her journeys and the many people she met along the way.

time out

In 1348 chivalry was born anew when King Edward III retrieved a garter dropped by one of the ladies in his court. The gesture is believed to have been the inordination of the British order of chivalry known as the Most Noble Order of the Garter.

> "… I SAY THAT YOU SHOULD NOT JUDGE SINNERS, BECAUSE YOU DO NOT KNOW THE JUDGMENTS OF GOD"
>
> ANGELA OF FOLIGNO (1248–1309), ITALIAN MYSTIC

The origin of the Most Noble Order of the Garter.

From Hedonism to Holiness

Foligno, Italy, January 4, 1309: The inspirational Angela of Foligno has died, aged about 60. The mystic nun will long be remembered for her amazing conversion, and for the vivid account of her visions, dictated to her confessor Father Arnold.

Angela's road to grace was not easy. She married at a young age and threw herself into life's pleasures, later saying that she lived a life of sin and dissolution. Sometime in 1285, when she was in her thirties, she had an epiphany, rejected her old lifestyle, and worked hard to understand the blessed mysteries. Inspired by the life and teachings of St Francis, and at the urging of Father Arnold, Angela joined the Third Order of St Francis. She also established a new branch of sisters, who, as well as adhering to the rules of the Third Order, also work among the community, helping the disadvantaged. When her family died, she embraced poverty, giving away all her possessions.

A woman working diligently at her loom.

Her personal account of her conversion and the visions that accompanied it, often referred to as *Memoriale*, is still read widely. In fact, her words carry an intensity that is unprecedented in mystical writings. In addition, over the years, Angela dictated letters to many people, instructing them in spiritual matters. There are hopes in the intellectual community that all her writings will be gathered together in the near future.

Salic Law Removes Jeanne's Right to Throne

France, January 1317: Since the death of Louis X in June last year, there has been much speculation about the succession. Louis has a daughter, Jeanne, the child of his first wife. His second wife, Clemence, was pregnant at the time of the King's

Salerno, Italy, 1300s: The famed Salerno medical school teaches a number of well-known female physicians, including Abella, Rebecca de Guarna, Mercuriade, and Margaritan.

Caltabellota, Sicily, 1302: The Peace Treaty of Caltabellota, brokered between the Angevins and the Aragonese, ends the 20-year-long War of the Sicilian Vespers.

England, 1305: Edward I standardizes the measurement of an acre.

Padua, Italy, c. 1305: Giovanni Pisano sculpts the *Madonna with Child* for the Arena Chapel.

Avignon, France, 1305: The pope establishes residency in Avignon, rather than the traditional papal seat of Rome. This is known as the Avignon Papacy, or the Babylonian Captivity.

Japan, 1307: Lady Nijo (Nakanoin Masatada no Musume) completes her autobiography, *Towazugatari* (*Confessions of Lady Nijo*).

Foligno, Italy, January 4, 1309: Angela of Foligno dies, aged 60.

France, June 1, 1310: Marguerite Porete is burned at the stake. Twenty-one theologians had declared her work *Mirouer des simples ames* heretical. Her refusal to obey the bishop's orders not to speak about her book leads to her death.

Poletains, France, 1310: Marguerite d'Oingt, prioress of the Carthusian sisters at Poletains, mystic, and writer, dies, aged about 70.

Mali, West Africa, 1312: Mansa Musa becomes King of the formidable Mali Empire.

Bannockburn, Scotland, June 23-24, 1314: The Scottish forces of King Robert the Bruce defeat the English.

Delhi, India, 1315: Advances in weaving and printing cotton make India the world's leading exporter of colorful cotton fabrics.

France, January, 1317: The Salic law, excluding women from succeeding to the throne, is invoked following the death of Louis X.

China, 1319: Painter, calligrapher, and poet Guan Daosheng dies, aged about 57. She often included a poem on her paintings.

Pamiers, France, July 1320: Beatrice de Planissoles, chatelaine of the Cathar town of Montaillou, appears before the Inquisition, accused of heresy.

Paris, France, 1322: The Faculty of Medicine at the University of Paris lays charges against Jacoba Felicie for practicing medicine without being qualified.

death, so determining who would be the next monarch of France and Navarre had to wait until the child was born. If a son, he would be the new King. Unfortunately, the infant boy, born last year, lived only a few days. This meant that the succession lay between Louis's young daughter and his brother, Philip, who has been acting as regent for the last six months.

In a decisive move, Philip has invoked Salic law and has loudly claimed the kingship for himself.

Salic law, which had its origins around the 490s, lays down a number of rules regarding inheritance, and it specifically excludes females, although a later amendment made an allowance for daughters to inherit where there were no sons. Despite the fact that Charlemagne revived the law

A woman swoons on hearing of her knight's death.

during his reign in the 700s, it gradually disappeared from the statute books.

Now, for the first time in memory, Salic law has been resurrected in order to ensure Philip's right to the throne. Although the law does not make any mention of royal succession, Philip has the support of many influential people at court. Also in his favor is the fact that at only five years old, Jeanne is clearly too young to rule in her own right.

Calligrapher-Artist at One with Nature

China, 1319: At the age of about 57, Guan Daoshang, the Chinese painter, calligrapher, and poet has died. Her painting style is characterized by elegant strokes, and her favorite subjects were bamboo groves, plum trees, and other scenes from nature. She sometimes incorporated her poetry into her paintings. Guan's *Bamboo Groves in Mist and Rain*, painted in 1308, is considered one of her best works.

Guan Daoshang, widely acknowledged as one of the great women artists, was the wife of renowned painter, Zhao Mengfu, whose works have been praised by Kublai Khan himself. Her son Zhao Yong is also a painter, and there is said to exist one art piece containing the work of all three family calligraphers.

Another Cathar Heretic

Pamiers, France, July, 1320: Beatrice de Planissoles, the chatelaine of Montaillou, is to appear before the Inquisition, which has been headed by Jacques Fournier, the bishop of Pamiers, for the past two years. She has been charged with heresy and blasphemy. Montaillou, in the south of France, has a large population of Cathars and the Church is eager to suppress further advances in Catharism.

On the charge of heresy, one witness, Guillaume Roussel, is expected to attest to Beatrice's doubts about the transubstantiation (the miracle whereby bread becomes the body of Christ), which suggests a Manichaean influence—Cathars combine Christianity with elements of Manichaeism, an ancient Persian religion—which is considered heretical. Cathars believe in spiritual, rather than physical, baptism, and they aim to purify themselves from the physical world.

Beatrice married Berenger de Roquefort in about 1294, and was married at one time to Otho Laglieze of Dalou,

but she also took a number of lovers. Among them were the heretic priest, Pierre Clergue, and the young priest, Barthélemy Amilhac, whose association with Beatrice has resulted in a charge of complicity in, and concealment of, heresy.

Interestingly, many people are saying that the popularity of Catharism—its followers refer to themselves as the "good people"—has been enhanced as a result of the exorbitant taxes that are levied on the people by the Church. Feeling ill-used by the Church's financial demands, many have embraced the alternative spiritual teachings offered by the Cathars, who are also known as Albigensians.

Beatrice has denied that she doubts the transubstantiation, and is expected to renounce her Cathar leanings. If she does this, she will probably be made to wear the yellow cross, the symbol of repentant heretics, for the rest of her life.

Marguerite d'Oingt

An Ottoman woman prostrates herself before the Sultan.

Kilkenny, Ireland, 1324: Alice Kyteler is tried by the Church for sorcery and witchcraft, and flees to England. One of her followers, Petronella de Meath, is burned at the stake.

Mexico, 1325: The city of Tenochtitlán is founded by the Aztecs as their capital.

Bologna, Italy, March 26, 1326: Anatomist's assistant Alessandra Giliani, who developed the method of injecting colored dyes into blood vessels, dies, aged 19.

Bursa, Byzantium, 1326: Ottoman forces take Bursa, and make it the capital of their empire. The founder of the empire, Osman, dies, and is succeeded by his son, Orhan.

India, 1326: The Hindu kingdom of Vijayanagara is established in southern India by brothers Harihara and Bukka Sangama.

London, England, January 25, 1327: Queen Isabella, wife of Edward II, becomes regent for her 14-year-old son, Edward III, after the overthrow of her husband.

Daidu (Beijing), China, 1327: Mongol military engineers complete the rebuilding of China's Grand Canal, which extends over 1,055 miles (1,700 km) from Hangzhou to Daidu.

Japan, 1333: Emperor Go-Daigo re-establishes imperial rule as the Kamakura Shogunate comes to an end.

Coimbra, Portugal, July 4, 1336: Queen Isabel of Portugal, wife of King Diniz and mother of King Afonso IV, dies, aged 65.

Berwick, Scotland, June 10, 1338: Lady Agnes Randolph, Countess of Dunbar, successfully defeats the Earl of Salisbury.

France, 1338: England's Edward III invades France.

Bruges, Belgium, June 24, 1340: The English fleet defeats the French at the Battle of Sluys.

Bavaria, 1342: Margaret of Carinthia (Margaret Maultasch) marries Louis, son of Emperor Louis IV.

Calais, France, August 1347: Philippa of Hainault, Queen Consort of England's Edward III, pleads to him successfully for the lives of six town leaders at the siege of Calais.

Avignon, France, 1347: Organized brothels are introduced. Forward thinking measures include regular medical checks for the working women, and assistance for the pregnant or sick.

Europe, 1347–1351: The Great Plague sweeps through Europe. The sisters of the Hotel Dieu in Paris continue to nurse the sick.

Philippa of Hainault

Woman Barred from Medicine

Paris, France, 1322: Opinions are divided on the role of women in medicine. On the one hand, many, especially women, are supportive of the caring attitudes and skills of female physicians; on the other hand, scientists and doctors are claiming that women should not be permitted to practice any manner of health care.

There have always been "wise women:" women whose healing skills have made them valued members of their communities. The famed Salerno Medical School in Italy even trains gifted women to be doctors. The legendary Trotula, author of definitive texts on women's health, was trained at Salerno over 200 years ago. In more recent times, the Salerno Medical School has taken on a number of women as students. The school maintains that women are eminently suited to caring for other women, particularly in matters of childbirth and other women's conditions. Of course, their interests often go beyond women's conditions. Abella, a Salerno graduate, has written authoritatively on black bile, and Mercuriade on fevers, so there is no doubt that some women are perfectly capable of becoming physicians.

However, this year, the Faculty of Medicine at the University of Paris laid charges against Jacoba Felicie for practicing medicine without being qualified. Jacoba is well known in Paris among the well-to-do women, who regularly consult her—often after seeing other doctors who have been unable to cure their maladies. Jacoba is a skilled midwife and healer who takes the pulses of her patients and tests their urine to assist in diagnosis. Her patients have acclaimed her skill in healing both internal and external injuries and wounds.

In spite of her obvious expertise in making the sick well again, the Faculty refuses Jacoba permission to practice medicine because of her gender. This comes at a time when there is a critical shortage of physicians in Paris, and many are greeting this decision with concern.

"She kept a stir in tower and trench, that brawling, boisterous Scottish wench; came I early, came I late, I found Agnes at the gate."

EARL OF SALISBURY, (ATTRIB.), ON LADY AGNES RANDOLPH, "BLACK AGNES"

Death by Fire for Heretic

Kilkenny, Ireland, November 3, 1324: Petronella de Meath, maid to the fugitive Alice Kyteler, has been burned at the stake as a witch and heretic. It is the first case in Ireland of death by fire for the crime of heresy, but Meath was not the primary target of the investigation. Alice Kyteler, 44, has that dubious distinction.

Dame Alice has been married four times, and before his death, her fourth husband, John le Poer, believed that he was being poisoned by his wife, a suspicion he imparted to his children. They, together with the children of Alice's other husbands, accused her of poisoning, her motive the enrichment of her only son, William. So she was taken before Richard Ledrede, the bishop of Ossory, who added the charges of blasphemy and witchcraft. He alleges that Dame Alice has regular meetings with the Devil himself, that she sacrifices living animals to him, and, worst of all, that she denies that Jesus Christ is the son of God.

Although she was taken into custody, Alice Kyteler's former brother-in-law, Roger Outlawe, the Chancellor of Ireland, is said to have assisted her escape from imprisonment, and arranged for her to be taken out of the country, possibly to England. The bishop remains keen to see justice and has pursued Dame Alice's followers. One of those followers, the unfortunate Petronella de Meath, confessed her guilt to the bishop, and was today burned alive as a witch.

After her husband's death, Isabel nursed the sick.

Death of Portugal's Peacemaker

Coimbra, Portugal, July 4, 1336: Queen Isabel, the mother of King Afonso IV, has died today, aged 65. Her skills as a peacemaker will be missed. More than once, Isabel has ensured peaceful outcomes to volatile situations.

The daughter of Pedro III of Aragon, Isabel married King Diniz of Portugal when she was just 12 years old and he was only 20. Although Diniz had many qualities, fidelity was not one of them. Isabel bore him a son and a daughter, but knew that her husband had fathered a number of other children. No one ever heard her criticize or complain about Diniz. A deeply religious woman, Isabel found solace in prayer and in doing good work among the people, particularly the poor and sick. She commissioned the building of an orphanage, a hospice, a convent, and some churches, and is even reported to have drawn up some designs for these projects herself.

In 1323, angered by the favoritism shown to his illegitimate half-brother by Diniz, Isabel's son, Afonso, engaged in a civil war against his father. Isabel rode into the midst of the battle and effected

The sisters of the Hotel Dieu in Paris are continuing to nurse victims of the Great Plague.

A Japanese woman gives birth while her husband prays for her well-being with the village priest.

**Queen Giovanna
of Naples and Sicily**

a reconciliation between her husband and her son. For this act, she became known as the "peacemaker."

When Diniz died in 1325, Isabel gave away all her possessions and entered the convent of the Poor Clares in Coimbra, where she spent the rest of her life caring for others. She has lived quietly there since then. But earlier this year she heard that her son, now Afonso IV, was marching against his son-in-law, Alfonso of Castile. Without hesitation, Isabel rode to Estremoz and convinced the warring parties to make peace. The undertaking of this mission weakened her, and today, the much-loved dowager Queen died.

Black Agnes Victorious

Berwick, Scotland, June 10, 1338: After a five-month siege by the Earl of Salisbury, Lady Agnes Randolph, Countess of Dunbar, has declared victory against England. "Black Agnes," nicknamed for her dark complexion, has been waging her own "war" against Salisbury at Castle Dunbar near the southeast border with England. England has been trying to conquer Scotland for some time now, but there was no joy in the English camp today when a woman put paid to their plans.

In January, aware that Patrick Dunbar was away with the Scottish army, the Earl of Salisbury arrived at Berwick. Patrick's wife, Agnes, locked the gates and rallied her men around her. In spite of battering rams and volleys of shots, Castle Dunbar remained impenetrable. At one point, a clearly desperate Salisbury told Agnes that he was holding her brother, John Randolph, hostage and that he would be executed if she did not surrender. Calling his bluff, Agnes declared that she would therefore inherit her brother's lands, so Salisbury could do as he pleased.

Days ago, Agnes received assistance from Alexander Ramsay and together they led a surprise attack on Salisbury's forces. This was the final straw, and much

to his chagrin, Salisbury finally admitted defeat. Agnes Randolph is being hailed as a woman of great courage and determination, a true Scottish heroine.

Philippa Saves Calais Leaders

Calais, France, August 1347: Philippa of Hainault, Queen Consort of England's Edward III, has successfully interceded with her husband and saved the lives of six Calais town leaders, who were about to be executed.

Having won the Battle of Crécy last year, Edward then laid siege to Calais, a town with strategic advantages, and well suited for receiving fresh supplies from England. The townspeople have valiantly tried to hold their own, but the prolonged encampment of English forces has led to severe food shortages, with many literally dying of starvation. When the English King declared that he would accept the town's surrender only if six town leaders agreed to become his hostages, six of Calais's most prominent citizens bravely volunteered, trusting that this act would

ensure provisions would be made available to the people of the city.

Edward made the hostages dress in simple clothes, wear nooses around their necks, and give him the keys to the city. There was no doubt in anyone's mind that he intended to have them executed.

Fortunately, Philippa, who is heavily pregnant, implored her husband, for love of her, to spare them. He could not refuse her request and the town leaders were freed. Philippa is a courageous woman—she has accompanied Edward on many of his campaigns, so she is no stranger to politics and warfare. Yet she is also known for her kind and generous nature, and her intervention on this occasion has had a happy outcome.

Giovanna Sponsors Holy Brothel

Avignon, France, August 1347: The Abbey, a new brothel for the exclusive use of Christians, has opened this month in Avignon, under the official patronage of Queen Giovanna (also known as Joan) of Naples and Sicily. In an effort to maintain control of prostitution, the notion of "holy brothels" has been introduced, and the Abbey is a fine example of this. It is run according to very rigorous rules, and the women who are employed there live in conditions similar to those in convents. In addition, they receive regular medical checks, and pregnant women are cared for until their confinement.

"Holy brothels" are usually located close to a church so that the working women are easily able to fulfill their religious duties. Prayer times are strictly adhered to. The Abbey is closed on Good Friday as a mark of respect.

Queen Philippa, who pleaded with her husband Edward III, has saved the lives of the burghers of Calais.

Jeanne de Bourbon

Mystic of Medingen Meets Her Maker

Dillingen, Germany, July 20, 1351: Margarethe Ebner, the nun whose revelatory writings have been widely circulated across Germany and Switzerland, has died, aged about 60. She is best known for her work, *Offerbarungen (Revelations)*, written about six or seven years ago.

Margarethe was born in Bavaria about 1291 and entered the Dominican convent of Maria Medingen at the age of 15. Political differences between Louis of Bavaria and Pope John XXII ultimately led, in 1324, to Louis's excommunication. The Pope then declared that Germany was under interdict, so the sacraments could not be given. Margarethe, as well as being deeply devout, was a keen observer of current events, and like many of the Dominican sisters, supported Louis, a benefactor of the convent. Her spiritual adviser, Father Heinrich von Nördlingen, a staunch supporter of Pope John XXII, left Germany rather than give up the sacraments.

It is because of these momentous events that we have Margarethe's writings today. During the long years of his exile, Heinrich and Margarethe corresponded regularly, and she informed him of the visionary experiences she had been granted. In the early 1340s, he encouraged her to write an account of her spiritual journey. This became *Revelations*, which includes a prayer asking for

> *"As the soul comes to know herself she also knows God better, for she sees how good he has been to her."*
>
> CATHERINE
> OF SIENA
> (1347–1380)

the grace of the sacraments the nuns were forbidden to receive. Heinrich distributed copies of her words across Switzerland, Germany, and the Netherlands, and Margarthe became known as the Mystic of Medingen, her words providing consolation and comfort to thousands.

Murder Ends Love Affair

Coimbra, Portugal, January 7, 1355: Inês de Castro, 29, long-time lover of Pedro, heir to the Portuguese throne, has been brutally murdered on the orders of King Afonso IV. She is reported to have been executed today at her home, Quinta das Lágrimas, although some say she had her throat cut at the nearby convent of St Clare. In any event it is a tragic end to a great, if scandalous, love affair.

Inês de Castro came from Spain to the Portuguese court as lady-in-waiting to Constance of Castile, Pedro's wife. Pedro and Constance had three children, including a son, Ferdinand. It is known that when

> ### time out
>
> French fashions are always in demand, and to keep up with the latest trends, English ladies often order small dolls from France that are dressed in the very latest styles. These mannequins are then passed on to their dressmakers.

Pedro first saw Inês, who was renowned for her beauty, he fell desperately in love with her, much to his father's disapproval. Afraid that Inês's Spanish connections would garner too much influence with the prince, the King banished her from court, but Pedro's feelings were not dimmed. Following Constance's death in 1345, Pedro set up house for his mistress. Inês bore Pedro four children, one of whom died in infancy. There are, however, two sons.

Afonso, concerned to secure the legitimate line of succession, had gone to great lengths to find another wife for his son, but Pedro refused to marry anyone but Inês. He even claimed that he secretly married Inês. The King's concerns are shared by members of the Portuguese court, who also hold deep-seated fears that the country may be subject to unwanted Spanish domination through Inês's family contacts. They successfully lobbied Afonso to do something drastic. Days ago, he ordered her death, sending his henchmen to Coimbra to do the deed.

Pedro, mad with grief, is said to be planning a rebellion against his father.

Infamous Isabella Dies

Hertford, England, August 23, 1358: Isabella Capet of France, mother of King Edward III, has died, aged about 66. The notorious Isabella was a daughter of France's Philip IV, and the Queen Consort of Edward II. She will no doubt live on in history as the woman who arranged for the removal from office and murder of her own husband, in 1327.

Isabella married Edward II in 1308, and although they had four children together, it was well known that Edward preferred the company of men. This led to many arguments and by the 1320s the royal couple's mutual dislike was evident. Isabella was also deeply angered by the favoritism that was shown to various members of court at the expense of

A pregnant woman; illustration from a 1356 treatise on medicine.

Key Events

Hangzhou, China, c. 1350: New techniques for roasting tea-leaves improve flavor and shelf-life.

France, 1350: Charles V of France marries Jeanne de Bourbon.

Dillingen, Germany, July 20, 1351: Margarethe Ebner, Dominican mystic, known for her correspondence with Heinrich von Nördlingen, dies, aged about 60.

England, 1351: The *Treason Act* is passed. Disloyalty to the monarch is considered high treason, while petty treason includes the murder of a husband by a wife.

Lan Xang (Laos), Southeast Asia, 1352: Fa Ngum establishes the Kingdom of Lan Xang (Kingdom of a Million Elephants), and founds his capital of Luang Prabang.

Gallipoli, 1354: The Ottoman Turks capture the peninsula, formerly a Byzantine possession.

Coimbra, Portugal, January 7, 1355: Inês de Castro is murdered by Afonso IV, father of her lover, Prince Pedro.

Pandrathan, Kashmir, India, c. 1355: Poet and mystic Lalla Ded, often known as "Mother Lalla," is born.

Poitiers, France, September, 1356: The English forces, under the leadership of Edward, the Black Prince, score a resounding victory over the French, and capture the French King, John II, his son, and a number of high-ranking nobles.

Hertford, England, August 23, 1358: Isabella Capet of France, daughter of France's Philip IV, Queen Consort of England's Edward II, and mother of Edward III, dies, aged about 66.

Europe, 1361: Though the continent has barely recovered from the last onslaught of plague, the deadly disease resurfaces.

Prague, July 11, 1362: Anne of Swidnica, Queen of Bohemia and wife of Holy Roman Emperor Charles IV, dies, aged 23.

Kashin, Russia, October 3, 1368: Russian princess Anna of Kashin, dies, aged over 85.

Nanjing, China, 1368: Rebel Zhu Yuanzhang defeats the Mongols in China and becomes the founding emperor of the Ming Dynasty.

Scotland, 1369: "Black Agnes," Countess of Dunbar, defender of her home against English forces, dies, aged 57.

Rome, Italy, July 23, 1373: Bridget of Sweden, founder of the Order of the Most Holy Savior (Brigittines), dies, aged about 70.

London, England, 1376: Alice Perrers, lady-in-waiting to Queen Philippa, and mistress of Edward III, interferes in court lawsuits and is banished by the Good Parliament.

Queen Isabella Capet entering the city of Paris.

others, and she deplored what she saw as poor treatment of the general populace.

When Isabella's brother, Charles IV of France, took back Edward's French possessions, Isabella returned to France where she helped to organize an invasion of her adopted country. In 1326, with her paramour Roger Mortimer, she defeated Edward, forcing his abdication in favor of their son, who was crowned Edward III in 1327 at the tender age of 14. Isabella and Mortimer appointed themselves regents for the new young King, and they also orchestrated the murder of Edward II.

These actions obviously had a profound effect on the young King. When Edward III came of age in 1330, he had Mortimer executed and banished his mother. Isabella spent the most of her remaining years in a Poor Clares convent.

Saintly Anna Leaves This Life

Kashin, Russia, October 3, 1368: Anna of Kashin, who has spent the long years since her husband's death serving God, has died. The daughter of Prince Dimitri Borisovich of Rostov, Anna married Prince Mikhail Yaroslavich of Tver in 1294, and had five children. In 1318, Mikhail was brutally killed by members of the Golden Horde, whose leader was Uzbeg Khan. Her two sons, Dimitri and Alexander, were also killed by the invading Mongols.

Following these personal tragedies, Anna decided to devote herself to God and moved into a nunnery in Tver. She spent her time assisting the poor and the sick, and providing comfort to the bereaved. Anna will be buried in the Church of the Blessed Virgin.

Brigittines Lose Their Founder

Rome, Italy, July 23, 1373: Bridget of Sweden, has died, aged about 70. She was the founder of the Order of the Most Holy Savior, which is also known as the Brigittines. Born into a wealthy family, Bridget, or Birgitta, married Ulf Gudmarsson when she was 13, and they had eight children. They were known and loved as a pious and charitable couple. During her time as a lady-in-waiting to Queen Blanche, Bridget became close to the royal family, and sometimes offered them spiritual advice.

Following the death of her husband in 1344, Bridget, like many another good woman widowed at a relatively young age, applied herself exclusively to religion. She wrote of the visions and revelations she had received from God, and when these writings were translated into Latin her fame grew. She often conversed with theologians and other holy men, and she advocated the return of the papacy from Avignon to Rome.

When Bridget founded the new congregation, the Order of the Most Holy Savior, in 1346, her patron, King Magnus, provided her with some financial assistance so she could establish a convent at Vadstena. Seeking confirmation for her order, Bridget traveled to Rome in 1349 and, apart from making a number of pilgrimages, she stayed there for the rest of her life. Pope Urban V finally confirmed the Brigittine order in 1370. Many are speculating that Bridget will be canonized in the not-too-distant future.

Italian noblewoman

Bridget of Sweden, founder of the Brigittines, with an acolyte.

Catherine of Siena

Parliament Pushes Perrers

London, England, 1376: The much-despised Alice Perrers, mistress of King Edward III and wife of Sir William de Windsor, has been banished from the royal court by the Good Parliament for interfering in lawsuits. Perrers came to the Plantagenet court in 1369 as a lady-in-waiting to Queen Philippa, and quickly became the King's mistress, bearing him a number of children. By all accounts, she is a greedy and ambitious woman who will stop at nothing to wield power and influence over the ageing King. She openly flaunts the jewels he gives her, and boasts of the grants of land she has received. What has brought her to the attention of the Good Parliament are her machinations in the matter of lawsuits—she has been actively promoting positive outcomes in lawsuits involving her friends and allies at court. For this alone, she is barred from court.

It has been an interesting few years in England, and the public perception that the government is corrupt is unshaken. Spending at court has been rampant and when the Good Parliament convened from April to July this year, one of its first actions was to impeach and imprison the King's chamberlain and financial officers, who were believed to be helping themselves to government money. The Good Parliament was conceived as a way to rid England of poor government policies, and to control taxes raised to finance war with France. Its name reflects its aim to reform corrupt behavior and re-establish a sense of propriety in government.

Knowing that Alice Perrers would suffer the opprobrium of the Good Parliament, Edward himself wrote them a letter pleading for mercy, but his appeal fell on deaf ears, and Perrers has left the court in disgrace. Prince John of Gaunt, the King's son, is known to dislike the Good Parliament, and many are watching current political events with interest.

Death of Catherine of Siena

Rome, Italy, April 29, 1380: Nun and mystic, Caterina Benincasa, who is better known as Catherine of Siena, has died, aged 33. She will be remembered as much for her role in having the papacy returned from Avignon to Rome, as for her wise counsel.

Catherine was born in Siena in 1347 and entered the Dominican order as a young girl. For a time, she lived as a recluse, but later left to work closely with the sick and infirm. Her mediation skills became well known, and in 1375, she was invited to go to Pisa to encourage its citizens to join the Crusades. That same year, Catherine received what she considered her greatest glory—the stigmata of Christ's wounds on her feet, hands, and heart, although she successfully prayed that the marks remain invisible.

Catherine lobbied to have the papacy returned to Rome. Based in Avignon in France since 1309, many had wanted the papacy to be restored to its original home in Rome. She wrote to Pope Gregory XI, and even went to see him personally. She also urged reform of the Church. Shortly before his death, Pope Gregory did, in fact, return to Rome, due in no small part to Catherine's entreaties.

Favored with divine visions, Catherine wrote a number of works of significant spiritual value, including her *Dialogue*, which contains details of her revelations. She will be buried in Rome.

Supporter of Anti-Pope Assassinated

Naples, Italy, May 12, 1382: Since the time of the Western Schism—the breakdown in the Church—political and religious loyalties across Europe have been divided. In Naples today, Queen Giovanna (also known as Queen Joan) was assassinated, a testament to the ruthless ambition of many powerbrokers.

Following the death of French-born Pope Gregory XI, Romans insisted that the next pope be Italian, and Urban VI was elected. His bad temper alienated many of the French cardinals who then elected their own pope, the Geneva-born Clement VII, known as the Anti-Pope. When Urban insulted Giovanna, she decided to back the Avignon papacy.

> *"JUST AS WOMEN'S BODIES ARE SOFTER THAN MEN'S, SO THEIR UNDERSTANDING IS SHARPER."*
>
> CHRISTINE DE PISAN (1365–1429), ITALIAN WRITER AND FEMINIST

Catherine of Siena has influenced the return of the papacy from Avignon to Rome.

Urban declared that she was no longer Queen of Naples and appointed Charles of Durazzo to rule instead. Charles entered Naples only days ago and Giovanna surrendered her authority, only to be cruelly strangled while at prayer.

Work Shows the Passion

Norwich, England, 1393: The anchoress and mystic known only as Julian of Norwich has written *Sixteen Revelations of Divine Love*, an account of a series of visions she received 20 years ago, in May 1373, while she was desperately ill. Also known as *A Book of Showings*, the work is a great addition to spiritual literature. Although she claims to be a simple woman, it is clear that Julian has an excellent understanding of theological principles.

In *Revelations*, Julian writes that when she was sick, a priest visited her, bringing a crucifix with him. Julian saw blood flowing from Christ's crown of thorns on that crucifix. Fifteen more showings of Christ's Passion and suffering were revealed to her. She discusses the Passion, the existence and nature of evil, and other philosophical and religious issues, in clear and eloquent language. Julian writes that for the 20 years between the showings and her documentation of them, she was learning "inwardly," working toward a closer communion with God. What distinguishes this work from others is that she says self-knowledge and knowledge of God are inextricably intertwined.

Julian herself is something of a mystery. Born about 1342, she joined the Benedictines and has lived for years as an anchoress at the church of St Julian in Norwich, from which she took her name.

Union in Scandinavia

Kalmar, Sweden, June 1397: At the town of Kalmar on the Swedish east coast, history was made when the Kalmar Union was formalized. The Kalmar Union joins the three kingdoms of Denmark, Sweden, and Norway under one ruler, although each country can keep its own laws and customs. Queen Margaret of Denmark has played a critical role in making this union a reality.

Margaret, who was born in 1353, is the daughter of Danish King Valdemar and widow of King Haakon VI of Norway. In 1380, Haakon died and Margaret took on the regency of Norway. When her father died in 1385, she became regent of Denmark for her son Olaf. When her son died in 1387, Margaret continued on as the ruler of both countries.

At the same time, in Sweden the people were becoming alarmed at the growing German influence in their land—their King, Albert of Mecklenburg, is German.

Isabeau of Bavaria on her wedding day.

Disaffected Swedish nobles turned to Queen Margaret for assistance. Together with Danish troops, they defeated Albert in February 1389, and Margaret became regent over Sweden. She is respected as a fair ruler and has promised to protect the rights, privileges, and political power enjoyed by Swedish nobles. She has also stated that Sweden would be ruled with Swedes in senior government positions.

Erik of Pomerania, Margaret's great-nephew, has just been elected King of Denmark, Sweden, and Norway. There are murmurings of discontent about this in parts of Sweden, as Erik is said to favor the strengthening of the monarchy at the expense of the aristocracy. However, as Erik has not yet reached his majority, Margaret will continue to govern the three kingdoms, her statesmanship and political acuity a hallmark of her reign.

Poland Loses Leader

Krakow, Poland, July 17, 1399: It has been less than one month since the Queen, Jadwiga, gave birth to her daughter, Elizabeth Bonifacia, who lived for just a week or so. Today Jadwiga, aged 25, joins her daughter in death, bringing the Polish Piast dynasty to an end.

Jadwiga was the daughter of Louis of Hungary, who took the Polish throne in 1370. When he died, his eldest daughter, Mary, ascended to the Hungarian throne, while 10-year-old Jadwiga ascended the Polish throne, and was crowned "King," an affirmation that she was a sovereign in her own right. In 1385 she married Jagiello of Lithuania, who promised to convert to Christianity. In spite of the large age difference—he was 34, she was 11—it was a good marriage.

With her husband's assistance, Jadwiga managed to reclaim territory that was taken by Hungary after her ascension to the throne. Well educated and multilingual, Jadwiga was deeply involved with political matters, and was a committed patron of the arts. She was a champion of the Church, and fostered education and science. One of Jadwiga's greatest legacies will surely turn out to be the Academy of Krakow, certainly one of the major intellectual centers of Europe.

Christine de Pisan

Jadwiga came to the Polish throne at 10 years of age, and ruled the country as "King."

St Cecilia

St Cecilia Adopted as Patron Saint of Musicians

Europe, c. 1400s: St Cecilia, who suffered martyrdom in the second century CE, has been adopted as the patron saint of music and musicians.

Cecilia, born in Rome, was a devout Christian from childhood. She was given in marriage by her parents to a Roman named Valerianus. After the wedding, when it came time to consummate the relationship, Cecilia told Valerianus that she was betrothed to an angel who would protect her from violation by a pagan. Valerianus asked to see the angel and Cecilia sent him to meet Pope Urbanus. He did as she asked and was baptized by the pope. When Valerianus returned to Cecilia an angel appeared to the couple and crowned them with roses and lilies. When Tiburtius, Valerianus's brother, heard what had happened he was also converted to Christianity.

Little else is known of Cecilia's life except that she praised God by playing musical instruments and singing.

Cecilia, Valerianus, and Tiburtius were all martyred. It is recorded that Cecilia was struck three times on the neck with a sword but survived for three days. As she was dying she asked the pope to convert her home into a place of worship. A church bearing her name does exist in Rome (at Trastevere). It was remodeled in the year 820 CE by Pope Paschal and contains the relics of St Cecilia.

Many artists, particularly musicians, have claimed St Cecilia as their muse.

Women Trained as Doctors in Korea

Korea, 1406: A medical training facility for women has been established in Korea. Female doctors will be able to treat the diseases suffered by women and also act as midwives. They will use a particular form of oriental medicine that is largely unpracticed in the west.

The training facility has been established by King Taejo, who has destroyed the last vestiges of the Buddhist Goryeo Dynasty and established a new "Chosun Dynasty." The new king is Confucian and has moved the capital from Kaesong, where the Buddhist influence is still strong, to Seoul.

The establishment of the medical training facility is intriguing because in Confucian societies women have low status. They have an obligation of subservience to their husbands, and after the death of the husband, to their eldest son.

time out

In 1438, Catherine de Vigri of Bologna, artist, writer, visionary, and abbess of an order of strictly enclosed Poor Clare nuns, writes her autobiography, Treatise on the Seven Spiritual Weapons.

Margaret of Denmark Dies

Copenhagen, Denmark, October 28, 1412: Margaret of Denmark, ruler of Norway, Denmark, and Sweden, and founder of the Kalmar Union, has died at the age of 59.

Margaret was born in 1353 at Vordingborg Castle in Denmark. In 1363, when only 10 years old, she married King Haakon VI of Norway, and seven years later she gave birth to a son, Olav.

When her father died in 1375, Margaret had her infant son declared the king of Denmark (in spite of what seem to be better claims to the throne by her older sister, her husband, and their son). In 1380 Margaret's husband Haakon died, and so just ten years old, Olav became king of Denmark and of Norway. Margaret was appointed as regent, and seven years later, when Olav died, Margaret became queen of both countries.

Margaret then turned her attention to Sweden where there was already an uprising against the unpopular king, Albert of Mecklenburg. In 1388, after having defeated Albert's army, Margaret became the queen of all Scandinavia. The following year Albert made an attempt to take back the throne of Sweden, but again Margaret's forces were victorious.

In 1397 Margaret summoned councils from Sweden, Denmark, and Norway to the Swedish town of Kalmar to ratify an act which made her great-nephew, Erik of Pomerania, king of Denmark, Norway, and Sweden. The councillors accepted Erik as their sovereign but, as he was only 15 years old, Margaret continued to be the true ruler of the three kingdoms for the remainder of her life.

Denmark, Norway, and Sweden had given up their sovereignty, but not their independence. In the following years Margaret proved herself to be a superb

The royal tomb of Margaret of Denmark, ruler of Norway, Denmark, and Sweden.

The Mosque of Herat, commissioned by Gawhar Shad.

Timurid Empire is famous. The entrances will be in the familiar Samarkand arch style but otherwise the mosque will be groundbreaking in its design. It will have four vaulted halls (iwans). Its main iwan will be decorated in pure white faience and topped by a spectacular dome. It will be flanked by two tile-decorated minarets that will be visible from many miles away. The other iwans will be colored soft pink and include large stylistic inscriptions.

Enamel bricks in various geometric designs will alternate with floral patterns and run around the entire courtyard of the mosque. Above this will be a band of calligraphy designed by Gawhar Shad's son, Baysunghur. This place of worship promises to be a truly magnificent structure.

Author of *City of Ladies* Dies

Paris, France, 1430: Writer and feminist, Christine de Pisan, has died, aged 66. Her literary works have challenged traditional attitudes to women.

De Pisan was born in Venice, but grew up in the court of King Charles V of France after her father accepted a position as the king's physician. As a child she spent many hours in the king's library learning languages and reading philosophy. Following the early death of her husband—she was only 24—Christine de Pisan started writing in order to support her three small children.

Her early works catered to the taste of the court, being love ballads and romantic poems. However, she became caught up in a literary debate revolving around *Romance*

of the Rose (a highly regarded poem written about 1230). She considered that its depiction of women as seducers was heinous and that the poem distorted the nature of female sexuality. The debate soon came to encompass the depiction of women in other literary works.

De Pisan went on to write two famous works regarding the role of women: *The Book of the City of Ladies* and *The Treasure of the City of Ladies*.

Her final work was entitled *The Tale of Joan of Arc* and celebrated the rise of a young woman who was destined to become a military leader. Christine de

Catherine of Valois

Folk heroine Joan of Arc led French troops into Orléans in 1429.

diplomat, maintaining the union by suppression of the opposition forces within the Kalmar Union and avoidance of foreign wars. Margaret died unexpectedly on board her ship in the Danish port of Flensburg.

Queen Gawhar Shad Commissions Mosque

Herat, Afghanistan, 1417: Queen Gawhar Shad (whose name in Farsi means "bright jewel") has commissioned the construction of a magnificent mosque in Herat. In common with many of the other buildings constructed during her reign, it will be designed by her favorite architect, Ghavameddin Shirazi.

Gawhar Shad is the wife of the third emperor of the Timurid Dynasty, Shah Rukh. In 1405, he moved the capital of the empire from Samarkand to Herat and attracted many artists and intellectuals to the court, including some of the world's greatest architects and artisans.

The mosque's facade will be covered in the mosaic tile decoration for which the

Europe, c. 1430: Guns of iron, cast in one piece, are constructed.

Florence, Italy, c. 1430: Donatello completes *David* in bronze. It is the first large nude statue of the Renaissance Period.

Rouen, France, May 30, 1431: Joan of Arc, known as the Maid of Orléans, is burned at the stake. She is 19 years old.

Seoul, Korea, 1431: King Sejong orders the publication of *Illustrated Conduct of the Three Bonds* to improve public morals.

Valladolid, Spain, 1432: One of the provisions listed in the Synod of Castilian Jews is that no one will have the right to impose a marriage against the will of either party.

Bruges, Belgium, 1434: Jan van Eyck paints his famous portrait of Giovanni Arnolfini and his wife, often called the *Arnolfini Marriage*.

Straubing, Germany, October 12, 1435: Agnes Bernauer, a baker's daughter who secretly married Albert, heir to the Bavarian duchy, is condemned to death as a witch, and is drowned in the Danube.

Naples, Italy, 1435: Giovanna II, who has been ruling Naples since 1414, dies, aged about 62.

Arboga, Sweden, 1435: A group of nobles from all over the country meet in the nation's first "parliament" as part of the rebellion against King Erik.

Netherlands, October 8, 1436: Jacqueline of Bavaria, also known as Jacoba, countess of Holland, Zeeland, and Hainault, dies, aged 35. She was the last of the Wittelsbach dynasty to rule Holland and Hainault.

England, c. 1436: Margery Kempe, mystic and traveler, publishes the first known autobiography in the English language, *The Book of Margery Kempe*.

England, 1439: The spectre of plague is ever-present, and among the measures to prevent the spread of disease is a ban on kissing, instituted by Henry VI.

Mexico, 1440: The Aztec emperor, Itzcoatl, dies. He is succeeded by his nephew, Montezuma (Moctezuma). Itzcoatl first came to power as a member of the Triple Alliance that defeated the Tepanecs.

Ghent, Belgium, 1447: Colette of Corbie, Flemish nun who imposed a stricter regime on Poor Clare convents, dies, aged 66.

England, 1448: Margaret of Anjou, wife of Henry VI, founds Queens' College, Cambridge.

Joan of Arc

French Heroine's Death by Fire

Rouen, France, May 30, 1431: Nineteen-year-old Joan of Arc, who led armies against the English occupiers of France and who claimed to have visions from God, has been burned at the stake as a heretic.

In 1415 the king of England, Henry V, took advantage of years of war and chaos in France to invade. By 1429 the English had possession of Paris and Reims and laid siege to Orléans, one of the few cities still loyal to the French Dauphin, Charles.

Joan was born in 1412 in the village of Domrémy. At the age of 12, she began receiving visions from saints who told her that she would expel the English forces and that the Dauphin would be crowned at Reims.

In 1429, disguised as a man, young Joan traveled through hostile territory to visit the Dauphin at Chinon. The Dauphin was so impressed with her belief in her visions and in him that he sent her with a relief expedition to the city of

The Dauphin granted her co-command of the army and she led it to Reims. On July 16, 1429 she entered the city and the Dauphin was crowned King Charles VII the next morning. However, fortune deserted her, and on May 23, 1430, she was captured at Compiègne. The English commanders turned her over to the Church, who put her on trial for heresy.

Today, just one year since those momentous events, France has indeed lost a true heroine.

Compulsory Marriage Banned

Valladolid, Spain, 1432: The Chief Rabbi of Castile, Don Abraham Benveniste, has called a synod of Iberian Jews at Valladolid. The delegates have passed a number of ordinances, one of which forbids the imposition of marriage on a Jew.

The ordinance reads, in part: "No one has the right to use an edict of the king or the queen, or any other lord or lady, or to otherwise compel, whether by persuasion or intimidation, a Jewess to accept a Jew, or a Jew to accept a Jewess in betrothal or marriage. Whoever transgresses this ordinance shall be declared anathema and excommunicated."

Other ordinances of the synod relate to a range of important issues, some of which include the education of children, the raising of taxes, and the sale of wine.

Jan van Eyck's portrait of the Arnolfinis is being widely acclaimed.

blonde hair. She captivated Albert but had too much self-respect to become his mistress, so they were married in secret in 1432.

Albert, the only son of Ernest, Duke of Bavaria, is entitled to his father's title and lands when he dies.

After the marriage, Agnes resided at Vohburg Castle. Albert's father was either of the opinion that the marriage was not legal, or else remained unaware of it, because he continued to make plans for his son to marry the daughter of Duke Erich of Brunswick. Albert was eventually compelled to tell his father that Agnes was already his lawful wife.

Not fazed by this knowledge, Ernest contrived for his son to leave Bavaria on state business. While Albert was away he arranged for Agnes to be arrested and charged with witchcraft.

A makeshift "court" quickly found her guilty and she was sentenced to death. On October 12 she was strapped to a device designed for drowning witches, and was plunged into the icy Danube River. It is reported that she was able to free herself from her restraints and swim to the bank. Arriving at the riverbank exhausted, Agnes attempted to clamber onto dry land but the executioner held her head forcibly under the water until the young woman drowned.

The horrible death of Agnes will no doubt cause a rift between Albert and his father, but whether it will endure is unlikely because of what is at stake—the inheritance of Bavaria.

Joan of Arc, who was burned at the stake, sought guidance from religion.

Orléans. She arrived there in April 1429 with borrowed armor and horse.

Abandoning the cautious strategy that had been adopted by the French war council, she attacked fortress after fortress, pressing the English troops back. Then on May 7, she led an assault on the main English stronghold, despite lack of support from the French commanders. During the battle she suffered a serious wound to her shoulder but returned to the battlefield to lead the final charge. The siege of Orléans was broken.

Baker's Daughter Drowned for Bewitching Nobleman

Straubing, Germany, October 1435: Agnes Bernauer, the baker's daughter who secretly married Albert, the heir to the Bavarian duchy, has been condemned to death as a witch by her father-in-law and drowned in the Danube River.

The date of Agnes's birth is not known with certainty. It is reported that she was a beautiful young woman with delicate features and magnificent

Death of the Queen of Naples

Naples, Italy, 1435: Giovanna II, also known as Joan or Joanna, ruler of Naples for 21 years, has died aged 62. Giovanna was the daughter of Charles III of Naples and Margherita of Durazzo. In 1414, after the death of her brother Ladislas, she became queen of Naples.

A year later, in the hope of securing an alliance with France, she married James of Bourbon. However, James sequestered the queen and tried to rule Naples alone. The people of Naples were enraged by this treatment and in 1416 they staged a rebellion. James was captured and imprisoned. In 1419 he was expelled from Naples and returned to France.

Giovanna would never marry again and, being childless, had to appoint an heir to the throne. Her choice was precipitated by the action of Louis III of Anjou who, in 1419, tried to invade Naples. In response, Giovanna declared Alfonso V of Aragon as her heir, her principal aim to obtain his support against Louis. In 1421 Alfonso entered Naples but his relationship with Giovanna deteriorated rapidly. He arrested her lover and tried to arrest the queen herself, but she managed to escape. In 1423 she met her former enemy, Louis III of Anjou, and retracted her declaration favoring Alfonso as her heir, instead naming Louis as her heir. Alfonso knew that he had been outmaneuvered and returned to Aragon.

The remaining years of Giovanna's life were relatively uneventful. She outlived her heir, Louis, and named his brother, René, as her successor.

Jacqueline of Bavaria Dies

Netherlands, October 8, 1436: Jacqueline of Bavaria, also known as Jacoba, has died today, aged 35.

Jacqueline was an only child. Her father, William VI, died in 1417 when she was 16 years old, and she inherited his lands and titles, becoming countess of Holland, Zeeland, and Hainaut and duchess of Bavaria-Straubing.

Her uncle, John of Bavaria, challenged her claim to these lands and a civil war ensued. In 1418, Jacqueline married John IV, Duke of Brabant, believing he would be of help in the struggle against her uncle. However John was weak and gave her no tangible support, and Jacqueline was forced to flee to England.

There she fell in love with Humphrey, Duke of Gloucester. She had her marriage to John annulled by the Avignon Pope, Benedict XIII, and married Humphrey

in October 1422. They traveled with an army to The Netherlands to restore Jacqueline to her former position.

Their mission did not succeed. Jacqueline was imprisoned and Humphrey quickly returned to England. Jacqueline escaped and continued to fight. However, in 1427 Pope Martin V declared that her marriage to John IV had been valid after all. This meant that her marriage to Humphrey was void and she could no longer rely on his support.

With no allies, her fight was over. In 1428 Jacqueline signed a treaty by which she kept her titles, but the administration

pilgrimages to Rome, Germany, and Spain. The book is already being hailed as the first autobiography written in English and is simply entitled, *The Book of Margery Kempe.*

Margery Kempe was born in Lynn, Norfolk. She married John Kempe in 1393 and gave birth to 14 children. In the book she describes her life before her conversion to Christianity: "My neighbors were very jealous of me, and wished that they were as well-dressed as I was. My only wish was to be admired."

After the birth of her first child she nearly died. It was at about this time that

Margaret of Anjou

Naples, Italy, the city ruled by Giovanna II from 1414 until her death in 1435.

of the region was handed over to her cousin, Philip III, Duke of Burgundy.

In 1434 Jacqueline married Francis van Borselen. They had two happy years together before she contracted consumption three months ago. Being childless, all her domains and titles pass to Philip.

Margery Kempe Writes Autobiography

England, c. 1436: Margery Kempe, an uneducated mystic and traveler, has published the story of her life including descriptions of raising 14 children, her attempts to start a business, and her

she claims to have started receiving visions of Jesus Christ. From that time on she railed against the pleasures of the world. In 1413 she and her husband took vows of chastity. She then made pilgrimages to holy sites in Europe and beyond.

She experiences many weeping fits and religious ecstasies and writes that, "On Sundays I receive the sacrament wherever time and place allows, and I weep and sob so violently that many people are struck with amazement that God had given me so much grace."

Being illiterate, Margery reportedly dictated her story to two scribes who have written it down for her.

Agnès Sorel

Joan of Arc Declared a Martyr

Paris, France, November 7, 1455: The conviction of Joan of Arc for heresy has been quashed, nearly a quarter of a century after her execution. A papal court has now described Joan as a martyr who was executed in pursuit of a secular vendetta.

Proceedings to nullify the original verdict were instigated by the Pope, Calixtus III, after he was petitioned by

"The day is short and the work is long."

FIFTEENTH-CENTURY PROVERB, ORIGIN UNKNOWN

King Charles VII of France, the Inquisitor-General Jean Brehal, and Joan of Arc's mother, Isabelle Romée. Since the English had been driven out of Rouen, access to the trial papers became available. A papal court investigated whether the trial and conviction of Joan of Arc had been handled according to ecclesiastical law. A panel of theologians analyzed testimony from 115 witnesses.

Joan was tried and executed in 1431 by French collaborators who recognized Henry VI as king under the English regency council. She was convicted of heresy, but it is now generally accepted that the motivation of the prosecutors was political rather than religious. In the final week of the trial Joan stopped

Joan of Arc in 1429. Executed for heresy in 1431, Joan is now a recognized saint.

dressing in male clothing and signed an abjuration in which she confessed to claiming falsely that she had visions from God.

However, several days later, she resumed dressing like a man. This was seen as a withdrawal of her earlier recantation, and she was sentenced to death. Joan was burned at the stake on May 30, 1431.

Royal Suicide

Vietnam, October 1459: Nguyen Thi Anh, the mother of the king of Vietnam, Le Nhan Tong, and effective head of state since 1451, has committed suicide.

Although her date of birth is not known with certainty, it is widely believed that Nguyen Thi Anh was born into a noble family in 1422.

A beautiful young woman, she became a consort to King Le Thai Tong at the age of 18 and gave birth to their son in 1441. A year later King Le Thai Tong died.

Le Nhan Tong was still an infant so his mother was officially named regent on his behalf. She was assisted by Trinh Kha, who had earlier been appointed as Imperial Councillor to her dead husband. Yet friction between Nguyen Thi Anh and Trinh Kha grew over many decisions involving the governing of Vietnam, and in 1451 Nguyen Thi Anh ordered the execution of Trinh Kha and his eldest son.

time out

Burgundian aggressors met with an unlikely enemy at the seige of Beauvais in 1470. Jeanne Laisne led a group of women armed with hatchets into a battle that will be commemorated by honors from King Louis XI himself.

Although Le Nhan Tong officially took control of the kingdom of Vietnam in 1453 at age 12, his mother continued to act as head of state.

The following years were relatively uneventful until, two days ago, 100 men led by the king's older half-brother, Nghi Dan, entered the palace late at night and killed the 18-year-old king. The following day, Nguyen Thi Anh, facing certain death at the hands of the coup leaders, committed suicide. She was 37 years old.

Elizabeth Woodville Crowned Queen

London, England, May 26, 1465: Elizabeth Woodville, who has been described as the most beautiful woman in England, has been crowned queen. It was only recently revealed that she married King Edward IV in secret last year.

Elizabeth had been a maid of honor to Margaret of Anjou, the wife of Henry VI. Elizabeth's first husband, Sir John Grey of Groby, was a Lancastrian supporter. He was killed at the second battle of St Albans in February, 1461. Edward IV had

Elizabeth Woodville meets with Cardinal Bourchier.

Jumièges, France, February 9, 1450: Agnès Sorel, official mistress of Charles VII, and said to be the model for artist Jean Fouquet's painting of the Virgin and Child, dies, aged 28.
Mainz, Germany, c. 1450: Johannes Gutenberg invents the printing press, with movable reusable blocks fashioned from metal.
Germany, 1451: Nicholas of Cusa invents concave lenses to correct near-sightedness.

Constantinople, Byzantium, 1453: The fall of Constantinople signals the end of the Byzantine era.
Rome, Italy, February 18, 1455: Artist Fra Giovanni da Fiesole (Fra Angelico) dies, aged about 59.
St Albans, England, May 22, 1455: The Battle of St Albans between Lancaster and York marks the beginning of the Wars of the Roses.
Paris, France, November 7, 1455: Charles VII and the family of Joan of Arc successfully petition Pope Calixtus III to overrule the verdict of heresy against the heroine.

Mainz, Germany, 1455: The first book printed by Johannes Gutenberg, the Bible, appears.
Vietnam, October, 1459: When her son King Le Nhan Tong is murdered in a palace coup, regent and effective ruler of Vietnam, Nguyen Thi Anh, commits suicide.
Bologna, Italy, March 9, 1463: Catherine de Vigri, known as Catherine of Bologna, dies, aged 49. A Poor Clare abbess and visionary, she wrote *Treatise on the Seven Spiritual Weapons*.

Westminster, England, May 26, 1465: Elizabeth Woodville, who married Edward IV in secret in 1464, is crowned queen.
Verona, Italy, 1466: Italian scholar, humanist, and correspondent Isotta Nogarola, dies, aged about 48.
Kyoto, Japan, 1467: Rival daimyo vying for power spark the breakout of the Onin Wars.
South America, 1471: Topa Inca (also known as Tupac Yupanqui) succeeds his father Pachacuti and continues the expansion of the Inca Empire.

Westminster, England, 1476: William Caxton sets up the first printing press in England. His first publication is *Dictes and Sayings of the Philosophers*.
Ghent, The Low Countries, August 18, 1477: Mary, the Duchess of Burgundy, marries Archduke Maximilian of Austria.
Spain, 1479: After five years of fighting the Portuguese in the War of the Castilian Succession, Isabella of Castile becomes queen of Spain, and her husband Ferdinand of Aragon becomes king.

many mistresses whom he has described as the merriest, the wiliest, and the holiest harlots in his realm, but the widowed Elizabeth Woodville refused to become a mere mistress. The king was reportedly captivated by her austere beauty but she insisted she "was too base to be his wife yet too good to be his harlot."

Eventually Edward relented and married her secretly on May 1, 1464, at her family home in Northamptonshire. Only the bride's mother and two other people were in attendance. A year later the secret was out in the open, and Elizabeth was crowned queen today in Westminster Abbey.

Two months earlier she had become patroness of the Queens' College, Cambridge, "as true foundress by right of succession." The college was founded in 1448 by by the previous queen, Margaret of Anjou. Elizabeth is currently drafting the college's first statutes.

Elizabeth is disliked by many in the royal court and is particularly detested by the king's brother, the Duke of Gloucester. Many resent the way she is using her position to bestow favors upon members of her family, including her two sons by her first marriage. Others accuse her of practicing witchcraft. It is said that she is able to entrance men by fluttering her eyelashes and some think she bewitched the king into marrying her. When an heir to the throne is born, no doubt these feelings will be suppressed.

Mary of Burgundy to Marry Maximilian

Ghent, The Low Countries, August 1477: Mary, the 19-year-old duchess of Burgundy, will marry Austrian Archduke Maximilian at Ghent on August 18.

Mary was born in Brussels in 1457, the daughter of the duke of Burgundy, Charles the Bold—so called because of his bravery. As an only child she became heiress to Burgundy, and other valuable

Isabella of Castile, the Queen of Spain.

lands in Europe. As a consequence, she has received many proposals of marriage. When her father died earlier this year, Mary immediately recognized that she was vulnerable and would need to wed one of her many suitors. Rejecting a proposal by her father's rival, Louis XI of France, to marry his son, she instead chose Archduke Maximilian of Austria, and a ring set with a diamond of enormous value seals the engagement.

Margaret of Anjou Dies

Anjou, France, August 25, 1482: Margaret of Anjou is dead, aged 53. In her final years she was a mere shadow of her former self and was often seen with her head bowed in melancholy reflection.

A Frenchwoman born in Lorraine in 1429, Margaret wed Henry VI of

England in 1445. However, it was eight years before they had a son—Edward of Westminster. The king had never been very heathy, and by the time of Edward's birth he had retreated into himself.

Richard, Duke of York, noting the king's condition, sought to depose him. In response, Margaret raised an army and the so-called "Wars of the Roses" began. There followed a number of battles between the two factions, the Yorkists and the Lancastrians. At the battle of Wakefield in 1460 both the Duke of York and the Earl of Salisbury were killed. Margaret had their heads displayed on the gates of the city of York. The following year, at the second battle of St Albans, she was briefly reunited with her husband. However, a series of Lancastrian losses followed and she fled to France.

Margaret returned to England to lead an army at the Battle of Tewkesbury in 1471. Her forces were defeated and her son was killed. She was imprisoned until 1478 when she was released to the French king. She spent her final years in Anjou where she will be buried.

Elizabeth Woodville

Margaret of Anjou with her husband, England's King Henry VI.

Joan of Portugal

Witch-hunter's Handbook Published

Cologne, Germany, May 9, 1486: The *Malleus Maleficarum (Hammer of Witches)*, a comprehensive witch-hunter's handbook, has been published in Germany today. The handbook was written by two Dominicans, Henrikus Kramer and Joseph Sprenger, and has quickly spread to all corners of Europe with the aid of the recently invented printing press. It provides guidance regarding the detection and punishment of witches and other evil creatures, and is based on a pronouncement in Exodus 22:18, "Thou shalt not suffer a witch to live."

The book is divided into three distinct sections. Part I explains why women are more susceptible to the lure of Satan than men. "Why is it that women are addicted to evil superstitions?" asks the *Malleus Maleficarum*. It then goes on to answer its own question. "Three vices appear to have a special hold over women: Infidelity, ambition, and lust. Therefore they are more than others inclined towards witchcraft." It also definitely states that it is a heresy not to acknowledge the existence of witchcraft. Part II describes the various forms that witchcraft can take, and Part III details the methods for detecting and destroying witches. Torture is acceptable (indeed, even encouraged) in order to obtain admissions of guilt.

Critics of the new book strongly maintain that it is little more than a license for misogynists to further persecute women, citing the passage, "What else is woman but a temptation to evil painted with fair colors!"

"YOUR COM-PLAINTS ARE HURTING MY EARS, FOR YOU SAY PUBLICLY AND QUITE OPENLY THAT YOU ARE NOT ONLY SUR-PRISED BUT PAINED THAT I AM SAID TO SHOW THE EXTRAORDINARY INTELLECT OF THE SORT ONE WOULD HAVE THOUGHT NATURE WOULD GIVE TO THE MOST LEARNED OF MEN."

LAURA CERETA (1469–1499), ITALIAN WRITER

An illustrated guide to the detection of witchcraft.

Caterina Cornaro arrives in Venice in 1489, after her expulsion from Cyprus.

Caterina Cornaro, Queen of Cyprus, Abdicates

Venice, Italy, February 1489: Caterina Cornaro, who has ruled Cyprus since 1474, has been forced to abdicate and to cede the administration of the island to the Republic of Venice.

A Venetian by birth, she became queen of Cyprus as a result of her marriage to James II Lusignan of Cyprus whom she had never met. They were married by proxy in 1468 when she was 14 and he was 28, but she did not travel to Cyprus for the formal marriage ceremony for another four years.

It was hoped that the marriage would end years of rancor between Venice and Cyprus; however, Caterina's husband died just a few months after the wedding ceremony in suspicious circumstances. Their infant son died a few months later, less than a year old. Many believe they were both murdered by Caterina's family.

Queen Caterina became sole ruler of Cyprus following these deaths. She was assisted in administration of the island by merchants and nobles, and demonstrated by her numerous conflicts with Venice that she was no puppet of her relatives. She developed a great affection for her subjects and they reciprocated her love.

However, this month she has been persuaded by the Cornaro family to cede Cyprus to Venice in exchange for a large estate at Asolo near Venice. She will also be allowed to retain her title, Queen of Cyprus. Those who were witness to her departure from Cyprus report that she dressed in black, and that her eyes were streaming with tears as she was led out of Nicosia on horseback. The entire population of the city could be heard weeping.

Caterina is still only 35 years old and intends to continue with her life in Italy by becoming a patron of the arts. Asolo is already gaining a reputation for literary and artistic excellence.

Queen Isabella Sponsors New World Voyage

Cadiz, Spain, September 25, 1493: Queen Isabella has sponsored a second voyage by Christopher Columbus to the New World. She has instructed Columbus to establish a colony in the recently discovered lands, which Columbus believes to be the eastern part of India.

In contrast to his first voyage where his expedition only had three ships, this time Columbus will be accompanied by 17 ships and more than 1,200 men. Earlier this year, Columbus returned from his first voyage, laden with gifts of gold and silver for the queen.

Queen Isabella has become a most influential monarch. Born on April 22, 1451, she never expected to rule. Her older half-brother became King Henry IV of Castile in 1454. He married Joan of Portugal the following year in spite of the fact that it was widely believed he was homosexual. Joan gave birth to a daughter, also named Joan, in 1462, but it seemed unlikely that the child was Henry's.

Henry implicitly acknowledged the illegitimacy of his daughter Joan when he declared his younger half-brother (Isabella's brother) Alfonso, as his heir. However, when Alfonso died in 1468, Henry then named Isabella heir to the throne of Castile.

Henry died six years later, on December 10, 1474, and Isabella showed her political astuteness by quickly crowning herself as queen of Castile. Afonso V of Portugal, now betrothed to Henry's "daughter" Joan, invaded Castile shortly afterward and declared his future wife to be the rightful queen. The war of the Castilian Succession ensued and was contested for the next five years.

After their eventual victory, Isabella and her husband, Ferdinand II of Aragon, set to work unifying their two realms. In 1480, they set up the *Cortes* of Toledo, which produced a codified set of laws for the new country.

Any conquests that Columbus makes in the New World will continue to consolidate this unified kingdom of Spain.

Queen Isabella and King Ferdinand farewell Christopher Columbus.

Shogun's Wife Dies

Japan, May 20, 1496: Hino Tomiko, the influential wife of the eighth shogun of the Muromachi shogunate, Ashikaga Yoshimasa, has died aged 56.

Born in Yamashiro Province in 1440, Tomiko married the shogun when she was 16 years old. Her husband showed little interest in political or administrative affairs, and Tomiko assumed the role of running the country.

When no heir was forthcoming, Yoshimasa passed the responsibilities of governing to his younger brother, Yoshimi. By the time Tomiko eventually did give birth to a son, Yoshihisa, in 1465, so much power had already been ceded to Yoshimi that two factions developed, one supporting Yoshimi, and the other upholding the succession of Yoshihisa. The resulting 11-year-long Onin War

was won by Yoshihisa, who eventually succeeded his father. Tomiko outlived both her husband and her son.

Nun Writes Guide to Fly-fishing

England, 1496: The *Boke of Saint Albans*, originally published in 1486, has been republished with a new section entitled *Treatyse of fysshynge wyth an Angle*, a guide to fly-fishing.

The 1486 edition was limited to hawking and hunting. There was no cover page, but authorship was attributed to "Julyans Barnes." The current edition acknowledges "Julyans Bernes" as author.

It is believed that both names refer to Juliana Berners, the prioress of the Benedictine abbey of Sopwell.

Juliana Berners was raised at court and later entered religious orders. However, even as a nun she retained her love of hunting and fishing. It is believed that she wrote the book in 1421, though it may not be all her own work. It would appear that it contains translations from similar French treatises.

The current edition is published by Wynkyn de Worde, who has become England's most famous publisher since the invention of the printing press 50 years ago.

Juliana Berners introduces the book with the words: "Truely to my best discretion it semeth good disportes and honest games in whom a man ioyeth without any repentaunce

after. Then foloweth it that good disportes and honest games: be cause of mannes fayre age and longe lyfe. And therfore nowe we wyll I chose of foure good dysportes and honest games, that is to wete of Haukyng, Huntyng, and fyshyng, and for foulyng."

Anne of Brittany Marries King Louis

France, January 8, 1499: Anne of Brittany has worn a majestic white bridal gown for her third wedding. In return for her hand in marriage her new husband, Louis XII, has recognized the autonomy of Brittany and his wife's title as the Duchess of Brittany.

Anne was born in 1477, the daughter of Duke Francis II of Brittany. Shortly after her birth, the French invaded Brittany and secured an undertaking from her father that Anne, as his heir, would only marry with the consent of the French monarch. Her father died 11 years later, in 1488.

Anne sought to renege on the undertaking of her father and pleaded for military assistance from Archduke Maximilian of Austria, King Henry VII of England, and King Ferdinand II of Aragon, but none was forthcoming. She even married Maximilian by proxy in the hope of securing assistance from Austria. Eventually, after being besieged for several months at Rennes, she capitulated. Her marriage to Maximilian was annulled and on December 6, 1491, she married Charles VIII of France.

The marriage was not a happy one. One of the many issues of contention was that Charles forbade Anne to use the title "Duchess of Brittany." None of their four children survived infancy.

When Charles died last year, Anne agreed to marry his successor, Louis XII, but only after his marriage to his first wife was annulled. We must hope that this third marriage will bring her comfort.

Anne of Brittany

The Land of the Shogun, a painting by the Japanese artist Sesshu.

Lucrezia Borgia Marries Again

Italy, December 1501: Lucrezia Borgia, the beautiful but notorious daughter of Pope Alexander VI (Rodrigo Borgia), has married Alfonso d'Este, Duke of Ferrara, and will be leaving Rome. This marriage, fiercely resisted by the Duke's family, is her third. Her first two marriages, made to further her powerful family's political and territorial ambitions, ended when their political value waned.

Lucrezia's first husband was Giovanni Sforza, Lord of Pesaro. She divorced him on the grounds of impotence. Her second husband, the handsome and much-loved Alfonso of Aragon, Duke of Bisceglie, was murdered, in spite of Lucrezia's attempts to protect his well-being.

Italy's Borgia family epitomizes the political and sexual corruption of the Renaissance Papacy, but Lucrezia Borgia's reputation as a heartless femme fatale is perhaps a little unfair, deriving from the association with her far more bloodthirsty and ruthless relatives.

Lucrezia Borgia

> *"I SHOULD HAVE NO COMPASSION ON THESE WITCHES; I SHOULD BURN THEM ALL."*
>
> MARTIN LUTHER
> (1483–1546) GERMAN
> RELIGIOUS REFORMER

Queen Isabella of Spain Dies

Valladolid, Spain, November 26, 1504: Isabella, Queen of Castile and wife of Ferdinand, King of Aragon, has died today at the age of 53. Known as "La Catolica" for her piety and orthodoxy, Isabella's marriage to Ferdinand united the territories of Castile and Aragon and led to the formation of modern Spain, ushering in a golden age of exploration and conquest for the country.

Dubbed "the Catholic Kings" by Pope Alexander VI, Ferdinand and Isabella were committed to the organization and unification of their new dominion and together established a highly effective co-regency. Their motto of equality was: *Tanto monta, monta tanto, Isabel como Fernando* ("They amount to the same, Isabella and Ferdinand").

As part of their efforts to establish centralized political, legal, and economic power and religious orthodoxy, Ferdinand and Isabella requested Pope Sixtus IV to authorize the Inquisition, and in 1483 Tomás de Torquemada became the first Inquisitor General in Seville.

In 1492, following years of lobbying, the noted navigator and explorer Christopher Columbus succeeded in convincing Isabella and Ferdinand to sponsor him in his quest to discover a sea route to China and India. His intention was to sail west around the world and reach Asia from the east, thus securing valuable access to trade. Columbus's subsequent discovery of the Americas laid the groundwork for Spain to establish its empire in the New World and become the first modern world power.

Surrounded by family members and courtiers, Isabella, Queen of Spain, lies on her deathbed.

French "Book of Hours" Is Completed

France, c. 1508: Anne, Duchess of Brittany and Queen Consort of Louis XII of France, has received *The Grand Hours of Anne of Brittany*, a book of hours commissioned from the master manuscript illuminator Jean Bourdichon, one of the most beautiful books ever created.

Known for her great intelligence and for her patronage of the arts, she is the only surviving child of Francis II, Duke of Brittany, and his wife Margaret Fois. Anne succeeded to her father's duchy on September 9, 1488.

Book of Hours.

In an attempt to preserve the autonomy of the duchy within France she allied herself with the powerful Maximilian of Austria, who married her by proxy on December 19, 1490. However, King Charles VIII of France, fearful that Brittany would pass into the hands of a foreign power, laid siege to Rennes and forced Anne to renounce her marriage and marry him instead, thus uniting Brittany with France.

The marriage produced four children, none of whom survived for very long. When Charles VIII died in 1498, Anne was only 21 years old and required by a previous agreement to marry his successor, Louis XII. This marriage has produced two surviving daughters, Claude and Renée. During the reign of Louis and Anne, the French court has established itself as a principal center of European art and culture.

Brazil, April, 1500: Portuguese explorer, Pedro Alvares Cabral, discovers a new landmass–Brazil.

Eastern Europe, 1500: War breaks out again between Lithuania and Russia, as Russia's Ivan III invades the neighboring country.

Varanasi, India, c. 1500: Mystical poet Kabir attempts to reconcile Muslim and Hindu communities.

London, England, November 14, 1501: Princess Catherine of Aragon marries Prince Arthur, older son and heir of Henry VII.

Italy, December, 1501: Lucrezia Borgia marries third husband, Alfonso d'Este, Duke of Ferrara.

Rome, Italy, 1501: A papal bull issued by Pope Alexander VI orders the burning of books that denounce the authority of the Catholic Church.

London, England, April 1502: Prince Arthur, heir to the Tudor Dynasty, dies, aged 16.

Tabriz, Persia, 1502: Shah Ismail I, having defeated his rival Alwand of the White Sheep, founds Persia's Safavid Dynasty.

Edinburgh, Scotland, August 8, 1503: Margaret Tudor, elder daughter of Henry VII, marries James IV of Scotland.

Florence, Italy, September 8, 1504: Michelangelo's magnificent statue *David* is completed.

Valladolid, Spain, November 1504: Isabella, Queen of Castile and wife of Ferdinand, King of Aragon, dies.

London, c. 1504: Thomas à Kempis's *De Imitatione Christi* appears in an English translation, the fourth book of which was translated by Lady Margaret Beaufort.

Netherlands, 1507: Margaret of Austria is appointed Regent of the Netherlands by her father Maximilian I, the Holy Roman Emperor.

France, c. 1508: Anne, Duchess of Brittany, Queen Consort of Louis XII of France, receives the *Book of Hours* which she commissioned from the master manuscript illuminator Jean Bourdichon.

Westminster, England, June 24, 1509: Henry VIII is crowned King, then marries his brother Arthur's widow, Catherine of Aragon.

Westminster, England, June 25, 1509: Lady Margaret Beaufort, Countess of Richmond and Derby, mother of Henry VII, dies, aged 68.

Florence, Italy, May 1510: Sandro Botticelli dies, aged about 65.

Venice, Italy, July 10, 1510: Caterina Cornaro, Queen of Cyprus, Lady of Asolo, dies, aged about 56.

Genoa, Italy, September 15, 1510: Italian mystic Catherine of Genoa dies, aged 53. She is remembered for her work among the poor and for her two treatises: *Trattato del Purgatorio* and *Dialogo*.

Catherine of Aragon and Henry VIII with the cardinals.

Coronation of Henry VIII and Queen Catherine

Westminster, England, June 24, 1509: King Henry VIII was crowned today and the nation rejoices. Young and energetic, the new King heralds a new era for England. Just two weeks ago he married Catherine of Aragon, the widow of his older brother Prince Arthur, and six years his senior.

Catherine is the youngest daughter of Spanish rulers Ferdinand II of Aragon and Isabella I of Castile. In 1501 she married Prince Arthur, eldest son of Henry VII. As the Prince of Wales, Arthur was sent to Ludlow Castle on the Welsh border. Catherine accompanied him. There they both succumbed to an epidemic of "sweating sickness," common among the English upper classes. Catherine was dangerously ill, but recovered to find herself a widow.

Not wishing to surrender Catherine's promised dowry and forgo the important alliance with Spain, Henry VII arranged for her to marry his second son, Henry. She testified that her short marriage to Arthur had not been consummated. On these grounds, Pope Julius II then issued a dispensation allowing Catherine to be betrothed to her husband's brother, a relationship that usually precludes marriage in the Catholic Church.

Rivalry between England and Spain and Ferdinand's refusal to pay the full dowry, as well as Henry VII's cooling enthusiasm for the match, has prevented the couple from marrying until Henry ascended the throne. Henry was by then under no obligation to marry Catherine, but appears to be genuinely in love with her and has chosen to honor the match.

Death of Lady Margaret Beaufort

Westminster, England, June 29, 1509: Lady Margaret Beaufort, the Countess of Richmond and Derby, and beloved mother of Henry VII, has died today, aged 68.

Lady Margaret can be said to be the mother of the Tudor dynasty. She was first married in 1450, as a very young child, to John de la Pole. Following the annulment of this marriage, she was married to Edmund Tudor, Earl of Richmond and half-brother to King Henry VI. Lady Margaret was only 13 years old and pregnant with Henry when Edmund died. This pregnancy at such a young age left her infertile.

Her third marriage was to Thomas, Lord Stanley, and made Margaret Countess of Derby, but she was usually known as the Countess of Richmond and Derby. Lady Margaret played an important part in bringing the disastrous Wars of the Roses to an end. After the battle of Bosworth Field, her son Henry, head of the Lancastrian party, became King in large part through her political strategies. He then united the warring houses of York and Lancaster through his marriage to Elizabeth of York, daughter of Edward IV.

Lady Margaret was a highly educated and extremely pious woman and a great benefactress. In addition to her many private works of charity the Countess was a generous patron of learning.

In 1502 she set up the Lady Margaret's Readership in Divinity at both Oxford and Cambridge universities, and through her generosity, God's College at Cambridge was refounded and enlarged as Christ's College.

She founded St John's College, Cambridge where her portrait hangs in the Great Hall, and the first women's college at Oxford, Lady Margaret Hall, is named in her honor. Her deep love of learning was clearly expressed through her ardent patronage of the early English press, and she commissioned works from some of the first printers, including William Caxton and Jan Wynkyn de Worde.

Margaret of Austria

time out

In 1500 an unprecedented event occurred in Switzerland, the result of a prolonged and difficult labor. Pig gelder Jacob Nufer performed an emergency caesarean section on his wife, who made a full recovery.

Lady Margaret Beaufort, mother of the Tudor dynasty, has died.

Goa, India, 1510: The Portuguese establish a trading colony at Goa, the first permanent European settlement in Asia.

Malacca, Malaya, August 24, 1511: The Portuguese fleet captures Malacca and gains control of the spice trade.

Panama, September 25, 1513: Vasco Nunéz de Balboa discovers the Pacific Ocean.

Edinburgh, Scotland, September 1513: Queen Margaret becomes Regent of Scotland on behalf of her infant son, James V.

Blois, France, January 1514: Anne, Duchess of Brittany, Queen Consort of Louis XII of France, dies aged 37.

Scotland, 1514: Queen Margaret of Scotland marries Archibald Douglas, Earl of Angus.

Netherlands, 1515: Margaret of Austria is reappointed Regent of Netherlands by her nephew Charles V, the Holy Roman Emperor.

Scotland, 1515: Scottish nobles take away the regency from Queen Margaret, and she and her husband, the Earl of Angus, flee to England.

France, 1515: Louise of Savoy, mother of King Francis, becomes Regent of France during his absence on campaign in Italy.

Greenwich, England, February 18, 1516: A daughter, Mary, is born to Henry VIII and Catherine of Aragon.

Wittenberg, Germany, October 31, 1517: Martin Luther, leader of the Reformation, nails his 95 theses to a church door.

Ferrara, Italy, June 24, 1519: Lucrezia Borgia dies, aged 39, much mourned by her husband and the people of Ferrara.

Mantua, Italy, 1519: Isabella d'Este rules Mantua after death of her husband Francisco Gonzago, as regent for their son, Federico.

Turkey, September 1520: Suleiman the Magnificent becomes sultan and the Ottoman Empire enters its most powerful period.

Bologna, Italy, c. 1520: Properzia de' Rossi wins a competition to sculpt doors for the Church of San Petronio and chooses for her subject in marble *Joseph and Potiphar's Wife*.

Tabriz, Persia, c. 1520: Persian mechanical engineer Hafez el-Esfahani invents two new types of water-mill.

Rome, Italy, January 1521: Martin Luther is excommunicated by Pope Leo X.

London, England, c. 1524: Margaret More Roper translates into English Erasmus's *A Devout Treatise upon the Pater Noster*.

Isabella d'Este

> " *REJOICE THAT*
> *HE WHO*
> *BESTOWS*
> *POWERS OF*
> *MIND*
> *(LARGITOR*
> *INGENII) AND*
> *GRANTS*
> *WISDOM TO*
> *MEN WHO ARE*
> *GREAT AND*
> *LEARNED IN*
> *THE LAW,*
> *SHOULD NOT*
> *HAVE DENIED*
> *TO THE FRAIL*
> *AND HUMBLER*
> *SEX SOME OF*
> *THE CRUMBS*
> *FROM THE*
> *TABLES OF*
> *WISDOM.*"

CHARITAS
PIRCKHEIMER, GERMAN
NUN, C. 1501

Anne, Duchess of Brittany, Dies

Blois, France, January 9, 1514: Anne, the Duchess of Brittany and twice the Queen Consort of France, has died at the age of 37. Married successively to two Kings of France, Charles VIII and Louis XII, Anne retained the title of Duchess of Brittany and reigned there as a sovereign duchess in her own right.

She remained passionately committed to the preservation of Breton independence and devoted her considerable energy and intelligence to the duchy's administration. During her life she was married three times and gave birth to 11 children, only two of whom, her daughters Claude and Renée by Louis, have survived.

In 1504, eager to keep Brittany out of French hands, Anne had arranged for Claude to marry Charles of Austria (the future emperor Charles V). Louis XII, however, had arranged instead a marriage between Claude and the next French heir, Francis of Angouleme. Anne refused to sanction the marriage, understanding that it would mean the final joining of Brittany to the crown of France.

The winter of 1513–14 was hard and cold, and the Duchess did not survive it. Her popularity was demonstrated at her elaborate funeral, which lasted for 40 days. Her heart was placed in an enameled gold reliquary and laid to rest in her parents' tomb at Nantes.

Although Claude will inherit Brittany from her mother, the independence of the duchy of Brittany will come to an end with Anne's death.

Queen Margaret Flees Scotland for England

Scotland, 1515: Queen Margaret of Scotland, eldest daughter of Henry VII of England and sister to Henry VIII, has fled Scotland for England with her

Margaret of Scotland with James IV.

husband Archibald, Earl of Angus. Her flight is the inevitable conclusion of a chain of events that began with her first marriage.

As a child of 12, Margaret was married by proxy to James IV, King of Scotland, and became Queen of Scots in 1502. This overt political match was made as part of the Treaty of Perpetual Peace between England and Scotland, concluded on the same day. In 1509, when Henry VIII ascended the English throne, he threatened this tenuous alliance by making war on France, an ancient Scottish ally. James IV was forced to invade England in order to honor the Auld Alliance and he met his death at the Battle of Flodden Field on September 9, 1513.

On his death Margaret became Regent of Scotland on behalf of her infant son James V. Her position, both as a woman and the sister of the enemy King, was extremely difficult, and a pro-French faction at court was soon promoting her replacement by John Stewart, Duke of Albany. Her considerable political skills enabled her to reconcile the opposing parties, but her good work was undone when she fell in love with, and secretly married, Archibald Douglas, Earl of Angus, on August 6, 1514.

This was a disastrous political move, for the marriage strengthened the pro-French faction and, according to the terms of the late King's will, meant that the Queen's position as Regent was forfeited. The Privy Council further ruled that she also forfeited her rights to the supervision of her children. Margaret responded by taking the young princes to Stirling Castle, but she was forced to surrender them to Albany on his assumption of the Regency in May 1515, and left Scotland soon afterward.

A Princess Is Born in Greenwich

Greenwich, England, February 18, 1516: A daughter was born today at the Palace of Palentia in Greenwich, to Henry VIII and

Anne, Duchess of Brittany, spent her life ensuring that Brittany retained its independence from France.

Catherine of Aragon. The infant, Mary, is their fourth child; none has yet survived infancy.

Catherine first became pregnant soon after their marriage, and a stillborn daughter was born prematurely in January 1510. This deep disappointment was soon followed by another pregnancy and Prince Henry, Duke of Cornwall, was born on January 1, 1511, and christened four days later. There were great celebrations for the birth of the young prince, an heir to the throne, but these were halted by the baby's death after just 52 days of life.

Catherine then had a miscarriage, followed by another short-lived son. It is hoped that Princess Mary may prove stronger than her siblings. Although the nation rejoices in the birth of a princess, it is greatly hoped that the Queen may soon provide the King with an heir. Catherine and Henry have proved a happy couple, despite the difference in their ages. Catherine is Henry's intellectual equal, and ruled well in his stead while he was away campaigning against the French from 1512–14.

Princess Mary will be baptized on Thursday, with Cardinal Thomas Wolsey standing godfather.

Ferrara Mourns the Death of Duchess Lucrezia

Ferrara, Italy, June 24, 1519: Lucrezia Borgia, devoted wife of Alfonso d'Este, Duke of Ferrara, has died of puerperal fever at the age of 39. This popular and much-loved Duchess, a loving wife to Alfonso and mother of his four children, will be mourned by her husband and the people of Ferrara.

Lucrezia was not always so well loved. The earlier part of her life was spent in Rome, where her family's name was a byword for lust, incest, cruelty, and even murder. Her scheming brother, Cesare, and their ruthless and powerful father, Pope Alexander VI, were certainly guilty of using bloody methods to achieve their political ambitions, but whether Lucrezia was as guilty as they were, or was merely used as their instrument, is a matter of ongoing debate. Alfonso's family, aware of the Borgias' unsavory reputation, initially resisted the marriage, but were soon won over by Lucrezia's considerable charm, grace, and virtuous character.

Within two years of her marriage, the Pope died and her brother Cesare was ruined, which left Lucrezia without the protection of the powerful Borgia family.

The studiolo of Isabella d'Este in Mantua, Italy.

Fortunately, she had proved herself worthy of her new family's love and respect, and her position was secure. As Duchess, Lucrezia established the Este court as a center of culture, encouraging visits by all the greatest poets, artists, and educated men of the time.

She was a generous and gracious patron to the artists working within the palace, and became known as "the good Duchess." One of the visitors, a Venetian poet called Pietro Bembo, became enraptured by the lovely Duchess and wrote adoring poems to her. They developed a close, and possibly romantic, friendship. Their correspondence shows her to have been a romantic woman of cultivated taste. Lucrezia will be remembered for her religious piety and patronage of the arts.

Commission for Properzia de' Rossi

Bologna, Italy, c. 1520: The sculptor Properzia de' Rossi has bested many male colleagues to win the prestigious competition to ornament the west facade of the Church of San Petronio in Bologna. She is to create three sibyls, two angels, and a pair of bas-relief marble panels. One panel will illustrate the subject of *Joseph and Potiphar's Wife*.

This work marks a move away from the complex and small-scale work, fashioned from stone-fruit pits, of her early career. Properzia de' Rossi, who studied under the Bolognese artist and master engraver Marcantonio Raimondi, is one of only around 30 female artists working in Italy today, and her skills as a sculptor make her even more unusual in this area.

English Translation of Popular Latin Text

London, England, c. 1524: Margaret More Roper, the eldest daughter of Sir Thomas More, the noted lawyer, humanist, and trusted adviser to King Henry VIII, has accomplished a remarkable feat of scholarship this year. Her admirable translation from Latin of *A Devout Treatise upon the Pater Noster*, the popular exposition of the Lord's Prayer by her father's friend Erasmus, is sure to assist the devotions of English Christians.

Such a worthwhile achievement lends powerful support to the argument for the value of the education of women, ably made by Richard Hyrde in the dedicatory letter to this volume. Margaret, educated in the classics and science, is considered an outstanding scholar and writer and Erasmus, an admirer of her work, has called her the "ornament of Britain."

Translation, particularly when it is of devotional treatises written by men, is considered the fruit of faith and seen as a proper occupation for a literate woman. Margaret herself would have preferred to study rather than marry, but her father convinced her that "one may spend a life in dreaming over Plato, and yet go out of it without leaving the world a whit better for having made part of it." She took his advice and married Will Roper.

Catherine of Aragon

Margaret More Roper (center) has translated Erasmus into English.

Angela Merici

Three Women and a Treaty

Cambrai, France, August 3, 1529: Today, three exceptional women have been instrumental in bringing about the end of hostilities between France and the Holy Roman Empire. Their efforts will put an end to the fighting between the forces of King Frances I of France and Emperor Charles V of Spain.

The treaty, which is called the Treaty of Cambrai, or " La Paix des Dames," has been negotiated by Louise of Savoy, the Regent of France, Margaret of Austria and Marguerite, Queen of Navarre.

Louise of Savoy has a brilliant understanding of all the intricacies of politics and diplomacy. She is the mother of King Francis, and his regent during his current absence. The King is incarcerated, having been captured by the forces of Charles V during the 1525 Battle of Pavia.

The two other women also share very close relationships with the feuding monarchs. Margaret of Austria, regent of the Netherlands, is Charles V's aunt and, during his minority, was his guardian. She is also an accomplished and seasoned negotiator. The third negotiator, Marguerite of Navarre, is a social justice advocate who calls herself "The Prime Minister of the Poor." She is the daughter of Louise of Savoy and the sister of King Francis.

Although the Treaty of Cambrai confirms Spanish (Habsburg) control in Italy, it does not exact the surrender of Burgundy to Charles. It is anticipated that this treaty will also bring about the release of King Francis.

Twelve Virgins Found Ursuline Order

Brescia, Italy, November 25, 1535: Today, in a small house in Brescia, near the Church

Angela Merici's vision urged her to found a religious order.

of St Afra, twelve women, bound by the noble aim of promoting family values and education, particularly for girls, have established a new religious order called the Ursulines. The order will also care for the sick and needy.

The order's founder is the religious leader Angela Merici. Merici believes that better Christian education is needed for young girls, and for several years has dedicated her time to teaching girls in her home, which she had converted into a school. She relates that one day she had a vision that revealed to her that she was to found an association of virgins who would devote their lives to the religious and scholarly training of young girls.

Born on March 21, 1474 at Desenzano, a lakeside town in Lombardy, Angela Merici became an orphan when she was only 10 years old. Shortly after the sudden death of her older sister, she joined the Third Order of St Francis and devoted herself to teaching children. Merici is a woman ahead of her times. Her plan for

training religious women without wearing a distinctive habit, taking solemn vows, or living in enclosure is decidedly contrary to today's prevailing notions. Yet, through her devotion and commitment to the betterment of society, Angela Merici has established herself as a candidate for sainthood.

Queen Jane Dies After Birth of Heir

Hampton Court Palace, Richmond, England, October 24, 1537: Just 12 short days after fulfilling her duty as wife to the King by producing a son and heir to the throne, Jane Seymour, third wife of Henry VIII has died. The Queen never recovered from complications following the arduous delivery of her son, Edward. Palace insiders have revealed that shortly after the birth she became feverish and then delirious. She managed to participate in her infant son's christening ceremony, weak and exhausted after her labor, but died soon afterward.

Jane Seymour, who was born about 1509, first came to court as a lady-in-waiting to King Henry VIII's first wife, Catherine of Aragon. When Anne Boleyn supplanted Catharine of Aragon in King Henry's affections, he broke from the

Reformationist ex-nun, Katherine von Bora.

Roman Catholic Church in order to marry her. Seymour continued as lady-in-waiting to the new Queen. Henry has been under great pressure to produce a male heir to the throne in order that the Tudor dynasty will continue. His loss of interest in Queen Anne stemmed from her failure to produce a son.

Anne Boleyn is condemned to death.

Henry became betrothed to Jane on May 20, 1536, the day after Anne Boleyn was beheaded, having been found guilty of the charges of bewitchment, incest, adultery, and treason. The King married Seymour on May 30, only 11 days after Boleyn's execution. Seymour was publicly proclaimed Queen on June 4, although she was never crowned.

Seymour's kind and gentle character was in distinct contrast to that of the sharp-tongued and flamboyant Anne Boleyn. Unlike her predecessor, Seymour shied away from national and political affairs, mindful that the last Queen lost her head when she meddled in politics.

Jane's body will be embalmed and laid to rest in the tomb at Windsor Castle. Her special status as mother of the heir to the throne will never be forgotten.

Abbess's Letter to Queen Confiscated

Geneva, Switzerland, 1539: An open letter, published in the form of a small book, and addressed to Queen Marguerite of Navarre, appealing for her support of religious freedom for women, has been suppressed by city officials. They claim that the book, called the *Epistre trés utile*, or "very useful letter," is subversive.

The author, the controversial Genevan Protestant reformer and theologian, Marie Dentière, believes that women should take a more active role in the Church. In addition, the letter contains a section called "Defense of Women," in which Dentière advocates women's right to interpret the Scriptures. She discusses the bold roles God gave to women, and cites Bible stories, such as the account of the mother of Moses who defied the law to protect her son. The letter further calls for an expulsion of Catholic clergy from France, and criticizes the foolishness of the Protestant clergy.

Dentière, a former nun and abbess, is a strong advocate of the need for the greater involvement of women in religious practice. She believes women and men are equally entitled to interpret the Scriptures and the practices of religion. The forward-thinking Marie Dentière, who plays an active role in Genevan religion and politics, has caused unease among her male colleagues because she does not conform to their opinions on the proper place of women in society. There are concerns that the anger her writings provoke among the authorities may result in a more repressive attitude toward women.

Leading Figure of the Renaissance Dies

Mantua, Italy, February 13, 1539: The First Lady of the Renaissance, Isabella d'Este, died today. She was 65 years old. The inventor, political ruler, patron of the arts, mother of seven children, and musician will be remembered for her remarkable contribution to Italian society. She not only supported great painters such as Titian, Raphael, and Da Vinci, but throughout her life served others, helping to better standards of living everywhere.

D'Este, who followed the principles for rulers set forth by Machiavelli, was related by birth or marriage to almost every ruler in Italy. She has influenced women all over the world and proved that they can be excellent and accomplished political leaders. A great diplomat and skilled negotiator, she has done much to make Italy the thriving place it is today.

Anne Boleyn

Portrait of Isabella d'Este by Giovanni-Francesco Caroto. She posed for many prominent artists.

Basel, Switzerland, 1536: Desiderius Erasmus, philosopher and humanist, dies, aged about 70.

Hampton Court Palace, Richmond, England, October 12, 1537: Queen Jane bears Henry VIII his long-desired son and heir, Edward.

Hampton Court Palace, Richmond, England, October 24, 1537: Queen Jane, third wife of Henry VIII, dies of complications arising from childbirth.

Rome, Italy, 1538: Vittoria Colonna, Marchesa di Pescara, publishes a collection of sonnets.

Geneva, Switzerland, 1539: Marie Dentière appeals to Queen Marguerite of Navarre to support religious freedom for women.

Mantua, Italy, 1539: Isabella d'Este patron of the arts, dies, aged 65.

Brescia, Italy, January 27, 1540: Angela Merici, founder of the Ursulines, dies, aged about 70.

Surrey, England, July 28, 1540: Catherine Howard marries Henry VIII, becoming his fifth wife. His fourth marriage, to Anne of Cleves, had been annulled.

Lima, Peru, June 26, 1541: Francisco Pizarro, Spanish explorer, dies, aged about 69.

London, England, February 13, 1542: Catherine Howard, fifth wife of Henry VIII, is executed for adultery.

Rome, Italy, July 1542: Pope Paul III establishes the inquisition into Protestantism.

Linlithgow, Scotland, December 14, 1542: Mary, the six-day-old daughter of James V of Scotland and his French wife, Mary de Guise, becomes Queen of Scotland.

Poland, March, 1543: Copernicus publishes *De revolutionibus orbium coelestium (On the Revolution of Heavenly Bodies)*, which contains his theory of heliocentric motion.

London, England, July 12, 1543: Catherine Parr marries Henry VIII in her third marriage and his sixth.

Japan, 1543: Portuguese traders introduce the first Western-style firearms into Japan.

England, 1544: Margaret More, scholar and daughter of Sir Thomas Moore, dies, aged about 39.

London, England, July 16, 1546: Poet Anne Askew is burned at the stake as a heretic.

Russia, January 16, 1547: Ivan IV is crowned the first Tsar of Russia.

Florence, Italy, 1547: Tullia d'Aragona publishes a book of verse examining women's notions of love and sexuality.

Odos en Bigorre, France, December 21, 1549: Marguerite of Navarre, patron of the arts and controversial figure, dies, aged 57.

Catherine Parr

Baby Queen for Scotland

Linlithgow, Scotland, December 14, 1542: A six-day-old baby girl is now the official ruler of Scotland. Mary, daughter of King James V of Scotland and his French wife, Mary de Guise, succeeded to the throne today, after the death of her 30-year-old father. It is believed King James's death was caused by his grief over the Scots' loss to the English at the Battle of Solway Moss. Medical experts claim, however, that he died from cholera. Sources also inform us that when James V heard the news of his daughter's birth, he despaired that it marked the end of the Stewarts' reign over Scotland.

Mary comes to the throne courtesy of a decree passed during the fourteenth-century reign of King James's ancestor, King Robert II of Scotland, stating that the Scottish Crown can only be inherited by males in the line of Robert's children (all sons). Females and female lines can inherit only after the extinction of male lines. Mary has ascended to the throne because, with the death of her father, there are no remaining direct, legitimate male descendants of Robert II.

There are rumors that Mary (who will now be known as Mary, Queen of Scots) will be betrothed to five-year-old Edward, the son of King Henry VIII of England, as soon as possible. This will ensure that their heirs inherit both the Kingdoms of Scotland and England.

King Henry Weds for the Sixth Time

London, England, July 12, 1543: Today, the twice-widowed and childless Catherine Parr has become King Henry VIII's sixth bride. The latest woman to take on the dangerous honor of being King Henry's Queen is the daughter of Sir Thomas Parr of Kendal in the Lake District, and his wife, Maud Green.

Catherine and Henry were married by Stephen Gardiner in the "Queen's closet" at Hampton Court Palace, with all the royal children present. The Queen has many admirable and attractive qualities. She is also as dedicated to finery and amusements as any of Henry's previous wives. She is respectable, well-educated, and wealthy, and although widowed two times is still 20 years younger than the King. Catherine is tall, vivacious, and witty, with a kind and sensible nature and an excellent record in caring for step-children and nursing elderly husbands.

Sources close to the royal court have revealed that Sir Thomas Seymour, flamboyant brother of the late Queen Jane, and uncle to Henry VIII's only male heir, was courting Catherine when she caught the eye of the King. Henry's first gifts to her were delivered on February 16, 1543, a year after the execution of his previous wife; Sir Thomas then wisely stepped aside. Catherine herself also graciously bowed to King Henry's attentions.

Henry VIII's tangled marital career has significantly aggravated England's turbulent political climate. His short-lived, politically motivated and unconsummated fourth marriage to the mysterious Anne of Cleves was annulled after he claimed he found her physically unattractive. His fifth marriage to Catherine Howard, 30 years his junior, ended in her execution for adultery and indiscretion. The court has been nervously anticipating the ageing King's next betrothal. As with his previous wives, the future Queen will play a critical role in England's religious and political arena.

Talented Scholar Dies

England, 1544: Margaret More Roper, the outstanding scholar, translator, writer, and eldest and favorite child of Sir Thomas More, has died. She was 39 years old. Trained in the classics, philosophy, and science, Margaret wrote elegant and graceful prose and verse both in Greek and Latin. She has translated a work by Erasmus on the Lord's Prayer into English and is credited with the amending of a Latin text by St Cyprian to recapture the original meaning. More also translated Eusebius from Greek to Latin.

In addition to her scholarly talents, she was a paragon of loyalty and familial love, shown through her unstinting efforts to comfort and honor her father during his imprisonment in the Tower of London. More and her husband, William Roper, were frequent visitors to her father's cell. When, in 1535, Sir Thomas More refused to bless the Reformation of King Henry VIII of England and swear to Henry as Head of the Church of England, he was beheaded. After her father's head was displayed on a pike for a month, Margaret More Roper purchased it and preserved it by pickling it in spices.

The erudite More was herself imprisoned for a time after her father's death when she revealed her plans to have his works published. More will be buried in St Dunstan's, Canterbury. She requested that her father's head be buried with her.

Margaret More Roper, with her father, Sir Thomas More.

Courageous Poet Burned at Stake

London, England, July 16, 1546: Today, the poet and member of the Reformed Church, Anne Askew, was burned at the stake after being charged twice with the crime of heresy. She is the first woman to be tortured in the Tower of London. Witnesses say that after months of torture on the rack, she was too crippled to walk to the stake and had to be carried to her execution on a chair.

Born at Stallingborough into a notable Lincolnshire family, she was forced by her father, Sir William Askew (Ayscough), to

England's Henry VIII, shown here with his six wives.

marry a Catholic man, Thomas Kyme, when she was just 15, as a substitute for her sister who had died. Anne, who bore two children, rebelled against her husband by refusing to adopt his surname. Her association with the Protestant Reform movement led her to be questioned by Church and government authorities in 1545. She was eventually released, but was tried again this year and tortured in an attempt to force her to implicate fellow reformers. However, she refused to abandon her Protestant faith or to incriminate her associates.

Anne Askew will be remembered for her courage and wit, which shine through in her writings, as well as her knowledge of the law and her subversion of male authority. Askew was a strong independent woman who has bravely presented these tumultuous times with an alternative model of Christian virtue.

Tullia Writes on Love

Florence, Italy, 1547: This year has been productive for Venetian socialite, poet, and philosopher Tullia d'Aragona, who has published a book of verse called *Rime della Signora Tullia d'Aragona et di diversi a lei*. The 44 verses are either addressed to d'Aragona or written about her by her many admirers. Her latest piece, the prose poem *Dialogue on the Infinity of Love*, examines women's sexual and emotional autonomy in exchanges of romantic love.

Never before has a woman dared to write on the topic of love; d'Aragona's entry into this male-dominated arena is unprecedented. Through her writings, she also links the issues of love and sex to the broader treatment of women. Thus the refined and entertaining d'Aragona is making a unique contribution to Italy's cultural and social history.

Marguerite's Death a Loss for France

Odos en Bigorre, France, December 21, 1549: France has lost an inspiring and brilliant feminine mind. The remarkable author and distinguished patron of humanists and reformers, Marguerite of Navarre, died today, aged 57.

Marguerite of Navarre's religious convictions and her status as a pioneer for women in the French literary scene have made her a controversial figure. She spent much of her life preoccupied with religious and ethical issues and became an activist for reorganization within the Catholic Church. She also inspired debate among theologians for her radical reform ideals. However, the conservative Paris university, the Sorbonne, disapproved of her outspokenness. In her later years, she

Claudia of France, wife of King Francis I.

withdrew from political life and devoted herself completely to letters and poetry.

The daughter of Charles d'Angoulême and Louise of Savoy, Marguerite was born on April 11, 1492, and was tutored from her earliest years by excellent teachers. She received a comprehensive education in Latin, Italian, Spanish, German, as well as Greek and Hebrew. When her brother, James I, ascended the throne, she became a major cultural influence and arranged for artists such as Leonardo da Vinci and Benvenuto Cellini to work at the King's court. In 1526, Marguerite traveled to Madrid to negotiate the Treaty of Madrid. A year later, she became the "Queen of Navarre" by marrying the much younger landowner Henri d'Albret.

During her time as an activist for reorganization within the Catholic Church, Marguerite called for a return to a focus on the Scriptures. She practiced the lifestyle that she preached and made a habit of regular prayer and daily meditation. She also procured asylum for religious activists, and composed poetry, including her first major work, "Marguerites de la Marguerite des princesses", which she published in 1547. A woman of both words and deeds, she will be fondly remembered not only for her friendliness, grace, and charity but also for her invincible strength of soul and prudence worthy of a philosopher.

Margaret of Austria

+ PLVS + VOVS + QV + MOY +

Marguerite of Navarre always dressed in mourning after the death of her infant son Jean in 1530.

Catherine de Medici

England Again Under Catholic Rule

London, England, July 19, 1553: Mary Tudor, the oldest daughter of King Henry VIII, has deposed her cousin, Lady Jane Grey, and has become the new Queen of England. Lady Jane was Queen for just nine days following the death of King Edward VI from tuberculosis.

King Edward, a Protestant, tried to prevent Mary, his devout Catholic half-sister, from succeeding him by proclaiming fellow Protestant, Lady Jane Grey, his successor in his will. Lady Jane's accession has now been deemed unlawful and thus Mary, who was born on February 18, 1516, becomes England's first Queen Regnant since 1141. She also automatically becomes the Head of the Church of England, but she has plans to convert England back to Catholicism.

The new Queen's first Act of Parliament will be to retroactively validate her parents' marriage. Mary and her father became estranged when he persuaded the Archbishop of Canterbury to annul his marriage to her mother, Catherine of Aragon, because she had given him no sons to continue the Tudor dynasty. To prevent a legal appeal from Catherine, Henry instigated a new law ending the Pope's jurisdiction over the Church in England, and making himself the head of the new Church of England. Mary was then deemed to be illegitimate and lost her place in the line of succession to Edward.

"WORLDLY COMFORT IS AN ILLUSION, NO SOONER YOU GET IT, IT GOES. I HAVE CHOSEN THE INDESTRUCTIBLE FOR MY REFUGE."

MIRABAI (1550–1574), INDIAN HINDU DEVOTEE

England's new queen, Mary, is a staunch Catholic.

Mary of Guise Assumes Regency in Scotland

Scotland, 1554: Former Queen Consort, Mary of Guise, has deposed the Earl of Arran, James Hamilton, as regent of Scotland, and will rule the country while her young daughter Mary, Queen of Scots, continues growing up in France with her future husband.

Born on November 22, 1515, Mary of Guise was Queen Consort of Scottish King James V of Stewart, who died in 1542. Their marriage was intended to further strengthen the Franco-Scottish alliance against England. Their sons died young, and their third child, Mary, was born six days before her father died.

Hamilton, a Protestant and pro-English party member, was next in line to the throne after the infant Mary, and so he was appointed as regent. In 1543, Hamilton negotiated her betrothal to England's Prince Edward, the son of King Henry VIII, who hoped the union would finally break Scotland's link with France. With Protestantism spreading, the Scottish Parliament approved the marriage under the Treaty of Greenwich, but the union failed to take place.

When French King Henry II of Valois suggested that Mary marry his son, the Dauphin Francis, Mary of Guise supported it. In 1548, the French Marriage Treaty was signed and five-year-old Mary was sent to live in France.

As regent, Mary of Guise plans to suppress Protestantism and further nurture the Franco-Scottish alliance.

time out

During the 1550s, the Irish warrior princess and pirate Graine Ni Maille, also known as Grace O'Malley, commands a fleet of ships that aims to protect the Irish coast from the threat of English invaders.

Death of Ottoman Sultan's Wife

Istanbul, Turkey, April 18, 1558: Roxelana, the wife of Ottoman Sultan Suleiman I, the Magnificent, died today, aged 58.

Roxelana was born Anastasia Lisovska in 1500 in Western Ukraine. She became known as Hurrem, or Roxelana, later in life. During a regular Crimean Tatar raid on Ukraine, she was captured and taken to the women's slave market in Istanbul, where she was selected for Suleiman's 300-strong harem.

Roxelana left the Topkapi Palace harem to become Suleiman's wife.

Libya, Africa, 1551: Ottoman forces invade and conquer Tripoli.

France, 1552: Catherine de Medici is appointed regent during her husband Henry II's absence at the siege of Metz.

London, England, July 10, 1553: Lady Jane Grey is placed on the throne by the Duke of Northumberland after the death of Edward VI.

London, England, July 19, 1553: Mary Tudor, daughter of Henry VIII and Catherine of Aragon, ascends to the throne.

London, England, February 12, 1554: Lady Jane Grey is executed at the Tower of London.

London, England, July 25, 1554: Queen Mary marries Prince Philip of Spain, but Parliament does not recognize him as king.

Scotland, 1554: Mary of Guise, Mary, Queen of Scots' mother, becomes regent of Scotland while the young queen is sent to France to marry the Dauphin, Francis.

Florence, Italy, c. 1554: Benvenuto Cellini completes his bronze statue of *Perseus and Medusa*.

France, 1555: Nostradamus publishes his *Book of Prophecies*.

China, January 23, 1556: A violent earthquake rocks Shaanxi Province; more than 800,000 perish.

India, 1556: Akbar becomes emperor of the Mughal Empire. He fosters religious tolerance.

Macau, China, 1557: Portuguese traders found the port city of Macau, the first European trading enclave in China.

Istanbul, Turkey, April, 1558: Roxelana Hurrem, wife of Suleiman the Magnificent, dies, aged about 58.

London, England, November 17, 1558: Elizabeth I ascends the English throne, following the death of her half-sister, Mary.

France, c. 1558: Marguerite of Navarre's collection of short stories is published posthumously under the title of *Heptameron*.

France, December, 1560: Catherine de Medici becomes regent of France for her son, Charles IX, after the death of her oldest son Francis II.

Leith, Scotland, August 19, 1561: Mary, Queen of Scots, widowed on the death of her husband, King Francis II of France, arrives in Scotland, aged nineteen.

Venice, Italy, 1561: Gabriele Fallopius publishes *Observationes anatomicae (Anatomical Observations)*.

France, January, 1562: The Edict of January, instigated by Catherine de Medici, recognizes limited rights for Protestants in France. Rejected by the Catholics, this leads to religious civil war.

Lady Jane Grey is executed at the Tower of London in 1554.

Koran, and a women's hospital near the women's slave market.

A spirited joyful woman, Roxelana soon became one of Suleiman's favorite concubines. This displeased his senior consort Gulfem, whose son, Mustafa, was considered heir to the throne. Roxelana convinced Suleiman to send Gulfem and Mustafa away in 1534, and shortly afterward she bore him a son, Selim, and became chief consort. She then made history by convincing the sultan to marry her. This broke 300 years of Ottoman tradition and caused something of an international stir. Islamic law allows a sultan to have four wives, but no sultan up to this time had ever married. Suleiman also allowed her to live at Topkapi Palace permanently, despite another tradition that when imperial heirs come of age, they and their mothers are sent away to govern a province of the Empire.

Roxelana bore five children and she remained Suleiman's only wife. She counseled her husband on affairs of state and encouraged him to control Crimean Tatar slave-raiding in Ukraine. She was involved in several major infrastructure projects and established charitable foundations that paid for a mosque, two schools devoted to study of the

England Returns to Protestant Rule

London, England, November 17, 1558: Elizabeth Tudor has become England's new queen following the death of her half-sister, Queen Mary I, this morning. People are rejoicing in the streets at the end of "Bloody Mary's" reign.

Mary had been attempting to re-establish England as a Catholic country. Her father, Henry VIII, had rejected the authority of the Pope and created the Church of England so he could divorce his first wife, Mary's mother, in 1533.

It is believed that Mary ordered the deaths of 300 religious dissidents during her 5-year reign, hence her nickname. She also caused major international unrest following her marriage to the Catholic Prince Philip (later King Philip II) of Spain, a rival country to England. The marriage was childless, and Philip returned to Spain in 1556.

Today, people are celebrating the accession of a Protestant Queen. Elizabeth is resourceful, determined, intelligent, and even-tempered. She will seek to heal religious divisions in England as soon as possible. Although she will support Protestants and encourage the further development of the Church of England, she will not follow in Mary's footsteps by persecuting those with differing beliefs.

Born on September 7, 1533, Elizabeth is the only surviving child of King Henry VIII and his second wife, Anne Boleyn. Elizabeth has never married, and many observers expect her to remain unwed. If she married, she would be compelled to hand power to her husband and serve as his Queen Consort, and she is unlikely to loosen her grip on power.

New Edition of the *Heptameron*

France, 1559: A second, more accurate version of the late Marguerite of Navarre's collection of short stories has been published today under the new title, *Heptameron*, a Greek word meaning "seven days." The *Heptameron* is a collection of 72 short stories written in French by Marguerite, Queen Consort of King Henry II of Navarre (also known as Marguerite of Valois). The collection was intended to comprise 100 novellas set over a 10-day period—the same format used by the fourteenth-century Italian writer, Giovanni Boccaccio, in his *Decameron*. But Marguerite died after completing the second story of the eighth day in 1549.

The manuscript was first published last year by Pierre Boaistuau, who made some changes. New publisher, Claude Gruget, has reinstated most of the omitted text but has not restored suppressed names. He has even added his own stories.

Elizabeth I of England

ANGOULÊME

CAPTIVITÉ DU ROI FRANÇOIS IER

MARGUERITE DE VALOIS
1492-1549

Marguerite of Navarre was a prolific writer.

London, England, 1563: Queen Elizabeth establishes the Church of England in law.

Rome, Italy, February 1564: Michelangelo (Michelangelo di Ludovico Buonarroti Simoni), painter, sculptor, and architect, dies, aged 88.

Scotland, July 29, 1565: Mary, Queen of Scots, marries her cousin Henry, Lord Darnley.

England, 1565: John Hawkins introduces tobacco to England from the New World, a year after bringing in the sweet potato.

London, England, 1565: Members of the Royal College of Physicians are allowed to perform dissections of the human body for the first time.

Anet, France, April 1566: Diane de Poitiers, influential mistress of Henry II of France, dies, aged 67.

Edinburgh, Scotland, June 19, 1566: Mary, Queen of Scots, gives birth to a son, James.

Istanbul, Turkey, September, 1566: Suleiman the Magnificent, Ottoman leader, dies, aged about 71. He is succeeded by his son, Selim II.

Avila, Spain, c. 1566: Teresa of Avila, Spanish mystic and founder of the Discalced Carmelites, writes *The Way of Perfection*.

Edinburgh, Scotland, May 15, 1567: Mary, Queen of Scots, marries the Earl of Bothwell at the Palace of Holyroodhouse.

Carberry Hill, near Edinburgh, Scotland, June 15, 1567: The forces of Mary, Queen of Scots, are defeated by the Scottish Protestant lords and Mary is imprisoned in Loch Leven Castle.

Scotland, July 24, 1567: Mary, Queen of Scots, is forced to abdicate the throne in favor of her infant son, who is declared James VI. She flees to England.

Scotland, May 13, 1568: James Stewart, Regent Moray and Protestant half-brother of Mary Queen of Scots, defeats Mary's forces at the Battle of Langside.

Rome, February 26, 1570: Queen Elizabeth of England is excommunicated by Pope Pius V with the papal bull, *Regnans in Excelsis*.

Japan, 1570: Nagasaki becomes the first Japanese port to open to overseas trade.

London, England, 1571: Queen Elizabeth opens the Royal Exchange.

Paris, France, August 24, 1572: In the St Bartholomew's Day Massacre over 8,000 Huguenots are killed.

Netherlands, December 1572: During the Siege of Haarlem, Kenau Hasselaer leads 300 women against the Spanish army.

France, 1574: Catherine de Medici again becomes regent of France.

Female Portrait Painter for Spanish Court

Sofonisba Anguissola

Madrid, Spain, 1559: Italian portrait painter, Sofonisba Anguissola, has been appointed court portrait painter and lady-in-waiting to Spain's new queen, Elizabeth of Valois, the third wife of King Philip II.

The artist was invited to join the court on the recommendation of the Spanish Duke of Alba, whose portrait she painted in Milan last year. In the Spanish court, she will produce regular portraits of members of the royal court and family.

Sofonisba Anguissola is the first female Italian artist to have achieved a degree of international recognition. There are few female painters of her talent and training, and her work has become highly sought after throughout Europe.

Born in 1532 in Verona, Italy, Anguissola was trained by Michelangelo Buonarroti, the revered sculptor, architect, and painter; Bernardino Campi, the respected portrait and Lombard school religious painter; and painter Bernardino Gatti.

Anguissola previously created many small devotional pictures, self-portraits and numerous portrait drawings and paintings, particularly of her family members. She has evolved a new style of portraiture involving subjects set in an informal way. One of her best-known works in this style is the 1555 painting, *The Chess Game*, depicting three of her sisters playing chess. The intimacy and spontaneity of such paintings is unprecedented, and they have become known as "conversation pieces." The artist says: "Life is full of surprises, I try to capture these precious moments with wide eyes."

> "IN EVERY RESPECT WE MUST BE CAREFUL AND ALERT, FOR THE DEVIL NEVER SLUMBERS."
>
> TERESA OF AVILA, C. 1566, *THE WAY OF PERFECTION*

Diane de Poitiers Dies in Exile

Anet, France, April 25, 1566: The Duchess of Valentinois and long-time mistress of the late King Henry II, Diane de Poitiers, died today, aged 67.

Diane was Henry's lifelong companion and the most powerful influence in his life, despite their 20-year age gap. She wielded great power at court, but was banished by Henry's wife, Catherine de Medici, after his death in 1559.

Born on September 3, 1499, Diane was 15 years old when she married Louis de Brézé, grandson of King Charles VII and servant to Henry's father, King Francis I, in 1515. Despite their 39-year age difference, they had a very happy marriage and she bore two daughters.

Diane served as lady-in-waiting to Henry's mother, Claude of France, and his grandmother, Louise of Savoy. She was later lady-in-waiting to Eleanor of Habsburg, King Francis I's second wife.

Diane de Poitiers and Henry II admire Jean Goujon's sculpture of Diana. Diane was a patron of the arts.

When his son Henry was 12 years old, Francis ordered Diane to educate him in court etiquette. Two years later, Diane's husband encouraged a marriage between Henry and Catherine de Medici, the great-niece of the Pope. They wed on October 28, 1533, when both were 14 years old. Diane's husband died a short time later and during 1538, Henry and Diane began the affair that lasted until his death.

Henry II became king in 1547, and relied on Diane for political advice. In 1548 she was accorded the title of Duchess of Valentinois as a sign of Henry's favor.

Teresa of Avila's *Way of Perfection*

Avila, Spain, c. 1566: The Spanish mystic and founder of the Discalced Carmelites, Teresa of Avila, has written a guide for the nuns of her new convent, entitled *The Way of Perfection*. The document conveys her directives and advice for obtaining a perfect, spiritual life through the power of resolute prayer.

Teresa founded the convent of Discalced Carmelite Nuns on August 24, 1562. The convent follows a reformed version of the Carmelite regime that reinstates strict earlier rules and also introduces new ones. These include the abandonment of material possessions and living in secluded poverty.

Teresa believes that leading a life of simple poverty allows her followers more time to focus on prayer. The nuns perform manual labor, fast, and have given up the comfort of shoes.

In *The Way of Perfection*, Teresa explains her concerns regarding the "harm and havoc" of the Lutheran movement in France. She laments the pain that God's people are inflicting on him through such attempts to reform the Catholic Church.

The document, which explores her own spiritual journey, also explains the importance of humility and deep introspection. *The Way of Perfection* advocates detachment from man-made things, fraternal love, and the importance of

Teresa of Avila aims to help her nuns follow the Lord's will.

personal solitude. The work was composed at night, so that the day's prayer was not interrupted.

Born in Avila, Spain, on March 28, 1515, Teresa entered the Carmelite Convent of the Incarnation at the age of 20. She experienced powerful mystical events after reading a book that instructed her on how to test her conscience and spirituality. She had bouts of spiritual rapture and felt she had made a union with God.

Mary, Queen of Scots, has abdicated the throne.

Abdication of Mary, Queen of Scots

Edinburgh, Scotland, July 24, 1567: Mary, Queen of Scots, has abdicated the throne in favor of her one-year-old son, James, following her kidnapping and imprisonment in the castle at Loch Leven last month by a group of nobles.

Queen Mary is desperately ill and has suffered a miscarriage. She was pregnant with twins, which were conceived when she was raped by James Hepburn, Earl of Bothwell, three months ago during another kidnapping ordeal.

On that occasion, April 24, Bothwell and a group of his supporters demanded that Mary marry him, and she agreed, hoping that their union might settle the violence between various noble factions. Bothwell's supporters signed a letter approving him as their leader, and he and Mary were married at the Palace of Holyroodhouse in May.

In June, the nobles became jealous of Bothwell's new power and rallied against him, sending their troops to meet Mary's soldiers at Carberry Hill. The nobles demanded that Mary abandon Bothwell and she surrendered herself to avoid a battle. She was taken to Loch Leven Castle and has been a prisoner there ever since.

Mary's life began disintegrating early last year. Her husband and cousin, Henry Stewart, Duke of Albany, commonly known as Lord Darnley, was becoming even more arrogant and power hungry, and increasingly resentful that Mary had denied him the Crown Matrimonial after their marriage in July 1565. He was also extremely jealous of her close friendship with her secretary, David Rizzio, whom he stabbed to death in front of her in March last year. Pregnant and terrified, Mary was held prisoner at the Palace until she convinced Henry to escape with her, and she gave birth to her son James on June 19 in Edinburgh Castle. On February 10 this year, Henry was found murdered and his house was blown up.

Queen Elizabeth Excommunicated

Rome, Italy, February 25, 1570: Pope Pius V has today issued a papal bull excommunicating the Queen of England, Elizabeth I. *Regnans in Excelsis* decrees that Elizabeth is "the servant of crime," and that the Catholics of England are "not to obey her or her orders, mandates and laws," on pain of facing excommunication—the ultimate disgrace—themselves.

Queen Elizabeth had established the Church of England in law in 1563, formalizing Henry VIII's actions in removing the Church from papal oversight. Since that time, the Catholics of England have been tolerated on condition that they remained loyal to Elizabeth and attended Church periodically.

Parliament is expected to react harshly to today's papal bull, particularly as it encourages Catholics to ignore English law. Catholics now face a choice between treason and excommunication.

Catherine de Medici Appointed Regent Again

France, May 30, 1574: Former Queen Consort, Catherine de Medici, has become Regent of France for the third time following the death today of her son, Charles IX.

Catherine's third son, Henry III, King of Poland, is next in line for the throne, but as he is living in Poland, Catherine has been appointed to the office of regent in his absence. Catherine was last regent of France from 1560 to 1563 during the minority of Charles IX. She was previously regent in 1552 when her husband, Henry II, was fighting in Metz.

Born in Italy on April 13, 1519, Catherine became Queen Consort after marrying King Henry II on October 28, 1533, when they were both 14 years old.

During her first regency in 1552, Catherine had little power and was consumed with jealousy over her husband's longtime mistress, Diane de Poitiers. When her husband died in 1559, she banished Diane.

Her second regency began in 1560 when her second son, Francis II, died, and Charles IX ascended the throne. This time, Catherine embraced her authority and has wielded considerable power ever since, even though she was regent for only three years.

In 1560, France was beset with religious divisions between Catholics and Protestants. Catherine, a Catholic, at first took a moderate view, even signing an edict allowing Protestants to worship publicly outside of towns and privately within them.

When a group of Protestants was massacred at a religious service in Champagne, the first of the French Wars of Religion began. Following an uneasy truce in 1563, the second war took place in 1567–68. The third war, in 1568–70, ended in the defeat of the Royal troops by the Protestants, led by the Admiral of France, Gaspard de Coligny.

Coligny gained significant influence over Charles IX, leading Catherine to conspire in his assassination. When the first attempt failed, she helped in the plotting of the Saint Bartholomew's Day massacres, in which Coligny and thousands of Protestants were killed. The massacre led to the fourth war, which ended with Henry III's election as King of Poland in May last year.

Kenau Hasselaer

As regent of France, Catherine de Medici regularly meets with foreign dignitaries.

Marietta Robusti Tintoretti

Pope Permits Artist to Promote her Work

Rome, Italy, June 5, 1575: Diana Scultori Ghisi today became the first female artist to be given permission by Pope Gregory XIII to sign her own name on her engravings. Until now only a select few artists—all men—have received written permission to sign their work. One is the great Michelangelo.

Diana requested papal approval to sign her work before moving to Rome from Mantua, where the printmaker's daughter was known as Diana Mantuana. In Rome her work is relatively unknown, so she intends to use her beautiful engravings to establish herself as an artist. Wife of the famous architect, Francesco da Volterra, many of her engravings feature work drawn by her husband. Her plan is to use the signed engravings to promote the family name and to secure future commissions for her husband and herself. Among her recent works are *St Jerome* and *Christ and the Adulteress*.

"I WILL MAKE YOU SHORTER BY A HEAD."

ELIZABETH I, QUEEN OF ENGLAND

Flemish Miniaturist Dies

London, England, June 23, 1576: Levina Teerlinc, famous for her exquisite tiny portraits, died today, aged about 65. She will be remembered as perhaps the finest miniaturist of her time.

When Elizabeth I ascended the British throne back in 1546, Teerlinc painted the young queen's portrait and presented it to her as a gift. Elizabeth was apparently so taken with the picture that she kept it in her private rooms as a personal keepsake. This is not surprising, given that Teerlinc's portraits are famous throughout Europe for their perfect detail, and the expressions she captures on the faces. Appointed to the English court of Henry VIII, Levina Teerlinc also painted portraits for Edward VI, Mary I, and Elizabeth. She was, by all accounts, an artisan of the very highest order.

Daughter of the famous miniaturist Simon Bening, Levina was born in Bruges about 1510. She was trained by her father, a well-known Flemish painter of the Ghent-Bruges school. Levina worked in her father's studio until she married George Teerlinc of Blankenberge and moved with him to England. She was appointed to the court of Henry VIII following the death of Hans Holbein the Younger. Unfortunately, many of Levina Teerlinc's paintings were destroyed in a big fire at Whitehall. Her surviving works include *Portrait of Lady Katherine Grey* and *Portrait of a Young Woman*.

time out

During 1575, William the Silent, the Prince of Orange, offers sovereignty of the Netherlands to Queen Elizabeth I of England in exchange for military and financial support, an offer she rejects.

Teresa of Avila has written *The Interior Castle*.

Warrior Queen Ready for War

Zazzua, Africa, 1576: Crowned queen of the African province of Zazzua following the death of her brother Karama, Amina—in her first official duty as queen—will lead a military operation to secure safe passage for traders to the region.

Queen Amina, who is about 43 years old, has taken the throne at a time when Zazzua, a province of Nigeria, is strengthening its position in western Africa and expanding its territory. Already renowned as a leading warrior of the Zazzua cavalry, Amina plans to force neighboring rulers to take on vassal status and allow traders safe passage. Zazzua is one of a number of city-states that dominate the trans-Saharan trade route. The area is famous for leather, cloth, kola, salt, horses, and some imported metals.

The military operation is set to take place in six months, and in the meantime Amina plans to build defensive walls around the city in an attempt to make it safer from invasion. Her warlike behavior already sets her apart from her late mother, Queen Bakwa of Turunku, whose reign was one of peace. Queen Amina joined the military when she was only 16, after her mother died and the crown passed to her brother.

Famous Spanish Conquistadora Dies

Santiago, Chile, 1580: Inés de Suárez, who made a name for herself as a *conquistadora*, died today, aged 73. She played a key role in the military operation to establish Santiago and is the only European woman who took part. She was part of the large expeditionary force which defeated the natives who fought the Spaniards' incursion into their lands.

Colorful feathered clothing shows the status of South American women.

Had it not been for her bravery, the 1541 expedition to secure Santiago may well have failed; certainly many more lives would have been lost. While carrying food and water to the troops, Inés saw their desperation and suggested that they behead the captured Indians, and set the heads rolling among the enemy troops. There was some objection to her plans from soldiers who wanted the prisoners spared, and kept as bargaining tools. De Suárez set the example by cutting off the first head. After all the prisoners had been decapitated, Inés, attired in mail and

helmet, went into the fray on her white horse. This added to the confusion caused by the rolling heads, and left the enemy demoralized. The Spanish went on to win the war. According to an eyewitness: "She went out to the plaza and put herself in front of all the soldiers, encouraging them with words of such exaggerated praise that they treated her as if she were a brave captain, instead of a woman masquerading as a soldier in iron mail."

In 1549 de Suárez married the captain of the Spanish army, Rodrigo de Quiroga, after which she led a much quieter life, dedicating her time to her home and various charities. Her husband went on to become governor of Santiago.

Catholic Crushed for Helping Priests

York, England, March 25, 1586:
Margaret Clitherow (née Middleton), aged 30, was put to death today for harboring fugitive Catholic priests. Last year, a law was passed in Britain which makes it a high treason offence for a Catholic priest to practice religion, and a felony for any person to assist a priest. Many "heretics" have since been put to death in England and Wales, but the victims' growing fame and inspiration as martyrs do not seem to be helping the cause of the nascent Church of England in the face of the outlawed—yet still very popular—Catholic faith.

Despite being brought up as a Protestant, Clitherow converted to Catholicism in 1574, soon after she wed York butcher John Clitherow. At the time, her confessor said she converted because she did not have faith in the ministers of the new Church of England, or in their doctrines—which she saw as departing from the word of God as laid out in the Bible. So Clitherow

ignored the law, allowing priests to shelter—and perform mass—in her home. Her trial, condemnation, and death sentence were carried out this morning. Clitherow was ordered to lie down between a rock and a wooden slab while heavy weights were dropped on her until her bones were crushed. Witnesses reported that her cries of "Jesus!" rent the air as she was dying.

Clitherow is survived by her husband and three children—Henry, William, and Anne. A shrewd businesswoman, she was an important part of the successful family business. Known by many as "the rose of York," she was also a fierce defender of her faith, which she practiced ardently, fasting four days a week and praying for one and a half hours every day.

Mary Herbert, Countess of Pembroke

Playing music was an essential skill for young women in the 1500s.

Key Events

English Channel, August 1588: The Spanish Armada is defeated in the English Channel.

India, 1587: Gulbadan Begum completes a memoir of her brother Humayun, the Mughal ruler.

Verona, Italy, 1588: Isabella Andreini, acclaimed *Commedia dell'arte* actress, publishes a pastoral play, *La Mirtilla*.

Blois, France, January 5, 1589: Catherine de Medici, wife of one, and mother of three kings of France, dies, aged 69.

France, April, 1589: Huguenot Henry of Navarre succeeds to the French throne, becoming Henry IV.

Bologna, Italy, 1589: Lavinia Fontana paints an altarpiece, *Holy Family*, for Philip II of Spain, a singular honor for a female artist.

Prato, Florence, Italy, February 2, 1590: Catherine dei Ricci, the Italian Dominican nun and mystic visionary, dies, aged 67.

Japan, 1590: Toyotomi Hideyoshi, successor to Nobunaga, successfully unites Japan.

Edinburgh, Scotland, January 1591: Midwife Agnes Sampson is burned to death as a witch.

Venice, Italy, 1591: Veronica Franco, famed courtesan, dies, aged 45. Her published verse *Terze Rime* and letters reveal the esteem in which she was held by the nobility.

Italy, 1592: The ruins of the Roman city of Pompeii are discovered.

China, 1593: Li Shizhen (or Li Shih Chen), medical researcher, dies, aged about 75. He wrote a comprehensive guide to the traditional Chinese remedies.

London, England, 1593: Mary Herbert, Countess of Pembroke and sister of Sir Philip Sidney, oversees the publication of her brother's work *The Countesse of Pembroke's Arcadia*, which he had dedicated to her in 1581.

Greenwich, England, 1593: Grainne (Grace) O'Malley, Irish warrior and pirate, petitions Queen Elizabeth at the royal palace in Greenwich for the release of her brother and sons.

Milan, Italy, 1596: 18-year-old Fede Galizia's *Portrait of Paolo Morgia* is praised for its realism and detail.

Korea, 1596: The first iron warships are built.

Nantes, France, April 1598: The Edict of Nantes is issued, allowing religious freedom to French Huguenot Protestants after years of persecution.

Isfahan, Persia, 1598: Shah Abbas names Isfahan his capital, and makes it a showplace of Persian islamic culture.

Elizabeth I

Scottish Queen Mary Loses Her Head

Northamptonshire, England, February 8, 1587: Mary, Queen of Scots, was beheaded today at Fotheringhay Castle by order of Queen Elizabeth. She was 44 years old.

Mary Stuart became Queen of Scotland when she was just six days old, and Queen of France when she was 16, a year after her marriage to the Dauphin, Francis, heir to the French throne.

When Francis died of an ear infection in 1560, Mary returned to Scotland to rule. There she met and later married her second cousin, Lord Darnley.

It was a fraught marriage. Darnley later turned on Mary with a group of conspirators, threatening his wife and murdering her secretary. Darnley was later found dead and Mary was implicated in his murder. Fleeing south, she sought shelter with Queen Elizabeth I. But fearing for her own throne, Elizabeth had Mary thrown into prison for 19 years. Mary's body will be laid to rest in Peterborough Cathedral.

Famous Actress Turns her Hand to Love Play

Verona, Italy, 1588: Actress and writer Isabella Andreini has published her first play, *La Mirtilla*. It is the first pastoral play to be published by a woman in Italy. Until now, Andreini has been known for her acting ability rather than her skill as a writer, although some of her poems have been published.

Isabella Canali joined Flaminio Scala's Compagnia dei Comici Gelosie company 10 years ago, when she was 16 years old, and married Francesco Andreini shortly afterward. The Gelosie company specializes in *Commedia dell' Arte*, although conventional dramas are also part of their repertoire. Isabella brought a new dimension of romance to the leading roles.

Isabelle Andreini's play is also about love, and features a strong female character who makes her own decisions. It is a pastoral play, written in verse. One of the characters argues that while "riches and wisdom are considered gifts of greater value, they are nothing like the delights of love, which have no equal."

As well as being a singer, actor, poet, and now playwright, Andreini is also a co-director of the Gelosi troupe with her husband, Francesco. Their children travel with the company, and may one day follow in their parents' footsteps.

Fontana to Paint on King's Altar

Bologna, Italy, 1589: Famous Italian painter Lavinia Fontana has been commissioned by Phillip II of Spain to paint an altar depicting the holy family. The commission is the first of its kind for a female artist in Europe and will add to Fontana's growing reputation.

Fontana is already widely regarded as one of the finest artists in Italy. Her paintings, which include a number of female nudes, have won her wide acclaim in the upper echelons of society, and she is one of the first women in western Europe to develop a career as an artist outside the confines of the court or convent. Daughter of the painter Prospero Fontana, Lavinia's work has caught the attention of Pope Paul V, and she is expected to move to Rome to take up a permanent position in his court.

Lavinia is married to artist Gian Paolo Zappi and they have 11 children. Their marriage is slightly unconventional in that Zappi takes prime responsibility for looking after the children and doing the housework, while his wife paints in her studio. Zappi also acts as her assistant, painting some of the minor details in the background of her portraits.

Italian Mystic Goes to God

Prato, Florence, Italy, February 2, 1590: Catherine dei Ricci, renowned for her mystical and miraculous life, died today. She passed away, after quite a long illness, at the Dominican convent of San Vincenzo in Florence, where she was perpetual prioress. She was 67 years old.

Born in Florence on April 23, 1590, as Alessandra Lucrezia Romola, dei Ricci showed religious tendencies early in her life. At the age of six she was sent to live with her aunt, Louisa dei Ricci, the abbess of the convent school of Morticelli. She entered the convent at the age of 13, and became a nun a year later despite stern opposition from her father. The quarrel became so serious that her father tried to remove her from the order. But when he attempted this, dei Ricci became deathly ill, and in the end he gave his consent for her to remain.

A painting by renowned Italian artist Lavinia Fontana.

In her early years, Catherine dei Ricci gained renown for her "supernatural favors." Not all of this attention was positive, however, and she endured a number of humiliating trials. With her holiness eventually vindicated, she went on to attain a number of important positions within the church. Her counsel was well regarded by princes and bishops, and she corresponded regularly with cardinals, three of whom became popes.

She will also be remembered for her intense meditations on the passions of Christ, which often saw her bleed spontaneously. At times a coral ring would appear on her finger while she was praying. She said it represented her marriage to Christ.

Many believe that dei Ricci is a saint. Some claim that she was capable of projecting her image hundreds of miles away, and that she could make herself invisible.

Isabella Andreini has published her first play, *La Mirtilla*.

Under the reign of King James, many women were accused of witchcraft.

Catherine de Medici

Scottish Healer Burnt for Witchcraft

Edinburgh, Scotland, January 16, 1591: Today, the Scottish healer and midwife Agnes Sampson was burnt to death for practicing witchcraft. She was found guilty of using magic to create the wild storms that endangered the life of King James and his wife Anne on their voyage home from Denmark last year.

Known as the "wise wife of Keith," Sampson lived and worked as a healer in a village in the Barony of Keith, East Lothian, Scotland. Sampson was one of 200 women in Scotland to be brought before a special tribunal headed by King James himself. Six women in Denmark had already been tried on the matter, all of them confessing that they used black magic to raise storms. During her trial, Sampson at first protested her innocence, but was later forced to confess, after "devil marks" were discovered on her body. She subsequently confessed to such a variety of remarkable crimes that at first James didn't believe her testimony, calling her a liar. Strangely, she had to convince him of her guilt, which she did by taking him aside and recounting what he had said to his queen on their wedding night.

On this evidence the king ordered that Sampson be taken to the scaffold on Castlehill, where she was garroted and burnt to death.

Queen Pardons Irish Woman Pirate

Greenwich, England, 1593: Upon their return to England, the notorious Irish pirate Grainne (Grace) O'Malley and her brother and sons have been pardoned by Queen Elizabeth.

Earlier this year, having tired of her life of seafaring plunder, Grace and her family returned to England to attempt to clear her name, and have their land returned. She had become a pirate when Sir Richard Bingham, the Governor of Connaught, took control of her estate following the death of her husband. By law, Grace claimed, she was entitled to one-third of the land, and she refused to leave. Bingham had her arrested and all her possessions confiscated. One of her three sons, Owen, was murdered by the governor's troops.

So, with her land taken, O'Malley and her family turned to the sea, which she had known and loved as a child, sailing with her father. She became known as a "notable traitoress" and "nurse to all rebellions in the Province."

She recently petitioned the queen for pardon and liberty, offering in return a pledge to attack the queen's enemies and defend her allies. The queen responded by sending her a list of questions about why she had become a criminal in the first place. Then Bingham, still Grace O'Malley's sworn enemy, heard of her appeal to the queen, and immediately retaliated by arresting her two sons, Murrough and Tibbott, and her brother, Donnell O'Piper. This action so angered O'Malley that she requested a private interview with the queen. The interview was granted and—in a move that amazed many in the court—Elizabeth not only pardoned the O'Malleys, but also granted a lifetime pension to Grace.

It is not known exactly what swayed the queen's decision, but Grace was born a noblewoman, which no doubt worked in her favor. Before being evicted by Bingham, Grace had owned a fleet of ships, as well as several islands and castles.

Isabella Clara Eugenia, Infanta of Spain and Portugal, and Archduchess of Austria.

Maria Eleonora
of Brandenburg

*"Though God
hath raised
me high, yet
this I count
the glory of
my crown:
That I have
reigned with
your loves."*

ELIZABETH I,
QUEEN OF ENGLAND,
1601

Acclaimed Actress Publishes Book of Poems

Pavia, Italy, 1601: Italian actress and author of the pastoral drama *La Mirtilla*, Isabella Andreini, has published a collection of 359 poems entitled *Rime*, illustrating her range of style, mastery of diverse genres, and not least, her views on court society.

After joining the traveling troupe of actors, Compagnia dei Comici Gelosi, at the age of 16, Isabella was soon improvising the group's scripts, and was writing sonnets which, by 1587, had found publication in various Italian anthologies. *La Mirtilla* appeared in 1588, and she has continued to write and correspond with scholars on classical themes while still traveling and acting with the Gelosi.

The Gelosi have performed at several royal functions. Two years ago the Gelosi went to Paris to entertain Henry IV and his Italian bride, Marie de Medicis.

In her own performances, Isabella Andreini has revolutionized the Italian stage, particularly in plays such as *The Madness of Isabella*, in which she tailored her role to highlight her own skills, such as speaking several languages, singing in French, and imitating the dialects of other characters in the play.

Isabella Andreini, the noted actress, has published a book of poetry.

Earlier this year Isabella was elected to the Accademia degli Intenti, a male-dominated Pavian intellectual association. She had begun compiling a collection of 148 fictional epistles, called *Lettere*, which reflected her views on art and life. This work has been set aside in deference to the demands of her theatrical life.

Virgin Queen Dies

Richmond, Surrey, England, March 24, 1603: Queen Elizabeth died this morning from blood poisoning. She was 69 years old.

Her passing may well be seen to have been hastened by the death of her dear friend, Robert Devereux, Earl of Essex, who was executed on Tower Green in February, 1601. Earlier this month she retired to Richmond Palace where she had been seen standing for hours on end, shunning bed rest. Increasingly frail, Elizabeth has refused to allow doctors to examine her. Witnesses have spoken of how, when Archbishop Whitgift was called to her bedside and spoke to her of heaven's rewards, the Queen reached out to squeeze his hand.

Eventually Elizabeth grew so weak that she was unable to argue with her ladies-in-waiting, and fell into a deep sleep from which she never awoke. She was England's monarch, through good times and ill, for 45 years, and the bulk of her subjects have never known another ruler.

Her passing was described as being "mildly like a lamb, easily like a ripe apple from the tree." The proclamation of her death was made by Robert Cecil, lord treasurer, first at Whitehall, then later at St Paul's Cathedral, and was received with silence and mourning on London's streets. She will be succeeded by King James VI of Scotland, who will also become King James I of England. Elizabeth's legacy is great and England is now a great power. English literature has been enhanced by such writers as William Shakespeare, Christopher Marlowe, Benjamin Jonson, and John Donne, while the explorers Sir Francis Drake, Sir Walter Raleigh, and Sir Richard Greville have sailed to new horizons. Elizabeth will also be remembered for the execution of her cousin, Mary, Queen of Scots, and for the defeat of the Spanish Armada.

Performance Spectacle Shocks Japan

Kyoto, Japan, 1603: A former *miko* (attendant) consecrated at the Izumo Shrine in the Shimane Prefecture, Izumo no Okuni is responsible for the creation of an innovative new dance and performance spectacle that is being called *kabuki*, a colloquial term meaning "to shock."

Accompanied by a troupe of women, Okuni was sent to Kyoto by her father to solicit alms through the performance of traditional songs and dance. However, her style of dancing and her shows of comic relief are being described as suggestive and even erotic. The dance troupe has established a theater along a dry riverbed near the town of Kitano.

Among the controversial performances is one that includes a provocative prayer dance to the goddess Amitaba. It is said to be an adaptation of the primitive devotional dance, *nebutsu odori*, in which the participants jump about to the rhythm of a ringing bell, accompanied by flutes and

time out

In May 1602, English explorer Captain Bartholomew Gosnold saw an island, reportedly covered in wild grapes, off the Massachusetts coast of America. He decided to name the island Martha's Vineyard, after his young daughter.

Izumo no Okuni's dance and performance spectacle, known as kabuki theater, has caused a sensation.

Midwifery Explained

Paris, France, 1609: Louyse Bourgeois, the royal midwife to Queen Marie de Medicis, has published what is believed to be the first ever written account on midwifery. It is entitled *Observations diverses sur la sterilité (Observations on Sterility)*.

Pocahontas

Born into France's middle class in 1563, little is known of Louyse Bourgeois's early years. In 1584 she married Martin Boursier, an army surgeon. After her family lost everything during the siege of Paris in 1589, Louyse sought certification as a midwife, and was soon admitted to the Guild of Midwives. She and her husband then purchased a house in the Rue Saint-André-des-Arts where she steadily increased her practice.

Having successfully delivered the children of one of King Henry's own physicians, she was formally selected as the royal midwife, traveling to Fontainbleau Palace outside Paris to be at the side of Henry's expectant Queen.

The heir to the throne was born healthy on September 27, 1601, and his mother suffered no complications. Since that auspicious delivery, Louyse has been in great demand among the aristocratic families of France, attending several births each week.

Bourgeois believes that a pregnant woman, whether a Queen or a mere commoner, is entitled to the right to a stress-free environment for childbirth. *Observations on Sterility* will, it is hoped, ensure that women receive the appropriate level of care and advice on matters of conception and also during childbirth, while at the same time helping to elevate the noble art of midwifery into a profession worthy of the respect of male physicians.

A midwife at work.

drums. The dance tells the story of two lovers, and has reportedly sent audiences into a frenzy, with its confrontational approach to public assumptions of decency and morality.

Okuni herself has been seen playing both male and female roles, and she is becoming known for her mastery of a number of parts, including samurai and Christian priests. Although the performances lack a credible plot, this has not proved detrimental, as the shows have a great deal of visual appeal, with their gaudiness, beauty, and profusion of color.

Expedition Leader Saved by 12-year-old Girl

Near Jamestown, North America, December 1607: After having been ambushed and taken prisoner by the Algonquin Indian chief Powhatan, Captain John Smith, one of the expedition leaders of the colony in Jamestown, Virginia, has reportedly had his life spared through the intervention of the chief's courageous 12-year-old daughter, Pocahontas.

After months of captivity Smith was due to be clubbed to death in a ritual ceremony. As he was made to place his head upon two great stones, Powhatan's daughter threw herself on Captain Smith, cradling his head in her arms and loudly imploring her father to relent.

Captain Smith's account has, however, been questioned. Some say it is possible that he may have simply misunderstood a traditional Algonquin ritual in which young Indian males undergo a "mock" execution prior to being "rescued" and having their life spared. Captain Smith has now returned to Jamestown.

London, England, 1611: Approved by King James, an official translation of the Bible is published.

Transylvania, January 1611: Elizabeth Báthory, Countess of Transylvania, is walled up in a room in her home, Castle Csejthe, accused of murdering hundreds of young women and using their blood to rejuvenate herself.

Kyoto, Japan, 1613: Izumo no Okumi, founder of kabuki theater, dies, aged about 40.

Russia, 1613: Mikhail Romanov comes to the Russian throne.

Jamestown, North America, April 5, 1614: Pocahontas, an Algonquin princess, marries John Rolfe, English tobacco farmer.

Rome, Italy, August 11, 1614: Artist Lavinia Fontana, one of the first women to have been elected to the Academy of Rome, dies, aged 62.

Castle Csejthe, Transylvania, August 1614: Elizabeth Báthory, Countess of Transylvania, is found dead in her walled-up room, aged 54.

Stratford-Upon-Avon, England, April 23, 1616: Playwright William Shakespeare dies, aged about 52.

Gravesend, Kent, England, March, 1617: Pocahontas, Algonquin princess, dies, aged about 22.

Constantinople, Ottoman Empire, London, England, 1617: Rachel Speght publishes a pamphlet—the first woman in England to do so under her own name. *A Mouzell for Melastomus* argues that woman is man's equal, as defined in Scripture.

Pontoise, France, April 18, 1618: Barbe-Jeanne Acarie, also known as Marie de l'Incarnation, dies, aged 52. She introduced the Order of Discalced Carmelites to France.

Provincetown, North America, November 21, 1620: The Pilgrims land in North America after a 65-day voyage from Portsmouth, England, in the *Mayflower*.

London, England, September 25, 1621: Mary (Sidney) Herbert, Countess of Pembroke, writer and patron of the arts, dies, aged 59.

Ndongo, Central West Africa, 1621: Nzinga, who is also known by her Portuguese name of Dona Ana de Souza, becomes Queen of Ndongo on the death of her brother.

Rome, Italy, October 15, 1622: Teresa of Avila, the founder of the Discalced Carmelites, is canonized by Pope Gregory XV.

Paris, France, 1622: After rebelling against her son, Louis XIII, Queen Marie de Medicis, former regent of France, is again a member of the King's council.

Mary Sidney

Death of the Hausa Warrior Queen

Hausaland, West Africa, 1610: The brilliant military strategist and undisputed ruler of Hausaland, Queen Amina, has died.

Within months of assuming the throne of the city-state of Zazzau in 1576, Amina began a series of military engagements, personally leading her cavalry through all her campaigns. She also exercised tight control over the trade routes connecting the western Sudan with Mali in the north and Egypt to the east. Hausaland now extends as far north as Kwararafa, and as far south as Nupe.

Queen Amina is credited with innovative approaches in protecting her soldiers: she had iron helmets and metal armor made for them to wear in battle, and she constructed her military camps behind fortified earthen walls. These walled forts are now found throughout Hausaland. After 34 years as Queen, Amina's legacy is a unified and peaceful territory.

> "SHE, SHE
> IS DEAD;
> SHE'S DEAD;
> WHEN THOU
> KNOW'ST THIS,
> THOU
> KNOW'ST HOW
> LAME A
> CRIPPLE THIS
> WORLD IS.
>
> JOHN DONNE,
> (1572–1631),
> ON 15-YEAR-OLD
> ELIZABETH DRURY

Bloodbath Countess Gets Just Reward

Transylvania, January, 1611: The Countess of Transylvania, Elizabeth Báthory, has been confined to a room in her residence, the Castle Csejthe, accused of torturing and murdering countless young women and using their blood to rejuvenate herself.

A group of soldiers led by Elizabeth's cousin, Count Cuyorgy, under orders from the Hungarian emperor, has raided Castle Csejthe and reportedly discovered the bodies of over 50 young girls. A dead girl, drained of blood, was found in the main hall. Another, whose body had been repeatedly pierced, was still alive. Several girls still within the grounds of the castle, in prison cells, exhibited signs of having been tortured. Nearly 50 bodies have been unearthed below the castle.

It is believed that the Countess took "blood baths" in the misguided hope of reversing her fading beauty.

An early interest in the occult seems to have encouraged her sadistic tendencies. With her husband, Count Ferencz, often away from home fighting forces of the Ottoman Empire, Elizabeth was free to pursue the torture and macabre punishing of her young servant girls.

After hearing the damning testimony of numerous witnesses and victims who had managed to survive their harrowing ordeals, the Royal Supreme Court found Elizabeth Báthory guilty of torture and murder. The principal evidence, however, came from her own servants, and others who had assisted the Countess in her murderous rampage, all of whom received the death sentence.

Pickpocket's Adventures Dramatized

London, England, 1611: A new play about the life and adventures of the notorious thief Mary Frith, entitled *The Roaring Girle,* has been published this year.

Written by Thomas Middleton and Thomas Dekker, the title character of Mary Frith, also known as Moll Cutpurse because of her habit of cutting purses in order to steal their contents, follows the life and exploits of the real-life cross-dressing pickpocket, the self-styled "governess of the underworld." Mary Frith herself is widely rumored to have been in the audience during several of the play's London performances.

Born in about 1584 to a shoemaker, Mary began work as a servant girl but was too boisterous and independent to stay in that profession for very long. Instead she began to dress in men's clothing, smoked tobacco, and was often observed to carry a sword. She turned to picking pockets, and on August 26, 1600, she and two other women were arrested for stealing a purse containing two shillings from the breast pocket of an unnamed gentleman.

In 1609 Mary Frith was again charged with stealing, this time from a house in Southwark. However, she was found not guilty by a jury reluctant to convict a woman of a capital offence. There are rumors that Mary has now set up shop in London, where she has been known to help out friends who need to "move" items quickly from their possession. Indeed, she may even be helping herself, as stories are circulating of her exploits as a highway robber!

The play *The Roaring Girle* has been published.

Isabella Brandt, as portrayed by her husband, Peter Paul Rubens.

Favored Portraitist of Several Popes Dies

Rome, Italy, August 11, 1614: The acclaimed portraitist and member of the prestigious Academy of Rome, Lavinia Fontana, has died at the age of 62.

Born in Bologna on August 24, 1552, she received extensive training in the arts from her father, the Mannerist painter Prospero Fontana. Young Lavinia soon excelled in the depiction of the female form as a graceful elongated figure, such as can be seen in her *Allegory of Music.*

Lavinia married Giano Paolo Zappi in 1577, and bore him 11 children, but she never ceased painting. She brought a fresh approach to devotional art. *The Holy Family,* for example, presents the Virgin Mary and Elizabeth center-stage looking at their sons, Jesus and John the Baptist, with a seemingly inconsequential Joseph observing them quietly in the background.

By the time she moved to Rome in 1603 she had become the portraitist of choice for the wealthy of Bologna, lauded for the detail and realism of her subjects. In Rome she became an official painter to the papal court of Pope Clement VIII. At his personal request, she began work on an altarpiece depicting the stoning of St Stephen the Martyr, which sits today in the church of San Paolo Fuori le Mura.

In 1611 a bronze portrait medallion of Lavinia was cast by the sculptor, Felice Antonio Cassoni. It showed her both in traditional profile and with the typical, untamed, flowing hair of an artist too immersed in work to care

Teresa of Avila was canonized in 1622 by Pope Gregory XV.

such as Edmund Spenser, Thomas Kyd, Christopher Marlowe, and Ben Jonson. William Shakespeare is reputed to have visited Wilton House on occasion.

After the death in 1586 of her beloved brother, the poet Sir Philip Sidney, Mary set herself the task of completing his paraphrasing and verse translations of the psalms, contributing 107 of the 150 psalms herself. She also edited his *Arcadia*.

Second only to Her Majesty as a *femme savante*, Mary retreated from public gaze when her husband died in 1601, and devoted herself solely to her family and writings.

Mary was primarily a translator of the works of others, and four of her translations have been published to date, most notably *A Discourse of Life and Death* by the French writer Philippe de Mornay, and *Antonius, A Tragedie*, also written in French, by Robert Garnier. *Antonius* was instrumental in bringing to the English way of writing the European tradition of citing Roman history in order to comment on contemporary politics.

Mary Sidney Herbert's reputation is best reflected in a portrait engraved by Simon van de Passe in 1618 in which she is depicted crowned with the laurel wreath of a poet, the first English woman ever to receive such recognition.

Mary will be buried in Salisbury Cathedral, not far from Wilton House.

The Return of the Queen

Paris, France, 1622: Having once rebelled against her son, Louis XIII, Queen Marie de Medicis, the former regent of France, has once again been restored to the King's favor and into his council.

Marie became regent for her son after the assassination of her husband, Henry IV, in 1610, and she soon began reversing many of the policies of her late spouse. The treasury surplus was drained in payments to a disaffected aristocracy, and in court extravagances. Marie was increasingly seen to be lacking in judgment, best illustrated by the elevation of her close friend, Concino Concini, to a prominent position in both the court and the royal council.

Concini was murdered and Marie was forced into exile in Blois in 1617 after a coup instigated by the 15-year-old Louis, who was eager to throw off the tutelage of his mother. Marie escaped exile in 1619 and became the rallying point of a fresh revolt, challenging the King in battle. It was only through the intervention of Bishop Richelieu of Lucon, loyal to young Louis, that the King and his mother were again reconciled. Last year the King permitted Marie to hold a small court at Angers, and she has now resumed her place on the royal council.

Elizabeth of France

about appearances. Cassoni's medallion was in honor of her significant contribution to the arts and in recognition of a career that was the equal of her male contemporaries.

Among her many sitters during her final years were the popes Gregory XIII and Clement VIII.

Lavinia Fontana leaves a large body of work, assuring her of a place in the history of portraiture and of large-scale works. She will long be admired and remembered for her attention to detail as well as for winning commissions normally only given to male artists.

Loss of Brilliant Scholar and Editor

London, England, September 25, 1621: The renowned author and patron of the arts, Mary (Sidney) Herbert, the Countess of Pembroke, died today at the age of 59.

Mary was born in Bewdley, Worcestershire, in 1561, the daughter of Sir Henry Sidney, the Lord Deputy of Ireland. She was invited to Queen Elizabeth's court in 1575 and it was there that she met Henry Herbert, Earl of Pembroke, whom she married in 1577. Together they set up a home in Wilton House in Wiltshire and had four children.

Throughout her life she worked to transform her home into an academic environment for the encouragement of writers and poets. This group, which came to be known as the Wilton Circle, is regarded as possibly the most important literary coterie in English history, because it included eminent writers

Queen Marie de Medicis, former regent of France, is back in favor with her son, King Louis XIII.

Louise de Marillac

Grand Old Lady of Portraiture Bows Out

Palermo, Italy, November 1625: Sofonisba Anguissola, the internationally famed artist, portraitist to the Spanish Court, and friend and colleague of the great Michelangelo, has died in Palermo, Sicily.

Born in Lombardy in 1532 to an Italian noble-man, Amilcare Anguissola, Sofonisba was the eldest in a family of six sisters and a brother. Her education was more fitting for a boy as she was taught Latin, Greek, the sciences, and the clavichord when it is considered more usual for females to learn needle-craft and the art of elegant dress.

In 1546 her father sent Sofonisba and her sister, Elena, to study under the tutelage of Mannerist painter and master of portraiture and devotional art, Bernardino Campi, as well as Bernardino Gatti, a follower of Corregio.

Sofonisba left for Rome in 1554 and became acquainted with Michelangelo. It was during this time that her paintings evolved from the elongated flowing lines of Mannerism to the more well-rounded and anatomically correct form practiced by Michelangelo and his adherents.

She soon began to develop a style all her own, painting scenes of everyday family life, and the common pursuits of the Italian aristocracy, which brought her great fame and many commissions.

The talented Flemish artist Anthony Van Dyck visited Sofonisba at her home in Genoa two years ago to paint what was to be the final portrait of the great artist prior to her retirement in Sicily. She died on the island yesterday at the grand age of 93.

time out

Sweden's Queen Christina was nicknamed the "girl king" for her temperament and dress style which had a masculine flavor. She was crowned at 5, and in 1649, at the age of 23, she abdicated to her cousin Charles X Gustav of Sweden.

Emperor Locks up Stepmother

Lahore, India, 1628: Nur Jahan, the widow of the former Mughal emperor, Jahangir, has been imprisoned by the new emperor, Shah Jahan, after a long and very bitter struggle for power. The new emperor is her stepson, her late husband's third son.

Following her father's death, 5-year-old Christina has become the new Queen of Sweden.

Born into an aristocratic Persian family in 1577, Nur Jahan was brought to the Mughal court as a lady-in-waiting. The moment the emperor laid eyes on her, he fell in love, and they were soon married. He bestowed upon her the title of Nur Mahal, which he later altered to Nur Jahan, the "Light of the World."

Despite being only one of a number of wives and concubines, within ten years Nur Jahan had managed to acquire all the rights of government and sovereignty that are accorded to the emperor, and she was the empire's de facto ruler up until the death of Jahangir in 1627.

Nur Jahan manipulated the emperor's dependence on drugs and alcohol in order to maintain her position. Governing through other males in order not to offend the tradition that women should not appear face to face with men in court, she controlled all the promotions and demotions within the royal government, and approved all appointments in her husband's name. Coins have been struck in her name, and she especially took a keen interest in the affairs of women. She modified their dress to take account of hot weather, provided land and dowries to orphaned girls, and encouraged poetry from the court women.

Her confinement by her stepson puts an end to Nur Jahan's considerable influence at court.

Lewd Performances Banned

Kyoto, Japan, 1629: To discourage licentiousness and a growing association with prostitution, the Tokugawa shogunate has issued a decree banning women from performing in kabuki theater. This move is aimed at preventing the further corruption of public morals.

The demise of *onna* (women) kabuki will, it is hoped, stress the importance of skill over beauty, and help to place a greater emphasis on drama and plot

London, England, March 27, 1625: King James dies, aged 58. He is succeeded by his son, Charles I.

Canterbury, England, June, 1625: Princess Henrietta Maria, the Catholic daughter of Henry IV of France, marries Charles, the Protestant King of England.

Palermo, Italy, November, 1625: Innovative Italian portrait painter Sofonisba Anguissola dies, aged 93.

Manhattan, North America, 1626: The Dutch West India Company buys the island of Manhattan for 60 guilders (around $24).

London, England, 1628: William Harvey publishes *On the Motion of the Heart and Blood in Animals*.

Lahore, India, 1628: Nur Jahan, widow of Jahangir, is a captive of her stepson, Shah Jehan.

Kyoto, Japan, 1629: Women are forbidden by the shogun to perform in kabuki theater.

Milan, Italy, 1630: Fede Galizia dies, aged 52. She is remembered for her colorful works of still life.

Bay of Naples, Italy, December 16, 1631: Mt Vesuvius erupts and more than 3,000 people die.

Rome, Italy, 1631: Papal Bull of Suppression closes the foundation set up by Mary Ward, the English Catholic, in which the nuns are not cloistered and whose main aim is to educate poor women.

Stockholm, Sweden, 1632: Five-year-old Christina inherits the throne of Sweden after the death of her father, Gustavus Adolphus II.

Paris, France, 1633: Louise de Marillac founds with Vincent de Paul the Sisters of Charity, a Catholic lay order which cares for the poor and sick women of France.

Haarlem, Netherlands, 1633: Portraitist Judith Leyster is the first woman to be admitted to the Haarlem Guild of St Luke.

Shimabara, Japan, 1636: The uprising of Christians ends in the slaughter of 30,000 rebels.

Massachusetts Bay Colony, New England, North America, March, 1638: Anne Hutchinson, a free thinker and believer in religious freedom, is tried, excommunicated, and banished, along with her band of followers.

London, England, 1638: Famous in Italy for her religious subjects, Artemisia Gentileschi is appointed court painter to King Charles I.

Ravenna, Italy, 1638: Artist Barbara Longhi dies, aged 86.

Quebec, New France (Canada), 1641: Marie Guyart, an Ursuline nun also known as Marie de l'Incarnation, establishes a convent in the French colony.

Cologne, Germany, July 3, 1642: Marie de Medicis, the widow of Henry IV of France, dies, aged 69.

Women's kabuki roles must now be performed by men.

rather than the increasingly sensual and rather erotic performances we have been witnessing in recent times.

It is accepted that the popular tradition of kabuki will continue, but it will now be exclusively the domain of males who will to write all the plays and perform all the roles. Known as *wakashu* kabuki, adolescent boys will play the female roles, and more attention will be given to stage sets to make a more colorful experience.

Papal Bull Closes Institute

Rome, Italy, 1631: In 1609, the Institute of the Blessed Virgin Mary was established in Saint-Omer in France by the English Catholic, Mary Ward, for the education of poor women. Mary, whose family are recusants living under persecution in Protestant England, steadfastly believed that she was led by the Holy Spirit to establish an order beyond the "cloister." This community, the members of which are often called "Loreto sisters," has now been found to be contradicted by the Council of Trent, which has decreed that religious women must remain strictly enclosed. A Papal Bull of Succession has been issued by Pope Urban VIII, which has resulted in the closure of the institute.

Mary Ward and her Sisters, supported by the English Jesuit, John Gerard, lived by the Jesuit constitutions, emulating the missionary zeal of the Jesuits while maintaining their independence from them. Also known as the "Jesuitesses" and admired by many for their fervor and good works, they set up schools and communities across London and throughout Europe. Despite their very tangible successes, the nuns were still viewed as women doing men's work. To remedy this, in 1629 Mary Ward went to Rome to present her ideas to the pope.

However, these pleas have fallen on deaf ears, with the Bull of Succession claiming in part that Mary's religious order is a real threat to the moral and intellectual fragility of women. Mary Ward herself was, for a time, imprisoned as a "heretic rebel and schismatic."

Faith More Important Than Good Deeds?

Massachusetts Bay Colony, North America, March, 1638: Anne Hutchinson, a Massachusetts Bay colonist and passionate advocate of religious tolerance and freedom of conscience, has been tried for sedition and for defying the colony's religious authorities. She, her family, and a small group of followers have been exiled south to the island of Aquidneck.

Hutchinson left England in 1634 with her husband and 15 children, following their minister, John Cotton, to the Massachusetts Bay Colony. Once established, she began inviting local women into her home for prayer and discussion. Anne expressed her personal views based on readings from scripture. Reacting against an excessive legalism that characterizes the churches throughout New England, she declared faith to be more important than works, and that a person led by the Holy Spirit is no longer bound by the law. Her discussions began to be perceived as sermons questioning fundamental

Puritan practices, which in turn led to her arrest and trial on charges of attempting to overthrow the government.

In this theocratic society where women are forbidden to preach and where any religious dissent is viewed as a crime punishable by hanging, Hutchinson faced the 49 men of the court alone and without legal representation. The governor of the colony, John Winthrop, described her as an "instrument of Satan," and the judges of the court continually undermined her defense by calling into question the legality of her right to speak out and express her deeply held religious views.

The Harvard professor, Reverend Peter Gomes, who was present at the trial, has stated that Anne Hutchinson repeatedly had the measure of even the best preachers and theologians over the course of the trial. It is hoped that her example as a pioneering advocate of the separation of church and state will pave the way for others who champion the expression of religious freedom in our increasingly Puritan society. However, it is much more likely that similar-minded people will keep their thoughts to themselves to avoid prosecution and banishment.

Princess Henrietta Maria of France

Ann Hutchinson and five of her children are killed in an Indian attack.

Key Events

England, 1642: England is plunged into civil war, as the "Cavalier" forces and the "Parliamentarian" forces engage in battle.
Paris, France, May, 1643: On the death of her husband, Louis XIII, Queen Anne becomes regent for their son, Louis XIV, aged five.
Long Island, North America, September, 1643: Anne Hutchinson, expelled from Massachusetts Bay Colony for espousing freedom of thought and religious belief, is killed in an Indian attack along with five of her children.

Peking, China, April 25, 1644: Zhu Youjan, the last Ming emperor, hangs himself as Manchu forces enter the Forbidden City.
Stockholm, Sweden, December 8, 1644: Christina comes of age and is officially declared Queen of Sweden.
Paris, France, 1645: Marie de Gournay, prolific writer, translator and editor of Michel de Montaigne's *Essais*, dies, aged 80.

Lahore, India, 1645: Widow of Mogul emperor Jahangir, Nur Jahan dies, aged 68. She was once the most influential woman in India.
Tainan, Taiwan, 1645: Pirate-patriot Zheng Chenggong establishes the Ming loyalist regime on Taiwan, and resists the newly established Qing (Manchu) Dynasty.
Baltimore, Maryland, North America, 1647: Unmarried Margaret Brent is the first woman in Maryland to own land in her own name.

Zaragoza, Spain, 1647: Maria de Zayas e Sotomayor publishes a second series of short stories entitled *Desengaños Amorosos*, which is a companion to her highly popular earlier work, *Novelas Amorosas y Exemplares*.
Maryland, North America, January, 1648: Margaret Brent asks the Assembly of Maryland for two votes—one for herself as a landowner, and one for Lord Baltimore whose interests she represents.
Agra, India, 1648: Work is completed on the Taj Mahal.

Westphalia, 1648: Queen Christina of Sweden helps to negotiate the Peace of Westphalia which results in the end of the Thirty Years' War.
London, England, January 30, 1649: King Charles of England, found guilty of treason, is executed. His son and heir, Charles I, is forced into exile in Europe. Oliver Cromwell becomes Lord Protector of England.
Paris, France, c. 1649: Madeleine de Scudéry, acclaimed author, establishes the *Salon de Samedi*.

Nur Jahan

Italian Artist Appointed to English Court

London, England, 1638: Artemisia Gentileschi, who stunned the art world with her interpretation of *Susanna and the Elders* in 1610 when the then illiterate young unknown artist was just 17, has been appointed court painter to King Charles.

Trained as a painter by her father who introduced her to the working artists of Rome, she was raped at the age of 19 by the Florentine artist, Agostino Tassi. Throughout the subsequent trial her own morality was continually called into question. Eventually Tassi was convicted upon the testimony of his own friends and associates who had heard him boast of the attack, although he served less than one year in prison for this crime.

In 1616 Artemisia was honored by becoming the first female admitted to the Academy of Design in Florence, made possible with the support of her Florentine patron, Grand Duke Cosimo II.

Artemisia's fame is best epitomized by the French artist, Pierre Dumonstier le Neveu, in his painting of her hand holding a paintbrush. The portrait of her by Jerome David carries the inscription "the famous Roman painter."

Earlier this year Artemisia Gentileschi moved to England to assist her father in the painting of the ceilings of the Queen's house in Greenwich. Since her arrival she has also been in great demand as a portraitist, and is currently in residence at the English court.

New Convent in New France

Quebec, New France (Canada), 1641: A new convent has been founded in the French colony of Quebec, New France, by Marie Guyart, an Ursuline nun who is also known as Marie de l'Incarnation.

Arriving in New France two years ago, commanded by a vision to become a missionary, Marie's ability as a business administrator enabled her to construct a convent and see it thrive against great financial odds.

Marie had been married to a silk maker who died in bankruptcy, and she left her 11-year-old son with her sister, despite objections from her family that she was abandoning her maternal responsibilities. She joined an Ursuline convent where later she volunteered for a program which the Jesuits had established, involving the sponsorship of a series of religious houses in Quebec to be run by women.

The End of an Era

Cologne, Germany, July 3, 1642: Today, at the age of 69, the once mighty Marie de Medicis, the former Queen Consort, Queen Regent of France, and the widow of King Henry IV, has died in poverty far away from her regal home. The daughter of Francesco de Medici, she was educated in Tuscany in the arts and sciences, and told by a seer while still in her youth that she was destined to become the Queen of France. Her uncle Ferdinand arranged for her to be introduced to King Henry IV of France, whose then wife, Margaret, had failed to produce an heir.

Marie de Medicis, shown here in her heyday, has died, aged 69.

After the pope annulled Henry's marriage in 1599, Henry and Marie were married in Florence on October 5, 1600. A son, Louis, was born within a year.

When an assassin murdered Henry in Paris in 1610, and his heir, now Louis XIII, was a mere eight years old, Marie was made regent. During her regency she brought artists into France from around the world, established artistic apprenticeships, and began a period of cosmopolitanism in Paris. Marie also fostered the Italian interests of her homeland, as well as those of Spain.

In 1617 Louis XIII was proclaimed of age to rule. He accused his mother of betraying the French people and had her imprisoned, and later sent into exile in Blois. After two years under house arrest, Marie escaped, and, in 1619, led a revolt against the King. Cardinal Richelieu negotiated a treaty which meant Marie was allowed to return to Paris and was again admitted to the King's council.

She rebelled once again, in 1630, and was again banished. This time she fled to Brussels. Louis forbade her to return to France, and for the next 11 years she lived the life of a wanderer in exile. In her final years, her wealth dwindled and she was forced to sell her beloved carpets and artworks to pay her many creditors.

The nuns in the new Ursuline convent in Quebec are doing good work in the community.

Queen Christina of Sweden helped to negotiate the Treaty of Westphalia, which is now being ratified.

Queen Anne of France

Woman Asks for Vote

Maryland, North America, January 1648: With the colony still in crisis from last year's Protestant revolt against the Catholic government, the influential Catholic landowner and single woman, Margaret Brent, has asked the Assembly of Maryland for two votes—one for herself and the other for Lord Baltimore (the proprietor of the colony), whose interests she represents.

Margaret Brent had been entrusted by the late Governor Calvert to pay a group of Virginian mercenaries brought in to quell the uprising. Calvert had pledged his estate and that of his brother, Lord Baltimore, as security for the soldiers' wages. Once peace had been established, the soldiers demanded their payment. In order to discharge this obligation, Brent exhausted all of Lord Calvert's personal estate, and as that proved inadequate, she also sold his cattle. Once paid, the soldiers dispersed, although many of them have indicated their intention of remaining in Maryland and becoming settlers.

When Margaret Brent demanded two votes in the Assembly earlier this month, the Provincial Court opposed her claim. However, although it declined to give her a vote, the Assembly did defend her stewardship of Lord Baltimore's estate, a situation with which he is unhappy!

It would appear that history has been made by Brent: this is the first recorded instance of a female in North America requesting the right to vote.

Emperor Builds Monument to Dead Wife

Agra, India, 1648: The Muslim emperor, Shah Jahan, has completed the construction of a mausoleum for his beloved wife, Mumtaz Mahal, at Agra in India. He has named it the Taj Mahal (Crown Palace), and it is already being regarded as one of the most beautiful monuments ever built by India's Mughal rulers.

Work began on the mausoleum back in 1633, two years after Mumtaz Mahal died in childbirth while accompanying Shah Jahan on an expedition to India's south. It has taken 20,000 workers over 15 years to construct.

On the day of her death, Shah Jahan cancelled all appointments and stayed in his rooms for eight days, refusing all food and drink. When he finally appeared, the warrior who had once cut down four brothers to inherit the throne emerged a broken man, speaking of the fragility of life and of his desire to renounce his title.

On her deathbed, Mumtaz Mahal is embraced by her husband, Shah Jahan.

It is said that his appearance altered. He seemed to be smaller, walked with a stoop, and his once lustrous black hair had turned white. His kingdom was ordered into mourning. Jewelry, music, amusements, and even brightly colored clothing were all banned.

Six months after her death, Mumtaz Mahal's body was brought to Agra, where a peaceful garden along the banks of a shallow river had been selected as the site for her mausoleum. There she was buried, and the imposing mausoleum has been constructed over her grave.

Literary Salon Attracts French Intellectuals

Paris, France, c. 1649: Madeleine de Scudéry, the acclaimed French author, has established the *Salon de Samedi* in Paris. It is certain to become a gathering point for French intellectuals, artists, and members of the nobility.

Born in Le Havre in northern France in 1607, Madeleine, the younger sister of dramatist Georges de Scudéry, moved to Paris where she was immediately accepted into the literary circle known as the Rambouillet coterie. However, it appears she has learnt from her friend and may well supplant Madame de Rambouillet as the leading Parisian literary hostess.

Madeleine's first novel, published in 1642 (under her brother's name), was *Ibrahim, or the Illustrious Bassa*. A four-volume work, its length was considered customary for the time. She has now commenced writing what is rumored to be a ten-volume work entitled *Artamenes, or the Grand Cyrus*. Large works such as these are becoming increasingly common in France, with readers appreciating the insights they provide into the private lives of the upper class.

From 1644 to 1647 she and her brother lived near Marseilles in the south of France, where Georges was appointed the captain of a local fortress. Upon returning to Paris she tried, unsuccessfully, to secure a position as a teacher while continuing to reside with her brother.

Though seemingly incapable of the exquisite prose of Madame de Sévigné, Madeleine's literary merits are nonetheless considerable.

Catalina de Erauso

Nun Soldier Dies

Cuetlaxia, New Spain, South America, c. 1650: Catalina de Erauso, also known as La Monja Alférez (the Nun Ensign), has died aged 55. Dressed in men's clothing, she fought as a soldier in King Philip IV's army in the New World.

Born in San Sebastian de Guipuzcoa, Spain around 1592, she fled a Basque nunnery at the age of 15, re-sewed her habit into men's attire, and joined the Spanish army, traveling to the New World in 1602 where she fought under the alias Alonso Diaz Ramirez.

Her adventures in Peru and Chile saw Catalina emerge as one of the great folkloric heroes of the Spanish-speaking world. She served in Chile in the conflict with the local Araucano Indians where it is said she fought the famous cacique Quispehuancha, whom she managed to unhorse in one-on-one combat and leave hanging from a tree.

Gradually she began to build an enviable reputation as a soldier, gambler, and duelist. Injured in an altercation while gambling, and believing she was dying, Catalina confessed that she was a woman and was confined to a convent for several years before being returned to Spain.

She arrived in Spain a hero and was given a full pardon by Philip IV. In 1630, bored by civilian life, she traveled to Mexico where she bought some mules and conveyed people from Mexico City to Santa Cruz. She became ill in Cuetlaxia and died. She has been buried in Orizaba.

"IL N'Y A PAS DE HÉROS POUR SON VALET DE CHAMBER. NO MAN IS A HERO TO HIS VALET."

ANNE BIGOT DE CORNUEL (1605–1694)

"MARRIAGE IS THE GRAVE OR TOMB OF WIT."

MARGARET CAVENDISH, DUCHESS OF NEWCASTLE, *NATURE'S THREE DAUGHTERS*

La Grande Mademoiselle Banished from Paris

Paris, France, October 1652: The cousin of Louis XIV, "La Grande Mademoiselle" Anne-Marie Louise d'Orléans, has been banished from Paris because of her

"La Grande Mademoiselle" pleads her case.

military support for the Fronde rebellion, the civil unrest that began in 1648.

Born at the Louvre in 1627, Anne-Marie's father is brother to Louis XIII and her mother, Marie de Bourbon, was heiress of the Duke of Montpensier. Marie died in childbirth, leaving her only daughter many titles together with immense land holdings that made Anne-Marie Louise the wealthiest woman in France.

It has been a momentous year for her. On March 27 she led an army that drove the token forces of the king from Orleans, and in July was in command of the Bastille.

In what has become known as the Battle of the Faubourg Saint Antoine, La Grande Mademoiselle ordered the Bastille's guns to be turned upon the royalist troops of Henri de la Tour d'Auvergne as they sought to destroy the army of one of the Fronde rebellion's leading noblemen, Prince de Condé, saving Condé's army from annihilation.

During the battle she established herself in the Hotel de Ville and acted as mediator between the opposing armies.

time out

During the Peasant Revolt in 1670, a former nun named Alyona leads a group of over 600 rebels that takes the Russian town of Temnikov. Soon after, she is captured by government forces and burned at the stake.

It was upon the victorious King's return to Paris earlier this month that La Grande Mademoiselle and her father were forced to flee into exile to their estate, Saint-Fargeau.

Christina Abdicates Her Throne

Stockholm, Sweden, June 6, 1654: Queen Christina of Sweden today abdicated her throne in favor of her cousin, Charles Gustav. Growing disaffection with Protestantism may be behind her decision, though rumors of any conversion to Catholicism have so far been unfounded.

Christina ruled as regent from the age of six when her father, King Gustavus II, was killed in the Battle of Lützen during the Thirty Years War. Upon turning 18 she inherited the throne. Count Axel Oxenstierna, who had governed until Christina was of age, continued as a member of the royal court in an advisory role. Perhaps

Queen Christina has announced her abdication.

Key Events

London, England, 1650: Anne Bradstreet's *The Tenth Muse Lately Sprung Up in America*, the first book of verse written by an American, is published to great acclaim.
Cuetlaxia, New Spain, South America, c. 1650: Catalina de Erauso, Nun Ensign, dies, aged 55.
Paris, France, October 1652: Anne-Marie Louise d'Orléans, Louis XIV's cousin, is banished from Paris.
Naples, Italy, c. 1652: Influential female artist Artemisia Gentileschi dies, aged about 62.

London, England, December 1653: Parliament collapses and a protectorate is established, with Oliver Cromwell as Lord Protector.
Stockholm, Sweden, June 1654: Queen Christina abdicates in favor of her cousin Charles Gustav.
London, England, 1656: Margaret Cavendish publishes *Natures Pictures Drawn by Fancies Pencil to the Life*, an autobiographical essay.
Agra, India, 1658: Shah Jahan is imprisoned by his son, Aurangzeb, who now assumes rule over the Mughal Empire.

Ville-Marie (Montreal), New France (Canada), 1658: Marguerite Bourgeoys opens the first school in Ville-Marie.
London, England, July 26, 1659: Mary Frith, "Moll Cutpurse," dies, aged about 75. In her infamous career she was an accomplished pickpocket, highwayman (she dressed in men's clothing), and receiver of stolen goods.
Heemstede, Netherlands, February 10, 1660: Judith Leyster, Dutch painter well known for her *Self Portrait*, dies, aged 50.

Paris, France, March 15, 1660: Louise, co-founder of the Company of the Daughters of Charity, dies, aged 68.
London, England, May 29, 1660: Charles II takes back the throne left vacant after his father's execution in 1649.
Brazil, 1661: The Dutch relinquish their hold on the country and the handover to Portugal is made official by the signing of a treaty.
Bologna, Italy, 1661: Marcello Malpighi becomes the first to view the capillary system.

London, England, May 21, 1662: Catherine of Braganza marries Charles II.
London, England, 1662: Charles II proclaims that in future women, not men, must play female parts on stage.
Matamba, Central West Africa, December 1663: Queen Nzinga of Ndonga and Matamba, dies, aged 80.

conscious of the "maleness" of her new role, she began to evolve a masculine identity that extended to the wearing of male attire and participating in male pursuits such as hunting.

During her reign she established a "Court of Learning" through her patronage of theater, music, and the arts. Arcangelo Corelli, the great Italian violinist and composer, dedicated his first printed sonatas to Christina.

She refused to marry, fearing that a union would destroy her freedom, and consequently has left no heirs.

Rumors of an interest in Catholicism go back to 1651 when it is said she initiated a series of meetings with Jesuits to discuss the faith and gain insight into some of the philosophical and religious questions that puzzled her. It is said she privately confessed her doubts regarding Lutheranism. Later that year she first announced, then later retracted, a decision to abdicate. She endorsed the Hapsburg King of Hungary as Holy Roman Emperor.

Her final years as queen have been plagued by interminable taxation and governance issues as well as difficulties in foreign policy. No reason has so far been offered from the palace to her subjects for her sudden abdication.

Catherine of Braganza Marries Charles II

London, England, May 21, 1662: Catherine of Braganza of Portugal, daughter of King John IV of Portugal and second great-granddaughter of Saint Francis Borgia, has married King Charles II in Portsmouth today after having been earlier married by proxy in Lisbon on April 23.

She brings with her the largest dowry ever known, including the cities of

Louise de Marillac, who founded the Daughters of Charity to help the poor, dies in Paris in 1660.

Tangiers in North Africa and Bombay in India under British control, as well as trading concessions throughout the Portuguese empire. In return England is expected to support Portugal against continuing hostility from Spain.

Catherine's Catholicism will however necessitate another ceremony, her faith preventing her from recognizing the validity of today's Anglican service.

Female Roles to be Performed by Women!

London, England, 1662: King Charles II has proclaimed that in future women are to play female roles on stage. Until now, female roles have been performed by boys.

This proclamation overturns hundreds of years of tradition, creating something of a stir. It is hoped this will not lead to equality or equal pay for women in the theater, although it is feared that some may use their new positions to achieve

intimate liaisons with titled gentlemen to increase their rather meager incomes.

Acting is still widely considered an immodest and unfeminine pursuit. The concept of female actors as intruders in a male world will be difficult to alter, and their vulnerability to gossip, and accusations of promiscuity is likely to bring them much hardship.

Others, however, are welcoming the proclamation after years of Puritan rule under Lord Protector Oliver Cromwell. Theaters across the country have been closed since 1642 when the Puritan Parliament decreed that the theater distracted a fragmented nation from its efforts to "avert the wrath of God."

Females have, of course, been playing female roles in countries such as Italy, Spain, and France for over 100 years. Charles's period of 20 years' exile in France has obviously tempered his views on the matter. Bored by the sameness of English theater, the King was heard to say not long after his return: "Where are all the actresses?"

Catherine of Braganza

Actress Lavinia Fenton in *The Beggar's Opera*. Women now play female parts on stage.

Key Events

England, 1663: Katherine Philips's translation of Pierre Corneille's play *La Mort de Pompée* is published.

Lancaster, England, 1664: Margaret Fell, "Nursing Mother" of the Quakers, writes *Women's Speaking, Justified, Proved, and Allowed of by the Scriptures*.

New York, North America, 1664: Known as New Amsterdam to the Dutch settlers, the English seize the area and rename it New York.

France, December 1665: Catherine de Vivonne, Marquise de Rambouillet, dies, aged 77.

Congo, Africa, 1665: King of the Kongo Empire, António I, is killed by the Portuguese at the Battle of Mbwila.

London, England, 1665: The Black Death (bubonic plague) strikes.

Bologna, Italy, 1665: Artist Elisabetta Sirani dies, aged 27. Renowned for the speed at which she painted, she leaves a large portfolio of work.

London, England, September 7, 1666: The Great Fire of London has consumed much of the city.

England, 1666: Katherine Philips, acclaimed poet known as Orinda, dies of smallpox, aged 32.

London, England, May 1667: Nell Gwynne as Florimel in John Dryden's *Secret Love*, is extolled by diarist Samuel Pepys for her comedic talent.

France, June 25, 1667: The first recorded blood transfusion is carried out by Jean-Baptiste Denys. He uses blood from a lamb to save the life of a young boy.

New France (Canada), North America, July 1667: A peace treaty is signed between the Iroquois people and the French.

China, 1668: The seven-year-old ban on foot binding is abolished.

London, England, September 1670: Aphra Behn's first play, *The Forc'd Marriage*, proves very popular.

Quebec, New France (Canada), April 30, 1672: Marie Guyart (Marie de L'Incarnation), founder of the Ursuline convent in Quebec, dies, aged 72.

Paris, France, 1672: Elisabeth-Sophie Cheron, portrait artist, is elected to the Académie Royale de Peinture et de Sculpture.

London, England, December 1673: Margaret Cavendish, dies, aged 50, and is buried in Westminster Abbey. She is one of England's most prolific writers, essayists, and poets whose work was published in her lifetime.

Copenhagen, Denmark, 1674: Leonora Christina writes her autobiography, *Memories of Woe (Jammers Minde)*, while imprisoned in the Blue Tower in Copenhagen.

Margaret Cavendish

Anti-colonial African Queen Nzinga Dies

Matamba, Central West Africa, December, 1663: Queen Nzinga, ruler of the south-west African kingdoms of Ndonga and Matamba and eternal thorn in the side of colonial Portuguese traders, has died in Matamba aged 80. Nzinga became Queen of Ndonga in 1624 and immediately began welcoming slaves that had fled the Portuguese. She called upon all Africans living under the rule of Portugal to rebel.

After meeting the Portuguese governor, a treaty was signed, which he was later to dishonor as Portugal's rapacious appetite for slaves continued unabated.

Nzinga formed an alliance with the Jaga people by marrying the Jaga chief and building an army that she then used to conquer the northern kingdom of Matamba and use as a base to continue her resistance to Portugal. Nzinga was also astute in forming alliances with Mbundu groups, forming a coalition in 1635 with the neighboring kingdoms of Kongo, Kasanje, Dembos, and Kissama.

Joined by thousands of slave soldiers, Nzinga also formed an alliance with the Dutch, who dispatched a militia at her request. She began to envision a grand African empire by taking advantage of the dissension that existed between the various European powers.

Her alliance with the Dutch came to nothing after they were driven from Luanda by the Portuguese in 1648, and by 1658 many of her supporters had either been lost or tired of what had become a decades-long struggle against colonial rule.

> *"WHEN WOMEN ARE SEEN WITH PEN IN HAND, THEY ARE MET IMMEDIATELY WITH SHRIEKS COMMANDING A RETURN TO THAT LIFE OF PAIN WHICH THEIR WRITING HAD INTERRUPTED, A LIFE DEVOTED TO THE WOMEN'S WORK OF NEEDLE AND DISTAFF."*
>
> ARCHANGELA TARABOTTI, WRITER AND NUN, 1654, VENICE, ITALY

"Manifesto" for Women's Rights

Lancaster, England, 1664: Margaret Fell—one of the founding members of the religious movement known as the Society of Friends or "Quakers," who was arrested earlier this year for holding religious meetings in her home and refusing to take the oath of allegiance—has written a work entitled *Women's Speaking Justified, Proved, and Allowed of by the Scriptures.*

The text, which Fell wrote while in prison, responds to the traditional view of the woman's role in the temptation story in Genesis, and the teachings of St Paul on the role of women within the church, including his exhortations against women as teachers of the faith. Margaret Fell's religious "manifesto" also acts as a persuasive challenge to the prevailing church doctrines asserting the prohibition son women as orators and ministers, and exemplifies the increasing role women are taking in religious debates, ministries, and in the growth of new religious movements across England.

Fell strongly refutes the notion that women are in any way subordinate to men, and she even asserts that those people who oppose women speaking on religious themes despise the message of the Lord Himself.

St Jerome, as painted by artist Elisabetta Sirani in 1650.

Margaret Askew was born in Lancashire in 1614. She married Thomas Fell in 1631. On returning home from a business trip in 1652 he found Margaret had met a Quaker, George Fox, who subsequently converted Margaret, their seven daughters, and the majority of their household to Quakerism. She ceased worshiping at St Mary's and soon rose to become a key figure in the Quaker movement.

Poet Raids Bookstores

England, 1664: The most widely-known poet of her generation, Katherine Philips ("The Matchless Orinda"), has withdrawn from bookstores several illegally printed works of her manuscript, *Poems by the Incomparable Mrs K.P.*, on the grounds that she had not sanctioned the copies.

The wife of the first Viscount Dungannon is still basking in the glow of last year's well-conceived translation of Pierre Corneille's *La Mort de Pompée.* Written while she visited her husband's estates in Ireland, the work went on to be performed in Dublin's famous Smock Alley Theatre, which subsequently led to a print run of 500 copies.

Her poetic style is simple, elegant, and straightforward, though it rarely strays from the conventional.

Marquise de Rambouillet Dies

France, December, 1665: Catherine de Vivonne, the Marquise de Rambouillet, has died, aged 77. Her much-imitated literary salon at the Hotel de Rambouillet was the first of its kind, where France's literary elite could meet with members

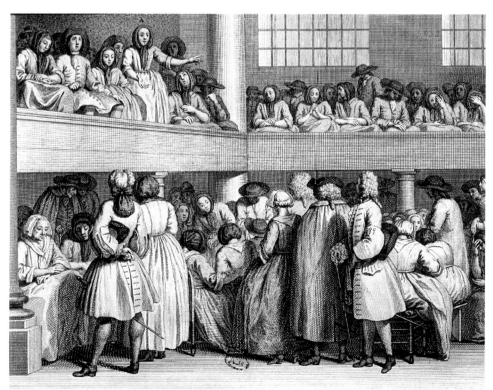

Margaret Fell champions Quaker women's rights to speak at public meetings.

of the nobility away from the various intrigues and politics of the court.

The daughter and heiress of the Marquis of Pisani, Jean de Vivonne, Catherine was born in Rome in 1588 and married at the age of 12 to the Vidame of Le Mans, Charles d'Angennes. Rather than immersing herself in the intrigues of the French court, she rearranged her house into a series of suites where people could meet and feel at home. Due to an illness that often saw her confined to her bed, she redesigned her bedroom, the famous Chambre Bleu, into a reception room where she could receive guests.

She freed herself from the royal court where protocol determined who could, and could not, attend court functions. Catherine invited France's most brilliant minds, many of whom were not members of the aristocracy, to her home, thus circumventing the societal mores that prevented those intellectuals from attending higher social circles.

Birth of Science Fiction

London, England, 1666: Margaret Cavendish, the Duchess of Newcastle, aristocrat and writer, has published a novel that blends science and fiction together for the first time. It is a satirical, imaginative tale of a young noblewoman's journey to a mythic world located deep in the Arctic wilderness.

The Blazing World opens with the kidnapping of an unnamed woman whose captors take her aboard a ship that unwittingly drifts into the Arctic Ocean. The young woman escapes in a lifeboat which itself drifts into a strange world of animal-like men who immediately enthrone her as Empress.

She then proceeds to entrust them with a host of different tasks. The Bearmen become her philosophers, the Birdmen her astronomers, the Fox-men her politicians, and so on.

The book represents an exposition of the author's own scientific and worldviews, and is a wonderfully peculiar work; a blend of science, fantasy, and feminist utopia. Her supporters are calling it a manifestation of a female mind frustrated by social mores and strictures. Her critics point to a supposed weak narrative style, bad spelling, and poor use of grammar.

One of eight daughters, Margaret was raised by her mother after the death of her father. Her family were Royalists who were forced to flee to France during the 1640s, returning to England after the restoration of Charles II to the throne. It was during this period of exile that she began to write. Her first book was a collection of poems entitled *Poems and Fancies*. Published in 1653, it was soon followed by various philosophical epistles and short fictional works.

Margaret Cavendish is a woman of firsts. She is the first woman in England to write mainly for publication, as well as the first woman ever to be allowed the chance to visit, though not be a member of, the Royal Society.

Leonora's Memories of Woe

Copenhagen, Denmark, 1674: Leonora Christina, Countess of Ulfeldt, who has been imprisoned in Copenhagen's infamous Blue Tower since 1663, has just completed an initial instalment of her life and ongoing incarceration in a moving account of her struggle entitled *Jammers Minde (Memories of Woe)*.

Already being hailed as one of the great autobiographies of Danish literature, it has been written under austere, even humiliating circumstances. The daughter of Christian IV, the former king of Denmark, Leonora Christina was imprisoned without charge or trial, and is said to have made her own ink by capturing the smoke from her candle on a spoon and writing on the back of discarded sugar wrappers. It is said that she was forced to bind her own manuscript, which also includes a collection of poems and prayers.

Leonora Christina has paid a high price for her marriage to Count Corfitz Ulfeldt. Accused by her half-brother Frederick III of plotting to kill the King and Queen, Ulfeldt and Leonora fled to Sweden in 1651 despite a trial that resulted in the Count being acquitted of all charges.

With the Swedish monarchy also distrustful of the scheming nobleman, they returned to Denmark in 1659.

Aphra Behn

In 1663, when Leonora was arrested in Dover, she was in possession of a letter written in a cipher that, had it been deciphered, would have implicated her husband as a conspirator against the king. Refusing to speak out against her husband or to give her consent to the abandonment of the family's property holdings in return for her freedom, Leonora has remained ever since a prisoner of the Danish state.

Her imprisonment is likely to continue despite her recently gained notoriety. Throughout the Ulfeldts's years of scheming against the monarchy, the couple left a paper trail of letters that unambiguously demonstrated their guilt. Written in Caesar codes, they were deciphered by an employee of the Royal Danish Chancellery, Zacharias Lund, a gifted mathematician who has decoded more than 50 letters sent between the Ulfeldts and the Swedish crown.

Nell Gwynne became an actress at 15 years of age.

Margaret Cavendish has published *The Blazing World*.

Lady Anne Clifford

Composer Strozzi Dies

Padua, Italy, November 11, 1677: One of the most prolific female composers of our time, Barbara Strozzi, has died, aged 58.

Born in Venice in 1619, the illegitimate daughter of the poet Giulio Strozzi, she never married and, remarkably for a woman of her time, managed to support herself financially from the sale of her many splendid musical works, and other business ventures.

Between 1644 to 1664 eight books of her vocal chamber music were published. They were primarily for solo soprano, ranging from lively duets and trios through to extended solo cantatas.

Though not a composer of operas, religious works, or purely instrumental pieces, Barbara Strozzi's body of work was nonetheless remarkable and varied. Her "Gaude Virgo," for instance, set for soprano voice, possesses a unifying refrain in a lively triple meter, sprinkled with extended melismas and written out ornaments, with a recurring bass line that imitates the vocal figurations.

At a time when many composers routinely fail to have their works published, Strozzi published over 100 works throughout the course of her life. Overflowing with ornamentation and expression, her compositional techniques are reflective of the monody that marks the music of our time, a reaction perhaps to the complexity of Renaissance polyphony.

"FROM THE FIRST DAWN OF LIFE UNTO THE GRAVE, POOR WOMANKIND'S IN EVERY STATE A SLAVE."

SARAH EGERTON
(1670–1723)

Italian Woman Receives Doctorate in Philosophy

Padua, Italy, June 25, 1678: Elena Cornaro Piscopia, a 32-year-old noblewoman who hails from Venice, has become the first woman in the world to be awarded a doctorate. It was granted in a ceremony at the University of Padua today.

The daughter of the Procurator of San Marco, the young Elena received an education the envy of many men. She began studying languages at the age of seven and was soon well versed in Latin, Greek, and Hebrew in addition to her native Italian. Her tutoring extended to mathematics, physics, and astronomy, though her greatest loves proved to be theology and philosophy.

Sent to the University of Padua by her father in 1672 to study toward a Doctorate of Theology, opposition from the Roman Catholic Church forced Elena to reapply, this time to the School of Philosophy.

Elena's examination had to be moved from the university to the Cathedral of the Blessed Virgin to accommodate all those who wanted to attend. Her answers dazzled her examiners, who asked her a series of questions from Aristotle's *Posterior Analytics and Physics*, the standard university text on natural philosophy and logic. It was later unanimously determined that her depth of knowledge and education reached far beyond that which is normally required for the awarding of her doctorate.

During the ceremony, Elena Piscopia was also awarded a teacher's cape, a poet's laurel crown, and a doctor's ring.

time out

On May 31, 1678, the first Godiva Procession was held as part of the Coventry Fair in England. It commemorated Lady Godiva's legendary ride, over 600 years ago, naked on horseback through the streets of Coventry.

Lily of the Mohawks Dies

Kahnawake, New France (Quebec), April 17, 1680: Missionary and virgin, Kateri Tekakwitha, died suddenly today, at the age of 24.

Kateri was the daughter of a Christian Algonquin woman and an Iroquois warrior. Known as Lily of the Mohawks, she lived in the midst of the debauchery and idolatry that characterizes the northern banks of the Mohawk River, spending her time doing good deeds.

When she was four, her parents and brother died of smallpox, and she was adopted by her aunts and an uncle who had just become chief of the Turtle clan. Smallpox ravaged her face and severely damaged her sight, leading her to shy away from marriage. In 1667 a group of visiting Jesuit missionaries who had been to Quebec to assist in concluding a peace treaty with the French stayed at her

Mary, daughter of James II, and her husband, William of Orange, accept the throne of England.

Sofia Alexeyevna, the Regent of Russia.

uncle's home. During their three-day stay Kateri first heard the Christian gospel.

Baptized at the age of 18 by Father Jacques de Lamberville, Kateri practiced her faith in the face of enormous opposition and hardship, and she was eventually forced to move from her uncle's lodgings to the town of Caughnawaga on the banks of the St Lawrence River.

Since the announcement of her passing today, large crowds have been gathering to pay tribute to her. A Christian Indian woman, Anastasia Tegonhatsihonga, has been quoted as saying Kateri Tekakwitha's extraordinary sanctity and remarkable virtue will long be honored by the French people and by the Jesuit community of which she was a part.

Hundreds of L'Incarnation Letters Published

Paris, France, 1681: Two hundred and twenty-one letters by Marie Guyart (Marie de l'Incarnation), founder of the Ursuline order in New France (Canada), have been published by her son, Claude.

Many were fundraising letters to the aristocracy in France, and there were also various reports written to the Jesuits and Ursulines in the city of Tours. The letters present a vivid picture of life in New France.

Arriving in Quebec from France in 1639, Marie became the first superior of the Ursulines in New France. She studied the local Indian languages, becoming so proficient in them that she compiled Algonquin and Ouendat dictionaries; she also wrote a catechism in the Iroquois language and was a prolific letter writer. As many as 12,000 letters by Marie Guyart may still be in existence.

Education for Young Women Established

Paris, France, 1686: Françoise d'Aubigné, Marquise de Maintenon and morganatic second wife of Louis XIV, has just established a school for the education of impoverished young women of the nobility in the town of Saint-Cyr near Paris.

Construction of the Maison Royale de Saint-Louis, now commonly known as Saint-Cyr, began in May last year under the watchful eye of the royal architect, Monsieur Mansart. It is an innovative attempt to provide the girls with an industrious and strict education in an atmosphere of dignity and piety.

Françoise d'Aubigné began her rise to power back in 1668 when a friend and mistress of King Louis XIV asked her to hide her newborn child, the offspring of the King. The task was completed with discretion and Françoise soon came to the notice of the King, being appointed governess to his children in 1669. Beautiful and witty, Françoise slowly grew in status, until she became Louis's advisor and confidant. Eventually she took the name of Maintenon (a nearby estate).

She consistently refused to become the King's mistress; after some years, they married in a secret ceremony in 1683.

Following the marriage, Madame de Maintenon began to exert great influence over Louis, slowly transforming his reign into something resembling a religious dictatorship that has seen an end to much of the revelry, comedy, dance, and many festivals that for so long had characterized royal life at Versailles.

Her influence over King Louis has, nonetheless, been grossly exaggerated by her many critics. For instance, she played no discernible role in last year's revocation of the Edict of Nantes, which has denied all rights to Protestants living within the borders of France. Much of her time now seems to be spent at the school of Saint-Cyr, where she is often seen taking refuge from the intrigues and restraints of the royal court.

Marquise de Maintenon

The Marquise de Maintenon has established a new school for girls.

London, England, April 16, 1689: Author, poet, and playwright Aphra Behn dies, aged 49.

Rome, Italy, April 19, 1689: Former Queen of Sweden, Christina, dies, aged 63.

London, England, 1689: The *Bill of Rights* caps the excesses and power of the monarchy, and the *Toleration Act* promotes tolerance of religious beliefs, although Catholics are excluded from the throne.

Ireland, July 1, 1690: Ousted English King James II is defeated by the forces of William III.

Paray-le-Monial, France, October 17, 1690: Margaret Mary Alacoque, nun and visionary, dies, aged 43.

Montreal, New France (Canada), October, 1692: Fourteen-year-old Marie-Madeleine de Verchères organizes her few companions to defend her father's fort for several days against attacking Iroquois.

Salem Village (Danvers), Massachusetts, North America, 1692: People convicted of witchcraft are hanged, and one man is pressed to death under heavy stones.

Madrid, Spain, 1692: Luisa Roldán is appointed Sculptor of the Chamber to Charles II, the first woman to hold this post.

Paris, France, April, 1693: Europe's wealthiest woman, "La Grande Mademoiselle," the Duchesse de Montpensier, dies, aged 66. She is famous for her *Mémoires*.

Neerwinden, Netherlands, July 29, 1693: Kit Cavanagh, disguised as a man, fights in King William III of England's army against the French in the Battle of Landen.

London, England, December 28, 1694: Queen Mary, wife of William III, dies of smallpox, aged 32.

Mexico City, Mexico, April 17, 1695: Sister Juana Inés de la Cruz, philosopher and advocate for women's education, dies, aged 46.

Paris, France, 1696: Acclaimed artist Louise Moillon dies, aged about 86.

London, England, 1697: *A Serious Proposal to the Ladies re Higher Education for Women* is published anonymously, but is known to be the work of philosopher Mary Astell.

Padua, Italy, February 1699: Elisabeth-Sophie Chéron, French artist and author, is elected to the *Accademia dei Ricovrati*.

Dunfermline, Scotland, April 22, 1699: Lady Anne Halkett, a Royalist wife, dies, aged 76. She wrote 21 volumes of *Meditations*, which expound her religious beliefs.

London, England, October 1699: Artist Mary Beale dies, aged 66.

Behn's Groundbreaking Novel Published

Margaret Mary Alacoque

London, England, 1688: Aphra Behn, the prolific dramatist and pioneer of the prose narrative style, has just published her latest work, a short narrative entitled *Oroonoko, or The Royal Slave*.

The novel is unique in that it depicts its central character, an African prince deeply in love with the beautiful Imoinda, as a rather "noble" savage, endearing him to her predominantly European audience. The novel also possesses an anti-colonial theme almost unheard of in literature, and is deeply philosophical.

In *Oroonoko*, Behn writes that slaves can and should be every bit as proud and noble as free men, in a work that portrays the African people favorably, to the point of glorification, and where white men are often shown as more savage than their African counterparts.

Behn was born in 1640 in the town of Harbledown outside Canterbury. Her first play, *The Forced Marriage*, was written in 1670 and performed at Lincoln's Inn Fields by the Duke's Company. This play was followed by *The Amorous Prince* (1671), *Covent Garden Drollery* (1672), and *The Dutch Lover* (1677). Her only tragedy, *Abdelazer*, was published in 1676. This was followed a few months later by *The Town Fop*.

Her most successful play, *The Rover*, was also published and produced in 1677, and saw the actress Nell Gwynne play the main role of the whore, Angelica Bianca.

Aphra Behn is widely regarded as the first fully professional female writer in the English language.

> *"One can find women who have never had one love affair, but it is rare indeed to find any who have had only one."*
>
> FRANÇOIS DE LA ROCHEFOUCAULD (1613-1680), FRENCH WRITER

Mexican poet and scholar, Sister Juana Ines de la Cruz.

The Salem witch trials saw at least 25 people executed and nearly 200 imprisoned.

Indian Slave's Witchcraft Confession

Salem Village (Danvers), Massachusetts, North America, March 1, 1692: An Indian woman named Tituba, a servant of the Reverend Samuel Parris in the town of Salem, Massachusetts, has become the first person to confess to being an active practitioner of witchcraft.

Parris moved to Salem in 1689 where he became Minister of Salem Village. Last year his young daughter Elizabeth began exhibiting strange behavior, similar to that of the Goodwin children four years earlier. Their laundress, Goody Glover, was arrested and tried for bewitching the children, and was subsequently hanged.

Elizabeth's bizarre behavior has since spread to other children in Salem including Anne Putnam Jnr and Elizabeth's 11-year-old cousin Abigail Williams. It is being claimed that Tituba prepared a "witch's cake," a mixture of urine and rye that was then fed to the family dog in the hope of uncovering the spirit responsible for bewitching the girls.

The Parris girls have accused Tituba of being responsible for their symptoms, after considerable pressure was brought to bear on them from local ministers and townspeople. Elizabeth also claimed to have been bitten, pinched, and been whispered to while asleep at home.

Accusations have also emerged that Tituba has been teaching Elizabeth and Abigail how to read palms, and telling them stories focused on black magic. In her confession, Tituba has claimed that she never meant either girl any harm and she professed her love for them. She also claimed that she was not the only witch in Salem, declaring that her acquaintances Sarah Good and Sarah Osborne were her co-conspirators and fellow practitioners of black magic.

Tituba has denied casting spells on the two Parris girls, claiming to have only a casual familiarity with witchcraft from her time in Barbados. By confessing, it is thought unlikely that Tituba will have to undergo the ordeal of a trial.

Young Woman Holds Off Native Assault

Montreal, New France (Canada), October 1692: A young girl and her two brothers, two soldiers, and an elderly man have held off an attack on her father's fort for over a week—until relief arrived from Montreal. A marauding band of Iroquois Indians has attacked the fort, which is near the banks of the St Lawrence River, just 20 miles (32 km) south of Montreal.

Marie-Madeleine Jarret de Verchères was born in Verchères on March 3, 1678, the daughter of the town's founder, Lord Francois-Xavier Jarret, and Marie Perrot. The fourth of 12 children, she was taught to read and write by her mother, and how to fire a musket by her father.

When the war between the French and the Iroquois broke out four years ago, Verchères became an easy target, and Madeleine's parents had defensive walls constructed around their tenants' log cabins and her father's house. With the recent summer passing without incident, Madeleine's parents decided to leave on business, and to gather supplies for the coming winter.

Encouraging those within the fort to fire their muskets and cannon, and make as much noise as possible, Madeleine convinced the Iroquois that the fort was well garrisoned and managed to hold out until reinforcements arrived.

Observers have reported that upon greeting the relieving French lieutenant, Madeleine exclaimed: "Monsieur, I surrender to you my arms."

Woman Disguised as a Man Fights for William III

Neerwinden, Netherlands, July 1693: In the recent conflict in Belgium being called the Battle of Landen, between the forces of England's King William III and the French army of Marshall Luxembourg, it has been discovered that a woman, disguised as a man, has taken part in the battle and been wounded.

The woman, Kit Cavanagh, also known by the name Mother Ross, was clothed as a dragoon and fought in the midst of the conflict that cost the lives of some 9,000 French and over 19,000 allied troops.

Known by her comrades as the "pretty dragoon," the spirited youngster from Dublin was lured to the battlefield by the "rough music" of cannon fire.

Pioneer of French Still Life Dies

Paris, France, 1696: One of the pioneers of French still life painting, Louise Moillon, has died of smallpox at the age of 80.

Louise's paintings are composed with painstaking attention to detail, with her finest works exhibiting a stillness and texture never before achieved in what is a much-overlooked genre. During her long

Margaret Mary Alacoque, nun of the Visitation Order, has died.

life the Parisian-born artist had worked for many distinguished patrons including King Charles I of England and many within the French aristocracy.

Born into an artistic family in 1610, she demonstrated a remarkable ability to draw and paint. Her father Nicolas Moillon, a notable art dealer and painter of still lifes, portraits, and landscapes taught her as a child but passed away when Louise was 10. Her mother soon

Queen Mary

married another artist who became Louise's second teacher and to whom she became apprenticed. She sold her first painting when she was 19 years old.

Over the course of her life, Louise's exquisitely rendered paintings have come to be widely admired for their quiet style, typified by *Still Life with Cherries, Strawberries, and Gooseberries* (1630), painted when the artist was just 20 years of age. Composed with a sharp eye aided by a meticulous hand, the painting's contemplative style is very different from the panache and sophistication of Moillon's Dutch counterparts.

Portraitist Mary Beale Dies

London, England, October 1699: Mary Beale, one of the nation's finest miniaturists and portraitists, has died at her home in Pall Mall, aged 66. The first native-born professional female painter to work in England, the eldest child of the Reverend John Craddock was born in Suffolk and grew up within an artistic environment thanks to her father's membership of the Painter Stainer's Company.

Mary married Charles Beale in 1652, and in 1654 she embarked upon a semi-professional career as a portrait painter. After fleeing London's Great Plague in 1665, she and her husband returned in 1670. Mary established a studio in Pall Mall and became friends with the court painter to Charles II, Sir Peter Lely.

It was during this period that her career in miniature portraits began in earnest. Miniatures, usually executed in watercolor or gouache, have become an invaluable aid in introducing people to one another, especially those who may be separated by vast distances. Members of the aristocracy often may arrange for couriers to carry a miniature of a daughter to a potential suitor.

Mary's patronage dwindled in recent years. Prompted by a declining income, she was forced to consider alternative materials on which to render her portraits, such as sacking, bed ticking, and even onion bags, though her characteristic refinement, sensitivity, and intimacy always shone through.

Mary Beale's last known portrait was of Samuel Woodforde in 1693, painted when the artist was 61 years old.

The Greengrocer by Louise Moillon, who will be remembered as one of France's greatest painters of still life.

Rosalba Carriera

La Roldana Reappointed Court Sculptor

Madrid, Spain, 1701: Señora Luisa Roldán (La Roldana), Spain's first acknowledged female sculptor, has been appointed Sculptor of the Chamber to the new king, Philip V, a continuation of her appointment to this prestigious position by his predecessor, Charles II.

La Roldana's assistance with her husband's work first brought her recognition. In 1686, she received her own commissions, sculpting wooden angels and prophets for the cathedral in Cadiz, and polychrome wooden statues of Cadiz's patron saints for the town council. These figures have thick locks of hair, billowing draperies, and dreamy-looking faces, with furrowed brows and parted lips.

time out

In December 1721, 20-year-old singer Anna Magdalena Wulken gave up a promising musical career to become the second wife of German composer Johann Sebastian Bach. She bore him 13 children.

In 1688, La Roldana and her family moved to Madrid, where she petitioned for the position of Sculptor of the Chamber, gaining the appointment in 1692. One of her first commissions was a wooden statue of St Michael for the Royal Monastery.

In the years since, La Roldana has produced her most innovative works, polychrome terracotta figure groups that previously existed only as elements of architectural decoration. These delicate works, which La Roldana calls her "jewels," are her favorite creations and have brought her much fame.

> *"THIRST OF WEALTH NO QUIET KNOWS, BUT NEAR THE DEATH-BED FIERCER GROWS."*
>
> ANNE FINCH, LADY WINCHELSEA, ENGLISH POET, 1713 *ENQUIRY AFTER PEACE*

Madame de Pompadour, by Rosalba Carriera.

The First Daily Newspaper

London, England, March 11, 1702: Editor Elizabeth Mallett today released the first issue of the world's first ever daily newspaper, *The Daily Courant*.

This single-sided two-column broadsheet will, she claims, "give news daily and impartially" and make no editorial comment, since its readers have "sense enough to make reflections for themselves," and will also focus on reporting the latest news and information from overseas.

Mrs Mallet reassures her readers that the informative newspaper will "spare the public at least half the impertinences which the ordinary papers contain."

Published in rooms above the White Hart Inn in Fleet Street, *The Daily Courant* will be eagerly devoured by the literate who make up over 45 percent of London's population, and be read aloud in coffee houses to audiences keen to hear the most up-to-date news.

The Daily Courant.

Numb.

Thursday, March 12. 1702.

From the Vienna Journal, Dated March 1. 1702.

Vienna, March 1.

THE Regiment of Huffars commanded by Major General Colonitz, confifting of 1000 Men, is on its March from Hungary towards Bohemia and the Empire; and feveral other Imperial Regiments are marching this way. Our new Levies are carry'd on with great Succefs, and Recruits are continually fending away to their refpective Regiments. We have Advice from Adrianople that the Sultan is in that City, and that my Lord Pagett, Embaffadour from England, is alfo arriv'd there from Conftantinople, and preparing to fet out for this Place in a few days. Count Teckely lives in fo Poor a Condition at Ifmid, otherwife call'd Nicomedia in Afia, the place to which he is banifh'd, that his Wife is reduc'd to Sell her Jewels for their Subfiftance; the Port having taken from them all their Eftate.

Copenhagen, Feb. 11. The French Embaffador is preparing for his Departure from hence, and feems very much diffatisfy'd with the Succefs of all his Negotiations at this Court: but chiefly, becaufe Seven new Regiments are raifing for the Service of the States General. There is a Report that the King intends in a fhort time to take a Journey to Holftein, and from thence to Norway.

From the Vienna Journal, Dated March 4. 1702.

Vienna, March 4. Our Forces defign'd for Italy continue their March thither with all Expedition, and our Army there will be much more Numerous this Year than it was the laft. The Levy-Money is diftributed to the Officers of the new Regiments of Huffars that are now raifing; and fome of them are to Serve in Italy, the others on the Rhine. Proveditore General Vorftern has laid up great Magazines of Provifions in the Countrey of Friuli; and having agreed with feveral Undertakers for the tranfporting of it from thence by the way of the Gulf of Venice towards the River Po; he has already fent into Italy by that means, about 60000 Bufhels of Oats, and 20000 of Wheat; fo that we do not in the leaft apprehend that our Army there can be in any Want of Provifions the next Campaign.

Warfaw, Feb. 19. We are fully convinc'd by two Letters which the King of Sweden has written to the Cardinal Primate, That that Prince is not in the leaft inclin'd to come to an Accommodation with us; which makes us fear that the Unfortunate breaking up of the Diet will foon be follow'd by a General Sedition. The hopes we were in that the Mufcovites would have given the Swedes fomeDiverfion on the other Side of Narva, are vanifh'd; nor will Oginski's Party be able to hinder them from taking Poffeffion of Birfa. And tho' the Affairs of Lithuania are Adjufted, it caufes but little Joy among us, fince we evidently fee that neither Party have yet laid afide their Animofities.

From the Harlem Courant, Dated March 18.

Bruxelles, March 15. The King has made the following Promotion of General Officers, who are to Serve in his Army in Flanders the next Campaign. Don Andrea Benites, heretofore Colonel of the

Guards of his Electoral Highnefs of Bavaria, the Count D' Autel, Governor of Luxemburg made Lieutenant Generals: The Counts of Gredonk and Toulongeon, the Barons of Winterfeld, Noiremont, Don John de Ydiaques, and Don tonio Amenzaga, Brigadiers, and the Sieur Ver[...] Engineer General. Orders given for the f[...] repairing the Caftle of *Ter Veur*, where an A[...] ment is to be got ready for the Duke of Burg[...] who is coming into this Countrey to Comma[...] Generaliffimo this Campaign. On Friday laf[...] Marquifs of Bedmar went to Ghent, where he receive on Sunday next, the Homage from the S[...] of Flanders in the Name of His Catholick Maje[...]

From the Amfterdam Gazette, Dated March

Vienna, March 1. The Emperour has refolv[...] diffofe of the Confifcated Eftates of the Hung[...] Rebels,and apply the Produce of them to the C[...] of the War; They are valued at three Millio[...] Crowns.

Francfort, March 8. The French Envoy [...] Speech to the Deputies of the Circle of Fran[...] in the Diet held at Nuremberg, having rudely [...] the Emperour with infringing the Peace, they [...] up without admitting him again into their Affem[...]

Harwich, March 10. At Six a Clock in the [...] ning Yefterday, fail'd the Eagle Pacquet-Boat w[...] Meffenger and an Exprefs for Holland: An [...] Morning a hired Smack fail'd with a Second E[...] for Holland.

London, March 12. The Right Honourab[...] Earl of Marlborough is declared Captain Gen[...] the Forces in England and Holland.

When the King's Body was laid out, ther[...] found a Bracelet about his Right Arm, wi[...] Queen's Wedding Ring on it. He was ope[...] Tuefday Morning, his Brain was in very good [...] but there was hardly any Blood left in the Bo[...] his Lungs were very bad.

ADVERTISEMENT.

IT will be found from the Foreign Prints,whic[...] time to time, as Occafion offers, will be men[...] in this Paper, that the Author has taken Car[...] duly furnifh'd with all that comes fromAbroad[...] Language. And for an Affurance that he w[...] under Pretence of having Private Intelligen[...] pofe any Additions of feign'd Circumftances [...] Action, but give his Extracts fairly and Impa[...] at the beginning of each Article he will qu[...] Foreign Paper from whence 'tis taken, that t[...] lick, feeing from what Country a piece o[...] comes with the Allowance of that Governmer[...] be better able to Judge of the Credibility an[...] neis of the Relation: Nor will he take upon [...] give any Comments or Conjectures of his ov[...] will relate only Matter of Fact; fuppofin[...] People to have Senfe enough to make Ref[...] for themfelves.

This Courant (as the Title fhews) will be P[...] Daily: being defign'd to give all the Materi[...] as foon as every Poft arrives: and is confin'd [...] the Compafs, to fave the Publick at leaft half [...] pertinences, of ordinary News-Papers.

LONDON. Sold by E. *Mallet*, next Door to the *King's-Arms* Tavern at *Fleet-Br*[...]

England's first daily newspaper is published by Elizabeth Mallett.

London, England, 1700: Philosopher Mary Astell publishes *Some Reflections of Marriage*, in which she argues the need for women to be educated.

Rome, Italy, 1700: Rosalba Carriera, miniaturist, and the first artist to paint on ivory, is elected to the Accademia di S. Luca.

Paris, France, 1701: Madeleine de Scudéry, famous saloniere, writer, and member of the Académie Française dies, aged 93.

Madrid, Spain, 1701: Luisa Roldán is appointed Sculptor of the Chamber to Philip V.

London, England, March 19, 1702: Anne, the sister of Mary II, becomes queen on the death of William III.

Lancashire, England, 1702: Aged 87, Margaret Fell Fox, the mother of Quakerism, dies.

London, England, March 11, 1702: Elizabeth Mallett publishes the first daily newspaper, *The Daily Courant*.

London, England, 1702: Catharine Cockburn Trotter, philosopher and playwright, publishes *A Defence of Mr. Locke's Essay of Human Understanding*.

Boston, North America, April, 1704: John Campbell publishes *The Boston News-Letter*, the first newspaper to appear on a regular basis in America.

Blenheim, Bavaria, August 13, 1705: The Battle of Blenheim is won by English, Austrian, and Dutch forces.

Hanover, Germany, August 22, 1705: Caroline of Ansbach marries George August of Hanover.

Amsterdam, Netherlands, 1705: Maria Sibylla Merian, publishes *Metamorphosis insectorum surinamensium.*

Ahmadnagar, India, March 3, 1017: Mughal emperor Aurangzeb Alamgir dies, aged 88.

Great Britain, May 1, 1707: England and Scotland unite under one ruler and one parliament.

Paris, France, 1707: Elisabeth-Claude Jacquet de la Guerre's second collection of compositions, *Pièces de Clavecin qui peuvent se jouer sur le viollon,* is published.

Düsseldorf, Germany, 1708: Rachel Ruysch and her husband, are appointed court painters to the Elector Palatine John William.

Poltava, Russia, July 8, 1709: Charles XII of Sweden is defeated by Peter I of Russia at the Battle of Poltava.

Malplaquet, France, September 11, 1709: Great Britain, Netherlands, and Austria defeat France, with enormous loss of life on both sides.

London, England, 1709: Susannah Centlivre writes and appears in *The Busybody*. The play is an enormous success, running for 13 nights.

London, England, 1709: Mary de la Rivière Manley is arrested for libel.

Madeleine de Scudéry

An Entirely English Monarch

London, England, April 22, 1702: Tomorrow is St Georges' Day, a fitting date for the coronation of England's new sovereign, Queen Anne. Although she is the daughter of James II, a Catholic, who is even now inciting rebellion in France, Her Majesty is nevertheless a strict Protestant. The *Act of Settlement*, passed in 1701, ensures that no Catholic can ever again ascend the throne of England.

Queen Anne said in a recent speech to Parliament: "As I know my heart to be entirely English, I can very sincerely assure you that there is not one thing … I shall not be ready to do for the happiness or prosperity of England." She hopes during her reign to unite England and Scotland under one rule and thwart her father's rebellion.

Her Majesty is 37 years old, and is married to Prince George of Denmark. Sadly, she is plagued by gout and has no living children. Should she die without issue, the Crown will pass to Sophia, Electress of Hanover.

Queen Anne in her coronation robes.

"Mother of Quakerism" Finds Peace

Lancashire, England, April 23, 1702: Today Mrs Margaret Fell Fox, called the "mother of Quakerism" by her peers, passed away at her home in Lancashire. The last words of the 87-year-old were "I am at peace."

Since her conversion to Quakerism in 1652 at the age of 38, Mrs Fell Fox has been a tireless advocate for religious freedom. As well as being a missionary, preacher, and teacher, she wrote at least 16 books and 27 pamphlets decrying ordained ministry, infant baptism, the eucharist, and other matters. Her most famous work, written while she was in prison in 1665, is *Women's Speaking Justified,* a scripture-based argument in favor of female ministers.

Before his death in 1658, her first husband, Judge Fell, allowed the Quakers to hold religious meetings at Swarthmoor Hall. This was courageous, since the Lord Protector Oliver Cromwell had made attendance at Church of England services compulsory, and imposed jail terms for illegal religious gatherings.

Soon after Charles II became king in 1660, Mrs Fell travelled to London to campaign for religious freedom and Quakers' release from imprisonment. Charles was sympathetic but did not want to antagonize the established clergy. In 1664, Mrs Fell Fox was arrested for holding Quaker meetings in her home. She was sentenced to life imprisonment and her property was forfeited, although in January 1665, Charles II returned Swarthmoor Hall to her son, and in 1668 secured her release.

On October 27, 1669, Margaret Fell married George Fox, founder of the Quaker movement. Shortly afterward she was again imprisoned for about a year for breaking the *Conventicle Act*, which forbade religious meetings of more than five people outside the auspices of the Church of England.

Mrs Fell Fox spent the rest of her life mainly at home, especially after 1691 when George Fox died. She will be remembered for her bravery and persistence in the face of persecution.

Proof: Insects not Born from Mud

Amsterdam, Netherlands, 1705: The noted entomologist Mrs Maria Sybylla Merian has taken the scientific world by storm with her new book, *Metamorphosis insectorum surinamensium.* Containing exquisite engravings on parchment, which have been colored by Mrs Merian and her daughter, this book describes the life cycles of 186 insect species. It contains information on plants these insects thrive on, ways in which caterpillars turn into butterflies and moths, and reproduction, proving that insects do not arise from the spontaneous generation of rotting mud—a theory still held by many.

Mrs Merian's groundbreaking work is the result of two years spent studying the flora and fauna of tropical Surinam. She explored uncharted territory and also recorded indigenous names of plants and their medicinal uses, until malaria forced her return to the Netherlands in 1701. Her study trip to South America was financed by Amsterdam's city fathers, who were impressed with her research into metamorphosis.

Mrs Merian's scientific investigations were sparked by studying other insect collections. In the preface to her book, she writes: "In these collections I had found innumerable other insects, but finally if here their origin and their reproduction is unknown, it begs the question as to how they transform, starting from caterpillars and chrysalises and so on." Born in Germany, the intrepid Mrs Merian has lived most of her life in the Netherlands. She is divorced with two daughters. This work is her third and most ambitious book to date.

Key Events

London, England, 1709: Elizabeth Elstob, the first woman to translate Anglo-Saxon, publishes *An English-Saxon Homily on the Birthday of St Gregory.*

Coalbrookdale, England, 1709: Abraham Darby uses coke instead of charcoal to fire his blast furnace, producing cheap cast iron.

Florence, Italy, 1709: Bartolommeo Cristofori invents the "pianoforte."

London, England, 1710: St Paul's Cathedral is completed.

Meissen, Germany, June, 1710: The first factory in Europe to produce Chinese-style hard paste porcelain begins operation.

Chelsea, England, c. 1712: Mary Astell establishes a charity school for girls.

Pennsylvania, North America, 1712: Hannah Penn becomes Acting Proprietor of Pennsylvania after her husband William has a stroke.

Utrecht, Netherlands, 1713: The War of the Spanish Succession is ended by the Treaty of Utrecht.

Zurich, Switzerland, c. 1713: Swiss miniaturist and portrait painter Anna Waser dies, aged about 39.

Hanover, Germany, June 8, 1714: Sophie, Electress of Hanover and next in line to the throne of Great Britain, dies, aged 84.

London, England, August 1, 1714: Queen Anne dies, aged 49. She is succeeded by George, Elector of Hanover.

Versailles, France, September 1, 1715: Louis XIV dies of gangrene, aged 76.

China, 1716: *The Kangxi Dictionary* of Chinese characters, named for the emperor who commissioned it, is published.

Greenwich, England, 1718: Edmund Halley discovers the true motion of "fixed" stars.

London, England, 1718: Lady Mary Wortley Montagu promotes the Turkish practice of inoculation.

London, England, 1719: Eliza Haywood's *Love in Excess, or, The Fatal Inquiry*, perhaps the first book to be described as a novel on its title-page, is a great success.

Paris, France, 1720: Rosalba Carriera, Venetian miniaturist, is elected to the Académie Française.

Jamaica, November 28, 1720: Female pirates, Anne Bonny and Mary Read, plead pregnancy to escape execution.

Edo (Tokyo), Japan, 1720: Shogun Yoshimune rescinds the law forbidding study of European books.

Haddonfield, West New Jersey, North America, 1721: Elizabeth Haddon Estaugh builds a Quaker meeting house, which becomes the focus for worship in the region.

Sophie, Electress of Hanover

English Novelist Cleared of Libel Charges

London, England, February 13, 1710: Mrs Mary de la Rivière Manley has been found innocent of a change of seditious libel, laid against her for her raunchy novel, *The New Atalantis*. This work describes how Astrea, goddess of Justice, is instructed by Lady Intelligence on human behavior, and witnesses scenes of adultery, seduction, and bigamy.

Despite Mrs Manley's insistence that her novel is fictitious, critics believe it is a thinly-veiled satire that accuses Whig politicians of sexual and political corruption, and a particularly pointed attack on Lady Marlborough, a confidante of Queen Anne, and her Whig husband John Churchill. Mrs Manley is a known ally of Robert Harley, leader of the Tories, and her previous novel, written in 1705, is also considered a political allegory attacking the Whigs.

Mrs Manley surrendered to the Secretary of State on October 29, 1709, after a warrant had been issued against her. She was released on bail on November 5. At her trial today at Queen's Bench Court, she was discharged after she denied that informants were supplying her with damaging information about Whig leaders, and insisted her work was entirely imaginative. Whatever the truth of the matter, it is predicted that six or seven editions will be needed to satisfy the public's demand for copies of *The New Atalantis*, and that this novel will help the Tories to gain more influence with the Queen.

New Charity School at Royal Hospital

Chelsea, London, England, 1712: Miss Mary Astell has announced the opening of a charity school, for daughters of pensioners, at the Royal Hospital. Supported by wealthy benefactors, the school aims to teach girls useful skills in order to help them gain employment. Miss Astell will be its headmistress. Long a proponent of education for women, Miss Astell has largely educated herself through reading and corresponding with learned men on theological matters.

A devout Christian, she came to the attention of society in 1694 when she wrote *A Serious Proposal to the Ladies for the Advancement of their True and Greatest Interest*, which advocated a boarding school where young ladies would learn to reason logically and make sensible decisions, rather than "make a fine show and be good for nothing." This book was a bestseller among the female population, and Queen Anne herself considered supporting such a school before being advised it would remind people too much of a Catholic nunnery.

In 1700, in *Some Reflections upon Marriage Occasioned by the Duke and Duchess of Mazarine's Case*, Miss Astell wrote that women's lack of education hindered them from choosing a good husband. In the third edition of this work, published in 1706, the author added a preface defending her book from critics, and asked: "If all men are born free, how is it that women are born slaves?"

Death of Famous Swiss Miniaturist

Zurich, Switzerland, 1713: The Swiss miniaturist, Anna Waser, has died from a fall, at the age of 39. This internationally acclaimed artist, who had received many commissions for portraits from Germany, London, and the Netherlands, also created pastoral scenes.

Miss Waser drew the world's attention when only 12 years of age as the result of her stunningly executed self-portrait. She subsequently studied under respected Berne artist Joseph Werner for four years before setting up her own business as a miniature painter in Zurich. From 1699 to 1702 she was employed as an artist at the court of Solms-Braunfels.

Her work includes an elegant silver-point drawing entitled *Ideal Head of a Woman*, created in 1711. This profile is drawn in the manner of antique busts but is more vibrant and realistic with its finely delineated hair and lively expression.

Queen's Letter Kills Electress

Hanover, Germany, June 8, 1714: Sophie, Electress of Hanover and heir to the British throne, died today, aged 84. She had just received a letter from England's Queen Anne, who believed the Electress was secretly planning to send her son, Georg, to England. Queen Anne wants nothing to do with her successors, and wrote that she would not tolerate Georg's presence.

The letter caused the Electress to depart from her habitual serenity. Only recently she had written, "I believe that I remain so long in this world because I keep my spirit calm," but confided to her friend, the Countess of Buckeburg, that she would die from the letter's emotional effects. Two days later, she passed away in the gardens at Herrenhausen. Elector Georg Ludwig of Hanover is now heir to the British throne.

The Electress was much respected as the intellectual and cultural focus of the court. She used her influence with her husband to have her friend Gottfried Liebniz (who invented the binary system and calculus) appointed as Privy Counselor of Justice. Liebniz once said: "In this region a courtier is not supposed to speak of learned matters, and without the Electress they would be spoken of even less." She will be sorely missed.

"Fierce Hellcat" Dies in Prison

St Jago de la Vega, Jamaica, April 28, 1721: Swashbuckling pirate Mary Read, and her

Hannah Penn becomes Acting Proprietor of Pennsylvania after her husband William has a stroke.

The notorious female pirates, Anne Bonny and Mary Read, pleaded pregnancy to delay execution.

Caroline of Ansbach

unborn child, today died of fever in prison. On November 28, 1720, Read and her equally aggressive associate, Anne Bonny, were convicted of "piracies, felonies and robberies ... on the high seas" and sentenced to hang. However, as both women were pregnant, their sentences were postponed.

Terrors of the Caribbean for over two years as crew members of Captain "Calico Jack" Rackham's pirate ship, Read and Bonny could defeat any man with sword and pistol. Stories of their bravery include Read's decapitating a fellow pirate to prevent the man she loved—a sailor on a captured ship—from being defeated in a duel. She was carrying her lover's child when she died. At their trial, a shipmate stated that these British women were both "fierce hellcats" who were "resolute and ready to board or undertake anything that was hazardous in the time of action."

Rackham's entire crew was captured in late October 1720 while anchored off Point Negril, celebrating victories by drinking rum. A British Navy man-o-war, headed by a Captain Barnet, surprised them. The men were too drunk to fight, so Bonny and Read alone fended off their attackers for over an hour.

Bonny reminded her lover Rackham of his behavior on that fateful night when he was allowed to see her before being hanged. She was heard to have said: "I'm sorry, Jack ... But if you had fought like a man, you would not now be about to die like a dog." As for Read, when asked at her trial if she believed hanging was too harsh a penalty for piracy, she said: "it is no great hardship."

For were it not for that, every cowardly fellow would turn pirate, and so unfit the sea, that men of courage must starve."

Smallpox Inoculations Attacked

London, England, 1724: Doctors and clergy are warning that inoculating people against smallpox contravenes the will of God. Today, one parish priest, John Birch, preached that smallpox is "a merciful provision ... to lessen the burthen of a poor man's family." The London College of Physicians is condemning the practice as taking the power of life and death out of God's hands.

Inoculation was introduced into England by Lady Mary Wortley Montagu after she observed its benefits in Turkey in 1717. She wrote: "People ... make parties for this purpose, and ... the old woman comes with a nut-shell full of the matter of the best sort of smallpox, and asks what vein you please to have opened." Impressed, Lady Montagu had her 6-year-old son inoculated in Constantinople. Her three-month-old daughter was the first person to be inoculated in England.

Lady Montagu contracted smallpox in 1715, which left her without eyelashes and with deeply pitted skin. In her work *Town Eclogues*, a collection of satirical poems published in 1716, she describes a woman whose life is ruined by the disfiguring disease. Since her return to London in 1718, Lady Montagu has tirelessly promoted inoculation, sending essays to magazines, writing to society leaders and persuading the royal family, the aristocracy, and prominent politicians, to have themselves and their children inoculated.

With foresight, Lady Montagu wrote from Turkey in 1717 that few doctors "have virtue enough to destroy such a considerable branch of their revenue for the good of mankind," and that she would have to "be patriot enough [to] war with them." Now the clergy are adding more weight to the debate, and opposition is mounting. Statistics which have been collected by the Secretary of the Royal Society reveal that between 1721 and 1723, 469 people had been inoculated. In 1724, the total number dropped to just 49. It remains to be seen whether Lady Montagu's influence in society can reverse the tide of public opinion.

Lady Mary Wortley Montagu, a strong advocate for inoculation against the disease smallpox.

Catherine,
Empress of Russia

Empress Catherine Dies

St Petersburg, Russia, May 17, 1727: The Empress Catherine, the first woman to rule Imperial Russia, died today at the age of forty-three. She had a meteoric rise through life, beginning as a peasant, progressing to become the wife of Peter the Great, and ending up as a respected and powerful leader.

Born Marta Skavronskaya, she grew up in Marienburg, raised by a pastor after she became an orphan. When the Russians captured Marienburg, she was taken prisoner and became the housekeeper of Prince Menshikov, who was later her ally. Attracted by her beauty and serenity, Peter the Great married her secretly in 1707 and openly in 1712. Catherine accompanied her husband on campaigns in the Russo-Turkish War of 1710–11, saving Peter and his army in 1711. Surrounded by Turkish troops, Catherine suggested using her jewels and those of other women to bribe Grand Vizier Baltaji, who subsequently allowed the Russians to retreat.

"The carping malice of the vulgar world; who think it a proof of sense to dislike every thing that is writ by Women."

SUSANNAH CENTLIVRE,
PLAYWRIGHT,
THE PLATONIC LADY,
1707

Peter the Great relied on his wife's shrewd counsel, her ability to calm his rages, and her nursing skills during his epileptic seizures. He crowned her Empress Consort in 1724 to rule by his side. After his death in 1725, Menshikov and the progressive faction, whom Peter had favored, feared a return to the rule of the entrenched aristocrats. They staged a coup and proclaimed Catherine the ruler.

During her time as empress, Catherine continued Peter's policies to modernize the country. She established the Russian Academy of Sciences, gave her name to Catherinehof near St Petersburg, and built that city's first bridges. Last year she established the Supreme Privy Council to help her rule. Menshikov was one of its members. Catherine will be buried in the cathedral of the St Peter and St Paul Fortress in St Petersburg. The new czar will be Peter the Great's grandson, Peter II.

Brilliant Female Physicist Joins University Staff

Bologna, Italy, May 1732: Laura Bassi, a philosophical debater and physicist, was this month awarded a doctorate by the University of Bologna and accepted the prestigious position of Professor of Anatomy. She is the first woman to be appointed as a university professor, and expected to be the next Professor of Physics. She is currently writing a treatise, criticizing the theories of Descartes, which reveals logical problems with the Cartesian system.

Gaetano Tacconi, her family's physician and a professor at the university, instructed Laura in philosophy and metaphysics from the age of 13 when she impressed contemporaries with her intellect. Cardinal Prospero Lambertini then persuaded her to defend 49 philosophical theses in Palazzo Pubblico against Tacconi and four other professors.

No doubt Laura Bassi's next intellectual achievement will also be impressive.

Woman Buried With Full Military Honors

London, England, 1739: Local legend Kit Cavanagh died earlier this year, aged seventy-eight. Her life story is certainly stranger than fiction.

After a four-year-long happy marriage, her husband Richard Walsh disappeared in 1692. Kit eventually received a letter from him—he had been conscripted into the army. Determined to find him, Kit left their three children with her mother, dressed as a man, and enlisted in the Duke of Marlborough's infantry.

Despite being wounded in the Battle of Landen, being captured by the French, and living closely with her fellow dragoons, no-one discovered Kit's secret. She loved the army and admitted she had "martial inclinations."

In 1704, she found her husband after the Battle of Hochstat. She swore him to secrecy and they continued fighting. Two years later, Kit was wounded and her gender was revealed. However, she was allowed to serve in Richard's regiment as a cook. Sadly, several months later Richard was killed at the Battle of Malplaquet.

Catherine Hayes and her lovers murdered her husband in 1725.

Empress Anna Ivanova, who died in 1740.

Venice, Italy, 1725: Antonio Vivaldi's *Four Seasons* (four violin concertos) are published.

London, England, May, 1726: Catherine Hayes is burned alive at Tyburn for the murder of her husband, John.

St Petersburg, Russia, May 17, 1727: Catherine, Empress of Russia, dies, aged 43.

London, England, 1728: James Bradley's star observations lead him to calculate the speed of light to be 183,000 miles (295,000 km) per second.

Paris, France, 1728: Pierre Fauchard publishes *The Surgeon Dentist*, the first dental textbook, and invents the word "dentist."

Dublin, Ireland, 1728: Irish Catholics lose the right to vote.

London, England, 1731: Kitty Clive establishes her comedic skills in Charles Coffey's ballad opera, *The Devil to Pay*.

Bologna, Italy, May, 1732: Laura Bassi is the first woman appointed to the staff of a European university (the University of Bologna).

Bury, Lancashire, England, 1733: John Kay invents the flying shuttle, speeding up the weaving process.

London, England, June 25, 1735: William Hogarth publishes his engravings with the protection of the *Engraver's Copyright Act*, which is passed the same day.

Paris, France, 1737: Philippe Buache uses contour lines to show elevation on maps.

Rome, Italy, 1737: The Blessed Catherine of Genoa is canonized by Pope Clement XII for her work with the sick.

Milan, Italy, 1738: The Italian mathematician Maria Gaetana Agnesi publishes *Propositiones philosophicae*.

London, England, 1739: Kit Cavanagh who, disguised as a man, fought under the Duke of Marlborough, dies, aged about 78.

St Petersburg, Russia, October 1740: Empress Anna Ivanova dies, aged 47.

Vienna, Austria, 1740: Maria Theresa becomes Archduchess of Austria on the death of her father, Charles VI, the Holy Roman Emperor.

France, 1740: Gabrielle-Emilie du Châtelet publishes *Institutions de physique*, which discusses the works of Leibnitz, Newton, and Descartes.

London, England, March 18, 1741: Pickpocket Jennie Diver is hanged after committing numerous offences.

St Petersburg, Russia, November 26, 1741: Elizaveta Petrovna, the daughter of Peter the Great, becomes czarina in a coup against the young Czar Ivan VI.

Germany, 1741: Dorothea Erxleben's request to study medicine at the University of Halle is granted.

When the war ended in 1712, Kit returned to London. She married a dissolute soldier named Davies. She started and lost several pubs in England and Ireland, ending up living on charity from rich members of the army and other admirers. The high esteem in which she was held was reflected in her burial: she was laid to rest in Westminster, with full military honors.

Pirate Ann Mills holds the head of a Frenchman.

Is "Pirate Ann" a Heroine?

Caribbean Sea, 1740: Reports have come in of a young female adventurer having acted with great bravery on the high seas.

The as yet unconfirmed story relates that Ann Mills (disguised as a man) was serving as a dragoon on the frigate *Maidstone* when some French sailors boarded her ship. Apparently, the entire crew was impressed with the way Ann fought the Frenchmen. A drawing doing the rounds shows "Pirate Ann" (not so well disguised) holding the severed head of a Frenchman. The drawing is quite probably anti-French propaganda.

Notorious Pickpocket Hanged at Tyburn

London, England, March 18, 1741: Jennie Diver, whose real name was Mary Young, was hanged today. She was driven to her execution in a mourning-coach, and wore a black dress and veil. A song written specially for the occasion states: "The crowds at Oxford stood to cheer as Mary passed alone to Tyburn Tree, her drop measured 18 inches (46 cm), my dear, 'tis the end of highway robbery."

A penniless Irish orphan, Mary went to London to make her fortune and was adopted by a gang of pickpockets. She was such a nimble-fingered thief that she became the gang's leader and was renamed Jennie Diver, "diver" being the colloquial term for pickpocket.

Jennie had had some education, and was attractive and well spoken. Dressed in finery, she mixed easily with the wealthy. It is said she attended church wearing two false arms, which remained in her lap. During prayers, she stole her neighbors' watches and jewelry.

Arrested and transported to Virginia in 1733 and then again in 1738, Jennie paid people to return her to London both times. But in January this year, she was caught trying to steal a purse from a young woman, and sentenced to death. She will live on as a character in John Gay's popular plays, *Beggar's Opera* and *Polly*, which have played consistently to packed audiences since they opened in 1728.

Peter the Great's Daughter Usurps Czar

St Petersburg, Russia, November 26, 1741: Last night, Elizaveta Petrovna, daughter of Peter the Great and Empress Catherine, usurped young Czar Ivan VI and his mother, Regent Anna Leopoldovna,

time out

In 1739, Englishwoman Joanna Stephens sells the recipe for her stone-dissolving remedies for £5,000. The "medicinal" powder combines crushed eggshells and dried snails; a potion and pills are also available.

by persuading the soldiers belonging to the Preobrazhenskii regiment to take up arms against them. She arranged for the regent and her children to be seized in their beds, then summoned all court officials, informing them that she was now the czarina. The coup was so swift and quiet that few people knew of it until late today.

Rumor has it that the regent planned to force Elizaveta to become a nun, prompting the coup. On April 25 next year she will be officially proclaimed czarina in the Dormition Cathedral of the Moscow Kremlin. Ivan and his mother will be exiled to Riga.

Renowned for her beauty and vivacity, as well as for her allegiance to her native Russians, Elizaveta says her reign will mark the end of the Prussian influence at the court that has been so unpopular during the reign of Ivan. She also vows to end capital punishment.

The 32-year-old Czarina is currently unmarried, though she has announced she is looking for a suitable husband.

Maria Theresa, Archduchess of Austria

The new czarina of Russia, Elizaveta Petrovna.

Claudine-Alexandrine
Guerin de Tencin

"[IT WAS] AN
ACT OF SIMPLE
HUMANITY."

FIONA MACDONALD,
1747, ON HER DECISION
TO RESCUE PRINCE
CHARLES STUART

Raunchy Novelist
Starts Monthly Journal

London, England, April, 1744: Last week Eliza Haywood, actor, playwright, and bestselling writer of amatory novels such as *Love in Excess*, launched her first edition of the monthly journal written by women for women, *The Female Spectator*.

This first issue contains essays that allegedly originate from readers' mail. As a popular novelist, Haywood has received many letters from female fans asking for advice on how women should conduct their lives.

In her journal, Haywood recommends women gain an education and make the most of available opportunities. She writes as four personas—Mira, Widow of Quality, Euphrosine, and The Female Spectator—and discusses such topics as marriage, children, reading, education, and appropriate behavior.

Her essay on education will doubtless spark a spirited response from one of her most savage critics, Alexander Pope, who has described her as, among many things, "a shameless scribbler." Haywood writes that men are opposed to educating women because they believe that "... if once they [women] have the capacity of arguing with us [men], where would be our authority!" She appeals to her readers that such reasoning betrays "an arrogance and pride in themselves, yet less excusable than that which they seem so fearful of our assuming."

Regardless of a backlash from her male critics, Eliza Haywood will have the last laugh. The first journal has sold very well, and her readers are eagerly awaiting the arrival of the next issue.

Male Midwife
Receives Doctorate

Glasgow, Scotland, 1745: William Smellie, from Lanark in southern Scotland, who has been teaching courses on obstetrics and midwifery for several years now, has received his medical doctorate from the University of Glasgow this year.

Having practiced medicine in Lanark for several years, Doctor Smellie became concerned with women's health before and during childbirth. His lecture notes contain information on a case where a very poor woman died of cold before she could deliver her baby.

He studied obstetrics in both Paris and London before setting up a small school in London in which he taught midwifery for five shillings. Doctor Smellie delivered poor women free of charge if his students were allowed to attend the delivery, and taught students using a leather-covered skeleton as a specimen.

Doctor Smellie's lecture notes make illuminating reading. He describes how the infant's head adapts to pelvic canal changes during birth, and how to revive an asphyxiated infant by inflating the lungs with a silver catheter.

His major achievement is pioneering the safe use of forceps. He has invented his own short wooden forceps based on the French model, and he advocates their use only after the baby's head enters the mother's pelvis. He controls their use by measuring the pelvis, and has introduced the diagonal conjugate measurement, measured by the fingers from the arch of the pubis to the sacrum.

Scottish Heroine
Freed from Prison

London, England, 1747: Flora MacDonald, the brave and beautiful lady who helped Charles Edward Stuart ("Bonnie Prince Charlie") escape from Scotland, has been freed from the Tower of London under a general amnesty. She was arrested in 1746 for helping Stuart—grandson of the unpopular Catholic and deposed king of England, James II—escape his pursuers by rowing him to Skye.

In 1745, Stuart landed in Scotland with plans to seize the throne of England. His father, James Stuart, had tried twice to invade Scotland and failed both times, and the son was destined to suffer the same fate. After his disastrous defeat at the Battle of Culloden in April last year, Stuart attempted to escape back to France with a bounty of £30,000 on his head. He ended up on the island of Benbecula in the Outer Hebrides, where Flora MacDonald's foster father commanded government troops and her fiancé, Allan Macdonald, was a military officer. Being a Jacobite sympathizer, she agreed to help the prince escape.

On June 20, 1746, Stuart and Flora, who was then 24, met for the first time and remained in hiding together for a week as they planned their escape.

Madame de Pompadour, mistress of Louis XV of France and a generous patron of the arts.

The prince was to be disguised as "Betty Burke," Flora's Irish serving-maid, dressed in a blue-and-white frock. Some say he kept his boots on and was nearly found out.

Flora and "Betty" crossed about 45 miles (72 km) by sea to Skye in a rowing boat, evading the watchful eyes of Hanoverian soldiers and bounty hunters. High winds caused tempestuous seas, and they were buffeted for days until they managed to land. Then they traveled overland to Portree where they parted company, and Flora returned home. Rumor has it that Stuart gave Flora a gold locket.

Boatmen's gossip reached soon official ears, and Flora was arrested and imprisoned. She was first sent to Dunstaffnage Castle, then to the Tower of London.

Now that she is free, Flora will marry her fiancé Allan Macdonald, and begin a new life in America.

Bonnie Prince Charlie farewells his rescuer, Flora MacDonald.

Indigo Production Boosts Economy

South Carolina, North America, 1747: The entrepreneur and plantation overseer, Mrs Elizabeth Pinckney, was today lauded by her fellow plantation owners for successfully growing indigo in South Carolina and exporting it to England. Mrs Pinckney has generously shared her knowledge of indigo cultivation with her neighbors, and this plant that produces a blue dye for fabric is now America's second-most profitable cash crop, after rice.

Mrs Pinckney has always been exceptional. At the age of 16 she was placed in charge of her father's three plantations near Charleston because he had to return to Antigua on business. She would start each day at 5 a.m., although she reports that a friend believed getting up so early would "spoil my marriage, for she says it will make me look old long before I am so." Not only did she successfully manage the plantations, she educated her slaves in reading, writing, and religion.

Always interested in botany, Mrs Pinckney experimented with growing flax, figs, and hemp. Around 1740, her father sent her indigo seeds from the West Indies. She began cultivating and creating improved strains of the plant, and producing commercial quantities of dye, which involved precise cutting and soaking of them, monitoring the liquid extracted from the leaves, and forming and drying cakes. An indigo-cultivator whom her father sent her tried to sabotage her crop, fearing competition with indigo grown in the West Indies; she dismissed him.

The first year Mrs Pinckney's plants were killed by frost and the second year they were eaten by worms; however, the third year the crop succeeded. This year, the colony has exported profitable amounts of indigo to England.

The amazing Mrs Pinckney has even found the time to have a family. In 1744, at the age of 22, she married Charles Pinckney who has supported her scientific efforts, and in 1745 she gave birth to their son, also called Charles.

Female Genius Simplifies Mathematics

Milan, Italy, 1748: This year, mathematician Maria Gaetana Agnesi published *Instituzioni analitiche ad uso della gioventù italiana (Institutions for the Use of Italian Youth)*, in which she simplifies differential calculus and other mathematical ideas.

Agnesi is already known as the author of the 1738 treatise *Propositiones philosophicae (Propositions of Philosophy)*, which contained 191 philosophical theses she disputed with experts, one of whom commented at the time: "She is … about twenty … much attached to the philosophy of Newton, and it is marvelous to see a person of her age so conversant with such abstract subjects."

Agnesi, a precocious child who spoke several languages, studied mathematics under Professor Ramiro Rampinelli, in Rome and Bologna. Her latest treatise has brought her more fame and praise. The Académie des Sciences in Paris states: "Order, clarity and precision reign in all parts of this work." It will be indispensable to students throughout Europe.

Doctor Demands Education for Women

Germany, 1749: Dorothea Erxleben, who is currently working as a doctor, has published *Rational Thoughts on the Education of the Fair*, in which she demands education for women. Although she has her own practice, which she took over from her father on his death in 1747, Frau Erxleben does not have a degree. She was educated in medicine by her father and her brother, read the latest textbooks, and studied and worked with her father, a respected physician.

Frau Erxleben is known as an innovator. In 1741, she petitioned King Frederick II to admit her to the University of Halle. Her petition was granted, and had she taken up the offer, she would have been the first woman to have received a tertiary education in medicine.

Frau Erxleben's duties as a wife and mother, and the need to work to support her family, have prevented her from attending university. However, her lack of academic qualifications has not prevented her from attracting many patients, despite complaints from male practitioners that she is a "quack."

Her treatise urges the government to give women books, lessons, and entry into schools. She also urges women to spend their time studying rather than indulging in gossip and paying unnecessary visits to friends and acquaintances.

Gabrielle-Emilie du Châtelet

Renowned Venetian artist, Rosalba Carriera.

Mariana Victoria
of Bourbon

Death of Marguerite de Launay, Baronne de Staal

France, June 15, 1750: The writer Marguerite de Launay, Baronne de Staal, died today at the age of 65 after leading an eventful life. She joined the household of the Duchess of Maine at Sceaux as a lady-in-waiting in 1710. A talented wit and writer, she became a favorite with the Duchess, and wrote comedies that were very well received.

The Duchess is married to Louis-Auguste de Bourbon, Duc de Maine, an illegitimate son of Louis XIV of France. When the king died, the Duc d'Orléans became Regent, and declared that illegitimate children had no claim to the throne of France and should rank less than other peers. Angered by the insult to her husband, the Duchess, along with de Launay, became involved in the Cellamare conspiracy, which sought to transfer the regency of France to the King of Spain.

On discovery of the conspiracy, de Launay and the Duke and Duchess were sent to the Place de la Bastille in Paris in 1718. De Launay wrote of this experience: "I heard half a dozen locks and bolts closing the door that shut me off from mankind. The first hour, which I spent gazing at my crackling fire, was the most desolate of all my imprisonment."

"I AM AS MUCH A WOMAN AS MY MOTHER EVER WAS, AND MY REAL NAME IS HANNAH SNELL."

"JAMES GRAY," THE FEMALE SOLDIER, REVEALING HER TRUE IDENTITY, 1750

Marguerite de Launay spent two years in the Bastille.

Freed after two years, Marguerite de Launay returned to the household of the Duchess, who had been freed a year earlier. In 1735, then over 50 years old, she married the Baron de Staal.

The Baronne has written her memoirs, which will be available once a suitable publisher has been found.

Famous Court "Flower Painter" Dies

Amsterdam, Netherlands, August 12, 1750: Renowned throughout Europe for her vibrant paintings of brightly lit flowers against dark backgrounds, artist Rachel Ruysch died today, aged 85.

Ruysch's talent was recognized by her father while she was young, so when she was 15 she was apprenticed to Willem van Aelst, a prominent Delft painter. Her talent grew, and her work drew the attention of the Elector Palatine, who invited her to Dusseldorf to be court painter. She held this position from 1708 until the elector's death in 1716.

After her return to the Netherlands, she continued painting in Amsterdam for prestigious clients. She was a prolific and well-respected artist and her paintings, selling for up to 1,000 guilders each, were sought after.

Ruysch is best known for paintings such as *Still Life With Bouquet of Flowers and Plums*, and *Still Life With Flowers on a Marble Tabletop*, which contain bright arrangements of roses, poppies, irises, carnations, and other flowers. Ruysch also painted insects on her flowers such as beetles, little flies, and caterpillars, which added a feeling of movement.

Married in 1693 to the portrait painter, Juriaen Pool, who died in 1745, Ruysch had 10 children in between her artistic assignments. Her works will continue to be valued in European markets.

time out

Revolution in Portugal has been narrowly avoided following the arrest of the Marchioness Leonor of Távora (an active political figure) and her husband, Francisco Assis, Count of Alvor. They were charged with treason and executed with their children.

Anne Appointed Princess-Regent

Netherlands, 1751: The eldest daughter of King George II of England and Queen Caroline, Princess Anne, was today appointed Princess-Regent of Friesland on the death of her husband, William IV of Orange, in October this year.

Princess Anne will rule in place of her late husband.

At only three years of age, their son, William V, future head of the principality, is too young to take the throne.

Princess Anne helped her husband run the country, and knows much about public affairs. She has the support of William Bentinck as well as other leaders of the Orangist party, and is considered to be the ideal regent for her son.

The Netherlands is currently in a great deal of debt, so one of the regent's first duties will be to manage the country's budget. It is quite probable that some of the military will be disbanded.

Hanover, Germany, March 16, 1750: Mathematician and astronomer Caroline Lucretia Herschel is born.
France, June 15, 1750: French writer Marguerite de Launay, Baronne de Staal, dies aged 65.
London, England, June 1750: A Royal Marine known as James Gray reveals that he is in fact a woman, Hannah Snell. The female soldier, who had fought in India, sold her story to the publisher Robert Walker.
Leipzig, Germany, July 28, 1750: Composer Johann Sebastian Bach dies, aged 65.

Amsterdam, Netherlands, August 12, 1750: Artist Rachel Ruysch dies, aged 85. She is best known for her still-life paintings of flowers, especially roses.
Mbunza (Namibia), c. 1750: Queen Kapango and her sister Queen Mate I form the two kingdoms of Mbunza and Uukwangali.
Portugal, 1750: Upon the death of his father, José I becomes King of Portugal. His wife, Mariana Victoria of Bourbon, becomes Queen Consort.

Copenhagen, Denmark, December 19, 1751: Louise, Queen of Denmark and Norway, dies, aged 27.
Luwu (Indonesia), 1751: Payung e-ri Luwu becomes the fourth consecutive woman on the throne of Luwu since 1713.
Netherlands, 1751: Princess Anne of Great Britain becomes Princess-Regent of Friesland on the death of her husband, William IV of Orange.
Versailles, France, February 10, 1752: Princess Henriette-Anne dies of smallpox, aged 24.

London, England, September 1752: Great Britain and her colonies adopt the Gregorian calendar; 11 days are deleted between September 2 and 14.
London, England, 1752: Poet and novelist Charlotte Ramsay Lennox publishes *The Female Quixote, or The Adventures of Arabella*.
London, England, 1752: Scottish obstetrician William Smellie publishes *A Treatise on the Theory and Practice of Midwifery*.
Uppsala, Sweden, 1753: Doctor Carl von Linné (Linnaeus) publishes *System plantarum*.

Halle, Germany, June 12, 1754: Dorothea Erxleben is the first woman to be awarded a medical degree in Germany.
Pennsylvania, North America, December 23, 1754: Queen Aliquippa, acknowledged leader of the Seneca tribe of Native Americans, dies. She had been an ally of the British during the French and Indian War.
Edinburgh, Scotland, 1754: Joseph Black discovers carbon dioxide, which he calls "fixed air."

Bestseller Runs to Second Edition

London, England, 1752: Charlotte Ramsay Lennox's bestselling novel, *The Female Quixote, or The Adventures of Arabella*, published this year, will run to a second edition, her publishers said. There are also rumors that the book will be translated into German, Spanish, and French.

The novel has been well received by critics and readers alike. Henry Fielding, who writes for the *Covent Garden Journal*, says that it is better than *Don Quixote*. Samuel Johnson believes Mrs Lennox to be one of the best writers of our time. He states that on dining with a trio of respected lady writers, "Three such women are not to be found; I know not where to find a fourth, except Mrs Lennox, who is superior to them all."

The novel describes the adventures of Arabella, a young heiress who thinks, after reading a surfeit of romantic fiction, that life is like a story. She believes all men are either trying to seduce her or fall in love with her. Eventually Arabella is cured of her delusions and learns that although it is exciting to invent one's own customs and manners, defying the established order leads to self-destruction.

Mrs Lennox's own life to date has been an adventure. Poverty brought her to London at the age of about 15 to be companion to the widowed Mary Luckyn, who was found to be insane. She then served as companion to Lady Isabella Finch, to whom her *Poems on Several Occasions*, written in 1747, is dedicated. Also in 1747, she married a Scotsman by the name of Alexander Lennox, who became bankrupt. They had two children.

Mrs Lennox had to continue writing for a living. Luckily, her acclaimed poem, "Art of Coquetry," was published in the *Gentleman's Magazine* in 1750, and gave her an entree into the literary world. In 1751, she wrote her first novel, which is titled *The Life of Harriot Stuart*.

Nicol Brown killed his wife by burning, in Edinburgh in 1750.

Female Doctor Awarded Medical Degree

Halle, Germany, June 13, 1754: Yesterday, practicing doctor Dorothea Christiane Erxleben became the first female ever to receive a medical degree.

Born in 1715, and originally taught by her father and brother, both doctors, Dorothea Leporin was given permission by the enlightened monarch, King Frederick II, to study at the University of Halle in 1741. Although her family duties following her marriage to deacon Johann Erxleben prevented her from actually attending any lectures, she established her own medical practice.

Last year, however, three male doctors brought a suit against Frau Erxleben for prescribing pharmaceuticals. Drugs can only be prescribed by academically trained physicians and Frau Erxleben, although a practicing doctor, did not have a degree. To confound her accusers, she wrote a thesis that deals, ironically, with the dispensing of pharmaceuticals, and criticizes doctors who cater to their patients' wishes for remedies such as purgatives and opiates, which produce immediate effects but do not cure the illness itself. She reported that she believes every illness needs time to be cured, and the body has its own powers that can assist the patient in the healing process.

Frau Erxleben defended her thesis in a final exam on May 6, 1754. Although she passed easily, the members of the medical faculty secured the sanction of the ministry at Berlin before awarding her the degree. Five weeks later she received her degree in medicine from the University of Halle.

Louise, Queen of Denmark and Norway

Hannah Snell, who joined the Royal Marines.

London, England, 1754: The controversial writer and cross-dressing actress Charlotte Charke, daughter of former poet laureate Colley Cibber, publishes her autobiography, *A Narrative of the Life of Mrs Charlotte Charke*.

St Andrews, Scotland, 1754: The Society of St Andrews Golfers is founded.

New York, North America, 1754: The King's College holds its first classes.

London, England, April 15, 1755: Samuel Johnson's *Dictionary of the English Language* is published. This influential work was more than eight years in the writing.

Paris, France, 1755: "Beauty and the Beast" author, Gabrielle-Suzanne Barbot de Villeneuve, dies.

London, England, May 15, 1756: Great Britain formally declares war on France, formalizing the existing conflict in the American colonies.

Russia, 1756: Empress Elizaveta Petrovna, daughter of Peter the Great, sides against Frederick II of Prussia in the Seven Years' War.

Venice, Italy, 1757: Painter and pastellist Rosalba Carriera dies, aged 81, having spent her latter years painting royal portraits.

Bayreuth, Prussia, October 14, 1758: Wilhelmine, Margravine of Brandenburg-Bayreuth, dies at 81. A talented musician, she was also responsible for many of the great buildings of the city.

Aranjuez, Spain, August 27, 1758: Barbara de Braganza, Queen Consort of Spain, dies, aged 46.

London, England, April 14, 1759: Composer George Frideric Handel dies, aged 74.

Quebec, Canada, September 13, 1759: James Wolfe and the British and American forces defeat Louis-Joseph, Marquis de Montcalm, and the French and Canadian forces. Wolfe dies in the battle and Montcalm is fatally wounded.

Spain, 1759: Charles III becomes King of Spain; his wife, Maria Amalia of Saxony, becomes Queen Consort.

France, 1759: French astronomer Nicole-Reine Lepaute, wife of the royal clockmaker, correctly predicts the return of Halley's comet.

Geneva, Switzerland, 1759: Writer and philosopher François Marie Arouet (Voltaire) publishes *Candide*.

Poland, 1759: Konstancja Czartoryska dies, aged 59. She was the mother of the last king of Poland, Stanislaw Poniatowski.

Charlotte Charke

Death of Loyal Native American Leader

Pennsylvania, North America, December 23, 1754: Today, Queen Aliquippa died, aged about seventy-five. A leader of the Seneca tribe of Native Americans, she was a loyal ally of the British during the current war, which European powers are waging to gain land in America.

In the 1740s, her tribe was living on the Ohio River in Pennsylvania, which both British and French colonists wished to control. Aliquippa, weighing up which country would treat her people better, decided on Britain. In 1748, she met Conrad Weiser, Pennsylvania's liaison between Native American people and the British, who had attended a meeting in nearby Logstown without visiting her village first. Once she reprimanded him, he rectified the error, giving her gifts, including gunpowder. He reported that she ruled with "great authority."

George Washington visited Queen Aliquippa in December 1753, stating that he gave her "a match-coat and a bottle of rum, which latter was thought much the better present of the two."

When the military explorer Céleron de Bienville came down the Allegheny River in 1749 to claim Ohio for France, Queen Aliquippa refused to receive him.

Aliquippa and her warriors traveled to Fort Necessity in 1754 to assist George Washington. Following the defeat of the British in the Battle of the Great Meadows, she moved her tribe to Aughwick Valley, where she died. Queen Aliquippa was an impressive leader to her people, and a good friend to the British.

published her children's fairytale in the magazine, *Le Magasin des enfants*. Her story is an abridgement of novelist Gabrielle-Suzanne Barbot de Villeneuve's tale for adults, *La jeune Ameriquain, et les contes marin (The Young American Girl, and the Sea Tales)*.

In the original 362-page novel, the author criticized arranged marriages. Her heroine, Beauty, said that many women must marry men worse than her Beast (a prince who has been transformed into an ogre). The author, whose novel won her the friendship of respected literary people, died in 1755.

Madame Leprince de Beaumont simplifies the long story, focusing on the power of Beauty's love for the Beast. Her love turns him back into a prince at the end of the tale.

Le Magasin de enfants is extremely popular with children, and an English translation is rumored.

Charlotte Charke Left "£5 and No More"

London, England, 1757: Controversial cross-dressing actress, playwright, novelist, and autobiographer, Charlotte Charke, has been left only £5 in her father's will.

Mrs Charke, who calls herself Mr Charles Brown, has been estranged from her father, former poet laureate Colley Cibber, for many years. Her autobiography, *A Narrative of the Life of Mrs Charlotte Charke*, was written in 1755 with the aim of ending the "painful separation from my once tender father." However, Mr Cibber continued to refuse to communicate with his daughter.

Maria Amalia of Saxony, Queen Consort of Charles III of Spain.

editions, and was serialized in installments in *The Gentleman's Magazine*.

From the age of 18, Mrs Charke has dressed as a man on stage (playing characters such as Roderigo in *Othello*) and in real life, identifying more with men than with women. Despite this, she married actor Richard Charke in 1730 when she was seventeen. Her only child, daughter Catherine, was born in December of that year and soon after, she and her husband parted company.

She became estranged from her father in 1736 when she joined Henry Fielding's company at the Haymarket Theatre. In the play *Pasquin*, she appeared as Lord Place, a character representing Mr Cibber, who was satirized for his fawning attachment to Robert Walpole. Furious, the offended father refused to talk to his daughter ever again.

Needing to work to support her own daughter, Mrs Charke took up several occupations as Mr Charles Brown, including puppeteer, valet to the Earl of Anglesey, sausage maker, tavern owner, pastrycook, farmer, and writer for the *Bristol Weekly Intelligencer*.

She was briefly imprisoned for debt, and has written many plays and a novel, *The History of Mr. Henry Dumont and Miss Charlotte Evelyn*.

Death of Margravine of Brandenburg-Bayreuth

Bayreuth, Prussia, October 14, 1758: The quite amazing woman who transformed Bayreuth into a miniature Versailles, Friederike Sophie Wilhelmine, sister of Frederick the Great, wife of Frederick, Margrave of Brandenburg-Bayreuth, and mother of Elisabeth, died today, aged 81.

Queen Aliquippa aided George Washington (center) at Fort Necessity during the French and Indian War.

Transformed Novel Popular with Children

Paris, France, 1756: Last week, Madame Jeanne-Marie Leprince de Beaumont

Mrs Charke's "account of my un-accountable life" was, however, a best-seller. A witty, entertaining, and at times breathtaking autobiography, it was published in book form in two

Resolving to put Bayreuth on the cultural map of Europe, the Margravine employed internationally acclaimed architects to construct beautiful buildings and landscapes in the new rococo style. The Italian architect, Galli de Bibienas, designed a theater in 1728, which was built in 1735. Other new buildings included a great opera house. The Bayreuth palace and summer residence were rebuilt, and a sunken garden was formed with interesting rock formations.

Keen also to make Bayreuth a center of learning and art, the Margravine founded the University of Erlangen, and invited the best European artists, poets, and composers to visit the court. Voltaire was one guest with whom the Margravine maintained an extensive correspondence about art, religion, and philosophy.

This woman of many talents was also a composer, a lutenist and harpsichord player, as well as a beautiful singer. She performed chamber music and scenic cantatas, which she had written herself, in the great hall of the palace in Bayreuth, and in 1740 wrote an opera, *Argenore*, which was performed for her husband's birthday. For this event she was composer, librettist, harpsichord player, coach, and artistic director.

The Margravine, who transformed the city from a backwater to a respected center of art and learning, leaves her autobiography, *Mémoires de ma vie*, in manuscript form.

Empress Elizaveta Leads Russia to Victory

St Petersburg, Russia, August 26, 1759: Empress Elizaveta Petrovna's critics, who urged her not to enter the Seven Years' War on the side of Austria but to support Frederick II of Prussia instead, have been proven wrong. Russia's gallant troops severely trounced the Prussians at the Battle of Kunersdorf on August 12 this year. Frederick II, known to his allies as Frederick the Great, commanding an army of 40,000 men, received his worst defeat yet after attacking a fortified position of 80,000 Russians and Austrians commanded by Generals Saltykov and Loudon. Rumor has it that Frederick is now contemplating suicide.

The Empress has consistently made the right decisions respecting Russia. In 1743, she made peace with Sweden on excellent terms, gaining land east of the Kymmene River, including the fortresses of Villmanstrand and Fredrikshamni. She has abolished certain local taxes, boosted local trade and industry, and opened the university in Moscow in 1755.

In 1756, Frederick the Great pushed aggressively into Europe, invading Saxony.

St Petersburg is home to Empress Elizaveta Petrovna, whose political astuteness is widely acknowledged.

War was declared in January 1757, the Empress siding with Austria, France, and Sweden against Prussia and England.

The Empress has personal reasons for disliking Prussia. She has not forgotten how the population suffered under Prussian favorites during the reign of previous rulers, and when she became Empress her imperial manifesto stated: "The Russian people have been groaning under the enemies of the Christian faith, but I have delivered them from the degrading foreign oppression."

Since becoming leader, she has surrounded herself with Russian officials. Frederick II's allies at court have tried to discredit them, including Alexius Bestuzhev-Ryumin, the former vice-chancellor, but to no avail. The Empress believes the King of Prussia is a threat to his neighbors, and wants Frederick's rank reduced to that of a prince-elector.

"We Could Not Have Done it Without Her"

France, 1759: In his article describing how three French astronomers—himself, Madame Nicole-Reine Lepaute, and Monsieur Alexis Clairaut—accurately predicted the return of Halley's comet to within one month, Monsieur Joseph Lalande, director of Paris Observatory, says he would never have taken on the volume of work without the invaluable assistance of colleague Madame Lepaute.

Monsieur Lalande writes that Madame Lepaute worked day and night for many months to calculate how the gravitational effects of Jupiter and Saturn would influence the comet's path.

Edmond Halley, for whom the comet is named, predicted in the seventeenth century that it would return in 1758 after a 76-year absence. Lalande employed

Madame Lepaute and Monsieur Clairaut to confirm that prediction. In September 1757 they released their findings. The comet returned in March this year.

Madame Lepaute married the royal clockmaker, Jean André Lepaute, in 1748. Herself fascinated by clocks, Madame Lepaute studied the oscillations of pendulums of different lengths. Her results were published by her husband in his *Traite d'horlogerie* in 1755.

Monsieur Lalande refuses to let Madame Lepaute rest. He has employed her to work with him on the Académie des Sciences's astronomical almanac for astronomers and navigators, which should be published around 1764.

Barbara of Braganza

Mademoiselle Catinon danced the role of Diana in the 1757 ballet *La Surprise de l'Amour*.

Lady Mary
Wortley Montagu

New Professor for Bologna

Bologna, Italy, 1760: The University of Bologna's innovative practice of hiring women as professors has paid off again today. The famous wax sculptress Anna Morandi has been appointed Professor of Anatomy.

Wax models of the human body and organs are vital in educating doctors as well as attracting tourists to this country. Signora Morandi's sculptures of the sense organs, female organs, brain, and cardio-vascular system are already very famous throughout Europe.

When wax modeler Ercole Lelli was commissioned by Pope Lambertini to produce a collection of exhibits for the University of Bologna's anatomy laboratory, he was assisted by the physician Giovanni Manzolini and his wife, Anna Morandi Manzolini.

Signora Morandi's models were the great success of the collection, being applauded by the London Royal Society and attracting attention from the press

"I shall be an autocrat: that's my trade. And the Good Lord will forgive me: that's his."

CATHERINE THE GREAT
(1729–1796)

for their attention to detail, accuracy, and finesse. Physician Luigi Galvani wrote that they set "the example to our and foreign men in moulding with equal skilfulness even … the most diaphanous parts, those that would almost escape from the sight …" Each model was accompanied by Signora Morandi's own detailed anatomical notes.

One of the new professor's sculptures, which will be vital in instructing her students, is a model of the human ear that can be taken apart to reveal all of its separate components.

Death of Empress Elizaveta Petrovna

St Petersburg, Russia, January 5, 1762: Today the dearly loved Empress, Elizaveta Petrovna, passed away at the age of fifty-two. She will be succeeded by her nephew, Grand Duke Peter Fedorovich, whom Elizaveta proclaimed as her heir in November 1742, and who will be crowned Czar Peter III.

Empress Elizaveta's achievements were many and varied. She gained land from Sweden and put fear into the heart of Frederick II of Prussia due to Russia's victorious campaigns in the current war. Of special note is Pyotr Alexandrovich Rumyantsev's capture of the Prussian fortress of Kolberg on Christmas Day 1761.

Domestically, she abolished capital punishment, so no-one was executed during her reign. She ordered the construction of many grand buildings in St Petersburg, including the Summer and Winter palaces and Smolmy Convent, all designed by Bartolomeo Rastrelli. Once finished, the new convent will house 120 noble orphan girls, each girl being given a separate apartment with a room for servants, a food cupboard, and a small kitchen space.

Archduchess of Austria, Maria Karoline.

The late Empress of Russia, Elizaveta Petrovna.

The Empress also contributed greatly to the country's education. She established the Academy of Fine Arts in St Petersburg and the University of Moscow. The university is of special interest, since it is, on the order of the Empress, open to nobles and commoners alike and tuition is free.

Empress Elizaveta will be buried in the Cathedral of the St Peter and St Paul Fortress in St Petersburg.

time out

In 1766 a French woman, Jeanne Baret, disguises herself as a man in order to circumnavigate the world while posing as her botanist husband's valet. The ship belonged to the French navigator, Louis Antoine de Bougainville.

First Female Editor in North America

Newport, Rhode Island, North America, August 22, 1762: Today Ann Smith Franklin was appointed editor of the *Newport Mercury*, the newspaper started by her son, James, in 1758. Mrs Franklin has taken over following his recent death, becoming the first ever female editor and publisher of an American newspaper. She has also taken on a partner, Samuel Hall.

Key Events

Bologna, Italy, 1760: Anna Morandi becomes Professor of Anatomy at the University of Bologna.
Paris, France, 1760: Jean-Georges Noverre's *Letters on Dancing and Ballet* is published, in which he promotes *ballet d'action*.
Strasbourg, France, December 1, 1761: Marie Grosholz is born. She later becomes famous as Madame Tussaud, when she opens her waxworks exhibition in London.
St Petersburg, Russia, January 5, 1762: Elizaveta Petrovna, Empress of Russia, dies aged 52.

England, August 21, 1762: Lady Mary Wortley Montagu, who introduced a form of smallpox inoculation in England, dies aged 73.
Newport, Rhode Island, North America, August 22, 1762: Ann Smith Franklin is appointed editor of the *Newport Mercury*, becoming the first woman editor of an American newspaper.
Moscow, Russia, September 22, 1762: Catherine II is crowned Empress of All Russia.

Gloucestershire, England, 1762: Seventeen-year-old Hannah More writes the play, *The Search After Happiness*.
Lyons, France, 1762: Claude Bourgelat establishes the world's first veterinary school.
Paris, France, February 10, 1763: The Treaty of Paris ends wars in both Europe and North America.
Newport, Rhode Island, North America, April, 1763: Publisher and editor of the *Newport Mercury*, Ann Smith Franklin, dies, aged 66.

Austria, November 27, 1763: Isabella of Bourbon-Parma, grand-daughter of Elisabeth Farnese and wife of emperor of Austria Joseph II, dies from smallpox, aged 21.
Quebec, Canada, June 21, 1764: The first issue of *The Quebec Gazette* is published by William Brown.
Lancashire, England, 1764: James Hargreaves invents the original spinning jenny with eight spindles.
London, England, February 9, 1765: Musician, singer, and composer Elisabetta de Gambarini dies, aged 33.

Austria, March, 1765: Empress Maria Theresa agrees to share power with her son Joseph II.
Benares, India, August 12, 1765: The Treaty of Allahabad gives the East India Company control of much of India.
Russia, 1765: Empress Catherine the Great allows freedom of worship across Russia.
Boston, North America, 1765: Thomas Fleet publishes *Mother Goose's Melodies*, based on the songs his mother-in-law, Elizabeth Foster Goose, sang to his son.

Women paint on fabric in a calico factory in Orange.

Mrs Franklin is no stranger to publishing. She ran a printing press from 1735, firstly with her husband, the brother of Benjamin Franklin, then with her son, James, and her two daughters, Mary and Elizabeth. Both daughters are highly trained and respected compositors.

Under her husband's pseudonym, "Poor Robin," Mrs Franklin wrote and printed a series of almanacs that parodied weather forecasters and those who predicted momentous events. In her 1741 almanac, she wrote the following forecast for the weather between October 20 and 23: "'Tis cold, 'tis cloudy, rain or hail, One of the four I hope won't fail."

Catherine II Crowned Empress of All Russia

Moscow, Russia, September 22, 1762: "Nice and noble stature, majestic pace, fine face and posture …" says the French ambassador, Monsieur de Ruliere, of the popular and charming Empress, who was crowned today as Ekaterina (Catherine) II. Supported by both nobles and guards, she overthrew her unpopular husband, Czar Peter III, in a bloodless coup on June 28. On that day, the streets of St Petersburg were thronged with an exultant public, who welcomed her with cries of "Viva!". The Senate took an oath of loyalty to her without delay.

Born on April 21, 1729, in the provincial town of Stettin, Germany, the daughter of Prince Christian of Anhalt-Zerbst, Catherine was named Sophie Augusta Frederika. She came to Russia in February 1744 at the invitation of Empress Elizaveta Petrovna, to be the bride of the future Peter III. They married on August 21, 1745, and she was christened into the Orthodox faith as Catherine.

Rumor has it that the marriage was not a success, and Czar Peter III certainly made a rather bad impression on the country during his short reign. He wished to re-establish the influence of Prussia on the court, and alienated nobles and army alike.

The coronation of the new empress has been most lavish. She traveled from St Petersburg to Moscow followed by 14 large sleighs and nearly 200 smaller ones. The grandest sleigh was a miniature palace on runners, containing a bedroom, living room, and library. Her coronation coach, the Romanov Carriage, is made of gold and was originally ordered by Peter the Great for his wife Catherine I, while her crown, made by skilled jeweler Jeremia Posier, is set with 5,000 Indian diamonds and a large red spinel weighing 398.72 carats, which was brought to Russia by Nicholas Spafary, the envoy to China from 1675 to 1678.

Catherine II will take up residence in the lavish Winter Palace, which was built by Empress Elizaveta Petrovna.

Lady Mary's Embassy Letters a Great Success

London, England, 1763: The letters written by Lady Mary Wortley Montagu while living in Turkey in 1718 and 1719 have been published posthumously in three volumes and are proving immensely popular. Multiple editions are forecast. Critic Edward Gibbon says of them: "What fire, what ease, what knowledge of Europe and Asia."

Lady Mary was best known for pioneering inoculation against smallpox in England, but was also a great satirist, helping her husband's political career by writing a newspaper that attacked the popular opposition paper *Common-Sense*. Her newspaper was called *The Nonsense of Common-Sense*. First brought out in 1737, the nine issues were avidly read. The issue of January 24, 1738, advised fellow female writers to: "Begin, then, ladies, by paying those authors with scorn and contempt who, with a sneer of affected admiration, would throw you below the dignity of the human species."

This was a dig at Alexander Pope, who viciously attacked Lady Mary's literary ability, wit, and even chastity in the popular press. His criticism so affected her husband's standing in parliament that she moved abroad in 1740. She lived in Italy and France until her husband's death in 1762, when she returned to England, dying soon afterward of breast cancer on August 21, 1762, aged seventy-three.

Lady Mary's last words, typical of such a spirited and resourceful woman, were: "It has all been very interesting."

Maria Leszczynska

Russia's new empress, Catherine II.

North America, 1765: Great Britain imposes the unpopular *Stamp Act* on the American colonies. The tax covers just about everything produced by the Americans, which leads to civil unrest.

Connecticut, North America, 1765: A group of women calling themselves the Daughters of Liberty boycotts British products.

New York City, North America, March 10, 1766: American botanist Jane Colden, who had classified more than 300 plant species, dies, aged 42.

Parma, Spain, July 11, 1766: Elisabeth Farnese, wife of Philip V of Spain, dies, aged 74.

Salzburg, Austria, 1766: Child prodigies, brother and sister Wolfgang Amadeus and Maria Anna Mozart, finish a three-and-a-half-year tour of Europe.

Copenhagen, Denmark, 1766: Sophia Magdalena of Denmark and Norway is married to Gustav III of Sweden by proxy.

Edo (Tokyo), Japan, 1766: Suzuki Harunobi uses up to 10 colored woodblocks to create his prints.

England, 1766: Singer and actress Susanna Maria Cibber dies.

Boston, North America, December 21, 1767: Slave Phillis Wheatley is the first African-American female to be published when one of her poems appears in the *Newport Mercury*.

Versailles, France, June 24, 1768: The wife of King Louis XV of France, Maria Leszczynska, dies, aged 65.

Trevecca, South Wales, August 24, 1768: Selina Hastings, Countess of Huntingdon, a convert to Methodism, establishes a theological college to train ministers.

Kathmandu, Nepal, September 25, 1768: Head of the house of Gorkha (Gurkha), Prithvi Narayan Shah, becomes first king of Nepal.

Derbyshire, England, 1768: Richard Arkwright invents the spinning frame, which makes very strong thread. The invention makes spinning a factory process rather than a cottage industry.

Vienna, Austria, 1768: Maria Karoline, Archduchess of Austria, marries Ferdinand IV of Naples.

London, England, 1768: The Royal Academy of Arts is formed, with Sir Joshua Reynolds the first president.

Glasgow, Scotland, January 5, 1769: James Watt patents an improvement to the steam engine.

New Zealand, October, 1769: The crew of the *Endeavour* become the first Europeans to land on New Zealand.

Dublin, Ireland, 1769: Brewer Arthur Guinness sends his popular darker beer, known at first as "porter," to England.

Maria Anna Mozart

Son to Rule Austria with Empress

Austria, March 1765: Empress Maria Theresa, Archduchess of Austria and Queen of Hungary and Bohemia, has announced that her son, Joseph II, will henceforth rule with her as co-regent and emperor. The Empress will continue to have sovereign control of affairs of state and her son's power will be limited. Rumor has it that she considers Joseph to be rather rash and arrogant.

The Empress has achieved much since she came to power in 1740. She established the first ever military academy in 1752 and an academy of engineering science in 1754. She also improved the efficiency of the medical faculty of the University of Vienna. She has reorganized the tax structure to ensure a predictable annual income for the government and army, and a centralized office now administers tax collection. In order to cut down on local corruption, elected mayors and town counselors must have their qualifications to hold office checked by the central government, and the powers of the guilds have been restricted.

With an abiding interest in agrarian reform, the Empress has improved and is still improving the lot of the country's peasants. She has created a system of obligatory, state-supported, public primary education, standardized landlords' fees, and endowed peasants with the status of free tenants so that they can move freely from place to place, marry without their lord's consent, and choose their own occupation.

The Empress also rules a large domain due to her excellent handling of foreign affairs. When threatened by Frederick II

of Prussia in both the War of Austrian Succession from 1740 to 1748 and the Seven Years' War from 1756 to 1763, she succeeded in holding onto her lands as well as attaining the title of Holy Roman Emperor for her husband Francis I.

The Empress is mourning the death of her dearly beloved husband, with whom she had 11 daughters and five sons.

America's First Female Botanist Dies

New York City, North America, March 11, 1766: North America's first female botanist, Jane Colden, passed away yesterday. She is survived by her husband, physician William Farquhar, whom she married in 1759, and a young child. She was only 42 years old.

Jane Colden was taught botany and the new system of classification developed by Swedish botanist, Carolus Linnaeus, by her Scottish father, Cadwallader Colden. She also learnt some Latin. Between 1753 and 1758, she cataloged and compiled specimens of, and wrote information on, more than 300 species of plants from the lower Hudson River Valley. In 1755, her father wrote to a contemporary that: "She has already a pretty large volume in writing of the description of plants ... [I] inclose some samples in her own writing, some of which I think are new Genus's."

A respected member of an international community that exchanged plants and information, Jane Colden corresponded with many other botanists in America and overseas. These included Alexander Garden of Charleston, South Carolina, who exchanged seeds and plants with her, and sent her descriptions of plants to other scientists. He wrote to another botanist, John Ellis, in March 1755 that: "not only the doctor himself is a great botanist, but his lovely daughter is greatly master of the Linnaean method, and cultivates it with assiduity."

Jane Colden was the first botanist to describe the gardenia, which she named after Alexander Garden. She also developed a technique for making ink impressions of leaves, and was a skilled illustrator of botanical specimens.

In 1758, John Ellis suggested to Linnaeus that he label a new plant *Coldenella* as a tribute to her. Linnaeus had already assigned the plant to the genus *Helleborus*, but he did praise Jane Colden's work.

It is rare for a woman to be taken seriously by men of science, but Jane Colden won the respect of her peers for her accurate, detailed studies of plants.

Elisabeth Farnese, former Queen Consort of Spain.

Power Behind Spanish Throne Dies

Parma, Spain, July 12, 1766: Yesterday, Elisabeth Farnese, wife of King Philip V of Spain and the power behind the throne for many years, died at 74 years of age. She and her ally, Cardinal Alberoni, influenced King Philip V to make daring and risky decisions affecting the future of Spain, not all of which paid off.

The daughter of the Duke of Parma, Elisabeth was the second wife of Philip V, marrying him in September 1714. An ambitious woman, she soon dominated her husband, who was very fond of her. They had seven children together.

One of Elisabeth's first decisions was to attempt to retrieve Sardinia and Sicily for Spain from their domination by Italy, which led to conflict with Britain, Germany, the Netherlands, and France. So vigorously did she enter into the war that she placed herself at the head of one division of the Spanish army. Spain was defeated, however.

As a result of a Spanish attack on Naples during the later War of the Polish Succession, Elisabeth's eldest son Don Carlos became King of Naples and Sicily in 1734 and her second son, Philip, became Duke of Parma.

Empress Maria Theresa will share power with her son Joseph II.

Elisabeth survived her husband by 20 years; however, she retired from court on the accession of her stepson, Ferdinand VI, in 1746, and wrote her memoirs, which were published in three volumes between 1746 and this year.

Child Prodigies Complete European Tour

Salzburg, Austria, 1766: The brilliant musical brother and sister, 15-year-old Maria Anna and 10-year-old Wolfgang Amadeus Mozart, have returned to Salzburg after three-and-a-half years touring Europe. Accompanied by their father, Leopold Mozart, himself a successful composer and violinist at the Salzburg court, the children have taken a number of major European musical centers by storm, including Stuttgart, Mannheim, Mainz, Frankfurt, Brussels, Paris, London, and Amsterdam.

Both Mozart children are prodigiously talented. Maria Anna, known to her family as "Nannerl," is an expert pianist and harpsichord player. Her brother Wolfgang plays the piano and violin and composes his own musical pieces. His father informs us that he composed his first minuet at the age of five and his first symphony at the age of nine.

Maria Anna and Wolfgang Amadeus Mozart.

Slave's Poem Published in Respected Newspaper

Boston, North America, December 21, 1767: Fourteen-year-old African slave, Phillis Wheatley, today had her poem, entitled "On Messrs. Hussey and Coffin," published in the *Newport Mercury*. The poem tells the story of two men who were saved from drowning through their faith in God, and shows an excellent knowledge of the classics and of vocabulary, as can be seen from this extract:

The late actress and singer, Susanna Cibber.

> Did Fear and Danger so perplex your Mind,
> As made you fearful of the Whistling Wind?
> Was it not Boreas knit his angry Brow
> Against you? or did Consideration bow?

Born in Gambia, Phillis was sold into slavery at the age of seven. She was named for the slave ship in which she came to Boston, Massachusetts, in July 1761, where John Wheatley, a merchant, purchased her as a domestic servant and companion for his wife.

The Wheatleys soon realized their charge was extremely intelligent. Mr Wheatley says that she had mastered the English language within 16 months of her arrival in America "to the great astonishment of all who heard her … As to her writing, her own curiousity led her to it …"

Phillis has also learnt Greek and Latin, as well as history, astronomy, geography, and British literature.

This remarkable girl recalls little of her birth family. She remembers seeing her mother pouring water to greet the rising sun, which could indicate that her African family is of the Muslim faith.

Phillis is a very talented poet and is fortunate in her patrons, the Wheatleys.

Countess Opens Theological College

Trevecca, South Wales, August 25, 1768: Selina Hastings, Countess of Huntingdon, is already well known for founding her own religious sect, a blend of Calvinism and Methodism, based on the teachings of George Whitefield and John Wesley. Known as the Countess of Huntingdon's Connexion, the sect retains ties to the Church of England.

Yesterday, on her birthday, the Countess opened a theological college to train ministers in her beliefs. Mr Whitefield preached at the opening, choosing as his text Exodus 20:24: "In all places where I record my name, I will come unto thee and bless thee."

A philanthropist who has helped those who are less fortunate than herself and opened several chapels in centers such as Brighton, Bath, and Worcester, the Countess is a devout lady whose religious zeal is now directed to education. Oxford and Cambridge, the only places where men can train for the ministry, are closed to dissenters, and in 1768, six students at Oxford were expelled for "their leanings toward Methodism." Concerned that those who feel as she does can receive no formal training, the Countess has therefore converted Trevecca House, an old stone structure dating back to 1176, into the new college.

The Countess has paid for renovations such as new floors and plastering, supplied furniture and books, and a silver communion set for the College Chapel.

Isabella of Bourbon-Parma

Sophia Magdalena of Denmark and Norway was betrothed to Gustav III of Sweden at the age of five.

Marie Antoinette

Amazon Adventurer Survives Jungle Terror

Cayenne, French Guiana, July 1770: Having conquered perils that are the contents of nightmares, Madame Isabel Godin was last week reunited with her husband after walking and traveling by dugout canoe through virgin jungle for more than 3,000 miles (4,828 km). This heroine, the first woman ever to travel the length of the Amazon River, has captured the imagination and acclaim of Europe.

Madame Godin, a Peruvian noble-woman, met her husband in Riobamba near Quito. A French mapmaker, he was sent to Ecuador in 1735 to measure a degree of longitude near the equator. The couple wed in December 1741, when Madame Godin was just thirteen. In 1749, Monsieur Godin tried to reach France to settle his family estate but was stranded in French Guiana for 20 years, due to political strife in Europe.

After their daughter died of smallpox at the age of 18, Madame Godin decided to join her husband. On October 1, 1769, she left Riobamba with her two brothers and nephew, and a French doctor and his traveling companion. Servants and 31 Indian porters brought the party to 41 persons. Porters were laden with fancy clothing, jewelry, china, and linen for Madame Godin's eventual move to France.

The party followed the Chambo River to Canelos, where some of them caught smallpox. The doctor and a servant went to seek help. After waiting for 20 days for their return, the party staggered on through the jungle, being bitten and stung by insects, one by one dying of hunger, thirst, or fatigue.

Eventually, Madame Godin was the only person from the original party left alive, an unimaginable situation.

> *"But what is a woman?— Only one of nature's agreeable blunders."*
>
> Hanna Cowley (1743–1809), from *Who's the Dupe?* Act 2, scene 2

Undaunted, she continued walking, surviving on water from plant leaves, eggs from birds' nests, and fruits. After eight days, she reached Bobonaza River, where native Indian people found her and cared for her. They then took her to a mission, from where she embarked on a 250-mile (402 km) river trip by canoe.

This amazing and inspiring woman, aged 41, is most deservedly revered for her bravery and determination.

Female Artist Elected to Royal Academy

Paris, France, 1770: Still-life artist Anne Vallayer-Coster was today elected to the Royal Academy of Painting and Sculpture, at 26 years of age. She is only one of four women ever to achieve the honor. The painting she submitted, *Musical Instruments*, showed passionate attention to detail.

It depicts a clearly legible music score and instruments that are minutely and accurately painted.

Anne Vallayer-Coster's paintings of flowers display the same powers of observation, intricacy, and liveliness.

Born on December 21, 1744, Mademoiselle Vallayer-Coster is the daughter of a Parisian goldsmith. She spent her child-hood working at Gobelins tap-estry factory where she learnt many skills from the craftspeople and artists. She had few lessons from professional artists, but she did study for some time with Madame Basseporte, a botanical illustrator, and Monsieur Vernet, a marine painter. However, she acquired most of the artistic skills needed to paint still-life depictions on her own.

time out

In 1779 the ship of Captain Charles Clerke and William Bligh received a stern farewell from the Queen of Kauai, who accused the mariners of infecting the women of Kauai with venereal disease, an affliction previously unknown to them.

The Toast of Paris Dies, Aged 60

France, 1770: The sparkling, athletic, and daring ballerina, Marie-Anne de Cupis de Camargo, known to her fans as La Camargo, has died at her home. She had retired from ballet in 1751 on a generous government pension.

Born in Brussels, La Camargo was trained by Françoise Prevost of the Paris Opera and became *première danseuse* in companies in Brussels and Rouen.

She made her Paris debut in May 1726 at the age of 16 in *Les Caractères de la Danse*, a ballet designed to exhibit a dancer's range and skills. La Camargo caused a sensation by leaping into the air and executing the *entrechat quatre*, a jump only before performed by men.

An overnight success, she shortened her skirts to above the ankle and wore slippers instead of heeled shoes. She also invented an undergarment to preserve her modesty during her jumps.

La Camargo specialized in *temps d'élévation*—jumps involving crossing and uncrossing the feet while in the air. Women at court, dreaming of having her grace and vivacity, copied her looped

One of numerous portraits of the great ballerina La Camargo.

Versailles, France, May 16, 1770: Marie Antoinette marries Louis, the dauphin of France.

Cayenne, French Guiana, July 18, 1770: The first woman to travel the length of the Amazon River, Isabel Godin, is reunited with her husband, mapmaker Jean Godin.

New Holland (Australia), August 22, 1770: Captain James Cook claims the east coast for Great Britain.

Paris, France, 1770: Painter Anne Vallayer-Coster is elected to the Royal Academy of Painting and Sculpture.

France, 1770: Ballerina Marie-Anne de Cupis de Camargo, known as La Camargo, dies, aged 60.

Kauai, Hawaii, 1770: Queen Kamakahelei of Kauai becomes the twenty-second Alii Aimoku, or ruler of the island.

France, 1770: Claude-Nicolas Ledoux is commissioned by King Louis XV to design a music pavilion at the Château de Louveciennes for the king's mistress, Madame du Barry. Ledoux's mother and godmother inspired and encouraged him to develop his drawing skills.

Rotterdam, Netherlands, 1771: Following the death of her husband, Marguerite Wolters continues his work as a spy for the British government.

Denmark, April 6, 1772: Queen Caroline Matilda and King Christian VII are divorced after she commits adultery with Johann Friedrich Struensee.

Java, Dutch East Indies, August 12, 1772: An avalanche caused by the volcanic eruption of Papadayan destroys about 40 villages and leads to almost 3,000 deaths.

Afghanistan, April 1773: Shah Durrani dies, aged about 50.

Boston, North America, December 16, 1773: Chests of tea are thrown overboard by rebellious colonists disguised as Indians.

London, England, 1773: Traders in company shares group together to form The Stock Exchange.

Canton, China, 1773: Opium is shipped from India to China.

Paris, France, 1773: Jean-Honoré Fragonard completes *The Progress of Love*, four paintings commissioned by Madame du Barry.

Liverpool, England, May 19, 1774: Shaker Ann Lee, accompanied by her husband and a small group, sails to New York in order to avoid religious persecution.

Edo (Tokyo), Japan, 1774: Sugita Gempaku produces the first Japanese translation of a European textbook on anatomy and medicine.

Paris, France, 1774: Madame du Barry is sent to Pont-au-Dames.

Kalisk, Poland, January, 1775: Nine elderly women, who had been accused of causing poor harvests, are burned as witches.

The 15-year-old Austrian princess, Marie Antoinette, and Louis, the dauphin of France, were married in the Royal Chapel at Versailles, France, on May 16, 1770. Here we see the blessing ceremony taking place.

the end of this month. Twenty-year-old Queen Caroline will be separated from her children and exiled to Hanover.

"Get Thee to a Nunnery," King's Mistress Told

Paris, France, 1774: The extravagant and beautiful Madame du Barry, mistress of King Louis XV, was today sent from court to the convent of Pont-au-Dames. The current sovereign, King Louis XVI, has promised to pay du Barry's creditors for the plethora of artworks, furniture, jewelry, and clothing she has acquired.

Madame du Barry became the king's mistress in 1769 and was his chief companion until his death. The king, charmed by her vivacity and playfulness, let her select which operas and plays would be performed at court, although she had little political influence.

Dauphine Marie Antoinette called Madame du Barry "… the silliest and most impertinent creature imaginable." Nevertheless, she was the darling of the painters, sculptors, and engravers who competed to reproduce her likeness and will no doubt miss her patronage.

Maria I of Portugal

hairstyle and employed her shoemaker. Artists vied to paint her portrait and many rich men vied to be her lover.

One of her lovers, the Comte de Clermont, persuaded her to retire from dancing between 1736 and 1741, after which she returned to the stage. She danced in 78 different operas or ballets during her impressive career.

Danish King Divorces English-born Queen

Denmark, April 6, 1772: Today, King Christian VII divorced Queen Caroline Matilda, sister to George III of England, for adultery. The marriage, which began in November 1766, was rumored to be unhappy, although the king fathered the Crown Prince, Frederick, born in 1768.

Queen Caroline also gave birth to a daughter in 1771 who is allegedly the child of Johann Friedrich Struensee, minister at the court, who became the

king's physician in 1769. A favorite of both the king and queen, Struensee practically ran the government from March 1771 to January this year, issuing 1,069 cabinet orders, more than three a day, most of which advocated sweeping reforms. He earned the enmity of many for bringing in new legislation far too quickly. He also sacked experienced government officials, substituting them with his favorites who knew little about running the country.

The affair between Queen Caroline and Struensee is said to have begun in 1770 after Struensee helped her nurse her young son through a serious illness. Cut off from most courtiers by her inability to speak Danish and by the enmity shown her by the dowager queen, Queen Caroline welcomed the friend, who then became a lover.

The couple were arrested in their respective bedrooms after a masked ball in January. Struensee will be executed at

The charming Madame du Barry, mistress to Louis XV.

Lexington, Massachusetts, North America, April 19, 1775: Local militiamen, alerted by Paul Revere, take a stand against British troops.

Philadelphia, Pennsylvania, North America, August 1775: An anonymous article appearing in *The Pennsylvania Magazine* calls for an end to discrimination against women.

London, England, 1775: Actress Sarah Kemble Siddons makes her debut at the Drury Lane Theater.

Moscow, Russia, March 28, 1776: Catherine II gives Petr Urosov permission to establish a theater and ballet company.

North America, May 1776: A strong advocate for women's right, Abigail Adams exchanges letters with her husband John, asking him "to remember the ladies" while drafting the Declaration of Independence.

Philadelphia, North America, July 4, 1776: Continental Congress adopts the Declaration of Independence, giving America freedom from British rule.

Philadelphia, North America, 1776: Betsy Ross (Elizabeth Griscom Ross Ashburn Claypoole) finishes sewing the first American flag.

New York State, North America, 1776: The Shakers (United Society of Believers in Christ's Second Appearing), led by pacifist Ann Lee, establish a community in Watervliet.

Portugal, 1777: Maria I becomes the first Queen Regnant of Portugal and Algarves. She had married her father's brother, Peter III, in 1760.

Bologna, Italy, February 20, 1778: Physicist and scholar, Laura Bassi, dies. She was the first woman lecturer in an Italian university.

London, England, 1778: Joseph Bramah patents his modern water closet with its improved flushing system.

London, England, 1778: *Evelina, or the History of a Young Lady's Entrance into the World* is published anonymously by Fanny Burney.

Hawaii, February 14, 1779: Captain James Cook, explorer, dies, aged 50.

Paris, France, February 1778: Anton Mesmer campaigns to have his theory of animal magnetism accepted as a valid healing process.

Ecuador, 1778: A revolt against the Spanish is led by female revolutionary Baltazara Chuiza.

Covent Garden, London, England, 1779: Martha Ray, a singer and the long-time mistress of John Montagu, fourth Earl of Sandwich, is murdered by Reverend James Hackman, a mentally unstable admirer. She leaves behind five children.

Abigail Adams

Article Calls for Fair Treatment of Women

Philadelphia, Pennsylvania, North America, August 1775: This month, the editor of *The Pennsylvania Magazine*, Thomas Paine, published an anonymous article, "An Occasional Letter on the Female Sex," which states that regarding women, men have always been "… at once their tyrant and their slave." The article relates that women have achieved much, but would achieve more if men honored them with equal civil rights and freedoms.

No stranger to controversy, in 1772 Mr Paine was dismissed from his job as an excise officer in England for lobbying for better wages. Since taking up the editorship of *The Pennsylvania Magazine* he has written and published articles calling for the abolition of slavery, cruelty to animals, and dueling.

Mr Paine has demonstrated his many skills by doubling the magazine's circulation in the first month after being appointed editor. He utilizes allegory and fable to bring the political and social world to life for his readers.

Many firmly believe that Mr Paine is the author of the article advocating rights for women. Although he writes freely about marginal issues, it could be that this topic is too sensitive for even a well-known rebel to handle openly.

Promising Actress Flops at Drury Lane

London, England, 1775: Actress Sarah Kemble Siddons, who has received rave reviews from provincial theaters, made her debut at Drury Lane last night. Her performance, as Portia in William Shakepeare's *The Merchant of Venice*, was ridiculed by the critics.

Mrs Siddons has worked in her father's traveling theater company since she was 12 years of age. While playing at Cheltenham in 1774, her portrayal of Belvidera in Thomas Otway's *Venice Preserv'd* won her acclaim as well as the attention of the theatrical producer, David Garrick. He sent a representative to see Mrs Siddons play Rosalind in Shakespeare's *As You Like It* in Worcestershire, and then offered her an engagement at Drury Lane.

Mrs Siddons says she was quite nervous about performing in such a large theater. She will have to improve or her contract will not be renewed at the end of the season.

"Remember the Ladies," Wife Pleads

North America, May 1776: Mrs Abigail Adams, the wife of John Adams, member of the Congressional Congress, has demanded he ensure that the interests of women are included in the new laws being drawn up to enable America to become independent of the British.

She has written to him stating, "I desire you would remember the ladies, and be more generous and favorable to them than your ancestors. Do not put such unlimited power into the hands of the husbands. Remember all men would be tyrants if they could."

Mr Adams replied by return post saying, "… we know better than to repeal our masculine systems," and his wife has retorted, "… whilst you are proclaiming peace and good will to men … you insist upon retaining an absolute power over wives."

Mr and Mrs Adams have been married since 1764, and have four children. They live in Boston, although Mr Adams's responsibilities have taken him to Philadelphia. Mr Adams tells us that his wife is a firm believer in educating women. He also says she is an excellent farm manager and mother, and is so successful in budgeting, planting, managing staff, and regulating livestock, as well as nursing and educating their children, that their neighbors inform him that he need not bother coming home.

In any event, Mr Adams will undoubtedly have to prepare himself for a lecture or two from his wife when he does return to Boston.

Jane Pope as Mrs Page in *The Merry Wives of Windsor*.

Mother Ann Establishes Shaker Community

Watervliet, New York State, North America, 1776: Mother Ann Lee, leader of the religious sect known as the Shakers, has announced that after purchasing land in Watervliet, her community will settle there. They have been living in New York City since 1774, following their arrival from England. However, America's imminent war has made many New York citizens distrust the English, and the Shakers have been accused of being spies and threatened with imprisonment.

Mother Ann assures us her people are pacifists, and just wish to live a clean frugal life marked by hard work.

The sect is named the Shakers or the Quaker Shakers (the group broke away from the Quaker movement in England) because its members shake and tremble during religious services, believing the Holy Spirit is purging them of sin. They are celibate, increasing their numbers by adopting orphans rather than having children of their own. They believe that earthly manifestations of God can be male and female, and that Mother Ann is the female embodiment of Jesus.

Mother Ann was born in Manchester, England, in 1736 and joined the Shaker movement in 1758. She rose to prominence in the organization through her gift of oratory. Her husband, whom she married in 1762, accepted her vow of celibacy after their four children died at birth, and joined the Shakers himself. They have since separated.

In England, Mother Ann and her followers were frequently imprisoned for

Actress Sarah Siddons, whose London debut was criticized.

American woman Mary Hays McCauley replaces her fallen husband John Hays as a cannon loader, 1778.

their beliefs. One time, Mother Ann was put in a cell so small that she could not stand or lie down, and was given no food for 14 days. She lived on wine and milk put into the bowl of a tobacco-pipe, the stem being inserted through the keyhole by her follower, James Whittaker.

Respected Professor of Experimental Physics Dies

Bologna, Italy, February 20, 1778: The first woman ever to work as a professor of physics at a European university died today aged sixty-seven. Born in 1711, Miss Laura Bassi became Professor of Anatomy at the University of Bologna in 1732. To commemorate her first lecture

in October of that year, the Senate of Bologna produced a medal in her honor.

Miss Bassi won the professorship of physics in 1733 soon after receiving her doctorate. Intrigued by the ideas of Sir Isaac Newton, especially his theories on light, optics, and motion, she was given special permission to view books in the Vatican dealing with these subjects.

In 1738, Laura Bassi married her colleague, Doctor Giuseppe Veratti, with whom she had 12 children. While raising her family, she lectured from home, and devised and conducted physical and electrical experiments to test Newton's ideas. She also lobbied the university for a salary increase to cover the money she spent on materials needed for her work.

In 1745, Laura Bassi was the only woman appointed as a member of an elite group of 25 scholars who would present a scientific paper to the pope each year. In 1757, the Academy of Science published two of her dissertations, "A Study of a Certain Kind of Trajectory Motion of Two Bodies on a Curve," and "Alternate Solutions to a Complex Hydrometrical Problem." Laura Bassi published a total of 28 technical papers on physics, hydraulics, mathematics, mechanics, and chemistry and other subjects.

In 1776, at 65, Miss Bassi was appointed Professor of Experimental Physics. Her husband became her official teaching assistant. As a deeply respected academic, Laura Bassi's salary in 1760, at 1,200 lire a year, was the highest paid to any professor in the university.

French ladies are embracing the fashion for extravagance.

The Writer of *Evelina* Is Revealed

London, England, 1778: Who among us has not yet read *Evelina, or the History of a Young Lady's Entrance into the World*? This wonderful witty novel, satirizing aristocrats and the working classes alike, has received glowing critical reviews, is the favorite novel of Queen Charlotte and the royal princesses, and has kept enthralled statesman Edmund Burke reading all night.

Thomas Lowndes published *Evelina* anonymously earlier this year, and the search for its author, rumored to be a man of substance, has been ongoing. The writer has now been revealed to be 26-year-old Fanny Burney, daughter of musical historian, Doctor Charles Burney.

Miss Burney began writing what she calls her "scribblings" when aged 10, and has kept a diary since then. Although she burnt her first manuscript, *The History of Caroline Evelyn*, in 1767, fearing disapproval from her father and stepmother, she did include some of it in *Evelina*.

Wishing to remain anonymous because she thought society would shun a female satirical novelist, Miss Burney copied *Evelina* in false handwriting before sending it to the publisher. She only received 20 guineas for her masterpiece. Miss Burney has since heard it being

Martha Ray

Novelist Fanny Burney, the author of *Evelina*.

discussed at dinner parties, in bookshops, even at the breakfast table, where her stepmother read out an advertisement promoting the novel.

Mr Burney says he is very impressed with his daughter's work. Modest Miss Burney, who refers to herself as a "nobody," thanks the critic, Doctor Johnson "…for such lenity to a poor mere worm in literature." This "nobody" will have to get used to being a "somebody," as she is now England's most celebrated novelist.

Sarah Siddons

> "I PRAISE
> LOUDLY, I
> BLAME SOFTLY."
>
> CATHERINE THE GREAT,
> (1752?–1796)
> EMPRESS OF RUSSIA

Archduchess of Austria, Maria Theresa, Dies

Austria, November 29, 1780: Maria Theresa, Archduchess of Austria, Queen of Bohemia and Hungary, and Holy Roman Empress, is dead at sixty-three.

Maria Theresa was the first woman to rule the Hapsburg Empire. Succession was previously through the male line and when she came to the throne in 1740 on the death of her father, Charles VI, her claim was disputed and the War of the Austrian Succession began. The Seven Years' War (1756–1763) further tested her, but she died with her empire consolidated and better administered than at the start of her reign.

Her many reforms included improved conditions for serfs, a uniform criminal code, the abolition of torture and a more universal system of education. Her son, Joseph II, is now ruler. Her daughter, Marie Antoinette, is Queen of France.

The late Archduchess of Austria, Maria Theresa.

Heroine Delivers Vital Information

South Carolina, USA, June 1781: Emily Geiger is the newest heroine of the American Revolution. Last week, General Greene was retreating from the forces led by Lord Rawdon in South Carolina, when he devised a plan to attack the British, if only he could get a message through to General Sumter to join him.

time out

New Orleans courtesans are big business. "Quadroons" (women with one black grandparent) must wear scarves to identify them as non-white. They are trained as courtesans by their mothers, and sold for handsome settlements.

The countryside was full of Whigs, who were friendly to the British cause and threatening death to any Whig spy. Eager to help, since her father John Geiger was too unwell to fight, Emily volunteered to take the message, because who would suspect a young woman traveling to visit her uncle?

General Greene gave her a letter for General Sumter, but he also told her what the letter contained so that she could repeat the message if the document were lost. After two days' travel, she was stopped by three British scouts and taken to the camp, where Lord Rawdon questioned her. She was not a confident liar and he decided to have her searched. In the short delay while a woman was found to search her, she tore up and swallowed the letter, and so nothing incriminating was found. She went on her way and faithfully delivered the message to General Sumter.

When asked about her ordeal, she complained of nothing except the difficulty of swallowing so much dry paper.

Woman Executed for Witchcraft in Switzerland

Glarus, Switzerland, June 17, 1782: Today, Anna Göldi, who has been accused of witchcraft, was executed in the small rural canton of Glarus.

The first large witch trial in Europe, in 1428, took place on Swiss soil. Many are asking why, in this age of enlightenment and reason, some people continue to hold on to the belief that neighbors—all too often elderly women without menfolk to protect or speak for them—are working magic that causes a cow's milk to dwindle, a child to fall ill, a house to catch fire, or any of the other normal accidents and misfortunes of daily life.

Anna Göldi was an uneducated servant who was charged with bewitching her master's child. There have been suggestions that she was probably tortured,

The women's regatta on Venice's Grand Canal has been popular for centuries.

since torture is still legal in Switzerland. Therefore, her confession may have been gained under duress.

Many commentators are calling for the Swiss Confederacy to act, as the Austrian government has done under the guidance of Empress Maria Theresa, to abolish

Austria, November 29, 1780: Archduchess Maria Theresa, dies, aged 63.

Clerkenwald, England, 1780: William Addis establishes the first company to mass produce toothbrushes.

Peru, 1780: Micaela Bastida Puyucahua, with her husband, Tupac Amaru, leads a revolt against the Spanish occupation of Peru.

Pennsylvania, USA, March 4, 1781: American philanthropist Rebecca Gratz is born.

South Carolina, USA, June 1781: Emily Geiger crosses British lines in North Carolina to deliver important battle instructions to General Sumter from General Greene.

Austria, September 1781: Emperor Joseph II abolishes serfdom, giving all subjects freedom to marry, own property, migrate, and work.

Glarus, Switzerland, June 17, 1782: Anna Göldi is executed for witchcraft.

Virginia, USA, September 6, 1782: Martha Jefferson, wife of Thomas Jefferson, dies, aged 34.

London, England, October 10, 1782: Sarah Siddons receives critical acclaim for her lead performance in *Isabella, or The Fatal Marriage* at the Drury Lane Theater.

Bangkok, Siam (Thailand), 1782: King Rama founds a new royal dynasty, and moves the Siamese capital from Thonburi to Bangkok.

Russia, April 8, 1783: Catherine the Great annexes the Crimea, thus gaining control over the northern coast of the Black Sea.

Paris, France, May 31, 1783: Portrait artists, Adélaide Labille-Guiard and Marie Louise Elisabeth Vigée-Le Brun, are admitted to the Royal Academy of Painting and Sculpture.

Annonay, France, June 4, 1783: Joseph and Etienne Montgolfier send a balloon to 6,562 ft (2,000 m), in the first hot-air balloon demonstration.

Scotland, 1783: Thomas Bell invents roller printing of fabric, a much faster process than block printing.

Spain, 1783: More anti-Gypsy laws are passed, continuing their persecution all over Europe.

Paris, France, April 26, 1784: Benjamin Franklin proposes daylight saving in a letter to *Paris Journal*.

Lyon, France, June 4, 1784: Opera singer Marie Elisabeth Thible becomes the first woman to "go aloft" in a hot-air balloon.

New York, USA, September 8, 1784: Ann Lee, founder of the Shakers, dies, aged 48.

London, England, December 1784: Writer and lexicographer Samuel Johnson dies, aged 75.

witchcraft as a criminal offence and ban judicial torture. In the neighboring republic-city of Geneva, the last trial and execution of a so-called witch took place in 1652, and in distant England, the last witch trial took place in 1712. Far from being severe, English judges have for decades laughed at the fanciful accusations brought in the name of witchcraft.

It may never prove possible to eliminate the superstitious fear and spitefulness that generate so many accusations of witchcraft, but many hope that Anna Göldi's case will be the very last occasion on which such accusations lead to an officially sanctioned execution.

French Academy Opens Doors to Female Artists

Paris, France, May 31, 1783: After 77 years of insisting on an exclusively male membership, the Royal Academy of Painting and Sculpture has finally admitted women this year, among them portrait painters Adélaide Labille-Guiard and Marie Louise Elisabeth Vigée-Le Brun.

It was only in 1706 that the academy banned women from its ranks, yet some members have resisted overturning this decision. Some people assert that those who object feel threatened by the high quality of some women's assured and delicately detailed works—particularly in the case of both Labille-Guiard and Vigée-Le Brun.

Labille-Guiard studied painting with the miniaturist François-Elie Vincent and later with his son, François-André, and with Maurice Quentin de la Tour. She has painted numerous portraits in pastels and more recently in oils. Labille-Guiard has her own studio and several female pupils.

Le Brun's father and first teacher was the well-known portraitist Louis Vigée. She is much in demand as a portrait painter to the nobility. Her entry into the academy was at first banned because of her marriage to the collector and art

A portrait of Louise-Elisabeth of France and her son Ferdinand, by Adélaide Labille-Guiard.

dealer, Jean Le Brun, but the patronage of Marie Antoinette, whose portrait she has frequently painted, has assured her place. Rumors of these two painters' antagonism have little foundation in their behavior, and appear to be the work of their jealous rivals.

Crimea Annexed by Russia

Russia, April 8, 1783: Catherine the Great has issued a formal manifesto annexing the Crimea—yet another blow to the Ottoman Empire. The Crimea has been independent for only nine years, since the Treaty of Kuchuk Kainarji ended the war between Russia and the Ottoman Empire.

By that treaty, Russia gained massive territories in the steppe along with access to the Black Sea. The Turks paid heavily with this loss of territory for their quickness to declare war on Russia in

1768, in support of a Polish revolt against the rule of Catherine's favorite, Stanislas.

Now Catherine has added the Crimea to Russia's territory, claiming that it is in a state of anarchy and knowing that as an independent nation it lacks the might to withstand her.

There are great military advantages to this annexation: Russia's hold on the Black Sea is confirmed and extended. At the end of the war, in 1774, the Russian navy had gained the right to sail on the Black Sea and through the Dardanelles. Now, with the Crimea in Russian hands, a Russian Black Sea fleet may be built up to rival the powers of France and England.

The Russian navy now poses a threat to the heart of the Ottoman Empire, the ancient city of Constantinople. Only time will tell how gigantic this ever-expanding Russian Empire will grow, at the expense of the Ottoman Turks.

Catherine the Great

An illustration commemorating Madame Thible's flight in Montgolfier's hot-air balloon, *Le Gustave*.

Key Events

St Petersburg, Russia, 1784: Ekaterina Dashkova becomes the first president of the Russian Academy of Science.

Phuket, Siam (Thailand), March 13, 1785: Sisters Kunying Jan and Kunying Mook assemble Siamese forces and fight off Burmese attack.

London, England, 1785: The East India Company publishes Charles Wilkins's translation of the *Bhagavad-Gita* from the Sanskrit.

London, England, 1785: Lady Emma Hamilton is portrayed as Circe by George Romney.

Kyoto, Japan, 1785: Reigen Eto, Japanese Zen painter and chief priest, dies, aged about 64.

Paris, France, May 31, 1786: Jeanne de La Motte is shown to be a swindler in the "affair of the diamond necklace."

Slough, England, August 1, 1786: Astronomer Caroline Herschel is the first woman to discover a comet.

Paris, France, 1787: Antoine-Laurent Lavoisier publishes the chemical nomenclature system devised with Antoine Fourcoy, Guyton de Morveau, and Claude-Louis Berthollet.

Port Jackson (Sydney), New South Wales, Australia, January 26, 1788: The 11 ships of the First Fleet arrive from England to establish a penal colony.

New Hampshire, USA, October 24, 1788: American writer, editor, and poet Sarah Josepha Hale is born.

Paris, France, July 14, 1789: Parisians storm the Bastille, releasing the prisoners.

Virginia, USA, August 25, 1789: Mary Ball Washington, mother of first US president George Washington, dies, aged 81.

France, September, 1789: Marie Louise Elisabeth Vigée-Le Brun begins a portrait of Madame du Barry.

Versailles, France, October 5, 1789: Around 7,000 armed women and their husbands march to the palace to demand that King Louis XVI return to Paris. Bread prices are extremely high, making it very hard for the poor to survive.

Versailles, France, October 6, 1789: Louis XVI agrees to leave Versailles for Paris.

Massachusetts, USA, December 28, 1789: American novelist Catharine Sedgwick is born.

Bordeaux, France, 1789: The choreographer and dancer, Jean Dauberval, presents the ballet later known as *La fille mal gardée*.

Paris, France, 1789: Marie-Anne Lavoisier illustrates her husband's *Traité élémentaire de chimie* (*Elementary Treatise on Chemistry*).

Paris, France, 1789: Louise du Pierry, the first woman professor of astronomy, dies, aged 43.

Lady Emma Hamilton

"LET THEM EAT CAKE."

MARIE ANTOINETTE (1755–1793), QUEEN OF FRANCE, 1789

Death of Mother Ann of the Shakers Announced

New York, USA, September 8, 1784: Ann Lee, leader of the Shakers, has died aged forty-eight. Not often does a man convince his followers that God lives incarnate in him; how extraordinary, then, for a woman to do so. Ann Lee's self-sacrificing and modest daily existence, the prophetic and visionary writings drawn from her accounts of spiritual visitations, and the miracles to which her followers attest, combined to convince the Shakers that she was Jesus Christ come again, the perfect embodiment of the Christian god in female form.

Ann was born in England on February 29, 1736, the daughter of a Manchester blacksmith. She married another local blacksmith, Abraham Standerin (sometimes Stanley), in 1762. Ann is said to have entered marriage reluctantly, convinced that celibacy was the true Christian path. Their four children all died at a very young age .

Four years earlier, she had joined a small religious community led by the Wardleys, known as the Quaker Shakers because of the ecstatic tremors that shook them at their meetings. These shakings were welcomed as an indication that the Holy Spirit was cleansing them from sin.

Ann Lee became a powerful speaker at these meetings, urging her hearers to practice celibacy and preach the faith more publicly. The local authorities responded by imprisoning her for blasphemy. By 1772 the group became known as Shakers and Ann became their official leader, often called "Mother Ann."

In 1774, she proclaimed her vision of a new Christian church to be founded in America. That year, seven believers accompanied Mother Ann and her husband to New York. The American Revolution brought new trials to the community, who were suspected of siding with the English. Mother Ann was imprisoned but was released when she guaranteed her neutrality. The first American converts have recently joined Mother Ann's community at Watervliet. All Shakers live together as brothers and sisters. They treat one another as equals, value simplicity in everyday living, and practice pacifism and strict celibacy.

A community of Shakers at worship in New York.

Phuket Saved By Sisters

Phuket, Siam, March 13, 1785: A victory against the odds has been achieved by the women of Phuket against the invading Burmese forces.

The town of Phuket must have seemed an obvious target for the invaders, who planned to take its inhabitants by surprise knowing that not enough men able to fight could be mustered to ward off such an attack. The recent death of Phuket's governor left the town still less capable of self-defense, or so it appeared, and the Burmese would have remembered their successful 1767 attack on Ayutthaya. Nevertheless, Phuket has not fallen. A British trader, Francis Light, was able to warn the population that an attack was imminent.

Two brave and intrepid women, the governor's widow, Kunying Jan, and her sister, Kunying Mook, gathered together what few fighting men they could. They also assembled several hundred women, dressing them as men and giving them makeshift weapons. This mixed band of warriors faced the invaders on the Phuket shore, knowing that if they failed, they were destined for slavery.

The Burmese invaders laid siege to Phuket for a month; however, the valiant resistance of the sisters and their forces has led to the abandonment of the siege.

King Rama is to break with protocol by bestowing on Kunying Jan the title Thao Thep Kasatri, which is usually reserved for those of royal blood, and Kunying Mook is to be given the title Thao Sri Sunthon.

In 1789, women march to Versailles to confront Louis XVI.

Verdict in Diamond Necklace Trial

Paris, France, May 31, 1786: With today's verdict, Jeanne de la Motte is revealed as the most brazen swindler ever to sully a queen's reputation. She was born Jeanne de Saint-Rémy de Valois, a true descendant of the Valois royal line, and her husband claims to be Count de la Motte.

La Motte persuaded many that she is a close friend of Marie Antoinette, a claim the queen denies. Her triumph was to convince Cardinal de Rohan, who knew that the queen disliked him, that Marie Antoinette wanted him to arrange for the secret purchase of a diamond necklace worth the price of a fighting ship, and was using La Motte as an intermediary. She caused affectionate letters to de Rohan to be forged in the queen's name. He failed to notice that the signature, "Marie Antoinette de France," was incorrect: royalty sign with their names only.

The besotted de Rohan attended a secret rendezvous in the Versailles gardens with the "queen"—actually a milliner employed by La Motte. He paid the first installment of the necklace's cost to La Motte, whose husband promptly fled France with it.

Scandal erupted when the jewelers sought further payment from the queen. Now de Rohan faces exile and La Motte is to be whipped, branded, and imprisoned for life. Though found innocent of the conspiracy, the queen has suffered a devastating blow to her reputation.

New Comet Discovered

Slough, England, August 1, 1786: From today Caroline Lucretia Herschel's discovery of a new comet means that women have firmly taken their place in the scientific

Washington receiving Instruction from his Mother.

Mary Ball Washington taught her son, George.

field of astronomy. Born in Germany, Miss Herschel arrived in England in 1772 to join her brother, Sir William Herschel, the Astronomer Royal.

Like her brother, Miss Herschel is musically gifted. However, rather than continue with the public duties of a singer, she chooses now to grind and polish telescope mirrors, maintain a meticulous record of observations made by herself and William, make mathematical calculations based on these observations, and scan the heavens for comets.

Mother of First US President Dies

Virginia, USA, August 25, 1789: Mary Ball Washington, George Washington's mother, has died. She was 81 years old.

Mary's Virginian parents, Joseph and Mary Ball, married in about 1708. Both had been married before and had children. Joseph died in 1711, three years after the birth of their daughter, Mary. Mary Ball then married a third husband who died shortly afterward, and she herself died when her daughter Mary was 12 years old. The child was left in the care of her guardian, George Eskridge, and her half-sister, Elizabeth.

When Mary grew up, her guardian urged her to marry a Virginian man of business by the name of Augustine Washington, a widower almost twice her age who had three children.

Following their marriage in 1731, they took up residence first at Pope's Creek Plantation on the Potomac River, then at Little Hunting Creek (since renamed Mount Vernon), and finally at Ferry Farm. On February 22, 1732, Mary gave birth to her first child, George. There were to be five more children, one of whom died in infancy.

Unexpectedly, in 1743, Augustine Washington died. Just as her mother had done, Mary Washington faced a difficult future. Unable to educate him in England, Mary sent George to stay with his half-brother, Lawrence, at Mount Vernon.

Mary did not, however, anticipate that Lawrence would suggest a career in the Royal Navy. Just as George was about to set out at the age of 14 to become a midshipman, Mary is said to have rushed to Mount Vernon to prevent this happening. Mary lived on at Ferry Farm until, in 1772, George moved her to a house in Fredericksburg.

While mother and son did not always agree, he spoke publicly of his gratitude toward her. The last time he went to visit his mother was in April this year, just before his inauguration as the first president of the United States of America.

Collaborative Effort?

Paris, France, 1789: Antoine-Laurent Lavoisier's *Traité elémentaire de chimie (Elementary Treatise on Chemistry)* is an extraordinary publication. It proclaims a newly discovered law of nature—the conservation of mass—from Lavoisier's observations that the total mass of matter involved in a chemical reaction in a closed system remains constant. But how much of this brilliant work should be attributed to his wife, Marie-Anne? Certainly she is responsible for the 13 illustrations of laboratory equipment in this book. Madame Lavoisier has acted as a laboratory assistant to her husband as well as sketching procedures.

The sciences are considered an occupation for which only male intellects are fit, and yet Madame Lavoisier has demonstrated women's capacity to comprehend and communicate science at its most advanced level. After her marriage she sought tuition in chemistry. She then translated the *Essay on Phlogiston* by the English chemist, Richard Kirwan, into French for her husband's benefit: it was this translation that gave Monsieur Lavoisier and his supporters the ammunition to attack the phlogiston theory.

Madame Lavoisier's hospitality has been enjoyed by such scientists and inventors as James Watt and Benjamin Franklin. In such a setting her championship of the Lavoisier system of naming elements and the law of conservation of mass is as bold as the ideas themselves.

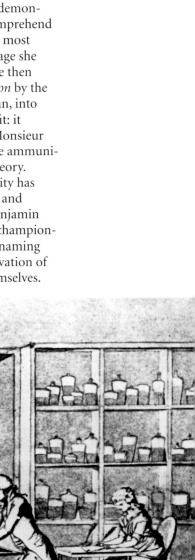

Madame du Barry

Madame Marie-Anne Lavoisier takes notes while her husband and his colleagues perform an experiment.

Mary Wollstonecraft

Quest for Equality Moves to the Netherlands

The Hague, Netherlands, April 1, 1792: The French Legislative Assembly has become used to the demands of revolutionary Frenchwomen, but today, it was a Dutch woman, Etta Palm Aelders, who voiced a passionate argument for equal rights for women, including the right to divorce.

Born in the Netherlands in 1743, Etta Aelders married Frenchman Ferdinand Palm in 1762, but was divorced soon after. Ten years later she moved to Paris, where she endowed herself with the title Baronne d'Aelders. Her first significant contribution to the debate about women's rights was her 1790 *Discourse on the Injustice of the Laws in Favor of Men, at the Expense of Women.* Etta's eloquence was coldly received by France's rulers, whose ideals of liberty, fraternity, and equality seem to apply only to men. Now she has brought the message to her homeland.

Wollstonecraft Fights for Women's Rights

London, England, 1792: *A Vindication of the Rights of Women,* Mary Wollstonecraft's new book, deplores the waste of so many women's lives. She takes issue with the philosopher Rousseau's disparagement of women as irrational beings. In Wollstonecraft's view, women's so-called inferiority arises from their poor education and the few opportunities allowed them in a world dominated by men.

Mary Wollstonecraft is a living example of how a woman may contribute to the world of ideas. When she was born in 1759, her family was prosperous, but her father was an over-optimistic businessman and a domestic brute. In 1784 Mary and her sisters tried to earn their living by setting up a school. When the school failed, Mary then became a governess in Ireland. She later returned to England, aiming to support herself by her writing. Employed as a translator, she acquired a political education through meeting such men as Thomas Paine. She also acquired an education in sexual desire when she became enamored of the artist, Henry Fuseli. She is said to have proposed a *ménage à trois*, a proposal he and his wife did not accept! Amid this turmoil Mary wrote her first political treatise, *A Vindication of the Rights of Men* (1790), in response to Edmund Burke's 1790 *Reflections on the Revolution in France.* Already her new book has drawn favorable attention; can it generate the changes in thinking that she so desires?

time out

On April 8, 1795, the Prince of Wales married his cousin, Caroline of Brunswick, in order to produce an heir. Repelled by his bride, the Prince became drunk and spent the night "under the grate where he fell," where Caroline left him!

The murder of Jean-Paul Marat by Charlotte Corday.

Execution Fever in Paris

Paris, France, October 16, 1793: Monarchists and republicans both have cause for grief this year in France. True Jacobins lament the assassination of one of their leaders, Jean-Paul Marat, at the hands of Charlotte Corday, 25, a woman from Normandy. A minor aristocrat, Corday supported the moderate Girondists in the Revolution and resolved to assassinate the man she thought was the leader of the rival Jacobins, believing that he was a savage beast leading the country inexorably toward civil war.

On July 13, Corday claimed to have news of a Girondist plot. Marat received her while lying in his bath, seeking some relief from a skin ailment, and it was there that she stabbed him in the heart. She was guillotined within the week. How futile was her act! Marat is now a martyr and Robespierre keeps the guillotine ever busier.

The guillotine's most recent victim is Marie Antoinette, the unfortunate Queen of France, whose crimes revolved around

Not even Marie Antoinette herself can escape execution.

Pitcairn Island, January 15, 1790: Fletcher Christian leads the *Bounty* mutineers and some Tahitians to settle uninhabited Pitcairn Island.

San Dominique (Haiti), August 22, 1791: Slaves in the French colony revolt against harsh conditions, burn plantations, and murder the owners.

France, September, 1791: Marie Gouze, also known as Olympe de Gouges, publishes *The Declaration of the Rights of Woman and the Female Citizen,* calling for more liberal rights for women.

Vienna, Austria, December 5, 1791: Composer Wolfgang Amadeus Mozart dies, aged 35.

Peking, China, 1791: The complete version of *Dream of the Red Chamber,* by Cao Xuegin, is published.

The Hague, Netherlands, April 1, 1792: Feminist Etta Palm Aelders calls for women's right to divorce.

Paris, France, September 3, 1792: French aristocrat, Marie-Louise, Princess de Lamballe, is killed by an angry mob. Her body is mutilated and her head impaled on a spike and carried about the streets of Paris.

Cornwall, England, 1792: William Murdock uses coal gas for lighting; it is the precursor of gas lighting.

London, England, 1792: Mary Wollstonecraft publishes *A Vindication of the Rights of Women.*

Paris, France, 1792: Highwayman Nicolas-Jacques Pelletier becomes the first French criminal to be guillotined.

Fiordland, New Zealand, 1792: First settling parties arrive; thus begins the country's integration with the global economy.

Paris, France, January 21, 1793: King Louis XVI is executed by guillotine.

Paris, France, July 17, 1793: Charlotte Corday is executed for the assassination, four days earlier, of the revolutionary writer Jean-Paul Marat.

Canada, July 22, 1793: Alexander Mackenzie is the first European to cross Canada from the Atlantic Ocean to the Pacific.

Paris, France, October 16, 1793: Queen Marie Antoinette is guillotined.

Paris, France, November 3, 1793: Marie Gouze (Olympe de Gouges), French campaigner for women's rights, is sent to the guillotine.

Rhode Island, USA, 1793: Hannah Slater is the first woman to file for a patent in the USA for her invention of a new way to spin thread.

Georgia, USA, March 14, 1794: Eli Whitney is granted a patent for his cotton gin invention.

Kiev, Russia, June 23, 1794: Catherine the Great allows Jews to settle in Kiev.

being born a Hapsburg, marrying the heir to the French throne, and living an extravagant self-indulgent life as Queen. Marie Antoinette had very little political acumen and, until her husband fell into depression, minimal influence on French politics, but she became a scapegoat for the country's financial troubles—from the size of the government's debts to the scarcity of grain in Paris.

Although much loved on her arrival from Austria to marry Louis-Philippe, she was soon cursed as Madame Déficit. She failed to persuade her husband to flee Revolutionary Paris until it was too late. The King and Queen were imprisoned in August last year. Louis XVI was pronounced guilty of treason on January 17, and almost immediately guillotined. Queen Marie Antoinette then suffered the anguish of having her son taken from her and placed into the dubious care of her enemies. Today, the Widow Capet, as she was contemptuously styled, made her last trip—this time, to the guillotine.

Feminist de Gouges Executed

Paris, France, November 3, 1793: In 1789, the French National Assembly issued the *Declaration of the Rights of Man and of the Citizen.* The rights laid down in this document pertain only to men, and in 1791 Olympe de Gouges published a response. Her *Declaration of the Rights of Woman and of the Citizen* call for women to have the vote and to have the right to hold public office. Indeed, she argues for full equality between the sexes and also advocates an end to slavery.

Olympe's declaration is convincingly argued, but not one of the all-male National Assembly would take a woman's political writing seriously. Unwisely, she appealed publicly to Marie Antoinette, hoping that royal patronage would help her cause. More unwisely still, she went on to criticize Robespierre, which resulted

Olympe de Gouges has been guillotined.

in her arrest, charged with having written works against the national interest and denouncing those in power. De Gouges was found guilty of attacking the sovereignty of the people in her writings and today she has been guillotined.

De Gouges was born Marie Gouze, the daughter of a Montauban butcher and servant, though she encouraged rumors that she was the illegitimate child of a local aristocrat. After a brief marriage, she moved, on the death of her husband, to Paris, where she changed her name, adding the aristocratic "de." She tried her fortunes as a playwright before her brief, spectacular, and catastrophic career as a champion of equal rights for women.

Jews to Live in Kiev

Kiev, Russia, June 23, 1794: Today's ukase issued by Empress Catherine II allows the Jewish population of Russia to reside in Kiev. Her earlier decree of December 23, 1791, set up a restricted territory, known as the Pale of Settlement for Jews, in the far west of Russia—this new decree now extends the Pale eastward. In centuries

gone by, when there were very few Jews living in Russia, no restrictions were put upon them, but as the Russian empire has grown westward over the last two centuries, and especially now that Catherine has annexed much of what was formerly Poland, the Jewish population has greatly increased in the west. The Pale of Settlement is a compromise between the hostility of the aristocracy and the Empress's wish for economic prosperity throughout the empire.

There have been many calls by other members of government to expel all Jews; Russia has had a sad history of persecution of the Jews. As an enlightened and tolerant monarch, Catherine has refused to persecute her Jewish subjects, though they must pay twice the amount of tax that Christians pay. While opening Kiev for settlement by Jews improves their position, it falls far short of the French government's recent decree of full rights of citizenship for all Jews in France. Catherine's policy also leaves Russian Jews clustered and thus highly vulnerable to persecution, should a future ruler prove less enlightened.

Charlotte Corday

Elizabeth Clendinning as Rosina in Frances Brooke's comic opera *Rosina*, first seen in 1782.

France, July 16, 1794: An optical telegraph line using Claude Charré's semaphore lighting begins operating between Paris and Lille.
London, England, 1794: Scottish chemist Elizabeth Fulhame publishes *An Essay on Combustion, with a View to a New Art of Dying and Painting, wherein the Phlogistic and Antiphlogistic Hypotheses are Proved Erroneous,* in which she discusses combustion and catalysis.
London, England, 1794: Ann Radcliffe publishes her fourth Gothic novel, *The Mysteries of Udolpho.*

Paris, France, March 31, 1794: French actress turned revolutionary Claire Lacombe is imprisoned. In 1793, with Pauline Léon, she established the feminist Société des Citoyennes Républicaines Révolutionnaires.
Milan, Italy, January 19, 1795: Maria Teresa Agnesi, composer and musician, dies, aged 74.
Paris, France, March 9, 1796: Josephine de Beauharnais marries Napoleon Bonaparte.

Edinburgh, Scotland, July 21, 1796: Poet Robert Burns dies, aged 37.
London, England, September 22, 1796: In a fit of lunacy, Mary Lamb, children's writer, kills her mother with a carving knife.
St Petersburg, Russia, November 17, 1796: Catherine the Great, empress of Russia, dies, aged 67.
London, England, September 10, 1797: Mary Wollstonecraft Godwin, writer and advocate of women's rights, dies at the age of 38, from blood poisoning, after giving birth to a daughter, Mary.

Germany, 1798: Alois Senefelder invents the printing technique of lithography.
Massachusetts, USA, 1798: *The Gleaner,* a collection of essays espousing reforms to women's education and other feminist issues, is published by Judith Sargent Murray.
Milan, Italy, January 9, 1799: Maria Gaetana Agnesi, linguist, mathematician, and philosopher, dies, aged 81. She was the sister of the composer Maria Teresa Agnesi.

Rosetta, Egypt, July, 1799: French soldiers find the Rosetta Stone.
London, England, 1799: The British Parliament passes the *Combination Act* to prevent workers joining together to improve conditions.
Bologna, Italy, 1799: Aged 21, Maria Dalle Donne is the first woman to graduate with a degree in philosophy and medicine.
Portugal, 1799: Queen Maria is declared mad and her son, João, becomes prince regent.

Josephine de Beauharnais

> "A LITTLE
> ALARM NOW
> AND THEN
> KEEPS LIFE
> FROM
> STAGNATION."
>
> FANNY BURNEY,
> 1796, CAMILLA

Ban on Women's Clubs

Paris, France, March 31, 1794: Women's political rights have suffered another blow with today's imprisonment of Claire Lacombe. In 1790, the cause of women's rights seemed quite promising. With the support of the Marquis de Condorcet, the Cercle Social (Social Circle) was established. The first political club to admit women, La Confédération des Amis de la Vérité (Confederation of the Friends of Truth), was also set up in 1790. Then, in 1793, La Société des Citoyennes Républicaines Révolutionnaires (Society of Republican Revolutionary Female Citizens) was founded by Pauline Léon, a chocolate worker, and Claire Lacombe, a provincial actress who had arrived in Paris in 1792. Lacombe had participated in the storming of the Tuileries.

The Society favored the Jacobins and endorsed the Terror. Its first action was to ask the National Assembly to legislate that all women should wear the tricolor cockade in public. This was effected, but the Society then fell out with the Jacobins over the laws concerning prostitutes. This was then followed by an attack by Society members on some working women who had not been wearing the cockade. The assaulted women complained to the Assembly, which responded by banning all women's political clubs.

On August 26, 1793, Lacombe defied the Assembly by addressing them about the membership of the army and the Constitution. She has now been arrested; French revolutionary women can only hope that her arrest is intended as a warning, and does not portend a forthcoming trip to the guillotine.

Musical Agnesi Dies

Milan, Italy, January 19, 1795: Maria Teresa Agnesi has died today. The younger sister of Maria Gaetana Agnesi, the mathematician, she was born on October 17, 1720 in Milan. As with her sister, her talents were exhibited by their father, Pietro Agnesi, to audiences in the family house; in her teens Maria Teresa was already a fine harpsichordist and singer. De Brosse himself praised her performance of her own compositions and those of Rameau.

In adult life she wrote many arias, a few concertos, and some keyboard pieces, but she is best known for her large-scale works for the stage. In 1747 the cantata pastorale, *Il ristoro d'Arcadia,* made its successful debut at Milan's Regio Ducale Teatro. Her other operatic works are *La Sofonisba, Ciro in Armenia, Il Re Pastore, La Insubria Consolata, Nitocri,* and *Ulisse in Campania.* For three of these she wrote her own librettos. It is reported that the Empress Maria Theresa enjoyed singing her arias. In 1776 *La Insubria Consolata* was performed as part of the celebrations for the engagement of Beatrice d'Este and the Archduke Ferdinand of Austria. In 1768 *Ulisse in Campania* was part of the marriage celebrations of Princess Maria Karolina and King Ferdinand of Naples.

Maria Teresa Agnesi herself married Pier Pinottini in 1752. The couple had no children.

Napoleon Marries

Paris, France, March 9, 1796: Today's marriage between Napoleon Bonaparte and widow Marie-Josèphe-Rose Beauharnais has all of Paris gossiping. Why has the lady (whom Napoleon likes to call Joséphine) agreed to marry this soldier? It is rumored that neither is known for their fidelity and people are wondering when they will tire of one another. And is it true that both bride and groom lied about their ages, Napoleon claiming to be older, Joséphine younger, than they really are? It is rumored, too, that Joséphine goes to the altar knowing that she is no longer able to conceive a child, while the general makes no secret of his hopes for a family. Against all this damaging gossip can be set the undeniable passion the general feels for his bride, which clearly outweighs his family's opposition to the match.

Napoleon himself tells a charming story about their very first meeting. Joséphine, the daughter of a Carribean plantation owner, had entered into a marriage of convenience with Alexandre, Vicomte de Beauharnais. The marriage was not happy and after they moved to Paris, Alexandre left her with their two young children while he pursued a political career. But he fell foul of the Jacobins and was imprisoned. Joséphine's efforts to save him only led to her own imprisonment. In 1794 he was guillotined, but when Robespierre fell from power, Joséphine was freed. Shortly after, a law was passed prohibiting private citizens to own weapons. According to Napoleon, Joséphine's son, Eugène, went to him to state his refusal to give up his dead father's sword. This idealistic gesture brought about the first meeting between the general and the widow. A spiteful rumor says that Joséphine is only marrying Napoleon because her most recent lover, Barras, no longer wished to pay her bills. Joséphine is known as a big spender, and her love of extravagance may put some pressure on their marriage.

Mary Campbell with her love, poet Robert Burns.

The End of an Era

St Petersburg, Russia, November 17, 1796: Empress Catherine II of Russia has always refused the title, "The Great," but this is how she will always be remembered. Born Sophie Auguste Frederica, daughter of the minor German Prince Christian Augustus, she entered an arranged marriage with Peter, the heir to the Russian empire.

One year before her 1745 wedding to Peter, the princess converted to Russian Orthodoxy, a matter of policy rather than conviction, and was renamed Yekaterina (Catherine). Peter was possibly impotent and when at long last a son was born, it was rumored that Catherine had conceived him with a courtier in order to meet the needs of the state.

The Paris home of Napoleon and Josephine in Rue de la Victoire.

St Petersburg, indeed all of Russia, is in mourning following the death of Empress Catherine the Great.

Mathematical Agnesi Leaves Us

Catherine the Great

Milan, Italy, January 9, 1799: Maria Gaetana Agnesi, sister of the musician Maria Teresa, has died today, aged 81. Some say that her Milanese father was a professor of mathematics but he was probably a wealthy man of business. He encouraged his oldest daughter's talents as a linguist and philosopher and often exhibited her fluency in Latin and philosophical thinking to academic audiences. This led to her first book, the 1738 *Propositiones Philosophicae.* However, her primary contribution to mathematics was her *Instituzioni analitiche ad uso della gioventú italiana,* in two volumes, which was published in 1748 and 1749. This would appear to be the first book on mathematics that has been written by a woman.

This work is a textbook which, rather than offering original findings, teaches differential and integral calculus by way of examples. In it she explains a *versiera* (turn), a particular mathematical curve that has become linked with her name, as it is called the "Agnesi curve."

Pope Benedict XIV awarded Maria Gaetana the position of honorary reader at the University of Bologna, and soon after, she was offered the chair of mathematics there. However, she never took up these academic posts. After her father's death in 1752, she chose not to pursue her mathematical studies but to devote herself to good works. She died today in one of the homes she had helped to establish for the poor, having given away all her wealth to the needy.

In 1762 the Empress Elizabeth died and Peter became Emperor, but immediately antagonized the army and nobility. Six months later, he was overthrown, then murdered, probably without Catherine's involvement. Catherine became Empress. Under her adept leadership, Russia has expanded its territories at the expense of the Ottoman Empire and Poland, and its influence spreads as far as Great Britain. Russian military power now rivals that of any other European nation.

Catherine has brought western ideas and art to Russia. Her personal collection of artworks is superlative. She gave refuge to the French philosopher Diderot, and cultivated the friendship of Voltaire. In 1767 she set up a legislative commission to codify Russian law following Enlightenment principles, but it has not had any practical outcome. The excesses of the French Revolution may have dampened her enlightened ideas of reform, for now, at the end of her rule, the Russian nobility has increased its powers over the serfs, been freed from taxation, and been given hereditary status. Catherine thought of passing the crown directly to her grandson, Alexander, but her death today at the age of 67 means that her inexperienced son, Paul, now rules the empire.

Essays on Equality of the Sexes

Massachusetts, USA, 1798: Judith Sargent Murray has acted very boldly in publishing *The Gleaner,* her collection of essays, plays, and a novel. Not only is this work written by a woman, sometimes masquerading as a male writer, but as well as addressing political and literary issues, the author mounts forceful arguments for the equality of women, and the necessity of providing the same good quality education for girls as for boys.

The general triviality of most women's lives is due to their poor education, Judith Sargent Murray claims. Her essay, "On the Equality of the Sexes," was first published in the *Massachusetts Magazine* in 1790, two years before Mary Wollstonecraft's incendiary 1792 work, *A Vindication of the Rights of Women.* Yet it is the English writer, not the American, who has so far won fame for championing women's capacities and rights.

Women love to meet and chat on the Boulevard Italien, a popular gathering place for Parisians.

Martha Washington

Can a Woman Ride to Victory?

York, England, August 25, 1804: Alicia Meynell, the first female jockey ever to compete in a horse race, today managed enough speed to stay in the lead for the first three-quarters of the four-mile York course, a feat she achieved despite the fact that she was riding sidesaddle.

Miss Meynell wore leopard and buff colors with blue sleeves and a riding cap. She was riding Colonel Thornton's horse, Ving-arillo, against Captain Flint on his horse, Thorn-ville. Alicia is rumored to be the Colonel's mistress, and he is said to have bet heavily on her success, helping to make her the pre-race favorite.

After the race, she accused Captain Flint of discourtesy, and threatens to take her complaint to the newspapers. Alicia Meynell has not been deterred from the sport, however, and hopes to compete again next year.

A Rooster, a Sheep, a Duck, and a Woman

Paris, France, 1805: Madame Sophie Blanchard has been appointed Chief Air Minister for Ballooning by Napoleon. It was only in 1783 that the first human beings flew in a balloon, safely tethered, at Versailles, and Monsieur Blanchard was the first person to fly untethered in Paris in 1784.

Madame Sophie Blan-chard is the first professional female balloonist, but she is not the first female balloonist: a tethered balloon ascent was made back in May 1784, by four intrepid women, and an untethered ascent was made later the same year.

time out

Swiss-born Marie Tussaud, having escaped the guillotine herself, was commissioned to create wax death masks of many of those who had been executed in France during 1792. Her wax-works became popular in Britain.

Emperor Napoleon with his wife, Josephine.

Sophie tells a romantic story of how her husband-to-be visited an inn more than a decade ago and was charmed by her mother. If she had a daughter, he said, he would return and marry her. In 1796, a year after his pioneer balloon crossing of the English Channel, he did indeed return to marry Sophie.

The Blanchards keep developing acrobatic and pyrotechnic displays to amuse and amaze the paying public. How far can such risky displays be taken, however, before a fatal accident occurs? The pair's bravado refutes the belief held in the early 1790s that balloon passengers would die from ascending to the heights they achieve. Some of Madame Blan-chard's admirers still remember the first balloon flight with living passengers, undertaken at Versailles in 1783. The world's first balloonists—a rooster, a sheep, and a duck—all survived.

Vive La Veuve's Champagne!

Champagne, France, 23 October 1805: The death of François Clicquot leaves his widow Nicole Barbe, la veuve Clicquot, in charge of a company with interests in banking, wool trading, and champagne production. Madame Clicquot already has plans to divest the business of its

> *"THE EDUCA-TION OF WOMEN MUST BE ENTIRELY FREE. WHEREVER OUR GENIUS LEADS US, THERE WE MUST BE ALLOWED TO WANDER IN THE FIELD OF KNOWLEDGE."*
>
> AMALIE HOLST, GERMAN FEMINIST, C. 1802

A display of hot-air balloons marks the coronation of Emperor Napoleon and Empress Josephine.

Connecticut, USA, September 6, 1800: Catherine Esther Beecher, American educator, is born.

Old Windsor, England, December 26, 1800: Writer and actress Mary Darby Robinson dies.

Virginia, USA, 1800: Martha Dandridge Custis Washington, the widow of George Washington, sets free all her slaves.

Madrid, Spain, c. 1800: Francisco Goya paints *La Maja Desnuda (The Nude Maja)*, one of his best-known works.

Philadelphia, USA, 1800: William Young designs shoes specifically for left and right feet.

South China Seas, 1801-09: Pirate Cheng I Sao, also known as Shi Xainggu, commands about 80,000 men and women as she terrorizes shipping in the South China Seas.

United Kingdom, January 1, 1801: The *Act of Union* between Ireland and Great Britain comes into effect.

St Petersburg, Russia, March 23, 1801: Paul I, Tsar of Russia, is assassinated and succeeded by his son Alexander.

Mexico City, Mexico, September 12, 1802: Antonio de León y Gama, Mexico's first archeologist, and the first European to record Aztec archeology, dies, aged about 67.

Germany, 1802: German writer Amalie Holst, a campaigner for specialist girls' schools, publishes *On the Capacity of Women for Higher Education*.

Paris, France, April 30, 1803: The French government sells its Louisiana Territory to the USA.

Ecuador, 1803: Rebel leader Lorenza Avemanay leads a revolt against Spanish forces.

Haiti, January 1, 1804: Jacques Dessalines declares Haiti a free republic after slaves mount a successful revolution against France.

Merthyr Tydfil, Wales, February 21, 1804: Richard Trevithick's steam locomotive begins operating.

York, England, August 25, 1804: Alicia Meynell becomes the first female jockey to compete in a horse race.

Paris, France, December 2, 1804: Napoleon Bonaparte crowns himself Emperor of France at Nôtre Dame Cathedral.

Malmaison, France, 1804: The Empress Josephine, wife of Napoleon, begins to collect rose plants, stimulating broad interest in the cultivation of roses.

Cape Trafalgar, Spain, October 21, 1805: Admiral Horatio Nelson leads the British Royal Navy to victory against France and Spain at the Battle of Trafalgar. He is fatally wounded.

**Empress Josephine
of France**

banking and wool-trading activities and to focus her energies on champagne.

She hopes to expand the acreage of the Clicquot vineyards and believes that she can take commercial advantage of the wars in Europe, once blockades are lifted, if she can move her goods quickly enough to make the first shipments of her quality champagne to her clients.

She also hopes to improve the wine's manufacture. Currently, champagne is sold cloudy in the bottle and must be decanted before drinking. It has so far been a problem how to remove the deposits that accumulate in the bottle as the champagne ages. Madame Clicquot is said to be experimenting with a new device that gradually tilts the bottles so that the deposits settle below the cork.

Marketing is another of her concerns. According to La Veuve, it is important not only to produce a great wine but also to render it instantly recognizable as coming from the house of Clicquot. She has not yet decided whether an identifying mark should be put on the cork, on the bottle itself, or perhaps on a label.

Sacagawea Paid Nothing

Hidatsa village, North America, August 17, 1806: After 16 months of journeying with explorers Meriwether Lewis and William Clark, it was revealed that Sacagawea, their Shoshone Indian interpreter, whose contribution to the expedition has been invaluable, has been paid nothing!

Sacagawea, whose name means "bird woman," joined the expedition team as the wife of its French-Canadian member Toussaint Charbonneau. Communications with the Shoshone passed via Sacagawea to Charbonneau, and then in French to François Labiche, who then translated the information into English.

Sacagawea was heavily pregnant when the expedition arrived at the Hidatsa village where she dwelt, looking for an interpreter, and on February 11, 1805, she gave birth to a son. Lewis assisted her through the pains of labor with a concoction made of crushed rattlesnake.

According to the expedition leaders, she showed "great courage and fortitude" when a boat was nearly overturned, saving "most of the light articles which were washed overboard." Sacagawea was the expedition's best help in communicating with the tribes they encountered and assuring them that they came in peace. She also advised on the best routes for the expedition.

The expedition ended for her today. Charbonneau was handsomely paid for doing very little, yet Sacagawea, without whom the expedition could not have succeeded, received nothing at all.

gawea acts as interpreter for Lewis and Clark.

Little Star Twinkles Brightly

Colchester, England, 1806: Writing for the enjoyment of small children is a task that many think easy and effortless but very few do well. Writing good poetry for children is a still rarer talent.

Rhymes for the Nursery, by Jane and Ann Taylor, is one of the most successful collections of poems for young children ever published. Possibly the most outstanding poem in the collection is the nursery rhyme "The Star," whose first line is "Twinkle, twinkle, little star." The poem is so simple and evocative that it is likely to enter the world treasury of best-loved nursery rhymes.

The sisters began writing verses for their family's enjoyment when they were very young. First Ann, and then Jane began to publish poems in *The Minor's Pocket Book.* The publisher enjoyed these contributions well enough to ask for more, and he published *Original Poems for Infants* by the Taylor sisters and other contributors in two volumes, in 1804 and 1805, followed by this 1806 publication.

The Taylor sisters' next project is reported to be writing enough hymns for a new book of hymns for children. Jane is also keen to try her hand at writing novels.

Charity Steel achieves freedom on her second attempt to escape slavery.

Key Events

Champagne, France, October 1805: Champagne maker François Clicquot dies. His widow, La Veuve Clicquot, takes over the business.

France, 1805: Madeleine-Sophie Armant Blanchard flies solo in gas-powered balloon flights, and from then on makes her living as a balloonist. Napoleon later appoints her official Aeronaut of the Empire.

London, England, October 7, 1806: Ralph Wedgwood patents "duplicate paper" (carbon paper), to be used with his "stylographic writer" to help blind people write.

Colchester, England, 1806: *Rhymes for the Nursery* by Ann and Jane Taylor is published; it includes "Twinkle, Twinkle, Little Star."

London, England, 1806: Joseph Bramah invents a machine to print successive numbers on banknotes for the Bank of England.

London, England, March 25, 1807: The *Abolition of the Slave Trade Act* is passed, outlawing the transport of slaves by British ships.

New Jersey, USA, 1807: The right of women to vote, granted in 1776, is revoked.

London, England, 1807: Brother and sister Charles and Mary Lamb write *Tales from Shakespeare.*

New Jersey, USA, 1807: Charity Steel achieves freedom on her second attempt to escape slavery.

USA, January 1, 1808: Congress bans the importation of slaves.

Weimar, Germany, 1808: Johann Wolfgang von Goethe publishes *Faust: A Tragedy.*

Vienna, Austria, May 31, 1809: Composer Franz Joseph Haydn dies, aged 77.

Connecticut, USA, May 1809: Mary Kies becomes the first woman to receive a US patent, for her technique of weaving straw for millinery use.

Maryland, USA, June 1809: Elizabeth Ann Seton founds the Roman Catholic Sisters of Charity of St Joseph.

Paris, France, 1809: Jean-Baptiste Lamarck publishes his *Philosophie zoologique,* outlining his theory of evolution.

Washington DC, USA, 1809: Dorothea (Dolly) Payne Todd Madison becomes the first First Lady to accompany her husband at his inauguration as President.

Parramatta, Sydney, Australia, 1809: Elizabeth Macarthur builds her absent husband's sheep farm into the biggest in the land.

Elizabeth Seton

Death of Angelica Kauffmann

Rome, Italy, November 5, 1807:
The funeral of Swiss artist, Angelica Kauffmann, promises to be as splendid as that of the great Italian artist, Raphael. The sculptor Canova is in fact using Raphael's funeral as a model for the procession of ecclesiastics and fellow artists in a fitting celebration of a long and prolific career as a historical artist and portrait painter.

Kauffmann was born in Switzerland in 1741 and grew up in Austria. A child prodigy as both artist and musician, she received her first commission as a painter at the age of eleven. Her father took her several times to Italy, where she became a popular portrait painter, especially among British visitors.

In 1776, emboldened by this success, she went to London where she developed a close friendship with Sir Joshua Reynolds. In 1786 she became a founding member of the Royal Academy of Arts, where she exhibited for over 30 years. She made an ill-judged marriage with a confidence trickster in 1767. In 1781, after his death, she enjoyed a much happier marriage with Antonio Zucchi, and moved to Rome with him.

The artist wished to win acclaim for her historical works, but her male figures were not convincingly masculine (for no respectable woman can study the nude male figure). Rather, it is expected that Angelica Kauffmann will be remembered as a fine painter of women's portraits.

Votes Denied to Women

New Jersey, USA, 1807: In a nation that prides itself on equality, how can it have happened that women, having been given the right to vote, are now to have that right rescinded?

In 1776, the State of New Jersey was a pioneer in granting women's suffrage and for the past 31 years women have enjoyed the vote with no ill effects. There has been no collapse of the State Constitution; New Jersey has not become ungovernable; husbands have not been deserted by their wives, nor have mothers neglected their children.

So, after so many years of sober success, many women are wondering why this right has now been denied them.

The American Declaration of Independence states that all "men are created equal;" and many maintain that

"LOVE IS THE WHOLE HISTORY OF A WOMAN'S LIFE; IT IS ONLY AN EPISODE IN MAN'S."

MADAME DE STAËL, ANNE LOUISE GERMAINE NECKER (1766–1817), FRENCH WRITER

Elizabeth Hartley in the 1805 production of *The Winter's Tale.*

it is an established rule of grammar that "man" here means "humankind," not simply members of the male sex. Additionally, if the idea of women's right to vote is so abhorrent, why did the State of New Jersey give the vote to women in the first place?

Some say that it was a mistake, that the State Constitution was poorly worded when it specified that adult "inhabitants" worth £50, who satisfied the residential requirement, could vote. Strictly interpreted, this phrasing allowed only single women the opportunity to vote, as married women are not permitted to own property in their own right.

Was it indeed a mistake, or were the New Jersey State Legislative delegates in 1776 more enlightened than their New York, Massachusetts, and New Hampshire counterparts? Were they thinking that all owners of property, as having an investment in the well-being of the State, should be entitled to vote? If women cannot be trusted with the vote, how is it that they are, and always have been, entrusted with the care and early education of their sons?

Women are calling on the legislators of New Jersey to rethink this unfair decision.

The Yorkshire Witch Hanged for Murder

York, England, March 20, 1809: Mary Bateman has been exposed as a confidence trickster, but the gullible public is clamoring to buy pieces of her skin for its supposed supernatural healing powers. The Leeds Infirmary will charge each spectator threepence to look at her corpse.

A Yorkshire farmer's daughter, she began working as a servant in the town of Thirsk in 1780 but lost many jobs for petty thievery; from 1787 she continued this pattern of behavior in York. In 1892 she married John Bateman, whom she defrauded. Operating as a fortune-teller in Leeds, she started to speak of "Mrs Moore" and "Miss Blythe," whose supposed supernatural powers she used to extract money from her victims. She also charged spectators to view eggs, supposedly laid bearing the words, "Christ is Coming."

In time most of her frauds were exposed. However, when a Mrs Perigo consulted her for "stomach flutterings," she took money from the credulous lady and her husband for over a year, eventually prescribing a powder to be taken daily with pudding. Mrs Perigo died not long after ingesting this powder. Some months later, after making more payments to Bateman, William Perigo inspected bags of "money" given to him as healing charms, discovering only rotting cabbage leaves and bad farthings.

The "Yorkshire Witch" was hanged today for the poisoning of Mrs Perigo.

Mary and Charles Lamb have published *Tales From Shakespeare.*

Marie Walewska is the close companion of Emperor Napoleon.

Dolly Madison

A Yankee Way with Hats

Connecticut, USA, May 1809: The people of Connecticut have long enjoyed a reputation for cleverness. Now Connecticut's Mary Kies is the first American woman to have her invention recognized by the US Patent Office. She has invented a new technique of weaving straw with silk that promises a most profitable application in the manufacture of straw hats.

The absence of patents hitherto registered by women has not been caused by a bias toward men or a lack of clever women. Rather, the law in many states prohibits married women from owning property in their own right, thus many women have not thought it worth their while to make the application.

Mary Kies's achievement has brought a congratulatory letter from the First Lady.

The Rise and Rise of a Pirate Queen

South China Seas, 1809: The pirates of the South China Sea are very different from the European and American notions of what a pirate should be. There are at least 70,000 of them, they obey strict rules of conduct, and they are currently under the control of a woman.

The pirate commander Cheng I Sao, also known as Shi Xainggu, who was formerly named Ching Shih, began her adult life as a prostitute but decided on a new career after her 1801 marriage to the well known pirate, Cheng I.

Together the couple assembled a confederation of pirates, fighting on the side of the Tay-Son during their rebellion. When this cause was defeated, Cheng I and his wife moved to South China, where their piracy proved spectacularly successful. Before Cheng I died in a storm in 1807, there were said to be 400 ships and 70,000 pirates under his command. These numbers have increased, and his widow rules the crews

of 200 sea-going junks, in addition to a vast number of coastal and river craft.

Following the death of her husband, Cheng I Sao promptly maneuvered herself into the position of command and, to keep the pirate business within the family, married her adopted son, Chang Pao, leader of one of her squadrons. She has set out strict rules for her men, with the death penalty for those who steal from friendly villages or try to defraud her treasury. Death is also the penalty for those who rape female captives, though the punishment for desertion or absence without leave is merely the loss of an ear.

So far her people have outfought all the forces that the authorities have sent against them. The only real threat that she faces, apart from the perennial dangers of the sea, is the possibility of a dispute arising within the ranks that sets pirate against pirate.

Merinos Rule!

Parramatta, Sydney, Australia, 1809: Great Britain has been sending her criminals to the Australian colonies for decades; today the colonies are sending a trouble-maker back to England.

In 1790 Lieutenant John Macarthur came to Australia with his family to join the New South Wales Corps. He has since made a name for himself as a hothead, and the colony has had enough of his antics. Rebelling against Governor William Bligh, John Macarthur has been sentenced to indefinite exile.

This leaves his capable wife, Elizabeth, in charge of the family's business ventures. The most cultured and well-bred of the New South Wales colony's female immigrants, she must now turn her attention toward questions of sheep breeding and wool quality.

In 1796 Lieutenant and Mrs Macarthur imported a new breed of sheep into the colonies, the fine-wooled merino from Spain, which they consider far more suited to Australian conditions than English breeds. They now have several thousand merinos in their flock at Elizabeth Farm and two years ago they began exporting their high-quality wool to England. Others imported merinos, but allowed them to cross-breed, and the quality of their wool soon deteriorated.

Perhaps John Macarthur's exile will turn to his advantage, in the end, for he plans to live in London where he can oversee the selling of the wool while his wife controls the day-to-day management of the farm. She will also have to ensure the obedience of the many convicts who work for her. She has already demonstrated all of these abilities during her husband's previous enforced absence. In 1801 he was sent to England after being caught dueling. While he was not then court-martialed, he did not return to the colony until 1805.

He is indeed a fortunate man to have such a loyal, forgiving, and gifted wife.

Macao authorities are always watching out for pirates, including the notorious female pirate Cheng I Sao.

Fanny Burney

Women on the Course

Musselburgh, Scotland, December 14, 1810: The game of golf probably originated in Scotland in the fifteenth century as a variant on the Flemish game, chole. It soon became popular with royalty; Mary, Queen of Scots, is said to have played a game of golf soon after the death of her husband, Lord Darnley, but otherwise this game has remained the province of men.

The Musselburgh Golf Club has just announced a prize for the best female golfer. January's competitors will come from the ranks of local fishwives, and the prize will be a fishing creel and basket, and some silk handkerchiefs. Some are already complaining that the prizes offered to the winner are too paltry. In comparison, the male golfers at Leith can win a silver cup.

"IT IS A TRUTH UNIVERSALLY ACKNOWLEDGED, THAT A SINGLE MAN IN POSSESSION OF A GOOD FORTUNE, MUST BE IN WANT OF A WIFE."

JANE AUSTEN, 1813, PRIDE AND PREJUDICE

Burney's "Cutting"

Paris, France, October 7, 1811: Fanny Burney is well known as a writer of satirical novels, from *Evelina*, which was first published anonymously in 1778, to her 1796 *Camilla*. Until last week, she seemed to be in danger of dying from breast cancer, but a successful operation has saved her life. Fanny Burney—Madame d'Arblay, since her marriage to General d'Arblay in 1793—first noticed a lump in her left breast when feeding her son in 1794. In the last year it has grown and caused great pain. The surgical response to such lumps, since ancient Egyptian times, has been to excise the lump, often by cutting off the entire breast. Admittedly, there are

time out

In June 1811, Frenchwoman Marie-Louise Christophe becomes Queen of the Caribbean island of Haiti, following the crowning of her husband, Henri Christophe, a former slave and the Haitian independence leader, as king.

surgeons now who argue that it is the lymph glands that should be removed, but Burney's surgeons performed a total mastectomy on September 30 with no painkillers except for some wine possibly mixed with a little laudanum. The patient remained conscious for almost all of the procedure, in excruciating pain throughout the "terrible cutting."

Burney has kept up an animated correspondence with her sister Susanna for the whole of her adult life. It is to be hoped that she will very soon feel well enough to resume writing and that eventually the account of her harrowing operation, indeed all her vivid accounts of her experiences, will be published so that the public can marvel and learn from the novelist's account of her own very eventful life.

When Napoleon is away from France, he writes to Josephine each day.

Astoria Survival Story

Oregon, USA, 1811: Word has come from Fort Okanogan that Marie Dorion, the native American wife of the Astoria expedition's interpreter, still lives. While the men were out trapping beaver, she stayed at the base camp. Friendly locals told her about the hostile Bannock tribe and she set off to warn her husband.

If women's competitions become popular, men at St Andrews may have to share the golf course.

Key Events

Paris, France, 1810: The Napoleonic Code prohibits abortion unless the mother's life is at risk.

Musselburgh, Scotland, December 14, 1810: Musselburgh Golf Club promises a prize for the best female golfer in the first recorded women's golf competition.

Connecticut, USA, June 14, 1811: Writer and abolitionist, Harriet Beecher Stowe, is born.

Batavia, Dutch East Indies, August 6, 1811: The British fleet captures Batavia, and wrests control of Java from the Dutch.

Paris, France, September 30, 1811: English writer Fanny Burney undergoes a mastectomy without anesthesia.

England, 1811: Jane Austen's first novel, *Sense and Sensibility*, is published anonymously.

Oregon, USA, 1811: Native American Marie Dorion is the only woman to be part of the Wilson Price Hunt Expedition from Montreal to Oregon.

Fort Manuel, South Dakota, USA, December 12, 1812: Sacagawea, Shoshone interpreter for explorers Lewis and Clark, dies, aged about 25.

Paris, France, 1812: Marie Boivin publishes her book on obstetrics and gynecology, *Mémorial de l'art des accouchments*.

Washington DC, USA, 1812: America makes a declaration of war against British North America.

Lyme Regis, England, 1812: Twelve-year-old Mary Anning discovers a 17-foot long fossil, later named *Ichthyosaurus*. She sells the fossil to Henry Henley for the sum of £23.

Peking, China, 1813: Li Ruzhen's novel *Jinghuayuan (Flowers in the Mirror)* envisions a world where sex roles are reversed.

Malmaison, France, May 29, 1814: Joséphine de Beauharnais, first wife of Napoleon Bonaparte, dies, aged 50.

London, England, December 27, 1814: Prophetess Joanna Southcott dies, aged 64.

Calais, France, January 15, 1815: Emma Hamilton, mistress of Lord Horatio Nelson, dies, aged about 50.

Sumbawa, Indonesia, April 11, 1815: The Tambora volcano eruption, the most powerful ever recorded, cause local devastation and affects northern hemisphere temperatures.

Waterloo, Belgium, June 18, 1815: The French forces are defeated at the Battle of Waterloo.

London, England, December 10, 1815: Ada Augusta King, mathematician and the daughter of English poet Lord Byron, is born.

Emma Hamilton

Three days later, Dorion found him and another man dead, and a third mortally wounded. Then she discovered that the Bannocks had killed and scalped all the other trappers from the expedition.

After nine days' travel through the snow with her two children, she built a shelter where she kept them alive for almost two months before hunger drove her to seek help. Some Walla Walla people found her wandering, partly snow-blinded, and brought all three to safety.

On the journey westward to Astoria, her courage had already been tested as they raced to establish a fur-trading post before the British did so. She was pregnant when she set off, but walked, carrying the children, until an extra horse could be brought for her. On the day she gave birth, the expedition went on. She caught up with the men the next day, riding her horse with all three children. A few days later, despite help from a friendly tribe, the baby died. Marie Dorion was silent and stoic throughout her ordeals, a model of resourcefulness, sense, and determination.

Open Southcott's Box Now!

London, England, December 27, 1814: There have been many self-styled prophets over the centuries of Christianity. Few have had such an impressive record of accurate short-term prophecy as Joanna Southcott and, now that she is dead, the public is entitled to know what as yet undeclared prophecies are stored in her box, tied with cords and sealed with seven seals. According to her followers, this famous box can only be opened during a national crisis in the presence of 24 bishops of the Church of England. So far no bishops have consented to attend such a ceremony.

Joanna Southcott was born in 1750 and until 1792 she led a quiet devout life as a servant. At 42 she began receiving prophetic messages, either from a voice addressing her or through automatic writing. Many have dismissed her words as lunatic, others have come to scoff but remained as disciples. In 1794 she was told that she was the Bride of the Lamb and this year the voice said that she would bear a son, Shiloh. She began to show all the signs of pregnancy despite her age (64) and more than 20 doctors confirmed that she was indeed pregnant. This month, all signs of pregnancy disappeared. Her followers assert that the child was born on Christmas Day and went straight to heaven.

Death of Nelson's Beloved Emma

Calais, France, January 15, 1815: Shunned by polite society, poor, and too fond of the bottle, Emma, Lady Hamilton died today in Calais. She had moved up the social ladder as the mistress of many men until she attracted the ardent attentions of Horatio Nelson. Shortly before he died, he made a will asking the British nation to provide for Emma and their daughter, Horatia. Their request is unlikely to be honored. Emma's progress upwards was dependent on her beauty, vitality, and talent for posing in dramatic attitudes.

Born Amy Lyon, the daughter of a Cheshire blacksmith, she went to London in her early teens, changed her name to Emma Hart and probably found employment striking attitudes at a disreputable "Temple of Health" before finding a protector, Sir Harry Featherstonhaugh. He quickly tired of her when she fell pregnant.

Her next protector was Charles Greville, who housed her in London and introduced her to the fashionable portrait painter, George Romney. Emma became his favorite subject, as herself, and as figures from myth and allegory. By 1785, Greville needed a rich wife to pay his debts and he offered Emma to his uncle, Sir William Hamilton, the diplomat and antiquarian, who lived in Naples. Emma went to Naples, expecting Greville to join her, but soon adjusted to life with Sir William, and in 1791 they married. He delighted in showing off his wife's Greek and Roman sculptural attitudes to visitors.

In 1793 she first met Nelson and in 1798 they probably became lovers, in a ménage à trois with her husband. Figures of celebrity and scandal, Lord Nelson, Sir William, and Emma returned to England, living together amicably until her the death of her husband. Nelson's death cut short her happiness and, after a period in debtors' prison, she left a hostile England to decline and die in Calais.

"Dido in Despair," a popular caricature of the late Emma Hamilton.

Key Events

London, England, January 1816: A month after her daughter is born, Annabella Milbanke leaves her husband Lord Byron.

Yorkshire, England, April 21, 1816: Novelist Charlotte Brontë is born.

St Cloud, France, July 5, 1816: Dorothea Jordan, Irish actress and long-time mistress of the Duke of Clarence (later King William IV) dies, aged 64.

London, England, July 1816: The waltz is introduced to the English court.

New York, USA, March 8, 1817: The New York Stock Exchange Board is established.

Paris, France, July 14, 1817: French writer Anne Louise Germaine de Staël, better known as Madame de Staël, dies, aged 51.

Winchester, England, July 18, 1817: English novelist Jane Austen dies, aged 41.

Valley of the Kings, Egypt, 1817: Giovanni Batista Belzoni discovers a number of ancient tombs, including the sepulcher of Seti I.

Bristol, England, 1817: John MacAdam develops a new way of building roads.

Canada, October 20, 1818: USA and Britain establish the boundary between Canada and the USA.

London, March 1818: Mary Wollstonecraft Shelley's Gothic novel *Frankenstein* is published.

Yorkshire, England, July 30, 1818: Writer Emily Brontë is born.

Quincy, Massachusetts, USA, October 28, 1818: Abigail Adams, wife of John Adams, second president of the United States dies, aged 73.

England, 1818: *Northanger Abbey* and *Persuasion,* both by Jane Austen, are published.

Singapore, February 1819: A port is established at Singapore.

London, England, May 24, 1819: Princess Victoria of Kent is born.

Istria, Italy, June 28, 1819: Prima ballerina Carlotta Grisi is born.

Leipzig, Germany, September 13, 1819: Pianist and composer Clara Wieck Schumann is born.

Warwickshire, England, November 22, 1819: English novelist, Mary Ann Evans (George Eliot), is born.

Virginia, USA, 1819: Slaves are banned from learning to read and write.

Madame de Staël

Byron Flees England and His Wife

Dover, England, April 25, 1816: Lord Byron leaves England today, perhaps forever. What a dismal exit after enjoying adulation as the most famous and handsome of young poets!

Lord Byron's friends do not understand just why he married the respectable Annabella Milbanke. No one believed that he would settle to a life of marital ordinariness. Her pregnancy and the birth of their daughter Ada did nothing to improve their troubled marriage and on January 15 this year, Annabella left London to return to her parents' home with the baby. In February her father formally requested a legal separation between Byron and Annabella.

By now rumors of the most lurid kind were circulating about Byron. It is beyond doubt that he treated her cruelly in word, if not in action. He repeatedly committed adultery during their short marriage. He had flaunted his affair with Lady Caroline Lamb in the face of society and the hysterical abandon with which his female admirers offered themselves to him would have afforded him a multitude of easy opportunities for infidelity.

A much more serious allegation is being voiced by Lady Caroline, angry at Byron's rejection of her; she says that he is enjoying an incestuous relationship with his half-sister, Augusta. Augusta and Byron were not brought up together and it was only in 1804 that they became close friends. Augusta's third child, born in 1814, was christened Elizabeth Medora Leigh, "Medora" being taken from the name of a heroine in Byron's *The Corsair*, but of course this is far from conclusive evidence of any illicit liaison.

Equally damaging are Caroline's insinuations of sodomy and it is perhaps the threat of being imprisoned for this criminal offence that has driven him abroad. British travelers are now likely to include in their tours of Europe a viewing—from a safe distance, to avoid possible moral contagion—of the notorious Lord Byron.

The Waltz: An Obscene Display

London, England, July 1816: Last week the Prince Regent gave royal approval to the waltz, a vulgar dance against which the guardians of public morality have already been fulminating.

This set of lascivious movements, in which the man presses his body against that of the woman, originated as a peasant dance but has been taken up with enthusiasm at the debauched courts of Europe, weary of the respectable pleasures of the minuet. It was hoped that the waltz might appear and disappear as a fad, but the Prince Regent's introduction of it as part of his recent ball probably guarantees its long life.

Respectable members of the public maintain that this dance compromises any woman naïve or corrupt enough to take part in it. They suggest that women who waltz jeopardize their chances of a good marriage, as their reputations will be sullied by allowing strange men to put their arms around their waists and clasp them tightly. Even Lord Byron, himself no model of respectability, has decried the waltz as giving seducers the opportunity to allow their hands to wander as they whirl their partners to the darker corners of a room.

The Times is denouncing the waltz as an "obscene display" that should be

Critics are warning that the waltz promotes lewd behavior.

"confined to prostitutes and adulteresses." Parents are being implored not to allow their daughters to waltz!

De Staël's Glittering Life Comes to an End

Paris, France, July 14, 1817: Anne Louise Germaine de Staël—daughter of Jacques Necker, intermittently finance minister for Louis XVI of France—died today.

The Swiss family managed to survive the beginning of the French Revolution, retreating to Coppet on Lake Geneva. Germaine's 1786 marriage to the Swedish ambassador Erik Magnus Staël gave her an entrée to French politics while also providing diplomatic safeguards. When France became too dangerous for political moderates, she went back to Coppet, then on to England where she held court over the moderate émigrés.

After the Reign of Terror, she returned to Paris, busying herself in opposition to Napoleon. Her liaison with the politician, Benjamin Constant, briefly gave her very real political power. Her 1802 roman à clef, *Delphine,* caused a stir and in 1803 Napoleon banished her from Paris, an event she had angled for. After visiting Germany, she provoked Napoleon to exile her again with her 1807 novel, *Corinne, or Italy*, and her 1810 study of Germany, *De l'Allemagne*. She secretly married a young officer in Coppet and, in the face of the persecution of her friends, went to Russia. In 1813 she enjoyed celebrity status in England before her final return to Paris.

Her books exemplify the sentimentalism and enthusiasm of the age. Her political influence was ultimately negligible. Her salon glittered. The sparkle gone, she may be forgotten by her fickle fans.

Lord Byron's Nottinghamshire home is empty, now that the poet has fled England following allegations of incest.

Two New Jane Austen Novels Published

England, December 1817: The novelist Jane Austen is dead, but we now have two new novels from her hand, *Persuasion* and *Northanger Abbey.*

Jane Austen began writing fiction in her youth.

The woman with such an acute eye for human folly in her novels has left little evidence of folly in her own life. Jane Austen was born on December 16, 1775, the second daughter of Cassandra Leigh and the Reverend George Austen, rector of the parish of Steventon, a small Hampshire village. She began writing comic, parodic fiction when she was 11 or 12 years old: it is sincerely to be hoped that the family will release these volumes for publication very soon.

By the time she was 25, she had written early versions of three of her novels, *Sense and Sensibility* ("Elinor and Marianne"), *Pride and Prejudice* ("First Impressions") and *Northanger Abbey* ("Susan"). *Northanger Abbey* was accepted for publication in 1803 but not published until this year. It is a romp through the lurid conventions of Gothic fiction; underlying the parody is Jane's characteristic moral probity, unflinchingly assessing each character. *Sense and Sensibility* was Jane Austen's first novel to be published, in 1811. It humorously and poignantly examines the cost of excessive romantic sensibility and the value of undemonstrative good sense.

Pride and Prejudice, published in 1813, the reading public's favorite, is a delightful study in the self-education of its proud and prejudiced hero and heroine. *Mansfield Park* (1814) attempts a less immediately appealing subject, a thoroughly good heroine. *Emma* (1816) is a wonderful study in self-deception and *Persuasion*, published just now, is a golden novel, its subject matter being a second chance at love.

Jane herself did not marry, though her family talk of an early love. She lived without pretension or fanfare, as obedient daughter, loving aunt and sister, and the most accomplished comic novelist in the English language.

Shelley's Monster Arises from a Dream

London, England, January 1, 1818: Informed sources say that the novel, *Frankenstein*, was published anonymously this year, was in fact authored by Mary Wollstonecraft Shelley.

It is concerned with the terrible creation of a living being from the body parts of corpses and the unspeakable outcomes of that act. The creative basis of the novel itself, while not as extraordinary as the source of Frankenstein's monster, is memorable in its own right.

In the summer of 1816, Mary (as yet unmarried) and her lover, the poet Percy Bysshe Shelley, were living in Switzerland with the poet Lord Byron, his physician John Polidori, and Clair Clairmont. The group enjoyed scaring themselves with German ghost stories, and on June 16 they challenged one another to write their own story of supernatural terror. Neither of the poets produced such a work but Polidori is working on a vampire story and Mary Shelley created the shocking and tragic tale of Frankenstein and his monster.

She says that inspiration came in the form of a vision, somewhere between sleep and waking, of "the hideous phantasm of a man … behold, the horrid thing stands at his bedside, opening his curtains." Some of the story's impetus came from Mary's interest in the experiments of the Italian scientist, Luigi Galvani, and some, perhaps, from her personal griefs over the death of her mother at her birth and her own dead infant.

Mary Shelley

Adams's Plea: "All Men Would be Tyrants"

Massachusetts, USA, October 28, 1818: Abigail Adams, the wife of the second President of the United States, died today of typhoid aged 74.

In 1764, this daughter of a Massachusetts Congregationalist minister, married a young lawyer, John Adams. Abigail endured lengthy periods of separation, managing their farm while he travelled the court circuits and later served as delegate to the Continental Congress. His diplomatic duties took them both to Paris in 1784 and England in 1785.

From 1797 to 1801, Abigail supported and advised John in his presidency of the United States. She championed women's education and, in a letter to her husband, argued for women's rights: "Do not put such unlimited power into the hands of the Husbands … all Men would be tyrants if they could." This is a sentiment shared by many women, and men would do well to heed Abigail's words.

The Adams mansion in Quincy, Massachusetts, where Abigail Adams died this year.

Tracing a Disease of the Blood

Caroline of Brunswick

Bonn, Germany, 1820: Hemophilia has long been a mysterious disease. Why do some infants develop massive bruising when they have only experienced the usual tumbles and collisions that are part of early childhood? Why are some children either unable, or slow, to stop bleeding? Why do sufferers develop joint pain? Is there any way to prevent their untimely deaths from accidents that would leave others almost unscathed?

The mysteries of hemophilia's cause and cure are yet to be understood, but the Canadian, Dr Christian Friedrich Nasse, has articulated a rule that only males are affected, and that the disease is inherited by male children from their mothers. This builds on the work of Dr John Otto who traced hemophilia or "hemorrhagic fever" through three generations of a New Hampshire family.

Once Nasse's rule becomes generally known, it may well produce difficulties for women. Already Christian doctrine lays heavy emphasis on the sinfulness of Eve. The knowledge that hemophilia is passed on through the female has the potential to reinforce misogynistic attitudes toward women, connecting this gender-linked inheritance to Eve's punishment in Genesis. Nasse's law, as is scientifically proper, attributes no blame to women for the transmission of hemophilia, but it is likely also to reinforce the belief that during conception the man contributes the vital spark of life and the woman contributes only the matter, that is, the body.

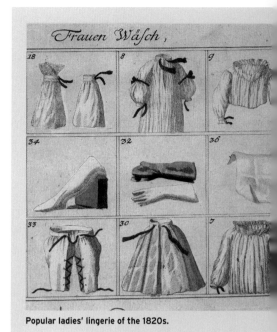
Popular ladies' lingerie of the 1820s.

> *"I SLEPT, AND DREAMED THAT LIFE WAS BEAUTY; I WOKE, AND FOUND THAT LIFE WAS DUTY."*
>
> ELLEN STURGIS HOOPER (1816–1841), AMERICAN POET

Louisa Chatterley in *The School for Scandal*.

America's First Saint?

Maryland, USA, January 4, 1821: Could Elizabeth Ann Seton become America's first saint? She was born on August 28, 1774 into the wealthy New York Bayley family, expected in due course to join high society, marry well, and entertain while her husband multiplied his fortune. The Bayleys were Episcopalian, but by the time Elizabeth Ann died today, she had converted to Catholicism, and pioneered parochial school education in America.

Little in her journey from Elizabeth Ann to Mother Seton was easy. In 1794 she married a successful businessman, William Seton, and had five children. William's shipping business went into bankruptcy, and then he fell victim to tuberculosis. They traveled to Italy for his health, but the Livorno authorities kept them for months in chilly quarantine. William's health became worse, and he died in Livorno in 1803.

time out

An ancient, armless statue of the goddess of love, Aphrodite, discovered on the Greek island of Melos has been given the name "Venus de Milo," and is already having a huge influence on contemporary sculpture.

With five children and few financial resources, Elizabeth was befriended by the Catholic Filicchi family and, with their support and instruction, by the time she returned to New York, had inwardly converted to Catholicism. Against her relatives' and friends' wishes she took her first communion in 1805. Impoverished and disowned by some of her family, she tried teaching at Episcopalian schools in New York, only to have some parents remove their children in protest. Then she was invited by the Reverend Louis Dubourg to start a Catholic girls' school in Baltimore. Saint Joseph's Academy and Free School opened in 1810 and is now run by members of a new religious order, the Sisters of Charity, over which Elizabeth presided for the rest of her life. As their numbers increase, the good works of the Sisters continue to multiply, and they now run the first Catholic orphanage in Philadelphia, and another in New York.

Bonn, Germany, 1820: Christian Friedrich Nasse discovers that hemophilia affects males only and is carried and inherited from females.

Maryland, USA, January 4, 1821: Elizabeth Ann Seton, founder of the Sisters of Charity, dies, aged 47.

Bristol, England, May 2, 1821: Hester Thrale, diarist, patron of the arts, and friend to writer Samuel Johnson, dies, aged 80.

London, England, August 21, 1821: Popular actress, playwright, and novelist, Elizabeth Inchbald, dies, aged 68.

London, England, August 7, 1821: Caroline of Brunswick, wife of King George IV, dies, aged 53.

South America, 1821: El Salvador, Guatemala, Honduras, Nicaragua, and Peru all gain their independence from Spain.

Troy, New York, USA, 1821: Emma Willard, educator and women's rights supporter, opens the first secondary school for girls.

England, 1822: Louisa Chatterley appears as Lady Teazle in Sheridan's *School for Scandal*.

Sussex, England, 1822: Mary Mantell discovers some fossilized teeth, later identified as belonging to the iguanodon, one of the first dinosaur discoveries.

Grenoble, France, 1822: Jean-François Champollion deciphers the hieroglyphs on the Rosetta Stone.

London, England, February 7, 1823: Ann Radcliffe, author of Gothic novels, dies, aged 59.

Spain, October 1, 1823: After French troops free Ferdinand VII and restore him to the throne, he revokes the nation's Constitution.

Jena, Germany, 1823: Johann Döbereiner produces fire by the interaction of air, hydrogen, and platinum. His "lighters" become popular accessories.

Vermont, USA, 1823: Alexander Lucius Twilight is the first African-American to graduate from college.

Dülmen, Germany, February 9, 1824: Anna Katharina Emmerick, a nun said to have received the stigmata of Christ, dies, aged 50.

Lima, Peru, February 10, 1824: Simón Bolívar is named as dictator of the new republic of Peru.

Missolonghi, Greece, April 19, 1824: Lord Byron, poet, dies, aged 36.

London, England, June, 1824: Nine-year-old Caroline Crachami, "the smallest person in history," dies.

Australia, 1824: Matthew Flinders's suggestion to name the Great South Land "Australia" is adopted.

Massachusetts, USA, 1824: Lydia Maria Child, novelist, journalist, and abolitionist, writes *Hobomok*, the first historical novel published in the United States. The book tells of the love between a Puritan girl and a native American.

Hester Thrale was a friend to many artistic people.

Dr Johnson's Friend, Mrs Thrale, Dead at 80

Bristol, England, May 2, 1821: Hester Lynch Piozzi, who died today, was better known as Mrs Thrale, the patroness and close friend of Dr Samuel Johnson. Mrs Thrale was born Hester Lynch Salusbury in Wales on January 16, 1741. She made a sensible, if initially reluctant, marriage to Henry Thrale, owner of a brewery. She enjoyed the company of the literary giants of her day, including Oliver Goldsmith, Edmund Burke, and Fanny Burney.

Hester first met Samuel Johnson early in 1765, and for almost twenty years she was his hostess, patroness, and confidante, until her husband died in 1781 and she decided to marry a second time for love. She chose an Italian, a Roman Catholic and a music teacher, Gabriel Piozzi, and on all these grounds London society judged the match unacceptable. Her decision estranged Dr Johnson and displeased her own daughters. Nevertheless, Hester married Piozzi in 1784 and found much happiness, first in traveling abroad with her new husband, then in attracting a fresh group of artistic celebrities into her social circle. She was a woman with a great gift for enjoying life. It is her 1786 book of reminiscences, *Anecdotes of the Late Samuel Johnson*, that is her major claim to fame, along with her 1789 *Observations and Reflections Made in the Course of a Journey through France, Italy, and Germany*.

A Passion for the Stage

London, England, August 1, 1821: It is quite an extraordinary feat for one person to succeed as novelist, actor, and playwright, especially when that actor is afflicted with a stammer. Elizabeth Inchbald, who was all these things, died today. Although she had published two novels, her earliest passion was for the stage. She ran away from her Suffolk home at the age of 19 to join the stage, making her debut as a very carefully enunciating Cordelia. Her acting, however, was better appreciated by provincial audiences than London audiences, and when her actor-husband died in 1779, she turned to playwriting to earn a living. Most of her plays are comedies, some are farcical and many are adapted from French originals. Possibly Elizabeth's best memorial is the choice of her play, *Lovers' Vows*, by Jane Austen in her popular novel, *Mansfield Park*, as a test of moral fortitude for Austen's characters.

The Injured Queen of England

London, England, August 7, 1821: "Here lies Caroline, the injured Queen of England." This is what the woman, whose treatment by her husband nearly brought down the monarchy, wanted on her tombstone.

In 1795, George, then Prince of Wales, was deeply in debt and agreed to marry on condition that Parliament paid his debts. Not only enamoured of the Countess of Jersey, he was also secretly married to Mrs Fitzherbert, ineligible as a royal bride because she was Catholic. Princess Caroline of Brunswick stood no chance, even before the prince recoiled from her at their first meeting, reportedly finding her ugly, coarse, and malodorous.

He got through his marital duties with the help of strong liquor. Nine months later, Princess Charlotte was born and the hostile couple separated. For many years, Caroline and George lived sexually scandalous lives, he at court and she, first in London, then in Italy.

When George III died in 1820, no one knew what would happen to Caroline. Would she be by her husband's side as the rightful Queen at the coronation? Could he persuade Parliament to pass a bill to divorce her? Would Caroline retaliate by exposing his affairs and secret marriage? The London mob sided with Caroline. George failed to obtain a divorce, and had the doors of Westminster Abbey barred against her at his coronation. Unwell when she suffered this humiliation, seventeen days later she was dead.

Elizabeth Ann Seton

Queen Caroline will be buried in her native Brunswick.

London, England, February 22, 1825: Poet Eleanor Anne Porden, wife of explorer John Franklin, dies, aged 29.

England, September 27, 1825: The first passenger steam railway in the world opens.

Southeast Asia, 1825: Indonesians revolt against the Dutch colonists in the Java War.

Nashoba, Tennessee, USA, 1825: Frances "Fanny" Wright sets her slaves free and establishes a multiracial community.

USA, 1825-29: Louisa Catherine Adams is the country's First Lady.

Germany, 1826: Georg Simon Ohm formulates the relationship between voltage, current, and resistance (Ohm's Law).

Greece, 1826: Educator, independence fighter, and writer, Evanthia Kairi, calls upon European women to come to the assistance of Greece, which is fighting for independence from the Ottoman Empire.

England, August 12, 1827: Poet, painter, and engraver William Blake dies, aged 69.

Dublin, Ireland, September 1827: Catherine McAuley founds the Sisters of Mercy, whose aims are to care for young girls and the sick.

Austria, 1827: Actress Therese Krones retires from the stage.

Mediterranean Sea, October 20, 1827: Russia, France, and Britain destroy the Turkish and Egyptian armada at the Battle of Navarino.

Peking, China, 1828: Painter Gai Qi dies, aged about 55. His paintings of beautiful women are much sought after by Chinese connoisseurs.

France, 1828: Spanish master painter Francisco de Goya dies, aged about 82.

Madagascar, 1828: Queen Ranavalona takes the throne of Madagascar.

South Africa, 1828: Shaka, founder and dictator of the Zulu empire, is murdered by his half-brothers.

Baltimore, Maryland, USA, July 1829: Mother Mary Elizabeth Lange founds the Oblate Sisters of Providence, the first black order of nuns in the United States.

Salzburg, Austria, October 29, 1829: Musician Maria Anna Mozart, known as Nannerl, dies, aged 78.

Calcutta, India, December 4, 1829: British authorities prohibit the practice of *suttee*, or widow-burning.

Stockbridge, Massachusetts, USA, December 28, 1829: Former slave Mum Bett, later known as Elizabeth Freeman, dies, aged about 80. In 1781, realizing her rights as an equal under the Constitution, she won her freedom in a celebrated court case.

Lydia Maria Child

Reclusive Author of Horror Novels Dies

London, England, February 7, 1823: Mrs Ann Radcliffe has finally and indubitably died. Her death has been falsely reported many times, including a report that her ghost walks. The woman who wrote the most influential novels of the late eighteenth century died from pneumonia at the age of 59. Wild rumors of her confinement to a lunatic asylum sprang from the reclusiveness of an author who suddenly stopped publishing, despite the critical and commercial triumph of her Gothic novels. She seems to have been an extraordinarily shy woman, with her husband, William Radcliffe, as her only friend and companion. As a result, Mrs Radcliffe's remaining years of life, after the 1797 publication of *The Italian*, have attracted the most lurid of speculations, as though she were a combination of the villain and heroine of her own novels.

The novelist was born Ann Ward on July 9, 1764. Little is known about her family except that her father was in trade as a London haberdasher. One of the few certain facts is her marriage to William Radcliffe, an Oxford graduate who turned to radical journalism. Mrs Radcliffe's first novels, *The Castles of Athlin and Dunbayne* and *A Sicilian Romance*, sit within the Gothic tradition pioneered by Horace Walpole's 1764 *Castle of Otranto*, and mingle with it picturesque evocations of Scottish and Sicilian landscapes and celebrations of the sensitive soul. It was with her third novel, the 1791 *Romance of the Forest*, that Ann Radcliffe attracted great critical acclaim, which led to an unprecedented payment of £500 for her next novel, *The Mysteries of Udolpho* (1794). *The Italian* was another success, but by now she was being attacked by critics as a blasphemer or a revolutionary. Her influence lives on in Lord Byron's brooding heroes, Shelley's rhapsodies, and Jane Austen's affectionate parody, *Northanger Abbey*.

Sad Little Victim of Freak Show Dies

London, England, June 1824: Very little about the life and death of the "Sicilian fairy" or "Sicilian dwarf," Caroline Crachami, stands up to scrutiny. She was supposedly born in Palermo, yet she has come to England not from Sicily but from Ireland, and it is from Ireland that her father has rushed to try to protect his daughter's corpse. The Dr Gilligan who has been exhibiting the unfortunate Caroline Crachami around the country is highly unlikely to be a medical doctor, and the father maintains that he was duped into letting Dr Gilligan have his daughter.

For a few months this year, Caroline has been represented as a curiosity of nature, a nine-year-old freak who is only 19½ inches (50 cm) tall, smaller than a newborn baby. Yet examination of the poor child's teeth indicates that she is no older than three! Even royalty craved the sight of this phenomenon. Gilligan disregarded the fact that Caroline was unwell and kept on with the exhibitions. Within a few months, she was dead from tuberculosis. Without the permission of her parents, the "doctor" sold her body for dissection. To the very end of her short life, the ill-fated child could not escape being put on exhibition; anatomist John Hunter had already done his work when her father arrived.

Caroline's short life and untimely death should provoke public outrage against the exhibition and exploitation of such unfortunate people.

Dramatic Call for Greek Independence

Greece, 1826: Perhaps in ancient Greece a city-state could win its campaigns simply in the field, but for contemporary

The fall of Missolonghi has prompted Evanthia Kairi's plea for help.

Greece to achieve its lengthy quest for independence from Turkish rule, Evanthia Kairi believes that much more than physical combat is needed.

The Greek fighters for independence are looking for material and moral support from the rest of Europe, and the writer and educator, Evanthia is using her eloquence both to inspire the Greek forces and to appeal to women's organizations outside Greece for help.

Now that the garrison at Missolonghi has finally fallen to Turkish forces, she has composed a play, *Nikiratos*, dedicated to the Greek women who gave their lives for the cause of independence. Once the struggle is over, Evanthia hopes to set up a school for war orphans on her home island of Andros.

House of Mercy Opens for Poor Women of Dublin

Dublin, Ireland, September 1827: The Dublin poor are rejoicing today as the doors of Catherine McAuley's House of Mercy open for the first time. Two hundred girls hope to enroll in the new Catholic school in Baggot Street, and there is provision also for destitute

Austrian actress Therese Krones retired from the stage in 1827.

women and orphans. All this is the result of Catherine McAuley's generosity, and the hope is that many other women will join the current volunteers and help to educate the poor.

Catherine McAuley has not always been a wealthy woman. Her father, James McAuley, was a well-to-do Dublin businessman and a Catholic, but after his death in 1783, five years after Catherine's birth, his widow Elinor gradually became burdened with many financial worries. Elinor died in 1798 and her three children were taken in by the Protestant Armstrong family.

Over the next five years, Catherine's brother and sister turned to the Protestant faith, but Catherine persisted as a Catholic. She was employed as a companion for a Mrs Callaghan; although the Callaghans forbade any religious images in their house, Catherine was allowed to instruct the Catholic servants, and also to teach at the nearby poor school. Her example of steadfast piety encouraged first Mrs Callaghan to convert to Catholicism, then her husband, just before he died. William Callaghan left a substantial fortune to Catherine McAuley, which has allowed the construction of her House of Mercy.

Widow-burning Banned

Calcutta, India, December 4, 1829: The British authorities in India have finally prohibited *suttee*. Centuries after the Portuguese banned the practice in Goa, long after the French and Dutch made

Actress Elise Hoefer in her dressing room.

it illegal, high-caste Hindu women in British India continued to burn themselves to death on their husbands' funeral pyres. To do so as a freely chosen act of love and respect might be seen as nobly self-sacrificial, but the British, and some Hindus, believed that a great many of these women were either coerced into the act by family and community expectations, or literally forced into the flames.

Lord William Bentinck, the current Governor-General of India, has taken time to weigh up what should be done. Christian missionaries have been putting pressure on the British government to act decisively, but it might prove alienating if Christian beliefs and practices are forced onto the Hindu population. A free-thinker might even question the right of Christians to assume their superiority over all other religious groups. Bentinck also had to take account of the possibility that the Indian soldiers in the army might mutiny again if suttee were banned. No such unrest has as yet followed the passing of the law rendering suttee illegal. However, some are asking what is to become of those widows, who are now abandoned to a protracted living death, despised, impoverished, segregated, now that they no longer have the option of a quicker death by fire.

A widow no longer has to throw herself on her husband's funeral pyre.

Slavery Ruled Unconstitutional

Stockbridge, Massachusetts, USA, December 28, 1829: Elizabeth Freeman, who died this day, was a woman bold enough to hold the Massachusetts Constitution to account. This Constitution, established in 1780, stated that "all men are born free and equal."

Elizabeth Freeman was an African-American slave, who was known then as Mum Bett, and she had not been treated as either free or equal. Her purchaser, Mr John Ashley, regarded her as his property. When Mrs Ashley tried to strike another slave with a heated kitchen shovel, Mum Bett intervened, she took the blow in the slave's place, and was scarred for life.

Elizabeth left the Ashley household and, early in 1781, took her case for freedom to an abolitionist lawyer, Theodore Sedgwick, who was happy to defend her and another male slave, Brom, as test cases. She did not argue mistreatment, rather she sought her freedom as a constitutional right.

John Ashley had favored the introduction of the new Constitution, and Mum Bett had heard discussions about the Bill of Rights and the Constitution when he held political meetings in his house. The jury found in favor of Brom and Bett, and this land-mark judgment eventually led to the abolition of slavery in Massachusetts. Mum Bett changed her name to Elizabeth Freeman and took up properly paid work as housekeeper for the Sedgwicks. As a cherished member of that family, she is to be buried in the Sedgewick family plot.

Maria Anna Mozart

Louisa Catherine Adams, United States First Lady from 1825-1829.

Maria Christina de Bourbon

Death of the Tragic Muse

London, England, June 8, 1831: The writers of books live on in their volumes, artists in their paintings, sculptors in their torsos and busts, but great actors can only live in the descriptions and depictions of others. Sarah Siddons, who died today, was the undisputed queen of the tragic stage, but what words or pictures can capture the queenliness of her presence on stage, the power of her acting or the richness of her voice?

She was born Sarah Kemble in Brecon on July 5, 1755. Her father, Roger Kemble, was an actor-manager and her brothers became actors, but her parents did not want Sarah to marry the actor William Siddons. Instead, she was sent to work as a maid and lady's companion in 1771.

In 1773 her parents finally allowed her to marry Siddons and she began attracting favorable notices for her performances in provincial theaters. In 1775, David Garrick engaged her for a London

> *"… IS IT TO BE UNDERSTOOD THAT THE PRINCIPLES OF THE DECLARATION OF INDEPENDENCE BEAR NO RELATION TO HALF OF THE HUMAN RACE?"*
>
> HARRIET MARTINEAU, 1837, BRITISH WRITER, *SOCIETY IN AMERICA*

time out

The Private Companion of Young Married People by Dr Charles Knowlton is published in 1832 to great outrage. It offers advice on practical birth control methods. The author is imprisoned for indecency, but the book is a bestseller.

season but her performance as Portia in *The Merchant of Venice* was a failure. Over the next six years Sarah refined her craft in the provinces, returning to London in 1782 to make a sensation as the heroine of Southerne's *Isabella*.

For 20 years, she reigned as queen of tragedy at the Drury Lane Theatre, specialising in William Shakespeare's tragic heroines. Macbeth's tormented queen was her most admired role (though some accused her of ranting). Sir Joshua Reynolds painted her as *The Tragic Muse*, and she achieved the acme of acceptance by polite society when she was invited to perform some readings at Buckingham Palace.

Sarah Siddons's farewell performance was as Lady Macbeth in 1812, but she has remained so dear to the public that many thousands are expected to line her funeral route, including every member of the Covent Garden and Drury Lane theatrical companies.

Polish Pianist Dies

St Petersburg, Russia, July 24, 1831: Learning to play the piano, students hope to move from the awkward and discordant to the smooth and accomplished. Maria Szymanowska went beyond mere accomplishment and achieved extraordinary acclaim as a piano virtuoso, enrapturing the courts of Europe and even gaining the writer, Goethe, as an admirer.

Born Marianna Agata Wolowska on December 14, 1789, in Warsaw, Maria's parents fostered her musical talent and education by inviting musicians visiting from abroad into their house. By 1810 Maria was giving public concerts as a pianist in Warsaw and Paris.

Then she married Joseph Szymanowski, who did not approve of these performances. Marriage thus restricted

Sarah Siddons was a true theatrical luminary.

her to a more domestic life—she occasionally gave concerts for a select few in her home and she also began composing. As with so many other female composers, most of her works are for solo piano or accompanied voice, and are intended to be performed in small venues.

After 10 years Maria separated from her husband and once more began giving public concerts in cities across Europe, from London to St Petersburg. Wherever she performed, her piano playing was received enthusiastically. One innovation that she introduced at her recitals was to perform her own piano pieces from memory, a feat that has astonished her audiences at least as much as the virtuosity of her playing. In 1828, Maria settled in St Petersburg where she was appointed to the post of court pianist. Sadly, she succumbed today to cholera.

The November Uprising was a rebellion against Russia.

Hero of the Uprising

Kapciamiestis, Lithuania, December 23, 1831: Countess Emilija Pliateryte (sometimes called Emily Plater) was born in 1806 in Vilnius, in the Grand Duchy of Lithuania, then part of the Russian Empire. During last month's November Uprising, Emilija, a fine horsewoman and sharpshooter,

Sterling, Massachusetts, USA, May 24, 1830: Sarah Hale publishes her collection of poems for children, including "Mary Had a Little Lamb."
London, England, June 8, 1831: Actress Sarah Siddons dies, aged 76.
St Petersburg, Russia, July 24, 1831: Polish pianist and composer, Maria Agata Szymanowska dies, aged 41.
Kapciamiestis, Lithuania, December 23, 1831: Emilija Pliateryte, the Lithuanian rebel leader and heroine of the November Uprising, dies while retreating from the enemy.

USA, 1831: Henry Blair patents a corn planter, becoming the second black person in the USA to be issued with a patent.
England, 1832: British writer Frances Trollope publishes *Domestic Manners of the Americans*, which comments on the people's rudeness and lack of respect. It also gives an unfavorable account of slavery.
Moscow, Russia, 1832: Ballerina Marie Taglioni dances *La Sylphide* at the Bolshoi Theater.

Montego Bay, Jamaica, 1833: Annie Palmer, a practitioner of black magic, is murdered in her sleep, possibly as revenge for allegedly murdering her three husbands.
Canterbury, Connecticut, USA, 1833: Educator Prudence Crandall admits black students to her girls' school. It is illegal to provide a free education to black students, and Crandall is imprisoned.
Spain, 1833: Maria Christina de Bourbon becomes regent for her daughter, the future Queen Isabella.

London, England, 1833: Scientist, mathematician, and astronomer Mary Somerville, who published *The Mechanism of the Heavens*, a translation of Pierre Laplace's *Celestial Mechanics*, in 1831, is admitted as an honorary member of the Royal Astronomical Society.
England, 1833: Parliament passes the *Slavery Abolition Act*, which grants all slaves in the British Empire their freedom.

London, England, July 25, 1834: The Society for the Promotion of Female Education in China, India, and the East is founded by missionary, David Abeel.
Varanasi, India, c. 1834: Lakshimi Bai, Rani of Jhansi and heroine of the independence movement, is born.
Illinois, USA, August 25, 1835: Ann Rutledge, reported to be the first and true love of Abraham Lincoln, dies, aged 22.
London, England, 1835: Wax worker Madame Tussaud opens a wax museum in Baker Street.

Ballerina Marie Taglioni brings an ethereal quality to *La Sylphide*.

formed a fighting group of made up of 280 riflemen, 60 cavalry, and hundreds of scythe-wielding peasants. Her forces captured Zarasai, and with another group took Ukmerge, but failed to win Vilnius. It is said that when General Chlapowski suggested she return home, she replied that she would not take off her uniform until her native land was freed.

Promoted to captain, Emilija refused to retreat to Prussia. Struggling to return to Lithuania, she fell ill and suddenly died in Justinava, a hero of the uprising.

Voodoo Battle at Rose Hall?

Montego Bay, Jamaica, 1833: Jamaicans have been scaring each other with tales of the white witch of Rose Hall, Annie Palmer, a woman who was possibly the Irish-English daughter of missionaries or perhaps French. She may have spent her childhood in Haiti where she learned voodoo, or else she was the child of an Irish missionary and a Haitian voodoo princess. Whatever her origins, all agree that she married John Palmer and moved to Jamaica to live with him in the plantation manor, Rose Hall. Some say that she was unhappy in her marriage, others that he found out she had a slave lover; all agree that she poisoned him.

Then Annie married two more men, each of whom died mysteriously. Autopsies were not performed. Rumor has it that Annie made her slaves bury these men, then forced the slaves into the graves to silence them. It seems that Annie enjoyed torturing slaves as well as sleeping with them.

Annie Palmer was found murdered in her bed, and some suspect that the father of a murdered female slave is responsible, having killed her to avenge his daughter's death. What happened in this house? Was there a voodoo battle at Rose Hall? Whatever the story, it shows the real cruelties inflicted on slaves by their thoughtless or sadistic owners.

Waxing Prosperous

London, England, 1835: To have survived the French Revolution is an achievement; to have memorialized it is the boast of Madame Marie Tussaud.

Marie was born in Strasbourg in 1761, the daughter of Johannes Grosholtz and Anna Walder. Her father died before her birth and her mother moved to Berne to keep house for Dr Philippe Curtius. The doctor's hobby was making anatomical models in wax, a pursuit that developed into wax portraiture. When he opened a wax museum in Berne, the Prince de Conti encouraged Curtius to move to Paris and offer his services at court as a portraitist. He was soon in vogue. He made a wax portrait of King Louis XV and opened a wax museum, Le Cabinet de Cire. To his aristocratic likenesses, he added death-masks of executed criminals.

Marie became his apprentice, showing great talent and modeling fine heads of eminent persons such as Voltaire and Benjamin Franklin. Through the Revolution the doctor and Marie generally prospered, though Marie was temporarily imprisoned. They busied themselves modeling ideal Revolutionary figures and death-masks of guillotine victims from the King and Queen to Charlotte Corday and Maximilien Robespierre.

When Dr Curtius died in 1794, Marie inherited his museum and she continued to exhibit, changing her display as politics changed. In 1795 she married François Tussaud, and in 1802 she transferred her waxworks to England, possibly to leave a bad marriage behind. In England her displays of heads from Revolutionary France, as well as death-masks of recently executed criminals were received with much enthusiasm.

Madame Tussaud's waxworks have been touring Britain for some 30 years, surviving near-disasters such as shipwrecks and fire. She has decided that the time has come to establish her amazing museum in a permanent location in London, at the corner of Baker Street. The museum's capacity to flourish and expand seems as boundless as the British public's insatiable appetite for history and horror.

Madame Tussaud in wax.

Frances Trollope

1835: Halley's Comet reappears.
Southern Africa, 1835: More than 10,000 Boers leave Cape Colony to found the republics of Natal, Transvaal, and Orange Free State. This mass migration becomes known as "The Great Trek."
Denmark, 1835: Hans Christian Andersen publishes his *Fairy Tales*.
Wyoming, USA, July, 1836: Narcissa Prentiss Whitman and Eliza Hart Spalding, traveling with their husbands, become the first European women to cross the Rocky Mountains.

France, 1836: Marie Lavoisier, editor, translator, illustrator, and collaborator with her husband, chemist Antoine Lavoisier, dies, aged about 78.
St Petersburg, Russia, February 10, 1837: Natalya Nikolaevna, wife of writer and poet Aleksandr Pushkin, is widowed when Aleksandr dies from wounds received in a duel while defending her honor.
England, 1837: Sir Isaac Pitman invents shorthand.
Canada, 1837: Black people are given the right to vote.

USA, 1837: Samuel Morse develops the telegraph and invents Morse Code communication.
UK, June 20, 1837: William IV dies and his daughter Victoria accedes to the throne of the United Kingdom of Great Britain, and Ireland.
Stockholm, Sweden, March 7, 1838: Soprano Jenny Lind, who becomes known as the "Swedish Nightingale," makes her operatic debut, as Agathe in Weber's *Der Freischütz*.
London, England, June 28, 1838: Queen Victoria is crowned in Westminster Abbey.

South Hadley, Massachusetts, August 1838: Mt Holyoke Female Seminary, established by Mary Lyon and one of the first colleges for women, has its first graduation ceremony.
Mt Blanc, France, September 4, 1838: Henrietta d'Angeville becomes the first woman to climb to the top of Mt Blanc, France.
Sydney, Australia, September 1838: Philanthropist Caroline Chisholm and her husband emigrate from England to further their philanthropic work.

Quetta, Afghanistan, 1838: The first Anglo-Afghan War erupts when the British governor of India attacks.
England, 1838: *Oliver Twist* by Charles Dickens is published in monthly instalments.
USA, 1838-39: Cherokee Native Americans are forced to relocate; they move westward on the brutal "Trail of Tears."
Staffordshire, England, January 29, 1839: Emma Wedgwood, youngest daughter of pottery manufacturer Josiah Wedgwood II, marries Charles Darwin.

Narcissa Whitman

Missionaries Climb Mountains

Oregon Territory, USA, July, 1836: Narcissa Whitman and Eliza Spalding are the first white women to cross the Rocky Mountains. Both have undertaken this daunting journey as missionaries and the wives of missionaries. Both experienced a calling to this vocation, although neither can have been prepared for the daily life of a missionary with its many challenges and disappointments, or the remoteness from other American families. It remains to be seen whether a childhood conversion—experienced by Narcissa during a revivalist meeting at 11—will prove strong enough to sustain such lonely endeavors.

To make the trip more uncomfortable, when Narcissa and her new husband, Dr Marcus Whitman, set out on the Oregon Trail, she discovered that their traveling companions were to be Eliza and her husband, Henry Spalding, a man whom Narcissa had previously rejected as a suitor. Eliza and Narcissa are unlikely to become close friends.

Narcissa's marriage to Marcus Whitman was not a love match. Wanting to set out as a missionary, she discovered that the American Board would not send her to try to convert the Native Americans unless she was married. The bride and groom had known one another for less than a week before their marriage on February 18, this year.

Nevertheless, this aspect of the missionary life seems to be happy enough for the Whitmans. Both women are reported to be coping well with the long, exhausting, daily horse-rides and poor food.

Which Lamb? Which Mary?

Boston, USA, 1837: Everyone now knows the nursery rhyme, "Mary Had A Little Lamb," from Sarah Hale's 1830 *Poems for Our Children,* but whose lamb is it? And whose poem? Sarah insists that the poem is entirely her own work and that the lamb existed only in her imagination.

However, Mary Sawyer Tyler, a woman from Somerville, Massachusetts, claims to have inspired the poem when a pet lamb followed her to school in 1815. Mary says that a young man then gave her a poem whose first lines were identical to those of the Hale poem. With no young man to question and the pet lamb undoubtedly long since eaten, Mrs Hale's case for authorship prevails.

Born Sarah Josepha Buell in Newport, New Hampshire, on October 24, 1788, Hale was the daughter of a Revolutionary War veteran turned farmer. In 1813 she married David Hale, a lawyer, and the couple had five children before he died

Soprano Jenny Lind is known as the "Swedish Nightingale."

nine years later in 1822. Sarah needed an income to support her family, and after trying millinery she turned to writing.

Her first book of poetry, *The Genius of Oblivion,* was published in 1823 with the financial backing of her husband's Freemason Lodge. In 1827 she was invited to edit the Boston-based *Ladies' Magazine* and now she is preparing to edit *Godey's Lady's Book.* Sarah Hale continues to promote the cause of women's education and publish only original contributions.

Duel Proves Nothing

St Petersburg, Russia, February 10, 1837: Duelling is not, as writers like to portray it, an age-old code of Russian aristocratic behavior but quite a novel institution, introduced in the eighteenth century from Western Europe. It originated in the medieval tournament and was believed, in its original context, to demonstrate the rights and wrongs of a dispute, based on the assumption that God would favor the side whose cause was good. It was clear, however, that even when tournaments flourished, might and right did not always coincide.

Duels in contemporary Russia are fought over questions of honor, including that of one's wife. Yet clearly no duel can uphold the reputation of a duellist's spouse. At best, it can attest to the duellist's skill as a pistol-shooter or swordsman, his bravery, and at times his willingness not to shoot

to kill. Yet there has been almost a mania for duelling among Russian aristocrats, including today's senseless killing of the great poet, Aleksandr Pushkin over an alleged slur to his honor—the accusation that his wife, Natalya Nikolaevna, had cuckolded him.

It is not known why Pushkin went ahead with the challenge to Georges d'Anthès. Two months ago Pushkin had challenged d'Anthès to a duel, but quickly retracted the challenge when he learned that d'Anthès was engaged to be married to Ekaterina Goncharova, Natalya's sister. D'Anthès had undoubtedly been pursuing Natalya, but rumors suggest that Pushkin's real rival was the tsar! The truth matters little, for in the end, a great poet's life is snuffed out, leaving only darkness and his written word.

No Man has Climbed Higher

Mt Blanc, France, September 4, 1838: Two women dispute the claim to have made the first female ascent of Mt Blanc. In 1808, an 18-year-old Chamonix maidservant, Marie Paradis, was dragged up to the summit, overcome with altitude sickness, and her climb was not counted as the first official ascent. Today, at age 44, Henrietta d'Angeville has managed to climb to the top despite an attack of altitude sickness, the first climb by "any woman capable of remembering her impressions," as she puts it. For the ascent she wore a large cloak, plaid trousers, a bonnet, veil, and boa. At the summit she wrote letters to her friends. She instructed her guides to lift her 4 feet (1.2 m) into the air so that she could reach a height greater than any male predecessor.

Mont Blanc has been conquered by a woman, Henrietta d'Angeville.

George Sand

Victoria is crowned Queen of the United Kingdom.

Long May She Reign

London, England, June 28, 1838: The coronation today of Queen Victoria is being compared everywhere with the coronation of Queen Elizabeth, almost 300 years ago. Will England become as great a power in the world now as it was then? Will its army and navy rule, as in Elizabethan times? Will its literature, art, and music enjoy a second Renaissance?

The Victorian Age begins with great popular goodwill toward this 19-year-old monarch, whose mother has so very carefully protected her from the scandals and dissipations of the court. It is widely hoped that Victoria will soon marry her German cousin, Prince Albert. Already observers have been very impressed by Victoria's collected regal behavior at the sad news of her royal uncle's death on June 20, 1837, and by her evident interest in political matters. Nevertheless, the new Queen understands that a monarch's duty is to be impartial, hard though this may prove for an ardent admirer of the Whigs and hater of the Tories.

Victoria has had to endure a couple of family difficulties on her way to the throne. The Queen's uncle, George, Duke of Cumberland, who would have been king now if male primogeniture rules of succession applied, is rumored to be longing to rule Great Britain, and has even sounded out the Duke of Wellington for his support in this suit. Yet such support is unlikely to be forthcoming.

Victoria's uncle, the late King, William IV, resented her mother's efforts to keep Victoria from the court and he made no secret of his determination to live until Victoria came of age and could rule in her own right, rather than with her mother as regent. The Queen celebrated her 18th birthday on May 24 last year, just a month before the King died, and so his wishes have been granted.

Many thousands of people have assembled in London's streets to witness the magnificent royal procession, as well as the free theater performances to be held afterward, along with tonight's fireworks and. May Queen Victoria's reign be long, happy and prosperous.

"Better Than a Dog"

Staffordshire, England, January 29, 1839: In 1836 Charles Darwin returned from his long sea voyage on the *Beagle* and gave thought to how he should shape the rest of his life. He was wondering whether or not to marry, and drew up a checklist of the advantages and disadvantages of the married state. Some of the disadvantages included worries about "wasting" his time, losing the freedom to go where he liked, and having less money to spend on books. The advantages included the prospect of companionship in his old age and someone to be "beloved and played with—better than a dog anyhow."

After careful reflection Darwin decided that the advantages prevailed, and made a proposal of marriage to his childhood friend and cousin, Emma Wedgwood. After a three-month engagement, they were married today at St Peter's Church. Emma is the youngest daughter of Josiah Wedgwood II and Elizabeth Allen. The Wedgwoods are a wealthy family, their fortune derived from the first Josiah Wedgwood's pottery business.

Emma and her sister Fanny, two years her elder, were nicknamed the Doveleys. The Wedgwood family is Unitarian and Emma's devout faith was strengthened when Fanny fell ill with cholera and died in 1832. She is a little concerned about Charles's dedication to scientific proof in matters spiritual. However dearly he loves Emma, Charles Darwin is unlikely to put Christian doctrine and faith ahead of his scientific efforts to collect, categorize, and account for the amazing diversity of plant and animal species in the world.

Chemist Antoine Lavoisier owed much of his success to the diligent work of his wife Marie (seated).

Caroline Chisholm

*"LITTLE DROPS
OF WATER,
LITTLE GRAINS
OF SAND,
MAKE THE
MIGHTY OCEAN
AND THE
BEAUTEOUS
LAND."*

JULIA A. CARNEY, 1845,
LITTLE THINGS

*"A WOMAN IS A
FOREIGN LAND,
OF WHICH,
THOUGH THERE
HE SETTLE
YOUNG,
A MAN WILL
NE'ER QUITE
UNDERSTAND
THE CUSTOMS,
POLITICS AND
TONGUE."*

COVENTRY KERSEY
DIGHTON PATMORE
(1823–1896), AN ANGEL
IN THE HOUSE

Government Finally Backs Caroline Chisholm

Sydney, Australia, 1841: Caroline Chisholm has been, for three years, a regular visitor to the Sydney wharves, meeting each ship that brings immigrants to the colony, and offering help to the newly arrived, unemployed female immigrants. Finally the Governor has agreed to support her philanthropic efforts, allowing her to use part of the old immigration barracks as a female immigrant house. This building can house more than 90 women, but it is Mrs Chisholm's hope that soon its services will no longer be needed. She is going to travel inland, seeking employment opportunities for these women in the Australian bush. Previously, during the time when her husband was posted to Madras by the East India Company, she set up a successful Female School of Industry for the Daughters of European Soldiers.

Sojourner Truth is Born

New York, USA, June 1, 1843: The name Sojourner Truth is a new one, adopted today by the woman formerly called Isabella Van Wagener. It sums up her plan to travel across the United States, spreading the truth that she says is revealed to her by the Holy Spirit.

Already Sojourner Truth has journeyed a long way from her humble origins as an African-American slave. She was born in about 1797 on a New York State plantation, daughter of Elizabeth and James Baumfree. She was sold in 1808, and then sold again. Her final purchaser, in 1810, was John Dumont, who treated her very cruelly. Five years later, Sojourner fell in love with a slave from another plantation whose owner beat him mercilessly when he caught them together, because the

child she was expecting would bring him no profit. In 1817 the Dumonts forced her to marry another slave. Several of their children were sold.

Although the young woman was well aware that slavery was to be abolished in New York State in July 1827, driven by unjust treatment she escaped in 1826, seeking refuge with the abolitionists Isaac and Mary Van Wagener, who bought out her freedom. Quakers helped her to win a court case to regain her son Peter, who was illegally sold to an Alabama purchaser. In 1829 she joined a New York religious group, known as the Retrenchment Society, as a housekeeper, where she developed her talents as a preacher. Now Sojourner Truth is ready to preach to the world.

Bliss for Barrett and Browning

London, England, September 19, 1846: Elizabeth Barrett and Robert Browning, the poets who have eloped, are now presumed to be on their way to Paris en route to an Italian retreat. They married a week ago at St Marylebone Parish Church, but have kept the marriage secret until now, Elizabeth returning home to Wimpole Street. Her father has long made it clear that he would not approve of any marriage partners for his children, and it is unlikely that Edward Barrett will ever forgive his daughter.

> ### time out
> On May 1, 1840, the world's first official adhesive postage stamp went into circulation throughout England. The Penny Black, which costs one penny, bears a depiction of 21-year-old Queen Victoria.

Indeed, the fact that she is physically capable of eloping is remarkable. Since 1841 she has been an invalid, confined to her room, unable even to walk to the door. She has been in delicate health ever since the age of 15, when she suffered an illness of the spine that had the doctors baffled. From childhood, Elizabeth was an ardent scholar with a particular love for classical Greek literature. She began writing as a child and her father paid for the publication of her first volume of poetry in 1820. So far she has published five collections of poetry which have pleased most readers, but in recent times, her father has become her harshest critic.

It is through her reading and correspondence that Elizabeth has kept in

The grand marriage of Queen Victoria and Prince Albert.

Key Events

London, England, January 6, 1840: Novelist Fanny Burney dies, aged 87.

London, England, February 10, 1840: Queen Victoria marries her cousin, Prince Albert of Saxe-Coburg-Gotha.

Canada, 1840: *Act of Union* unites upper and lower Canada.

USA, 1840: The *Selected Letters* of former First Lady, Abigail Adams, who died in 1818, published.

USA, 1840: The Austrian Romantic ballerina Fanny Elssler begins her American tour.

Sydney, Australia, 1841: Philanthropist Caroline Chisholm establishes the Female Immigrants House, providing shelter and employment for women arriving from the United Kingdom.

Paris, France, 1841: *Giselle,* the first great Romantic ballet, premières.

Connecticut, USA, 1841: Educator Catherine Esther Beecher publishes *A Treatise on Domestic Economy for the Use of Young Ladies at Home and at School,* which examines women's roles in society.

Paris, France, March 30, 1842: French artist Elisabeth Vigée-Lebrun, known for her work in portraiture, dies, aged 86.

France, 1842: Cristina Trivulzio, Princess Belgioioso, publishes the first of her works on the Catholic Church, *Essai sur la formation du dogme catholique.*

New York, USA, June 1, 1843: Former slave Isabella Van Wagener changes her name to Sojourner Truth, and becomes an evangelist and an advocate for oppressed people in America.

London, England, June 1843: Queen Victoria formally proclaims Hong Kong a British crown colony.

England, 1843: Ada Byron Lovelace translates and annotates *A Sketch of the Analytical Engine,* a work by Italian mathematician Luigi Menabrea on Charles Babbage's analytical engine.

England, 1843: Brunel's SS *Great Britain* is launched, the first iron screw-propelled steamship.

New Zealand, 1843: The Maoris revolt against the British.

China, 1844: Chinese pirate and former prostitute Cheng I Sao dies, aged about 59. She is said to have commanded over 2,000 ships.

Ireland, 1844: Francis Rynd, physician, invents the hypodermic syringe and administers the first subcutaneous injection.

Hampshire, England, March 22, 1845: Cassandra Austen, sister of novelist Jane Austen, dies, aged 72.

Bologna, Spain, September 7, 1845: Soprano Isabella Colbran, wife of Italian composer Gioacchino Rossini dies, aged 61.

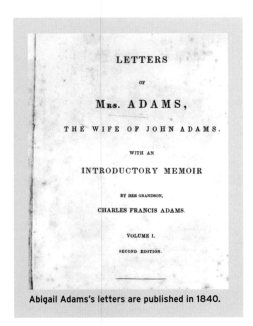

Abigail Adams's letters are published in 1840.

touch with contemporary culture and intellectual life. One of the authors she discovered was the aspiring poet Robert Browning, and she enjoyed his "Bells and Pomegranates" series of plays and poems so much that she made favorable mention of them in her ballad, "Lady Geraldine's Courtship." In January 1845 he responded with a letter, then another, and although Elizabeth had become a recluse, by May she had allowed Robert Browning to visit her. The blissful couple states that their courtship took place mainly through correspondence—almost 600 letters. It was Elizabeth's father's refusal to permit her to winter in Italy on doctors' advice that precipitated the elopement.

Death of a Mendelssohn

Berlin, Germany, May 14, 1847: Fanny and Felix Mendelssohn were brother and sister, both musical prodigies and prolific composers. Yet Felix's career as a composer was encouraged, while Fanny was allowed, for much of her life, to shine only in a restricted social circle. Her parents, Abraham and Lea Mendelssohn, gave her the same excellent musical

education as her brother, but discouraged her from public performances, however brilliant her talents. Even her brother discouraged her from publishing her works under her own name, though he did publish some of her songs as part of his own Opus 8 and 9. The restrictions placed on her as a performer meant that her creativity found its outlet at first in solo piano pieces and lieder, such as could be performed at home.

In 1829, at the age of 24, Fanny married Wilhelm Hensel. With his encouragement, she launched a series of more ambitious salon concerts with a choir and a group of musicians. The range of her compositions increased to include oratorio and cantata. In 1839 Fanny and her husband spent a happy year in Italy, far from the restrictions of life in Berlin. Finally Fanny began to publish her works under her own name. Her sudden death has left the project unfinished. There is now speculation that her family will release the compositions that still remain unpublished.

Fanny Mendelssohn was a true creative force.

Mary Lamb, Collaborator and Killer

London, England, May 20, 1847: Only now that Mary Lamb has died are her friends willing to reveal the true facts about her madness. For many years, Mary Lamb has been portrayed to the world as her brother's protector as they amicably shared a house. Now it can be revealed that Charles Lamb was made Mary's legal guardian in 1797 when she was found unfit to stand trial after killing her mother and attempting to kill her father. On September 22, 1796, Mary stabbed her mother to death with a carving knife at the dinner table, then threw a fork at her father, injuring him slightly, before being restrained. She had already shown signs of mental illness.

There have been suggestions that the manic state in which she attacked her parents was brought on by stress. Mania has since been her lifelong companion. Mary's life before this point had been very restricted. Her father had worked as a manservant to Samuel Salt, a member of parliament and a lawyer, but after his employer's death, he and his wife lived with Mary and their son Charles in a very small set of rooms. Mary worked as a mantua-maker, and had the onerous responsibility of caring for her invalid mother, with no prospect of escape to an independent life or marriage. Her murderous deed freed her from the drudgery of this existence. After a stay in a private madhouse in Islington, she was released into her brother's care (even though he too had recently been mentally ill). For the rest of his life, until he died in December, 1837, brother and sister lived together. Mary was able to recognize the symptoms of incipient mania and she regularly committed herself to the madhouse until she was well enough to return home. Her best-known work is the 1807 *Tales from Shakespeare*, written in collaboration with her brother.

Elizabeth Barrett

Ireland, 1845-50: Potato blight causes famine, and begins mass migration to Britain and the USA.
Lowell, Massachusetts, USA, February 1846: Labor leader Sarah Bagley becomes the first female telegrapher at the new telegraph office.
London, England, September 12, 1846: Poet Elizabeth Barrett secretly marries Robert Browning.
USA, 1846: The editor of *Godey's Lady's Book*, Sarah Josepha Hale, begins a 17-year campaign to establish the Thanksgiving holiday.

New York, USA, January 30, 1847: Virginia Clemm Poe, who married her cousin, the writer Edgar Allan Poe, at the age of 14, dies aged 24.
Germany, May 14, 1847: Pianist, composer, and sister of composer Felix Mendelssohn, Fanny Cecilia Mendelssohn Hensel dies, aged 42.
London, England, May 20, 1847: Writer Mary Lamb, who co-wrote *Tales From Shakespeare* with her brother and guardian, Charles Lamb, dies, aged 82. In 1796, she killed her mother with a carving knife.

Edinburgh, Scotland, November 15, 1847: Scottish obstetrician James Simpson uses chloroform to alleviate labor pain during childbirth.
London, England, September, 1847: Opera singer Jenny Lind creates the role of Amelia in Verdi's *I Masnadieri*.
England, 1847: Charlotte Brontë publishes *Jane Eyre*, her sister Emily *Wuthering Heights*, and youngest sister Anne *Agnes Grey*.
Lowell, Massachusetts, USA, 1847: The women's labor union, the Lowell Female Industrial Reform and Mutual Aid Society, is founded.

New York, USA, July 19, 1848: Abolitionists and feminists, Lucretia Mott and Elizabeth Cady Stanton, convene the first women's rights convention, addressing issues including a woman's right to divorce.
Massachusetts, USA, November 23, 1848: The Female Medical Educational Society is established.
Massachusetts, USA, 1848: Astronomer Maria Mitchell becomes the first woman to be elected to the American Academy of Arts and Sciences after her discovery last year of a comet.

New York, USA, January 23, 1849: English-born Elizabeth Blackwell becomes the first woman to graduate from medical school.
Yorkshire, England, May 28, 1849: Novelist Anne Brontë dies, aged 29.
Portugal, 1849: Antónia Gertrudes Pusich publishes a magazine devoted to women's rights.

Charlotte Bronte

Pain-free Childbirth!

Edinburgh, Scotland, November 15, 1847: Women everywhere are rejoicing as news spreads of the first childbirth rendered painless through ether and, more recently still, the use of a superior anesthetic—chloroform. Ether's power to render the mind senseless to pain has been known for some time, but it was only last year that William Morton demonstrated its usefulness in dentistry. This January, the innovative surgeon Sir James Simpson successfully anesthetized a woman in childbirth with ether, but the substance is flammable and irritates the mouth and nose. Today, he gave the first public demonstration of anesthesia using chloroform, which has none of these problems (though its long-term effects remain unknown).

The benefits of anesthetics are obvious, yet already opposition is mounting. Some are arguing for pain as a useful diagnostic tool, but others say that this has nothing to do with the amputation of limbs or difficult childbirths.

Others argue that experiencing pain is morally beneficial; this would seem to be the opinion of men who have never given birth or suffered the agonies of major surgery. Yet others claim that God has wisely imposed the pangs of childbirth on women as punishment for Eve's sin, and that to remove the pain is to tamper with God's intent. But surely God imposed the effort of labor, not its attendant agonies, on womankind, and to alleviate those agonies is a work of compassion, as amply demonstrated today.

Sing on, Nightingale!

Stockholm, Sweden, December, 1847: What a triumphant year for Jenny Lind, who is widely known as the "Swedish Nightingale." Having enraptured her Viennese audience as Marie in *La Fille du Regiment,* she came to London and made her debut as Alice in *Robert le Diable,* performing in the presence of Queen Victoria and Prince Albert. Informed sources report that the Queen was delighted with the Swedish Nightingale's voice and acting, and the London public acclaimed her even more highly when she sang Amelia in *I Masnadieri,* a part written for her by Giuseppe Verdi.

Her provincial tour of Britain has been a further success, delighting audiences from Glasgow to Exeter, from Norwich to Liverpool.

These triumphs are all the sweeter because in 1841 she strained her voice and there was thought to be some danger that she might be prematurely ending her singing career. It was the excellent work of singing teacher Manuel García in Paris that rescued her voice, when he prescribed a period of silence and then almost a year of singing lessons before she returned to the Stockholm stage. Miss Lind is now thinking of retiring from the operatic stage after only five years of glory, to the great disappointment of her devotees, but she promises that she will continue to sing in oratorio and perform in concerts. Seeking new worlds to conquer, Jenny Lind is very likely to undertake an extensive concert tour of the United States of America.

Miss Mitchell's Comet

Massachusetts, USA, 1848: Accolades are flowing to Maria Mitchell, the discoverer of "Miss Mitchell's comet." Her life has not been unlike that of Caroline Herschel, the first woman to discover a comet 61 years ago. Like Caroline Herschel, Maria Mitchell had a very close association with another astronomer in her immediate family and learned from him how to use the telescope and to take measurements from the stars. Maria was born on Nantucket Island, Massachusetts, in 1818. Her father, William Mitchell, was a Quaker

Maria Mitchell's astronomy skills have been recognized.

schoolmaster and it was from him that she received some of her early education. Educated as well as any boy, she followed her father's example by becoming a schoolmistress herself, before she turned to librarianship as a profession.

William Mitchell was responsible for regulating ships' chronometers, by way of celestial observations and measurements, for the whaling ships of Nantucket. Maria helped with this and also with her father's work for the United States Coast Survey, which made use of stellar observations. By now highly adept with a telescope, on October 1, 1847, Maria Mitchell discovered the comet that was soon given her name. For a short time, another astronomer was credited with this, but his comet-spotting came two days after hers. Among the honors she has received for this discovery is her election to the American Academy of Arts and Sciences. She is its first female member.

The Fight for Equality Goes On

New York, USA, July 19, 1848: In 1840 the men in charge of the World Anti-Slavery Convention in London refused to allow

The pains of childbirth are now a thing of the past, with Dr Simpson's anesthetic coming to the rescue.

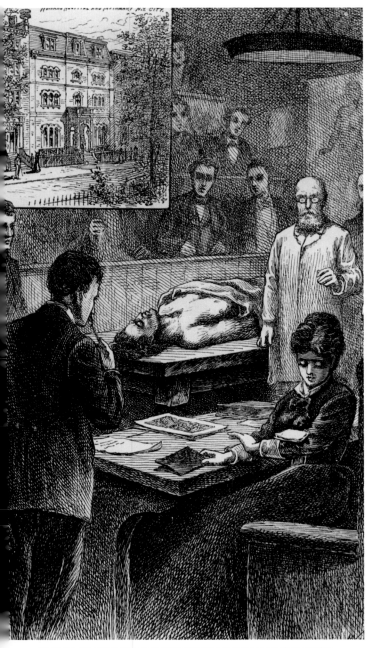

Elizabeth Blackwell has made history by graduating in medical studies.

Lucretia Mott

women delegates to participate. They had to sit in segregation from the men. This blatant display of misogyny has inspired two of its victims, the delegate Lucretia Mott and audience member Elizabeth Cady Stanton, to organize a Women's Rights Conference at Seneca Falls in New York State.

The first women's rights meeting to be held in the United States, it has passed resolutions affirming women's rights of all kinds, including the right to vote in elections. "We hold these truths to be self-evident, that all men and women are created equal," is Mott and Stanton's correction to the American Declaration of Independence, as voiced in their Declaration of Sentiments.

Both women recall specific realizations that inspired their campaign. Lucretia Mott, born into a Nantucket Quaker family and well educated in the Quaker tradition, became a teacher and soon discovered that male teachers were paid twice as much as women. It was Elizabeth

Stanton's father, an attorney, who unwittingly provided his daughter with her early insights into inequity, via his law books. She read a host of laws that openly deny women the rights freely afforded to men. Elizabeth Stanton refuses to be known as Mrs Henry Stanton. For these fighting spirits, the quest for equality shapes their whole life.

First Female Doctor

New York, USA, January 23, 1849: Another advance has been made by women today with Elizabeth Blackwell's graduation from Geneva College as a doctor. She is the first woman to graduate from medical school. Her family came to the United States from England in 1832 when she was 11 years old. Her father, a sugar refiner, was a committed abolitionist. Elizabeth was committed to a medical career but was rejected by Yale, Harvard and all New York City and Philadelphia medical schools. When she looked beyond the cities to New York State and applied to the Geneva College, the faculty asked its students to vote on her application and the students voted her in, believing it was a hoax. She has had to fight prejudice and condescension all through her medical training, so she can be proud of her achievement.

A Sad Year for the Brontës

Yorkshire, England, May 28, 1849: This has been a terrible 12 months for the Brontë family. The Reverend Patrick Brontë must be deploring the bleakness of the Yorkshire climate which has helped destroy the health of yet another of his daughters, Anne, who died today. Already the parsonage family has endured the death from cancer of Patrick's wife, Maria, in 1821, shortly after they moved to the village of Haworth. In 1852 Patrick's two oldest daughters, Maria and Elizabeth, fell ill and died of tuberculosis after enduring harsh conditions and poor food at school.

Their sister, writer Charlotte Brontë, has described these conditions with passionate indignation in her pseudonymously published novel, *Jane Eyre*.

Now delicate Anne has died of tuberculosis, despite her last-minute trip to Scarborough in the hope that the change of climate might keep her alive. Anne published two novels, the 1847 *Agnes Grey* and the 1848 *The Tenant of Wildfell Hall.* It is believed that she returned home in June 1845 from her position as governess to the Robinson children because of her brother Branwell's indiscreet behavior in the same household, to which she had recommended him as a tutor. Branwell had long been the most troubled of the Brontë children, knowing that he was wasting his talents, and scandalizing the district with his amours. After a possible liaison with Mrs Robinson, and then a decisive rejection from her, he took to laudanum and drink, and suffered delirium tremens. Masked by his addictions was the family scourge, tuberculosis. He died on September 24, 1848. His sister Emily, whose novel *Wuthering Heights* was published in 1847 to no great critical acclaim, caught cold at his funeral and died on December 19.

Now only Charlotte remains, author of the extraordinarily popular *Jane Eyre*, published under the name of Currer Bell in 1847. May her life be long and healthy!

Branwell Brontë painted his sisters—Anne, Emily, and Charlotte.

Florence Nightingale

> "IT'S BUT
> LITTLE GOOD
> YOU'LL DO
> A-WATERING
> LAST YEAR'S
> CROP."
>
> GEORGE ELIOT
> (MARY ANN EVANS),
> 1859, ADAM BEDE

Creator of Frankenstein Dies

London, England, February 1, 1851: Mary Shelley is dead, leaving one surviving son and an immortal novel, *Frankenstein, or the Modern Prometheus*. She was the daughter of philosopher William Godwin, and the campaigner for women's rights, Mary Wollstonecraft, who died shortly after the birth of their daughter. They had gone against their principles and married in order to make Mary's birth legitimate.

Mary grew up as her father's devoted daughter, educated from his library, acquainted with the Godwin circle of radical thinkers. It was there that she met Percy Bysshe Shelley, a married poet. She followed what she considered to be Godwinian principles of free love in eloping with Shelley, but earned her father's lasting disapproval.

It was while the couple were staying with Lord Byron in Geneva that they challenged one other to write a ghost story, a challenge that resulted in *Frankenstein*. Mary and Shelley married in 1816 but found the married state not altogether happy; but after his death by drowning in 1822 she idealized him and set herself the task of editing his works, a labor unaided by the hostility of Shelley's father. Mary managed to support herself by writing more novels, including *Mathilda* (which deals with father-daughter incestuous attraction), and the end-of-the-world story, *The Last Man*. Dutiful daughter, mother, and widow though she was, it is for the sheer terror and horror of her creation, Frankenstein's monster, that Mary Shelley will be best remembered.

time out

In June 1850, *Harper's* magazine is launched in New York City, USA. It contains articles by journalists, politicians, and other writers, and also features the latest in women's fashions.

Harriet Tubman is helping slaves to escape north to Canada.

Mary Shelley's legacy to literature is *Frankenstein*.

Railroad to Freedom

Ontario, Canada, 1851: Born into slavery in Maryland, Harriet Tubman was accustomed to being whipped as a child. Yet even when she was brain-injured from a blow to the head, given by an overseer when she refused to help tie up a would-be runaway, she maintained her spirit of independence and resolve.

This spirit serves her well as she begins her self-appointed task of leading more fugitive slaves to freedom in Canada. She herself escaped in 1849, aided by abolitionists in the Underground Railroad network. Now, promising to shoot any escapees who wish to turn back, she has set off, despite her blackouts, on what she plans will be the first of many trips to the South to conduct slaves northward to Canada, the land of freedom.

Will This Book Bring War?

Massachusetts, USA, March 20, 1852: Harriet Beecher Stowe has been astonished by the hostile reactions from the southern American states to her book, *Uncle Tom's Cabin, or Life Among the Lowly*. While the people of the North weep over the ordeals of her black characters, in the South she is accused of presenting an utterly untrue picture of slavery. She has even received a severed black ear in a letter. In response, she is currently preparing a new book, to be called *The Key to Uncle Tom's Cabin*, which will assemble the facts on which her accounts were based.

Harriet did not come from an abolitionist family. She was born in 1811, the daughter of the Reverend Lyman Beecher, a Congregationalist minister, in Connecticut. In 1832, Beecher moved with

UNCLE TOM'S CABIN;

OR,

LIFE AMONG THE LOWLY.

BY

HARRIET BEECHER STOWE.

VOL. I.

ONE HUNDRED AND FIFTH THOUSAND.

BOSTON:
JOHN P. JEWETT & COMPANY
CLEVELAND, OHIO:
JEWETT, PROCTOR & WORTHINGTON.
1852.

Uncle Tom's Cabin has caused a national stir.

his family to Cincinnati to become president of Lane Theological Seminary. Harriet worked as a teacher and began to write and publish. Across the Ohio River was the slave state, Kentucky, and it was then that she first met escaped slaves, visited a plantation, and began forming abolitionist views. In 1836 she married Calvin Stowe, a professor of theology. The family was not rich and she wrote to supplement their income.

In 1850, the *Fugitive Slave Act* was passed into law, giving legal responsibility to the northern authorities for returning escapees, and in 1851, Harriet experienced a vision during a church service of a bleeding slave being whipped to death. With her husband's tearful encouragement, this developed into *Uncle Tom's Cabin*, published first in weekly instalments and now as a two-volume book.

Such is the power of Stowe's narrative that she is likely to sway public opinion in the North decisively against compromise on the issue of slavery. *Uncle Tom's Cabin* may in future years be seen as the book that brought about an American civil war.

George Sand's Own Story

Paris, France, 1855: George Sand is the nom-de-plume of Amantine Aurore Lucile Dupin, who was born in 1804. Her father was an aristocrat and her mother a commoner. She was partly raised by her grandmother at her Nohant estate, and many of her novels are set nearby in the Berry region of France.

In 1822 she married Baron Dudevant. The couple had two children before separating. Aurore's income diminished upon separation, and before long she attempted a career as a journalist, before collaborating, in 1831, with Jules Sandeau on a novel, *Rose et Blanche*. Her mother-in-law asked her not to pollute the Dudevant name as a writer and so she devised the name "George Sand" from the name of her early collaborator and lover, Sandeau. Along with a male name, she adopted men's clothing; she had first discovered the freedom of dressing as a man when learning to ride a horse.

Sand has been a prolific and popular novelist, writing stories on themes of love and socialism; her talents are best displayed in her shorter works. Dressing as a man, she behaves like another Byron in the ardor of her love affairs and the suddenness of their endings. Among her lovers have been the composer Frédéric Chopin and the novelist Alfred de Musset. The publication this year of her autobiography *Histoire de ma vie (Story of My Life)* builds on the success of her 1842 *Un Hiver à Majorque (A Winter in Majorca)*, which dealt with her liaison with Chopin.

Harriet Beecher Stowe

Florence Nightingale tends wounded soldiers in the military hospital at Scutari in the Crimea.

Crimea, Russia, 1855: Florence Nightingale reforms British military hospitals.

London, England, 1855: Sewers are modernized after the fourth outbreak of cholera.

France, 1855: Novelist and writer Amantine Aurore Lucille Dupin de Francueil, better known as George Sand, publishes her autobiography.

Massachusetts, USA, 1855: Women's rights advocate and abolitionist, Lucy Stone, marries Henry Blackwell, but retains her own name, the first woman to do so.

France, April 1856: Gustave Flaubert publishes the controversial novel *Madame Bovary*, and the following year is charged with crimes against morality.

China, 1856: The Second Opium War; French forces join British.

Balaclava, Crimea, Russia, 1856: Jamaican nurse Mary Seacole, also known as "Mother Seacole," funds and builds the British Hotel for soldiers during the Crimean War.

Paris, France, 1856: Treaty of Paris ends the Crimean War.

India, 1856: The Hindu Widows Re-Marriage Act allows Hindu widows to remarry.

Meerut, India, May 10, 1857: Native Indian troops begin an uprising (Sepoy Mutiny).

New York, USA, May, 1857: Elizabeth Blackwell, Emily Blackwell, and Marie Zakrzewska establish the New York Infirmary for Women and Children.

Madagascar, November, 1857: Queen Ranavalona foils the plot by her son to overthrow her and seize the throne.

London, England, 1857: The *Divorce and Matrimonial Causes Act* makes divorce without parliamentary approval legal. It also gives women some property rights.

Lourdes, France, February 11, 1858: Fourteen-year-old Marie Bernarde (Bernadette) Soubirous sees visions of the Virgin Mary.

England, September 1859: Lady Jane Franklin's years of searching for her husband, Arctic explorer Sir John Franklin, and his crew, come to an end with the return of the *Fox*.

London, England, 1859: Novelist George Eliot (Mary Anne Evans) publishes *Adam Bede*.

London, England, 1859: Charles Darwin publishes *On the Origin of Species by Means of Natural Selection*.

St Petersburg, Russia, 1859: Social reformers Anna Filosova, Nadezhda Stasova, and Mariya Trubnikova found an organization offering cheap housing and schooling to women and their children.

Elizabeth Siddal

Mary Seacole Needs Help

Balaclava, Crimea, Russia, July, 1856: Mary Jane Seacole is returning to England, destitute, after spending her money on helping wounded soldiers in the Crimean War. She was born in Jamaica, probably in 1805, daughter of a Scottish soldier and a free Jamaican mother. Her mother kept a boarding-house for invalid soldiers in Kingston and Mary first learned about healing by watching her mother tend the sick. In about 1822 she set herself up as an independent trader and in 1836 she married Edwin Seacole, who died eight years later. She alternated between commerce and healing, making a name for her skills during the 1850 Jamaican cholera outbreak and the 1851 New Granada epidemic.

When Mary heard of the Crimean War, she went to England to volunteer as a nurse, but was repeatedly turned away because of her skin color. Having been rejected in person by Florence Nightingale, she decided to use her own money to build and open the British Hotel and general store near Balaclava. There she tended all those in need, whether or not they could pay, and she treated casualties from both sides of the battlefield.

Once peace was declared this year, she fell into financial difficulties since her hotel's stock of provisions was no longer marketable. Now Mary Seacole is likely to be declared bankrupt. Can anything be done for the woman who has done so much for others?

Hope for Hindu Widows

Calcutta, India, 1856: After successfully banning the practice of *suttee* (widow-burning), the British government in India has been mindful of the plight of higher-

Mary Seacole nursed casualties of the Crimean War.

caste widows, forbidden to remarry, deemed unlucky by their families, often poorly treated, and sometimes forced into beggary and prostitution. Many widows had been married at a very young age to elderly men; widowed as children, theirs was the worst plight.

Isvararachandra Vidyasagara, the great Sanskrit scholar, has been advocating the legal right of higher caste widows to remarry. Rather than arguing for legal innovation, he has been demonstrating that nowhere do the ancient Sanskrit texts ban Hindu widows from remarriage. Now his arguments have borne fruit in the *Hindu Widows Remarriage Act*.

It remains to be seen how many Hindu widows will actually remarry. Opposition is strong among orthodox Hindu men. Given the option of marrying a virgin or a widow, many men will choose the virgin. And can a widow be assured that she is being chosen as a lifelong companion and not for financial advantage by a man bent on polygamy? Since widows are enjoined to shave their heads, how many will attract a loving suitor? Vidyasagara is urging his son to marry a widow and proposes to help financially with other widows' remarriages, hoping to set a positive precedent.

Married Women Gain Rights

London, England, 1857: Caroline Sheridan's marriage to George Norton was disastrous: her husband beat her, tried to implicate her in an adulterous relationship with the Prime Minister and then attempted to blackmail him.

He denied Caroline her earnings and access to her children, even when one of them was dying. Having no legal redress, Caroline became a vigorous campaigner, first for maternal custody rights, and then for reform of divorce and property laws. Her efforts have led to the 1857 *Divorce and Matrimonial Causes Act*.

Before now, wives in England had no independent legal existence and could not own property. Divorce was possible for men through a costly, lengthy, ecclesiastical and civil procedure, but was virtually impossible for women. The new act allows for a civil divorce procedure and gives courts the power to order ex-husbands to pay maintenance to their divorced wives. A husband who has deserted his wife can no longer claim her earnings. A divorced or legally separated wife recovers the property rights she had before marriage, and regains a legal identity. The grounds for divorce are now, however, more onerous for the woman, who has to prove not only that her husband is adulterous but also that he has committed incest, bigamy, bestiality, rape, sodomy, extreme cruelty, or desertion.

Ranavalona's Revenge

Madagascar, November, 1857: The plot by Prince Radama to overthrow his mother, Queen Ranavalona, has been discovered. Many are surprised that the queen has not taken revenge on her son, saying that he was misled by others. Instead she has expelled all Europeans from Madagascar.

She has long persecuted Christianity in the kingdom, but her son had secretly been attending Catholic masses, and in 1854 he wrote to Napoleon III asking for military help to overthrow the government. The French emperor did not send troops, but it is only this year that the plot has been uncovered.

Ranavalona, 50, whose original name was Rabodoandrianampoinimerina, is the widow of former king, Radama. She was adopted into the royal family by King Andrianampoinimerina and married his son. Radama was a pro-Western monarch, who imported Western military technology along with printing presses and missionaries. He died in 1828, in highly suspicious circumstances, and his wife immediately took power, having all rival claimants to the throne killed. Because royal succession passed through the male line, she declared herself a man. Her son is considered by the people of Madagascar to be the child of her dead husband, despite the impossibility of this parentage by a dead father. She undid most of her husband's Westernizing, reinstituted slavery, and, in 1835, expelled all missionaries. Since then, she is thought

A new law has given Hindu widows the right to remarry.

The grotto at Lourdes, where Bernadette has seen the Virgin Mary.

to have had half the island's population killed for their Christian beliefs, inventively varying their executions (being eaten by dogs, or thrown off cliffs). Ranavalona had a particular European favorite, Joseph-François Lambert, who set up armaments factories for her, but even he, however, has suffered now that her son's plot has been revealed.

Miracles at Lourdes?

Lourdes, France, July 28, 1858: The Catholic Church is investigating a series of visions of the Blessed Virgin Mary, reported to have occurred to a 14-year-old Basque girl. Marie Bernarde Soubirous, known as Bernadette, is the oldest child of a poor family, reduced in 1856 to living in a tiny dark room formerly used as a prison cell, in the town of Lourdes. Bernadette went out with friends on February 11 this year to collect firewood and saw her first vision of a Lady. Vision followed vision, the people of Lourdes flocked to witness, and the police interrogated Bernadette at length. The Lady revealed herself as the "Immaculate Conception" by March 25. Her message speaks of prayer and penance. Miracles of healing are now being reported from Lourdes.

Lady Franklin's Success

London, England, September, 1859: Lady Jane Franklin has at last learned the fate of her husband, Sir John. He set off in 1845 on an Arctic expedition and it is only now that one of the ships that she commissioned to search for him—the *Fox*—has returned with definite proof that he perished in 1847, his ship trapped

in the ice. According to Lady Jane, the documents that the searchers brought back show that her husband definitely proved the existence of the North-West Passage. It is greatly to her credit that she financed several expeditions to search for her husband despite 14 years of disappointments.

Lady Jane herself has led an adventurous and sometimes controversial life. She is the daughter of John Griffin, a silk merchant. Her mother died when she was three, and Griffin took his daughter on his travels through much of England and Europe, when she formed the habit of keeping detailed travel diaries. In 1828 she married John Franklin, already an established Arctic explorer, and lived with him in the Mediterranean. While he commanded HMS *Rainbow*, she was able to tour Turkey, Egypt, Syria, the Holy Land, and Greece, surviving encounters with brigands, an earthquake, and a hurricane.

The Franklins' dream was to discover the North-West Passage, but for this they needed Admiralty backing, which was not forthcoming in the 1830s. Instead, Sir John was offered the governorship of Van Diemen's Land. There Lady Jane campaigned for such causes as improved conditions for prostitutes and Aborigines, earning her the hostility of respectable white society in the colony. In 1843 the Franklins were recalled from Australia and Sir John was finally given Admiralty backing for his Arctic expedition. Lady Jane plans to travel as much as she can for the remainder of her own life.

A Triumvirate of Givers

St Petersburg, Russia, 1859: The current efforts of Anna Filosova, Nadezhda Stasova, and Mariya Trubnikova to set up an organization offering cheap housing and schooling in St Petersburg is part of a very long tradition of female Russian philanthropy. More recently, philanthropy has come to be accepted as a secular virtue. Catherine the Great set an example of social intervention in the late eighteenth century with her orphanages and schooling for aristocratic girls, while Empress Mariya, wife of Catherine's successor, focused her efforts in the early nineteenth century on women of the lower classes.

The idea that charity is one of the most admirable qualities of the Russian noblewoman has been enhanced now that Emperor Nicholas has died. At the beginning of his reign, the Decembrists (aristocrats who attempted a revolt) were banished to Siberia. Some of their wives chose to accompany them. Now, after the emperor's death, the surviving exiles are returning, and the self-sacrificing heroism and good works of these women have been widely publicized.

Mariya Trubnikova is the daughter of one of these exiled Decembrist families, born in Siberia in 1835. Anna Filosova is a liberal aristocrat, born in St Petersburg in 1837, and Nadezhda Stasova, the third of the "triumvirate," as the women are being referred to, was born in 1822, and is the daughter of a St Petersburg court architect. The women have founded a Society for Cheap Lodging in St Petersburg, directed towards women fleeing abusive relationships, and widows with orphans. They have also set up sewing workshops for women, and are vigorous campaigners for women's education.

Lady Jane Franklin

Captain McClintock and his party from the *Fox* receive helpful information from Eskimos.

Rosa Bonheur

Death of the Tarantula Dancer

New York, USA, January 17, 1861: Today, Lola Montez died of pneumonia. Her autobiography is not to be trusted, nor are the multitudes of stories about her life. Even her date of birth and parentage are disputed. She was, it is believed, born on February 17, 1821, in Grange, County Sligo, Ireland. Lola's mother was an Irish parliamentarian's illegitimate daughter and her father, Edward Gilbert, was a soldier. She was christened Eliza Rosanna Gilbert. The family moved to India in 1823; her father died there and her mother remarried. At age five, Eliza returned to Britain for her schooling.

"THERE IS NO MORE FRUITFUL SOURCE OF FAMILY DISCONTENT THAN A HOUSEWIFE'S BADLY COOKED DINNERS AND UNTIDY WAYS."

ISABELLA BEETON, 1861, ENGLISH WRITER

Lola Montez led a life of adventure and scandal.

In 1839 her mother came to England to arrange her daughter's marriage, but Eliza chose instead to elope with Lieutenant Thomas James. The marriage was short-lived as both partners were unfaithful. Eliza reinvented herself as a Spanish dancer, and after some training in Spain, went to London, using the name Lola Montez. Her London debut was not a success, but she went on to tour the

European capitals with outrageously suggestive dances. She was reputed to be the mistress of many, including Franz Liszt. In 1846, currently without a lover, she visited Munich, claiming to be a Spanish noblewoman. King Ludwig of Bavaria became infatuated with her and for over two years she wielded great political influence until she was exposed as an adventuress. When she left, the King abdicated.

After a brief marriage to a London Guards officer, Lola went back to the stage, performing her brazen Tarantula Dance without underclothes for the delectation of American and European audiences. She made another short-lived marriage in 1853, then, in 1855 she caused a huge scandal on the Australian goldfields, horse-whipping an editor for his newspaper attack on her. Yet by 1857 Montez's theatrical allure was fading and after many unsuccessful comebacks, she went to New York where she lived the rest of her days.

Tz'u-Hsi Takes Power in China

Peking, China, November, 1861: Had Tz'u-Hsi been a character in a novel, the author would probably have been accused of creating a wildly unlikely storyline. This remarkable woman, now wielding power in China, was born on November 29, 1835, the daughter of a minor Manchu family; she was known in her youth as Yehenara. Her father was a government clerk who rose to the modest height of provincial administration.

At the age of 16, Tz'u-Hsi was chosen to be one of the Emperor Hsien Feng's concubines. Among the many wives and concubines of the Emperor, she ranked low, first named a concubine of the fifth rank, and then promoted to the fourth rank. On April 27, 1856, she gave birth to

T'ung Chih, the Emperor's only son and thus heir to the Chinese empire. She was promoted at once to the third rank, then to the second. The Emperor died in 1861 and the small boy became Emperor in his place, but at age five he could not rule. A regency of eight was set up by Hsien Feng to rule after his death until the boy was 17 years old. Tz'u-Hsi, as Dowager Empress, has now seized absolute power with the help of Prince Kung, the late Emperor's brother. The choice given to her opponents was to comply with her demands, commit suicide, or face the executioner. This is a bloody beginning to her reign.

time out

In February 1862, "The Battle Hymn of the Republic" was published in *Atlantic Monthly*. The words were penned by abolitionist Julia Ward Howe. Set to music, it soon became a popular song with Union forces in the American Civil War.

A Model Life

London, England, February 11, 1862: The lovely Elizabeth Siddal is dead at the age of just 32. The overdose of laudanum that took her life may have been taken by accident or deliberately—she was distressed by the stillbirth of her child last year.

Elizabeth Siddal modeled for this work by by D. G. Rossetti.

Key Events

London, England, May 16, 1860: Anna Isabella (Annabella) Milbanke Byron, briefly married to Lord Byron, and the mother of mathematician Ada Byron Lovelace, dies, aged 60.
London, England, 1860: The first professional school of nursing (the Nightingale Training School) is opened in St Thomas's Hospital.
Vladivostok, Russia, 1860: A port is founded on the Sea of Japan.
New York, USA, January 17, 1861: Irish-born dancer Lola Montez, dies, aged 39.

Florence, Italy, June 29, 1861: Poet Elizabeth Barrett Browning dies, aged 55.
South Australia, Australia, 1861: Suffragist Catherine Helen Spence publishes *A Plea for Pure Democracy*, advocating women's rights and asking for proportional representation.
Peking, China, 1861: Tzu-Hsi, the Emperor's concubine, becomes regent for her son.
Russia, 1861: The serfs are emancipated.

Spain, 1861: Writer and feminist Concepción Arenal publishes her groundbreaking treatise, *The Woman of the Future*.
USA, 1861-65: American Civil War.
USA, 1865: Clara Barton, Civil War nurse, is placed in charge of tracing the fate of 30,000 missing men of the Union Army.
London, England, February 11, 1862: Elizabeth Siddal, artist and artists' model, dies, aged 32.

Philadelphia, USA, 1862: Emeline Horton Cleveland becomes chief resident at the Women's Hospital, where she later develops training courses for nurses.
USA, April 9, 1863: President Abraham Lincoln issues his Emancipation Proclamation, declaring that all slavery must end.
Geneva, Switzerland, 1864: The International Red Cross is formed.
Massachusetts, USA, 1864: Rebecca Lee Crumpler becomes the first African-American woman to receive a medical degree.

London, England, February 6, 1865: Cookery writer Mrs Isabella Beeton dies, aged 28.
Como, Italy, April 1, 1865: Soprano Giuditta Negri Pasta dies, aged 68.
Washington DC, USA, April 14, 1865: President Abraham Lincoln is assassinated.
London, England, June 1865: *Alice's Adventures in Wonderland* by Lewis Carroll (Charles Dodgson) is published.
England, July 2, 1865: William Booth forms the Salvation Army.

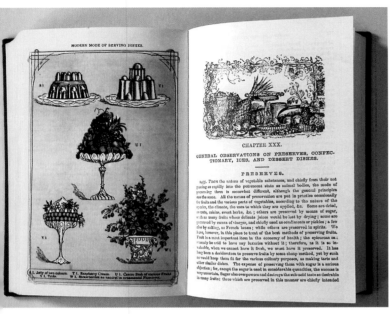

Mrs Beeton's invaluable *Book of Household Management*.

Siddal was the incarnation of female beauty—tall and slender, with a magnificent column of a throat and a glorious head of copper-colored hair. She is said to have been spotted working as a milliner, and quickly became Dante Gabriel Rossetti's favorite model. In 1852 she posed as Ophelia for John Everett Millais, reportedly lying in cold water for hours without the least complaint.

Elizabeth herself began to sketch and paint, taking lessons from Rossetti. In 1860 Rossetti and his seriously ill muse married. The grief-stricken artist plans to bury his poems with his wife.

Queen of the Kitchen Dies

London, England, 6 February, 1865: Today one of the best known English writers, Isabella Beeton, died of puerperal fever, resulting from the birth of her fourth son. She was 28 years old. The multitudes of women who own and treasure her *Book of Household Management* have made her name a household word. "Mrs Beeton" has a solution, it seems, for every household difficulty, a recipe for every occasion, and eminently sensible advice for the management of household servants from housekeeper to nursemaid, from butler to footman. Less lavish households are not neglected, either.

Mrs Beeton's book makes no pretence of being totally original. It is a miscellaneous collection of materials from other writers such as Eliza Acton, as well as Mrs Beeton's own ideas. Her promise is that she has tested every recipe in her own kitchen. She was born in Cheapside, London, in 1836, the oldest in a family of 21 children. After her father died, her mother remarried and Isabella helped with managing the household. Having married editor Samuel Beeton, she became increasingly involved with the writing and editing of his *Englishwoman's Domestic Magazine. The Book of Household Management* was first published in monthly parts in this magazine; as a book it continues to sell spectacularly well. In 1858 she followed her own advice about active charity, opening a soup kitchen for poor children during a particularly difficult winter.

Italian Civil Code Disappoints Women

Italy, 1865: The new liberal government of unified Italy has introduced a civil code this year, based on the familiar Napoleonic Code. For the most part, the Pisanelli Code confirms the rights of men, denying women such civil rights as the right to vote or to hold public office. Within a family, authority is vested in the male head of the household. Married women are not permitted to undertake property transactions, nor can they enter the commercial world without their husband's consent (this is known as marital authorization). A married woman cannot live separately from her husband, must take on her husband's citizenship, and must acquiesce in her husband's choice of where to live.

Except where a husband's adultery is extremely blatant concubinage, only women can be found guilty of adultery, an aspect of the legislation open to abuse by malicious husbands. When the head of a household dies, issues of inheritance are to be settled by a family council without women's input. Women have no rights of custody over their children, and have power to make decisions for their children only when the father is absent for an extended period (in cases of imprisonment, desertion, or emigration).

This means that it is more legally and economically advantageous for a woman *not* to marry. As it stands, the Pisanelli Code is biased well and truly in favor of fathers and husbands, to the righteous indignation of all thinking women.

Clara Barton

Annie Etheridge, Civil War nurse and "brave soldier in petticoats."

Key Events

Finland, December 31, 1865: Novelist and feminist Fredrika Bremer dies, aged 64.

Paris, France, 1865: Artist Rosa Bonheur is the first woman to receive the Légion d'Honneur.

Germany, 1865: Feminist Luise Otto-Peters helps establish the General Union of German Women.

Italy, 1865: The Pisanelli Code is enacted, entrenching men's rights and women's subservience.

USA, 1865: An estimated 4 million slaves are freed after the defeat of the South in the Civil War.

Ohio, USA, February 1866: Lucy Hobbs becomes the first woman to graduate as a dentist.

London, England, June 7, 1866: The first petition for women's suffrage is presented to Parliament.

Andros, Greece, 1866: Educator and independence advocate Evanthia Kairi dies, aged 69.

Canada, 1867: The Dominion of Canada is created by the *British North America Act.*

Toronto, Canada, 1867: Emily Howard Stowe, the first female doctor in Canada, practices medicine illegally after being declined permission to sit the Canadian exams required for foreign practitioners.

Germany, 1867: Karl Marx publishes *Das Kapital*, a critical analysis of capitalism.

Stockholm, Sweden, 1867: Alfred Nobel, chemist and industrialist, invents dynamite.

France, 1867: Sophie Frémiet Rude dies, aged 70.

Tokyo, Japan, 1868: Women, banned from the stage since 1629, are now permitted to perform in kabuki theater.

Massachusetts, USA, 1868: Elizabeth Cabot Cary Agassiz publishes *A Journey in Brazil.*

Massachusetts, USA, 1868: *Little Women*, a novel about life in New England, by Louisa May Alcott, is published.

Egypt, 1869: The Suez Canal opens.

Nelson, New Zealand, 1869: "Femina" publishes *An Appeal to the Men of New Zealand*, calling for women's rights to be recognized.

New York City, USA, 1869: The National Woman Suffrage Association is established by feminists Susan B. Anthony and Elizabeth Cady Stanton.

The Vatican, Italy, 1869: The Roman Catholic Church prohibits abortion at any stage of pregnancy.

Princess Victoria
of England

1,499 Women Say Yes

London, England, June 7, 1866: The first petition for women's suffrage has been presented to the British Parliament with 1,499 signatures. The women responsible for organizing this petition have learned much from American abolitionist campaigners, but it is not at all clear that they have learned enough about strategy. The petition asks for all women be granted suffrage. The group that decided on the wording of this request was split on the question whether to ask for suffrage for all women as being fully equal to men, or whether to take a more modest approach, asking in the first instance for the vote for single, divorced, and widowed women, in the understanding that a further petition, claiming suffrage for married women also, would be presented after the success of this one. Such a partial request would have built on the success of the 1857 *Divorce and Matrimonial Causes Act,* legislation that has had no adverse consequences, and would be less likely to stir up complete opposition than the petition in its current form.

The ammunition for opponents of women's suffrage is all too copious, both in the legal differentiation between single and married women in Britain, and also in the firm belief held by the majority of men that a married woman's place is in the home, where she should be mindful only of her domestic duties. By opting for universal women's suffrage, the campaigners may have denied themselves even a partial extension of the vote.

One of the organizers of the petition is Barbara Bodichon, an experienced campaigner for women's rights and co-founder of *The Englishwoman's Review.* Bodichon also founded the Women's Suffrage Committee. Helen Taylor, John Stuart Mill's stepdaughter, held different views about the committee's tactics and it was her close connection with Mill, needed to champion the cause of women's suffrage in Parliament, that has ensured that her views prevailed.

"THE HAPPIEST WOMEN, LIKE THE HAPPIEST NATIONS, HAVE NO HISTORY."

GEORGE ELIOT
(MARY ANN EVANS),
ENGLISH AUTHOR
1860

Toronto Welcomes First Woman Doctor

Toronto, Canada, 1867: Dr Emily Howard Stowe is returning to Canada in order to set up the country's first female doctor's medical practice, now that she has graduated from medical school in the United States. Toronto women are welcoming this move, because at last they have the opportunity to consult a woman on matters so intimate that they have been reluctant to consult a male doctor. It is hard to believe that the Canadian authorities—all male—are refusing Dr Stowe

Women and children in the coal-sifting room at the Blanzy mine, Saone-et-Loire, France. Coal has been mined in this area since the fifteenth century.

a license to practice medicine. She says she will work as a doctor illegally until they see the folly of their decision.

Ontario's College of Physicians and Surgeons stipulates that any doctor who trained in the USA, as Dr Stowe has, must train further in Ontario and pass an admissions examination—but no Ontario medical school will accept a woman as a student.

Emily Stowe was born on May 1, 1831, in Norwich, Upper Canada, the oldest daughter of Solomon Jennings and Hannah Howard. Belonging, as she did, to a Quaker family, she received a good education, going to a co-educational school. As a young girl, she studied homeopathic medicine, apprenticed to Dr Joseph Lancaster, but she later became a teacher in Brantford. In 1856 she married John Stowe, a carpenter and carriage-maker, and they had ten children. He fell ill with tuberculosis and went to a sanatorium in a vain attempt to recover his health. Emily decided to become a doctor, possibly because teaching provided too little income for the family, possibly because her husband's illness rekindled her interest in medicine. Since no Canadian medical school would admit her, she trained in homeopathic medicine at the New York Medical College for Women. She returns to Toronto eager to champion women's rights and to legitimize her medical practice.

Women in Kabuki Theater Again?

Tokyo, Japan, 1868: Although kabuki originated as a woman's dance, created at the start of the seventeenth century by

Izumo no Okuni in Kyoto, women have been banned from performing in kabuki since 1629. At that time, the Tokugawa shogunate gave as its reason for banning *onna* (women's) kabuki the strong link between woman actors and prostitution. This ban promptly led to the setting up of *wakashu* (adolescent male troupes) kabuki, hotly sought after by Japanese samurai, and in 1652 these troupes of boy actors were also banned. For over two centuries, *yaro* kabuki has been the only form allowed (all parts acted by adult males), and the *onnagata* (female impersonators) have become extraordinarily refined in their acting methods.

Now, with the fall of the shogunate and the Meiji Restoration, the laws excluding women from kabuki have been rescinded. It remains to be seen whether the public will accept women actors playing female parts, or whether the acting conventions of the *onnagata* are too firmly established and too beautiful in their own right to be abandoned. Another challenge to contemporary kabuki is how, if at all, to deal with

Women have returned to the kabuki stage.

Elizabeth and Louis Agassiz journeyed through Brazil by steamboat.

western clothing and western concepts. Is kabuki to remain faithful to its repertoire of classic drama, or is it to modernize? Government censorship of kabuki content is likely to continue, whichever path the drama takes.

A Journey in Brazil

Massachusetts, USA, 1868: The publication of Elizabeth and Louis Agassiz's *A Journey in Brazil* is the latest achievement in their busy lives. Elizabeth was born on December 5, 1822. Her father was a lawyer who abandoned his struggling legal career to make several not very successful forays into business, in conjunction with some family members. By 1832 the family was living in Boston where Elizabeth was educated at home because of her delicate health. It was here that she met the Swiss scientist, Louis Agassiz, who had come to Boston to chair the Lawrence Scientific School at Harvard University. Louis was a widower, considerably older than Elizabeth, and the father of three children.

They married in 1850 and Elizabeth determined to play more than a domestic role in his life. In the mid-1850s, following financial problems, she opened the Agassiz School for the young women of Cambridge, who were, of course, barred from entry to Harvard University. The school gave them access to the Harvard faculty, and to Louis himself. Once their finances improved, the school was closed, as both Louis and Elizabeth were eager to travel on scientific expeditions. Elizabeth has stated, however, that the cause of higher education for women is one that she will continue to pursue.

In 1865, Louis and Elizabeth Agassiz set off on the Thayer expedition to Brazil. Elizabeth had already published a children's book, *A First Lesson in Natural History,* in 1859. On this Brazilian journey she wrote many lively letters "partly for the entertainment of her friends, partly with the idea that [Louis] might make some use of [them] in knitting together the scientific reports of [his] journey by a thread of narrative." Now that this goal has been accomplished, and *A Journey in Brazil* is likely to gain a far greater readership than any totally science-based account.

Louisa Alcott's Masterpiece

Massachusetts, USA, 1868: When Louisa May Alcott was asked to write a realistic girls' story, she agreed without enthusiasm and plodded her way through the writing of *Little Women.* Now that it is finished, she finds it "simple and true" and already the American public is agreeing with her verdict. *Little Women* is a charming, touching, and humorous fictionalization of the lives of Louisa and her sisters, their mother and neighbors (though the absent father is not a close counterpart to her real-life father, Amos Bronson Alcott). Louisa is already thinking about a second volume, and the public may well demand more stories about the March family.

With this book, she has moved children's novels away from the previous dreary emphasis on morality. There is no absence of moral challenge in this book, but it is dealt with as a young girl might experience it in real life, and there is not always a totally clear right path. Louisa has been writing for children ever since her 1855 *Flower Fables.* In 1867 she began editing the children's magazine, *Merry's Museum.* She has also written some works for adult readers. Louisa, whose health was permanently damaged from her time as a nurse during the Civil War, writes to support not only herself but also her parents, for her father, the transcendental educator, is notoriously impractical.

Louisa May Alcott

Who is Femina? The Public Has a Right to Know!

Nelson, New Zealand, 1869: *An Appeal to the Men of New Zealand,* a compellingly argued claim for women to be given all political rights enjoyed by men, has been published under the nom-de-plume of "Femina." Femina has been campaigning for women's rights for almost 20 years as a contributor to the *Nelson Examiner,* and it is understood that she was influential in the passing of the 1860 *Married Women's Property Protection Act.*

But just who is Femina? Her political agenda appears to be exactly the same as that of Mary Ann Muller, who emigrated from England in 1850, although it is well known that Mrs Muller's husband, who is Nelson's resident magistrate, is a staunch opponent of women's rights. Only the editor of the *Nelson Examiner,* Charles Elliott, knows Femina's true identity, and he is refusing to disclose it.

Révolte à Bruges èn 1436 by French artist Sophie Rude (1797–1867).

Death of an Educator

Emma Willard

Troy, New York, April 15, 1870: The death occurred today of the eminent educator, Emma Willard. The girls' secondary school which she founded in 1821 as the Troy Female Seminary still continues to flourish.

Born in Berlin, Connecticut, she was educated locally, and at 16 took on the role of teacher. Over the years she set about improving the ordinary methods of teaching, seeking to make subjects interesting to her pupils. She was 22 years old when she married widower, Dr John Willard; she then stopped teaching to raise the doctor's children and their own infant. However, the family fell upon hard financial times, and Emma returned to teaching, this time opening a school for young women in the family home. Her husband supported this move.

She published *A Plan for Improving Female Education*, a considered and cautious document. While Emma was prepared to argue that women were "the companions, not the satellites of men," she was careful to avoid pushing the notion that women were intellectually equal with men—a proposal that would have been in no way acceptable to a male audience at that time.

By 1819 Emma had moved her school to new premises, leased at Waterford, New York. But the establishment was underfunded, and within a few years was in serious financial difficulty. The endeavor was rescued by a grant from the Troy Common Council and additional funds were raised by public subscription; as a result, the Troy Female Seminary, the first secondary school for girls in the United States, came into being, with an enrolment of 90 students.

Emma published many school books, with the subjects ranging from history, geography, and health, to morals. As a result of a visit to Europe she published her well-received *Journal and Letters from France and Great Britain*. Willard will long be remembered for her contribution to girls' education.

> "WE ASK JUSTICE, WE ASK EQUALITY, WE ASK THAT ALL THE CIVIL AND POLITICAL RIGHTS THAT BELONG TO THE CITIZENS OF THE UNITED STATES, BE GUARANTEED TO US AND OUR DAUGHTERS FOREVER."
>
> DECLARATION OF RIGHTS FOR WOMEN, 1876

time out

The game American poker is taking over the world with rumors that Queen Victoria herself began lessons on how to play in 1871 under the instruction of the American ambassador to the Court of St James.

Princess Pauline de Metternich, noted socialite.

Married Women to Retain their Earnings

London, England, 1870: The British Parliament has passed the *Married Women's Property Act* for the purpose of providing relief to married women who are earning an income from any employment, trade, or occupation in which they are presently engaged.

Up until now a woman has had to surrender legal ownership of all her possessions upon marriage. In effect her existence was suspended, and her personality was incorporated into that of her husband. A married woman had no legal right to any income she brought to the marriage, and her husband could deal with such money in any way he chose. Previously, married women had to rely on a small annual allowance granted by a husband at his discretion, or settled before marriage, to meet personal expenses— so-called "pin money."

This new act allows a married woman to keep and control any earnings she makes, including income received in consequence of literary, artistic, or scientific undertakings. These reforms have been a long time coming.

Caroline Norton campaigned for married women's rights in the 1850s, and in 1869 John Stuart Mill published his pamphlet *The Subjection of Women*, in which he argued that the situation regarding married women's lack of financial independence was an injustice needing the earliest remedy.

Not all property rights sought by the English women's rights movement have been granted by this legislation. There is already agitation to gain even further relief for married women.

Caroline Norton

Matterhorn Vanquished by a Female

Switzerland, August 22, 1871: The deadly Matterhorn has again been conquered. But this time it has been climbed by a woman. Today, Lucy Walker, the indomitable English alpinist, is the first woman to reach the summit of this towering 14,693 ft (4,478 m) mountain.

Troy, New York, USA, April 15, 1870: Emma Willard, educator and founder of the first secondary girls' school in the United States, dies, aged 83.
New York, USA, 1870: Susan Smith McKinney Steward is the first African-American graduate of the New York Medical College for Women, and the third African-American doctor.
UK, 1870: The *Married Women's Property Act* is passed, allowing women to keep their own earnings and to inherit personal property.

The Matterhorn, Switzerland, 1871: English mountaineer Lucy Walker becomes the first woman to scale the Matterhorn.
Paris, France, 1871: Mary Putnam Jacobi graduates from the Ecole de Médécin, the second woman to do so.
Naples, Italy, November 28, 1872: Scottish scientist and feminist Mary Somerville dies, aged 92. Her 1834 book *The Connection of the Physical Sciences* won her respect in the scientific community. Her last book was published when she was 89.

New York, USA, 1872: Social reformer Victoria Woodhull is nominated for President of the United States.
Florence, Italy, 1872: Aurelia Cimino Folliero de Luna established a journal that calls for legal reforms to women's rights.
Avignon, France, May 8, 1873: British philosopher, economist, and supporter of women's rights, John Stuart Mill, dies, aged 66.
Massachusetts, USA, August 19, 1873: Helen Blanchard invents the first zigzag stitch sewing machine.

London, England, 1873: The *Custody of Infants Act* allows British divorcees access to their children.
France, 1873: After her imprisonment after the fall of the Paris Commune, Louise Michel is deported to New Caledonia.
Cleveland, Ohio, USA, 1874: The Woman's Christian Temperance Union is founded.
Hanoi, Vietnam, 1874: French occupation.
Washington DC, USA, March 1, 1875: The *Civil Rights Act* implements equal rights in public housing.

England, 1875: Emma Paterson and Edith Simcox become the first female delegates to the Trades Union Congress.
Philadelphia, USA, March 10, 1876: Scottish-American inventor Alexander Graham Bell transmits his voice via the first phone.
Nohant, France, June 8, 1876: Novelist George Sand (Amantine Aurore Lucile Dupin) dies, aged 72.

She made the climb accompanied by a small party, which included her father, Frank Walker. They were assisted by the famous Swiss guide, Melchior Anderegg.

This is not the first time Lucy Walker has come to the notice of the public, and she is certainly well known among the climbing fraternity. In 1864 she was the first woman to scale the Balmhorn; over subsequent years she established herself as the dominant female climber, making ascents of the Wetterhorn, the Lyskamm and, in 1869, of the Piz Bernia.

She was introduced to the challenge of mountaineering by her father. An accomplished climber, he encouraged Lucy to climb, suggesting that it would help cure her rheumatism.

Walker is a woman of formidable size, who, curiously, sustains herself during ascents by relying on a diet of sponge

Louise Michel is arrested after the fall of the Paris Commune.

cake and champagne. Unlike some female alpinists, who opt to climb in trousers, she prefers to make her ascents in a dress.

Her latest feat has drawn criticism from some male quarters, where the view is generally held that ladies are better served by limiting themselves to gentle walks among the foothills.

Death of Pre-eminent Scientist

Naples, Italy, November 28, 1872: The death has been announced today of the noted scientist and staunch feminist, Mary Fairfax Somerville. She was 92 years old.

This extraordinary woman was self-educated. Her father, Sir William George Fairfax, held the view that girls were best occupied by attending to needlework and similar pursuits. Despite this attitude, she taught herself geometry and algebra.

In 1812 William Somerville, a cousin, became Mary's second husband. Her first husband had died some years earlier after three years of marriage. William was supportive of his wife's studies, and when he was elected to the Royal Society he introduced her to leading scientists, both in London and on visits to Paris.

Commissioned to translate Laplace's *Mécanique Céleste*, Mary took four years over the task. The finished work, *The Mechanism of the Heavens*, was more than a translation; it incorporated an extensive explanation of the mathematics used by Laplace. The work brought her much critical acclaim. It was followed in 1834 by *On the Connection of the Physical Sciences*, and later, *Physical Geography* (1848), and *On Molecular and Microscopic Science* (1869).

By 1838 Mary and her husband had moved to Naples. She had already been awarded a civil pension by the British Prime Minister, Sir Robert Peel, and been elected to the Royal Astronomical Society. This long-time supporter of

women's education and suffrage certainly made a valuable contribution to science.

Female President for the USA?

New York, USA, 1872: Victoria Woodhull has been nominated by the Equal Rights Party as its candidate to seek the presidency of the United States of America. Her running partner is to be Frederick Douglass, a former slave.

Although American women do not have the right to vote, it is a peculiarity of the system that there is nothing to prevent them running for public office.

In her election platform she proposes that all bills, having received presidential approval, or having been enacted by Congress, must be directed to the Registrar of United States Law and then passed to each state or territory, to be voted on by the people. In this way, Woodhull seeks to wrest control from those who currently possess the political power—capitalists. An advocate of free love, and the first woman stockbroker in the country, Woodhull is someone to watch.

Mary Somerville

Victoria Woodhull, presidential candidate, and her sister.

Queen Victoria

Women Pray for Liquor Store Closures

Cleveland, Ohio, USA, November, 1874: After a year of planning the Woman's Christian Temperance Union has come into being, holding its first national convention here on November 18. Annie Wittenmyer was elected president. The organization has as its objective control of the consumption of alcohol. It advocates abstinence and seeks a prohibition on the sale of alcohol.

The movement has come about following a lecture on temperance given last year by Dr Dio Lewis at Hillsboro. Inspired by what they heard, a number of local women, under the leadership of Eliza Thompson, joined together to form the Woman's Temperance Crusade. They mounted a campaign aimed at the closure of every saloon, local store, and drugstore where liquor was being sold. Their tactic was to enter the premises, praying and singing hymns, with a view to shaming the proprietors into closing the establishment. If denied entry, the women would kneel outside the establishment, singing and praying until such time as the dealer capitulated. Following its initial success, the Woman's Temperance Crusade rapidly spread throughout the states of Ohio and New York. Esther McNeil organized the women of Fredonia, New York, with her group adopting the name Woman's Christian Temperance Union. A national conference was quickly arranged.

The WCTU is committed to non-violence, believing its objective can be achieved through unity and prayer. The

> "WOMAN MUST NOT DEPEND UPON THE PROTECTION OF MAN, BUT MUST BE TAUGHT TO PROTECT HERSELF."
>
> SUSAN B. ANTHONY, WOMEN'S RIGHTS ACTIVIST, JULY, 1871

temperance movement has long been strong in this country. The Independent Order of Good Templar, dedicated to promoting abstinence from consumption of alcohol, was founded in New York in 1851, and has some branches overseas. The WCTU, however, is the first of its

Eleanor Vere Boyle's *Beauty and the Beast*.

kind, being organized by women with an entirely female membership.

The WTCU has taken a white ribbon bow as its emblem and the motto "For God and Home and Native Land." There is a strong move afoot to establish reading rooms for women, and to present anti-drinking programs in schools.

First Women Delegates to the TUC

Glasgow, Scotland, October, 1875: The annual assembly of the Trade Union Congress held this month at Glasgow has, for the first time, admitted two women delegates. Both women, Emma Paterson and Edith Simcox, have long been engaged in the struggle to advance the rights of women workers.

Edith Simcox has a well-established reputation as an educator and author. She has written on a broad range of subjects—her article on the influence of John Stuart Mill's writings should be of particular interest to all those engaged in the struggle to improve the social and economic position of workers. One reviewer of her literature has categorized her as a "scientific rationalist." She is well known as a lecturer at workmen's clubs, and has had the practical experience of managing a small cooperative shirt-making enterprise.

Emma Paterson, one-time secretary of the Women's Suffrage Association, and founder of the Women's Protective and Provident League, has as her stated objective the formation of unions for every trade in which women work. She faced some initial resistance from male trade unions, whose membership was of the opinion that women should not be in the workforce. She is, however, opposed to the idea of protective legislation exclusively for women, mindful that as yet women have no direct political influence in the framing of such laws.

Notorious Novelist George Sand Dies

Nohant, France, June 8, 1876: The death occurred today of Amantine Aurore Lucile Dupin, Baronne Dudevant, the prolific novelist, who is better known to her readers as George Sand. Her first work, *Rose et Blanche*, was co-authored with her lover Jules Sandeau; published in 1831, it appeared under the pseudonym, Jules Sand.

Her next novel, *Indiana*, was published in 1832 under the name George Sand. In it she asserted a woman's right to love and independence; the book was criticized for its "immoral tendency." Many works followed in quick succession, and were well received in France. She also built up a following in Great Britain, where one

Members of the Woman's Christian Temperance Union stage a prayer vigil outside a saloon.

The novelist George Sand has died, aged 72.

reviewer remarked, "George Sand is undoubtedly the most gifted and original female writer of her country and times."

The writer had been pressured into an unhappy marriage with Baron Dudevant, which she endured for eight years, after which she moved to Paris where she at first tried to support herself by painting. Later she turned to writing.

A passionate and independent woman, George Sand became notorious for her free-wheeling lifestyle. She wore men's clothes, smoked cigars, and had a number of very public affairs. Scorning many of the social norms of the time, she attacked the Church and was contemptuous of conventional marriage. She was a staunch republican and supporter of socialism.

Her novels promoted ideals of spiritual and sensual love. Her later rustic novels drew inspiration from her love of the countryside, and these are probably her best works. She challenged the accepted literary roles ascribed to characters. Writing to a critic, she commented that if not yet understood, some day she would be. In addition, she said, "I have opened the way for other women." Her public will certainly mourn the fact there will be no more new works from her.

Empress Victoria

London, England, January 1, 1877: Her Majesty, Queen Victoria, has assumed the title "Empress of India." The event has been marked by the holding of a magnificent Imperial Assemblage at Delhi, India, which was attended by local princes, chiefs, and nobles.

The announcement of the new title received a mixed response in Great Britain. For some time, Queen Victoria had expressed a deep desire to take a title that would reflect more accurately her position with regard to her various colonial possessions. Earlier, the style "Empress of Great Britain, Ireland, and India" had been considered, but it was soon abandoned as problematic.

Prime Minister Disraeli, while sympathetic to her Majesty's desire to assume a title reflecting dominion over India, was cautious in advancing her claim. He realized that Parliament was initially less than supportive of the idea. Some government members saw it as a dangerous precedent—a harbinger of a return to an intrusive monarchy; yet others demanded to know why the title "queen" was no longer considered adequate.

The members of the House of Lords were equally unenthusiastic. Eventually, however, when persuaded to view the additional royal title as a symbolic and personal measure, rather than a practical and political one, they supported the introduction of the *Royal Titles Act.*

In India, the more politically aware questioned the worth of whole process. Many felt that title and "mere pageantry" served as a poor substitute for the grants of land to natives. Yet, in spite of the criticism, there is no denying that Queen Victoria, Empress of India, is delighted with her new title!

Black Beauty Tells His Tale

England, November 24, 1877: The Norwich printers, Messrs Jarrold, have today published a book that has been written by a horse!

The title page of this new work identifies it as the eponymous autobiography of "Black Beauty," which, we are told, is "translated from the Equine" by Anna Sewell.

Anna Sewell is a resident of Old Catton, Norfolk, and we may safely guess that this book is the work of her own hand. This is her first effort at authorship, though her mother, Mary Wright Sewell, is well known as a writer of juvenile literature.

Miss Sewell believes there is far too much abuse of animals, and the message of *Black Beauty,* which is aimed at young readers, is to treat horses, and indeed all animals, with kindness. Unfortunately Miss Sewell herself is in indifferent health, and it is not known whether she will continue her writing career.

Acquittal on Assassination Charge

St Petersburg, Russia, April 1878: An excited crowd outside St Petersburg Circuit Court cheered and shouted "Bravo," on hearing of the acquittal of Vera Zasulich. She had been charged with the attempted murder of General Fyodor Trepov, governor of the city.

When General Trepov ordered the whipping of a political prisoner who failed to remove his hat in his presence, Zasulich decided to exact revenge. She considered whipping a cruel and illegal act, corporal punishment having been abolished many years previously. Using the pretence of presenting a petition to the general, she gained access to his reception room, where she produced a pistol, then shot and wounded him.

Zasulich was already well known to the authorities as a result of her close association with the revolutionary, Sergi Nechaev. In 1870 she had been imprisoned without trial for a year, and subsequently remained under police surveillance for a further four years.

Her case excited much public sympathy, and a number of prosecutors declined to present any evidence against her. Eventually the trial commenced on March 31. Testimony was given as to the conditions under which political prisoners are held, together with details of her own miserable existence as a political suspect. After a short deliberation the jury pronounced her not guilty.

George Eliot

In the 1870s, Harriet Beecher Stowe went on a reading tour of the USA.

No Abbey Burial for George Eliot

London, England, December 22, 1880: The author George Eliot, who died today after a short illness, will not be buried in Westminster Abbey's famous "Poet's Corner." George Eliot, the *nom de plume* of Mary Ann Evans, considered the greatest English author since Dickens, was at one time engaged in an "irregular" relationship with journalist George Henry Lewes. In light of her disregard for orthodox religious conventions, her husband, John Cross, whom she married earlier this year, has decided against approaching the Dean of Westminster Abbey to seek the interment of his wife there.

George Eliot

> "Do not go where the path may lead, go instead where there is no path and leave a trail."
>
> MARY ANN EVANS WRITING AS GEORGE ELIOT (1811–1880), ENGLISH NOVELIST

In 1844 Mary Ann Evans, as she then was, turned to writing as a translator for David Strauss, a German theologian and writer, rendering his *Das Leben Jesu* into English. She received no credit and little payment for this effort. She then acted as editor for the *Westminster Review*. By 1854 she was living with George Lewes, who arranged to have one of her stories published in *Blackwood's Magazine*. She adopted the name George Eliot for its publication, and published her first novel, *Adam Bede*, in 1859. The London *Times* declared it "a rare first novel." Many works followed, most notably *Silas Marner, Romola, Middlemarch,* and her final novel, *Daniel Deronda*. Eliot, who was 61, will be buried in Highgate Cemetery in north London.

time out

In Iowa in 1881, heroic teenager Kate Shelby braved the wreckage of a flood-damaged bridge from which a train had toppled. She battled a torrential downpour to reach a telegraph office and warn trains of the hazard ahead.

Religious Order Founded

Cadogno, Italy, 1880: Francesca Cabrini, well known locally as a devout lady, has moved a step closer toward fulfilling her ambition of establishing a Christian mission to the Chinese with the founding of the Missionary Sisters of the Sacred Heart of Jesus.

Appointed as administrator of the Cadogno Orphanage in 1874, Cabrini took her vows as a nun in 1877 and was soon made prioress of the order of nuns. Mother Frances Xavier Cabrini was then given a mandate from the local diocesan authorities to form a separate religious institute; this she has done with seven young nuns, who have taken their vows under her instruction.

The rules of the new order stress modesty, humility, and daily silence. Mother Cabrini hopes to be in the mission field in the near future, spreading the Gospel and tending to the poor and needy in homes, hospitals, and prisons.

Death of Queen of the Desert

Damascus, Syria, August 11, 1881: The current outbreak of cholera in Damascus has claimed the life of a remarkable woman: Jane Digby el Mezrab, wife of Sheikh Abdul Midjuel el Mezrab.

Married under Muslim law, Jane Digby had been with her husband for the past twenty years. Sheik el Mezrab was not her first husband; she had been married three times previously. Her first husband, whom she married in 1824, was Lord Ellenborough, a man many years her senior. Finding him less than attentive, she had engaged in numerous liaisons.

Divorced in 1830, by an Act of Parliament, she moved to Munich where she became a favorite of King Ludwig. There she also met, and in 1832 married, Baron Venningen. This relationship, too, turned out to be short-lived.

The Priory, in St John's Wood, London, was George Eliot's home from 1863 to 1878.

Kansas, USA, November, 1880: Kansas becomes the first US state to legislate against the consumption of alcohol, introducing prohibition following a referendum.

London, England, December 22, 1880: Novelist George Eliot (Mary Anne Evans) dies, aged 61.

Cadogno, Italy, 1880: Francesca Cabrini founds the Missionary Sisters of the Sacred Heart of Jesus.

St Petersburg, Russia, March 13, 1881: Reforming tsar Alexander II is assassinated by a revolutionary organization, the People's Will.

Transvaal, March 23, 1881: The Boers are conceded self-government following numerous victories in bloody battles.

Damascus, Syria, August 11, 1881: British adventurer Jane Digby el Mezrab, known for her romantic affairs and marriage to a sheik, dies, aged 74.

Western India, 1881: Writer and social reformer Pandita Rambai testifies to the Hunter Commission regarding the need for women's education. The following year she founds a home for widows.

London, England, January 25, 1882: Novelist and essayist Virginia Woolf is born.

Berlin, Germany, March 24, 1882: Robert Koch presents his discovery of the cause of tuberculosis.

Amsterdam, Netherlands, 1882: Doctor Aletta Jacobs begins to prescribe birth control methods to her patients.

London, England, 1882: Eleanor Ormerod, who has recently published a report on crop pest the turnip fly, is appointed as consultant entomologist to the Royal Agricultural Society.

Sunda Strait, Dutch East Indies, August 27, 1883: The Krakatoa volcano erupts, killing 36,000 people.

Michigan, USA, November 26, 1883: Former slave, abolitionist, and women's rights campaigner, Sojourner Truth, dies, aged about 86.

Bayreuth, Germany, 1884: Following the death of her husband, composer Richard Wagner, Cosima Wagner, daughter of the composer Franz Liszt, assumes directorship of the Bayreuth Festival.

USA, 1884: Writer and activist Helen Hunt Jackson publishes *Ramona*, noting the poor treatment of Native Americans.

Paris, France, May 22, 1885: Two million mourners attend the funeral of writer Victor Hugo.

Bombay, India, December, 1885: The Indian National Congress is formed after lobbying by British civil servant Allan Hume.

Burma, 1885: Queen Supayalat, who has ruled since 1878, and her husband Thibaw, are forced to leave Burma when British forces invade.

She went on to fall in love with a Greek nobleman, Count Theotoky, marrying him and moving to Greece, but not before her previous husband, the Baron, had fought a duel with the Count.

In Greece, Jane caught the eye of King Otto, and her marriage to Theotoky ended in divorce. After another failed relationship with an Albanian general-turned-bandit, she traveled to the Middle East.

At the age of 46 Jane fell in love with Sheik el Mezrab. She adopted Bedouin-style dress and became an inveterate smoker of the hookah. With her husband she lived half the year in the desert, in Bedouin tents, the other half in the palace they had built in Damascus.

She became a close friend of Isabel Burton, wife of Sir Richard Burton, the British adventurer, explorer, writer, and, for a time, British consul in Damascus. Isabel Burton described Jane as "a most beautiful woman."

The Sheik's tribesmen regarded Jane as their queen, and she sometimes galloped at the head of horsemen as they engaged in warfare with other Bedouin tribes. She was renowned, too, for the excellence of the sheep and horses she bred.

Truth be Told: She Was a Woman

Michigan, USA, November 26, 1883: No more will the voice of Sojourner Truth be heard advocating justice and equal rights for women and enslaved African-Americans. This unique champion of women's causes and abolitionism has died at the ripe old age of 86 years.

Born into slavery in New York State in about 1797, she boldly took her freedom, escaping before emancipation became law in 1827. At first she saw her mission as spreading the Christian message, but in time she focused her boundless energies on securing the rights of women in a male-dominated society, and gaining freedom and recognition for those still bound in slavery.

She was a forceful public speaker. While attending a Women's Rights convention in Ohio, hearing some ministers of religion claim men had the right to dominate the "weaker sex," she stood to her full height, showed her arms, well-muscled by years of hard labor, and demanded simply, "Ain't I a woman?"

At the outbreak of the Civil War, she made numerous speeches in support of the Union, and visited President Abraham Lincoln on a number of occasions. She agitated for the federal government to grant land in the West to the emancipated slaves, and actively supported the National Freedmen's Relief Association and the Freedmen's Bureau.

She had been cared for by her daughters in her final years.

Eleanor Ormerod

The Royal Agricultural Society, whose members are shown here at a country meeting, has appointed Eleanor Ormerod as consultant entomologist.

Key Events

Mannheim, Germany, January 29, 1886: Karl Benz patents the Tri-car, the world's first automobile.

Athens, Georgia, USA, May 8, 1886: Doctor John Pemberton develops Coca-Cola, a cola-based health tonic.

London, England, June 8, 1886: The Irish Home Rule Bill, tabled by William Ewart Gladstone as he leads his third government, is defeated and an election is called.

New York City, USA, October 28, 1886: President Cleveland dedicates the Statue of Liberty, a gift from France.

USA, 1886: Women's rights activists Susan B. Anthony, Elizabeth Cady Stanton, and Matilda Gage publish the third in their three-volume work, *The History of Woman's Suffrage,* a collection of writings about the women's movement in the USA.

Paris, France, 1886: Astronomer Dorothea Klumpke begins work at the Paris Observatory.

Japan, 1886: Feminist and social reformer Yajima Kajiko helps to establish the Japanese branch of the Woman's Christian Temperance Union.

Pennsylvania, USA, 1886: Anandibai Joshee graduates from the Women's Medical College of Pennsylvania, the first Indian woman to qualify as a doctor.

London, England, November 2, 1887: Soprano Jenny Lind, the "Swedish Nightingale," dies, aged 67.

London, England, December, 1887: Arthur Conan Doyle's first Sherlock Holmes story, *A Study in Scarlet,* is published.

Boston, USA, March 6, 1888: Novelist Louisa May Alcott, best known for *Little Women,* dies, aged 56.

Rochester, New York, USA, September 4, 1888: George Eastman's camera, the Kodak, is patented.

Denmark, 1888: Swedish playwright August Strindberg's *Miss Julie* premieres, scandalizing audiences with its themes of class and desire.

Brazil, November 16, 1889: A republic is proclaimed after a coup.

England, 1889: Garden designer Gertrude Jekyll meets architect Sir Edward Luytens, and begins to design gardens for his houses.

Poland, 1889: Revolutionary and journalist, Rosa Luxemburg, flees to Switzerland to avoid arrest for her left-wing affiliations and activities.

New York City, USA, 1889: Barnard College, part of Columbia University, is established to provide education for women.

Naples, Italy, 1889: Soprano Gemma Bellincioni is selected to play in *Cavalleria Rusticana* next year.

Helen Hunt Jackson

Wagner Plays On

Bayreuth, Germany, 1884: Cosima Wagner, widow of composer Richard Wagner and daughter of composer Franz Liszt, has presented a posthumous performance of the Ring Cycle at the Festival Theater (Festspielhaus), in Bayreuth. Under her guidance, this year's festival has been a cultural and financial success.

The presentation of the Bayreuth Festival has always presented a challenge because of Richard Wagner's demands for authenticity in the form of live animals on stage and elaborate costumes and scenery. These and other factors created a singular financial burden on the organizers.

Finances proved to be a problem from the very beginning. Bayreuth lacked a suitable venue, and it was necessary to design, construct, and fund an appropriate performance space.

From the inception of the Festival, the Wagners sought to achieve musical excellence and a sound financial return. The former objective was readily met—attending the inaugural Festival in 1876, Russian composer Piotr Tchaikovsky wrote, "Something has taken place today at Bayreuth which our grandchildren and their children will remember."

Always protective of her husband and his works, Cosima took control of the Festival after his death in February last year. She said of their relationship, "Fate laid it on me." She has already proved to be a better manager than her husband, and despite some misgiving from others

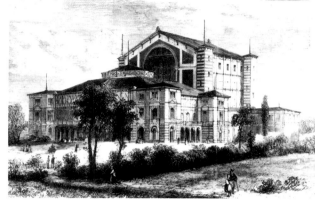

The Festival Theater, Bayreuth, saw its first performance in 1876.

involved in the event's organization, this year's success augurs well for a profitable continuance of the Festival.

Ramona a Revelation!

USA, 1884: Helen Hunt Jackson's romantic novel, *Ramona*, provides an opportunity for the general reader to gain an insight into the appalling conditions experienced by Native Americans. Long an advocate of Native American rights, Hunt is already well known in political circles as a result of her scathing documentation of the manner in which treaties with the Indians have been broken and promises ignored.

Her research, published in *A Century of Dishonor*, in 1881, was sent to every member of the US Congress. The Department of the Interior then commissioned her to undertake a survey of Indian tribes in southern California. The result was a 56-page document, "Report on the Conditions and Needs of the Mission Indians."

Helen Hunt Jackson has now reworked and added to the material from her 1881 publication to produce *Ramona*. By so doing this, she hopes to broadcast her

reformist message to a larger audience. The novel is proving extremely popular.

She has not always been involved with such weighty matters, having earlier established a reputation as a writer of children's stories and poetry. However, during a visit to Boston some years ago, she heard Chief Standing Bear and a female member of his tribe, Bright Eyes, speak about the mistreatment of the Ponca Indians of Nebraska. She became friends with Bright Eyes, and it is believed that she used her as a model for the protagonist of her novel.

Queen's Reign Ends in Smoke

Burma, 1885: The cheroot-smoking Queen Supayalat and her husband, the deposed King Thibaw, have departed Mandalay. The city, where tension had been building for a long time, is now under the control of the British expeditionary forces.

Thibaw came to the throne of Burma in 1878. He married his two half-sisters: Supayagyi and her younger sister, Supayalat. Supayagyi took up residence in the Chief Queen's apartment, but Supayalat, ignoring royal protocol, moved directly into the King's quarters and usurped her sister's position as chief wife. Immediately, King Thibaw came under Supayalat's spell, and, at her prompting, had many of his relatives murdered, lest they threaten his hold on the throne. The British representative in Mandalay lodged a protest, but this was ignored.

The King developed a partiality for strong liquor and this provided Supayalat with an opportunity to act in his stead. She had her son designated Crown Prince and heir apparent, but the child died.

Thibaw and Supayalat further annoyed the British, who had held the southern portion of Burma as a dominion since 1824, by entertaining proposals from France relating to trade and commerce.

In September, 1884, believing themselves threatened, the King and Queen planned the murder of their political opponents, most of whom were already held in prison. A jailbreak was contrived. With the warders turning a blind eye, waiting troops shot the escapees, and the prison was set alight. It is estimated some 300 prisoners perished.

This brought no direct response from the British. However, a dispute between the Bombay-Burma Trading Company and the Burmese Government was seen to provide the British Indian authorities with an excuse to commence hostilities in Burma. Mandalay was eventually taken by British forces on November 28, 1885.

Queen Supayalat and King Thibaw have been exiled to Ratnagari, India.

Cosima Wagner is pictured with her husband, Richard Wagner (center), and her father, Franz Liszt.

Susan B. Anthony (left) and Elizabeth Cady Stanton.

A Work in Progress

USA, 1886: Three women's rights activists have released the third volume of *The History of Woman's Suffrage*. The work is the result of the combined authorship of Susan B. Anthony, Elizabeth Cady Stanton, and Matilda Gage.

The initial volume appeared in 1881, volume two followed in 1882, and volume three has been published this year. Copies have been distributed, free of charge, to all schools and libraries.

This prodigious undertaking is the brainchild of Susan B. Anthony, raised in a Quaker family with activist traditions, who decided to compile a record of the campaign to win the vote for women. She was joined in this undertaking by Elizabeth Cady Stanton, the pair having founded the National Woman's Suffrage Association in 1869.

Matilda Gage, the third member of the group, is the founder of the Woman's National Liberal League. Although perhaps the least well known of the three as an activist, Gage has a solid reputation as a writer, and has added literary touches to the work, leaving the organizational side of matters to her colleagues.

Initially, publishers were not interested in the project, so Anthony invested her own money, and, with the further help of a bequest, saw the first volume of the book into print.

It is suggested that a further volume may need to be written before the question of women's suffrage is resolved.

Western Model for Japanese Reform

Japan, 1886: Inspired by the effectiveness of the Woman's Christian Temperance Union in the United States, Yajima Kajiko, a Christian lady living in Tokyo, has founded a local association modeled

on the American group. Her organization, Fujin Kyofukai (Women's Reform Society), while conscious of the dangers of immoderate use of alcohol, has charged itself with a campaign against prostitution, concubinage, and other abuses arising from Japan's patriarchal system.

Under Japanese law, women are prohibited from becoming involved in any political association and cannot attend Parliament. With the voices of Japanese women thus muffled and their overt political conduct greatly restricted, Yajima Kajiko's Women's Reform Society is an organization through which they may seek to mobilize public opinion in support of their objectives.

A First for India and Pennsylvania

Pennsylvania, USA, 1886: On March 11, Anandibai Joshee received her degree from the Women's Medical College of Pennsylvania. She is India's first woman doctor. She intends to undertake an internship at Boston's New England Hospital for Women and Children.

The graduation was attended by her husband, Gopalrao, and many notables, including Pandita Ramabai, the well-known advocate of Hindu women's education, who is a relative.

Anandibai was born into an aristocratic family. While her father encouraged her to learn to read, her mother was a traditionalist who did not approve of such progressive ideas.

Anandibai's father did, however, subscribe to the custom of childhood marriage for girls; at the age of nine she became the bride of Gopalrao Joshee, a 27-year-old widowed postmaster. Joshee intended that his new bride should receive an education, and she learned English and Sanskrit. Anandibai herself made the decision to study medicine.

Attempts to study in America failed, until Anandibai came under the patronage of Mrs Theodocia Carpenter of Philadelphia, who arranged her passage to New York. Anandibai was able to commence her studies at the Women's Medical College in 1883.

Shortly afterward, Gopalrao Joshee arrived in America to lecture on Indian culture. To the embarrassment of his wife's supporters, he was dismissive of most things American. Anandibai, for her part, acknowledged that reform of her homeland's patriarchal society was desirable, but supported many of the traditions and customs of India.

"Home, Sweet Home" No More!

England, November 2, 1887: One of the sweetest voices ever heard has been silenced. Jenny Lind, the world-renowned "Swedish Nightingale," died today at her home in the Malvern Hills, Shropshire.

Lind was accepted as a student into the Swedish Royal Opera at the age of nine. By her early 20s, she had established herself as Europe's leading soprano. Hans Christian Andersen was one of many who fell under her spell; he proposed, and was (kindly) rejected, not once, but three times. It is said he wrote "The Emperor's Nightingale," "The Angel," and "The Ugly Duckling" as tributes to Miss Lind.

In the course of her career, she came to England and sang before Queen Victoria and members of the Royal family. The Queen was impressed, saying: "She has a most exquisite, powerful and really quite peculiar voice."

Lind retired from the operatic stage in 1849, but continued performing as a concert artist. She was persuaded to tour North America, and wildly enthusiastic crowds greeted her arrival in New York. Her rendition of the song, "Home, Sweet Home," made it the most popular song in America. Her appearances in Canada were also warmly received.

While in Boston she married Otto Goldschmidt, her accompanist. The couple returned to Europe, settling in Dresden, before Lind decided to move to England. By 1858 she had virtually retired, and finally gave her last concert at the age of 63. She took up the position of Professor of Singing at the Royal College of Music, London, but had been in failing health for some time.

Gemma Bellincioni

In her prime, Jenny Lind was the leading soprano of Europe.

Blithe Bly Shrinks World

New York, USA, January 25, 1890: Police officers were obliged to clear a path for a smiling Nellie Bly as she disembarked from her train at Jersey City today, having hurtled around the world in the record time of 72 days, 6 hours, and 11 minutes. Her editor at the *New York World* had set this intrepid reporter the mammoth task of circling the globe in under 80 days—a record ascribed to the fictitious Phineas Fogg by the English author Jules Verne in his famous novel *Around the World in Eighty Days*. By rail, road, and sea, Miss Bly has traversed the world in a shorter time than any previous adventurer, the task rendered all the more difficult by the fact that only three days were allowed for her to prepare for the journey.

Nellie Bly, who was born Elizabeth Cochrane, has built a reputation as an unortho- dox reporter. She obtained her first job in journalism as the result of her impassioned response to an item in the *Pittsburgh Dispatch* that had proposed that women were only good for housework and raising children. Impressed, the editor commissioned her to write a series of articles on working women. Later, moving to the *New York World*, Nellie reported on the treatment of the insane by having herself committed to an asylum. The resulting article, "Ten Days in a Mad- house," exposed the abuses suffered by inmates of the city's mental institutions.

Prepared to place herself in risky situations to uncover a good story, she posed as a country girl to report on the techniques that criminals use to lure young women into prostitution. Nellie Bly was also talented enough to pass herself off as a chorus girl in order to write a story on the seedy side of stage life. Her many adventures in the city provided her with the gritty material for her exciting novel, *The Mystery of Central Park*.

Science Suffers a Loss

Stockholm, Sweden, February 10, 1891: Sonya Kovalevsky, the first female member of the Russian Academy of Sciences and a renowned mathematician, died today after a short illness. Her claim to fame lies not only in being the world's first female professional math- ematician; Kovalesky is also noted for her considerable literary skills—she was a writer of both fiction and non-fiction.

A lifelong interest in politics and current events did not distract Sonya Kovalevsky from the pursuit of a scientific education. Back in 1867, Russian universities did not formally admit women as students. At this time, Kovalevsky traveled with her husband to Germany where she enrolled at the University of Heidelberg. Later she studied privately under the direction of Profes- sor Karl Weierstrass, at Berlin.

Professor Weierstrass was deeply impressed with her work, so much so that he advised her to present her re- search material to the faculty as a PhD dissertation. The award of a doctorate to a woman was almost without precedence, but the University of Göttingen was pre- pared to consider her workn, and in 1874 awarded her PhD, *summa cum laude*.

In April, 1883, Kovalevsky's husband committed suicide. Having settled his affairs, she took up a lectureship at the University of Stockholm and was later appointed assistant professor, another first for a woman. In December, 1888, the Academy of Paris awarded her the Prix Borodin for her work. Her death today, at the age of just 41, is a big loss to the scientific community.

Editor Leaves Town

Memphis, Tennessee, USA, April, 1892: Ida Wells-Barnett, the African-American campaigner for racial justice and part- owner of the newspaper *Memphis Free Speech*, has received news while she has been away that the *Free Speech* printing presses have been destroyed by a white mob, which has also declared an intent to lynch her should she return to Memphis.

These actions follow an editorial she wrote during March, condemning the

Souvenir postcard of Queen Victoria's family, c. 1890.

lynching of three local black businessmen after a week of racial disturbances that appear to have been engineered largely by a white business rival.

In her editorial Wells-Barnett stated, "The city of Memphis has demonstrated that neither character nor standing avails the Negro if he dares protect himself against the white man or becomes his rival." She advised local African-Americans to "leave a town that will neither protect our lives and property." Many followed her advice; Ida Wells-Barnett now has no option but to do the same.

Fanny Kemble was a leading figure of the British stage.

Death of Acclaimed Actress

London, England, January 15, 1893: Fanny Kemble, the actress whose appearances on stage could prompt a riot of enthusiasm, passed away quietly today at her London home. She was 83 years of age. Born into a theatrical family, Fanny first came to public notice for her portrayal of the doomed heroine in Shakespeare's *Romeo and Juliet*. She later wrote a successful historical drama, *Francis I*, in which she played the leading role.

In order to assist her family, which was beset by financial troubles, Fanny Kemble traveled to America for a series of appearances that she hoped would raise sufficient funds to reduce the family's debt. An immediate hit, some critics acclaimed her the best actress they had ever seen.

In 1834 Fanny married Pierce Butler, heir to a Georgia plantation. But she soon found that neither the American way of life, nor her husband, whom she bitingly referred to as "my lord and master," were to her liking, and the conditions suffered by the plantation slaves horrified her. She set out her feelings on these subjects in her *Journal of Residence in America*, which was published in 1835.

Fanny Kemble resumed her acting career in 1847, and toured America and Britain giving readings of Shakespeare's plays. Having divorced her husband in 1849, she wrote another book, *Journal of a Residence on a Georgia Plantation*, a denunciation of slavery published during the American Civil War, when it was used to advance the Union cause.

A New Stage for Avril

Paris, France, April 20, 1893: A new act at the Jardin de Paris is being cleverly advertised in a new style of art!

Jane Avril, a dancer already very well known to patrons of the Moulin Rouge for her performances of the can-can, has been engaged by the Jardin de Paris, a café-concert establishment, as the feature act. Artist Henri de Toulouse-Lautrec has created a magnificent poster, in the *Art-Nouveau* style, to advertise the event; it portrays Avril in mid-dance, giving one of her famous high kicks.

Life has not always been kind to Jane Avril. She grew up abused by both her father and drunken mother. She ran away from home but was detained by authorities and, deemed to be insane, she was committed to a hospital for the mentally disturbed. Later, at a social function given for the staff and inmates, she performed a solo dance with such grace and sensitivity that she convinced those who saw her that she was fit for discharge.

In Paris, Jane worked doing odd jobs, only performing her dance in local clubs whenever an opportunity arose, until she was strongly encouraged by the writer René Boylesve to pursue a full-time dancing career. He suggested she abandon her own name—Jeanne Beaudon—and adopt the stage name she now uses.

Jane Avril was employed by the Moulin Rouge when it opened in 1889.

Annie Oakley

Jane Avril, as painted by Toulouse-Lautrec.

Harriett Beecher Stowe

A First for New Zealand Women

New Zealand, September 19, 1893: In a historic move, the Governor today signed into law the *Electoral Act,* which includes an extension of the franchise to women. It has been a long hard battle, but at last women are to be admitted a direct voice in the government of the colony. Now, any woman over the age of 21 years, natural born or naturalized British subject, and resident in the colony for 12 months, is entitled to vote.

In the Parliament, Sir John Hall and Sir Robert Stout have been supporters of this landmark reform, but no one has worked harder to achieve the present result than Mrs Katherine Sheppard. Long associated with the Christian Temperance Union, Mrs Sheppard has strongly advocated the involvement of that movement in other matters of social concern, beyond just the practical consideration of temperance. It is her conviction that "all that separates, whether of race, class, creed, or sex, is inhuman, and must be overcome."

Two years ago, Katherine Sheppard organized a petition in favor of women's suffrage, which the Temperance Union presented to Parliament. It received some support, but no action was forthcoming.

> *"When a woman isn't beautiful, people always say, 'You have lovely eyes, you have lovely hair.'"*
>
> ANTON CHEKHOV
> (1897), *UNCLE VANYA*

Another petition followed, again without a positive result. Earlier this year, Mrs Sheppard presented yet another petition, this one bearing over 30,000 signatures, which represents one-quarter of all adult women in the colony. This sizable document caused something of a stir in the Parliament when it was unrolled in the debating chamber for all members to see.

With only ten weeks to go before the general election, Mrs Sheppard is busily organizing the enrolment of women voters. The Wellington *Evening Post*, a strong supporter of the women's suffrage movement, has distributed application for enrolments forms with today's copy of the newspaper, and carries the banner headline, "Register! Register! Register!"

Dress Reformer Dies

Iowa, USA, December 30, 1894: Amelia Bloomer, feminist activist, newspaper proprietor, and advocate of female dress reform, has died today at her home, at 76 years of age.

The founder and editor of the *Lily* (1849–1855), a newspaper "devoted to the interests of woman," Amelia was a champion of issues of social justice, including women's suffrage and access to education. She also promoted sensible women's apparel. In the 1850s, clothing for women was extremely uncomfortable, and even undergarments could weigh up to 14 pounds (6.5 kg).

Noting the comfortable outfit worn by another feminist, Elizabeth Miller— a pair of Turkish pantaloons and a short overskirt—she deemed this a liberating costume, and, in the *Lily*, championed its adoption for general wear. She and fellow campaigners for women's rights began wearing the garment that now bears her name—"bloomers."

Amelia Bloomer models her comfortable outfit.

A Woman and a Lasting Impression

Paris, France, March 2, 1895: The final Impressionist art exhibition was held some years ago, and today Impressionism appears to be on its last legs, particularly with the announcement that one of the final exponents of this style of painting, Berthe Morisot, died, aged 81 years.

Morisot was a pioneer in what came to be called the Impressionist movement, which challenged the conventions and traditions of the orthodox art establishment. Along with others in the movement, she suffered as a consequence, her work receiving scant recognition from the jurors at the influential Paris Salon.

As a young girl, Berthe had studied painting under Geoffroy-Alphonse Chocarne, but his adherence to orthodoxy prompted her to seek out another tutor, Joseph Guichard, who proved a more relaxed teacher, allowing her to experiment and find her own style.

When she took seriously to painting, Berthe Morisot had to contend with the predominantly dismissive attitude with which the majority of male artists viewed the work of their female counterparts. There were, of course, exceptions. Berthe had adopted an innovative unorthodox style, which had been labeled by art critics "Impressionism," and she soon found support from artists Manet and Degas, who painted in the same style.

With the passage of time, the Impressionist school experienced dissent within its own ranks, with some preferring to submit to the Salon as per the custom, while others, Berthe Morisot among them, choosing to exhibit independently.

Berthe Morisot's work was taken up by the art dealer Paul Durand-Ruel, and he showed her paintings in art galleries in Paris and New York. One critic remarked, "That young lady does not waste time on reproducing a host of boring details.

Berthe Morisot, in an 1869 painting by her friend, Édouard Manet.

When she has a hand to paint she simply applies as many brushstrokes as there are fingers and the job is done!"

In later years Morisot's art came to be accepted for its unmistakable merit, *In the Dining Room* becoming one of her best known and reproduced works.

No More Binding for Pity's Sake

Shanghai, China, 1895: Once again, locals and Christian missionaries have forcibly expressed opposition to the practice of

The Meers Sisters' perform a daring bareback riding equestrian act.

female foot binding. A group of Western women in this city, led by Mrs Archibald Little, have established a "Natural Foot Society," and have written to the Dowager Empress Cixi to seek her support in their endeavor to bring foot binding to an end. The Society "invites the help and sympathy of those who are moved by considerations ethical, economic or simply by pity."

Tradition has it that during the rule of Emperor Li Yu (961–975 CE), his favorite consort had enchanted him by performing a graceful dance atop a golden lotus pedestal, with her feet wrapped in silk binding for support. Other court ladies quickly adopted the silken binding as a fashion. In time, however, it became the practice to bind the feet so tightly as to cause deformation of the toes and an acute arching of the foot.

Chinese reformers have previously tried to halt foot binding, so far in vain. Missionaries now accept only girls with unbound feet as students in their boarding schools, and some Christian churches have even excluded women with bound feet from attendance at religious services. Whether any of this will counter the local belief that a girl with large feet is destined to a life of ill fortune remains to be seen.

Hawaii No Longer a Monarchy

Honolulu, Hawaii, December, 1896: Lydia Kamekeha Liliuokalani, former Queen of Hawaii, who was sentenced to five years' imprisonment on a charge of neglect of duty (misprision), has been released and granted a pardon by President Dole, head of the Provisional Government. Upon her release, Liliuokalani sailed straight to the United States of America.

From the time she came to the throne in January 1891, the Queen's reign had been a troubled one. Her Prime Minister, John Stevens, believed annexation by the United States was necessary in order to

sustain the local economy. Liliuokalani disagreed and moved to strengthen the monarchy. This was countered by the formation of a provisional government, which declared not only that the Queen was an "insurgent" who had "rebelled against her own government," but that she was no longer monarch. On January 16, 1893, American troops entered Honolulu and took control of government buildings. Liliuokalani protested to President Cleveland, who, while expressing regret at America's involvement, did nothing to rectify matters. The Queen's situation worsened when a search conducted by the provisional government found guns, ammunition, and bombs buried in the garden of her home. She was arrested, and, on January 24, 1895, was forced to sign an act of abdication. Sentenced to imprisonment, she was allowed to serve the sentence confined to two rooms of her house.

Once in the United States, Liliuokalani intends to protest again to President Cleveland regarding what she terms the "theft" of her country.

The Atom is Reassessed

Paris, France, 1898: Prepare to add three new words to today's scientific lexicon: radioactivity, polonium, and radium. Marie Curie, a well-regarded scientist conducting research in the School of Physics at the Sorbonne, has submitted a preliminary paper to the Academy of Science, in which she describes the behavior of uranium as displaying, as she terms it, radioactivity.

As part of her doctoral studies, Marie Curie has been investigating the rays emitted by uranium. She believes that these electrical rays could have an atomic property. The current scientific understanding is that the atom is the most elementary

particle, but her study hints at a complex inner structure within the atom itself.

Assisted in this work by her husband Pierre Curie, a noted physicist, the couple has discovered that pitchblende is more radioactive than pure uranium. They have separated two substances from the pitchblende, one containing mostly bismuth, the other barium. In the bismuth they have detected a new element, which Marie has named "polonium" after her native Poland, while the barium fraction contained an element that the scientists have named "radium." Although the chemical properties of these two new elements are dissimilar, both exhibit a strong radioactivity.

The scientific community is likely to remain skeptical of these findings until Marie and Pierre Curie have succeeded in isolating samples of pure radium and polonium—an arduous task in which these two brilliant scientists are now very actively engaged.

Queen Liliuokalani of Hawaii

Marie and Pierre Curie take a break from their groundbreaking scientific research.

Carrie Chapman Catt

Women Called to the Cause

Dublin, Ireland, October 1900: Ireland's women, who have always been excluded from the country's nationalist organizations, now have an organization of their own. Actress and social activist, Maud Gonne, has founded a women's group, Inghinidhe na hÉireann (Daughters of Ireland), with the objectives of establishing an independent Ireland, encouraging Irish literature, and actively discouraging English culture in Ireland.

Maud Gonne is equally well-known to nationalists and the British authorities. She assisted tenants in their campaign for a reform of the land tenure system, and was recently involved in the formation of the Irish Transvaal committee, which supports the Boer cause in South Africa. During Queen Victoria's visit to Ireland this year, Gonne organized a "Patriotic Children's Treat" to counter festivities arranged for the royal visit.

New Opportunity for Women to Study Medicine

Tokyo, Japan, 1900 : Women who wish to follow a medical career now have an opportunity to undergo training in the newly opened Tokyo Women's Medical

"Ours is the old, old story of every uprising race or class or order. The work of elevation must be wrought by ourselves or not at all."

FRANCES POWER
COBBE
(1822–1904),
JOURNALIST AND
SOCIAL ACTIVIST,
ON WOMEN'S SUFFRAGE

School (Tokyo Joigakko), Japan's first medical school for women. Dr Yoshioka Yayaoi, herself a qualified and licensed medical practitioner, has opened this new institution. She believes that "medicine is a noble profession, suited to women."

It has always been difficult for women in Japan to enter the medical profession. Though permitted to take the medical examination, obtaining professional training locally has been a problem. Dr Yoshioka Yayaoi was fortunate in being permitted to study at the Saisei-Gakusha school of medicine, and received only the twelfth medical license to be granted to a woman in this country. Medical training has recently been rendered even more difficult, with the reintroduction of the prohibition against women attending medical schools, which would have forced intending female students to travel overseas to obtain their qualification.

Dr Yoshioka Yayaoi has been able to follow in the footsteps of her father and two brothers, all of them respected medical practitioners, but it has been a very difficult undertaking.

She has expressed the hope that the Women's Medical School will not only provide excellent medical training for the next generation of doctors, but will serve the additional function of improving the status and independence of women.

Actress Ethel Barrymore with her brothers John (left) and Lionel.

The Victorian Age has come to an end.

Close of a Reign

Cowes, England, January 22, 1901: Thousands of Londoners gathered outside Mansion House today as the Lord Mayor appeared at an upper window and announced to the silent crowd the death of Queen Victoria. He read out a telegram from the King, Edward VII, which said: "My beloved mother has passed to her rest." Her Majesty had reigned for almost 64 years, longer than any other British monarch. At the news of her death, church bells tolled, and places of entertainment ceased their performances.

The Queen was at Osborne House on the Isle of Wight at the time of her death. After her last breath was drawn, members of the Royal Family, who had been at her bedside, knelt and kissed the hands of the new King in a gesture of fealty.

Her Majesty ascended the throne on June 20, 1837. She married her cousin, Albert, son of the duke of Saxe-Coburg-Gotha, in February of 1840. A true love match, the couple had nine children. When Prince Albert died in 1861, the Queen went into deep mourning, and wore black for the rest of her reign.

Victoria's time on the throne has seen many changes to society, as well as great scientific and technological advances. During her reign, the British Empire has doubled in size. The Queen became Empress of India in 1876.

Dublin, Ireland, March–April 1900: Revolutionary and actress Maude Gonne founds the nationalist organization, Inghinidhe na hEireann, the Daughters of Ireland.
New York, USA, May 15, 1900: Florence Parpart and Hiram Layman invent the street cleaning machine.
Tokyo, Japan, 1900: Dr Yoshioka Yayoi establishes the Tokyo Joigakko, the Tokyo Women's Medical School, the first training college in Japan for women doctors.

New York, USA, 1900: Activist and feminist Carrie Chapman Catt succeeds Susan B. Anthony as president of the National American Woman's Suffrage Association.
Cowes, England, January 2, 1901: After a 64-year reign, Queen Victoria dies, aged 82.
China, September 7, 1901: The end of the Boxer Rebellion is negotiated.
UK and Canada, December 12, 1901: Italian Guglielmo Marconi transmits wireless telegraphic signals from Cornwall to Newfoundland, a distance of 2,232 miles (3,593 km).

Broadway, New York, USA, 1901: Actress Ethel Barrymore appears on Broadway in *Captain Jinks of the Horse Marines*, her first starring role.
Australia, 1901: Miles Franklin (Stella Maria Sarah Miles Franklin) publishes *My Brilliant Career*.
Gournia, Crete, 1901: American archeologist Harriet Boyd begins excavating Minoan ruins at Gournia.
Massachusetts, USA, May 12, 1902: Dr Marie Zakrzewska, co-founder of the New York Infirmary and the New England Hospital for Women and Children, dies aged 72.

Australia, June 12, 1902: Revised electoral laws give Australian women the right to vote and to stand as candidates in elections.
New York City, USA, October 26, 1902: Women's rights activist Elizabeth Cady Stanton dies, aged 86.
Victoria, Australia, December, 1902: Journalist and women's rights activist, Vida Goldstein becomes the first female candidate for the Australian parliament. Earlier this year, she founded the journal *The Australian Woman's Sphere*.

London, England, 1902: Physicist Hertha Marks Ayrton publishes *The Electric Arc*, and is the first woman nominated a Fellow of the Royal Society of London, a distinction denied her because she is married.
England, 1902: Beatrix Potter publishes *The Tale of Peter Rabbit*.
Hamburg, Germany, 1902: The Union for Women's Suffrage is founded by a group of women including Lida Heymann and Anita Augsburg.

Her reign was, in the main, peaceful. Though there were disturbances in the Empire, British troops were involved in only one European conflict: the Crimean War (1854–1856). The Queen was a keen supporter of her troops and instituted the Victoria Cross as an award for bravery.

Queen Victoria was a talented artist and writer and, unusually for a reigning monarch, published two books, *Leaves from the Journal of our Life in the Highlands* (1868) and *More Leaves* (1884).

Archeologist Announces Important Finds

USA, 1902: A most resolute and self-assured woman, Miss Harriet Boyd has concluded a national lecture tour, during which she told of her exciting archeological discoveries on the island of Crete.

Miss Boyd, who teaches archeology and modern Greek at Smith College, is the discoverer of a Minoan town at Gournia that dates from the Early Bronze Age (3000 BCE). She has been excavating on the island of Crete since 1900. Before that, she had discovered houses and tombs from the Geometric period (900 BCE) at Kavousi. This success brought her work to the attention of the Secretary of the American Exploration Society, which provided funding for her further work on Crete.

Returning to the island in 1901, Miss Boyd was able to employ a force of over 100 workers for the excavations at Gournia. She is certainly the first woman to have directed a major archeological dig. The Gournia excavation unearthed more than 70 double-storied stone houses, a small palace complex, paved roads, and a large quantity of pottery.

On her return home earlier this year, Harriet Boyd delivered an address to the American Archaeological Institute, giving details of her finds. She is the first woman to have addressed members of the Institute, and this august body has declared her discoveries to be of "great interest and importance."

Harriet Boyd intends to continue her work at Gournia next year.

Peter Rabbit in Color

England, 1902: A small, privately published children's book, relating the adventures of a rabbit called Peter, appeared late last year. Its author, Beatrix Potter, made it available to her young readers at the price of a halfpenny; as she explained, "Little rabbits cannot afford to spend 6 shillings."

The *Tale of Peter Rabbit* has now proved so successful that it has been taken up by the publishing house Frederick Warne & Co., who have further commissioned Miss Potter to reproduce her black and white illustrations in full color. The book will be printed in a small format, the better to fit into little hands.

Beatrix Potter has had some earlier publishing success, with a charming book of verse, and her illustrations being used for Christmas cards. She has a decided talent for capturing on paper the likeness of the small animals that inhabit our countryside. Although residing with her family in London, she has spent considerable time in the country, particularly in the Lake District, of which she is very fond.

She admits having owned, at various times, mice, rats, lizards, and, of course, rabbits. But Potter's interests extend beyond fauna to flora, and her excellent research paper, "On the Germination of the Spores of Agaricinae," has been read to the Linnean Society in London.

Current reports indicate that sales of the little book are doing very well.

Elizabeth Cady Stanton

The Nobel Prize was awarded to Marie and Pierre Curie.

Author and illustrator, Beatrix Potter.

Massachusetts, USA, January 6, 1903: Margaret Knight receives a patent for her improvements to the rotary engine.

Kishinev, Russia, April 16, 1903: Officials under Tsar Nicholas II stoke peasants' anti-Semitic feelings and a bloody pogrom results in the deaths of hundreds of Jews.

Toronto, Canada, April 30, 1903: Dr Emily Howard Jennings Stowe, suffragette and the first woman to practice as a doctor in Canada, dies, aged 72.

Bancroft, Omaha, USA, May 26, 1903: Susette La Flèche Tibbles, also known as "Bright Eyes," dies, aged 49. The daughter of the last Omaha chief, she was one of the first women to promote the rights of Native Americans.

Deadwood, South Dakota, USA, August 1, 1903: Frontierswoman and star of Buffalo Bill's Wild West Show, Calamity Jane (Martha Jane Cannary Burke), dies, aged 51.

Alabama, USA, November 10, 1903: Mary Anderson invents the windshield wiper.

Manchester, England, October 1903: Suffragettes Emmeline and Christabel Pankhurst found the Women's Social and Political Union.

Stockholm, Sweden, December 10, 1903: Marie and Pierre Curie share the Nobel Prize in Physics with Henri Becquerel for their work on radioactivity.

Chicago, Illinois, USA, 1903: Factory worker Agnes Nestor is elected president of the International Glove Workers Union of America.

Havana, Cuba, February 5, 1904: US troops withdraw from Cuba.

Aceh, Dutch East Indies, April 3, 1904: Dutch colonial forces kill over 500 Achenese in 30-year Aceh War.

Ireland, April 5, 1904: Frances Power Cobbe, Irish writer on theology and ethics, and social reformer, dies, aged 81.

Edinburgh, Scotland, October 7, 1904: Travel writer Isabella Bird Bishop dies, aged 72.

Ain Sefra, Algeria, October 21, 1904: Swiss-born explorer Isabella Eberhardt dies, aged 27. She had traveled extensively through Africa dressed as a man.

Washington DC, USA, December 6, 1904: Theodore Roosevelt's Corollary to the Monroe Doctrine, invoked to force the Dominican Republic to pays its debts, sees the USA take on the role of international policeman.

Dublin, Ireland, 1904: Dramatist Lady Augusta Gregory becomes a director of the Abbey Theatre, which she co-founded with poet W. B. Yeats.

Massachusetts, USA, 1904: Helen Keller becomes the first deaf and blind person to graduate from a college when she completes her studies at Radcliffe.

Calamity Jane

Women on the Move

Hamburg, Germany, 1902: The campaign for women's votes in Germany is likely to take a radical turn with the founding of the Union for Women's Suffrage. Until now the majority of feminist groups have managed to avoid militancy and have disassociated themselves from disruptive mass action. The leadership of the Union of Women's Suffrage has indicated that it is likely to adopt more forceful tactics.

Lida Heymann and Anita Augsburg are among the leadership of the Union. Heymann has been closely associated with the Women's Welfare Association, an organization that fought against regulated prostitution.

Augsburg, also active in the movement to ban regulated prostitution, believes that moderate feminists are not taking the movement forward. The Union of Women's Suffrage intends to forcefully accelerate the campaign for the vote.

Calamity Jane toured for a time with Buffalo Bill's famous Wild West Show, showing off her horsemanship.

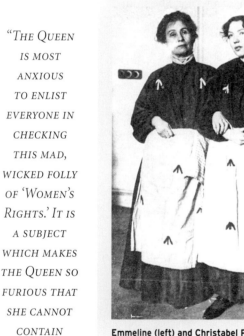

Emmeline (left) and Christabel Pankhurst.

> *"THE QUEEN IS MOST ANXIOUS TO ENLIST EVERYONE IN CHECKING THIS MAD, WICKED FOLLY OF 'WOMEN'S RIGHTS.' IT IS A SUBJECT WHICH MAKES THE QUEEN SO FURIOUS THAT SHE CANNOT CONTAIN HERSELF."*
>
> QUEEN VICTORIA
> (1819–1901),
> ENGLISH QUEEN

A Legend in Her Lifetime

Deadwood, South Dakota, USA, August 1, 1903: Calamity Jane is an American name that immediately conjures up myriad tales, some tall, some true.

Born Martha Jane Cannary, in Princeton, Missouri, in 1853, Calamity Jane earned her better-known name during the Indian War of 1873, when she was serving as a scout with the cavalry under the command of Captain Egan. When he was shot in a skirmish, she lifted him onto her horse and delivered him safely back to the fort. He declared his rescuer "Calamity Jane, the heroine of the plains."

It is not clear how long Calamity Jane served with the army, but having been in uniform, she felt perfectly at home in men's clothes. This helped to disguise her gender when she later worked as a stagecoach driver, and drove ox-teams, carting supplies and machinery to the mining sites during the gold rushes in South Dakota. Jane also worked for a time as a Pony Express rider, carrying the US mail between Deadwood and Custer cities. She had a reputation for being quick with a gun and deadly with a whip, and with these skills, she toured with Buffalo Bill's Wild West Show for some years.

But the legend is no more. Calamity Jane died today at the Calloway Hotel, near Deadwood. She was 51 years old.

Is it Legal?

Victoria, Australia, December 1902: Members of the Federal Parliament have challenged the Minister of Home Affairs, Sir William Lyne, arguing against the eligibility of women to become federal legislators. The Minister has dismissed their concerns, which is just as well, since Miss Vida Goldstein, a longtime activist in the quest for women's suffrage, has been nominated as a candidate for a Senate position in the upcoming Federal election. It is her view that the *Uniform Federal Franchise Act,* introduced in June this year, gives her the right to stand for election. She seeks to represent Victoria, a state that has not yet granted the franchise to women.

Miss Goldstein's name appears along with those of 17 male candidates for the election to be held on December 16. She is the first woman to stand for parliament in Australia, and is an independent candidate, declining to seek endorsement from any of the established political parties.

The young teacher, educated at the Presbyterian Ladies College, is deeply committed to countering the oppression of women in the wider community. She founded the monthly paper, the *Australian Women's Sphere,* which addresses not only local social and political issues, but also reprints many articles concerning the women's movement in other countries. As a member of the United Council for

Vida Goldstein is a candidate for the Australian Senate.

Women's Suffrage, Vida Goldstein has traveled to Washington DC, representing Australia and New Zealand.

No More Traveling for Isabella

Edinburgh, Scotland, October 7, 1904: Undaunted by a lengthy and serious illness, the noted travel writer, Isabella Bird Bishop, had her suitcases all packed in readiness for another overseas trip when she died today in Edinburgh, just a week short of her seventy-third birthday.

Her first voyage, at the age of 22, was undertaken to improve poor health. The trip from her home in Yorkshire was to Canada through the northern states of America. Upon her return she wrote an account of her travels: *An Englishwoman in America*, published by John Murray. The book sold well. Subsequent trips to New Zealand, Australia, Hawaii, and Japan all resulted in the publication of travel narratives, and Isabella Bird soon established a firm reputation as a serious geographer and anthropologist.

When not traveling, Isabella Bird resided in Edinburgh, and it was there that she became a member of the Royal

Isabella Bird Bishop, travel writer and geographer.

Scottish Geographical Society. In 1833, the year that London's Royal Geographical Society admitted members of other societies to its ranks, it was discovered that, for the first time ever, it suddenly counted women among its membership. The Royal Society decided that no new women members would be accepted, although those existing members, such as Isabella, would not be excluded.

At the age of 50, Isabella Bird decided to marry Dr John Bishop, who had attended her during an illness. Married life was difficult for the wanderer at first, but during this time she set down the records of her earlier journeys from Japan, through China, Hong Kong, and the Malay States. Her recollections were published as *The Golden Chersonese and the Way Thither*. When her husband died in 1886 after only five years of marriage, Isabella resumed her travels.

Motivated by her charitable instincts, Isabella Bird Bishop had funded the establishment of small cottage industries in poverty-stricken areas of the Western Highlands, and during her travels she also established a number of mission hospitals in India and China.

Lady Augusta, Star of Irish National Theater

Dublin, Ireland, December 27, 1904: Those Dubliners who wondered what was afoot at the old Mechanics' Institute in Abbey Street now have their answer. Tonight saw the opening of the Abbey Theatre in the refurbished building. The directors, Lady Augusta Gregory, William Butler Yeats, and Edward Martyn, intend the Abbey to function as the Irish National Theatre.

The project, funded by Miss Annie Horniman, a friend of poet W. B. Yeats, had grown out of an earlier venture, undertaken by Lady Gregory, Yeats, and Martyn, which saw the formation of an Irish Literary Theatre. This establishment presented performances in Dublin from May, 1899, and featured the first production of a play spoken in Gaelic; a second play followed in 1902.

Lady Gregory is deeply interested in Irish history and folklore, and is a fluent Gaelic speaker. She has authored books about ancient Irish epics, and, in collaboration with Yeats, has written two plays, *Cathleen ni Houlihan* and *The Pot of Broth*. She is also a strong supporter of self-government for Ireland.

In the past Lady Gregory's anti-British stance has been noted with some disapproval by her neighbors, such as the time when she refused to light a bonfire on her property to mark the celebration of Queen Victoria's jubilee.

The opening program at the Abbey Theatre has met with general approval. Two pieces were presented: Lady Gregory's play, *Spreading the News* and *On Baile's Strand*, by Yeats.

A Unique Honor

Massachusetts, USA, 1904: An important battle has been won, and a blind and deaf young woman has achieved a unique feat. Helen Keller, whom illness left deaf and blind before her second birthday, has graduated with a Bachelor of Arts degree, awarded with honors, from Radcliffe College. She is the first deaf and blind person ever to achieve this.

For the first seven years of her life, Helen was uneducated. Her parents, unable to communicate with her, and with her conduct becoming increasingly uncontrollable, in desperation sought the help of Dr Alexander Graham Bell, well known for his work with the deaf. Acting on his advice, Helen's parents approached the Perkins School for the Blind, which arranged for Miss Annie Sullivan, herself partially sighted, to move into the Keller household and act as Helen's tutor. After a slow and difficult start, Annie taught Helen a system of manual communication, and Helen mastered Braille. She was also taught a style of written alphabet, especially devised for use by blind people.

At the age of 13, Helen Keller wrote a lively account of her visit to the Chicago World's Fair, and it was published in a youth magazine in December 1893. The article was so well received that Helen decided to become a writer. She studiously prepared to take the entrance examination for Radcliffe College, the women's school attached to Harvard University, an otherwise all-male institution. Her tutor, Annie Sullivan, had to be constantly at her side, translating the lectures into the special manual alphabet that Helen used to learn her lessons.

Apart from her studies, Helen has also written an autobiography, *The Story of My Life*, and has had a collection of essays published. She is known for her advocacy for the provision of improved methods of education for the blind and deaf.

Frances Power Cobbe

Helen Keller has graduated from Radcliffe College.

Emmeline Pankhurst

Research Shows Gender Inherited

Massachusetts, USA, 1905: Research undertaken by the Carnegie Institute biologist, Nettie Stevens, looks set to end the long-standing scientific debate as to whether sex is determined by heredity or other factors. Miss Stevens has found that the gender determination of the common mealworm, *Tenebrio*, is the result of X and Y chromosomes.

Miss Stevens will next investigate the presence of similar chromosomes in a range of insects. Many believe her work will produce the evidence to show that chromosomes also influence human gender traits.

The breakthrough has pushed Miss Stevens into the forefront of modern science. Although little known until now, she has had a stellar career as a research

scientist. She showed early signs of brilliance when she completed the four-year course at Westfield Normal School, Massachusetts in less than half the allotted time and graduated top of her class. She went on to Stanford University, obtaining a BA in 1899 and an MA in 1900. She obtained her PhD in 1903 at Bryn Mawr College where she was influenced by the work of the then head of the Biology Department, Edmund Wilson, and his successor, Thomas Hunt Morgan.

Her interest in the biology of sexual determination stems from time spent at Theodor Boveri's lab at the Zoological Institute at Würzburg, Germany. Boveri was working on the problem of the role of chromosomes in heredity.

First Woman Winner of Nobel Peace Prize

Stockholm, Sweden, 1905: Leading pacifist and writer Baroness Bertha von Suttner has become the first ever woman to be awarded the Nobel Peace Prize. The Baroness, who exerted a long-standing influence on Alfred Nobel, was briefly his secretary, and it is understood she played a major role in his decision to include a peace prize among the many bursaries in his will. She has been widely regarded as sharing the leadership of the peace movement with the "apostle of peace," Frédéric Passy.

Born Countess Kinsky in Prague to an impoverished aristocratic family, she took a post in Vienna as teacher-companion to the four daughters of the von Suttner household. It was here she met the youngest son of the family, Baron Arthur Gundaccar von Suttner. The two married in 1876, against his family's wishes. Both earned their livings as writers until they became involved in the International Arbitration and Peace Association and

Nobel Peace Prize winner, Bertha von Suttner.

> *"STRANGE HOW BLIND PEOPLE ARE! THEY ARE HORRIFIED BY THE TORTURE CHAMBERS OF THE MIDDLE AGES, BUT THEIR ARSENALS FILL THEM WITH PRIDE!"*
>
> BERTHA VON SUTTNER (1843–1918), PACIFIST

Isadora Duncan's dancing offends the Germans.

promised to promote its principles of arbitration before armed conflict.

Baroness von Suttner first came to prominence in 1889 with the publication of her novel, *Die waffen nieder! (Lay Down Your Arms!)*, in which the heroine suffers the horrors of war. The book was painstakingly researched, and so real that it made a huge impact on the reading public, launching her career as an activist. She went on to forge an international reputation as editor of the international pacifist journal *Die waffen nieder!*, named after her book. Baroness von Suttner retired in 1899.

Although grief-stricken at the death of her husband in 1902, Baroness von Suttner has shown herself determined to carry on with their joint work. For the past three years, she has led a reclusive life in Vienna. emerging only to conduct peace missions. She continues to write.

time out

Karl Nessler, a young hairdresser from Germany, has revolutionized hairstyling with the development of the permanent wave in 1906. It has been introduced in Britain and is taking off in a big way!

St Petersburg, Russia, January 22, 1905: One hundred thousand workers march to the Tsar's Winter Palace to present a petition. Cossack troops open fire, killing 100.
London, England, July 8, 1905: May Sutton (USA) becomes the first non-Briton to win at Wimbledon.
Dublin, Ireland, November 28, 1905: Sinn Fein, a group of nationalists aiming to unite Ireland, is formed.
Massachusetts, USA, 1905: Nettie Stevens publishes her finding that gender is determined by a particular chromosome.

Stockholm, Sweden, 1905: Writer and pacifist, Bertha von Suttner, is the first woman to win the Nobel Peace Prize.
Berlin, Germany, January 4, 1906: American dancer, Isadora Duncan, is forbidden to dance when police label her work obscene.
London, England, January 31, 1906: Suffragette leader Emmeline Pankhurst warns that women are impatient with waiting for the right to vote and are ready to take radical action to advance their cause.

Tahiti, February 8, 1906: A fierce typhoon inundates the Pacific kingdom, killing 10,000 people.
Rochester, New York, USA, March 13, 1906: Suffragette and civil rights campaigner, Susan B. Anthony, dies, aged 86.
San Francisco, USA, April 19, 1906: More than 1,000 people are killed and the city is devastated in the aftermath of an earthquake.
Dunedin, New Zealand, August 26, 1906: Educator Learmonth White Dalrymple, campaigner for women's education, dies, aged 79.

Russia, November 2, 1906: Bolshevik Leon Trotsky is exiled to Siberia for revolutionary activities. Anti-tsarist feelings run high after Nicholas II suspends the Duma.
Paris, France, 1906: Marie Curie is appointed Professor of General Physics in the faculty of sciences at the Sorbonne, the first woman to hold the post.
St Petersburg, Russia, 1906: Anna Pavlova is named prima ballerina at the Maryinsky Theater.

England, 1906: Economist Beatrice Potter Webb and her husband Sidney Webb publish the first volume of their nine-volume work, *English Local Government*.
Rome, Italy, January 1907: Educator and doctor, Maria Montessori, opens her first school, using her own teaching techniques.
London, England, February 13, 1907: Police repel suffragettes attempting to storm Westminster.
Helsinki, Finland, March 15, 1907: Finland is the first European country to give women the right to vote.

New Zealand Education Advocate Dies, Aged 79

Dunedin, New Zealand, August 26, 1906: Learmonth White Dalrymple, advocate for women's education, has died at Ashburn Hall. She will be best remembered for her determined seven-year campaign to establish New Zealand's first girls' school, the Otago Girls High School—also claimed as the first girls' school in the Southern Hemisphere.

When Otago Boys' High School opened in 1863, the local paper mooted the idea of a "companion institute for girls." Miss Dalrymple took up the cause, battling local apathy and antipathy. Despite many setbacks, she finally won the support of influential men such as the speaker of the provincial council, Major J. L. C. Richardson. The school opened on February 6, 1871, with 78 pupils, the number rising to 130 by the end of the year. It quickly developed a reputation for academic excellence.

Miss Dalrymple then turned her attention to lobbying for the inclusion of women in the planned University of Otago. Again she received the support of Major Richardson, who was chancellor when the university opened in July 1871. On August 8, 1871, the council voted unanimously to admit women, the first university in Australasia to do so.

Her final years were devoted to the Women's Christian Temperance Union. Toward the end of her life her health and memory began to fail and she returned to Dunedin. She will be buried at Palmerston North.

Montessori Opens Experimental School

Rome, Italy, January, 1907: It was a big day for the 60 children from Rome's impoverished inner-city San Lorenzo district today when they joined Dr Maria Montessori at her Casa dei Bambini, or "Children's House." With the opening of her school,

The innovative educator, Dr Maria Montessori.

Dr Montessori looks certain to revolutionize early childhood education with her "scientific approach" to teaching.

Dr Montessori insists: "children teach themselves." A medical practitioner and a member of the university's psychiatric clinic, she has spent considerable time researching the way children learn. From her observations, she has concluded that they have an almost effortless ability to absorb knowledge from their surroundings, as well as an abiding interest in manipulating materials. As a result, she has developed a new, more relevant style of teaching, her innovative methods based on a hands-on learning style that encourages children to move at their own pace and explore independently. Every piece of equipment, every exercise, and every method Dr Montessori has developed has been based on this principle.

Dr Montessori has now given up her university chair and her medical practice to further the self-creating process of the child. In recent years, she has devoted herself entirely to the study of the way children learn. This was sparked by her work with children considered "mentally retarded" or "uneducable."

Dr Montessori first came to prominence when she graduated as one of Rome's first female physicians in 1896.

Finland Leads the Way by Giving Women the Vote

Helsinki, Finland, March 15, 1907: Finland went to the polls today, the first European nation to grant women the right to vote.

Nineteen women have been elected members of parliament. Nine are from the Social Democratic Party, and 10 are from centrist and right-wing parties. All are regarded as competent politicians who have been working within their own parties to improve women's status and promote social welfare legislation.

Finland is only the third country in the world to recognize women's voting rights. New Zealand pioneered the woman's vote in 1893, and Australia gave its women voting rights in 1902. In 1869, Wyoming Territory in the United States was the first place in the world to give votes to women.

Anna Pavlova

A Finnish woman casts her vote in Helsinki.

Transvaal, March 22, 1907: Mohandas Gandhi vows a campaign of passive resistance if restrictive racial legislation is introduced.

Stuttgart, Germany, August, 1907: Indian nationalist Madame Bhikaji Cama unveils her design for the Indian flag.

China, September 8, 1907: Sun Yat-sen founds the Kuomintang Party.

Brussels, Belgium, 1907: British nurse Edith Cavell is appointed Head of Nursing at the Birkendael Institute.

Massachusetts, USA, February 21, 1908: American sculptor, Harriet Goodhue Hosmer, dies, aged 77.

New York, USA, March 8, 1908: Thousands of women march to demand suffrage, better pay, and an International Women's Day.

Detroit, USA, August 12, 1908: Model T Ford production begins.

Mt Huascarán, Peru, September 2, 1908: American Annie Smith Peck is the first person to climb the highest peak in the Peruvian Andes.

London, England, October 31, 1908: The Olympic Games end; more than 2,000 athletes participated, including about 35 women.

Peking, China, December 2, 1908: Three-year-old Pu Yi is crowned Emperor of China.

Dresden, Germany, December, 1908: Having devised coffee filter papers, Melitta and Hugo Bentz found the Melitta Bentz Company.

Oregon, USA, 1908: In the case of Muller v. Oregon, the US Supreme Court upholds state restrictions of women's working hours.

Antarctica, January 9, 1909: Ernest Shackleton's party is forced to turn back 97 miles (156 km) from the South Pole, as food supplies run low.

New York, USA, January 29, 1909: The world's tallest building, the 50-story Metropolitan Life Insurance building in Manhattan, is completed.

Constantinople. Turkey, April 26, 1909: Sultan Abdul Hamid II is deposed.

Boston, Massachusetts, USA, October 22, 1909: Harvard Law School excludes Inez Mulholland.

Stockholm, Sweden, 1909: Swedish writer Selma Lagerlöf is the first woman to be awarded the Nobel Prize for Literature.

Buenos Aires, Argentina, 1909: Peruvian writer and campaigner for Indian rights, Clorinda Matto de Turner, dies, aged about 57.

New York, USA, 1909: Canadian-born Florence Nightingale Graham changes her name to Elizabeth Arden and opens her first beauty salon on New York's Fifth Avenue.

Edith Cavell

Indian Nationalist Unveils New Flag

Stuttgart, Germany, August, 1907: In front of an audience of more than 1,000 delegates of the International Socialist Conference, Indian nationalist Madame Bhikaji Cama today unveiled her revolutionary design for the Indian flag.

A frail figure dressed in a colorful sari, Madame Cama shouted: "This flag is of Indian Independence! Behold, it is born! It has been made sacred by the blood of young Indians who sacrificed their lives. I call upon you, gentlemen to rise and salute this flag of Indian Independence. In the name of this flag, I appeal to lovers of freedom all over the world to support this flag."

The tricolor flag that Madam Cama unfurled had green, saffron, and red stripes. Red represented strength, saffron indicated victory, and green stood for boldness and enthusiasm.

First Woman Arrested for Smoking

New York, USA, January 22, 1908: Miss Katie Mulcahey, 29, became the first woman to be arrested and jailed for smoking today when she lit a cigarette in front of a policeman and stated: "No man shall dictate to me."

Miss Mulcahey was making a stand against the ordinance passed last week by the New York Board of Aldermen prohibiting public smoking by women, a move that was welcomed by the National Anti-Cigarette League.

Many people believe the board was misguided and that children should be the number one target. There has long been widespread concern over the health and moral wellbeing of the increasingly high numbers of children taking up the habit. The 100,000-strong National Anti-Cigarette League has made children its main focus since its formation in 1901.

Over the last few years, a number of American states have been working on various cigarette control measures. In spite of intense and sustained pressure from the tobacco lobby, both Wisconsin and Nebraska banned cigarette sales in 1905, and in the same year, the state of Indiana went so far as to prohibit anyone from even owning a cigarette.

Last year, the states of Arkansas and Illinois banned cigarette sales, although the Illinois Supreme Court soon struck down the Illinois law on a technicality, a decision that prompted the National Anti-Cigarette League's high profile superintendent, Lucy Page Gaston, to mount a counter-campaign; however, her fight was unsuccessful.

"Today the two hundred million men in our country are entering into a civilized new world ... but we, the two hundred million women, are still kept down in the dungeon."

QUI JIN
(c. 1870–1907),
CHINESE WRITER
AND REVOLUTIONARY

Strikers Want International Women's Day

New York, USA, March 8, 1908: An estimated 15,000 women left their jobs today in the garment industry of New York City's Lower East Side and took to the streets, marching under banners that protested against child labor, slave wages, and terrible sweatshop working conditions. They adopted the slogan "Bread and Roses," with bread symbolizing economic security and roses a better quality of life.

The rally was organized by Branch No 3 of the New York City Social Democratic Women's Society. Organizers declared the event a victory for women everywhere and promised that they would push to have the day made an International Women's Day, a day set aside for demonstrations in support of women's suffrage.

The clothing workers say they typically work up to 15 hours a day and are paid by the piece. They have to pay for needles, thread, electricity, and even the crude boxes they have to sit on because there are no chairs. They are issued harsh fines for being late and for damaged work. Children also work long hours.

Annie Smith Peck designs her own climbing shoes.

The rally follows a series of smaller walkouts held over recent months. In spite of numerous arrests and heavy fines, as well as beatings by police and hired thugs, the women, many of whom are teenagers, have continued to protest. Middle and upper class women inspired by the strikers have lent their support and have also been arrested.

This is not the first rally for New York's female clothing workers. More than half a century ago, a march was held to protest against dire working conditions and low wages. During that rally, the women were attacked and dispersed by police. Seventy women were arrested.

The demonstration led to the formation of the first female labor union two years later, in a bid by the women to protect themselves from exploitation and gain basic rights in the workplace.

Peck is First Climber to Conquer Andean Peak

Mt Huascarán, Peru, September 2, 1908: The first reports have come through confirming that the 58-year-old climber from America, Annie Smith Peck, has become the first person to reach the north peak of Peru's Mt Huascarán, 22,205 feet (6,768 m) high.

It has taken nearly a decade and no fewer than six attempts for Miss Peck to conquer what she believes to be the highest summit in the Western Hemisphere. However, accurate measurements are yet to be taken.

The reports are suggesting that the climb was far more difficult than Miss Peck had expected, with poor weather conditions, including snowstorms, which made the ascent a "nightmare." One of Miss Peck's two Swiss-born guides has lost a hand and part of a foot to frostbite.

Annie Peck's name hit the headlines in 1895 when, after several attempts, she became only the third woman ever to scale the Matterhorn in the Swiss Alps, and the first to make the climb in trousers rather than in a cumbersome skirt.

She has frequently complained about climbing dress and equipment, which, because it is designed for men, is often ungainly and ill-fitting for women. Miss Peck designs her own mountain shoes and has them made to order.

A good friend of Miss Peck's said that she attributed her remarkable physical strength, endurance, and courage to time spent as a child in competition with her three older brothers.

Annie Smith Peck was born in Providence, Rhode Island, on October 19, 1850. She has enjoyed a distinguished academic career, including gaining a master's degree from the University of

More and more American women are joining the fight for their rights. In 1908 they seek the establishment of an International Women's Day.

Selma Lagerlöf

Michigan and completing advanced study in Germany and Greece. She was made a professor of Latin at Purdue University, becoming one of the first women in the United States to attain the rank.

Selma Lagerlöf Wins Nobel Prize in Literature

Stockholm, Sweden, 1909: The Swedish novelist, Selma Lagerlöf, has become the first woman to win the Nobel Prize for Literature. Known around the world for her children's book: *Nils Holgerssons underbara resa genom sverige, (The Wonderful World of Nils)*, she was awarded the prize "in appreciation of the lofty idealism, vivid imagination and spiritual perception that characterize her writings."

Miss Lagerlöf's work is deeply rooted in Nordic legends and history. She has rejected the realistic movement that has dominated Swedish literature since the latter part of the nineteenth century, and writes in a romantic and imaginative manner about the peasant life and the landscape of northern Sweden.

The Nobel prize is awarded annually to an author from any country who, in the words of Alfred Nobel, has produced "the most outstanding work of an idealistic tendency." This generally refers to an author's work as a whole, not to an individual book, though individual works are sometimes cited in the awards. Each year, the Swedish Academy decides who, if anyone, will receive the prize.

Miss Lagerlöf worked as a country schoolteacher in Landskrona for almost ten years, and as part of her work with children she was able to develop her storytelling skills, drawing on the legends she had learned herself as a child. It was here she began her first novel, *The Story of Gösta Berling*. She submitted the first chapters to a literary competition, and won a publishing contract for the book.

Clorinda Matto de Turner Dies

Buenos Aires, Argentina, 1909: The controversial Peruvian writer, publisher, and campaigner for Indian rights, Clorinda Matto de Turner, died at her home today in Buenos Aires. She was 57 years old.

She was a pioneer of indigenous literature in Peru, and is regarded as one of that country's most influential writers. Throughout her life, Matto de Turner has been a radical figure and much of her work has provoked strong reactions in her homeland.

Matto de Turner was known for a series of novels as well as for the translation of the Gospels into Quechua. She published her three best-known novels between 1889 and 1895: *Birds Without a Nest*; *Character*; and *Heredity*. Her most famous novel, *Birds Without a Nest*, sparked outrage when it was published in 1889 because of its unsparing exposé of small town officials, judicial authorities, and priests, and their oppression of the native peoples of Peru.

As a result, Matto de Turner was excommunicated by the Catholic Church, and her effigy was burned by crowds protesting against the book. Ultimately, however, the novel proved to be strongly influential and Peruvian President, Andres Avelino Caceres, credited it with inspiring him to pursue some badly needed reforms.

Matto de Turner also founded the magazine, *El Recreo*, and edited the newspapers, *La Bolsa*, *El Perú Illustrado*, and *El Búcaro Americano*. She has lived in exile in Argentina for the past 14 years, having been forced by the government to leave Peru because of a controversial story she published in *El Perú Illustrado*.

A Princess in Dreamland, by British artist Elizabeth Stanhope Forbes.

Elizabeth Blackwell

A Life Devoted to Health Care Reform

Sussex, England, May 31, 1910: Trail-blazing physician and educator Dr Elizabeth Blackwell died today, aged eighty-nine.

Miss Blackwell moved from England to New York City with her family when she was eleven. Although she was born into a wealthy family, they were plunged into poverty with the death of her abolitionist father in 1838, prompting her to establish a private school.

After she had pursued informal medical training, she sought admission to a medical school in 1847 and was accepted, virtually by accident, at Geneva College, New York, after all of the major schools had declined. Despite vocal criticism and social rejection by locals and by the other students, she finished top of her class in 1849 and became both the first woman to graduate from a medical school and America's first qualified woman physician.

Elizabeth Blackwell further pursued her studies in England and France, but contracted an eye infection that left her blind in one eye, which prevented her from becoming a surgeon. Upon her return to New York she was not accepted by any of the city's hospitals and was not permitted to rent quarters from which to run a private practice.

After publishing a series of lectures, she opened a dispensary, in 1853, in a New York slum district. Her sister, Emily, who had also qualified as a physician, helped her turn the dispensary into the New York Infirmary for Women and Children.

In 1868, following discussions with Florence Nightingale, Miss Blackwell set up the Women's Medical College, which was known for its rigorous training. She moved to Great Britain the following year, opened a prosperous private practice, assisted in establishing the National Health Society, and was later appointed professor of gynecology at the London School of Medicine for Women.

"IN THE BEGINNING, WOMAN WAS TRULY THE SUN. AN AUTHENTIC PERSON. NOW SHE IS THE MOON, A WAN AND SICKLY MOON, DEPENDENT ON ANOTHER, REFLECTING ANOTHER'S BRILLIANCE."

HIRATSUKA HARU (RAICHO), 1911, LAUNCHING THE FEMINIST LITERARY JOURNAL, *SEITO*

Healing Lamp Extinguished

London, England, August 13, 1910: The Lady with the Lamp, Florence Nightingale, passed away in London today, aged ninety. The only woman to receive the prestigious award, the Order of Merit, she is credited as the founder of modern professional nursing as we know it.

Miss Nightingale was named for the Italian city of her birth, in which her British parents were then living. She devoted her early life to learning and, at the age of 16, believed she had a revelation from God, indicating some as yet unknown mission in life.

She began training as a nurse in 1850, and became superintendent of a minor institution for sick but wealthy women in 1853, where she undertook administrative reform. Yearning for more meaningful work, she found it in the context of the Crimean War. In 1854, she was appointed to head up the nursing of wounded British soldiers in the military hospitals in Turkey. Upon arrival she found the hospitals rife with rats and fleas, water supplies grossly deficient, sanitation appalling, and doctors hostile. She ordered the men's clothing washed outside the hospital and requisitioned 200 scrubbing brushes. The behavior of some the nurses caused her to bar them from the wards after 8.00 p.m., so she personally attended to all of the sick, as well as shouldering the formidable burdens of administration, correspondence, report-writing, and personal illness. Miss

Gabrielle Ray in *The Merry Widow*.

An artist's impression of Florence Nightingale caring for soldiers wounded in the Crimean War.

Egypt, February 21, 1910: Prime Minister Boutros-Ghali is assassinated.
Worldwide, May 20, 1910: Halley's Comet passes within 13 million miles (21 million km) of Earth. In France and Russia, the comet's passing is thought to be responsible for the poor weather this year.
Sussex, England, May 31, 1910: Dr Elizabeth Blackwell, the first woman to graduate from an American medical school, dies, aged 89. Her sister, Dr Emily Blackwell, dies in September at 83.

South Africa, May 31, 1910: The Union of South Africa comes into being as a British dominion. Boer War hero Louis Botha is Prime Minister, but is already challenged by many Boers for being too pro-British.
London, England, August 13, 1910: Nurse Florence Nightingale dies, aged 90.
Skopje, Eastern Europe, August 26, 1910: Agnes Gonxha Bojaxhiu (Mother Teresa of Calcutta) is born.
Greece, October 18, 1910: Eleftherios Venizelos becomes Prime Minister of Greece.

Boston, Massachusetts, USA, May 21, 1911: Scottish-born astronomer, Williamina Paton Stevens Fleming, who found 10 novae, 52 nebulae, and hundreds of variable stars, dies at 54.
Kansas, USA, June 9, 1911: Carry Nation, famous axe-wielding temperance activist dies, aged 64.
Paris, France, June 13, 1911: Tamara Karsavina dances in *Petrushka*.
Peru, July 16, 1911: American mountaineer, Annie Smith Peck, aged 61, climbs to the top of Mt Coropuna, where she is said to have planted a banner declaring "Votes for Women."

Machu Picchu, Peru, July 24, 1911: American explorer Hiram Bingham rediscovers the ancient Inca city.
Stockholm, Sweden, December 10, 1911: Marie Curie is the recipient of an unprecedented second Nobel Prize, this time for chemistry due to her work on radium.
South Pole, December 14, 1911: Norwegian Roald Amundsen, reaches the South Pole. Both poles have been conquered in just three years.

Nanking, China, December 29, 1911: Leader of the revolutionary forces, Sun Yat-sen, is elected president of a provisional government.
France, 1911: Feminist, anthropologist, and cross-dresser, Madeleine Pelletier, publishes *L'Emancipation sexuelle de la femme* (*The Sexual Emancipation of Women*).
USA, 1911: Writer Edith Wharton publishes her novel, *Ethan Frome*.
Japan, 1911: The writer and feminist known as Raicho founds the all-women's journal *Seito*.

Nightingale also fought ultimately successful battles with officials over the extent of her authority. She transferred directly to the Crimean front in 1855.

Miss Nightingale returned to England a hero, but would not accept a public reception. In England she devoted herself to the broader issue of the general welfare of British servicemen. After securing an interview with Queen Victoria, she succeeded in initiating two Royal Commissions, which resulted in the establishment of the Army Medical School and a Sanitary Department in the India Office.

The popularity of the Lady with the Lamp led to a public subscription of £45,000, which she used in 1860 to set up the world's first professional school for nurses. She also worked hard to improve conditions in workhouses.

Largely an invalid confined to her home from 1857, Florence Nightingale devoted herself exclusively to her causes, maintaining her influence via correspondence across vast distances and meetings at her house. She became entirely blind in 1901.

A Perfect Day for Mrs Jacobs-Bond

Chicago, Illinois, USA, December 12, 1910: Carrie Jacobs-Bond's song, "(The End of) A Perfect Day," has broken all records as the highest-selling sheet music item of all time, confirming her place as the world's most successful female composer. In recent years, Mrs Jacobs-Bond has sung at the White House before President Roosevelt and, in London, with Enrico Caruso.

However, things have not always been so comfortable for the songwriter, whose husband died after a fall on ice in 1894. She then moved to Chicago, where she rented rooms and struggled with poverty and rheumatism, publishing her first book of songs in 1901

with a loan from singer Jessie Bartlett Davis. She and her son set up the Bond House publishing company. Her fortunes have been aided by her recent decision to lease her songs out to recording companies.

Petrushka Surprises

Paris, France, June 13, 1911: Noted Russian ballerina, Tamara Karsavina, has appeared in a new and controversial work performed by Serge Diaghilev's Ballets Russes. The troupe was formed in Paris two years ago and Karsavina's dancing partner is Vaslav Nijinsky. Choreography is by Michel Fokine.

Diaghilev commissioned the music, known as *Petrushka*, from the young and little-known composer Igor Stravinsky, who studied under Rimsky-Korsakov, after he heard a performance in St Petersburg of one of his compositions.

The experimental ballet has received favorable reviews from most critics, although it has prompted others to express nostalgia for Miss Karsavina's more traditional work in classics such as *Giselle* and *Swan Lake*. Some of the audience appeared puzzled and even annoyed by Mr Stravinsky's composition, which can seem discordant and harsh to some enthusiasts of classical music. The ballet concerns a puppet who comes to life and develops the capacity to love, rather like the legend of Pinocchio, perhaps more familiar to our

The Ballet Russes' Karsavina and Nijinsky.

> ### time out
>
> In Philadelphia, USA, in 1912, 15 women are fired for dancing the Turkey Trot during their lunch break. Some people consider the dance, probably introduced in 1909 by Louise Gruenning and John Jarrott, to be sexually suggestive.

readers. It is being performed at the Théâtre du Chatelet.

Radical New Journal

Tokyo, Japan, December, 1911: A new literary journal in Japan is causing a stir. Named *Seito*, it is dedicated exclusively to the writings of women. The title translates as *Bluestocking's Journal*, a reference to an eighteenth-century group of British women who sought to institute intellectually inclined evenings of literary conversation to replace the more conventional card-playing, which was usually associated with women's entertainment.

Seito's motto is "In the beginning, woman was truly the sun," a reference to traditional Japanese belief that the deity linked with the sun is female, and also suggesting the links between this group and their Occidental suffragette colleagues. This more political aspect of the magazine has begun to surface under the leadership of founder, Hiratsuka Haru, who uses the pen name of Raicho and is influenced by the writings of Swedish feminist Ellen Key. The journal's recent discussion of women's private behavior and women's rights is causing outrage in some sectors of Japanese society.

Carry Nation

Ellen Key, who inspired Raicho.

Key Events

Savannah, Georgia, USA, March 12, 1912: Juliette Gordon Low starts the American Girl Guides.

Atlantic Ocean, off Newfoundland, April 14, 1912: The liner *Titanic*, on its maiden voyage, strikes an iceberg and sinks. About 1,500 people perish.

Stockholm, Sweden, July 15, 1912: Australian swimmer, Sarah "Fanny" Durack, wins the 100 meter (109-yard) freestyle, the only individual swimming event for women at the Olympic Games.

India, 1912: Poet and feminist, Sarojini Naidu, publishes *The Bird of Time*.

Istanbul, Turkey, January 23, 1913: Young Turks overthrow the Ottoman government in a coup.

Tuskegee, Alabama, USA, February 4, 1913: Civil rights pioneer Rosa Parks is born.

Auburn, New York, USA, March 10, 1913: Harriet Tubman dies, aged around 93. She led more than 300 slaves to freedom from the South on the "Underground Railroad" during the 1860s.

Canberra, Australia, March 12, 1913: The foundation stone for the new Australian capital is laid.

Epsom, England, June 4, 1913: Emily Davison is struck by a horse when she runs onto the Derby track in order to gain publicity for the suffragette cause.

Finland, December 24, 1913: Women's rights advocate Alexandra Grippenberg dies, aged 56.

Norway, 1913: Norwegian women are granted the right to vote.

USA, March 31, 1914: Actress Pearl White stars in the first of the film serials, *The Perils of Pauline*.

New York, USA, March, 1914: Margaret Sanger publishes *The Woman Rebel*, a journal promoting contraception.

USA, May 9, 1914: The first Mother's Day is announced by President Woodrow Wilson, to recognize the contribution to society made by mothers.

Montevideo, Uruguay, July 6, 1914: Delmira Agustini, Uruguayan poet, is murdered.

Sarajevo, Bosnia, June 28, 1914: The heir to the Austrian throne, Archduke Franz Ferdinand, is assassinated.

Europe, August 2, 1914: Germany, having declared war on Russia on August 1, invades Luxembourg.

London, England, August 4, 1914: Britain declares war on Germany as German troops invade Belgium.

Turkey, November 5, 1914: France and Britain declare war on Turkey.

Russia, 1914: Princess Eugenie Shakhovskaya becomes one of Russia's women military pilots.

Harriet Tubman

Marie Curie Awarded Second Nobel Prize

Stockholm, Sweden, December 10, 1911: Marie Curie has become the first person to receive two Nobel Prizes after she was granted this year's award in Stockholm for chemistry. It will sit on her mantelshelf along with a Nobel Prize for Physics, which she was jointly awarded in 1903, with her husband Pierre Curie, and Antoine Henri Becquerel, for their research into the phenomena of radiation.

According to the official citation, Madame Curie received this year's prize for the discovery of the chemical elements radium and polonium, and for her work in determining the properties of radium.

This distinction has come upon the heels of a seemingly remarkable decision this year by the Académie des Sciences to deny her a place among its ranks. Madame Curie applied for the vacant seat last November but lost out to Edouard Branly, who is known for his work on wireless telegraphy.

The decision is thought to be somewhat political, insofar as it reflects the support of French patriots and Catholics for Branly and that of progressive forces for Polish-born Madame Curie, whose sex and foreign birth still arouse suspicion in some quarters.

The year has had other strains. A scandal arose in the press while she was in Belgium attending a physics conference, centering on the publication of what were said to be intimate letters between Madame Curie and another physicist, Paul Langevin. The letters are deemed to have sullied the name of Madame Curie, who has been depicted as a home-wrecker and, falsely, as a Jew. Upon her return from Belgium she found an angry mob outside her home. Monsieur Langevin has taken part in a duel with a journalist over the accusations.

Eighteen Guides Show American Girls the Way

Savannah, Georgia, USA, March 12, 1912: Mrs Juliette Gordon Low has organized 18 girls into the United States's first troop of American Girl Guides, just two years after the inception of the Girl Guides in Great Britain. She is highly qualified for the undertaking, as she is a personal friend of boy scout and girl guide founder Robert Baden-Powell and his sister Agnes.

Mrs Low has chosen Savannah as the location for the US foundation of the organization as she was born here to a prominent local family in 1860. While young, she lost much of the hearing in one ear when an earache was treated with silver nitrate. She then lost most of the hearing in the other ear when her eardrum was burst trying to remove a grain of rice that lodged there during her marriage to another prominent Savannah scion, William Low, in 1886.

The couple spent much of their time in Great Britain, where they befriended the Baden-Powells. Mr Low died in 1905 in the midst of divorce proceedings, leaving all of his money to another woman. Mrs Low went on to form a girl guide troop in Scotland then another two in London before returning to bring the cause to the United States. Mrs Low says that the purpose of the guides is to train girls in

Juliette Gordon Low, American Girl Guides founder.

citizenship, good conduct, and outdoor activities. The guides vow to observe a code of good behavior, to participate in community service projects, and to develop their skills by earning badges in a broad range of activities.

Gold Medal Winner Nearly Didn't Make it to Olympics

Stockholm, Sweden, July 15, 1912: Baron Pierre de Coubertin would be horrified. The founder of the modern Olympic Games made it clear he thought the role of women was only to encourage excellence in their sons.

Despite this, women competed in the more decorous sports (tennis, golf, and croquet) at the second Olympic Games in Paris in 1900. Archery was added in 1904, and figure skating in 1908. This year has seen the inclusion of equestrian events, platform diving, and two swimming events: the 100 meter (109-yard) freestyle and the 100 meter (109-yard) freestyle relay. In all, 57 of this year's 2,406 athletes were women.

Two of those 57 were from Australia: Sarah "Fanny" Durack and Mina Wylie, two swimmers from Sydney who are both friends and fierce competitors. Back in Australia, the New South Wales Ladies' Amateur Swimming Association forbids

Controversial scientist and Nobel Prize winner, Marie Curie, is questioned by journalists.

Sarah "Fanny" Durack (right) and Mina Wylie.

women from competing in events at which men are present. However, when Miss Durack set world records in the 100 meter (109-yard) and 220 meter (240-yard) freestyle events earlier this year, followed closely by Miss Wylie, the public began to call for their inclusion in the Olympic team. The Amateur Association finally agreed to let them compete, but it would not pay for them to go.

This prompted a successful public appeal for funds; luckily for Australia, as Miss Durack has set a new world record in one of the heats for the 100 meter (109-yard) final (the only individual event for female swimmers) and she has now won the final, with Miss Wylie in second place.

Miss Durack's medal is one of only two gold medals for this Australian team and it is also the first gold ever for an Australian woman.

Near Riot as Women March for Suffrage

Washington DC, USA, March 3, 1913: An estimated 8,000 women have marched up Pennsylvania Avenue to publicly promote the cause of women's suffrage. The timing of the parade was clearly calculated to maximize publicity as the eyes of the nation make ready for tomorrow's inauguration of the new president, Woodrow Wilson.

In this the marchers were successful because the streets of the national capital were crowded with visitors and members of the press. Many onlookers proved hostile, with the atmosphere becoming ugly and riotous at times. Some bystanders blocked the marchers' way, with others spitting on and assaulting them.

The parade was organized by the National American Woman Suffrage Association (NAWSA). Its congressional committee seeks an amendment to the US Constitution that would make it illegal to deny the vote to any person based on their sex.

The chairman of the committee, Alice Paul, has recently returned from England, where she was doing settlement work and where she became involved with the Women's Social and Political Union, known for undertaking similar tactics, such as marches, demonstrations, and extreme measures designed to provoke arrests and publicity. The 26-year-old Miss Paul was born into a prosperous Quaker family and graduated from Swarthmore College, where she studied social work.

Miss Paul was imprisoned three times in the United Kingdom for her suffragist activities and, while in jail, went on a hunger strike. So extreme are Miss Paul's views that it is understood she is planning on leaving NAWSA because she finds it too tame. Apparently, she wishes to set up a more radical organization.

National Day Proclaimed in Honor of Mothers

USA, May 8, 1914: Following a joint resolution by Congress today, President Woodrow Wilson has proclaimed this Sunday as Mother's Day. The announcement represents the culmination of a campaign started by Miss Anna Jarvis eight years ago.

Miss Jarvis was the daughter of Mrs Anna Jarvis of Virginia, a social worker and activist who organized women to help the wounded in a non-partisan way during the Civil War, and who encouraged the mothers of soldiers from both sides to meet after hostilities officially ceased. Like Julia Ward Howe, the author of the "Battle Hymn of the Republic" and the 1870 Mother's Day Proclamation, she supported calls for a Mother's Day tied to the cause of pacifism.

Following her mother's death in 1905, Anna Jarvis began tirelessly campaigning for a national day to honor all mothers. Numerous states, beginning with Miss Jarvis's own West Virginia, have adopted the concept, which was today declared a national day, to be observed on the second Sunday of each May, so as to coincide with the commemoration of Mrs Anna Jarvis's death.

Poet of Passion Shot by Former Husband

Montevideo, Uruguay, July 6, 1914: The young Uruguayan poet, Delmira Agustini, has been murdered in Montevideo. Miss

Agustini, the daughter of Italian immigrants, was widely considered an important and promising contributor to Latin American literature.

A student of French painting and music, Miss Agustini has been writing poetry since the age of ten. She made contributions to the literary magazine, *La Alborada*, reflecting her place in a literary circle that included fellow Uruguayan poets, Julio Herrera y Reissig and Leopoldo Lugones.

As a poet she was greatly impressed by another leading light of Spanish-language literature, Rubén Darío, an influential, Nicaraguan-born writer who settled in El Salvador, and whose speculative work drew on recent experimental French poetry. Darío has stated that in his view, Miss Agustini was the only woman to express herself as a woman since the sixteenth-century saint, Teresa of Ávila. He refers to her sensual subject matter, which focuses on the heated passions and desires of women.

Miss Agustini has published several volumes of verse, including *Cantos de la mañana* (*Morning Songs*) and *El libro blanco* (*The White Book*). Her latest volume, *Los cálices vacíos* (*Empty Chalices*), is dedicated to Eros, the god of love, but it seems the deity was an unpredictable patron, for it was passion that led to the poet's death. The 27-year-old was today shot twice through the head by her former husband, who then turned the gun on himself. The couple were married last August but separated only a month later. They were divorced last month.

Pearl White

Emily Davison is remembered by her suffragist friends.

Virginia Woolf

Women, Workers of the War

UK, March 18, 1915: Today Lord Asquith's Liberal government has made an appeal to women to redouble their contribution to the war effort. This call comes after comments from the British Commander-in-Chief, Field Marshal Sir John French, regarding the recent disaster at the battle of Neuve Chapelle in Artois, France. There, an offensive against the German army had to be abandoned after three days with less than 2 miles (3 km) of enemy territory regained. In the fighting, 11,200 British and Indian soldiers lost their lives. In the field marshal's opinion, this terrible loss was in part due to a shortage of shells.

In response, the government has called upon patriotic women to support our courageous men at the front. Women are required not only to nurse those men injured in battle but to join the army in clerical and other non-combat roles. The government stressed that it is imperative for women to work in munitions factories to increase the vital supply of arms and shells for the troops.

The chronic shortage of able-bodied men is also leading to the employment of women in a wide range of civilian jobs in order to keep the nation operating, and to maintain supplies of food and other basics. Women are needed to work in government departments, public transport, offices, factories, as farm laborers, and even to shift goods on the docks.

Unions are not averse to women taking up these critical positions in this time of dire need, so long as they will relinquish them again as soon as the present conflict is over. As women are often paid less than half the wages that men receive, unionists are also insistent that businessmen do not turn this saving into rampant profit-making.

The Board of Trade would like every woman who is willing to work to register with them as soon as possible.

timeout

In October 1916, American birth control advocate Margaret Sanger opens the first birth control clinic in the United States, in Brooklyn. Some nine days later, it is raided by police, and Sanger is briefly imprisoned.

Heeding government appeals for their help, these British women are at work in a munitions factory.

Edith Cavell has been executed by German forces.

Brave Nurse Faces Firing Squad

Brussels, Belgium, October 12, 1915: British nurse Edith Cavell was executed at dawn today by a German firing squad.

Arrested on August 4, Edith Cavell was suspected of aiding the escape, to neutral Holland, of those Allied soldiers trapped when German forces occupied Belgium on August 20 last year. She was held in solitary confinement for over nine weeks. During this time it is said that her captors tricked her into confessing, stating that by doing so she would save the lives of those arrested with her. She subsequently admitted to assisting more than 200 men.

Cavell was holidaying in England when war was declared, but quickly returned to her position as matron of the Berkendael Institute in Brussels, a teaching hospital for nurses, believing that her skills would be needed more than ever. The Institute became a Red Cross hospital, treating patients of all nationalities. Although Cavell knew she should remain neutral, she hid Allied soldiers before they were guided across the border, believing they would have been shot otherwise. She tended to those soldiers herself, so that no other nurses would be incriminated.

Edith Cavell was sentenced to death only three days ago, giving little time for appeals for mercy. Last night she told the prison chaplain that, "Standing as I do in

Key Events

North Sea, February 4, 1915: Germany declares blockade; U-boats attack Allied and neutral shipping. Britain retaliates with the seizure of all goods bound for Germany.
Gallipoli Peninsula, Turkey, February 19, 1915: Churchill orders a bombardment of Turkish positions to divert the Turks from Caucasian objectives.
UK, March 18, 1915: The government appeals for women to take up jobs in industry, as men depart for war.
Atlantic Ocean, May 7, 1915: German U-boats torpedo the *Lusitania*.

Italy, May 22, 1915: Italy joins the Allies, having quit the Triple Alliance.
Warsaw, Poland, August 4, 1915: The Polish capital falls to Germany.
Brussels, Belgium, October 12, 1915: Found guilty of assisting Allied prisoners to escape custody, British nurse Edith Cavell is executed by a German firing squad.
Berlin, Germany, November 25, 1915: Einstein's General Theory of Relativity is published.
The Hague, Netherlands, 1915: International Women's Congress for Peace discusses ways to end the Great War.

California, USA, 1915: Appointed one of America's first sworn police-women in 1910, Alice Stebbins Wells founds the International Police-women's Association.
England, 1915: *The Voyage Out* by Virginia Woolf is published.
Dublin, Ireland, May 1, 1916: The Easter Uprising of republicans is put down by British forces. An Irish Republic is declared. Constance Markiewicz, Irish patriot, fights against the British, is arrested, and charged with treason.

The Somme, France, July 1, 1916: The first day of the new Western Front offensive claims over 58,000 casualties, one-third fatalities.
Montana, USA, November 6, 1916: Jeannette Pickering Rankin is the first woman elected to Congress.
Petrograd, Russia, December 30, 1916: "Mad monk" Rasputin is murdered.
Alberta, Canada, 1916: Feminist and social activist Emily Ferguson Murphy becomes the first female magistrate of a court in the British Empire.

Manitoba, Canada, 1916: Women in the Prairie Provinces win provincial voting rights.
Puerto Rico, March 2, 1917: Puerto Rico becomes a US protectorate, with all citizens awarded American citizenship.
Ohio, USA, March 13, 1917: Lizzie Dickelman is issued a patent for her invention of the grain storehouse.
Washington DC, USA, April 6, 1917: The USA declares war on Germany. The discovery of the "Zimmerman Note," outlining German designs on the Americas, was a deciding factor.

view of God and Eternity, I realize that patriotism is not enough, I must have no hatred or bitterness towards anyone." A heroine of the Allied cause, Cavell's name will long be remembered.

International Association for Policewomen

California, USA, 1915: Alice Stebbins Wells, one of the first policewomen in the United States, has formed the International Policewomen's Association. The association aims to promote the use of

Bird Millman, celebrated tightrope walker, in 1915.

female officers, and to provide an arena in which they can exchange ideas.

In 1909, Wells presented a petition to the Los Angeles city council asking them to employ a policewoman. As a social worker, she saw a pressing need for women to work as police officers with female and juvenile criminals. Convinced, in 1910 the council asked her to take on the task.

Following her historic appointment, Wells spoke publicly in more than 100 cities to encourage the enlistment of policewomen. Two were appointed in Los Angeles in 1912 and 10 in Chicago in 1913, creating a growing need for the association Wells has helped to found.

Irish Patriot Charged with Treason

Dublin, Ireland, May 1916: Earlier this month, Countess Constance Markiewicz was charged with treason against Britain for her part in the Easter Uprising. The Countess, wife of a Polish count and the daughter of the explorer Sir Henry Gore-Booth, spent much of her childhood on her father's Irish estate where, despite her life of privilege, she grew up with a great sympathy for the Irish people.

The Easter Uprising began on April 24, when around 1,250 militant Irish rebels attempted to take over Dublin. Patrick Pearse proudly declared an Irish Republic from the steps of the captured General Post Office. But the rebels were soundly defeated, after six days of fierce fighting, by 16,000 British troops.

Lieutenant Markiewicz of the Irish Citizens Army was second in command to Michael Mallin at St Stephen's Green. When British soldiers fired on the rebels from the surrounding buildings with machine guns, Markiewicz returned fire, and succeeded in wounding one of them. The Irish retreated into the Royal College of Surgeons where they held out against the British, and only gave up their arms when presented with a written order from Pearse, who had already surrendered.

Constance Markiewicz was marched with the other rebels to Dublin Castle, from where they were taken to Kilmainham Jail. She was tried and given a death sentence, which was later commuted due to her gender. However, her fellow rebel leaders have not been not so lucky. They are due to be executed very soon.

Mata Hari Executed for Spying

Vincennes, France, October 15, 1917: Today the infamous exotic dancer, Mata Hari, was driven from Saint-Lazare Prison to the cavalry grounds on the outskirts of Paris and shot at dawn by a firing squad.

Mata Hari, the Malay stage name of Dutchwoman Margaretha Zelle, gained attention in 1905 when she performed in Paris posing as an Eastern temple dancer. Audiences were shocked by her daring sensual dancing. She appeared in night-clubs across Europe, but in recent times the novelty of her act has lost its appeal.

Over the years Mata Hari took many military men as lovers. As a citizen of neutral Holland, she traveled freely across borders. She is said to have admitted to British intelligence officers to spying for France. Arrested on February 13, Mata Hari, accused of being a double agent for Germany, was blamed for giving secrets to the enemy that led to the loss of thousands of lives. Her public trial on July 24 attracted great crowds. Despite protestations of innocence, she was condemned to death, and her appeals for clemency were rejected.

Eyewitnesses report she died bravely, refusing a blindfold or to be tied to the stake. She even blew a kiss at the firing squad as the order to shoot was given.

Constance Markiewicz

The dancer and spy, Mata Hari.

Washington DC, USA, May 19, 1917: Belva Ann Lockwood, who in 1879 became the first woman admitted to practice before the US Supreme Court, dies, aged 86.

Vincennes, France, October 15, 1917: Dutch dancer and double agent, Mata Hari, is executed by the French.

Egypt, December 15, 1917: Arabic scholar, traveler, and horsewoman, Lady Anne Blunt, daughter of Ada Lovelace, dies, aged 80.

Los Angeles, USA, December 25, 1917: Ida Forbes invents the electric hot water heater.

Hollywood, USA, 1917: Theda Bara stars in the the film *Cleopatra*.

Ireland, May 17, 1918: Eamon de Valera, leader of Sinn Féin, and 500 nationalists are imprisoned on grounds of colluding with Germany.

Canada, May 24, 1918: Female citizens over 21 are allowed to vote.

Victoria, Australia, June 17, 1918: Feminist and women's rights leader, Henrietta Dugdale, dies, aged 91.

Ekaterinberg, Russia, July 16, 1918: The Romanov dynasty ends with the execution of Tsar Nicholas and his family by Bolsheviks.

Japan, November 1918: Deguchi Nao, founder of the Omoto religion, dies, aged 81.

Worldwide, November 11, 1918: The Great War comes to an end.

Berlin, Germany, 1918: Austrian physicist Lise Meitner, working with Otto Hahn, isolates the element protactinium.

Austria, Canada, Estonia, Germany, Hungary, Latvia, Poland, Russia, and the United Kingdom, 1918: Women are granted the right to vote.

Paris, France, February 14, 1919: At the Paris Peace Conference, 27 nations vote for the establishment of a League of Nations.

Moscow, Russia, March 4, 1919: Lenin convenes the *Third International*, with the goal of international Communist revolution.

Hollywood, USA, April 17, 1919: Mary Pickford, Douglas Fairbanks, D. W. Griffith, and Charlie Chaplin found United Artists to produce their own motion pictures.

London, England, July, 1919: Wimbledon resumes after the war. Frenchwoman Suzanne Lenglen wins the women's title.

Rawalpindi, India, August 8, 1919: The end of the third Anglo-Afghan War is negotiated.

London, England, November 28, 1919: US-born Lady Nancy Astor becomes the first woman Member of Parliament.

Chicago, USA, December 21, 1919: Lithuanian-born American anarchist, Emma Goldman, is deported from the United States to Russia.

Theda Bara

Death of Horse-breeder Lady Anne Blunt

Egypt, December 15, 1917: Lady Anne Isabella King Blunt died today, aged 80. Lady Anne was born on September 22, 1837, to William King, first Earl of Lovelace, and Lady Ada Lovelace, the daughter of poet Lord Byron and Lady Annabella Byron. As Lady Anne's mother was often busy with her scientific studies, Lady Byron largely raised her granddaughter.

In 1869 Lady Anne married the poet Wilfrid Blunt. The horse-loving couple founded studs in Egypt at Sheykh Obeyd near Cairo, as well as in England. They traveled widely, making several trips to the Middle East from the late 1870s and buying numerous pure Arabian horses, a breed that at that time was in danger of extinction. Their Arabians have founded bloodlines around the world that are known for their strength and endurance.

Lady Anne decided to separate from her husband in 1906 when one of his numerous mistresses moved in with him. Their English stud was divided, with Lady Anne taking Crabbet Park. Aided by her capable daughter, Judith Blunt-Lytton, Lady Anne achieved great success with her breeding program. She now spent her winters at Sheykh Obeyd, not returning to England again after 1915.

Apart from her immeasurable contributions to the world of horse breeding, Lady Anne was an accomplished writer and published two books based on the journals of her Middle Eastern travels. She was also a gifted artist and violinist, and spoke French, German, Italian, Spanish, and Arabic.

"I AM A WOMAN WHO ENJOYS HERSELF VERY MUCH; SOMETIMES I LOSE, SOMETIMES I WIN."

MATA HARI
(1876–1917),
DUTCH DANCER
AND SPY

Death of the Founder of Omoto Religion

Kyoto Prefecture, Japan, November 6, 1918: The founder of the Shinto-based Omoto religion, Deguchi Nao, has died peacefully at her home. She had collapsed earlier in the day and her family sent out messages to Omoto followers who prayed for their leader.

Omoto's story begins in 1892, when Deguchi Nao, a 55-year-old widow who had lived in poverty all her life, dreamt that she met two divine figures. Afterward, Nao was apparently possessed by the god Ushitora. While in a trance, she spoke the god's pronouncements in a loud masculine voice, even when, on occasion, she attempted to stop her mouth from moving.

Many believed she was insane, and she was detained in the house of one of her sons-in-law. But here the illiterate woman began to write the god's teachings clearly on paper with a brush. This convinced those who witnessed the writings that a spirit was working through her. In her remaining years she was to write 200,000 words, none of which she could read.

When, through her, the god predicted the Sino-Japanese War of 1894, the religion began to gain many followers.

Omoto promises a spiritual golden age, and its followers live simply and practice a form of meditation.

The husband of her daughter Sumiko, Onisaburo Deguchi, succeeds Deguchi Nao as leader of Omoto.

Lady Astor, the first woman to take a seat in the House of Commons.

Physicist Isolates Protactinium

Berlin, Germany, 1918: The physicist Lise Meitner, alongside chemist Otto Hahn at the Kaiser Wilhelm Institute, has isolated the first long-lived isotope of element 91, the radioactive protactinium.

Lise Meitner was born in November 1878 in Vienna. Her parents believed that education was extremely important and after Meitner finished school at the age of 13, they hired private tutors for her. She entered the University of Vienna in 1901 to pursue her passion for science. The courses she could take were limited by which lecturers would allow women in their classes, but Meitner still managed to gain her doctorate in 1906.

In 1907, the young physicist moved to Berlin where she began to collaborate with Otto Hahn in the Chemical Institute of the Kaiser Wilhelm Institute. There she worked as an unpaid research assistant supported by her parents until 1912. At first, propriety had to be maintained, so Meitner worked separately from her male colleagues, in the basement. In 1913, she began her first paid job, as assistant to Professor Max Planck at the University of Berlin, and became a member of the Chemical Institute. Meitner volunteered as an x-ray technician during the war, and although Hahn was in the army, the two were able to meet to continue their work.

This year, Meitner has been appointed the head of the Radiophysics Department

The Women's Battalion of Death, known as Yashkas, Russia, 1917.

Emma Goldman

At last, millions of women have the right to vote.

at the Physics Institute, where she will be continuing her scientific research.

Millions of Women Gain the Vote

Austria, Canada, Estonia, Germany, Hungary, Latvia, Poland, Russia, and the United Kingdom, 1918: The long, sometimes bitter, struggle for women's suffrage had had only limited success by the time of the outbreak of the Great War. This year has seen women win the right to elect and be elected in several nations.

Many women have gained the vote due to the massive political changes that swept through Europe in the final throes of the war—in particular the break-up of the Russian, German, and Austro-Hungarian empires. In the new republics of Russia, Germany, Poland, Estonia, Latvia, Austria, and Hungary, women now have similar voting powers to their menfolk.

During the war, many campaigners for women's suffrage in the United Kingdom refocused their efforts on supporting their nation as army medical staff, clerks, and workers on the home front. Women worked in industry, including in munitions factories, and kept their nation functioning by taking up roles previously occupied by men.

Their efforts earned them grateful respect; as *Punch* magazine noted of British women in 1916, the nation "never for a moment supposed they would be anything but ready and keen when the hour of need struck."

The *Representation of the People Act* came before the British parliament this year. Women over the age of 30 with property were granted the right to vote and stand for election. The first opportunity to exercise this new right came in December. Prominent Irish freedom fighter, Countess Constance Markiewicz, released from jail in 1917 under a general amnesty for those who had participated in the Easter Uprising, was elected as Britain's first female parliamentarian. Following Sinn Féin policy, she refused to take her seat.

This year, Canada has also extended the powers of its women in the political process. It looks as though the United States will soon follow suit, with amendments to the Constitution partially through the long process of being ratified by Congress.

In future politicians will have to consider women in a new light.

Shocking Victory at Wimbledon

Wimbledon, England, July 1919: Frenchwoman Suzanne Lenglen has won the Ladies' Singles at the first Wimbledon Championships since the outbreak of the Great War. Lenglen, 20, defeated seventimes winner, British-American Dorothea Douglass Chambers, 40, in a grueling match, 10-8, 4-6, 9-7.

Before the hostilities, Suzanne Lenglen had reached the French Championship final, and then won the World Hard Court Championships.

It was clear to Wimbledon spectators that the graceful Frenchwoman was able to move freely in her lightweight (and very revealing!) dress. Her opponent, on the other hand, was wearing a longsleeved, high-necked shirt and a long skirt with petticoats. Although Lenglen's

Suzanne Lenglen demonstrates her amazing forehand.

attire helped her game, the audience was shocked by the sight of her forearms and lower legs, not to mention the brandy she sipped from the flask offered by her father and coach, Charles Lenglen.

Anarchist Deported from America

Chicago, USA, December 21, 1919: Emma Goldman and 247 other Russian resident aliens have been deported on board the *Buford*, dubbed the "Soviet Ark" by the press. Under recently created acts, the Justice Department can deport any alien previously convicted of two crimes. Having been jailed three times, Goldman certainly qualifies.

Born in the Russian Empire in Kaunas, Lithuania, in 1869, Goldman moved with her family at 13 to St Petersburg to escape Jewish pogroms. There she was exposed to revolutionary ideas while working in a corset factory. In 1886, Goldman immigrated to the United States. Working in the textile industry, she was deeply shocked by conditions in what she had expected to be a land of prosperity and freedom. Inspired by radical speakers, she became an anarchist.

Goldman was first arrested in 1893 for inciting the unemployed to riot and was imprisoned for a year. In 1906, she began publishing the anarchist magazine *Mother Earth* with her lover and fellow anarchist Alexander Berkman. Suspicious of her ideals, the US government revoked her residency status in 1908.

In 1916 Emma was arrested for distributing information about birth control—which she sees as a way of reducing dangerous abortions—and jailed again.

Once released, Goldman encouraged defiance of the draft. These actions led to her third arrest in 1917, this time along with Berkman. The government raided their offices, seizing subscription records for *Mother Earth* and Berkman's journal, *Blast.* Attorney-General Alexander Palmer then used these records in order to identify other radicals.

On November 7 this year, the second anniversary of the Russian Bolshevik Revolution, the US Justice Department arrested thousands of people, including the recently released Emma Goldman and Alexander Berkman.

During her deportation hearing, Palmer's assistant, J. Edgar Hoover, said Goldman was "one of the most dangerous anarchists in America." Berkman is to be deported along with "Red Emma," as Goldman is being referred to in the nation's newspapers.

Despite some ideological differences, Emma Goldman is prepared to support the Bolshevik government in Russia.

Susan B. Anthony

American Women Win Right to Vote

USA, August 26, 1920: Women across America are now legally entitled to vote. The Nineteenth Amendment to the United States Constitution was ratified today, with the Secretary of State signing it into law.

For more than 50 years, American suffragettes have campaigned long and hard for this legal breakthrough, none more so than Susan B. Anthony, whose name will be forever associated with what is known as the "Anthony Amendment." Anthony didn't live to see her fellow American women win the right to cast their vote in political elections (she died in 1906) but until the very end of her life she maintained a staunch optimism that her 60 years of activism would result in change.

As far back as the 1850s, Anthony and other women's rights activists were holding public rallies, writing letters, marching on government buildings, convening hunger strikes, and getting arrested in their bid to lobby for constitutional revision. In 1869, Wyoming became the first state to pass a referendum on the extension of full voting rights to women. Slowly, more and more states followed suit, and while each small victory was celebrated by the suffragettes, they realized that, in order to make a real impact, they needed to push for change at a national level.

The amendment was first introduced to Congress in 1878, but was defeated by 34 votes to 16. It was presented again and again to Congress in following years, with no advance. Then on May 21, 1919, the House of Representatives finally passed the amendment, quickly followed by the Senate. Just over a year later, Tennessee became the thirty-sixth state to approve the amendment, which meant three-quarters of the states were in favor, paving the way for the constitutional change that now sees every American woman granted the right to choose their representatives in government.

Soprano Dame Nellie Melba.

Japanese Suffrage Group Founded

Japan, 1920: Two Japanese women have founded an organization that will press for social reform and suffrage. The women's rights activists Raicho Hiratsuka and Fusae Ichikawa established the New Women's Association (called Shinfujin Kyokai in Japanese), the first body of its kind in Japan to give voice to ordinary women. Its members include teachers, nurses, reporters, and housewives. One-third of the people at the official launch of the association were men who feel that, with the new liberalism that has arisen since the end of the Great War, Japanese society needs to move on from its old oppressive traditions. The New Women's Association has the stated aim of petitioning the Diet (Japanese parliament) to enact legislative change, allowing Japanese women the right to vote and attend political meetings.

Britain's First Family Planning Clinic Opens

London, England, March 17, 1921: Birth-control advocate Dr Marie Stopes has opened Britain's first family-planning clinic, aimed at giving women advice and information on contraception and reproductive health. Called The Mothers' Clinic, it offers a free service to married women, enabling them to make informed decisions about the size of their family.

The clinic's opening was conducted with little fanfare; the Church, the medical establishment, and the wider public are all of the view that birth

> "AS LONG AS YOU KNOW MEN ARE LIKE CHILDREN, YOU KNOW EVERYTHING."
>
> COCO CHANEL, FRENCH DESIGNER (1883–1971)

Japanese women are demanding better wages and the right to vote in parliamentary elections.

Key Events

USA, January 16, 1920: The 18th Amendment officially bans beer, wine, and liquor.

San Remo, Italy, April 25, 1920: The League of Nations gives Britain a mandate over Mesopotamia and Palestine.

Geneva, Switzerland, June 13, 1920: The first International Feminist Conference opens.

Chelmsford, England, June 15, 1920: Australian soprano Nellie Melba makes the first advertised radio broadcast at Marconi headquarters.

USA, August 26, 1920: American women gain the right to vote.

Ireland, December 14, 1920: The British government partitions Ireland into two separate territories, following Bloody Sunday (November 21), when 26 people were killed.

Japan, 1920: The New Women's Association is established, calling for equal rights for Japanese women.

Mongolia, March 13, 1921: Mongolia expels the Chinese after 200 years.

London, England, March 17, 1921: Author and women's rights advocate, Marie Stopes, opens Britain's first family planning clinic.

Panama, April 20, 1921: The Colombian Treaty grants Colombia free access to the Panama Canal and $25 million in exchange for US possession of the strategic waterway.

Paris, France, May 1921: Gabrielle "Coco" Chanel unveils Chanel No. 5.

Russia, August 4, 1921: Lenin appeals for Western aid to combat a famine that is sweeping the country.

San Francisco, USA, September 9, 1921: Actress Virginia Rappe dies from a ruptured bladder after allegedly being raped by silent film star Roscoe "Fatty" Arbuckle.

USA, September, 1921: Bessie Coleman returns to America, the first African-American woman to be licensed as a pilot, having learned to fly in France.

Ireland, December 6, 1921: Southern Ireland becomes a free state under the dominion of Britain. The eight counties in the north forming Ulster remain part of the UK.

Fontainebleau, France, 1921: French composer, conductor, and teacher Nadia Boulanger is appointed to the staff of the American Conservatory.

Hollywood, USA, 1921: Sisters Lillian and Dorothy Gish star in D. W. Griffith's film Orphans of the Storm.

New York, USA, 1921: Margaret Sanger establishes the National Birth Control League.

USA, 1921: Edith Wharton's novel The Age of Innocence, published last year, wins the 1921 Pulitzer Prize for fiction.

Recording artist, blues singer Bessie Smith.

Edith Wharton

control should not be practiced at all, much less openly promoted.

Dr Marie Stopes was almost single-handedly responsible for setting up the clinic and used her own money to fund it. Her interest in family planning was sparked when her first marriage made her acutely aware that her sex life was not what it should be. She had the marriage annulled on the grounds that it was never properly consummated. Scottish-born Stopes later married again and wrote a taboo-busting sex manual called *Married Love*, which caused an outcry when it was published in 1918, because it suggested sex should be as satisfying for women as for men. Her female readers loved the book and sent Stopes hundreds of letters asking for more advice on birth control, prompting her to establish The Mothers' Clinic.

On the other side of the Atlantic, nurse Margaret Sanger has founded the National Birth Control League in New York. Much like Stopes, Sanger's goal is to educate women on the methods of preventing unwanted pregnancies.

Coco Chanel Designs Fragrance

Paris, France, May 1921: Fashion designer Gabrielle "Coco" Chanel has launched her first perfume, Chanel No. 5. In 1920,

Chanel fell in love with Grand Duke Dimitri Pavlovich, of Russia's Romanov family. He advised her that, unlike the French perfumes that quickly evaporated and faded, the perfumes used by the Russian court had a greater intensity.

Pavlovich introduced Coco Chanel to the perfume chemist and Russian émigré Ernest Beaux. The pair started collaborating on developing a fragrance and, after much research, Beaux came up with a perfume based on 80 individual scent components and evoking the snowy environs of his homeland that Coco believed captures the spirit and ethos of her Parisian fashion house. The fragrance is the first to use a high concentration of aldehydes, which are synthetic aromas that heighten the scent of the natural ingredients. Ylang ylang and iris are among the flowers evident in the perfume's top note, fading to rose and jasmine, then revealing base notes that include sandalwood and vanilla.

Chanel has designed the perfume's bottle herself, and has opted for a clear, rectangular vessel sealed with a stopper that shows just the fragrance's name in simple black print against a white background. This is vastly different from the decorative ornate shapes favored by other fragrance makers. The perfume is named No. 5 for its release in May, the fifth month of the year.

Gish Sisters Star Together in Film

Hollywood, USA, 1921: The thespian sisters Lillian and Dorothy Gish are sharing star billing playing two young girls caught up in the turmoil of the French Revolution in director D. W. Griffith's latest film, *Orphans of the Storm*. The women, both acclaimed Hollywood actresses, draw on their affection for each other to turn in

outstanding performances. In fact, Lillian Gish is generally regarded as one of the most gifted actresses in Hollywood, thanks to her extraordinary ability to convey subtle emotions on screen.

Lillian and Dorothy grew up in Ohio. They inherited a love of the theater from their mother, who turned to stage acting to support her children after the girls' father abandoned them. As soon as they were old enough, the Gish sisters also began performing on stage.

In 1912, the actress Mary Pickford, a long-time friend, introduced Lillian and Dorothy to the director D. W. Griffith—shortly afterward they won studio contracts and began appearing in Griffith's films.

Orphans of the Storm is the tale of two girls brought up as sisters; Dorothy plays Louise, who is blind. The sisters head to Paris during the French Revolution, in a bid to visit a doctor who is able to restore Louise's sight. The two girls become separated when Lillian's character, Henriette, is abducted by an aristocrat and she finds herself facing both the guillotine and a difficult struggle to reunite with her sister.

An exciting film that runs for over two hours, *Orphans of the Storm* will further enhance the Gish sisters' reputation.

> **time out**
>
> Two aeronautical women struck up quite a deal in 1921! Neta Snook "Snookie" Southern is the first woman to run a commercial airfield in the USA and is teaching Amelia Earhart to fly for the price of a few Liberty bonds.

Lillian and Dorothy Gish star in the epic *Orphans of the Storm*.

Ahmedabad, India, March 18, 1922: Mahatma Gandhi is sentenced to six years in prison for civil disobedience.
India, April 5, 1922: Writer, women's rights advocate, and social reformer Pandita Ramabai dies, aged 64.
Northern Iraq, June 18, 1922: Led by Sheikh Mahmud, Iraqi Kurds revolt, demanding independence or autonomy from Baghdad.
Valley of the Kings, Egypt, November 26, 1922: Lord Carnarvon and Howard Carter open the tomb of Tutankhamen.

Moscow, USSR, December 30, 1922: The Union of Soviet Socialist Republics is proclaimed, tying together Russia, White Russia, Ukraine, and Transcaucasia.
USA, 1922: Emily Post publishes *Etiquette in Society, in Business, in Politics and at Home*.
Fontainebleau, France, January 9, 1923: New Zealand-born writer Katherine Mansfield dies, aged 34.
Paris, France, March 26, 1923: After 50 years in the theater, la divine Sarah Bernhardt dies, aged 79.

London, England, April 26, 1923: Lady Elizabeth Bowes-Lyon marries Albert, Duke of York.
London, England, July 7, 1923: Frenchwoman Suzanne Lenglen wins her fifth consecutive Wimbledon singles championship.
Lausanne, Switzerland, July 24, 1923: The Near East Treaty establishes peace between Greece and Turkey.
New York, USA, August, 1923: Bessie Smith's recording of "Downhearted Blues" sells over 750,000 copies in six months.

Angora (Ankara), Turkey, October 29, 1923: Leader of the nationalist movement that brought an end to the Ottoman Empire, Mustafa Kemal has been elected president of the new Turkish republic.
New York, USA, November 6, 1923: El Dorado Jones is issued a patent for her invention of the engine muffler, which is designed to cut car engine noise.
Cairo, Egypt, 1923: Pioneering feminist Huda Sh'arawi founds the Egyptian Feminist Union.

England, 1923: Mystery writer Dorothy L. Sayers publishes *Whose Body?*, featuring Lord Peter Wimsey.
USA, 1923: Bacteriologists Gladys Dick and her husband George Dick publish their findings that scarlet fever is caused by the streptococcus bacteria.
USA, 1923: Poet Edna St Vincent Millay is the first woman to win the Pulitzer Prize for Poetry.
Denmark, 1924: Politician Nina Bang is appointed Minister for Education. She is the world's first woman cabinet minister.

Indian Feminist Dies

Emily Post

India, April 5, 1922: Pandita Ramabai, India's foremost champion of emancipation for women, has died today, aged 64. A woman of great courage and many achievements, she penned a feminist manifesto, converted from Hinduism to Christianity, translated the Bible into Marathi (her first language), and established a refuge for child widows and other people in need.

Born into a Brahmin family in Maharashtra on April 23, 1858, Ramabai was educated by her father, a Sanskrit scholar. At the time, few Indian girls had even a basic level of literacy, but Ramabai went on to become a scholar in her own right, her special area of study being the *purana*, Sanskrit tales dating from ancient times. She was honored in Calcutta with the title "Saraswati" (goddess of wisdom).

At the age of 22, Ramabai married a Bengali lawyer, creating quite a stir in Hindu society, as he was not Brahmin. Her husband died not long after they had married and, unwilling to accept the social limitations placed on widows in Hindu society, she caused yet more scandal by becoming a Christian.

In 1887, while studying in England, Pandita Ramabai published *The High Caste Hindu Woman*, in which she railed against child marriage, wife murder, and the social stigma that is associated with widowhood. Then, in the 1890s, she visited America, and wrote *Pandita Ramabai's American Encounter*, which included in it a call for Indian women to be granted the same liberties as she observed American women receiving.

Ramabai's Mukti Mission opened in Bombay in 1889, with two high-caste child widows the first to benefit from her benevolence. In 1895, she bought land in Maharashtra and relocated the mission there. By 1901, the mission was supporting 2,000 girls and women, and in 1902, a center for boys was opened nearby. Now, following her death, Ramabai's work assisting Indian widows, orphans, and special-needs children is certain to continue through the Mukti Mission.

> "MY CANDLE BURNS AT BOTH ENDS; IT WILL NOT LAST THE NIGHT; BUT AH, MY FOES, AND OH, MY FRIENDS—IT GIVES A LOVELY LIGHT."
>
> EDNA ST VINCENT MILLAY, "FIRST FIG" (1920)

Manners Manual Published

USA, 1922: Minding one's manners has become a little more manageable with this year's publication of Mrs Emily Post's book, *Etiquette in Society, in Business, in Politics and at Home*. Drawing on the many experiences from her privileged upbringing, Post has turned her hand to writing following her divorce from her husband, the businessman Edwin Post.

The book offers a wealth of practical advice, covering everything from appropriate greetings for business associates—"When a lady goes to a gentleman's office on business, he should stand up to receive her, offer her a chair, and not sit down until after she is seated"—to the finer points of what is, and is not, acceptable in polite American society today—"One who is rich does not make a display of his money or his possessions. Only a vulgarian talks ceaselessly about how much this or that cost him."

Post's impeccable manners have been cultivated from the earliest age. Emily was born in Baltimore in 1872, the only child of architect Bruce Price, who designed one of America's first gated communities, and Josephine Price, who came from a wealthy mining family. After attending an exclusive New York girls' school, she made her debut into society in 1892, her beauty and charm winning her many admirers. Post met her husband at an exclusive ball; they married soon after and had two sons together. Receiving little alimony in her divorce from him, she wrote a number of novels set in high society, a travelog, and had several stories published in reputable magazines.

Having been brought up to believe that women from a wealthy background should marry rather than work, Post has found herself enmeshed in a successful career. In 1921, an astute publisher noted the rise in numbers of upwardly mobile Americans and prosperous immigrants, and commissioned Emily Post to produce this comprehensive guide on how to behave in American society.

The incomparable actress Sarah Bernhardt.

Death of Sarah Bernhardt

Paris, France, March 26, 1923: France—indeed the world—is today in mourning after one of its brightest and most popular stars, actress Sarah Bernhardt, died at the age of 79. Bernhardt, who for the last years of her life was confined to a wheelchair after the loss of a leg through gangrene, is said to have passed away in the arms of her son, Maurice.

One of her best-loved performances was as Marguerite Gautier in Dumas's *La Dame aux Camélias*. She also played Joan of Arc, and toured both Europe and America with a production of *Hamlet*, in which she took the title role. The famed actress gained notoriety for her curious habit of sleeping in a coffin (usually only when a photographer was present); she was a consummate self-promoter.

Born in Paris on October 23, 1844, Bernhardt grew up with little financial security. Her first break came at the age of 15, when a friend of her mother paid for her to study at the Conservatoire de Musique et Déclamation.

After several years as a successful stage actress, Bernhardt appeared in the film

Paulette Duval, French actress, arrives in America.

Suzanne Lenglen wins fifth consecutive Wimbledon singles championship.

Lady Elizabeth Bowes-Lyo[n]

Tosca in 1906, but was unhappy with her performance. Her 1911 movie, *Camille*, was a success, yet it was the following year's *Queen Elizabeth* that she was most pleased by. It is claimed she cried, "I am immortal! I am a film!" upon watching it. She continued to act (in a seated position) almost until her death.

Cause of Scarlet Fever Pinpointed

USA, 1923: Dr Gladys Dick has discovered the bacterium that causes scarlet fever. Working in conjunction with her husband, Dr George Dick, she has published the results of her research showing that a toxin produced by a strain of the streptococcus bacterium causes the disease.

Scarlet fever is a childhood illness that begins with a sore throat and is characterized by a red rash that starts on the neck and spreads across the whole body. It has been recognized as a disease since 1675, but until now its cause was unknown.

The two doctors first came to their conclusion after injecting a volunteer with blood-borne streptococcus; the patient went on to develop scarlet fever. These findings will pave the way for further research into immunization against this disease.

Female Poet Wins Pulitzer Prize

USA, 1923: Edna St Vincent Millay has become the first woman to be awarded a Pulitzer Prize for Poetry. Her collection, *The Harp-Weaver and Other Poems*, clinched the win for this 31-year-old poet. Extremely popular for its blend of liveliness, romanticism, and subtle social commentary, particularly on feminist issues, Millay's work reflects the views of her generation. Her poetry recitals always attract appreciative audiences.

Millay was born in Maine to a poor immigrant Irish family and showed an early interest in poetry—by 15 she had had several works published in magazines and anthologies. Her talents were more widely recognized after her lengthy poem *Renascence* was published in 1912; this won her a scholarship to Vassar College. During the Great War, she read her poetry on the radio in support of the war effort. Then, after the war, she moved to New York's Greenwich Village and immersed herself in its bohemian buzz. One line from her poetry—"My candle burns at both ends"—captures the intensity of this period of her life.

As well as being known for her poetry, Millay is frequently the subject of scandal and gossip. In 1920 she refused literary critic Edmund Wilson's proposal of marriage, then in 1921 she had a brief relationship in Paris with American sculptor Thelma Wood.

Her collection *A Few Figs from Thistles* (1920) is also widely admired.

First Woman Cabinet Minister Appointed

Denmark, 1924: Nina Bang has become the world's first female cabinet minister. She has been appointed Denmark's Minister for Education in the country's first Social Democratic government.

Nina Bang has worked long and hard to gain this position of power. Even as a child, she expressed an interest in politics and ensured that her views were known. One of the few women to be admitted to Copenhagen University, she studied history and became interested in the writings of Karl Marx.

In 1895, she married Gustav Bang and together they joined the Social Democratic party. Then, in 1898, she moved away from history and became a journalist, writing articles that focused on politics and the plight of female workers. Meanwhile, Bang helped to develop social policy for the party. She became a member of the Social Democrats' executive committee in 1903 and soon rose to be deputy of the party, as well as its spokesperson on both financial matters and the welfare of Denmark's women and children.

An accomplished public speaker, Nina Bang has traveled widely and met many prominent international socialists. Upon taking up her ministerial post, she has announced that her primary goals are to democratize Denmark's education system and to lift the standard of teacher training. She expressed a desire that the nation's teachers be trained to educate their students in personal, health, and social matters.

DIE ÜBERLEBENDEN   KRIEG DEM KRIEGE!

A dramatic anti-war poster designed in 1924 by Käthe Kollwitz, whose son was killed in the Great War.

Women's Education Pioneer Mourned

Rose Scott

Kent, UK, April 22: All academia is today mourning the death of Lucy Caroline Lyttelton Cavendish. A descendant of William the Conqueror and maid of honor to Queen Victoria, Cavendish worked tirelessly to ensure access to education for girls from all social strata.

A major benefactor of the Girls Public Day School Company—responsible for establishing day schools for middle-class girls—Lucy's commitment to women's education was recognized with the Presidency of the Yorkshire Ladies Council for Education and appointment to the 1894 Royal Commission on Secondary Education. Also of note was the decision in 1904 by Leeds University to award Lucy Cavendish, the first ever woman recipient, an honorary degree of Doctor of Laws for notable service to education.

Women's World's Fair a Great Success

"GENTLEMEN PREFER BLONDES."

ANITA LOOS, AMERICAN AUTHOR (1893–1981)

Chicago, USA, April 26: The official closing by Vice President Charles G. Dawes yesterday marked the end of a successful Women's World's Fair. The fair, opened on April 18 by First Lady Grace Coolidge, was the initiative of Helen Bennett, manager of the Chicago Collegiate Bureau of Occupations.

Bennett's major motivations were twofold. First, her aim was to raise awareness of the contributions by women and the opportunities available to them in all areas of society including science, industry, the arts, and literature. Secondly, she wished to raise funds and support for the Republican Party women's organizations.

An all-female board was incorporated, with Louise de Koven Bowen as President. Edith Rockefeller McCormick, a board

French singer and comedienne, Mistinguett.

timeout

There's just no stopping the fussin' and flappin' that the Charleston is causing. Young woman are now dancing it either on their own or with a partner in speakeasies, dance halls, and at parties all over the USA.

member, wrote of the fair, "[It] marks the passing of the drooping, useless hothouse lily of Queen Victoria's reign and glorifies that nonetheless beautiful flower, the red rose of modern woman, eager, joyous, purposeful."

In the last eight days, the fair attracted more than 160,000 visitors who were entertained and informed by over 280 booths celebrating the diversity and contribution of women in the workforce. The fair's credibility was apparent through the participation of such big corporations as Illinois Bell Telephone Company, major national and regional newspapers, manufacturers, and banks.

A strong representation from related women's groups included the Women's Trade Union League. The WTUL has been a dynamic force over the last 20 years in the movement of women workers into trade unions, the lobbying for protective legislation, and the fight for women's suffrage.

Although figures are being finalized, confident predictions that the fair has made about $50,000 bode well for its social relevance as an ongoing annual concern in the future.

Socialite Poet Suffers Stroke

Massachusetts, USA, May 12: Controversial poet, patron, and socialite, Amy Lowell, died today. She had been suffering from a troublesome hernia and was advised to stay in bed. She ignored this advice and suffered a massive cerebral hemorrhage.

Born February 9, 1874, to the wealthy and prominent Lowell family in Brookline, Massachusetts, Lowell was educated by a governess before attending a series of private schools. A university education was not considered "proper" for a Lowell daughter and so Amy set about educating herself, availing herself of the thousands of volumes in the family library and collecting her own books—an interest that was to become a lifelong habit. Amy soon developed a fascination with poetry and, in particular, the work of John Keats.

Amy Lowell will be missed at social and cultural events.

New York, USA, January 9: English-born pianist and composer Ethel Leginska makes her conducting debut at Carnegie Hall, when she conducts the New York Symphony Orchestra.
Peking, China, March 12: Sun Yat-sen, the "father of the republic," dies, aged 58. His political philosophy, the Three Principles of the People, is highly influential.
Tennessee, USA, March 23: The teaching in schools of Charles Darwin's theory of evolution is banned in favor of creationism.

Indiana, USA, April 14: Twenty-eight-year-old Madge Oberholtzer dies of complications following her abduction, rape, and torture by the leader of the Ku Klux Klan. Klan membership numbers drop as a result.
Chicago, USA, April 18–25: The Women's World's Fair is held, showcasing women's achievements and ideas in science, industry, and the arts. Over 160,000 people visit the fair.

Sydney, Australia, April 20: Australian feminist and suffragist Rose Scott dies, aged 77.
England, April 22: Lucy Caroline Lyttelton Cavendish, advocate for women's education, dies, aged 83. She was the first woman to be awarded an honorary degree by Leeds University.
Germany, April 25: Field Marshal von Hindenburg is elected president.
Chicago, USA, April 25: The official closing by Vice President Charles G. Dawes of the Women's World's Fair.

Massachusetts, USA, May 12: Poet Amy Lowell dies, aged 51.
The Vatican, May 17: St Thérèse of Lisieux, who died in 1897, is canonized by Pope Pius XI.
South Africa, June 29: The parliament legislates to prohibit non-whites from working in skilled and semi-skilled jobs.
Olyphant, Pennsylvania, USA, August 6: Loretta Perfectus Walsh dies, aged 29. She was the first woman to serve in the US armed forces in a capacity other than nurse, and saw active duty in the Great War.

Auckland, New Zealand, August 19: Feminist and trade unionist Harriet Morison dies, aged 63. In 1888, she established New Zealand's first trade union for women.
Locarno, Switzerland, October 16: Germany and France sign a peace treaty, seven years after hostilities ended, recognizing a demilitarized zone along the Rhine.
Paris, France, October 17: Nineteen-year-old African-American dancer Josephine Baker is the toast of Paris due to her erotic dancing in *La Revue Nègre*.

Women Ku Klux Klan members march through the streets of Washington DC.

reader in Woolf's major themes of prevailing social mores. In particular, these include her ideas regarding the role of women and her disdain for the current treatment of mental illness. The book has aspects of the autobiographical: Woolf's recurrent battles with depression, which surfaced following the death of her mother, Julia, in 1895, are well known.

Woolf is a founding member of the avant-garde Bloomsbury Set, a group of intellectuals—artists, writers, economists, and art critics—who are causing quite a stir in the worlds of art and literature.

St Thérèse of Lisieux

Premature Death of True Patriot

Pennsylvania, USA, August 6: Loretta Perfectus Walsh, the first woman to serve on active duty in the US Navy, and the first woman to serve in any of the US armed forces in a non-nurse occupation, has died of unknown causes, aged 29.

Loretta enlisted in the Navy on March 17, 1917—prompted by the escalation of German Navy hostilities toward all ships, including those flying the US flag. Less than two weeks later, Congress approved Woodrow Wilson's declaration of war. Clearing the path for about 13,000 female yeomen (F), or "yeomanettes," she served actively until July 1919, then continued on inactive reserve status until her enlistment period ended in March 1921.

The yeomanettes enabled the freeing up of thousands of male troops for deployment overseas—a need predicted by the Secretary of the Navy, and instrumental in his support for the enlistment of females. Although women have served previously in the military as nurses, they were civilian employees and little recompensed. That yeomanettes were accorded the same benefits and rates of pay as their male counterparts illustrates the efficacy of the Navy's decision, recognizing the service to their country that Loretta and her fellow female yeomen offer.

She had been working on a biography of Keats for some years before her death.

Lowell mostly lived the life of a wealthy socialite, giving and attending parties and organizing entertainments. But after her parents died, Amy took over her father's civic duties, particularly those of supporting education and libraries.

It is, however, her devotion to, and promotion of, the Imagist poetry movement in America, and her prolific output of poetry, for which she is best known. The much traveled Lowell was popular on the lecture circuit and renowned for her eccentricities, such as her maroon automobile and maroon-liveried chauffeur, her preference for mannish clothes, and her cigar smoking.

Her poetry and her support of many of America's best-known poets will be sorely missed. Amy Lowell's secretary, traveling and living companion, actress Ada Dwyer Russell, will continue to live in the home they shared.

Virginia Woolf's Modernist Approach

England: Many are describing Virginia Woolf's new novel *Mrs Dalloway* as the female rejoinder to Joyce's *Ulysses*. Yet the comparisons to Joyce will probably amuse Woolf, as her family had earlier rejected the opportunity to publish *Ulysses*.

Woolf has embraced the developing modernist approach, using a stream of consciousness technique that lets readers immerse themselves in the character's thought processes. While the splintered sentence structure and disjointed interior monologs are at times disconcerting, the overall effect succeeds in engaging the

Josephine Baker

Pioneer of Women's Movement Dies

Auckland, New Zealand, August 19: Harriet Morison, a pioneer of women's rights in all facets of New Zealand society, passed away today aged 63.

Morison had experienced, first hand, the appalling conditions and exploitation of women workers during the time she was employed as a tailoress. This was the catalyst for her involvement—at the age of 26—in the development of the Tailoresses' Trade Union, and a lifetime of service on behalf of women's rights. The union, with Morison at its head, was successful in raising the basic wage and improving working conditions.

For Morison it was a natural progression from the trade union movement to her involvement in, and advocacy for, the women's suffrage movement, which was most vehement in the Dunedin area. In 1892, Morison was one of the organizers of the Women's Franchise League and she traveled the country exhorting other women and groups to join in the fight.

Harriet Morison's approach was often described as evangelical, and indeed, she spent some time as a lay preacher and Chairwoman of the Unitarian Church. Harriet's strong belief in the rights of women stemmed from what she believes is the fundamental Christian principle of social justice and equity.

In 1906 Morison became the first woman inspector of factories and, from 1908 to 1921, was the head of the Women's Employment Bureau in Auckland. Throughout her time in public service, Morison was constantly under pressure

"IF YOU DO NOT TELL THE TRUTH ABOUT YOURSELF, YOU CANNOT TELL IT ABOUT OTHER PEOPLE."

VIRGINIA WOOLF
ENGLISH AUTHOR
(1882–1941)

from the establishment, and her resignation in 1921 followed years of apparent acrimony from the Labour Department bureaucracy. Hopefully other women will now step up and carry on Morison's legacy across New Zealand.

"Goddess" Stops Paris

Paris, France, October 17: Ever since Miss Josephine Baker sashayed onto the stage at Théâtre des Champs Elysées two weeks ago, she has been the center of Parisian nightlife. As the star of the new *La Revue Nègre*, nineteen-year-old Baker is causing a sensation with her barely-there dresses, incredibly sensuous dance routines, and her obvious facility for comedy.

Josephine, with the exotic looks of her African slave and Apalachee Indian descent, leads a cast direct from Harlem, New York. Blending jazz and exotic dance, the show has caught the imagination of the city, but there is no doubt it is Baker they come to see. Those in enraptured attendance have included Pablo Picasso and a clearly smitten Ernest Hemingway.

Her trademark Charleston dancing, refined at the famous Cotton Club, will no doubt see Baker hot property well into the foreseeable future.

Naidu Named National Congress President

Kanpur, India: Sarojini Naidu has been elected President of the Kanpur Session of this year's National Congress—the first woman ever to hold this position.

The daughter of a scientist-philosopher father and a poet mother, Sarojini Naidu's journey to the presidency follows an extraordinary life. Matriculating to Madras University at the age of 12, the already multilingual Naidu's formative years were spent in the company of intellectuals, poets, and revolutionaries. At 16 years of age, she received a scholarship from Hyderabad College to study overseas, and was admitted to Kings College and later Girton College, Cambridge. Poor health and disenchantment with the rigid English education system, however, forced her to leave and, after briefly traveling through parts of Europe, she returned home.

In 1898, with the full agreement of her parents, Sarojini Naidu, a Brahmin, married Govindarajulu Naidu, a non-Brahmin— a courageous step for a young woman in a society that did not sanction inter-caste marriages. The couple now has four children.

Following the partition of Bengal in 1905, Naidu joined the Indian Independence Movement. Although continuing to write poetry—most notably *The Golden Threshold, The Bird of Time,* and *The Broken Wing*—Naidu became more concerned with the nation's freedom. The influence of freedom leaders and advocates, Gopalakrishna Gokhale and Mohandas Gandhi, led to her give up writing and devote herself entirely to social issues, including the emancipation of Indian women, Hindu–Muslim unity, and the Independence of India.

Following service as the Home Rule Party's ambassador to England in 1919, Naidu returned to India in 1920 to join Gandhi's Non-Cooperation Movement. The movement's resistance to the government, through non-violent civil disobedience, was a direct response to the Rowlatt Acts—British legislation that imposed many authoritarian restrictions upon the Indian population.

Naidu's most recent posting prior to the Presidency was as a delegate of the Indian National Congress to the East African National Congress.

Tacke Finds "Missing" Element

Berlin, Germany: The German chemist and physicist Ida Tacke, in collaboration with Walter Noddack and Otto Berg, has just announced the discovery of element 75 which they have called "rhenium." Rhenium, named for the Latin word for the Rhine River, fills a periodic table vacancy left by Dmitri Mendeleev.

Tacke was born in 1896 in the village of Lackhausen, Germany. She was able to take advantage of new laws, enacted after the Great War, finally allowing women to attend university in Germany and earn advanced degrees. Tacke studied chemistry and received her PhD in 1921 from the Berlin Technical University. After her graduation, she worked for private enterprise for the next four years, first with Allgemeine Electrical Works and then with Siemans-Halske.

Ida Tacke returned to public research with the Imperial Physico-Technical Research Office where she was encouraged by the head of chemistry, Walter Noddack, to focus her research on the elusive missing elements—a formidable assignment considering the fact that the Research Office was merely a government

American anthropologist Osa Johnson with Lumbwa women.

Daredevil stuntwoman, Alice Van-Springsteen.

Mary Pickford

a mixture of good fortune and perseverance. Born in Buckinghamshire, England, in 1900, she entered Newnham College, Cambridge, in 1919 to study botany, physics, and chemistry.

Her fortuitous attendance at a lecture about a recent solar eclipse, by astrophysicist Arthur Eddington, changed the direction of Payne's interests and from that moment on she devoted herself to astronomy. Although unable to change her major from physics, due to astronomy's identification as a branch of mathematics, Payne continued to attend Eddington's lectures and read widely on the subject. Having convinced Eddington of her ability and desire to pursue astronomy, he offered her access to the Observatory's Library and its avenues to astronomical research.

After her graduation from Cambridge, Cecilia Payne was determined to find a career in the astronomical field, so she applied for, and received, a research fellowship to study at the Harvard Observatory. At Harvard, the young astronomer had at her disposal a huge archive containing literally hundreds of thousands of stellar spectra plates, possibly best described as wavelength 'photographs' of stars.

Put simply, astronomers have been attempting to determine the composition of stars by comparing their differing spectral planes with those of known chemicals. Payne however, through her analysis of these planes and with reference to the relatively new field of quantum physics, suggests that spectra vary due to temperature and not composition. It is from this innovative premise that Cecilia advocates the theory that stars are composed almost entirely of hydrogen and helium.

School for Study of Ancient Music

Paris, France: The respected musician and educator, Wanda Landowska, has established the Ecole de Musique Ancienne (The School of Ancient Music) at Saint-Leu-la-Fôret, which is not far from Paris. Wanda Landowska is renowned for commissioning the manufacture of new harpsichords, writing insightful papers promoting them, and performing various compositions—particularly the works of Bach—to

wide acclaim. Between 1905 and 1909 she wrote a number of scholarly articles which were published in book form in 1909 as *Musique Ancienne*. With her exploration of musical history and her passion for the harpsichord she is credited with single-handedly reviving the instrument's popularity.

Wanda was born in Warsaw in 1879, and began playing the piano at 4 years of age. Her parents were musicians; her mother spoke six languages and founded the first Berlitz School in Warsaw. Wanda studied at the Warsaw Conservatory with Aleksander Michalowski and then, at 17, went to Berlin to complete her studies in piano with Moritz Moszkowski. She took lessons in composition from the German composer Heinrich Urban.

Wanda Landowska at one of her beloved harpsichords.

After moving to Paris in 1900, Landowska married Henri Lew, who encouraged her to explore the music of the seventeenth and eighteenth centuries. That Wanda Landowska now directs her worthy efforts to a School of Ancient Music seems only natural.

laboratory and incomparable to the likes of Cavendish's or the Curies' resources.

Working alongside Walter Noddack and Otto Berg, Ida Tacke's approach to identifying the new element followed a different path from those before her. Researchers had previously attempted to extract elements from ores, but Tacke employed the use of spectroscopy and a formula advocated by British scientist, Henry Moseley. The basic premise of the formula suggests that atomic number and frequency of emitted X-rays correspond.

"Accidental" Astronomer Awarded PhD

Cambridge, Massachusetts: Astronomer Cecilia Payne has become the first person ever to be awarded a PhD in astronomy from Harvard University. Her doctoral thesis, *Stellar Atmospheres, A contribution to the observational study of high temperature in the reversing layer of stars,* has been hailed as the most brilliant PhD thesis ever written in astronomy. Payne's path into the field of astronomy has followed

Ellen Key

A Musical Match

Berlin, Germany, January: Austrian singer and actress Lotte Lenya married German composer Kurt Weill this month. Lenya is already well known for her stage work and Weill has been called one of the best young composers of his generation.

Lotte Lenya was born Karoline Wilhelmine Blamauer in 1898 or 1899. At the age of about 13, she began training as a ballet dancer in Zurich, Switzerland, remaining there for the duration of the war. She proved an apt pupil and was soon being given roles at the Schauspielhaus (the Playhouse), under the direction of Richard Revy. By 1916, young Lotte was made a full member of the ballet company and two years later was appearing as a soloist. She also took acting lessons and performed in dozens of plays. Lenya sometimes appeared in dancing roles in various operettas, including the popular *The Merry Widow*. In 1921, she moved to Berlin where she felt there were more artistic opportunities for her talent. It was hard going at first, but Lenya was determined to succeed.

> *"It is only the women whose eyes have been washed with tears who get the broad vision that makes them little sisters to all the world."*
>
> DOROTHY DIX
> (ELIZABETH MERIWETHER GILMER)
> (1870–1951), US JOURNALIST AND WRITER, *DOROTHY DIX, HER BOOK*, 1926

Berlin's cafés are a focus of intellectual life.

Two years ago, Lotte Lenya was introduced to Kurt Weill. He has a love for musical theater, and his first opera, *Der Protagonist*, is expected to open later this year. There is no doubt that the partnership of Lenya and Weill will produce some truly memorable music.

In *The Torrent*, her first American film, Greta Garbo portrays an opera singer.

Woman Shoots Il Duce

Rome, Italy, April 7: Italian leader Benito Mussolini was today the victim of an assassination attempt. As Il Duce was leaving the International Congress of Surgeons, to whom he had given an address, a woman fired a pistol at his head from close range. Fortunately, Mussolini had tossed his head back to acknowledge the crowd, so the bullet passed across his nostrils. He was only mildly injured and having been attended to by a doctor, he was declared fit.

Mussolini was overheard to have said, "Fancy. A woman!" before leaving the scene of the incident. So who is this

woman? She is the Honorable Violet Albina Gibson, an Irishwoman, whose brother is Baron Ashbourne, son of the late Lord Chancellor of Ireland. Violet Gibson is estimated to be about 50 years old, and by all accounts, suffers from insanity. Sources reveal that she spent

time in a mental asylum during 1923. Even her family acknowledges that she has a mental illness.

After she fired her pistol, Gibson was attacked by the angry mob, and sustained cuts and bruises before police moved in to arrest her. Mussolini himself directed the crowd to leave Gibson alone. At this stage it appears that he is unlikely to press charges against the woman. She will most probably be deported.

Education Was Ellen's "Key"

Strand, Sweden, April 25: Swedish writer, educator, and feminist Ellen Key has died

Mecca, Hejaz, January 8: Abdel-Aziz ibn Saud takes the title of King of the Hejaz, stating his intention to rename his kingdom Saudi Arabia.
London, England, January 27: John Logie Baird demonstrates his invention, "television," to the Royal Institute.
Berlin, Germany, January: Austrian singer and actress Lotte Lenya marries composer Kurt Weill.

Canada, January: Canada joins the Commonwealth of Nations.
Turkey, February 17: Under the modernizing influence of Kemal Ataturk, new civil, criminal, and law codes based on European systems are adopted by Turkey.
Hollywood, USA, February 21: *The Torrent*, with Swedish actress Greta Garbo in her first starring Hollywood role, is released.

Rome, Italy, April 7: Irishwoman Violet Albina Gibson attempts to assassinate Mussolini, but the Italian leader suffers only an injured nose.
London, England, April 21: A daughter, the Princess Elizabeth, is born to the Duke and Duchess of York.
Sweden, April 25: Swedish feminist and educator Ellen Key dies, aged 77.
Calcutta, India, April: Sectarian riots between Muslims and Hindus erupt, injuring hundreds.

Broadway, New York, USA, April: Actress Mae West is arrested for obscenity when *Sex*, the play she wrote, directed, and stars in, opens on Broadway.
England, May 12: Paralyzing general strike, precipitated by the walkout of coal miners, ends.
Barcelona, Spain, June 9: Architect Antoni Gaudi dies, aged, 74, after being run over by a tram.
Paris, France, June 14: American painter Mary Cassatt dies, aged 82.

Arizona, USA, June: Having disappeared, presumed drowned, in May, evangelist Aimee Semple McPherson reappears, claiming to have been kidnapped and drugged. Although the evidence does not support her claim, she gains worldwide publicity for her evangelical tours.
Kingsdown, England, August 6: US swimmer Gertrude Ederle becomes the first woman to swim the English Channel and sets a new record of 14.5 hours.

today, at the age of 77. Key's views on education have long been the subject of discussion among teachers, philosophers, and parents. She will be most remembered for her book *The Century of the Child*, which was first published in Sweden in 1900. By 1909, it had been translated into nine European languages including English, and in 1916 it was translated into Japanese. This year, 36 editions of that book have been published in Germany alone. It is clear that Key's views are having an influence on educators around the globe.

Key believed that children should learn responsibility from an early age, and that they should be made aware of life's sometimes harsh realities. Her aim was that every child should receive a liberal education and grow up to be a thinking individual. Key is quoted as saying, "Education can give you a skill, but a liberal education can give you dignity." She stressed the importance of child-rearing, focusing on the critical role of motherhood, a point she made forcefully in her 1896 article "Female Psychology and Female Logic." Attracted by the principles of the socialist movement, Key also felt that because bringing up children is so important to society, it should be subsidized by the government.

Ellen Key was born in 1849 into a household that encouraged liberal thinking. She read extensively, and Nietzsche, Mill, Goethe, Spencer, and Rousseau were among her favorite thinkers. She first worked as a teacher in Stockholm, but in the middle of the 1880s she also began to write. Her published articles discussed such subjects as politics, religion, art and literature, women's rights, marriage, and education. By 1903, she had decided to be a full-time writer.

Among the many influential works she wrote, *Love and Marriage* (1911), *The Woman Movement* (1912), and *The Younger Generation* (1914) are still widely read.

Mae's Risqué Play

Broadway, New York, USA, April: After a successful initial Broadway run, *Sex*, the play written, directed by, and starring blonde bombshell Mae West, has been raided, and West charged with obscenity. The cast was also arrested and West was sentenced to 10 days in jail. Although the play is a comedy—West is known for her use of innuendo and dry humor—the show has been deemed immoral. She is accused of corrupting America's youth. The play's very title is considered to be offensive, and the fact that West plays a Canadian woman of loose virtue has authorities in a lather.

Mae West has been performing in vaudeville for a number of years now, and she is keen to make her mark both on the Broadway stage and in film, so she is not particularly concerned with the charges or even her recent stint in prison. She was released from jail two days early for good behavior, and she is well aware that the case has provided her with a good deal of free publicity. While in jail, she is said to have charmed both prison staff and inmates—after all, it is not often that a celebrity spends time behind bars, especially for a piece of entertainment. Her comic skills and clever use of double entendre are certain to keep Mae West in the public spotlight.

Death of Mary Cassatt

Paris, France, June 14: The art world is mourning the death today of American painter Mary Cassatt, who was 82. Born in 1844, Cassatt studied at the Pennsylvania Academy of Fine Arts in Philadelphia, USA. She first visited Paris in 1866 and, apart from a couple of brief periods back in the US, spent most of her adult life in France. During the 1870s, Cassatt encountered the works of Edgar Degas and Berthe Morisot, and she became involved in the Impressionist movement, exhibiting with them four or five times between 1879 and 1886.

Cassatt was particularly drawn to the image of mother and child, exploring the theme in a number of her paintings. She was also became interested in printmaking, following an exhibition of Japanese prints in Paris, but failing eyesight over the last decade or so effectively put an end to her creative work.

Mae West

time out

Over 100,000 mostly female fans lined New York's streets to catch a glimpse of the casket of Rudolph Valentino, dead at 31. In his short career, the screen idol had captured the hearts of millions of women with his Latin charm.

The Coiffure was produced in 1891 by Mary Cassatt.

Key Events

Transvaal, South Africa, August 22: The discovery of massive reserves of diamonds brings 50,000 people to the region.

Hankou, China, September 6: Nationalist Kuomintang troops, led by General Chiang Kai-shek, capture the strategic treaty port of Hankou. The northern troops have retreated and there is fear that Peking will fall.

New Zealand, September 9: The *Maori Arts and Crafts Act* revives traditional Maori skills.

Greenville, Ohio, November 3: Sharpshooter and former member of Buffalo Bill's Wild West Show, Annie Oakley, dies, aged 66.

Japan, December 25: Hirohito becomes Emperor following his father Yoshihito's death, ending the Taisho period.

London, England: Turkish novelist and feminist Halide Adivar Edib publishes her English-language autobiography, *Memoirs*, which describes recent Turkish history, her pacifism, and the struggle for women's emancipation.

Yorkshire, England: After disappearing for several days, British crime writer Agatha Christie is found in a hotel, claiming to have suffered amnesia.

Berlin, Germany: Austrian physicist Lise Meitner is appointed professor of physics at the University of Berlin, the first woman in Germany to attain this position.

Boston, Massachusetts, USA: Mathematician and logician Christine Ladd-Franklin receives her PhD in mathematics from Harvard University.

New York, USA: The Lucy Stone League successfully fights for the right of married women to be granted copyright in their own names.

New York, USA: Dancer and choreographer Martha Graham founds her own dance company.

Paris, France: Fashion designer Coco Chanel creates the little black dress.

Stockholm, Sweden: Italian novelist Grazia Deledda wins the Nobel Prize for Literature.

New York, USA: Poet, critic, and wit Dorothy Parker publishes her collection of poetry, *Enough Rope*.

Tamil Nadu, India: Social reformer E. V. Ramasany Naicker founds the Self-Respect Movement. One of his aims is for women to be more independent.

Paris, France: "Esthetic surgeon" Dr Suzanne Noel publishes *La Chirurgie Esthétique, Son Rôle Social*, which describes the importance of cosmetic surgery.

London, England: Ballerina Ninette de Valois founds the Academy of Choreographic Art.

Aimee Semple McPherson

Sister Aimee in Abduction Scandal

Arizona, USA, June: When charismatic evangelist Aimee Semple McPherson went swimming last month and did not return, it was assumed that she had drowned, and a huge search was undertaken to find her body. On June 20, the plot thickened when her mother received a ransom note demanding $500,000 for her return. Three days later, McPherson herself turned up on the Arizona–Mexico border, claiming to have been kidnapped, drugged, and held hostage in a hut in the desert, only managing to escape her captors at an opportune moment, and then walking through the desert for more than 12 hours. A huge contingent of reporters has covered the story since her alleged abduction.

Yet many doubt the story's veracity. No hut could be located in the vicinity, and McPherson was suffering neither dehydration nor sunburn. Her shoes weren't dusty and, possibly most significantly, she was not wearing a swimsuit. She was also wearing a watch that everyone agreed she was not wearing while swimming.

McPherson, who was born in 1890, began preaching across America in her late teens. In 1921, she settled in Los Angeles, basing her evangelical ministry there. She designed and built the Angelus Temple, funding the construction from the proceeds of her preaching. She operated a radio program to help spread her Christian message and she later founded the Foursquare Church. She is fondly known as Sister Aimee.

There are rumors that McPherson faked her abduction so she could spend time with her lover in Carmel, California, but McPherson denies this. She has a devoted band of followers who are standing by her. It is likely, however, that a grand jury investigation will be instigated

"FOUR BE THE THINGS I AM WISER TO KNOW: IDLENESS, SORROW, A FRIEND, AND A FOE."

DOROTHY PARKER, AMERICAN WRITER, *ENOUGH ROPE*, 1926

to determine the truth of the matter. Whatever the outcome of that hearing, Aimee Semple McPherson has garnered more free publicity than she could ever have imagined.

Swimmer Proves Women's Abilities

Kingsdown, England, August 6: In an amazing feat of endurance and swimming ability, American Gertrude Ederle has today become the first woman to swim the English Channel. Not only that, but she has set a new record of 14.5 hours, beating the previous record by no less than two hours.

Nineteen-year-old Gertrude Ederle has already made a name for herself as a swimmer. From 1921 to 1925, she set a total of 29 US and world records for swimming. At the 1924 Olympic Games, she was part of the gold medal-winning 400 m relay team, and she also won two bronze medals. Ederle started swimming long distances about five years ago. Last year, she swam the 21-mile (34 km) distance between the Battery, in Manhattan, and Sandy Hook, New Jersey.

Ederle has maintained that women could do anything men could, and today she has proved it. Only five men have successfully swum the English Channel, and Ederle has bettered their times. The Channel is a perilous body of water—there are cross-currents and strong tides, and inclement weather is common. Today was no exception. When she set off from Cap Gris-Nez, France, at 7.08 this morning, conditions were rough. After 12 hours in the water, Ederle's trainer wanted her to give up, but the plucky teenager refused, and finally walked ashore on the Kent coast at Kingsdown at 9.35 tonight and straight into the history books.

Anemia Claims Famous Markswoman

Greenville, Ohio, USA, November 3: Annie Oakley, legendary sharpshooter and long-time member of Buffalo Bill's Wild West Show, has succumbed to anemia. She died today, aged 66.

Phoebe Ann Moses was born in Ohio in 1860, and helped support her family by shooting small game animals. Nicknamed "Little Sure

Gertrude Ederle trains for her English Channel swim.

Shot" by Chief Sitting Bull, Oakley began her professional life at the age of about 16 when she entered and won a shooting contest in Cincinnati against noted marksman Frank Butler. The pair married soon after and began performing in vaudeville shows. Butler was the star, and Annie acted as his assistant. But he soon acknowledged her superior talent and they changed roles—he became her manager and assistant.

In 1885, the Butlers joined Buffalo Bill Cody's famous traveling show. Such was Oakley's precision that she could shoot the ash of a cigarette held in someone's

BUFFALO BILL'S WILD WEST.
CONGRESS, ROUGH RIDERS OF THE WORLD.

MISS ANNIE OAKLEY,
THE PEERLESS LADY WING-SHOT.

Annie Oakley was one of the stars of Buffalo Bill's Wild West Show.

mouth. She could shoot a 10-cent coin at 90 ft (27 m) in the air. She was equally adept with a rifle, a pistol, or a shotgun, so it was no surprise that she quickly became the show's star attraction.

The Wild West Show toured extensively around the country and overseas, appearing at Queen Victoria's golden jubilee celebrations in 1887. The show went to France, Spain, and Italy, bringing the American frontier to European audiences. From then on, Annie Oakley's international reputation was assured.

The Butlers left Cody's show in 1901, wishing to lead a more settled life. Oakley continued to perform, appearing in the 1902 stage show *The Western Girl*. Later she joined the Young Buffalo Wild West, her shooting skills undimmed by middle age. In 1922, Annie Oakley decided to make a comeback, but she was injured

THE DAILY NEWS, SATURDAY, DECEMBER 11, 1926.

MRS. CHRISTIE DISGUISED.

Mrs. Agatha Christie as she was last seen (centre), and (on left and right) how she may have disguised herself by altering the style of her hairdressing and by wearing glasses. Col. Christie says his wife had stated that she could disappear at will if she liked, and, in view of the fact that she was a writer of detective stories, it would be very natural for her to adopt some form of disguise to carry out that idea.

How Agatha Christie may have disguised herself when she disappeared.

DISARMIN GERMA

"NOT COMI

BRITISH AD HOLD UP L

From Our Special C

The agenda of the League of Nations finished, and to-morro hoped, will be devote sions regarding Leagu man armaments. It i however, that a Sunda necessary.

The British, French, and Belgian Foreign M morning, and endeavor outstanding differences

That, however, they Conference of A

Dorothy Parker

PhD a Long Time Coming

Baltimore, Maryland, USA: Forty-four years after writing the dissertation that fulfilled the requirements for a PhD in Mathematics, mathematician and logician Christine Ladd-Franklin has at last been awarded her doctorate by Johns Hopkins University. An exceptional scholar, Ladd-Franklin attended Vassar College. She then spent some years teaching before returning to do postgraduate work in mathematics and logic—she was the first woman admitted to study at Johns Hopkins University.

While there, she was entitled to receive the remuneration accorded to university "fellows," but was not allowed to use the title because of her gender. It was while she was at Johns Hopkins that she wrote her PhD, which the university refused to award, again because of her gender.

Christine Ladd-Franklin pursued a career in mathematics because physics was denied her, as women were not being allowed to enter science laboratories. It is fitting that the university has at last granted this brilliant woman the honor she has long deserved.

Italian Woman Wins Nobel Prize

Stockholm, Sweden: "For her idealistically inspired writings which with plastic clarity picture the life on her native island and with depth and sympathy deal with human problems in general." These words encapsulate the connections between people and places that are the hallmarks of the work of this year's winner of the Nobel Prize for Literature, Italian novelist Grazia Deledda.

Deledda was born in Nuoro, Sardinia, in 1871. She received private tuition in Italian and French, but had little other formal education. She was, however, an avid reader, which provided her a base on which she could nurture her own writing ambitions. While in her early teens, she penned a number of short stories, some of which were published in magazines in Rome and Milan.

Her first novel, *Fior di Sardegna (Flower of Sardinia)*, was published in 1892 when Deledda was only 21. Her first major critical success came in 1903 with the publication of *Elias Portolú*, a moving novel about a shepherd who falls in love with his brother's fiancée. Her 1904 book *Cenere (Ashes)* was made into a film in 1916 with Eleonora Duse in the lead role.

In 1900, Deledda married Palmiro Madesani with whom she has two children. During that year they moved to Rome, where they have lived ever since, but Sardinia has always been close to her heart and still plays a critical part in her works.

in a car accident and has been in poor physical condition since. The death of this champion shooter closes a chapter on America's Wild West.

Turkish Novelist Publishes Memoirs

London, England: Turkish novelist, nationalist, and feminist Halide Adivar Edib has published—in English—her autobiography, *Memoirs*, which describes in detail recent Turkish history, plus her own views of pacifism and the struggle for women's emancipation. Having fallen out of favor with the Turkish government, Edib is currently living in exile in England with her second husband, Dr Adnan Adivar.

Halide Adivar Edib is one of the new Turkish Republic's foremost feminists. Born in 1884, she was educated at Istanbul's American College for Girls. She then taught history before being appointed to the University of Istanbul in 1918, where she taught literature. Passionately nationalistic, she and her husband served as soldiers during the Turkish War of Independence.

She has already written a number of works, one of which, 1922's *Atesten Gömlek (The Daughter of Smyrna)*, was translated into English, but this is the first time Edib has published in English. She is keen for Westerners to understand the problems facing the new Turkey, particularly the problems faced by Turkish women. *Memoirs* is an account of Edib's childhood and her first marriage, which ended in divorce because of her husband's polygamy. She provides details about the nationalist movement, and explains why she is a pacifist. Edib paints a clear picture of some of the issues that relate to the cultural clashes between East and West. Her autobiography is sure to strike a chord.

An artist captures the hubbub and glamor of London's West End.

Clara Bow

Girl Scouts Lose Their Leader

Savannah, Georgia, USA, January 17: The founder of the American Girl Scouts, Juliette Gordon Low, has died today, aged 66, having succumbed to breast cancer. She will be remembered for her historic words of March 12, 1912—"I've got something for the girls of Savannah, and all of America, and all the world, and we're going to start it tonight!" She was, of course, referring to the establishment of the Girl Scouts, which began with a group of 18 girls under the name American Girl Guides. In 1911, Low had met Sir Robert Baden-Powell, founder of the Boy Scouts and Girl Guides in England, and immediately formulated plans to set up the same thing in the United States.

One of the reasons behind the great success of the Girl Scout movement is that Low insisted that it be open to girls from all backgrounds, including girls

"NOBODY'S INTERESTED IN SWEETNESS AND LIGHT."

HEDDA HOPPER
(1885–1966), AMERICAN
ACTRESS AND GOSSIP
COLUMNIST

with disabilities. Juliette Low herself suffered from deafness, but never let this affliction stop her from achieving her goals. Girl Scouts get plenty of physical and mental exercise, taking on character-building activities and learning independence and resilience in the process. Low maintained that these activities prepared girls for adulthood, either as wives and mothers, or as working women in the professions.

For the past 15 years, Low, known to her friends as Daisy, worked tirelessly to promote and improve the Girl Scout movement. Low's vision has had a tangible impact on the girls of America.

Juliette Gordon Low founded the Girl Scouts in 1912.

Conference in India

Poona, India, January: This month has seen the founding of the All India Women's Conference, in Poona, an initiative of Irish-born feminist and suffragette Margaret Cousins, who has lived in India since 1913. Cousins has enlisted a number of prominent social activists to assist at the conference, including Kamaladevi Chattopadhyay, Rajkumari Amrit Kaur, Sarala Ray, and Dorothy Jinarajadasa, among others.

The conference aims to bring together women of different castes, religions, and economic status from all over the subcontinent. Conference attendees are discussing issues important to women, such as education for girls, the age of marriage, maternity leave, child welfare, and housing. Cousins, who founded the Irish Women's Franchise League in 1908, is a well-known suffragette and was once imprisoned in London for engaging in feminist projects. Although she is the driving force behind the

All India Women's Conference, she wants it to be run entirely by Indian women.

One of the leading members of the conference is Kamaladevi Chattopadhyay, who was born into wealth and educated at London University. In spite of her privileged background she has a strong desire to improve the lot of ordinary women in India. This is a sentiment shared by Rajkumari Amrit Kaur, who is also an advocate for India to cut its colonial ties with Britain. All involved in this historic undertaking are hoping that the conference will be taken to other cities, thus making it a truly national women's movement.

time out

Mae West, must you? Undeterred by the closure of her play *Sex* and her arrest for "corrupting the morals of youth," the buxom blonde opens and stars in her new production, *The Drag*, a show about homosexuality.

Clara Bow Has "It"

New York, USA, February 15: Novelist Elinor Glyn coined the term; director Clarence Badger made it into a film; and 21-year-old actress Clara Bow has brought it to life—"It." The new film *It* has just been released and already Miss Bow is being called the "It Girl." What is this "It"? It is pure, unashamed sex appeal, something Clara Bow has in abundance. Charming, vivacious, and full of fun, Bow steals every scene of the movie and she is sure to become the brightest star in Hollywood's firmament.

Clara Bow made her screen debut, playing a flapper, in 1922's *Beyond the Rainbow*. Since then, she has appeared in dozens of films, playing salesgirls and waitresses. But she has proved that she has serious acting ability in films such as *Mantrap, Free to Love,* and *Grit*. In *It*, Bow plays Betty Lou Spence, a shop girl who is romantically interested in the shop's owner, played by Antonio Moreno. The film is entertaining, and is the perfect vehicle for Bow's vibrant personality.

Bow has had a tough upbringing. She was born in Brooklyn, New York, her

Clara Bow is one of Tinseltown's brightest lights.

mother was constantly ill, and her father is said to have been abusive. Clara got her big break when she won a fame and fortune contest, the first prize of which was a part in a motion picture. She has not looked back. Her first reviews, received when she was just 16, remarked on her confidence and enthusiasm.

Bow is rumored to have embraced a real Hollywood lifestyle *and* some of its leading men—unsubstantiated reports suggest that she has had affairs with actors John Gilbert, Gary Cooper, and Gilbert Roland, among others. Whether this is true or not matters little. With *It*, Clara Bow has become a role model for young women seeking adventure and a certain amount of freedom from society's strictures.

Juliana Turns 18

The Hague, Netherlands, April 30: Under the terms of the Dutch constitution, Princess Juliana has to be ready to succeed to the throne by the age of 18. Today, she comes of age and is now theoretically entitled to assume the throne in the event of the death of her mother, Queen Wilhelmina. In two days' time, she will be officially installed in the Council of State, the body advising government.

One of the princess's first duties in her new role will be to visit the small town of Borculo, which has suffered cyclone damage. She will also be expected to attend the opening of Parliament. Although she has now entered public life, Princess Juliana is intending to study law and literature at Leiden University this year.

The End for Lizzie Borden

Fall River, Massachusetts, USA, June 1: Lizzie Borden, whose trial and acquittal of the murder of her parents made her a household name, has died, aged 66. In August, 1892, Lizzie's father and stepmother were hacked to death in their home. Suspicion immediately fell on Lizzie, then aged 32. She was at home at the time, and the fact that relations between members of the Borden family were unhappy was well known in the community.

Lizzie was arrested by the police and put on trial for double homicide, but she maintained that she was in the barn at the time of the murders. Press reports fuelled the public's imagination, and there were suggestions that Lizzie murdered her stepmother in one room, then killed her father in another. After that, according to her accusers, she cleaned the ax and burned her blood-stained clothes.

The trial began in June 1893 and lasted two weeks. Newspaper reports at the time commented on the accused woman's lack of emotion, and she was universally condemned. However, one witness backed up Lizzie's story of being in the barn at the time of the murders, and this, together with the judge's summation that most of the evidence in the case was circumstantial, led to her acquittal.

Unfortunately for Lizzie Borden, the murderer was never found. Ostracized by the community in which she lived, she died a lonely woman.

Willa Cather

Lizzie Borden was dogged by accusations of murder.

Tamara de Lempicka

> "WE MAY NOT
> ALL BREAK THE
> TEN COM-
> MANDMENTS,
> BUT WE ARE
> CERTAINLY ALL
> CAPABLE OF IT.
> WITHIN US
> LURKS THE
> BREAKER OF
> ALL LAWS …"
>
> ISADORA DUNCAN,
> (1878–1927), AMERICAN
> DANCER

Countess of Courage

Dublin, Ireland, July 15: Freedom fighter and politician Constance Gore-Booth, Countess Markiewicz, died today, at the age of 59. A most remarkable woman, Markiewicz spent her life fighting for women, the poor, and, significantly, the rights of Ireland against Britain.

She was born in 1868, and joined the women's suffrage movement while in her twenties. She studied art in London and Paris, where she met her future husband, Count Casimir Markiewicz.

The couple settled in Dublin, where Constance became active in women's rights, joining a revolutionary group, the Daughters of Erin, and set up a youth branch of the Irish republican movement. She also became involved in nationalist politics. When she demonstrated against a visit to Ireland by King George V in 1911, she was arrested for the first time. During the 1916 Easter Uprising, when Irish rebels declared that Ireland was a republic, Constance was appointed second-in-charge to Michael Mallin.

She was later charged with treason and sentenced to death, a sentence commuted to life imprisonment because she was a woman. At her trial, she famously said, "I did what was right and I stand by it." Released in the 1917 amnesty, Constance campaigned against the conscription of Irish men into the British army.

Jailed again in 1918, this feisty woman decided to stand for the British Parliament. She won her seat, but as a member of Sinn Fein refused to go to London, preferring to join the Parliament in Dublin, where she became the Minister for Labor. During the Irish Civil War, the countess took part in the fighting and was arrested again. Her republican sentiments kept her in trouble with the authorities, but she never wavered in her dedication. Although she was born into privilege and then married into it, Constance

Margaret Sanger focuses on world population issues.

Constance Markiewicz, the first woman elected to the British Parliament, although she never took up her seat.

Gore-Booth Markiewicz never lost her sense of civic and republican duty.

Sanger Organizes Population Conference

Geneva, Switzerland, August-September: The first World Population Conference has just been held in Switzerland. Organized by American birth control advocate Margaret Sanger, the conference examined the nature, makeup, and impact of the world's population on the social, economic, and political structures in which we live today.

Margaret Sanger is well known for her work in the birth control movement. She was greatly concerned with the high rate of self-induced abortions, many proving fatal to the mother, and worked hard to educate women about their choices in life, including contraception. *What Every Girl Should Know*, published in 1920, goes into great detail about puberty, menstruation, reproduction, and pregnancy, so women can learn how their own bodies function.

Sanger established the American Birth Control League in 1921, and two years later, she opened the first legal birth control clinic in the country. She has not been without her critics. Many people see her as lewd and unprincipled, and the Catholic Church has denounced her work. She is, however, changing the way women see their options.

The World Population Conference is another innovation from Sanger. At the end of the conference, a decision was made to establish a permanent international organization to study and report on the world's population and the problems that face us all. The new body will probably be known as the International Union for the Scientific Study of Population.

Isadora Dances in a Better Place

Nice, France, September 14: In a horrific freak accident, the famed American dancer Isadora Duncan was killed today when her scarf became caught in the wheel of her automobile and her neck was broken. She was 49. Duncan will no doubt be remembered as the inventor of "modern dance," her free unfettered style and characteristic bare-footed performances changing the way we think about dance. She often wore her hair loose, and her flowing Grecian-style costumes gave her a vitality not evident in more traditional forms of dance.

Isadora Duncan was born in San Francisco in 1878. Her father was a poet, her mother a musician who nurtured in young Isadora a love of music. The works of some of the great composers, including Tchaikovsky and Chopin, were the inspiration behind Isadora's performances.

Isadora Duncan poses with pupils at one of her dance schools.

ROBES DU SOIR, de JEANNE LANVIN

Use of embroidery sets apart the designs of Jeanne Lanvin.

Duncan first danced publicly in San Francisco, but her talents were unappreciated. At the turn of the century, she moved to Europe where she could more easily express herself in dance, and there she was well received. For a time in the early 1920s she lived in Russia.

Her unconventional approach to dance extended into her personal life—Duncan had two children, by two different men, although she married neither of them. Tragically, both children drowned in 1913. She did marry once. Her husband, Sergei Esenin, left her after a year or two. In 1925, he committed suicide.

Duncan founded dance schools in Germany, Russia, and the USA. Her passion for music and dance remained undimmed to the end.

Bringing Blacks and Whites Together

New York, USA, October: Civil rights campaigner and writer Mary White Ovington has just published a book of biographical sketches of 20 leading African-American men and women. Entitled *Portraits in Color*, it includes items on Marcus Garvey, W. E. B. DuBois, and Lucy Laney. It is another feather in the cap of this committed social activist. Born in 1865 into a family that supported the rights of women and had been involved in the anti-slavery movement, Ovington dedicated her life to campaigning for civil rights for America's black citizens.

In 1911, having studied the employment, health, and housing conditions endured by black New Yorkers, she published *Half a Man: A Study of the Negro in New York*, an indictment of white America's treatment of its black brothers and sisters.

History was made following the 1908 Illinois race riots—in which scores of black people were killed and injured—when Ovington was inspired by socialist author William Walling to rally to the black cause. Along with Henry Moskowitz, Ovington and Walling organized a national conference to discuss the rights of African-Americans. This led to the formation of the National Negro Conference in 1909, which ultimately became the National Association for the Advancement of Colored People (the NAACP). Many prominent citizens, black and white, joined the NAACP, including notable civil rights campaigner Mary Church Terrell and anti-lynching activist Ida Wells-Barnett.

Ovington served as the executive secretary of the NAACP and later became the organization's chairman. The NAACP fights against racism and segregation, and focuses particularly on the issues of housing, education, employment, and health. Members also work toward educating people against racial violence.

Apart from her involvement in the NAACP, Mary White Ovington has also found time to write several books, including *How the National Association for the Advancement of Colored People Began* (1914) and *The Upward Path* (1919), an anthology aimed at African-American children. Ovington hopes that her new work will show something of the contribution made to the wider US community by African-Americans.

Finland Appoints Female Minister

Helsinki, Finland: Finland has its first female government minister. In 1906, Finland became the first European country to give women the right to vote and to stand for election to Parliament, but it has taken until now for the first woman minister to be appointed. Miina Sillanpää, 60, is the new Minister for Social Affairs. She is expected to concentrate on women's issues, particularly the plight of single mothers, and the well-being of children.

Miina Sillanpää is well qualified to assume this responsibility. In her youth, she worked in factories and as a maidservant. She later became active in Finland's women's movement. Her success at this level is an inspiration to women to achieve their aspirations.

Liberal Education Espoused by the Russells

West Sussex, England: Social activist, feminist, and educator Dora Black Russell and her husband, philosopher and mathematician Bertrand Russell, have opened a progressive private school, Beacon Hill, in West Sussex. Its aim is to provide children with a liberal education. Bertrand Russell does not favor a strictly academic approach to education, and Dora strongly believes in democratic and cooperative methods of teaching, saying that the combination of these ideals will result in pupils becoming mature, disciplined, and inquiring young adults. So committed are the Russells to their new school that their own children, John, 6, and Kate, 4, will be educated there.

Dora Russell, 33, has long been known for her progressive views. An advocate for girls' education, she deplores the inequities in the education system. She is also known for her rather liberal views on other social issues—she espouses birth control and is one of the founders of the Workers' Birth Control Group. She also promotes more sexual freedom for women, a view she expressed in her 1925 book *Hypatia: Women and Knowledge*.

Although the couple has established the school together, it is thought that Dora Russell will assume the major responsibility for curriculum development and pedagogical approaches.

Dora Black Russell

FLORENZ ZIEGFELD PRESENTS

SHOW BOAT

ADAPTED FROM EDNA FERBER'S NOVEL OF THE SAME NAME

BOOK & LYRICS BY
OSCAR HAMMERSTEIN 2nd
MUSIC BY
JEROME KERN

ENSEMBLES & DANCES BY
SAMMY LEE
SETTINGS BY
JOSEPH URBAN

Make Believe
Can't Help Lovin' Dat Man
Ol' Man River
Why Do I Love You?
Bill
You Are Love
SELECTION

T. B. HARMS COMPANY
NEW YORK

Show Boat, featuring the song "Ol' Man River," has been a hit.

Margaret Mead

*"A FLOWERLESS
ROOM IS A
SOULLESS
ROOM, TO MY
WAY OF THINK-
ING; BUT EVEN
ONE SOLITARY
LITTLE VASE OF
A LIVING
FLOWER MAY
REDEEM."*

VITA SACKVILLE-WEST
(1892–1962), ENGLISH
WRITER

Infamous Murderess Executed at Sing Sing

New York, USA. January 13: Ruth Snyder, aged 32, died in the electric chair yesterday evening after being found guilty of murdering her husband, Albert Snyder. New Yorkers awoke to the *Daily News* headline "Dead!" above a controversial photograph of her last moments. It was taken by newspaper photographer Tom Howard, who had a camera strapped to his ankle. Right to the end Ruth Snyder was news. Her sensational trial and the days leading up to the execution have kept reporters in a frenzy.

Ruth, a striking blonde, apparently tired of her husband and embarked on a series of affairs until she met Henry Judd Gray, an insignificant corset salesman. They conspired to kill Albert and take off with his $48,000 life insurance policy. After several botched attempts, in March last year they were finally "successful." The pair bludgeoned Albert to death.

However, their plan to make the murder appear the result of a robbery

was a failure, and the lovers were arrested. Loyalty did not run deep, and at the subsequent trial, both accused the other of the murder. Sentenced to death, the pair was sent to Sing Sing Prison.

Ruth Snyder is the first woman to be executed by electrocution in Sing Sing Prison since 1899, and the first woman to be executed by Robert Elliott, the Sing Sing executioner.

time out

The British parliament finally extends full franchise to women 21 and over. Voting rights had been delayed since 1918 when the female population had been greater than the male and fears were held that a woman's party might dominate Britain.

Sing Sing Prison was the scene of Ruth Snyder's final moments.

Winter Gold at 15

St Moritz, Switzerland, February 19: Sonja Henie, aged 15, capped her brilliant career in ice skating to win an Olympic gold medal this week at the Winter Games. Six of the seven judges awarded Sonja first place for her interesting technique and innovative choreography routines.

Four years ago at the previous games, she was placed eighth in the same event. In 1926 at the world championships she came second. Sonja has been skating since she was six and is the youngest Olympic skating champion ever. Wearing a short skating skirt and with her blonde hair flying, Sonja wowed the spectators as she skimmed over the ice to Olympic gold. She will certainly go far in the skating world.

Revolutionary Executed

China: Xiang Jingyu, a pioneer of the women's movement in China, was executed in Hong Kong by the Kuomintang (the National People's Party of China).

Born in Xupu in 1895 to a wealthy father who believed in education,

Sonja Henie, Olympic gold medal winner.

she was sent to the Hunan School in Changde, where she excelled. In 1916 she returned home to rebuild the Xupu Girls' School, which had been destroyed by a flood, becoming the school's principal. She encouraged girls to attend the school, and worked to eradicate the practice of foot binding. She believed education of the individual was the best way to achieve social change.

In the early 1920s, she went to France to study, and married Cai Hesun, a Marxist and member of the Chinese Communist Party. Subsequently Xiang Jingyu's beliefs became more radical; she now accepted that class struggle was the way to change society. Returning to Shanghai, she became head of the Women's Bureau, encouraging women to participate in politics and protecting the interests of women workers. In 1925 she helped to form the China Women's Federation.

After her marriage collapsed, she studied in Moscow. Last year she was assigned by the Party to work in Wuhan. However,

UK, January 5: The British government introduces the aged pension of 10 shillings per week for people over 65 on a low income.

Dorchester, England, January 11: Author Thomas Hardy dies, aged 87. His ashes are to be interred in Westminster Abbey.

New York, USA, January 12: Found guilty of murdering her husband, Ruth Snyder is executed.

Oakland, California, USA, January 28: Astronomer Dorothea Klumpke Roberts is the first member of the Eastbay Astronomical Society.

Darwin, Australia, February 22: Aviator Bert Hinkler completes the first solo flight from England.

St Moritz, Switzerland, February 19: Norwegian figure skater Sonja Henie wins her first Olympic gold medal at the Winter Olympic Games.

Denmark, March 26: Nina Bang, Danish politician and the world's first female government minister, dies, aged 61.

Turkey, April 29: Premier Mustafa Kemal introduces the Latin alphabet in preference to the Arabic.

Oxford, England, April: The final volume of the *Oxford English Dictionary* is published. The project was initiated in 1879.

USA, May 11: The first commercial television broadcasts begin with three 90-minute sessions per week.

Amsterdam, Netherlands, May 17–August 12: The IX Olympic Games introduces women's athletics and gymnastics.

London, England, June 14: Suffragette Emmeline Pankhurst dies, aged 69, weeks before British women finally gain the right to vote.

Carmarthenshire, Wales, June 18: Aviatrix Amelia Earhart crosses the Atlantic from Newfoundland in 21 hours.

UK, July 3: Women are granted the right to vote in Great Britain.

London, England, July 21: Acclaimed British stage actress Ellen Terry dies, aged 80.

Lucknow, India, August 30: Dissatisfied with the adoption of the Nehru Plan, the Independence of India League is established under the leadership of Jawaharlal Nehru, son of the author of the plan.

London, England, September 15: Bacteriologist Alexander Fleming makes a discovery while studying *Staphylococcus* bacteria; *Penicillium notatum*, a mold growing on some specimens, has killed the bacteria.

Dresden, Germany, September 16: German women's rights leader Marie Stritt dies, aged 72.

Illinois, USA, September: Blues singer Ma Rainey (Gertrude Pridgett) makes a hit recording, "Leaving this Morning."

Canadian Ethel Catherwood won gold in Amsterdam.

the tenuous cooperation between the Kuomintang and the Communists broke down, many Communists and left-wing Kuomintang members were killed. Xiang Jingyu continued to promote Communist Party ideals, but it was inevitable that she would be arrested, and we now know that she has been executed.

Women at the IX Olympic Games

Amsterdam, Netherlands, May 17–August 12: Athletes gathered in Amsterdam to compete in the IX Olympic Games. Of these athletes, 290 are women, almost double that of prior Olympics. Women are now allowed to compete in athletic and gymnastic events (although they have taken part in swimming, archery, figure skating, tennis, golf, and fencing in the past). For the first time, the Olympic flame was lit at the opening ceremony, and an added touch involved the athletes from Greece entering the stadium first with the team from the Netherlands, the host nation, coming in last.

History is being made in other ways as the results come in from Amsterdam. In the five new track events for women, 16-year-old American Betty Robinson won gold in the 100 meters, going on to win silver in the 4 × 100 meters relay. Halina Konopacka became the first Polish female to win gold with her record-breaking throw in the discus event. Having jumped for gold in the high jump, Canadian Ethel Catherwood cheered on her teammates to gold in the 4 × 100 meters relay.

To loud roars of approval from the crowd, the Dutch women took gold in the Team Combined Exercises; Italy had to settle for silver and Great Britain bronze.

Some competitors showed signs of exhaustion after the 800 meters race, perhaps justifying earlier criticism that the race would be too strenuous for women. The gold medal in that event was won by Linda Radke from Germany.

Clothing for the women competitors has been an important consideration. Women wear long shorts and blouses for the athletics, while blouses, tunics, long bloomers, and stockings are worn to hide womanly curves in the gymnastics.

Building on the success of women at these Games, we must hope that there will be more female participants at the next Games in four years' time.

First Woman to Fly the Atlantic

Carmarthenshire, Wales, June 18: Aviatrix Amelia Earhart joined Wilmer Stultz and Louis E. Gordon in crossing the Atlantic Ocean today. They arrived in Wales in the Fokker F7, *Friendship*, 21 hours after taking off in Newfoundland. Amelia is the first woman to cross the Atlantic in an airplane.

The flight was the idea of Amy Guest, an American living in London, who, unable to take part in the flight herself, arranged for publicist George Putnam to find a suitable substitute. Amelia seemed the most appropriate woman, with her knowledge of flying, good looks, and personality. Her duties involved keeping the flight log. Today's flight is indeed a high point in aviation history, following on from Australian aviator Charles Kingsford-Smith's successful ground-breaking flight across the Pacific.

Amelia's introduction to flying was a ride with barnstormer Frank Hawks in 1920. Flying with Frank impressed her so much that she said, "As soon as I left the ground, I knew I myself had to fly." Within a short time she took her first flying lesson, and quickly gained her pilot's license. Six months later she had bought her first plane. She built up her flying time, and in 1922 Amelia broke the women's altitude record when she ascended to 14,000 ft (4,267 m). Today she has another record under her belt.

Amelia Earhart

Russian emigrés gather together in Parisian cafes.

Moscow, USSR, October 1: The beginning of Stalin's first five-year plan. Farms are made collectives and heavy industry is expanded.
Addis Ababa, Ethiopia, October 7: Ras Tafari is crowned King. For the last 10 years, he has shared power with his aunt, Empress Zauditu.
Boston, USA, October 12: The iron lung, a machine enabling a person to breathe, is used for the first time on a child with infantile paralysis.

USA, November 18: Walt Disney's short cartoon film *Steamboat Willie* introduces Mickey Mouse.
Illinois, USA, November 27: Marjorie Joyner invents the permanent hair wave machine.
Nanking, China, November: The Kuomintang government headed by Chiang Kai-shek gains international legitimacy, signing treaties with 12 countries.
Rhodesia, December: British archeologist Gertrude Caton-Thompson begins her excavations of the ruins of Great Zimbabwe.

London, England, December: An appeal against the banning of Marguerite Radclyffe-Hall's *The Well of Loneliness* fails.
Sydney, Australia: Feminist Adela Pankhurst Walsh, daughter of Emmeline Pankhurst, founds the Australian Women's Guild of Empire, which assists working-class women.
China: Xiang Jingyu, feminist and head of the Communist Party's Women's Bureau, is executed.
England: Novelist Virginia Woolf publishes *Orlando*, an examination of the meaning of gender.

Europe, 1928-29: Dancer and choreographer Bronislava Nijinska creates the ballets *Nocturne, Bolero, Le Baiser de la Fée* and *La Valse*, all for ballerina Ida Rubinstein.
Jerusalem, Palestine: Golda Myerson is elected secretary of the Histadrut Women's Labor Council.
Puerto Rico: Women are granted the right to vote.
Hollywood, USA: Gloria Swanson stars in *Sadie Thompson*, a film adaptation of W. Somerset Maugham's story "Rain."

USA: Bacteriologist Alice Evans becomes the first woman to be elected president of the Society of American Bacteriologists.
USA: Psychologist Leta Hollingworth, who works with women and children, publishes *The Psychology of the Adolescent*.
USA: Anthropologist Margaret Mead publishes *Coming of Age in Samoa*.
USA: Artist Georgia O'Keeffe paints *White Calla Lilies with Red Anemone* and *Black Petunias*.

Votes for Women

Emmeline Pankhurst

United Kingdom, July 3: Women all over Britain are celebrating after the Equal Franchise Bill was passed this morning, giving women over 21 the right to vote. It has been a long struggle with many suffering privation and even death in their quest to achieve this goal.

A memorable contributor to the cause was Emmeline Pankhurst who, in 1903, founded the Women's Social and Political Union with her daughters Christabel and Sylvia. Unlike the supporters of the earlier movement, they used militant means to advance their cause, becoming known as suffragettes—their motto, "Deeds, not words." Many were arrested for disrupting public meetings and damaging public property. Notable acts included that of Mary Richardson, who was arrested for damaging—with a meat chopper—the Diego Velázquez painting *Rokeby Venus* in the National Gallery.

More tragically, Emily Davison was killed when she ran in front of King George V's horse on Derby Day. Many women were sent to prison, where they conducted hunger strikes, which resulted in forced feeding. In 1913 a new law—known as the "Cat and Mouse Act"—was passed to allow police to release prisoners until they regained their health, and then re-arrest them so they completed their sentences. Militant tactics by the suffragettes gave the cause a bad name but also highlighted women's dissatisfaction with their lack of franchise.

"WE HAVE TO FREE HALF OF THE HUMAN RACE, THE WOMEN, SO THAT THEY CAN HELP TO FREE THE OTHER HALF."

EMMELINE PANKHURST, (1858–1928), BRITISH SUFFRAGETTE

During the Great War, militant activity among the suffragettes stopped, although peaceful action continued. With so many men at the Front there was a shortage of labor, and many women at this time went out to work. Taking on men's traditional roles showed lawmakers how capable women could be, and gave new vigor to the struggle for equal franchise.

Sadly Emmeline Pankhurst, who had fought so hard for this day, did not live to see it. She passed away just over three weeks ago, aged 69.

Ma Rainey's New Hit

Illinois, USA, September: "Blues" fans are lining up for "Leaving this Morning," the latest recording from Ma Rainey, the "Mama of the Blues." Accompanied by her Tub Jug Washboard Band, Ma Rainey's new record will delight this style's aficionados.

Born Gertrude Pridgett, she began singing at 15 in a talent show. She became known as Ma Rainey after she married showman and singer Pa Rainey in 1904. Together the Raineys traveled, singing "blues songs" on the vaudeville circuit throughout the southern states of America.

On stage, Ma Rainey cuts a flamboyant figure, with her sequins and diamonds, and a necklace of gold coins around her neck. When she starts to sing, her powerful contralto voice rises and falls in her inimitable style.

Since signing a contract with the Paramount company in the early 1920s, a number of her songs have been recorded. Among these, "Farewell Daddy Blues," "Blame it on the Blues," "Don't Fish in My Sea," "Misery Blues," and "Little Low Mama" have proved popular.

During her career, Ma Rainey has worked with many well known jazz musicians, including Louis Armstrong, Coleman Hawkins, Tommy Ladnier, and Fletcher Henderson.

Her wide following is due no doubt to radio broadcasts and the gramophone. The blues, a new type of music with its roots in the Deep South, has caught on, not only in America but also in Europe. With its haunting melodies and eloquent lyrics telling tales of love, hardship, disappointment, and uncertainty, it speaks to everyone.

Ma Rainey belts out songs that audiences love.

Gloria Swanson Plays Sadie Thompson

Hollywood, USA: Gloria Swanson took on one of the more controversial roles in her career when she decided to play a prostitute in her latest film, *Sadie Thompson*. Her portrayal of Sadie, who is transformed from happy-go-lucky whore to a browbeaten penitent, is outstanding and no doubt she will be nominated as Best Actress in next year's Oscars.

Gloria Swanson plays the lead role in the movie *Sadie Thompson*.

Adapted from W. Somerset Maugham's short story "Rain," the film tells of prostitute Sadie Thompson, who sails to Samoa. Unable to leave Pago Pago for Apia, the small group of passengers is forced to stay together in close quarters. Unfortunately for Sadie, one of these is a zealous missionary, Reverend Davidson, who feels compelled to reform her.

A moving role for Swanson—with luck her next film will also showcase her talent.

New Secretary for Women's Labor Council

Jerusalem, Palestine: Golda Myerson has agreed to become secretary of the Women's Labor Council of the Histadrut, the large voluntary labor organization for workers, also known at the General Federation of Jewish Labor. Histadrut was founded in 1920 as a trade union, and its aims are to take care of the rights of workers. By 1927 more than half of the Jewish working population of Palestine held membership.

Ellen Terry as Portia in *The Merchant of Venice.*

Born in Kiev, Russia, Golda had an early life of hardship and privation. Her family emigrated to America in 1906 and settled in Milwaukee, Wisconsin, where Golda attended school. With ideas of becoming a teacher, Golda spent one year at teacher training college where she also become involved with the Milwaukee Labor Zionist Organization.

In late 1917, Golda married Morris Myerson, and as married women are not allowed to be teachers, she left that profession and worked fulltime for the Labor Zionist movement. In 1918, Golda went to Philadelphia for the inaugural meeting of the American Jewish Congress, where she was the youngest delegate to attend the convention.

In 1921, the Myersons decided to emigrate to Palestine and join a kibbutz. Golda's day-to-day duties included raising the chickens and fruit picking, but she also became active in kibbutz politics and this led to her being chosen as the kibbutz representative in the Histadrut. After three years on the kibbutz, Golda and Morris left and moved first to Tel Aviv, where their son was born, and then to Jerusalem, where two years ago their daughter was born.

During this time, Golda remained involved with the Histadrut. On accepting the position of secretary of the organization's Women's Labor Council, Golda will be setting up house in Tel Aviv, although it is not certain whether her husband will also move. His work will perhaps keep him in Jerusalem.

Digging at Great Zimbabwe

Rhodesia, December: British archeologist Gertrude Caton-Thompson began her excavations of the stone ruins of Great Zimbabwe earlier this year. Situated in southern Rhodesia, this large site had been considered to be the remains of an ancient Caucasian civilization, but now this theory is causing controversy among archeologists. Some, including Caton-Thompson and David Randall-MacIver, who wrote *Medieval Rhodesia* (1906), believe the ruins to be African in origin.

The site, which extends over 1,800 acres (728 hectares) has three main areas: the "Hill Complex," "Great Enclosure," and "Valley Ruins." All areas contain ruins of large stone constructions made with huge blocks of granite; there are also remains of mud-brick and earthen structures. Such a complex could have supported a considerable Shona population.

Caton-Thompson, who was born in 1888, studied at Cambridge University and the British School of Archeology in Egypt. From 1924 to 1926 she and Elinor Wight Gardner, a geologist, began a survey of the Northern Faiyum depression in the western desert south of Cairo. Caton-Thompson has continued to work in this region as a field director until now.

During her current excavation, Caton-Thompson will be classifying pottery, iron implements, and other archeological items as well as directing stratigraphic studies of the ruins in Great Zimbabwe. Due to the controversy over the origins of this area it will be interesting to see what developments occur during this dig.

Novelist Loses Appeal

London, England, December: *The Well of Loneliness* remains banned after an appeal against the verdict of obscenity failed this month. Novelist and poet Marguerite Radclyffe-Hall, who writes as Radclyffe Hall, is the book's author.

Published in August this year, the novel explores love between an older woman and a young girl. Explicit lesbian overtones, although written with sympathy and restraint, combined with the message that people should understand and tolerate such behavior, proved abhorrent to the conservative British public.

An article in the *Sunday Express* on August 19 condemned the book as shameless. The publishers were ordered by the Home Secretary to withdraw it from sale. The resulting trial banned the book on the grounds of obscenity, and all copies ordered to be destroyed. However, the book continues to have high sales in France and the United States, where attempts to ban it have failed.

Radclyffe-Hall is a well-established figure in the literary world, having published several volumes of poetry before turning to fiction. Her novels, which include *Adam's Breed, The Forge,* and *The Unlit Lamp,* have all been received with critical success.

A colorful figure, Radclyffe-Hall is quite open about her "invert" nature. *The Well of Loneliness* is, however, her first novel to deal overtly with lesbianism.

Ida Rubenstein

Among the latest French fashion collections, colorful sashes and ribbons add glamorous highlights.

Lillie Langtry

English Stage Beauty Dies at 75

Monte Carlo, Monaco, February 12: The very public life of famed British stage actress and one-time royal mistress, Lillie Langtry, ended in Monte Carlo today. The "Jersey Lily" will be buried on the island of Jersey in the English Channel this week.

Born Emilie Charlotte Le Breton in 1853, but always called Lillie for the luminous quality of her skin, in 1874 she married the well-to-do Edward Langtry, and persuaded him to move to London. In fashionable society she quickly became renowned for her beauty and intelligence, and came to the attention of Edward, the Prince of Wales. He was captivated by her, and they embarked on a barely concealed affair. Such were her charms that the prince was not the only one entranced; playwright Oscar Wilde once said of her: "I would rather have discovered Lillie Langtry than America."

When Langtry eventually fell out with the prince, however, her welcome in the salons and drawing-rooms of society London disappeared. She discovered that her husband was in financial distress, and that she herself was almost bankrupt—so, after befriending the French actress Sarah Bernhardt, Lillie decided to take to the stage to earn a living, a highly unusual step for an upper-class Englishwoman. She soon earned a name as a skilled actress, and attracted yet more admirers when she toured the United States.

Langtry continued her stage work until 1917, and along the way wrote a novel, published an autobiography, and invested in several businesses, including a racing stable. She also acquired a new, wealthier, and titled husband, Hugo de Bathe, in 1899 after divorcing her first husband.

Lillie Langtry is survived by her daughter, Jeanne Marie, as well as the thousands of photographs of her, collected by her adoring public, which depict her at the height of her fame.

"I DO NOT REGRET ONE MOMENT OF MY LIFE."

LILLIE LANGTRY (1853–1929), BRITISH ACTRESS

Mary Pickford stars in *Coquette,* her first talkie.

Silent Leading Lady Makes Leap to Talkies

Hollywood, USA, March 30: "America's Sweetheart" of the silent film era, Mary Pickford, takes the lead role in *Coquette,* a new talking picture released today.

A star of popular silent films including *The Poor Little Rich Girl* and *Rebecca of Sunnybrook Farm,* in her first talkie Mary Pickford plays Norma Besant, a beautiful Southern belle with more admirers than she can handle, until she is caught in the arms of her favorite beau, Michael Jeffrey (John Mack Brown), of whom her father heartily disapproves.

Pickford is not only known for her screen work. Along with performer and filmmaker Charlie Chaplin, her husband Douglas Fairbanks, and film director D.W. Griffiths, she established the United Artists film distribution company. The founders all seek greater control over their creative output. In the past, she has produced many of her films through her Pickford Film Corporation. Already there

is talk of Pickford being nominated for Best Actress for *Coquette* at the second Academy Awards next year. The first-ever ceremony is scheduled to take place in May this year in Los Angeles, but *Coquette* will not be eligible to be nominated for an award until next year.

But will Pickford make the transition to talking pictures that some stars have found so challenging? Will her vocal technique be good enough? Her fans are in no doubt— their heroine is up to the task.

Actress Marries Baseball Legend

New York, USA, April 18: Actress Claire Merritt Hodgson had an earlier start than usual yesterday when she married New York Yankees baseball star Babe Ruth at 5:45 in the morning. The early start aimed to deter crowds from interrupting the ceremony, and to give Ruth time to prepare for the Yankees' game against the Boston Red Sox, but the weather was on the bride's side—rain postponed the game until today and allowed the wedding party to continue. At today's game against the Red Sox, Ruth hit a home run and, as he arrived

Babe Ruth poses with Claire Hodgson and his daughter.

Key Events

Los Angeles, USA, January 2: Twenty-two-year-old pilot Evelyn "Bobbi" Trout sets a new women's solo endurance record when she flies non-stop for 12 hours and 11 minutes.
Yugoslavia, January 6: Alexander I takes direct control of the Kingdom of the Serbs, Croats, and Slovenes, renaming it Yugoslavia.
Calcutta, India, January 6: Nineteen-year-old Sister (later Mother) Teresa goes to India with the Sisters of Loreto, where she becomes a teacher at St Mary's High School.

Belgium and USA, January: Two comic strip characters make their debut: Hergé's *Tintin,* and Popeye, drawn by Elzie Segar.
Rome, Italy, February 11: Mussolini and the Papacy sign the Lateran Treaty, creating the Vatican and re-establishing the sovereignty of the Pope after 60 years of tension.
Monte Carlo, Monaco, February 12: British stage actress Lillie Langtry, who gained notoriety through her affair with the Prince of Wales, dies aged 75.

Hollywood, USA, March 30: The film *Coquette* is released, starring Mary Pickford in her first "talkie."
New York, USA, April 17: Actress Claire Hodgson marries baseball star Babe Ruth.
Picardy, France, April 24: Journalist and feminist Caroline Rémy de Gueghard, known as Séverine, dies, three days before her 74th birthday.
Brussels, Belgium, May 4: Screen actress Audrey Hepburn is born.

Los Angeles, USA, May 16: The first Academy Awards ceremony is held at the Roosevelt Hotel in Hollywood.
Berlin, Germany, May 17: Soprano Lilli Lehmann, known for her performances of Wagner's operas, dies aged 80.
London, England, June 10: Margaret Bondfield becomes Britain's first female Cabinet minister, in the new Labour government of Prime Minister Ramsay MacDonald.
Frankfurt, Germany, June 12: World War II diarist Annelies Marie Frank, known as Anne Frank, is born.

Southampton, New York, USA, July 28: Jacqueline Bouvier (Kennedy Onassis) is born.
London, England, August 5: Death of Dame Millicent Fawcett, feminist and suffragist.
Baarn, Netherlands, August 10: Women's rights activist, campaigner for birth control, and the first Dutch woman to qualify as a physician, Dr Aletta Jacobs, dies aged 75.
Jerusalem, Palestine, August 31: Jewish access to the Wailing Wall causes a violent Arab uprising, leaving 500 dead.

at third base, tipped his cap and blew a kiss toward his wife in the stands.

The record-breaking baseballer met Hodgson in Washington DC in 1923 when he attended a play called *Dew Drop Inn* with a friend. Hodgson had a small role in the production, and she caught Ruth's eye. She accepted an invitation from Ruth's friend to meet the "sultan of Swat," and their on-again-off-again romance has been a staple of newspaper gossip ever since.

The union between 34-year-old Ruth and the 31-year-old actress is not without controversy, however. Four years ago, Ruth separated from his first wife, Helen Woodford—with whom he had adopted a child—who died in a house fire in January this year. Hodgson, a native of the southern state of Georgia, was herself a widow: her husband, Frank, died in 1922.

First Academy Awards Ceremony Held

Los Angeles, USA, May 16: The Academy of Motion Picture Arts and Sciences held its first Academy Awards ceremony this evening at the Hollywood Roosevelt Hotel. The President of the Academy, Douglas Fairbanks, hosted the event and presented awards celebrating not only the performers in motion pictures, but also the talents of those behind the cameras, including directors, writers, cinematographers, and art directors.

Although the event was not one of suspense—the winners have been publicly known for three months—the Academy looks forward to it becoming a prestigious annual event.

In the Best Actress category, silent screen star Janet Gaynor won an award for her performances in three movies: *Seventh Heaven*, *Sunrise: A Song of Two Humans*, and *Street Angel*. The other two nominees were Louise Dresser for *A Ship*

Street Angel earned a Best Actress award for Janet Gaynor.

Comes In, and Gloria Swanson for *Sadie Thompson*. Emil Jannings was named Best Actor for his performances in *The Way of All Flesh* and *The Last Command*.

Seventh Heaven won two other awards, for Best Director and Best Writing (Adaptation), while *Sunrise* triumphed in the Best Picture (Unique and Artistic Production) and Best Cinematography categories. The award for Best Picture (Production) was given to *Wings*, which stars Clara Bow.

With talking pictures now on the rise, next year's Academy Awards are tipped to be radically different. The event will no doubt include exciting newcomers to the filmmaking scene, which is experiencing a period of unprecedented change.

time out

New York ladies do more than lunch when Abby Aldrich Rockefeller holds a luncheon to raise money and establish the Museum of Modern Art (MoMA). As the Museum's primary patron she has donated over 2,000 works.

Britain's First Female Cabinet Member

Mary Pickford

London, England, June 10: From draper's assistant to first female member of Cabinet—Margaret Bondfield has come a long way in 42 years. Today she was named the Minister of Labour in Ramsay MacDonald's Labour government, and is the first woman to hold a Cabinet position in the history of Britain. "In the name of the whole country we greet her in the new position she is to fill," Prime Minister MacDonald said in his welcoming speech.

With little formal schooling behind her, Bondfield rose through the ranks of the trade union movement, joining the National Union of Shop Assistants soon after its formation. In 1898 she became its Assistant Secretary and was the only female delegate at the Trades Union Congress of 1899.

Margaret Bondfield has served as Labour member of Parliament for Northampton since 1923.

Margaret Bondfield talks to fellow Labourite, Sidney Webb.

London, England, October 18: Canadian magistrate and women's right campaigner, Emily Ferguson Murphy, and four other women, bring the "Persons Case" to the Privy Council in Britain, which rules that the word "person" covers both men and women.

New York, USA, October 24: The "Black Thursday" stock market crash wipes millions off the value of shares.

Valley Stream, New York, USA, November 2: Female aviators found an association of women pilots. Its first secretary is Louise Thaden.

New York, USA, November 7: The Museum of Modern Art opens, confirming the significance of avant-garde artists this century.

Philadelphia, USA, November 12, 1929: Film actress and later Her Serene Highness of Monaco, Grace Kelly, is born.

Montlhéry, France, December 18: Racing car driver Hélène Delangle, known as Hellé Nice, breaks the land speed record for women.

Lahore, India, December: Violence between Hindus and Muslims leads to the All India Congress calling for independence from Britain.

Paris, France: Twenty-one-year-old Simone de Beauvoir is the youngest person to qualify as a philosophy teacher in France. This year she also meets Jean-Paul Sartre, a fellow philosopher.

Macau, South China Seas: Female pirate Lai Choi San, who commands 12 ships, begins her pirating career.

Ecuador and Romania: Women in Ecuador and Romania are granted the right to vote.

Dakar, Senegal: Writer and feminist Mariama Bâ is born.

India: The government passes the *Child Marriage Restraint Act*, proposed by Harbilas Sarda at the urging of Mahatma Gandhi, which raises the minimum age of marriage for girls to 14.

London, England: Novelist Virginia Woolf publishes the feminist essay *A Room of One's Own*, which originated from lectures she gave the year before at Cambridge University.

USA: Social reformer Katharine Bement Davis, a former head of New York City's Department of Correction, and the first woman to head a municipal agency, publishes *Factors in the Sex Life of Twenty-Two Hundred Women*, the culmination of nine years' survey work.

Millicent Fawcett

> "A WOMAN
> MUST HAVE
> MONEY AND A
> ROOM OF HER
> OWN IF SHE IS
> TO WRITE
> FICTION."
>
> VIRGINIA WOOLF, 1929,
> A ROOM OF ONE'S OWN

Dutch Birth Control Reformer Dies at 75

Baarn, Netherlands, August 10: One the world's first advocates of birth control and family planning, and a prominent international campaigner for women's rights, Dr Aletta Jacobs, died today at the age of 75.

Born in 1854, the daughter of a doctor, Jacobs decided to follow her father's career very early in life, and was granted special permission to study at university. She became the Netherlands' first qualified female medical doctor—despite the resistance of some of the teachers at her university—in 1878. Dr Jacobs opened the world's first family planning service in the Netherlands in 1882. She was a key inspiration for other international birth control reformers, including the United States' Margaret Sanger and Scotland's Marie Stopes, who both traveled to the Netherlands to meet with Dr Jacobs.

Dr Jacobs did not just concern herself with medical matters, however; she also campaigned for women's rights in all spheres. After she attempted to enroll to vote in 1883 and was rejected, she helped to establish the Vereeniging voor Vrouwenkiesrecht (Woman Suffrage Alliance) and campaigned tirelessly with international suffrage organizations to agitate for worldwide changes. In 1904 she co-founded the International Woman Suffrage Alliance (IWSA), which drew members from all over the world. The Netherlands finally granted women the right to vote in 1919. During the Great War, she was also a prominent advocate for peace and an end to the war.

One "Person" Now Equals Two Genders

London, England, October 18: A landmark decision in Britain's Privy Council has enshrined the right of Canadian women to participate fully in their political system. Until today, it was deemed that the word "persons," as used in the *British North America Act 1867*, the statute that established Canada as a nation, referred only to men. Today, however, five Canadian women's rights reformers—Emily Ferguson Murphy, Nelly McLung, Irene Parlby, Louise McKinney, and Henrietta Muir Edwards—won their battle to have women recognized as "persons" under the Act, allowing them to stand for election to the Canadian Senate.

The women first brought their motion to the Supreme Court of Canada, which allows any five citizens to challenge a point of constitutional law. When the court decided last year that the words "qualified persons" in the Act referred only to men, Murphy's group persuaded Prime Minister William Lyon Mackenzie King to take their case to the highest court of appeal: the Judicial Committee of the British Privy Council. Today's result was a unanimous reversal of the Canadian Supreme Court's decision. On behalf of the Committee, Viscount Sankey declared that not allowing women to take public office was "a relic of days more barbarous than ours."

The group's success is not altogether surprising, considering the distinguished legal pedigree of its driving force, Emily Ferguson Murphy. The prominent lawyer has campaigned for women's legal rights for women for more than 20 years. She was a key member of the Equal Franchise League, an advocate of property rights for women, and the first woman in the British Empire to hold the position of police magistrate when, in 1916, she was appointed to preside over a new court for cases involving female defendants.

The "Persons Case," as it has become known, is a watershed for the rights of women in Canada, and a resounding triumph for the reformers.

Women Pilots Band Together

Valley Stream, New York, USA, November 2: Female aviators today inaugurated their own organization for licensed women pilots. Plans for the new association, which is yet to be named, were formed when a group of female pilots—Amelia Earhart, Gladys O'Donnell, Ruth Nichols, Blanche Noyes, Phoebe Omlie, and Louise Thaden—met at the conclusion of the National Women's Air Derby earlier in the year and decided to group together. An invitation was issued to the 117 licensed female aviators in the United States. "It need not be a tremendously official sort of an organization," stated the invitation letter, "just a way to … discuss the prospects for women pilots … and to tip each other off on what's going on in the industry." Eighty-six of the 117 pilots have joined the new association.

Today's meeting officially launched the association. Louise Thaden, the 23-year-old winner of the Women's Air Derby, was elected its secretary. The Derby was established this year to allow women to compete in the air, with competitors racing from Santa Monica to Cleveland, a distance that takes several days to cover. Thaden, who earlier in the year held the records for altitude, endurance, and speed all at once, only began flying in 1927 when she started working for the Travel Air Company. She won the Derby in a Travel Air plane.

Fastest Woman Driver in the World?

Montlhéry, France, December 18: Dancer, model, cabaret star, and … racing-car record-breaker? Hellé Nice, the glamorous Frenchwoman with a daring disposition, today broke the land-speed record for women at the Montlhéry racetrack just outside Paris. In her Bugatti race-car, she managed, on her

Ocean liners are a popular mode of transport for the well-to-do in the 1920s.

Wedding celebrations continue, but child marriage is outlawed.

fastest lap, to reach an incredible speed of 122.85 mph (197.70 km/h); over 10 miles (16 km), her car averaged a speed of 121.95 mph (196.26 km/h). On the back of today's outstanding success, Nice now has plans to tour the United States as an exhibition driver.

Mariette Hélène Delangle was born in a village in northern France in 1900, the daughter of the local postman. These modest beginnings scarcely foretold the success Hélène would soon achieve. While still in her teens, she moved to Paris and began a career as a dancer and, famously, a nude model, becoming Hélène Nice in the process. But her love of fast cars—and the fast life—got the better of her and, after touring her cabaret act successfully for several years, she turned her efforts to motor racing, changing her name to Hellé Nice in the process.

Earlier this year, on June 2, Nice won the Grand Prix at the Journée Féminine de L'Automobile—the most respected women's racing event in the world—in a specially made Omega Six race-car. Coached by experienced French racing driver Marcel Mongin, she undertook a regime of strength-building exercise and track training to achieve her win. And, in true Nice style, she took the time to touch up her make-up—still sitting in the car— before meeting reporters and photographers at the end of the race. A week later she won the Actor's Championship, a less

serious race in which any actor or performer can compete, after only a week of training in a new machine, a powerful Bugatti T43A. Considering that racing is a sport whose greatest stars are always in danger of bone-shattering accidents, Nice's boldness and skill are even more remarkable.

Indian Legislation to Protect Child Brides

India: At the urging of Mahatma Gandhi, the Indian government has passed the *Child Marriage Restraint Act,* which prohibits the marriage of girls under 14 years of age and is due to come into force on April 1 next year. Gandhi's campaign to introduce the legislation began when the 1921 Indian census figures were released. These figures showed that 600 brides were aged between one month and 12 months old. He urged politician Harbilas Sarda to introduce the Bill, which was passed today.

The Act sets out the punishments (which include imprisonment) to be meted out to would-be husbands (if aged over 18), parents or guardians of child brides, and for any person who performs an illegal child

marriage. The courts have also been given the power to issue injunctions to stop planned illegal marriages taking place.

An Income of Woolf's Own

London, England: Feminist and novelist Virginia Woolf has just published an essay, *A Room of One's Own,* based on two lectures she delivered at Cambridge last year. The author of *Mrs. Dalloway, To the Lighthouse,* and, most recently, *Orlando,* takes as her subject "women and fiction," and ranges over the role of women in fiction, and in writing fiction.

Female writers, according to Woolf, work under a different set of limitations than do male authors: "one would say that women's books should be shorter, more concentrated, than those of men, and framed so that they do not need long hours of steady and uninterrupted work. For interruptions there will always be." Another of her contentions is that women require privacy—that is, rooms of their own—to write, and enough money to afford the time to do it.

Woolf is well placed to know the value of an independent income: in *A Room of One's Own* she admits that without the annuity left to her by an aunt—"for no other reason than that I share her name"—her own creative life would be much more constrained.

Virginia Woolf

Greta Garbo chats with the director on the set of *Anna Christie*—her first talkie—which will be released next year.

Death of Cosima Liszt

Cosima Wagner Liszt

Bayreuth, Germany, April 1: Cosima Liszt has died at the age of 92. The daughter of Hungarian composer-pianist Franz Liszt and wife of German composer Richard Wagner, Cosima Liszt gained worldwide recognition in her own right as the director, for 31 years, of the annual Bayreuth Festival of Wagner's operas.

Liszt was born out of wedlock in the town of Bellagio, Italy, to Countess Marie d'Agoult, an author who used the pen-name Daniel Stern. In 1857, Liszt married one of her father's students, piano virtuoso and conductor Hans von Bulow, with whom she had two daughters, Daniela and Blandine. Her father had earlier introduced Cosima to Richard Wagner, and after her marriage to von Bulow she came into frequent contact with the German composer, who was 24 years her senior and still married to Minna Planer.

Wagner and Liszt became lovers in 1863 and five years later they set up house together in a villa on the shore of Lake Lucerne, Switzerland. Their three children, Isolde, Eva, and Siegfried, were born before Liszt's divorce from von

> *"A GIRL WHOSE CHEEKS ARE COVERED WITH PAINT / HAS AN ADVANTAGE WITH ME OVER ONE WHOSE AIN'T."*
>
> OGDEN NASH (1902-1971), AMERICAN WRITER

Bulow cleared the way for their marriage in 1870. The family moved to Bayreuth where in 1876 Wagner inaugurated the Bayreuth Festival, an enterprise that was passionately supported by Liszt. After her husband's death in 1883, Liszt took over as musical director of the Festival, a duty she discharged until the outbreak of the Great War in 1914.

Nurse Gets Off to Flying Start

time out

American Mary Ware Dennett, whose sex education and contraception pamphlets were judged "obscene" last year, wins an appeal against that judgment. The result has been hailed as a boost for freedom of speech in the USA.

California, USA, May 15: Registered nurse Ellen Church today pioneered what promises to be a career for women in the flying industry when she used her medical experience in a novel way to become the world's first airline stewardess. She will tend to the comfort of passengers on board a Boeing Air Transport flight between Oakland and Chicago.

Born in rural Cresco, Iowa, on September 22, 1904, Church developed a fascination with flying while watching planes perform at the county fair. After graduating from Cresco High School, she studied nursing, then went to work in a San Francisco hospital, indulging her childhood passion by learning to fly in her free time.

When Church initially approached Steve Stimpson at Boeing Air Transport, she applied for the position of pilot. Although Stimpson rejected Church's application, he was persuaded by her suggestion that placing nurses on board planes could help allay the public's fear of flying. Boeing was already planning to hire stewards, as some European airlines have done, but with airsickness common due to bumpy conditions, Church argued that nurses were better qualified to care for sick and frightened passengers.

Boeing headquarters finally agreed to give Church's idea a three-month trial.

Sarojini Naidu, Mahatma Gandhi on Salt March.

She was hired as head stewardess and asked to recruit seven other nurses who met the airline's requirements. Church and her recruits are to be paid $125 a month for their services.

White South African Women Enfranchised

Johannesburg, South Africa, May 19: White women in South Africa have been granted the right to vote, ending a struggle that was officially launched in 1907 when a meeting of the Women's Christian Temperance Union endorsed the formation of the Cape Women's Enfranchisement League. One of the League's most notable leaders was Olive Schreiner, author of the 1883 novel *Story of an African Farm*, and a passionate advocate for the equality of the sexes. It was this same passion, however, that prompted Schreiner to resign from the League when it decided against broadening its struggle to include black South African women.

Cosima Liszt was director of the Bayreuth Festival.

England, January: Engineer Frank Whittle submits a patent for the first turbojet engine.

New York, USA, February 25: *The International Review*, starring Gertrude Lawrence, premieres.

London, England, March 14: Plans to build a tunnel from England to France are approved by the Channel Tunnel Committee.

USSR, March 16: Joseph Stalin begins a terror campaign to eradicate wealthy farmers.

Turkey, March 28: The name of the city of Constantinople is officially changed to Istanbul.

Bayreuth, Germany, April 1: Cosima Liszt, daughter of composer Franz Liszt and wife of composer Richard Wagner, dies aged 92.

Dandi, India, April 6: After completing his 100-mile (161-km) Salt March, Mahatma Gandhi defies the British salt tax laws by evaporating sea water to make his own salt.

China, April 23: Nationalists and Soviet Communists challenge General Chiang Kai-shek's efforts to control China.

Berlin, Germany, May 13: Educator and women's rights campaigner Helene Lange dies, aged 82.

California, USA, May 15: Nurse Ellen Church is hired as the first airline stewardess, flying the route between San Francisco and Chicago.

Johannesburg, South Africa, May 19: White women in South Africa now have the right to vote.

Darwin, Australia, May 24: British aviatrix Amy Johnson arrives in Darwin 19 days after commencing her solo flight from London.

Cincinnati, USA, June: Sarah E. Dickson is ordained as the first female Presbyterian elder in the country.

Lambeth, England, August 14: The Church of England reluctantly accepts the use of contraception.

New York, USA, October 14: Singer Ethel Merman appears in her first starring role, in *Girl Crazy*, by George and Ira Gershwin.

Ithaca, New York, USA, August 24: Natural historian, conservationist, and illustrator Anna Botsford Comstock dies, aged 75.

In 1911 a similar group, the Women's Enfranchisement Association of the Union (WEAU), was established by a small group of suffragists in the city of Durban. From its inception, the WEAU was also an exclusively white movement, attracting its members from the ranks of educated English-speaking women, including such prominent figures as Lady Rose-Innes and Edith Woods. In its early days, the WEAU held meetings and wrote newspaper articles to encourage others to support its cause, but as a moderate, non-confrontational movement, it was regarded with indifference by lawmakers, who maintained that politics was the domain of men and that a woman's place was in the home.

It was not until the 1920s, a decade when Afrikaner women workers began to enter the labor force, that the issue of women's enfranchisement was accorded greater credibility and respect. In 1921,

the WEAU managed to garner more than 54,000 signatures to a petition, which was then presented to the government of Prime Minister Jan Smuts. However, the government deferred any decision, promising to revisit the subject in the future. The issue was finally addressed when Prime Minister J. B. M. Hertzog established his Pact government in 1924 and subsequently undertook to pass legislation giving white women the same voting rights as white men.

High-Flyer Touches Down in Darwin

Darwin, Australia, May 24: Young British aviatrix Amy Johnson today became the first woman to fly solo from England to Australia when she landed her De Havilland Gipsy Moth in Darwin after a 19-day journey through sandstorms, monsoon rains, and blistering heat.

Born on July 1, 1903, in Kingston upon Hull, Johnson attended Boulevard School before moving on to the University of Sheffield and graduating with a Bachelor of Arts in economics. She learned to fly at the London Aeroplane Club while working as a legal secretary in the city, gaining her pilot's license in July 1929. Just months later, after showing an unusually keen interest in the mechanical side of flying, she became the first woman in Britain to gain a ground engineer's license.

Earlier this year, with only 75 hours of flying time to her credit, Johnson managed to secured the financial backing of Lord Wakefield in a bid to challenge and break the England to Australia solo flight record. The present record was set in 1928 by Australian Bert

Gertrude Lawrence

Hinkler, who made the journey in just 15 days. Johnson set off from Croydon, South London, on May 5. Although delays caused by unscheduled stops, including several crash landings, saw her fall four days short of her record-breaking goal, her long-distance flying feat has guaranteed her a prominent place in the history of world aviation.

Woman Becomes Presbyterian Elder

Wisconsin, USA, June: The Presbyterian Church in Wauwatosa, Wisconsin, has today ordained Sarah E. Dickson as the nation's first female Presbyterian elder. The groundbreaking move comes less than a week after the General Assembly of the Presbyterian Church in the USA voted to approve a resolution brought by a 1929 conference of women, who maintained that the church could best be served by allowing the full participation of both sexes without discrimination except as to ability and capacity.

According to reports, the Assembly's decision was very well received. When it was announced that women could now be leaders within the church, every member of the Session of Wauwatosa offered to resign if by his resignation a vacancy could be created for Miss Dickson as an elder.

Norma Shearer stars in *The Divorcée*, 1930.

Amy Johnson has set a new record for women flyers.

Key Events

New York, USA, November 16: Greta Garbo's first talkie, *Anna Christie*, is released. Garbo's first screen words are: "Gimme a vhisky ..."

New York, USA, December 31: The collapse of the Bank of the United States, which has 60 branches in New York alone, leacs to a run on banks throughout the country.

The Vatican, December 31: The papal encyclical *Casti Connubii* reaffirms the Catholic Church's ban on contraception, apart from the natural rhythm method.

USA: Mildred Wirt Benson, under the pen name Carolyn Keene, publishes *The Secret of the Old Clock*, the first of her mystery books for children featuring Nancy Drew.

England: The National Birth Control Council is founded by Helena Wright, providing information to married women about contraception.

Georgia, USA: Feminist and anti-racism campaigner Jessie Daniel Ames founds the Association of Southern Women for the Prevention of Lynching.

Shanxi, China: Englishwoman Gladys Aylward and another female European missionary open an inn, with the idea of converting travelers to Christianity.

USA: Aviatrix Anne Morrow Lindbergh, wife of Charles Lindbergh, is the first woman to be granted a glider pilot's license.

Russia: The Zhenotdel (Women's Department), set up by Communist Alexandra Kollontai to look after the "needs of women," including child care, housing, and employment, is closed down.

London, England: Polish-born dancer and ballet producer, Marie Rambert, establishes the Ballet Club at the Mercury Theatre. Within a decade, it becomes known as Ballet Rambert.

South America: Uruguayan poet Juana de Ibarbourou publishes *La rosa de los vientos*.

USA: Anthropologist Margaret Mead publishes *Growing up in New Guinea*.

Western Desert, Egypt: British archeologist Gertrude Caton-Thompson begins her survey and excavations of Kharga Oasis.

England: Crime writer Agatha Christie publishes *Murder at the Vicarage*, which introduces her amateur detective Miss Jane Marple.

China: The Kuomintang government passes legislation intended to promote gender equality.

Greta Garbo

> "PRAY FOR THE
> DEAD, AND
> FIGHT LIKE
> HELL FOR THE
> LIVING."
>
> MARY HARRIS (c. 1837–
> 1930), AMERICAN UNION
> ORGANIZER

Garbo Talks

New York, USA, November 16: The promise of the promotional catchphrase "Garbo Talks!" was realized today when silent screen star Greta Garbo made her talking picture debut in *Anna Christie*, Metro-Goldwyn-Mayer's screen adaptation of Eugene O'Neill's 1922 play.

Born Greta Gustafsson in Stockholm, Sweden, in 1905, Garbo studied acting at the Royal Dramatic Theater between 1922 and 1924. During this time, she was discovered by director Mauritz Stiller, who changed her surname to Garbo and gave her an important role in the Swedish film *The Atonement of Gosta Berling* (1924). When Stiller was hired by MGM in 1925, Garbo accompanied the director to the United States and was also put under contract by the studio. In 1926, she played the lead role in her first American film, *The Torrent*, and then went on to establish her star quality in such films as *The Temptress* (1926), *Flesh and the Devil* (1927), *Love* (1927), *A Woman of Affairs* (1928), and *The Kiss* (1929), MGM's last silent production.

With the screening of *Anna Christie* today, a spellbound audience finally heard Garbo utter her first film words: "Gimme a vhiskey, ginger ale on the side. And don't be stingy, baby!" Delivered in a throaty Swedish accent, Garbo's opening lines in her 14th film signal a seamless transition to the sound era for one of Hollywood's most celebrated silent stars.

National Birth Control Council Formed

England: A new organization, the National Birth Control Council, has been formed. Its aim is to promote information and open discussion about birth control "so that married people may space out/limit their families and thus mitigate the evils of ill health and poverty." Until now, wealthy women have been able to pay for contraception, but the poor have had no choice, often being forced to bear children they cannot afford or have illegal backstreet abortions that risk their lives. Indeed, according to figures compiled by the Council, some 450 women die each year while undergoing abortions in England and Wales alone.

The Council's founder, Dr Helena Wright, has written a number of works dealing with sex instruction, including *The Sex Factor in Marriage*, which was published this year. Born in 1887, Wright trained at the London School of Medicine for Women, qualifying as MRCS (Eng.) and LRCP (Lond.) in 1914, and as MB, BS the following year. Later, while she was practicing at the Bethnal Green Hospital,

she met her husband, Peter Wright, a surgeon in the Royal Army Medical Corps. After the end of the Great War, the couple traveled to China, where they worked as medical missionaries until 1927.

Wright continued to pursue her goal of promoting sexual health despite the opposition of the Catholic Church and other Christian denominations, all of which have traditionally condemned the use of artificial birth control. However, on August 14 this year, the Church of England became the first denomination to relax its stand when delegates to the Lambeth Conference of Bishops of the Anglican Church passed a resolution that allowed the use of contraception "where there is a clearly-felt moral obligation to limit or avoid parenthood." Despite this concession, the Catholic Church remains steadfast in its teaching that any act that deliberately inhibits the natural power of marital love to generate life is "an offence against the law of God and of nature."

Not in Our Name

Georgia, USA: Attendees at a conference organized by Jessie Daniel Ames, the tireless crusader for equality of both the sexes and races, have voted to form a new organization called the Association of Southern Women for the Prevention of Lynching (ASWPL). Twenty-six women attended the conference, with 12 forming the nucleus of the ASWPL, most of them prominent members of the Southern states' Protestant churches.

Ames has been a leader of a number of organizations in the past. She first became sensitive to the inequalities suffered by women after her husband died in 1914, leaving her a widow at age 31 and forcing her into the male-dominated world of business to support her three children. Two years later, she made her entry into the world of public politics as organizer of the Georgetown Equal Suffrage League. She went on to become

The brutal practice of lynching will be challenged by a new organization formed by Jessie Daniel Ames.

Anne Morrow Lindbergh, wife of Charles, is the first woman to obtain a glider pilot's license.

treasurer of the Texas Equal Suffrage League in 1918, the year that finally saw passage of legislation allowing women to vote in state primaries, and, in 1919, she became the first president of the Texas League of Women Voters.

In 1922, as her concerns broadened to include the rights of black people, Ames was appointed to chair a women's committee of the newly formed Texas Interracial Commission. It was through this work that she was alerted to an alarming rise in lynchings throughout the South.

Dedicated to eradicating the brutal practice, Ames now plans to launch a public campaign to expose the fallacy of lynching's "chivalrous" rationale. The perpetrators argue that they are merely defending the honor of Southern white women, but according to statistics presented by Ames, just 29 percent of the 204 lynchings between 1922 and 1929 involved allegations of crimes against white women. Ames and her organization also have plans to engage in action at the county level by enlisting the help of local groups and lobbying sheriffs to prevent lynching before it occurs.

Room at the Inn

Shanxi, China: An inn has been opened by two European women missionaries who hope to spread their Christian message by offering travelers nightly entertainment in the form of Bible stories.

One of the women, 30-year-old Gladys Aylward, herself an intrepid traveler, only recently arrived in mountainous Shanxi province. Convinced that she was called by God to preach the Gospel, she set out from London earlier this year to journey to China via the Trans-Siberian Railway, undeterred by the fact that Russia and China were waging an undeclared war. After some narrow escapes in the midst of hostilities, she then secured sea passage from Vladivostok to Japan, where she boarded another ship bound for China. Aylward then braved further travel by train, bus, and finally mule before reaching her destination.

Zhenotdel Shuts Down

Russia: The Zhenotdel, established in 1919 as the world's first government department for women, has been shut down in accordance with the official view that it has achieved its goal of improving the conditions of women's lives. Inessa Armand was the first director of the department, but within a year the role passed to the Zhenotdel's main supporter and founder, Communist revolutionary Alexandra Kollontai, the most prominent woman in the government at the time.

Born into a liberal aristocratic family in 1872, Kollontai rejected her privileged background when she joined the Russian Social-Democratic Workers' Party in 1898. Initially a Menshevik, she aligned herself with the Bolsheviks in 1914. After the Bolsheviks came to power in 1917, she was appointed Commissar for Public Welfare, a position she used to initiate reforms aimed at ensuring education for women and securing their participation in the workforce. Kollontai also championed such causes as easy divorce, legal abortion, and ensuring that children born out of wedlock gained equal rights with children born in marriage.

Kollontai remained director of the Zhenotdel until 1921. From 1923, however, the Party effectively exiled her to ambassadorial positions in Norway, Mexico, and Sweden.

Although precluded from playing an active role in the politics of women's policy in her homeland, Kollontai's campaign lives on in her published writings, most notably *Love of Worker Bees* and *A Great Love*.

Agatha Christie Puts a Woman on the Case

England: Prolific mystery writer Agatha Christie has published a new novel, *The Murder at the Vicarage*, in which Miss Jane Marple, an elderly woman from the quaint little English village of St. Mary Mead, matches wits with the killer to solve the crime and make her fictional debut as a shrewdly inquisitive amateur detective. The author's most enduring sleuth to date, retired Belgian policeman Hercule Poirot, with his waxed moustache and "little grey cells," was introduced in her first novel, *The Mysterious Affair at Styles*, published in 1920.

Christie was born Agatha Miller in 1890. She did not attend school as a child, being educated at home by a governess and tutors. In 1914, she married Archibald Christie, a fighter pilot in the Great War, and while working as a nurse during his absence she made the decision to write detective fiction. The couple divorced in 1928 and Christie remarried this year to archeologist Max Mallowan.

In creating Miss Marple, Christie says she was inspired by another of her characters, the sister of Dr Sheppard in her popular 1926 novel *The Murder of Roger Ackroyd*. Although Christie does not expect to keep writing novels about Miss Marple as she has with Poirot, the intuitive St. Mary Mead sleuth is a triumph of writing skill and promises to rival the eccentric Belgian detective in the reading public's affections.

Agatha Christie

Alexandra Kollontai founded and once headed the now disbanded Zhenotdel.

The World Mourns Anna Pavlova

Lupe Velez

"To follow without halt, one aim; there is the secret of success. And success? What is it? I do not find it in the applause of the theater; it lies rather in the satisfaction of accomplishment."

ANNA PAVLOVA,
1881–1931, RUSSIAN
BALLET DANCER

The Hague, Netherlands, January 23: The world is grieving after the sudden death of the elegant and passionate Russian ballerina, Anna Pavlova. She died early this morning of pleurisy, just three weeks before her fiftieth birthday. Pavolova was in the middle of her farewell tour.

In accordance with ballet tradition, tomorrow's performance will proceed as scheduled, with a single spotlight circling the stage in her place.

Anna Pavlova was born in St Petersburg, Russia, on January 31, 1881, and trained under some of the greatest teachers of the day. She was 10 years old when she danced her first performance as a cupid in Marius Petipa's *A Fairy Tale.* She exploded into the public's attention in 1901 when she played Nikya in *La Bayadère*—a role her tutor Mathilde

time out

On November 30, *The Joy of Cooking* by Irma S. Rombauer is published in the United States; she pays for the 3,000 copies herself. Her mix of recipes and "casual culinary chat" prove to be very popular with American women.

Kschessinska thought she would fail in because of her lack of strong technique. Her delicate frame and ethereal air enchanted audiences and made her ideal for romantic roles such as her resounding 1906 performance as Gisele.

Her most famous piece was the Dying Swan from *Carnival of the Animals* by Camille Saint-Saëns, choreographed for her by fellow dancer Michel Fokine. Pavlova once said: "If I can't dance, I would rather be dead."

Pavlova spent her last years living in London with her husband and manager Victor Dandre. She will be greatly missed by her millions of fans around the world. Her funeral will be held in London's Russian Orthodox Church and her cremated remains will be buried in Golders Green Cemetery.

Legendary Russian ballerina, Anna Pavlova.

Australia Loses a Golden Voice

Sydney, Australia, February 23: Dame Nellie Melba, the first Australian opera singer to achieve international recognition, died today of septicemia, aged 69 years. With an angelic voice that was remarkable for its pure even tones and range of nearly three octaves, Melba is most famous for the role of Mimi in Puccini's *La Bohème.*

Dame Nellie Melba was born Helen Porter Mitchell on May 19, 1861. Melba is a contraction of Melbourne, her native city. In 1887, Melba made her operatic debut in Brussels as Gilda in Verdi's *Rigoletto.* Within a few years, she was heralded as one of the most accomplished sopranos of her time, performing in Paris, London, and New York. In 1918, she was appointed a Dame Commander of the Order of the British Empire and was elevated to Dame Grand Cross in 1927. Between 1904 and 1926 she made almost 200 recordings and became the

Australia's famous opera singer, Dame Nellie Melba.

first internationally renowned artist to participate in direct radio broadcasts. Dame Nellie Melba also established a singing school at the Melbourne Conservatorium of Music in Albert Street, where she taught free of charge.

Melba was married for 20 years to Charles Nisbett Frederick Armstrong. They had one son. After many "retirements," she gave her last concerts in Australia in 1928, performing in Sydney, Melbourne, and Geelong. Dame Nellie has been described at various times in her career as temperamental, a canny businesswoman, and a kindly friend. She will be remembered not only for her outstanding contribution to Australian opera, but also for two dishes created by French chef Auguste Escoffier in her honor—peach Melba and Melba toast.

Her state funeral will be conducted from Scots Church, Melbourne. A funeral motorcade will follow the service and she will be buried in Lillydale Cemetery.

Key Events

Iraq, January 6: Archeologists unearth a 550 BCE royal palace at the ancient city of Ur.

The Hague, Netherlands, January 23: Anna Pavlova, famous ballerina, dies, aged 49.

Noank, Connecticut, USA, February 7: Aviator Amelia Earhart marries publisher George Palmer Putnam.

Sydney, Australia, February 23: Australian soprano Dame Nellie Melba, dies, aged 69.

Washington DC, USA, March 3: President Hoover signs an act declaring that the national anthem will be "The Star-Spangled Banner."

Washington DC, USA, March 14: Ida Harper, journalist, suffragist, and biographer of Susan B. Anthony, dies, aged 80.

India, March 25: Racial riots in Cawnpore kill hundreds in a throat-slitting bloodbath.

Chicago, USA, March 25: Feminist, journalist, and anti-lynching campaigner Ida Wells-Barnett dies, aged 68.

Madrid, Spain, April 14: King Alfonso XIII abdicates the throne and flees the country, and the Republic of Spain is proclaimed. Niceto Alcalá Zamora takes over the presidency under a provisional government.

Eretz, Israel, April 16: Hebrew poet Rachel Bluwstein, known simply as Rachel the Poet, dies, aged 41.

London, England, April 30: Editor, feminist, and physician Harriet Clisby dies, aged 100.

Morristown, New Jersey, USA, August: The Seeing Eye, a school for training guide dogs for the visually impaired, founded by Dorothy Harrison Eustis, moves from Nashville to New Jersey.

London, England, September 7: King George V takes a £50,000-a-year pay cut to help deal with the economic crisis.

Manchuria, September 18: Japan invades Manchuria in a surprise attack, thus violating the Kellogg-Briand pact.

Phoenix, Arizona, USA, October: Winnie Ruth Judd allegedly shoots Agnes Anne LeRoi and Hedvig Samuelson, cuts up their bodies, and sends them in her baggage to Los Angeles where they are discovered a few days later.

Women in France are still without the right to vote.

Rachel the Poet's Life Cut Short

Eretz, Israel, April 16: The Russian-born Hebrew poet Rachel Bluwstein—known simply as Rachel the Poet—died today at a sanatorium for tuberculosis patients. She was just 41 years old.

Rachel's haunting lyrical poems, echoing her feelings of longing and loss, were influenced by French imagism, Biblical stories, and the literature of the Second Aliyah pioneers (Russian immigrants to Palestine during the period 1904–1914). Published in the Hebrew newspaper *Davar* on a weekly basis, her poetry quickly became popular with the Jewish community in Palestine.

Rachel was the granddaughter of a Kiev rabbi. Following the wish expressed in her poem "If Fate Decrees," she will be buried in the Kinneret cemetery in a grave overlooking the Sea of Galilee.

Women's Justice Advocate Dies at 100

London, England, April 30: The trailblazing editor, feminist, and physician Harriet Clisby died today, four months away from her one-hundred-and-first birthday. Born in St James's, London—"very near the palace"—her family moved to South Australia when she was just eight years old.

As a young woman, Harriet developed a strong social conscience and established a community home for the rescue of women prisoners. At the same time, she was pursuing a career as a journalist, and in 1861 she collaborated with writer Caroline Dexter to publish a science, literature, and art magazine, *Interpreter*. It was the first magazine in Australia published by women.

Unable to train as a doctor in Australia or England, Clisby eventually moved to New York and entered the Medical College and Hospital for Women founded by Dr Clemence Sophia Lozier, a homeopathic physician and feminist. Clisby became one of America's first women physicians when she gained her medical degree in 1865. In 1871, she moved to Boston, founding the Women's Educational and Industrial Union, now one of Boston's primary service providers and advocacy organizations for women.

Not long after her retirement, Clisby founded L'Union des Femmes in Geneva, Switzerland. In her last years, Clisby continued to lead a productive life, keeping abreast of modern movements and giving drawing-room lectures on spiritual and medical subjects.

Ray of Hope for Spanish Women

Spain, October 16: Bullying, philandering, and financially incompetent husbands can now be shown the door after a divorce law was passed today allowing full dissolution of marriage. Following Alfonso XIII's peaceful departure from the throne in April, the freely elected Constitutional Cortes introduced a number of reforms, including this divorce law. Government has also taken steps to positively transform the lives of women, such as allowing them to vote and hold public office.

This new government (the Azaña Regime) presents a unique political opportunity for forces seeking democratic reformist solutions to Spain's multiple problems. Repressive family laws, stereotypical social expectations, and limited opportunities for women have been some of the key issues at the center of Spain's ideological conflict.

Now, Spanish women are rejoicing as this flash of freedom from the oppression of the past allows their concerns to become visible for the first time and gives them far more control over their lives. Spanish women owe much to the tireless crusading of warriors for women's rights such as Dolores Ibárruri (known as La Pasionaria) who founded the Organization of Anti-Fascist Women.

This new period in Spanish history is being heralded as the beginning of the Second Republic.

Irene Dunne

Academy Award winner Marie Dressler, as Min in the film *Min and Bill*.

Nobel Peace Prize for Social Activist

Jane Addams

Oslo, Norway, December 10: Today, pacifist social worker Jane Addams became the first American woman to receive the Nobel Peace Prize. At times a controversial figure, and often criticized for her anarchist and socialist views, she is a fiery advocate for labor reform that governs working conditions for children and women, as well as an active advocate for world peace. She is also a charter member of the National Association for the Advancement of Colored People.

Addams grew up in the small community of Cedarville, Illinois. In 1889, inspired by Toynbee Hall in the London slums, she co-founded one of the first settlement houses in the USA—Chicago's Hull-House—which still provides services for immigrants to Chicago from all over Europe. Hull-House offers a range of services, such as legal aid, child care, vocational skills, and English classes.

Over the years, Addams has supplemented Hull-House funding with revenue from lecture tours and articles. Her first book was published in 1910 while her 1912 autobiography, *Twenty Years at Hull-House*, met with huge success.

After the 1893 depression, Addams also directed her efforts at the root causes of poverty. She began lobbying the State of Illinois to protect immigrants from exploitation, limit the working hours of women, mandate schooling for children, recognize labor unions, and provide for industrial safety.

Addams was also an active participant in the peace movement, and in 1915 organized the Women's Peace Party and the International Congress of Women, which both made serious diplomatic attempts to prevent international conflict.

"I DO NOT BELIEVE THAT WOMEN ARE BETTER THAN MEN. WE HAVE NOT WRECKED RAILROADS, NOR CORRUPTED LEGISLATURE, NOR DONE MANY UNHOLY THINGS THAT MEN HAVE DONE; BUT THEN WE MUST REMEMBER THAT WE HAVE NOT HAD THE CHANCE."

JANE ADDAMS,
NOBEL PEACE PRIZE
WINNER, 1931

When the US joined the war in 1917, she continued her work for peace despite criticism from some quarters and her expulsion from the Daughters of the American Revolution. In 1919 she was elected first President of the Women's International League for Peace and Freedom, a position she continues to hold.

Aerodynamics Get a Lift

Gottingen, Germany: A young woman engineer with considerable mathematical talent has solved a niggling aerodynamics equation. Irmgard Lotz, a doctor of engineering at the Aerodynamische Versuchsanstalt in Göttingen, has solved a problem pertaining to wing lift distribution that leading German aerodynamicists, Ludwig Prandtl and Albert Betz, had been struggling with for some time. The practical uses for Lotz's equation are considerable. Together, Lotz and her colleagues Prandtl and Betz have made substantial advances in methods for the prediction of aerodynamic pressures on bodies, wings, and turbine blades.

Lotz was born to Osark Lotz and Dora Grupe in Hameln, Germany, on July 16, 1903. Her father was a traveling journalist and her mother worked in the Grupe family construction business. It was through her visits to building sites that Lotz developed a fascination with construction. She also went with her family to watch airship tests being conducted by Count von Zeppelin near her home. Her interest in mathematics was encouraged by her father, also a mathematician of considerable talent.

She is fond of saying that she chose a career in engineering because she wanted "a life which would never be boring—a life in which new things would always occur." At only 28 years old, this talented young woman has a bright future ahead.

New Company for British Ballet

London, England: A promising new ballet company has been founded in London. The Vic-Wells Ballet Company is the initiative of dancer and ballet teacher Ninette de Valois, or "Madam" as she is affectionately referred to by colleagues. De Valois created her repertory ballet

Sissinghurst, home of the writer Vita Sackville-West.

company, the Academy of Choreographic Art, in 1926 as an offshoot of the Royal Ballet School.

This year, her company moved to the Sadler's Wells Theatre and was renamed the Vic-Wells Ballet School. It feeds dancers into the newly formed Vic-Wells Ballet Company. The determined and creative de Valois attributes her resolve to her two years of experience dancing with Sergei Diaghilev's Ballets Russes.

Buck's *Good Earth* a Masterpiece

USA: Novelist Pearl S. Buck's critically acclaimed bestseller *The Good Earth* has touched the imagination of the American

Ninette de Valois interspersed her ballet classes with choreography.

Pearl S. Buck, author of *The Good Earth*.

The Lloyd Triestino shipping line encourages women to join one of their cruises to exotic locations.

Vita Sackville-West

More Votes for Women

Spain, Portugal, Chile, and Ceylon: The international women's suffrage movement is gaining momentum this year the countries of Spain, Portugal, Chile, and Ceylon all grant women the right to vote.

As part of the reforms currently sweeping the country, Spanish women can now vote and hold public office. This demonstrates a genuine commitment to democracy on the part of Spain's new leaders.

Neighboring Portugal has also given women the right to vote, but this right is subject to educational level restrictions. Only those women with university degrees or high school education will be eligible to vote.

These are remarkable advances in two countries where "machismo," or exaggerated masculine superiority, has held sway for centuries. This attitude is strongly associated with traditional Catholic doctrine and has long contributed to women's subordinate social position.

In Chile, women's suffrage has been a subject of much public debate since the 1920s, yet Chilean suffragettes have had to battle not only masculine opposition but also a feminine lack of interest in political matters. However, as women integrate in greater numbers into the working world, their need to move from passive citizenship to real participation in the political system has never been greater. This year, in a tentative move to acknowledge the rights of women, General Carlos Ibáñez del Campo has introduced a decree-law into the Chilean legislation that gives women who own property the right to vote in municipal elections.

In Ceylon, the Donougmore Constitution has implemented a landmark reform and introduced universal adult suffrage. Women here are now entitled to vote and be elected to the national legislature, called the State Council, and to municipal and urban councils. However, they still do not have the right to vote or be elected to town councils and village committees.

Whitney Museum Founded

New York, USA: When the New York Metropolitan Museum of Art turned down her offer to donate her 25-year collection of modern artworks, wealthy philanthropist Gertrude Vanderbilt Whitney established her own museum. The new Whitney Museum of American Art, which currently houses a core group of 700 art objects, includes the work of American revolutionary artists such as John Sloan, as well as realist painters such as Edward Hopper and Thomas Hart Benton. Mrs Whitney has plans to purchase other art objects for the museum to provide a more thorough overview of American art in the early decades of this century.

The Whitney Museum grew out of the Whitney Studio Club, which was established at 147 West Fourth Street in 1914 as a facility where young artists could exhibit their works.

Mrs Whitney's tremendous wealth has enabled her to become a patron of the arts and a keen advocate and supporter for the advancement of women in art. A talented sculptor, she maintains studios in Greenwich Village and in Passy, a fashionable Parisian suburb.

She studied at the Art Students League in New York, then with August Rodin in Paris. Her works receive critical acclaim in Europe and the United States. Mrs Whitney started the collection now housed in the Whitney Museum while she was studying.

Sculptor and philanthropist Gertrude Vanderbilt Whitney has founded her own museum.

public. Published this year, her remarkable story chronicles the fictional life of Chinese peasant farmer Wang Lung and his rise to prosperity in feudal China. The symbolism of the earth as an agent of life, health, and prosperity dominates the book, which has been highly praised for its exquisite storytelling and compelling portrait of Asian women. It gives a graphic view of the social and political upheavals in early twentieth century China and also breaks new ground by introducing American readers to a long-ignored alien landscape and people. Although an "outsider," Buck demonstrates a remarkable sensitivity toward the idiosyncrasies of Chinese culture, and represents her Chinese characters with great empathy and compassion.

The story is based on Buck's own experiences and observations as a missionary daughter in China. The sixth of seven children, she was born during her parents' year of home leave from China. Buck grew up speaking Chinese and was educated at home by her mother and a Chinese tutor. As a child, she belonged to two worlds—an American missionary world and the world of Chinese custom and traditions.

The Good Earth is the first of a planned trilogy. This ground-breaking masterpiece is predicted to be a strong contender for next year's Pulitzer Prize.

Lady Gregory

America's First Female Senator

Arkansas, USA, January 12: History was made in Arkansas today when Democrat candidate Hattie Wyatt Caraway became the first woman elected to the US Senate. Senator Caraway was temporarily granted the Senate seat late last year when her husband, Thaddeus Caraway, died. Her electoral success allows her to fill the position for the remainder of her husband's original term of office.

Hattie Caraway, aged 52, was born in Bakerville, Tennessee, and graduated in 1896 from Dickson Normal College. She met her husband when they were both students.

Senator Caraway is a proud housewife who raised the couple's family and helped to run their Arkansas farm while her husband pursued a career, first in law then politics. She states that since the introduction of women's suffrage 12 years ago, she has always seen it as her duty to vote.

> "YOU MUST MAKE YOUR OWN BLUNDERS, MUST CHEERFULLY ACCEPT YOUR OWN MISTAKES AS PART OF THE SCHEME OF THINGS."
>
> MINNIE MADDERN FISKE (1865–1932), AMERICAN ACTRESS

Hattie Wyatt Caraway, the first female US Senator.

Although she is a strong supporter of prohibition, Senator Caraway has no plans to make any speeches from the floor. While some doubts have been raised regarding a woman's capacity to carry out such a serious role, she declares that she is a student of her husband's career and takes her duties and responsibilities as a public servant very seriously.

Broadway Loses Prominent Star

New York, USA, February 15: One of the country's best-known stage actresses, Minnie Maddern Fiske, has died of heart failure in New York, at 66 years. "Mrs Fiske," as she was known, took to the stage as a small child and never left. Born in New Orleans, she played a central role in introducing a number of controversial plays to American audiences, including those of Henrik Ibsen, and a stage adaptation of *Tess of the D'Urbervilles* (1897). The latter led to the first of her two screen roles, after which she turned her back on the silver screen.

Mrs Fiske also wrote a number of plays, and was active in a number of causes including animal welfare, opposing prohibition, and supporting Alfred Smith in the 1928 presidential election. Well known for her versatility as an actress, she made her final appearance on the stage in 1930.

time out

Miriam Underhill, 32, has gone over-mountain with Alice Damesme in what is the first all-female expedition to the top of the Matterhorn. Underhill has already conquered the Torre Grande and the Jungfrau.

Formidable Irish Literary Figure Dies

Galway, Ireland, May 22: The famous Coole Park estate is in mourning today. For the last 40 years, many of the leading lights in the Irish literary revival movement, such as W. B. Yeats, George Bernard Shaw, J. M. Synge, and Sean O'Casey, met at the estate. However, none was more central to

the movement, albeit less well known, than the estate's owner, Lady Isabella Augusta Gregory, who died of breast cancer at her home today, aged eighty.

A native of County Galway, Ireland, Lady Gregory was born in 1862 into an upper class family. At just 18 years of age, Isabella married Sir William Gregory, 35 years her senior, fell in love with his library, and soon began writing. In the 1880s, she and her husband conducted a literary salon in London that was attended by the likes of Henry James, Robert Browning, and Lord Tennyson.

Originally a rather strong supporter of a union between Ireland and England, Lady Gregory became an ardent cultural nationalist and Republican during the 1890s after researching Irish history. It was at this time that she began organizing Irish language lessons for local schoolchildren and collecting Irish folk tales for publication.

With poet W. B. Yeats and playwright Edward Martyn, Lady Gregory founded the Irish Literary Theatre in 1899 and the Irish National Theatre Society in 1904. The latter found its home in the famous Abbey Theatre of Dublin. Lady Gregory

Helen Hayes, Best Actress winner for this year.

Key Events

Amelia Earhart and US ambassador to Britain after her transatlantic flight.

Recognition for Brilliant Mathematician

Zurich, Switzerland, September: German mathematician Emmy Noether will address this year's International Mathematical Congress in Zurich, the first woman to address this prestigious body. The honor has been bestowed in recognition of her outstanding achievements in algebra.

Owing to her gender, Miss Noether, the daughter of a distinguished mathematician, was not permitted to enroll in higher mathematical studies until 1904 when the rules were changed. She received her doctorate in 1907 and gained a strong reputation through her publications. She moved to Göttingen in 1915 where the faculty at Göttingen University were divided over the issue of allowing a woman to teach. Consequently, she was not formally admitted until 1919. Since then, she has gained a reputation as the most creative abstract algebraist of her times.

Annie Smith Peck

remained a director of the Abbey until her retirement in 1928. By that time she had written some 40 plays for production at the Abbey, though they caused less interest than the plays of O'Casey and Synge, whose *Playboy of the Western World* caused a riot on its opening night in 1907 in Dublin.

Lady Gregory and Sir William had one son, who was killed while serving as a pilot in World War I, inspiring a well-known poem by Mr Yeats, "An Irish Airman Foresees His Death."

Greatest Athlete of All Time a Woman?

Los Angeles, USA, August: Outstanding athlete Mildred "Babe" Didrikson has dazzled the sporting world with her prowess at this year's Olympic Games in Los Angeles.

The career of this young woman began in earnest last year when she led the team of the Employers Casualty Insurance Company of Dallas, Texas, to victory in the Amateur Athletic Union (AAU) Basketball Championship.

Then, earlier this year, she blitzed the sporting world at the AAU track-and-field Championships in Illinois. Despite the fact that she was its only member, her "team" still came first (the second-place team had 22 competitors). Miss Didrikson entered eight of the ten events, winning five outright and tying for first place in another. She set five world records in the space of a few hours. This outstanding effort earned her a place in the US Olympic team, although being a woman she was permitted to compete in only three events.

Participating in the Olympics Games, she won gold medals in the 80-meter (262 ft) hurdles and the javelin. Controversially, she was relegated to second place in the high jump after tying for first place when the judges deemed her new "Western Roll" technique suspect.

Born of Norwegian immigrants to the United States, Mildred says she earned the nickname "Babe" because of her baseball prowess. She is also accomplished in softball, swimming, tennis, diving, rifle-shooting, roller-skating, and bowls.

Mildred "Babe" Didrikson wins Olympic gold in the javelin.

Octogenarian Mountain Climber

Gorham, New Hampshire, USA, September 19: Feel like you're getting a bit old? Well, here's some news to make you feel even older. Miss Annie Smith Peck, aged 81, today reached the top of Mount Crescent in New Hampshire's White Mountains—an elevation of 3,280 feet (1,000 m).

Still, that's nothing new for Miss Peck. In 1908, at the age of 57, she climbed to the 21,812-foot (6,648 m) summit of Mount Huascaran in the Andes. In her honor, the mountain was renamed Cumbre Ana Peck.

Annie Peck was born in 1850, in Providence, Rhode Island, and has worked as an archeology professor at a number of universities. She recently published *Flying over South America: Twenty Thousand Miles by Air*, a book about her 1930 trip to South America.

Hollywood, USA, September 30: Stage actress Katharine Hepburn makes her film debut in *A Bill of Divorcement*, directed by George Cukor and starring John Barrymore.

Zurich, Switzerland, September: German mathematician Emmy Noether is the first woman to present a lecture at the International Mathematical Congress.

Iraq, October 3: Iraq gains independence from its British-imposed rule under a treaty granting the UK certain privileges.

USA, October 21: Shirley Temple, aged four, makes her film debut in *The Red-Haired Alibi*.

USSR, November 9: Nadezhda "Nadya" Alliluyeva, the wife of Joseph Stalin, dies, aged 30.

London, England, December 8: Garden designer Gertrude Jekyll dies, aged 89.

Pretoria, South Africa, December 30: Suspected of poisoning two husbands in order to collect their life insurance, and found guilty of poisoning her son for reasons not clear, Daisy de Melker is hanged.

USA: Laura Ingalls Wilder publishes *Little House in the Big Woods*, the first in her series of *Little House* books, describing her childhood in the Midwestern frontier.

England: British composer Elisabeth Lutyens writes the music for the ballet *The Birthday of the Infanta*.

Germany: Film-maker Leni Riefenstahl co-writes, directs, and appears in *Das Blaue Licht (The Blue Light)*, which brings her to the attention of Adolf Hitler.

London, England: Lilian Wyles becomes the first woman Chief Inspector of the Metropolitan Criminal Investigation Department.

Japan: Feminist, birth control campaigner, and politician Kato Shidzue founds the Women's Birth Control League of Japan.

Brazil, Uruguay, and Thailand: Women are granted the right to vote.

India: Independence fighter Rani Gaidinliu is arrested by the British colonial government and sentenced to life imprisonment.

Lake Placid, USA: Norwegian-born figure skater Sonja Henie wins the European skating championship in Paris, the world title in Montreal, as well as another Olympic gold medal at Lake Placid.

Hollywood, USA: Helen Hayes wins Best Actress for her debut sound film, *The Sin of Madelon Claudet*, at the Academy Awards.

Shirley Temple

Hollywood Claims Another Victim

Los Angeles, USA, September 20: The final twist in the tragic tale of Peg Entwistle unfolded today when she was cremated at Hollywood Memorial Park. The actress's damaged body was found two days ago beneath the "H" of the iconic "Hollywoodland" sign. Police say that, almost two days prior, she had climbed to the top of the 50-foot-high (15 m) letter "H" and leapt to her death.

A suicide note was published in the *LA Times* yesterday in hopes that it would aid in the identification of the body. It read: "I am afraid I am a coward. I am sorry for everything. If I had done this a long time ago, it would have saved a lot of pain. P. E." Miss Entwistle's body was subsequently identified by her uncle, with whom she was living on Beachwood Drive.

Lillian Millicent (Peg) Entwistle was born in Wales in 1908. Her mother died in England and in 1922 Peg emigrated to New York City with her father who soon after died in a traffic accident. Left destitute, Miss Entwistle pursued a career on the Broadway stage but last year, after appearing in seven consecutive financial flops, which she apparently took personally, she headed for Hollywood.

After appearing briefly in a play opposite minor movie actor Humphrey Bogart, she landed a role in the RKO film *Thirteen Women* (which was released on the day of her death). Unfortunately, the test screenings did not go well and cuts to the film saw the actress's role reduced. She was not invited to the premiere,

which has received poor reviews. After drinking alcohol, Miss Entwistle told her uncle she was going to the local drugstore and then out to meet friends; however, she did not return.

The final cruel and bizarre twist came to light today in the form of a letter posted the day before her death, offering Peg a leading theatrical role in which her character would have committed suicide in the final act. Her death follows only two weeks after the gunshot suicide of producer-director-writer Paul Bern.

Arrested Rebel Leader a Girl

Pulomi, India, October 17: A contingent of the paramilitary force known as the Assam Rifles, led by a Captain MacDonald, has raided the village of Pulomi in the state of Manipur and arrested Indian rebels fighting the British. The principal figure in the drama is a 16-year-old girl named Rani Gaidinliu. She became a leader of the messianic, anti-colonial movement last year after the arrest and execution by British authorities of Haipou Jodonang, regarded by his followers not only as a political leader, but also as something of a healer, prophet, and Messiah. Jodonang's execution was for the murder of four men—murders he attributed to Gaidinliu.

Although the rebel movement's main concerns relate to local Indian culture, values, and society, it is its larger political aims that concern British authorities. There are fears that the group has links with the wider independence movement associated with the Indian National

> *"I WANT TO BE ALONE."*
>
> GRETA GARBO,
> SWEDISH ACTRESS,
> *GRAND HOTEL* (1932)

American actress Billie Dove retires this year.

Congress. It is understood that rebels encourage followers to refuse to pay any taxes, to disobey officials and interpreters working for the British, and to defy the requirement that villagers supply food and porters for the British and show deference by removing headgear in the presence of white men.

Some villages have requested an exemption from taxes on the grounds that they have paid tribute to the rebels. British officials insist this tribute is being used to fund armed rebellion. Collective fines have been imposed on villages for refusing to cooperate with British demands. A reward was offered for Gaidinliu's arrest; however, it is understood that she has had strong support among the local people.

Ironically, Gaidinliu was interviewed by Mr Higgins, the political agent of Manipur, after he had Jodonang arrested, but Higgins took no action against what appeared to him to be merely a surly, unimpressive 16-year-old girl. Gaidinliu is expected to face trial soon.

Soviet Leader's Wife Dies

USSR, November 9: Nadezhda Alliluyeva, the wife of Soviet leader Joseph Stalin, has died, aged 30, in her bedroom in Moscow. According to the press announcement, she passed away suddenly due to illness. However, there are rumors that the death was a suicide by gunshot.

Some say that the death followed an argument between husband and wife at a Communist Party dinner. It is understood that the couple had a troubled marriage and that the General Secretary of the Communist Party had engaged in extramarital affairs. It is not known if this played a role in events, but it is said that Stalin is shaken and distressed.

Illustration for *Let the Hurricane Roar*, Rose Wilder Lane's story about her mother Laura.

Adolf Hitler campaigns for votes from German woman.

"Nadya," as she was known, was the Soviet leader's second wife. They married when she was 17 and he was 41 years old. The couple met in 1911 when Stalin was on the run after escaping from exile in Siberia. He was offered shelter by Nadya's father, fellow Marxist and railroad worker Sergei Alliluyev and his wife Olga.

Following the Communist Revolution of 1917, Nadya traveled to Moscow and worked as a confidential code clerk in the office of the then Communist Party leader, Vladimir Lenin. Known for her

Nadya Alliluyeva and her daughter Svetlana.

unadorned appearance (in keeping with Bolshevik values), she married Stalin in 1919. They have two young children.

Woman Hanged for Murdering Son

Pretoria, South Africa, December 30: Pretoria Central Prison was the scene today of the execution of Daisy de Melker, following a trial that generated intense public interest. Only the second woman ever to be hanged in South Africa, she was found guilty of murdering her 20-year-old son, Rhodes.

Born in 1886, Daisy de Melker was married three times, on each occasion to a plumber. Her first husband, William Cowle, became ill in 1923 after ingesting some Epsom salts proffered by his wife. Wracked with pain, he began screaming when touched, frothed at the mouth, became blue about the face, and then died. The doctor was suspicious as to the cause of Cowle's death; however, an autopsy concluded the cause of death to be a brain hemorrhage. As Cowle's widow, de Melker received the sum of £1,795 from her husband's will.

Exactly three years after Cowle's death, she married Richard Sproat. The following year he died a death similar to that of Cowle's, while consuming beer at home with his wife. The doctor declared the death was due to cerebral hemorrhage. No autopsy was performed. This time, as Sproat's widow, she inherited over £4,500.

In February last year, Daisy de Melker walked many miles to a distant pharmacy where, using a former married name, she purchased arsenic. Within a week her son became ill and died after drinking coffee from a flask prepared by his mother. The doctor declared cerebral malaria the cause. His mother received £100 from her son's life insurance policy.

However, the month following Rhodes's death, Richard Sproat's brother became suspicious and spoke to the police. The three bodies were exhumed and traces of strychnine were found in the husbands' bones, while arsenic was detected in the son's corpse, in the coffee flask, as well

as in the nails and hair of Rhodes's friend, James Webster, who had temporarily become ill after drinking a small amount of Rhodes's coffee.

When de Melker was arrested, the pharmacist recognized her photograph in the newspaper and testified to her arsenic purchase. While circumstantial evidence was strong, the husbands' deaths were not conclusively proved. However, it was found that Rhodes had died of arsenic poisoning at his mother's hand. Her exact motive in killing her son is unknown.

Sonja Henie

New Look for Britain's Investigative Police

London, England: History has been made in the ranks of the British police force with the appointment of the first woman, Lilian Wyles, to the position of Chief Inspector of the Metropolitan Criminal Investigation Department (CID).

Miss Lilian Mary Elizabeth Wyles was born in 1885, the talented daughter of a brewer. After serving as a nurse in the Great War, she enrolled in the Women's Special Police Patrols, which had been created on a temporary basis because of a shortage of manpower. By the time the "Women Police" folded, Wyles had attained the rank of sergeant and managed to transfer as an officer to the CID in 1921.

Her appointment was not popular with the men of the Department and she was generally given menial work to do. Matters improved with colleagues and her range of duties increased, owing to her refusal to criticize her superior officer during an investigation of police methods in the Savidge case of 1928. This case concerned the arrest of Miss Savidge and MP Sir Leo Money when they were found by police in Hyde Park in a manner deemed an affront to public decency.

While female athletes stay at a luxury hotel, an Olympic Village houses male athletes.

Fay Wray

Fay Wray is King Kong's Leading Lady

Hollywood, USA, March 2: When actress Fay Wray auditioned to be King Kong's leading lady, little did she know that her leading man would be big, black, and hairy. When producer Merion Cooper told her she'd have the "tallest, darkest leading man in Hollywood," Fay thought she'd be starring opposite Clark Gable.

In the crucial scene of the blockbuster *King Kong*—which premiered today—a screaming Wray is held precariously in the hand of the giant mutant ape atop the Empire State building as airplanes attack them. The actress struggles and swoons voluptuously—all the way to an anticipated box office hit, which the RKO studio hopes will save it from bankruptcy. Wray certainly shows talent for acting as a vulnerable yet sexy woman with an impressive set of vocal cords.

Wray's screen career started when she scored a small role at the age of 16 in

"It's better to be looked over than overlooked."

MAE WEST (1893–1980), AMERICAN ACTRESS

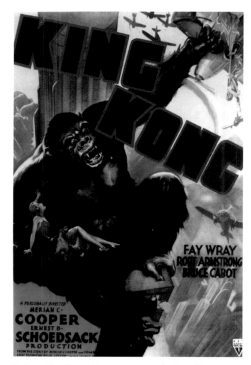

Actress Fay Wray stars opposite a giant gorilla.

Gasoline Love, which was not a hit. Two years later she gained another role in *The Coast Patrol,* which again was not a hit but did raise her profile. From 1926, Fay's career prospects improved as she started to be offered regular work in westerns and horror movies. It wasn't until 1927, when Wray starred in the lead role of Mitzi Schrammell in *The Wedding March,* that she announced herself as an actress of some *gravitas.*

It would not surprise if, at the end of Wray's career, the role for which she is most remembered is Ann Darrow—the tiny screaming damsel caught in the hand of the rampaging King Kong.

Worth a Mint and Making History

Washington DC, USA, May 3: On January 5, 1925, Nellie Tayloe Ross was inaugurated as the first female governor in US history. This was the first of numerous "firsts" in Tayloe Ross's life. Today, President Franklin D. Roosevelt appointed her as the first female director of the US Mint.

Although Tayloe Ross comes from a prestigious family on both sides—and is well educated, having attended both private and public schools—she started her early working life as a two-year-trained kindergarten teacher in Omaha, Nebraska. In 1902, she married lawyer William Bradford Ross and had four sons—twins George Tayloe and James Ambrose in 1903, Alfred Duff in 1905, and William Bradford in 1912. Although she did strive to improve her intellectual development as an active member of the Cheyenne Woman's Club, Tayloe Ross believed her role in married life was to be at home supporting her husband and looking after her sons.

From 1902 her husband practiced law in Cheyenne, Wyoming, and ran for

This year's World Women's Professional Billiards Championships winner, Miss Joyce Gardner.

political office. In 1922, he was elected Democratic Governor of Wyoming. Unfortunately, his tenure in this position was cut short by his death on October 2, 1924, due to complications arising from surgery to remove his appendix.

It was not until her husband's death that Tayloe Ross's political light began to shine. Her husband's party needed a representative to run for governor, less than one month after his passing. At first Tayloe Ross was not keen, but relented and, despite lacking in political experience, won as a Democrat in a Republican-dominated election. Although nominated for a second term by her party, Tayloe Ross was defeated in 1926.

After this defeat, Tayloe Ross campaigned for the Democratic presidential

time out

Having proved her excellence at basketball, and track and field (including high jump, long jump, hurdles, javelin, discus throw, and five-shot put), 22-year-old Babe Didrikson decides to become a champion golfer, and begins taking lessons.

Key Events

Rochester, New York, USA, January 9: Engineer and business-woman Kate Gleason dies, aged 67. She was the first female member of the Society of Mechanical Engineers.
Berlin, Germany, January 30: Recha Freier founds Support for Jewish Youth, an organization to help young Jews find employment, and provide for refugee children.

USA, February 17: Blondie Boopadoop marries Dagwood Bumstead in the popular comic strip *Blondie.*
Hollywood, USA, March 2: Actress Fay Wray appears with a giant gorilla in the motion picture hit *King Kong.*
Germany, March 22: The first Nazi concentration camp at Dachau, near Munich, begins operation.

Germany, March 23: Adolf Hitler becomes dictator of Germany after the Reichstag grants him full powers, less than two months after he was appointed Chancellor of Germany.
Germany, April 11: The Nazis decree "non-Aryans" to include anyone descended from non-Aryan, particularly Jewish, parents or grandparents.
Scotland, May 2: A bizarre creature is reportedly seen in Loch Ness.

Washington DC, USA, May 3: President Roosevelt appoints Nellie Tayloe Ross the first female director of the US Mint.
Paraguay, May 10: Paraguay declares war on Bolivia.
Moscow, Russia, June 20: German-born politician and women's rights activist Clara Eissner Zetkin dies, aged 75.
Providence, Rhode Island, USA, June 24: African-American soprano Sissieretta Joyner Jones, dies at 64 years of age.

Tervete, Latvia, June 25: Writer Anna Brigadere dies, aged 71.
UK, July 7: Doctors announce that they have been able to isolate the influenza virus.
Poona, India, August 23: An emaciated Mahatma Gandhi is released from hospital, five days into a fast protesting his exclusion from working with untouchables while in prison. Earlier in the year he had been on a three-week hunger strike to protest the poor treatment of lower castes.

nominee, Franklin D. Roosevelt. Now that Roosevelt holds power, Tayloe Ross's efforts have been rewarded.

A Woman for All Women

Moscow, Russia, June 20: When Clara Eissner Zetkin passed away today at the age of 75, Germany and the world lost a prominent member of communist, socialist, and feminist organizations. Zetkin believed that equality for women could be achieved if a class revolution, based on Marxist principles, overthrew the capitalist system.

One of Clara's earliest influences was her mother, Josephine Vitale Eissner, who was a strong believer in equal rights for women. From 1875, at the age of 15, Clara was educated at Schmidt and Otto's Van Steyber Institute in Leipzig, where she further educated herself on the principles of socialism.

In 1878, Clara met another major influence on her life and ideology—Ossip Zetkin from Odessa in Russia. Initially, Ossip Zetkin acted as a political mentor by introducing Clara to the principles of Karl Marx and Friedrich Engels. Later he became her de facto partner and the father of her two sons.

Throughout her life Zetkin remained active in many political parties including the Independent Social Democratic Party of Germany (USPD), and the Spartacist League, which she co-founded in 1916 and which later became the Communist Party of Germany (KPD). Her belief in, and dedication to, women's affairs led her to form the social-democratic women's movement in Germany. Zetkin worked for many prominent German left-wing organizations, such as the solidarity group Rote Hilfe (Red Aid).

Zetkin was strongly opposed to the Great War, and was arrested several times for anti-government statements and actions. At times she proved unpopular with some feminists due to her socialist

Women's rights activist, Clara Eissner Zetkin.

convictions. Earlier this year Adolf Hitler banned the Communist Party of Germany from the Reichstag, forcing Zetkin into exile in the Soviet Union.

Swansong for Soprano "Black Patti"

Providence, Rhode Island, USA, June 24: Sissieretta Joyner Jones, the famous soprano known as "Black Patti," passed away today from cancer at the age of sixty-four. Joyner Jones lived a life full of career highs—and some lows, arising from the widespread chauvinistic policy which did not allow African-American singers to perform in many venues.

Joyner Jones strongly disapproved of her nickname—which was supposedly complimentary, based as it was on the prima Italian soprano, Adelina Patti. However, the name stuck, whether she liked it or not.

Her career started early when, at five years old it was noted that she had a beautiful voice. When Sissieretta sang at Boston's Music Hall, she attracted the attention of concert managers Abbey, Schoffel, and Grau. Later in her career she sang at the Chicago World Fair in 1893 and in Madison Square Gardens.

In 1883, at the age of 14, Sissieretta married news dealer and hotel bellman David Richard Jones. However, in 1898 the marriage ended in divorce.

Although Joyner Jones performed in many venues and became the highest-paid African-American artist of her time, her career was frustrated by the racism that often barred her from performing in top venues such as the Metropolitan Opera in 1896. So, Joyner Jones formed a troupe of artists of varying backgrounds, which performed all over the country. Her last performance was at the Lafayette Theater in New York City in October 1915.

Annie Wood Besant

Writer Leaves Forests of Fantasy

Tervete, Latvia, June 25: Latvian writer Anna Brigadere passed away today at the age of 71, after a lifetime of writing dramas, comedies, and autobiographies.

Her plays have the feeling of fairytales, and one of her most famous works is *The Tale of Spriditis*, a play about a young peasant boy's adventures in the forest. Spriditis suffers under the hand of a nasty stepmother who harasses him endlessly and forces him into drudgery. He leaves in search of the Land of Happiness. Through his adventures Spriditis realizes that he can only be happy in his native land.

Brigadere lived and wrote in the rather beautiful and ancient Latvian village of Tervete, surrounded by an inspiring forest of ancient pine trees.

Englishwoman Molly Taylor makes artificial eyes.

New Zealand, September 13: Elizabeth McCombs becomes New Zealand's first female Member of Parliament.

Adyar, India, September 20: The British-born social reformer and theosophist Annie Wood Besant dies, aged 85.

Turin, Italy, September 24: A crowd of 25,000 people flocks to see the Turin Shroud.

County Meath, Ireland, October 2: British artist Elizabeth Thompson Butler, known for her depictions of British military battles, dies at 86.

Tujunga, California, USA, October 5: French-born film actress Renée Adorée dies of tuberculosis at 35 years of age.

Edmonton, Alberta, Canada, October 17: Lawyer, suffragist, social activist, and member of Canada's "Famous Five," Emily Ferguson Murphy, dies, aged 65.

New York, USA, November 27: Jazz singer Billie Holiday makes her first studio recording with band leader Benny Goodman.

Washington DC, USA, December 5: The prohibition against intoxicating liquor ends. The repeal of the law goes into effect after Utah becomes the 36th state to ratify it.

France: American writer Gertrude Stein publishes *The Autobiography of Alice B. Toklas*, which is, in fact, her own autobiography.

New York, USA: Journalist Clare Boothe is appointed editor of *Vanity Fair*.

Germany: Gertrud Scholtz-Klink is appointed Reich women's leader and head of the Nazi Women's League. She urges all Aryan women to bear more children for Germany.

Portugal: Portugal's new constitution declares that everybody is equal, "except for women, the differences resulting from their nature and for the good of the family."

Washington DC, USA: Frances Perkins is appointed Secretary of Labor by President Roosevelt, becoming the first female US Cabinet member.

USA: Senator Hattie Caraway is the first woman to chair a senate committee, the Committee on Enrolled Bills.

Renée Adorée

British Military Artist Dies

County Meath, Ireland, October 2: The renowned British war artist, Elizabeth Thompson Butler, passed away today at her daughter Viscountess Gormanstown's castle in County Meath.

She was born in 1846 and her father, a cultured man, educated her and her sister Alice, mostly in Italy. From 16 to 18 years of age, Thompson Butler studied at the South Kensington School of Art. Then, in October 1868, she went to study in Florence under the great teacher and artist Belucci. Initially she painted portraits and landscapes, but when she saw paintings inspired by the Franco-Prussian War in France she returned to England and began painting military scenes. She resumed studies at South Kensington, and observed the autumn maneuvers of the British Army in 1872.

Thompson Butler sold one of her sketches titled *Soldiers Watering Horses* to a Mr Galloway of Manchester, who became a patron. She was already a well-established military artist when she painted *The Roll Call*, a work which highly impressed the Prince of Wales, and his mother Queen Victoria.

During the 1870s, Thompson Butler was one of the most popular and high-profile artists in Britain, appealing to patriotic sentiments but also attracting much critical acclaim. She declared: "I never painted for the glory of war, but to portray its pathos and heroism." Eminent critic John Ruskin was moved to confess that she had single-handedly changed his opinion that "no woman could paint." Although her work sold well, she failed in her bid to be elected as an associate to the Royal Academy in 1879.

In 1877 she married Colonel William Butler, a distinguished soldier and Irish patriot who later became a lieutenant general and received a knighthood. When he passed away in 1910, she remained in Tipperary. She painted scenes from the Great War and donated the proceeds to war charities. In her later years she lived with her daughter at Gormanstown Castle. Thompson Butler was the mother of six children, five of whom survive her.

War painting by Elizabeth Thompson Butler.

Billie Holiday: A Bright New Star

New York, November 27: Up-and-coming jazz singer Billie Holiday made her recording debut today, with the song "Your Mother's Son-in-Law," led by jazz musician and bandleader Benny Goodman. Well-connected jazz writer and producer John Hammond reported: "She is the greatest singer I have ever heard."

Holiday's early life was certainly not easy. The illegitimate daughter of a teenage mother and a neglectful teenage father, Billie spent several years in a Catholic reform school, due to truancy—and her report that she had been raped. Although she was supposed to stay at the school until adulthood, a friend of the family secured her release after two years.

Scarred by her experiences as a child, Holiday moved with her mother to New York in 1928. But life was just as difficult for her there, especially when Holiday's mother discovered their neighbor in the act of raping her daughter. The rapist, Wilbert Rich, was sentenced to just three months' jail.

Born Eleanora Fagan, Holiday took her professional pseudonym from Billie Dove, an actress, and her father Clarence Holiday. She started singing in Harlem clubs for tips in the 1930s. Legend has it that when the penniless Holiday sang "Body and Soul" with her emotive and poignant voice, she reduced the audience to tears. It was in one of these Harlem clubs—reportedly Monette's—that the talent scout John Hammond discovered her earlier this year.

Jazz singer Billie Holiday.

Stein's *Alice B. Toklas* Tops Bestseller List

France: Earlier this year American writer Gertrude Stein published her autobiography, (misleadingly titled) *The Autobiography of Alice B. Toklas*. It is already her first bestseller.

Born in Allegheny, Pennsylvania, on February 3, 1874, Stein was one of three children in a wealthy German-Jewish immigrant family. She has lived off a stipend from her family until recently, but will not need to depend on that in future. She did not start off as a writer; in her early years, she studied at the Johns Hopkins Medical School for two years, but did not graduate.

In 1902, Stein moved to France where she became a writer and collected the work of cubist and experimental artists. Her Paris salon attracted many famous artists and painters, including Pablo Picasso and Henri Matisse, as well as writers Mina Loy and Ernest Hemingway.

Hitler Appoints Woman to Promote Male Superiority

Germany: Adolf Hitler has appointed Gertrud Scholtz-Klink as the Reich women's leader, and head of the Nazi Women's League. A mother of six, she is well suited to her task of promoting male superiority and encouraging women to bear more children.

Married to a factory worker at the age of 18, Scholtz-Klink was considered by the national socialist Nazis to be a perfect candidate, due largely to her classic, if plain Germanic looks. She joined the Nazi Party and became the leader of the women's section in Berlin in 1929.

Scholtz-Klink is a very strong speaker, and in one of her speeches declared: "The mission of woman is to minister in the home and in her profession to the needs of life from the first to last moment of a man's existence." Her primary role will be to encourage German women to work hard for the good of the Nazi government, which is almost exclusively led by men. She is also quoted as saying: "No Nazi woman will ever be motivated to work for money. Serving men is our only wish," and: "Though our

American writer and patron of the arts, Gertrude Stein.

Gertrud Scholtz-Klink addresses a group of women at a Nazi rally in Nuremberg, Germany.

Senator Hattie Caraway

adolescents of Eastern Jewish extraction were losing their jobs. Freier was quick to pinpoint the reason as anti-Semitic rather than economic, having suffered some anti-Semitic bigotry herself when she was a very young girl living in the small town of Silesia.

So on January 30 this year, on the day of Adolf Hitler's ascent to power, Freier founded the aid organization Support for Jewish Youth. She plans to take young men to Palestine in order to both build their personalities and develop the country. The task is enormous because it involves selecting and preparing the teenagers for their new life in Palestine, raising money for the trip, and organizing appropriate documents.

Freier is encountering a great deal of opposition, from both inside and outside the Jewish community. Some Jewish parents believe that there is no real threat to Jews in Germany at this time, and that Zionist organizations only want professionals who will work for the betterment of Palestine. Yet Freier is unstoppable in her conviction that these adolescents—many of them refugees from the Nazi government—must be saved. When she needed money and documents to take the first group of six teenagers to Palestine, she wasn't afraid to coerce or embarrass others to achieve her ends.

A most dedicated social activist, Recha Freier currently travels between Berlin and Palestine, making useful contacts and raising more money to help her reach her goal of rescuing 10,000 children.

weapon be but a wooden spoon, it must become as powerful as other weapons."

Although she supposedly holds a high position, Scholtz-Klink has no real political clout in the organization because virtually all decisions are made by men. However, Hitler believes that women are crucial to the success of the Aryan "race," and he is encouraging them to breed. It is Scholtz-Klink's primary role to stimulate them to do just that.

First Woman Appointed to US Cabinet

Washington DC, USA: President Franklin D. Roosevelt has appointed Frances Coralie Perkins to the position of Secretary of the Department of Labor, making her the first woman to serve in the US Cabinet.

Perkins, the daughter of Frederick W. Perkins and Susan Bean Perkins, was born in Boston, Massachusetts, on April 10, 1882. She graduated from Mount Holyoke College and worked as a social worker and then a teacher. She gained a master's degree in sociology from Columbia University in 1910, after which she became Executive Secretary of the National Consumers' League (NCL). Perkins has served on numerous boards for the New York state government.

Witnessing the Triangle Shirtwaist factory fire in New York in 1911, in which 146 workers died, pushed Perkins to help improve workers' hours and conditions.

When Perkins married Paul Caldwell in 1913, she kept her maiden name and fought in court for her right to do so. In 1918 Governor Al Smith asked her to join the New York State Industrial Commission, making her the first female member.

In 1929 Franklin D. Roosevelt became Governor of New York, and appointed Perkins as his Industrial Commissioner.

Failed presidential candidate Alfred Smith warned him at the time: "I have always thought that, as a rule, men will take advice from a woman, but it is hard for them to take orders from a woman." Roosevelt ignored this advice then, as he has now. One of Perkins's first battles will be to improve the working conditions of American women.

Recha Freier Rescues Jewish Children

Berlin, Germany: When Recha Freier's husband, Moritz Freier, was the chief rabbi of Berlin, she noticed that many

US Secretary of Labor Frances Perkins greets President Roosevelt.

Botanist Elizabeth Britton Dies, Aged 76

Hélène Boucher

New York, USA, February 25: American botanist and bryologist, Elizabeth Gertrude Britton, has died at her home in New York. Britton was the driving force behind a successful campaign by the Torrey Botanical Club to create a botanical garden in New York. It was incorporated in 1891 and her husband became the first director of the 250-acre (100 ha) garden in Bronx Park in 1896.

The Brittons married in 1885 when they were both members of the Torrey Club. Mrs Britton's first specialty was bryology (the study of mosses). She published 346 scientific papers between 1881 and 1930 and was the unofficial curator of mosses at Columbia College. She later became curator of mosses at the botanical garden and founded the Sullivant Moss Society, which became the American Bryological Society. The moss genus *Bryobrittonia* is named for her, as are 15 other plant species.

Britton was born on January 9, 1858, in New York City, and as a young girl moved to Cuba with her family, where they owned a sugar plantation. She attended schools in Cuba and New York, and in 1875 graduated from Normal College, New York City.

> *"Nothing in life is to be feared. It is only to be understood."*
>
> MARIE CURIE (1867–1934), NOBEL PRIZE-WINNING SCIENTIST

Britton was a founder of New York's Botanical Gardens.

Hail of Bullets Slays Bonnie and Clyde

Bienville Parish, Louisiana, USA, March 23: Infamous criminals 23-year-old Bonnie Parker and her partner 25-year-old Clyde Barrow were mown down in a hail of bullets at about 10 a.m. today on a lonely stretch of road near their hideout in Bienville Parish, Louisiana. Their deaths are the final chapter in a three-year reign of terror that saw the Barrow gang terrorize banks and store owners in five states—Texas, New Mexico, Oklahoma, Missouri, and Louisiana.

Bonnie and Clyde were shot by a posse of four Texan and two Louisiana officers led by Captain Frank Hamer, who ambushed them as Clyde stopped his stolen Ford V8. The officers opened fire with an estimated 130 armor-piercing rounds from their military-style weapons. Clyde was killed instantly by a head shot, but Bonnie did not die as easily. The posse reported her uttering a long horrified scream as bullets tore into the car.

Controversy surrounds the incident because the posse did not call out a warning or order the duo to surrender. Gang members W. D. Jones and Ralph Fults said they had never seen Bonnie carry or fire a gun, and described her role as purely logistical. One of the officers said the posse opened fire with the automatic rifles while the Ford was still moving, then used the shotguns. "There was smoke coming from the car, and it looked like it was on fire. After shooting the shotguns, we emptied the pistols at the car, which had passed us and ran into a ditch about 50 yards [46 m] on down the road. It almost turned over. We kept shooting at the car even after it stopped."

Bonnie Parker and her partner in crime, Clyde Barrow.

Young Aviatrix Breaks England–Australia Record

Darwin, Australia, May 23: New Zealand aviatrix Jean Batten arrived in Darwin today after a record-breaking solo flight from London, which took 14 days, 22 hours, and 30 minutes. She beat the previous record, set by Amy Johnson, by more than four days.

This was the third attempt for the 25-year-old, who only six weeks ago was being mocked by London's Fleet Street press for her second failed attempt, when she ran out of fuel in the skies over Rome. "Try Again, Jean," suggested one newspaper headline.

Batten's third attempt did not look promising. Her plane, a patched-up Gipsy Moth, was almost five years old. She ran into severe weather near Burma and five hours out of Rangoon found herself in the middle of a huge tropical storm with her fuel supply running too low for her to turn back. With visibility at next to zero and a flooded open cockpit, she just made it to an airfield.

Batten has held her solo pilot's license for only five years. As soon as she received her license, she sought financial backing for a solo England–Australia trip, but with her lack of experience and no track record nobody took her seriously.

Crowds greet Jean Batten on her arrival.

Undeterred, she went on to learn aircraft maintenance, studied meteorology and navigation, and gained enough flying hours to receive a commercial license.

She made her first attempt two years ago, but in Baluchistan was forced down by a sandstorm, making a blind landing and damaging the propeller.

Dionne Quintuplets Born

Callender, Ontario, Canada, May 28: In what is being described as a miracle birth, identical female quintuplets were born today at their parents' modest farm house at Corbeil, near Callender. The chances of having identical quintuplets are said to be one in 57 million. The five sisters have been named Cécile, Yvonne, Marie, Annette, and Emilie.

Together the babies weighed less than 14 pounds (6.4 kg), and each one could be held in an adult palm. They were placed near an open stove to keep them warm, and mothers from surrounding villages brought breast milk for them. The quintuplets arrived two months prematurely to mother Elzire and father Oliva Dionne with the assistance of Dr Allan Roy Dafoe and two local midwives, Mme Legros and Mme Lebel.

Some say the parents have been approached by fair exhibitors who want to display the children on tour. It is not uncommon to see premature babies displayed in this way, but this would be the first time that quintuplets have been shown.

Nuclear Pioneer Marie Curie Dies at 66

Savoy, France, July 4: The discoverer of radium and twice Nobel Prize-winner, Marie Curie, died today, from leukemia—thought to be a consequence of her work.

Curie was born Maria Sklodowska in 1867 in Warsaw, Poland, the daughter of a secondary school teacher. She moved to Paris in 1891 to study physics and math at the Sorbonne university. Here she met and married her teacher, Pierre Curie. The Curies' work focused on radioactive substances. They found that uranium ore, or pitchblende, contained much more radioactivity than could be explained solely by the uranium content. The Curies began a search for the source of the radio-

time out

Six-year-old Shirley Temple charms audiences in her latest film *Bright Eyes*, singing "On The Good Ship Lollipop." The film proved to be a timely success for the ailing studio Fox, with audiences flocking to the box office.

activity and discovered two highly radioactive elements, radium and polonium—named for Mme Curie's home country. They won the 1903 Nobel Prize for Physics, shared with fellow French physicist Antoine Henri Bacquerel, who had discovered natural radioactivity in 1896. In 1906, Pierre was tragically killed when he was run over by a horse-drawn wagon. Marie took his place as Professor of General Physics in the faculty of sciences, becoming the first female director of a research laboratory. She continued her work on radioactive elements and won the 1911 Nobel Prize for Chemistry for isolating radium and researching its chemical properties. In 1914, she helped found the Radium Institute in Paris, and was the institute's first director. Described as quiet, dignified, and unassuming, Marie Curie was held in the highest regard by scientists throughout the world. She was a member of the Conseil de Physique de Solvay from 1911, and since 1922 has been a member of the Committee on Intellectual Cooperation within the League of Nations.

Constance Cummings

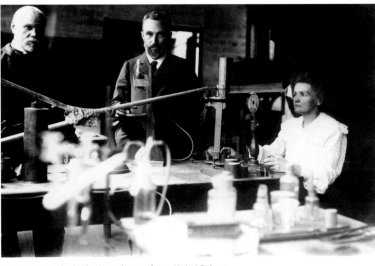

Professor Marie Curie, the winner of two Nobel Prizes.

Key Events

Marseilles, France, October 9: Croatian and Macedonian extremists assassinate King Alexander of Yugoslavia and French foreign minister Louis Barthou.
China, October: The communist Red Army commences a great northward march, retreating from southeastern China after being encircled by General Chiang Kai-shek's nationalist forces and suffering heavy losses.
England, November 11: Evangeline Booth is elected.

New York, USA, November 26: The Supreme Court deems "Little Gloria" Vanderbilt's mother an unfit parent, and the child is placed in the custody of her aunt, Gertruce Vanderbilt Whitney.
France, November 30: French aviatrix Hélène Boucher, 26 years of age, is killed when her plane crashes during a training flight.
Turkey, December 5: Turkish women are granted the right to vote and stand for election.

Hollywood, USA: Constance Cummings plays opposite Spencer Tracy in the film *Looking for Trouble*.
Ohio, Michigan, Kentucky, Tennessee, USA: Florence Ellinwood Allen is the first female judge appointed to the sixth circuit court of appeal.
USA: Danish writer Karen Blixen publishes *Seven Gothic Tales*, under the pen name Isak Dinesen.
Cuba, Brazil, Portugal: Women are granted the right to vote, although some restrictions are still in place in Portugal.

India: Indian lawyer and writer Cornelia Sorabji publishes her memoir *India Calling*.
Hollywood, USA: Oscar-winning actress Katharine Hepburn surprises her fans by playing a tomboy faith healer called Trigger Hicks in the film *Spitfire*.
England: British sculptor Barbara Hepworth sculpts *Mother and Child*.

Paris, France: Irène Curie, daughter of Marie and Pierre, and her husband Frédéric Joliot publish their findings on the synthesis of new radioactive elements. They are nominated for the Nobel Prize for Chemistry.
USA: Birth control campaigner Margaret Sanger publishes *Code to Stop the Overproduction of Children*.
Berlin, Germany: Painter and pacifist Käthe Kollwitz, whose work focuses on social injustice, paints *Death and the Woman*.

Catherine Breshkovsky

Women's Suffrage Pioneer Dies, Aged 87

Christchurch, New Zealand, July 13: Suffragist Kate Malcolm Sheppard, who spearheaded the campaign that resulted in New Zealand becoming the first country to grant women the vote, has died.

Born in England and migrating to New Zealand in 1869, Sheppard led the quiet life of a typical middle-class wife to Walter, and mother to son Douglas, until she became involved in the Women's Christian Temperance Movement. She threw herself into the work, but it was not long before she transferred her energies to another crusade—women's right to vote. She traveled widely, overcoming her natural timidity to speak at public gatherings, and bringing to her audiences new ideas from the American and British suffrage movements. It took Sheppard and her fellow activists almost seven years to get a bill before parliament.

On September 19, 1893, the bill was tabled. Sheppard presented a petition—which was 766 feet (233 m) long and contained more than 27,000 signatures. This was no mean achievement, given that the entire New Zealand population was less than one million. The petition was unrolled in a room to awed silence. Mrs Sheppard announced that the Bill had been passed with the words: "The news is being flashed far and wide, and before our earth has revolved on her axis every civilized community within the reach of the electric wires will have received the tidings that civic freedom has been granted to the women of New Zealand."

"I KNOW I'LL PASS AWAY LIKE THE OTHERS. I'M NOT THAT EXCEPTIONAL."

HÉLÈNE BOUCHER
(1908–1934), AVIATOR
AND STUNT PILOT

Death of Revolutionary "Little Grandmother"

Prague, Czechoslovakia, September 12: The Russian revolutionary known as "Babushka" (Little Grandmother) has died in Czechoslovakia, aged ninety.

Born Yekaterina Konstatinova Breshko-Breshkovskaya near Vitsyebsk, Mme Catherine Breshkovsky left her wealthy husband and child at the age of 26 to join followers of anarchist Mikhail Bakunin at their Kiev Commune. As a Narodnik revolutionary, she was imprisoned in St Petersburg, and in 1878 exiled to Siberia. Following her release in 1896, Breshkovsky founded the political society the Social Revolutionists. As a result, she was again threatened with imprisonment. In 1900, she fled to Switzerland and then traveled to the United States where she lived during 1904 and 1905.

After returning to Russia for the unsuccessful revolution of 1905, she was again imprisoned and banished to Siberia between the years 1907 and 1910.

Breshkovsky had made a considerable impact while she was in America. Author Mark Twain was among many intellectuals who in 1907 put their name to an unsuccessful petition submitted to the Russian ambassador to the USA, Baron Rosen, seeking clemency.

During the 1917 revolution, she was released from Siberia by the head of the Russian provisional government, Aleksandr Kerensky, and was enthusiastically welcomed back in Petrograd. But her role in the Kerensky government ended with the seizure of power by the Bolsheviks in the revolution. Breshkovsky was again compelled to flee and in 1919 moved to Czechoslovakia, where she remained until her death.

Dietrich Flops in *The Scarlet Empress*

Hollywood, USA, September 14: Josef von Sternberg's film *The Scarlet Empress,* starring German-born actress Marlene Dietrich as Catherine the Great, has opened to small houses and is being tipped as a financial flop. The movie has received generally poor reviews despite the fact that a few are predicting that it will become a seminal work. It is the sixth collaboration between director Sternberg and the world's highest-paid actress.

The Scarlet Empress is a sumptuously designed, visually powerful study of a woman who progresses from innocent youthfulness to scheming maturity in order to survive. Von Sternberg discovered Dietrich in Germany in 1930, when he saw her performing in the cabaret *Zwei Kravatten*, and he cast her in his

Marlene Dietrich and John Lodge in *The Scarlet Empress.*

1930 film *Der Blaue Engel (The Blue Angel).* Even before the movie was completed, von Sternberg offered a rough cut to his American studio, Paramount, which immediately signed Dietrich for a series of movies, the first being *Morocco,* in which she played a cabaret singer in love with a legionnaire. This was followed by *Dishonored* in 1931, in which she portrayed a prostitute who becomes a Great War secret agent, and then *Shanghai Express, Grand Hotel,* and *Blonde Venus.*

First Female International Salvation Army Chief

England, November 11: The newly elected international Commander-in-Chief of the Salvation Army is Evangeline Booth, the first woman to hold the position. She will be based in London.

British-born Booth has successfully led the American Salvation Army for 30 years. She is best known for expanding social services by establishing hospitals for unmarried mothers, soup kitchens,

International Commander-in-Chief of the Salvation Army, Evangeline Booth.

Composition, by French artist Marie Laurencin, features the pastel shades typical of her artwork.

Katharine Hepburn

emergency shelters, homes for the aged, and support services for the unemployed. During her first Christmas season in New York, Booth was appalled to discover that there were 70,000 children going to school without breakfast. She quickly got to work, and on Christmas Day that year, the Salvation Army provided meals for 30,000 people. While in America she took out American citizenship and changed her name from Eva to Evangeline.

Booth was born in 1865 in the North London suburb of Hackney, the seventh of eight children of William Booth and Catherine Mumford, who that year had founded the Christian Mission (renamed the Salvation Army in 1878). She showed signs of being a gifted public speaker and preacher at an early age. In 1887, at 21, she became the officer of the corps in Marylebone, West London. She was appointed Field Commissioner of Great Britain in 1888, serving in the post until 1891, when her father appointed her to train cadets in London. In 1896, she was appointed Territorial Commander of Canada and rose to the rank of field commissioner. She became head of the Army's international training college, and was Commander of the Salvation Army in London for five years.

Aunt Wins Custody of "Poor Little Rich Girl"

New York, USA, November 26: The Supreme Court today deemed "Little Gloria" Vanderbilt's mother an unfit parent, and placed the child heiress in the custody of her aunt, philanthropist and sculptor Gertrude Vanderbilt Whitney.

In what has been a bitter and sensational public custody battle before Judge John F. Carew, the court has heard a series of allegations concerning the scandalous lifestyle of Gloria Morgan Vanderbilt, widow of the railroad mogul Reginald Vanderbilt, who, it was maintained, neglected little Gloria—dubbed by the media "poor little rich girl." However, commentators have noted that much of the evidence was conjecture and hearsay, and was more concerned with the elder Gloria's use—or misuse—of the child's $4 million trust fund, and less with the actual care of the daughter. Little Gloria, a descendant of shipping baron Cornelius Vanderbilt, became heiress to the trust fund upon her father's death from alcohol poisoning when she was 17 months old.

For five hours in court, the elder Gloria listened tight-lipped as family nurse Emma Keislich, unkindly known as "Dodo," denounced her with relish as "a cocktail-crazed dancing mother, a devotee of sex erotica, and the mistress of a German prince." The child's aunt, Mrs Vanderbilt Whitney, has claimed that Little Gloria sometimes did not see her mother for months on end. At other times, she and Dodo lived in Paris, Monte Carlo, Biarritz, or London with her mother, her mother's twin sister Thelma—then mistress of the Prince of Wales—and her mother's lover Gottfried Hohenlohe-Langenburg, a destitute German prince and great-grandson of Queen Victoria. Little Gloria apparently feared and hated the prince. She sent postcards from Europe to her grandmother Morgan saying that her mother was so bad she wished she could run away.

It has been suggested that, being a child bride herself, the elder Gloria was completely unprepared for adult responsibilities as a widow of means.

Pacifist Paints *Death and the Woman*

Berlin, Germany: The latest work by German painter and pacifist Käthe Kollwitz, *Death and the Woman*, looks like being one of her most powerful and controversial yet. Kollwitz, whose work focuses on social injustice and the plight of the poor, has long been a thorn in the side of Adolf Hitler and the Nazi Party.

Her first important works, produced around the turn of the century, were two separate series of prints, entitled *Der weberaufstand (Weavers' Revolt),* and *Bauernkrieg (Peasants' War).* The death of her youngest son in the Great War profoundly affected her, and she expressed her grief in another cycle of prints with the themes of a mother protecting her children, or the mother with a dead child. Her latest series of lithographs, *Death,* treats the theme with ever starker and more powerful forms that convey a sense of anguish and drama. They have titles such as *Death and the Woman, Departure and Death*, and *Death Seizes the Children.*

Kollwitz's work has been driven by the miserable conditions of the urban poor, which she has seen first-hand through her physician husband's Berlin clinic. It has been said of Kollwitz's art that the viewer is unable to turn away without feeling guilt, and is forever haunted by her powerful recognition of truth.

"Little Gloria" Vanderbilt with her aunt.

Ma Barker

Amelia Earhart Sets Another Record

The Pacific, January 11: Today the daring Amelia Earhart became the first person to successfully fly solo over the Pacific Ocean. Her route carried her from Honolulu, Hawaii, to Oakland, California, and was so smooth and uneventful a ride that she passed the last few hours of her flight listening to a radio broadcast from the Metropolitan Opera House in New York City. As usual Earhart flew her Lockheed Vega 5b, which she calls "old Bessie, the fire horse."

Earhart's trouble-free, record-setting flight over the Pacific stands in sharp contrast with the disastrous Dole Air Race of 1927 in which 10 pilots lost their lives competing to be the first air crew to fly from Oakland to Honolulu.

Earhart's success over the Pacific comes just three years after she became the first woman to fly solo across the Atlantic Ocean. In recognition of that achievement, the United States Congress awarded Earhart the Distinguished Flying Cross, the French government presented

"DON'T PUT YOUR DAUGHTER ON THE STAGE, MRS WORTHINGTON, DON'T PUT YOUR DAUGHTER ON THE STAGE."

NOEL COWARD (1879–1973), ENGLISH AUTHOR AND SONWRITER

her with the Legion of Honor, and she received the Gold Medal of the National Geographic Society from the hand of President Herbert Hoover.

She is said to be planning a solo run from Los Angeles to Mexico City this spring, and there are rumors that Earhart's ambition is to be the first woman to fly around the world.

Ma Barker Goes Down Fighting

Lake Weir, Florida, USA, January 16: A lengthy gun battle ended today with the death of 63-year-old Ma Barker and the suicide of her youngest son Fred Barker. FBI agents had traced the Barkers to a rental cottage at Lake Weir, Florida, where they surrounded the house, then called on the Barkers to surrender. Ma and Freddie replied with a blast from a machine gun.

After six hours of nearly non-stop gunfire, the cottage fell silent. Inside, Ma Barker lay dead with three bullet wounds in her body. Fred lay nearby; he had been wounded 14 times but rather than be taken alive, he killed himself. The FBI agents estimated that they had fired 1,500 rounds of ammunition at the house. No FBI men were injured.

Ma Barker was born in Ash Grove, Missouri, in 1873. Her name was Arizona Donnie Clark, but her family and friends called her Kate. In 1892 Kate married George Barker. They had four sons: Herman, Lloyd, Arthur,

time out

The Irish government makes it illegal to advertise, promote, or sell any form of artificial birth control. But this is unlikely to deter Dr Marie C. Stopes, who continues to open family planning clinics in Great Britain and may soon open one in Ireland.

Nobel Peace Prize winner Jane Addams.

and Fred. Kate doted on her children, refusing to let George discipline them. It is uncertain whether George Barker walked out on his family or was thrown out by his wife. It is certain, however, that in the years after their father's departure, the Barker boys grew up as juvenile delinquents. Usually Ma Barker could get her boys off by storming into the police station and either playing the grief-stricken mother or launching into a shrieking tantrum that terrified the police.

The FBI claims that Ma Barker was the mastermind who encouraged her boys to trade petty crimes for bank robbery and kidnapping. There is no hard evidence for this charge. Nonetheless, Ma Barker did travel with her sons on their crime sprees. She may not have been a criminal, but she was undoubtedly an accomplice.

Six-year-old Shirley Temple Wins an Oscar

Hollywood, California, USA, February 27: On Oscar night the Academy of Motion

Aviator Amelia Earhart is the first person to fly solo over the Pacific Ocean.

Libya, Africa, January 1: The Italian colonies of Kyrenaika and Tripoli are joined as Libya.

Florida, USA, January 16: Members of the notorious Barker gang, led by Ma Barker, are killed by FBI agents during a shootout at Lake Weir.

The Pacific, January: Aviator Amelia Earhart flies solo from Hawaii to California, becoming the first person to fly solo over the Pacific. Later this year, she flies solo from Mexico City to Newark.

Hollywood, USA, February 27: Six-year-old actress Shirley Temple is presented with a special Academy Award for her performance in 1934's *Bright Eyes*.

Berlin, Germany, March 16: Germany denounces the disarmament clauses of the Versailles Treaty, resuming military conscription.

Bryn Mawr, Pennsylvania, USA, April 14: German-born mathematician Emmy Noether, whose work in algebra has been much admired, dies, aged 53.

USA, April 22: Elsa Lanchester stars in *The Bride of Frankenstein*, released today.

Middlesex, England, April: An aircraft-locating device, "radar," is patented by Scottish physicist Robert Watson-Watt.

Philadelphia, Pennsylvania, USA, May 3: Children's book illustrator Jessie Willcox Smith dies, aged 71.

Chicago, USA, May 21: Jane Addams, social worker and Nobel Peace Prize winner, dies, aged 74.

Moscow, USSR, August 20: The Seventh World Congress of the Communist International calls for the USSR and all communists to unite with democracies against their common enemy, the fascist dictatorships.

Washington DC, USA, August 31: As tensions mount in Europe, Congress passes the first of its Neutrality Acts designed to keep the USA out of foreign conflict.

Venice, Italy, August: The movie adaptation of Leo Tolstoy's *Anna Karenina*, starring Swedish actress Greta Garbo, is the highlight of the Venice Film Festival.

Srinigar, Kashmir, August: Swiss-born journalist, photographer, and adventurer Ella Maillart arrives in Srinigar after a seven-month journey from Peking via the Silk Road, her mission to have explored Chinese Turkestan.

Nuremberg, Germany, September 15: The Nuremberg decree legalizes the Nazi persecution of Jews.

Picture Arts and Sciences presented six-year-old actress Shirley Temple, a rising star in Hollywood, with a special Juvenile Award, "In grateful recognition of her outstanding contribution to screen entertainment during the year 1934." Shirley appeared in nine films last year, including *Little Miss Marker*, but the unique award, which was invented for the child star, emerged primarily from

up entirely of children ages three to five. Shirley's performance of "She's Only a Bird in a Gilded Cage" wowed audiences and critics alike.

The Juvenile Award was not the only time Shirley Temple took the spotlight at the Academy Awards: later in the evening she presented the Oscar for Best Actress to Claudette Colbert.

Mathematician Emmy Noether Dies

Bryn Mawr, Pennsylvania, USA, April 14: Emmy Noether, the mathematician Albert Einstein eulogized as "the most significant creative mathematical genius thus far produced since the higher education of women began," died during or shortly after surgery at a hospital near the campus of Bryn Mawr College.

Noether was born in 1882 in the town of Erlangen, Germany, to a well-to-do Jewish family. As a child mathematics fascinated her; at the time, however, women were barred from enrolling in German universities. By 1904, the policy had changed and Noether was matriculated at the University of Erlangen. Three years later, the university granted her a doctorate in mathematics.

In spite of her advanced degree, no German university would accept a female professor. It was not until 1919 that Noether was offered a teaching job, at the University of Göttingen. By that time she became interested in ring theory, a field of mathematics that is essential in algebraic geometry.

In 1933, to escape the Nazis, Noether emigrated to the United States where she joined the faculty of Bryn Mawr College.

Noether's death came as a shock to her friends, colleagues, and students because she had told no-one that she was about to undergo

an operation, and no-one knows what medical condition the surgeons were attempting to correct.

Hoodoo Life in America

Philadelphia, Pennsylvania, USA: Philadelphia publisher J. B. Lippincott has released a new work by Zora Neale Hurston, an author and trained ethnographer who has united her two interests in *Mules and Men*, a book that combines folktales with descriptions of the voodoo (or "hoodoo," as it is called in the book) traditions of the African-American inhabitants of the southern states of the US.

Hurston's main source for her book was her own experiences growing up in the entirely African-American town of Eatonville, Florida. And while she brings into play her study of ethnography and anthropology, *Mules and Men* wears its learning lightly, not least because Hurston writes in a style that imitates local speech patterns, a choice that may get her into trouble with some readers.

Elsa Lanchester

Shirley Temple with Bill "Bojangles" Robinson.

her heart-tugging performance in one of the biggest box office hits of 1934, *Bright Eyes*. Shirley played the daughter of a housemaid who has died in an auto accident. The haughty, well-to-do family who employed her mother agrees to care for the orphan until she can be placed in a suitable home. One of the high points of the movie is Shirley's bouncy performance of "On the Good Ship Lollipop."

Shirley was only three years old when she made her movie debut in *Glad Rags to Riches*, a one-reeler with a cast made

The brilliant mathematician Emmy Noether.

Key Events

Baden, Germany, September: Chemist and physicist Ida Tacke Noddack publishes a paper proposing that atoms are split into large fragments, a theory denigrated by the scientific community.
Yenan, China, October 20: Mao Tse-tung concludes the Red Army's Long March.
Weimar, Germany, November 8: Elisabeth Förster-Nietzsche, sister and literary executor of Friedrich Nietzsche, dies, aged 89.

New York, USA, November 23: Former managing editor of *Vanity Fair*, Clare Boothe, marries the founder and publisher of *TIME* magazine, Henry Robinson Luce.
Chicago, USA, November: Katharine Kuh opens her art gallery, which showcases modern American and European art.
Greensburg, Pennsylvania, USA, November: Helen Richey, hired as the first woman airplane pilot, resigns her position after months of ostracism by her male colleagues.

New York, USA, December 5: Mary McLeod Bethune founds the National Council of Negro Women.
Pennsylvania, USA: African-American writer and anthropologist Zora Neale Hurston publishes *Mules and Men*, a study of the African-American people of the southern American states.
USA: Aviator Anne Morrow Lindbergh publishes *North to the Orient*, describing her flights across Alaska, Canada, China, and Japan with her husband Charles Lindbergh.

Myanmar (Burma): Women are granted the right to vote.
England: The British novelist Ivy Compton-Burnett publishes *A House and its Head*.
New York, USA: American anthropologist Margaret Mead publishes *Sex and Temperament in Three Primitive Societies*, which challenges long-held assumptions about gender.
Paris, France: Edith Piaf, who becomes known as the "Little Sparrow," makes her singing debut.

USA: Laura Ingalls Wilder's *Little House on the Prairie*, a children's novel based on her pioneering family's experiences, is published.
Persia: Persia officially changes its name to Iran to gain favor with Germany; "Iran" is derived from the word "Aryan."
UK: Dame Lilian Barker is appointed Assistant Commissioner of Prisons, with special responsibility for female prisoners, and begins working toward reforming the women's prison system in the United Kingdom.

Ella Maillart Survives Journey to Turkestan

Margaret Mead

"ALWAYS REMEMBER THAT YOU ARE ABSOLUTELY UNIQUE. JUST LIKE EVERYONE ELSE."

MARGARET MEAD
(1901–1978)
AMERICAN
ANTHROPOLOGIST

Srinigar, Kashmir, August: Her skin red, raw, and chapped by mountain winds and desert sun, the intrepid Ella Maillart, aged 32, has arrived in Srinigar, Kashmir, after a seven-month, 3,500-mile (5,630 km) trek through some of the most dangerous places on Earth. Accompanied by Peter Fleming, 28, the world-renowned correspondent for *The Times* (London), Maillart explored Chinese Turkestan.

This vast region declared its independence from China in 1933; however, within a year the forces of Chiang Kai-shek's Nationalist government crushed the rebellion and closed the borders to all visitors. Since then, no news of what is happening inside Turkestan has reached the outside world.

Maillart came to China in 1934 on assignment for the French newspaper, *Le Petit Parisien*, to file reports on Japanese-occupied Manchuria. While there she ran across Fleming and the Swedish explorer and geographer Sven Hedin. When Maillart said she wanted to visit Chinese Turkestan, Fleming offered to go along, and Hedin volunteered to plan their itinerary. Hedin's route took Maillart and Fleming to Tibet, across the arid 350-mile (560 km) Tsaidam Plateau, then to the city of Sinkiang where they picked up the old Silk Road and followed it through

The adventurer Ella Maillart has traveled in many remote and rarely visited places across the world.

Turkestan into Kashmir, ending their adventure in Srinigar. Hedin admitted that if Maillart and Fleming followed his itinerary they would run the risk of encountering bandits, Communist

troops, and typhus epidemics, yet his route had one significant advantage: the Chinese government considered it so dangerous that it hadn't thought to close it to travelers.

This is certainly not the first time Maillart has put her life at risk to satisfy her wanderlust and get a good story; she has already trekked through the Caucasus Mountains and explored the Soviet republics of Kazakhstan and Uzbekistan. There is talk that both Maillart and Fleming plan to publish books about their experiences in Chinese Turkestan.

Noddack Finds Flaw in Fermi's Theory

Baden, Germany, September: Chemist and physicist Ida Tacke Noddack has published a paper in *The Periodical for Applied Chemistry (Zeitschrift fur Angewandte Chemie)* in which she reveals a flaw in physicist Enrico Fermi's innovative method for producing artificial radioactive substances by using neutrons to split the nuclei of uranium atoms. Fermi believed that by bombarding the uranium atoms he had created a new element which he called Element 93. In her paper, Noddack argues that the only way to determine if a new element has been created is through chemical analysis; something that Fermi, as a physicist, failed to do.

To date, Noddack's peers have ignored her critique of Fermi's work, while the scientific rumor mill is whispering that Fermi stands a good chance of winning a Nobel Prize.

As one of the first German women to study chemistry, Noddack is accustomed to defying convention. With her husband, Walter Noddack, she has claimed to have found two elements missing from the periodic table: rhenium and masurium. Rhenium has been accepted by the scientific community, but because other scientists have not been able to replicate the experiments that the Noddacks used to identify masurium, that "element" remains in scientific limbo.

Meanwhile, because Ida is Jewish, the Noddacks are considering emigrating from Nazi Germany.

Student Debuts in Controversial Opera

New York, USA, October 11: Last night at the Alvin Theater, George Gershwin's opera, *Porgy and Bess*, opened with a cast

Greta Garbo and Fredric March in a scene from *Anna Karenina*.

made up entirely of African-Americans. The performances were dazzling, but the absolute stand-out was the 23-year-old soprano, Anne Wiggins Brown, who sang the role of Bess. This is Brown's first professional role; technically, she is still a graduate student at the Juilliard School. She has a voice and stage presence that are made for opera, yet the professional opera companies in America are closed to African-American singers. It is for this reason that Brown has made her debut on Broadway.

Out of respect for Brown's great talent Gershwin actually changed the title of his opera. Originally he had called it *Porgy*, but while the show was in rehearsal he invited Brown to a neighborhood café for "a glass of orange juice." There he told her that he had decided to rename his opera *Porgy and Bess*.

Anne Wiggins Brown was born in 1912 in Baltimore, Maryland. Her father, Harry Brown, was a prominent physician in the city. Her mother, Mary Wiggins Brown, was a passionate music lover; she taught all of her daughters how to sing. The four Brown girls grew up performing in concerts and plays for Baltimore's African-American community.

When she completed high school, Brown applied to the Peabody School of Music, but was rejected because of her race. Juilliard did accept her, however; she was one of two African-American students at the prestigious New York music school.

Nonetheless, Gershwin's *Porgy and Bess* has generated much controversy among African-Americans. Brown's own father has complained to her that the opera perpetuates stereotypes of African-Americans as violent, ignorant, and sexually promiscuous. Brown replied that she thought Gershwin had taken a slice of life from a poor African-American neighborhood in South Carolina and "rendered it superbly."

Death Claims Nietzsche's Nazi Sister

Weimar, Germany, November 8: Elisabeth Förster-Nietzsche, younger sister and literary executor of the philosopher Friedrich Nietzsche, has died, aged 89.

Though once close, brother and sister avoided each other after Elisabeth married Bernhard Förster, a fanatical anti-Semite. In 1887, two years after their marriage, Elisabeth and Bernhard led five German families to Paraguay to found an Aryan colony that they imagined would revitalize German culture. The colony failed, and Bernhard took his own life by drinking a cocktail of morphine and strychnine.

In 1893 Elisabeth returned to Germany where she found her brother suffering from a mental collapse. As Nietzsche's writings began to reach a wide audience, his sister became his foremost promoter and publicist. On Nietzsche's death in 1900, Elisabeth became the executor of his literary estate and founded the Nietzsche Archive to protect her brother's papers and foster his ideas.

Elisabeth's hatred for the Jews and her unshakeable belief in the superiority of the Aryan race led her in 1930 to become an ardent supporter of the Nazi Party. To "prove" that Friedrich Nietzsche was a precursor of the Nazis, Elisabeth distorted passages from her brother's work and published them in a book entitled *The Will to Power*.

High-ranking representatives of the Nazi government will attend Elisabeth Förster-Nietzsche's funeral, including Adolf Hitler.

Artwork by Jessie Willcox Smith.

Helen Richey Forced Out of Pilot's Job

Greensburg, Pennsylvania, USA, November: Only months after she was hired as a pilot by Central Airlines, a commercial air carrier based in Greensburg, Pennsylvania, Helen Richey has been forced out of her job by the all-male pilots' union. Richey was the first woman ever hired as a professional pilot.

Born in 1909 in McKeesport, Pennsylvania, Richey showed her unconventional streak early. She was the only schoolgirl to walk around town in pants. At age 20 she took flying lessons, and became so enthusiastic about flying that once she acquired a pilot's license her father, Joseph B. Richey, McKeesport's superintendent of schools, bought her an airplane.

In 1932, Richey and a co-pilot, Frances Marsalis, set a flying endurance record, remaining in the air for nearly 10 days. To safeguard their record they even arranged to have their plane refueled in midair. Two years later, Richey took first place in the first National Air Meet for women aviators. That same year she was hired by Central Airlines.

From her first day on the job, Richey encountered harassment and ostracism from male pilots who did not want a woman working with them. The Airline Pilots Association, the union for professional aviators, refused to let Richey join and then forced her to give up her job.

Margaret Mead Takes a Swipe at Gender Issues

New York, USA: American anthropologist Margaret Mead has published a new book that is likely to generate as much controversy as her *Coming of Age in Samoa*. The new work, which is called *Sex and Temperament in Three Primitive Societies*, challenges several long-held assumptions about gender.

Traditional thinking has held that male aggression and female passivity are biologically determined, that these behaviors are not acquired as little boys and little girls grow up. Yet in Papua New Guinea in the western Pacific, Mead found three societies that do not fit the mold. Among the Tchambuli people, the women are dominant; they are the providers, while the men sit around all day adorning themselves. The men of the Mundugumor people are very aggressive, very warlike, and so are the Mundugumor women. As for the Arapesh people, Mead found both the men and women tend to be passive and non-confrontational.

Mead set off a firestorm of debate in 1928 with the publication of *Coming of Age in Samoa*, a work in which she

contrasted the social mores of Samoa and the United States, and their impact particularly upon teenagers. She argued that with their permissive view of sex, their broad social network in which the society is more important than any individual family, and their complete ignorance of the strictures of the Judeo-Christian moral code, the Samoans were a happier and psychologically a much healthier people than Americans.

Some of Mead's severest critics are her fellow anthropologists. The renowned Edward Sapir, Chairman of the Department of Anthropology at Yale University, is said to have characterized Mead as "a pathological liar" and her work on sex, gender roles, and social structures as the product of wishful thinking rather than scientific field research.

Mary McLeod Bethune

A Star is Born

Paris, France: Regulars at Gerny's, the Paris nightclub owned by Louis Leplée, were introduced recently to a thrilling new

Singer Edith Piaf, also known as "The Little Sparrow."

talent, a 20-year-old singer named Edith Piaf. As the diminutive chanteuse, who stands only 4 feet 8 inches (142 cm) tall came on stage, Leplée introduced her to the audience as *La Môme Piaf* (The Little Sparrow, or The Sparrow Kid).

Piaf has been a street singer, crooning in the Pigalle, Ménilmontant, and the Paris suburbs. On the night of her debut at Gerny's, Piaf was obviously nervous, and as she stepped into the spotlight the audience gave her a cool reception. Her singing, however, brought the crowd to their feet, and she left the stage to cheers and raucous applause.

Conchita Cintrón

> *"IT IS BETTER
> TO DIE ON YOUR
> FEET THAN
> LIVE ON
> YOUR KNEES."*
>
> DOLORES IBÁRRURI
> ("LA PASIONARIA")
> SPANISH COMMUNIST
> LEADER, 1936

Groundbreaking Foreign Correspondent Dies at 50

Paris, France, January 6: The American journalist and writer Louise Bryant, who was best known for her articles on radical political and feminist themes, died today in Paris, aged fifty.

Bryant first became involved with politics and women's rights issues while completing a degree at the University of Oregon, and later became an active suffragist. In 1909, she married Paul Trullinger, a Portland dentist, and began a career as an illustrator and editor for the *Spectator*, a local paper. Chafing under the restrictions of her marriage, a love affair with socialist and activist John Reed, whom she met in 1914, offered her escape into an exciting, intellectual world.

Bryant followed Reed to New York in 1915 where she joined a group of radicals associated with the journal *The Masses*. In September 1917, Bryant married Reed, also a journalist with *The Masses*, and the couple traveled together to Moscow. For the next six months they reported on Bolshevik and Communist Party activity in Russia. The lectures she gave upon returning to the United States were gathered into a collection and in 1918 published as *Six Red Months in Russia: an Observer's Account of Russia Before and During the Proletarian Dictatorship*.

Bryant caused some controversy with her sympathetic portrait of Russian socialism, writing that "Socialism is here, whether we like it or not—just as woman suffrage is here—and it spreads with the years." Bryant was with Reed in Moscow in 1920 when he died of typhoid. She continued her career as a journalist from 1920 to 1923 and remarried in 1926. However, she was already starting to suffer from Dercum's disease—a debilitating and disfiguring illness which causes painful lumps to appear over the body—and her marriage ended in divorce.

She spent her final years in Paris, writing and experimenting with sculpture. Just before her death, a postcard to a friend showed her devotion to Reed's memory: "If I get [to heaven] before you do or later—tell Jack Reed I love him."

> **time out**
>
> German film-maker and photographer Leni Riefenstahl released her film *Olympia*, a study of the Berlin Olympic Games. The political climate ensured the games were eventful, but her film is said to be the best sports documentary ever made.

Journalist Louise Bryant lectured on Russian socialism.

Divorce for Pickford and Fairbanks

Hollywood, California, USA, January 10: Screen star and film industry entrepreneur Mary Pickford (43) today announced her divorce from Douglas Fairbanks, Sr. (52) after 15 years of marriage. It is believed that Pickford will retain "Pickfair," the couple's mansion in the San Ysidro Canyon near Los Angeles.

Pickford met and fell in love with Fairbanks when they were starring in silent films. They were both married to other partners at the time, but within three weeks of Pickford's divorce from Owen Moore in 1920, the couple married. They formed United Artists together with Charlie Chaplin and D. W. Griffiths, and Pickford became one of the most powerful women in Hollywood.

Her marriage to Fairbanks has by all accounts been in trouble for some time, although nobody is saying for certain what went wrong. After their official

Mary Pickford and Douglas Fairbanks in happier times.

separation in mid-1933, there were several rumors of alcoholism and affairs; Fairbanks has also been linked to English beauty Lady Sylvia Ashley. Although once one of the most famous couples in Hollywood, Pickford and Fairbanks have not matched their early screen successes since the late 1920s. Their influence behind the scenes, however, has continued. "Pickfair" is still the setting for numerous lively social events featuring key players in the Hollywood film scene, and United Artists continues its work in film production and distribution.

Reputation of Women in Bullfighting Heightened

Lima, Peru, January: Fifteen-year-old Conchita Cintrón came out as a force to be reckoned with at the Festival Hipico Taurino, which was held in the

Paris, France, January 6: American-born journalist and feminist Louise Bryant dies, aged 50.

Hollywood, USA, January 10: Screen legend Mary Pickford divorces Douglas Fairbanks.

Lima, Peru, January: Chilean-born *torera* (female bullfighter) Conchita Cintrón has her first public bullfight.

Madrid, Spain, February 16: Dolores Ibárruri, Communist Party politician, is elected to the Cortes (parliament).

Germany, March 7: France decides a large military force will be needed after German troops reoccupy the Rhineland.

France, March 16: Journalist, actress, and founder of the feminist journal *La Fronde*, Marguerite Durand, dies, aged 72.

Berne, Switzerland, March 19: Actress Ursula Andress is born.

Birmingham, England, April 16: Nurse Dorothea Waddington, convicted of murdering two patients with morphine, is hanged.

Vienna, Austria, May 5: Marianne Hainisch, founder of the Austrian women's rights movement, dies, aged 97.

Abyssinia, May 5: Abyssinia is taken by Italy, crumbling under the weight of the massive offensive.

USA, May 14: The film *Show Boat* is released, starring Irene Dunne and Allan Jones.

Tokyo, Japan, May 21: Sada Abe, a former prostitute, is arrested after wandering the streets of Tokyo for three days with her dead lover's penis and scrotum in her hand.

Vienna, Austria, May 28: Bertha Pappenheim dies, aged 77. Known as "Anna O," she was a patient of Sigmund Freud and Doctor Josef Breuer, and a subject in their book *Studies on Hysteria*.

Berlin, Germany, August 1: The Games of the XIth Olympiad open. Hitler temporarily abstains from his actions against Jews.

Athens, Greece, August 4: Prime Minister General John Metaxas leads a military coup and establishes a dictatorship.

Rome, Italy, August 15: Writer and Nobel Prize winner Grazia Deledda dies, aged 64.

London, England, August 31: Elizabeth Cowell is the first female announcer on the new BBC television service.

London/North America, September 4-5: British-Kenyan aviator Beryl Markham flies solo across the Atlantic Ocean from east to west.

London, England, September 21: J. R. R. Tolkien's book *The Hobbit* is published.

Bullfighting is attracting more women participants.

Marianne Hainisch

Plaza de Acho in Lima this month. Performing publicly in the bullfighting ring for the first time, Conchita astonished aficionados of the sport. Although women have competed in bullfighting for several years, this new young *torera* has lifted their profile considerably.

This Puerto Rican-American "gringa," who has made Peru her home, has been training in horseback-riding for several years but has only recently begun to learn the art of *rejoneo*, which is a Portuguese style of bullfighting from horseback with a short spear.

Under the tutelage of the Portuguese bullfighter Ruy da Cámara, and with the help of her mare Mizraut, Conchita drew accolades from the festival crowd when she won second place in the women's riding events.

However, it was in the *rejoneo* that she showed unique skill. As one local newspaper reported, "At the Festival Taurino, the attractive and graceful Miss Conchita Cintrón stood out … and it was clear that this young girl possesses the necessary skills to perform these difficult maneuvers."

With this success behind her, Conchita plans to leave in a few months for Lisbon, Portugal, to test her skills in the birthplace of *rejoneo* bullfighting. The tour is expected to last most of the summer. Conchita will be accompanied on her travels by her teacher.

"La Pasionaria" Wins Seat

Madrid, Spain, February 20: Spain's national elections, held on February 16, resulted in 17 leaders of the Communist Party being elected to the Cortes (parliament). Among these politicians is Dolores Ibárruri, a long-time activist who enthusiastically supports the "Popular Front" policy—an electoral coalition of left-wing parties formed to stand against right-wing leaders—which is largely responsible for the Communist Party's electoral success.

Since the February 16 election result, Ibárruri, representing the Azurias region, has intensified her campaign for the release of political prisoners. Her actions at Oviedo jail, where she negotiated with the prison director and addressed a crowd of about 20,000 gathered outside the jail, has today resulted in the mass release of all political prisoners at Oviedo. When her train arrived back in Madrid, she was greeted by an enthusiastic crowd of vocal communist supporters.

Ibárruri has been active in the Spanish Communist Party since its formation in 1921. In the following decade her political work and journalism distinguished her as a central figure in the party. In 1930 she was elected to the party's Central Committee and in 1931 she joined the editorial board of the communist newspaper *Mundo Obrero (Workers World)*. In 1932, she was elected the party's Secretary of Women's Affairs. Imprisoned many times in the past, she has twice this year already been imprisoned by right-wing government forces for agitation. Her nickname, *La Pasionaria* ("The Passion Flower"), is proving to be more than apt.

Death of a Tireless Campaigner

Vienna, Austria, May 5: The founder of the National Council for Women (NCW) in Austria, Marianne Hainisch, has died, aged 97, in Vienna. Hainisch was an early advocate for the education of women, and campaigned from the 1860s onward to have Austrian grammar school and university places opened up to women.

In 1899, she was elected Honorary Vice-President of the International Council of Women (ICW), becoming its Honorary President by 1930.

Hainisch took a central role in the new Austrian NCW and helped initiate inquiries into women's health, employment rights, education, and suffrage, as well as advocating pacifism and disarmament in Austria. Her son, Michael Hainisch, an independent politician, was President of Austria from 1920 to 1928.

The newly released movie musical, *Show Boat*, stars Irene Dunne as Magnolia Hawks and Allan Jones as Gaylord Ravenal.

Spain, October 1: General Franco is appointed commander-in-chief of the rebel forces in the civil war after capturing Toledo.

New York, USA, October 20: Annie Sullivan Macy, the teacher best known for her work with deaf and blind girl Helen Keller, dies, aged 70.

London, England, November 16: Edward VII announces his intention of marrying Mrs Wallis Simpson.

Hollywood, USA, November 17: Austrian-American contralto Ernestine Schumann-Heink dies, aged 75.

UK, November 20: New *Matrimonial Causes Act* permits divorce, but only on grounds of drunkenness, incurable insanity, cruelty, desertion, or imprisonment on death row.

London, England, December 12: Prince Albert is proclaimed King George VI after his brother Edward VII abdicates the British throne.

China, December 12-25: Nationalist general Chiang Kai-shek is kidnapped in an attempt to force him to negotiate with the Communists against their enemy, Japan.

Washington DC, USA, December 30: First Lady Eleanor Roosevelt's daily syndicated newspaper column called "My Day" has been running for one year. She uses the column to express her opinions on a range of topics, including the plight of the poor.

Spain: Dancer Antonia Mercé, whose stage name is La Argentina, after the country of her birth, dies at 48 years of age. She is often referred to as the "Flamenco Pavlova."

Denver, USA: The first Tampax tampons are sold in the US. Tampons had been patented by Dr Earle Haas in 1929.

Belfast, Ireland: Social reformer, writer, and promoter of birth control and sex education in the United Kingdom, Dr Marie C. Stopes, opens the Mother's Clinic, the first family planning clinic in Ireland.

London, England: Writer and painter Phyllis Pearsall creates and publishes *A to Z: The Atlas and Guide to London and Suburbs*.

England/USA: Russian-American novelist Ayn Rand publishes *We, the Living*, which describes life in Russia under Soviet rule. Other important novels released this year include *The House of Incest* by Anaïs Nin, *Jamaica Inn* by Daphne du Maurier, and *Nightwood* by Djuna Barnes.

London, England: Laura Knight is the first woman to be admitted into the Royal Academy of Arts.

Geisha's Crime Causes Sensation

Bertha Pappenheim

Tokyo, Japan, May 21: Former geisha and prostitute Sada Abe was today charged with manslaughter after being found in Tokyo holding her dead lover's severed penis and testicles. Early reports say that 32-year-old Abe and her lover Kishida Ichizo had hidden themselves away at Masaka Inn in northern Tokyo for over a week, but that after days of sex and experimenting with asphyxiation, Abe strangled her lover with a piece of string. She then cut off his penis and scrotum and wrapped them in paper.

She was found today by police—three days after Ichizo's death. It is rumored that she was arrested at an inn in Shinagawa, where she was planning to commit suicide.

Sada Abe's father sold her to a geisha house when she was a troubled 16-year-old, but at 21 she left to become a *shogi* (licensed prostitute). Six years later she took work as a waitress and occasional prostitute. It was while she was waitressing that she met Ichizo and they started the passionate affair that would ultimately end his life.

Upon the discovery of Ichizo's body, newspapers avidly followed the search for Abe, and reporters and curious onlookers converged on the inn where the lovers held their final rendezvous. Since her arrest, crowds have been gathering outside

> "UNEMPLOY-MENT INSUR-ANCE IN MANY HOMES IS ALL THAT STANDS BETWEEN MANY A FAMILY AND STARVATION."
>
> ELEANOR ROOSEVELT, US FIRST LADY, 1936

Cecilia Colledge at the Berlin Olympic Games.

the police station where she is being held. Her forthcoming trial will no doubt keep her in the headlines for some time yet.

BBC TV Employs First Women Presenters

London, England, August 31: Today, during one of the BBC's test broadcasts from Alexandra Palace in London, people saw for the first time a female presenter appear on the television screen. Elizabeth Cowell made her first appearance today in the high-definition broadcast direct to onlookers at the Radiolympia exhibition. The exhibition is an annual event which

Elizabeth Cowell is BBC TV's first female announcer.

features live shows and an opportunity for the public to meet their favorite radio announcers. As a bonus, for the last five days exhibition attendees have been able to watch the BBC's groundbreaking television broadcasts.

Elizabeth Cowell and Jasmine Bligh were chosen from a pool of 1,200 eager female applicants. The requirements for the positions were charisma, diplomacy and tact, personality, a pleasant "mezzo" voice, and visually attractive features. The applicants also had to be unmarried.

The test broadcasts have featured a range of programs including music, film excerpts, and news. A variety program, "Here's Looking at You," features singer Helen McKay and other guests.

The BBC is planning a regular television service to be launched early next year. These test broadcasts will give the fledgling presenters a taste of the spotlight where, unlike radio broadcasters, they will have to perform physically as well as vocally for their new audience.

Helen Keller's Teacher and Friend Dies

New York, USA, October 20: Annie Sullivan Macy, the inspirational teacher who gave Helen Keller the ability to read and write, has died today in the home she shared with Keller. She was 70 years of age. Macy had been in a coma for six days, tended daily by her former student and friend who still refers to Macy as "Teacher."

Macy herself suffered from blindness as a child and attended the Perkins Institution for the Blind for six years. Her sight was restored after two operations and, upon her graduation at age 20, she accepted a position to teach the blind, deaf, and mute seven-year-old Helen Keller. Her successes in teaching the girl to "finger speak"—a technique which Macy herself had learned at school—have been widely reported over the 49 years of their partnership. Macy and Keller were due to receive the Roosevelt Memorial Association Medals for outstanding achievement on October 27, an honor conferred for "cooperative achievement of heroic character and far-reaching significance."

Over the last few years, Macy had begun to lose her sight again, and just before her death Keller had been teaching her to read Braille. In a statement to the press, Keller expressed her sense of loss, saying that Macy "is free at last from pain and blindness. I pray for strength to endure the silent dark until she smiles on me again." Macy's funeral will be held on October 22 at Park Avenue Presbyterian Church.

Edward Abdicates for Mrs Simpson

London, England, December 11: King Edward VIII of England yesterday ended a week of fierce speculation in the local press by submitting his abdication to Parliament in order to marry the American socialite Mrs Wallis Simpson.

Edward VIII and Mrs Wallis Simpson will marry soon; they will be the Duke and Duchess of Windsor.

Annie Sullivan Macy and her pupil Helen Keller, who went on to become a writer and public speaker.

United Feature Syndicate (UFS). Since then, she has published six columns a week without missing a single one.

The aim of her column is to offer a portrait of the daily life of a First Lady, and provide a forum for the issues that concern her. And it has succeeded! After an initial appearance in 20 newspapers, by year's end this has tripled to 60 papers, including some unashamedly anti-Roosevelt publications. What makes her journalistic feat even more noteworthy is that this year has been an election year and Mrs Roosevelt has been actively campaigning on behalf of her husband, as well as attending to her usual community and social duties.

The subjects Mrs Roosevelt has talked about during the year have been both personal and political. From daily life at the White House and family events to sometimes controversial explorations of social issues such as poverty, race relations, and prison reform, she has left no stone unturned in describing the world as she sees it. Charitable causes, women's rights, post-Depression work programs, the Spanish Civil War, the arts, the perils of fame, and economic policy are only some of the topics she has touched on.

Her May 8 column, which lamented the terrible conditions at a Training School for Delinquent Girls she visited, and her subsequent hosting of a party at the White House for the girls—regardless of their race—have ruffled some conservative feathers, as have her exhortations for social reforms and racial reconciliation. However, the popularity of "My Day" has withstood the critics' barbs, and looks set to continue for some time to come.

Antonia Mercé

English Artist Creates Map of London

London, England: How long does it take to walk 3,000 miles (4,828 km) and navigate 23,000 streets around London in order to draw a map? For artist Phyllis Pearsall, it took a year of walking for up to 18 hours a day. The result is a book of maps called *A to Z: The Atlas and Guide to London and Suburbs*. Instead of trying to encapsulate the whole of London in one map, Pearsall divided the city into sections to produce her ground-breaking guidebook.

Unable to find a publisher willing to take on her book, Pearsall began her own company and published it herself. After convincing the head of newsagent chain W. H. Smith to stock the guide, Pearsall hand-delivered 250 copies to outlets in a wheelbarrow. Such has been the book's popularity that within seven days of receiving their first batch, the newsagent at Victoria Station had sold out.

Although the relationship between the unmarried Prince of Wales (as he was until January this year) and Simpson has been front-page news in the United States for some time, the news was only released in England over the last month, and has caused a public furor. Despite the fact that Simpson has been granted a preliminary decree of divorce from her second husband, Ernest Simpson, she is unable to remarry until next year—and both the Church of England and the political establishment have made clear their strong objections to a twice-divorced woman becoming Queen of England.

So today, the momentous and irrevocable decision was made and the king has abdicated, preventing any children he and Simpson may have from succeeding to the throne.

In his abdication speech broadcast today, the Duke of Windsor—as he will now be known—professed his allegiance to his brother and restated the reason for his dramatic decision: "I have found

it impossible to carry the heavy burden of responsibility and to discharge my duties as king … without the help and support of the woman I love."

Surprisingly, little is known of Mrs Simpson. She met the former Prince of Wales in 1930 when she and her husband became part of the prince's elite social circle. It is thought that their affair began about two years ago.

Now, with the king's abdication—the first voluntary abdication in English royal history—the couple will be free to begin life as a married couple next year.

A Year of the First Lady's Daily Thoughts

Washington DC, USA, December 30: The end of 1936 marks a new anniversary for the extremely busy US First Lady, Eleanor Roosevelt. On December 30 last year, Mrs Roosevelt—wife of President Franklin D. Roosevelt—launched her new newspaper column, "My Day," with

Ekaterina Geladze

"Men seldom make passes at girls who wear glasses."

DOROTHY PARKER
(1893–1967)
AMERICAN AUTHOR

Death of Psychoanalyst

Göttingen, Germany, February 5: As word of the passing of Lou Andreas-Salomé spread across this Prussian university town today, professors and students went into mourning. At Göttingen's Gestapo headquarters, however, Hitler's thugs are planning to mark Salomé's death by raiding her house, hauling her library out into the street, and burning every volume.

A Russian-born Jew, Salomé was a writer, an intellectual, and a psychoanalyst, but she was most famous for her avant-garde romantic adventures. At the age of 17 she enchanted her tutor, a Dutch pastor named Hendrik Gillot, who swore he would divorce his wife if she would consent to marry him. At age 21 she formed a threesome (which may or may not have been sexual) with the author Paul Rée and the philosopher Friedrich Nietzsche. When she was 26 she married a linguistics scholar, Carl Friedrich Andreas, with the understanding that they would never have sex together, but she could have as many lovers as she liked. The unconventional arrangement suited the couple: they remained together until Andreas's death in 1930. At 36 years of age Salomé took as her lover the 21-year-old poet Rainer Maria Rilke. She corresponded with Sigmund Freud, but apparently never made love to him.

In the end, Salomé found no comfort in her eventful life. "If I let my thoughts roam I find no-one," she lamented. "The best, after all, is death."

First-time Novelist Wins Pulitzer

New York, USA, May 3: The accolades keep coming for *Gone With the Wind*. Today author Margaret Mitchell learned that her best-selling novel has won a Pulitzer Prize. Mitchell, who is a first-time novelist and life-long Georgian, based her book on the stories of her elderly relatives who had lived through the Civil War.

As for the book itself, it was published almost by chance. Mitchell had written most of the novel while bedridden, recuperating from a broken ankle. In 1935, she met Macmillan publisher Howard Latham, and after escorting him around Atlanta, agreed to let him read her manuscript. Recognizing that he had a blockbuster in his hands, Mr Latham sent Mitchell a contract and an advance check.

Since publication in June 1936, *Gone With the Wind* has sold nearly 1.3 million copies.

Joseph Stalin's Mother Dies

USSR, May 13: The only person who could get away with calling Joseph Stalin by his childhood nickname, "Soso," died today. Ekaterina Geladze,

Actor Clark Gable reads Margaret Mitchell's prize-winning book.

the serf whose son grew up to become one of the most powerful and feared men in the world, was 79 years old.

She was born in 1858 in what is now the Soviet Republic of Georgia. At the age of 16 she married Vissarion Dzhugashvili, by whom she had three sons. The youngest one, Joseph, born in 1878, was the only child to survive infancy. Sometime before 1888 Vissarion left his wife and never returned.

In order to support herself and Joseph, Ekaterina hired herself out as a washerwoman, seamstress, and housecleaner. She dreamed of her boy becoming a priest, and tried to put money aside for his education. It appears likely that she achieved her goal thanks to the financial assistance of the Pismamedov family, wealthy Jewish merchants who employed Ekaterina as a housekeeper. In 1894, Joseph entered the Tiflis Theological Seminary and remained there until 1899 when he was expelled, supposedly for his involvement in revolutionary activity.

In one of their very last conversations together Ekaterina asked her son, "Joseph, who exactly are you now?"

"Remember the czar?" Stalin replied. "Well, I'm like the czar."

Ekaterina was not overly impressed. "You'd have done better," she responded, "to become a priest."

time out

Civil unrest and riots have broken out in Albania following King Zog I's decree that women are now forbidden to wear veils and burkas. The unmarried Muslim declared himself king almost 10 years ago.

"Blonde Bombshell" Dies from Kidney Failure

Los Angeles, USA, June: Hollywood sex goddess Jean Harlow died on June 7 of kidney failure, only days after she collapsed on the set of the film *Saratoga*. She was 26 years old.

Harlow's death is a blow to the executives at Metro-Goldwyn-Mayer who had groomed their "Blonde Bombshell" to

Moscow, USSR, January 23: The trial begins of 17 leading Communists accused of participating in Leon Trotsky's plot to overthrow Joseph Stalin's regime and assassinate its leaders.

Göttingen, Germany, February 5: Russian-born writer and psychoanalyst Lou Andreas-Salomé dies, a few days before turning 76.

India, April 1: The British Parliament's *Government of India Act*, aimed at transforming India's governmental system, comes into effect, giving provincial governments greater authority.

Hollywood, USA, April 27: Janet Gaynor and Fredric March star in *A Star is Born*.

New York, USA, May 3: Author Margaret Mitchell wins a Pulitzer Prize for her debut novel *Gone With the Wind*.

New Jersey, USA, May 6: The German airship *Hindenburg* bursts into flame while mooring, killing 36 people.

London, England, May 12: The coronation of King George VI and Queen Elizabeth takes place at Westminster Abbey.

USSR, May 13: Ekaterina Geladze, the mother of Joseph Stalin, dies, aged 79.

South America, May 26: The Chaco War between Bolivia and Paraguay comes to an end.

Vienna, Austria, June 2: Soprano Nuri Hadzic stars in the première of the opera *Lulu*, written by Austrian composer Alban Berg.

Los Angeles, USA, June 7: Actress Jean Harlow dies, aged 26.

Washington DC, USA, June 25: The *National Fair Labor Standards Act* rules in favor of a minimum wage law for both women and men.

South Pacific Ocean, July 2: Aviator Amelia Earhart disappears between New Guinea and Howland Island near the end of a round-the-world flight.

Peking, China, July 28: Japanese forces complete their occupation of the city following an initial strike on July 7 at Lukochiao.

USA, July: The American Medical Association now teaches students about birth control and the various forms of contraception.

Saint-Brice-sous-Forêt, France, August 11: American-born novelist Edith Wharton dies, aged 75.

Jean Harlow starring in the 1936 movie *Libeled Lady*.

Jean Harlow

take the place of such fading MGM stars as Norma Shearer and the increasingly reclusive Greta Garbo.

Ash blonde was the natural color of Harlow's hair. She achieved her trademark platinum blonde look by applying, every week, a mixture of peroxide, ammonia, Clorox bleach, and a detergent known as Lux Flakes. The result was such a distinct, glamorous shade of blonde that as a publicity gimmick Howard Hughes offered $10,000 to any beautician who could reproduce Harlow's precise shade.

Born Harlean Carpenter in Kansas City, Missouri, on March 3, 1911, Jean Harlow was discovered on the lot of the Fox Studios; she was sitting in her car, waiting for a friend who had an appointment at Fox, when some studio executives spotted her and asked the 16-year-old beauty if she were interested in a movie career. After a series of bit parts in silent movies, Harlow landed her first substantial role in *Hell's Angels*, a talkie produced by Howard Hughes. The critics panned her performance, but her raw sex appeal created a sensation among moviegoers. Soon she was starring in movies opposite Clark Gable, James Stewart, William Powell, and James Cagney.

Although Jean Harlow married three times, William Powell was the great love of her life. At her funeral a single gardenia bearing an unsigned note that read, "Good night, my dearest darling," was placed in her hands. Mourners assumed the token was from Powell, who had paid $25,000 to have Harlow laid to rest in a lavishly decorated private tomb in Hollywood's favorite cemetery, Forest Lawn Memorial Park.

Earhart Vanishes

South Pacific Ocean, July 2: Renowned aviator Amelia Earhart failed to arrive as scheduled on Howland Island today, and all attempts to contact her via radio have failed. Earhart was on the final leg of her round-the-world flight.

After departing from Lae, New Guinea, Earhart and her navigator, Fred Noonan, maintained radio contact with the US Coast Guard cutter, *Itasca*, which was anchored at Howland. The pair made their last position report when they were near the Nukumanu Islands, about 800 miles (1,300 km) from Lae.

Officials report that Earhart and Noonan have not been heard from since.

The aircraft's radio was malfunctioning. Apparently the radio crew of the *Itasca* could hear Earhart clearly, but she could not hear their transmissions. During one transmission to the ship Earhart and Noonan said they had sighted Howland Island and were preparing to land. In fact, they were still at least 5 miles (8 km) from the island. In an effort to guide the aviators to their true destination, the captain of the *Itasca* ordered the engineers to generate a great black plume of smoke from the ship's oil-fired boilers, but to no avail.

The sky near Howland was cloudy today. Experienced aviators have observed that other pilots have mistaken shadows cast by clouds on the surface of the ocean for islands. If Earhart and Noonan made that mistake, the chances of finding them alive are very slim indeed.

Aviator Amelia Earhart flies over the Golden Gate Bridge in Oakland, California.

Clarksdale, Mississippi, USA, September 26: Bessie Smith, considered the greatest blues singer of all time, dies, aged about 42.

China, September 29: General Chiang Kai-shek unites forces with his rival, Communist Mao Tse-tung, against the Japanese.

Baku, Azerbaijan, October 15: Actress Pamphylia Tanailidi, accused of being a spy, is executed.

New York, USA, December 27: Mae West is banned from radio broadcasts by NBC on the grounds of indecency.

Ireland, December 29: The new Irish Constitution comes into force and the Irish Free State officially becomes Eire.

New York, USA, December: *Ruth Wakefield's Toll House Tried and True Recipes*, which includes her famous Toll House cookies, is published.

Vienna, Austria: Anna Freud, the daughter of Sigmund Freud, publishes *The Ego and the Mechanisms of Defence*.

China: Song Qingling, widow of Sun Yat-sen, organizes the China Defence League, providing medical care to rural Chinese.

Denmark and England: Danish writer Isak Dinesen (Karen Blixen-Finecke) publishes *Out of Africa*.

Cambridge, England: British chemist Dorothy Crowfoot Hodgkin is awarded a doctorate from Cambridge University.

Paris, France: Acclaimed choreographer Bronislava Nijinska creates one of her most famous ballets, *Chopin Concerto*.

Uttar Pradesh, India: Vijaya Lakshmi Pandit is the first woman to be given a government portfolio.

Paris, France: Nobel Prize winner Irène Joliot-Curie is appointed professor of science at the Sorbonne.

Manchuria: The Japanese invade. Thousands of girls and young women are abducted and forced into having sex with Japanese soldiers.

The Philippines: Women are granted the right to vote.

Edinburgh, Scotland: Jessie Chrystal MacMillan, the first woman to graduate in science from the University of Edinburgh, lawyer, and suffragette, dies, aged 55.

New York, USA: German-born American psychoanalyst Karen Horney publishes *The Neurotic Personality of Our Time*.

Anna Freud

*"LIFE IS ALWAYS
A TIGHTROPE
OR A FEATHER
BED. GIVE
ME THE
TIGHTROPE."*

EDITH WHARTON
(1862–1937)
AMERICAN NOVELIST

Empress of the Blues Dies from Injuries

Clarksdale, Mississippi, USA, September 26:
Just hours after being seriously injured in a car accident, blues singer Bessie Smith died at the Afro-American Hospital in Clarksdale, Mississippi. She was about 42 years old.

Smith was born into a desperately poor family in Chattanooga, Tennessee. The precise date is unknown, but the two most common birth dates suggested are sometime in July 1892, or April 15, 1894. While still a child, she became a street performer: Bessie sang while her brother Andrew played the guitar. In 1912 she joined the Moses Stokes theater company—but as a dancer, not a singer. Smith developed a close friendship with another member of the company, blues singer Ma Rainey, who had a profound influence on Smith's future career.

By 1920 Smith was singing the blues in vaudeville, and was popular in the South and along the eastern seaboard of the United States. She cut her first recording in 1923 with Columbia Records, "Down-hearted Blues"(with "Gulf Coast Blues" on the flip side). The record sold nearly 800,000 copies and made her a star. She went on to record with the era's greatest jazz musicians, including Coleman Hawkins and Louis Armstrong. At the time of her death, Smith was trying something innovative, incorporating some of the sounds of swing into her performance of the blues.

England versus Australia during this year's women's Test series. England retained the Ashes.

Mae West Banned

New York, USA, December 27:
In response to public outrage and pressure from decency-in-broadcasting advocacy groups, television network NBC has banned actress Mae West from the airwaves.

On December 12, West appeared as a guest star on "The Chase & Sanborn Hour," more popularly known as "The Edgar Bergen and Charlie McCarthy Show," the most listened-to broadcast on radio, reaching a national audience of approximately 8 million homes. West appeared in two sketches that night, first playing Eve in a "Garden of Eden" skit, and later reminiscing with Charlie McCarthy (a ventriloquist's dummy) about their last romantic encounter.

True to form, West "vamped" her lines in both sketches, and although the Charlie McCarthy skit was more sexually suggestive, it was the much tamer "Garden of Eden" skit that enraged the listening public, perhaps because West addressed the Serpent as "my palpitatin' python."

West has long been a lightning rod for the censors. Her first starring role on Broadway came in 1927 in a play called *Sex*, which she wrote, produced, and directed. Police arrested the entire cast, and West was sentenced to 10 days in jail for public obscenity. Since 1932 West has worked in Hollywood where she has often put her own salacious spin on her lines.

Though it may appear harsh, the NBC ban is unlikely to derail the career of a woman who thrives on controversy.

Dorothy Crowfoot Hodgkin Awarded PhD

Cambridge, England: One of the world's most innovative chemists, Dorothy Crowfoot Hodgkin, has been awarded a doctorate from Cambridge University.

Hodgkin was born in 1910 in Cairo, Egypt. Her father was an archeologist and classics scholar, her mother an archeologist, specialist in textiles, and botanist. Hodgkin's interest in science began early: as a child, she and her sister used a mineral analysis kit to study interesting pebbles they found in the garden of their home in Khartoum, Sudan.

Dorothy was 15 when her mother gave her a copy of Sir William Henry Bragg's *Concerning the Nature of Things*, a landmark book which discusses how X-rays could be used to study atoms and molecules.

Hodgkin entered Oxford University, enrolling at Somerville College, where she studied physics and chemistry. After graduating from Oxford, she attended

The famous American blues singer, Bessie Smith.

Cambridge University to study with John Desmond Bernal, a protégé of Sir William Henry Bragg. Hodgkin and Bernal pursued their shared interest in the relatively new science of X-ray crystallography, which tries to determine the structure of molecules in a substance to understand the practical uses of that substance, particularly in medicine. Since 1934, Hodgkin has been studying the complex molecular structure of insulin.

This year she and Thomas Hodgkin, who is a historian, were married.

Advocate of Women's Rights Dies

Edinburgh, Scotland: Jessie Chrystal Macmillan, the first woman to graduate with a degree in science from Scotland's distinguished University of Edinburgh, and the first woman to plead a case before the British House of Lords, has died. She was 55 years old.

Born in Edinburgh in 1882, daughter of a wealthy tea merchant, Macmillan began her education at St Andrews, then she transferred to the University of Edinburgh where she received a master's degree in 1900. In her appearance before the House of Lords in 1908, Macmillan argued that women with university degrees should be permitted to vote. The Lords rejected her appeal.

In spite of this setback, Macmillan remained devoted to the cause of women's rights. She was especially active in trying to overturn the law that stripped a British woman of her citizenship if she chose to marry a foreigner.

Perhaps the most pressing issue for women during the early years of the twentieth century was suffrage. From 1913 to 1920, Macmillan was secretary of the International Woman Suffrage Alliance. During that period she helped organize the International Congress of Women, which met in the Hague in 1915 to discuss how women could play a greater role in politics and in society at large.

During the Great War, Macmillan worked to relieve the suffering of Belgian refugees, and helped draw up a list of proposals intended to stop the war. After the war, Macmillan served as a delegate to the 1919 Paris Peace Conference.

Macmillan became a lawyer in 1924. She ran for parliament in 1935 but was defeated.

Out of Africa and into the Bookstores

Denmark and England: Isak Dinesen, author of the popular *Seven Gothic Tales*, has just published a memoir of the years she spent running a 6,000-acre (2,430 ha)

The Great Ziegfeld won Best Picture this year.

coffee plantation in British East Africa. Titled *Out of Africa*, Dinesen (the pen name of Baroness Karen Blixen-Finecke; she married her cousin Baron Blixen-Finecke) offers her readers an intimate account of her life in Africa, including her close friendship with her chief servant, a Somali named Farah, and her romance with big-game hunter Denys Finch Hatton.

Unlike other colonial writers, Dinesen insists that the most profound difference between Europeans and Africans is not race but historical experience. European civilization is now largely mechanized and commercial, while the African civilizations are still primarily pastoral and agricultural. Dinesen is enchanted by traditional life in Africa, but fears that the temptation to adopt European technology will destroy the old ways forever.

Another Political First for the Nehru Family

Uttar Pradesh, India: In a sharp break with tradition, Vijaya Lakshmi Pandit has been elected to the legislative assembly of the United Provinces of India. Pandit is the first woman to hold elective office in India. She will serve as minister for self-government and public health in Uttar Pradesh.

Pandit belongs to a family that for decades has been in the forefront of the struggle for Indian independence. Her father, Motilal Nehru, was twice president of the Congress Party, and chaired the commission that produced the Nehru Report (1928), the first Indian constitution. Because the Nehru Report called for dominion status by which India would remain a member of the British Empire, it was rejected by activists who insisted on complete independence and absolute sovereignty for India. Ironically, one of those activists who rejected the Nehru Report was Pandit's brother, Jawaharlal Nehru, the most charismatic proponent of the Indian independence movement.

After 1916, the Nehru family formed a political partnership with Mahatma Gandhi. Under his influence they gave up western-style clothing and dressed in traditional Hindu garb. The entire family became politically active, taking part in mass demonstrations of public disobedience. As a result Pandit, her mother, her sisters, and her brother Jawaharlal have all been arrested by the British and served several prison terms.

Vijaya Lakshmi Pandit

Danish writer Isak Dinesen on safari in British East Africa, where she ran a coffee plantation for many years.

Rosa Mayreder

"FASHION EXISTS FOR WOMEN WITH NO TASTE, ETIQUETTE FOR PEOPLE WITH NO BREEDING."

QUEEN MARIE OF ROMANIA (1875–1938), BRITISH-ROMANIAN ROYAL, 1938

Pioneer of Native American Rights Passes

Washington, USA, January 25: Gertrude Simmons Bonnin was better known as Red Bird (Zitkala-Sa in the language of the Sioux). She became the voice of many tribes, and was a tireless campaigner for Native American causes right up until her death today at sixty-one.

Born on the Yankton Reservation in South Dakota in 1876, she remained in the local school until she was eight, when she was sent to a Quaker academy, White's Institute, in nearby Wabash, Indiana. Her "white" education continued at Earlham College, where she won a prize for oratory. As a teacher at the Carlisle Indian School in Pennsylvania, she harbored a strong desire to be a writer, as well as a talent for the violin (which she fostered at the Boston Conservatory and which led to her composition of an opera based upon the Plains Sun Dance). Her short fiction was published by the prestigious *Harper's* magazine, and *Atlantic Monthly* ran her autobiographical essays.

When Red Bird returned to the reservation, marrying a Sioux named Raymond T. Bonnin in May, 1902, and having a son in 1903, her work as an activist began. She taught for the United States Indian Service, a division of the Federal Bureau of Indian Affairs, which promoted an "assimilationist" policy of mainstreaming Native Americans. Ultimately, Red Bird felt that she could achieve more for her people through civil rights activism.

In 1916 she moved to Washington DC, where she was particularly adroit at using women's networks to generate interest in Native American rights and welfare. Thanks to her efforts, President Hoover's administration convened a commission in 1928 to investigate conditions on the reservations. The findings prompted swift action under Franklin Roosevelt's New Deal. Red Bird's legacy also includes the founding of the Council of American Indians.

And the Oscar Goes to...Luise Rainer

Hollywood, USA, March 10: The popular acclaim for Pearl S. Buck's *The Good Earth* has not stopped with her best-selling novel. The blockbuster movie that was based upon it has this year hit Oscar gold.

Luise Rainer has won Best Actress for her depiction of O-lan, a peasant girl beset by hardship. A German-Jewish refugee, Rainer identified with the role of the displaced victim of oppression. The film also won Oscars for best director, editor, cinematography, and production. Rainer and the cast, including Paul Muni as Wang Lung, wore a new type of make-up designed to evoke Asian faces.

The Oscar was the second in back-to-back wins for Rainer, who captured best actress honors the year before for her role in *The Great Ziegfeld.*

time out

The *New York Post* fires its financial reporters and replaces them with Sylvia Porter, who is to carry out all their duties as well as write her own column. She uses the byline S. F. Porter to keep her gender under wraps.

Luise Rainer proudly holds her Oscar for Best Actress.

Rape and Mass Slaughter in Nanking

Nanking, China, March: Much more than just a metaphor for one of the most devastating examples of wartime atrocity, the "Rape of Nanking" has seen the literal raping of more than 20,000 Chinese women and young girls, most of them subsequently murdered.

The city of Nanking fell to the Japanese on December 13 last year and the period since then has been filled with horror, as recent reports have revealed.

Japanese soldiers, intoxicated not only by alcohol but by the suspension of discipline and morality, have roamed the city in packs of a dozen or more looking for women to assault. Many women who somehow survived the initial attacks were rounded up by Japanese soldiers, on orders from the infamous General Iwane Matsui, as well as Prince Asaka, an uncle of Emperor Hirohito, and pressed into service in brothels.

The carnage has taken on unprecedented proportions. The city had been flooded with more than 100,000 refugees who had fled the marauding Japanese invaders over the past months. These people have been shot on sight.

Since the fall of the city, at least 300,000 civilians and soldiers have been killed. Eyewitnesses have related how some people were lined up and used for machine-gun target practice, while others were methodically bayoneted and left in the street to die. The Nanking Red Cross has reported that they have buried more than 40,000 bodies.

Key Events

London, England, January 3: The government plans to provide all schoolchildren with gas masks.

Vienna, Austria, January 19: Women's rights campaigner and writer, Rosa Mayreder, dies, aged 79. She was a former head of the International Women's League for Peace and Liberty.

Washington, USA, January 25: Gertrude Simmons Bonnin, also known as Zitkala-Sa (Red Bird), writer and campaigner for Native American rights, dies, aged 61.

London, England, January: Art collector, Peggy Guggenheim, opens the Guggenheim-Jeune art gallery. Her first exhibition shows works by Cocteau.

Oxford, England, February: The drug, diethylstilbestrol (DES), is synthesized.

Saudi Arabia, March 3: Oil is discovered in Saudi Arabia.

Hollywood, USA, March 10: Luise Rainer wins the Best Actress Academy Award for her performance in *The Good Earth,* based on the novel by Pearl S. Buck.

Nanking, China, March: Japanese troops slaughter up to 300,000 civilians and prisoners of war in a massacre.

Paris, France, April 7: Suzanne Valadon, artist and model for Degas, Renoir, and Toulouse-Lautrec, among others, dies, aged 73.

Toronto, Canada, May 26: Soprano Teresa Stratas is born.

Berlin, Germany, June 20: Communist resistance activist, Liselotte Hermann, convicted of treason, is beheaded, a few days before her twenty-ninth birthday.

USA, June: The *Helen Keller Journals* are published, in which Keller recalls four decades with her teacher and friend Anne Sullivan Macy.

Doncaster, England, July 20: Film and television actress, Diana Rigg, is born.

Miami, Florida, USA, July 21: Janet Reno, the first female Attorney-General of the USA, is born.

Rome, Italy, August 3: Mussolini introduces his anti-Semitic laws into Italy, following the lead of his German allies.

Hollywood, USA, August 26: Norma Shearer plays the title role in *Marie Antoinette* opposite Tyrone Power and John Barrymore.

Zagreb, Croatia, September 21: Writer Ivana Brlic-Mazuranic, twice nominated for the Nobel Prize for Literature, commits suicide, aged 64.

Czechoslovakia, October 5: Hitler's army marches into Czechoslovakia.

Hollywood, USA, November 1: Margaret Lockwood and Michael Redgrave star in Alfred Hitchcock's movie, the suspense thriller *The Lady Vanishes.*

The End of an Era: Model and Muse Dies at 73

Paris, France, April 7: Where would art be without its muses? The history of painting in Europe would look vastly different if the face of Suzanne Valadon were deleted from its pages.

Valadon held her pose for an astonishing three generations of great painters in Paris, and gave birth to a major figure of the third (the painter Maurice Utrillo was her illegitimate son).

Helen Wills-Moody

Thousands of recruits have joined the Women's Auxiliary Territorial Service, formed this year to provide the British army with cooks, cleaners and signalers.

She began life as Marie-Clementine Valadon, a laundress (also the illegitimate daughter of a laundress) and seamstress whose side jobs included a period as a circus acrobat at a time when such artists as Seurat, Lautrec, Degas, Picasso, and others were turning to acrobats and clowns for their subject matter. She was in the studio often enough to pick up a few technical pointers of her own, and soon began painting.

Valadon posed (and more) for the influential muralist, Puvis de Chavannes, who discovered her. Her smoldering beauty inspired the Impressionist painter Pierre Auguste Renoir, as well as the Post-Impressionist master Henri de Toulouse-Lautrec, and the Modernist star Pablo Picasso. She was a dear friend of Degas, who, when she first began making her own paintings, bought three of her works at one of her highly successful gallery exhibitions, starting in 1915. She was also the lover of the inventive Modernist composer Erik Satie.

Suzanne Valadon's legacy also includes giving birth to a major artist. Her son was Maurice Utrillo, whose streetscapes of Montmartre carved a special niche in the School of Paris, a group that included Marc Chagall, Joan Miro, Henri Matisse, Amadeo Modigliani, and, of course, Pablo Picasso. Utrillo was unfortunately one of the most violent alcoholics of Montparnasse, and Valadon in her later years, especially during her 14-year-long marriage to a respectable banker named Paul Moussis, did her best to keep him out of jail. Valadon's funeral was attended by the new generation of the School of Paris, including Picasso, Georges Braque, and Andre Derain.

Prominent Writer Commits Suicide

Zagreb, Croatia, September 21: Ivana Brlic-Mazuranic, one of the most popular writers in Europe at one time, has taken her own life. She was 64 years of age.

Born in Ogulin on April 18, 1874, Brlic-Mazuranic was the accomplished scion of a renowned Croatian family, the granddaughter of Ivan Mazuranic, poet and statesman, and the daughter of Vladimir Mazuranic, a prominent lawyer and historian. In 1892 she allied her famous family with another of Croatia's leading political families by marriage. Her husband, Fabroslav Brlic, was a lawyer and government official, himself related to the writer Ignjat Alojzije, and the journalist and politician Andrija Tokvart Brlic.

Brlic-Mazuranic's first published works were in French. She gained international fame for her stories and was dubbed the "Croatian Hans Christian Andersen" after her popular collection, *Tales of Long Ago,* was published in 1916. Widely translated, she was nominated for a Nobel Prize for Literature in 1931 and 1938, and in 1937 became the first woman ever elected to the Croatian Academy of Sciences and Arts.

She had six children, for whom the books she wrote were educational texts, and critics agree that her insight into the minds of children was extraordinary. Her insight makes it all the more astonishing that she would take her own life.

Norma Shearer as Marie Antoinette in the film of the same name.

Key Events

Pennsylvania, USA, November 8: Crystal Bird Fauset is the first African-American woman elected to a state legislature.

Berlin, Germany, November 9: Jewish shops, homes, and synagogues are looted and destroyed as Hitler puts into practice throughout Germany his anti-Jewish policies.

Stockholm, Sweden, December 10: American author, Pearl S. Buck, wins the Nobel Prize in Literature for her novel, *The Good Earth.*

East London, South Africa, December 22: Naturalist Marjorie Courtenay-Latimer identifies a coelacanth, a fish thought to be extinct, when it is hauled up in a fishing trawler.

London, England, December: Gracie Fields stars in the musical comedy film, *Keep Smiling.*

New York, USA: Doctor Dorothy Hansine Andersen discovers that cystic fibrosis is a distinctive disease, and begins working on a means of diagnosis.

Buenos Aires, Argentina: Chilean-born poet and feminist, Gabriela Mistral (Lucila Godoy y Alcayaga), publishes *Tala,* dealing with themes of motherhood and childhood.

Bolivia and Uzbekistan: Women are granted the right to vote.

China: Former actress and later notorious political figure, Jiang Qing, marries Mao Tse-tung.

England: Physician, feminist, and politician Edith Summerskill establishes the Married Women's Association, which is aimed at achieving equality in marriage.

Harlem, New York, USA: Jazz singer Ella Fitzgerald records "A-Tisket, A-Tasket," a huge hit.

Dublin, Ireland: Revolutionary, actress, and feminist, Maude Gonne, publishes a memoir, *A Servant of the Queen.*

Shanxi Province, China: When Japanese forces invade the region, British missionary Gladys Aylward leads nearly 100 children to safety on a 27-day trek.

Hollywood, USA: Fashion designer Edith Head is the first woman chief designer in a major movie studio.

Bamburgh, Scotland: One hundred years after Grace Darling heroically rescued shipwrecked passengers off the Scottish coast, the Grace Darling National Memorial Museum opens to commemorate her bravery.

Norway: Women are permitted to join the military services.

California, USA: American tennis champion Helen Wills-Moody, who won this year's women's singles title at Wimbledon, announces her retirement from the sport.

Gracie Fields

Legislator Breaks the Color Barrier

Pennsylvania, USA, November 8: Crystal Bird Fauset has today been elected to the Pennsylvania State Legislature, representing Philadelphia's thirteenth district, and making history as the first African-American woman to be elected as a state legislator. The moment is all the more dramatic because more than two-thirds of the voters in her district are white.

Born in 1894, Crystal Bird's path to elected office followed a distinguished record in public service. In 1927, she had taken a staff position on the new Inter-racial Section of the American Friends Service Commission. She said she was interested "in having people of other racial groups understand the humanness of the Negro wherever he is found."

During literally hundreds of speaking engagements over the next year, from Philadelphia to New York, Washington, Boston, Baltimore, and Indiana, her message reached audiences totaling more than 40,000 listeners (and drove her nearly to exhaustion).

The Philadelphia Democrats invited Crystal Bird to become their candidate for the Pennsylvania House of Representatives earlier this year.

Biologist's Discovery: Giant Fish is New Species

East London, South Africa, December 22: One fisherman's prize catch may prove a biologist's dream come true. For the young scientist and curator of the provincial museum of East Londen, a small coastal town in the Eastern Province of South Africa, the hold of a fishing trawler may turn out to hold a treasure.

Marjorie Courtenay-Latimer had been informed of the capture of a strange fish by a local fishing captain named Hendrick Goosen. Today, she took a taxi down to the dock to greet Goosen's trawler, and below a pile of sharks on the deck she spotted a blue fin, the first glimpse of what she would describe as "the most beautiful fish I had ever seen, five feet long, and a pale mauve blue with iridescent silver markings."

She knew at once that the giant fish was a most unusual find, and sent a sketch of the mysterious specimen to a colleague. The fish, formerly seen only in fossils millions of years old, was confirmed to be a coelacanth, which was previously believed to be extinct.

Breakthrough Made in Cystic Fibrosis

New York, USA: Scientists have drawn closer to unraveling a baffling disease with the publication of Doctor Dorothy Hansine Andersen's very important findings on abnormalities of the pancreas and lungs, naming the combination cystic fibrosis.

Doctor Hansine Andersen is an American physician who gained her Bachelor of Arts degree from Mount Holyoke College in 1922, and earned her medical degree from the prestigious Johns Hopkins University four years later. She was on the faculty of the University of Rochester and then joined the Columbia College of Physicians and Surgeons, where she works at the Babies Hospital of the Columbia-Presbyterian Medical Center in uptown Manhattan.

Her next challenge is to develop a method for diagnosing the disease, and to find ways of treating it and hopefully curing it.

Aylward Leads Children to Safety

Shanxi Province, China: Gladys Aylward is an unlikely heroine in many ways. The daughter of a postman, she was born in the London suburb of Edmonton on February 24, 1902. At 14, she became a parlor maid. Four years later, during a revival meeting, she discovered her calling, and in her mid-twenties applied for mission work. She was rejected for a posting in China on the grounds that her academic background was not sufficient.

Physician, feminist, and politician Edith Summerskill works tirelessly to improve the lives of women in England.

It took a back door to get her into China, offered in the form of a position as personal assistant to an older missionary, Jeannie Lawson, who could not even pay Aylward's passage. So with two pounds nine pence in savings, she booked steerage and began the long voyage to Yangchen, a remote town in the mountains of Shanxi province, southwest of Beijing. The mission was housed in an old inn that served the trade route along which mule caravans passed.

When Mrs Lawson was injured in a fall and died, Aylward was left alone to care for the mission. It had by now become a sanctuary for children and refugees from a particularly chaotic time in Chinese history. The province had become a battleground across which various heavily armed factions waged war, including the Japanese, who were closing in on Peking along with the warlords and Communist troops contending for domestic sovereignty.

Aylward and her brave Chinese cook, a stalwart partner in her struggle, found themselves besieged by the great tide of refugees. From 20 orphans, most of them small children, they soon found themselves tending to around 100 children and dozens of injured Chinese adults, including soldiers.

Gladys Aylward's commitment to the local people prompted her to become a citizen of China in 1936. She was known as Ai-weh-deh (a phonetic transcription of her last name that happens also to pun on "Virtuous One.")

The refugee crisis reached breaking point this year. In addition, the Japanese placed a bounty on Aylward's head (for spying). Tipped off about an imminent

Marjorie Courtenay-Latimer has identified the coelacanth.

One hundred years ago, 22-year-old Grace Darling rowed through raging seas to rescue shipwrecked passengers off the coast of Scotland. Her heroism has been commemorated with the opening of a museum.

Paramount Picks Edith Head as Design Chief

Hollywood, USA: From its rough-and-ready days as a boomtown in the Roaring Twenties, not unlike the gold rush of an earlier moment in California history, Hollywood has been a man's world, where only the toughest survived. Women may have been stars on-screen, but with few exceptions they were strictly supporting cast in the power structures of the major studios.

Gabriela Mistral

So heads were certainly turned today when Edith Head was named chief designer at Paramount Pictures, the town's most powerful studio.

Edith Claire Posener studied art at the Otist Art Institute and the Chouinard School of Art, after gaining a master's degree in romance languages in 1920. In 1923 she began working at the Paramount studios as a sketch artist for Howard Greer, and was later promoted to designer, under Travis Banton.

The announcement that she will take over from Banton, her mentor, is a tribute

raid by Colonel Linnan, a local warlord, Aylward decided to cast the fate of the children in her care on a desperate trek across the mountains to the ancient capital of Xian. The seemingly impossible 100-mile (160 km) march to safety took 27 days and left many of them, including Aylward, on the brink of death from fatal illnesses (including typhus and pneumonia) and totally exhausted.

Nobel Goes to Pearl S. Buck, Laureate of China

Stockholm, Sweden, December 10: The first Nobel Prize in Literature awarded to a woman has been conferred on Pearl S. Buck, the controversial American novelist whose sagas of contemporary China have drawn crowds to bookstores and ignited

Pearl S. Buck receives news of her Nobel Prize.

floor fights in Congress between members with differing views on China.

Buck snared the Pulitzer Prize in 1932 for *The Good Earth*, her idealistic novel trumpeting the virtues of Mao Tse-tung's ideals for the "New China." Filled with a quasi-religious zeal and intimate knowledge of China's landscape and people (Buck's parents were missionaries and she grew up in Zhenjiang, a small city on the Yangtze River), it was the opening volume in an ambitious historical fiction trilogy called *The House of Earth*, completed in 1935 (the other volumes were *Sons* and *A House Divided*).

The trilogy leapt to the top of the bestseller lists and became a flashpoint in the political debate over whether the west should support Mao and the Communists or the Kuomintang ("Nationalist") Party of Chiang Kai-shek, which had decamped to the island of Taiwan.

Buck's tear-jerking and thrill-packed saga presented to a mass audience in the United States her heroic version of Mao's quest to change Asia. Some considered it propaganda, but most concede that Buck's novels, two volumes of memoirs, and translation of the Chinese classic, *All Men Are Brothers* (1933), succeeded in opening a door to Chinese culture, which for decades had been misunderstood in the west.

Buck was born Pearl Comfort Sydenstricker in Hillsboro, West Virginia, in 1892, but her first memories were of her childhood in China. She married John L. Buck in 1917, and they went through a very public and painful divorce in 1934.

Winning the two top accolades in all of literature, a Pulitzer Prize and the Nobel Prize, is a remarkable achievement.

Edith Head has changed the status quo in Hollywood.

to her extraordinary work ethic, which may also have contributed to her failing marriage to Charles Head.

She has so far designed costumes for Clara Bow, Mae West, Frances Farmer, and Dorothy Lamour, among a host of others. The sarong she created for Dorothy Lamour in *The Jungle Princess* has altered fashion history.

Tallulah Bankhead

New Play Outfoxes Playwright's Family

Broadway, USA February 16: Lillian Hellman's new play, *The Little Foxes*, opened last night on Broadway. It stars the notorious actress Tallulah Bankhead in the lead role of Regina. The title of the play is taken from chapter 2, verse 15 of the Old Testament book, Song of Solomon:

Take us the foxes, the little foxes that spoil the vines: for our vines have tender grapes.

A story of avarice and a woman who knows no boundaries when it comes to achieving her ends, *The Little Foxes* promises to be one of this season's successes. Hellman makes no secret of the fact that the play's characters are based on her family; it is thought that Regina is modeled on her grandmother, Sophie.

Lillian Hellman's previous successes include *The Children's Hour* (1934), a play about the revenge that a rebellious girl wreaks on the two headmistresses of her boarding school when she announces they are lesbians; and *The Dark Angel*, Hellman's adaptation of the Guy Bolton novel for the movie that stars Frederic March and Merle Oberon.

First Lady's Protest Concert

Washington DC, USA, April 10: A decision by the Daughters of the American Revolution (DAR) in January to deny world-renowned African-American opera star, Marian Anderson, an engagement at Constitution Hall so enraged First Lady Eleanor Roosevelt that she resigned from the DAR. Then she set about arranging for one of the world's greatest contraltos to sing for her thousands of fans.

Yesterday, Marian Anderson sang to an audience of 75,000 on the steps of the Lincoln Memorial. Anderson began the concert singing "America," which she followed with an Italian aria. Next came

"WRITING IS NOT AN AMUSING OCCUPATION. IT IS A COMBINATION OF DITCH-DIGGING, MOUNTAIN-CLIMBING, TREADMILL AND CHILDBIRTH. WRITING MAY BE INTER-ESTING, ABSORBING, EXHILARATING, RACKING, RELIEVING. BUT AMUSING? NEVER!"

EDNA FERBER,
AMERICAN WRITER
A PECULIAR TREASURE

Marian Anderson sings at Lincoln Memorial in April.

"Ave Maria," composed by Franz Schubert, and then three of her favorite African-American spirituals, "Gospel Train," "Trampin'," and "My Soul is Anchored in the Lord." She also included "Nobody Knows the Trouble I've Seen."

Anderson's illustrious career began in 1925 when, at the age of 28, she won first prize in the New York Philharmonic voice competition. The following year she left for Europe and returned in 1930 to perform at Carnegie Hall. Since then she has toured Europe, Africa, and South America where she was a box-office sensation.

It was her manager, impresario Sol Hurok, who decided it was time that Anderson sang at a major hall in the nation's capital. But he had not reckoned with the clause in the contract that stipulated that the hall was for concerts by "white artists only, and for

no other purpose." The resignation of Mrs Roosevelt from the Daughters of the American Revolution was followed by those of other prominent women.

Star of *Marta of the Lowlands* Dies

New York, USA, April 19: The Polish-born actress Bertha Kalich, star of New York's Yiddish theater scene, died yesterday, at the age of sixty-four. Kalich, who was born in Lemberg, was known for her roles as women of the world on both stage and screen. Her most famous parts were in Henrik Ibsen's *A Doll's House*, Sardou's *Fedora*, Maurice Maeterlink's *Monna Vanna*, and Àngel Guimerà's *Marta of the Lowlands*. In the latter she starred in both the original stage version and the film alongside Wellington A. Playter as the love interest Manelich.

Described as a "dramatic actress of exceptional talent," Kalich also won great acclaim for her role as Ophelia in Shakespeare's *Hamlet*.

Bertha Kalich will be buried at the Mount Hebron Cemetery, in New York.

Billie Holiday's Powerful Protest Song

New York, USA, April: Billie Holiday first sang her new song "Strange Fruit" at Barney Josephson's Café Society, New York's first integrated nightclub, in March. However, her record company, Columbia, refused to record her singing it. Now, 24-year-old Holiday has persuaded Milton Gabler, the owner of a small record label, Commodore Records, to put out the song.

Since it was first heard, this protest song, written by Lewis Allan, has caused a great deal of controversy, partly because the composer and lyricist,

time out

The movie of Clare Booth Luce's play *The Women* is finally released. The screenplay for this hilarious exposé of women's maneuvers and manipu-lations was written by Anita Loos.

Paris, France, January 12: Romanian-born soprano Hariclea Darclée dies, aged 78.

Melbourne, Australia, January 29: Writer, scholar, and feminist Germaine Greer is born.

Washington DC, USA, January: The Daughters of the American Revolution refuse to let African-American singer Marian Anderson perform at Constitution Hall.

New York, USA, February 15: Lillian Hellman's new play *The Little Foxes* opens on Broadway with Tallulah Bankhead in the lead role.

Hollywood, USA, February 23: Bette Davis wins the Academy Award for Best Actress in the 1938 film *Jezebel*, co-starring Henry Fonda.

Czechoslovakia, March 16: The German army occupies Prague, and Czechoslovakia becomes a Nazi protectorate.

Spain, April 1: Franco declares the end of the Civil War.

New York, USA, April 18: Polish-born actress Bertha Kalich, a star of the city's Yiddish theater scene, dies, aged 64.

Oslo, Norway, April 20: Gro Harland Brundtland, later prime minister of Norway and director of the World Health Organization, is born.

New York, USA, April: Jazz singer Billie Holiday records "Strange Fruit," an anti-lynching song written by Lewis Allan (Abel Meeropol).

Cambridge, England, May 6: Dorothy Garrod is appointed the Disney Professor of Archeology at Cambridge University, the university's first woman professor.

Rome, Italy, May 22: Mussolini signs a military pact with Hitler, obligating Italy to fight alongside Germany.

Florida, USA, June 4: The USA denies entry to the *St Louis*, a ship carrying 907 Jewish refugees, after it is turned away by Cuba.

Sheffield, England, June 5: British novelist Margaret Drabble is born.

Britain, July: The Women's Land Army is re-formed after disbanding at the end of the Great War.

New York, USA, July 22: Jane M. Bolin is the first African-American woman to be appointed as a judge.

Europe, September 3: Britain and France declare war on Germany in accord with treaty obligations to Poland, followed by Australia, New Zealand, and India.

Fukushima Prefecture, Japan, September 22: Mountaineer Junko Tabei, the first woman to reach the top of Mt Everest, is born.

Poland, September 29: The Nazis and Soviets divide up Poland. More than 2 million Jews reside in Nazi-controlled areas, and 1.3 million in the Soviet area. Warsaw surrenders.

Judy Garland as Dorothy in the popular film *The Wizard of Oz*.

Kahlo's Self-Portrait

Mexico City, Mexico: Frida Kahlo, the renowned Mexican artist who painted her first self-portrait in 1926, has painted a double self-portrait which she calls *The Two Fridas*. Kahlo paints in the style of Mexican ex-voto, a Catholic tradition in which the painting is done as an offering of thanks for salvation from adversity. However, Kahlo's paintings are not expressions of gratitude, rather they are depictions of traumatic events in her own life.

The Two Fridas conveys Kahlo's anguish over her divorce from her husband, artist Diego Rivera. The Frida on the right sits in traditional Mexican costume, holding a picture of Diego as a child. Her exposed heart is whole.

The Frida on the left is dressed in a Victorian lace wedding dress and holding a pair of scissors, her bisected heart dripping blood onto her lap. The painting has also been described as representing the conflict felt by those known as *mestizos* whose heritage is a mix of Mexican and European. Kahlo's father is German and her mother has a mixed Mexican-Spanish background.

Kahlo has painted *The Two Fridas* for the International Exhibition of Surrealism, to be held in Mexico City next year.

New Theory on Neuroses

New York, USA: Psychoanalyst Karen Horney has published *New Ways in Psychoanalysis,* following on from her highly successful *The Neurotic Personality of our Time,* published two years ago. In this new book Horney describes the ways that neuroses function as a peculiar struggle for life under adverse conditions. Horney continues to expand on her theory that diverges from Freud's biological orientation and places emphasis on culture and interpersonal relationships. She explains that neuroses are a result of adverse conditions in the environment as a whole, and especially in the family, which, she says, create a basic anxiety against which a child defends itself by developing strategies of defense that are self-alienating, self-defeating, and in conflict with each other.

As Karen Horney continues to work in the field of psychoanalysis and explores these theories, we can expect that she will produce more works of great interest.

Marjorie Kinnan Rawlings

such as whooping cough bring to families, especially the poor who are not able to afford medical help. They will continue to work in the field developing vaccines that help prevent childhood diseases.

New Element Identified

Paris, France: After a number of false claims by other scientists, it appears that Marguerite Perey of the Curie Institute in Paris has discovered a new element. It has been known until now as element 87, and while Perey at first thought to call it catium, she has now decided it will be given the name francium and assigned the symbol Fr. This element is the first naturally occurring element to have been discovered since rhenium in 1925.

Perey isolated francium when studying the radioactive decay of the element actinium. Actinium and other radioactive elements break apart spontaneously, and when this happens they give off energy and particles, thus forming new, simpler elements. Perey's research showed that while 99 percent of actinium atoms decay into thorium, the remaining one percent decays into a different element. Chemists in Russia, England, the United States, and France have claimed the discovery of this element over the years; however, all these claims were found to be erroneous.

There is debate about how rare this element is. Some say it is the second rarest element in the crust after astatine; others that is the rarest element found on Earth's surface and that there may be only about half an ounce (15 g) of it in existence.

Perey has been working at the Radium Institute, founded by Marie Curie and her husband Pierre Curie, for many years.

Frida Kahlo and Diego Rivera, with Kahlo's painting *The Two Fridas* hanging on the wall in the background.

Mrs Patrick Campbell

British Feel the Pinch from Food Rationing

London, England, January 8: Severe shortages have caused the introduction of food rationing in Great Britain, as German submarines attack convoys of merchant ships carrying food and other imports to Great Britain from the United States. Accordingly, the Ministry of Food has announced that supplies of sugar, butter, lard, ham, and bacon will be very strictly controlled, and from now on consumers must redeem government-issued coupons to obtain these products.

It is anticipated that other foods such as eggs, milk, and fruit may soon be added to the list, along with such necessities as soap and clothes. The ministry stated that restaurants, cafés, and pubs serving meals will not be rationed by customers' coupons. Instead, they will receive permits for rationed foods on the basis of the number of meals they serve. People with relatives or friends in friendly countries such as Australia, Canada, or the USA may receive food parcels without affecting their ration entitlements. People are urged to harvest wild rosehips and other edible wild plants, and hand them in to regional Women's Institute collection centers.

Food preparation will be difficult, but the home economics skills of British women have been well developed over many years of lean times since the Depression, so they will be particularly well placed to cope with rationing. The ministry has recognized that such expertise will be a vital strategic asset on what it calls "the kitchen front."

> *"IT ISN'T WHERE YOU CAME FROM, IT'S WHERE YOU'RE GOING THAT COUNTS."*
>
> ELLA FITZGERALD (1917–1996), AMERICAN JAZZ SINGER

Wartime shortages have led to food rationing in Great Britain.

Southern Epic Scoops Pool

Hollywood, USA, March 1: David O. Selznick's American Civil War blockbuster *Gone With the Wind* dominated last night's Academy Award presentations, winning seven of 13 nominated categories. Along with the prestigious Best Picture and Best Director, it was also saluted in the categories of Best Screenplay, Color Cinematography, and Art Direction. As expected, the brilliant performance of British-born Vivien Leigh as heroine Scarlett O'Hara gained the Best Actress prize, but—surprisingly to many—Clark Gable as the ultra-urbane Rhett Butler was pipped for Best Actor. Hattie McDaniel, playing Mammy, won Best Supporting Actress, becoming the first African-American to win an Oscar.

Last year's gala première in Atlanta, Georgia, was blighted by racial politics. As Georgia is a segregated state, "Hi-Hat" McDaniel and the other African-American cast members were not invited. Clark Gable threatened to boycott the première unless McDaniel and the others were able to attend, later relenting after McDaniel persuaded him to go.

Vivien Leigh and Hattie McDaniel in *Gone with the Wind*.

McDaniel, a well-respected and seasoned radio and screen star, has been criticized for playing maids and other subordinate, stereotypical roles—but in fact she has long worked behind the scenes to battle racism and discrimination. She said: "I'd rather play a maid f or $700 a day than be one for $7 a day."

At the awards ceremony, the loudest ovation of the evening went to McDaniel. After giving her acceptance speech she broke down in tears of joy and left the stage. She has said that her favorite expression is "Humble is the way."

Gone With the Wind is the longest Hollywood movie ever made, and many are saying it is also the best. Rhett Butler's "Frankly my dear, I don't give a damn!" and Scarlett's poignant famous last words, "Tomorrow is another day…," are destined to achieve cinematic immortality.

Death of a Nobel Laureate

Sweden, March 16: Swedish writer Selma Lagerlöf, who in 1909 became the first woman to win the Nobel Prize for Literature, has died in Sweden at 81 years of age. In his Nobel presentation speech, Claes Annerstedt, president of the Swedish Academy, said: "The greatness of her art consists precisely in her ability to use her heart as well as her genius to give to the original peculiar character and attitudes of the people a shape in which we recognize ourselves."

Lagerlöf was born in Östra Emterwik, Sweden, and brought up on Mårbacka, the family estate, which she left in 1881 to attend teachers' college in Stockholm.

She was a gifted child and a voracious reader—she read her first novel at the age of seven, and the entire Bible by the age of ten. She achieved fame in 1891 with her first novel, *Gösta Berlings saga (The Story of Gösta Berling)* and quit teaching in 1895 to write full-time. In 1914 Lagerlöf became the first female member of the Swedish Academy, the body that awards the Nobel Prize.

Her other publications include: *Antikrists Mirakler (The miracles of Anti-Christ)*, 1897; the children's book *Nils Holgerssons underbara resa genom Sverige (The Wonderful Adventures of Nils)*, 1906; and the historical trilogy *Löwensköldska ringen (The Ring of the Löwenskölds)*, 1925, *Charlotte Löwensköld*, 1927, and *Anna Svärd*, 1928. Her reminiscences under the title *Mårbacka* appeared from 1922 to 1932. Mårbacka will be preserved as a museum.

Selma Lagerlöf.

Sweden has lost a great writer in Selma Lagerlöf.

roles included Ophelia in *Hamlet* (1896) and the title role in *Hedda Gabler* (1907). Her verbal *bon mots* were legendary, including (of homosexuals): "Does it really matter what these affectionate people do—so long as they don't do it in the streets and frighten the horses?" Despite the death of her husband in 1900, she continued to use "Mrs Patrick Campbell" as her stage name, and was affectionately known as "Mrs Pat."

Acclaimed Actress "Mrs Pat" Dies

Aquitaine, France, April 9: The highly acclaimed British stage and film actress Mrs Patrick Campbell (Beatrice Stella Tanner) died today in Pau, France. The feisty thespian is perhaps most famous for her role as Eliza Doolittle in the original 1914 London production of *Pygmalion,* which George Bernard Shaw wrote for her.

From 1888 to 1930 Mrs Campbell pursued a rich and varied stage career in London and on Broadway, before moving to Hollywood. Her many celebrated stage

time out

Eleanor Roosevelt, possibly the USA's most progressive first lady, uses her position publicly to personally endorse birth control. Her stance has not endeared her to America's Catholic population.

Anarchist "Red Emma" Passes

Toronto, Canada, May 14:
The Lithuanian activist and anarchist Emma Goldman, widely known as "Red Emma," has died of a stroke in Toronto, aged seventy. Goldman was born in 1869 and grew up in Russian-controlled Kaunas, Lithuania, where her Jewish family ran a small inn. After suffering discrimination the family moved to St Petersburg in 1882. Poverty forced

Goldman to leave school after six months and work in a glove factory, where she was introduced to the concept of revolutionary violence as a tool for social change.

In 1885 she went to Rochester, New York, where she worked in a textile factory and joined the New York anarchists, becoming an agitator against tyrannical employers. She was jailed in 1893 for incitement to riot in New York after saying, "Ask for work. If they do not give you work, ask for bread. If they do not give you work or bread, take bread." She won increasing international fame for her stirring speeches, and addressed anarchist conferences in Paris (1899) and Amsterdam (1907).

In 1906 she founded the anarchist monthly *Mother Earth*, and in 1917 was fined $10,000 and jailed for two years for opposing military recruitment. In 1919, Goldman was deported to Russia but returned to the United States in 1924 to work in urban slums. She published an autobiography, *Living My Life* (1931), and several anarchist works.

Vivien Leigh

Lithuanian activist, the late "Red Emma" Goldman.

Paris, France, June: Following the German occupation of France, scientists Irène Joliot-Curie and her husband Frédéric Joliot send their heavy water to England for safekeeping, and hide their stockpile of uranium. They also apply for patents for the utilization of atomic energy, and win the Barnard College Gold Medal for meritorious service to science.

USA, June: The 23-year-old writer Carson McCullers causes a stir in the literary world when she publishes *The Heart is a Lonely Hunter.*

London, England, June: Princess Juliana of the Netherlands is sent to Canada to establish a government-in-exile.

Hollywood, USA, July 26: The movie *Pride and Prejudice,* based on Jane Austen's novel, opens. It stars Greer Garson, Laurence Olivier, and Maureen O'Sullivan.

Coyoacán, Mexico, August 21: Soviet leader Leon Trotsky is assassinated with an ice-pick.

Lascaux, France, September 12: Four schoolboys discover Paleolithic paintings in a cave.

Berlin, Germany, September 27: Japan, Germany, and Italy sign a 10-year pact.

London, England, September: Buckingham Palace is bombed several times with the royal family in residence.

London, England, November 7: The Women's Corps, which reports to the Free French Forces, is established.

UK, November 30: Germany mass-bombs regional cities Glasgow, Birmingham, Coventry, Manchester, and Sheffield.

Hollywood, USA, December 1: *The Philadelphia Story,* starring Katharine Hepburn, Cary Grant, and James Stewart, is released.

England, December 17: Amateur mathematician Alicia Boole Stott dies, aged 80.

Hollywood, USA: Photographer Ruth Harriet Louise, MGM studio's official photographer and the only female portrait photographer working in Hollywood, dies of complications in childbirth, aged 37.

New York, USA: Founding member of the American Civil Liberties Union, Elizabeth Gurley Flynn, is expelled for being a Communist.

USA: The Equal Rights Amendment to the constitution, proposed in 1925, is endorsed by the Republican Party.

Greece: Journalist and women's rights campaigner Kalliroe Parren dies, aged about 79.

USA: American anthropologist Ruth Benedict publishes *Race: Science and Politics,* in which she attacks racism and other forms of bigotry.

Katharine Hepburn

Danish Painter Marie Krøyer Dies at 72

Stockholm, Sweden, May 25: Famous Danish painter Marie Martha Mathilde Triepcke Krøyer Alfvén, better known as Marie Krøyer, has died in Stockholm. Marie studied under various artists in Copenhagen, and debuted at Charlottenborg in 1888. Shortly after coming to Paris alone in December 1888—a daring move for a respectable young woman—Marie met artist and leading Danish cultural figure Peder Severin Krøyer and, after a whirlwind romance, married him in 1889 in Germany.

Willful and talented enough to overcome the inherent prejudices against a female artist, Marie Krøyer produced and exhibited numerous oils and watercolors, and designed furniture for rich and influential people. She divorced Peder in 1905, married Swedish composer Hugo Alfvén in 1912, and divorced him in 1936.

Dutch Princess Sets Up Government in Canada

London, England, June: Princess Juliana of the Netherlands has been sent to Canada by her mother, Queen Wilhelmina, to establish a government-in-exile. Last May 10, without warning—and despite repeated protests from the Dutch protesting their neutrality—the German army entered the Netherlands, killing thousands and forcing surrender within days. One of the Nazis' key objectives was to capture the Dutch royal family, but Wilhelmina managed to escape to England with Juliana and her family.

With England itself now facing invasion, the queen has decided to send the crown princess to safety in Canada with her husband of three years, Prince

"AUTHENTICITY IS SOMETHING I ALWAYS TRY TO AVOID."

DALE MESSICK, CARTOONIST, 1940

Princess Juliana and Queen Wilhelmina.

Bernhard zur Lippe-Biesterfeld, and their two daughters. Wilhelmina will stay in London to encourage the Dutch resistance. They all plan to return to the Netherlands if Germany loses the war.

Brenda Starr Breaks the Male Cartoonist Barrier

Chicago, USA, June 30: A new cartoon heroine has appeared in the Sunday comics section of the *New York Daily News* and other newspapers across the United States. Dale Messick has created *Brenda Starr, Reporter*, featuring a glamorous and adventurous newspaper journalist whose appearance is based on movie star Rita Hayworth.

Other female cartoonists have achieved success, including Edwina Dumm with *Little Orphan Annie*, but in the male-dominated world of cartooning, Messick is the first female artist to be syndicated. Messick said she wanted to produce a strip with a female protagonist who travels and has adventures more glamorous, exciting, and romantic than most reporters actually experience.

Originally named Dalia, Messick changed her first name to overcome the prejudice of male editors. She produced a number of strips with titles such as *Mimi the Mermaid, Peg and Pudy, Streamline Babies, Weegee,* and *The Strugglettes,* but none was accepted for publication.

Finding a publisher for *Brenda Starr, Reporter,* was not easy. Messick wanted to approach Joseph M. Patterson, publisher of the *New York Daily News* and head of the *Chicago Tribune-New York News* syndicate, but Patterson had said he wants nothing to do with women cartoonists,

"having tried one once." Patterson's girl Friday, Mollie Slott, is a friend of Messick and presented "Dale's" work to her boss.

Buckingham Palace Has Been Bombed

London, England, September 15: Queen Elizabeth, consort of King George VI, has responded defiantly to this week's German bombings of Buckingham Palace, saying: "Now I can look the East End in the face."

Last week Germany's Luftwaffe began conducting heavy, nightly bombing attacks on British centers. The air raids have caused great damage to much of London and other cities, started major fires on the London docks, and have so far killed more than 400 people. On September 10 the Buckingham Palace quadrangle and swimming pool were hit

Queen Elizabeth and King George VI survey the damage caused to Buckingham Palace.

by bombs, shattering many windows but leaving the royals unharmed. Two nights ago the palace chapel was destroyed, and coverage of this event has already been shown in cinemas. The king and queen were filmed inspecting their bombed home, the smiling queen immaculate in hat and matching coat. It shows the common suffering of rich and poor, and the determination of the royals to boost national morale by remaining with their subjects through this present danger.

It appears that the Nazis are targeting Buckingham Palace in the belief that its destruction will destroy the nation's will to resist. Air raid shelters have proved to be totally inadequate in the face of this bombing blitz, and the London populace has been taking nightly refuge in underground railway stations.

Activist Elizabeth Gurley Flynn attends a Communist Party rally.

Joan Fontaine

"Rebel Girl" Expelled

New York, USA: Activist and feminist Elizabeth Gurley Flynn, known as "the rebel girl" has been expelled from the American Civil Liberties Union (ACLU), despite being one of its founding members. The board has deemed that her membership of the Communist Party renders her unfit to retain her position. Introduced by her parents to socialism, Flynn was 16 when she gave her first speech, "What socialism will do for women," at New York's Harlem Socialist Club.

She was expelled from high school in 1906 for her political activities. The following year Flynn became a full-time organizer for the Industrial Workers of the World (IWW), organizing campaigns to support lowly paid and exploited workers in various industries all over the United States. Flynn was arrested ten times during this period, but never convicted. Author Theodore Dreiser described her as "an East Side Joan of Arc." During the IWW's Massachusetts textile strike of 1912, Flynn fell in love with anarchist organizer Carlo Tresca, living with him for the next 12 years. In 1917 she founded the International Liberty Defense League (later the Workers' Liberty Defense Union).

In 1920, she co-founded the ACLU, and served on the board until her expulsion. She became active in the campaign to free two anarchists, Nicola Sacco and Bartolomeo Vanzetti, who were charged with murder. Though the case was an international *cause célèbre,* the two were executed in 1927 despite a lack of evidence—and the confession of another man. In 1936, Flynn joined the Communist Party and wrote a feminist column for its journal, *The Daily Worker.* Two years later she was elected to the national committee.

Flynn made her first speech as a communist at Madison Square Garden, New York, in 1937. She still writes a column for the *Daily Worker,* and is chair of the Communist Party's Women's Commission.

Women's Land Army Recruitment Lags

Britain: The British government has expressed great concern over the slow recruitment rate in the Women's Land Army, which was re-formed in July last year after being disbanded at the end of the Great War. With the German navy controlling the Atlantic and preventing food and other supplies from reaching Britain, and in the face of the bombing blitz of London and other areas, women are being recruited to perform rural work which would normally be done by the men who are now serving in the armed forces.

Many women, attracted by glamorous recruitment posters of fashionable women having fun, are surprised at the nature of the work. In reality it is hard physical labor, at times demeaning and disheartening. Many are experiencing loneliness and language difficulties, especially those posted to unfamiliar locations such as Wales.

Applicants must be between 18 and 40 years old, and able to work full-time on farms anywhere in Britain. Remuneration is 32 shillings for a 48-hour week, with eight pence per hour overtime. Tasks include growing crops and tilling the land, rat-catching, caring for animals, and general farm maintenance work. Some work on fruit farms or market gardens, while "timber Jills" work in forests, felling, pruning, and planting trees.

All members receive training and a uniform of poplin shirts, a green pullover, brown corduroy breeches, brown socks, a three-quarter length overcoat, and a khaki felt cowboy-type hat.

Women are finding the Land Army less than glamorous.

The queen has responded to advice that she should emulate other wealthy people by sending her daughters to Canada until the war is over, saying: "The children will not leave unless I do. I shall not leave unless their father does, and the king will not leave the country in any circumstances whatsoever."

Death of a Geometrician

England, December 17: The self-educated amateur geometry pioneer Alicia Boole Stott has died, aged eighty. She is best known for coining the term "polytope" (a convex, four-dimensional solid) and for achieving a remarkable grasp of four-dimensional geometry at a very early age.

In 1890 Alicia married actuary Walter Stott, who noted that her "hobby" of identifying four-dimensional objects in hyperspace closely resembled the work of brilliant Dutch mathematician Pieter Schoute. After Alicia sent him pictures of her work, Schoute came to England, where they worked together for many years. He persuaded her to publish her findings, *On Certain Series of Sections of the Regular Four-dimensional Hypersolids,* in 1900.

Stott discovered that there are six regular polytopes in four dimensions, and that they are bounded by 5, 16, or 600 tetrahedra; 8 cubes; 24 octahedra, or 120 dodecahedra. She created three-dimensional central cross-sections of all the six regular polytopes, using her own methods since, amazingly, she had never learned analytic geometry.

She also made attractively colored cardboard models of all the sections. Her father, George Boole, proved that Aristotelian logic can be represented by algebraic equations, and is known as the founder of mathematical (or "Boolean") logic. From 1930 Stott worked with the eminent mathematician H. S. M. Coxeter, who admired her.

WINTER ISSUE No.II

Wonder Woman

Final Flight for Amy Johnson

London, England, January 5: Famed British aviator, Amy Johnson, is feared drowned today after the plane she was flying for the Air Transport Auxiliary went down in the Thames estuary. There is no sign of her body and little hope of survival. Johnson was determined to carry out her duty despite poor weather conditions.

Determination marked Johnson's life. She received countless accolades, including a CBE in 1931, and she made many "firsts" in the world of flight. The first woman to receive a licensed engineer's certificate from the Air Ministry in 1927, she attempted, three years later, to break Bert Hinkler's 1928 England-to-Australia record. Although not record-breaking, her solo flight received much attention, including comments from King George V. In 1931 Johnson flew to Tokyo via the Soviet Union in 78 hours, 50 minutes.

A 1932 flight from Kent to Cape Town was particularly notable as she beat her

"HAD I BEEN A MAN, I MIGHT HAVE EXPLORED THE POLES OR CLIMBED MOUNT EVEREST, BUT AS IT WAS, MY SPIRIT FOUND OUTLET IN THE AIR."

AMY JOHNSON
(1903–1941)
BRITISH AVIATOR

A Russian women's brigade ready for the harvest on a collective farm in the USSR.

Amy Johnson farewells her aviator husband, James Mollison.

husband, aviator James Mollison's, record by 10 hours. The two high flyers were married on July 29, 1932 and made the first direct flight from the UK to the USA together. They divorced in 1938, but Amy Johnson's love of the air continued, and in 1939 she even wrote a book, *Skyroads of the World*.

Suspect Princess's Hysterical Arrest

Palo Alto, California, March 9: Yesterday, in her Palo Alto apartment, Princess Stephanie Hohenlohe of Hungary was arrested by officers from the Department of Immigration on orders from Washington. Her 26-year-old son Franz and her attorney Joseph Bullock were present at the time.

Bullock stated that Princess Stephanie was in such a state of distress and anxiety that she had to be literally half-carried from the apartment.

The princess arrived in the USA from London on a Hungarian passport on December 22, 1939. A member of the royal circle in the old Austro-Hungarian imperial monarchy, the princess is a close friend of Captain Fritz Wiedemann, the German Consul-General in America. Reports from Britain paint the princess as a Nazi sympathizer, but she has denied claims that she is a Nazi spy. Her arrest is not unexpected—immigration officials had issued her with a deportation warrant in January of this year. Although her request to have her visitor's permit renewed was not granted, two extensions were given on grounds of ill health due to hysteria. However, an appeal against the deportation was denied last week.

The princess's future destination remains under a cloud. Her attorney, Mr Bullock, vehemently claims that, in spite of his best efforts, he could not find a country that would issue her a visa.

Virginia Woolf's Suicide

Sussex, England, April 19: Last night the body of 59-year-old British novelist and essayist Virginia Woolf was found in the River Ouse, ending the speculation surrounding her disappearance from her country residence on the morning of March 28. Today the coroner announced that it was death by suicide—the writer had walked into the water with her pockets weighted down by stones.

Born in 1882, the third daughter of writer and editor Sir Leslie Stephen, Woolf grew up in a house frequented by writers and thinkers. Together with her sister Vanessa, she moved to Bloomsbury, London, after their father's death in 1904. Here they gathered around them a lively group of young intellectuals, among them the art critic Clive Bell, whom Vanessa married, and author Leonard Woolf, who became Virginia's husband.

time out

During a Nazi attack on the town of Babi Yar in the USSR, Grunie Melamud miraculously survives by digging her way out of a trench full of corpses. She later joins the Red Army and earns eleven medals for bravery.

Leonard and Virginia ran the successful Hogarth Press from 1917 until 1938. Woolf herself was a prolific, diverse and original writer. From her first novel, *The Voyage Out*, written in 1915, to her most recent works, she innovated the form, style, and content of the English novel. She also provided sharp literary criticism and contributions to current debate through her essays.

Despite her success, Woolf's life was filled with tragedy. In just over ten years she lost her mother, half-sister, father, and in 1906, her beloved brother, Thoby. Virginia had long suffered from acute bouts of mental distress, perhaps made worse when two of her homes were recently bombed in German air-raids.

Virginia left a note for her husband, who was present at the coroner's hearing today. In it, she wrote, "I cannot go on any longer in these terrible times."

Hannah Arendt Reaches Safety of America

New York, USA, May: The safe arrival of writer Hannah Arendt in New York City is a cause for rejoicing, as thousands of German Jews and other refugees continue to flee Nazi-occupied Europe. The fall of France last year saw the displacement of many such "stateless" Germans.

Hannah Arendt had fled Germany for Paris after her burgeoning academic career was quashed by the Nazi government in 1933. Having been trained under philosophical luminaries such as Rudolf Bultmann, Karl Jaspers, and the more dubious character Martin Heidegger, she escaped to Paris where her intellectual pursuits were accompanied by a growing political activism, particularly in relocating German Jewish youths to Palestine. She and her husband, Heinrich Blucher, join a growing, yet well-established

Virginia Woolf appeared on the cover of *Time* in 1937.

community of exiled writers and intellectuals now residing in New York City.

Kiwi Women Rise to the Challenge

New Zealand, June 26: New Zealand is showing what "total warfare" means to a country of only 1.6 million. The Minister for Industry has revealed that the number of women enlisted in the recently-formed Women's War Auxiliary is already over 10,000. Since the declaration of war, New Zealand women have eagerly stepped into new roles at military bases, on farms, and in factories. Women's overtime work in factories alone has doubled in the last six months, as New Zealand seeks to supply blankets, uniforms, and, of course, cheese for Great Britain's war needs.

Marlene Dietrich

Ginger Rogers and James Stewart with Oscars.

The Women's War Auxiliary seeks to coordinate already existing efforts to provide aid for overseas troops, transport services at home, and much-needed labor for the "land army" keeping New Zealand's farms running at full productivity.

Petrishchevo, USSR, November 29: Zoya Anatolyevna Kosmodemyanskaya, a Russian partisan volunteer, is captured and killed by Nazi troops.

London, England, November: Vera Lynn's radio show makes her the sweetheart of the British troops.

Minnesota, USA, December 5: Australian nurse Sister Elizabeth Kenny's new treatment for infantile paralysis is approved.

Honolulu, Hawaii, December 7: Japanese planes make a surprise attack on the US fleet at Pearl Harbor.

Europe, December 8: Hungary and Romania declare war on Britain. Britain reciprocates.

Washington DC, USA, December 8: The USA, Britain, Australia, and New Zealand declare war on Japan. Congresswoman and pacifist Jeanette Rankin casts the only vote against US involvement in World War II.

Central America, December 11: Cuba, Costa Rica, Nicaragua, and the Dominican Republic declare war on Germany and Italy.

USA, December 11: The USA reciprocates Germany's and Italy's declarations of war.

Europe, December 12: Hungary, Romania, and Bulgaria declare war on the USA.

London, England, December 18: The *National Service Act* is passed, conscripting all women aged between 20 and 40 to register for war work.

Hong Kong, December 25: Japan seizes Hong Kong.

St Petersburg (Leningrad), USSR, December 25: Over 3,000 people have starved to death since the German siege on the city began in September.

USA, December: Wonder Woman first appears in *All Star Comics #8*.

France: French photographer Dora Maar models for her lover, Pablo Picasso. The painting *Dora Maar au Chat* is considered a masterpiece.

Ethiopia: Emperor Haile Selassie and Empress Menon return from exile.

France: An independent women's volunteer corps is created within the French Air Force.

Panama: Women win the right to vote.

South Africa: Elizabeth Tshatshu of the AmaNtinde line becomes acting paramount chief of the Xhosa Tribe.

USA: Marlene Dietrich stars in *The Flame of New Orleans*.

Marina Tsvetaieva

Exiled Poet Dies Unrecognized

Elabuga, USSR, August 31: One of the Soviet Union's most talented and prolific poets was found dead this morning in the town of Elabuga—Marina Ivanova Tsvetaieva had hanged herself.

Tsvetaieva, though born in Moscow in 1892, had never been able to make Russia her home. Her husband, Sergei Efron, had fought in the White Army during the revolution of 1917–1920, and Tsvetaieva and her family had been forced to live as émigrés in Prague, Berlin, and Paris during the 1920s and 1930s. Tsvetaieva's lyric poems, often involving reminiscences of pre-revolutionary Russia, or pro-White Army sentiment (such as the epic *The Swan's Encampment*) were often published outside of the Soviet Union. In her native country Marina was largely unrecognized, and indeed ostracized as a writer.

While living in the émigré communities, Tsvetaieva enjoyed a string of romantic and intellectual friendships, many of which have been mythologized in her poems. Yet she often found it just as difficult to gain acceptance within the émigré communities as she had found it in Moscow. This was further aggravated by the fact that her husband was forced to leave Paris and return to Russia after being implicated in a murder investiga-

tion. In 1939 Tsvetaieva also left Paris for Moscow. However, dramatically, earlier that year her husband was killed by the Soviet Secret Service, and their daughter, Alya, was taken to prison.

After the invasion of the USSR by Germany, Tsvataieva was evacuated to Elabuga, and there, unemployed and alone, she has taken her own life.

New Book Brings Ocean to Life

New York, USA, October 31: Biologist Rachel Carson's debut book about ocean life, *Under the Sea-Wind*, was released today and is sure to make waves. Three natural environments are examined in the new book—the shores, the open sea, and the sea bottom—and Carson introduces her readers to the fascinating creatures that inhabit these worlds in a manner that combines the precision of a biologist and the lyrical pen of a poet.

Rachel Carson, currently a biologist on the staff of the United States Bureau of Fisheries, was born in 1907 in rural Pennsylvania. With dreams of becoming a writer she enrolled as an English major at Pennsylvania College for Women in 1925, before switching her focus to biology halfway through her degree. In 1929 she was honored with a scholarship to undertake an MA in zoology at Johns Hopkins University, Maryland. Carson took advantage of both her literary and scientific talents when she was hired by the Bureau of Fisheries in 1935 to write a series of radio programs on marine life called "Romance under the Waters." Carson continues her scientific storytell-

How Green Was My Valley, starring Maureen O'Hara.

Women all over the world are joining the Armed Forces.

ing in *Under the Sea-Wind*. Her text is complemented by Howard Frech's eight beautiful full-page illustrations, and an invaluable 40-page glossary.

Brutality and Bravery at Execution of Woman

Petrishevo, USSR, November 29: Today, Zoya Anatolyevna Kosmodemyanskaya, barely 18 years of age, was hanged, having been brutally interrogated and then tortured by German troops in the Russian town of Petrishevo, which is just 43 miles (70 km) outside of Moscow.

Kosmodemyanskaya was allegedly involved in a raid by saboteurs on German troop quarters in Petrishevo, when she was discovered and apprehended by a group of German soldiers.

The young partisan volunteer, who wore a man's uniform and kept her hair cropped short, was marched barefoot through snow toward a makeshift gallows erected by German troops in the village square. Blood dripped from her lips, and she showed signs of bruising, burns, and severe mistreatment. A tin of gasoline and a sign saying "Guerilla" were draped from her neck. This gave the German photographer, who was busy at the scene, plenty of chances for photographs.

Despite her body being broken, Zoya's spirit remained remarkably strong. She managed to avoid giving her captors her name—defiantly saying "Tanya" instead. Standing upon the gallows, with her feet resting on the suitcases and boxes that supported her, she shouted at her captors with chilling bravery, grit, and determination: "You hang me now. But I am not alone. There are 200 million of us. You can't hang us all!" To her Soviet compatriots, who had been forced into the village square to watch the execution, she cried, "Comrades! Cheer up! Smite the Germans! Burn them!"

Zoya Kosmodemyanskaya had indeed been involved in burning German troop quarters and horse stables, and she had successfully cut a German field-telephone wire while behind enemy lines.

The body of the courageous young woman, who left secondary school just last year, will hopefully find a resting place back in Moscow. German intentions are, however, to leave her bayoneted body exposed for weeks to come as a warning against further partisan activity.

"Sincerely Yours" Makes Vera Lynn Sincerely Loved

London, England, November: There is a very sweet sound to be heard above the clamor of war—it is the voice of popular British singer Vera Lynn, "the Forces' Sweetheart", as she is fast becoming known. Lynn's BBC radio program "Sincerely Yours" is now broadcast to troops overseas as well as to audiences at home. The program showcases ballads sung by Lynn and her quartet (such as the popular 'We'll Meet Again" and "The White Cliffs of Dover"), but perhaps more importantly, it provides a vital link between the two very disparate worlds of soldiers abroad and families at home. Vera Lynn reads aloud personal messages from girls to their soldier sweethearts overseas, giving the program its poignant title; in turn she and the quartet perform the songs most requested by soldiers stationed abroad.

Vera Lynn bolsters the morale of British troops.

Further, this year, Lynn has been busy performing in person at military camps around England.

Vera Lynn began charming with song well before the start of the war. Born Vera Margaret Welch on March 20, 1917, in East Ham, London, she chose to adopt her grandmother's maiden name of Lynn as her stage name. By the age of seven, Lynn was performing in local working-men's clubs. At 15 she was a vocalist with the Howard Baker Orchestra, and at 18 she made her first radio broadcast with the Joe Loss Orchestra. In 1936 Vera Lynn recorded her first solo record, "Up the Wooden Hill to Bedfordshire." From 1937, she worked almost exclusively with Bert Ambrose's acclaimed Ambrose Orchestra. She met Ambrose's clarinet and tenor sax player, Harry Lewis, and they married in 1939. Lewis then became her manager. In 1940 Lynn went solo.

Vera Lynn clearly demonstrates that entertainment and morale are a vital part of the war effort, as is the BBC's decision to maintain radio broadcasting during wartime.

Rankin Casts Single Vote Against War

Washington DC, USA, December 8:
Applause in the House for pro-war speeches quickly turned to hisses today as the Republican Congresswoman Jeannette Rankin said a firm "no" to a resolution declaring war with Japan. At 12.30 p.m. President Roosevelt addressed a joint session of the Senate and House. Despite the brevity of his speech—just six minutes and 30 seconds—his words were overwhelmingly convincing: "I ask that Congress declare that since the unprovoked and dastardly attack by Japan on Sunday, December 7, a state of war has existed between the United States and the Empire of Japan." The entire assemblage, including Cabinet and the Supreme Court, rose and cheered.

By 1.10 p.m. the vote was in, and by 4.15 p.m. the resolution was signed. The vote was 82–0 in the Senate, and 388–1 in the House. Jeanette Rankin stood out as the single dissenter in the united crowd.

Rankin was the first woman elected to the House of Representatives in 1917. She is well known for her pacifist views, having served with various peace groups, such as the Women's International League for Peace and Freedom, the Women's Peace Union, and the National Council for the Prevention of War. Today Jeannette Rankin refused to participate in interviews and waited in a phone-box until crowds had dispersed.

Woman-power to the Rescue

London, England, December 18:
Following weeks of often heated debate, Parliament today passed the *National Service Act (No.2)*, which among other measures provides for the legal conscription of all unmarried women between the ages of 20 and 31.

Eligible women will be required to choose between serving in the armed forces (through already-existing agencies such as the Women's Royal Naval Service or the Auxiliary Territorial Service), or engaging in industrial or farm work (through the Women's Land Army). The demand for female munitions factory workers also continues to grow as Britain seeks to strengthen its defenses for war with Germany, and now Japan.

Empress Menen

Jeannette Rankin, a lone voice in the Congress.

Earlier this month, the Minister for Labor, Mr Bevan, told Parliament that since the outbreak of war over a million women have already been transferred to work on munitions. The labor of volunteer women will remain crucial in civil-defense work dealing with air-raids. However, under the new legislation, we may expect to see more women operating anti-aircraft guns and radar stations, alongside those already administering first aid and running canteens.

Compulsory conscription of women has been seen as inevitable by some commentators—though not without controversy—ever since Sir William Beveridge's report recommending the measure was circulated last year. The registration of all women with the government since spring of this year also helped smooth the way to conscription.

Women laborers in London prove that woman-power works!

Carole Lombard

Murder Suspected in Communist's Death

Mexico City, Mexico, January 5: Actress, photographer, and former Communist Party member, Tina Modotti, has died aged 45, supposedly of a heart attack—but there is some speculation she was murdered by former lover and Russian assassin, Vittorio Vidali.

Italian-born Modotti emigrated to America in 1913 and began an acting career in 1917. She moved to Mexico City with her lover, American photographer Edward Weston, in 1922 and together they produced the country's first Modernist photographic images. In 1926, after Weston left, Modotti joined the Mexican Communist Party, using her art to make political statements. She began an affair with Vidali, and in 1930 was deported on suspicion of conspiring to assassinate President Pascual Ortiz Rubio. Modotti and Vidali then worked for Stalin in Moscow and fought in the Spanish Civil War. Modotti re-entered Mexico secretly in 1939 and abandoned Communism.

"THIS IS NOT THE END. IT IS NOT EVEN THE BEGINNING OF THE END. BUT IT IS, PERHAPS, THE END OF THE BEGINNING."

ANNE FRANK, GERMAN JEW IN HIDING, DIARY, NOVEMBER 9, 1942

Carole Lombard Killed in Plane Crash

Nevada, USA, January 17: American movie star Carole Lombard is among 22 people confirmed dead after the TWA plane in which she was traveling last night crashed in the Potosi Ranges near Las Vegas and burst into flames. Search parties were organized as soon as news of the crash reached officials. Lombard's husband, Clark Gable, flew to the scene where he waited at the foot of the mountain in the faint hope that there might have been survivors.

Also among the dead are Lombard's mother, Elizabeth Peters, and her press agent, Otto Winkler. The trio were returning from Indianapolis to California after raising $2.1 million in war bonds in Indiana.

e del lavoro. - Negli stabilimenti per la produzione di guerra le donne italiane la attende, assidue, sostituendo con cosciente dedizione la maestranza maschile.
(Disegno di A.Beltrame)

Illustration of Italian women workers in munitions factory.

Born Jane Alice Peters on October 6, 1908, Lombard's career began at age 12 when she was spotted by a film director in a Los Angeles street.

As the film industry moved from silent to talking pictures, Lombard's breezy sexy voice landed her several roles and a contract with Paramount Pictures.

Lombard starred in 42 movies including classic screwball comedies such as *Hands Across the Table* (1935), *My Man Godfrey* (1936), and *Nothing Sacred* (1937). A brilliant bright comedienne, she managed to look elegant and beautiful even after being drenched with buckets of water or having pies thrown in her face. She received one Academy Award nomination for Best Actress for her role in *My Man Godfrey*.

time out

In Chicago, USA, the *Negro Digest* becomes a regular publication and when First Lady Eleanor Roosevelt includes a piece she penned entitled 'If I Were a Negro,' the sales soar more from 3,000 to 100,000.

Women Swell Ranks of US Military

Washington DC, USA, May 15: In the newly-created US Women's Army Auxiliary Corps (WAAC), women will be allowed to serve in paid non-combat positions with a military rank. The new Auxiliary Corps is the first female military unit other than the Army Nurse Corps. It will allow skilled women to take on essential service jobs such as switchboard operations and typing, thus freeing up more men for combat roles.

The new law was signed by President Franklin D. Roosevelt today. The Bill was passed in the House with 249 votes to 86, and the Senate passed it yesterday with 38 votes to 27. An initial recruitment goal of 25,000 in the first year has been set, but the Army will provide up to 150,000 auxiliaries with food, uniforms, living quarters, pay, and medical care. This starkly contrasts with World War I, when female war workers had to obtain their own food, shelter, and medical care, and received no disability or pension benefits. Today's event follows a debate among politicians and the American community. The Bill was first introduced in May last year by Massachusetts Congresswoman Edith Nourse Rogers, but failed to gain serious attention until after the Japanese attack on Pearl Harbor. A key proponent of the Bill, Army Chief of Staff General George Marshall, said the Army was wasting time and money training men for clerical roles when skilled women were available. Another key advocate is First Lady Eleanor Roosevelt.

US Congress Women's Army Auxiliary Corps.

husband was already a faculty member. Undeterred, she joined the team as an unpaid assistant.

Scharff Goldhaber was born in Mannheim, Germany, on July 14, 1911. She was interested in science at a young age and studied physics at the University of Munich, saying: "I want to understand what the world is made of." She also studied at Freiburg, Zurich, and Berlin universities before starting her thesis with Walther Gerlach at Munich.

When the Nazis came to power in 1933, life became very difficult for Jews. However, although she felt ostracized by university staff, Scharff Goldhaber stayed and finished her PhD in 1935. She moved to London and worked as a research associate with George P. Thomson at

Responding to an encyclical from Dutch Catholic bishops criticizing the deportation of Jews and the expulsion of Jewish children from Catholic schools, the Nazis have arrested all Dutch Catholics of Jewish extraction.

Stein was born into an Orthodox Jewish family on October 12, 1891, in Breslau, Prussia. Although respecting her family's faith and her mother's openness toward God, she was an atheist as a teenager and much more interested in academic studies. As one of the country's first women admitted to university, Stein studied philology and philosophy and later became a teacher. Her interaction with Christian intellectuals led to her Catholic conversion in 1921. Stein went on to become a well-known philosopher,

Una Marson

Although Congresswoman Rogers wanted women to have equal pay and benefits, the Army would not accept women directly into its ranks and have agreed to form a separate women's unit where women will receive a military rank, although it will not be equal to a male rank, and will not carry the same pay and entitlements.

Unpaid Assistant Makes Breakthrough Discovery

Urbana, Illinois, USA, May 18: An unpaid German physicist working as an assistant in the University of Illinois Physics Laboratory has made an historic scientific discovery by establishing that neutrons are emitted in spontaneous nuclear fission. Gertrude Scharff Goldhaber submitted her findings for publication today, but they will be classified by the US Government and will not be published while the war is in progress. Although she joined the staff of the university after her marriage in 1939, Scharff Goldhaber was not allowed a paid position due to nepotism rules because her

Anne Frank's diary was published as *The Diary of a Young Girl* and eventually translated from its original Dutch into many languages. It became one of the world's most widely read books.

Imperial College, before moving to Illinois with her new husband in 1939, just before the outbreak of war in Europe.

Carmelite Nun among Jewish Deportees

Echt, Netherlands, August 2: Carmelite nun, philosopher, and women's advocate, Edith Stein, and her sister Rosa, also a Carmelite nun, were arrested by Nazi troops today.

teacher, and author. When, in 1933, the Nazis forced Stein to give up teaching, she entered the cloistered Carmelite Order in Cologne, taking the name Teresa Benedicta of the Cross. With the Nazi threat worsening, she entered the Carmelite convent at Echt in the neutral Netherlands in 1938, and her sister joined her there. When the Nazis invaded, the sisters planned to move to Switzerland, but were arrested before they were able to flee.

Key Events

Auschwitz, Poland, August 9: Carmelite nun, Edith Stein, is executed by Nazis.

USA, August 11: Actress Hedy Lamarr and composer George Antheill patent a shield for wireless radio communications.

Dieppe, France, August 19: A nine-day Allied offensive takes out key German infrastructure.

Auschwitz, Poland, August 19: French-Jewish author Irène Némirovsky dies in a camp, leaving a novel, *Suite Francaise*, about a village occupied by Nazi forces.

Boisrenard, France, September 24: Andrée Borrel and Lise de Baissac are parachuted into occupied France, the first female Special Operations Executive (SOE) agents to do so.

USA, September: Nancy Love is appointed to direct the new Women's Auxiliary Ferrying Squadron (WAFS).

Volgograd (Stalingrad), USSR, October: German aerial attacks kill thousands of civilians and destroy 80 percent of the city area.

Theresienstadt, Europe, October 9: Elise Richter, Austrian professor, is deported to a concentration camp.

Papua New Guinea, November 2: Australian troops take Kokoda after surviving horrific conditions of steep inclines, mud, and malaria, while fighting on the Kokoda Track.

UK, November 6: Women are allowed into church without hats.

Morroco and Algeria, North Africa, November 8: A major Allied invasion of North Africa, Operation Torch, is launched.

USA, November 23: The US Coast Guard Women's Auxiliary is formed.

Minnesota, USA, December 17: The Sister Kenny Institute for trainee nurses and physiotherapists opens.

USA, December: Superintendent of the Army Nurses Corps, Julia Flikke, becomes the first woman colonel in the US Army.

USA: Black author Margaret Walker Alexander writes her famous poem, "For My People."

USA: Aviator Beryl Markham publishes her memoirs, *West With the Night*, although many speculate it was written by her husband, journalist Raoul Schumacher.

USA: Mary McCarthy publishes her first novel, *The Company She Keeps*.

New York, USA: Dawn Powell publishes her novel *A Time to be Born*.

USA: J. Howard Miller paints an image of a factory worker for Westinghouse, with the slogan "We can do it!"–an image commonly dubbed *Rosie the Riveter*.

Dominican Republic: Women win the right to vote.

Warsaw, Poland: Irena Sendler poses as a nurse and persuades women that children will be safer if smuggled out of the Warsaw Ghetto.

Hedy Lamarr

A Shield for Wireless Communications?

Hollywood, USA, August 11: Austrian actress Hedy Lamarr, and American concert pianist and composer George Antheil, today took out a US patent on a "Secret Communication System."

The controversial device combines musical technology with military components. It relies on slotted paper rolls similar to piano rolls to synchronize the frequency changes in transmitters and receivers, creating a frequency-hopping spread spectrum. The device could potentially allow high-altitude observation planes to steer torpedos from above. The Navy has rejected the invention, saying the mechanism is too big to fit inside a torpedo, but Antheil insists it could be made smaller and has implored the Navy to reconsider, given Germany's superiority in naval weaponry.

Hollywood neighbors Lamarr and Antheil devised their shielding device during a conversation about military weaponry and radio control for torpedos. Lamarr learned about military technology from her former husband, arms dealer Fritz Mandl. Antheil studied military history, and as a musician developed a unique mechanical-like sound using a piano, electric bells, airplane propellers, and sirens. Lamarr told Antheil about her idea for "frequency hopping" and Antheil suggested a way to achieve rapid synchronized frequency changes.

"ONE COULD SAY THAT IN CASE OF NEED, EVERY NORMAL AND HEALTHY WOMAN IS ABLE TO HOLD A POSITION. AND THERE IS NO PROFESSION WHICH CANNOT BE PRACTICED BY A WOMAN."

EDITH STEIN (1891–1942), GERMAN NUN

Novelist's Tragic Ending

Auschwitz, Poland, August 19: Renowned Jewish author, Irène Némirovsky, died in the gas chambers today, but has left behind a legacy with a partly finished

Nancy Love is appointed to command the new Women's Auxiliary Ferrying Squadron (WAFS), in the USA in September.

Ingrid Bergman and Humphrey Bogart star in *Casablanca*.

novel entitled *Suite Française*, documenting the tragic life of Jews in France over the past two years. The novel is now in the possession of her oldest daughter, 13-year-old Denise.

Irène Némirovsky was born on February 11, 1903, in Russia, and her family lived in France from 1919. A talented and educated writer, Némirovsky published her first novel, *David Golder*, in 1929. It was an enormous success, as was her next novel, *Le Bal*, in 1930. Némirovsky became part of the literary set and had many friends, some of whom were anti-Semitic.

Némirovsky married a banker, Michel Epstein, in 1926 and had two daughters: Denise in 1929, and Élisabeth in 1937. By this time, Némirovsky had published 11 books.

Némirovsky converted to Catholicism in 1939 but her books were banned due to her Jewish heritage. When Germany invaded France, the couple's friends deserted them. They fled to the French village, Issy-l'Evêque, where Némirovsky began writing *Suite Française*. Intended as a four-volume piece, the first

two volumes cover the Jewish exodus from France and the initial Nazi occupation between 1940 and 1941.

Although official records claim Némirovsky died of typhus, she and her husband both died in the gas chambers. However, their children have been spared.

Agents Parachuted into France

Boisrenard, France, September 24: Lise de Baissac and Andrée Borrel, Special Operations Executive agents, have been dropped by parachute into occupied France to assist the French Resistance in the fight against Nazi Germany. The first female agents to be parachuted into France, they landed in Boisrenard late this evening. Borrel, 22, will travel on to Paris and de Baissac, 37, will proceed to Poitiers.

In June, 1940, France signed an armistice with Germany that divided the country into occupied and unoccupied zones, and allowed Germany 60 percent control. Then, in July 1940, the Special Operations Executive was initiated by the British Government to help French people who wanted to keep fighting the Nazis.

In April this year, British Prime Minister Winston Churchill gave approval for Special Operations Executive women to go into Europe, as it is believed that women are less conspicuous and can be used as couriers and wireless operators.

Effective Methods of Treating Polio

Minnesota, USA, December 17: The Sister Kenny Institute for trainee nurses and physiotherapists opened today in Minneapolis. Named after pioneering Australian polio nurse, Sister Elizabeth Kenny, the Institute will train medical professionals in Kenny's unique methods of treating infantile paralysis.

Kenny has saved and improved the lives of thousands of children with her simple methods, which were initially lambasted by US and Australian medical authorities, but which are now generally accepted and applauded around the world as extremely effective.

Last year, the National Foundation for Infantile Paralysis publicly backed Kenny's methods, and she now plans

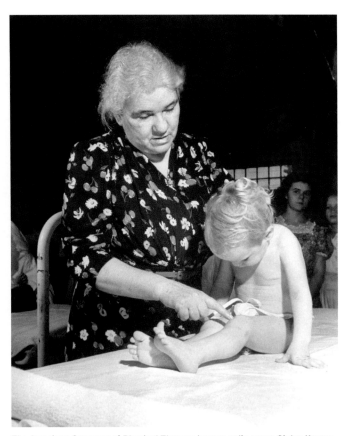
The American Congress of Physical Therapy honors polio nurse Sister Kenny.

Children out of Warsaw Ghetto

Warsaw, Poland, December: A Polish woman posing as a nurse has been risking her life to smuggle Jewish children out of the Warsaw Ghetto, with scores of children already saved from inevitable death in the Nazi extermination camp at Treblinka.

Irene Sendler, a member of the Polish Underground, has been working with terrified parents in the ghetto to gain their trust and permission to take their children and place them in the care of Polish families, orphanages and Catholic convents. She is keeping their coded names and new identities in a hidden jar with the intention of reuniting the children with any family members who are left after the war.

The Warsaw Ghetto was created in October 1940, and is being used by the Nazis to hide captured Jews. About 5,000 people are dying in the ghetto every month from starvation or disease. In December last year, the Nazis began a policy of killing all Jews in Europe, starting with those in Poland. The Treblinka extermination camp was built in July this year and by September more than 300,000 Jews had been transported there.

After the 1939 invasion, appalled by the horrors of the Nazi regime, Sendler began arranging food, clothing, money, and medicine for Jewish people at canteens run by the Social Welfare Department where she worked as a social worker. She later joined the Polish Underground organization, Zegota, or Council for Aid to Jews.

As a departmental employee, Sendler has a permit to enter the ghetto and visits daily with food, medicine, and clothing. She has been smuggling the children out in sacks, ambulances, garbage cans, potato sacks, and coffins. This month, Zegota nominated Sendler to manage its children's department, and has given her the code name Jolanta.

US Army Appoints First Female Colonel

USA, December: Colonel Julia Flikke is the first female in US military history to gain the rank of colonel. Her commission has been made possible by Public Law 828, which authorizes commissions for nurses in grades from second lieutenant to colonel in the Army of the United States. Under the same law, Army nurses will now receive pay equal to officers of comparable grade without dependents

Born in Wisconsin on March 16, 1878, Flikke took up nursing after the death of her husband. She studied nursing in Illinois, and graduated in 1915, then completed further studies in education and administration.

Colonel Flikke began her military career with the Army Nurse Corps in 1918, serving at the US Army General Hospital in New Jersey. As Chief Nurse of the Augustana unit, she nursed wounded soldiers in France.

In 1920, she became a first lieutenant and worked in the Philippines and China. She returned to the USA in 1922 and became Chief Nurse at Walter Reed General Hospital in Washington, DC, where she remained for 12 years.

In 1927, she was promoted to the rank of captain and in 1934, Flikke transferred to Houston, Texas, as Chief Nurse at Fort Sam Station Hospital, returning to Washington, DC in 1937 to become Superintendent of the Army Nurse Corps. The new rank changes her position to Chief of the Army Nurse Corps.

Beryl Markham

to set up more treatment and training clinics across the entire USA, allowing others to train in her methods.

Sister Kenny treated her first polio patient as a bush nurse in 1911. Shocked by the sight of the paralyzed toddler, she sought the advice of a doctor who told her the disease was incurable and to do "the best you can." Kenny put strips of blankets in boiling water, wrung them out and applied them to the child's aching deformed muscles. It eased the pain and the child slept. When she woke, the child cried out, "I want them rags that wells my legs."

Traditional polio treatment involves immobilizing paralyzed limbs with casts and splints, but Kenny argues that the muscles are in spasm, not paralysis, and can be relieved with hot packs and physical therapy to stimulate and re-educate them.

Born on September 20, 1880, Kenny grew up in Queensland, Australia. She first learned about the human musculoskeletal system as a teenager after breaking her wrist and convalescing with Dr Aeneas McDonnell, who showed her books on bones and muscles.

Kenny's methods for treating polio gained attention during the 1930 epidemic, and during 1935–1940 she set up clinics across Australia and England. She came to Minneapolis in 1940, and again faced a skeptical medical establishment. However, with a polio epidemic underway, doctors could not continue to ignore her proven methods, which are now widely practiced.

Mary McCarthy publishes her first novel, *The Company She Keeps.*

Eleanor Rathbone

Deadly Coda for Red Orchestra

Germany, February 16: Today, American-born teacher and translator, Mildred Harnack, 40, was guillotined by the Nazis at Plötzensee Prison, near Berlin. Her husband, Arvid Harnack, was hanged there last December. The couple were founding members of an organization dubbed "Red Orchestra" by the Gestapo, which began as a group of intellectuals debating politics, and evolved into an anti-Hitler resistance movement with around 200 members. The Red Orchestra sent information on Nazi plans to America and Russia, published an underground newsletter revealing Nazi atrocities, and helped dissidents and Jews escape from Germany.

Mildred Harnack was originally sentenced to six years' hard labor, but Hitler himself ordered that she be re-tried, and she was given the death penalty. Harnack was devoted to Germany, having lived and taught there for many years. Her last weeks in prison were spent translating verses by Goethe into English, despite the effects of torture and illness.

"MILLIONS LONG FOR IMMORTALITY WHO DON'T KNOW WHAT TO DO WITH THEMSELVES ON A RAINY SUNDAY AFTERNOON."

SUSAN ERTZ 1943,
ANGER IN THE SKY

Hitler's SS Gives Husbands Back

Rosenstrasse, Berlin, Germany, February 27–March 6: When the last of the estimated 10,000 Jews living in Berlin were rounded up last week, Joseph Goebbels, head of the city's Nazi Party, separated about 1,700 men related to non-Jewish (or Aryan) Germans and detained them in Rosenstrasse 2–4, the Jewish welfare office. The official line was that these men would be sent to labor camps, but in reality they were expected to end up at Auschwitz.

The SS and Goebbels were taken by surprise when groups of women—wives and relatives of the detained men—began appearing at Rosenstrasse demanding the return of their menfolk. They initially came in small groups, but the number of protesters kept growing so that there was always a group of women outside the door. Night and day, the women made their peaceful protest, even in the face of gun-toting Gestapo officers. With cries of "Give us our husbands back!", the women steadfastly insisted that their husbands be released. They resisted the

MGM's musical *Girl Crazy* has been a hit.

guns and the threats of arrest. After a very wearying week, the women's efforts have now borne fruit.

Wishing to avoid violence against the women, as well as any associated public-relations backlash, Goebbels has released all the detained men and ordered that the two dozen men already sent to Auschwitz be returned immediately. It is a stunning victory for the women.

Until recently, Jews married to Aryans have been largely exempt from Hitler's "final solution," the mass murder of Jews. Yet, with marriage between Aryans and Jews portrayed by the Nazis as a protest against Hitler's dream of racial purity, many intermarriages have ended in divorce. This "Rosenstrasse protest" is the first public protest by ordinary German women against the deportation and death of Jews. Privately, Goebbels is commenting that he will "finish the job" of ridding Berlin of Jews within a month, but this remains to be seen.

Prisoners arrive at Auschwitz concentration camp, intended destination of the men detained at Rosenstrasse.

Tripoli, Libya, January 23: British forces capture Tripoli.

Stalingrad, USSR, February 2: Axis troops surrender to the Red Army.

Germany, February 16: Member of the Red Orchestra resistance group, Mildred Harnack, is executed for treason.

London, February 16: The British government accepts the principle, long championed by Member of Parliament Eleanor Rathbone, of paying a child allowance to parents.

Rosenstrasse, Berlin, Germany, February 27–March 6: In the only protest of German people against the Nazis, women campaign against the imprisonment of their Jewish husbands. The group of 1,700 men is released.

Texas, USA, March 21: Cornelia Fort crashes her plane and becomes the first American woman to die flying a military aircraft.

Kentucky, USA, March 26: Elsie Ott is the first American woman to receive an Air Medal for her services as an army nurse.

Austria, March 30: Sister Restituta Kafka is beheaded by the Nazis for putting up crucifixes in a hospital.

Izieu, France, April: Sabina Zlatin opens a farmhouse to hide Jewish children from Nazi capture.

England, April 30: Writer and social reformer Beatrice Potter Webb dies, aged 85.

USA, May 29: Norman Rockwell's painting "Rosie the Riveter" appears on the cover of the *Saturday Evening Post*.

USA, May 30: Play commences in the newly formed All-American Girls Professional Baseball League, founded by Chicago Cubs owner Philip K. Wrigley.

Italy, July 25: Premier Benito Mussolini is ousted. A new Italian government under Marshal Pietro Badoglio places him under arrest.

Kharkov, USSR, August 1: Renowned Soviet fighter pilot Lilya Litvyak is shot down by German planes over Kharkov.

USA, August 5: Jacqueline Cochran is appointed to direct the newly formed Women Airforce Service Pilots (WASP), a merger of the Women's Auxiliary Flying Squadron and the Women's Flying Training Detachment.

Italy, August 17: Allied forces occupy Sicily. With North Africa already under occupation, the Allies now control the Mediterranean Sea.

Canberra, Australia, August 21: Dame Enid Lyons and Dorothy Tangney are the first women elected to the Australian Federal Parliament.

A Women's Auxiliary Ferrying Service pilot in action.

Woman Military Pilot Dies on Duty

Texas, USA, March 21: Cornelia Fort, 24, today became the first American woman to die while flying a military aircraft. Fort, a pilot with the Women's Auxiliary Ferrying Service (WAFS), died when the plane she was taking to an air base in Texas was clipped by another plane and plummeted from the sky.

Fort learned to fly in 1940 and became the first female flight instructor in her native Tennessee. By 1941, she was teaching members of the armed services how to fly. In December that year, while instructing a student at Pearl Harbor, Fort grabbed the plane's controls to avoid being hit by what turned out to be a Japanese plane. That event cemented her desire to serve her country.

After the Japanese attack on Pearl Harbor, women pilots were approached to assist in the war effort by ferrying planes from factories to airfields. This freed male pilots for active duty. Fort and her fellow female civilian pilots have had to endure a great deal of animosity from their male counterparts who feel that women should not be employed as pilots. The evidence has shown, however, that these women pilots are extremely capable and competent.

The WAFS has 28 female pilots, led by Nancy Love. They often fly in adverse conditions, including flying in open cockpits in bitterly cold temperatures, often without radio contact. Fort's death is a great loss to the fledgling air service.

Indefatigable Nurse Honored with Medal

Kentucky, USA, March 26: "For meritorious achievement while participating in an aerial flight." With these words, Brigadier-General Fred Borum today awarded army nurse Lieutenant Elsie Ott the Air Medal, the first received by a woman.

In January this year, while stationed in Karachi, Pakistan, Ott was instructed to accompany five seriously ill patients on an evacuation flight to the USA, a distance of more than 7,500 miles (12,000 km). The patients were suffering from various conditions—one had tuberculosis, another had polio, and yet another had multiple bone fractures. Along the way, at a stopover in Ghana, she took on another 11 patients.

time out

Russian-born author and philosopher Ayn Rand publishes *The Fountainhead*, which is loosely based on the life of architect Frank Lloyd Wright. Her libertarian convictions are proving to be core values in modern American life.

Single-handedly—the only health professional on the plane—Ott set up a miniature flying hospital complete with cots strapped to the floor. She managed all aspects of the patients' care. From Karachi to Florida, by way of Arabia, Ethiopia, Sudan, Ghana, South Africa, Brazil, and Puerto Rico, Ott tended her patients with little time to rest. When the flight finally ended, she demonstrated her consummate leadership skills by unloading her charges into ambulances and personally cleaning out the plane.

In spite of the inordinate demands on her time, Ott also managed to take notes on the flight, and she is expected to make some recommendations to her superiors regarding improving procedures for future medical evacuations.

Beatrice Potter Webb Dies

Beatrice Potter Webb

England, April 30: Writer, socialist, and social reformer, Beatrice Potter Webb, died today, aged 85. She wrote extensively on a number of social issues—among them equal pay for women and an analysis of the capitalist economic model.

Born in 1858, Webb embraced the notion that the good of the community came before the good of the individual and wrote about this in her 1891 publication, *The Cooperative Movement in Great Britain*. In 1892 she married economist and socialist Sidney Webb, a leading figure in the Fabian Society, a socialist intellectual organization. Together they produced books on the trade union movement and industrial democracy. In 1895, when the Fabian Society inherited £10,000, the Webbs proposed that a new university be built. This was the beginning of the now famous London School of Economics and Political Science.

In 1913 Beatrice helped establish *The New Statesman*, a weekly publication covering the political issues of the day. During the 1914–18 war she maintained her involvement in politics by serving on various government committees. In the last few years, Beatrice Webb supported Soviet ideals of health and education.

The Oscar for Best Actress went to Greer Garson for *Mrs. Miniver*.

Italy, September 12: Italy surrenders unconditionally to Allied forces.
China, September 13: General Chiang Kai-shek is elected president of the Republic of China.
USA, September 30: The Women's Army Corps is formed, affording women the same status as other army services, and replacing the Women's Auxiliary Army Corps.
Paris, France, September: After months of listening and flirting with German officers, spy Jeannie Rousseau has enough information to send a detailed report on V-2 rockets to England.

Italy, October 13: Marshal Badoglio declares war on Germany.
Italy, October 14: Allied forces take control of southern Italy.
Lyon, France, October 21: Lucie Aubrac, together with others in her French Resistance group, frees her husband Raymond Aubrac from Nazi imprisonment.
Paris, France, October 22: Actress Catherine Deneuve is born.
Lebanon, November 22: France grants Lebanon independence.
Auschwitz, Poland, November 30: Diarist and letter writer Etty Hillesum dies.

Cairo, Egypt, December 1–4: The USA, Britain, and China sign the Cairo Declaration, a joint plan to force Japan to surrender.
Lancashire, England, December 22: Author and artist Beatrix Potter dies, aged 77. She is best known for *The Tale of Peter Rabbit*.
USSR, December 31: Soviet troops force the Axis powers to retreat from the central area of the Eastern Front in Belarus (White Russia).

Boston, USA: Doctor, chemist, and social reformer Alice Hamilton publishes her autobiography, *Exploring the Dangerous Trades*, which outlines her work studying industrial and occupational diseases.
USA, December: More than 486,000 women are employed in the aircraft industry.
New York, USA: Betty Smith's coming-of-age novel, *A Tree Grows in Brooklyn*, is published, and becomes a bestseller.
USA: Physicist Elda Emma Anderson is recruited to help further develop the atomic bomb at Los Alamos.

USA: George Papanicolaou and Herbert Traut publish "Diagnosis of Uterine Cancer by the Vaginal Smear," which paves the way for Pap smears to become a routine way to detect cervical cancer.
Paris, France: Artist Françoise Gilot meets Pablo Picasso.
France: The Rochambelles Corps is created. It consists of nurses and first-aid personnel, and through it female staff will take part in campaigns in Tunisia, France, Italy, and Germany.

Girls at the Bat!

Jacqueline Cochran

USA, May 30: With many young men now away serving in the armed forces, Philip K. Wrigley, owner of the Chicago Cubs, has devised a radical way of maintaining interest and crowd support for baseball—he has established the All-American Girls Professional Baseball League. A new set of rules, a mixture of baseball and softball regulations, has been written to accommodate the new league. Most rules are the same as those for the major league, but with a few modifications such as reduced infield distances and a slightly smaller ball. Underarm pitches are also permitted.

To gain the public's interest in girls' baseball, prominent sportsmen have been recruited as coaches, and an attractive sports tunic has been designed for the players. Today the initial two games were played—one in Rockford, Illinois, the other in Racine, Wisconsin. It will be interesting to see what these girls can do with a bat!

"WORK IS THE BEST OF NARCOTICS, PROVIDING THE PATIENT BE STRONG ENOUGH TO TAKE IT."

BEATRICE POTTER WEBB (1858–1943), WRITER, SOCIALIST, AND SOCIAL REFORMER

Soviets Lose Second Female Ace

Kharkov, USSR, August 1: It took eight German pilots flying state-of-the-art Messerschmitt fighter planes to bring down the brilliant Soviet fighter pilot Lilya Litvyak, aged just 22. Sometimes called the "White Rose of Stalingrad," she was shot down in her YaK-1 aircraft over Kharkov today. In her short but successful life as a combat pilot, Litvyak shot down at least 12 enemy aircraft—the first (a Junkers Ju88) in September last year. Earlier this year, she was attacked by four Messerschmitts. She shot down two of them and drove the other two fighters away. Such was her reputation that German pilots are said to have tried to avoid her unless flying in a group.

Women have been an integral part of the Soviet Union's fighting forces since October, 1941, many serving at the front or in the skies. Lilya Litvyak was a member of the 586th Fighter Regiment, an all-female team led by pilot Marina Raskova. This group of talented female Soviet fighter pilots have been defending Russia throughout the war. Only last month, another gifted air ace—Katya Budanova, 27—also lost her life, in an attack by three enemy fighters. Their superior aeronautical skills led Litvyak and Budanova to be transferred to other regiments, where they flew and fought alongside their male counterparts.

TIME photographer Margaret Bourke White took photographs of the US attack on Tunis from this Flying Fortress bomber.

Women Elected to Australian Parliament

Canberra, Australia, August 21: Two women have made history today as the first women to be elected to the Australian Federal Parliament. Dame Enid Lyons, from Tasmania, won a seat in the House of Representatives as a member of the conservative United Australia Party and is the first woman to be elected to the Lower House. Dorothy Tangney, a member of the Australian Labor Party from Western Australia, is the first woman to be elected to the Senate. Although on opposite sides of the political fence, these two women are sure to make their marks.

Dame Enid, 46—widow of Joseph Lyons, prime minister of Australia from 1932 until his death in 1939—is a popular figure with voters. A mother of 12, she managed to combine motherhood with official duties during her husband's time as prime minister, when she divided her time between the prime minister's official residence in Canberra and her home in Tasmania. In 1937, Lyons was made a Dame Grand Cross of the Order of the British Empire. It is expected that Dame Enid will focus her parliamentary attention on issues surrounding families, such as maternity care and widows' pensions. She is a strong advocate for women in government.

Senator Dorothy Tangney, 32, is a former school teacher. She first stood for the Senate in 1940 but was unsuccessful. An advocate of social reform, she has a deep interest in health and education. She is expected to seek increased public funding for the nation's universities.

Although women have stood for election to the Australian Federal Government before (notably the suffragist Vida Goldstein, who first stood in 1903), it has taken until these elections for women to

Lilya Litvyak (left), Katya Budanova (center), and another female Soviet pilot prepare for combat.

take their place in Parliament and play a part in deciding the nation's future.

Lucie Gets Her Man

Lyon, France, October 21: In a daring undertaking, French Resistance forces today freed their leader, Raymond Aubrac, and about a dozen other Resistance members from Gestapo custody. It was the culmination of months of careful planning by Raymond's wife Lucie.

Lucie Aubrac was born in 1912 and spent her early adult years as a teacher.

A young girl reads one of Beatrix Potter's many books.

She married Raymond Samuel in 1939. Like many French people, the couple became increasingly concerned with the rise of Nazism. When France surrendered to Germany in 1940, and the French Vichy government came into being, she and her husband took the name Aubrac to avoid anti-Semitic persecution. Soon afterwards, they joined the Libération-Sud, one of a number of resistance groups fighting against the Germans, and have been active in the movement ever since. Together with Emmanuel d'Astier, they also run an underground newspaper.

On June 21 of this year, a group of Resistance fighters, including Raymond Aubrac and Jean Moulin, were captured by the Gestapo. The resourceful Lucie, pregnant with her second child, went to see the local Gestapo commander, Klaus Barbie, claiming she was not married and was carrying Raymond's child. She begged Barbie to allow her to marry Raymond in prison before his execution and thus make her unborn baby legitimate.

Barbie's agreement made the next part of the plan possible. In order to see Lucie, Raymond was brought to Gestapo headquarters from Montluc Prison, where he has been held these past four months. On

the way back to prison, the truck carrying Raymond was ambushed by Lucie and her team, freeing the captives.

There is talk that the Aubracs, whose wartime change of identity has now been revealed, may move to London until hostilities cease.

Peter Rabbit's Creator Dies

Lancashire, England, December 22: Beatrix Potter, who created such lovable characters as Peter Rabbit, Squirrel Nutkin, Mrs Tiggy-winkle, and Benjamin Bunny, died today, aged 77. Potter was more than a writer of children's stories; she was also an accomplished artist and, for the last 30 years or so, a successful farmer and conservationist.

When Beatrix Potter published *The Tale of Peter Rabbit* in 1902, she had no idea how it would change her life. The great success of that book gave her the financial freedom to purchase land in her favorite part of the world, England's Lake District. In 1903 she bought her farm, Hill Top, where she wrote and illustrated some of the best-loved of her 23 books, including *The Tale of Tom Kitten*, and *The Tale of Jemima Puddle-duck*.

Potter was born in 1866 to wealthy parents, and spent much of her childhood with governesses, rather than other children. Inspired by family holidays in the Lake District and Scotland, she gained a love of animals and plants, and expressed this in watercolor drawings. Encouraged by family friends, in 1890 she created a set of greeting cards which she sent to a German publisher. The rest, as they say, is history. Her first book, *The Tale of Peter Rabbit*, was published privately in 1900 and commercially two years later. Twenty-two more books followed in the space of twenty years.

In 1905, Potter became engaged to Norman Warne, the son of her publisher, but he died soon after. In 1913, at the age of 47, she married Lake District solicitor William Heelis. Together they began breeding Herdwick sheep. With royalties from her books, and an inheritance from her parents, she continued to buy property in the area with a view to conservation. It is thought that her estate will probably be left to the National Trust.

Women Flying High in Aircraft Industry

USA, December: This year has been a peak year in the American aircraft industry, which has been steadily increasing production since 1940. There are now 81 factories involved in producing aircraft across the nation, and the workforce numbers more than 2.1 million, of whom more than 486,000 are women. At Willow Run, Michigan, the country's largest aircraft manufacturing plant, 38 percent of the staff are women.

Betty Smith

With many men away at war, American industries are having to look further afield for employees, and the image of Rosie the Riveter is helping industry recruit women into jobs traditionally seen as being in the male domain. The aircraft industry has been hiring women for some years now. Initially wives and widows of military men were given priority, but there are plenty of single women also being accepted. Some say women are preferred over African-American men.

With women now an established part of the workforce, new labor policies are being developed, taking into account issues such as women's pay, child care, and job training. However, it is no secret that management assumes that most women will give up their positions when the war is over and men return to their old jobs.

It's Our Fight Too!

Rosie the Riveter encourages women into the workforce.

Eva Duarte

Sparks of Passion at Fundraiser

Argentina, January 22: Juan Perón, the Secretary of Labor in the Argentinian government, appears to have been be smitten by a woman half his age. Perón, 48, met the stage, film, and radio actress Eva Duarte today at a charity event organized to raise funds for the victims of the earthquake that struck San Juan on January 15. Eva Duarte was one of a group of actors who last week walked through San Juan's streets with collection boxes, encouraging local people to donate money to aid the victims of the earthquake. A source said that Perón seemed overcome by the force of Duarte's words, her strong voice, fragile appearance and fiery eyes. Duarte comes from rural Argentina and, at age 15, made her way to Buenos Aires to pursue her career.

Spiritualist Arrested for Séance

Portsmouth, England, January 19: A séance conducted by Scottish spiritualist Helen Duncan was raided by police today in

"Parents can only give good advice or put them [children] on the right paths, but the final forming of a person's character lies in their own hands."

Anne Frank (1929–45),
DIARY ENTRY FOR
JULY 15, 1944

American Red Cross workers land in France to help Allied forces there.

Portsmouth, home port of Britain's Royal Navy. Witnesses reported that the séance was interrupted by the blast of a whistle blown by a plainclothes policeman. He and an accompanying naval lieutenant attempted to stop the "ectoplasm" they saw coming out of Duncan's mouth, believing it to be a trick made with a white sheet. However, they were unable to touch it and a subsequent search of the rooms failed to find any evidence of such a sheet. Duncan and three members of her audience were taken into custody.

Helen has been in great demand over the last few years among people who have lost family members while on active duty, and her séances are said to offer great comfort. However, her spiritual activities have been attracting the attention of a skeptical and increasingly suspicious establishment. In November, 1941, she informed an audience that the spirit of a sailor from the battleship HMS *Barham* appeared to her announcing that he had gone down with his vessel. It turned out that the *Barham* had been sunk a few days previously—with the loss of most of her crew—but the government had not yet reported the loss. The sinking was officially revealed a few months later.

There is a great deal of speculation brewing about the real motive behind today's raid, including a fear that she might reveal the date of the imminent D-Day operation, the invasion of France. At the Portsmouth Magistrates' Court today, Duncan was charged with the crime of vagrancy, which carries a maximum fine of five shillings.

There are rumors, however, that the authorities are determined to lay more serious charges. These may include conspiracy, and contravening the *Witchcraft Act* of 1735, which has not been used for a century. It is likely she may also be charged under the *Larceny Act* for taking money under false pretences.

Duncan's supporters have already started a defense fund.

During the US attack on Truk Island, Japanese soldiers massacred one hundred "comfort women."

Girls and Women Massacred on Truk

Truk Island, The Carolines, February 18: Early reports following the American attack on Japanese forces on the island of Truk in the Carolines describe a hideous scene. Around a hundred women (most of them so-called "comfort women"—girls forced into prostitution by Japanese Forces) were machine-gunned after they sought shelter in a dugout behind the Japanese naval base where they worked.

According to reports, the Japanese, fearing that the "comfort women" would be an embarrassment should they fall into American hands, decided to kill

Argentina, January 22: Juan Perón meets Eva Duarte at a charity event.
Portsmouth, England, January 19: Helen Duncan is arrested after holding a séance in Portsmouth. Her accurate pronouncement on the sinking of a British warship had aroused suspicion.
Berlin, Germany, January 21: Allied bombing leaves the city in ruins.
Birmingham, Alabama, USA, January 26: Radical and writer Angela Davis is born.

January 27: The siege of Leningrad is lifted; over 640,000 people died during the 900 days of the siege.
Truk Island, The Carolines, February 18: Japanese soldiers massacre a hundred women (mostly girls forced into prostitution) in a dugout behind the naval base on Truk Island.
USSR, February 1: A new USSR constitution allows Soviet republics to conduct their own armies and negotiations.
Eatonton, Georgia, USA, February 9: Writer Alice Walker is born.

Hungary, March 23: A German puppet government is created in Hungary after German occupation on March 22.
Izieu, France, April 6: Sabina Zlatin's children's home, where Jewish children found refuge, is raided by Klaus Barbie's Lyon Gestapo.
Broadway, New York, USA, April 12: Lillian Hellman's play, *The Searching Wind,* has its first performance.
France, April 21: The *Comité Français de Libérations National* pronounces the ordinance which grants women the right to vote.

Rome, June 4: Rome is liberated by Allied forces.
Japan, June 15: The USA begins heavy bombing of Kyushu, Japan.
Iceland, June 17: Iceland breaks free of Danish rule, becoming a republic.
Natzweiler, Germany, July 6: SOE spies Vera Leigh, Sonia Olschanezky, Andrée Borrel, and Diana Rowden, are executed by the Nazis.
Rastenburg, East Prussia, July 20: Count von Stauffenberg, German officer, plants a bomb in an attempt to assassinate Hitler. The bomb explodes, but Hitler survives.

India, August 11: An advance by Allied troops forces the Japanese to retreat to Burma.
Paris, France, August 23: Citizens and the French Resistance assist Allied forces in taking Paris.
Buchenwald, Germany, August 27: Princess Mafalda of Savoy dies after being seriously wounded during an American bombing raid on a munitions factory in Buchenwald concentration camp.

Jewish refugees at Fort Ontario line up to receive towels and soap.

Aimee Semple
McPherson

of Jewish refugees interred behind barbed wire, at Fort Ontario—a former army training base close to the city of Oswego, New York State—to be granted US citizenship. Gruber escorted the refugees into the United States earlier this year, following a special invitation from President Franklin D. Roosevelt.

Ever since the rise of Nazism in the 1930s, the US Congress had imposed a quota on Jewish immigration to the United States from Europe. When, in early 1944, Congress refused to lift the quota, President Roosevelt, acting by executive authority, "invited" 1,000 Jewish refugees in liberated Italy to visit America as his guests. Gruber was sent to Italy to secretly meet them and accompany them to the USA. To ensure her safety during the mission, Gruber was given an honorary rank of general. This meant that, if she were captured, she would be treated as a prisoner of war rather than executed as a civilian spy.

Once safely in Italy, Gruber boarded the army troop transport *Henry Gibbins* with 982 refugees—men, women, and children—and 1,000 wounded American soldiers. Throughout the potentially dangerous voyage across the Atlantic, she recorded the survival stories of the refugees. She told them, "You are the first witnesses coming to America. Through you, America will learn the truth of Hitler's crimes." She took notes as the refugees told their stories, often having to stop because her tears blurred the ink in her notebook. The grateful refugees call Gruber "Mother Ruth."

US government agencies are arguing about whether the refugees should be allowed to remain in the country, but for the moment at least, the people are safe from deportation behind the barbed wire of Fort Ontario. Gruber, who was born in 1911 in Brooklyn, New York City, one of five children of Russian Jewish parents, says the mission has been a life-changing experience. She intends to continue the fight for Jewish people living under oppressive governments.

First AA Woman Fights Prejudice

USA: The new National Council on Alcoholism and Drug Dependence (NCADD) has turned Marty Mann's dream into a reality. Determined to educate the country and eliminate the stigma surrounding alcoholism, she has joined forces with the Yale School of Alcohol Studies to establish the NCADD, which provides education, information, help, and hope to the public, advocating prevention, intervention, and treatment for those suffering from alcoholism.

Recent scientific research describes alcoholism as a biochemical abnormality, not a symptom of moral decay, and recognizes it as a disease which manifests itself as "an allergy of the body coupled with an obsession of the mind." Mann advocates that alcoholism be viewed as a public health problem and therefore a public responsibility and that the alcoholic be viewed as a sick person who can be helped and is worth helping.

The elegant Mann, who regularly sweeps people off their feet with her charm and intellect knows about the disease from firsthand experience. Born into a wealthy family in Chicago, she was blessed with beauty, brains, and a forceful will. At 14, Mann was diagnosed with tuberculosis. After several years of private care, she recovered, only to have another disease assert itself. Mann's early signs of alcoholism eventually led to round-the-clock drinking, a personal crisis, and, finally, institutionalization. Once Mann attended her first meeting of Alcoholics Anonymous (AA) in 1939—the first women ever to do so—the real healing began.

Her triumphant recovery and commitment to eliminate ignorance of alcoholism is powering an historic change in our society. Mann is a persuasive speaker, who continues to inspire other female alcoholics. Even audiences initially skeptical of her message—that an alcoholic is a sick person who can be helped—have ended up enthusiastically supporting her.

Through the NCADD and Mann's vision and leadership, the attitude of America toward alcoholism is starting to change. The problem of alcoholism is moving from being a moral issue to one of public health.

King of Siam Story an Instant Bestseller

Michigan, USA: Novelist Margaret Landon's book *Anna and the King of Siam* is a runaway success with the American public. The book, published this year, is the story of a British governess engaged by the King of Siam to help him communicate with foreign governments and tutor his children and favored concubines.

A mixture of truth and fiction, this entertaining book weaves meticulously researched facts with beautifully imagined scenes. Based on the diaries of Anna Leonowens, a British governess in the Royal Court of Siam during the 1860s, the story mainly concerns the culture clash between Imperialist Victorian values of the British Empire and the autocratic rule of Siam's King Mongkut. There is already discussion about making the story into a film.

Female partisans in Yugoslavia take part in a training exercise.

Queen Wilhelmina

Auschwitz Liberated

Poland, January 27: Soviet forces have liberated Auschwitz, the largest concentration camp complex established by the Nazi regime. Auschwitz played a central role in Adolf Hitler's plan to exterminate the Jews of Europe. More than a million Jewish men, women, and children from many different European countries were put to death in the gas chambers since the main camp began functioning in 1940.

When Soviet soldiers entered Auschwitz today, they found only a few thousand emaciated survivors. Investigations revealed that thousands of prisoners had been killed in the preceding days, while tens of thousands of others had been forced to march westward as the German SS authorities evacuated the complex in the face of the rapid Soviet advance. The retreating Germans also tried to obliterate traces of mass murder at the complex, but the Soviets have already uncovered abundant evidence of such crimes.

"DARE TO DREAM, AND WHEN YOU DREAM—DREAM BIG."

HENRIETTA SZOLD
ISRAELI PIONEER
(1860–1945)

"I AM IN THE WORLD TO CHANGE THE WORLD."

KATHE KOLLWITZ
ARTIST AND PACIFIST
(1867–1945)

A Red Cross team tends concentration camp survivors.

Founder of Hadassah Dies

Palestine, February 13: American Jewish scholar and Zionist leader Henrietta Szold died of pneumonia today at the Hadassah Medical Center in Jerusalem, the hospital she worked so hard to create. She was 85.

Szold was born in 1860 in Baltimore, Maryland, the daughter of a rabbi. After leaving high school, she worked as a teacher before enrolling in the Jewish Theological Seminary in New York. She became executive secretary of the Jewish Publication Society in 1893—a position she held until 1916—translating, editing, and indexing many significant Jewish works throughout that time.

It was while visiting Palestine in 1909 that Szold became a committed Zionist. A year later, she was appointed secretary of the Federation of American Zionists and in 1912 she went on to found Hadassah, the Women's Zionist organization, serving as its president until 1926. One of her finest achievements was to set up the American Zionist Medical Unit, which sailed for Palestine in 1918 to reform medical care in the region. In 1920, Szold herself moved to Palestine to direct operations, which included the establishment of a nursing school, dental school, medical school, clinics, and hospitals.

In 1933, while working with Hadassah in Palestine, Szold began work on another of her memorable projects, initiating the Youth Aliyah agency, which has since

Szold helped rescue children from Germany.

time out

The versatile Babe Didrikson Zaharias is named the Associated Press Woman Athlete of the Year, for her achievements on the golf course this time. She also won this award in 1932, that time for track and field.

been credited with rescuing thousands of Jewish children from Nazi Germany and other European countries.

Lena Baker Goes to the Electric Chair

Georgia, USA, March 5: African-American Lena Baker today became the first woman to be put to death in the State of Georgia's electric chair. Baker was convicted of the 1944 murder of her former employer, Ernest B. Knight, a gristmill owner who had hired her to care for him after he broke his leg in a fall.

Born at the turn of the century in the small community of Cotton Hill, near Cuthbert, Baker had known little else but hard work and grinding poverty when Knight, a white man 23 years her senior, offered her employment. It wasn't long before a sexual relationship developed between the two. According to local reports, Knight soon took to imprisoning Baker in the gristmill for several days at a time.

On August 14 last year, Baker's trial convened at the courthouse in Randolph County under the jurisdiction of Judge Charles William "Two Gun" Worrill, so dubbed because he kept two pistols on the bench. In her testimony, Baker explained how Knight had locked her in the mill on Sunday, April 30, while he went to a church singing. Upon his return, he refused to let her

Key Events

Poland, January 27: Soviet forces seize the Auschwitz concentration camp to find thousands of starving prisoners near death; most prisoners had already been herded out of the camp by the SS.
USSR, February 4–11: At a conference in Yalta, President Roosevelt, Prime Minister Churchill, and Marshal Stalin finalize their plans for the defeat of Germany.
Palestine, February 13: Henrietta Szold, US Zionist, feminist, and founder of Hadassah, dies at age 85.

Germany, February 14: The city of Dresden lies in ruins after massive bombing by Allied forces.
Bergen-Belsen, Netherlands, March: Diarist Anne Frank dies of typhus.
Netherlands, March: Queen Wilhelmina returns to her home country briefly.
Georgia, USA, March 5: African-American Lena Baker is denied clemency by the State of Georgia, and executed for the murder of her former white employer. She was tried and sentenced in one day by an all-male, all-white jury.

Los Angeles, USA, March 7: Ingrid Bergman wins the Best Actress Academy Award for her performance in *Gaslight*.
USA, March 8: The first African-American nurse to serve in World War II, Phyllis Mae Daley, receives her commission in the US Navy Nurse Corps.
Warm Springs, Georgia, USA, April 12: President Franklin D. Roosevelt dies. Harold S. Truman is sworn in as US president.

Netherlands, April 17: Dutch resistance fighter Hannie Schaft (known as "The Girl with the Red Hair") is executed by the Nazis.
San Francisco, USA, April 25: Heads of government meet to establish the United Nations, the organization that is to replace the League of Nations. It will officially come into existence on October 24.
Milan, Italy, April 28: Mussolini and his mistress, Clara Petacci, are strung up for public display after being shot dead by partisans.

Germany, April: Allied forces liberate Nazi concentration camps, finding starved, critically ill captives and grounds piled with rotting corpses.
Berlin, Germany April 30: German test pilot Hanna Reitsch flies a Luftwaffe general into Berlin to meet with Hitler, dodging Soviet anti-aircraft fire.
Berlin, Germany, April 30: As Soviet forces move to take Berlin, Hitler commits suicide in his bunker by shooting himself. His newly wed wife, Eva Braun, poisons herself and dies.

Ingrid Bergman in Oscar-winning form in *Gaslight*.

was executed today by German occupation forces. She was 24 years of age.

Jannetje Johanna Schaft was born in Haarlem on September 16, 1920. After finishing high school, she studied law at the University of Amsterdam until 1943, when her refusal to sign a declaration of allegiance to the German occupation authorities left her no choice but to discontinue her studies and return home to Haarlem. There, under the name Hannie Schaft, she joined a resistance organization with close ties to the Dutch Communist Party. As she became more and more active in the movement, she worked as a weapons courier, gathered information about German military activity, committed acts of sabotage, and carried out a number of attacks on Germans, collaborators, and traitors. She was hated by the Germans.

Heavily disguised, Schaft was captured by chance while distributing illegal newspapers on March 21 this year. She was transported to German headquarters and after days and nights of interrogation, her identity as "The Girl with the Red Hair" was confirmed. Today, with the south of the Netherlands already liberated and the end of the war in sight, Schaft was taken to the dunes near Overveen, where she was shot dead by her captors and buried in a shallow grave.

Mission Accomplished

Berlin, Germany, April 26: Test pilot Hanna Reitsch today accomplished her most daring feat to date when she flew Luftwaffe General Robert Ritter von Greim into the besieged city of Berlin to meet with Adolf Hitler, evading heavy anti-aircraft fire to land her Fieseler Storch aircraft on a shell-pocked street near the Brandenburg Gate.

Reitsch was born in Hirschberg, Silesia, on March 29, 1912. While attending medical school in 1932 she took the decision to pursue a career in flying and soon went

on to become the first woman to cross the Alps in a glider. In 1937, after graduating to powered aircraft, she was posted to the Luftwaffe testing center at Rechlin, where she became a test pilot on the Junkers Ju 87 Stuka and Dornier Do 17 projects. She was also one of the few pilots to test the world's first fully controllable helicopter, the Focke-Achgelis Fa 61.

As World War II progressed, Reitsch was assigned more difficult missions, including testing the rocket-propelled Messerschmitt Me 163 Komet. It was on her fifth Me 163 flight, in 1942, that she was forced to crash-land, and, although badly injured, she managed to sketch out

Clara Petacci

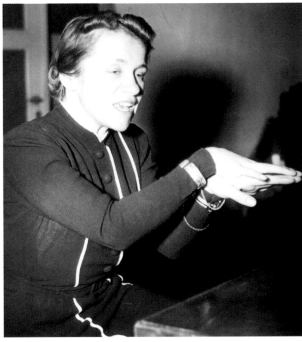

Hanna Reitsch is one of Germany's leading test pilots.

a report before losing consciousness. After recovering, she went on to test a manned version of the V-1 rocket bomb.

In 1941 Reitsch was awarded the Iron Cross First Class, the first female recipient during World War II. She is also the only woman to have been awarded the Luftwaffe Combined Pilot and Observer Badge with Diamonds.

leave, despite her pleas to be let free, and the two began to argue. In Baker's words, they then "tussled" over a pistol, which discharged, hitting Knight in the head and killing him instantly.

The trial lasted less than a day, and the all-white male jury took less than an hour to return a verdict of guilty. Baker was sentenced to death but was later granted a 60-day reprieve to allow the Board of Pardons and Parole to review the case. Clemency was denied by the Board, and she was taken to Reidsville State Prison in February this year to await execution by electrocution. Baker went to her death today still proclaiming her innocence: "What I done, I did in self-defense, or I would have been killed myself."

The Girl with the Red Hair

Netherlands, April 17: Dutch resistance fighter Hannie Schaft, nicknamed "The Girl with the Red Hair" by the Germans,

Netherlands, May 2: Queen Wilhelmina returns to a liberated area of her country. She is known as the "Mother of the Resistance."
Reims, France, May 7: Germany signs an unconditional surrender after the foreign minister gives notice in a radio broadcast.
London, England, May 8: Crowds of spectators jam London's streets to hear Churchill's broadcast announcing the war in Europe will end at midnight. Around 50,000 gleeful revellers take to the streets—singing, dancing, and embracing.

Japan, June 21: American troops take Okinawa after two months of intense fighting.
New Mexico, USA, July 16: The first atomic bomb is successfully tested in the desert near Alamogordo.
London, England, July 26: Winston Churchill loses the British general election to Clement Attlee, leader of the Labour Party, who wins a landslide victory.

Japan, August 6: The United States drops an atomic bomb on the city of Hiroshima. On August 9, another atomic bomb is dropped on the city of Nagasaki.
Japan, September 2: Japan signs an unconditional surrender to the Allied powers.
Yokohama, September 5: Iva Toguri d'Aquino, who some have identified as "Tokyo Rose," is arrested for broadcasting pro-Japanese wartime propaganda.

Boston, USA, September 26: Harvard Medical School's first class of women is enrolled in the university.
Nuremberg, Germany, November 20: Hitler's collaborators, including Hermann Goering and Rudolf Hess, stand trial for war crimes.
USA, December: President Truman appoints Eleanor Roosevelt as a delegate to the General Assembly of the newly created United Nations.

Stockholm, Sweden, December: Chilean poet Gabriela Mistral wins the Nobel Prize for Literature. She is the first Latin American to win this prestigious prize.
San Francisco, USA: Artist Georgia O'Keeffe paints *Pelvis Series Red with Yellow*.
USA: The Pulitzer Prize for Drama goes to Mary Coyle Chase for the play *Harvey*.
Italy, Japan, and the Dutch East Indies (Indonesia): Women win the right to vote.

Gabriela Mistral

Hitler and Braun in Suicide Pact

Berlin, Germany, April 30: Adolf Hitler and Eva Braun committed suicide together today, less than 24 hours after they were married in a brief civil ceremony at the Führerbunker in Berlin.

The couple met in 1929 while Braun was working for Heinrich Hoffman, the official photographer for the Nazi party. In the early days of their relationship, she twice attempted suicide, and it was after her second attempt in 1935 that Hitler bought her a villa in Munich near his home, also providing her with a Mercedes and a chauffeur for her personal use. By 1936, she was acting as hostess at Hitler's

"Tokyo Rose" has been arrested.

Adolf Hitler and Eva Braun committed suicide a day after their wedding.

"THIS CAN'T LAST. THIS MISERY CAN'T LAST. I MUST REMEMBER THAT AND TRY TO CONTROL MYSELF. NOTHING LASTS REALLY. NEITHER HAPPINESS NOR DESPAIR. NOT EVEN LIFE LASTS VERY LONG."

NOEL COWARD/DAVID LEAN'S *BRIEF ENCOUNTER* (1945), QUOTE FROM LAURA JESSON

Berghof at Berchtesgaden, in Bavaria, whenever he was in residence, although they seldom appeared in public together.

Earlier this month, Braun traveled to Berlin to be with Hitler, refusing to leave him as the Russians closed in on the city. In accordance with Hitler's wishes, their bodies have been cremated in the Reich Chancellery garden.

Mother of the Resistance Returns

Netherlands, May 2: Queen Wilhelmina today made a triumphant return to her liberated homeland after spending the last five years in exile in Britain. When Nazi Germany invaded the Netherlands on May 10, 1940, and met with rapid success, the queen initially planned to travel to the southern province of Zeeland and coordinate further resistance from the town of Breskens, hoping to remain there until the arrival of reinforcements. Zeeland soon came under heavy attack from the Luftwaffe, however, and within three days she made the decision to withdraw

with her family to Britain, where she assumed leadership of the Dutch government in exile. On May 14, 1940, all Dutch troops, except those in Zeeland—who held out until May 19—surrendered to the German invasion forces.

Although Wilhelmina was not a physical presence in the difficult and dangerous years that followed, she proved to be a source of great moral support and inspiration to the resistance against the German occupation of her country. She communicated eagerly awaited late-night messages to her people via Radio Oranje, vehemently condemning Adolf Hitler as "the arch-enemy of mankind," and dismissed her prime minister when, doubting an Allied victory, he sought to negotiate a separate peace with the Nazis. Nor was she spared danger herself while in Britain. During the Blitz, she narrowly escaped death when a bomb badly damaged her country home, killing several of her guards.

The queen's experience, knowledge, and fortitude as a monarch also earned her admiration and respect among world leaders throughout the war years, with British Prime Minister Winston Churchill describing her as "the only real man" among the governments in exile in London. In 1944, in recognition of her role as a prominent symbol of Dutch freedom, Queen Wilhelmina became only the second woman to be inducted into the British Order of the Garter.

A Rose by Many Other Names

Yokohama, Japan, September 5: What's in a name? Trouble, as Iva Toguri d'Aquino discovered today when she was arrested by United States Army authorities after being identified in press reports as the woman behind the voice of "Tokyo Rose," the infamous World War II Japanese radio propagandist.

Born Ikuko Toguri in Los Angeles on July 4, 1916, Aquino was raised by her immigrant parents to consider herself American and was a popular student at her school. After graduating from the University of California with a degree

in zoology, she traveled to Japan to visit family, but found herself stranded there after Japan's attack on Pearl Harbor on December 7, 1941.

Aquino was forced to support herself, and took Japanese language lessons before eventually obtaining work as a typist with the Domei News Agency. Later, she found employment with Radio Tokyo, where she became a broadcaster on the "Zero Hour," a radio program aimed at demoralizing American forces serving in the South Pacific. Using the alias "Ann" and then "Orphan Ann," Aquino taunted her listeners and played popular songs as part of Japan's psychological warfare campaign to inculcate among American forces a sense of the terrible hardships they were enduring and pointless sacrifice in the face of superior Japanese forces.

Following the Japanese surrender on September 2, two American reporters searching for "Tokyo Rose" discovered Aquino's involvement in such broadcasts and offered to pay her for exclusive interview rights. Aquino agreed and signed a contract that identified her as the troops' notorious radio protagonist.

The case against Aquino remains problematic, however, because at no time did she refer to herself as "Tokyo Rose" on air. The name was, in fact, invented by the American forces and could have applied to any number of female voices emanating from the Japanese-controlled radio stations. Questions also remain about Aquino's motivation, because she never agreed to renounce her American citizenship, even when she married Felipe Aquino, a Portuguese citizen of Japanese-Portuguese ancestry.

In a Class of their Own

Boston, USA, September 26: Harvard Medical School today enrolled its first class of women. This event ends nearly a century of advocacy that began in 1847, when Harriot Hunt, a practicing physician who had trained through an apprenticeship, wrote to the dean of the medical faculty requesting a more scientific education. While her request was denied, it marked the first of numerous applications from women and physicians of both sexes, who wanted women to be placed on an equal footing with male students and so obtain the best medical tuition possible.

The school's decision to allow the entry of women students today was the direct

First racial and now gender barriers have fallen at Harvard, with the enrolling of women in the medical school.

achieve formal recognition until 1914, when she won a national literary prize with the work *Sonnets of Death*. The first volume of her collected poems, *Desolation*, was published in 1922, followed by *Tenderness* (1925), *Questions* (1930), and *Tala* (1938). Among the central themes of her poetry are nature, betrayal, death, love, sorrow, and Latin American identity.

The publication of her works significantly assisted Mistral's advancement in her career as an educator. In 1921 she was appointed principal of Santiago High School, Chile's most prestigious secondary school for girls, and in 1922 she was asked to help reform schools and libraries in Mexico. She was rewarded for these achievements in 1923, when the Chilean government gave her the title "Teacher of the Nation."

Meanwhile, Mistral's stature as poet and educator was gaining wider attention on the international scene, and she found herself invited to attend and address conferences in the United States and Europe. Between 1925 and 1934, she lived mainly in France and Italy, writing numerous articles for newspapers and magazines, and also working for a League of Nations organization, the League for Intellectual Cooperation. In 1933 she entered the Chilean Foreign Service, serving as an ambassador-at-large for Latin American culture before moving on to represent Chile as honorary consul in a variety of countries, including the USA and Spain.

Eleanor Roosevelt

result of a report presented by a subcommittee of the Administrative Board at a special faculty meeting on May 22 last year. The report found that male students could gain from learning to accept women as equals, and that the lower paid areas of medicine, routinely avoided by men, could gain from the expertise of married women doctors who did not need to support their families. Central to the report, however, was the argument that the quality of a medical class as a whole would be enhanced significantly if the lowest group of male students were to be replaced by a superior group of women.

The recommendations of the report were accepted almost unanimously by the faculty. On June 5 last year, the Corporation, the main governing board, voted in agreement, and on September 25 the Board of Overseers endorsed the vote.

Woman of the World

Washington, DC, USA, December: President Harry S. Truman has appointed former First Lady Eleanor Roosevelt one of the members of the United States delegation to the first session of the United Nations General Assembly, to be held in January next year. Her appointment comes just eight months after the death of her husband, Franklin D. Roosevelt, on April 12.

During her husband's long presidency, Eleanor Roosevelt was an active First Lady

who held weekly press conferences, wrote columns for national newspapers, and made numerous trips around the nation to look at ordinary people's living and working conditions. A champion of the poor and oppressed, she argued against all forms of discrimination.

A long-time pacifist, Roosevelt nevertheless embraced the cause of Allied victory when the nation entered World War II in 1941, visiting England and the South Pacific to promote goodwill among the Allies and raise the morale of American soldiers serving overseas.

A Poet Laureate for Latin America

Stockholm, Sweden, December: Chilean poet Gabriela Mistral has become the first Latin American to receive the Nobel Peace Prize for Literature. Acknowledging the honor in her acceptance speech, Mistral said: "At this moment, by an undeserved stroke of fortune, I am the direct voice of the poets of my race and the indirect voice for the noble Spanish and Portuguese tongues."

Mistral was born Lucila Godoy y Alcayaga in the Andean village of Vicuña on April 7, 1889. She published some early poems while working as a teacher but did not

French newspaper *Libération* marks the end of World War II.

Georgia O'Keeffe

Ship Arrives with Cargo of GI Brides

New York, February 4: Early this morning, the SS *Argentina* steamed into New York's ice-clogged harbor carrying, for the first time, not returning US servicemen from the war in Europe but the women they had married overseas.

The ship left Southampton, England, on January 26, carrying 456 women (and one man) who had married US personnel during the war, as well as their 173 babies and young children. They hail from England, Scotland, Wales, Malta, and Northern Ireland. They are the first of an expected 70,000 wives who will make the crossing.

The women spent the week before the voyage at Tidworth Army Base having physical examinations, watching films about their new homeland, and being instructed about ship life. As the wives left England, they were filled with mixed emotions—they were leaving behind their families and homelands but would soon be seeing their husbands again. Many were excited about the prospect of living in the United States.

The voyage started well and the women enjoyed walking on the decks of the former ocean liner. There were films to watch

> *"MEN AREN'T ATTRACTED TO MY MIND, THEY'RE ATTRACTED BY WHAT I DON'T MIND."*
>
> GYPSY ROSE LEE
> (1914–1970),
> AMERICAN ACTRESS

Ethel Merman stars in *Annie Get Your Gun*.

GI brides and babies do lifejacket drill on board the SS *Argentina*.

and organized games to take part in. On day three, however, there was a bad storm. Many women were seasick and the crew had a busy time looking after ill passengers and their children. One little boy, Francis Hardiman Jr., tumbled from his bunk in the rough weather and received a nasty cut to his forehead.

However, in the early hours of this morning all of the women's difficulties were forgotten. The commander of the *Argentina*, Commodore Thomas N. Simmons, had called ahead and made a request for a special welcome, and New York had obliged: For the first time since the start of the war, the Statue of Liberty was lit up. After many years living in blackout conditions, the GI brides were thrilled to see the lights of New York City.

Northside Center for Childen Opens

New York, USA, March: This month, a center offering much-needed psychological services to black children and their families in Harlem has opened in a basement apartment on 158th Street. Doctor Mamie Clark, the first black woman to be awarded a doctorate in psychology from Columbia University (and only the second black person after her husband, Doctor Kenneth Clark), is the founder and director of the new Northside Center.

During her studies, Doctor Clark worked extensively with young black children and found that frequently they have very low self-esteem. One test she employed involved offering 3-year-old black children a choice between a black or a white doll to play with, and seeing that they most often chose the white doll, she concluded they already saw their skin color negatively.

After finishing her studies, she worked at the Riverdale Home for Children, a residence for homeless black girls. She became aware of the total lack of psychological services for black children in the Harlem neighborhood. She and her husband asked existing agencies to extend their services to black children, but they met with no success. As a consequence, they have decided to open their own agency offering free psychological assessment and assistance.

Doctor Clark's own family has provided the funds to pay the rent on the apartment and furnish it. The psychologists, psychiatrists, social workers, and doctors at the center are volunteers.

Southampton, England, January 26: The first official boatload of GI brides sails on the SS *Argentina*.
London, England, January 30: The first meeting of the United Nations General Assembly is held.
Fulton, Missouri, USA, March 5: Winston Churchill makes a speech, "Sinews of Peace," in which he warns the western powers of the dangers of Soviet expansion and refers to an "iron curtain" descending across Europe.

Paris, France, March 6: France recognizes Vietnam as a free state within the Indochina Federation.
New York, USA, March: Doctor Mamie Clark founds the Northside Center for the assessment of child development.
Los Angeles, USA, March 7: Joan Crawford takes the Oscar for Best Actress in the title role of *Mildred Pierce*. Muriel Box, with her husband, Sydney Box, wins the Oscar for the Best Original Screenplay for *The Seventh Veil*.

Australia, April 11: The War Crimes Commission reports that Japan routinely committed acts of torture on Australian prisoners of war.
Geneva, Switzerland, April 18: The League of Nations is dissolved.
USA, May 1: Emma Clarissa Clement is named Mother of the Year. She is the first black woman to be given the honor.
San Francisco, USA, May 2-4: Nine guards are taken hostage by inmates at Alcatraz prison; five people are killed.

New York, May 15: Georgia O'Keeffe gives the first solo exhibition by a female artist at New York's Museum of Modern Art.
New York, USA, May 16: Irving Berlin's musical, *Annie Get Your Gun*, opens on Broadway. Ethel Merman stars as Annie Oakley. The song "There's No Business Like Show Business" is a hit.
USA, May 25: Patty Smith Hill, credited with writing "Happy Birthday to You," dies at age 78.

London, England, May 30: The organic farming charity, the Soil Association, is founded. It is inspired by Lady Eve Balfour's 1943 book *The Living Soil*.
Italy, June 3: Italy abolishes its monarchy after a referendum and becomes a republic.
Argentina, June 4: Juan Perón is inaugurated as Argentina's first president. His wife, Eva, is fondly known as Evita by the people of Argentina.

Joan Crawford means business in *Mildred Pierce*.

Best Actress Oscar for Joan Crawford

Grauman's Chinese Theater, Los Angeles, USA, March 7: Joan Crawford has received the Academy Award for Best Performance by an Actress for the title role in the film *Mildred Pierce*. The film has been a huge hit with critics and audiences.

Crawford plays a woman determined to support her children during the Great Depression. Hard-working Mildred Pierce, separated from her unemployed husband, becomes a restaurant owner. However, financial success does not bring happiness. Mildred's daughter is contemptuous of her working mother. Their relationship ends in disaster.

Crawford's award follows a lull in her career. She had been regarded as a "has been," and her

contract with MGM was terminated in 1943. *Mildred Pierce* was only her second film for her new studio, Warner Bros. Her place back among the first rank of Hollywood stars now seems assured.

First Black Mother of the Year

USA, May 1: Emma Clarissa Clement was today called from a church meeting to the one telephone in the Negro section of Springfield, Kentucky, to be told by her daughter that she had been named America's Mother of the Year by the Golden Rule Foundation. She is the first black mother to receive the award.

Seventy-one-years-old Mrs Clement, widow of the late George Clement, bishop of the African Methodist Episcopal Zion Church in Louisville, has been selected for having been, according to the citation, "a mother of children who are devotedly serving their country and their people, a partner in her husband's ministry in his lifetime, a social and community worker in her own right."

Born in 1874, Mrs Clement was raised in a poor family, but she completed her school education and trained as a teacher.

Her husband did not earn a lot as a black minister, but each of her seven surviving children (a son died in infancy) completed their higher education, supported through their schooling by their mother, who kept a warm and orderly home and supplemented the family's income by teaching music. Her children have all gone to achieve outstanding success: Rufus Clement is the President of Atlanta University, three are college professors, one is a chaplain who served in World War II, one is a Red Cross field director still serving in Italy, and one works as an organizer for a church missionary society.

time out

Right-wing populist politician Juan Perón has been elected President of Argentina. He was aided and abetted in no small part by his second wife, Maria Eva de Duarte (Eva Perón or Evita), who is a popular public figure.

Georgia O'Keeffe Show

New York, USA, May 15: This evening a solo exhibition devoted to the paintings of Georgia O'Keeffe opens at America's premier modern art gallery, the Museum of Modern Art. She is the first female artist to be so honored. The exhibition consists of 57 of her works, spanning thirty years of her career.

Born in 1887 in Wisconsin, O'Keeffe spent some of her childhood in Virginia, and trained in Chicago, New York, and Virginia. She mainly worked in a strictly representational style until in 1912 she took a summer course taught by Alon Bement. He introduced her to the ideas of Arthur Wesley Dow, who believed art was an individual's expression of feeling. His ideas freed O'Keeffe to discover her own style. In 1916 the photographer and patron of artists Alfred Stieglitz saw some of her charcoal drawings and exclaimed, "Finally, a woman's feeling on paper!" He promoted her work and soon became her companion, the two marrying in 1924.

O'Keeffe's work is typified by pared-back realism blended with abstraction—images of flowers, bones, and other objects float in landscapes, especially of her beloved southwest, where she spends much of her time.

Mary Lou Williams

The Seventh Veil won Best Original Screenplay at the Oscars.

USA, June 20: The motion picture *Anna and the King of Siam*, starring Irene Dunne and Rex Harrison, premieres.

New York, June: Mary Lou Williams's *Zodiac Suite* is performed by the New York Philharmonic Orchestra at Carnegie Hall.

Germany, June–September: One hundred thousand Jews have left Poland for displaced peoples' camps in Germany.

Marshall Islands, July 1: The USA tests a 20,000-ton atomic bomb at Bikini Atoll.

Philippines, July 4: The nation gains independence from the USA, and becomes known as the Republic of the Philippines.

Paris, France, July 5: The bikini debuts at a fashion show.

Vatican City, July 7: The first American saint is canonized: Mother Frances Xavier Cabrini.

USA, July 14: Doctor Benjamin Spock's book on how to raise children, *The Commonsense Book of Baby and Child Care*, is published.

Paris, France, July 27: Author and poet Gertrude Stein dies at age 72.

India, August 19: Up to 4,000 Muslims and Hindus die during days of religious riots in Calcutta.

Nuremburg, Germany, October 1: The International Military Tribunal finds 22 Nazi leaders guilty of war crimes.

USA, October 19: Wartime economy on skirt length ends. Order L85 now allows dressmakers to increase the length of women's skirts and dresses.

England, October: The Royal Commission on Equal Pay recommends men and women civil servants receive equal pay for equal work.

Siessen, Germany, November 6: Sister Maria Innocentia Hummel, whose artwork inspired the famous Hummel figurines, dies at age 37.

Oslo, Norway, December 10: Emily Greene Balch, founder of the Women's International Committee for Permanent Peace, co-wins the Nobel Peace Prize.

Indochina, December 19: Communist leader Ho Chi Minh attacks the French in Hanoi, prompting the beginning of a new war.

Liberia and Yugoslavia: Women win the right to vote.

USA: The winner of the Houghton Mifflin prize for poetry, *North and South*, by newcomer Elizabeth Bishop, is published.

Paris, France: Prostitutes are forced on to the streets as "La Loi Marthe Richard" dictates the closure of brothels.

Irene Dunne

Soil Association Founded

London, England, May 30: The inaugural meeting of a new charitable foundation, the Soil Association, was held today. It is made up of farmers, scientists, and nutritionists who believe that plant, animal, and environmental health, and therefore human health, can be traced to farming methods. They advocate natural farming methods and question the use of chemicals such as the pesticide DDT, stating, "…we may well be upsetting the whole balance of Nature. We are like schoolboys rat-hunting in a munitions dump with a flame-thrower."

The Soil Association came about due to research undertaken by some of its founders. From 1935 to 1939, Doctor George Williamson and Doctor Innes Pearse surveyed 950 families through the Peckham Health Club in south London and found that education about exercise and nutrition could prevent ill health.

In 1939 Lady Eve Balfour and Alice Debenham, two Suffolk farmers, began a long-term farming experiment, the Haughley Experiment, to follow up the connections made by scientists between human health and plant and animal nutrition. Lady Eve published their early findings in 1943 in her book *The Living Soil*, the success of which has prompted the formation of the Soil Association.

The association aims to promote natural farming, to conduct further research, and to collate information gathered around the world by other researchers.

America's First Saint

Vatican City, Italy, July 7: Pope Pius XII has today canonized Mother Frances Xavier Cabrini (1850–1917) in recognition of her holiness and service to humanity. She is the first American citizen to become a saint.

She was born Francesca Cabrini in a village near Milan, Italy, the youngest of 13 children. Born premature, she was a sickly child, and continued to be in frail health for the rest of her life. After finishing school and gaining a teacher's certificate, she attempted to join two orders of nuns. Both times she was refused as

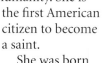

Mother Cabrini.

it was thought her poor health would not withstand the austere life of a nun. Instead the young woman became a teacher in a public school in 1872 and, in 1874, the administrator of the Cadogno Orphanage. She and five other women working there created their own order, taking their vows in 1877. She became known as Mother Cabrini. The Church authorities shut the orphanage in 1880, and the nuns founded the Missionary Sisters of the Sacred Heart of Jesus in an old Franciscan convent.

In 1887 Mother Cabrini went to Rome, seeking permission to take her mission to China, a long-held dream. Pope Leo XIII, however, did not agree to this, instructing her instead to work among the thousands of poor Italian immigrants in America.

She and her sisters arrived in New York in March, 1889. In time, they established orphanages, schools, and hospitals across not only the United States, but also in Europe and South America. In 1909 she became a naturalized American citizen.

Fourteen years after her death, Mother Cabrini was beatified, the first step on the path to sainthood.

Gertrude Stein leaves an important literary legacy.

Cancer Claims Gertrude Stein

Paris, France, July 27: Gertrude Stein, the American poet and author, died of colon cancer today in the American Hospital of Paris. She was 72.

Stein is well known in literary circles for her modernist, experimental writing, which critics likened to the painting style of artists such as Picasso. In turn, she had a great influence on many writers, most notably Ernest Hemingway.

Born in 1874, Stein grew up between the United States and Europe. She studied medicine but did not graduate. In 1903 she moved to France where she spent much of the rest of her life, remaining there during both world wars. Her Paris salon attracted many writers and painters. Her first major public success came with the publication of *The Autobiography of Alice B. Toklas* in 1933, named for her long-time lover and supporter.

Early Death for Figurine Designer

Siessen, Germany, November 6: Sister Maria Innocentia, whose pictures of innocent children inspired the famous Hummel porcelain figurines, has died today of tuberculosis, aged only 37 years, at the Franciscan Convent at Siessen.

Born Berta Hummel on May 21, 1909, in Masing, Bavaria, the talented artist attended the Munich Academy of Fine Arts where she graduated top of her class in 1931. She then joined the Franciscan Convent of Siessen where she became a teacher and continued to draw and paint, particularly children. In 1934 Hummel took the veil and the name Sister Maria Innocentia. Her drawings and paintings of children were turned into postcards and books. The funds from their sale supported the work of the convent.

Franz Goebel, head of a struggling porcelain factory in Oesalu, saw the pictures and approached the convent for permission to create figurines based on them. Production began in 1935 under Sister Maria Innocentia's supervision.

The Nazis took over the Siessen Convent in 1940. Sister Maria and the few remaining nuns were confined to the basement, short of fuel and food. Their only source of income was the proceeds from her artworks.

Sister Maria Innocentia first showed signs in 1936 of the illness that was to take her life. The harsh conditions of wartime life worsened her fragile health. After French troops liberated the convent, she was finally diagnosed with tuberculosis. The disease was too advanced for her to make a recovery. The Hummel pictures and figures are her legacy, and they will no doubt become collectors' items.

Nobel Peace Prize Awarded to Americans

Oslo, Norway, December 10: The Nobel Peace Prize has been awarded to Emily Greene Balch, 76, long-time worker for peace and international understanding.

She shares the award with fellow American, John R. Mott, of the Young Men's Christian Association.

In 1889 Balch became one of the first graduates from Philadelphia's prestigious Bryn Mawr College, and in the following years continued her economic studies, focusing on poverty and social justice, in Paris, Berlin, and America. She joined Wellesley College as a staff member in 1896. By 1913 she had become a professor of economics and sociology.

With the outbreak of World War I in 1914, Balch concentrated her efforts on bringing about peace. In 1915 she was a delegate to the International Congress of Women in The Hague, Netherlands, where she was instrumental in creating proposals that were presented to the leaders of the warring nations. During this time she co-founded the Women's International Committee for Permanent Peace, later the Women's International League for Peace and Freedom, with Jane Addams (who received the Nobel Peace Prize in 1931) and others. She continued to stand against America's involvement in the war and when her commitments to her peace work grew, the trustees of Wellesley College terminated her position.

Between the wars, Balch often worked with the League of Nations. In the 1930s she aided refugees escaping from Nazi-governed Germany. Nazi atrocities and the onset of war caused her, reluctantly, to set aside some of her pacifist beliefs, stating that people had every right to defend themselves against horrific mistreatment, all the while working to try and bring about peace.

In presenting the award, Gunnar Jahn, chairman of the Nobel Peace Prize committee, noted that her "lifelong indefatigable work for peace…has taught us that the reality we seek must be earned by hard and unrelenting toil in the world in which we live…"

Controversy Over "Closed Houses"

Paris, France: In France in 1804 it became illegal for prostitutes to solicit on the street, while brothels, known as "closed houses," were legalized. According to law, closed houses had to be away from main thoroughfares, at least 100 yards (100 m) from schools and churches, and were not allowed to advertise their services. Only women were permitted to run them, although they could have the financial backing of men. Prostitutes had to be registered with the police and be checked

4-H Clubs reach out to young people in rural America.

regularly for venereal disease by doctors. This system attempted to circumvent criminal involvement, improve public health, and above all, avoid offence by hiding prostitution behind closed doors.

On April 13 of this year "La Loi Marthe Richard" (the Marthe Richard Law) came

into being and ruled that closed houses must be shut down. While prostitution was not outlawed, brothels were. The law was named for one of its chief proponents, Marthe Richard, who experienced life in a closed house firsthand as a prostitute before her marriage in 1915. She is now a member of the French National Assembly.

Politicians and others opposed to brothels claim that many of the women were often treated violently and worked in virtual slavery, being unable to leave the premises and made to pay off impossibly high debts to brothel owners for their keep. Brothels also offered a false sense of security when it came to health. Doctors have admitted that, for a price, diseased women were often passed fit to work.

Of recent concern is that during the war brothels were taken over by the German occupying force. Many people believe that information about the Resistance was passed to the Germans within brothel walls. This is something else Marthe Richard is familiar with, though during World War I she spied *for* France, not against it.

With French prostitutes now walking the streets again, the controversy about closed houses seems far from over.

Emily Greene Balch

This hotel is one of many used by Parisian prostitutes, who can no longer operate from brothels.

"Red" Ellen Wilkinson

Social Reformer Takes Own Life

London, England, February 6: Trade unionist and politician "Red" Ellen Wilkinson has died from an overdose of barbiturates, aged 65. It is understood that Wilkinson had been depressed for some time by the slow pace of the social reforms she was pushing for, especially in the area of public education.

Many regard the *Free Milk Act*—free milk for all schoolchildren—which she managed through Parliament last year, as the culmination of a long career of public service.

Wilkinson was born in Manchester in 1891 to a conservative-voting textile worker and his wife, Ellen. The girl discovered socialism at an early age, and by 16 had joined the Independent Labor Party after hearing socialist and adult suffragette, Kathleen Glasier, speak.

Nicknamed for both the color of her hair and the shade of her politics, Ellen Wilkinson led a prodigiously productive life of social activism. She ran her local branch of the Fabian Society, a socialist intellectual organization, and was a pacifist during World War I. She became a Manchester City councilor, and then made the move into national politics as the Labor Party's Member of Parliament for Middlesborough, and later for Jarrow. She organized the famous Jarrow hunger marches in 1936 which saw thousands of starving, unemployed workers walk to London from the northeast of England. It was a turning point in British social history.

> *"WOMEN WANT LOVE TO BE A NOVEL, MEN WANT IT TO BE A SHORT STORY."*
>
> DAPHNE DU MAURIER (1907–89), ENGLISH WRITER

Another important victory was the introduction of the *Hire Purchase Act* in 1938 to protect working-class people who had paid part of the price of goods but lost them when their payments went into arrears.

The Times said in fitting tribute that had she lived longer "… there is little doubt that the children of England and Wales would have had reason to bless her name. She … would have seen to it in fact, as well as promise, [that] no child would be denied the opportunity that was his due."

American Women's Suffrage Founder Dies

New York, USA, March 9: Feminist Carrie Lane Chapman Catt, one of the founders of the US women's suffrage movement, and one of the instigators of the Nineteenth Amendment granting women the right to vote, has died, aged 88.

A dynamic speaker and tenacious organizer, Catt was a powerful force in American politics in the early 1900s. In 1900 she became president of the National American Woman Suffrage Association, succeeding 80-year-old activist Susan B. Anthony.

Later, she took the fight for women's rights to the world stage, forming the International Woman Suffrage Association. She served as international president from 1904 to 1923 and was active as honorary president until the time of her death.

Catt continued to speak out in her last years. She backed working women's causes, supported pacifism, and lobbied for relief for Jewish refugees.

time out

Dr Lillie Rosa Minoka-Hill has been given the Outstanding American Indian of the Year Award for her contributions to the health care of her people. Dr Minoka-Hill works among the Onedia tribe in Wisconsin.

Sudden Death of Willa Cather

New York, USA, April 24: One of the most important American novelists of the early twentieth century, Willa Cather has died aged 73 of a cerebral hemorrhage at her home in New York. She will be remembered by the public mostly as a chronicler of the pioneering American West, for which she drew on her own experiences growing up in Nebraska.

Willa Cather was a journalist, editor, and novelist. She wrote 12 novels, the best known being *My Antonia* (1918), *O Pioneers!* (1913), *The Song of the Lark* (1915), and *Death Comes to the Archbishop* (1927). In 1922 Cather won the Pulitzer Prize for *One of Ours*.

She graduated from the University of Nebraska in 1895. She had first arrived there in male dress, answering to the name William. While in college, she fell passionately in love with fellow student and athlete, Louise Pound.

Olivia de Havilland wins an Oscar for her role in *To Each His Own*.

London, England, February 6: Trade unionist and politician "Red" Ellen Wilkinson dies of an overdose of barbiturates, aged 65.

Paris, France, February 10: Peace treaties for Italy, Finland, Hungary, Romania, and Bulgaria are signed.

Germany, February 20: The state of Prussia is abolished and becomes part of the newly formed Federal Republic of Germany and German Democratic Republic.

New York, USA, March 9: Carrie Lane Chapman Catt, feminist and political activist, dies, aged 88.

Los Angeles, USA, March 13: Olivia de Havilland wins the Best Actress Academy Award for her performance in *To Each His Own*.

Los Angeles, USA, March 21: Premere of the movie *The Egg and I*, a romantic comedy starring Claudette Colbert, Fred MacMurray, and Marjorie Main.

Washington DC, USA, April 16: The *Army-Navy Nurse Act* is passed by US Congress, granting permanent commissions and officer status to female military nurses.

New York, USA, April 24: Writer Willa Cather dies, aged 73.

Connecticut, USA, April: Six doctors are sacked from three Catholic hospitals for supporting a bill which would allow them to provide birth control information to a patient whose life might be endangered by pregnancy.

Tokyo, Japan, May 3: Japan's new constitution guarantees women's equality.

London, England, May 9: The first laundrette in Britain opens in Queensway for a six-month trial.

London, England, May 23: Britain agrees to the plan proposed by Lord Mountbatten, the Viceroy of India, to divide India into two states—one for Muslims and one for Hindus.

Jerusalem, Palestine, March-May: A Bedouin shepherd finds mysterious religious scrolls in Qumran on the Dead Sea.

Paris, France, March-May: Christian Dior launches the "New Look." The British government requests women boycott the trend for long skirts to avoid wasting material.

Amsterdam, Netherlands, June: The diary of a young Dutch Jewish girl, Anne Frank, is published.

China, July 1: General Chiang Kai-shek mobilizes his troops across the country to fight the Communists.

New Zealand, July 10: The government decrees that in official correspondence the word "native" will be replaced by the word "Maori."

Paris, France, July 11-13: Europe's foreign ministers meet to draw up a plan for European post-war recovery.

In many of her works Cather created strong female characters who had the courage and vision to face all obstacles in their difficult lives. However, she never wrote openly on lesbian or gay themes.

She published little in her later years. In her last novel, *Sapphira and the Slave* (1940), she looked at the relationships between African-American women, and mothers and daughters.

Willa Cather spent the last 40 years of her life with her companion, Edith Lewis, in New York. She will be buried at Jaffrey, New Hampshire, on the hillside spot she selected.

British Government Backs Down on Hem Lengths

Paris, France, March–May: In Britain, the government has softened its stance against the new longer skirt lengths, which it considers a waste of scarce material in these years of post-war rationing. The change of heart follows the news that Princess Margaret, a fashion leader in Britain, wore a flounced skirt to a recent social event.

The Board of Trade had asked women to boycott the new fashion, prompted by Parisian designer Christian Dior's new, very feminine range which focuses on soft rounded shapes, full, billowing skirts, and nipped-in waists. Now, however, a Board spokesman has said, "We cannot dictate to women the length of their skirts."

Dior, a 30-year-old couturier, made a big impact on the world fashion scene in February when he launched his first collection of 90 designs. Some of Dior's skirts had up to 45 yards (41 m) of fabric in them. However, he said women were tired of sacrifice and the shabby uniform-like clothes they had of necessity been wearing. The style has been dubbed the "New Look" following a comment made by Carmel Snow, the editor of US fashion magazine *Harper's Bazaar*.

Dior staged a private presentation for the British royal family, although it is

The New Look marks a shift from a post-war austerity.

understood that at first King George VI forbade the young princesses, Elizabeth and Margaret, from wearing the New Look in case they set a bad example at a time when rationing was still in force.

The house of Dior has been inundated with orders. It seems that glamor has returned to fashion!

Two Divas Have Emerged

Verona, Italy and Sydney, Australia, August: Two sopranos with all the hallmarks of greatness made their debuts this month. Maria Callas stunned audiences in the title role in *La Gioconda* at the Arena di Verona in Verona, Italy, while Joan Sutherland appeared to great critical acclaim in *Dido and Aeneas* in Sydney, Australia.

Callas, who was born in New York in 1923, built a formidable reputation in Greece, where she

lived with her mother and sister from the age of 14. Two years ago, she left Greece two months short of her 22nd birthday. By then she had given 56 performances in seven operas and had appeared in some 20 recitals. Dubbed by Italian fans "La Divina" for her sublime voice, Callas promises much, thanks to a great dramatic talent and an impressive *bel canto* technique. Leading Italian opera conductor Tullio Serafin described Callas in *La Gioconda* as "amazing—so strong physically and spiritually; so certain of her future. I knew ... this girl, with her courage and huge voice, would make a tremendous impact."

Meanwhile, on the other side of the world, 21-year-old Joan Sutherland was showing her precocious talent as an outstanding coloratura soprano in her singing debut as the tragic heroine Dido in a concert performance of Henry Purcell's *Dido and Aeneas*.

The term coloratura is derived from "color" and refers to a soprano with a high range and the vocal agility to sing trills, rapid passages, and other vocal musical embellishments.

Opera lovers are sure to be thrilled by these two wonderful new divas.

Carrie Lane Chapman Catt

Anne Frank's just-published diary tells of her life hiding from the Nazis.

Haifa, Palestine, July 18: The *Exodus*, a ship loaded with nearly 4,500 Jewish Holocaust survivors, is refused refugee status by the UK.

Verona, Italy, August 2: Maria Callas makes her operatic debut in Amilcare Ponchielli's *La Gioconda*.

Dutch East Indies, August 3: A UN-brokered ceasefire comes into effect between Indonesian and Dutch military forces.

Egypt, August 12: Women's rights activist and nationalist Huda Shaarawi dies, aged 68.

India, August 15: The newly formed countries of Pakistan and India gain independence after 163 years under British rule.

New Zealand, August 23: The first post-war assisted migrants arrive on New Zealand shores.

Sydney, Australia, August: Soprano Joan Sutherland debuts as Dido in Purcell's *Dido and Aeneas*.

Hungary, September 1: The Communists win the election.

Amritsar, India, September 24: Violence explodes in India when 1,200 Muslim refugees heading for Pakistan by train are slaughtered by Sikh troops and civilians.

Argentina, September: Women win the right to vote.

India, October 22: Tribal forces in Pakistan invade the Indian border state of Kashmir.

London, England, November 12: Baroness Emmuska Orczy, author of *The Scarlet Pimpernel*, dies aged 82.

London, England, November 20: Princess Elizabeth, daughter of King George VI, and Lieutenant Philip Mountbatten marry.

New York, USA, December 3: Premiere of Tennessee Williams's play, *A Streetcar Named Desire*, starring Jessica Tandy as Blanche DuBois and Marlon Brando as Stanley Kowalski.

Stockholm, Sweden, December: Gerty Cori and her husband Carl Ferdinand Cori win the Nobel Prize in Physiology or Medicine.

Florida, USA: *The Everglades, River of Grass*, by Marjory Stoneman Douglas, is published.

1946-47: American golfer Babe Didrikson wins 17 straight golf tournaments around the world.

USA: The book *Goodnight Moon*, by Margaret Wise Brown, is published.

China: China's new constitution comes into effect, giving women the right to vote.

London, England: Rebecca West publishes *The Meaning of Treason*, an account of the Nazi war crimes trials in Nuremberg.

Baroness Emmuska Orczy

Egyptian Activist Ends Her Fight

Egypt, August 12: Egyptian feminist and nationalist Huda Shaarawi has died, aged 68. For many, she is best remembered for taking off her hijab as a political act at a Cairo railway station in 1923, along with fellow activists Nabawiya Moussa and Ceza Nabarawi.

However, it was her work in forming the Egyptian Feminist Union (EFU) and in opening up relations with international women's groups that had the most lasting impact on the lives of the women of her country. She was president of the EFU up until the time of her death. It was an organization dedicated to women's rights, especially in the areas of education and health. Importantly, it campaigned for the government to impose a minimum marriageable age—something in which Shaarawi had a personal interest.

Born in 1879 into a wealthy family, she was raised and educated in the traditional harem system and at the age of 13 was married off to her cousin. The couple divorced seven years later.

Shaarawi used her wealth and position in Cairo society to great effect. In 1908 she established a philanthropic society offering social services for poor women and children. In 1910 she founded a girls' school that taught academic subjects instead of the conventional "women's subjects," such as midwifery, that were all that was available at the time. In 1914 she founded the Intellectual Association of Egyptian Women.

She involved the women's movement in Egypt's struggle for independence from British control. Shaarawi saw it as a way for women to take greater control of their lives and to play a part in the political life of the nation. In 1919, the same year she formed the EFU, She organized the largest anti-British demonstration that Egypt had ever seen. However, following independence in 1922, the new government not only denied women their rights, it banned them from the opening of the Parliament. Shaarawi led a group to picket the event.

Shaarawi forged links between the EFU and the International Women's Suffrage Movement, and the EFU played a major part in helping to establish the All Arab Feminist Union.

Argentine Women Join the Voting Elite

Argentina, September: Argentina has been added to the list of those countries where women can vote in elections, when the Argentine government this month passed Law No. 13.010.

The new legislation has been heavily backed by the president's wife, Eva Perón, a major promoter of women's civil and political rights in Argentina. Eva Perón founded the charity, the Eva Perón Foundation, as well as the nation's first large-scale women's political party, the Female Perónist Party. This ensured a network of Perónist women throughout the country.

This year, a number of countries have extended voting rights to women. Most notable of these is China, where a new

constitution, promulgated by Chiang Kai-shek's government in January, enables all of the country's adults to vote. The law comes into effect in December. Other countries to give women the vote this year include Bulgaria, Malta, Nepal, Pakistan, and Singapore. In Mexico, women have been given the right to vote in elections at the municipal level.

Scarlet Pimpernel Author Dies

Henley-on-Thames, England, November 12: Baroness Emmuska Orczy, the British novelist best remembered as the author of *The Scarlet Pimpernel*, has died, aged 82, at her home in Henley-on-Thames.

Baroness Orczy wrote detective and historical novels. She was also a painter of note, and her works were exhibited at the Royal Academy, London.

She was born in Hungary, the only daughter of Baron Felix Orczy, a well-regarded composer and conductor, and friend of Wagner and Liszt. She moved with her parents to Brussels and then to London. She married artist and writer Montague Barstow in 1894, and together they produced book and magazine illustrations, and published an edition of Hungarian folktales.

Baroness Orczy began her career as a writer by contributing detective stories to various magazines. In 1903 she and her husband wrote a play called *The Scarlet Pimpernel*, based on one of her short stories. In 1905, before the play was produced, she re-wrote it as a full-length novel under the same title.

The play was very successful and ran for four years in London, breaking many stage records. It was translated and produced in other countries. Its success generated huge sales for the novel.

The Scarlet Pimpernel is set against the background of the French Revolution. Its hero, Sir Percy Blakeney, masquerades as an effete English aristocrat while secretly conducting heroic deeds helping French aristocrats escape the guillotine. It continues to attract a readership today.

Princess Elizabeth Weds

London, England, November 20: Britain's 21-year-old Princess Elizabeth today married Prince Philip of Greece and Denmark, recently created Duke of Edinburgh, at Westminster Abbey with all the pomp and fanfare one would expect from the wedding of the next-in-line to the throne.

Huge crowds gathered to watch the princess arrive on the arm of her father, George VI. She wore a dress designed by Norman Hartnell. She was followed by her pages, Prince Michael of Kent and

> "THERE ARE WHOLE PRECINCTS OF VOTERS IN THIS COUNTRY WHOSE UNITED INTELLIGENCE DOES NOT EQUAL THAT OF ONE REPRESENTATIVE AMERICAN WOMAN."
>
> CARRIE LANE CHAPMAN CATT (1859–1947), AMERICAN FEMINIST AND POLITICAL ACTIVIST

British royalty was out in force for the marriage of Princess Elizabeth and Lieutenant Philip Mountbatten.

Rebecca West

The two lived and worked in Buffalo until 1931 when Carl left to become a professor at Washington University in St. Louis, Missouri, where Gerty was hired as a research associate. Despite her equivalent degrees and comparable research experience, it was not until 1943 that she was given a faculty position. She became full professor earlier this year.

The awarding of the Nobel Prize caps a full career dedicated to science.

Landmark Book on Florida's Everglades

Florida, USA: A new book promises to be a landmark environmental work on the Everglades of Florida, America's largest subtropical wilderness. *The Everglades, River of Grass,* by Marjory Stoneman Douglas, examines the vast wetland in all its facets—the diversity of its wildlife, the history of the native peoples of the area, and the explorers who traveled there. What makes this book so important is the author's explanation of the role of the Everglades as the region's watershed, and the fact that it addresses modern civilization's impact on its fragile ecosystem.

The book is highly readable thanks to Marjory Douglas's descriptive, fluid prose and her skill at portraying the strange beauty of the region.

Marjory Douglas has lived in Miami, South Florida, since 1915, when Miami was a town of a mere 5,000 inhabitants. She has been dubbed the "mother of the Everglades." An environmentalist, activist, feminist, and independent thinker, she is known for her tireless, ground-breaking efforts to protect the region.

Gerty Cori and Carl Ferdinand Cori win the Nobel Prize in the Physiology or Medicine category.

Prince William of Gloucester, both wearing kilts in the royal tartan, and behind them, eight bridesmaids led by her sister, Princess Margaret, and cousin, Princess Alexandra of Kent. Prince Philip was accompanied by his best man, Lord Milford Haven.

The couple left Westminster Abbey together and then later appeared on the balcony of Buckingham Palace. They will honeymoon at Broadlands, the historic house in Hampshire owned by Philip's uncle, Lord Mountbatten.

Elizabeth met Philip when she was 13, while playing tennis. It is understood that it was love at first sight on her part for the 18-year old Philip, then a cadet in the Royal Navy. Throughout her teens she remained devoted to the good-looking young man, whom she called "my Viking prince" because of his blond hair and blue eyes. The couple became secretly engaged last year, and the official announcement was made in June this year.

Her choice of husband has not been without controversy and met with some opposition from her family, given that Philip is Greek Orthodox, with no financial resources behind him, and has sisters who had married Nazi supporters. It is rumored that the princess's mother, Queen Elizabeth, opposes the marriage, even referring to Philip as "the Hun."

Prince Philip renounced his claim to the throne of Greece and since then has been known simply as Lieutenant Philip

Mountbatten—the surname being an Anglicized version of his mother's German family name, Battenberg.

After their honeymoon the royal couple will live at Clarence House in St. James's Palace.

First American Woman to Win Science Nobel Prize

Stockholm, Sweden, December: Gerty Cori, jointly with her husband, Carl Ferdinand Cori, has won the Nobel Prize in Physiology or Medicine for their discovery of "the course of the catalytic conversion of glycogen"—the cyclical process used by muscle cells to make and store energy.

Understanding this process of sugar metabolism—known as the Cori cycle—promises to help future management and treatment of diabetes.

Cori has become the first American woman to win a Nobel Prize in science; indeed, only the third woman to receive the honor in a science discipline, following in the footsteps of Marie Curie and Irène Joliot-Curie. As with the previous female winners, Cori is a co-recipient of the prize with her husband. Also sharing this year's award is Bernardo Houssay, an Argentinian physiologist who has been conducting studies in the same field.

Gerty Cori was born in 1896 in Prague. She and her husband moved to America in the early 1920s, and in 1928 they both became US citizens.

Margaret Wise Brown is the author of Goodnight Moon.

The title of the book comes from a line in the second paragraph of the first chapter: "The miracle of the light pours over the green and brown expanse of saw grass and of water, shining and slow-moving below, the grass and water that is the meaning and the central fact of the Everglades of Florida. It is a river of grass."

Loretta Young

First African-American Joins Army Nursing Corps

USA, February 12: A nurse from the Lincoln School for Nurses, in the Bronx, New York, has become the first African-American to be admitted to the Army Nursing Corps.

Nancy Leftenant was born in the town of Goose Grease, South Carolina, one of 13 children of James and Eunice Leftenant. In her late teens, she worked as a maid for a year to save the $100 required for nursing school.

She first reported for duty as a reservist army nurse in February, 1945, with the rank of second lieutenant, and 11 months later was promoted to first lieutenant. Her status as a reserve, however, prevented her from serving in the army's regular nurse corps.

She was sent to Fort Devens Army Hospital, near Boston, where she and 36 other African-American nurses took part in a program to determine their suitability to care for white patients (previously, black nurses were assigned only to black patients). Leftenant worked 12-hour shifts, six days a week in a ward of 40 patients, all casualties of the war.

Segregation of the races, entry quotas,

"The great comfort about being a woman is that one can always pretend to be more stupid than one is, and no one is surprised."

FREYA STARK
(1893–1993),
BRITISH TRAVEL
WRITER

Juliana is now queen of the Netherlands.

and gender discrimination have persisted in all arms of the US military since the cessation of hostilities in 1945.

Protest Against Boeing Organized

Seattle, USA, April–September: A leading member of the Socialist Workers Party (SWP) and an assembly-line technician for the Boeing corporation, Clara Fraser, has achieved nationwide notoriety in an ongoing dispute with the aircraft manufacturer's management. She was involved in organizing a mother's brigade of protestors complete with baby strollers to walk the picket line at Boeing's plant in Seattle.

Her innovative approach to labor dis-sent comes on the back of her successful campaign for increased involvement of women in the International Association of Machinists, and the granting of first-class union membership to African-American workers.

When Boeing let an April 16 deadline pass for the choosing of arbiters in the long-running dispute over contractual negotiations, Clara Fraser and her fellow workers of the Machinists Union District Council voted to strike on April 22. Strike sanction was granted by the International Association of Machinists six days later.

Requests to the district court to grant an injunction requiring Boeing to negotiate went unheeded.

On September 13, Clara Fraser and the Machinists Union returned to work after a third of the union's original 14,000 members had given way in the face of Boeing's continual refusal to bargain or heed the requests of the National Labor Relations Board.

It is believed that Boeing took back the workers because of pressure from the US government over delays in the production

time out

The Queen of the Netherlands, Wilhelmina, has abdicated the throne, which she has occupied since 1890 when she was only 10. She is to be succeeded by her only daughter, Juliana.

of the B50 bomber, combined with the financial burden caused by losses of more than $170,000 a day.

Born Clara Goodman in Boyle Heights, East Los Angeles, in 1923, Clara Fraser was raised in a multi-ethnic, working-class neighborhood. Her mother was a liberal socialist who worked for the Ladies Gar-ment Workers Union and her father was an anarchist and member of the Teamsters Union. Clara graduated from UCLA in 1944 with a Bachelor of Arts in literature and education, briefly gaining work in Hollywood as a screenwriter before joining the SWP.

Together with her husband, Clara moved to Seattle in 1946 to build an SWP branch there. Clara Fraser has long been in the fore-front of social change and the pursuit of civil rights, combining a Marxist philosophy with grassroots activism.

Women at last Admitted to Degrees at Cambridge

Cambridge, England, July 4: Cambridge University today admitted women to full degrees. The decision to do so was taken last December by the university's all-male governing body in the face of growing public pressure.

A student works toward her degree at Cambridge.

Burma, January 4: At 4.20 a.m. Burma is granted independence by Britain. Astrologers choose this auspicious timing.
Indonesia, January 17: The Renville Truce Agreement is signed by UN representatives, proposing a truce between the Netherlands and the Republic of Indonesia along the Van Mook Line.
New Delhi, India, January 30: Mahatma Gandhi is assassinated by Nathuram Godse, a fanatical Hindu.
Ceylon (Sri Lanka), February 4: Ceylon is granted independence.

USA, February 12: Nancy Leftenant becomes the first African-American to enter the Army Nursing Corps.
Prague, Czechoslovakia, February 27: The Communist Party of Czechoslovakia seizes full power in a coup; democratic politicians are taken prisoner.
Los Angeles, USA, March 20: Loretta Young takes out the Oscar for Best Actress for her role in the 1947 movie *The Farmer's Daughter.* Celeste Holm receives the Best Supporting Actress award for her role in *Gentlemen's Agreement.*

New Zealand, April: The New Zealand Women's Army Corps is incorporated into the New Zealand regular army.
Seattle, USA, April–September: Activist Clara Fraser organizes a strike against Boeing, and pressures the Machinists Union to represent women and minorities.
Tel Aviv, Israel, May 14: The state of Israel is proclaimed.
South Africa, May 26: The Afrikaner National Party, with its apartheid manifesto, wins the election.

London, England, June 10: A surgeon at Guy's Hospital performs the first open-heart operation.
Washington, DC, USA, June 12: With the introduction of the *Women's Armed Services Integration Act,* women are granted permanent status in the nation's armed forces.
Toronto, Canada, June 24: The Toronto School Board grants female teachers pay equal to that of males.
London, England, June 24: Dame Lillian Penson is named vice-chancellor of the University of London.

Cambridge, England, July 4: Cambridge University admits women to full degrees for the first time.
USA, July 5: The first episode of the radio show *My Favorite Husband,* with Lucille Ball, is aired on CBS.
London, England, July 5: The government introduces the National Health Service, which gives free health care to all.
USA, July 7: Six female reservists are sworn in to the regular US Navy, the first women to do so since the introduction of the *Women's Armed Services Integration Act.*

The *US Women's Armed Services Integration Act* grants women permanent status in the military.

Since the 1870s, women in England have had increasing access to university classes, but higher education for women has remained a controversial agenda. Although women studying at Cambridge University attended the same lectures and passed the same exams as male students, they still were not granted a degree. This long-overdue reform gives women the equality of status so long campaigned for.

Pioneers in university education for women were women's colleges associated with Cambridge, most notably Newnham (founded in 1871) and Girton (1873). They have offered examinations since the 1880s and awarded degrees since 1921.

The question of awarding degrees to women first arose in 1897 and caused much excitement in the national press. The consensus at the time, however, was an overwhelming belief that there should be no "mixed colleges."

It is expected that Cambridge's female students will adopt the current academic dress. Square caps will continue to be worn, although some changes may be required to be made to the gown's sleeves, which may have to be closed so that in summer, when women wear short-sleeved dresses, bare shoulders are kept covered in an appropriate manner.

At long last women who have achieved in academia will be openly rewarded.

Comedienne Lucille Ball in New Radio Series

USA, July 5: A new radio sitcom starring Lucille Ball and Richard Denning, titled *My Favorite Husband,* aired tonight on CBS Radio.

Sponsored by Jell-O, the half-hour show features the middle-class lives of Liz Cugat, a socially prominent woman, and her husband George, a successful banker. They live at 321 Bundy Drive in fictitious Sheridan Falls.

The weekly show revolves around the Cugats' everyday lives, with Liz tending to get herself into annoying scrapes which George has to resolve.

The people behind the show include the writing team of Madelyn Pugh and

Margaret Chase Smith campaigns for election.

Bob Carroll Jr., and Jess Oppenheimer, the producer/director. *My Favorite Husband* appears to have sparked something in Lucille's acting—her talent as a comedienne is being taken to a new high by performing in front of a live audience. Of added interest, the actors are made to wear costumes, and the radio show is treated more as a theatrical experience. This show provides the red-headed star with a means to give her listening public many hours of comic entertainment.

Lucille Ball

National Health Service Established

London, England, July 5: Equality in health care for women across England has taken a giant leap forward today with the introduction of the National Health Service (NHS), bringing together hospitals, medical practitioners, and community-based services under a single national organization. Funded by the taxpayer, this service will be free of charge to all.

A special priority service organized by local authorities has also been established for expectant mothers and young children. Prior to today, access to a doctor was a free service that applied predominantly to male workers on low wages, though not necessarily to the wives and children of these men.

The NHS was set up by the Labour Government that achieved a landslide victory three years ago, in 1945. Aneurin Bevan, as Minister of Health, is responsible for the Department of Health, which will be running the new organization. However, with an increasing number of expectant mothers wanting to have their babies born in the safe environment of a hospital, coupled with the development of complex forms of surgery, and a growing demand for increasingly expensive drugs, it is expected that the Department of Health may be forced to introduce fees to cover the system's unforeseen and already escalating costs.

Suffragette Rheta Childe Dorr Dies

Winifred Wagner

Pennsylvania, USA, August 8: Known as one of the great muckrakers of her time, the journalist and suffragette Rheta Childe Dorr has died at her home in Bucks County, Pennsylvania.

She was born in Omaha, Nebraska, 80 years ago. In 1890, soon after graduating from the University of Nebraska, she moved to New York City.

Her account of the rise of suffrage clubs and trade unions in the United States and Europe, *What Eight Million Women Want* (1910), brought her to the attention of the nation. The book sold half a million copies.

In 1912 she went to Paris to assist the noted feminist Emmeline Pankhurst in the writing of her autobiography, and in 1917 traveled to Russia to observe the 1917 Communist revolution. She penned *Inside the Russian Revolution* (1917) from memory after her notes were confiscated by the Russian authorities as she tried to leave the country. In it she laid bare her disillusionment with the nation's political leadership and what she called the "barbarism" of Lenin and his cronies.

During World War I she also visited her son, who was serving in France. She subsequently published many wartime articles, including *A Soldier's Mother in France* (1918).

"AS FAR AS I'M CONCERNED, LOVE MEANS FIGHTING, BIG FAT LIES, AND A COUPLE OF SLAPS ACROSS THE FACE."

EDITH PIAF
(1915–1963),
FRENCH SINGER

Fanny Blankers-Koen and Alice Coachman Win Gold

London, England, August: Fanny Blankers-Koen, the 30-year-old athlete from the Netherlands and mother of two, has become the star of the London Olympic Games by winning four gold medals. The USA's Alice Coachman has also made history by becoming the first African-American woman to win gold at an Olympic Games.

Blankers-Koen, who is nicknamed the "Flying Housewife," won her gold medals in the 80 meters hurdles, the 100 meters and 200 meters sprints, and the 4 x 100 meters relay. Already the world record holder in the long jump and high jump, she was probably deprived of even further Olympic glory by a rule that limits female athletes to a maximum of three individual track and field events.

She won the final of the 80 meters hurdles in an Olympic record time of 11.2 seconds—she already holds the world record at 11.0 seconds. Including heats and finals, Blankers-Koen was to run 12 times in only nine days. She won her fourth gold medal in the 4 x 100 meters relay running the anchor leg and catching Australia's Joyce King in the last two strides of the race.

As a child, Alice Coachman, the great American high jumper, was barred from using public sports facilities in her native Georgia because of her race. At these Olympics, she defeated her nearest rival, the British jumper Dorothy Tyler, to win the gold medal in the high jump, setting a new Olympic record of 1.68 m (about 5½ ft). King George VI personally presented her with her gold medal.

Alice Coachman has dominated the women's high jump in the United States for over a decade, winning the Amateur Athletic Union outdoor high jump championship from 1939 through 1948. However, it is Blankers-Koen who holds the world record but who was unable to compete in the event at these games.

At these London Olympics, both women have made outstanding contributions to the track and field events.

Princess Elizabeth poses with her first child, Charles.

"Axis Sally" Indicted for Treason

Washington, DC, USA, September 10: Mildred Gillars, aka "Axis Sally," has been indicted on charges of treason. An American citizen from Portland, Maine, she broadcast propaganda over the airwaves to US soldiers from Berlin during World War II.

After the war, Gillars disappeared into Europe's throngs of displaced persons. In 1946 she was picked up and taken to an internment camp after spending three weeks in a US hospital. She managed to obtain a pass which permitted her to gain residence in the French zone of Berlin, but was later arrested when traveling to Frankfurt to have the pass renewed, and flown to the United States, where she was imprisoned in Washington, DC's district jail on August 21 this year.

Today she was charged with 10 counts of treason and engaging in "psychological warfare" by a federal grand jury. If convicted of these charges, she faces up to 30 years' imprisonment.

She was born on November 29, 1900. Her parents divorced when Mildred was six, and her mother later married Doctor Robert Bruce Gillars, a dentist. Mildred graduated from high school in 1917 and held a succession of dead-end jobs.

After failing at a career in vaudeville and musical comedy, she moved to Germany in 1935 where she found work with

Fanny Blankers-Koen wins one of her four gold medals at the Olympics.

Radio Berlin as an announcer and actress. Calling herself "Midge at the Mike" but dubbed "Axis Sally" by American soldiers, she began her propaganda broadcasts on December 11, 1941. She was heard across Europe, the Mediterranean, North Africa, and the United States until her final broadcast on May 6, 1945.

Her most famous broadcast was her so-called "Vision of Invasion" of May 11, 1944, beamed to US troops in the south of England who were preparing for the upcoming D-Day landings along the beaches of northern France. In it, Gillars played the role of an American mother who had had a dream that her son, a participant in the Allied invasion force, never made it to the beaches, dying aboard his burning transport ship as it tried to cross the English Channel.

This broadcast and others like it will very likely come back to haunt Mildred Gillars when her trial begins.

First Novel of Activist Dorothy West Published

Martha's Vineyard, Massachusetts, USA, October: Dorothy West, the writer, editor, and grande dame of the New York literary movement known as the Harlem Renaissance, has published her first novel.

The Living is Easy is a largely autobiographical work exploring the racial, economic, and social tensions present in the African-American community as shown in the lives of a fictional Boston family. West's central character, Cleo Judson, is a beautiful Southern African-American woman who moves to Massachusetts to work in the home of her white benefactors. The manipulative Cleo marries the hardworking Bart and proceeds to create her own domain in which she rules over largely benign, servile males.

The book attempts to create a "raceless" world that reflects the postwar optimism of many African-Americans, giving the characters the attributes, aspirations, social concerns, and dilemmas faced by their white contemporaries.

West was born in Boston on June 2, 1907, one of 22 children. She began to write in 1914 at the age of seven, and in 1926 her story "The Typewriter" took her to New York after it was awarded second prize in a contest.

Settling in New York, she soon became involved in what was to become known as the Harlem Renaissance, a group of young African-American writers, including Langston Hughes, who nicknamed West "The Kid."

In 1934 she founded and became editor of *Challenge*, which was among the first magazines to provide a forum for realistic literary portrayals of African-Americans.

In South Korea, women win the right to vote.

When it was forced to close, she went to work for the Federal Writers' Project for the Work Project Administration (WPA) until the mid-1940s, prior to settling in Martha's Vineyard.

Avant-garde Poet Publishes New Work

England, November: British author and poet Edith Sitwell has just added to her extensive publications with the appearance of a book of poetry entitled *Song of the Cold.*

Born in 1887 in Scarborough, Yorkshire, and raised by aristocratic parents, she first came to the attention of the literary world as the editor of a poetry anthology called *Wheels,* which featured not only her work but that of her brothers as well. Famous for her wit and her penchant for

dressing in elaborate costumes, her friends include Aldous Huxley and T. S. Eliot.

The abstract nature of her poems often makes Sitwell's work extremely difficult for readers to understand, but her literary legacy to modern poetry is not in dispute. Her poems reveal her dedication to feminism, and love for the complex cycles of nature. Her style has been described as contemptuous of the idyllic quietism of the so-called Georgian poets. This new collection of poems will be appreciated by her many admirers.

Edith Sitwell

Human Rights Declaration Adopted by UN

Paris, France, December 11: After one final marathon debate that lasted well into the evening, the Universal Declaration of Human Rights was yesterday adopted by the United Nations. The declaration was presented for adoption by the driving force behind it, Eleanor Roosevelt, the former US First Lady.

Forty-eight nations voted in favor of the declaration, eight countries abstained, and two were absent. Its final acceptance without dissent is a testament to the hard work of the Commission on Human Rights and its chairman, Mrs Roosevelt, who says "[it] may well become the international Magna Carta of all men everywhere." Three years in the making, it guarantees all people equality and dignity regardless of color, race, or economic status.

Mrs Roosevelt has long been a champion of social reform. As First Lady, she forever changed the role of the president's wife, often speaking on women's issues and bringing the plight of the oppressed to the president's attention.

Eleanor Roosevelt, pictured with a colleague, chaired the United Nations Commission on Human Rights.

Conchita Cintron

Evita's New Feminist Party Hopes to Inspire Women

Argentina, July 26: Today, first lady Eva Perón founded the Partido Peronista Feminino (the Peronista Feminist Party), and it is now expected that the number of women seeking political office will grow.

Evita, as the president's wife is fondly known, is recognized for her work, not just with women's groups, but also with the poor and disadvantaged. She has been involved with the trade union movement, and a few years ago she established the Eva Perón Foundation, which helps build hospitals, schools, orphanages, and aged care homes. She also works in an unofficial capacity with the government, seeking better working conditions for the lower paid. She intervenes personally in labor disputes to seek favorable outcomes for working class men and women.

Eva Perón, the former actress who married President Juan Perón in 1945, has also been actively campaigning over the last few years for women's right to vote, a goal finally achieved only two years ago. She is now encouraging all Argentinian women, not just those from wealthy and educated backgrounds, to participate in politics, and to use the power of their collective voice to improve the lot of women. The Peronista Feminist Party is the first large female organization in the country devoted to political issues.

Evita is its first president, and has already convinced many women, who might otherwise have remained indifferent to politics, to take a more active interest in national affairs.

"ONE IS NOT BORN A GENIUS, ONE BECOMES A GENIUS; AND THE FEMININE SITUATION HAS UP TO THE PRESENT RENDERED THIS BECOMING PRACTICALLY IMPOSSIBLE."

SIMONE DE BEAUVOIR,
1949,
THE SECOND SEX

Mourners at the funeral of Margaret Mitchell.

Scarlett's Creator Dies

Atlanta, Georgia, USA, August 16: Author Margaret Mitchell has died, five days after being hit by a car. She was 48. *Gone With the Wind*, her unforgettable civil war saga, was published in 1936 and won the Pulitzer Prize the following year, and in 1939 the motion picture version of her sprawling epic novel was released to great critical and popular acclaim. Starring Vivien Leigh as Scarlett O'Hara and Clark Gable as Rhett Butler, the film scooped the pools at the Academy Awards ceremony, winning a record ten Oscars, including Best Picture and Best Leading Actress.

Margaret Mitchell was born in Atlanta in 1900 to a family that included many civil war veterans. Her father was a lawyer, her mother a suffragist. Reportedly a headstrong girl, she defied convention by becoming a journalist, writing regularly for the *Atlanta Journal*.

She married sportsman Berrien Upshaw in 1922, only to divorce him two years later. In 1925 she married journalist John Marsh. It was while recovering from an ankle injury in the late 1920s that she wrote the book many have compared with Tolstoy's epic *War and Peace*.

First American Woman to Head Diplomatic Mission

USA, October 12: For the first time in American history, a woman has been appointed to head a diplomatic mission. President Harry Truman named Eugenie Moore Anderson, 40, the United States ambassador to Denmark.

Born in Iowa, the daughter of a Methodist minister, she married artist John Pierce Anderson in 1930 and they spent some years living in New York where Eugenie studied music at the famed Juilliard School. She and her husband have two children.

After several years, the family moved back to Red Wing, Minnesota. It was there, in her husband's home town, that Eugenie Anderson became involved in politics. She joined the Minnesota Democratic-Farmer-Labor Party (DFL) in 1944, where she developed an interest in international matters—she often spoke publicly about foreign policy. Anderson was also involved with the League of Women Voters and had connections with many social and civic groups.

In 1948, Anderson was selected to the Democratic Party committee. She also became the Minnesota delegate to the Democratic National Convention in Philadelphia, where she lent her support to Harry Truman and Hubert Humphrey. Up until now, she has been practically unknown outside Minnesota, but her appointment as Danish ambassador means that Eugenie Anderson's name will certainly be more widely known across America. Described as frank and unassuming, she has already charmed the Danes by learning their language.

Eva Perón hopes to encourage more involvement by women in politics.

Maori Woman Elected to Parliament

New Zealand, November 29: Iriaka Ratana was today elected to the New Zealand parliament, having received more than 9,000 votes. She is the first Maori woman to have a seat in the nation's legislative body. Not all Maoris will celebrate her win—her decision to stand for election was opposed by many traditional Maoris who do not believe that women should assume positions of leadership. However, Iriaka Ratana has overcome this resistance, winning by a comfortable margin.

Ratana was born Iriaka Te Rio in 1905. In her teens she worked as an entertainer in a number of Ratana troupes, touring with them to Europe, Britain, and Japan. In 1925, she became the second wife of Tahupotiki Wiremu Ratana, founder of the Ture Wairua, the Ratana Church, which preached the gospels and aimed to give Maori a political voice. When he died in 1939, Iriaka married Matiu Ratana, a son of her first husband. Together they worked a dairy farm.

When Matiu's brother, a member of parliament, died in 1945, Matiu was elected in his place. Meanwhile, Iriaka farmed the land and raised her children, but when her husband died accidentally in 1949, she decided to stand in his place. She was so confident of winning that she vowed to stand as an independent unless the Labour Party endorsed her.

Despite being pregnant with her seventh child (which is due next month), Iriaka Ratana campaigned well. She is expected to focus her energies on welfare matters, including improved training and education for Maori youth.

Mixed Marriages Banned

South Africa: Marriage between whites and people of other races is now strictly forbidden by one of the first acts of parliament passed since last year's elections. The *Prohibition of Mixed Marriages Act No. 55* is intended to ensure that whites marry only whites. The Afrikaner National Party, under the prime ministership of Dr Daniel Malan, has long had an agenda of racial segregation, and many are commenting that there will be plenty of laws coming into effect over the next 12 months that will essentially make any form of racial discrimination legal.

Malan and his party are keen to guarantee that political, economic, legal, and social dominance falls squarely on white shoulders. There is speculation that the government will enact laws restricting the rights of blacks to own property or even to be present in certain areas.

Already, contact between the races is actively discouraged. Since the early 1940s, the Afrikaner National Party has campaigned on a platform of *apartheid*, or "apartness," and they are determined to make this philosophy an integral part of South African law. It is expected that people will soon be formally classified according to their race—white, black, colored, native, or Asian.

Although the new law forbids marriage between these races, the reality is that of all the marriages registered since 1946, only about 75 have been mixed. Almost 30,000 have been white marriages.

Well-deserved Honor for a Great African-American

Haiti: The Haitian Medal of Honor and Merit has been awarded this year to the prominent black leader and educator, Mary McLeod Bethune. She is the first woman to receive this prestigious tribute.

Bethune was invited by President Dumarsais Estime to join in the celebrations of the 1949 Haitian Exhibition. While she was there, he presented her with the Medal, the highest honor that the Republic of Haiti can bestow.

Mary McLeod Bethune, 74, is one of America's greatest women leaders. One of 17 children born to a former slave couple, she originally hoped to be a missionary in Africa, but soon realized that there were plenty of problems being faced by black people in her own country. Dedicated to education and to human rights, Bethune has spent her life putting her ideals into action. In 1904 she opened a school for African-American girls in Florida; in 1923, it merged with a men's institute and became one of the few colleges for black students in the United States. Bethune also lobbied for universal suffrage, traveling door-to-door in 1912 to raise awareness of the issue, an action that brought unwelcome attention from the Ku Klux Klan, whom she defied.

This strength of character has served her well since. A former president of the National Association of Colored Women, she also founded the National Council of Negro Women. She was the director of Negro Affairs in the National Youth Administration from 1936–1944, making her one of the first black women to head a federal agency. In 1940 she was the vice-president of the National Association for the Advancement of Colored People.

She has also served as a consultant to the Secretary of War regarding the selection of female officers, and is often asked to advise the government on issues relating to African-Americans.

Mary McLeod Bethune has achieved many great things for black Americans, especially women. The Haitian Medal of Honor and Merit has gone to an extremely worthy recipient.

Mary McLeod Bethune

Elizabeth Taylor, Mary Astor, June Allyson, Margaret O'Brien, and Janet Leigh in *Little Women*.

Agnes Smedley

Brooks First African-American to Win Pulitzer

New York, USA, May 1: In a first for the Pulitzer Prize, African-American poet Gwendolyn Brooks was today declared winner of the poetry section of the prestigious awards. Brooks's award, presented for her 1949 collection of poems *Annie Allen*, is the first in any category ever given to an African-American person.

The 33-year-old poet has already garnered recognition for her work from highly respected quarters. Her first volume of poetry, *A Street in Bronzeville* (1945), established her reputation as a talented poet who did not shy away from the harsh realities of African-American lives, and she was subsequently awarded two Guggenheim Fellowship grants to continue her writing.

Although Brooks was born in Kansas, the family moved to Chicago soon afterward, and she regards Chicago as her home town. Many of her poems are set there. Encouraged by her parents, she began writing at an early age, and had her first poem published at the age of 13.

"You can be up to your boobies in white satin, with gardenias in your hair and no sugar cane for miles, but you can still be working on a plantation."

BILLIE HOLIDAY (1915–1959), AMERICAN JAZZ SINGER

Annie Allen is a connected series of poems that follows a woman's life from childhood to adulthood. In her review of the book in January this year, the *New York Times*' Phyllis McGinley said that when Brooks "writes out of her heart, out of her rich and living background, out of her very real talent, then she induces almost unbearable excitement."

New Chinese Marriage Laws Take Effect

China, May 1: As of today, Chinese women have more rights in marriage, as the new *Marriage Law of the People's Republic of China* comes into effect. Article 1 of the Act abolishes the feudal marriage system, in which women are considered the property of their husbands, replacing it with the "New Democratic marriage system, which is based on free choice of partners, on monogamy, on equal rights for both sexes, and on protection of the lawful interests of women and children." The Act gives women full divorce rights.

As well as redefining marriage as a union between two equals, the new law explicitly forbids polygamy, concubinage, arranged marriages, and child marriages. A woman must be 18 years of age, and a man 20, before they are legally allowed to marry. Remarriage after divorce is permitted, and women can now inherit their husbands' property.

Accused "Soviet Spy" Journalist Dies Mid-book

Oxford, England, May 6: Agnes Smedley, the journalist and author once accused by General Douglas MacArthur—but soon cleared of the charge—of being a Russian spy, has died, aged 56.

A controversial figure, Smedley first made her name in journalism reporting from China in 1928–41. She flagged her radical beliefs early. After spending her childhood in Osgood, Missouri and in Trinidad, Colorado, she married Ernest Brudin and moved to California, where she began to take an interest in socialist ideas. While in her twenties she worked briefly with the anarchist Emma Goldman. But in 1919, after a spell of imprisonment for her political affinities, Smedley left the United States.

Until 1928 she lived in Berlin with Indian nationalist leader Virendranath Chattopadhyaya, before going to China as a correspondent for the German newspaper *Frankfurter Zeitung*. Traveling across the country, she wrote for many newspapers and publications around the world and published several books on Chinese Communism—an ideology she responded to enthusiastically.

During the 1937–38 Sino-Japanese war she traveled with the Eighth Route Army and reported her experiences in her book *China Fights Back* (1938). She returned to the United States in 1941, lecturing,

The gown in which actress Elizabeth Taylor married hotel magnate Conrad Hilton was a gift from MGM.

Mildred Burke, world's champion lady wrestler.

touring, and writing about her Chinese experiences, until General MacArthur accused her of being a Soviet secret agent. Smedley called this a "despicable lie," and it was retracted by the Army six days later. She left for England not long afterward, and was writing a biography of Chinese leader Chu Teh at the time of her death.

Lillian Ross Article Shows Hemingway in a New Light

New York, USA, May 13: A profile of the American novelist Ernest Hemingway, published today in *The New Yorker*, is a warts-and-all portrait guaranteed to provoke readers' reactions. Written by 22-year-old journalist Lillian Ross, the article is entitled: "How Do You Like It Now, Gentlemen?" and contains a blow-by-blow description of Ross's interaction with Hemingway and his wife, Mary, during a brief visit the famous couple paid to New York last year. The piece has already become a talking-point for its portrayal of Hemingway. Rather than

conduct a starstruck interview with one of America's greatest writers, Ross paints him using a humorous, observational brush, transcribing his utterances and actions in detail. Using imagery almost entirely based around baseball, shooting, and boxing, Hemingway is, by turns, hilarious, bombastic and endearingly childlike. In literature, he claims he has "beaten" Turgenev and de Maupassant, "but nobody's going to get me in the ring with Mister Tolstoy;" Marlene Dietrich, whom he calls "the Kraut," pays a visit; Hemingway eats caviar and oysters, and drinks copious amounts of champagne; he shops for a coat, punching his own stomach to show the shop clerk how fit he is; and he explores the Metropolitan Museum, toting a hip flask all the way.

While Hemingway's life has been under the microscope since the 1920s, comparatively little is known about Lillian Ross herself. Born in 1927, and a native of New York state, Ross became a staff writer on *The New Yorker* last year.

McCarthy's Fear Campaign Condemned by Senators

Washington DC, USA, June 1: Margaret Chase Smith today led a group of seven Republican senators to publicly condemn the anti-Communist campaign of fellow Republican Senator Joseph McCarthy.

McCarthy's allegation in February this year that the US State Department harbored 205 Communists—and that, furthermore, he knew all their names— thrust him into the political spotlight, and provoked widespread discussion across the United States.

The dissident senators' "Declaration of Conscience," delivered in the Senate today by Senator Smith, accused "certain elements" in the Republican Party of trying to win favor by "the selfish political exploitation of fear, bigotry, ignorance, and intolerance." While not specifically naming those "certain elements," Smith

nevertheless clearly pointed the finger at McCarthy's tactics. "The American people are sick and tired of being afraid to speak their minds lest they be politically smeared as 'Communists' or 'Fascists' by their opponents," she continued.

Although strongly anti-Communist herself, Senator Chase lamented the fact that, as a result of McCarthy's actions, "freedom of speech is not what it used to be in America."

While arguing that the Democratic administration was also damaging the nation, Smith's Declaration nevertheless did not mince words regarding the shortcomings of her own party: "It is clear that this nation will continue to suffer as long as it is governed by the present ineffective Democratic administration. Yet to displace it with a Republican regime embracing a philosophy that lacks political integrity or intellectual honesty would prove equally disastrous to this nation."

During her 10 years in politics so far, Senator Chase—who represents the constituents of Maine—has become known for taking an independent stance on many issues, even voting with the Democrats on several occasions.

Evangeline Booth

Thailand's new King Phumiphon and his fiancée.

Dover, England, August 8: Florence Chadwick sets a new women's record for swimming the English Channel.
London, England, August 15: Princess Elizabeth gives birth to her second child, a girl.
USA, August 24: Judge Edith Sampson becomes the first African-American to be named a delegate to the United Nations.
Calcutta, India, October 7: A nun known as Mother Teresa establishes the Missionaries of Charity.
New York, USA, October 13: Premiere of *All About Eve*.

Austerlitz, New York, USA, October 19: Poet Edna St Vincent Millay dies at the age of 58.
Canberra, Australia, October 24: The Commonwealth Court of Conciliation and Arbitration determines a basic female wage, which is set at 75 percent of the basic male wage.
North Korea, November 28: China joins forces with the North Koreans in the Korean War.

USA, November 30: President Truman says the United States is giving "active consideration" to the use of atomic bombs in Korea.
Tibet, December 19: The Dalai Lama flees Chinese-occupied Tibet after the invasion of his country on October 21.
England: Catherine Cookson publishes her first book, the autobiographical *Kate Hannigan*.
England: Elizabeth David inspires British housewives with her *Book of Mediterranean Food*.

Boston, USA: Felicia Kaplan publishes her first book, *Mink on Weekdays*.
USA: Judith Merril publishes the sci-fi nuclear war thriller, *Shadow on the Hearth*.
England: Elizabeth Jane Howard publishes her diaristic novel, *The Beautiful Visit*.
New York, USA: South African author Doris Lessing's first novel, *The Grass is Singing*, is published in the United States.
Thailand: King Phumiphon Aduldet is formally crowned Rama IX.

USA: Babe Didrikson is named Female Athlete of the Half-century by Associated Press.
London, England: At King's College, Maurice Wilkins and Rosalind Franklin produce the first pictures of DNA.
England: Grace Robertson makes an exclusive freelance arrangement with *Picture Post* to document daily life in Britain with her camera.
India: Women are granted the right to vote.
Haiti: Women are granted the right to vote.

Edna St Vincent Millay

Women Admitted to Harvard Law Program

Boston, USA, August 1: In what may prove an historic decision, Harvard University Law School has agreed to let women enter its law program from next year, though Louis A. Toepfer, the Director of Admissions, remarked that the university was "not enthusiastic" about the change.

"We didn't feel we needed women, but could find no reason for excluding them," he told the *Christian Science Monitor* today. Harvard's is the oldest law school in the United States, and women seeking admission will be expected to pass the university's Legal Aptitude test.

Toepfer indicated that he expects about a dozen women to take places in the School next year.

"THE GREAT ACHIEVEMENT OF THE HARPER EMPIRE IS THE WOMEN IT HAS MADE."

MARTHA MATILDA HARPER (1857–1950), BUSINESSWOMAN

Beauty and Franchising Entrepreneur Dies

Rochester, New York, USA, August 3: The first person to establish a franchise system of business, Martha Matilda Harper, died today, leaving behind her a business legacy that has benefited thousands worldwide in the last 60 years.

Harper, born in Canada in 1857, began her working life as a domestic servant in Rochester, New York, at the age of seven. As a young woman, she began developing her own hair tonic in her spare time, believing that commercially available

hair-cleaning products were in fact damaging to the hair. By the age of 31 she had developed alternative products of her own and had saved enough money to open the Harper Method Shop in Rochester, New York, where she could make and sell her shampoo and skin products. Her own hair, which reached to the floor, featured in her advertising.

Although Harper came up with other ideas—she invented the first reclining chair for hair and beauty treatments, and popularized the concept of a beauty salon (instead of hairdressers visiting clients at home)—it was her invention of the franchise system which was, overall, her most influential contribution to business. In 1891, she set up a second shop, which was owned by a "franchisee," but whose staff were trained and monitored by Harper herself. Others followed. Over the years she encouraged women from many different backgrounds to become franchisees, and provided training for all new owners. At her peak, she had over 500 shops around the world.

English Channel Swim Breaks Women's Record

Dover, England, August 8: Californian swimmer Florence Chadwick today clocked in as the fastest woman ever to swim the English Channel, breaking the previous women's record by over an hour. In an impressive display of stamina and determination, the 31-year-old made the difficult crossing from Cap Gris Nez in France to Dover in England in 13 hours and 20 minutes, smashing Gertrude Ederle's 1926 record and falling only two hours short of the men's record.

Chadwick has been a long-distance and rough-water swimming champion in her home country for well over a decade. After winning her first race—a six-mile swim across the San Diego Channel—aged 11, she went on to break records wherever she could. At one Californian junior swimming meet in 1934, she broke both the junior and senior records in the 300-meter medley—at the age of 12.

Today's record-breaking swim began at around 2:30 this morning (French time). Chadwick

set out with another American swimmer, 17-year-old Shirley May France, but the younger girl flagged and had to abort her swim some miles from the English coast.

Taking only sugar for sustenance, Chadwick seemed to have stamina to spare. As she finished her swim she was heard to say, as she made it to shore, "I feel fine and am quite prepared to swim back!" She then boarded a boat back to France, accompanied by her father.

Chadwick completed much of her training for the self-funded swim—which cost her and her family $5,000—in the Persian Gulf, close to where she has been working as a secretary for an American oil company in Saudi Arabia.

Mother Teresa's New Order Takes to the Streets

Calcutta, India, October 7: After working in the slums of Calcutta for two years, relying on donations to teach the city's poorest children, the Catholic nun known as Mother Teresa has widened her charitable and religious reach by officially establishing the Order of the Missionaries of Charity of Roman Catholic nuns.

The Order aims to relieve the suffering of the poor worldwide—not just in India. Pope Pius XII has given the group his official sanction, and today the Constitution of the new Order was read out to a large congregation gathered in Calcutta.

The Missionaries of Charity, so far consisting of a group of 11, will take a vow of extreme poverty. Its novitiates will spend most of their time in the streets of Calcutta, begging for food for the most needy and undertaking religious and teaching duties. At today's service, Father Celeste Van Exem said that members of the new Order "are resolved to spend themselves unremittingly in seeking out, in towns and villages, even amid squalid surroundings, the poorer, the abandoned, the sick, the infirm, the dying; in taking care of them assiduously and instructing them in the Christian Doctrine."

Although she is not Indian by birth, Mother Teresa has spent the last 21 years in Calcutta, teaching and helping the poor. Born in 1910 to an Albanian family, she worked with the Sisters of Loreto in a convent school in Calcutta for 17 years.

She left two years ago, with the blessing of the Loreto Sisters, in order to help people in the slum district of Motijhil, one of the city's poorest areas. Setting up an open-air school between the huts, she drew the letters of the Bengali alphabet into the dirt for her pupils. It was this work that inspired her to initiate the Order of the Missionaries of Charity to continue her work with the impoverished and needy.

Princess Elizabeth and Prince Philip celebrate the birth of daughter Anne.

Celeste Holm, Bette Davis, and Hugh Marlowe star in the 20th Century Fox film *All About Eve*.

Babe Didrikson

Award-winning Poet Found Dead in Her Home

Austerlitz, New York, USA, October 19: Edna St Vincent Millay, the celebrated Pulitzer Prize-winning poet, died in her home near Austerlitz this morning, aged 58, after suffering a heart attack. Discovered by a caretaker in the afternoon, Millay had been dead for at least six hours, according to medical experts.

It was a sudden and lonely end for a poet whose work has been hailed by critics since she published her first volume of poetry, *Renascence and Other Poems*, in 1917. Millay began writing as a child, and had her first poem published when she was 14 years old. She grew up poor, but in her teens her poetry attracted the notice of a wealthy benefactor, who helped secure her a place at Vassar College when she was 21. After graduating, she moved to Greenwich Village in New York—the centre of bohemian life and art in the 1920s—and began to support herself by some theatre acting and by writing, often publishing short stories under the name Nancy Boyd.

Her second volume, *A Few Figs from Thistles* (1920), gained her wider attention, particularly for the poem "First Fig" in which she included the line, "My candle burns at both ends," which became something of a catchcry for her admirers. But it was *Ballad of the Harp-Weaver* that won Millay the Pulitzer Prize for verse in 1923, and cemented her fame as one of her generation's finest poetic voices.

For the rest of her life she continued to write—poetry, plays and an opera libretto—and lend her name to social causes, most notably the 1927 campaign to free accused murders Sacco and Vanzetti. Since her husband, Dutch businessman Eugen Jan Boissevain, died last year, Millay has lived alone in the isolation of the Berkshire Hills, not far from the border of Massachusetts.

Male Wage Decision Makes Women Less than Equal

Canberra, Australia, October 24: A wage decision in Australia's Commonwealth Court of Conciliation and Arbitration has increased the basic wage for male workers—and in a landmark development, has set the female basic wage at 75 percent of the male wage, replacing the 54 percent previously awarded 19 years ago. The campaign, launched by the Australian Council of Trade Unions (ACTU) and supported by other unions, led to an increase of the basic wage from £7 to £8 2s, of which women will now receive three-quarters.

In the so-called Basic Wage Case, which began last year, the ACTU initially campaigned for equal pay for women, but Justices Kelly, Foster and Dunphy disagreed with this proposal. In his judgment, Justice Alfred Foster argued that equal pay for women would strain the economy; that the "productivity, efficiency, needs and the responsibilities etc. of females were substantially less than that of males in the community;" and that increasing the spending power of "young unmarried females" would "disturb the economy," disadvantaging men and their families.

Some women will receive a pay rise, but those working in industries such as the metal trades are unlikely to support this new decision. Nor will it be popular with other women who were employed in war industries, and who still receive up to 90 percent of the male wage. They now face losing that extra income.

Marcel Blistene's film *Etoile sans lumière (Star without Light)* features chanteuse Edith Piaf.

Ilse Koch

Second Sentence Sticks for Witch of Buchenwald

West Germany, January 15: A German court today sentenced infamous war criminal, Ilse Koch, popularly known as "the Witch of Buchenwald," to the maximum penalty possible under the German constitution: life imprisonment with hard labor. The 44-year-old mother of three was convicted on counts of incitement to murder and physical mistreatment of prisoners within the Buchenwald concentration camp. The court president, Georg Maginot, called her a "ruthless and hard-headed women" who had "done everything in her power to worsen the condition of these poor tortured men." Koch was married to the concentration camp commander, Karl Koch, and was herself an overseer at the camp. Insufficient proof was given to support claims that Mrs Koch had selected prisoners and murdered them for their tattooed skin; but the court did not doubt that she had had decorative lampshades made out of human skin.

> *"ONE CANNOT ACCOMPLISH ANYTHING WITHOUT FANATICISM."*
>
> EVA PERON,
> (1919–1952), FIRST LADY
> OF ARGENTINA

Head of BBC Children's Television Frida Lingstrom's creations Andy Pandy, Looby Lou, and Teddy.

Born in Dresden, Germany, Ilse Koch is the daughter of a farmer. Her first job was in a factory and she later worked as a librarian. She met Karl Koch in 1936 when she was employed as a secretary and guard at the Sachsenhausen concentration camp not far from Berlin. Today is the second time Koch has been sentenced to spend her life in prison. A United States court handed down the same sentence in 1947, but it was subsequently reduced to four years due to lack of evidence.

Koch was not present at the trial today. She remained locked in a padded cell at the Aichach women's prison in a reportedly hysterical state.

Historic Hanging at Pentridge

Melbourne, Australia, February 19: Crowds gathered outside the walls of Pentridge Prison in Victoria, Australia today while inside the prison, the first hanging of a woman in Victoria in 56 years took

place. At 8 a.m. Jean Lee was sent to the scaffold for the murder of William "Pop" Kent. She was followed two hours later by her accomplices, her boyfriend Robert David Clayton, and an acquaintance, Norman Andrews.

Not surprisingly, the trial and hangings have aroused much public attention and discussion. While it seems most people applauded the death sentence, groups such as the Labor Women's Organising Committee have expressed sympathy for the divorced single mother.

"Jean Lee," born Jean Wright, was used to brushes with the law. Lee had appeared frequently in Sydney courts on charges relating to offensive behavior, not helped by her work in prostitution.

In late 1949 she traveled to Melbourne with Robert Clayton, who had recently been released from prison, and the pair teamed up with Norman Andrews, whom Clayton had met while in jail. The trio met 73-year-old part-time bookmaker, William "Pop" Kent at Carlton's University Hotel. Having gained access to his Dorrit Street boarding house, they reportedly bashed him, tortured him, and strangled him. It seems money was a motive. While in custody Lee initially

Ethel Rosenberg, sentenced to death with her husband Julius for spying.

confessed to the crime, but later retracted her confession. After a five-day trial in March last year Lee and the two men were found guilty and sentenced to death. On receiving the sentence Lee reportedly cried out, declaring her innocence. She was 31 years old.

Arendt Confounds Hitler and Stalin

New York City, USA, March: This month the first major work written and published in America by renowned German-born philosopher, Hannah Arendt, hit the shelves across the country. *The Origins of Totalitarianism* seeks to come to terms with the magnitude of the evil represented by both Nazi Germany and Stalinist Russia. Arendt controversially equates the two regimes as "totalitarian" despite their ideological differences and bloody opposition to one another during the last war.

Arendt's analysis is, nevertheless, as profound and moving as it is scholarly and complex. The author was herself a refugee from Nazi Germany in 1933, and her own experiences and emotions seep through the pages, whether she is analyzing Greek political philosophy or giving detailed accounts of concentration camp torture and propaganda.

Garland Bowled Over by Crowd at Palladium

London, England, April 10: Diminutive screen star Judy Garland was a huge hit on stage last night with her first live performance at the London Palladium. For 35 minutes Garland sang popular songs from her film career, concluding the night fittingly with "Over the Rainbow." The thunder of applause from the audience was almost too much for Garland, who fell over when taking bows. It was a rare slip from a consummate professional.

Garland's career began early, when she was still a child, with her family act, "The Gumm Sisters," later called "The Garland Sisters." Her performance as Dorothy in the MGM film *The Wizard of Oz* (1939) at the age of 16 won her an honorary Academy Award.

time out

In Meridian, Mississippi, USA, Paula Ackerman serves temporarily as a rabbi after the death of her rabbi husband. She is the first woman known to have performed rabbinical functions in the United States.

Joyce's Muse Dies Far from Ireland

Zurich, Switzerland, April 10: Today Nora Barnacle, wife of Irish author James Joyce, died in Zurich from uremic poisoning. A beautiful woman, Nora is also reputed to have served as a model for her husband's fictional characters. It has been noted that Nora's speaking and writing style resembles Molly Bloom's stream-of-consciousness soliloquy, which concludes Joyce's groundbreaking modernist novel *Ulysses*.

Nora first met Joyce in 1904, when she was working as a Dublin chambermaid. The date of their first romantic evening out together, June 16, 1904, was later chosen by Joyce as the date on which the action of *Ulysses* takes place.

In October 1904 the unwed couple left for the Continent, settling in Trieste, Austria where their first child, Giorgio, was born. During World War I the family settled in Zurich and lived in relative poverty while Joyce continued to write *Ulysses*. After the war the growing family moved to artistically thriving Paris, and there Nora learnt her third language.

In 1931, the couple were married in England, but with the approach of the Nazis in 1939, they again settled in Zurich. In January 1941 James died suddenly from a perforated ulcer. Nora remained in Zurich with her son nearby, and it is believed she will be buried near her husband in Fluntern Cemetery.

Judy Garland

Judy Holliday, Broderick Crawford, and William Holden in the George Cukor film *Born Yesterday*.

London, England, August 15: The first Miss World competition, initially called the Festival Bikini Contest, is won by Miss Sweden.

San Francisco, USA, September 8: Forty-nine nations sign a peace treaty with Japan.

Dover, England, September 11: Florence Chadwick swims the English Channel in both directions.

Wellington, New Zealand, September 24: The Maori Women's Welfare League holds its first conference.

Mexico City, Mexico, October 15: Doctor Carl Djerassi develops a synthetic oral contraceptive.

USA, October 15: The first episode of *I Love Lucy* goes to air.

California, USA, October 24: Doctor Albert Bellamy, Head of Radiological Services, assures residents that test explosions of a hydrogen bomb near Las Vegas will cause no ill effects.

London, England, October 25: Winston Churchill becomes Prime Minister again after winning the election against the Labour Party.

Vatican, October 29: Pope Pius XII cautiously sanctions the use of the rhythm method as a natural form of birth control.

New York, USA, November 13: Ballerina Janet Collins becomes the first black artist to perform at the Metropolitan Opera House.

USA, November: Deborah Kerr and Robert Taylor star in the movie epic, *Quo Vadis*.

Los Angeles, USA, December 23: Premiere of the film *The African Queen*, starring Katharine Hepburn and Humphrey Bogart.

Connecticut, USA: Marion Donovan patents the "Boater," a precursor to the first fully disposable diaper.

Jerusalem, Israel: The *Women's Equal Rights Law*, which prohibits gender discrimination, is passed.

Florida, USA: Brownie Wise is appointed Vice-President of the Tupperware Plastics Co.

England: The BBC broadcasts a very successful serial adaptation of Edith Nesbit's *The Railway Children* for Children's Hour, produced by Dorothea Brooking.

England: The British comic *Girl* is published, the first to be aimed specifically at the female market.

England: Frida Lingstrom, creator of children's classics Andy Pandy, Looby Lou, and Teddy, becomes Head of BBC Children's Television.

Geneva, Switzerland: The World Health Organization publishes *Maternal Care and Mental Health*.

New York, USA: American photographer Eve Arnold becomes the first woman to work for the celebrated Magnum agency.

Althea Gibson

International Consensus on Equal Pay for Women

Geneva, Switzerland, June 29: Today could prove to be a landmark day for workers worldwide—after weeks of deliberation, the General Conference of the International Labour Organization (ILO) voted to adopt the proposed Equal Remuneration Convention. Delegates from the ILO, an international agency founded over thirty years ago, have been engaged in heavy talks in Geneva for the past two weeks. The Convention proposes a standard of equal pay for men and women for work done of equal value.

The adoption of the Convention was by no means guaranteed as it had to be adopted by a two-thirds vote of the plenary session, and many governments represented at the conference feared the increase of their wage expenses. Only last week the British Labour Government turned down a Civil Service proposal for equal pay for men and women working for the government.

Like many resolutions of the new international organizations, the Convention is not legally binding if countries do not ratify the proposals into law. However, the ILO's Equal Remuneration Convention does express a growing international consensus that men and women engaged in work of the same value should receive the same pay. Such an expression will prove to be useful ammunition for trade unions and women's groups fighting for equal pay around the world.

German delegates to People's Constitutional Assembly, Geneva.

Californian Conquers English Channel

Dover, England, September 11: Today was a day of double firsts for Californian swimmer Florence Chadwick. She is the first woman in history to cross the English Channel from England to France and the first woman to successfully cross the channel both ways. Last year Chadwick broke the women's record for the France–England crossing, finishing in just 13 hours and 20 minutes.

Florence Chadwick, first woman to swim the English Channel in both directions.

Fog and darkness proved no obstacle today for the tenacious 32-year-old, who is currently working as a secretary. She started swimming at St Margaret's Bay near Dover and, following a zigzag course to use the channel tides to her advantage, finished barely out of breath 16 hours and 22 minutes later at Sangatte, France. While flares lit up the sky as Chadwick began at Dover, only a small group of schoolchildren were present to see her arrive in Sangatte this morning. She immediately got into a boat with her father, a San Diego policeman who is probably her proudest supporter.

Chadwick came close to record time for today's swim, falling just 51 minutes short of British man, Tom Blower's record. Although she was disappointed at not breaking the record, Chadwick joins an elite group of distance swimmers. It has been estimated that around 200 swimmers have tried the England to France crossing, and only five have succeeded.

In the boat on the way back to Dover, the super swimmer showed that she was human after all as she drifted off to some well-needed sleep.

Maori Women Unify to Tackle Urbanization

Wellington, New Zealand, September 24: Today witnessed the inaugural conference of the newly established Maori Women's Welfare League. Already the League is garnering much enthusiasm as Maori women have long seen the need for such a national organization to deal with the problems arising from the large-scale Maori migration to New Zealand's cities. The League's motto is fitting—"Tatau Tatau"—which means "Let us be united." The League stands united by its members' common goals: to promote fellowship between Maori women; to work for the welfare of Maori communities, especially in the areas of women's and children's health, education and housing; to foster and pass on Maori arts and crafts; and to maintain and preserve Maori culture. The promotion of fellowship between Maori and non-Maori women is also considered an important objective. The 90 female delegates have chosen Whina Cooper to be the first President of the League. Born Hohepine (Josephine) Te Wake in 1895 in the northern Hokianga region, Whina is a highly respected businesswoman and community leader whose views are often sought by government officials.

The need for a national league for women was seen afresh in 1945 when Maori welfare officers were employed under the New Zealand government's *Maori Social and Economic Advancement Act*. One senior officer suggested the establishment of a forum to allow direct dialogue with women outside the primarily male world of tribal committees. With this in mind, the Maori Women's Welfare League brings together previously existing organizations for Maori women, such as the Maori Health League (since 1936), and the many welfare committees that were started in the 1940s.

Today the Maori Women's Welfare League stands as a powerful political, social, and cultural force in its own right, and a hopeful indicator of the future improvement of race relations in this growing Pacific nation.

"Natural" Contraception Gets Papal Assent

Vatican, October 29: Catholic men and women around the world will take note of the speech given yesterday by Pope Pius XII before the National Congress of Italian Obstetricians and the Italian Catholic Union of Midwives. The Pope offered an historic qualification to the Church's opposition to all forms of birth control by conceding that husbands and wives may resort to the "rhythm method" if serious reasons compel them.

Twenty years ago, in an atmosphere of changing sexual mores and trends, church bodies around the world began to reconsider the ethical quandary represented by contraception. The Anglican Lambeth Conference of 1930 issued a statement cautiously in favor of contraception, and the following year the Protestant Federal Council of Churches in America offered a similar declaration. The Catholic Church, however, maintained a strong and uncompromising resolution against all forms of birth control.

In 1930, Pope Pius XI issued the encyclical *Casti Connubii,* reasserting that the primary purpose of sex is the conception of children. Anything that frustrated this purpose was declared to be a sin against nature. Yesterday, Pope Pius XII reiterated his disgust at the "culture of pleasure" which has divorced the sexual act from reproduction. However, in what

is an important concession, he granted that husbands and wives may exercise their right to use the "rhythm method" to limit the size of their families where necessary. The restriction of sex to times of least fertility is seen as a "natural" form of contraception and thus morally preferable to other "artificial" methods.

The Pope stopped short of actually advocating use of the rhythm method. While he advised against one partner choosing to withhold sex unilaterally, he cautiously said it was valid for both parties to choose not to "use" their "marital right" in times of fertility.

Plastic Party Fantastic

Florida, USA: Until recently Tupperware was a little-known product that stayed on the shelves of department stores. But with the recent appointment of Brownie Wise as Vice-President of the Tupperware Plastics Co., the cleverly designed plastic homewares are off the shelves and finding their way into kitchens across America.

The secret of the product's success lies in the new method of selling it. Through a scheme called "The Hostess Party Plan," the product is being sold by women to groups of women within the walls of their own homes. More successful than door-to-door sales, the scheme draws on women's social networks, and a system of sales incentives. Although Wise has no formal training outside of YMCA

secretarial school, she seems to have an uncanny understanding of the needs and aspirations of women today, and this has sent sales figures through the roof.

Born in 1913, Wise moved to Florida with her mother when her son became ill. For a time she and her mother sold Stanley Home Products door-to-door, until the young entrepreneur thought of a better method: she called it "Patio Parties." Among the products they sold was Poly-T (Tupperware), making use of the new technology of plastics. Sales were enough to catch inventor Earl Tupper's attention, and under Wise, they should continue to rise. Both the Tupperware brand and the woman behind its success have caught America's attention.

Deborah Kerr

Tupperware enthusiasts sometimes wear their containers as hats.

A Mother's Touch Crucial to Good Mental Health

Geneva, Switzerland: Today a high-level report was released by the World Health Organization (WHO), under the auspices of the United Nations, stating that a lack of connection between a mother and child in infancy results in a poor state of mental health for the child and the adult that child later becomes. In 1948, the United Nations commissioned a study into the needs of homeless children around the world. The WHO looked specifically at the mental health aspects of the problem and the result is *Maternal Care and Mental Health*.

Dr John Bowlby, the author of the report, demonstrates the negative mental-health effects of separating a child from its mother, then proposes remedies, largely focusing on social measures to keep families together. Even a less-than-perfect parent is found to be better than no parent at all. Bowlby explores the various causes of family failure and where institutions like foster homes are inevitable, he offers psychological advice. The report reiterates the social and, indeed, political impact of maternity.

The Festival Bikini Contest, now dubbed the Miss World competition, at the Empire Rooms, London.

Maria Montessori

One Less Star

New York, USA, January 8: The American astronomer Antonia Maury has passed away at the age of 84. Maury, the granddaughter of J. W. Draper and niece of Henry Draper, both pioneering astronomers, invented a brand new system of star classification. The scientific community failed to give it the recognition it deserved until much later in Maury's life.

Born in 1866, Maury was educated at home before she moved on to study at Vassar College, graduating with honors in astronomy and physics in 1887. A year later, she was employed by astronomer Edward Charles Pickering, her uncle's successor at Harvard College Observatory, to assist in the observation and classification of selected bright northern stars. Finding the classification system too simple to handle the complexity of the spectra, Antonia Maury devised her own system, adding three subdivisions to classify the width and distinctness of the stars' lines. Pickering, however, refused to use her new system at Harvard, prompting her to leave his group in 1892 without completing the study.

While the dispute hurt her career, one person who acknowledged the value of Maury's work was noted Danish astrophysicist Ejnar Hertzsprung, who applied her classification to verify his discovery of giant and dwarf stars. Despite Hertzsprung's early endorsement, Maury's system did not gain full acceptance until 1943 when, at the age of 77, she was awarded the Annie J. Cannon Prize by the American Astronomical Society.

> *"I CANNOT AND WILL NOT CUT MY CONSCIENCE TO FIT THIS YEAR'S FASHIONS."*
>
> LILLIAN HELLMAN (1952–1984), AMERICAN PLAYWRIGHT, IN A LETTER TO THE COMMITTEE OF UN-AMERICAN ACTIVITIES

Russian Revolutionary Dies

Moscow, USSR, March 9: Feminist revolutionary Alexandra Kollontai has died just a few weeks short of her eightieth birthday. Initially a Menshevik, Kollontai joined the Bolshevik party in 1914 and it was not long before she became a prominent member of the government following the 1917 revolution.

A leading advocate for women's liberation, Kollontai played a major role in establishing the Zhenotdel, or Women's Department, and she also published numerous works addressing policies relevant to women. However, she became increasingly critical of the Communist Party, and was effectively sidelined when she formed a left wing faction known as the Workers' Opposition.

From 1922, Kollontai was assigned work that was outside her homeland, becoming Ambassador to Norway in 1923, and later serving as Ambassador to Mexico and Sweden. Alexandra was also a member of the Soviet delegation to the League of Nations.

Women's rights advocate Alexandra Kollontai.

A Life Devoted to Learning

Noordwijk aan Zee, Netherlands, May 6: Maria Montessori, the Italian physician, scientist, and developer of the now well-known Montessori Method of child education, has died at 81 years of age.

Born in the town of Chiaravalle in 1870, Maria Montessori graduated from medical school in 1896 to become Italy's first woman physician. In 1901, she returned to university to study psychology and philosophy, and in 1904 she was appointed professor of anthropology at the University of Rome. Two years later, she gave up her university chair and her medical practice to work with 60 young children in Rome's San Lorenzo district, establishing her first "Children's House," a specially prepared environment that allowed the children to absorb knowledge simply from their surroundings. Montessori's keen observations of these children's learning processes led her to conclude that children can teach themselves at their own pace without adult intrusion—a conclusion that became the basis of all her educational methods, including teacher training.

Maria Montessori visited the United States in 1913, the year that Alexander Graham Bell and his wife Mabel founded the Montessori Educational Association at their home in Washington, DC. She then went from strength to strength. In 1938, she opened the Montessori Training Center in Laren, Netherlands, and in 1947 she established the Montessori Center in London.

In recognition of her lifelong pursuit of educational reform, Maria Montessori was nominated for the Nobel Peace Prize in 1949, 1950, and 1951.

Anne Frank Published in English

USA, July 16: Bookstores today released the first English-language version of

New York, USA, January 8: Antonia Maury, American astronomer, dies. Maury's system for classifying stars plays a vital role in the discovery of giant and dwarf stars.
USA, January: Backyard nuclear fallout shelters are proliferating all around the country.
Greece, February 1: *Gynaika*, the first Greek women's magazine, is published.
Sandringham, England, February 6: King George VI dies. His 25-year-old daughter, on safari in Kenya, accedes to the throne as Elizabeth II.

California, USA, March 4: Film stars Ronald Reagan and Nancy Davis are married in the San Fernando Valley.
Moscow, USSR, March 9: Russian revolutionary and socialist feminist Alexandra Kollontai dies.
Washington DC, USA, April 3: Queen Juliana of the Netherlands becomes only the second woman to address a joint session of Congress; the first was her mother, Queen Wilhelmina, in 1942.
Vietnam, April 26: France seeks UN aid in Vietnam if China gets involved in its conflict against the Viet Minh.

Noordwijk aan Zee, Netherlands, May 6: Maria Montessori, physician, scientist, and educator, dies.
Cambridge, England, May: Rosalind Franklin, working alone at King's College, makes a clear X-ray photograph of the wet form of DNA. Her revolutionary photograph demonstrates that the structure of the DNA molecule is a helix, but Franklin keeps the photo in a drawer.
East Germany, June 1: East Germany closes access to West Germany from midnight. Now, only permit holders may enter.

London, England, June 2: Edith Evans stars as Lady Bracknell in the film adaptation of Oscar Wilde's play, *The Importance of Being Earnest*.
USA, June 5: Doris Day records the hit single "When I Fall in Love."
USA, July 16: *The Diary of a Young Girl* by Anne Frank, who died during the war, is published in English.
Argentina, July 26: Eva "Evita" Perón, dies, aged 33.
Cairo, Egypt, July 26: King Farouk I abdicates following a military coup by General Gamal Abdel Nasser's Free Officers, a nationalist group.

New York, USA, September 6: British actress Gertrude Lawrence dies while starring on Broadway in *The King and I*. She was 54.
USA, October 3: *Our Miss Brooks*, formerly a radio show, premieres on television, starring Eve Arden.
Australia, October 3: The British atomic bomb is tested in the remote Monte Bello Islands off the northwest coast of Western Australia.
California, USA, October 11: Researchers announce the discovery of a polio vaccine that is suitable for large-scale manufacture.

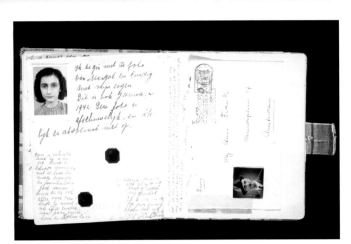

Anne Frank's diary tells the story of a young Holocaust victim.

Anne Frank's *The Diary of a Young Girl*, in which entries in the form of letters to "Kitty" describe the day-to-day experiences of eight Jews who were hiding in Nazi-occupied Amsterdam during World War II. The diary was initially published in the Netherlands in 1947, two years after the bright adolescent author died of typhoid fever in the notorious Bergen-Belsen concentration camp.

Anne Frank was born in the German city of Frankfurt in June 1929. Following the Nazis' rise to power in 1933, the Frank family left Germany to settle in Amsterdam, where Frank's father, Otto, became the managing director of a food import business with a warehouse and office on Prinsengracht Canal. When Germany invaded the Netherlands in 1940, Frank's father prepared a secret hiding place in the top back portion of the premises; the family fled there in July 1942 after Anne Frank's older sister, Margo, received an order to report for deportation. Within a short time, they were joined by Mr and Mrs Van Daan and their teenaged son, and several months later, by a middle-aged Jewish dentist named Dussel.

The eight inhabitants of the hiding place remained effectively imprisoned together for over two years. They were provided with food and other necessities by friends who worked in the company's office, but conditions were cramped and they were forced to endure strict silence during the day while the business of the firm was conducted downstairs.

Suddenly, in August 1944, their hiding place was raided by the German secret police and all eight inhabitants were transported to Dutch transit camp Westerbork, and from there they were taken to the concentration camp at Auschwitz in Poland.

Of the Frank family members, only Otto Frank survived. His daughter's diary, left behind during the police raid, was presented to him when he returned to Amsterdam from Auschwitz in 1945.

Argentina Loses a Leading Lady

Argentina, July 26: Argentina was plunged into mourning today following the announcement that First Lady Eva Perón, affectionately known as "Evita," had succumbed to cancer at age 33. Recently proclaimed the Spiritual Leader of the Nation, Perón last appeared in public on June 4 during the inauguration ceremonies for her husband's second presidential term.

Perón was born Eva Duarte in the rural village of Los Toldos on May 7, 1919. At the age of 15, she escaped to Buenos Aires where she pursued a career as a radio, stage, and film actress. In 1944, she met Colonel Juan Perón, and became his second wife in 1945, the year before he assumed the presidency.

As First Lady, Perón undertook numerous charitable and feminist works. She established the Eva Perón Foundation, an organization that builds homes and schools for the poor, and also provided free medical care to citizens. In addition, she legalized divorce, secured women's enfranchisement, and created the Female Perónist Party, the first large women's political party in the country's history.

In 1951, she was nominated for the vice-presidency, but solid opposition from the military and her own declining health prevented her candidacy. Adored by the working classes, the women's party, and unions, Eva Perón was nevertheless disliked by the military and the elite, who suspected that she was using her public position to further her personal ambitions. Evita is gone now but her memory will live on.

time out

The words "pregnancy" and "pregnant" cannot be used on American television, but that hasn't stopped comedienne Lucille Ball from making her own pregnancy part of her show. Hers is the first pregnancy shown on television.

Doris Day

Thousands gather for the funeral for Eva Perón in Buenos Aires.

Key Events

Ontario, Canada, October: Project Magnet, which was set up to investigate Canada's UFO sightings, reports that there is a "substantial probability of the real existence of extra-terrestrial vehicles."

Eniwetok Island, Pacific Ocean, November 6: The USA explodes its first hydrogen bomb on a Pacific island, blasting it apart.

Kenya, November 8: Prominent Kenyan nationalist leader, Jomo Kenyatta, is among hundreds of people rounded up as suspects in the Mau Mau terrorist uprising.

Nice, France, November 13: Margaret Wise Brown, American author of the classic children's story, *Goodnight Moon*, dies.

London, England, November 25: Agatha Christie's whodunit *The Mousetrap* premieres in the West End, starring Richard Attenborough and Sheila Sims.

Denmark, December 1: Revealed: Former GI George William Jorgensen Jr has undergone a sex change, and is now Christina Jorgensen.

Denver, Colorado, USA, December 2: The delivery by caesarean section of Gordon Campbell Kerr becomes the first ever publicly televised birth. His mother, Lillian Kerr, receives a $100 defence bond for her efforts, broadcast on a 49-station NBC network.

New York, USA: Chilean Ana Figueroa becomes the first woman appointed to the United Nations Security Council.

South Korea: Louise Yim (Yim Yongshin), the county's first female MP, becomes the Founding Chairperson of the Women's Party.

Tokyo, Japan: Kinuyo Tanaka stars in director Kenji Mizoguchi's newly released film, *The Life of Oharu*.

UK: *Excellent Women*, a novel by Barbara Pym, is published.

Philadelphia, Pennsylvania, USA: Rear Admiral Grace Murray Hopper, US naval officer and mathematician, is part of the team that invents the first computer compiler.

New York, USA: Nineteen-year-old puppeteer Shari Lewis wins the Arthur Godfrey television talent scout show on CBS.

Mexico City, Mexico: Amalia Hernández founds the Ballet Folklórico de México. Her aim is to preserve the country's colorful dance traditions.

USA: Maureen Connolly is named Associated Press Female Athlete of the Year, after winning both the US Open and Wimbledon tennis championships.

Paris, France: Jacqueline du Bief wins the gold medal at the World Figure Skating Championships.

England: Mary Norton wins the Carnegie Medal in Literature for her children's book *The Borrowers*.

Television Debut For Miss Brooks

Shari Lewis

USA, October 3: The popular radio program *Our Miss Brooks* made the transition to television today when it premiered on CBS with largely the same cast, including Eve Arden in the title role of Miss Connie Brooks, the sharp-witted English teacher at the fictional Madison High School.

Since the situation comedy was launched on radio in 1948, it has not only generated good ratings but also accolades from many professional educators who have applauded Arden for her work in humanizing the American teacher. Indeed, such is the realism of Eve Arden's portrayal of Miss Brooks—a woman who is single, smart, and pursuing what many consider to be an unglamorous career—that the star has been made an honorary member of the National Education Association.

"ONLY, OF COURSE, THERE'S A FASHION IN THESE THINGS, JUST LIKE THERE IS IN CLOTHES. MY DEAR, HAVE YOU SEEN WHAT CHRISTIAN DIOR IS TRYING TO MAKE US WEAR IN THE WAY OF SKIRTS?"

AGATHA CHRISTIE 1952, *THEY DO IT WITH MIRRORS*

Our Miss Brooks, starring Eve Arden, looks set to become a huge hit with television audiences.

George is Now Christine

Denmark, December 1: "Ex-GI becomes blonde bombshell!" shrieks the front-page headline in today's *New York Daily News,* as young American army veteran George William Jorgensen creates a big media frenzy back home, amid the breaking news that he has undergone successful male-to-female gender reassignment surgery in Copenhagen.

George Jorgensen was born to Danish immigrant parents in The Bronx, New York City, on May 30, 1926. Raised as a Lutheran, he was a thin and frail little child who shied away from fistfights and rough games, feeling like a "miserable misfit" because he was outwardly a boy yet secretly yearned to be a girl.

After graduating from the Christopher Columbus High School in 1945, George was drafted into the United States Army. He served 14 months as a clerk before returning to New York. It was then that his lonely journey towards transsexual surgery began. Upon learning that such a process was possible, he researched the subject thoroughly, studying photographs and scrutinizing all the reading material he could find about sex hormones and glandular imbalances. When he discovered that surgical procedures were being carried out in Scandinavia, he set sail in 1950 for Sweden. During a stopover to visit relatives in Copenhagen, however, he discovered that gender reassignment surgery was also available to approved patients in Denmark.

The two-year transformation from George to Christine was overseen by Dr Christian Hamburger, and involved hormone replacement therapy as well as a series of surgical procedures. Earlier this year, while she was recuperating in her hospital bed in Copenhagen, 26-year-old Christine Jorgensen wrote a long letter, explaining what she had done, to her parents back in New York. In it she said: "Nature made a mistake, which I have had corrected," she told them. "I am now your daughter." They cabled a swift and supportive response: "We love you more than ever."

Suzanne Flon plays dancer Myriamme Hayam in this year's motion picture, *Moulin Rouge.*

A Dramatic Entrance

Colorado, USA, December 2: When Gordon Campbell Kerr made his entry into the world at Denver's Colorado General Hospital today, weighing in at 5 pounds 7 ounces (3.3 kg), he became an instant television star on a 49-station NBC network, courtesy of the pharmaceuticals manufacturers Smith, Kline & French. Physicians at American Medical Association (AMA) meetings have previously observed childbirth over closed-circuit hookups, but today's delivery of baby Gordon is the first such event ever telecast for the general public.

AMA members and the commercial sponsors decided to feature a caesarean delivery on the program, acknowledging the irrefutable fact that natural childbirth cannot be scheduled with any precision. Baby Gordon's 38-year-old mother, Mrs Lillian Kerr, wife of a sergeant stationed at Fitzsimons General Hospital, has two other children, both born by caesarean section—an obstetric history that certainly facilitated the doctors' task of setting the time and date for the third procedure to be performed.

Television viewers—including the anxious expectant father John Kerr, who was watching a set in the hospital basement—were treated to the sight of Mrs Kerr on the operating table surrounded by doctors and nurses in tight formation. After a brief explanation of what was about to occur, the fetal heartbeat resounded over the air before the picture abruptly cut to the hospital's modern facilities for the treatment of premature babies. Apart from the medical team, the television crew and attendant newsmen were the only people to witness the actual abdominal incision and the speedy extraction of the baby from his mother's womb. The television viewers were returned to the scene just in time to see a wailing baby Gordon's umbilical cord tied, his mouth drained of mucus, and drops placed in his eyes. For her part in today's television drama, Mrs Kerr is to receive a $100 defence bond.

Amazing Grace

Philadelphia, Pennsylvania, USA: United States naval officer, mathematician, and computer scientist, Grace Murray Hopper, has lived up to her nickname of "Amazing Grace" with the invention of the first compiler, an intermediate program that translates English language instructions into the language of a target computer.

Hopper was born Grace Brewster Murray in New York City on December 9, 1906. After graduating from Vassar with a BA in mathematics and physics in 1928, she pursued her graduate education in those subjects at Yale, receiving her MA in 1930 and PhD in 1934. She began teaching mathematics at Vassar in 1931, achieving the status of associate professor in 1941.

Hopper resigned her Vassar post to join the Navy WAVES in 1943. Commissioned as a lieutenant in 1944, she was assigned to the Bureau of Ordnance Computation Project at Harvard University where she worked as one of the early programmers of the Mark I calculator. When World War II ended in 1945, Hopper was already working on the Mark II version of the machine, and she was appointed to the Harvard faculty as a research fellow. Although no longer on active duty with the Navy, she remained in the reserves, and took on yet another job in 1949, this time with the Eckert-Mauchly Computer Corporation as part of the team developing the UNIVACI.

A Brilliant Career

Tokyo, Japan: Audiences across Japan are applauding the outstanding performance of actress Kinuyo Tanaka in director Kenji Mizoguchi's newly released film, *The Life of Oharu.* Tanaka plays the title role in the period drama, which is an adaptation of playwright Sakiku Ibara's seventeenth century classic farce about a woman's fall from imperial courtesan to beggar.

Born in Shinomoseki in 1910, Tanaka left the world of light opera at the age of 14 to eventually become one of the most

Kinoyu Tanaka, a shining star of Japanese cinema.

successful actresses in the Japanese film industry. After making her debut at the Shochiku studio in 1924, she went on to establish her star status in such light-hearted silent productions as *Young Miss* in 1930. Despite the studio's concerns about her accent, her future popularity was ensured by her critically acclaimed performance in Japan's first talking picture, Heinosuke Gosho's *The Neighbor's Wife and Mine,* released in 1931.

In the early 1940s, Kinuyo Tanaka began what has become an extensive period of collaboration with director Mizoguchi, who has provided her with a platform to shed her image as the "eternal girl" by offering her more challenging roles, including that of Oharu. Following a visit to Hollywood in 1949, Tanaka took another step to refresh her career when she severed her connection with the Shochiku studio to work freelance, a move that now allows her to choose her own directors and films.

Little Mo Takes Another Title

USA: Young American tennis sensation, Maureen "Little Mo" Connolly, had added another title to her rapidly expanding collection with the announce-

ment that she has been named Associated Press Female Athlete of the Year for the second year in a row.

Little Mo Connolly was born in San Diego, California, on September 17, 1934. At age 10, she began playing tennis on the municipal courts of San Diego under the watchful eye of her coach Wilbur Folsom, who encouraged her to switch from left-handed to right. Later, Connolly became a student of the notoriously demanding coach, Eleanor "Teach" Tennant, and at age 14 became the youngest player to win the US national championship for girls under 18, her first major title.

With a great competitive spirit and a game characterized by speed, accuracy, baseline power, and an especially strong backhand, Connolly has now surged ahead to dominate women's tennis both at home and internationally. Last year, at the age of 16, she defeated Shirley Fry to become the youngest woman player to win the prestigious US national singles title at the West Side Tennis Club in Forest Hills, Queens.

This year, Little Mo Connolly not only successfully defended her US title, overcoming Doris Hart in straight sets, but she also claimed her first women's singles championship at Wimbledon with a straight-sets victory over fellow American Louise Brough Clapp.

Jacqueline du Bief

Marilyn Monroe and Richard Widmark feature in *Don't Bother to Knock.*

Vijaya Lakshmi Pandit

Kinsey's Report on Female Sexuality Published

Philadelphia, USA, September 14: A highly controversial report on female sexuality, *Sexual Behavior in the Human Female*, has been published today by Dr Alfred C. Kinsey and his research staff at the Kinsey Institute at Indiana University.

Dr Kinsey and his staff interviewed almost 6,000 women, gathering data for this groundbreaking study on subjects such as premarital sex, female orgasm, and masturbation.

Research for the book began in late 1948 amid the shadows of the ongoing debate surrounding Kinsey's earlier publication, *Sexual Behavior in the Human Male* (1948), which has since gone on to sell more than 200,000 copies.

Sexual Behavior in the Human Female is divided into three parts: "History and Method," which is devoted largely to a rebuttal of the criticism of his work on male sexuality; "Types of Sexual Activity Among Females," which focuses on sexual development of females from childhood through to puberty, and "Comparisons of Male and Female."

Dr Kinsey has used his accumulated data to argue that women are no less sexual than men. He found that 50 percent of his respondents had participated in premarital sex, 26 percent had extra-

"To make oneself an object, to make oneself passive, is a very different thing from being a passive object."

SIMONE DE BEAUVOIR (1908–1986), FRENCH WRITER AND FEMINIST, IN *THE SECOND SEX*

analysis of the contentious and much-anticipated report.

There are some media outlets, however, that are refusing to publicize the book's launch, and many more conservative publications are coming out in defense of what they perceive as the sanctity of American womanhood.

Woman Elected President at UN

New York, USA, September 18: Indian politician, diplomat, and former Ambassador to the United States, Vijaya Lakshmi Pandit, has become the first woman to be elected President of the United Nations General Assembly. A staunch follower of Mahatma Gandhi, she was imprisoned several times during the 1930s and 1940s.

Vijaya Pandit was born in 1900, into one of India's most prominent political families. Her father, Motilal Nehru, was a former President of the Indian National Congress and her brother, Jawaharlal Nehru, is currently Vice-President of the Executive Council and Member of External Affairs. Elected to the Legislative Assembly of India's United Provinces in 1937, Vijaya Pandit became the first Indian woman to hold a cabinet post when she was appointed Minister for Local Self-Government and Health later that same year. She was President of the All-India Women's Conference from 1941 to 1943.

Vijaya Lakshmi Pandit was elected late this afternoon after the Assembly opened its eighth session by postponing a consideration of Communist China's claim to a UN seat.

The UN's first female president won the vote over Thailand's Prince Van Waithayakon by 37 votes to 22.

President of the UN General Assembly, Vijaya Lakshmi Pandit.

they expect the first human being to have been conceived through the artificial insemination of deep-frozen male sperm cells to be born within the next three months. It is expected that the child will be born without complications, and X-rays of the mother's womb indicate that the fetal skeleton is developing normally. Though artificial insemination has been successful in the past, this is the first time that the insemination of a human being using frozen semen has been a success.

Doctors at the University of Iowa Medical School have also announced that two other women have conceived with the implantation of frozen sperm cells, although their pregnancies are not as advanced, and are still being monitored.

Time Honors America's Favorite Grandma

USA, December 28: Anna Mary Robinson, the quintessential American folk artist who is better known as Grandma Moses, and who completed her first painting at the age of 76 when crippling arthritis meant she could no longer hold a needle to embroider, appears on this week's cover of *Time* magazine.

The much loved Grandma Moses paints nostalgic works that portray the contentment and joys of rural life. She imbues with luminous color and truth simple tasks such as maple sugaring, candlestick making, berrying, and the making of apple butter.

Kinsey's study of female sexuality is the subject of much coffee-table conversation.

marital encounters, and 62 percent had engaged in masturbation. Yet the book is more than mere data and sociological observations. It has a scientific basic, and grand science at that. It is detailed research that should be studied so that we can learn more about ourselves.

Five of the country's most prominent national magazines, *Time, Colliers, Life, Newsweek,* and *Woman's Home Companion,* have hit the newsstands today with considered articles featuring detailed

Frozen Sperm Successfully Implanted

Iowa, USA, December 3: Scientists from the University of Iowa today announced that

This refreshingly self-deprecating artist is not, however, one to elevate her own art. Almost all her works are produced in the corner of her upstairs bedroom at her home in the small town of Eagle Bridge in upstate New York. Two small windows provide light during the day and a single 150-watt, wall-mounted light bulb illuminates her pine-planked, circa 1762, tilt-topped easel at night.

Grandma Moses is proud of the fact that she is a frugal artist who paints in batches in order to save paint. Lining up

The paintings of Grandma Moses evoke the American countryside.

her masonite boards, she first paints blue skies, then white clouds, and finally green mountains. She uses leftover house paint, and even scavenges around for surfaces to paint on. She sees her works as "products", much like the preserves she sold as a farm wife. One early work was painted over a section of canvas used to repair the cover of a threshing machine.

Born in 1860 on a farm in New York's Washington County, Anna Mary Robertson left home at the age of 12 to work on a neighbor's farm. Quite a few decades later, in 1938, a New York engineer and art collector named Louis Caldor noticed several of her works selling for $3 to $5 in a drug store in Hoosick Falls. He impulsively bought them all. The following year her paintings were part of an exhibition of "contemporary unknown painters" at New York City's Museum of Modern Art. She did not remain "unknown" for long.

The Second Sex Available in USA and Britain

UK and USA: Simone de Beauvoir's feminist masterpiece, *The Second Sex*, was published throughout Europe in 1949. And now, the work of this French author and philosopher has been released across the United States and Great Britain.

In the book, de Beauvoir argues two primary assertions: First, that one is not born a woman, one "becomes" one; and secondly, that throughout all known societies, women are seen by men as the "other" sex, and therefore as less than fully human simply because they are not male. She has also stirred considerable controversy with her claim that the "wife–mother" destiny is a myth conceived by men to deny women their freedom.

Born into a bourgeois Catholic family in Paris in 1908, de Beauvoir turned her back on marriage and, in 1929, enrolled to study philosophy at the Sorbonne. During this time she met and became friends with the existentialist, Jean-Paul Sartre. They soon became lovers. In 1939 she received a teaching post in Marseilles, and in the autumn of 1943 she published her first novel, *She Came To Stay*, which is a fictionalized account of her complex relationship with Sartre and a young student, Olga Kosakiewicz.

The Second Sex is sure to become a foundation work in contemporary feminism. It is an intensely philosophical work, exploring Freudian, Marxist, and Hegelian themes in an attempt to uncover the historical definition of woman as "the other" of man. The work is not without its critics, who have openly referred to de Beauvoir as a "nymphomaniac" and to the book as "dispassionate."

New Text on Plant Anatomy Published

New York, USA: Noted pioneer of plant biology Katherine Esau has just published *Plant Anatomy*, a dynamic new work that brings to life the structure of plants. The book is likely to become the standard text on plant biology for many years to come. Born in Russia in 1898 and educated in Moscow and Berlin, Esau emigrated with her parents to the United States in 1921, settling in the Mennonite community of Reedley, California. Her extraordinary contributions to plant anatomy can be traced to the beginning of her graduate studies at the University of California at Berkeley, after having worked at the Spreckels Sugar Company in Salinas where she was involved in the development of a sugar beet resistant to the curly-top virus. Katherine Esau received her doctorate in botany from the University of California in 1931 and since then has become one of the world's most celebrated plant anatomists, recognized primarily for her contributions to paleobotany, morphology, and embryology, as well as her studies on the structure and development of phloem.

She began writing the manuscript for her 735-page *Plant Anatomy* in the late 1940s while at the University of California, Davis campus, close to her home at 237 First Street where she lived with her mother and father.

Already being hailed as a structural botanist's bible, *Plant Anatomy's* developmental approach and thorough cataloguing of plant structures has resulted in a textbook that is almost single-handedly revitalizing the discipline of plant anatomy throughout the world.

Simone de Beauvoir

Rita Hayworth plays the title role in the hit film *Salome.*

Judy Garland

Queen Elizabeth II Visits Australia

Sydney, Australia, February 3: Accompanied by her husband, the Duke of Edinburgh, Queen Elizabeth II arrived at Sydney's Farm Cove at 10.30 this morning and received a tumultuous greeting from the estimated one million people lining the streets, and the half a million crowding every foreshore vantage point from the Heads to the Sydney Harbour Bridge.

For the very first visit of a reigning monarch to Australia, Queen Elizabeth wore a champagne chiffon dress printed in gold with a tinge of green, setting off her complexion, which is somewhat paler than is suggested by her photographs and portraits. Australian women are eager to see what latest fashions the young, glamorous monarch has brought with her from London and Europe.

Her Majesty's program is a demanding one. She is scheduled to visit every capital city with the exception of Darwin, and 70 country towns. She will give 100 speeches and will travel 10,000 miles (16,000 km) by air and 2,000 miles (3,220 km) by

road. Automobiles belonging to the Royal Visit Car Company are expected to log over 500,000 miles (805,000 km).

The royal yacht *The Gothic* sailed into a beautiful, sunlit Sydney Harbour this morning flanked by six vessels from the Australian Navy and a flotilla of private boats, ferries, and yachts dubbed the "armada of mischief." Small craft, instead of remaining to the rear of the escort ships, darted ahead, weaving across the bow of the royal yacht.

For the coming two months until her eventual departure from Fremantle in Western Australia, it is estimated almost three-quarters of the Australian population will take the opportunity to demonstrate their support and loyalty to the Commonwealth. With television not yet available in Australia, many people will be traveling unheard of distances to catch a glimpse of their new monarch.

A special agency has been created within the Prime Minister's Department to coordinate all arrangements for Her Majesty's national tour.

Doris Day Has Number 1 Hit

USA, March 6: The popular song "Secret Love," written for the film *Calamity Jane* by Sammy Fain and Paul Francis Webster, and beautifully performed by the singer and movie star Doris Day, has reached Number 1 on the Cash Box charts.

Doris Day was born on April 3, 1924 in Ohio to German immigrant parents. Her wholesome girl-next-door image, combined with a seemingly effortless ability to sing, dance, and play both dramatic and comedic roles, has seen her become one of America's most hardworking actresses of recent times.

Doris Day starred as Calamity Jane in last year's film.

An auto accident in 1937 meant the young Doris Mary Ann von Kappelhoff was forced to abandon her dream of a dancing career. So she went on to sing for the big bands of Bob Crosby, Barney Rapp, and Les Brown before starting her own solo career in the late 1940s.

Calamity Jane has catapulted Doris Day to international stardom. "Secret Love" was recorded in a single take at the Warner Brothers studio under the watchful eyes of Ray Heindorf, Jack Warner's musical director.

Wife of Russian Defector to Remain in Australia

Darwin, Australia, April 20: The wife of the defecting Russian diplomat Vladimir Petrov has been seized from Russian couriers by Australian Security Intelligence Organization (ASIO) agents at

> *"A CAREER IS A WONDERFUL THING, BUT YOU CAN'T SNUGGLE UP TO IT ON A COLD NIGHT."*
>
> MARILYN MONROE (1926–1962), AMERICAN ACTRESS

The Queen with the Australian Prime Minister.

Groton, USA, January 21: USS *Nautilus*, the first atomic submarine, is launched today by First Lady Mamie Eisenhower.

Sydney, Australia, February 3: Over one million well-wishers turn out to greet Queen Elizabeth II as she sails into the harbor on her first royal trip to the country.

UK, February 12: A report by the British Standing Committee on cancer says cigarette smoking is directly linked to lung cancer.

USA, March 6: Doris Day reaches Number 1 on the Cash Box charts with her song "Secret Love."

Hollywood, USA, March 25: From *Here to Eternity* wins eight Academy Awards.

Johannesburg, South Africa, April 17: Rachel (Ray) Simons forms the Federation of South African Women with others such as Helen Joseph, Lillian Ngoyi, and Amina Cachalia. This is the first attempt to establish a broad-based women's organization in this country.

Darwin, Australia, April 20: Evdokia Petrov, Soviet Union spy, elects to defect with her husband, Vladimir Petrov.

New York, USA, May 13: Broadway musical *The Pajama Game* premieres today. Actress and dancer Carol Haney shoots to instant fame for her role as Gladys Hotchkiss.

Paris, France, May 25: Eighteen-year-old author Françoise Sagan wins the Prix des Critiques for her first, somewhat scandalous novel *Bonjour Tristesse*.

London, England, May: Irish-born British philosopher and author, Iris Murdoch, publishes her first novel, *Under the Net*.

New Guinea, June 10: A hitherto unknown tribe of 100,000 people is found.

Ohio, USA, July 4: Marilyn Sheppard, aged 31 and pregnant, is found brutally beaten to death at her home near Cleveland. Amid extensive publicity, her husband Dr Sam Sheppard is accused, tried, and jailed for the murder.

UK, July 4: Food rationing ends, with meat finally removed from the list nearly nine years after the end of World War II.

Ulanbataar, Mongolia, July 7: Sühbaataryn Yanjmaa ends nine months as acting President of Mongolia. She is the first modern woman to take the role of head of state of a country.

Mexico City, Mexico, July 13: Artist Frida Kahlo dies. Her final painting is an incomplete portrait of Joseph Stalin.

Darwin airport, and has made a last-minute decision to defect to Australia with her husband.

Mrs Evdokia Petrov has been under virtual house arrest in the Soviet Embassy in Canberra ever since news of her husband's intention to defect became public on April 4. Last week Soviet couriers arrived in Australia to return her to the Soviet Union, and today a large crowd of fiercely anti-Communist Eastern European migrants and supporters gathered at Sydney's Mascot Airport to protest against her departure.

Vladimir made his fateful decision to defect on the day his KGB successor arrived in Australia. It is understood his wife was unaware of his decision.

Fearful of the opposition party's claims of abandoning Mrs Petrov, the Australian Prime Minister, Robert Menzies, ordered ASIO officials to intercept her at Darwin airport when the aeroplane landed for refueling. At the airport, her Russian guards were wrestled and disarmed, and Mrs Petrov was spirited away.

Irish Philosopher Publishes Novel

London, England, May: *Under the Net* is the first novel of the Irish-born philosopher Iris Murdoch, who is described as possessing great wit, inventive power, and a knack for producing absurd incidents.

The novel is dedicated to the French novelist Raymond Queneau, and tells of the adventures of frivolous drifter Jake Donaghue and his opportunistic ability to live off the generosity of his friends.

Iris Murdoch's engaging style of prose conveys the sheer happiness she finds in the endless flow of talk from one friend to another, her deep love of the creative processes of writing, and her joy in the invention of stories.

time out

The Miss America pageant, which originated in 1921 in Atlantic City, is televised for the first time this year. The national competition is open to young women and assesses the contestants' beauty, poise, and talent.

Although lacking in the complexity and strength one might expect, this fast-paced tale with its well-developed characters and detailed settings is replete with considerations of moral and philosophical issues. Born in Dublin in 1919, Iris Murdoch's youth was characterized by an inner serenity and an immense capacity for pleasure. Despite often depicting the ravages of anxiety and destructive passions in her novels, there is little evidence she suffered from them herself. Murdoch attended Somerville College at Oxford where she studied philosophy and the classics, and joined the Communist Party during World War II, although she resigned after becoming disenchanted with its ideology. She then worked for the United Nations Relief and Rehabilitation Administration from 1944 to 1946. In 1948, she was elected as a fellow of St Anne's College, Oxford.

Unknown Author Bursts onto Literary Scene

Paris, France, May 25: An unknown 18-year-old author who dropped out of the Sorbonne after failing her first-year literary exams has exploded onto the French literary scene by winning the Prix des Critiques for her precocious debut novel, *Bonjour Tristesse (Hello Sadness)*.

Françoise Sagan, the youngest of three children of an industrialist from the Lot district of southwest France, has written a remarkable novel telling the story of a bored, manipulative 17-year-old girl who destroys a series of relationships between her father and various women.

The book's irreverent tone, subversive subtexts, and emotional rawness and intimacy have shocked the French public, and found an echo among young people in their search for identity and meaning.

However, some see her as a superficial novelist, writing about the sexuality and budding emotions of a young woman while lacking the maturity and profundity of an experienced author who could properly analyze the causes and effects of her feelings. Others see her success as the beginning of the end of serious philosophical treatises within the context of fiction, with a post-World War II generation that has escaped a major conflict, only to be confronted with the possibility of nuclear annihilation, more than ready to embrace a lightening up of the pretensions of literature.

The manuscript for *Bonjour Tristesse* was 200 pages long, and typed with two fingers on a dilapidated typewriter in only 32 days. It is likely to make Françoise Sagan independently wealthy. Her small advance on the novel was quickly spent on a black sweater and several rounds of whiskey for her friends.

Frida Kahlo

Author Françoise Sagan with her publisher.

Geneva, Switzerland, July 20: War in Indochina ends with the signing of the Geneva Accords.

Paris, France, August 3: Sidonie-Gabrielle Colette, French actress, librettist, novelist (the *Claudine* series), and critic, dies. Her body is interred in Le Père Lachaise Cemetery in Paris.

Christchurch, New Zealand, August 28: Two teenage girls, Juliet Hulme and Pauline Parker, are found guilty of murdering Juliet's mother in a brutal bashing.

Ontario, Canada, September 8: Sixteen-year-old Marilyn Bell is the first person to swim across Lake Ontario.

USA, September 13: Alicia Patterson, founder and editor of *Newsday*, appears on the cover of *Time* magazine after the tabloid wins its first Pulitzer Prize.

Drummoyne, NSW, Australia, September 19: Author (*My Brilliant Career*) and feminist Miles Franklin dies, leaving provision for an award for Australian literature.

Hollywood, USA, September 29 : Judy Garland stars in the movie musical *A Star is Born*.

New York, USA, October 7: Marian Anderson is the first black soloist to be hired by the Metropolitan Opera.

USA, October 7: Marilyn Monroe and Joe Di Maggio are divorced, just nine months after their marriage.

Egypt, October 19: Egypt and Britain agree to terms over the Suez Canal.

Alabama, USA, November 30 A woman is struck by an 8 lb 8 oz (4 kg) meteorite as she sleeps on her sofa, suffering only bad bruising.

USA, December: Swanson and Sons' new TV dinner–a ready-to-heat meal of turkey and vegetables–costs 98 cents.

USA: Babe Zaharias wins the US Women's Open Golf Tournament, and is also named Associated Press Female Athlete of the Year.

New Delhi, India: Aruna Asaf Ali helps to establish the National Federation of Indian Women (NFIW), the women's wing of the Communist Party of India. The NFIW is intended to be a radical alternative to existing women's organizations.

Bogota, Colombia: Women are granted the right to vote.

Paris, France: Couturier Coco Chanel reopens her design house, which was closed in 1939 with the onset of the war.

New Mexico, USA: Georgia O'Keeffe paints *My Last Door*, an abstract image of a patio door that has fascinated the artist for a number of years and inspired many variations.

Georgia O'Keeffe

Century's "Most Liberated Woman" Dies

Paris, France, August 3: Highly acclaimed French journalist, playwright, and literary giant Sidonie-Gabrielle Colette, whose hand famously froze into a permanent writer's cramp in her mid-seventies—the result of a lifetime of writing—has died at 81 years of age.

Born in 1873 in Saint-Sauveur-en-Puisaye in Burgundy, France, and once

> "WHAT A WONDERFUL LIFE I'VE HAD! I ONLY WISH I'D REALIZED IT SOONER."
>
> COLETTE
> (1873–1954),
> FRENCH AUTHOR

Colette, one of France's most prolific writers.

called "the most truly liberated woman of the twentieth century," Colette will become the first woman in the history of France to be given a state funeral.

Her legacy of over 50 books, mostly autobiographical, as well as plays, operas, and films, often dealt with the conflict of women's yearning for sexual expression and their desire for true independence.

In Paris, Colette's fine skills as a writer were first encouraged by Henri Gauthier-Villars, known as Willy, a would-be writer she married when she was 20 years old. She wrote a series of racy tales describing schoolgirl crushes and rebellious tomboyish pursuits (the *Claudine* series), which Willy published under his own name and which became very successful.

Colette and Willy were feted by the bourgeoisie and the avant-garde of Paris, and Colette soon became acquainted with a circle of prominent lesbian writers that included Renée Vivien and Natalie Clifford Barney. In 1906, after 13 years of marriage, she divorced Willy and became a music-hall performer.

By the 1920s, Colette had achieved success as a novelist, and by the 1930s, she was writing confronting novels about homosexuality, sadism, and masochism,

such as *The Pure and the Impure*, which the author considered her finest work.

To her wider audience, however, it is the short 1945 novella *Gigi*, published when the author was 72 years old, for which she is best remembered. In 1951, *Gigi* was turned into a Broadway musical starring Audrey Hepburn, whom Colette personally selected for the role.

Colette married twice more and had a number of romantic liaisons, including some lesbian affairs. She had one daughter. A sometimes controversial person, Colette will be remembered as much for her individualty as her writing.

Toronto Schoolgirl Conquers Lake Ontario

Ontario, Canada, September 9: A plucky 16-year-old Toronto schoolgirl, Marilyn Bell, has today become the first person in history, male or female, to swim across Lake Ontario. Competing in the Canadian National Exhibition event, Marilyn stepped into the water at Youngstown, New York, just after 11 pm last night alongside the Canadian swimmer Winnie Roach, who swam the English Channel three years ago. Roach was forced from the lake's water in the early hours of this morning, as was the race favorite, the 34-year-old Florence Chadwick.

Canadians stayed awake throughout the night listening on their radios as the petite, freckled winner of this year's Atlantic City swimming marathon battled appalling conditions that forced her to swim much further than the 32-mile (51-km) course across the lake. Marilyn Bell persevered under the supervision of her coach in the face of lamprey eels and

high waves to triumphantly reach the Toronto shoreline of Lake Ontario at 8 pm this evening, 20 hours and 57 minutes after entering the water.

Newspapers printed extra editions and radio stations announced hourly updates on Bell's progress, creating a mild hysteria that resulted in more than 100,000 people gathering to greet the young swimmer as she finally emerged from the water, overwhelmed with fatigue.

The first person to conquer Lake Ontario learnt to swim at an early age at Port Credit, Ontario's Lakeshore Swimming Club, under the guidance of its founder, Gus Ryder. The patriotic young Canadian was quoted as saying that she "did it for Canada," and her phenomenal accomplishment is expected to shatter once and for all any remaining myths of the "fragile female."

Alicia Patterson: Editor, Publisher, Maverick

USA, September 13: Alicia Patterson, the editor and publisher of the most profitable and fastest-growing tabloid newspaper in the United States today—Long Island's *Newsday*—is featured on this week's cover of *Time* magazine.

Born on October 15, 1906, in Chicago, daughter of the founder of the *Daily News*, Joseph Medill Patterson, Alicia was cautioned by her father that conservative Long Island readers would never accept a tabloid newspaper. Nevertheless, the woman whose only prior experience in journalism was incurring a libel suit at the *Daily News* and being fired by her father, purchased the defunct *Nassau Daily Journal* with her husband Harry

Alicia Patterson, founder and editor of *Newsday*, with her editorial team.

F. Guggenheim on April 5, 1940. She renamed it *Newsday*, and henceforth set out to violate every convention of sedate, respectable journalism, preferring to run stories on suburban gambling rackets and celebrity arrests, rather than reporting on tea parties and fundraisers.

Newsday possesses a distinctive layout all its own, sporting only three columns rather than the usual five-column format. By 1942 its breezy, irreverent style saw its circulation climb to over 30,000, in the process overtaking its only Long Island competitor, the *Nassau Daily Review-Star*. It also carries more advertising than any other US daily newspaper and over the last 14 years has become as indispensable as the automobile for many Long Islanders.

Earlier this year the paper won its first Pulitzer Prize for a series of articles on the corrupt union leader William DeKoning.

Soprano Marian Anderson joins the Metropolitan Opera.

Author Bequeaths Literary Award to Nation

Sydney, NSW, Australia, September 19: It has just been revealed that the great Australian author and feminist Miles Franklin, who passed away today at the age of 74, has established a bequest in her will to be known as the Miles Franklin Literary Award.

The "Miles Franklin," as it is being referred to, is to be awarded annually to any published play or novel portraying Australian life. The literary award is accompanied by a second, but no less unprecedented, bequest of the author's entire personal and literary collection to Sydney's Mitchell Library.

Stella Maria Sarah Miles Franklin was born in the southern alpine region of New South Wales in October 1879, and grew up on the family farm, Brindabella. Franklin was only 20 years old when she penned the Australian classic *My Brilliant Career* (1901), causing much consternation among her friends and family, many of whom were convinced they saw themselves portrayed in the book.

After its publication Franklin worked for a while as a nurse, a handmaid, and as a freelance journalist for the *Sydney Morning Herald* and the *Daily Telegraph*. The critical and commercial success of *My Brilliant Career* led to requests urging her to continue writing, though subsequent successes eluded her.

On April 7, 1906, Franklin set sail for the United States, with her mother's financial support, in the hope of finding further literary glory.

In Chicago she found work with the National Women's Trade Union League, and was appointed its press officer during the Garment Worker's Strike of 1910–11. Her life as an author was unknown to her fellow workers. Franklin wrote in secret, continuing to submit short stories, plays, and novels to publishers who continued to routinely reject them.

Miles Franklin traveled to London in 1915, and in the early 1920s published a series of novels that detailed her family history in Australia under the engaging pseudonym, Brent of Bin Bin.

Franklin returned to Sydney in 1932, and four years later won the S. H. Prior Memorial Prize with *All That Swagger*.

Once again a celebrity, this indomitable, sociable, witty, yet vulnerable artist went on to publish books almost until the day she died. The income expected to be generated from her bequest will be used to finance prizes for the overall improvement and betterment of Australian literature, and to honor the great art of storytelling. It confirms that Miles Franklin was a woman who was certainly well ahead of her time.

Coco Chanel is Back in Business

Paris, France: In the hope of boosting lagging perfume sales, designer Gabrielle "Coco" Chanel has reopened her Paris design house, which she closed in 1939 at the outbreak of World War II.

In contrast to today's full-skirted "New Look," the new house of Chanel couture features classic suit jackets made from highly textured tweeds, and accessories such as quilted handbags.

Credited with revolutionizing the world of women's fashion with her elegant modern styles, the famous "little black dress," trousers for women, and braid-trimmed suits, Coco Chanel still

represents the last word in sophistication and impeccable taste. Born outside Paris in 1883, Chanel was orphaned at six and raised by two aunts in the province of Auvergne. At 16, she went to Paris and quickly developed an appreciation of the habits and tastes of the Parisian elite. In 1914 she opened a millinery boutique, which in five short years grew to be one of the leading fashion houses of Paris.

Pauline Parker

Indian Organization Furthers Women's Rights

New Delhi, India: Aruna Asaf Ali, a heroine of India's freedom struggle, has helped to establish the National Federation of Indian Women (NFIW).

A network of organizations and individual activists, the NFIW is designed to facilitate an egalitarian society in which India's women will have equal access to food, shelter, health, education, and property in an environment in which women's rights are no longer dependent upon caste, class, or religious background.

An ardent socialist, Aruna Asaf Ali was born Aruna Gangulee on July 16, 1909, in Haryana province and was educated in Lahore. She became a prominent leader in the Quit India movement launched by Mahatma Gandhi in 1942.

Agatha Christie at her play, *The Spider's Web*, in London.

Mother Katherine Drexel

Women in Civil Service to Receive Equal Pay

London, England, January 31: A need to increase the number of females working in Britain's civil service, combined with a push to eliminate it as an election issue, are the best guesses behind the Conservative Government's decision today to agree to provide women in the service with equal pay to men.

Conservative MPs were instrumental in defeating equal pay bills in 1936 and again in 1944, and no official explanation has so far been offered for the change of policy.

After the Labor Party announced in January 1954 that it would pursue the implementation of equal pay should it win government, pressure from white-collar unions and the feminist Equal Pay Campaign Committee have combined to force a reversal of the Conservatives' long-standing history of steadfast opposition to equal pay proposals.

"I DID NOT GET ON THE BUS TO GET ARRESTED...I GOT ON THE BUS TO GO HOME."

ROSA PARKS (1913–2005), CIVIL RIGHTS ACTIVIST, USA, ON REFUSING TO GIVE UP HER BUS SEAT TO A WHITE MALE

Death of Mother Drexel, the "Millionnaire Nun"

Pennsylvania, USA, March 3: Philadelphia heiress and founder of the Sisters of the Blessed Sacrament for Indians and Colored People, Katharine Drexel, has died at 96 years of age.

Sometimes referred to by the media as the "millionaire nun," Drexel was born on November 26, 1858, the daughter of a prominent Philadelphia banker. Her mother died shortly after giving birth, and a few years later her father married Emma Bouvier. Emma is credited with first planting within Katharine the seeds of religious conviction.

Emma died in 1883 after a long battle with cancer, and when the young Katharine's father passed away in 1885

she was left with a considerable fortune, wealth which allowed her to travel.

Katherine had witnessed the appalling conditions and treatment of Native Americans on a trip to the US Northwest territories with her father a year before he died. The following year she donated money to the St Francis Mission on South Dakota's Rosebud Reservation.

time out

Civil unrest erupts in Alabama after Rosa Parkes is arrested for refusing to stand for a white passenger on the bus. Thousands of other African American citizens join her protest and bus companies quickly feel the impact.

She traveled to Rome in 1887 and had an audience with Pope Leo XIII during which he encouraged her to become a missionary. This confirmed her own inner calling to service, and in May 1889 she began a six-month postulancy at the Sisters of Mercy Convent in Pittsburgh. In November 1889 she took the religious name Sister Mary Katharine, and pronounced her final vows on February 12, 1891. Later that same year she founded the Sisters of the Blessed Sacrament.

In 1915 Mother Drexel purchased an abandoned university in New Orleans and built Xavier Preparatory School,

which was America's first preparatory school for African-Americans. In North Carolina she donated $4,000 for renovations to a church provided that several rows of pews were set aside for African-American parishioners.

Her legacy is a profound one. Today there are more than 60 mission schools staffed by over 500 Sisters scattered across the country, catering to the educational needs of Native and African Americans.

Live Broadcast Captures Nation's Imagination

New York, USA, March 8: Last night a nationwide audience of up to 75 million viewers sat down in front of their television sets to a color production of the stage musical *Peter Pan*, broadcast live from Broadway.

The telecast drew a 68 percent audience share, making it by far the most-watched show in the short history of television. The figure is all the more remarkable considering it was achieved against the country's most popular television show, *I Love Lucy*.

Peter Pan stars (left to right) Mary Martin, Kathy Nolan, Joseph Stafford, and Robert Harrington.

London, England, January 31: The government agrees to give women in the civil service equal pay to men.

Johannesburg, South Africa, February 9: Police forcibly evict 65,000 black Africans, razing their homes and forcibly resettling them in new black townships.

Alabama, USA, March 2: Sixteen-year-old African American Claudette Colvin is arrested for refusing to give up her seat on a bus to a white passenger.

Pennsylvania, USA, March 3: Mother Katharine Drexel, a Philadelphia heiress turned Catholic nun, dies. She gave away most of her considerable fortune in her work with Native and African Americans.

New York, USA, March 7: The Broadway musical version of *Peter Pan*, starring Mary Martin, is televised for the first time by NBC to the largest audience to date.

Los Angeles, USA, April 7: Theda Bara (Theodosia Goodman), silent screen sex symbol, dies.

Michigan, USA, April 12: The results of the field trials of Jonas Salk's polio vaccine reveal that the vaccine is effective.

USA, April 16: The McGuire Sisters' single "Sincerely" enjoys its tenth week at No. 1.

West Germany, May 5: West Germany reverts to its pre-war sovereign state.

Warsaw, Poland, May 14: The Warsaw Pact, a mutual defense agreement between Eastern European nations, is signed.

Daytona Beach, USA, May 18: Mary McLeod Bethune, educator and civil rights leader, dies at 79 years of age.

London, England, July 13: Ruth Ellis is hanged after she is found guilty of shooting her lover, racing driver David Blakeley.

California, USA, July 17: Walt Disney opens Disneyland, an amazing 243 acre (98 ha) amusement park.

California, USA, July 20: The body of missing schoolgirl Stephanie Bryan is found in a shallow grave. The 14-year-old had been missing since April 28.

New Zealand, August 2: Publications containing sex or violence are burned by publishers following raids.

California, USA, August 5: Carmen Miranda, Portuguese/Brazilian singer and actress, dies.

New York, USA, August 13: Soprano Florence Easton dies.

Argentina, September 19: President Juan Perón is ousted and hides out in a gunboat in Buenos Aires harbor.

San Francisco, USA, September 21: The Daughters of Bilitis is formed to improve the status of lesbians and to provide a social alternative to bars.

This—the first-ever musical version of *Peter Pan*—is produced by veteran Jerome Robbins, stars Mary Martin in the title role, and has been running at New York's Winter Garden theatre since last October 20.

The production was originally intended to have only a few incidental songs, with music and lyrics by the inexperienced team of "Moose" Charlap and Carolyn Leigh, but Robbins—realizing the potential of the project—turned to the established team of Jule Styne, Betty Comden, and Adolph Green to add additional songs and turn it into a full-blown Broadway musical.

Mary Martin has been a much-loved star of stage and screen in London and the United States since she burst upon the scene in 1939 with her role in the Paramount movie *The Great Victor Herbert*. She won the 1950 Tony Award (which honors Broadway stage actors) for "best performance by a leading actress in a musical" for her starring role in Rodgers & Hammerstein's *South Pacific,* and is widely tipped to repeat the feat this year with *Peter Pan.*

Silent Screen Legend, Theda Bara, Dies

Los Angeles, USA, April 7: Theda Bara, Hollywood's first publicity-created superstar who enthralled audiences with her portrayals of bejeweled, gothic-looking, female seductresses, died today from abdominal cancer in California Lutheran Hospital in Los Angeles. She was 69.

Born Theodosia Goodman in Cincinnati, Ohio on July 20, 1885, she was discovered by Twentieth Century Fox studios, who changed her name to Theda Bara, an anagram for "Arab Death," in an attempt to create a character who could destroy a man with a single sexy glance. Theda Bara was to be a very different star from the multitude of sweet-faced innocents of the time.

Theda Bara, silent screen sex symbol.

Fox publicists concocted a mysterious and totally fictitious past for the young actress, claiming she was born in the Sahara Desert in the very shadows of the Sphinx. Her first starring role was in the box-office success *A Fool There Was,* which made her an instant star. From 1915 to 1919 Theda Bara made 39 films on a salary that began at $150 a week and soared to $4,000 a week at the height of her career in 1919.

Post-World War I cultural mores saw her popularity dwindle, and Fox dropped her contract. She returned to the stage with little success in the 1920s and 1930s, and wrote an as-yet unpublished autobiography titled *What Women Never Tell.*

Ruth Ellis Hanged at Holloway Prison

London, England, July 13: Ruth Ellis, the 28-year-old mother of two and Soho hostess who was found guilty of shooting her lover, David Blakeley, outside the Magdala Tavern in Hampstead Heath, was hanged today at London's Holloway Prison.

Ellis suspected Blakeley was having a clandestine affair with a friend's nanny. Lying in wait for him outside the tavern, Ellis shot Blakeley. She was still holding the smoking .38 caliber revolver in her hand and standing over Blakeley's lifeless body when arrested by an off-duty policeman. She was taken to Hampstead police station where she made a calm, detailed confession to the killing.

Her trial at London's Old Bailey began on June 20, and only lasted a day and a half. Though entering a plea of not guilty, she later went on to confirm under cross-examination that she had every intention of killing Mr Blakeley. The jury took only 14 minutes to return a verdict of guilty.

Following the verdict, Ellis was taken to Holloway Prison's Condemned Suite where warders guarded her around the clock. At 9:01 this morning her hands were pinioned behind her back and she was walked the 15 ft (4.5 m) to the gallows where a white cotton hood was placed over her head. What followed took only 15 seconds, and reports confirmed that her death was instantaneous.

Carmen Miranda

Ruth Ellis was hanged for murdering her lover.

London, England, September 23: Barbara Mandell is the first female newsreader on British television.
UK, September 26: Birdseye frozen fish fingers appear in stores.
USA, October 3: A new children's television program, *The Mickey Mouse Club,* starts on ABC TV.
New York, USA, October 5: A stage adaptation of *The Diary of Anne Frank* opens at the Cort Theater.
USA, October 6: The drug LSD is made illegal.

London, England, October 31: Princess Margaret announces she will not marry Captain Peter Townsend because he is divorced.
Chelsea, England, October 31: Fashion designer Mary Quant opens a clothes shop called Bazaar.
New York, USA, October: Kay Thompson's book *Eloise,* about a mischievous six-year-old who lives at the Plaza Hotel, is published.
Alabama, USA, December 1: Rosa Parks is arrested in Montgomery for refusing a bus driver's order to give up her seat to a white man.

New York, USA, December 6: After seven weeks on the program, psychologist Doctor Joyce Brothers becomes the second person and only woman to win the top prize on the CBS game show *The $64,000 Question.*
USA, December 29: The 13-year-old singer Barbra Streisand makes her first recording, "You'll Never Know."
Cannes, France: American actress Grace Kelly meets Prince Rainier of Monaco at the Cannes Film Festival in May. Their engagement is announced in December.

London, England: Dame Evelyn Sharp becomes the first woman permanent secretary in the civil service as Head of the Housing Ministry.
Canada: The Canadian Army and Navy begin to recruit women for regular service, not just reserves.
London, England: The Women of the Year Lunch and Assembly at the Savoy Hotel is founded by Tony (Antonella) Lothian, Odette Hallowes, and Georgina Coleridge.

New York, USA: Anne Morrow Lindbergh's *Gift from the Sea,* a meditation on women's lives in the twentieth century, is published.
Toronto, Canada: With no leagues for girls, 8-year-old Abigail "Abby" Hoffman cuts her hair and joins an ice hockey team disguised as a boy, "Ab" Hoffman. The ploy is discovered when she is required to submit her birth certificate in order to compete in a major game.
Norway: The "Ice Woman," explorer Louise Arner Boyd, is the first woman to fly over the Arctic Circle.

Mary Quant

Lesbian Civil Rights Movement is Born

San Francisco, USA, September 21: A lesbian association named the Daughters of Bilitis has been formed in San Francisco by four female couples led by Phyllis Lyon and Del Martin, with a view to providing a social alternative to the traditional homosexual bar scene, as well as to providing relief from repetitive police raids and their associated stigma.

The name "Daughters of Bilitis" comes from French author Pierre Louys's *Songs of Bilitis,* which is a series of love poems exchanged between two women.

The Daughters of Bilitis is very likely the world's first organization that is openly committed to lesbian empowerment and visibility. Its launch in today's McCarthyist era, where homosexuals can be fired from their jobs and where it is illegal in every state in the union to be in a same-sex relationship, is a heroic attempt to alter America's perception of what it means to be homosexual.

"A KISS CAN BE A COMMA, A QUESTION MARK OR AN EXCLA-MATION POINT. THAT'S BASIC SPELLING THAT EVERY WOMAN OUGHT TO KNOW."

MISTINGUETT
(1875–1956),
FRENCH DANCER AND
SINGER, *THEATRE ARTS*

Princess Margaret Cancels Wedding Plans

London, England, October 31: Princess Margaret today announced she has called off her plans to marry the divorced Royal Air Force Captain Peter Townsend.

Interrupting the BBC's evening programming, Princess Margaret said that while a civil ceremony was possible

Princess Margaret will not marry Peter Townsend.

providing she relinquish all rights of succession, her overriding duty to the Commonwealth and to the Church of England's teaching that Christian marriage is indissoluble has seen her place those considerations before all else. Her decision was made official just four days

Kay Thompson's book *Eloise* is published. The talented writer, actress, and singer/songwriter has been entertaining for decades.

ago in a visit with the Archbishop of Canterbury, Doctor Geoffrey Fisher.

Group Captain Townsend, who was once equerry to King George VI, met and fell in love with the young princess when Margaret was just 22 years old and he a divorced man twice her age. In the spring of 1953 the couple informed the Queen of their plans to marry.

Their plans were made public in Britain by a tabloid newspaper while the Princess and the Queen Mother were overseas in Rhodesia. By the time Princess Margaret had returned to England, Peter Townsend had been encouraged by Palace advisers to accept an overseas posting to Brussels for a period of two years as air attaché at the British Embassy.

The Queen has been put in an awkward position. As Head of the Church of England, she cannot be seen to approve of a marriage between a divorced man and her own sister. Public opinion, however, is overwhelmingly in favor of the marriage, with 95 percent polled saying the personal happiness of Princess Margaret and Peter Townsend should be all that matters.

Princess Margaret Rose was born at Glamis in Scotland on August 21, 1930.

Mix 'n' Match Designer Challenges Status Quo

Chelsea, England, October 31: Chelsea's King's Road has further ensconced itself

as the Main Street of London fashion with the opening of a new fashion house called Bazaar by dynamic young designer Mary Quant, who had no formal business training or even a shred of experience in selling high fashion.

Quant's Bazaar is already developing a reputation for its surreal window displays and quirky mix of clothes, jewelry, and accessories in the midst of a haute couture neighborhood catering to the well-heeled and middle-aged.

Quant rejects the concept of haute couture. A contemporary of her clients rather than a product of another generation, her designs are classless, bold, and within the price range of young consumers. They epitomize today's modern British women, liberating them from the restraints of the cardigan and the long skirt with the introduction of slimmed down, elongated men's shirts for women to be worn over tights and under PVC raincoats. A sleek bob haircut completes the new look.

Mary Quant was born on February 11, 1934, in Kent and studied illustration at Goldsmith's College. She opened Bazaar on the first floor of a small three-story building called Markham House at 138A King's Road, and sells the sort of clothes she herself wants to wear: tights, funky dresses, and bras called Booby Traps.

Doctor Joyce Brothers Becomes TV's Quiz Queen

New York, USA, December 6: Psychologist Joyce Brothers has today become only the second contestant and the first woman to walk away with television's ultimate quiz show prize on *The $64,000 Question,* by answering seven questions on the subject of boxing.

Although the topic is considered to be an exclusively male domain, Brothers began studying boxing encyclopedias to please her husband, Milton. Her decision to remain at home to raise their newborn daughter Lisa reduced the couple's income and therefore provided her with the incentive to approach the show's producers, who liked to match contestants with unlikely topics, in this case the attractive female psychologist and the brutal "art" of boxing.

Born Joyce Diane Bauer in New York City on October 29, 1929, Brothers is the

Television quiz winner Dr Joyce Brothers.

daughter of two middle-class attorneys and grew up in Far Rockaway, Queens. She received a Masters of Arts in Psychology from Cornell University in 1949 before enrolling at Columbia University to study behavior and personality, going on to become an assistant in psychology and teaching at Hunter College. In 1953 she earned a PhD for her work on anxiety disorders and escape behavior.

Inaugural Event Highlights Women's Achievements

London, England: Three remarkable women have been the driving forces behind this year's inaugural Women of the Year Lunch and Assembly at London's Savoy Hotel. It brings together distinguished working women to share views on a wide range of important issues.

Odette Churchill with her new husband early this year.

Tony (Antonella) Lothian, the well-known journalist and broadcaster; Odette Churchill (née Hallowes), the nurse who fought with the French underground in World War II and was tortured by the Nazis; and journalist Georgina Coleridge shared a passion to create an event that would celebrate the achievements of women who had distinguished themselves in their respective careers.

At the lunch and assembly, 500 women were honored, equally, for their contributions. The three women wanted to honor those women who were not in the public spotlight, women who worked quietly within their own communities as cooks, cleaners, foster parents, and so on.

From a young age, Tony Lothian was passionate about social justice. She once wrote: "Childhood loneliness was lifted by daydreaming, nearly always about my leading a campaign against injustice."

Sharing a common belief that "excellence is genderless," these women have defied the skeptics and established a forum that it is hoped will recognize and applaud the outstanding achievements of women of all backgrounds and walks of life for many decades to come.

Louise Boyd, First Woman to See the North Pole

Norway: The pioneering and intrepid Arctic explorer Louise Arner Boyd, aged 67, has chartered a DC-4 with a Norwegian crew and returned from a 16-hour, non-stop, privately financed flight over the geographic North Pole.

Despite a long-held aversion to flying, it was the only way she could fulfill her lifelong dream of reaching the pole. With her she carried the flag of the Society of Women Geographers.

Boyd was born in 1887 into a wealthy family in San Rafael, California. By the age of 32 she had outlived her parents and two older brothers to become the sole inheritor of the family fortune.

Her passion for polar exploration began in 1924 when she sailed to the Arctic aboard a Norwegian cruise ship. In 1928 Boyd led an exploration to find the Norwegian explorer Roald Amundsen, who had disappeared while searching for the Italian explorer Umberto Nobile who himself had crashed while aboard a dirigible somewhere over the Arctic.

Her search took her across approximately 10,000 miles (16,000 km) of Arctic wilderness, from Franz Josef Land in the east to the Greenland Sea in the west. Despite not finding any trace of Amundsen, Boyd was awarded the Chevalier Cross of the Order of St Olav by the Norwegian Government, the first non-Norwegian to receive the honor.

In 1931 she returned to the Arctic to lead a scientific expedition to Greenland's fiord region to catalogue and photograph plant and animal life on De Geer Glacier and study glacial formations. Four more trips to the region were to follow prior to the start of World War II, including trips in 1937 and 1938 which were sponsored by the American Geographical Society and led to the discovery of submarine ridges between Jan Mayen and Bear Islands.

In 1941 Boyd was sent to Greenland by the US Government's National Bureau of Standards to study the effects of polar magnetism on radio signals and to secure data on radio-wave propagation. The voyage took her up the west coast of Greenland and down the coast of Baffin Land and Labrador.

Her experiences in Greenland became the subject of two books: *The Fjord Region of East Greenland* (1935), and *The Coast of Northeast Greenland* (1948).

Grace Kelly

American actress Bette Davis played Queen Elizabeth I in this year's movie *The Virgin Queen*.

The living conditions on these voyages to Greenland aboard the *Veslekari* were primitive. Boyd and her secretary Mrs Roche were the only two women on board. There was no running water, baths, or showers. Heavy seas continually crashed over the ship's decks.

When she wasn't exploring the Arctic, Louise Boyd lived a comfortable life in San Francisco at Maple Lawn, the family home, where she continued to work for the Bureau of Standards and was the chairman of the San Francisco chapter of the American Red Cross.

Doris Day

"Dear Abby" Launches

San Francisco, California, USA, January 9: Today the *San Francisco Chronicle* launches a new column called "Dear Abby." We invite readers of all ages to submit questions on any life issues to the column's writer, Pauline Esther Friedman Phillips, who will write under the pseudonym "Abigail Van Buren."

Phillips has a twin sister, Esther Pauline Friedman Lederer. The pair grew up in Sioux City, Iowa, and are very close. They even had a joint wedding in 1939. The parallels in their lives continue today, with Lederer also an advice columnist at the *Chicago Sun-Times.* Lederer began writing her column last year under the pseudonym, "Ann Landers."

Phillips created her pseudonym by combining the biblical character, Abigail, with the name of former US President, Martin Van Buren.

> "UNDER THIRTY-FIVE A MAN HAS TOO MUCH TO LEARN, AND I DON'T HAVE TIME TO TEACH HIM."
>
> HEDY LAMARR
> (1913–2000),
> AMERICAN ACTRESS

Pauline Friedman Phillips as advice columnist Dear Abby.

Female Suffrage Granted in Egypt

Cairo, Egypt, March 3: Women have been granted the right to vote in parliamentary elections and run for public office for the first time in Egyptian history after an elections law was formally passed today.

Today's new law follows the declaration of Egypt's first Republic Constitution on January 16, which established a presidential government system and alluded to women's suffrage by saying that Egypt's citizens would be "equal in front of the law."

Voting will not be compulsory for women, like it is for men, and they will have to apply to vote and provide evidence of their literacy.

The right to vote is another win for the women of Egypt, who have enjoyed greater freedoms since the 1952 Revolution, when King Farouk I and the Egyptian monarchy was overthrown in a military coup d'état led by the Free Officers Movement on July 23. The Movement comprised a group of army officers who blamed the King for Egypt's failure in the 1948 war against Israel, and was led by Colonel Gamal Abdel Nasser, now Egypt's prime minister.

Women's rights in Egypt have been championed by two groups: the Bint El-Nil (Daughter of the Nile) Union, established in 1948 by Doria Shafik, and the Egyptian Feminist Union, set up in 1923 by Huda Sha'rawi. They advocate not only women's suffrage, but also education, employment and controls on polygamy.

Cackling Comedienne Wows Audiences

San Francisco, California, USA, March: A 38-year-old mother of five has been wowing audiences for a year at the renowned Purple Onion nightclub with her side-splitting comedy routine.

Audiences love the outlandish housewife character Phyllis Diller portrays, with her untamed hair, eccentric costumes, heavy make-up, cackling laugh, and a long cigarette holder always in hand. Self-deprecating monologues often refer to her fictitious husband, "Fang," and her numerous facelifts. With very

Phyllis Diller's comedy routine is a smash hit.

few single comedians on the circuit, not to mention females, Diller is a hit and will continue performing at the Purple Onion indefinitely.

Grace Kelly Marries Her Prince

Monaco, April 19: American movie star, Grace Kelly, has married Prince Rainier III of Monaco in a grand religious ceremony at Saint Nicholas Cathedral in Monaco-Ville, Monaco, today. The wedding follows a civil ceremony conducted yesterday by the president of the Monaco Supreme Court in the Palace of Monaco. It is a Monaco tradition that a civil marriage ceremony must precede the religious one.

Kelly, who will now be known as Princess Grace, wore an ivory gown designed by Academy Award-winning costume designer, Helen Rose, of MGM. More than 600 people attended the wedding, and about 30 million people watched it on television. The couple, who have been together for about

time out

Patricia Highsmith, the American novelist, pathological liar, and stalker-of-women writes possibly her most famous novel, *The Talented Mr Ripley*, about a murderous male homosexual who is both a stalker and a liar.

San Francisco, California, USA, January 9: Abigail Van Buren begins her career as advice columnist Dear Abby on the *San Francisco Chronicle.*
Cyprus, January 12: British troops are sent to quell the rising tension between Greeks and Turks.
UK, January 26: Heroin imports and exports are made illegal.
West Virginia, USA, January 28: Iva Toguri D'Aquino, the woman most identified as "Tokyo Rose," is released from prison by the US Federal Prison Bureau after serving over six years for treason.

Melbourne, Australia, February 21: Dawn Fraser wins a gold medal in the 100 meter freestyle at the Olympic Games in Melbourne.
Cairo, Egypt, February 27: Women are granted the right to vote and the right to nominate themselves for membership of the National Assembly.
Paris, France, March 17: Irène Joliot-Curie, French scientist, and daughter of Marie and Pierre Curie, dies. Jointly with her husband, Irène was awarded the Nobel Prize for Chemistry in 1935.

Rome, Italy, March 25: The Treaty of Rome is signed, which removes tariff barriers and establishes the European Common Market. Signatories to the Treaty are France, West Germany, Belgium, the Netherlands, Luxembourg, and Italy.
San Francisco, USA, March: Comedian Phyllis Diller's popularity at the Purple Onion continues.
New York, USA, April 2: The soap operas *As the World Turns* and *The Edge of Night* premiere on CBS.
Monaco, April 19: Grace Kelly marries Prince Rainier III.

Washington DC, USA, June 1: Doris Day signs a $1 million recording contract with Columbia Records.
New York, USA, June 29: Marilyn Monroe and playwright Arthur Miller are married.
USA, June 29: Deborah Kerr and Yul Brynner star in *The King And I.*
Israel, June: Golda Meir becomes Israeli foreign minister.
Paris, France, June: Tennis player Althea Gibson becomes the first African American to win a Grand Slam singles title.

London, England, July 5: The Clean Air Bill is passed today in a bid to remove the threat of the city's toxic "pea soup" smogs.
Pretoria, South Africa, August 9: Over 20,000 women march to petition the Prime Minister against the introduction of Pass Laws.
USA, August 31: Marilyn Monroe teams with Don Murray in the movie *Bus Stop.*
London, England, August: *This is Tomorrow*, an art exhibition featuring the new "Pop Art" style, is put on at the Whitechapel Gallery.

15 months, will spend their honeymoon cruising the Mediterranean on Rainier's yacht.

Born on November 12, 1929 in Philadelphia, Pennsylvania, Kelly is considered one of the world's most beautiful women. She won a Best Actress Academy Award and Golden Globe for her performance in the 1954 film, *The Country Girl*. She also received a Golden Globe for Best Supporting Actress in the 1953 film, *Mogambo*. Among her other films are Alfred Hitchcock's *Dial M for Murder* (1954) and *To Catch a Thief* (1955). Her last two films, *The Swan* and *High Society*, will be released in the USA next week and in July respectively.

Kelly will now leave the movie-making industry and devote herself to Monaco.

Oscar winner Anna Magnani stars in *The Rose Tattoo*.

Natural Childbirth Association Established

London, England, May: A young mother who placed an advertisement in a London newspaper calling for help to form a women's group advocating natural childbirth has set up the Natural Childbirth Association.

Prunella Briance, 30, received an overwhelming response to her advertisement, indicating that many women are interested in UK obstetrician Dr Grantly Dick-Read's philosophy that childbirth should be natural with as little medical intervention as possible.

Dick-Read has been widely criticized for his books and teachings advocating that mothers should have primary control of the birthing process, not doctors. Briance was inspired to form the group not only by Dick-Read's work, but also because of her own bad experience giving birth in a hospital.

Dick-Read argues that women feel greater fear about giving birth due to a lack of support and information. This fear makes the pain of labor worse. Expectant mothers also do not have choices, and pain relief and episiotomies have become routine.

The Association's philosophies are that women should be encouraged to try natural childbirth and that it should

preferably take place at home, or in a specially-designed maternity ward that is homey and comfortable. Husbands should be allowed in delivery rooms and breastfeeding should be self-regulated.

The Association will provide support and information to pregnant women and new mothers.

20,000 March Against Pass Laws

Pretoria, South Africa, August 9: More than 20,000 women led by anti-apartheid activist, Lilian Ngoyi, marched to the Union Buildings today to petition Prime Minister Johannes Gerhardus Strijdom against the proposed extension of Pass Laws to women.

The march, organized by the Federation of South African Women, was one of the largest demonstrations ever seen in South Africa. Federation president, Ngoyi, bravely took thousands of petitions right to the Prime Minister's door. They were accepted by his secretary.

The Pass Laws, introduced in 1952, extended the *Native Urban Areas Act* of 1923, making it compulsory for all non-white males aged above 15 to carry pass books at all times. The books contain their fingerprints, photo, address and employment details, as well as permits for entering certain places. Any man found without a pass can be imprisoned. Now the government wants to extend these laws to women.

Lilian Masediba Ngoyi was born in Pretoria in 1911. As a young adult, she worked in a clothing factory and joined the Garment Workers Union. In 1952, she joined the African National Congress Women's League, and became president in 1953. When the Federation of South African Women was formed in 1954, Ngoyi became a national vice-president, and was elected president this year. She is a powerful orator and source of inspiration to many women.

Irène Joliot-Curie

Actress Grace Kelly marries Prince Rainier III.

Key Events

USA, September 25: The first transatlantic telephone cable commences functioning.
Texas, USA, September 27: Mildred (Babe) Didrikson Zaharias, famed athlete, dies of cancer, aged 42.
Illinois, USA, October 17: As breastfeeding rates in the US drop, the first meeting of La Leche League, an organization which promotes breastfeeding, is convened with seven founding members.
USA, October 18: Ruth Alice Kistler gives birth to a daughter. At 57, she is the oldest woman to bear a child.

Budapest, Hungary, October 25: The Soviets open fire with machine guns on men, women, and children, with estimates of up to 3,000 killed.
Egypt, October 29: Israel invades Egypt, entering via the Sinai Peninsula toward the Suez Canal.
Cairo, Egypt, October 31: French and British forces bomb military airfields after a 12-hour ultimatum to Egypt and Israel to withdraw troops is ignored.
Egypt, November 8: The UN imposes a cease-fire in the Suez Canal that will take effect at midnight.

UK, December: Electric trains replace steam trains between London, Liverpool, and Manchester.
Montgomery, Alabama, USA, December: The bus boycott begun by the arrest of Rosa Parks is ended.
Texas, USA: Bette Nesmith Graham introduces the best-selling correction fluid, Mistake Out.
New York, USA: Grace Metalious writes *Peyton Place*.
New York, USA: Physicist Chien-Shiung Wu disproves the law of conservation of parity.

California, USA: Phyllis Lyon and Del Martin publish *The Ladder*, the first national lesbian periodical.
Ottawa, Canada: The Canadian government passes a law granting women equal pay for "identical or substantially identical" work as men.
London, England: In Britain, legal reforms say that women teachers and civil servants should receive equal pay to men.
Minnesota, USA: Scotchgard, the fabric protector invented by Patsy Sherman, appears in stores.

Wales, UK: Jan Morris, Welsh essayist and travel writer, authors her book *Coast to Coast* based on traveling around America.
New York, USA: Maria Callas, US-born Greek soprano, makes her debut at the Metropolitan Opera House in New York City.
France: Brigitte Bardot stars in *And God Created Woman*, directed by her husband Roger Vadim. The role earns her the title of "sex kitten."
England: Dodie Smith writes the children's novel *101 Dalmatians*.

League Formed for New Mothers

Franklin Park, Illinois, USA, October 17: As breastfeeding rates across America drop to 20 percent, seven local women have formed an organization called La Leche League to promote breastfeeding and provide information and support to new mothers.

The League's first meeting was held tonight at the home of Mary White. The other founding members are Marian Leonard Tompson, Viola Brennan Lennon, Mary Ann Cahill, Betty Wagner Spandikow, Edwina Hearn Froehlich and Mary Ann Kerwin.

The League aims to educate women on the health benefits and emotional joys of breastfeeding. It says there is a mandate for the organization, with fewer American women choosing to breastfeed due to misinformation and social pressures. The League will hold meetings, distribute information, and provide telephone support for new mothers who are interested in breastfeeding.

A large factor in declining breastfeeding rates is the mass promotion and production of infant formula, which is seen as convenient, and a sign of modern motherhood. Breastfeeding

Dr Chien-Shiung Wu

"The only tired I was, was tired of giving in."

ROSA PARKS
(1913–2005),
CIVIL RIGHTS ACTIVIST

Mass promotion and production of infant formula sees a dramatic decline in breastfeeding.

mothers are increasingly being seen as uneducated and old-fashioned, with breastfeeding in public and in the workplace becoming taboo.

The League says breastfeeding is the most effective and nutritious way to feed a baby, and also promotes a profound bond between mothers and their babies. It says there are many women in society who would like to breastfeed their babies, but they have no idea how to do it, with little or no support or information available.

Salacious Novel's Sales Skyrocket

New York, USA, October 24: More than 100,000 copies of *Peyton Place*, the most

Grace Metalious, author of *Peyton Place*, sets record sales of over 100,000 copies in one month.

controversial book of our time, have been sold since its release just one month ago.

The extraordinary success of the book, written by New Hampshire wife and mother of three, Grace Metalious, is attributed to its salacious, titillating content. With most first novels averaging 3,000 sales a month, *Peyton Place* has set an incredible new record.

Although critics have labelled the book "trash" and branded Metalious a "Pandora in Blue Jeans" and "purveyor of filth," Americans appear mesmerized by the novel and its explicitly sexual storyline. The book remains on the *New York Times* bestseller list.

Born Marie Grace de Repentigny on September 8, 1924, Metalious is enjoying her fame and fortune following a life of poverty. Although she insists the book is fiction, there is speculation it is based on her home town of Gilmanton, and two other towns in New Hampshire's Lakes Region. Locals are mortified by the notoriety the book has brought upon them, and are very resentful of Metalious.

The book documents the sexual awakening of three women: Constance Mackenzie (a lonely, conservative woman), her illegitimate adolescent daughter, Allison, and her employee, Selena Cross. Themes include hypocrisy, social inequality, lust, adultery

and murder. Metalious wrote the book, originally titled *The Tree and the Blossom*, last year.

Parks Sparks Win for Civil Rights

Montgomery, Alabama, USA, December 21: The 382-day bus boycott sparked by the arrest of Rosa Parks, an African-American woman who refused to give up her bus seat for a white man, has ended today. The US Supreme Court has upheld a ban on racial segregation on public buses.

On November 13, the Supreme Court upheld a District Court decision that Montgomery's racial segregation laws were unconstitutional, and the court order was finally served on city, state, and bus company officials in Montgomery yesterday.

The bus boycott has captivated the country and established a young pastor, Martin Luther King Jr, as a national symbol of black civil rights.

The boycott began on December 5 last year following Parks' arrest four days earlier. On December 1, Parks, a seamstress, boarded a bus and sat in the first row of the colored section. As the white section filled up, the driver demanded she surrender her seat for a white man. After years of witnessing and experiencing such discrimination, Parks suddenly felt defiant, and she refused to move. She was arrested, charged and thrown in jail.

Supporters rallied around her and a bus boycott was organized for the day of her

Althea Gibson wins the Grand Slam singles title.

Rosa Parks (center), whose arrest set the bus boycott in motion.

Golda Meir

trial. Despite the rain, more than 40,000 blacks participated. Parks was convicted and fined, and that afternoon the Montgomery Improvement Association was formed, with Luther King as president. The boycott has continued ever since.

In February, civil rights lawyers Fred Gray, Clifford Durr and E. D. Nixon filed a federal lawsuit challenging racial segregation with the District Court. In June, the court ruled that segregation was unconstitutional, but an appeal kept the law intact until the Supreme Court's decision in November.

Born Rosa Louise McCauley on February 4, 1913, Parks is a quiet, dignified and intelligent woman. She is married to barber Raymond Parks, and both are volunteers of the National Association for the Advancement of Colored People.

Scientist Proves Nature Not Symmetrical

New York, USA: A Chinese-American physicist has stunned the scientific world by disproving one of the fundamental laws of nature: The conservation of parity. Dr Chien-Shiung Wu of Columbia University has conducted a revolutionary experiment that shows the laws of nature are not always symmetrical in terms of left and right.

For 30 years, physicists have believed that all objects and their mirror images behave the same way, just with the left and right sides reversed. Wu's work shows that, at least in radioactive decay, identical nuclear particles do not always act alike.

Associate Professor Wu designed her experimental test for fellow Chinese-American physicists, Tsung-Dao Lee and Chen Ning Yang, who had theorized that parity was not conserved in weak interactions among nuclear beta decay, and needed a test to prove it.

The previously accepted view was that beta particles, emitted by a radioactive nucleus, are ejected in any direction regardless of the nucleus' spin. But in her experiment, using atoms of the radioactive isotope, cobalt-60, Wu observed that the beta particles were ejected mostly in one direction, depending on the nucleus's spin. If conservation of parity was correct, an equal number of particles would have been ejected in each direction.

Born in China in 1912, Wu studied physics at Nanjing University and completed a PhD at the University of California, Berkeley. She married in 1942 and worked as an assistant professor at Smith College, Massachusetts before moving to Princeton University, becoming its first female physics instructor.

In 1944, the US government invited Wu to work on the top secret Manhattan Project at Columbia University, which produced the atom bomb. Wu contributed by helping to develop a uranium enrichment process that produced fuel for the bomb. She remained at Columbia as a research scientist and became an associate professor in 1952.

Scotchgard Now in Supermarkets

Minnesota, USA: Scotchgard, a revolutionary fabric protector and stain blocker, which was accidentally invented by a young local female scientist, has hit supermarket shelves across America.

Research chemist Patsy Sherman discovered the Scotchgard formula in 1953 while working for the 3M corporation. Just 21 years old and in her first job since graduating from Gustavus Adolphus College, Sherman had been assigned to work on fluorochemicals.

One day in the laboratory, Sherman and her colleague, Samuel Smith, were working on a new type of rubber for aircraft fuel hoses when an assistant dropped a bottle containing a fluorochemical-latex emulsion that Sherman had made. It splashed on the assistant's canvas shoes. Despite washing with soap and solvents, the mixture could not be removed, and the liquids applied to it simply beaded and ran off.

Sherman quickly realized the commercial value of a chemical that could be applied to fabric to prevent soiling. Like other fluorochemicals, the mixture was inert, meaning not chemically active. It was clear, and resistant to oil and water.

Sherman was born on September 15, 1930 in Minneapolis. At school she had an aptitude for science and was stunned by the results of a test that predicted she would be a housewife. She insisted on taking the male version of the test, which showed a career in chemistry or dentistry.

Brigitte Bardot stars in *And God Created Woman*.

Anne Frank

Jean Peters and Howard Hughes Tie Knot in Secret

Nevada, USA, January 12: Actress Jean Peters, best known for her film roles as a feisty independent woman, married billionaire industrialist Howard Hughes today in a top secret ceremony at Tonopah's Mizpah Hotel in Nevada.

Jean Peters, a onetime schoolteacher from Ohio, won a popularity contest in 1946 that brought her to Hollywood for a screen test. Signed up by 20th Century Fox, she made her debut with Tyrone Power in *Captain from Castile*.

Hughes first met the popular leading lady at a party in 1946 but it was another eleven years, during which time Peters briefly married Stuart Cramer, before they tied the knot.

> *"Dying is an art, like everything else. I do it exceptionally well. I do it so it feels like hell. I do it so it feels real. I guess you could say I've a call."*
>
> SYLVIA PLATH
> (1932–1963),
> AMERICAN POET

Actress Jean Peters has married Howard Hughes.

Author of *Little House on the Prairie* Dies

Missouri, USA, February 10: Author Laura Ingalls Wilder died today, aged 90, at her home in the Ozarks, Missouri. She is remembered fondly by the millions of readers of her "Little House" books—a series of historical novels for children which were largely based on her own childhood in a pioneering family on the American prairies. Born February 7, 1867 in a log cabin in Wisconsin, most of Laura's childhood was spent traveling in a covered wagon with her parents and three sisters. Her father saw himself as a pioneer, moving West in search of unsettled land. After a couple of unsuccessful attempts at farming and after working in various jobs, he eventually brought the family to the new town of De Smet in South Dakota where they settled.

time out

'China's Great Leap Forward' is getting women out of their homes and away from their children so they can work more productively in the fields. Childcare and domestic work has also been collectivized.

Laura was a shy child but a very good student, especially in English and history, and at the age of fifteen she obtained her teaching certificate and began to teach. In 1885 she married Almanzo James Wilder, a farmer. They had one daughter, Rose, who would later recall how entranced she was by her mother's stories of growing up on the prairies.

It was Rose who, as an adult, encouraged her mother to write down her stories for other children to enjoy. *Little House in the Big Wood*, published in 1932 to great acclaim, was followed by *Little House on the Prairie* in 1935. *These Happy Golden Years*, Laura's eighth "Little House" book, was published in 1943.

So popular are these books about a bygone era in American history that for years fans have been visiting the sites Laura wrote about and calling in on their favourite author at her Ozark Mountain farm.

Anne Frank's house has a secret annex at the back.

Foundation Hopes to Save Anne Frank's Sanctuary

Amsterdam, Netherlands, May 3: Today the Anne Frank Foundation was established by Otto Frank to raise sufficient funds to purchase and restore the Amsterdam building at Prinsengracht 263 in which he, his wife Edith, and daughters Margot and Anne hid from the Nazis during World War II. Due for demolition to make way for a factory, the building came to the public's attention in 1955 when the Dutch newspaper *Het Vrije Volk* initiated a campaign to have it listed as a protected property. Many prominent Amsterdam citizens as well as the general public are supporting the Foundation and its goals.

It was in a secret annex at the back of the building at Prinsengracht 263 that the Frank family, together with the van Pels family and Fritz Pfeffer, hid from the Nazis for just over two years. Never allowed outside and forced to be quiet during the day while the warehouse employees worked below, Anne Frank found refuge in writing her now famous diary. Disarmingly honest, Anne reveals her intimate thoughts and the small details of the world around her. The diary ends

London, England, January 10: Prime Minister Anthony Eden resigns due to ill health. His deputy Harold Macmillan takes his place.

Nevada, USA, January 12: Actress Jean Peters marries billionaire industrialist Howard Hughes.

Missouri, USA, February 10: Laura Ingalls Wilder, author of the *Little House on the Prairie* books, dies.

England, February 16: The "Toddlers' Truce" (an arrangement whereby no TV broadcasts were made between 6 pm and 7 pm, to allow parents to put their children to bed) is abolished.

London, England, February 28: Cancer experts express health concerns about Australians exposed to radiation from British atomic tests.

USA, February: *Annie Oakley*, a Western television series that fictionalized the life of the famous sharpshooter, ends a three-year run.

West Africa, March 6: The Gold Coast and Togoland become Ghana, gaining independence from Britain.

London, England, April 1: A spoof on the BBC's *Panorama* fools the public into believing that spaghetti is grown on trees in Switzerland.

Egypt, April 10: The Suez Canal re-opens to all shipping.

Chicago, USA, April 15: Ray Kroc's McDonald's franchise celebrates its second anniversary.

Jordan, April 25: King Hussein declares martial law in the aftermath of a failed coup earlier this month.

Amsterdam, Netherlands, May 3: Otto Frank establishes the Anne Frank Foundation.

US, May 6: "The Ricardos Dedicate a Statue"—the last episode of the sixth and final season of the *I Love Lucy* television show–was aired today.

London, England, July 6: Althea Gibson becomes the first black tennis player to win a Wimbledon singles title, defeating fellow American Darlene Hard 6-3, 6-2.

Alabama, USA, July 16: Anti-segregationist Juliette Hampton Morgan dies by her own hand.

Tunisia, July 25: Tunisia abolishes its monarchy, becomes a republic.

London, England, June 26: The Medical Research Council releases a report highlighting the link between smoking and lung cancer.

Philadelphia, USA, August 5: Dick Clark hosts the first episode of *American Bandstand* on ABC TV.

Juarez, Mexico, September 17: 22-year-old actress Sophia Loren and producer Carlo Ponti wed by proxy as two male attorneys stand in for the couple.

California, USA, September: Oceanographers Roger Revelle and Hans Seuss reveal that the oceans cannot absorb all the carbon dioxide being released and that this will lead to global warming.

in August 1944 when the families were discovered and sent to concentration camps in Germany. Otto Frank was the only one to survive.

On his return to Amsterdam he was given Anne's diary which had been kept safe during the war years. The diary was first published in Dutch in 1947, with an American edition published in 1952.

Spokeswoman Against the Evils of Segregation Dies

Alabama, USA, July 16: Juliette Hampton Morgan was this morning found dead in her bed, an empty bottle of sleeping pills beside her. She left a note that said, " I am not going to cause any more trouble to anybody." She was just 43.

Juliette Hampton Morgan, a white woman, was born in 1914 into a privileged southern family. She graduated in 1934 from the University of Alabama with a degree in English literature and political science and became a librarian at Montgomery's Carnegie Library. In 1952 she was made Director of Research at Montgomery Public Library.

With a keen sense of justice and fairness, Morgan became aware during her daily bus trips to work of the abuse black passengers received. Outraged, she began writing eloquent letters to the local newspaper arguing that segregation was un-Christian and wrong. During World War II she continued her criticism of the treatment of black bus passengers, writing that if a man was good enough to die for his country, he was good enough to have a seat on a bus. She strongly supported the 1955 Montgomery Bus Boycott against segregation on public buses, writing many letters to the *Montgomery Advertiser*.

Her actions raised the fury of some white citizens. She received death threats, obscene phone calls and hate mail. Even some of her own friends called her mad, and as a result of her strong public views

Newlyweds Sophia Loren and Carlo Ponti.

she become increasingly estranged from friends, former students, colleagues, neighbors and even her own mother.

Eventually she was driven from her job by the Mayor of Montgomery, who threatened to withhold funding to the library if she didn't resign. The next day, overcome by anxiety and depression, Morgan took her own life.

Atlas Shrugged Howled Down by Critics

US, October 12: Ayn Rand's novel *Atlas Shrugged* was published today to scathing reviews. Critics have been clamoring to point out that it is poorly written and contains an unrealistic view of the world. The conservative magazine *National Review* accuses Rand of atheism, while John Chamberlain of the *New York Herald Tribune* describes the book witheringly as "Ayn Rand's Political Parable and Thundering Melodrama."

Well known for her previous novel *The Fountainhead*, which was published in 1935 and was highly successful, Ayn Rand is no stranger to controversy and criticism. Born in 1905 in St Petersburg, Russia as Alissa Rosenbaum, Ayn Rand experienced the harsh realities of the Soviet system first hand. Hating the oppressive life of the Soviet Union, she migrated to the USA in 1926.

It was as a result of her early experiences that she developed her philosophy of "rational individualism." In a note included as an afterword to *Atlas Shrugged* she states: "My philosophy, in essence, is the concept of man as a heroic being, with his own happiness as the moral purpose of his life, with productive achievement as his noblest activity, and reason as his only absolute."

She is an advocate of a laissez-faire capitalism where government's role is to protect the rights of each person, their liberty and their property, and not to control business or commerce.

Ayn Rand

Wimbledon champion Althea Gibson.

USSR, October 4: The space age begins as the USSR launches the first satellite to orbit Earth, *Sputnik I*.

Montecatini, Italy, October 24: Fashion designer Christian Dior dies of a heart attack after choking on a fishbone and is succeeded by his assistant, Yves Saint Laurent.

New York, USA, October: Ayn Rand publishes *Atlas Shrugged* to negative reviews and good sales figures.

New York, USA, November 27: Jacqueline Kennedy, wife of John F. Kennedy, gives birth to their daughter Caroline Bouvier Kennedy.

Essex, England, December 17: Writer Dorothy Sayers dies.

Las Vegas, USA, December 29: Singers Steve Lawrence and Eydie Gormé marry.

USA, December: *The Cat in the Hat* by Theodor Seuss Geisel (Dr Seuss) is published.

Cambridge, England, October: Astrophysicists show that all of the elements except the very lightest are produced in stellar interiors.

Illinois, USA: Margaret Hillis founds the Chicago Symphony Chorus.

USA: Dorothy Parker, American writer and poet best known for her caustic wit, wisecracks, and sharp eye for twentieth century urban foibles, begins writing book reviews for *Esquire* magazine.

California, USA: Adaline Kent, surrealist sculptor, dies in an automobile accident and bequeaths $10,000 for an annual award to a promising California artist.

New York, USA: *Memories of a Catholic Girlhood* by Mary McCarthy is published.

USA: A pill developed for treating menstrual problems is approved by the FDA in America.

Berlin, East Germany: Ruth Werner, who had channeled atomic bomb secrets to the Soviets under the code name Sonya during World War II, publishes *An Unusual Girl*.

London, England: *Voltaire in Love*, by Nancy Mitford, is published.

Illinois, USA: The newly established breastfeeding organization La Leche League brings Dr. Grantly-Dick Read, childbirth expert, to speak to a packed house at a local high school.

Manchester, England: Mary Stott sets up the *Guardian's* women's page and becomes its first editor.

Japan: The first Japanese women's weekly magazine, *Shukan Josei*, is published.

New York, USA: Gypsy Rose Lee publishes an autobiography, *Gypsy*.

California, USA: Stripper Annie Banks, after legally changing her name to Tempest Storm, signs a $100,000 contract in San Francisco to tour the burlesque circuit.

Creator of Peter Wimsey was Translating *Paradiso*

Nancy Mitford

Essex, England, December 17: Distinguished writer Dorothy Sayers, best known to the general public for her Lord Peter Wimsey detective novels, died today aged 60.

Born in 1893, Sayers was a keen and gifted student, winning a scholarship in 1912 to Somerville, the Oxford women's college. She graduated with first class honours in modern languages in 1915, and in 1916 published her first work, a collection of poetry titled *Op I*. She worked as a teacher in France and Yorkshire and was a reader for the Oxford publishers, Blackwells. In 1926 Sayers married journalist Captain Oswald Arthur Fleming. He died in 1950.

Sayers published the first of her Peter Wimsey novels, *Whose Body?* in 1923. The eleventh and last, *Busman's Honeymoon*, was published in 1937. The main protagonist, Wimsey, is an elegantly dressed man-about-town who solves perplexing murder cases for a hobby. The cases he investigates involve an imaginative array of murder weapons and methods—a cat with poisoned claws, poisoned tooth fillings, a dagger made of ice.

With the success of her Wimsey books, Sayers achieved financial security and the means to pursue her principal passions of theology and literature. She was a prolific writer, producing poetry, short stories, scholarly essays, and a number of plays—including the notorious *The Man Born to be King* for the BBC in December 1941. This play caused such an outcry that Prime Minister Winston Churchill was swamped with letters demanding that the play be banned because Christ and the other characters spoke in colloquial English, including American slang.

> *"THIS IS NOT A NOVEL TO BE TOSSED ASIDE LIGHTLY. IT SHOULD BE THROWN WITH GREAT FORCE."*
>
> DOROTHY PARKER, 1957, ON AYN RAND'S *ATLAS SHRUGGED*

Sayers translated a number of works including the *Song of Roland* from Old French. She wrote *Begin Here: A War-time Essay*, and the seminal work on theology and creativity, *The Mind of the Maker*. She was working on a translation of *Paradiso*, the third volume of Dante Alighieri's *The Divine Comedy*, when she suffered a heart attack and died.

Stars Made the Elements

Cambridge, England, October: *Reviews of Modern Physics* has just published a groundbreaking article, "Synthesis of the Elements in Stars," by Margaret Burbridge and her colleagues, Geoffrey Burbridge, William Fowler, and Fred Hoyle.

The authors show that all elements, from carbon to uranium, are created through a series of nuclear reactions that take place inside stars. The process starts with hydrogen and helium, which are the lightest and the very first elements to be produced in the Big Bang. Through fusion of the nuclei of these lightest elements, a heavier element is created which in turn creates an another heavier element, and so on. This constant process of one element converting into another eventually ceases when the star becomes immensely heavy and runs out of nuclear fuel. Its immense weight causes it to implode and then explode under the massive pressure to become a supernova.

Margaret Burbridge, who was born in England on August 12, 1919, began work with her three colleagues in Cambridge, England, in 1954. They moved to the United States in 1955 to work at the Kellogg Radiation Laboratory and the Mount Wilson Observatory.

Margaret Hillis to Direct Chicago Symphony Chorus

Illinois, USA: Margaret Hillis has been recruited from New York by Fritz Reiner, the Director of the Chicago Symphony Orchestra, to establish and direct the Chicago Symphony Chorus.

Born on October 1, 1921, in Kokomo, Indiana, Margaret Hillis has wanted to be an orchestral conductor ever since she was eight years old—a seemingly impossible ambition considering that at that time the profession was entirely made up of men. Hillis learned to play piano, trumpet, horn, saxophone, and string bass, and studied at Indiana University, Julliard, and with Robert Shaw—one of America's choral innovators. With orchestral conducting still dominated by men, Hillis took up choral conducting, and has as a result become the director of the first professional symphony chorus in America.

Mary McCarthy Looks Back With Candor

New York, US: Writer, critic and left-wing social commentator Mary McCarthy has published *Memories of a Catholic Girlhood*, a collection of candid stories about her childhood.

Born in Seattle in 1912, she was orphaned at the age of six and, with her three younger brothers, was sent to live with a paternal great aunt and uncle. Her life with them is the focus of *Memories of a Catholic Girlhood*, in which she bitterly recollects the cruel treatment she received, especially her uncle's vicious criticism and physical abuse.

Life improved considerably, however, when at the age of 12 she was sent to live with her maternal grandparents. It was from her grandfather that she developed an awareness of social and political issues.

Mary McCarthy's prose is both candid and precise.

After graduating in 1933 from the liberal arts college Vassar, in New York, McCarthy began writing reviews and articles. A politically active and widely respected liberal intellectual, she is a frequent contributor to left-leaning magazines such as *The Nation* and *The New Republic*. As part of the *Partisan Review* circle she is considered a cutting-edge social and political commentator. She is a vocal critic of both McCarthyism and Communism. Although thankful for her Catholic classical education, she calls herself an atheist.

Mary McCarthy has won a number of prestigious literary awards, among them the Horizon prize (1949) and a Guggenheim fellowship (1949–50).

Dorothy Parker is seldom short of an opinion.

A pregnant Jacqueline and John F. Kennedy.

Oral Contraceptive Gets Limited FDA Approval

USA: The Food and Drug Administration (FDA) has approved the use of Enovid for the treatment of severe menstrual disorders, and has stipulated that the drug label must carry the warning that Enovid will prevent ovulation.

Enovid, which contains the hormones estrogen and progesterone, was developed by Gregory Pincus and John Rock as a birth control pill.

Trials of the medication as a contraceptive have been carried out in Puerto Rico, Haiti and Mexico City, but scientists have been unable to carry out large-scale trials in the United States because of the anti-birth control laws in Massachusetts and many other states.

The idea of using hormones to control ovulation and fertilization was initially proposed by the Austrian Ludwig Haberlandt in 1931. He discovered ovarian extracts given to mice orally inhibited fertility; however, the ovaries of more than 2,000 pregnant pigs were needed to produce just a few milligrams of progesterone. Then in the 1940s, the chemist Russell Maker showed that large quantities of progesterone could be extracted from Mexican yam. Nine years later, Vienna-born chemist Carl Djerassi joined Maker's company Syntex to work on a pill for women suffering menstrual problems, and in 1951 Syntex patented norethindrone. However, its potential as a birth control pill was not realised at the time.

Meanwhile in the United States, Margaret Sanger of the Planned Parenthood Federation of America was urging Gregory Pincus to develop a contraceptive pill. In 1952 Pincus joined forces with the gynaecologist John Rock and by 1954 they were ready to test their new pill on humans. Under the guise of a fertility study, Rock and Pincus began the first human trials on 50 women. The trial was a success—not one woman ovulated.

Because of continuing strong opposition to birth control measures, it has been difficult to set up and run clinical trials of the new medication in the United States. What this means in practice is that Enovid cannot be approved by the FDA as a means of preventing pregnancy.

However, it is expected that many American women will be developing "severe menstrual disorders" in the foreseeable future.

Gypsy Rose Lee

The Guardian Creates New Page for Women

Manchester, UK: Mary Stott has been appointed the editor of *The Guardian's* first women's page. The talented Mrs Scott hopes that under her editorship the page will become a platform for women's voices and concerns.

The daughter of two journalists, Stott recalled being "a most dislikable child," describing herself as "plain and charmless, with disastrously straight hair and thick glasses." She left school and went to work at the *Leicester Mail* at the age of 17. As a young, female journalist in a gruff, masculine environment she was barely tolerated, and after two years she was assigned to the *Mail's* women's page, in the belief that this spelled the end of her imagined career as a "proper journalist." However, she went on from that position to work at the *Bolton Evening News*, and later at the Co-operative Press in Manchester, where she edited the two pages of the weekly *Co-op News*. Then in 1945, she was offered a "real" journalist's job as a sub-editor on the *Manchester Evening News*, where she remained until 1950.

It was her skills as a "real" journalist that attracted *Guardian* editor Alastair Hetherington's attention and led to Scott being offered an editorial position with the paper. She is expected to bring industry and dedication to the job.

Models wearing garments from the new Christian Dior collection.

Connie Francis

Last "Coming Out" Party at Buckingham Palace

London, England, March 18: The last of the British debutantes curtseyed to Queen Elizabeth at Buckingham Palace today, signaling the end of a 200-year tradition. A rite of passage for many women from the British aristocracy and upper class, "coming out," as it was known, was a ceremony to mark a girl's emergence from the schoolroom and into society, and in search of a husband.

The girls performed a choreographed walk as they were each presented to the Queen. Instituted by Queen Charlotte, wife of George III, at the end of the 18th century, the original purpose of coming out was to display aristocratic young women to eligible bachelors.

From now on the Queen will entertain a cross-section from society at garden parties, a practice that is felt to be more in keeping with today's world.

"A 41-INCH BUST AND A LOT OF PERSEVER- ANCE WILL GET YOU MORE THAN A CUP OF COFFEE—A LOT MORE."

JAYNE MANSFIELD (1933–1967), AMERICAN ACTRESS

Fairy Tale Ends as Shah Divorces Childless Wife

Tehran, Iran, March 22: A deeply saddened Shah of Iran yesterday announced his divorce from his Empress, Soraya Esfan- diary Bakhtiari. The end of the fairytale marriage has come because after seven years, the beautiful Soraya has yet to produce an heir to the throne. It is understood that the Shah, who wept as he made the announcement, is still very much in love with his young wife and regrets having to make this move.

Born in 1932 to an Iranian business- man, Khalil Esfandiary, and his German wife Eva Klein, Soraya met the Shah in London when she was just 16. The Shah had recently divorced his first wife, Queen Fawzia, sister of Egypt's former King Farouk, because, although she had given birth to a daughter, she had not produced a son. Now, Soraya has herself failed to bear any children at all.

Empress Soraya fled Iran after the end of her marriage.

During their seven years of marriage, Soraya sought treatment for infertility in Switzerland and France but without success. It had been suggested to her that she allow the Shah to take a second wife but she is reported to have said that she "could not accept the idea of sharing her husband's love with another woman."

Since fleeing Iran in February Soraya is understood to have been staying with her parents in Cologne, Germany. The Shah is believed to have sent his wife's uncle to visit her in an attempt to persuade her to return, but the unhappy Empress refused.

The Empress released a statement in which she announced that "in the interest of the future of the State and of the welfare of the people in accordance with the desire of his Majesty the Emperor I sacrifice my own happiness, and I will declare my consent to a separation from His Imperial Majesty."

It is believed that the former Empress will eventually settle in France, and that her sad but duty-bound husband will confer on her the title of Princess.

Sweater Girl's Daughter Accused of Murder

Beverly Hills, California, USA, April 5: Police have alleged Cheryl Crane—the 14-year- old daughter of actress Lana Turner (known affectionately as "The Sweater Girl")—murdered her mother's boy- friend Johnny Stompanato in their home yesterday, Good Friday. Stompanato, a well-known mobster and former United States marine, was reportedly possessive and abusive toward Turner, and Cheryl claimed to be protecting her mother when she stabbed Stompanato.

Turner started dating Stompanato following her divorce from her fourth husband. He is known to have worked as the bodyguard of gangster Mickey Cohen, and to have had connections with the underworld. Turner is said to have been frightened for her life.

Turner was the pin-up girl of many of the forces during World War II and many still admire her, despite the fact that most of her recent films have been box office flops. Her best-known films to date are *Ziegfeld Girl*, *Johnny Eager*, *The Postman Always Rings Twice* and those she has made with Clark Gable, including *Honky Tonk*, *Somewhere I'll Find You*, and *Home- coming*. Her most recent movie is *Peyton*

Lana Turner (center) with ex-husband Stephen Crane.

Place, the adaptation of Grace Metalious's novel about the personal dramas and endless intrigues of small-town America.

Cheryl, Turner's only child by former husband Stephen Crane, was taken to the police station. District Attorney William B. McKesson has announced an inquest to take place next week. Cheryl faces life imprisonment if found guilty of murder.

Passing of the Woman Who Unravelled DNA

London, England, April 17: British scientist Rosalind Elsie Franklin, who is credited with the discovery of the molecular structure of DNA, died yesterday of ovarian cancer. Properly known as deoxyribonucleic acid, DNA is one of a class of large molecules responsible for the transference of genetic characteristics. Thanks largely to pioneering work by Franklin, it is now known to have a helical structure.

DNA, a double helix.

After gaining her doctorate in chemistry in 1945, Franklin worked with Jacques Méring at the State Chemical Laboratory in Paris (1947–1950), where she became proficient at X-ray crystallography. These studies led to research on graphite which proved invaluable for the coal industry.

In 1951 she was offered a place at King's College, London, where she worked on the structure of DNA. However there was a misunderstanding about her role and she found herself working alongside scientist Maurice Wilkins, who found it difficult to work with a woman and was hostile towards her. Franklin persevered, working alone on a very thorough, and

therefore slow, analysis of DNA that finally produced one extremely clear photograph of DNA in its wet form (Photo 51), which definitely showed a helix. She also identified the location of phosphate sugars in DNA.

Maurice Wilkins secretly copied Franklin's work and showed it to his colleague James Watson, who was working on a similar project at Cavendish Laboratory in Cambridge. Watson and his colleague Francis Crick used Franklin's data to formulate a theory of DNA's structure and publish it in the scientific journal *Nature*.

It is important to recognize the role played by Rosalind Franklin in this discovery, which may well revolutionize our understanding of human genetics.

Doctors Use Sound Waves to Look Inside the Body

London, England, June 7: Results published in the authoritative medical publication *The Lancet* today are likely to change the way obstetrics is practiced. The article "Investigation of Abdominal Masses by Pulsed Ultrasound" cites a dramatic case where ultrasound saved the patient's life by revealing a large, operable, ovarian cyst in a woman who had previously been diagnosed with an inoperable stomach cancer. Ultrasounds are very high frequency sound waves, inaudible to the human ear, that are directed at an object. The sound waves bounce back in a pattern that can be produced as an image, known as a scan, on a television screen.

Professor Ian Donald, who holds the position of Regius Chair of Midwifery at the University of Glasgow, is the author of the article. He has also held appointments at various London hospitals, and his early research focus was on newborns with respiratory problems. This led to an interest in machines designed to help

time out

In Morocco women have been given the right to choose their own husbands. They do not, however, have the right to transmit citizenship to their children, a right that is still restricted to males.

babies with breathing difficulties that earned him the nickname "Mad Donald" among his colleagues. Donald became interested in the idea that sonar could be used for medical diagnosis in 1955 and has been experimenting with its use. With the help of a technician, Tom Brown from the Kelvin & Hughes Scientific Instrument Company, he began an intensive investigation into the value of ultrasound in diagnosing conditions of the abdomen. His article reports the results. Ultrasound was first used medically in 1947 by Dr George D. Ludwig, who located gall stones using ultrasound. It is believed that ultrasound will one day revolutionize the treatment of women during pregnancy because of the ability to diagnose multiple pregnancies or complications such as placenta praevia or fetal abnormality.

Mitzi Gaynor

Oscar winner Joanne Woodward in *The Three Faces of Eve*.

New York, USA, September 20: The lesbian group Daughters of Bilitis forms a New York chapter with Barbara Gittings as president.
London, England, October 21: The *Life Peerages Act* entitles women to sit in the House of Lords for the first time. Baroness Swanborough, Lady Reading, and Baroness Barbara Wooton take their seats.
USSR, October 31: Boris Pasternak, the author of *Dr Zhivago*, refuses his Nobel Prize in Literature because he is angry about his expulsion from the Union of Soviet Writers.

USA, November 18: Susan Hayward stars in *I Want to Live!*, the true story of a prisoner facing execution.
California, USA, November 22: Actors Janet Leigh and Tony Curtis become the proud parents of a baby daughter, Jamie Lee Curtis.
New York, USA, December 26: Mezzo-soprano Eva Gauthier dies.
UK, December: The ban on portraying homosexuality in the theater is lifted.
USA, December: Popular toys with children this year include hula hoops and the new Lego bricks.

London, England: Claudia Jones founds *The West Indian Gazette*, the first black newspaper in Britain.
London, England: Hilda Harding becomes the first woman bank manager, taking charge of Barclays in Hanover Street.
England: Ultrasound becomes available to examine unborn babies.
Reims, France: Cyclist Elsy Jacobs from Luxembourg wins the Elite Women's World Road Championships and Balina Ermolaeva becomes the first women's World Sprint Champion.

Ottawa, Canada: Blanche Margaret Meagher becomes the first woman to be appointed as a Canadian ambassador. She is posted to Israel.
New York, USA: Ketti Frings's adaptation of the Thomas Wolfe novel *Look Homeward, Angel* wins the Pulitzer Prize for Drama and Frings is named "Woman of the Year" by the *Los Angeles Times*.
Kobe, Japan: *Shufu no Mise Daisei*, a Japanese supermarket, opens in Sanbomiya, and is soon imitated.
London, England: Publication of Mary Renault's *The King Must Die*.

Japan: Sue Sumii publishes *The River With No Bridge*.
Illinois, USA: *The Womanly Art of Breastfeeding* is published as a loose-leaf booklet by La Leche League. Founders had planned to distribute separate chapters by mail, but soon realized that most mothers needed all the information at once.
USA: There are 320 registered women architects in the USA, equal to 1 percent of the total number of registered architects in the country.
Australia: Nancy Cato's *All the Rivers Run* is published.

African Social Worker Marries Nelson Mandela

Elizabeth Taylor

"I THINK I MARRIED TROUBLE."

NELSON MANDELA, 1958

Transkei, South Africa, June 19: Nomzamo Winifred (Winnie) Madikizela, a young social worker, and Nelson Mandela, African National Congress (ANC) member, were married today in a Methodist service. Madikizela admitted that at first she was in awe of Mandela, having heard so much about his activities, but in the year they have been working together with the ANC, a romance has developed. Mandela is 40, his bride is 18.

Winnie comes from the Eastern Cape of South Africa. Her parents, who had eight children, were both teachers, but her mother died when she was only nine years old. With the support of her father and other relatives, she went to school in Shawbury and gained a diploma in social work, becoming the first black professional social worker in South Africa. Working at the Baragwanath Hospital she has become acutely aware of the enormous gap between the privileged white minority and the very poor black majority, and has recently completed a

study that found that one in a hundred black babies die unnecessarily at birth. An active member of the ANC, she has been a political prisoner.

The bride will live at her husband's home in Soweto outside Johannesburg, where they must comply with strict legal constraints arising from the so-called "treason trial" in which he is currently involved. Two years ago, the South African government arrested 156 political leaders in a police swoop and charged them with high treason, which carries the death penalty. Nelson Mandela was among those charged. The trial is continuing.

Susan Hayward plays real-life alleged murderer Barbara Graham in *I Want to Live!*

Winnie and Nelson Mandela.

Women's Rights Advocate Has History on Her Side

New York, USA, August 14: Historian and human rights campaigner Mary Ritter Beard died today at the age of 72. She once said: "The volumes which record the history of the human race are filled with the deeds and the words of great men… the twentieth century woman…questions the completeness of the story."

Beard set out to redress that imbalance, writing a number of books about the role of women in society, and was a pioneer in women's rights at work.

Born in Indianapolis, Indiana in 1876, Mary Ritter was one of six children. At 16 years old, she entered university, studying political science, languages and literature. In 1900, she married Charles Austin Beard and they moved to England, where she became involved in the British women's suffrage movement. Three years later, after moving back to New York, a daughter was born, but Beard continued to take an interest in women's suffrage, and in 1907, she began working for the Women's Trade Union League.

Between 1910 and 1912 she edited *The Woman Voter*, and was also involved in the union for women textile workers in New York. At the same time she began a publishing career which was to last the rest of her life. Her first book, *Woman's Work in Municipalities*, was followed by *A Short History of the American Labor Movement* (1920). She also wrote with her husband Charles, but it is her own titles that pioneered the field of women's history. *Understanding Women* (1931), *America Through Women's Eyes* (1933), and *Women as a Force in History* (1946) are among her most memorable.

Woman Launches London's First West Indian News

London, England: Since arriving in England three years ago, Claudia Jones, feminist, community leader, Communist, black nationalist, political activist, and journalist, has worked with London's African-Caribbean community. Now Jones has launched *The West Indian Gazette*, a newspaper for this community.

Jones has long been involved in black rights and Communism. Born Claudia Cumberbatch in Trinidad in 1915, she moved to New York with her family in 1922 as a result of the economic downturn, but the Great Depression threw them into poverty. At the age of 17, she contracted tuberculosis as a result of the family's poor living conditions.

Despite these problems Jones was a brilliant student. While working in a factory she began to write a column for a Harlem periodical. In 1936 she joined the Youth Communist League (YCL) and took up a position with *The Daily Worker*, the newspaper of the Communist Party. She proved to be an eloquent speaker and an excellent writer and put her skills to use serving the National Council of the YCL.

In 1943 she became editor of *Spotlight*, the monthly journal of American Youth for Democracy. Her political work focused

Ketti Frings, Pulitzer Prize-winning Woman of the Year.

on helping immigrants and unemployed youth. In 1946, she helped to organize a demonstration protesting the slaying of two black youths in Freeport, Long Island, and in the years following World War II fought against the oppression of black working class women. All this brought her to the attention of the FBI. In 1948 she was arrested on immigration charges—later shown to be unfounded— and she was arrested again in 1951 for "advocating" the overthrow of the US government. In 1955, she was deported from the United States and went to Britain rather than returning to Trinidad.

Claudia Jones's new project, *The West Indian Gazette*, aims to provide a forum for discussion of civil rights and to report news items of a kind often overlooked by the mainstream media.

Golfer Jessie Valentine Scores Another Trophy

Norfolk, England: Popular Scotswoman Jessie Valentine added the title of British Ladies Amateur Golf Champion to her impressive résumé when she won the championship tournament held at Hunstanton Golf Club in Norfolk, England. Valentine was rated as one of the favorites, but her victory was a close one. She beat Elizabeth Park by a single hole.

Born in Perth, Scotland in 1915, Valentine (née Anderson) is recognized as one of the greatest women golfers of our time. She has won the British Ladies' title twice before, in 1937 and 1955, and has won tournaments in France and New Zealand. She has won the Scottish Ladies' Amateur Championship no less than six times. During World War II she drove a truck and was held in great esteem by golfers in the United States.

Trend-setting Songster Leaves this World

New York, USA, December 26: From Eva Gauthier's debut in 1917, when she sang the first Stravinsky songs ever performed in the USA, to 1923 when she made history by including six jazz pieces in her concert at New York's Aeolian Hall, to 1924 when, with skirts at knee-length, she sang the songs of a great unknown, George Gershwin, the tiny mezzo-soprano surprised and often shocked her audiences.

Gauthier studied in London, Paris, and Rome, but settled in New York some time around 1914. Considered one of the most flamboyant and innovative singers of her time, she was passionate about the music of Francis Poulenc, Igor Stravinsky and Achille-Claude Debussy. She was also the first woman to introduce jazz and Asian music to America.

In 1910, she married a Dutchman and went to live with him in Java. There she discovered batik gowns and oriental jewelry, and fell in love with Javanese folk music, which she added to her repertoire. She divorced her husband and returned to New York where she continued to explore new music. In 1924, 25-year-old George Gershwin made his first public appearance as both a composer and pianist in a concert with Gauthier that included several of his compositions as well as the work of Jerome Kern, Irving Berlin, and Walter Donaldson. Perhaps because of the stir this concert caused in musical circles, orchestra leader Paul Whiteman commissioned Gershwin to write a work for piano and orchestra— the famous "Rhapsody in Blue."

Eva Gauthier died today, but her memory will live on in the effect she had on others, especially through her eclectic combination of influences—music from Java, jazz, songs so old no one else was singing them, and songs so new that no one else dared sing them in public— songs that have changed the American musical landscape for all who follow.

Japanese Woman Writer Champions the Underclass

Japan: Sumii Sue, an outspoken advocate for victims of discrimination, has written an article for the magazine *Buraku*. Called "*Hashi No Nai Kawa*" (The River With No Bridge), it will eventually become part of a multi-volume novel. Among other things, it exposes prejudices against the burakumin, an underclass of butchers,

leatherworkers, and grave diggers who, in Buddhist eyes, are unclean, though no valid reasons exist for this prejudice. Though the Edict of Emancipation in 1871 stipulated that the burakumin should receive equal treatment, discrimination and low living standards continue.

The article tells a story, set in 1908, in which two young Japanese people are so harassed by their classmates and teachers that when they grow up they determine to do something about this gross prejudice. The story of the burakumin is one that continues today.

Though born in Nara prefecture, which is home to many burakumin communities, Sumii does not belong to this underclass. After graduating from Haramoto Women's School she worked for Kodansha publishers, but was not happy with her employer's treatment of women and resigned. She married a political activist and moved with him to rural Japan where she had four children. During this time Sumii wrote a number of novels and stories for young people. When her husband died last year she began to write what she hopes will be an eight-volume work.

Sarah Vaughan

Janet Leigh with baby daughter Jamie Lee Curtis.

Barbie

Ana María Matute Wins Spain's Nadal Prize

Barcelona, Spain, January 6: Ana María Matute, the Spanish author acclaimed for her delicate prose, and for tales of suffering drawn from her experiences as a pre-adolescent during the Spanish Civil War, has won Spain's prestigious literary award, the Nadal Prize, for her novel *Primera memoria (First Memory)*.

The Premio Nadal has been awarded annually by the editorial house Ediciones Destino every January 6 since 1944, when Carmen Laforet became its inaugural recipient for her novel *Nada (Nothing)*.

The most prominent female writer of twentieth-century Spain, Matute was born in Barcelona on July 26, 1926, and was just 10 years old when the first shots were fired in the Spanish Civil War (1939) that saw General Franco rise to power.

Matute, considered a spokeswoman for her generation, has prospered as a writer under the General's oppressive military dictatorship. Her novels often reflect the violence, poverty, and loss of innocence of Spain under Franco.

> *"Once in his life every man is entitled to fall madly in love with a gorgeous redhead."*
>
> LUCILLE BALL (1911–1989), ACTRESS AND COMEDIENNE

Oscar for Best Actress goes to Susan Hayward.

Gabrielle Renard, painter's model and director's mentor.

Friend to Two Generations of Renoirs Dies

California, USA, February 26: Gabrielle Renard, nanny to the director Jean Renoir and model to the painter Pierre-August Renoir, who was known to place a brush into the arthritic hands of the Impressionist master in his old age, has died at her home in Beverley Hills, Los Angeles. She was 80 years of age.

Gabrielle came to the Renoir house at the age of 15 to help raise the painter's son, Jean. The nanny and child became so close that Renoir would often paint them engaged in everyday activities. In *Gabrielle and Jean* (1895), the two are seen playing contentedly together with miniature figures. *Gabrielle, Jean and a Girl* (1895) shows Jean sitting in Gabrielle's lap, reaching for an orange being offered to him by a neighbor.

Jean Renoir fled to the United States from war-ravaged Europe in 1940, and became a successful film director. In 1955, following her husband's death, Gabrielle moved to Beverley Hills to be near Jean.

time out

It would seem that the catchphrase "the customer is always right" applies in Britain, where open soliciting on the street can gain prostitutes a night in jail but their clients cannot be charged.

Sexy New Doll Is a Hit with Young Consumers

New York, USA, March 9: A new doll called "Barbie", modeled after the popular European "Lilli" dolls with their skimpy, tight clothes and curvaceous bodies, has been unveiled at the American Toy Fair in New York City. It sells for $3, and comes with pearl hoop earrings, stiletto heels, black eyeliner, and hand-sewn clothes.

Barbie's creator and marketer, Ruth Handler, was inspired to design a doll for children similar to the Lilli doll of Europe, which began life as a cartoon character in a daily newspaper called the *Bild-Zeitung*, after watching her own daughter, Barbara, grow uninterested in playing with the traditional dolls of babies and children. Handler felt that today's young girls need dolls that can act out future roles and help them to imagine what they themselves may grow up to be.

The Barbie doll represents glamour and independence in an age when the majority of American women stay at home to cook, clean, and care for their children. It may succeed in turning five-year-old girls into serious consumers, and be destined to become an American cultural icon.

Ruth Handler was born in Denver, Colorado, of Polish immigrant parents on November 4, 1916, and married Elliot Handler in 1938. In 1945 they founded the Mattel toy company and began making and selling picture frames. A Mattel executive, Jack Ryan, purchased the rights to the Lilli doll and began the task of giving her the perfect body. Her joints were modified, and gone were her bee-stung lips and heavy eyelashes. "Barbie" weighs in at a very sprightly 11 ounces (312 grams), is 11½ inches (29 cm) tall, and possesses moveable head, arms, and legs.

Key Events

Cuba, January 2: Revolutionary leader Fidel Castro has seized power as president. Incumbent General Fulgencio Batiswta resigns.

Alaska, USA, January 3: Alaska is admitted as the 49th state of the USA, with Juneau as its capital.

Barcelona, Spain, January 6: Writer Ana María Matute wins the country's prestigious Nadal Prize.

Nepal, February 18: Nepal's first national parliamentary election is held. Nepali women are allowed to vote, but are segregated from men.

Cyprus, February 19: Cyprus gains independence in an agreement signed by Britain, Turkey, and Greece.

California, USA, February 26: Gabrielle Renard, artist's model to French painter Pierre-August Renoir, and nanny and mentor to his son, film-maker Jean Renoir, dies at her home in Beverley Hills.

Zimbabwe (Rhodesia), February 27: A state of emergency is declared as violent outbreaks are feared.

New York, USA, March 9: The Barbie doll is unveiled at the American Toy Fair by the Mattel toy company.

New York, USA, March 11: *Raisin in the Sun*, the first Broadway play by a black woman, Lorraine Hansberry, opens at Ethel Barrymore Theater.

USA, March 29: Premiere of the movie *Some Like it Hot*, starring Marilyn Monroe and Jack Lemmon.

Arizona, USA, April 9: Acclaimed architect Frank Lloyd Wright dies at the age of 91.

Tokyo, Japan, April 10: Prince Akihito marries a commoner, Michiko Shoda.

New York, USA, April 22: British ballerina Dame Margot Fonteyn arrives in New York after spending 24 hours in a Panamanian prison.

West Germany, May 1: The five-day working week is introduced.

Toronto, Canada, May 8: The use of the strap as punishment in Canadian schools is banned.

New York, USA, May 21: The musical *Gypsy*, based on the memoirs of burlesque artist Gypsy Rose Lee, opens at the Broadway Theater.

Havana, Cuba, May 23: Ofelia Miriam Ortega becomes the first Hispanic woman ordained in the Presbyterian Church.

London, England, May 28: Johnson and Bart's musical *Lock Up Your Daughters* premieres in London at the Mermaid Theatre.

London, England, June 11: Unveiling of the hovercraft–a new vehicle that goes on both land and sea.

New York, USA, June 18: *The Nun's Story*, starring Audrey Hepburn, Peter Finch, and Edith Evans, premieres.

The "Michiko boom" has had an impact worldwide.

Commoner Marries Heir to Imperial Throne

Tokyo, Japan, April 10: In what has been described as one of the happiest days in postwar Japan, Japanese Prince Akihito has married 24-year-old Michiko Shoda, the daughter of a successful industrialist and the first commoner in 2,600 years to marry an heir to the imperial throne.

Michiko Shoda was born on October 20, 1934, in Tokyo, and in 1953 entered the University of the Sacred Heart where she earned a Bachelor of Arts in English literature. She met Prince Akihito on a tennis court at Karuizawa in 1957, but did not come to the attention of the media until August 1958. With no suitable bride for the Prince to be gleaned from the Japanese aristocracy, she soon became the center of a "Michiko boom" and her popularity has reached unheard

of extremes. Many Japanese people believe she can bridge the gap between the imperial family and the populace.

Prima Ballerina Released from Panamanian Prison

New York, USA, April 22: After spending 24 hours in a jail cell in Panama City, the acclaimed British ballerina Dame Margot Fonteyn has been mobbed by journalists after arriving, amid much speculation, at New York's La Guardia airport.

Her husband, Doctor Roberto Arias, is still in hiding somewhere in Panama, suspected of involvement in a conspiracy to topple the Panamanian Government. It is claimed Doctor Arias was planning to storm the National Guard barracks in the town of Chorrera with weapons including automatic rifles and grenades concealed in a buoy below the waters surrounding the Pearl Islands.

Dame Margot told waiting reporters she does not know where her husband is or whether or not he is safe.

Yesterday she was detained by Panamanian officials in Balboa harbor on the Panama Canal, having been apprehended on the fishing boat the couple had set out in the day before to go fishing. It is as yet unclear what light Fonteyn can shed on her husband's disappearance or the alleged plot against the government.

Born in Reigate, England, on May 18, 1919, Dame Margot began dance classes at the age of four before traveling with her father to Shanghai where she received lessons from the Russian George Goncharov. At 14 she returned to London to study at the Sadler's Wells Ballet School, debuting in 1934, at the age of 15, as a snowflake in *The Nutcracker*.

A wealth of dance roles soon followed, including *Swan Lake*, *Giselle*, and *The Sleeping Beauty*, but it was her collaboration with the choreographer Sir Frederick Ashton that gave her what she was later to recall as her happiest moments on

stage, in ballets such as *Apparitions* and *The Wise Virgins*. As first ballerina in George Balanchine's Ballet Imperial during the war years, she performed throughout England and Europe. She entertained Allied troops in Brussels and proved herself to be Britain's most versatile and complete dancer, exhibiting a once-in-a-generation ability to perform the most difficult choreography with disarming ease and grace.

Dame Margot was freed today after the intervention of Sir Ian Henderson, the British High Commissioner. Her release was also welcomed in a speech by Foreign Secretary, Ernest Bevan, in the House of Commons in London.

Dame Margot, who refused to answer questions about the situation in Panama, concluded today's interview by saying she has every intention of returning there to be reunited with her husband.

Marilyn Monroe

Margot Fonteyn and Roberto Arias were married in Paris in 1955.

Key Events

Brussels, Belgium, July 2: Prince Albert marries Italian princess Paola Ruffo di Calabria at the Royal Palace.
New York, USA, July 15: Jazz singer Billie Holiday dies from cirrhosis of the liver.
Olduvai Gorge, Tanzania, July 17: Doctor Mary Leakey discovers the oldest known hominid skull, dubbed "Nutcracker Man."
USA, September 25: The 37-year-old advertizing executive Helen Gurley marries film producer David Brown (aged 43).

Colombo, Sri Lanka (Ceylon), September 26: Prime Minister Solomon Bandaranaike dies in hospital after being shot by a Buddhist monk, Talduwe Somarama.
South Africa, October 17: De Beers announces the manufacture of synthetic diamonds.
New York, USA, November 16: Rodgers and Hammerstein's musical *The Sound of Music* opens.
Tehran, Iran, December 21: Farah Diba marries the recently divorced Shah of Iran, becoming his third wife, and Empress of Iran.

Washington DC, USA: The Newbery Medal is won by Elizabeth George Speare for her historical novel *The Witch of Blackbird Pond*.
Rome, Italy: After working as a design assistant at Guy Laroche in Paris, Valentino Garavani, better know as Valentino, returns home to open his own studio.
New York, USA: Abstract expressionist artist Lee Krasner paints *Cool White*. It is a difficult year for the artist: Her mother dies and there are problems with her late husband Jackson Pollock's estate.

Kathmandu, Nepal: The Family Planning Association of Nepal (FPAN) is founded to increase support for sexual health and rights.
Virginia, USA: The Du Pont Company develops a new fabric, Lycra®, at its Waynesboro plant.
New York, USA: Anna Balakian writes *Surrealism: The Road to the Absolute*, an exposition of surrealist literature and art.
New York, USA: Joyce Ballantine Brand, commercial artist, creates the Coppertone Girl for Coppertone suntan lotion.

North Carolina, USA: Pantyhose, which give the appearance of stockings without garters, garter-belts, or corsets, are introduced by Glen Raven Mills.
Ontario, Canada: Betty Oliphant and Celia Franca found the National Ballet School of Canada in Toronto.
Maine, USA: Landscape architect Beatrix Farrand dies, aged 87.
Brasilia, Brazil: Clairvoyant Tia Neiva founds Valley of the Dawn, a sect of 2000 mediums that incorporates Egyptian, Inca, Aztec, Catholic, and Afro-Brazilian rituals.

Lee Krasner

Greatest Jazz Singer of Our Age Dead at 44

New York, USA, July 15: The life and tumultuous times of the lady whom many people consider to have been the greatest jazz singer of all time, Billie Holiday, came to an end today in New York City's Metropolitan hospital. She died from complications caused by years of alcohol and heroin addiction.

Born Eleanora Fagan to a 13-year-old mother and a 15-year-old father in Philadelphia on April 7, 1915, Holiday spent an impoverished childhood in Baltimore before moving to New York with her mother in the late 1920s.

She successfully auditioned as a feature singer at a Harlem speakeasy, and was the hottest property in the New York borough by the age of 20 when the jazz writer John Hammond Senior saw her perform. He wrote that she was the greatest singer he'd ever heard, and by 1933 Holiday was recording with the likes of Benny Goodman, Duke Ellington, and Lester Young, who nicknamed her "Lady Day" and with whom she would make some of her greatest recordings.

She became one of the first black vocalists to sing with a white orchestra when she worked with Artie Shaw and his orchestra in 1938, but felt that singing with a big band was too restricting and decided to pursue a solo career.

> *"The difficult I can do today. The impossible will take a little longer."*
>
> BILLIE HOLIDAY
> (1915–1959),
> JAZZ SINGER

"Lady Day" shone despite her personal troubles.

Valley of the Dawn, a sect of mediums in Brazil.

Holiday opened at the Greenwich Village club Café Society in January 1939, and was a regular there for the next nine months, during which time she sang her classic protest song against the horror of black lynching, "Strange Fruit." The song became a nightly ritual, and some commentators claim it marks the birth of the modern civil rights movement—the first unmuted cry against racism.

"Strange Fruit" was a watershed in Holiday's career, marking her transition from exuberant jazz singer to a storyteller singing of pain and loneliness.

At the same time as her singing career was on the way up, Holiday's personal life was spiraling out of control. By the time of the breakup of her disastrous marriage to Jimmy Monroe in the early 1940s, she was an opium user and heroin addict. Seemingly unable to distance herself from men who systematically mistreated her, she began to drink heavily and was jailed in 1947 on drug charges after a highly publicized trial.

Her addictions and lifestyle affected the quality of her later recordings, though she did return to Columbia last year to record the haunting "Lady in Satin."

Fossil Find Suggests We All Came from Africa

Olduvai Gorge, Tanzania, July 17: At an archeological site in the Olduvai Gorge in northern Tanzania, the English paleoanthropologist Doctor Mary Leakey has discovered hundreds of skull fragments belonging to what is believed to be an early hominid. This important find has put Africa at the center of the world's fossil map.

Called "Nutcracker Man" and estimated to be over 1.7 millions years old, the skull will be reconstructed by Leakey and her team in the coming months. The rebuilt skull seems destined to change the minds of those who still cling to the belief that humans evolved in Asia.

The Olduvai Gorge is a deep ravine within the Great African Rift Valley. Over the years it has given up a complex catalogue of early human activity including a butchery site, human footprints estimated to be 3 million years old, and animals such as sabre-toothed cats and dwarf elephants. The varying density of human bone fragments, tooth shapes, and cranium capacities found at Olduvai Gorge have led Leakey to conclude that a new genus in the hominid family has been discovered.

One of the most renowned fossil hunters, Mary Douglas Leakey was born in London on February 6, 1913, and spent her childhood in south-west France, a region rich in archeological sites and prehistoric art. Expelled from two Catholic schools in the years following the sudden death of her father, she met the anthropologist Louis Leakey at Cambridge University in 1933 and they were married three years later.

In the decades since, the famous couple have worked on many excavations throughout East Africa and are building a reputation as the pre-eminent archeologists and anthropologists of our time.

Fairytale Wedding Gives Iran its First Queen

Tehran, Iran, December 21: His Imperial Majesty Mohamed Reza Shah Pahlavi has today married 21-year-old Farah Diba. The fairytale wedding in Tehran's Marble Palace has catapulted the beautiful young Empress to international celebrity status.

Farah Diba was born in Tehran on October 14, 1938. Her father, Sohrab Diba, was an Iranian army officer and law graduate of the Sorbonne. Her mother, Farideh Diba, supervised her education, sending Farah to study at the École d'Architecture in Paris and instilling in her a lifelong love of architecture.

While studying in Paris, Farah was invited to meet the Shah, who was in France on a private visit, and took the opportunity to complain to him that Iranian currency restrictions for students studying abroad made life very difficult.

A year later she repeated the complaint to a relative of the Shah who arranged for them to meet over tea. The Shah was so impressed by Farah that he proposed to her, and she accepted. Today, accompanied by an escort of imperial lancers, she arrived to meet her groom in the Marble

The Shah of Iran's wedding to 21-year-old Farah Diba.

Palace's Hall of Mirrors wearing a 33 lb (15 kg), jewel-laden Dior wedding gown. Set in her tiara was the famous 60-carat, tear-shaped Noor-ol-Ain diamond surrounded by pink, clear, and yellow diamonds in a stunning setting designed by Harry Winston.

Children's Author Wins Newbery Medal

Washington DC, USA: *The Witch of Blackbird Pond*, the second novel of the American author Elizabeth George Speare, has won the Newbery Medal.

The novel tells the story of one girl's opposition to the excesses of her Puritan surroundings. Kit, a 16-year-old free-spirited girl from Barbados, is forced to live with relatives in the small town of Wethersfield, Connecticut. Unable to adjust to a life of rules and restrictions, she retreats to the meadows where she meets and befriends an old Quaker woman named Hannah.

Hannah is known in town as "The Witch of Blackbird Pond," and Kit is told by her uncle that she can no longer visit her. But when an epidemic strikes the town and Hannah is accused of practicing witchcraft, Kit helps her escape. Incurring the wrath of the townspeople, Kit becomes the focus of their retribution and is herself put on trial, forcing her to make a choice between what is in her heart—loyalty to her friend—and her sense of duty to a Puritan lifestyle.

Elizabeth Speare has lived her entire life in New England. Although possessing the impulse to write from an early age, she didn't pick up a pen until her two children were in junior high school. She started with magazine articles, then moved on to novels.

Born in Melrose, Massachusetts, on November 21, 1908, she had a happy childhood of picnics, hikes, concerts, and summer trips to the shore with her family. She received a Master's degree in English from Boston University and worked as a teacher before meeting her future husband, Alden Speare. They moved to Connecticut, where they raised their two children, Alden Junior and Mary.

The Newbery Medal, the nation's highest award for children's literature, has been awarded every year since 1922 by the Association for Library Service to Children.

Death of Great American Landscape Architect

Maine, USA: The landscape architect whose work represented the very pinnacle of her craft, Beatrix Farrand, has died at the age of 87 at her home in Bar Harbor, Maine.

Born in New York in 1872, the lone female founder of the American Society of Landscape Architects began her career while living in her mother's brownstone apartment in New York, designing gardens for the elite citizenry of the area. By the age of 27 she was creating walled and formal gardens for some of the country's most notable families, including the Rockefellers. In 1912 she designed a landscape plan for Princeton University's Graduate College, and the following year married Max Farrand, chairman of the history department at Yale University.

Her greatest work, however, remains the gardens of the Bliss family home at Dumbarton Oaks in the Washington DC suburb of Georgetown. French, Italian, and English traditions come together in what is regarded as one of the world's great gardens, and a fitting testament to Farrand's vision and artistry.

Coppertone's Pin-up Girl Owes Success to Mom

New York, USA: A three-year-old girl named Cheri Brand has become symbolic of endless summers, and an unlikely poster girl for an advertising campaign by the Coppertone sunscreen company.

Cheri's mother, the commercial artist Joyce Ballantyne Brand, is responsible for her daughter's sudden celebrity status. Ms Brand was paid $2,500 to come up with the image of a pig-tailed girl with a dog pulling down the bottom of her swimsuit, and in the process displaying a decidedly un-tanned patch of skin.

"She worked cheap and was convenient," according to Ms Brand. The cocker spaniel was drawn from recollections of a neighbor's dog.

Audrey Hepburn

Mary Martin in *The Sound of Music* at the Lunt-Fontanne Theatre, New York.

Loretta Lynn

Acclaimed Author Dies in Poverty

Florida, USA, January 28: The author and anthropologist Zora Neale Hurston, doyenne of the 1920s Harlem Renaissance movement, has died penniless and in relative obscurity after suffering a stroke at her home in Fort Pierce. She was 69.

Hurston first came to prominence in the African-American community with the publication of short stories in black literary magazines. Her first novel, *Jonah's Gourd Vine*, published in 1934, was a critical success. It was followed later that decade by *Mules and Men*, which investigated voodoo practices in the black communities of New Orleans and Florida, and *Their Eyes Were Watching God*, a luminous and haunting novel that tells the story of an African-American woman's quest for love and sensuality.

Born in the small town of Notasulga, Alabama on January 7, 1891, Zora was the fifth of eight children. Her father was a carpenter and Baptist preacher and her mother a schoolteacher. When Zora was a year old the family moved to Eatonville,

"A MAN IN LOVE IS INCOMPLETE UNTIL HE HAS MARRIED. THEN HE'S FINISHED."

ZSA ZSA GABOR, AMERICAN ACTRESS, NEWSWEEK

Florida, the first incorporated black municipality in the United States. While at school there, she grew to love writing.

Her mother died when Zora was a teenager and she was forced to leave school. Later, a woman for whom she worked arranged for Zora to attend high school, and after graduating in 1918 she attended Howard University, where she continued writing, and began entering literary competitions.

In 1925 she moved to New York and became involved in the Harlem Renaissance. The fact that she received financial sponsorship from wealthy white New York patrons brought her much criticism from the Black Arts Movement.

Hurston's career faltered in the mid-1940s. Despite being acquitted of molesting a ten-year-old boy, the damage to her reputation lingered and she drifted into depression. Her 1948 novel *Seraph on the Suwanee* was a critical failure, and by the early 1950s Zora Hurston, a woman with a utopian vision who believed African-Americans could win their sovereignty from white America, was earning a living as a house cleaner in Florida.

"Queen of Comedy" Files for Divorce

California, USA, March 4: After years of enduring the infidelities and excessive drinking of her husband Desi Arnaz, Lucille Ball has today filed for divorce. This comes just one day after taping the final episode of *The Lucy-Desi Comedy Hour,* and brings the curtain down on one of America's most public couples.

The two met in 1940 on the set of the RKO picture *Too Many Girls*, and were married in November of the same year. Their marriage was at times tempestuous. Ball, the comedienne, is said to be conservative and uncomfortable among people she doesn't know, whereas the Cuban vocalist, Arnaz, has a reputation as a fun-loving extrovert.

Lucille Ball and Desi Arnaz in happier times.

Lucille Ball was born in Jamestown, New York, on August 6, 1911. After dropping out of high school she began a modeling career that saw her become the 1933 Chesterfield Cigarette Girl.

Ball's popular television show, *I Love Lucy,* ran for six seasons, from 1951 to 1957 and made her a household name. The third season episode in which Lucy gave birth to the couple's on-screen son, Little Ricky, saw 44 million people tune in, making it the most-watched single episode in American television history.

Over 20 Million Watch First Televised Royal Wedding

London, England, May 7: Yesterday Princess Margaret married the Cambridge graduate and aspiring photographer Anthony Armstrong-Jones at Westminster Abbey. The first royal wedding to be televised, it attracted an estimated audience of 20 million people.

The Princess arrived at the abbey looking resplendent in a silk wedding dress designed by Norman Hartnell. Its classic, uncluttered style featured an elegant V-neck bodice and was complemented by a satin-bound silk tulle veil.

Oscar for Best Actress goes to Simone Signoret.

Princess Margaret weds Anthony Armstrong-Jones in the first royal wedding to be televised.

Jane Goodall

Closed circuit television relayed pictures to all corners of Westminster Abbey, allowing all of the 2,000 guests to witness the ceremony taking place in the abbey's sanctuary. The Archbishop of Canterbury presided over the service, after which the bride and groom traveled with the royal family to Buckingham Palace. There, they appeared on the balcony to wave to a cheering throng of onlookers.

Later in the evening the Princess and her husband, now the Earl of Snowdon, Viscount Linley of Nymans, headed to Battle Bridge Pier on the River Thames where they boarded the Royal Yacht *Britannia* for their six-week honeymoon in the Caribbean.

"Most Powerful Woman in the World" Dies

Bucharest, Romania, June 14: Ana Pauker, once described by *Time* magazine as "the most powerful woman in the world," has died in her bed, aged 67. At the height of her power, she was the leading Communist in the Soviet satellite nations that

time out

Harper Lee publishes a tale of racial cruelty in America's deep south. Entitled *To Kill a Mockingbird*, it tells the story of a black man wrongly accused of raping a white woman.

stretched from the Adriatic to the Baltic. She is said to have had seven telephones in her office, one of which was a direct line to the Kremlin.

Pauker came from an impoverished background. The granddaughter of a Jewish orthodox rabbi, she was born in a tiny Moldavian village in 1893. She became a member of the Romanian Communist Party in 1920 after her marriage to Marcel Pauker, and was appointed to its Central Committee in 1922.

After being arrested in 1925 she fled to the USSR where she worked for the Comintern until 1939. In 1944 she re-entered Romania on the back of a Soviet tank to become Foreign Minister in the new Soviet-imposed government. A puppet of Soviet Communism, Pauker's Romania was often little more than a political battle of wills between her own Muscovite faction and the opposing Prison faction led by Georghiu-Dej, who used the rising tide of anti-Semitism within Soviet policy to convince Stalin to move against the Pauker faction. Finally, in May

1952, Ana Pauker's faction was purged and she was put on trial in February 1953. After the death of Stalin in March she was placed under house arrest.

Naturalist Hopes to Shed New Light on Chimpanzees

Tanzania, July 4: The English naturalist and zoologist, 23-year-old Jane Goodall, has arrived in Kenya's Gombe Stream Reserve at the behest of the famous anthropologist Louis Leakey to realize her dream of studying the little-known lives of chimpanzees.

Her intention is to track and record the habits of chimpanzees, using such unorthodox techniques as constructing a banana feeding station to lure them into the open for easier and more thorough observation. Goodall also intends naming the chimps rather than simply giving them a number.

Goodall has been quoted as saying she expects to find that chimpanzees possess behaviors and emotions falsely believed to be unique to humans.

Ana Pauker in her prime, as Romanian Foreign Minister.

New York, USA, September 25: Mrs. Emily Post, for many years a leading authority on all matters of etiquette, dies at the age of 86.
Addis Ababa, Ethiopia, September 27: Sylvia Pankhurst, social activist and prominent British suffragette, dies at the age of 78.
New York USA, October 4: Angela Lansbury and Joan Plowright star in *A Taste of Honey* by Shelagh Delaney. Written when the author was still a teenager, the play focuses on a working-class girl who rejects her ordinary surroundings.

London, England, October: Poet Sylvia Plath publishes her first book of poems, *The Colossus*.
USA, November 9: John F. Kennedy is elected president of the USA, narrowly defeating Richard Nixon.
UK, November 10: Penguin Books sells out of D. H. Lawrence's 1928 novel *Lady Chatterley's Lover* on its first day of release.
New Orleans, Louisiana, November 14: Six year-old Ruby Bridges is the first African-American child to attend a whites only school in Louisiana.

Toronto, Canada, November 24: Grand Duchess Olga Alexandrovna, the last surviving sister of Tsar Nicholas II, dies, aged 78.
England, December 7: Granada Television broadcasts the first episode of "Coronation Street."
Sweden, December 10: US Chemist Willard F. Libby is awarded the Nobel Prize in Chemistry for developing carbon dating techniques.
California, USA: The Daughters of Bilitis hold the first National Lesbian Conference in San Francisco.

Sydney, Australia: Painter Judy Cassab wins the Archibald Prize for her portrait of Stanislaus Rapotec.
England: British sculptor Barbara Hepworth casts the hollow bronzes *Figure for Landscape* and *Archaeon*.
Jonquiere, Quebec, Canada: The breastfeeding association, La Leche League, establishes its first group outside the USA.
Wirral, England: Maureen Nichol establishes the National House-wives' Register, for "housebound wives with liberal interests and a desire to remain individuals."

USA: American teen Brenda Lee hits number one with her song *I'm Sorry*.
Brisbane, Australia: Madam Chao Feng from the National Women's Federation of China, and Madame Roesijati R. Sukardi from the Indonesian Women's Organization, attend meetings of International Women's Day committees.
Copenhagen, Denmark: This year marks the 50th anniversary of International Women's Day, and delegates from 73 countries attend a conference to mark the occasion.

Sirimavo Bandaranaike

World's First Female Prime Minister Elected

Colombo, Ceylon, July 22: Sirimavo Bandaranaike, the bereaved widow of Solomon Bandaranaike, who took over the leadership of the Sri Lanka Freedom Party (SLFP) after her husband was assassinated by a Buddhist monk last year, was sworn in yesterday as the world's first female prime minister.

The election of the SLFP is the result of the leader of the United National Party's (UNP) Dudley Senanayake's failure to establish a coalition after elections in March, in which the UNP received only 50 of the 151 seats contested. In the second round of polling the SLFP, led by Bandaranaike, captured 75 seats and has formed government in a coalition with Marxist parties. Bandaranaike is expected to continue her husband's policies, such as the nationalization of major enterprises, the creation of a comprehensive welfare state, economic independence, and the pursuit of a non-aligned foreign policy. However, her determination to press ahead with nationalist, pro-Buddhist policies and her goal of making Sinhalese the official language of this tiny island is expected to cause bitter resentment among the Tamil minority in the north.

Sirimavo Bandaranaike was born into one of the country's leading feudal families on April 17, 1916, and was educated by Roman Catholic nuns at a convent in Colombo. In 1940 she married Solomon Bandaranaike, the founder of the nationalist Sri Lankan Freedom Party and was dubbed "the weeping widow" when, as leader of the party in opposition after his

"NO ONE CAN MAKE YOU FEEL INFERIOR WITHOUT YOUR CONSENT."

ELEANOR ROOSEVELT,
US FIRST LADY

"WOMEN SPEAK BECAUSE THEY WISH TO SPEAK, WHEREAS A MAN SPEAKS ONLY WHEN DRIVEN TO SPEECH BY SOMETHING OUTSIDE HIMSELF — LIKE, FOR INSTANCE, HE CAN'T FIND ANY CLEAN SOCKS."

JEAN KERR,
THE SNAKE HAS ALL
THE LINES

American teen Brenda Lee hits number one.

Sylvia Pankhurst, imprisoned for inciting the armed forces "to mutiny and lawlessness," on her release in 1921.

death, she pledged to honor his vision and continue with his socialist policies if elected to government.

Sirimavo Bandaranaike's election win is so unprecedented that some of the world's media are unclear as to what title to give her. London's *Evening News* has suggested that perhaps she should simply be called a stateswoman. They also noted that her victory was "…a suffragette's dream come true."

Suffragette Sylvia Pankhurst Dies in Ethiopia

Addis Ababa, Ethiopia, September 27: Sylvia Pankhurst, the pioneering campaigner for women's suffrage, and outspoken advocate for the restoration of Ethiopian independence, has died, aged 78.

Born in 1882 in Manchester, Sylvia grew up in a world of social activism. Her parents, Doctor Richard Pankhurst and Emmeline Pankhurst, both members of the Independent Labor Party, were also active in the suffrage movement, as was her sister Christabel.

Hoping to become a painter, Sylvia won a scholarship to the Manchester School of Art in 1900. She went to Venice in 1902, returning to London in 1904 to study at the Royal College of Art in South Kensington. In 1906, however, she began working alongside her mother and her sister for the Women's Social and Political Union. She broke with the group in 1914 due to its promotion of arson attacks.

Sylvia founded a group of suffragettes known as the East London Federation of Suffragettes and was the owner and editor of their weekly newspaper, *The Women's Dreadnought*. In addition to campaigning for women's rights, she was a founder and

editor of four newspapers, wrote and published 22 books, and was a tireless activist in numerous international solidarity organizations.

Although she was a founding member of the British Communist Party, the 1930s purges under Stalin caused her to become disillusioned with Communism, and she devoted her remaining years to fighting the iniquities of racism and fascism.

When Ethiopia was overrun by fascist Italy in 1935, Sylvia rallied to its support by publishing a newspaper, the *New Times and Ethiopia News*. The paper remained in circulation for over 20 years and at its height sold 40,000 copies a week with a readership that extended from Ethiopia to the West Indies.

Segregation Ended by Six-year-old Girl

New Orleans, Louisiana, USA, November 14: A six-year-old African-American girl, Ruby Bridges, began school today at New Orleans's William Frantz Elementary School. She was escorted by four federal marshals and surrounded by a crowd of protestors who hurled abuse and displayed racist and intimidating placards.

Ruby was born in Mississippi in 1954 and then moved to New Orleans. The National Association for the Advancement of Colored People (NAACP) contacted Ruby's parents and asked if they would be willing to allow their child to participate in the integration of schools in New Orleans. Her parents, believing they had an obligation to challenge a discriminatory and unconstitutional education system, agreed.

In response to the new situation, white parents pulled their children out of the school, and are threatening to keep them

Not everyone is glad to see the end of segregation.

when her father was the ruling autocrat, has died in poverty at her tiny home in Cooksville.

A petite, fragile, and deeply religious woman, Olga was born on June 14, 1882 in the Alexander Palace in Peterhof, Russia. She worked as a nurse at the Russian front during World War I, but fled to the Crimea in the wake of the 1917 Revolution with her second husband, Nicholas Koulikovsky, and her mother before escaping to Denmark by boat in February of 1920.

From Denmark they moved with their two sons to Canada where Olga indulged her love of painting. Over the course of her lifetime the Grand Duchess was to paint over 2,000 works, mostly medium-sized water-colors, many of them immersed in the subdued light and colors of Russia and exhibiting serenity, a love of nature and a sensitive eye for composition.

After the death of her husband two years ago, Olga moved from their house to an apartment over a barbershop. She will be buried alongside her husband at York Cemetery in Toronto.

First Woman in 20 Years to Win Archibald Prize

Sydney, Australia: Judy Cassab, the Hungarian-born artist who migrated to Australia in 1951 to escape war-torn Europe, has been awarded this year's Archibald Prize for her portrait of the artist Stanislaus Rapotec. Cassab is the first woman in 20 years to win the much-coveted award.

Born in Vienna in 1920 to middle-class Hungarian Jewish parents, Cassab was raised by her grandmother after her parents separated in 1929. She took refuge in Budapest during the war when her husband was sent to a labor camp. Most of her family, including her mother and grandmother, died at Auschwitz.

Reunited with her husband Jancsi Kampfner after the war, Cassab came to Australia with him and their two young sons. Although her world has remained a fragile one, she has managed to scale the heights of artistic achievement at a time when female artists are struggling for recognition. In 1953 she held her first solo exhibition at Sydney's Macquarie Galleries, and in 1955 she won the Perth Prize for her portrait of Michael Kmit. She has since established herself as one of Australia's premier painters of abstracts and portraits.

Sculptor's Hollow Bronzes Break New Ground

England: The British sculptor Barbara Hepworth, considered one of the country's great artists of this century, has cast two unorthodox, groundbreaking bronze figures, *Archaeon* and *Figure for Landscape*.

Though not as renowned as her friend, the sculptor Henry Moore, Hepworth is generally considered by critics to be every bit as influential. Born in Wakefield, West Yorkshire in 1903, she studied at the Leeds School of Art and went on to the Royal College of Art on a senior scholarship. She was a finalist in the Prix de Rome in 1924, finishing runner-up to her future husband, John Skeaping.

Hepworth's earliest work was naturalistic, but her interest in formal elements led her increasingly toward abstraction and to a focus on the interplay between mass and space. Her concept of piercing a solid bronze mass with a hole, thus making the object more transparent, is best seen in *Figure for Landscape*, an abstract shape suggesting a human figure whose hollow interior paradoxically achieves a greater prominence than the surrounding bronze.

Wilma Rudolph

at home for the entire school year if the status quo is not reinstated. Ruby will be in a class of two—herself and her teacher, Barbara Henry, the first white teacher Ruby Bridges has ever seen. The woman originally designated to be Ruby's teacher resigned rather than teach a black child, but Henry, when invited by the superintendent of schools to teach classes in an integrated school, immediately agreed.

Ruby's classroom has been stripped bare save for its blackboard. Barbara Henry says her first task will be to work with Ruby to redecorate the classroom with Ruby's artwork—the school having offered no assistance or support.

The first African-American child to desegregate an elementary school may not have other children to play with at her new school, but her extraordinary teacher has declared she is determined to fill Ruby's days with a love of learning and an awareness of the importance of compassion and tolerance.

Farewell to the Last Grand Duchess

Toronto, Canada, November 24: Grand Duchess Olga Alexandrovna, the youngest child of Tsar Alexander III of Russia and sister of Tsar Nicholas II, the only Romanov sibling born "in the purple"

British sculptor Barbara Hepworth in her studio.

Emily Greene Balch

Supreme Unknowns on the Move to Motown

Detroit, USA, January 15: Four promising female African-American backing singers have been signed by Motown Records at their Hitsville studios today. Motown's owner Berry Gordy is said to be undecided about the virtues of the unknown quartet of working-class girls, but chose to sign them at the urging of Smokey Robinson, Motown's hit-making rhythm and blues soul singer.

Three of the four singers, Florence Ballard, Mary Wilson, and Diana Ross, first performed together as a quartet with Betty McGlown. Called the Primettes, they accompanied a trio of male singers, the Primes, which included Eddie Kendricks, Paul Williams, and Kell Osborne.

The Primettes first approached Motown in the summer of 1960. Berry Gordy was impressed, but felt they were too young,

"… LET US HASTEN ALONG THE ROAD, THE ROAD OF HUMAN TEN-DERNESS AND GENEROSITY. GROPING, WE MAY FIND ONE ANOTHER'S HANDS IN THE DARK."

EMILY GREENE BALCH
(1867-1961),
NOBEL PEACE PRIZE
WINNER

and suggested they come back to see him again after graduating from high school. For months the group continued to show up at Motown's headquarters after school, to no avail. Betty McGlown left the group and a new singer, Barbara Martin, replaced her. In the summer of 1960 persistence finally paid off when the Primettes were chosen as backup singers for Mabel John. Soon they were on a salary of $2.50 a week— split four ways. December of the same year saw the group record some material of their own, including the single "I Want A Guy." Now, at the behest of Smokey Robinson, they are part of the Motown family. Berry Gordy, however, has asked for a name change. A list of alternatives was presented to the group, and Florence Ballard, over the objections of Diana Ross, chose the last name on Gordy's list. From tomorrow the Primettes will be known as the Supremes.

time out

Housewives across the United States have gone on strike for peace. They've downed their dish towels, dropped their mops, and are asking governments to "End the arms race, not the human race."

The once-struggling Primettes, now Motown Supremes.

Hollywood Farewells its First Non-White Star

Santa Monica, California, USA, February 2: Anna May Wong, born in the Chinatown district of Los Angeles on January 3, 1905, died today of heart failure, at the age of 56. She was the first Asian-American woman to become a film star, and one of only two non-white actors to be regularly cast in starring roles in Hollywood.

A woman possessed of exceptional beauty and a smouldering sensuality, Wong stole the camera from Gilda Gray in *Piccadilly* (1929), and at 5 ft 7 inches (170 cm) was taller than Marlene Dietrich in *Shanghai Express* (1932). Despite often playing stereotypical roles as a "dragon lady" or "innocent lotus flower," she brought to the screen a subtlety and grace that garnered her a legion of adoring fans stretching from Shanghai to London.

An aura of the exotic surrounded Anna May Wong.

In the late 1920s Anna May Wong became the darling of Europe, and it is rumored was even invited to be the first Chinese woman to be presented to the British court. In 1934, the Mayfair Mannequin Society of New York voted her the World's Best Dressed Woman.

Her success was all the more remarkable given the ethos of the time. In 1924 the US Congress passed the *Immigration Exclusion Act* barring Chinese immigrants from entering the United States. Chinese-Americans were not permitted to testify in court against whites, and people of Chinese descent faced the indignity of special taxes that applied to no other segment of the community.

Wong toured extensively on the stage throughout Europe and America, and in the early 1950s starred in her own television series, *The Gallery of Madame Liu-Tsong*, using her own birth name for the title character. A spirited and independent woman, she never married.

USA, January 9: Nobel Peace Prize recipient Emily Greene Balch dies.
Detroit, USA, January 15: A female singing group, The Primettes, are asked to change their name to something else when they sign with Motown Records. They choose to be known as The Supremes.
Katanga, Congo, January 18: After less than a year as prime minister in the newly independent nation, Patrice Lumumba is brutally murdered, and several western countries are implicated in his death.

London, England, January 31: The contraceptive pill goes on sale.
California, USA, February 2: Film actress Anna May Wong dies.
Belgium, February 15: A Boeing 707 crashes, killing 73 people, including 18 figure skaters from the USA.
Canberra, Australia, February: A new *Matrimonial Causes Act* establishing "no fault" divorce comes into effect.
London, England, March 2: Yesterday, cellist Jacqueline du Pré made her debut to critical acclaim.

USSR, March 10: Boris Pasternak's lover, Olga Ivinskaya, appeals to the authorities to repeal her detention in a Soviet gulag.
Nice, France, March 13: At the age of 79, Pablo Picasso marries 37-year-old Jacqueline Rocque.
USA, March 13: Mattel's popular Barbie doll gets a boyfriend, Ken.
Charleston, England, April 7: Vanessa Bell, artist, interior designer, and sister of novelist Virginia Woolf, dies, aged 81.

South Vietnam, April 10: Staunch anti-Communist President Ngo Dinh Diem is re-elected. His Catholic faith, nepotism, and authoritarian rule have made him unpopular with the mostly Buddhist population.
Cuba, April 20: Yesterday 1,400 US-backed Cuban exiles landed at the Bay of Pigs hoping to overthrow the government of Fidel Castro. The invasion was repelled with over 200 killed, sparking a major diplomatic incident with the USA.

Havana, Cuba, May 1: Fidel Castro proclaims Cuba a socialist country.
Columbia University, New York, USA, May 1: Harper Lee wins the Pulitzer Prize for fiction for her novel, *To Kill a Mockingbird*.
New York, USA, May 8: Former editor of *Harper's Bazaar*, Carmel Snow, dies aged 74.
Dominican Republic, May 30: After a 31-year rule, ruthless dictator General Trujillo is assassinated with the assistance of the CIA.

Jacqueline du Pré's first cello teacher was her mother.

Teen Cellist Captivates Audience at Wigmore Hall

Wigmore Hall, London, England, March 2: Last night 16-year-old cellist Jacqueline du Pré made an astonishing debut with the BBC orchestra playing Elgar's *Concerto for Cello in E minor.* In front of a packed house, du Pré played on a 1672 Antonio Stradivarius, given to her by an unknown admirer.

Born in Oxford on January 26, 1945, this young girl, who shows such intensity and and plays at such a high level of technical perfection, could sing in tune before she could talk. She was given her first cello when only four, and by the time she was seven was studying at London's Guildhall School of Music. She has won many local music competitions alongside her sister, flautist Hilary du Pré, and at the age of 10 she won the international Suggia-Cello Prize. Jacqueline du Pré's main teacher, since 1955, has been the respected cellist William Pleeth.

Zhivago's "Lara" Pleads for Release

USSR, March 10: The lover of epic novelist Boris Pasternak, Olga Ivinskaya, has today asked Soviet authorities to repeal her detention. She was first arrested, tortured and interred in a Soviet prison camp in 1949 in a failed attempt by Stalin to persuade Pasternak to abandon his epic novel, *Dr Zhivago.* Its heroine, Lara, was modeled on Ivinskaya. After her release in 1953 she resumed her relationship with Pasternak, and during the last 14 years of his life, Ivinskaya was his closest companion and greatest love, providing constant inspiration for his writing until his death on May 30, 1960. Two days after his death, the KGB raided Ivinskaya's home seizing papers and letters, and arrested Invinskaya on smuggling charges. She is still being detained.

Bloomsbury Founder Dies

Charleston, England, April 7: Vanessa Bell, painter and interior designer whose bohemian style of decorating broke with what she often called the oppressive Victorian styles of the past, has died of heart failure at her farmhouse. She was 81 years of age.

Born in May 1879 in Hyde Park Gate, Vanessa began taking drawing classes when she was in her teens. After the death of her father in 1904 she traveled to Paris. Upon returning to London she studied at the Slade School of Arts, receiving her first commission in April 1905 after exhibiting a painting at the New Gallery.

Later that year she launched her Friday Club, a regular association of artists who met regularly at her home on Gordon Square. This group was to evolve into the famous Bloomsbury Group, with her sister Virginia Woolf, whose works had been gaining in popularity and critical acclaim, at its center. An exhibition of post-Impressionists including Cézanne, Van Gogh, and Manet at London's Grafton Gallery profoundly influenced Bell, and in August of 1912 she sold her first painting, *The Spanish Model.*

After marrying Clive Bell in 1907, Vanessa soon began an affair with art critic Roger Fry before meeting and falling in love with the gifted painter Duncan Grant, with whom she lived for the remainder of her life. She continued to live and work in London for the next three decades as an interior designer and increasingly respected painter.

Tragedies beset her life in the 1930s and 1940s. Roger Fry, to whom she had remained close, died in 1934, and in 1937 her son Julian was killed in the Spanish Civil War. Then in 1941 her famous but emotionally fragile sister Virginia ended her own life. Vanessa Bell's legacy remains her paintings, whose vivid, impressionistic explorations of color and profound sense of geometric design have contributed immeasurably to the evolution from post-Impressionism to Modernism.

Vanessa Bell

Oscar winner Elizabeth Taylor in *Butterfield 8.*

Montgomery, Alabama, USA, May: White pro-segregation residents attack the "Freedom Riders," a multiracial group touring the southern states.

Stüttgart, Germany, July 19: African-American Wilma Rudolph sets a new world record for the 100-meter dash.

Berlin, Germany, August 13: East German troops begin erecting a wall to divide East from West Berlin.

Ndola, Rhodesia, September 18: UN Secretary-General Dag Hammer- skjold dies in a plane crash in suspicious circumstances.

Zurich, Switzerland, September 27: US poet H.D., aka Hilda Doolittle, dies, aged 75.

New York, USA, October 14: *The Prime of Miss Jean Brodie*, by Muriel Spark, appears in *The New Yorker* magazine.

New York, USA, October 16: *Mastering the Art of French Cooking*, by Julia Child, Simone Beck, and Louisette Bertholle, is published.

Novaya Zemlya, USSR, October 30: Russia explodes the world's largest nuclear bomb, provoking worldwide condemnation. At 58 megatons, it is 4,000 times more powerful than the bomb dropped on Hiroshima in 1945.

USA, November 1: An estimated 50,000 women across the USA stage a strike for peace, imploring governments to "End the arms race, not the human race."

Saigon, South Vietnam, December 11: Following President Kennedy's pledge to increase military aid to South Vietnam, 400 US troops land in Saigon.

USA, December 13: US folk artist Grandma Moses dies, aged 101.

USA, December 14: President Kennedy establishes the President's Commission on the Status of Women.

Albuquerque, New Mexico, USA: Thirteen women pass the same rigorous tests as the "Mercury 7" men passed to become astronauts.

USA: *Academic Women* by Professor Jessie Barnard published.

New Zealand: *Faces in the Water* by Janet Frame published.

USA: *New Mathematical Library*, a series edited by Anneli Cahn Lax, commences.

New York, USA: *Shadows on the Grass*, a memoir by Isak Dinesen, is published by Random House.

USA: *Witch Doctor's Apprentice* by Nicole Hughes Maxwell, an account of the author's time in the Amazon jungle studying medicinal plants, is published.

Harper Lee Wins Pulitzer Prize with Debut Novel

Harper Lee

Columbia University, New York, USA, May 1: Author Nelle Harper Lee has won the Pulitzer Prize for fiction for her debut novel, *To Kill a Mockingbird*. Already a great popular success, the book tells a harrowing but ultimately uplifting story in which purity and innocence, and simple goodness, rise above the racial prejudices, ingrained bigotry, and injustices present in American society.

Set in the fictional town of Maycomb, Alabama in the 1930s, the book covers three years in the life of its narrator, Jean Louise "Scout" Finch, who lives with her older brother Jem and their widowed father Atticus. Atticus Finch is asked to defend an African-American accused of raping a white woman. His impassioned defense of the accused, Tom Robinson, makes him a focal point for the town's fear and mistrust of African-Americans. But this only strengthens his own moral convictions and highlights his efforts to pass those convictions on to his children.

A second plot line tells the story of Scout and Jem's fascination with a local recluse, Boo Radley, whom the father of Robinson's accuser attempts to kill on Halloween. Their growing friendship with Radley reveals that he, like Tom Robinson, is an innocent, simple man misunderstood and shunned by his community. Black Tom Robinson and white Boo Radley are symbolic of the "mockingbird" in the book's title, which is taken from the saying, "It is a sin to kill

"GIVE ME A GIRL AT AN IMPRESSION-ABLE AGE, AND SHE IS MINE FOR LIFE."

MURIEL SPARK,
THE PRIME OF MISS JEAN BRODIE

a mockingbird." In the southern states the mockingbird is seen as a creature with purity of heart and a selfless character.

Harper Lee was born in Monroeville, Alabama, in 1926, and studied law at the University of Alabama. Fortunately for the literary world, however, she had a change of heart. Just six months before completing her studies she traveled to New York to pursue a literary career, and in 1959 she accompanied Truman Capote to Kansas as a research assistant on a so-called non-fiction novel Capote is writing on the murder of a Kansas farming family, with the working title, *In Cold Blood*.

During the 1950s Lee wrote several essays and short stories, and it was one of these that her agent encouraged her to develop into a novel. Lee quit her job as an airline reservations clerk and in 1957 submitted a manuscript to the J. B. Lippincott Company.

Despite their initial criticism that the work was too episodic, they encouraged her to do a rewrite, and with the help of one of Lippincott's editors, *To Kill a Mockingbird* was finally released in 1960.

Harper Lee is the first woman to win the Pulitzer Prize since 1942. The novel has won praise from readers and critics alike, and to date has sold a staggering 500,000 copies and has been translated into ten languages.

"The Black Gazelle" Sets a New World Record

Stüttgart, Germany, July 19: The French call her *La Perle Noire*, the Black Pearl, and the Italians know her as *La Gazella Nera*, the Black Gazelle. In Stüttgart today, these superlatives and others are being bestowed upon the great African-American track and field star Wilma Rudolph, who ran a world record time of 11.2 seconds in the 100 meters to become the fastest woman in history.

When this extraordinary African-American, now confirmed as the world's premier female track and field athlete, was born prematurely, the twentieth of 22 children on June 23, 1940 in Clarksville, the prospects of her one day becoming the darling of a US Olympic team seemed an improbable dream. As a child, Wilma suffered many illnesses, including scarlet fever, measles, and double pneumonia. Unable to be treated in Clarksville's whites-only hospital, she was nurtured throughout her childhood by her mother Blanche. When it became apparent that Wilma's left leg and foot were partially deformed her mother drove her to a black medical college on the grounds of Nashville's Fisk University where she was diagnosed as having polio and fitted with leg braces.

American Wilma Rudolph, fastest woman in the world.

With her family providing all the necessary physical therapy, Blanche Rudolph drove the 100-mile (161 km) round trip to Nashville twice a week for two years until, at age 12, her daughter was finally able to walk unaided. She still had to wear corrective shoes, but in high school she began taking them off to play basketball barefoot with her siblings and friends, and eventually she stopped wearing them altogether.

Wilma also joined the basketball team, and soon began setting state records for highest score. Nicknamed "Skeeter" by her coach, she led her junior high school team to a state championship, and though she was known at school for sleeping a lot—and when she wasn't sleeping, reading in bed—Wilma nevertheless found time to excel in track and field events. In fact, she was so outstanding that she eventually won a place on the US Olympic team.

At the age of 16 she won a bronze medal in the 4×100 meters relay at the 1956 Melbourne Olympics, and at the 1960 Rome Olympics she became the first female in the United States to win three gold medals, winning the 100 meters, 200 meters, and the 4×100 meters relay, running the anchor leg. In 1960 and again this year she has been voted the Associated Press's Female Athlete of the Year.

Wilma Rudolph's persistent triumphs over societal and physical adversity have made her an inspiration to all Americans, regardless of color.

US folk artist Grandma Moses dies, aged 101.

Author Muriel Spark wins high praise from the critics.

Author Hailed as Virtuoso

New York, USA, October 14: Today's issue of *The New Yorker* magazine has been entirely given over to a new novel, *The Prime of Miss Jean Brodie*, by Scottish author Muriel Spark. The magazine's reviewer, John Updike, describes Spark as one of the few writers on either side of the Atlantic with the daring and resources to alter the world of fiction and put the reader in touch with the "happiness of creation," while the academic Frank Kermode has praised Spark as a remarkable virtuoso, herself in her prime.

Set in the strictly conservative Marcia Blaine School for Girls in Edinburgh, Scotland, the book tells the story of Jean Brodie, an outspoken, feminist teacher able to elicit unquestioning devotion from her female students, and who considers herself to be above criticism from her faculty colleagues. Her students, known as the Brodie set, soon find themselves increasingly isolated from other students as they become enmeshed in their teacher's self-indulgent world of intrigue and mystery, with fatal consequences.

Muriel Spark was born in Edinburgh in 1918. In 1930, aged 12, she received the prestigious Walter Scott prize for a poem entitled "Out of a Book." Her years at Edinburgh's strict James Gillespie's School for Girls undoubtedly provided her with much of the material she needed to re-create the fictional world of rigid conformity against which Miss Jean Brodie so passionately rebels.

American Women Rally Against Nuclear Threat

USA, November 1: An estimated 50,000 woman in 60 cities across the United States, fearful of the possible effects of nuclear proliferation on the short- and long-term health of their children, have staged an inaugural Women Strike For Peace (WSP) rally.

Marching beneath banners bearing slogans such as "End the arms race—not the human race," and "Let's live in peace, not pieces," the women are calling for nuclear disarmament and an end to the stockpiling of weapons.

The day-long protest also hopes to highlight the dangers of high levels of irradiation in milk, and to draw public attention to the recent increase in size and frequency of nuclear tests by the US and Soviet governments.

Today's protest began as a series of telephone calls between concerned housewives a mere six weeks ago. This fledgling group is rapidly becoming more structured and well organized, and is prepared to use its influence with consumers by, among other things, encouraging them to put letters in their milk bottles threatening to cancel their deliveries if the milk isn't decontaminated. The group is also asking women to send their children's baby teeth to their senators on Capitol Hill, with a request that they be measured for levels of strontium 90, an isotope present in radioactive fallout.

Young women are waging a literacy campaign in Cuba.

Female Astronauts on the Horizon

Albuquerque, New Mexico, USA: At a training base outside Albuquerque, known as the Lovelace Clinic, a group of 13 women, most of whom are professional pilots, have passed the same series of tests faced by the original "Mercury 7" astronauts.

Jan Dietrich, future woman astronaut?

The first woman invited to join the training program, which was devised by Doctor William Randolph Lovelace II, was Geraldyn Cobb, who performed so well in the tests that she was invited to help recruit more women to participate. Eventually 25 women ranging in age from 23 to 41 years underwent four days of rigorous testing. Thirteen have today been chosen for training at the National Aviation Centre in Pensacola, Florida.

Novel Reveals Dark Side of Psychiatric Institutions

New Zealand: New Zealand novelist, poet and short-story writer Janet Frame has published a new book, *Faces in the Water*. The book mixes fact with fiction, drawing on Frame's own experiences in mental asylums to create the book's central character, Estina Mavet.

Frame was diagnosed with schizophrenia at the age of 20 and spent eight years in various psychiatric institutions before the diagnosis was withdrawn. *Faces in the Water* is a compelling and damning indictment of institutional ill-treatment and demoralization of mental patients and society's failure to address the issue.

Janet Frame was born in Dunedin on New Zealand's South Island in 1924 and made her debut as a writer in 1951 with *The Lagoon*, a collection of short stories that won the Hubert Church Memorial Award. Her first novel, *Owls Do Cry*, was published in 1957.

Isak Dinesen

"School of the Air" Founder Dies

Sue Lyon

Woodville, South Australia, February 4:
Educationist and trade union official, Adelaide Laetitia Miethke, has died at her home, aged 80. Miethke was born on June 8, 1881 at Manoora in South Australia. She became a teacher and in 1915 founded the Women Teachers' League.

Her speech at the Women's Non-Party Political Association conference, arguing that "technically gifted girls should have a chance of developing their bent," made a positive impression and in 1916 she was appointed the first female vice-president of the South Australian Public School Teachers' Union.

In 1924 Miethke was provided with an opportunity to implement her theories about the education of girls when she was appointed inspector of schools. A number of "central schools" was established with an emphasis on vocational skills; mornings were devoted to academic subjects while the afternoons were spent learning practical skills considered useful for girls.

Miethke became South Australian state president of the National Council of Women in 1934, and national president in 1936. She was appointed an Officer of the Order of the British Empire in 1937.

> *"I DO NOT REGRET ONE PROFESSIONAL ENEMY I HAVE MADE. ANY ACTOR WHO DOESN'T DARE TO MAKE AN ENEMY SHOULD GET OUT OF THE BUSINESS."*
> — BETTE DAVIS, THE LONELY LIFE

Oscar winner Sophia Loren in *Two Women*.

In 1941 she retired as inspector of schools and as president of the National Council of Women. The following year she founded the Woodville District Child Welfare Association that established four new pre-schools, and in 1951 she established Adelaide Miethke House for country girls studying in Adelaide.

During World War II Miethke administered the South Australian Children's Patriotic Fund and directed its fundraising efforts. After the war she used the remaining money to fund the Royal Flying Doctor Service. In 1946, while traveling to Alice Springs with a doctor, she was struck by the isolation of children in the outback, so she devised and established the world's first School of the Air using radio communication between teachers and children on remote homesteads. The school began operating from Alice Springs on September 20, 1950, with the children using pedal-powered wireless sets.

The First Lady's televised tour involved nine tons of equipment and 54 technicians.

First Lady's Televised Tour of the White House a Hit

USA, February 15: Yesterday, three out of four television viewers in the United States watched "A Tour of the White House with Mrs John F. Kennedy." The program was so popular it will be shown again in a few days and will be broadcast around the world later in the year. Hundred of millions of people will see the tour, making it the most widely viewed television documentary of all time. At a time when women are expressing dissatisfaction with their limited domestic roles, Jacqueline Kennedy is a figure of fascination. She has toured the world with her husband and has been seen on television conversing with Soviet leader Nikita Khrushchev, chatting with French President de Gaulle in French, and delivering speeches in Latin America in Spanish.

time out

Helen Gurley Brown's *Sex and the Single Girl*, an immediate bestseller, encourages women to have a career, achieve financial independence, pursue the single life, and stop agonizing about their looks.

Key Events

Ranrahirca, Peru, January 11: Whole villages are destroyed and 4,000 people perish in a massive landslide of rocks and ice.
Paris, France, January 21: Director Nadine Marquand and actor Jean-Louis Trintignant announce the birth of their daughter, Marie Trintignant.
Woodville, South Australia, February 4: Activist, educationist, and trade union official Adelaide Laetitia Miethke dies.
USA, February 14: Jacqueline Kennedy leads a televised tour of the White House.

Argentina, February 25: Sister Maria Ludovica de Angelis, of the Buenos Aires Children's Hospital, dies, aged 81.
Garden City, Michigan, USA, March 1: A new discount department store called Kmart opens.
Algiers, Algeria, April 20: Head of the OAS, General Raoul Salan, is captured, ending the anti-colonial uprising in Algeria and France.
USA, April 29: In a paper for the American Medical Association, Dr Helen Glaser draws attention to the problem of adolescent glue-sniffing.

Athens, Greece, May 14: Princess Sophia of Greece weds Prince Don Juan Carlos of Spain.
Laos, May: US troops are deployed to fight the communist group Pathet Lao, which captured Nam Tha.
Kent, England, June 2: Poet and novelist Vita Sackville-West dies at the age of 70.
USA, June 13: The controversial movie, *Lolita*, is released in cinemas. Directed by Stanley Kubrick, the film stars James Mason and Sue Lyon in the lead roles.

New York, USA, June: Rachel Carson's *Silent Spring* is serialized in *The New Yorker*.
Algeria, July 3: Two days after the Algerian people vote in a referendum on independence, France's President de Gaulle severs 132 years of colonial ties.
Hollywood, USA, August 5: Marilyn Monroe is found dead, aged 36.
Jamaica, August 6: Jamaica becomes independent within the British Commonwealth; Alexander Bustamente of the Jamaica Labour Party is the first prime minister.

USA, August 7: The US Food and Drug Commissioner warns doctors that women may risk blood clots when taking the oral contraceptive, Searle's Enovid. In the past year, 28 women are known to have developed clots, and six of them have died.
New York, USA, August 15: The Netherlands signs the *New York Agreement*, ceding West New Guinea to Indonesia.

Soon after her husband became President, Mrs Kennedy launched a campaign to redecorate the White House. She chose the new furnishings and led fundraising efforts. When the project was nearing completion she agreed to conduct a televised tour of the residence.

The tour gives a fascinating insight into what is both the private home of her family and a public space close to the heart of all Americans. There was a real sense of intimacy as Jacqueline Kennedy described the decor and its significance in America's cultural heritage.

Toward the end of the program, President Kennedy appeared for a short interview during which he praised his wife's restoration efforts.

Princess Sophia Marries Heir to Spanish Throne

Athens, Greece, May 14: Princess Sophia has renounced her right to the throne of Greece and converted from Greek Orthodoxy to Roman Catholicism in order to marry Prince Don Juan Carlos, the heir to the throne of Spain.

Princess Sophia was born in Athens on November 2, 1938. Her family was exiled from Greece during World War II and she spent her early years living in London and Cairo. The family returned to Greece in 1946 and her father acceded to the throne a year later when her uncle, George II, died. Having attended school in Germany she undertook tertiary studies in Athens. She is reportedly fluent in at least five languages. She is also a keen sportswoman, and in 1960 represented Greece in sailing at the Olympics. Princess Sophia met Prince Juan Carlos during a cruise in the Mediterranean in 1954.

Princess Sophia weds Prince Don Juan Carlos of Spain.

Writer and Gardener Vita Sackville-West Dies

Kent, England, June 2: Vita Sackville-West, poet, novelist, and garden designer, died today, aged 70. Born into an aristocratic family in Kent in 1892, she married the journalist, Harold Nicholson, in 1913.

Sackville-West's best known works include the narrative poem, *The Land*, which won the Hawthornden Prize in 1927, and *Collected Poems*, which was awarded the same honor in 1933. She is the only writer to have won the Hawthornden Prize twice. Of her novels the two most highly regarded are *The Edwardians* (1930) and *All Passion Spent* (1931). In 1946 she was made a Companion of Honour for services to literature.

She was also famous for her unconventional lifestyle and numerous affairs. She began an affair with another writer, Violet Trefusis, when both girls were still in their teens. Even after both women married, they still took regular holidays together in Paris where Vita dressed as a man when they went out in public. They wrote a novel together, *Challenge*, whose male protagonist, Julian, had the same name Vita used when disguised as a man.

During the 1920s Sackville-West began an affair with Virginia Woolf, whose novel *Orlando* was inspired by their relationship.

In 1947 she started writing a weekly gardening column for the *Observer*. She also designed the most visited gardens in England, at Sissinghurst Castle.

Vita Sackville-West

Hazards of DDT Exposed

New York, USA, June: A book written by marine biologist Rachel Carson, exposing the hazards of pesticides, has been serialized in *The New Yorker*.

Underlying Rachel Carson's book is a love of nature.

The book, *Silent Spring*, traces the effects of pesticides through the food chain. Carson argues that DDT does not just kill insects; it is also toxic to humans and other animals.

Rachel Carson was born on a small farm in Pennsylvania in 1907. Despite growing up in poverty she had a brilliant academic record and became one of the first women ever to be hired by the US Government as a marine biologist. She has been concerned about the profligate use of pesticides since the 1940s.

Berlin, Germany, August 17: Eighteen-year-old East German Peter Fechter is the first person to be shot and killed while attempting to cross the Berlin Wall to the West.

Phoenix, Arizona, USA, August 26: Sherri Finkbine's Swedish abortion ignites a storm of controversy.

Rungstedlund, Denmark, September 7: Writer Isak Dinesen dies, aged 77.

Könnersreuth, Germany, September 18: Mystic Therese Neumann dies.

Oxford, Mississippi, USA, October 1: Three die and 50 are injured as riots beak out at the University of Mississippi after the first African-American is admitted as a student.

Vatican City, October 11: Pope John XXIII convenes the first session of the second Vatican Council.

India, October 26: Indian and Chinese troops engage in heavy fighting over the disputed border region of Arunachal Pradesh.

Cuba, October 28: Seven days of escalating tension bring the world to the brink of nuclear confrontation before the USA and USSR reach a compromise.

New York City, USA, November 7: Former first lady and United Nations delegate Eleanor Roosevelt dies, aged 78.

Netherlands, November 28: Former Queen of the Netherlands, Wilhelmina, dies, aged 82.

Massawa, Eritrea (Ethiopia), December 19: A group of police desert the Ethiopian force to join the Eritrean Liberation Front, formed in 1961 in response to Ethiopia's UN-sanctioned annexation of the strategically important nation.

England: The Pre-school Playgroups Association is founded.

California, USA: Dolores Huerta helps to unionize the state's farm workers, reputedly among the most exploited in the United States.

New York City, USA: The first international conference on intra-uterine devices is held.

Strasbourg, France: Marguerite Perey is admitted to the Académie des Sciences.

London, England: *The Golden Notebook*, an experimental feminist novel by Doris Lessing, is published.

USA: *Sex and the Single Girl* by Helen Gurley Brown is published.

USA: *Capitalism and Freedom* by Milton Friedman, a landmark book on economic thinking, is published.

Marilyn Monroe

Marilyn Monroe Found Dead

Hollywood, USA, August 5: Troubled actress and sex symbol Marilyn Monroe, 36, has been found dead at her home.

The star's housekeeper, Eunice Murray, became concerned when she arrived for work this morning and found the house locked. She called a doctor who broke into the bedroom where he discovered Miss Monroe's body lying naked on the bed with an empty bottle of sleeping pills nearby. The coroner says that the circumstances indicate suicide.

Miss Monroe's behavior had become increasingly erratic in recent months. She was fired by Fox Productions two months ago for her repeated absences from the set of the film *Something's Got to Give.* She conducted a lengthy interview with *Life,* in which she expressed bitterness at being labeled a dumb blonde and said how much she loved her audience.

Marilyn Monroe was born Norma Jeane Mortenson on June 1, 1926. She appeared in 30 films in a career lasting over 15 years, including *Some Like it Hot,* for which she won a Golden Globe for Best Actress in a Comedy. Her last major public appearance was when she sang "Happy Birthday, Mr President," at a televised birthday party for President John F. Kennedy in May this year.

"IF I HAD TO LIVE MY LIFE AGAIN, I'D MAKE THE SAME MISTAKES, ONLY SOONER."

TALLULAH BANKHEAD (1903–1968), AMERICAN ACTRESS

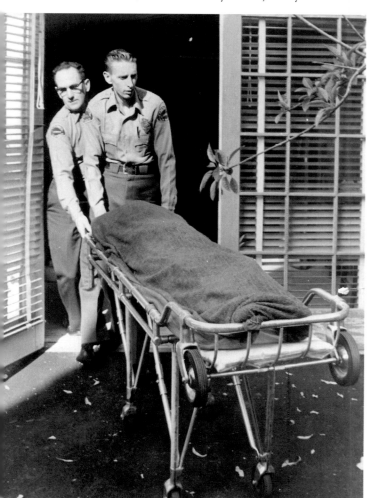

Marilyn Monroe's death will sadden millions.

TV presenter Sherri Finkbine with her daughter Lucy.

TV Presenter Causes Storm Over Abortion

Phoenix, Arizona, USA, August 26: Sherri Finkbine, an actress and children's television presenter, has returned to the USA after having an abortion in Sweden. She decided to abort her fifth child after taking the drug thalidomide for morning sickness during the first few weeks of her pregnancy. Finkbine's doctor advised her that there is growing evidence that thalidomide is responsible for severe fetal deformities and recommended that she have an abortion.

The abortion was scheduled to take place at a Phoenix hospital a few days later. While she was waiting, Mrs Finkbine told her story to a reporter from a local paper, as a warning to other women about the dangers involved in taking thalidomide. Publication of the story was met with a storm of controversy. The hospital, fearing criminal liability, reversed its position and the procedure was abruptly canceled.

Mrs Finkbine and her husband took the case to the Arizona State Supreme Court but their appeal was dismissed.

There was increasing public pressure on the couple from various sources not to terminate the pregnancy but Mrs Finkbine was resolute, saying that she didn't want to have to look after a disabled child, possibly without arms or legs, in addition to the four children she already has to care for.

Eventually she traveled to Sweden where the procedure was performed. It has been reported that the fetus had no legs and only one arm. Mrs Finkbine's supporters say that this justifies her decision not to proceed with the pregnancy. As a result of the controversy, she has been fired from her job.

Death of German Mystic Therese Neumann

Konnersreuth, Germany, September 18: The German mystic, Therese Neumann, has died after suffering a cardiac arrest.

Therese Neumann was born into a poor but very devout Catholic family in Bavaria on Good Friday in 1898, the first of 11 children. During World War I her father gave her a picture of Therese of Lisieux and Neumann began to pray for her beatification.

In 1918, while fighting a fire on her father's farm, she injured her back and over the next few days had several falls resulting in blindness and partial paralysis. She was confined to bed for an extended time and developed terrible bedsores. But she continued to venerate Therese of Lisieux and on April 29, 1923, the day Therese of Lisieux was beatified, Neumann's sight was restored. Two years later, when Therese of Lisieux was finally canonized, Neumann was cured of her paralysis and bedsores.

On the first Friday of Lent in 1926 Neumann had a vision of Jesus in the Garden of Gethsemane. Soon afterward she developed a wound slightly above her heart that trickled blood. On the second Friday of Lent, she had another vision of Jesus. This time he was being crowned with thorns. Over the rest of Lent she experienced the entire passion of Christ through her visions. Terrible agonies and wounds accompanied the visions, appearing on her body in places that corresponded with the wounds of Jesus (stigmata). Neumann continued to have these visions and suffer the stigmata for the rest of her life.

Neumann claimed that since the 1920s she had abstained from food and drink apart from the consecrated wafer (the Holy Eucharist) taken daily at mass.

Single Girls Are Sexy

USA: A guidebook for single women who want to pursue a "rich, full life of dating," as well as having a career and financial independence, has been published. The author, Helen Gurley Brown, assures the single woman that she is "the newest glamour girl of our times" and admonishes her to "work with the raw material you have, namely you, and never let up."

The book, *Sex and the Single Girl,* has been causing some controversy due to its underlying message that sex is an important and natural part of a single woman's life. It is seen as contributing to what is being called the "sexual revolution."

The book is understood to be semi-autobiographical. Helen Gurley was born to a poor family in rural Arkansas in 1922.

Author Helen Gurley Brown surrounded by some of the men involved in her novel, *Sex and the Single Girl*.

Woman Admitted to Académie des Sciences

Strasbourg, France: Marguerite Perey, best known for discovering and isolating the 87th element in the Periodic Table, francium, has been admitted to the French Académie des Sciences. She is the first woman to become a member.

Marguerite Perey was born in 1909 in Villemomble, France. As a teenager she was interested in becoming a doctor but her father's death left the family without the necessary resources, so she studied physics instead. In 1929 she accepted a three-month job at the Institut du Radium, as an assistant to Marie Curie, but stayed on after the job expired and the two women became firm friends. When Curie died in 1934, Perey vowed to continue her mentor's research.

In 1939 she discovered the radioactive element she named francium in honor of her country. The following year, she accepted a position at the Centre National de la Recherche Scientifique. In 1949 she became professor of nuclear physics at the University of Strasbourg, where she founded what later became the Centre de Recherches Nucléaires.

Perey has unfortunately been diagnosed with cancer. Her illness will prevent her from attending the admission ceremony.

Dolores Huerta

Her sister was paralyzed by polio and her father died in an elevator accident when she was 10 years old.

She began work at the age of 18 and had nearly 20 secretarial jobs before an astute employer gave her a job in the copywriting department. From there her career took off and in 1938 she accepted a job with the Los Angeles firm Kenyan & Eckhardt that made her one of the highest paid professionals in her field. In 1959 she married David Brown, vice president of 20th Century Fox.

Dolores Huerta Backs Farm Workers Association

California, USA: Dolores Huerta has joined union leader Cesar Chavez to found the National Farm Workers Association. She will attempt to unionize Latino farm workers so they can collectively bargain with their employers.

Doris Lessing's *The Golden Notebook*, an experimental feminist novel, is published.

Dolores Huerta was born Dolores Clara Fernandez on April 10, 1930 in New Mexico but moved to California with her mother Alicia and her two brothers after her parents' divorce. They settled in the agricultural region of the San Joaquin Valley. Her mother initially worked two jobs as a cook to support the family, but eventually became the owner of two hotels and a restaurant. Dolores and her siblings grew up in one of them. Farm workers and their families often stayed at the hotels for free.

Dolores experienced racism as a teenager. On the night of VJ Day (Victory over Japan), August 15, 1945, her brother was viciously beaten in a racist attack.

She attended school in Stockton before becoming the first member of her family to receive a higher education and be awarded a teacher's certificate.

Recognizing the needs of farm workers, she left her job as a teacher to found the Agricultural Workers Association in 1960. Of her decision to quit her teaching job she later said, "I quit because I couldn't stand seeing kids come to class hungry and needing shoes. I thought I could do more by organizing farm workers than by trying to teach their hungry children."

She is a tireless lobbyist and in 1961 she succeeded in obtaining the removal of citizenship requirements for pension entitlements, public assistance programs, and disability insurance.

Other successes have included the introduction of legislation allowing people the right to vote in Spanish and the right to take the driver's license examination in languages other than English. Now she has turned her attention to giving farm workers a collective voice and greater bargaining power.

Former first lady Eleanor Roosevelt dies, aged 78.

Poet Sylvia Plath Takes Own Life

Edith Hamilton

London, England, February 11: Troubled American poet, Sylvia Plath, was found dead after committing suicide in the kitchen of her Fitzroy Road apartment. Her two children were found unharmed.

Although widespread literary fame has not so far accompanied the publication of Plath's poetry, she did receive critical acclaim for her first published volume of poems, *The Colossus*, published in England in 1961. Reviewing the collection, the London *Times* said the "presences" in her poems were "most forcefully conjured up in brilliantly apt words, often with a lot of humor as well." Her poetry has been published in many magazines and journals in the USA and the UK, and she was rumored to have been working on an autobiographical novel and a new series of poems before she died.

Despite a stunning academic career at Smith College in Boston, then at Cambridge University, where she studied under a Fulbright Scholarship, Plath's psychological health had been precarious for some time. She had her first nervous breakdown while attending college in Boston, and periods of severe depression marked her life, informing profoundly the themes and imagery of her work.

Plath, 30, was married to well-known English poet Ted Hughes, the father of her two children. The couple separated last summer after six years of marriage.

" SHUT MY EYES AND ALL THE WORLD DROPS DEAD; I LIFT MY EYES AND ALL IS BORN AGAIN."

SYLVIA PLATH (1932–1963), AMERICAN POET.

An airplane crash claims the life of country music singer Patsy Cline–seen here with fellow country singers.

Chien-Shiung Wu, hailed as "Queen of Physics" for her work in experimental atomic physics.

Trailblazing Country Star Cline Dies in Plane Crash

Camden, Tennessee, USA, March 5: The singer credited with bringing country music to the mainstream, Patsy Cline, died this evening in an airplane crash in Tennessee at the age of thirty-one.

Country stars Hawkshaw Hawkins and Cowboy Copas, as well as Cline's manager Randy Hughes, were also killed in the crash. Cline achieved her breakthrough success in 1957, when her song "Walkin' After Midnight" almost made it to the top of the US country music charts. She became a regular on the radio show, *Grand Ole Opry*, and two more hits—"Falling to Pieces" and "Crazy"—followed in 1961. In the last two years she has had a string of top-ten hits, gaining success on the pop music charts as well as the country music scene.

The Feminine Mystique into Fourth Printing

New York, USA, April: A new book published last month lifts the lid on the unhappiness and dissatisfaction of American wives and mothers. According to the *Los Angeles Times*, Betty Friedan's *The Feminine Mystique* "will cause at least an uproar and possibly a revolution." The book was born when Friedan—journalist, writer, wife, and mother—interviewed female college graduates for a magazine article in 1957. She discovered that even these most educated women saw themselves primarily

Congo, January 15: Secessionist leader of breakaway Katanga province, Moise Tshombe, is forced to reunite with the Congo under intense pressure from the UN and other African states.
Paris, France, January 29: President de Gaulle vetoes Britain's entry into the European Economic Community and is supported by Germany's Chancellor Adenauer.
London, England, February 11: Writer Sylvia Plath commits suicide, aged 30.

Paris, France, February 15: A plot is uncovered to assassinate President de Gaulle, one of numerous attempts on his life in the past year.
Tennessee, USA, March 5: An airplane crash claims the life of country music singer Patsy Cline.
Atlantic Ocean, April 10: The nuclear-powered submarine, USS *Thresher*, is lost off Cape Cod with 129 men on board.
New York, USA, May 6: Barbara Tuchman receives a Pulitzer Prize for *Guns of August*.

Jakarta, Indonesia, May 18: Sukarno, hero of the struggle against the Dutch in the 1940s, declares himself president for life.
USA, May 20: *Newsweek* magazine hails Chinese-American Chien-Shiung Wu as "Queen of Physics."
Washington DC, USA, May 31: Author Edith Hamilton dies, aged ninety-six.
London, England, June 3: Christine Keeler's affair with Secretary of State for War, John Profumo, leads to his resignation after he admits misleading Parliament.

Washington, DC, USA, June 10: The *Equal Pay Act* is passed by Congress.
USSR, June 16: Valentina Tereshkova becomes the first woman in space.
USA, June 17: The Supreme Court rules that the Lord's Prayer and bible recitation should be banned from public schools, after a challenge by Madelyn Murray.
Berlin, Germany, June 26: West Berliners gather to hear US President Kennedy's speech denouncing Communism. "Ich bin ein Berliner," he states.

London, England, July 8: Australian Margaret Smith, 21, wins the Wimbledon singles title.
London, England, July 31: The *Peerage Act* permits female and Scottish peers to sit in the House of Lords.
Washington, DC, USA, August: Following her husband's suicide, Katharine Graham assumes presidency of the *Washington Post*.
Mexico: Madre Lupita, co-founder of the congregation of the Servants of St Margaret Mary and the Poor, dies, aged 85.

The Miracle Worker stars Anne Bancroft.

Minister Resigns Over Affair with Model

London, England, June 3: Creating a scandal that will shake British politics to its foundations, British Secretary of State for War, John Profumo, today resigned from Parliament after admitting he had sexual relations with the now 21-year-old model, Christine Keeler—despite his assertion in March this year that there was "no impropriety whatsoever" in his "acquaintanceship" with Keeler. Keeler, who was 19 when she met Profumo, had an affair with the prominent Conservative politician in 1961, after also engaging in a sexual relationship with Russian diplomat, Yevgeny Ivanov.

Profumo's admission today was set in motion in March by Keeler's disappearance midway through a trial against another of her ex-lovers, John Edgecombe, who was charged with shooting at Keeler on December 14 last year. Keeler's disappearance prompted questions in the House of Commons about Profumo's possible role in the affair, which he vehemently denied any knowledge of at that time. Little is known about Keeler, or her reaction to today's events. Born in 1942, she left home at 16 for London, where she found work at a cabaret club and met Stephen Ward, an osteopath with wealthy connections. It was through Ward that Keeler met Profumo, and embarked on their brief but now significant liaison.

time out

Margaret Murray, one of Britain's own historic treasures has died at the age of 100 shortly after the publication of her autobiography, *My First Hundred Years.* Murray was an archeologist, anthropologist, and suffragette.

First Woman in Space

Moscow, USSR, June 17: "Russian blonde in space" proclaimed the *Chicago Tribune* today, as news came through from the USSR that the first woman to enter orbit around the Earth had made it through her first night in space. Twenty-six-year-old Soviet cosmonaut, Valentina Teresh-

kova, was launched as pilot of *Vostok VI* yesterday from the Tyuratam Space Station, and is expected to be in orbit for around three days.

Junior Lieutenant Tereshkova's first report from space, using her call sign "Seagull," confirmed that all was well: "I see the horizon. A light blue, a beautiful band. This is the Earth. How beautiful it is!" The Soviet public celebrated the news today, and Premier Nikita Khrushchev expressed pride that "a girl from the land of Soviet" had entered the record books as the first woman in space.

Vostok VI is one of two Soviet craft currently undertaking space missions; Vostok V, piloted by Lieutenant-Colonel Valery Bykovsky, was launched three days ago, and it is thought the two pilots may attempt a meeting while in orbit. Another goal of the mission is to assess the physical effects of space travel on women.

Tereshkova, a former factory worker, was inspired by the feats of Soviet cosmonaut, Yuri Gagarin. She took up parachuting in 1959, and two years later was accepted into space training. For the past 18 months Tereshkova has been working intensively towards her position as pilot of the Vostok VI.

Christine Keeler

in relation to their husbands and children—and it didn't make them happy. So she looked further into "the feminine mystique," which she believes dictates that "the highest value and the only commitment for women is the fulfillment of their own femininity." The logical end of this view, Friedan says, is "Occupation: Housewife", rather than a model of womanhood which allows women to be independent, creative, and personally fulfilled.

The book also includes a damning refutation of psychiatrist Sigmund Freud's view of women as "inferior, childish, helpless, with no possibility of happiness unless [they have] adjusted to being man's passive object."

The Feminine Mystique is certainly causing a stir, with letters to newspapers revealing both unreserved support and opposition to Friedan's ideas. W. W. Norton, the book's publisher, is already advertising its fourth printing, proclaiming it "The book that's causing all the talk," while *Life* magazine has predicted it will "provoke the daylights out of almost everyone who reads it."

Valentina Tereshkova becomes the first woman in space.

Cheddington, England, August 8: Approximately £2.6 million in cash and jewelry is seized in a daring train robbery.

Washington, DC, USA, August 28: Martin Luther King delivers his "I have a dream..." speech.

Neuilly, France, September 11: Painter Suzanne Duchamp dies, aged 74.

Aberdeen, San Diego, USA, September 14: The US's first surviving quintuplets are born to Mary Ann Fischer.

Birmingham, Alabama, USA, September 15: A bomb explodes in the Sixteenth Street Baptist Church, killing four black schoolgirls: Addie Collins, Denise McNair, Carol Robertson, and Cynthia Wesley.

Malaysia, September 16: Malaysia is formed by unifying Singapore, Malaya, North Borneo, and Sarawak.

Hollywood, USA, October 1: The extremely costly epic, *Cleopatra*, starring Richard Burton and Elizabeth Taylor, is a box-office dud, with audiences dismissing it as dull and overblown.

Paris, France, October 11: "The Little Sparrow," Edith Piaf, dies of cancer, aged 47.

Australia, November 1: Indigenous men and women are granted the right to vote in Australian elections.

Dallas, USA, November 22: President Kennedy is assassinated; Lyndon B. Johnson is sworn in as President less than two hours after the tragedy.

New York USA: Barbara Epstein and Robert Silver found the *New York Review of Books*.

South Vietnam, November: Madame Nhu, sister-in-law and spokeswoman for assassinated despotic leader, Ngo Dinh Diem, is refused the right to return to the country by the new military government.

Stockholm, Sweden, December 10: Maria Goeppert-Mayer wins the Nobel Prize for Physics jointly with Hans D. Jensen for "their discoveries concerning nuclear shell structure."

Boston, USA: Julia Childs' *The French Chef* airs for the first time on American television.

Detroit, Michigan, USA, December 14: The "Queen of Harlem Blues," Dinah Washington, dies, aged 39.

South Africa, December, 1963: Journalist and activist, Ruth First, departs for exile in England after 117 days in solitary confinement.

USA: Betty Friedan publishes *The Feminine Mystique*.

USA: Hannah Arendt's *Eichmann in Jerusalem: A Report on the Banality of Evil* is published.

Leeds, England: Pianist, Fanny Waterman, founds the Leeds International Pianoforte Competition.

Madalyn Murray Wins School Religion Case

Madre Lupita

Washington, USA, June 17: In a controversial decision bound to divide the USA, the US Supreme Court today ruled that the forced reading of the Lord's Prayer or any passages from the Bible is no longer allowed in American public schools at the start of each day. In an eight-to-one decision, the Court decided that requiring biblical texts to be read in public schools violated the US Constitution's First Amendment, which states that Congress cannot make laws decreeing the establishment of a religion.

The case came about after a campaign by the atheist, Madalyn Murray, who objected to the requirement by the Baltimore school board that public schools begin each day with Christian readings. The case went all the way to the Supreme Court, and its decision will now apply to other US states that enforce similar policies.

Murray, a psychiatric social worker who cares for her two children as a single parent, began her campaign after discovering in 1960 that her then 14-year-old son, William, was being teased by the other children at school for asking to be excused from the morning Bible readings. According to Murray, her son encouraged her to "stand up for [her] convictions." With the help of contributions from supporters all over the world, and while earning money by writing for various journals and publications, she took on the three-year case, which the decision today finally concluded.

"WHATEVER WOMEN DO THEY MUST DO TWICE AS WELL AS MEN TO BE THOUGHT HALF AS GOOD."

CHARLOTTE WHITTON
(1896–1975),
CANADIAN POLITICIAN.

The 20-year-old Australian Margaret Smith wins the Wimbledon singles title at her third attempt.

First Australian Wins Wimbledon Singles Title

London, England, July 8: Tennis ace, Margaret Smith, became the first Australian to win a Wimbledon women's singles title today when she defeated reigning title-holder, Billie Jean Moffitt.

In front of a center court crowd of 17,000 enthusiastic spectators, Smith triumphed over Moffitt in straight sets: 6-3, 6-4. Even a last-minute comeback by the young American champion couldn't stop the formidable 20-year-old Australian from winning the tournament in only 50 minutes.

Smith turned professional in 1961, and since then has won all the major women's singles titles in the world, including last year's Australian Open, French Open, and US Open singles titles. Later today she also won the mixed doubles event with partner Ken Fletcher, but failed to take out a third title when she and Robyn Ebbern lost the women's doubles final to Americans Maria Bueno and Darlene Hard.

Cancer Claims the "Little Sparrow"

Paris, France, October 11: Aged only 47, French singer Edith Piaf died in her Paris home this morning. Known worldwide for her unique voice and emotionally powerful renditions of songs like "Non, je ne regrette rien" ("No, I Do Not Regret Anything") and "La vie en rose" ("Life Through Rose-Colored Glasses"), Piaf's personal story has become almost as famous as her voice.

Edith Giovanna Gassion began her life in poverty, and in her early years traveled around France and Belgium with her father, an acrobat, as he tried to scrape a living by performing on the streets, and lived for a time in a brothel with her grandmother. She began singing while on the road with her father. She had a daughter in 1933, when she was just 18, but the child died within two years from meningitis. When Louis Leplée, the owner of the Paris club, Gurney's, discovered the young Piaf singing on the street in 1935, her fortunes took a turn for the better. Leplée recognized her talent, nicknaming her "La Mome Piaf" ("Kid Sparrow"), and taking her from the streets to the stage and then into the recording studio.

Despite her growing success, Piaf's life was never short of tumultuous events. Passionate affairs gone wrong, murdered lovers, drug use, and a series of physically debilitating car accidents dogged her successes from the 1940s and into the post-war period, when she finally made

Cleopatra, starring Richard Burton and Elizabeth Taylor.

Edith Piaf

her name with American audiences. In the 1950s she starred in films and plays, and continued recording her trademark songs of love and loss, but bouts of illness interrupted her performing career.

Despite a stunning comeback in 1960, resulting in the best-selling recording, *Live at the Olympia*, and her marriage to 27-year-old singer Théo Sarapo last year, her health continued to decline.

South Vietnam's "First Lady" in Exile After Coup

South Vietnam, November: The sister-in-law of the assassinated Vietnamese leader, Ngo Dinh Diem, Madame Nhu, has been refused permission to re-enter South Vietnam by the new military government. The former president Diem was killed on November 2 during a coup. Madame Nhu's husband, Ngo Dinh Nhu, was also killed during the coup, while Madame Nhu was touring the USA. The coup was initiated by a group of soldiers who opposed Diem's regime.

Although Diem's leadership had been gradually losing US backing during the last six months, Madame Nhu has continued in exile in the USA, and the new South Vietnamese government has since allowed her children to join her in Los Angeles. It is thought she will move with her family to Europe if she continues to be refused entry into her own country.

The "Queen of Harlem Blues," Dinah Washington.

Madame Nhu played a key role in the government of Diem after he became the first president of South Vietnam in 1955. Although her official position was as "hostess" for Diem—and unofficial "first lady" of South Vietnam—she has always been a very public figure, declaring her anti-American sentiments and her dislike of Buddhists openly, prompting her father, the Vietnamese ambassador to the USA, to publicly state earlier this year that his daughter showed "no respect."

Controversy over Madame Nhu's role in the anti-Buddhist violence in South Vietnam earlier this year has punctuated her tour of the USA. Demonstrations, picketing, and even egg- and rock-throwing have accompanied her public appearances; Buddhists and anti-Communists are both opposed to her outspoken views.

Nobel Prize for American Scientist

Stockholm, Sweden, December 10: For the first time since Marie Curie's success in 1903, the Nobel Prize for Physics has been awarded to a woman, Dr. Maria Goeppert-Mayer, for her work with Dr. Hans D. Jensen on the structure of the nuclear shell. The team shared their award with Eugene Paul Wigner, a quantum physicist, at today's ceremony in Stockholm, presided over by King Gustav VI Adolf of Sweden.

Goeppert-Mayer, 57, is a native of Germany who emigrated to the USA in the 1930s with her husband and fellow scientist Joseph Mayer. She found a position at an American university initially difficult to

come by, but during World War II was invited to join a secret team at Columbia University to develop fuel for an atomic bomb. Goeppert-Mayer felt personally conflicted about her work, and was relieved that she was not a part of the team that developed the bomb used in the Allied attacks on Japan.

After the war, Goeppert-Mayer took a position at the Argonne National Laboratory at the University of Chicago, and began to investigate the nature of the nuclei of various atoms. After publishing a paper on the subject in 1949, she started a collaboration with Hans Jensen, who had independently reached the same conclusion—that each nucleus had a "shell" of protons and neutrons circling it, and when certain "magic numbers" of these particles were present, an atom became more stable. Together they published a well-received book, and today's Nobel Prize comes more than ten years after their findings first appeared in print.

Goeppert-Mayer's initial reaction to the prize was disbelief. "Is it really true?" she said when she first heard the news. "Good, I've always wanted to meet a king," she added.

Anti-apartheid Activist Freed

South Africa, December: South African activist and journalist, Ruth First, was today released from 117 days in prison, after being arrested in August and charged under the notorious 90-Day Law in South Africa.

First, 38, is a member of the South African Communist Party and has campaigned publicly against South Africa's apartheid laws and government repression for over a decade, working alongside organizations such as the African National Congress (ANC) since the early 1950s. She has been involved in several left-wing and banned publications, but despite official suppression has managed to keep publishing anti-government articles and speeches by ANC members for the last decade.

Although not arrested in July this year with other prominent anti-government activists, including Nelson Mandela and Govan Mbeki, First was later imprisoned in August under the 90-Day Law, which allows the government's security forces to hold anyone suspected of treason in detention for 90 days without charge, without access to a lawyer, and in solitary confinement. It is thought that she will relocate to England with her family in the near future to avoid persecution in her home country, and to continue her political work.

LIFE

McNAMARA'S MISSION; MME. NHU ON THE ROAD

VIETNAM CLIMAX

The 117-Day Zero-Calorie Diet

OCTOBER 11 · 1963 · 25¢

The new military government of South Vietnam refuses to allow Madame Nhu to return.

Fannie Lou Hamer

Hamer the Heroine

Atlantic City, New Jersey, USA, August 22: Civil rights leader, Fannie Lou Hamer has today co-founded the Mississippi Freedom Democratic Party (MFDP). Hamer challenged the all-white Mississippi delegation at the Democratic National Convention because she believed the delegation did not accurately represent all Mississippians. She was a strong speaker and her speech in front of the Credentials Committee was televised, reaching a large audience across America.

Hamer passionately explained what happened to African-Americans who wanted to exercise their right to vote and how they were intimidated. She spoke from first-hand experience. On June 3, 1963 Hamer, who worked for the Southern Christian Leadership Conference and the Student Nonviolent Coordinating Committee, was taken to Montgomery County Jail. She said: "Three white men came into my room. One was a state highway policeman…they made me lay down on my face and they ordered two Negro prisoners to beat me with a blackjack. That was unbearable. The first prisoner beat me until he was exhausted, then the second Negro began to beat me. I had polio when I was about six years old. I was limp. I was holding my hands behind me to protect my weak side. I began to work my feet. My dress pulled up and I tried to smooth it down. One of the policemen walked over and raised my dress as high as he could. They beat me until my body was hard, 'til I couldn't bend my fingers or get up when they told me to. That's how I got this blood clot in my eye—the sight's nearly gone now. My kidney was injured from the blows they gave me on the back."

Her brave action to get up and speak after such terrifying intimidation led to the Democrats making a decision that no future delegation would be seated if their state denied voting rights to its citizens.

A Life of Laughter

Hollywood, USA Aug 27: Comedian Gracie Allen has died of a heart attack. Allen, who played the daffy partner to her husband George Burns's straight man on *The George Burns and Gracie Allen Show,* had a long and successful career in vaudeville, radio, television, and film.

There is some disagreement as to when Allen was born, with estimates ranging from 1895 to 1906. Her husband claimed he himself did not know how old she was. Allen said her birth certificate was destroyed by the earthquake and great fire of San Francisco in 1906.

"I SINCERELY DOUBT THAT ANY OPEN-MINDED PERSON REALLY BELIEVES IN THE FAULTY NOTION THAT WOMEN HAVE NO INTELLEC-TUAL CAPAC-ITY FOR SCIENCE AND TECHNOLOGY."

CHIEN-SHIUNG WU (1912–1997), PHYSICIST, SPEAKING AT A 1964 CONFERENCE ON WOMEN AND SCIENCE

Her career started early in 1909, when she began performing with her sister in a vaudeville act. She started performing with Burns in 1922 touring the vaudeville circuit. In 1926 she entered into a controversial marriage with Burns. Despite their different religions—Burns was Jewish and Allen, Catholic—they were married for over 38 years.

On October 12, 1950, the couple's show premiered on television, employing a similar format to their radio show. The show played for eight seasons and ended on September 22, 1958, when, due to ill health, Allen retired. In that time she was nominated six times for an Emmy as best actress and comedian.

Allen's character was very popular and she is remembered as an excellent comedic actress.

Women Victorious at Tokyo Olympics

Tokyo, October 24: At the closing ceremony, we consider the contribution of women to international sport in these games.

Mary Rand has become the first British woman to win a gold medal in Olympic competition. Rand won the medal for the long jump with a jump of about 22 ft (6.76 m). It was a successful Olympics for Rand who also won silver in the pentathlon and bronze as a member of the British team in the 4 x 100-meter relay. Speaking before the games, Rand said: "What I would love to do at the Olympics would be to win with a world record."

When Rand competed in Rome in 1960 as Mary Bignal, she was ranked as the favorite, but Rand ran through the long

Comedian Gracie Allen dies, aged 71.

jump twice, leaving her in ninth place. So it was not without some apprehension that she competed and won in Tokyo.

A new sport was introduced in the Tokyo Olympics, volleyball. Although volleyball began in the United States, the women's competition was won here by the home team of Japan.

In swimming, Australian Dawn Fraser won her third successive gold medal for the 100-meter freestyle. Born on September 4, 1937 in Balmain, New South Wales,

At the Tokyo Olympics, Dawn Fraser wins her third successive gold medal for the 100-meter freestyle.

Charlotte, Grand Duchess of Luxembourg, abdicates in favor of her son Jean.

Dame Edith Sitwell

she is a popular icon in her home country. A legend in the pool, she has won eight Olympic medals and eight Commonwealth medals over the course of her outstanding career.

Fraser began her swimming career when she was 16 years old. Only three years later, in 1956, she was competing in the Melbourne Olympic Games. It was here that she won her first Olympic Gold for the 100-meters freestyle. When she entered this same event at the 1960 Rome Olympics, she claimed victory a second time. Winning this event in Tokyo four years later has made her the first female athlete in history to win the same event three years in a row.

Grand Duchess Abdicates

Luxembourg, November 12: Charlotte, Grand Duchess of Luxembourg, has abdicated in favor of her son, Jean. This abdication was a natural progression after several decades of rule.

Forty-five years earlier, Charlotte's sister, Grand Duchess Marie-Adelaide, abdicated because she was considered to be too interested in the political affairs of Luxembourg. When Charlotte took over her position, she assured her government and the nation in her accessional speech that she would remain above political affairs, a policy that has clearly endeared her to her people.

The Grand Duchess, married to Prince Felix of Bourbon-Parma, had six children: Prince Jean (1921), Princess Elizabeth (1922), Princess Marie-Adelaide (1924),

Princess Marie-Gabrielle (1925), Prince Charles (1927) and Princess Alix (1929).

When World War II began, the Grand Duchess was forced to go into exile rather than be captured by the German Army, which invaded the Grand Duchy on May 10, 1940. Although Charlotte and her family spent some time in the United States, she settled in London and soon became the focus of hope for the people of occupied Luxemburg by sending regular radio broadcasts on the BBC.

It wasn't until the end of the war on April 14, 1945 that the Grand Duchess was able to return home to her people. She was given a wonderful welcome.

Poet's Passing

England, December 9: Poet Dame Edith Sitwell has died of a cerebral hemorrhage. Sitwell's earliest literary influence was her governess, Helen Rootham, also an aspiring poet. She did not get on well with her father, Sir George Sitwell, or her mother, Lady Ida Emily Augusta Denison. Sitwell said: "My parents were strangers to me from the moment of my birth."

Sitwell left home to live in London with Helen Rootham, a life-long companion, in 1913. It was here that she started her literary career and she also began to publish poetry. Her first volume, *The Mother and Other Poems*, came out in 1915. She also started an avant-garde literary anthology named *Wheels*.

In 1923, she gave her first public performance of a series of abstract poems, *Façade*, which she recited behind a screen

through a megaphone accompanied by music. Her audience received this very unusual performance with bemusement and great interest.

Sitwell never married, though it is believed that she became emotionally attached to a homosexual painter, Pavel Tchelitchew. In 1932, Sitwell moved to Paris with Rootham, who had contracted cancer, and stayed there until Rootham passed away in 1938.

Sitwell wrote several successful books. Two were about Queen Elizabeth I of England: *Fanfare for Elizabeth* (1946) and *Queen of the Hive* (1962).

She will be remembered as an intriguing woman who was not afraid to explore different media for her art.

Woman Wins Nobel Prize for Chemistry

Stockholm, Sweden, December 10: Dorothy Crowfoot Hodgkin has been awarded the Nobel Prize for Chemistry for her research on the structure of vitamin B-12. Only two other women have previously won the Nobel Prize for Chemistry: Madame Curie and Irene Joliet-Curie. Hodgkin was born on May 12, 1910. By the age of 10, she was already interested in chemistry. She studied at both Oxford and Cambridge, obtaining her doctorate from Cambridge University in 1937. Using X-ray analysis, she played a major role in determining the structure of penicillin and vitamin B-12. She paved the way for work decoding the structures of proteins.

Dorothy Crowfoot Hodgkin wins Nobel Prize.

Dawn Fraser Named Australian of the Year

Dawn Fraser

> "BEING A WOMAN HAS ONLY BOTHERED ME IN CLIMBING TREES."
>
> FRANCES PERKINS (1882–1965), US CABINET MINISTER AND FEMINIST

Canberra, Australia, January 15: Champion sprint swimmer Dawn Fraser is named Australian of the Year for 1964, a year which saw her claim gold in the 100-meters freestyle at Tokyo to become the only competitor in her sport to win the same event in three consecutive Olympic Games. The historic Tokyo victory came despite a car accident earlier in the year that killed her mother and left the swimmer battling serious neck and spine injuries. Born in the Sydney suburb of Balmain on September 4, 1937, Fraser was discovered at an early age by swimming coach, Harry Gallagher, who offered to train her for free. In 1956, she qualified for the Olympic Games in Melbourne, where she won a gold medal in the 100-meters freestyle, setting a new world and Olympic record, and a gold medal in the 4 x 100-meters freestyle relay. At the 1960 Rome Olympics, she again dominated the 100-meters freestyle and took silver in the 100-meters freestyle and medley relays.

Two years later, she earned further accolades when she became the first woman to break the 1-minute barrier for the 100-meters freestyle. Over the course of her outstanding swimming career, Fraser has also collected eight medals from the Commonwealth Games and 39 world records, 27 of them individual. In addition, she currently holds the record for the most Olympic medals won by an Australian. Her greatest handicap to date has been her naturally rebellious spirit, which has frequently led her into conflict with officialdom. Assorted indiscretions saw her fall foul of authorities at the 1960 Rome Games, and her troubles escalated in Tokyo last year amid allegations that she climbed a flagpole in Emperor Hirohito's palace and took an Olympic flag.

time out

Forty-year-old Viola Liuzzo, a leading white civil rights leader, is shot to death in her moving car in April by a Ku Klux Klansman in a car traveling beside hers. Her black co-driver, Leroy Moton, is also shot but survives.

Dawn Fraser wins the gold medal in the 100 meters.

Cosmetics manufacturer Helena Rubinstein.

Cosmetics Queen Finally Retires

New York, USA, April 1: Helena Rubinstein, pioneering cosmetics manufacturer, patron of the arts, philanthropist, and avid collector, has passed away today at the age of ninety-four. Energetic to the end, the Polish-born businesswoman never stopped working, even when her health was failing.

At 20, two years after her arrival in Australia from Poland, Rubinstein opened a modest shop in Melbourne from which she dispensed a single product, her Crème Valaze, at the same time offering individual instruction to women on how to care for their skin. As the business prospered, she expanded to London in 1902, Paris in 1906, and then to New York in 1912, eventually creating an international cosmetics empire that earned her a reputation as a major force in the world of business. Rubinstein also earned a reputation as a philanthropist and patron of the arts. Over the years, numerous artists painted her portrait and she accumulated an eclectic range of pieces including modern painting and sculpture, African sculpture, and Egyptian antiquities. In 1953, she established the Helena Rubinstein Foundation, which today provides funds to organizations connected to health, rehabilitation, and medical research. The foundation also offers generous support to the American Israel Cultural Foundation.

In 1959, Rubinstein officially represented the cosmetics industry in the United States at the American National Exhibition in Moscow. Last year, she published her memoirs in a book called *My Life for Beauty*.

Canberra, Australia, January 15: Champion swimmer, Dawn Fraser, is named Australian of the Year.
London, England, January 30: A state funeral is held for wartime leader, Sir Winston Churchill, who died six days ago, aged 91.
Canada, February 15: The red and white maple leaf flag is adopted.
New York, USA, February 21: Firebrand black nationalist leader, Malcolm X, is assassinated by two members of his former organization, the Nation of Islam.

New York City, March 2: The movie version of Rodgers & Hammerstein's Broadway hit, *The Sound of Music*, starring Julie Andrews, premieres at the Rivoli Theater.
USA, March 11: A collection of reviews by Pauline Kael, *I Lost It at the Movies*, is published by Little, Brown & Co.
New York, USA, March 25: The opera *Lizzie Borden* premieres.
Sri Lanka, March 27: The world's first elected woman prime minister, Sirimavo Bandaranaike, is voted out in favor of Dudley Senanayake.

Danang, South Vietnam, March 31: The first US troops are sent to Vietnam to protect the US air base at Danang. In February, American bombers began to pound Vietcong positions in the north.
New York, USA, April 1: Cosmetics manufacturer and entrepreneur, Helena Rubinstein, dies in her 90s.
Hollywood, USA, April 6: Julie Andrews wins the Best Actress Oscar for *Mary Poppins*.
Glenville, Illinois, USA, April 10: Actress Linda Darnell dies in a house fire, aged 47.

Canberra, Australia, April 29: Prime Minister Menzies commits 1,000 Australian troops to fight in South Vietnam.
New York City, USA, May 14: Politician Frances Perkins dies, aged 83.
Dominican Republic, May: The USA sends 14,000 troops to the Caribbean island after civil war breaks out in April following a coup.
USA, June 7: Use of contraceptives by married couples is finally legal in the state of Connecticut, after a landmark Supreme Court decision.

New York, USA, June 7: Film star Judy Holliday dies of breast cancer, aged 43.
Algeria, June 19: Independence hero and Prime Minister, Ahmed Ben Bella, is deposed in a bloodless coup led by Colonel Boumedienne.
Tokyo, Japan, June 22: Japan and South Korea sign a treaty of basic relations, normalizing relations for the first time since Japan annexed the Korean peninsula in 1910. Japan agrees to pay $800 million in compensation.

Politician Frances Perkins at the age of 83.

Frances Perkins Dies

New York, USA, May 14: Frances Perkins, the nation's first woman cabinet member, has died. An early feminist and committed advocate for working people, Perkins served as Secretary of Labor under President Franklin D. Roosevelt from 1933 to 1945, leading the fight against the Great Depression and playing a major role in formulating New Deal legislation. She also oversaw the abolition of child labor, and the enactment of minimum wage and maximum hour legislation.

Perkins finally resigned her position to head the United States delegation to the International Labour Organization Conference. When she returned to the US, she served on the Federal Civil Service Commission until her retirement in 1952, following which she continued an active life of teaching and public speaking. She also published two books: *People at Work* (1934) and *The Roosevelt I Knew* (1946).

The Shrimp in Hot Water

Melbourne, Australia, October 30: Melbourne's conservative establishment was scandalized today when British model, Jean Shrimpton, attended Derby Day wearing a sleeveless white dress with a hemline some 4 inches (10 cm) above the knee. Derby Day is a major fixture of Melbourne's famous Spring Racing Carnival, the social and fashion event of the year, and the 22-year-old model unwittingly caused further affront to Flemington Carnival conventions by failing to wear the customary hat, gloves, and stockings.

The highest paid model in the world, Shrimpton gained international fame as the original face of Yardley cosmetics. She has appeared on countless fashion magazine covers and was named Model of the Year by *Glamour* in 1963. Known as "The Shrimp," a nickname she hates, and billed as the most beautiful girl on earth, she is currently on a two-week promotional visit to Australia, sponsored by a local synthetic fiber company and the Victorian Racing Club.

Amid today's furor, speculation is now rife about Shrimpton's scheduled appearance at the Melbourne Cup next week, when she will again present prizes for the "Fashion on the Field" contest. Meanwhile, the model herself, more attuned to the pulse of Swinging London, has expressed surprise at Melbourne's conformity to dress codes, particularly in blistering 94°F (34°C) heat. As for what she might wear to Australia's most famous racing event next week, a resigned Shrimpton concedes, "I suppose I'll have to give it a lot more thought."

Woman of Action

Vietnam, November 4: American photojournalist, Dickey Chapelle, has been killed by a landmine while on patrol with a platoon on the front lines of the Vietnam War. Chapelle is the first member of the press to be killed in the war and the first American woman reporter ever to be killed in action. She was 47 years old.

Born Georgette Meyer in Shorewood, Wisconsin in 1919, Chapelle named herself "Dickey" after her favorite explorer, Admiral Richard Byrd. She undertook her first foreign assignment during World War II, when she was posted with the United States Marines as a correspondent for *National Geographic*. Due to her tenacity, she was subsequently embedded in the fighting forces of a number of different nations, including rebel groups in Algeria, Cuba, Hungary, and South Vietnam. After taking up parachuting at the age of 40 in order to access difficult terrains, she became the first woman reporter to receive Pentagon approval to jump with American troops.

During her career, Chapelle collected numerous awards, including the 1963 Press Photographer's Association "Photograph of the Year" award for her picture of a combat-ready marine in Vietnam. A strident anti-Communist, she also engaged in annual lecture tours, hoping to raise support among the American public for the struggle against Communist insurrections in other countries around the world.

Jean Shrimpton

The musical *Mary Poppins* stars Julie Andrews.

Auckland, New Zealand, July 25: Shirley Ann Lawson gives birth to the world's first set of quintuplets as a result of fertility treatment.
Washington DC, USA, July 30: US Congress amends the *Social Security Act*, establishing Medicaid, which funds various family programs.
USA, July: The first edition of *Cosmopolitan*–edited by Helen Gurley Brown–author of *Sex and the Single Girl*–hits the stands.

Vermont, USA, August 8: Horror fiction author, Shirley Jackson, dies.
Singapore, August 9: Serious racial tensions between Malays and Chinese force Singapore to declare independence from Malaysia.
Los Angeles, USA, August 15: Six days of rioting leaves 34 people dead and over 1,000 injured. The trouble began when a black motorist was arrested in the Watts area.
Kashmir, September 6: The Indian army invades West Pakistan in response to earlier incursions by Pakistani soldiers.

Hollywood, California, USA, September 8: Actress Dorothy Dandridge dies of an antidepressant drug overdose, aged 41. She was the first African-American nominated for the Best Actress Oscar for her role in *Carmen Jones*.
London, England, September 19: Dusty Springfield, the "white lady of soul," is voted best female singer in Britain.
USA, September 27: Silent film star Clara Bow dies of a heart attack, aged 60.

New York City, USA, October 15: Thousands attend the latest anti-war protest as movement gains favor.
Melbourne, Australia, October 30: British model Jean Shrimpton shocks the world and sets a new trend by wearing a mini-skirt and no gloves to a Melbourne horse race meeting.
USA, October: Patricia Harris becomes the first African-American ambassador when she takes a post in Belgium.
USA, November 8: Soap opera, *Days of Our Lives*, premieres on TV.

Rhodesia, November 11: World-wide condemnation greets Prime Minister Ian Smith's decision to sever links with Britain and maintain white-minority rule.
London, England, December 10: As Maria Callas gives her last performance in *Tosca* at the Royal Opera, Australian Joan Sutherland takes the mantle as supreme diva.
Tonga, December 15: Salote Tupou, former Queen of Tonga, dies, aged 65.
London, England December 23: Barbara Castle becomes England's first female Secretary of State.

Dusty Springfield

Tonga Mourns Beloved Monarch

Tonga, December 15: Tonga is in mourning today following news that Queen Salote Tupou has passed away after a long illness. She was 65.

Just 18 years old when she ascended the throne in 1918, the Queen's reign has been marked by unity and stability, with schools and other public assets built, public health improved, crops diversified, and tourism developed, earning her the love and respect of her people. Queen Salote also won the affection of people all around the world when she attended the 1953 coronation of Queen Elizabeth II in London, riding through the streets in an open carriage in the pouring rain as a symbol of respect for the new monarch.

"I WOULDN'T KNOW HOW TO HANDLE SERENITY IF SOMEBODY HANDED IT TO ME ON A PLATE."

DUSTY SPRINGFIELD
(1939–1999),
BRITISH SINGER

Barbara Castle Promoted

London, England, December 23: Barbara Castle has been promoted to the position of Minister for Transport in the government of Labour Prime Minister Harold Wilson. A committed socialist aligned with the left wing of the party, Castle relinquishes her post as Minister for Overseas Development, the portfolio she was assigned following Labour's victory in the 1964 general election.

Educated at Bradford Girls' Grammar School and St. Hugh's College, Oxford, Castle always aspired to be a journalist and a politician. In 1937, she helped establish the *Tribune*, a weekly paper whose declared aim was to recreate the Labour Party as a truly socialist organization. During World War II, she worked as housing correspondent at the *Daily Mirror*, and in 1943 she delivered her first speech at the Labour Party national conference. The following year, she was selected for one of two Blackburn seats, a constituency she continues to represent in the House of Commons.

A proven Cabinet performer, Castle is expected to inject new dynamism into her latest portfolio. Already, she has signaled that she will be scrutinizing such issues as speed limits, compulsory seat belt use, and breathalyzer tests for suspected drunken drivers.

General Union of Palestinian Women Founded

Middle East: A new organization, called the General Union of Palestinian Women (GUPW), has been established to officially represent and promote issues affecting women in Palestine and in exile. The GUPW will carry out its operations within the larger framework of the Palestinian Liberation Organization (PLO), an umbrella body founded at an Arab League summit in June last year to provide a more unified and legitimate channel for Palestinian nationalism.

As part of the broader PLO, the overall goal of the GUPW will be to mobilize Palestinian women to join in the long struggle of their people for the establishment of an independent secular state on their national soil. In pursuit of this goal, the organization will focus on developing programs to help raise the standard of women's health and education, and also to enhance the opportunities for women to be included in economic activities. At the same time, the GUPW will work to increase the political awareness of women within Palestinian communities and encourage them to begin participate in decision-making processes.

Delayed Reaction

Australia: *The Man Who Loved Children*, a novel by Australian author Christina Stead, has been attracting widespread critical acclaim since it was recently reissued with an introduction by American poet, Randall Jarrell. The novel was poorly received when it was published in 1940 and has gone largely unrecognized for the past 25 years.

Born in the Sydney suburb of Rockdale on July 17, 1902, Stead has lived something of a wandering life, traveling to London in 1928 and living there for two years before relocating to Paris.

Later, she moved to Spain, and then headed for the United States when the Spanish Civil War erupted in 1936. In the years that followed, she worked in Hollywood as a screenwriter for MGM studios, contributing to *Madame Curie* and the John Wayne war movie *They Were Expendable*.

She also spent two years as an instructor and tutor at the Workshop in the Novel at New York University.

Throughout her travels, Stead's passion for writing has remained paramount. Her first novel, *Seven Poor Men of Sydney*, was published in 1934, followed by *The Beauties and Furies* (1936) and *House of All Nations* (1938). After the initial release of *The Man Who Loved Children* in 1940, she wrote several other novels, including *For Love Alone* (1944), *Letty Fox: Her Luck* (1946), *A Little Tea, a Little Chat* (1948), and *The People with the Dogs* (1952).

Actress Dorothy Dandridge dies of an overdose.

Hollywood Farewells Three Leading Ladies

USA: This year saw Hollywood bid farewell to three talented leading ladies: Linda Darnell, who was killed in a house fire on April 10, Judy Holliday, who succumbed to breast cancer on June 7, and Dorothy Dandridge, who died of a drug overdose on September 8.

Barbara Castle, first female Secretary of State in the UK.

The first edition of *Cosmopolitan*–edited by Helen Gurley Brown–hits the stands.

Joan Sutherland

role in film came in 1953 when she played opposite Harry Belafonte in the all-black drama *Bright Road*. The following year, she was catapulted to the heights of Hollywood stardom when she played the title role in *Carmen Jones* and became the first African-American woman to receive an Academy Award nomination for Best Actress. Despite her fame, she had trouble finding further suitable projects, and it was 1959 before she secured her next great role as Bess in *Porgy and Bess*, a performance that earned her a Golden Globe Award.

From this point on, Dandridge's life seemed to unravel. Faced with the breakdown of her second marriage and the financial losses of a failed business investment, she turned to alcohol and antidepressants.

She made only one more film, *Malaga*, and in 1963 she declared bankruptcy. Suffering from a severely injured ankle requiring pain medication, it may never be known if the tragic overdose that claimed her life was accidental or intentional.

Known as the girl with the perfect face, Linda Darnell was born Monetta Eloyse Darnell in Dallas, Texas on October 16, 1923. At age 13, while appearing with a local theater company, she was discovered by Hollywood talent scouts who then arranged for a screen test. Once her age was revealed, however, she was rejected. She was just 16 when she returned to Hollywood in 1939 to make her film debut in *A Hotel for Women*, but it was her third film, *Star Dust*, released in 1940, that set her career in motion. Other quality films followed, including *My Darling Clementine* (1946), *Forever Amber* (1947), and *A Letter to Three Wives* (1949). Her final appearance on the silver screen was in her 46th film, *Black Spurs*.

On April 10 this year, Darnell had been visiting a friend in Chicago when she fell asleep while smoking in bed, sparking the fire that killed her. In a tragic twist of irony, she had been watching a television rerun of her signature film *Star Dust* earlier the same evening.

Still mourning the loss of Darnell, Hollywood was saddened to learn of the passing of Judy Holliday just two months later. Born Judith Tuvim on June 21, 1921 in New York City, Holliday made her start in show business as a member of a group called The Revuers. As her career burgeoned, she changed her name to Holliday and headed for Hollywood, but her first film, *Greenwich Village* (1944), was a box office failure, and after appearing in two more films that year she returned to

New York and the stage. In 1945, Holliday received the Clarence Derwent Award for best supporting actress for her performance in the Broadway production, *Kiss Them for Me*. The following year, 1946, she opened to rave reviews in the stage comedy, *Born Yesterday*; and when Columbia Pictures purchased the screen rights, she was signed to play the same role, which would earn her the Oscar for Best Actress in 1950. She went on to star in such comedies as *It Should Happen to You* (1954) and *The Solid Gold Cadillac* (1956). Her last film, *Bells Are Ringing*, was released in 1960, the year she was diagnosed with cancer. After five years battling the illness, Holliday died in New York City on June 7 this year, just three weeks short of her 44th birthday.

Hollywood was hit by further bad news on September 8, when Dorothy Dandridge was found lying on the bathroom floor in her home, dead from an overdose of antidepressants. Born on November 9, 1922 in Cleveland, Ohio, Dandridge entered show business in the 1930s, performing in a song-and-dance team with her sister. As a teenager, she won small roles in a number of films, but virtually retired from performing after her marriage in 1942. When the marriage ended in 1951, she returned to the nightclub scene as a solo singer, opening at The Mocambo, and later performing at sophisticated venues in London, Rio de Janeiro, San Francisco, and New York. Dandridge's first starring

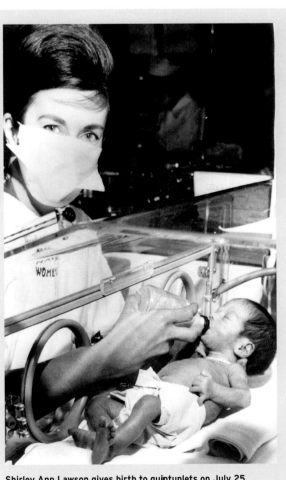

Shirley Ann Lawson gives birth to quintuplets on July 25.

You Can Never Be Too Thin...

London, England, August 27: Readers of *Woman's Mirror* were astonished to discover a striking model on the cover of their magazine—a wide-eyed waif with very long eyelashes and an almost painfully thin build. This newcomer to the world of high fashion modeling goes by the name Twiggy (what could be more appropriate?). Her given name is Lesley Hornby, and she is just three weeks shy of her seventeenth birthday. She was born in the London suburb of Neasden. Her father is a master carpenter; her mother worked as a sales clerk at Woolworth's. But now for the question everyone is asking: what is Twiggy's weight? She stands 5 feet, 4 inches tall (1.62 cm), and weighs 91 pounds (41 kg).

She was discovered working in a hair salon by Nigel Davies, a Mayfair hairdresser with ties to the fashion industry. He launched the girl's career, urged her to go by Twiggy, her old childhood nickname, and then changed his own name to Justin de Villeneuve.

With her child-like figure, short hair, and androgynous appearance, Twiggy has become the model of choice for designer Mary Quant's line of "mod" style clothing, which is not aimed at full-figured women. In all likelihood, next season's fashion shows will be dominated by Twiggy, and others trying to imitate her distinctive under-nourished look.

Margaret Sanger Dead at 86

Tucson, Arizona, USA, September 6: Margaret Sanger, who coined the term "birth control" and asserted that every woman was "the absolute mistress of her own body," died today in Tucson, Arizona. She was 86 years old, and just eight days shy of her 87th birthday.

It is thought that the experiences of Sanger's mother, Anne Purcell Higgins, who had 18 pregnancies, influenced her decision to become an advocate for birth control. In 1912 Sanger began working in the slums of New York's East Side, where she distributed *Family Limitation*, a pamphlet on birth control. Such activities

Family planning advocate Margaret Sanger.

were risky; under the Comstock Law of 1873, printed material about contraception was deemed obscene and distributors of such material were subject to arrest and imprisonment.

In 1915 she opened a family planning clinic in Brooklyn. Police raided the clinic and arrested Sanger; she served 30 days in jail. In the years that followed she continued to publish pamphlets and periodicals about birth control, women's health, and sexuality. In 1921 she was the founder of the American Birth Control League. It was kept afloat by generous grants from John D. Rockefeller, Jr, who insisted that his gifts remain a secret.

Although she will be best remembered as a family planning advocate, Ms Sanger took other moral positions that her supporters find hard to defend. For example, she believed in sterilizing criminals and people who suffered from hereditary physical or mental disabilities.

Yet in spite of the fierce opposition she encountered when she first began to teach family planning techniques to poor women, by the time of her death, easy access to birth control information and products in the United States and elsewhere is almost universal.

Joan Baez Joins Civil Rights Demonstration

Grenada, Mississippi, USA, September: Folk singer and political activist, Joan Baez, has joined Dr Martin Luther King, Jr. and members of the Southern Christian Leadership Conference in trying to protect black elementary and high school children from roving bands of Ku Klux Klan-led armed gangs. The thugs were attacking the students with baseball bats,

Mia Farrow

"You make me feel like a natural woman."

ARETHA FRANKLIN (1942–), AMERICAN SINGER

Model Twiggy appears on the cover of *Woman's Mirror*.

Joan Baez joins civil rights demonstration.

pipes, and bullwhips to keep them from attending what had been previously a whites-only public school.

For Baez, the catalyst occurred on the first day of school, September 12, when 250 children were viciously attacked as they tried to enter the school buildings. Police officers on the scene laughed as they watched the melee and did nothing to save the children.

Baez has a long history of activism, dating back to high school when she refused to join a school-mandated air raid drill. Like other folk singers, such as Pete Seeger, she has managed to blend her music with her politics. During a 1962 concert tour she went to college campuses throughout the American South where she insisted that if any of the audiences were racially segregated, she would not go on stage. Since 1964, to protest US military involvement in Vietnam, she has withheld a percentage of her income tax.

Meanwhile in Grenada, as violence escalates against the schoolchildren, as well as anyone who attempts to protect them, including journalists who film and report on the events, a federal court judge has issued an injunction ordering state police to keep the white mobs from any attacks on black students. It is a victory for the civil rights activists, but Baez and SCLC personnel refuse to leave Grenada until the situation is stable and the rights of the black students to attend desegregated public schools are guaranteed.

Cosmetics "Empress" Elizabeth Arden Dies

New York City, USA, October 19: Elizabeth Arden, the woman who made cosmetics not only respectable, but essential for all women, has died. She was 87 years old.

Born Florence Nightingale Graham in Woodbridge, Ontario in 1878, Arden traveled to Paris in 1912 to study facial massage and other skincare treatments as they were practiced in French beauty salons. She also began to learn about makeup, and when she returned to the United States she brought along a collection of rouges and other powders and sold them in her beauty salon. Next she consulted with a Swiss chemist to create face cream and skin tonic—the first cosmetics ever made whose results had been tested in a scientific laboratory. It was the beginning of a cosmetics empire than spanned the globe; during the 1930s the name Elizabeth Arden—her business name—was almost as well-known outside the United States as the famous Coca-Cola.

Arden continually adapted her line of products to fit the times. During World War II, she manufactured a shade of lipstick called Montezuma Red for women in the armed forces (the lipstick matched the red in their uniforms).

At the time of her death there were 100 Elizabeth Arden salons around the world. The estimated value of her estate is between $30 and $40 million.

NOW Pledges to Bring Women into Public Life

Washington, DC, USA, October 29: Four months after it was born in anger and frustration in a Washington DC hotel room, the National Organization for Women (NOW), has returned to the city of its birth to hold its first national conference. Of the 300 women and men who have registered as charter members, only 30 are attending the conference. Nonetheless, the attendees adopted a Statement of Purpose written by Betty Friedan, author *The Feminine Mystique* and one of the founders of NOW. In this founding document the members have pledged "to bring women into full participation in the mainstream of American society now, exercising all the privileges and responsibilities thereof in truly equal partnership with men."

Nigerian Woman's First Novel a First for Africa

Lagos, Nigeria: Flora Nwapa has become the first Nigerian woman to publish a novel. Nwapa's book, *Efuru*, is the story of a beautiful Ibo woman who lives in a small village in West Africa. She is strong-minded and a successful entrepreneur, but what she longs for is a child. Everything goes well for Efuru except her family life, her neighbors begin to gossip about her, suggesting that she has been cursed by the spirits, and Efuru herself wonders if spirits are acting against her.

Nwapa was born in 1931 in the town of Oguta in southeast Nigeria to wealthy parents who sent her to University College in Ibadan and then to the University of Edinburgh, where she earned a degree in education. She wrote her first novel while juggling her responsibilities as an educator and civil servant. Nwapa has become a source of pride for women in Nigeria, with critics are hailing her as the mother of modern African literature.

Nelly Sachs

Sheila Scott returns to Heathrow after flying solo around the world with a new speed record of 189 hours.

The Sarah Bernhardt of Opera

Inverurie, Scotland, January 3: With the death of Mary Garden, the world of opera has lost a grande dame and arch-diva of the old school. She was a clear-headed businesswoman who would wring every last dime out of an opera house manager before agreeing to sign a contract, and a headstrong performer who insisted upon singing her role in French, even if the language of the opera was Italian or German.

Garden was born in Aberdeen in 1874. When she was six years old, she and her family emigrated to the United States, settling in Chicago. During the last 30 years of her life she lived in Scotland.

Garden studied music in Chicago and then in Paris where in 1900 she made her debut in the title role of Gustave Charpentier's opera *Louise*. Later Claude Debussy selected her to sing the female lead in his opera, *Pelléas et Mélisande*. She went on to sing such classic roles as Violetta, Tosca, and Carmen, but it was her racy interpretation of the title role in Richard Strauss's *Salome* that caused a sensation. In a eulogy that was also an assessment of her personality and career, *New York Times* music critic, Harold Schonberg, described Garden as "lively, indomitable, glamorous, witty, imperious, publicity-minded, capricious and a great artist on top of all that."

Mary Garden

> "MOST WOM-EN'S MAGAZINES SIMPLY TRY TO MOLD WOMEN INTO BIGGER AND BETTER CONSUMERS."
>
> GLORIA STEINEM (1934–), FEMINIST

Stalin's Daughter Defects to the United States

New Delhi, India, March 9: In a move that has shocked the world and created an uproar at the highest levels of the Soviet government, Josef Stalin's daughter, Svetlana Alliluyeva, has walked into the US embassy in New Delhi and formally requested political asylum. Chester Bowles, the American ambassador to India, has granted her request.

Alliluyeva had traveled to New Delhi about two months ago on a mission of compassion, bringing home the ashes of an Indian Communist, Brajesh Singh, whom she had befriended while he was in Russia being treated for emphysema. After Singh's death, she received permission to take his ashes back to his family so they could be scattered in the Ganges River.

In the Soviet Union, Alliluyeva was a member of the *nomenklatura*, an elite group of Communist Party members who enjoy luxuries and privileges denied to the ordinary Russian. As Stalin's daughter, she had access to the highest level of the Soviet administration. When she gave up her teaching job to raise her children full-time, the government granted her a pension. By Soviet standards, Alliluyeva's life was an easy one. Yet there are stories of her father making her life a misery.

Her mother, Nadezhda Alliluyeva, died when Svetlana was six years old. Some say she killed herself; other reports claim that Stalin had his wife murdered, or that he had murdered her himself. At the age of 16 Alliluyeva fell in love with Alexei Kapler, a 40-year-old Jewish filmmaker. Stalin forbade the budding love affair, and later had Kapler exiled for ten years to an industrial city near the Arctic Circle.

Alliluyeva leaves behind two children, 22-year-old Joseph and 17-year-old Ekaterina. The Soviet government can be cruel to the families of defectors, so what will become of Stalin's grandchildren is very uncertain.

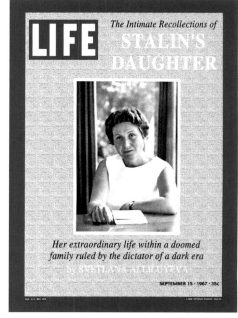

Josef Stalin's daughter, Svetlana Alliluyeva.

time out

Franca Viola defies the traditions of Sicily where a woman who is raped is considered "ruined" and must then marry her rapist. In her case it was a rejected suitor and in December she is to marry a different man of her own choosing.

Elizabeth Taylor in *Who's Afraid of Virginia Woolf?*

Indictments in Thalidomide Scandal

Aachen, Germany, March 14: The top executives of Chemie Grünenthal, the company that manufactured thalidomide, a drug to offset morning sickness in pregnant women, have been indicted

Sacramento, USA, January 2: Former film actor, Ronald Reagan, is sworn in as Governor of California.

Scotland, January 3: Scottish opera legend Mary Garden dies, aged ninety-two.

Cape Kennedy, USA, January 27: Astronauts Virgil "Gus" Grissom, Ed White, and Roger Chaffee, die in *Apollo* spacecraft fire.

New York City, USA, February 22: Barbara Garson's satirical play, *MacBird*, premieres.

India, March 9: Josef Stalin's daughter, Svetlana Alliluyeva, seeks political asylum at the US embassy.

Connecticut, USA, March 11: Soprano Geraldine Farrar dies, aged eighty-five.

Aachen, Germany, March 14: Executives of Chemie Grünenthal are charged over Thalidomide drug, which caused deformities in babies.

Cornwall, England, March 29: Armed forces bomb stricken oil tanker, *Torrey Canyon*, which ran aground, spreading oil on beaches in France and the UK.

Athens, Greece, April 21: Right-wing army officers under Colonel George Papadopoulos seize power, deposing George Papandreou.

Las Vegas, USA, May 1: Elvis Presley marries Priscilla Beaulieu.

Canberra, Australia, May 27: Australians vote for a proposal to count Aboriginal people in the national census.

Wimbledon, England, June: Billie Jean King wins all three possible titles at Wimbledon: women's singles, women's doubles, and mixed doubles.

London, England, June 7: Queen Elizabeth meets the Duchess of Windsor, healing the 30-year rift caused by Edward VII's abdication.

New York City, USA, June 7: Critic and author Dorothy Parker dies, aged seventy-three.

California, USA, June 15: Governor Reagan signs the *Therapeutic Abortion Act*, legalizing abortion in certain circumstances in California.

Middle East, June 10: The six-day war between Syria and Egypt comes to an end as Israel finally observes a UN ceasefire.

Virginia, USA, June 12: The US Supreme Court rules that Virginia's ban on interracial marriage is unconstitutional in its ruling of the *Loving vs. Virginia* case.

Hawaii, USA, June 20: Actress, Nicole Kidman is born.

New Orleans, USA, June 29: Film actress Jayne Mansfield is killed in a car accident; her three children survive in the back seat.

London, England, July 8: Vivien Leigh, the screen beauty who immortalized Scarlett O'Hara in *Gone with the Wind*, dies at fifty-three.

for rushing the drug into distribution before it had been adequately tested for side effects. Between 1957 and 1961, there were at least 10,000 cases of women giving birth to infants with flipper-like arms and feet, no ears, defective eyes, and mal-formed internal organs.

As early as 1959 doctors were reporting these shocking results to executives at Chemie Grünenthal, yet the company ignored the reports. In September 1960, Chemie Grünenthal applied to the Food and Drug Administration for permission to sell thalidomide in the United States. The case was assigned to Frances Kelsey, a trained pharmacologist, who suspected thalidomide might be dangerous for children, pregnant women, and their developing fetuses. Missing from the drug company's application was information on the effects of thalidomide on the human metabolism, chronic toxicity studies, and other essential data. Six times Kelsey requested additional data, and six times the manufacturer refused to comply. Consequently, Kelsey rejected the application to market the drug in the USA. Once the dangers of thalidomide were revealed, Kelsey was hailed in the *New York Times*, *Life* magazine, and hundreds of other publications as a heroine for preventing the drug's use.

Priscilla Marries The King

Las Vegas, Nevada, USA, May 1: The Arabian Nights-themed Aladdin Hotel on the glitzy Las Vegas Strip was the setting for the wedding of 22-year-old Priscilla Beaulieu and the King of Rock 'n' Roll, Elvis Presley, age thirty-two.

Priscilla Beaulieu marries Elvis Presley.

Although born in Brooklyn, New York, Beaulieu and her family have moved often, a consequence of her father's career as an officer in the United States Air Force. In 1959, when Priscilla was 14 years old, the Beaulieus were stationed in Wiesbaden, West Germany. There she met a handsome young soldier, Elvis Presley. In spite of a ten-year age difference, Priscilla and Elvis began dating; the couple has always maintained that their relationship was platonic.

Priscilla has married a multi-millionaire: since 1960, Presley's 27 movies have grossed approximately $130 million, his record sales $150 million. But she may have caught Elvis as he begins the downward spiral of his career. His movies, with their weak repetitive plots and vapid songs, are passé. And his act, which was edgy and cool in the 1950s, pales in comparison to such hard-driving, sexually charged bands as The Doors, Jefferson Airplane, and the Grateful Dead.

Billie Jean King Takes Three Titles at Wimbledon

Wimbledon, England, June: One of the most dynamic champions in women's tennis, Billie Jean King, has swept all three available titles at Wimbledon: women's singles, women's doubles, and mixed doubles. A fast, aggressive, intensely competitive right-handed player who likes to rush the net, she has been quoted often as saying that it takes guts to win.

King first came to Wimbledon in 1961 when she was 17 years old; on that occasion she walked away a doubles champion. Since then she has scored six more Wimbledon championships, including an incredible upset in 1962 in which she defeated Margaret Court Smith, the number one tennis player in the world. King criticized the United States Lawn Tennis Association, denouncing the practice of top players being paid under the table to guarantee entry into tournaments. Of her success King says, "Victory is fleeting. Losing is forever."

Geraldine Farrar

Billie Jean King wins all three titles at Wimbledon.

Port Harcourt, Nigeria, July 16: The Igbo (Ibo) people of Nigeria set up the separate state of Biafra in the oil-rich south-east of Nigeria, initiating civil war between Nigerian forces and the rebels.
New York City, USA, July 31: Feminist author Elizabeth Wurtzel is born.
Beijing, China, August 30: Red Guards set fire to the British Mission in Beijing and bar all members from leaving without permission.

Bolivia, August 31: Argentinean-born guerrilla and disciple of Che Guevera, Haydee Tamara Bunke Bider, is killed by Bolivian soldiers in an ambush.
Cambridge, England, September: Astronomical research student Jocelyn Bell discovers pulsars.
USA, September 11: *The Carol Burnett Show* premieres on American television.
Villa Grande, Bolivia, October 10: The body of Ernesto "Che" Guevara is put on display after he is shot by troops in Bolivia.

Oakland, California, USA, October 20: The fifth day of anti-Vietnam War protests sees 4,000 demonstrators battling police. Four days ago folk singer Joan Baez was arrested at a sit-in at a military induction center in Oakland.
England, October 27: In England, Scotland and Wales, under medical supervision and in certain circumstances, abortion is legalized.
South Vietnam, November: General Westmoreland is heavily fortifying Khe Sanh in preparation for attacks on the Ho Chi Minh Trail.

Portsea, Australia, December 22: Australian Prime Minister Harold Holt drowns while swimming in rough seas off Cheviot Beach.
New York City, USA, December 28: Muriel Siebert wins a seat on the New York Stock Exchange, the first woman to do so.
New Zealand: The National Council on the Employment of Women is established.
USA: Diane Arbus takes her famous *Identical Twins* photograph.

London, England: Dame Cicely Saunders establishes St. Christopher's Hospice, revolutionizing the way the medical profession deals with the dying.
USA: Denise Levertov publishes *The Sorrow Dance*, a book of poetry about the Vietnam War and the death of her sister.
San Francisco, USA: Marjorie Fiske Lowenthal's *Aging and Mental Disorder* is published by Jossey-Bass Inc.

Vivien Leigh

Ban on Interracial Marriage Unconstitutional

Washington, DC, USA, June 12: It took a ruling from the Supreme Court of the United States, but the marriage of Mildred Jeter and Richard Perry Loving is lawful at last.

Jeter, a black woman, and Loving, a white man, were residents of the state of Virginia in the late 1950s when they decided to marry.

Under Virginia's *Racial Integrity Act of 1924*, it was unlawful for a white person to marry a non-white person, so the couple traveled to Washington DC for their wedding. When they returned home to Virginia, they were charged with violating the state's racial integrity legislation. In court, Jeter and Loving pleaded guilty and were sentenced to a year in prison. However, the sentence was suspended for 25 years provided the couple moved out of the state of Virginia.

Jeter and Loving relocated to Washington DC, where in 1963 they initiated the first in a series of lawsuits to overturn their conviction. The basis of the argument was the Fourteenth Amendment of the US Constitution that requires all states to guarantee to all their citizens equal protection under the law. In recent years the Fourteenth Amendment has been used successfully to dismantle racial segregation legislation.

Today, in a unanimous decision, the nine justices of the Supreme Court ruled in favor of Jeter and Loving and declared Virginia's *Racial Integrity Act of 1924* unconstitutional. In handing down the ruling on this landmark civil rights case, Chief Justice Earl Warren wrote, "Marriage is one of the basic civil rights of man, fundamental to our very existence and survival…Under our Constitution, the freedom to marry, or not marry, a person of another race resides with the individual and cannot be infringed by the State."

> *"I DO KNOW THAT GOD CREATED US EQUAL AND WE'RE NOT LIVING UP TO IT."*
>
> JAYNE MANSFIELD, (1932–1967), ACTRESS

Ban on interracial marriage is found unconstitutional.

Astronomical research student Jocelyn Bell discovers pulsars after studying scans from quasars.

Cambridge Graduate Student Discovers Pulsars

Cambridge, England, September: Jocelyn Bell, a graduate student at the University of Cambridge, has discovered rotating neutron stars that give off electromagnetic radiation in the form of radio waves or signals. Because the signals have a regular pulse they have come to be called pulsars, although initially Bell and her thesis advisor, Antony Hewish, gave the radio signals the more whimsical name of "Little Green Men."

Bell, who grew up in Northern Ireland, has nurtured a lifelong love for astronomy and physics. As a graduate student in astrophysics at the University of Cambridge she met Hewish, who then invited Bell to join a team of professors and graduate students who were building a radio telescope in order to study quasars. The completed telescope scanned and registered its findings on three-track pen recorders that generated 96 feet (29 m) of chart paper daily. It was while analyzing the print-out that Bell discovered something odd—she called it "a bit of scruff." It was only after determining that the "scruff" wasn't a quasar, or a star, or something man-made that Bell realized she had found something new in the universe.

Publisher Helen Vlachos Eludes Greek Junta

Athens, Greece: Helen Vlachos, publisher of two Athens newspapers, *Kathimerini* and *Messimvrini*, has escaped house arrest and fled to London. Vlachos is a political and social conservative and a staunch

Premiere of *The Carol Burnett Show* on television.

anti-Communist—exactly the kind of person Greece's military junta wants on their side. She ran afoul of the colonels when, to protest the country's harsh censorship laws, she refused to publish her newspapers any longer.

When she fled Vlachos left behind her home, her wealth, her position in Greek society, and her husband. In response, the junta has stripped Vlachos of her Greek citizenship, and barred her husband from leaving the country.

According to Vlachos, since the coup of April 21, 1967, the colonels have maintained their power over the people of Greece through blacklists, widespread surveillance, the brutal torture of prisoners, and purges of "anti-national elements" in the universities and even in the Greek Orthodox Church.

"Personally," says Vlachos, "I think that the only way of getting rid of these little fascists is from another coup."

Revolution in Care for the Dying

London, England: "You matter because you are you," says Cicely Saunders OBE, "and you matter to the last moment of your life." Building upon that philosophy, Saunders has established St. Christopher's Hospice, a place where the terminally ill will find compassionate care, medication to help control the pain and symptoms associated with their illnesses, and social, spiritual, and psychological counseling for themselves and for their family and friends. And treatment here is free.

The idea for St. Christopher's began 21 years ago. Saunders was a registered nurse caring for David Tasma, a Polish Jew who had escaped the Warsaw Ghetto and emigrated to England where he had

found work as a waiter. In 1948 he was dying, and Saunders was his nurse. They fell in love. When Tasma died, he left Saunders his entire estate—£500. She knew she wanted to use the windfall to help the terminally ill, but the idea of opening her own hospice had not yet occurred to her.

In 1957 Saunders became a doctor and the following year went to work at St. Joseph's Hospice in east London, where for seven years she cared for the patients and studied pain control. By now she was developing her ideas for a unique type of hospice.

Throughout the early 1960s, Cicely Saunders added fund-raising to her long list of commitments. Building began in 1965; today the doors of St Christopher's Hospice are open to anyone who needs palliative care.

Years ago Saunders, a committed Christian, read this verse from Psalm 37, "Commit thy way unto the Lord; trust also in him; and he shall bring it to pass." A revolution in the care of the dying has indeed come to pass.

Nineteen-Year-Old Publishes First Novel

Tulsa, Oklahoma, USA: Thethousands of teenage boys who have made *The Outsiders* one of the hottest novels of the year might be surprised to learn that the author of their favorite book is a young woman, 19-year-old Susan Eloise Hinton.

Hinton adopted the byline S. E. Hinton so that male readers would not think that her novel was about "girl stuff." She began writing her book when she was 15 years old. It was completed about a year later, and this year The Viking Press published the book, Hinton's first novel.

S. E. Hinton set *The Outsiders* in Tulsa, Oklahoma, which is her hometown, and based the gangs the Greasers and the Socs (pronounced "soashes") on two antagonistic groups that dominated her own high school's social scene.

The main character of the novel is 14-year-old Ponyboy Curtis, the youngest of three orphaned boys who belong to the Greasers, a tightly knit group of boys and young men who come from families at the bottom of Tulsa's economic and social ladder. Their arch-enemies are the rich-kid Socs—short for Socials. The main action of the novel comes when a Soc is killed in a knife fight with a Greaser.

Teenage readers have responded very strongly to the book; they apparently like the slangy dialog, the melodramatic plot, and the sense of loyalty that binds the Greasers together. The book skilfully explores notions of friendship, conflict, and fitting into society.

Anne Bancroft Stars in *The Graduate*

New York, USA, December 21: It seems there's no stopping the current trend in Hollywood to produce edgy, unconventional movies. (The past few years have seen the genre-defying *Dr. Strangelove* and *The Good, the Bad, and the Ugly*, among others.) Now, in *The Graduate*, director Mike Nichols upsets traditional beliefs about love and marriage, youth, and middle age, and the quests for sex and success.

A very boyish-looking Dustin Hoffman plays Ben, a kid fresh out of college (in real life Hoffman is 30 years old). While Ben is utterly confused about what he should do with his life, the wife of his father's business partner, Mrs. Robinson, played by Anne Bancroft, is planning to complete Ben's education in a way he has never imagined.

Bancroft, who was born in the Bronx, New York, in 1931, has played on Broadway, television, and of course film. Hoffmann plays the title role in *The Graduate*, but it's Bancroft who dominates the movie, giving a brilliantly nuanced performance of a jaded, unsentimental, sexually voracious man-eater. In the movie's soundtrack she even gets her own song, "Mrs. Robinson," written by Paul Simon and sung by Simon and Garfunkel.

Diane Arbus

Anne Bancroft as Mrs Robinson in *The Graduate*.

Tallulah Bankhead

"Protest is when I say this does not please me. Resistance is when I ensure what does not please me occurs no more."

ULRIKE MEINHOF,
(1934–1976), ACTIVIST,
KONKRET MAGAZINE

Striking Ford Employees Awarded Pay Rise

Dagenham, Essex, England, June 30: The Ford strike that began on June 7 is over. A group of 850 women employed as sewing machinists at the company's Dagenham factory went on strike for equal pay. The dispute spread to the Ford plant in Liverpool, and had the backing of the engineering and transport unions.

The strike was precipitated by the company's job re-classification policy. Under the new grading, five classes were introduced: A, B, C, D, and E, with E being the highest. Salaries were then set according to grade. Many people were unhappy with what they felt were vast inequities in the system. The skilled women machinists were placed in Grade B, while men working in occupations of equal or lesser skill were awarded the higher C grading.

During the three weeks, the striking women virtually stopped production at the Ford plants until Employment Minister Barbara Castle was called in. An agreement was reached; the machinists will receive 92 percent of male C-grade wages. Although not a total victory, it is a big step in the move toward equal pay for women in the UK.

Pope Paul VI bans the use of contraceptives by Catholics.

Papal Encyclical Bans Birth Control

Vatican City, Italy, July 25: Since the contraceptive pill came onto the market in 1960, it has proved to be an effective and convenient form of birth control, freeing millions of women from the fear of unwanted pregnancy.

It is little wonder, then, that many Catholics are bitterly disappointed at Pope Paul VI's encyclical entitled *Humanae Vitae* (*On Human Life*, subtitled *On the Regulation of Birth*), which was released today.

Because of the reforms initiated by the Vatican II Council, such as the modernization of the Mass, the relaxation of the rules on fasting and abstinence, and the lifting of some restrictions on inter-faith marriage, it was naturally assumed that the Pope would adopt a more liberal attitude to the Catholic Church's traditional bans on artificial contraception. However, despite the efforts of medical advisers who argued that the pill was a more reliable and scientific version of the Church-approved "rhythm" method, Pope Paul stands firm on the Church's position on artificial birth control.

The encyclical presents a view of the sanctity of Christian marriage. It states: "Artificial contraception denies that human lovemaking is designed to be open to conception. In doing so it touches the very core of the marriage union and is therefore wrong." It goes on to say: "Man, growing used to contraceptive practices, may lose respect for the woman and come to the point of considering her as a mere instrument of selfish enjoyment, and no longer as his respected and beloved companion."

Some Catholics will accept the teaching, but given the response so far, many will choose to ignore it, and others will no doubt launch a vehement protest, despite the fact that to go against the Church's laws would be to commit a serious sin.

Sheep Awarded "Miss America" Crown

Atlantic City, New Jersey, USA, September 7: Feminist demonstrators have disrupted this year's Miss America beauty pageant in a multi-pronged guerrilla-theater attack, which included the crowning of a live sheep and the auction of a mannequin puppet.

The protest was organized by the women's liberation group, New York Radical Women. They believe all women are hurt by beauty competitions, which affirm that looks are the most important thing about a woman. They say that women are made to feel inferior if they do not measure up to Miss America standards. The group wants to "attack the male chauvinism, commercialization of beauty, racism, and oppression of women symbolized by the pageant." The women sang songs parodying the contest and the idea of selling women's bodies. They ceremoniously crowned a live sheep as Miss America 1968, singing, "Ain't she sweet, making profits off her meat."

Sixteen women smuggled in a banner reading WOMEN'S LIBERATION. They unfurled it in the front row of the balcony, shouting "Freedom for Women,"

Jacqueline Kennedy marries Aristotle Onassis.

Physicist Lise Meitner was best known for her analysis of Nobel Laureate Otto Hahn's work.

Shirley Chisholm

and "No More Miss America," as the outgoing Miss America made her farewell speech. Items they considered symbols of female oppression—bras, high heels, girdles, curlers, and tweezers—were thrown into a "Freedom Trash Can."

This outrageous campaign against the iconic Miss America pageant has brought the press out in droves, and put women's liberation on front pages worldwide.

Eminent Physicist Lise Meitner Dies

Cambridge, England, October 27: Eminent Austrian-born physicist Lise Meitner has died, aged 89. She was born in Vienna on November 7, 1878, the daughter of a successful and prosperous lawyer. She gained a doctorate from Vienna University in 1906 for her thesis on the conduction of heat in homogeneous solids. It was the experimental and highly theoretical treatise involving analysis of research by the great British physicist J. C. Maxwell.

Meitner moved to Berlin in 1907, where she collaborated with the eminent physicist, Otto Hahn, for the next 30 years. They discovered the first long-lived isotope of a new element, protactinium, and also achieved uranium fission. But Hahn failed to recognize that the uranium atoms were actually disintegrating, and in 1939 Meitner—having fled to Sweden from Germany because of her Jewish heritage—correctly identified the process, in partnership with her nephew, Otto Frisch, who coined the term "nuclear fission" to describe it. Many people say Meitner should have shared the 1944 Nobel Prize with Hahn, who received all the credit for their discovery.

Albert Einstein called her "the German Madame Curie" but she was always extremely modest and unassuming. "I am not important, why is everybody making such a fuss over me?" was one of her well-known remarks. Regarding a Hollywood plan to make a movie about the development of fission and the atomic bomb, she declared to a studio executive: "I would rather walk the length of Broadway in the nude than see myself in a movie."

Triumph and Turmoil at Mexico City Olympics

Mexico City, Mexico, October 27: The closing ceremony of the Games of the XIX Olympiad was held today. Even before competition began, the Games were fraught with disturbance and political upheaval. Since the decision was made to

Mexico City hosts the XIX Olympic Games.

hold the Olympics in the Mexican capital, students have taken to the streets, protesting that the money spent on the Games should have been channeled into social welfare. The high altitude was also an issue, inhibiting the performance of many athletes.

Finally, two black American sprinters, Tommie Smith and John Carlos, were suspended from the US team for raising their fists in the Black Power salute during the national anthem.

For many female athletes, however, 1968 was a watershed year. For the first time, the Olympic torch was lit by a woman: Mexican 400-meter runner Norma Enriqueta Basilio Satelo.

Sixteen-year-old Debbie Meyer from the USA won the 200 m, 400 m, and 800 m freestyle events, becoming the first swim-mer to win three individual gold medals. Runner Wyomia Tyus, a 23-year-old student at Tennessee State University, also won a total of three gold medals. In addition, she became the first woman to retain her 100 m title.

Australians, too, found their way into the record books. Maureen Caird won the 80 m hurdles just two weeks after her seventeenth birthday, defeating her countrywoman Pam Kilborn to become the youngest ever Australian to win Olympic gold.

The triumphs of Czech gymnast Vera Caslavska were hard won and especially gratifying. Branded as a political extremist by the Communists, she was forced to go into hiding just weeks before the commencement of the Games, severely hampering her chances. Nevertheless Caslavska will take home three gold medals and one silver.

Poisoned Sea Exposé Hits Bestseller List

Japan: The Japanese writer and activist Michiko Ishimure has published a book protesting against the dumping of mercury in Minamata Bay on the southern island of Kyushu. *Kukai Jod—Waga Mina-mata (Pure Land—Poisoned Sea)* publicizes the pollution of the bay by the Chisso Corporation since 1908 when it set up a carbide plant followed by the release of methyl mercury from 1932, and subsequent cover-ups and denials. "Minamata disease," or mercury poisoning, causes numbness and loss of coordination, progressive loss of all senses and the ability to walk, speak, or write. In later stages it results in severe body malformations and death. Ishimure's view is that Minamata disease symbolizes the sickness of Japanese society. Her book is already a bestseller, and has stimulated concern and support for victims of the disease.

Sharon and *Sea Sharp II* Cross the Pacific

Maureen Catherine Connolly

San Diego, California, USA, July 26: Sharon Sites Adams, 39, today became the first woman to make a solo voyage across the Pacific Ocean. Her 6,000 mile (9,655 km) trip from Yokohama to San Diego in the Mariner 31-class sailing boat *Sea Sharp II* took 74 days, 17 hours, and 15 minutes. She survived six gales, saying, "I was terrified in every one of them."

Adams grew up in Oregon and took her first sailing lesson in California in October, 1964, at the age of 34, after being attracted by an advertisement for a sailing school. The following year she sailed solo to Hawaii in the original 25 ft (7.6 m) *Sea Sharp*. She has sailed to numerous South Pacific islands, climbed an erupting volcano, and encountered several cannibal tribes—staying overnight with one, which had had no previous contact with the outside world. She has also sailed across Lake Titicaca in the Andes, the world's highest lake.

She has said, "I think one of the big things I want to prove with my sailing is that a woman should not be precluded from doing anything. A woman should not be precluded from going to the moon." Ironically, she reached the Californian coast just as Neil Armstrong stepped on the Moon—her small step for womankind echoing his giant leap for mankind.

> "WE HAVE ALWAYS SAID THAT IN OUR WAR WITH THE ARABS WE HAD A SECRET WEAPON—NO ALTERNATIVE."
>
> GOLDA MEIR (1898–1978), ISRAELI PRIME MINISTER, *LIFE* MAGAZINE

Barbra Streisand wins an Oscar as the popular singer and comedian, Fanny Brice, in the movie *Funny Girl*.

Birth Control Pill is Safe

Washington DC, USA, September 4: The US Food and Drug Administration has today issued a report stating that the contraceptive pill (birth control pill) is safe, despite the slight risk of fatal blood-clotting.

The first birth control pill (Enovid) was approved by the USFDA and released commercially by G. D. Searle in 1960, after a decade of clinical testing. Women were quick to adopt this new and effective method of contraception: In 1962, about 1.2 million women had been prescribed the pill, and this number more than quadrupled by 1965.

Only one year after the birth control pill was released, there were reports of serious side effects such as heart attacks, strokes, and blood clots. However in 1962, G. D. Searle claimed there was no conclusive evidence that these health issues were a direct result of the pill.

In 1965, the USFDA commissioned Johns Hopkins University in Baltimore to determine the prevalence of the side effects. Simultaneously, the FDA Advisory Committee on Obstetrics and Gynecology performed its own study.

The most recent research has concluded that the risks of stroke, heart attack, and blood clots were linked to the levels of estrogen, and that the pill can be safer, yet just as effective, with only half the amount of estrogen contained in earlier pills.

Alexandra David-Néel Reaches Final Nirvana

Digne, France, September 8: Alexandra David-Néel, the multi-talented writer, adventurer, and Buddhist scholar, has died at the age of one hundred. Born Louise Eugénie Alexandrine Marie David, in Paris, on October 24, 1868, to a socially prominent family, she once said, "I learned to run before I could walk!"

An acclaimed opera soprano, active anarchist, religious reformer, and brave explorer who traveled in western China for some 14 years, Alexandra David-Néel undertook a spiritual search that led her from a youthful interest in socialism and Freemasonry to the teachings of the great sages of India, culminating in her initiation into the esoteric tantric rites of Mahayana Buddhism.

She married railroad engineer Philippe Néel in Tunis in 1904, and from 1903 to 1911 lived in London and Paris, studying and writing. David-Néel traveled to India in 1911 to further her interest in Buddhism, and was the first European woman granted a private audience with the Dalai Lama—the spiritual ruler of Tibet—who was living in exile in northern India after fleeing Tibet when the Chinese invaded in February, 1910.

For two years, David-Néel lived alone in a cave on top of a 13,000 ft (4,000 m) mountain, inspired, not discouraged by isolation, cold, and hunger. After she emerged in 1916, she learned the local language and visited and studied at many sacred and secluded monasteries, one of which provided her with a 15-year-old attendant boy named Yongden. In 1924, after a perilous year-long journey with Yongden across the Himalayas, Alexandra became the first European woman to reach "the forbidden city" of Lhasa—at a time when foreigners were prohibited. Throughout her many subsequent years of journeying in northern India and all over China, Yongden accompanied and assisted her, remaining with her until his death in France in 1955.

Louise de Vilmorin, the French novelist, poet, and journalist, died in December this year.

David-Néel published over 40 books about Eastern religion, philosophy, and her travels. Her teachings influenced many westerners, including beat writers Jack Kerouac and Allen Ginsberg.

Union Gets its Teeth into Colgate

Chicago, USA, September 26: After a long, drawn-out legal process, Thelma Bowe and other female employees of the Colgate-Palmolive company today won the right to work in positions previously open only to men—provided they can meet the physical requirements of the position. The suit, originally filed by the International Chemical Workers Union more than two years ago, claimed that companies do not have the right to segregate jobs on the basis of gender by limiting women to less strenuous jobs.

The three Appeals Court judges agreed, ruling that companies may not use discriminatory job classification systems. For example, if a weight-lifting limit is used as a standard, it must apply to both genders, and women must be given the opportunity to demonstrate their ability to perform the job.

Champion Skater and Screen Star Dies

Oslo, Norway, October 12: Sonja Henie, 57, the pioneering figure skater turned Hollywood star, has died from leukemia during a flight from Paris to Oslo.

Henie was born on April 8, 1912, in Kristiania, Norway, the daughter of Wilhelm Henie, an affluent fur trader and one-time world cycling champion. From the age of two she was taught by a series of experts, including the famous Russian ballerina Tamara Karsavina. At the age of nine, Henie won Norway's national amateur skating championship. She took the figure skating gold medal in the 1928, 1932, and 1936 Winter Olympics, and in 1927—at the age of 15—won the first of an unprecedented ten world figure skating championships. She also won six consecutive European championships.

She was the first figure skater to wear a short skirt, and to make use of dance choreography. Her innovative skating techniques and her glamorous disposition transformed skating permanently, and hastened its acceptance as a legitimate Olympic sport. Henie's act became so popular that police had to be called out to control crowds in several cities, including Prague and New York. She was also an accomplished tennis player.

Following the 1936 Olympics, Henie took up a career as a screen and stage actress. She was based in the United States but also had highly successful shows in Norway in 1953 and 1955. Her hit movies included *One in a Million* and *Sun Valley Serenade*. In 1938 she published her autobiography, and in 1941 became a US citizen. In 1956 Henie and her third husband, Niels Onstad, settled in Oslo and amassed a large collection of modern art that forms the basis of the Henie-Onstad Art Center.

Sonja Henie is regarded as one of the greatest figure skaters in history, and became one of the world's wealthiest women. She will be buried on a hilltop overlooking the Art Center that bears her name.

Sharon Tate Killed by "The Family"?

California, USA, November: Police have conducted jail interviews with Susan Atkins—imprisoned in connection with a car theft—after she boasted to fellow inmates that she was responsible for the recent murder of film actress Sharon Tate. Tate and five others were brutally slain last August 9, at 10050 Cielo Drive, Benedict Canyon—the home Tate shared with her husband, Polish-born film director Roman Polanski. She was eight-and-a-half months pregnant.

Atkins openly admitted that she carried out the massacre—

along with several other members of a quasi-religious sect known as "The Family"—under orders from its charismatic leader, Charles Manson, who is reputedly a drug supplier to members of California's music and film industry.

The sensational murders sent shockwaves of paranoia throughout the Los Angeles community—a relieved Polanski, hearing of Atkins's confession, admitted that at times he had suspected various of his friends and colleagues of some involvement in the slaughter.

Polanski and Tate married in London on January 20, 1968, after having met in 1967 while working on Polanski's *The Fearless Vampire Killers*. After gaining a series of small parts in the early 1960s in the TV series *Mr Ed* and *The Beverly Hillbillies*, Tate featured in several films, including *The Eye of the Devil*, *Don't Make Waves*, and this year's *The Wrecking Crew*. Tate has been nominated for this year's Golden Globe award New Star of the Year—Actress, for her recent performance in *Valley of the Dolls*.

Liv Ullmann

Sharon Tate with her husband, Roman Polanski.

The late Sonja Henie in one of her many movie roles.

Tragic Death of Horror Actress

Betty Friedan

Lisbon, Portugal, August 18: The 27-year-old Spanish horror movie star, Soledad Miranda, was killed today in a car accident on the road between Estoril and Lisbon, Portugal. She was traveling in her new convertible car with her racing car driver husband when they were involved in a collision with a small truck. Soledad's side of the car was crushed and she suffered serious fractures to the skull and spine. She was taken to the Hospital of the Red Cross in Lisbon where she died a few hours later. Her husband, who survived with minor injuries, was driving. She leaves behind a young son.

Described as the most painfully beautiful woman who ever lived, Soledad appeared in many horror films over the past decade—her haunted, enigmatic beauty ensuring her a prominent place in the genre. She also had a brief stint as a pop singer in Spain.

The daughter of Portuguese parents, she started her career as an 8-year-old, performing flamenco. She made her film debut at 16, and during the following years appeared in more than 30 classics, comedies, and B-movies. Her big break came when she was spotted by legendary Spanish horror movie director Jesus Franco, who cast Soledad in such cult classics as *Count Dracula* and *Vampyros Lesbos*. Her last movie was *The Devil Came from Akasava*.

"This woman's place is in the House— the House of Representatives."

BELLA ABZUG, AMERICAN POLITICIAN, CAMPAIGN SPEECH

Betty Friedan leads Women's Strike for Equality through the city of New York.

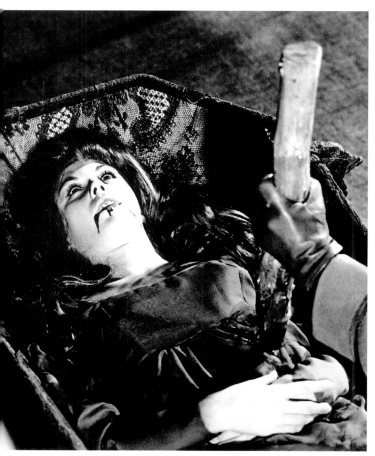

Horror movie actress Soledad Miranda.

Women's Lib Icon Leads Strike

New York, USA August 26, 1970: Feminist crusader and author of *The Feminine Mystique*, Betty Friedan, today led the "Women's Strike for Equality" protest in New York City on the 50th anniversary of women's suffrage in the USA.

The strike, the largest women's protest in US history, was sponsored jointly by the National Organization for Women (NOW)—an organization Friedan started in 1966—and the Women's Equity Action League (WEAL). The protest involved sit-ins, lunch-hour rallies, and a street march down Fifth Avenue in New York. Before the march, Friedan made a point of lunching at Whyte's, a downtown restaurant formerly open to men only.

Tens of thousands of woman marched down Fifth Avenue with Friedan in the lead. Carrying signs and banners with slogans such as "Don't Cook Dinner — Starve a Rat Tonight!" and "Don't Iron While the Strike is Hot," women of all ages, along with a number of sympathetic men, marched down the street to cheering crowds. The march ended with a rally in Bryant Park where Friedan, Gloria Steinem, Bella Abzug, and Kate Millett all gave passionate speeches.

The Feminine Mystique is widely regarded as one of the most influential books of the twentieth century. It has made Friedan famous and established her as one of the chief architects of the women's liberation movement. Published in 1963, it has been credited with igniting the contemporary women's movement and, as a result, transforming the social fabric of the United States and other countries around the world.

Hijacker Leila Khaled Released

London, England, September 30: Popular Front Liberation of Palestine (PLFP) hijacker, Leila Khaled, was today released from Ealing prison by Prime Minister Edward Heath in exchange for 56 western hostages.

Her departure ends a three-week international crisis sparked by the PLFP's hijacking on September 6 of four airliners inside Jordanian territory. The PFLP announced that the hijackings were designed "to teach the Americans a lesson because of their long-standing support of Israel." Two planes were taken to Dawson's Field, a former RAF base in the middle of the Jordanian desert. A third was blown up in Cairo after the passengers and crew were released.

Meanwhile, Patrick Arguello and Leila Khaled were attempting to hijack an El Al flight from Amsterdam. Their mission failed when Israeli sky marshals shot Arguello and overpowered Khaled. The plane made an emergency landing at Heathrow Airport, London, where Arguello died and Khaled was arrested.

Three days later, the group demanded Khaled's release by hijacking a fifth plane —a BOAC flight from Bahrain. With more than 300 hostages—65 of them British and American—the hijacking created a major international crisis.

Initially the PFLP delivered a 72-hour ultimatum but, after some frantic diplomacy via an Arab intermediary, they agreed to an extension to the deadline. Six days into the crisis, the majority of the hostages—mostly women and children—were released unharmed. However, the hijackers were impatient and on

Popular Front for the Liberation of Palestine member Leila Khaled, the notorious hijacker, is released.

12 September delivered a graphic warning by blowing up three empty planes. That act, seen around the world on television, spurred the British Government to act. Prime Minister Edward Heath said that Britain had no choice but to go public with its intentions to free Khaled.

Khaled first came to international attention after she took part in a 1969 hijacking of a TWA flight from Rome to Tel Aviv. The international press became enthralled by the romantic idea of an exotic 24-year-old freedom fighter. Before the second hijacking Khaled underwent cosmetic surgery to alter her appearance.

Joplin Dies of Overdose

Los Angeles, USA, October 4: Blues-rock singer Janis Joplin has been found dead at the Landmark Hotel in Hollywood from a suspected overdose of heroin and whiskey. She was 27. Many believe Joplin, with her powerful bluesy voice, was on the brink of major stardom. At the time of her death she was working on a new album, to be called *Pearl*, with the Full Tilt Boogie band. Among the songs she had already recorded were "Mercedes Benz" and "Me and Bobby McGee," written by her lover Kris Kristofferson. With her distinctive voice, she became an overnight success after appearing at

the Monterey Pop Festival in 1967. Her use of drugs throughout her career was legendary. She was a heavy drinker, with a liking for the popular bourbon Southern Comfort.

Joplin will be cremated in the Village Memorial Park Cemetery, Westwood, California. Her ashes will then be scattered over the Pacific Ocean and along Stinson Beach.

Italy Legalizes Divorce

Rome, Italy, October 9: The Italian Senate has passed the First Fortuna bill, which will legalize divorce in Italy and end a bitter battle between the Roman Catholic church and the State. Although divorce is an issue that affects both men and women, it has come to be regarded as a women's issue over the past decade—a decade that has seen Italian women fight for equal rights.

Until the passing of this bill, Italy was one of the last remaining western nations to hold out against any form of legal divorce, and many believed it was inevitable that any moves to allow divorce would cause great conflict in this conservative, Catholic country. Although the bill was passed by only a slim margin, the result is being seen as a severe defeat for the Catholic hierarchy and the Vatican. It confirms a trend toward secularization in Italy, and highlights the reality of women's changing status in Italian society.

Italy's new divorce law, however, is tough by European standards. A five-year

Janis Joplin dies of an accidental drug overdose.

legal separation is required before courts will grant a divorce that is mutually agreed to by husband and wife, while a seven-year waiting period is mandatory for a contested divorce. The law states that the break-up of a marriage is permissible when "the spiritual and material communion between spouses can no longer be maintained or reconstructed."

The bill has prompted further calls for a revision of the 1929 concordat forged between the Mussolini government and the Vatican, which established Catholicism as Italy's official religion, and which still regulates Church–State relations.

Germaine Greer

After a series of groundbreaking operations and treatment, a former soldier is the first man to become a woman.

Female Eunuch Raises Storm

England, December: Australian feminist provocateur Germaine Greer has sent a shock wave around the world's dinner tables with the publication of her first book, *The Female Eunuch*.

The book claims to expose the truth about gender inequality. Greer argues that sexual liberation is the key to women's liberation, stating that women have become separated from their libidos. She says the typical suburban existence, with its focus on consumerism and the nuclear family, represses women sexually, devitalising them, and rendering them "eunuchs." Worse still, women are oblivious to how much men hate them and how much they have been taught to hate themselves.

Currently a lecturer in English at the University of Warwick, Greer earned a PhD from Cambridge University in 1968.

Swiss Women Win Vote

Glenda Jackson

Geneva, Switzerland, February 7: The results of an historic referendum today will see Swiss women given the right to vote in federal elections for the first time ever. The men of Switzerland voted in a clear majority (621,403 in favor, and 323,596 against) to amend the federal constitution and extend the franchise. Switzerland was one of the last western European nations to have restricted the vote to men. Until today it remained in the company of Saudi Arabia, Jordan, and Kuwait, which have not yet extended the vote to women. Times had been slowly changing in Switzerland, however, where some cantons and municipalities had already granted women the vote in local elections.

Just 12 years ago, in a national referendum on the same issue, the results were almost entirely the reverse, with 654,924 against and 323,306 in favor of giving the vote to women. Given the state of Swiss law, today's vote is welcomed by many women. In some parts of the country, women still require a husband's consent to take out a loan, apply for a passport, or accept a job.

> *"Freud is the father of psychoanalysis. It has no mother."*
>
> GERMAINE GREER
> (1939–), WRITER AND
> FEMINIST

Groups such as the Swiss Association for Women's Suffrage see today's victory as the first step in a gradual program of legal reform. It is expected that 1.5 million women will vote in this autumn's elections, outnumbering the 1.2 million men.

Over 300 Women Admit to Abortions

Paris, France, April 5 : Today 343 French women made their private pasts public knowledge as part of a campaign to change the conservative French stance on abortion. Their bold admission, "I am one of them. I have had an abortion," was put into print in a radical manifesto in the independent left-wing magazine *Nouvel Observateur*. The signatories included many actresses and writers, such as Simone de Beauvoir and Catherine Deneuve. In speaking out, the women risk potential imprisonment, but it is for this very reason they see the need to act. The 1923 law that currently applies in France provides for between six and 24 months imprisonment as well as a sizeable fine for obtaining an abortion. Although the law is not always enforced, it is usually the more economically disadvantaged who suffer under it. Those not wealthy enough to travel to England or Switzerland, where safe abortions are more readily available, must act in secret—not only breaking the law, but also facing grave physical danger. Despite the prohibition, the French abortion rate is high.

time out

After a referendum in Switzerland, woman have finally been given the right to vote. It is expected that 1.5 million women will vote in the incoming autumn elections, outnumbering the male voters.

Severine, representing Monaco, wins the Eurovision Song Contest.

Ike and Tina Turner's "Proud Mary" hits No. 4.

The manifesto seeks not only the legalization of abortion, but also the provision of free services to safely perform them. The declaration comes as part of a lively current debate on the topic. Recently a bill was approved in the National Assembly that authorized abortion in special circumstances such as rape, or if birth would endanger the mother. The Episcopate of the French Roman Catholic Church condemned the bill, while the Mouvement de Liberation des Femmes is behind the current campaign to request that the bill be taken even further to cover other cases.

Vietnamese Peace Warrior Sets Herself on Fire

Saigon, South Vietnam, May: A teenage Buddhist nun today joined a growing list of peace radicals who have resorted to self-immolation in protest at the continued US military presence in Vietnam. Nguyen Thi Co, aged 17, burned herself to death inside a pagoda in the South Vietnamese village of Cam Li. Self-immolation—effected by dousing one's self with flammable liquid and then lighting a match—has, over the last

Paris, France, January 10: French fashion designer Gabrielle (Coco) Chanel dies, aged 87.
Berlin, Germany, January 31: Telephone services between East and West Berlin are re-established after 19 years.
Geneva, Switzerland, February 7: Switzerland gives women the right to vote in federal elections.
USA, February 13: The six-part TV miniseries *Elizabeth*, Glenda Jackson's tour-de-force as the fiercely independent Elizabeth I of England, debuts.

London, England, February 15: The decimal system of currency is introduced. The previous system was in place for 1,200 years.
Liechtenstein, February 28: The tiny country's male electorate refuses the vote to women.
London, UK March 6 : 4,000 women protesters march from Hyde Park to Downing Street in the UK's biggest women's liberation demonstration.
USA, March: Janis Joplin's hit song "Me and Bobby McGee" is released posthumously.

USA, March: Ike and Tina Turner's "Proud Mary" peaks at No. 4 on the popular music charts.
Dubin, Ireland, April 3: Severine, representing Monaco, wins the Eurovision Song Contest with the song "Un banc, un arbre, une rue."
France, April 5: The *Manifeste des 343* is published, in which 343 French women, including some celebrities, risk arrest for declaring publicly that they have undergone abortions.

North Pole, April 5: Canadian Fran Phipps becomes the first woman to reach the North Pole.
Hollywood, USA, April 15: Glenda Jackson wins the Academy Award for Best Actress for her performance in *Women in Love*.
Saigon, South Vietnam, May: Buddhist Nguyen Thi Co immolates herself to protest the Vietnam War.
London, UK June 8: Members of the Women's Institute convene for the 50th AGM of the National Federation of Women's Institutes.

California, USA, June: Computer "floppy disks" are developed by IBM to store data.
Wimbledon, England, July 2: Nineteen-year-old Evonne Goolagong wins Wimbledon title, beating fellow Australian Margaret Court 6-4, 6-1.
New York, USA, July 10: Gloria Steinem addresses the first meeting of the National Women's Political Caucus, formed by US feminists Steinem, Betty Friedan, Fannie Lou Hamer, Congresswoman Bella Abzug, and others.

decade, become a recurring action among Buddhists, both men and women, who oppose governmental oppression and the continuance of war in Vietnam.

In 1966, a veritable wave of self-immolations was provoked by the example of well-respected middle-aged nun, Thich Nu Thanh Quang, who burned herself to let the world know of the tragedy of what she saw as "a war without reason." While some Buddhists oppose this form of political radicalism, self-immolation is never seen as an act of suicide or escape, but rather one of strength and moral purity. Vietnamese Buddhism revolves around the themes of compassion, wisdom, and involvement.

For twentieth-century Vietnamese women who feel frustration at the suffering caused to their people by the decades of war, the principles of compassion and involvement have come to mean active opposition to all forms of warfare. Self-immolation is understood as doing something for the suffering of other people by making their plight known to the world.

Nguyen Thi Co was an active follower of "engaged Buddhism" (expressed most notably in the writings of the international leader, Thich Nhat Hanh). While we are yet to see whether such protests will prove politically successful in ending the war, many Buddhists hold these women as peace heroes, and believe they will escape reincarnation and become bodhisattvas as a result of their actions. A bodhisattva is one who postpones entry into nirvana in order to help others to attain enlightenment.

Australian Teenager Takes Wimbledon Title

Wimbledon, England, July 2: It took just 62 minutes today for 19-year-old Evonne Goolagong to be crowned the new queen of the Wimbledon court. Goolagong vied for the Wimbledon title with fellow Australian Margaret Court, beating the

Evonne Goolagong wins at Wimbledon.

senior player 6-4, 6-1. Just last year, this graceful girl from the outback town of Barellan in New South Wales, was knocked out in the first round of the prestigious competition.

Goolagong's overjoyed coach, Vic Edwards, was not entirely taken by surprise with her success. He first saw her potential at age nine, and believes the young champion still has room to grow. Goolagong's victory today marks the highest peak of achievement for Aboriginal women in international tennis.

Death at Memorial Concert

Chicago, USA, August 27 : Jazz musician Lil Hardin Armstrong died while performing at her piano today in the Civic Center Plaza, Chicago. Her death comes just seven weeks after that of her ex-husband, famous jazz trumpeter Louis Armstrong. In a bizarre coincidence Hardin, 73, was performing "St Louis Blues" at the

televised memorial concert for Armstrong when she collapsed and reportedly suffered a heart attack.

One of the most prominent woman in early jazz, Lil Hardin played piano, composed, and arranged for most of the important New Orleans bands. She was married to Louis Armstrong for 14 years, from 1924 to 1938, and is generally credited with both encouraging the young Armstrong and being influential in shaping his early career.

Hardin played for Sugar Johnny's Creole Orchestra and then Freddie Keppard's Original Creole Orchestra before leading her own band at Dreamland Café in Chicago. She joined King Oliver's Creole Jazz Band in 1921 where she met Armstrong and became his second wife.

Despite their increasing musical success, the couple's marriage was rocky and ended in divorce, although they remained friends for life.

Lil appeared in several Broadway shows, and in the late 1930s reinvented herself as a swing vocalist, recording 26 vocal sides for Decca records. Back in Chicago in the 1940s, Lil played as a

Coco Chanel

Lil Hardin Armstrong's musical career began in the 20s.

soloist in nightclubs. She continued to record sporadically up until 1963, often with the old gang of New Orleans and Chicago musicians. She was working on an autobiography when she died.

UK, July 16: Terry Clark, who has passed the Football Association's referee's exam, becomes one of a handful of women referees.
South Africa, July 25: Christiaan Barnard performs the first combined heart-lung transplant.
Newport, USA, July 26: British sailor Nicolette Milnes-Walker is the first woman to sail solo across the Atlantic, from Wales to Newport, Rhode Island, in 45 days.
The Moon, July 30: Apollo 15 lands a four-wheeled "moon buggy" and astronauts drive 17 miles (27 km).

USA, August 1: The Sonny and Cher Comedy Hour premieres on TV.
Paris, France, August 1: French swimmer Christine Caron wins the 100m backstroke event at the Nautic Stadium Georges Vallerey in Paris
London, England, August 4: Sheila Scott lands at Heathrow after making the first solo light-aircraft flight around the world, equator to equator over the North Pole.
Australia and New Zealand, August 18: Australia and New Zealand announce they will pull troops out of Vietnam by December.

Chicago, USA, August 27: Jazz musician Lil Hardin Armstrong, ex-wife of Louis Armstrong, dies onstage while playing "St Louis Blues" at a televised memorial concert for Armstrong, just seven weeks after his death.
Vatican City, October 20: Barbara Ward is the first woman to address the Vatican Council.
Belfast, Ireland, November 10: Two Belfast women are tarred for dating British soldiers, and a Catholic girl in Londonderry is also tarred for her intention to marry a British soldier.

London, UK November 10: Women's libbers demonstrate outside the Royal Albert Hall, London, during the Miss World contest.
Alberta, Canada, November 12: Canadian flight attendant Mary Dohey saves the lives of passengers and crew when her Air Canada flight is hijacked.
California, USA, November 15: Intel produces the first micro-processor.
Hong Kong, November 28: Jane Hwang Hsien Yuen and Joyce Bennett are the first women to be ordained as Anglican priests.

London, England: Erin Pizzey sets up the Chiswick's Women's Aid, a pioneering shelter for battered women.
France, December 20: A group of doctors form Médecins Sans Frontières to assist the people of the Biafra region of Nigeria. They form the group in frustration at the neutrality of the Red Cross.
France: Exiled Greek actress and singer, Melina Mercouri ,publishes her autobiography, I Was Born Greek.
Vatican City: Barbara Ward is first woman to address Vatican Council.

Barbara Ward

First Woman to Address Vatican

Vatican City, October 20: Today, England's Barbara Ward (Lady Jackson), became the first woman ever to address a Synod of Bishops at the Vatican. One of the themes on the Vatican's agenda was that of "Social Justice in the World."

Ward, who is a Roman Catholic, achieved two historic firsts by being both the first woman and the first layperson ever to address such a Synod. In her speech she called on the Roman Catholic Church to take seriously the international problems of injustice, poverty, and need; and to mobilize its 500 million members to pressure governments as well as set an example for change.

Ward is a renowned expert on world development. She is currently the Albert Schweitzer Professor of International Economic Development at Columbia University, and has consulted, lectured, and written extensively on international economics and politics.

Ward graduated in politics, philosophy, and economics from Oxford in 1935. After serving briefly with the British Ministry of Information, she was invited to join the staff of *The Economist* in 1939, and became foreign editor in 1940. She married her Australian husband, Commander Robert Jackson, in 1950 and they have one son.

In a sign of the slowly expanding role of women in the Church, Ward's expertise and energy led to her part in the recent formation of the Pope's special Commission for Justice and Peace.

> "USUALLY I OBJECT WHEN SOMEONE MAKES OVER-MUCH OF MEN'S WORK VERSUS WOMEN'S WORK, FOR I THINK IT IS THE EXCEL-LENCE OF THE RESULTS WHICH COUNTS."
>
> MARGARET BOURKE-WHITE (1904–1971), PHOTOGRAPHER AND WAR CORRESPONDENT

Melina Mercouri publishes her autogiography, *I Was Born Greek.*

Shaved and Tarred for Love

Belfast, Northern Ireland, Nov 10: Last night Mary Doherty, a 19-year-old Catholic woman from Belfast, was subject to an almost medieval attack from her compatriots. Picked up and forced into a car while walking along the street, Miss

Women outside London's Albert Hall protest against the Miss World contest.

Doherty was reportedly taken to the Bogside Catholic ghetto in Londonderry, where she was strapped to a lamp post. A group of 80 women jeered and taunted "Soldier lover! Soldier lover!" while one of them shaved off Miss Doherty's hair. Tar was then poured over her as she reportedly wept and pleaded for mercy. She was left strapped to the lamp post for around 30 minutes while a photographer took photos.

Miss Doherty was attacked for being romantically involved with a British soldier named John Larter, serving with the Royal Anglian regiment. She was engaged to marry him next month, although there are reports that she has changed her mind following the attack.

The incident comes in a growing climate of hatred, as many Catholics begin to resent the presence of British soldiers in their districts. Only two years ago, Catholics relied on British soldiers for protection from their Protestant neighbors. However, resentment has grown over midnight searches of houses, the internment and interrogation of Catholics, and what is seen as unfair protection of Protestants during marches. The attack on Doherty comes just days after another Londonderry female factory worker was seized and forcefully removed of her hair, also for seeing a British soldier. The women responsible wish to send a clear warning to other Catholic women of Northern Ireland that private relations with British soldiers will lead to public shame and will not be tolerated.

Flight Attendant Soothes Hijacker

Alberta, Canada, November 12: No amount of training on the ground could have prepared Air Canada flight attendant Mary

Dohey for the ordeal she faced today in the sky. It started as a routine day for the crew of the flight from Vancouver to Montreal. After the plane left Alberta, Dohey was seized by a man in a black hood claiming to be carrying dynamite. Holding the crew at gunpoint, he told them that the plane must fly to Ireland. Describing himself as a member of the Irish Republican Army, the 27-year-old from Calgary also demanded $1.5 million in ransom money.

Under extreme pressure, Dohey remained calm throughout the ordeal, and consistently put her passengers' lives and those of her fellow crew members before her own. The plane briefly touched down in Great Falls, Montana, to pick up $50,000 ransom money. Remarkably, after taking off again, Dohey managed to persuade the hijacker to allow the plane to return to Montana to let all the passengers and some of the crew leave the aircraft safely. Although she was free to leave at this point, Dohey chose to stay on the plane to placate the crazed man.

The conflict came to a dramatic close when another crew member hit the hijacker over the head with a fire ax. Without Dohey's presence of mind, the safety of the 118 passengers and crew was by no means certain. She prevented the incident with the increasingly unstable hijacker from escalating.

Women Priests Ordained in Hong Kong

Hong Kong, November 28: This evening, school principal Jane Hwang Hsien Yuen, along with head of the Hong Kong Branch of the Church Missionary Society, Joyce Bennet, participated in an historic ordination service. They are the first women to be ordained as Anglican priests

Glenda Jackson is one of the stars of *Women in Love*.

Sheila Scott

following a recent decision made by the Anglican Consultative Council.

The Council, which met in Kenya, voted that it would be "acceptable" for a bishop to ordain a woman with Diocesan approval. It was by no means a unanimous decision; the result was passed by a tight vote of 24–22. Key figures within the Church of England still oppose the move.

Chilean Women Fight Tear-Gas with Pots and Pans

Santiago, Chile, Dec 3: Last night, the city of Santiago came to a standstill as around 5,000 women took to the streets of the nation's capital to protest food shortages and the ongoing visit of the Marxist Cuban leader Fidel Castro.

At its peak, the protest march stretched along four blocks, with women filling every space on the street. Women of all ages, from middle and working classes, beat pots and pans, and chanted slogans against Castro and the current leftist leader of Chile, Dr Allende. The protestors were drawn from the ranks of the Chilean National Party as well as the Christian Democratic Party, both of which are critical, indeed hostile, toward the left-wing Popular Unity Coalition of Dr Allende.

The women, who began peacefully, encountered opposition from both pro-government protesters and the police. Pro-government demonstrators—mostly young men—hurled rocks at them and waved their leftist red-and-black flags in support of Allende. The police, who were surprised by the number of women participating, also moved in on the protestors as they neared the Presidential Palace. Eventually the police fired tear-gas grenades into the crowd of women. They used the same treatment in turn on the

pro-government rioters. However, even after the police had cleared the city using water cannons rioting continued into the night.

In this most violent of political demonstrations against Allende's incumbency, a total of 88 people were injured from tear-gas grenades, gun-shot wounds, and assaults. This mass protest by Chile's women shows the instability of the present regime and the frustration felt by many at the Marxist leadership's inability to address the critical food shortage.

Door Wide Open for Battered Women

London, England: Thanks largely to the enterprise and responsiveness of Englishwoman Erin Pizzey, a previously derelict house in Hounslow, London, is fast becoming a place of refuge for abused women with nowhere to go.

Pizzey and her team of women originally established the house as a "drop-in" style center for women with children who—like Pizzey herself—needed to find energy and support in meeting the everyday challenges of marriage and child-raising. Pizzey and her friends were motivated to start a group of their own after they became disillusioned with the broader women's movement, which they felt was more concerned with politics than with the basic needs of women and children. The local council granted them the use of No. 2 Belmont Terrace as a base, and the women set about renovating the small house themselves. What Pizzey didn't

predict was that the house would soon become a refuge for a growing number of abused wives.

The change in direction came with a knock on the door from a visibly battered woman claiming she had no one else to help her. The pioneering Pizzey has since discovered that the need for such a refuge is overwhelming. Just weeks after the first request for help, around 40 women and children have been squeezed into the four-room home.

Pizzey is at the forefront of a growing public concern with what has been

British sailor Nicolette Milnes-Walker is the first woman to sail solo across the Atlantic.

traditionally kept a private subject—marital violence. Some see Pizzey's refuge, the first of its kind in England, as a harbinger of many more. Such help is seen as a welcome supplement to the feeble protections afforded to women under the law.

Erin Pizzey sets up a pioneering shelter for battered women.

Angela Davis

Shirley Chisholm's Double First for the Democrats

New York, USA, January 25: Shirley Chisholm today formally announced her Democratic candidacy for US president, becoming only the second African-American woman to run for the presidency.

Last July, Ms. Chisholm, the Congressional representative from New York's Twelfth District, announced she was considering running for President. Today she formally became the first woman and

Shirley Chisholm will run for the US presidency.

> *"I AM WOMAN HEAR ME ROAR / IN NUMBERS TOO BIG TO IGNORE."*
>
> HELEN REDDY, "I AM WOMAN"

the first African-American to seek the Democratic Party nomination for the nation's highest office. Several other women (and African-Americans) have previously run on minor party tickets, and Republican Senator, Margaret Chase Smith, campaigned for the 1964 Presidential nomination, but Chisholm's candidacy is a double first for the Democrats. Born in New York of West Indian parents, Chisholm became the first black woman to sit in Congress in 1968, after serving in the New York Assembly for four years. The Brooklyn Democratic Party machine did not support her Presidential nomination, but she succeeded nonetheless. Her campaign slogan

was "Unbossed and unbought." Chisholm has insisted that she is not the "women's candidate," but she has always been a strong advocate of women's rights. Last year she was one of the four founders of the National Women's Political Caucus, and has often said that during her 20 years in politics "I have met far more discrimination because I am a woman than because I am black." Indeed, Shirley Chisholm has been so outspoken over women's rights that she has been criticized for neglecting black issues.

Angela Davis No Killer, Court Declares

San Jose, California, USA, June 4: After just 13 hours' deliberation, an all-white jury today found 28-year-old black militant, Angela Davis, not guilty on all charges of murder, kidnapping, and criminal conspiracy. The announcement set off such an emotional uproar that Judge Richard E. Arnason threatened to clear the courtroom.

Davis, having shown little emotion through the 13 weeks of the highly publicized trial, burst out sobbing after the last verdict had been announced. "This is the happiest day of my life," she said later.

The charges were lodged in August, 1970, after 17-year-old Jonathan Jackson smuggled guns into a courtroom in San Rafael, Marin County, California, giving them to three black convicts. They then attempted to escape, using a judge, an assistant district attorney, and three women jurors as hostages.

The judge died in the getaway van, along with Jackson and two of the three would-be-escapees. The judge, who had a shotgun taped to his neck, was shot in the head with a blast from the weapon, and also received a chest

time out

Carole King's album *Tapestry* is on top of the charts for a year and sells 10 million copies in the USA alone. Tracks include immortals like "You've Got a Friend," "A Natural Woman," and "Will You Love Me Tomorrow?"

wound from a bullet that many say must have been fired from outside the van. Trial evidence showed that either shot could have been fatal. The smuggled guns were registered in Davis' name.

The jurors were cheered loudly as they left the courtroom for the final time today, and later Davis met them in the pressroom, hugging each in turn.

Women's Voices Heard Loud and Clear

USA, July: The feminist magazine *Ms.*, which has been making occasional appearances as an insert in *New York* magazine, has hit the newsstands as a monthly, stand-alone publication.

When *Ms.* debuted last December, carrying articles on such subjects as "the housewife's moment of truth," sexism in the English language, and abortion, the syndicated columnist James J. Kilpatrick sneered that the tone of the magazine

Gloria Steinem names *Ms.*, the feminist magazine.

Copenhagen, Denmark, January 15: Margrethe II is crowned Queen of Denmark—the first Danish queen to succeed directly to the throne under the new Act of Succession.
New York, USA, January 25: Shirley Chisholm announces her Democratic candidacy for president, becoming the second African-American woman to run for the US presidency.
Washington DC, USA, March 22: The Equal Rights Amendment is sent to the states for ratification after passing both Houses of Congress.

USA, March 24: Francis Ford Coppola's cinematic masterpiece about a Mafia family, *The Godfather*, opens.
Madrid, Spain, March: Maria del Carmen Martinez-Bordiu y Franco, grand-daughter of General Franco, marries Don Alfonso, Duke of Anjou and Cadiz.
World, March: The El Niño weather pattern is seen to reverse trade winds on the equator.

Hayman Island, Australia, April 22: Sylvia Cook becomes the first woman to row across any ocean with John Fairfax. They left San Francisco, USA, on April 26, 1971.
New York, USA, April 30: Seven nuns are arrested at St. Patrick's Cathedral for disrupting a Mass in an anti-war protest.
New York, USA, May: Barbara Tuchman wins her second Pulitzer Prize for non-fiction for *Stilwell and the American Experience in China*, published in 1971.

San Jose, California, USA, June 4: Angela Davis is acquitted on charges that she supplied guns for a shooting at Marin County Courthouse in 1970.
Washington, D.C., USA, June 17: Five men are arrested breaking into the Democratic National Committee offices in the Watergate Hotel.
Geneva, New York, USA, June 24: Bernice Gera becomes the first woman to umpire a professional baseball game.
USA, July: *Ms.* magazine goes monthly. The first issue hit the newsstands in January.

New York, USA, August: Juanita Morris Kreps becomes the first woman on the board of directors of the New York Stock Exchange.
North Vietnam, August 22: Jane Fonda, actress and anti-war protester, makes an address to American servicemen in Vietnam.
New York, USA, August 30: Yoko Ono performs with John Lennon in the "One to One" charity concert at Madison Square Garden.
Munich, Germany, September 6: Palestinian terrorists kill 11 members of the Israeli Olympic team.

was a "C-sharp on an un-tuned piano," and a note "of petulance, of bitchiness, or nervous fingernails screeching across a blackboard."

The title came from a friend of feminist crusader, Gloria Steinem, who in turn heard it in a radio interview.

The term "Ms." was conceived in 1961 by Sheila Michaels, who was illegitimate, and sought a title that reflected her situation. She was not "owned" by a father and did not wish to be "owned" by a husband. Men go by "Mr.," which gives no indication of marital status, and etiquette and business practice demands that women use either "Miss" or "Mrs.," but many women do not wish to be defined by their marital status. For the growing number of women who wish to keep their own maiden name after marriage, neither Miss nor Mrs. is technically correct.

The stated aim of *Ms.* magazine is to achieve "…a just and safe world where power and possibility are not limited by gender, race, class, sexual orientation, disability, or age."

Actress-Activist Takes on Nixon Over Vietnam

North Vietnam, August 22: Hollywood star Jane Fonda has sparked controversy with a radio speech criticizing the USA for its involvement in the Vietnam War.

Fonda has been in North Vietnam for several weeks, making speeches and issuing photos and media releases. However, her actions have received only scant coverage in the USA, with many perceiving her actions as an unpatriotic, even treasonous display of comfort to the enemy. But the Nixon Administration has dismissed calls for any legal action against Ms Fonda.

Jane, daughter of actor Henry Fonda, made her stage debut in 1955, playing alongside her father in *The Country Girl*. She married film director, Roger Vadim,

Jane Fonda protests against the Vietnam War.

in 1965, and starred in his films, *La Ronde* (1964) and *Barbarella* (1968), an eroti-fi fantasy. In the latter, she plays a scantily clad cartoon-style heroine.

Last year Fonda won the Academy Award for Best Actress, playing a prostitute in the murder mystery, *Klute*.

She has long been engaged in political activism in support of the civil rights movement, and in opposition to the Vietnam War.

In 1969, along with other celebrities, she supported the occupation of Alcatraz Island, which was intended to call attention to Native American issues.

Today's speech included the words: "One thing that I have learned beyond a shadow of a doubt since I've been in this country is that Nixon will never be able to break the spirit of these people; he'll never be able to turn Vietnam, north and south, into a neo-colony of the United States by bombing, by invading, by attacking in any way."

Jane Fonda's speech was broadcast widely on North Vietnam radio, and follows the withdrawal 10 days ago of

the last American ground troops from Vietnam. However, 43,000 Air Force along with vast support personnel still remain in the country.

Tiny Russian Wins Hearts Worldwide

Munich, Germany, September 11: The tiny Soviet gymnast, Olga Korbut, has completed a highly successful Munich Olympics program, captivating hearts worldwide and winning one silver and three gold medals.

Korbut stands only 4 feet 11 inches tall (1.5 m), weighs 90 pounds (41 kg), and was the smallest of all the Olympic competitors. Her pigtails make her appear even younger than her 17 years.

She has helped the Soviet team to a gold medal in the women's gymnastic team event, and she has also won individual gold medals on the balance beam and the floor exercise. Despite losing her balance and subsequently falling off the uneven parallel bars, she also won the silver medal in this event.

Olympic gymnasts are generally in their mid-20s, but Olga's success may lead to an increase in the number of much younger and more diminutive competitors in future Olympics.

Annemarie Renger

Tiny Olga Korbut is the darling of the Munich Olympics.

Key Events

Munich, Germany, September 11: Tiny Soviet gymnast, Olga Korbut, takes home one silver and three gold medals from the Munich Olympics.
New York: Playwright Cynthia Buchanan publishes her novel *Maiden*.
USA, October: Helen Reddy's "I Am Woman," reaches number one on the popular music charts.
Nashville, USA, October: Loretta Lynn becomes the first woman to win the Country Music Association's Entertainer of the Year award.

United Nations, November 15: Jeanne-Martin Cissé of Guinea is elected the first woman president of the United Nations Security Council.
Bolivia, November 16: Lydia Gueiler Tejada becomes Bolivia's first woman president—in a caretaker role.
West Germany, December 13: Annemarie Renger becomes the first female president of the West German Bundestag.
Austria: Hertha Firnberg is elected the first Austrian minister for science and research (SPO - social democrat).

Greenwich, England: British astronomer, Margaret Burbidge, becomes the first woman director of the Royal Observatory at Greenwich, although without the traditional honorary title of Astronomer Royal.
USA: Health food guru, Adele Davis, publishes *Let's Have Healthy Children*.
Sweden: Harriet Andersson, Ingrid Thulin, and Liv Ullmann star in Ingmar Bergman's film *Viskningar och rop* (*Cries and Whispers*).

Ahmedabad, India: Ela Bhatt forms the Self-Employed Women's Association, to help lower class female workers.
United Kingdom: Ann Oakley's classic survey of women's social position—*Sex, Gender and Society*—is published.
Washington DC, USA: Dr. Barbara Sizemore is elected superintendent of schools for the District of Columbia public school system, making her the first African-American woman to head the public school system of a major city.

New York, USA: Finland's Helvi Linnea Sipila becomes the highest-ranking woman in the UN Secretariat as Assistant Secretary General for Social Development and Humanitarian Affairs.
Cape Town, South Africa: Yvonne Bryceland, with her husband Brian Astbury, founds the Space Theatre, the country's first racially integrated theater.

Ingrid Thulin

Women's Work Deserves Equal Pay

Canberra, Australia, December 15: After many decades of agitation by women through the unions and the broader women's movement, the Australian Arbitration Commission today ruled in favor of the principle of equal pay for men and women who perform work of equal value.

The newly elected Whitlam Labor Government supported the submission to the Commission by the Australian Boot Trades Employees' Federation and other unions, as did the National Council of Women, the Union of Australian Women, as well as the Women's Liberation Movement.

The decision means there can no longer be lower rates of pay for women doing the same work as men—teachers, for example. But most women remain in segregated occupations where it is difficult to make pay comparisons with male workers, in jobs like nursing, childcare, and aged care.

Female Public Health Leader Sacked

"The worker must have bread, but she must have roses, too."

ROSA SCHNEIDERMAN
(1882–1892), POLISH-
BORN US UNION
LEADER

Egypt: The Egyptian government has dismissed its Director of Public Health Education, Nawal El Saadawi, after the publication of her book *Women and Sex*, which addresses women's issues including the inferior status of women in the Arab world.

Swedish director Ingmar Bergman with some of his leading ladies.

The book speaks out against the common practice of genital infibulation, or surgical closure of the female labia majora by sewing them together to seal off the genitalia, leaving only a small hole for the passage of urine and menstrual blood. This is usually carried out on girls at around the onset of puberty (as it was to Saadawi), supposedly to ensure

Self-Employed Women's Association (SEWA) clothes stall.

chastity. It is usually performed along with clitoridectomy, or removal of the clitoris and labia minora. These practices are euphemistically known as female circumcision, and are intended to render women less sexual.

Saadawi attracted the antagonism of highly placed political and theological authorities, who fear that her ideas will attract the support of Arab women, who enjoy far less power and freedom than their male counterparts.

Saadawi was born in 1931 in the small village of Kafr Tahla, one of nine children. Her father was a government official in the Ministry of Education who had fought against the British in the 1919 revolution. He was unusually progressive, in that he sent his daughters—as well as his sons—to school. Ms. Saadawi studied medicine at Cairo University. Her writings include a collection of short stories, *I Learned Love* (1957), and novels, *Memoirs of a Woman Doctor* (1958), *The Absent One* (1969), and *Two Women in One* (1971). *Women and Sex* is her first work of non-fiction.

None of these books have been translated into English, but Saadawi's case has nonetheless attracted worldwide publicity, and outraged many observers. The

magazine, *Health*, which she founded in 1969, and edits, has also recently been banned.

"Untouchables" Enjoy Union Power

Ahmedabad, India: Ela Bhatt, teacher, lawyer, and social activist, has formed the Self-Employed Women's Association (SEWA) in Ahmedabad, northern India. It is a trade union specifically designed to help lower class female urban workers to obtain access to low-cost credit and education. Since 1968, Bhatt has headed the women's section of the successful and very well-organized Textile Labor Association (TLA) in Ahmedabad.

Last year Bhatt received the International Diploma of Labor and Cooperatives from the Afro-Asian Institute of Labor and Cooperatives in Tel Aviv, Israel. Upon her return to Ahmedabad, Bhatt undertook to organize the city's lowest-paid women into a trade union under the auspices of the TLA.

The organization includes weavers, stitchers, cigarette rollers, food vendors, firewood and wastepaper collectors, junksmiths, handcart pullers, and road construction workers. Most are subject to high rents for stalls and the tools of their trade, and also to routine exploitation by moneylenders, employers, and officials. In Ahmedabad, 97 percent of these women live in slums, 93 percent are illiterate, and most are in debt.

Under India's rigid caste system, almost all such workers are classified as "untouchable"—the lowest of the low—and are not protected by any laws. Many of these workers are related to employees in the textile or other industries.

Initially the government objected to the registration of the union because, it said, legally a union is only for employees and not for the self-employed.

Bhatt, however, has convinced the government that a union exists for the economic development of its members, not just for protection against any exploitation by employers.

SEWA plans to develop health, death, and maternity benefit schemes, and set up cooperatives of various trade groups. They are developing new tools, designs and techniques, and are engaging in bulk buying and promotional marketing. Other plans include the establishment of schools, training programs, and a dedicated bank for SEWA members, allowing them some financial freedom.

Model Bianca Jagger and her rocker husband Mick were supporters of Angela Davis.

Female Astronomer Reaches the Stars, Almost

Greenwich, England: The eminent British astronomer, Margaret Burbidge, has become the first female director of the Royal Observatory at Greenwich, but has not been granted the honorary title of Astronomer Royal which traditionally accompanies the post. That honor has been given to male radio astronomer Martin Ryle, a decision that has stirred outrage in many quarters.

Burbidge received her PhD in astronomy in 1943, and began to research galaxies by linking spectrographs to telescopes. She applied for a Carnegie Fellowship in 1945, but was turned down because the position involved work at Mount Wilson Observatory, California, from which women were barred. In 1948 she married theoretical astrophysicist Geoffrey Burbidge, and in 1953 they began

research in collaboration with distinguished astronomers Fred Hoyle and William Fowler. They proved that all elements in the universe, except the very lightest, are created by nuclear processes inside stars.

In 1955, Ms Burbidge finally gained access to Mount Wilson by posing as her husband's assistant. When management found out, they allowed her to stay only if she and her husband lived in a separate cottage on the grounds, rather than using the men's dormitory.

Last year Burbidge turned down the prestigious Annie J. Cannon Award of the American Astronomical Society because it was awarded to women only, saying, "It is high time that discrimination in favor of, as well as against, women in professional life be removed."

Challenge to Gender Basis of Discrimination

United Kingdom: Ann Oakley, the British sociologist and feminist, has published *Sex, Gender and Society,* a groundbreaking analysis of the social position of women in the present day.

Oakley's thesis is that in order to eliminate discrimination against women, we need a way of distinguishing the social treatment of men and women from the biology of sex. She aims to provide a critical tool for the emerging academic discipline of women's studies, and to invalidate the social inequality that results from translating the biological difference between the sexes into a value judgment, which almost invariably concludes that women are inferior to men.

The book accepts the basic biological differences, but regards an upbringing that grooms girls exclusively for the role of wife and mother as a process that hinders a young woman's development as an individual of varied powers and wide interests.

Oakley speaks out against cultural ideals and stereotypes of masculinity and femininity, and also, at the structural level, the sexual division of labor in institutions and organizations.

She says: "While our society is organized around the differences rather than the similarities between the sexes, these two extremes of mas-culinity and femininity will recur, so apparently confirming the belief that they come from a biological cause. Whatever biological cause there is in reality, however influential or

insubstantial it may be, thus...becomes increasingly a rationalization of what is, in fact, only prejudice."

New Theater to Tackle Apartheid

Cape Town, South Africa: Yvonne Bryceland and her husband Brian Astbury, along with highly regarded black playwright and actor Athol Fugard, have opened the Space Theatre, the country's first racially integrated theater.

Hertha Firnberg

The groundbreaking principle of the theater is that anyone—black, colored, or white—may attend as an audience member or audition for an acting role. This is a revolutionary concept in strictly segregated South Africa, and it is difficult for those who are unaware of the full horrors of apartheid to appreciate just how subversive this policy will appear to many. Taboos such as nudity and inter-racial relationships will be explored, and cross-racial issues dramatized.

Actor and producer, Bryceland, began her career as a stage actress in Cape Town in the late 1940s, and first worked with Fugard in 1969, when she starred in his work, *People are Living There,* and later in *Boesman and Lena,* Fugard's play about a homeless black couple.

The theater's first production will be Fugard's *Statements After an Arrest Under the Immorality Act.*

Author of *Maiden,* playwright Cynthia Buchanan.

The South African *Immorality Act* contains laws that prohibit almost all forms of inter-racial contact. However, the penalties for infringement are much greater for black people than they are for white people.

The Space Theatre troupers hope that their egalitarian practices on integration may, over time, infiltrate the wider South African society, and eventually help lead to the complete downfall of apartheid in the country.

Franco's granddaughter marries into the deposed Spanish royal family when she weds the grandson of King Alfonso XIII.

1973

1970s

Roberta Flack

Supreme Court Hands Down *Roe v. Wade* Decision

Washington DC, USA, January 22: In March 1970 an anonymous pregnant 21-year-old known as Jane Roe sued Dallas District Attorney Henry Wade to allow her to have an abortion in Texas, where the procedure is illegal. She argued that as she was single and poor she did not wish to raise the child and couldn't afford to travel to a state where abortions were legal. She also asked the court not to prosecute other women who procured abortions in Texas.

The court granted Roe the right to an abortion on the grounds that the law violated her constitutional right to privacy with her doctor, but it refused to ban future prosecutions. Roe and her attorneys decided to take the case further.

The matter reached the Supreme Court in December 1971, by which time Roe's baby had been born and adopted out. However, as the circumstances had the potential to be repeated, it was decided to go ahead. Judgment was postponed because the judges wanted the complicated case reheard.

Today seven judges have voted in favor of Roe and two against. The final statement said that laws against abortion are unconstitutional as they violate a woman's right to privacy, but that this right is the primary concern only in the first trimester. In the second and third trimester the state has an interest in the health of the woman and, as late abortion is more dangerous, it cannot be allowed except where not to do so would endanger her life. Also, in the third trimester the unborn child can survive outside the mother's body and, as its life would be at risk, it cannot be aborted except where the mother's life is in danger.

The decision overturns state laws forbidding abortion; nonetheless, the debate between pro-choice and pro-life camps looks set to continue.

> *"BEING AN OLD MAID IS LIKE DEATH BY DROWNING, A REALLY DELIGHTFUL SENSATION AFTER YOU CEASE TO STRUGGLE."*
>
> EDNA FERBER (1885–1968), AMERICAN WRITER

The US Supreme Court decision overturns state laws on prohibiting abortion.

Pakistan's First Woman Governor

Pakistan, February: This month Begum Rana Liaquat Ali Khan has been appointed Governor of Sindh Province, making her Pakistan's first female governor. Begum Rana is the widow of Nawabzada Liaquat Ali Khan, Pakistan's first prime minister, and has been a prominent figure in the nation since its early days.

Born in 1905, Begum Rana graduated with a master's degree in economics from the University of Lucknow in 1929, and went on to become a professor of economics. She married in 1932, and she and her husband were active in the Muslim League.

Liza Minnelli wins an Academy Award for *Cabaret*.

In 1942, when there was fear that Japan would invade India, Begum Rana trained Muslim women as first-aid workers. In 1947, she organized women to give aid to Muslim refugees flooding into the newly formed Pakistan from India and for women to train in defense.

Begum Rana founded the All Pakistan Women's Association in 1949. Despite criticism by Muslim conservatives, it became a prominent welfare agency that promoted women's education and their right to economic independence.

After her husband's assassination in 1951, Begum Rana became the first Muslim woman ambassador, posted first to the Netherlands and then Italy.

Recently, Prime Minister Ali Bhutto has supported equal rights for women, and now Pakistanis have elected one of the nation's most capable women, Begum Rana, to a high government position.

time out

Russian-born American Ida Rosenthal, dressmaker and businesswoman, widely credited as the inventor of the brassiere, dies on March 23. She was co-founder of Maidenform, the first company to standardize cup sizes.

Key Events

Washington DC, USA, January 22: In the historic *Roe v. Wade* decision, the US Supreme Court overturns state laws prohibiting abortion.
Paris, France, January 27: The US and Vietnamese combatants in the Vietnam War sign a peace accord.
Pakistan, February: Begum Rana Liaquat Ali Khan is appointed as the first female Governor of Sindh Province.
Denver, Colorado, USA, February: Pilot Emily Howell Warner becomes the first woman to join the flight crew of a US airline.

USA, March 4: Roberta Flack wins the Record of the Year Grammy Award for "Killing Me Softly."
London, England, March 26: Ten women brokers are admitted to the London Stock Exchange.
Los Angeles, California, USA, March 27: Liza Minnelli wins Best Actress award for her role in *Cabaret*.
New York, USA, April 4: The two 110-story towers of the World Trade Center are completed.

Luxembourg, April 7: Anne Marie David, representing Luxembourg, wins the Eurovision Song Contest with her song *"Tu te reconnaitras"* ("Wonderful Dream").
Taft, Oklahoma, USA, April 16: Leila Foley becomes the first black woman mayor of an American city.
Mandal, Uttar Pradesh, India, April: The Chipko Movement is born when a group of village women prevent the logging of their local forest by throwing their arms around the trees and refusing to move.

Florida, USA, May 14: NASA launches its first crewed space station, *Skylab*.
Cannes, France, May: Italian director Lina Wertmuller's film is nominated for a Golden Palm award at the Cannes Film Festival.
USA, June 1: Jeanne Holm becomes the first female major general in the US Air Force.
London, England, June 21: The first board meeting of Virago Press, "the first mass-market publisher for 52 percent of the population—women," conceived the previous year by Carmen Callil, takes place.

Santa Monica, California, USA, July 2: American actress Betty Grable, whose legs had been insured for $1 million each, dies.
Moscow, USSR, August 16: The US children's TV series "Sesame Street" is denounced as "veiled neocolonialism" by the Kremlin.
London, England, August 17: The first use of a "CAT" scan heralds a breakthrough in medical imaging.
Santiago, Chile, September 11: A bloody military coup led by General Pinochet results in the death of Marxist president Salvador Allende.

Emily Howell Warner, US Commercial Pilot

Denver, Colorado, USA, February: This month Frontier Airlines employed Emily Warner as the first woman flight crew-member in a US commercial airline company since 1934. In that year, Helen Ritchie was hired, then fired after two months when her male colleagues wouldn't allow her to join their union.

At 17, Warner wanted to be a steward-ess, but her ambition to become a pilot was ignited when she was invited to view the cockpit during a flight.

In 1958 she began to take flying lessons, working as a receptionist at the flying school to pay for them. Over the next 14 years she gained her private, commercial, and transport pilot licenses and became a qualified flight instructor, aviation school chief pilot, flight school manager, and pilot examiner.

She attempted to gain a position as a commercial pilot in 1967, approaching airlines again and again, in the meantime watching men she had trained getting jobs. In 1972 she applied to Frontier Airlines when they employed an instructor she knew who had less experience than her. At this time women were entering industries formerly closed to them, and the growing commercial airline industry needed pilots. Frontier was willing to consider Warner; however, despite her experience she was the only applicant asked to pass a flight simulator test before she was accepted.

So far Warner's new colleagues have been cautiously welcoming, an improve-ment on the hostile reception Ritchie received.

London Stock Exchange Finally Admits Women

London, England, March 26: Although the London Stock Exchange's admission rules never specifically excluded women from becoming members, before now none has been accepted.

For years, women in the financial industry applied pressure to be admitted to gain the business advantages it pro-vides. In May 1971, the members voted 1,287 to 955 against doing so. By January 1972, mounting contro-versy forced the Stock Exchange to state that "no suitable candidate has ever been refused admission to membership." Female applicants were still unsuitable because the Exchange's new building had no facilities for women.

On February 1 it was announced that women could become members, primarily because the London Stock Exchange will merge with regional exchanges that already have female members. Today, for the first time, ten women members entered the London Stock Exchange.

Ten women brokers are admitted to the London Stock Exchange.

Women of Mandal Village Save Their Trees

Mandal, Uttar Pradesh, India, April: In Uttar Pradesh, people—usually women—rely on the Himalayan forests for fodder, wood for fuel, medicinal plants, and, in times of hardship, fruit and edible tubers.

The deep forest soils also absorb water, preventing floods and landslides during the monsoon. The water they soak up emerges in springs throughout the year. With the mass clearing of forests, land-slides have become more frequent and springs are vanishing.

In the last century, conflict over this resource has increased. First foreign colonists took wood for manufacturing, and these days the Indian Government grants licenses to do so. The local people have steadily lost access to the forests.

This April, the women of Mandal village took matters into their own hands. While the villagers had been denied permission to use some trees to make agricultural tools, the government granted a license to a company to fell trees to make sporting goods. Axemen arrived while the village men were away at a meeting. The village women ran to the forest and begged the axemen to spare the trees. When threatened by the contractors, the women embraced the trees, saying they would die with them. Unsure of what to do, the axemen left.

Embracing trees to save them has a long history in India. In around 1730, a woman named Amrita Devi led a group of village women to save trees that the Maharaja of Jodhpur wanted felled. After soldiers killed a number of women, the maharaja spared the trees.

Protests against large-scale logging have been growing. At a meeting in 1972 the poet Ghanasyam Raturi composed a poem about this embracing, known as *Chipko* in Hindi, of the trees. Events in Mandal seem to indicate that his words have been translated into action.

Rachael Heyhoe-Flint

Houston, Texas, USA, September 20: Billie Jean King beats Bobby Riggs in the "Battle of the Sexes," 6-4, 6-3, 6-3, in front of 40 million television viewers.
Sydney, Australia, October 20: Queen Elizabeth II opens the Sydney Opera House, declaring it "one of the wonders of the world." It cost 14 times the original estimate.
Philippines, October 29: Cecilia Muñoz-Palma becomes the first woman justice appointed to the Supreme Court.

England, October: Renowned English cellist Jacqueline du Pré is diagnosed with multiple sclerosis.
USA, November 6: Computer whiz Patricia Wiener patents one of the first memory systems to be contained on a single silicon computer chip.
New Jersey, USA, November 7: Sylvia Pressler, hearing examiner for the New Jersey Civil Rights Division, rules that Little League Baseball must admit girls into its programs.

London, England, November 14: Princess Anne marries Captain Mark Phillips.
Melbourne, Australia, November 25: State Supreme Court judge Justice Marilyn Warren is appointed Vic-toria's Chief Justice, the first woman to fill the position in Australia.
USA, November: Erica Jong's *Fear of Flying* is published.
New York, USA, December 10: Mexican lawyer and politician Maria Lavalle Urbina is awarded a United Nations Human Rights Prize.

Vancouver, Canada: Canada's first rape crisis center opens.
San Francisco, USA: Margo St James founds the sex workers' rights group, COYOTE (Call Off Your Old Tired Ethics).
Israel: Shulamit Aloni establishes the Ratz Party (Movement for Citizens' Rights and Peace).
England: Cricketer Rachael Heyhoe-Flint becomes television's first woman sports commentator.
France: Lebanese poet Nadia Tuéni is awarded the Prix de l'Académie Française.

England: Alicia Markova, sometimes called "the miniature Pavlova," is named a governor of the Royal Ballet. She was born in England as Lilian Alicia Marks, but Serge Diaghilev changed her name during her time with the Ballets Russes.
Los Angeles, California, USA: Canadian-born pathologist Elizabeth Stern Shankman links prolonged oral contraceptive use with cervical cancer.
USA: Danielle Steel publishes her first novel, *Going Home*.

Virago Press Founded

Erica Jong

London, England, June 21: Last year, the Australian-born Carmen Callil, who runs a small publicity company, dreamt up the idea of establishing a publishing house with books exclusively by and for women.

Today Callil and the two women who began publishing the feminist magazine *Spare Rib* last year, Rosie Boycott and Marsha Rowe (also Australian), held the first official board meeting of their new publishing venture, Virago Press, in her kitchen.

Their goals for Virago are clear. At present most popular writing by and for women is romantic fiction. More serious women's books other than established classics are considered too radical for mainstream publishers. Virago aims to fill the gap by bringing feminist ideas to a wider audience and being "the first mass-market publisher for 52 percent of the population—women."

Princess Anne weds Captain Mark Philips.

First Female Justice for Supreme Court

The Philippines, October 29: Cecilia Muñoz-Palma today was appointed as the first female justice of the Supreme Court of the Philippines, indeed of any supreme court in the world.

Muñoz-Palma is used to breaking new ground. She studied at the College of Law of the University of the Philippines where she was the first woman president of the Law Student Council. She graduated in

1937, topping the bar exams. In 1947 she became the Philippines' first female prosecutor. She gained her master's degree in law from Yale University in 1954 and became the Philippines' first female district judge.

Muñoz-Palma is not driven by personal ambition. As a young woman she contemplated becoming a nun and believes her considerable gifts and opportunities were granted to her by God to serve others.

During her undergraduate years Muñoz-Palma campaigned for the right of women to vote, a cause that was successful in 1937. This was also the year she married lawyer Rodolfo C. Palma. He and the couple's three children have continued their support for her career through the years.

President Marcos, who imposed martial law last year, appointed Justice Muñoz-Palma under the advice of the Secretary of Justice, long viewed as loyal to the president.

However, in light of Justice Muñoz-Palma's independent and outspoken career, her performance in her new role will be scrutinised with considerable interest.

Cellist Jacqueline du Pré's Mystery Illness Diagnosed

England, October: It has been announced that renowned British cellist Jacqueline du Pré, 28, has multiple sclerosis.

Du Pré comes from a musical family and her older sister Hilary is a well-known flautist. When Jacqueline was four years old and being taught music by her pianist mother Iris, the child heard a cello on the radio and asked for "one of those." Her parents obliged and Iris began to teach her daughter with simple tunes she wrote herself. At the age of five, du Pré began lessons and soon showed talent. At ten, cellist William Pleeth began to teach her. In 1961, at 16, Jacqueline made her solo debut and, one year later, she made her concert debut with the BBC Symphony Orchestra playing Elgar's *Cello Concerto*.

From then on du Pré has been in great demand, performing all over the world and becoming famous not only for her technical ability but also for her passionate interpretation. In 1967 she married pianist and conductor Daniel Barenboim,

English cellist Jacqueline du Pré is diagnosed with multiple sclerosis.

and the couple have often performed together, with Barenboim conducting or accompanying du Pré.

For some time du Pré's difficulties performing have been causing comment in the music world. It is reported that the musician has been losing sensation in her fingers, feeling numbness in her legs, weakness in her back, and blurred vision. On occasion she has been unable to lift her instrument. During part of 1971 and 1972 she took a break from performing, and for a time separated from her husband. When she returned to playing, several concerts were cancelled due to an unnamed illness.

Now that multiple sclerosis has been diagnosed, there is speculation that du Pré may not be able to play again. The disease attacks the central nervous system and can lead to severe disability and death.

Mexican Lawyer Awarded UN Human Rights Prize

New York, USA, December 10: On Human Rights Day, Maria Lavalle Urbina has been announced as a recipient of the United Nations Prize in the Field of Human Rights for her work for the rights of women and children in Mexico and around the world.

Lavalle Urbina began her career in 1926 as a teacher in the state of Campeche. In 1944 she was the first woman in

Campeche to receive a Bachelor of Laws degree, and moved to Mexico City to pursue her legal career.

From 1947 to 1954 Lavalle Urbina was the first female magistrate of the Superior Court of Justice of the Mexican Federal District, where she became known for her defense of human rights.

From 1954 to 1964 Lavalle Urbina was head of the Department of Social Planning and was involved with organizations promoting social justice, such as the Alliance of Women and the Mexican Academy of Education. In 1963 she was recognized for her services when she was named Mexico's Woman of the Year.

In 1964 Lavalle Urbina became one of two of the first women in the Senate of Mexico and in 1965 the first woman to preside over it.

Lavalle Urbina has taken her commitment to legal, educational, family, and women's issues into the international arena, representing Mexico in the UN's Commission on the Status of Women (1957–1968) and the Organization of American States' Inter-American Commission of Women (1965).

Aloni's New Ratz Party in Israel's Elections

Israel, December: Knesset elections were due to be held in October. However, on October 6, the date of this year's holy Yom Kippur, Egypt and Syria began an invasion of lands taken by Israel in 1967's Six Day War. Israel succeeded in defending itself, though sustaining heavy losses, and a ceasefire occurred on October 26.

The elections have been postponed until December 31.

Golda Meir's Alignment government has been accused on one hand of being unprepared and of mismanaging the defense, and on the other of not striving to make peace with the Arab states.

During the year cracks have been appearing in the leftist Alignment. For instance, after seriously disagreeing with the leadership, Shulamit Aloni, a Mapai member since 1959 and Knesset member between 1965 and 1969, departed.

Within 48 hours she started the Movement for Citizens' Rights and Peace, known as the Ratz Party. Aloni is an outspoken lawyer with a commitment to education and legal aid. Her party seeks lasting peace with the Palestine Liberation Organization and the Arab states, and is against continued Israeli control of the Gaza Strip and the West Bank. Ratz supports civil rights, including those for Palestinians and women.

The party believes the state should be separate from religion. It remains to be seen whether Israelis will vote for the hawks or the doves, and whether the fragmented left will hold onto power.

Support Group for Sex Workers

San Francisco, USA: This year Margo St James has founded an advocacy and support group for sex workers called COYOTE. James worked as a prostitute herself and has studied law. She chose the name COYOTE because novelist Tom Robbins once called her a "coyote trickster" at a party. The acronym COYOTE stands for Call Off Your Old Tired Ethics, which neatly sums up the group's stand on these issues.

St James has founded the group because she believes that workers in the sex industry—including prostitutes, sex phone workers,

Legendary film actress Marlene Dietrich shakes hands with the public after her performance at the Espace Cardin Theater in Paris.

Alicia Markova

strippers, and pornography models and performers—need to speak up to gain the same rights, protections, and respect as other workers. While sex workers are often victimized and abused, the law is prejudiced against them, sees them as criminals, and offers no protection when crimes are committed against them.

The organization is calling for the decriminalization of prostitution, pimping, and pandering when conducted by consenting adults. Instead, it says that laws against forcing others into sex work or having sex should be strictly enforced. Sex workers should have the same protection of the law as they go about their job as workers in other industries. COYOTE is now offering sex workers legal advice.

At a personal level, COYOTE offers counseling to sex workers, recognizing that they are often drug users and are frequently the victims of violence and abuse. If people working in the sex industry wish to find other work, COYOTE also gives them advice on how to go about it.

One of COYOTE's first aims is to commence action to have repealed the Californian law that quarantines prostitutes when they are arrested and insists that they have a medical examination for venereal disease before they can be released. COYOTE views this rule as making prostitutes the scapegoats for sexually transmitted disease when, in fact, the group believes that prostitutes are responsible for the transmission of few cases in the community.

Performer Josephine Baker still wowing the crowds at 66.

Arlette Laguiller

> "WHO KNOWS
> WHAT WOMEN
> CAN BE WHEN
> THEY ARE
> FINALLY FREE
> TO BECOME
> THEMSELVES?"
>
> BETTY FRIEDAN
> (1921–2006),
> AMERICAN FEMINIST

"The Three Marias" Beat Censorship Charges

Portugal, May: Feminist authors Maria Isabel Barreno, Maria Teresa Horta, and Maria Velho de Costa, collectively known as "The Three Marias," have had charges against them dropped. The trio were arrested in June 1972, each facing a jail sentence of up to two years for publishing their book *New Portuguese Letters*, which Portuguese censors claimed was an "abuse of the freedom of the press" and would "outrage public morals."

The book is a new interpretation of the seventeenth-century work, *Letters of a Portuguese Nun*, which details the correspondence of a young nun to a French army officer who had seduced her and then promptly vanished. The Three Marias collaborated to create a work that had many parallels to the original book and contained fictional letters, essays, and poems that made comment on the lack of equality modern Portuguese women face. In particular, The Three Marias—all mothers and in their thirties—rail against the oppression of motherhood, marriage, and the religious traditions so prevalent in Portugal.

"In *Letters of a Portuguese Nun*, it was a nun who was cloistered," Barreno told

Glenda Jackson wins an Academy Award for the comedy *A Touch of Class*.

Time magazine in 1973. "In [our book], it is all women. The social institution that shackles them worst is the role of mother. Society idealizes the role, of course, but the idealization masks the slavery of it."

The Portuguese government banned the sale of the book in 1972, and confiscated copies already printed.

A new law was created that made it possible for authors to be charged if their work—which is only judged by censors after publication—is deemed subversive or inflammatory. But it was the arrest of the three authors that brought the plight of the Three Marias to world attention.

Feminists across the world were appalled that the women should be silenced in this manner. America's National Organization for Women took up the cause, and women across the United States staged protests targeted at Portugal's representatives in their nation. The dropping of charges against the Three Marias has feminists everywhere proclaiming a victory for freedom of speech.

timeout

A Mesopotamian melody, the oldest existing tune in the world, is played on an 11-string lyre for the first time in over 3,000 years. It was deciphered by Anne Kilmer, an Assyriologist at Berkeley University, California.

Isabel Perón Named President

Argentina, July 1: At 43 years of age, Isabel Perón has today become the first woman to be named President of Argentina and Latin America's youngest head of state. She has been sworn in as the nation's leader after the death of her 78-year-old husband, President Juan Perón.

In a state broadcast made just three days before his death, Perón—known to

Isabel Perón, 43, becomes the first female president of Argentina.

Argentines as "Isabelita"—announced that the president had handed power to her because he was "conscious that his state of health prevents him directly attending to government affairs until his recovery."

A dancer before she met her husband in 1956, Isabel Perón abandoned her showbusiness career to become his personal secretary and live with him in Madrid. The couple married in 1961. During his exile she became an emissary for her husband, traveling to Argentina to promote support for the ousted president and the Peronist political candidates he was aligned with.

She had been the nation's vice-president since October 1973, when her husband was returned to power after 18 years in political exile. As Juan Perón's third wife, she had long lived in the shadow of his second wife, Eva Perón, who was adored by many Argentines and who died of uterine cancer in 1952, aged 33. Isabel Perón has inherited several problems in taking on the leadership of Argentina, including a beleaguered economy and an increasingly violent political opposition.

"Mama" Cass Elliot Dies

London, England, July 29: "Mama" Cass Elliot, singer and former member of the pop group The Mamas and the Papas, was today found dead after suffering a heart attack in her hotel room. She had been in England performing her sell-out solo concerts at the London Palladium.

Elliot is perhaps best known for the songs she recorded with The Mamas and the Papas, including 1965's "California

"Mama" Cass Elliot is found dead in her hotel room.

Dreamin'," "Monday Monday" (1966), and "Dream a Little Dream of Me" (1968). Elliot launched her solo career in 1968, and went on to record nine albums

before her death. Her fans adored her distinctive alto voice, but some had expressed concern in the early 1970s that her voice was audibly weakened through the crash dieting she subjected her body to. She openly talked—and sometimes even joked—about her weight and eating disorders, which had plagued her since her teens and are thought to be a reason behind her heart attack.

Legend had it that Elliot's vocal range improved after she was hit on the head with a metal pipe. She later verified this story, telling *Rolling Stone* magazine in 1968: "It's true, I did get hit on the head by a pipe that fell down and my range was increased by three notes. They were tearing this club apart ... workmen dropped a thin metal plumbing pipe and it hit me on the head and knocked me to the ground. I had concussion ... and a bad headache for two weeks, [then] all of a sudden I was singing higher."

It is believed Elliot died in her sleep. She was 32 and is survived by her seven-year-old daughter, Owen.

Spanish Women Win Bullfighting Rights

Spain, August: After a three-year fight in the Spanish Supreme Court, Angela Hernández has won her battle to overturn legislation that prevents women from competing in bullfighting contests on an equal footing with their male counterparts. The ruling declares obsolete a 1908 law that decreed bullfighting by women "improper and contrary to civilized manners and all delicate sentiment."

In the eighteenth century, women did fight bulls—and some of these *toreras,* as they are known, were captured in sketches by the great Spanish artist Francisco Goya. The 1908 ruling forced women who wanted to compete in bullfights to do so in other nations, such as Portugal or Latin American countries. Prior to the new law coming into effect,

the only way a woman could face a bull in the bullring was on horseback. Now, a man is no longer required to enter the ring to finish off the bull—the female bullfighter is permitted to complete the contest just as a *matador* would.

Anne Sexton

Mounties No Longer Male-Only

Saskatchewan, Canada, September 18: Thirty-two women have today commenced training to become uniformed members of the Royal Canadian Mounted Police (RCMP).

On May 23, RCMP Commissioner M. J. Nadon called for applications from women interested in conducting regular police duties. The resulting all-female Troop 17 is made up of women from right across Canada. They have assembled at the RCMP depot in Regina, Saskatchewan, for six months of training.

As far back as the 1890s, women have held roles with the RCMP—but usually it was as prison warders and escorts for female inmates. In the early twentieth century, more women became employed by the RCMP as lab and fingerprint technicians, and Doctor Francis McGill (who is sometimes referred to as the "first female Mountie") was widely acknowledged for her work for the force in the areas of medical science and forensics.

Until today, Canadian women have not been permitted to become officers of the RCMP. The move to open up fully-fledged female membership follows a recommendation from the Royal Commission on the Status of Women. The new female recruits attracted much media attention at their induction ceremony, where they were required to sign their names and kiss the Bible before the cameras. Once they complete their training, the female members of the RCMP are to wear the Mounties' distinctive red serge jacket with a skirt, high heels, and a clutch bag.

Ottawa, Canada, September 16: Renaude Lapointe becomes the first woman speaker of the Senate.

Saskatchewan, Canada, September 18: The first women recruits for the Royal Canadian Mounted Police arrive for training.

Melbourne, Australia, September: Australia's first rape crisis center opens in Collingwood.

Boston, USA, October 4: Poet Anne Sexton commits suicide, aged 45.

Oklahoma, USA, November 13: Nuclear plant worker Karen Silkwood is killed in a car crash.

Hadar, Ethiopia, November 24: The "Lucy" hominid skeleton, believed to be three million years old, is found.

Germany, November 29: Terrorist Ulrike Meinhof is sentenced to eight years in prison.

Darwin, Australia, December 24-25: Sixty-six people die and thousands are injured as Cyclone Tracy devastates the Northern Territory.

Central African Republic, December: Elizabeth Domitien becomes the country's first woman prime minister.

Antarctica, Winter: Biologists Mary Alice McWhinnie and Sister Mary Odile Cahoon are the first women to spend a winter on the frozen continent.

France: Philosopher and feminist Simone de Beauvoir becomes president of the French League for Women's Rights.

USA: Lithuanian-born archeologist and feminist Marija Gimbutas publishes *Goddesses and Gods of Old Europe*, a book that challenges the traditional concepts of the origins of western civilization.

Jordan: Women get the right to vote and be elected to office.

London, England: Nadine Gordimer wins the Booker Prize for *The Conservationist*.

USA: Marabel Morgan's bestselling book *Total Woman* advises housewives to pamper and submit to their husbands.

Norway: Politician Eva Kolstad becomes the first woman leader of a Norwegian political party, Venstre.

Los Angeles, USA: Glenda Jackson wins her second Academy Award for Best Actress in *A Touch of Class*.

Houston, USA: Anita Martini becomes the first female journalist to report from a professional sportsmen's locker room.

France: Author and journalist Françoise Giroud becomes secretary of state for the status of women.

New York, USA: Billie Jean King establishes the Women's Sports Foundation.

New York, USA: New Zealand lyric soprano Kiri Te Kanawa makes a widely acclaimed debut at New York's Metropolitan Opera as Desdemona in Verdi's *Otello*.

Nuclear Whistleblower Dies in Crash

Ulrike Meinhof

Oklahoma, USA, November 13: The death today of nuclear power plant worker Karen Silkwood in a car crash has immediately raised the question: Was this an accident or was she murdered? Silkwood was on her way to meet with a *New York Times* reporter and a union representative about safety violations at the Kerr-McGee plutonium plant when the one-car accident occurred.

She was making the journey to hand over documentation that supported her claim that the company had been negligent with quality control and that official operational records had been falsified. Just hours after the accident, it became evident that the documents she was transporting were missing.

Silkwood had been employed as a metallography lab technician at the power plant and was an active member of the Oil, Chemical and Atomic Workers' Union. She was involved in criticizing her employer's safety procedures and had been gathering evidence to back her claims. Following one strike at the plant, the number of union members fell, which prompted Kerr-McGee to set about organizing an employee vote on stripping the union of its status as a collective bargaining agent.

It was this move that saw Silkwood appointed to the union's bargaining committee. As part of her duties, she studied the plant's health and safety standards—and found them lacking. She reported to the committee that she had uncovered several major problems, including leaks, spills, and substandard production of fuel rods.

Just days before her death, during a check for personal radiation exposure, she recorded a positive response. Two days later, the contamination appeared to have worsened, with high levels of radiation on her right ear, neck, and arms. A test of Silkwood's apartment found significant levels of radiation there, too, all of which added to her resolve to fight for better safety conditions at the Kerr-McGee plant. Silkwood was 28 years old and mother to three children.

"THE EQUATION OF FEMALENESS WITH HOUSE-WIFERY IS BASIC TO THE STRUCTURE OF MODERN SOCIETY."

ANN OAKLEY, 1974,
THE SOCIOLOGY OF
HOUSEWORK

Button slogans reflect the flowering of feminism.

German Terrorist Imprisoned

Germany, November 29: Ulrike Meinhof, a key figure in the Baader-Meinhof militant group, was today sentenced to eight years in prison for attempted murder. Her incarceration follows many years of involvement with bombings and bank robberies across Germany.

Meinhof was born in 1934 and became politically active when a teenager. At 23, she joined the Socialist German Student Union and took part in protests against national re-armament and nuclear weapons. She became a member of the German Communist Party two years later, even though it was illegal to do so, and then began working as editor of the left-wing *konkret* magazine.

Her articles for *konkret* quickly became increasingly militant. She began to incite action among her readers with statements such as this: "If one sets a car on fire, that is a criminal offence. If one sets hundreds of cars on fire, that is political action."

It was through *konkret* that she came to meet fellow activist Andreas Baader. In 1968, he was convicted of arson-bombing a Frankfurt department store. On May 14, 1970, Meinhof was among the group of people who helped free Baader from police custody. In the process of extricating Baader, Meinhof and her associates shot a librarian and wounded two officers.

From this point on, the German media tagged the group "Baader-Meinhof" (although it is also called the Red Army Faction) and a 10,000 deutschmark reward was announced for the capture of Meinhof. Retreating even further into a life of guerilla warfare, she bombed German buildings, robbed banks, and even tried unsuccessfully to kidnap her twin daughters, with a view to taking them to Palestine to live. Enthusiastic about sharing her views, Meinhof continued to contribute articles and manifestos explaining her ideological standpoint until she was finally apprehended on June 15, 1972.

Tennis Star to Foster Young Sportswomen

New York, USA: Billie Jean King, one of America's greatest tennis players, has set up the Women's Sports Foundation to raise the profile of up-and-coming sports-women. Long regarded as an outstanding sportswoman herself, King has fought hard to bring to public attention the inequalities experienced between the genders when it comes to sporting prize money, status, and opportunities. Her impeccable sporting credentials include

Kiri Te Kanawa in Verdi's *Otello* at New York's Metropolitan Opera.

20 Wimbledon titles (six of which are singles titles). She has also won the US Open, Australian Open, and French Open, and was ranked the world's top female tennis player five times between 1966 and 1972. King also became the first female athlete to earn in excess of $100,000 in sporting prize money.

In 1973, King became involved in what was billed as a "Battle of the Sexes" when former tennis champ Bobby Riggs challenged her to a match, asserting that even a 56-year-old man such as himself could beat a leading female player.

The match—which took place in Houston, Texas, in September 1973—created much public interest and was broadcast across the world. King, who was 29 at the time, thrashed Riggs 6-4, 6-3, 6-3. After the match, the *New York Times* reported: "Most important perhaps for women everywhere, she convinced skeptics that a female athlete can survive pressure-filled situations and that men are as susceptible to nerves as women."

This year, King also became the first woman to coach a professional team that included male players. She has said: "I like putting money back into what made my

Biologists Mary Alice McWhinnie and Sister Mary Odile Cahoon are the first women to spend a winter at McMurdo Station, on the frozen continent of Antarctica. They will study how tiny, shrimp-like krill survive the icy waters.

Nadine Gordimer

life, and tennis has been great to me." As well as supporting successful sportswomen, the Women's Sports Foundation will also play a role in educating young women about the important benefits of physical activity.

Women to Endure Antarctic Winter

Antarctica, Winter: American biologists Mary Alice McWhinnie and Sister Mary Odile Cahoon are the first women to spend an entire winter in Antarctica. They are based at McMurdo Station, America's research base in Antarctica, where McWhinnie is chief scientist.

The extremes of temperature are unlikely to be a shock to McWhinnie who, prior to this appointment, has spent more than a decade working on Antarctic research ships. Cahoon is acting as McWhinnie's assistant in her mission to study krill (tiny, shrimp-like creatures) with a view to understanding how and why they can survive in icy waters.

The two women are joined at Mc-Murdo Station by 128 men spending a winter on the frozen continent.

Goddess Book Causes Controversy

Los Angeles, USA: Lithuanian-born and US-based archeologist and feminist Marija Gimbutas has caused a stir with the publication of *Goddesses and Gods of Old Europe*. The book by the UCLA professor challenges the traditional concepts of the origins of western society by asserting that European prehistoric culture was female-focused and that in these earliest civilizations a Mother Goddess was revered as the giver of all life.

She uses her own cultural experiences of growing up in Lithuania and substantiates her views with her extensive research in the fields of archeology, ethnography, folklore, and linguistics.

Gimbutas studied Indo-European language and culture in Lithuania, and gained a PhD in Germany before fleeing the war in Europe. In 1950, she became a research fellow at Harvard University, where she concentrated on Eastern European prehistory. After moving to UCLA in 1963, Gimbutas began conducting major excavations of Neolithic sites in Europe. It was during these expeditions that she uncovered a number of ancient symbols and objects which she feels support her premise that some prehistoric European societies built their spiritual rituals around the existence of a female creator or goddess.

Feminists around the world have been quick to seize upon Gimbutas's book, pointing out that lessons can be learned from the ancient civilizations she describes—they were peaceful and appeared to practice equal social, spiritual, and sexual rights between the genders. Some of her peers take a different view, though—asserting that the arguments Gimbutas offer are weak and that she has ignored scientific findings that do not fit with her view.

Nadine Gordimer Wins Booker Prize

London, England: South African novelist Nadine Gordimer has won the prestigious Booker Prize for her novel, *The Conservationist*. Like her preceding novels, *The Conservationist* is set in—and comments upon—a society that has been oppressed by apartheid.

Her lead character, Mehring, is a white South African who appears on the surface to be quite liberal. He is a landowner who believes he is conserving his farm, but what he is really doing is exploiting it. Parallels can be drawn between what happens on Mehring's land and more broadly in South Africa.

While Mehring thinks of himself as a wealthy sophisticate, his colonialist tendencies become apparent through his sexual proclivities when he picks up a young black girl and takes her to a disused mine, only to be confronted by the African guards at the mine. But when the corpse of a black man is found on his farm, Mehring finds himself identifying with the unknown man. He buries him but cannot forget the experience—and so this disenfranchised African begins to haunt Mehring, in effect colonizing his mind.

The Conservationist has been greatly lauded as one of Gordimer's most profound and poetic novels.

This year, the Booker Prize has been jointly awarded to Gordimer and to England's Stanley Middleton for his novel *Holiday*.

Françoise Giroud becomes France's secretary of state responsible for the status of women.

Margaret Thatcher

UK Conservative Party Elects Female Leader

England, February 11: Margaret Thatcher, the former Tory Education Minister in the Heath Government and the opposition's spokesperson on the environment, has just been chosen as leader by the Conservative Party after she defeated Ted Heath 130 votes to 119 in the first ballot of a party-room vote last week.

Thatcher becomes the first female leader of a western political party, and the first woman to serve as Leader of the Opposition in the House of Commons.

Her election signals a turn to the right for the Tories, who have chosen to overlook the centrist Willie Whitelaw, who only managed to poll 79 votes compared to Thatcher's 146 in the all-important second ballot. The remaining three candidates, Sir Geoffrey Howe QC, James Prior, and John Peyton, trailed with 19, 19, and 11 votes respectively.

Thatcher's election is something of a surprise. She had few outspoken supporters and many of her views are not widely held within the party. Historically, the

"LIFE IS TOO SHORT TO STUFF A MUSHROOM."

SHIRLEY CONRAN, BRITISH AUTHOR, *SUPERWOMAN*

conservative leaders emerge from the party's center-left faction, such as Whitelaw, and Margaret Thatcher is firmly entrenched within the party's free market right.

Margaret Thatcher was born in the town of Grantham, Lincolnshire, on October 13, 1925. She was educated at Somerville College and Oxford University where she became the first woman president of the Oxford University Conservative Association.

Despite running unsuccessfully for parliament in 1950, she nevertheless managed to increase the Conservative vote in her district by 50 percent. The following year she married Denis Thatcher, the director of a paint firm.

Thatcher entered parliament as the member for the north London constituency of Finchley in 1959, and throughout the party's years in opposition during the 1960s, served continuously as a shadow minister and established herself among the party's elite. Thatcher was elected shadow spokesperson for education in 1969, and when the Conservatives won the 1970 general election, she entered cabinet as Education Minister.

Her influence and her rise within the Conservative Party increased despite her constant struggle with popularity in the eyes of voters, summed up in an infamous headline by the *Sun* newspaper in 1972 when it bluntly labeled her "the most unpopular woman in Britain."

Thatcher's tenure as Education Minister was a tumultuous period characterized by student radicalism and personal vilification of her in the media. The Heath Government continually lurched from one crisis to the next, constantly issuing policy reversals and becoming one of the most interventionist governments in UK history.

Barbra Streisand with film producer Jon Peters.

The party's defeat last year, amid a legacy of industrial turmoil and high inflation, has led to many within its ranks hoping for a new leader to emerge who will give the party a fresh start and some semblance of hope when the next general elections are due in 1979.

Spain's Alicia de Larrocha Wins Second Grammy

USA, March 1: Alicia de Larrocha, the legendary Spanish pianist whose performances have been an inspiration to guitarists around the world for over 50 years, has won her second Grammy Award for Best Classical Performance for Soloist with Orchestra for two concertos by Ravel and Fauré's *Fantaisie*. The most enduring contributions to the world of music by this most formidable artist are undoubtedly her unparalleled advocacy of Spanish and Catalonian composers, where her impeccable taste, polished technique, and mastery of textures and rhythms can be heard in her classic interpretations of the music of Granados, Falla, and Albéniz. Her recordings of Mozart and French impressionist music

Ellen Burstyn wins an Oscar for *Alice Doesn't Live Here Anymore*.

United Nations, January 1: The United Nations proclaims the International Year of the Woman.
France, January 17: Minister of Health Simone Veil achieves the legalization of abortion.
England, February 11: Margaret Thatcher becomes Tory leader and the first woman to lead a major British political party.
USA, March 1: Barbra Streisand's "The Way We Were," from the movie of the same name in which she starred, wins Song of the Year at this year's Grammy Awards.

USA, March 1: Spanish pianist Alicia de Larrocha wins her second Grammy Award, for Best Classical Performance for Soloist with Orchestra. Her first was in 1974 for Best Classical Performance for Soloist without Orchestra.
Beverly Hills, Los Angeles, USA, March 14: Oscar-winning actress Susan Hayward dies of cancer.
Stockholm, Sweden, March 22: Austrian vocalist Getty Kaspers and the group Teach-In, representing the Netherlands, win the Eurovision Song Contest with the song "Ding-a-Dong."

Riyadh, Saudi Arabia, March 25: King Faysal is assassinated in the palace by his nephew, who has a history of mental illness.
USA, April: *Jaws*, a terrifying film about a man-eating shark by Steven Spielberg, opens.
New York, USA, April 7: Soprano Beverly Sills makes her Metropolitan Opera debut in Rossini's *The Siege of Corinth*.
Los Angeles, USA, April 8: Ellen Burstyn wins Academy Award for Best Actress for the 1974 movie, *Alice Doesn't Live Here Anymore*.

Paris, France, April 12: American-born singer and dancer Josephine Baker, who became a major European star in cabaret, musical theater, and film, dies.
Saigon, Vietnam, April 30: Saigon falls to the North Vietnamese, ending 30 years of war and uniting North and South Vietnam.
The Himalayas, May 16: Deputy leader of an all-woman Japanese expedition, Junko Tabei, 35, is the first woman to climb Mt Everest and with her Sherpa guide, is the 36th person to reach the summit.

New York, USA, May 20: The First Women's Bank is chartered in New York City.
New Delhi, India, June: Prime Minister Indira Gandhi declares a state of emergency to retain power after a High Court conviction for election fraud.
Lyons, France, June 2: Some 150 French prostitutes occupy a church to protest against violence and police repression.
USA: Betty Friedan is named Humanist of the Year by the American Humanist Association.

are also highly regarded. Born on May 23, 1923, in Barcelona, de Larrocha is an artist of outstanding interpretive insight. She made her first public appearance at the age of five, and at 11, she performed Mozart's *Coronation Concerto* with the Madrid Symphony Orchestra.

De Larrocha made her first tour of Europe in 1947, and her first appearance in the United States was in 1955 when she performed with the Los Angeles Philharmonic Orchestra. In 1959, in addition to a hectic touring schedule, she took over as the Musical Director of the Academia Marshall in Barcelona.

Susan Hayward Dies of Brain Cancer

Beverley Hills, California, USA, March 14: Hollywood motion picture legend Susan Hayward, who gave one of the great screen performances in her 1958 Oscar-winning role of convicted murderer Barbara Graham in the film, *I Want To Live!*, has died of brain cancer in Beverly Hills. She was 57 years old.

Her condition, first diagnosed in 1972, is suspected of having stemmed from her work on the set of the 1956 film *The Conqueror*, which was shot in the Utah desert only a short distance from a nuclear test site that was in full use at the time. Hayward's co-stars in the film, John Wayne and Agnes Moorehead, also died of cancer.

Susan Hayward was born Edythe Marrenner on June 30, 1917, in Brooklyn, New York, and will be buried beside her last husband, Eaton Chalkley, a former FBI investigator who died in 1966, in the cemetery of Our Lady of Perpetual Help Catholic Church in Carrollton, Georgia, adjacent to the Hayward family farm.

Susan Hayward made a career of playing strong women who invariably met tragic ends. Her popularity peaked

time out

Recent statistical surveys of South East Asian Nations have revealed that women in Thailand outnumber men three to one when it comes to owning and running their own businesses.

in the 1950s, but she continued making films throughout the 1960s. Her final film was *Valley of the Dolls* in 1967.

Josephine Baker Dead At 69

Paris, France, April 12: Josephine Baker, the singer and dancer known the world over as the "Black Venus" and the "Creole Goddess," and recipient of over 1,500 marriage proposals, has died quietly in her sleep of a cerebral hemorrhage.

She was born on June 3, 1906, in St Louis, Missouri, the daughter of a washerwoman and a vaudeville drummer. By the time she was 12 years old, she was cleaning houses and working as a babysitter for wealthy white families in the city. Baker went from performing in skits with a touring band in 1919, to being one of the most photographed women in the world by 1927. She become an instant success for her erotic dancing and for appearing practically nude on stage. Her stage shows became legendary, and she would often combine her performances with civil rights activism, often refusing to play at venues that would not allow an integrated audience. In later shows in Paris, she was often accompanied on stage by her pet cheetah, Chiquita, who was adorned with a diamond collar.

Baker played to standing ovations almost until her death. Just four days ago, she thrilled Princess Grace of Monaco and Sophia Loren with a triumphant performance at Paris's Bobino Theatre. She had become a citizen of France in 1937.

Josephine Baker was found dead in her bed, surrounded by copies of rave reviews of her performance from an enraptured French media.

Junko Tabei the First Woman to Climb Everest

The Himalayas, May 16: Junko Tabei, a Japanese mountain climber and leader of an all-female climbing club called the Ladies Climbing Club: Japan, has become the first woman to stand on the top of the world.

Responding to a challenge from a Japanese newspaper looking for women to form the nucleus of an Everest expedition, Tabei applied and was chosen to lead the assault, despite having just given birth to a daughter. She immediately began giving piano lessons to help raise the $5,000 necessary for expenses.

Tabei and her team literally had to claw their way to the summit after an avalanche had roared through their campsite. Upon their descent, Nepalese women showered the women with apples as a sign of appreciation. A victory parade is planned in the streets of the capital, Kathmandu, and the King of Nepal will meet her to offer his congratulations.

Susan Hayward

Hearse containing the body of the US-born dancer and singer Josephine Baker.

Key Events

Shaanxi Province, China, July 11: Archeologists find 6,000 life-size terracotta statues of warriors, together with horses, chariots, and weapons, dating from 221-206 BCE.
Mauritania, August 22: Toure Aissata Kane is the first woman to attain cabinet rank, as Minister for the Protection of the Family and for Social Affairs.
Sacramento, California, USA: "Manson family" member Lynette Alice "Squeaky" Fromme attempts to assassinate President Gerald Ford and is arrested.

Forrest Hills, New York, USA, September 6: Czech tennis player Martina Navratilova, aged 18, asks for asylum in the US.
The Vatican, September 14: Mother Elizabeth Ann Seton (1774-1821) becomes the first native-born American to be canonized by the Roman Catholic Church.
UK, October: Rock group Queen release their innovative song "Bohemian Rhapsody."
Rome, Italy: Women demonstrate for reform on behalf of the Italian Women's Movement.

Iceland, October 24: Around 25,000 housewives, 90 percent of the nation's women, strike for the day to call attention to the low value placed on women's work.
Tanzania, October 30: British paleontologist Mary Leakey announces her discovery of 3.75-million-year-old human remains.
USA, November: Bill Gates and Paul Allen form a business partnership called "Micro-Soft."
Madrid, Spain, November 22: Juan Carlos de Borbón is proclaimed King of Spain following Franco's death.

Ethiopia: Youdith Imre is appointed the country's first female ambassador, to Denmark, Sweden, Finland, Norway, and Iceland.
Tehran, Iran: Shirin Ebadi, who was the first woman judge in Iran, becomes president of the Tehran City Court.
England: Agatha Christie kills off her famous detective Hercule Poirot in the book *Curtain*.
USA: Ariel and Will Durant publish the eleventh book, *The Age of Napoleon*, in their Story of Civilization series.

Mozambique: Women win the right to vote and be elected to office.
Ireland: Bernadette Devlin McAliskey serves on the national executive of the Irish Republican Socialist Party, which she co-founded last year.
Toulon, France: French-born filmmaker Babette Mangolte wins the Prix de la Lumière at the Toulon film festival for *What Maisie Knew*.
Barbados: Barbadian public health official Nita Barrow is named medical commissioner of the Pan American Health Organization.

Acclaimed Fungal Researcher Dies

Simone Veil

USA, June 24: The pioneering bacteriologist Elizabeth Lee Hazen who, along with Rachel Fuller Brown created the world's first non-toxic antifungal antibiotic, nystatis, has died at 89 years of age.

Last month, the two researchers were the first women to receive the American Institute of Chemists' Chemical Pioneer Award for their discovery of nystatis in 1950, which has since been effective in treating disabling fungal infections, and skin and mucous membrane diseases and fungal growth in livestock feed.

Hazen was born in Mississippi in 1885 and came to work in the New York State Department of Health in 1930. Rachel Brown was born in Springfield, Massachusetts, in 1898, and after completing a degree in chemistry and bacteriology at the University of Chicago in 1924 moved to the Albany, New York, headquarters of the Department of Health.

Their collaborative search for a broad-spectrum antibiotic was made possible by the efficiency of the US Post Office. Hazen would culture organisms found in soil samples in her New York office, and if any activity was detected in vitro against certain fungi she would post the samples to Brown in a mason jar.

Of all the hundreds of soil samples sent to Hazen from across the globe, one was eventually found to contain a substance the two researchers initially named *Streptomyces noursei*, and later renamed nystatis in honor of New York State and the NY State Division of Laboratoies and Research.

Hazen and Brown remained active in fungal research, discovering another two fungicidal antibiotics, though neither could be adapted for medical use. At age 70, Hazen co-authored a guide to fungal research titled *Laboratory Identification of Pathogenic Fungi Simplified*.

> "I WASN'T REALLY NAKED. I SIMPLY DIDN'T HAVE ANY CLOTHES ON."
>
> JOSEPHIN BAKER (1906–1975), AMERICAN DANCER

Manson Follower Points Gun at President Ford

Sacramento, California, USA, September 5: A long-time member of Charles Manson's "family," Lynette Alice "Squeaky" Fromme, left her home in Stockton, California, this morning and traveled to Sacramento's Capital Park dressed as a nun, with the apparent intention of assassinating the visiting US President Gerald Ford.

Carrying a .45 Colt automatic pistol in a leg holster, she took aim at the President as he was leaving the Senator Hotel on L Street. At 9.57 a.m. Fromme made her way through a small crowd of people until she was just 2 feet (0.6 m) from the President, before pulling the trigger.

Lynette Fromme, a follower of Charles Manson, being led away after her failed attempt to kill President Ford.

Witnesses have said that they heard a "click," but apparently there was no bullet in the chamber. Others claim that a Secret Service agent jammed his finger behind the trigger before Fromme had the chance to discharge it. All agree that the gun was pointing downwards, somewhere between the President's knee and waist. Fromme was also heard to say that she deliberately ejected the round that was in the chamber before leaving her home earlier this morning and traveling to the hotel.

Four bullets were later found in the handle of the gun, though none was in the chamber. Fromme either had no intention of actually harming the President, or she simply forgot to jack back the slide and push it forward to inject a bullet into the chamber for firing.

Fromme was born in Santa Monica, California, on October 22, 1948. The oldest of three children, she had a miserable childhood and left home after only barely graduating from high school.

Encouraged to return home, she attended El Camino Junior College before another argument with her father over the definition of a word saw her finally leave home and never return.

She met Charles Manson while she was living at Venice Beach and was immediately drawn into his "family," moving with the group to the ranch of 80-year-old George Spahn.

After Manson was imprisoned for the murder of Sharon Tate and the La Biancas, Fromme became head of the "family." She moved to San Francisco when Manson was in San Quentin, and then moved again to Stockton near Sacramento when he was transferred to Folsom Prison.

Fromme is likely to be convicted of attempting to assassinate the President, which carries a maximum sentence of life imprisonment.

Vatican Canonizes First Native-born American

The Vatican, September 14: Mother Elizabeth Ann Seton, founder of the first American religious community for women and the nation's first Catholic orphanage, has today become the first

Nuns attending the canonization of Mother Elizabeth Ann Seton.

native-born American to be canonized by the Roman Catholic Church.

Born on August 28, 1774, two years before the American Revolution, Elizabeth Bayley Seton grew up among the New York upper class and enjoyed all the trappings of high society. At 19, she married the wealthy William Seton, and together they had five children. When he died of tuberculosis, Elizabeth, aged 30, suddenly found herself destitute with five young children to raise.

Raised as an Episcopalian, she later converted to Catholicism in 1805, and started a school in Baltimore at the suggestion of the president of Baltimore's St Mary's College, and soon plans were begun to establish a Sisterhood. Elizabeth Seton took her vows of poverty, obedience, and chastity on March 25, 1809.

Though struck down with tuberculosis, Mother Seton continued to oversee and nourish the children in her care. By 1818 the Sisterhood had two orphanages and another school. She died in Emmitsburg, Maryland, in 1821, aged 46.

Mother Seton was declared venerable on December 18, 1959, and was beatified on March 17, 1963.

Cambridge Gains First Female Vice-Chancellor

Cambridge, England: Rosemary Murray, the administrator, academic, JP, and Liveryman of the Goldsmith's Company, at a time when very few women hold such positions, has today become the first female vice-chancellor of the 765-year-old University of Cambridge.

After full degree status was awarded to women studying at Cambridge in 1948, Murray was instrumental in the founding of the campus's female college, New Hall, at a time when the university had the lowest percentage of female undergraduates of any learning institution in the United Kingdom. Murray was elected president of New Hall and remains in that role today.

Her contribution to public life outside of university life is impressive. After thirty years a justice of the peace, she became the first woman to be elected Deputy Leader of the County. Her public service involvement has extended to membership on the Wages Council and the Armed Services Pay Review Board.

Rosemary Murray was born in 1913 and studied chemistry at Lady Margaret Hall, Oxford. She taught chemistry at Royal Holloway College and Sheffield University prior to World War II, during which time she enrolled in the Admiralty Signals Department and was promoted to the rank of officer in the Women's Royal Naval Service. After World War II

Agatha Christie autographing French editions.

she moved to Girton College and then became a demonstrator in chemistry. In 1948 Murray took an active part in the meetings of the Third Foundation for Women.

Iran Appoints First Female Judge

Tehran, Iran: Shirin Ebadi, a graduate of Tehran University and Iran's first female judge, whose outspoken demands for reform have often seen her at odds with the nation's clerics, has become President of Bench 24 in the Tehran City Court.

Born into a family of academics in the northwestern city of Hamedan in 1947, Ebadi began to serve as a judge in 1969, after receiving her law degree in just three and a half years from Tehran University. In 1971, she also received a doctorate with honors in private law.

Ebadi is on record as a representative of Reformed Islam, and will use her position to further basic human rights such as religious freedom, freedom of speech, and gender equality. She is also a supporter of basic rights for members of the Baha'i faith, a religious minority that has been suppressed within Iran since its foundation.

Booker Prize for Ruth Jhabvala

England: The Anglo-Indian author Ruth Prawer Jhabvala has won this year's Booker Prize for her love story contrasting the romances of two

women living parallel lives in 1920s and 1970s India, *Heat and Dust*. The novel tells the story of Olivia, an extremely bored colonial wife in India, who finds herself suffocating amid the constraints and protocols ascribed her as the wife of an English civil servant. She then meets and begins an affair with an Indian prince, becomes pregnant, has an abortion, and finally abandons her husband. Fifty years later the book's narrator, the step-granddaughter of Olivia, journeys to the subcontinent to lay the ghosts of this family scandal to rest.

Jhabvala was born in Germany in 1939, and traveled to England with her parents when she was 12. After graduating from Queen Mary College, London University, she married the Indian architect, C. S. H. Jhabvala and moved to Delhi. Her first novel, *To Whom She Will*, was published in 1955. She also began submitting short stories to *The New Yorker*. *Get Ready for Battle* (1962) is a portrait of middle-class everyday life in modern Delhi that mocks the self-seeking, ego-driven personalities of many of its central characters. The Booker Prize is one of the world's most prestigious literary awards, and is given by the National Book League of the UK to the best novel written in English by a citizen of the Commonwealth or the Republic of Ireland.

Betty Friedan

Italian Women's Movement march for pre-school and curriculum reform in Rome.

Rosi Mittermaier

The Queen of Crime Dead at 85

Wallingford, England, January 12: Dame Agatha Christie DBE, the prolific and wildly popular mystery writer, has died at age 85 at Winterbrook House in Wallingford, Oxfordshire. Christie is one of the most innovative and influential mystery writers of all time, with more than one billion copies of her novels sold in English, and another billion or so in the 103 languages into which her books have been translated.

In addition to being the creator of the detectives Hercule Poirot and Miss Marple, Christie wrote the stage play that has had the longest continuous run in London theatrical history, *The Mousetrap*, which opened November 25, 1952, and is still running. Many of her novels and short stories have been made into movies—most famously *Witness for the Prosecution* (1958), starring Charles Laughton, Marlene Dietrich, and Tyrone Power, and *Murder on the Orient Express* (1974), with Albert Finney heading an all-star cast.

Christie was born in Torquay, Devon, which became the setting for many of her stories. During World War I she worked in a pharmacy where she learned all about poisons, and then drew on that information for many of the murders in her novels. It is believed that Christie left two completed manuscripts, both Miss Marple stories, which should be published soon.

"WAR SETTLES NOTHING…TO WIN A WAR IS AS DISASTROUS AS TO LOSE ONE."

— DAME AGATHA CHRISTIE (1890–1976) BRITISH CRIME WRITER, *AN AUTOBIOGRAPHY*

Alpine Skier "Gold-Rosi" Wins Again!

Innsbruck, Austria, February: West German alpine skiing champion Rosi Mittermaier has thrilled her country and the world by winning gold medals in the women's downhill and the slalom, and a silver medal in the giant slalom at the Winter

Louise Fletcher in One Flew Over the Cuckoo's Nest.

Olympic Games in Innsbruck, Austria. Her German fans are calling her "Gold-Rosi."

Mittermaier delivered thrilling performances. In the downhill race she won by half a second; in the slalom by a third of a second. At the giant slalom, two days later, the crowd was cheering her on to become the first woman to win gold in all three alpine skiing events, but Kathy Kreiner soon showed that she was the skier to beat as she blazed across the finish line with a time of 1:29.13. Then Mittermaier began her run. Halfway through the course she was a half second ahead of Kreiner, but at one of the lower gates she lost her lead, finishing just an eighth of second behind Kreiner and taking the silver medal in the event.

Nonetheless, Mittermaier's performance at Innsbruck has been nothing short of incredible. She has been racing on the

time out

"Slap your wife and she'll know you love her," is the official word from the Kenyan Parliament, where a motion to forbid wife-beating has been defeated.

World Cup circuit for 10 years, and raced in the 1968 and the 1972 Olympics, yet this is the first time Mittermaier has won a major downhill event.

Pat O'Shane First Aboriginal Barrister

Australia, February 6: Patricia O'Shane, a former high school teacher, has become the first Aboriginal Australian to be admitted to the bar. O'Shane was born in Mossman, Queensland, in 1941, of an Irish father and an Aboriginal mother. The family was very poor, living in a tent with a dirt floor and no running water. During primary school, O'Shane often fought with other children after receiving severe racial abuse. It was not unusual for her to come home with a black eye or a bloody nose. But she gave as good as she got, and by the time she entered secondary school she realized she could be just as effective—and intimidating—with words, as she had been with her fists.

At the end of high school O'Shane won a teacher's scholarship and studied at Queensland Teachers' Training College, then at the University of Queensland.

In the 1960s, O'Shane taught at Cairns State High School before pursuing a career in law. Some of her colleagues from that time have often described her as "aggressive" and "volatile." A story is told of O'Shane dragging a disruptive student out of her classroom by his ear. However, she was highly thought of.

In 1973 the Federal Government awarded O'Shane an Aboriginal study grant, and she enrolled in Law at the University of New South Wales. In a ceremony at the New South Wales Supreme Court, O'Shane joined the ranks of Australia's barristers.

Wallingford, England, January 12: Agatha Christie, mystery writer, dies, aged 85.

New York, USA, January 13: Sarah Caldwell becomes the first woman conductor at the Metropolitan Opera.

London and Paris, January 21: Two Concorde jets take off on their first commercial flights.

Innsbruck, Austria, February: West German Rosi Mittermaier turns in the greatest Olympic performance by a female alpine skier at the Winter Olympic Games.

Australia, February 6: Patricia O'Shane becomes Australia's first Aboriginal barrister.

Croydon, England, February 7: Joan Bazeley is the first woman to referee an all-male football match.

USA, February 8: Jodie Foster stars as a teenage prostitute opposite Robert De Niro in Martin Scorsese's film *Taxi Driver*, released today.

Cambridge, Massachusetts, USA, February 21: Susan Estrich becomes first woman president of the prestigious *Harvard Law Review*.

San Francisco, USA, March 20: Patty Hearst, heiress and former hostage, is found guilty of armed robbery, after being kidnapped.

California, USA: Louise Fletcher wins Academy Award for *One Flew Over the Cuckoo's Nest*.

March 24: President Isabel Perón, who succeeded her late husband Juan in 1974, is overthrown by a military junta. She is to be charged with corruption.

Brighton, England, March 26: British cosmetics entrepreneur Anita Roddick opens The Body Shop.

California, USA, April 1: Two college dropouts, Stephen Wozniak and Steven Jobs, form the Apple Computer Company.

San Francisco, USA, April 7: Genentech, the first commercial company engaged in genetic engineering, is established.

New York, USA, May: Poet and author Gwendolyn Brooks is the first woman and first African-American elected to the 250-member National Institute of Arts and Letters.

USA: Shere Hite publishes *The Hite Report*, analyzing women's sexuality.

Montreal, Canada, July: Romanian Nadia Comaneci is the first gymnast to earn a perfect score of 10, at the Summer Olympic Games. She goes on to receive seven perfect scores during the competition.

Entebbe, Uganda, July 4: Israeli commandos storm the airport to free 105 hostages being held by terrorists. Three hostages were killed, as was Israeli commander, Colonel Y. Netanyahu.

Canberra, Australia, July 8: Senator Margaret Guilfoyle becomes the first woman Federal Cabinet minister.

Sarah Caldwell

Patty Hearst is found guilty of armed robbery.

Patty Hearst Found Guilty

San Francisco, California, USA, March 20: Patty Hearst, newspaper heiress, one-time hostage, and fugitive terrorist, has been found guilty of armed robbery. On April 14, 1974, Hearst joined four members of the Symbionese Liberation Army (SLA) in an armed hold-up at the Sunset branch of the Hibernia National Bank in San Francisco. During the robbery, two people were shot. Ironically, one of Hearst's closest friends as a child had been Patricia Tobin, whose family founded Hibernia National Bank.

Security cameras at the bank caught an enthusiastic, even euphoric Hearst, armed with an assault rifle, shouting commands and obscenities at frightened bank customers and employees. During her trial, celebrated defense attorney F. Lee Bailey argued that in response to the physical, psychological, and sexual abuse

she suffered during the two months she was held captive by the SLA, Hearst had come to sympathize with her captors, and aligned herself with their revolutionary agenda. This psychological condition resembles Stockholm Syndrome, a term coined by psychiatrist Nils Bejerot after a 6-day hostage siege following a Swedish bank robbery in 1973. Bailey went on to argue that Hearst's participation in the bank robbery was not truly voluntary, and that she had been brainwashed and intimidated into taking part in the crime. He brought a host of psychiatrists and mind-control experts to bolster his case, but many of these expert witnesses failed to apply their scientific theories directly to Hearst's case. Further complicating the defense was Hearst's refusal to testify against other members of the SLA, which struck many observers as a clear sign that she sided with the revolutionaries of her own free will.

In the end the jury refused to believe that a well-educated young woman from a privileged background could have been psychologically pressured into joining a gang of terrorists. After deliberating for 12 hours, the jury found Hearst guilty of armed robbery.

A Natural Beauty is Born

Brighton, England, March 26: Inspiration, necessity, and social conscience have led Anita Roddick to open a remarkable new store. When her husband Gordon Roddick said he dreamed of traveling from New York to Buenos Aires on horseback, Anita encouraged him to go. But with two small daughters to raise, she desperately needed to find a way to make a living. And so The Body Shop was born. The Body Shop's line of cosmetics is small—

only 15 products at the moment. But by offering cosmetics that are all-natural and have not been laboratory-tested on animals, Roddick has tapped into a growing worldwide interest in environmental, health, and animal rights issues.

The shop is also encouraging customers to return their used containers to the shop to be refilled at a discount, in order to save money and reduce the environmental impact of the packaging.

Roddick is hoping to open more shops soon, based on a co-operative franchise model. She hopes that The Body Shop marks the beginning of a new trend—commerce with a conscience. She is quoted as saying, "the original Body Shop was a series of brilliant accidents."

Poet Gwendolyn Brooks on the back steps of her home in Chicago.

New York, USA, July 12: Barbara Jordan becomes the first woman and the first African-American to address a political convention, the Democratic National Convention.
Italy, July 30: Tina Anselmi becomes the first woman in the Italian Cabinet, as Labor Minister.
Brisbane, Australia, August: Australian squash player Heather McKay wins the inaugural Women's World Open Championship.
East Sussex, England, August 21: Mary Joy Langdon becomes the first female firefighter in Britain.

Forrest Hills, New York, USA, August 21: Transsexual Renée Richards (formerly Richard Raskind) is barred from competing in the US Tennis Open.
Beijing, China, September 9: Mao Zedong, father of the Chinese revolution, dies, aged 82.
USA, September 22: The television series *Charlie's Angels* premieres.
China, October 6: Jiang Qing, widow of Mao Zedong, and the rest of the Gang of Four, are arrested in China for reportedly plotting a coup.

New York, USA, October 6: Barbara Walters appears as the first woman co-anchor on an American network evening news program, on ABC, partnered with Harry Reasoner. Her contract is for $1 million a year over the next five years.
USA, November 3: Sissy Spacek and Piper Laurie star in Brian DePalma's film *Carrie*, released today.
London, England, December 1: The punk band Sex Pistols cause a furor by swearing on live TV.
Sweden: Karin Söder is the first female Minister for Foreign Affairs.

World: Thailand's Princess Prem Purachatra is elected president of the International Council of Women.
England: Islamic scholar and writer Charis Waddy publishes *The Muslim Mind*, giving insight into Muslim beliefs, family life, and women's rights. She was the first woman graduate of Oriental Languages at Oxford University.
Paris, France: Historian Hélène Ahrweiler is elected the first woman president in the 700-year history of the Sorbonne.

Jaipur, India: Indian politician Gayatri Devi, born Princess Gayatri Devi of Cooch Behar and until 1970 the Maharani of Jaipur, publishes her memoir, *A Princess Remembers*.
Los Angeles, USA: Paige Rense, editor-in-chief of *Architectural Digest*, is named Woman of the Year by the *Los Angeles Times* for her dynamic editorial policies.
Colombia: María Elena Jimenéz de Crovo, the first woman to serve as Colombia's Minister of Labor and Social Security, is named Ambassador to Mexico.

Women Rule at the Summer Olympics

Barbara Jordan

Montreal, Canada, July: From the moment Queen Elizabeth II opened the Montreal Summer Olympics, women have seized the spotlight at these games.

The darling of the crowd, as well as the international media, was the 14-year-old Romanian gymnast, Nadia Comaneci. Her routine on the uneven bars won her a perfect 10—a first in the history of the Olympics, and she went on to achieve an astonishing six more perfect scores. Comaneci's number one competitor at the Games was Nellie Kim of the USSR. Kim came away with three gold medals—for the team competition, the vault, and the floor exercise. For the vault, Kim was also the first to be awarded a perfect 10. And during the floor routine she wowed the crowd and the judges by performing a double back salto—another first in women's events at the Olympics.

One of the most dramatic moments of the Games came during the small-bore rifle three-position event, in which men and women compete against each other. No woman had ever won a medal in the event. Initially it appeared that the two Americans, Margaret Murdock and Lanny Bassham—a man—had tied for the gold. After examining the targets more closely, the judges decided that Bassham's marksmanship was slightly

Margaret Murdock is the first markswoman in history to win an Olympic medal.

better, and awarded him the gold medal. Bassham, however, disagreed with the decision. At the awards ceremony, as the US national anthem was being played, Bassham insisted that Murdock share the victory platform with him.

Congresswoman Jordan Opens National Convention

New York, USA, July 12: Saying, "We believe in equality for all and privileges for none," Representative Barbara Jordan of Texas delivered the keynote address at the Democratic National Convention today.

Jordan is the first woman and also the first African-American from either political party to deliver the keynote address at a national convention, but this achievement is only the latest in a long line of "firsts" for the congresswoman.

In 1966, she was elected to the Texas Senate—the first African-American woman to win a seat in the state legislature, and the first African-American to serve in the Texas Senate since 1883. Jordan's election to the United States House of Representatives in 1972 set another record—she was the first African-American woman from one of the old Confederate states

to be elected to Congress. Thanks to the backing of her fellow Texan, former President Lyndon Johnson, Jordan was appointed to the powerful House Judiciary Committee.

She rose to prominence during the Watergate scandal when she delivered a nationally televised speech calling for the impeachment of President Richard Nixon for his part in the affair.

Sharing the spotlight with Jordan at the Democrats' convention is Representative Marie Corinne "Lindy" Boggs of Louisiana, who is chairing the convention—another first in American politics.

Transsexual Barred from Playing in US Open

Forrest Hills, New York, USA, August 21: The United States Tennis Association (USTA) has refused to permit transsexual Renée Richards (formerly Richard Raskind) to compete in the US Tennis Open as a woman. USTA officials argued that gender reassignment surgery does not alter a person's genetic make-up, and that Richards still possesses the normal strength of a male player, giving her an unfair physical advantage over other female players.

In the late 1960s Raskind began receiving hormone treatments in preparation for the sex-change operation. Dressed as a woman, Raskind traveled to Casablanca, Morocco, to see Dr Georges Burou, a gynecologist renowned for his innovative gender reassignment surgical techniques. At the last moment, however, Raskind canceled the surgery and returned home to the United States. In the years that followed, Raskind married and fathered a son, the marriage later ending in divorce. In 1975, at the recommendation of transsexism pioneer Harry

Nadia Comaneci achieves excellence with a perfect 10 in gymnastics.

Benjamin, Raskind scheduled another sex change operation with surgeon Roberto C. Granato, Sr. Following surgery Richards started a new life for herself in Newport Beach, California. After competing in several women's tennis tournaments, a newspaper reporter published a series of articles claiming that Richards was a man masquerading as a woman.

Richards has played tennis since childhood, captaining the high school tennis team at the Horace Mann School in New York City, and the men's tennis team at Yale. In 1972, Raskind qualified

Renee Richards (formerly Richard Raskind).

for the finals of the men's national 35-and-over championships. Since her gender assignment surgery, Richards has decided to put aside her career as an eye surgeon and become a full-time professional tennis player.

As for the ban from the US Open, Richards has said she will challenge the USTA ruling in court.

Heather McKay is Unbeatable!

Brisbane, Australia, August: Squash player Heather McKay, one of Australia's—and the world's—greatest athletes, has won the inaugural Women's World Open Championship. McKay's win comes as no surprise to her fans, as she has won every Australian Women's Squash Championship competition from 1960 to 1973, and this year scored her 14th consecutive win at the British Women's

Open. Nor has she not lost a single competitive match during this period, a record which has probably never been, and may never be equaled.

McKay is more than a natural athlete; she is a prodigy. All her opponents have learned from painful experience that she can get to balls they think will be beyond her. And when she returns volleys, the ball often flies so fast that her opponents find that they can't get anywhere near it. In terms of on-court performance, McKay is a strict perfectionist. "Good technique doesn't fall down," she says, "even when you're tired."

Mao's Widow and Her Allies Arrested

China, October 6: Less than a month after the death of Mao Zedong, his widow Jiang Qing and three of her associates, Wang Hongwen, Yao Wenyuan, and Zhang Chunqiao, known collectively in China as "The Gang of Four," have been arrested and charged with attempting to foment a military coup in Beijing and Shanghai. As all news reports from China must be vetted by the Communist Party's propaganda ministry, it is impossible to say with any degree of certainty why Jiang Qing and her three associates have fallen from power.

Jiang Qing was a film and stage actress in the 1930s, but gave up the theater in 1938 and joined the Communist Party in Yan'an, where she met Mao. They married, and after the Communist Revolution of 1949, Mao assigned his wife to work in the Ministry of Culture. In 1966, when he launched the Cultural Revolution, Mao placed Jiang Qing in charge of implementing the numerous radical changes to Chinese life. Through her Red Guard units, groups of militant, often fanatical students—many of them only teenagers—Jiang Qing oversaw a reign of terror in which millions of Chinese were imprisoned and many more publicly humiliated, injured, or killed, and countless works of art were destroyed. Under Jiang Qing's leadership only works with revolutionary and Maoist themes, such as the *Red Detachment of Women* ballet, could be performed. Privately, however, she has always enjoyed classic and foreign movies; her favorite is said to be *Gone With the Wind*.

In recent years, as China's leaders have begun to open up to the outside world (witness President Richard Nixon's visit to China in 1972), the violent, destructive methods of rule endorsed by Jiang Qing and her political allies have fallen out of favor. The next step in the drama is sure to be a show trial in which all four of the "conspirators" will be found guilty.

Hollywood Star Rosalind Russell Dies

Los Angeles, USA, November 28: Rosalind Russell, who made a career playing tough, unconventional, outspoken, free-spirited women, has died of breast cancer at the age of 69. Her death comes just three weeks after the passing of Patrick Dennis, author of *Auntie Mame*, which became one of Russell's most famous roles.

Her movie career began in 1934 when she signed with Universal Studios. But within days MGM made her a better offer. In order to escape her contract and dump Universal, she turned up for work in dowdy clothes and pretended to be a ditzy starlet who didn't understand complicated things like contracts. The Universal executives fell for it, "sacked" her, and she signed with MGM. During the 1930s, Russell was a secondary player whom MGM executives used as "a replacement threat" for one of their top stars, Myrna Loy. Every time Loy made unreasonable salary demands, MGM threatened to replace her in her next movie with Russell.

Among Russell's most memorable films are *His Girl Friday* (1940), *My Sister Eileen* (1942), *Picnic* (1955), and *Gypsy* (1962.) Russell also performed on Broadway, most famously in the musical comedies *Wonderful Town* and *Auntie Mame*. Her numerous *bon mots* include: "Acting is standing up naked and turning around very slowly." Russell was nominated for four Oscars, and won four Golden Globe Awards and a Tony.

Jiang Qing

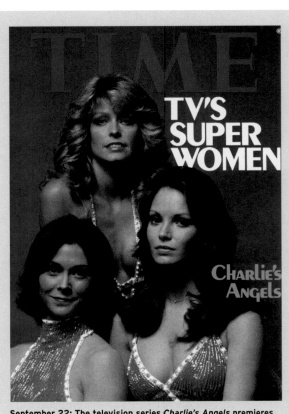

September 22: The television series *Charlie's Angels* premieres.

Bette Davis

Anais Nin, Mistress of Erotica, Dies

Los Angeles, USA, January 14: Anais Nin, the unconventional novelist and diarist of Spanish, Catalan, Cuban, and Danish descent, died today of cancer, aged 73. Famous for her many sexually-explicit journals which span more than 60 years, she was also one of the first women in modern Europe to explore the realm of erotic writing. Her beautifully written journals which she began writing when she was 11 years old, have been praised for their unusual depth of analysis, honesty and insight.

Nin was born in Neuilly, France and moved to New York City with her mother and two brothers when her parents separated. While still a teenager, she abandoned formal schooling, began working as a model and later studied psychotherapy. Nin was also known for her colorful life and for her lovers, who included Henry Miller, Edmund Wilson, Gore Vidal, and Otto Rank. She was married to banker and artist Hugh Guiler of New York, who tolerated her affairs. Then, in 1955, she entered into a second marriage to the much younger Rupert Pole in California. Largely ignored until the 1960s, she is now regarded as a most inspirational feminist writer and a source of inspiration for women who challenge conventional gender roles. In 1973, she received an honorary doctorate from Philadelphia College of Art. Nin's body will be cremated, and her ashes scattered over Santa Monica Bay.

> "I'VE BEEN
> UNDRESSED BY
> KINGS / AND
> I'VE SEEN SOME
> THINGS / THAT
> A WOMAN AIN'T
> SUPPOSED TO
> SEE/
> I'VE BEEN TO
> PARADISE / BUT
> I'VE NEVER
> BEEN TO ME."
>
> CHARLENE,
> "I'VE NEVER BEEN
> TO ME"

Presidential Pardon for "Tokyo Rose"

Washington DC, USA, January 19: History was made today when former "Tokyo Rose," Iva Toguri d'Aquino, was granted a full and unconditional pardon—and the nation's apologies—by President Gerald Ford. It is the first time in American history that such a pardon has been conferred after a treason conviction.

Found guilty of aiding the Japanese by broadcasting morale-damaging propaganda during World War II, she was sentenced to 10 years in prison. Her highly publicized 1949 trial was a travesty of justice, with prosecutors publicly defaming her as a traitorous siren while pressuring witnesses to commit perjury and to conceal evidence of her innocence. For more than 25 years the Federal Government successfully concealed the truth—the woman prosecuted as "Tokyo Rose" was a genuine American heroine who aided prisoners of war in Japan and subverted Japanese efforts to undermine Allied troop morale in the Pacific.

Twenty-seven years after her conviction, two witnesses who testified against her admitted they had been coached by the prosecutor and had testified under extreme duress.

Toguri's pardon is the outcome of a concerted campaign, led by a group of journalists, to clear her name. They contended that Toguri had been the victim of racism and wartime hysteria and had lobbied tirelessly for a complete re-examination of her case.

Iva Toguri d'Aquino was "Tokyo Rose."

Eighth Grammy for First Lady of Song

Los Angeles, USA, February 19: The tireless performer Ella Fitzgerald won another Grammy today—her first since 1962—for Best Jazz Vocal Performance in *Fitzgerald and Pass…Again.* Fitzgerald, who is acclaimed for her peerless technique and wide vocal range, is accompanied on the Grammy-winning album by guitarist Joe Pass. This is the second album the pair has recorded together since 1973. The winner of countless awards, Fitzgerald won four Grammy awards in 1959 and, in 1967 at the age of 50, won a another Grammy for Lifetime Achievement.

Shy and reserved off stage, Fitzgerald is completely at home in the spotlight.

Ella Fitzgerald wins her first Grammy Award since 1962.

New York, USA, January 7: Australian Rupert Murdoch purchases the *New York Post*.

Los Angeles, USA, January 14: Anais Nin, novelist and diarist, dies, aged 73.

Saudi Arabia, January: Princess Misha is executed for eloping and marrying a man of her own choice rather than one of her father's.

Washington DC, USA, January 19: Iva Toguri d'Aquino, who was found guilty of treason in 1949 as "Tokyo Rose," is pardoned by President Gerald Ford.

Washington DC, USA, January: Patricia Harris becomes the first African-American woman to serve in a Cabinet post.

Los Angeles, USA, February 19: Ella Fitzgerald wins her first Grammy Award since 1962, for Best Jazz Grand Vocal Performance

USA, March 2: Bette Davis is the first woman to be given the Life Achievement Award by the American Film Institute.

New Delhi, India, March 22: Indira Gandhi quits politics following a crushing defeat in the elections.

Los Angeles, USA, March 29: Lina Wertmuller is the first woman to be nominated for an Oscar as Best Director, for *Seven Beauties.*

Liverpool, England, April 2: 21-year-old Charlotte Brew is the first woman to ride in the Grand National steeplechase.

Buenos Aires, Argentina, April 30: Mothers of children who have disappeared hold a rally at the Plaza de Mayo.

Indianapolis, Indiana, USA, May: Driver Janet Guthrie is first woman to qualify for the Indianapolis 500.

Switzerland, May 2: Dr. Elisabeth Blunschy becomes the first woman president of the National Council of Switzerland.

USA, May 25: Carrie Fisher stars in the spectacular film *Star Wars*, which is released today.

Spain, June: Communist leader Dolores Ibárruri, exiled for 38 years during Spanish dictator Franco's regime, is re-elected to Parliament.

UK, June 7: Week-long celebrations commemorating Queen Elizabeth's 25 years on the throne commence.

London, England, July 7: Marie Myriam, representing France, wins the Eurovision Song Contest with the song "L'oiseau et l'enfant."

Santo Domingo, Dominican Republic, July 16: Janelle Penny Commissiong, representing Trinidad-Tobago, is the first black woman to win the Miss Universe title.

Northamptonshire, England, August: British parasitologist and world expert on fleas Miriam Rothschild hosts the first international flea conference. More than 100 flea experts attend.

Faye Dunaway in her Academy Award-winning performance in the 1976 movie, *Network*.

La Passionaria Re-elected to Parliament

Spain, June: The impassioned orator champion of women's rights, and Communist leader, Dolores Ibárruri, fondly known as La Passionaria, has been re-elected to Parliament in Spain's first free elections for 41 years.

After 38 years in exile in Russia, Ibárruri returned to her homeland in May, one month after the PCE (Partido Comunista de España,) was legalized. Her election completes a political circle that began half a century ago when she was one of 17 Communist Party members elected to Parliament. A skilled propagandist, Ibárruri was almost alone in the party hierarchy in demanding that women be treated as men's equals, and that women's economic and political emancipation should be a primary goal of the Communist movement.

Dolores Ibárruri

After the civil war, Ibárruri was among the tens of thousands of fellow Republicans who fled Franco's Spain. Like many other Communists, Ibárruri found refuge in the Soviet Union, where, apart from brief spells abroad, she lived for the next 36 years. In the early 1960s, she was granted Soviet citizenship. Her political work was recognized during these years and she received an honorary doctorate from the University of Moscow. In addition, she received the Lenin Peace Prize (1964) and the Order of Lenin (1965). Her autobiography *No Pasarán (They Shall Not Pass)*, was published in 1966. Ibárruri's triumphant homecoming following Franco's death in 1975, and her success in this election is seen as a sign that Spain's war wounds are finally healing and that the country is ready to move on in its endeavor to allow a more liberal society.

She is also a talented improviser, and her unique voice reaches well beyond the jazz world, attracting the adoration of international audiences from all walks of life.

Mothers of Missing Children Challenge Government

Buenos Aires, Argentina, April 30: Fourteen women, desperate to discover the whereabouts of their missing children, gathered today in front of the Presidential Palace in the Plaza de Mayo. They came bearing a letter to Argentina's leader, General Jorge Rafael Videla, asking him where their children were. One of the women has been looking for one of her sons and her daughter-in-law for over six months.

Since the military junta took power last year, regular disappearances have occurred across class and age lines, but most of the kidnapped are young blue-collar workers and students, including pregnant women. There are concerns that many have been killed by government agents.

Motivated by a force more powerful than fear for their own lives—the love of their children—these women, who met in the waiting rooms of police stations while trying to discover the whereabouts of their children, have taken extraordinary risks in today's despotic political climate.

There is no doubt that their unprecedented show of solidarity and their demand for social justice will raise the hackles of the government.

Although the women are first and foremost desperate to find their children alive, their other agenda is truth and justice. We have been told that the demonstrators plan to meet every Thursday to highlight their plight. These brave women are traversing repressive social boundaries in a society where they are expected to be silent. But they are determined to continue. The fate of the rally's organizers in these politically turbulent times remains to be seen.

time out

Women in Argentina unite in protest at the disappearance of sons and loved ones jailed as political prisoners. Despite victimization and harassment, the women, who number over 2,500, are keeping vigil.

Key Events

English Channel, September: Canadian swimmer Cindy Nicholas is the first woman to complete a round-trip, non-stop solo swim across the English Channel.
Paris, France, September 16: Maria Callas "La Divina", the American-born Greek opera star whose life was as dramatic as her stage roles, dies.
New York, USA, September 29: Eva Shain becomes the first woman to referee a world heavyweight fight, between Muhammad Ali and Ernie Shavers at Madison Square Garden.

Washington DC, USA, October 11: Carolyn R. Payton becomes the first woman and first African-American to serve as director of the Peace Corps.
Washington DC, December 3: Karen Farmer becomes the first African-American to be admitted into the Daughters of the American Revolution.
Stockholm, Sweden, December 10: American nuclear physicist Rosalyn Yalow wins the Nobel Prize for medicine for her work in the 1950s in developing radioimmunoassay of peptide hormones.

Oslo, Norway, December 10: Mairead Corrigan and Betty Williams share the postponed 1976 Nobel Peace Prize.
New York, December 16: The General Assembly of the United nations adopts a resolution calling for a day to be observed by member states as International Women's Day.
California, USA: Jane Goodall and Genevieve, Princess di San Faustino, co-found the Jane Goodall Institute for Wildlife Research, Education, and Conservation.

Baltimore, USA: Oprah Winfrey becomes co-host of the morning TV talk show *People Are Talking*.
Ireland: Mary Harney, aged 24, becomes the youngest member of the Irish Senate.
Australia: Colleen McCullough publishes *The Thorn Birds*.
USA: Conservative anti-feminist Phyllis Schlafly publishes *The Power of the Positive Woman*.
Paris, France: Leading international dancer Violette Verdy (born Nelly Guillerm) becomes the first woman director of the Paris Opera Ballet.

Beijing, China: Conductor Zheng Xiaoying, China's first woman orchestra conductor, becomes head conductor at Beijing's Central Opera Theatre.
Israel: Miriam Ben Porat becomes the country's first female Supreme Court judge.
Canada: Sandra Lovelace, an Aboriginal woman from Tobique Reserve in New Brunswick, appeals to the UN Human Rights Commission against the *Canadian Indian Act*, which gives native status through the male head of the household.

Rosalyn Yalow

Saudi Princess Misha Executed for Adultery

Saudi Arabia, July 15: The execution of a young Saudi princess has sparked public outrage and reignited the debate about the treatment of Islamic women. Sources say that Princess Misha, after eloping and marrying a commoner, was executed by members of her own family.

Misha was the daughter of a member of Saudi Arabia's ruling family—one of 2,000 princesses belonging to the House of Saud—which intermarries to protect family interests. She had been attending the American University in Beirut when she fell in love with and married a relative of the Saudi ambassador to Lebanon. After being summoned by her family back to Riyadh to marry a much older man, she attempted to fake her own drowning and was caught trying to escape with her husband. Misha was publicly executed on the orders of her grandfather, Prince Muhammad bin Abdul Aziz, by gunshots to the head, after being charged with adultery. Her lover, who was not recognized by the King as her legal husband, was executed.

There is no clear evidence that an actual trial of the princess or her lover took place. Traditionally, a woman guilty of sexual offences is punished by her own family to restore their sense of family

honor. In this case, the royal family was also enforcing its own rules forbidding dalliance with commoners.

The incident has captured the imagination of the public and also aroused a sense of indignation over the denial of a freedom western women take for granted—the right to choose one's own partner and marry for love. The tragic fate of Princess Misha also illustrates the extraordinary confusion created by the ruling family's attempt to modernize the country without losing grip on power, or alienating conservative religious opinion.

Canadian Swimmer Breaks Channel Speed Record

English Channel, September: A 20year-old Canadian woman has set the English Channel round-trip speed record. Cindy Nicholas, the first woman to complete a double crossing of the English Channel, has taken an astonishing 10 hours off the previous record.

The crossing took the stoic Nicholas just 19 hours and 55 minutes. This solo, nonstop swim is another achievement in the young swimmer's stellar career, and has earned her the title "Queen of the Channel." Nicholas began competitive swimming when she was six years old in Scarborough, Ontario, Canada, and has set several Canadian age group swimming records, mostly in butterfly.

Her first marathon achievement was at age 16, when she attained provincial fame by swimming across Lake Ontario in 15 hours and 10 minutes. This crossing bettered all previous records— for both men and women. One year later, she made her first English Channel crossing, setting another record for the crossing from France to England. In 1976, she became the women's world marathon-swimming champion.

The inspiring Nicholas, who plans to study law, has a tremendous future ahead of her. Her combination of pragmatism and endurance is sure to serve her well,

Naturalist Miriam Rothschild working in her lab.

both in the arena of law and the world of competitive swimming. She is a fine example of a woman striving to achieve her dreams and succeeding through hard work and dedication.

Death of La Divina, Maria Callas

Paris, France, September 16: Maria Callas, the Greek-born American opera star whose life was, at times, as tragic and passionate as her stage roles, died today of heart failure. The dramatic coloratura soprano—perhaps the best-known opera singer of the post-World War II period—combined an impressive *bel canto* technique with great talent and dramatic flair. An extremely versatile singer, her repertoire ranged from the *bel canto* operas of Bellini and Rossini, to Verdi and Puccini, and, in her very early career, the musical dramas of Wagner. Her quite remarkable musical and dramatic talents led to her being hailed worldwide as La Divina (The Divine Woman).

Callas's life was as distinctive and colorful as her voice and she endured many struggles and scandals over the course of her career. Born in New York, as a young girl Callas enjoyed listening to gramophone records and radio programs, and took piano as well as singing lessons. She received her musical education in Greece and established her career in Italy. Her dramatic mid-career weight loss turned her from a stout woman into

Maria Callas led a life as dramatic as her roles on stage.

a glamorous icon, but there is much speculation from disappointed fans that this may have contributed to her vocal decline and premature end of her career. Reports of her diva behavior, her supposed rivalry with Renata Tebaldi, and her love affair with shipping tycoon Aristotle Onassis, have filled press columns to the point where it often seemed that her dramatic life and personal tragedies overshadowed her remarkable talents. Her artistic achievements, however, were such that eminent conductor and composer Leonard Bernstein called her "The Bible of Opera."

After Onassis's marriage to Jacqueline Kennedy, widow of assassinated American president John F. Kennedy, Callas suffered a breakdown. She later made several attempts to resurrect her career, but her voice was a mere shadow of its former self. She will, however, be remembered for the power and distinctive timbre of her voice, her dramatic presence, and her fastidious musicianship.

Irish Housewives Win Nobel Peace Prize

Oslo, Norway, December 10: Two Irish housewives who became spokespeople for the nation's outrage at the ongoing violence and mindless killing of innocent victims have been jointly awarded the postponed 1976 Nobel Peace Prize. In today's presentation speech, Egil Aarvik, Vice-Chairman of the Norwegian Nobel Committee, spoke of the women's bravery and commitment to the cause of peace in Northern Ireland.

The Nobel Laureates, Mairead Corrigan and Betty Williams, met after a tragic incident on a Belfast street last August 8, in which three children of Corrigan's sister, Anne Maguire, were killed by a car driven by Danny Lennon, an IRA member who was fatally shot by British troops while trying to make his getaway. Williams witnessed the event and, within two days, had obtained 6,000 signatures on a petition for peace and gained widespread media attention. Williams and Corrigan then organized a peace march to the graves of the children, which was attended by 10,000 Catholic and Protestant women. At the end of August, the two women led 35,000 people onto the streets of Belfast, petitioning for the end of violence and permanent peace between the republican and loyalist factions.

Both women believe the most effective way to end the conflict is through re-education rather than violence, and the movement they founded has become

Mairead Corrigan and Betty Williams share the Nobel Peace Prize for 1976.

known as the Community of Peace People. Today, Aarvik praised Williams and Corrigan for taking the first steps along the road to peace in a country where terror and violence have become a way of life. He added that they have given fresh hope to those who thought that all hope was gone. Williams and Corrigan have become spokeswomen for the silent and innocent victims of war, especially women and children, and are also inspirational models for ordinary people actively promoting the causes of tolerance and peace.

UN Adopts International Women's Day

New York, December 16: Today a long tradition of struggle for equality, justice, peace, and development is at last being recognized. The United Nations General Assembly has adopted a resolution proclaiming the United Nations Day for Women's Rights and International Peace to be observed on any day of the year by member states, in accordance with their historical and national traditions. In adopting this resolution, the General Assembly recognizes the role of women in peace efforts and development, and urges an end to discrimination and increased support for women's full and equal participation. International Women's Day will mark the story of ordinary women as makers of history, and is rooted in centuries-old struggles of women to participate in society on an equal footing with men.

Paris Opera Ballet's First Woman Director

Paris, France: Internationally acclaimed dancer Violette Verdy made history this year when she was appointed the Paris Opera Ballet's first female artistic director. Verdy comes to the position with a very impressive artistic pedigree. In 1971, Le Chevalier de l'Ordre des Arts et des Lettres was bestowed upon her by the

French Government.

Like most great ballerinas, Verdy—born Nelly Guillerm—began her training as a small child. Born in Pont-L'Abbé, France, Verdy began her dancing career in 1945 as a soloist in Roland Petit's famed Ballets des Champs-Elysées. She went on to dance with Les Ballets de Paris and toured the United States for the first time in 1953.

Five years later, Verdy was invited by Lincoln Kirstein and George Balanchine to join the New York City Ballet (NYCB) as principal dancer, a position she held for 18 years until her retirement from the stage in 1976. While she was with NYCB, Balanchine created many roles for Verdy, including *Emeralds*, *Tchaikovsky Pas de Deux*, *La Source*, and *Sonatine*. On two separate occasions in 1976, President and Mrs. Ford invited Verdy

Phyllis Schlafly

Violette Verdy, the first woman director of the Paris Opera Ballet.

to dance at the White House and at the Capitol for state functions. Choreography is also close to Verdy's heart, and this is reflected in a children's book she wrote called *Giselle: A Role for a Lifetime*. Verdy's extensive dance experience and exceptional artistic generosity of spirit will serve her well in her trailblazing new role where she will bring the Paris Opera Ballet to the forefront of dance.

Iris Murdoch

American Women Take Back the Night

San Francisco, USA, November 19: This evening, some 3,000 American women, chanting slogans such as "no more profits off women's bodies," staged the nation's first Take Back the Night march, filling the streets and blocking off traffic as they wound their way through the red-light district of San Francisco. The candle-lit march coincided with a conference that was organized by the Women Against Violence in Pornography and Media, and served as a symbolic statement of their commitment to stop "…the tide of violence against women in all arenas," and to demand "…that perpetrators of such violence be held responsible for their actions and be made to change."

The San Francisco event comes two years after the first Reclaim the Night march was held in Belgium by women attending the International Tribunal on Crimes Against Women. Other such marches have since been held in Rome, where around 10,000 women marched through the center of the city to protest escalating rape statistics, and in West Germany, where the women marchers demanded "…the right to move freely in their communities at day and night without harassment and sexual assault." Last year, British women singing protest songs simultaneously took to the streets in 11 towns stretching from Manchester to Soho as a reaction to the Ripper Murders in Leeds.

Helen Suzman wins the UN's Human Rights Award.

Helen Suzman Wins UN Human Rights Award

United Nations, December 10: South African politician and anti-apartheid campaigner, Helen Suzman, has been named winner of the United Nations' Human Rights Award. Since entering the South African parliament in 1953, Suzman has been a courageous champion of human rights, tenaciously fighting to keep liberal values alive in the face of a white-imposed system of racial segregation formalized in 1948.

Born Helen Gavronsky in Germiston, Transvaal, Suzman attended Witwatersrand University, where she trained to be an economist and statistician. At age 20,

she married Dr. Moses Suzman, giving birth to their two daughters before returning to her university as a part-time lecturer in 1944. She left academic life in 1952, a year before she was elected to parliament as a member of the United Party. In 1961, she switched to the liberal Progressive Party, and over the next 13 years served as its sole representative in the South African legislature.

During those 13 years, Suzman was the only parliamentary voice of opposition to the injustices of apartheid. She alone defended human rights, equal opportunity, and rule of law, speaking out against oppression and the practice of detention without trial. The only representative willing to regard disenfranchised black South Africans as part of her constituency, she investigated the situation of those dispossessed of their homes and land, attended political trials, and visited political prisoners. Due to her persistence, prison authorities finally allowed political detainees to receive books and study materials.

As South Africa's best-known woman politician, Suzman has used her position to harass apartheid ministers and bureaucrats at every opportunity, and to voice her fierce opposition to apartheid in order to capture the attention of the media and inspire support for the cause. Her efforts have not only earned her the gratitude of all oppressed black people within her own society, but also the recognition and respect of the international community.

Rideout vs Rideout

Salem, Oregon, USA, December 27: Today, a jury of eight women and four men acquitted John J. Rideout, the first man in modern American history to face trial for raping his wife. The verdict, reached after three hours of deliberation, was based on reasonable doubt that force was used. As one jury member later revealed, "We didn't know who to trust. There were so many conflicting stories."

Oregon is now one of only three states that do not recognize "marital privilege" as a defense against rape, and for four days the jury heard graphic testimony about the couple's sexual relations.

Greta Rideout testified that her husband demanded sex up to three times a week and violent sex once a week, and that he frequently kicked and hit her. On the day in question, she said her husband became very angry when she refused his demand for sex and then a physical fight began in the presence of their two-year old daughter. According to Greta Rideout, she submitted after her husband ordered the child to leave the room, when

Julia Child and co-author Simone Beck pose in Julia's kitchen in Cambridge, Massachusetts in June 1970.

began beating her, hitting her especially hard in the jaw. John Rideout told a different story. He admitted to hitting his wife but said she hit him first. He insisted that he apologized for striking her, after which they kissed and made up before having voluntary sexual intercourse. Testimony given by other witnesses also cast doubt on Greta Rideout's honesty as well as her motives for accusing her husband of rape. On the other hand, the physician who attended Greta

by Franco Zeffirelli. In 1960, she began her international opera career with a series of debuts at some of the leading opera houses, singing Lucia to great acclaim in Paris, performing the title role in *Alcina* in Venice, and then later repeating the role in her US debut at the Dallas Opera. The following year, she sang the role of Lucia in her debut appearances at Milan's La Scala and also at the New York City's Metropolitan Opera. Hailed around the world as La

Chrstina Crawford Tells All

Hannah Arendt

USA: Readers and reviewers continue to reel following the publication of Christina Crawford's scathing memoir, *Mommie Dearest*, in which she portrays her adoptive movie-star mother, Joan Crawford, as a cruel and manipulative alcoholic. The release of the startling tell-all tome comes just a year after the famous actress died, leaving a will that disinherited Christina and her brother Christopher "…for reasons which should be well known to them."

In her book, Christina Crawford alleges that she was the victim of child abuse, recounting several instances of her mother's destructive drunken rages, including one occasion when her mother physically attacked her. Contending that her mother was both overbearing and unbalanced, Crawford describes another incident when her mother launched into a vicious tirade after discovering wire coat hangers in her daughter's closet.

She also accuses her mother of being more interested in her career than in her children, even suggesting that her mother may have adopted her four children solely for publicity purposes.

Crawford's shocking exposé is the first of its kind and the reaction has been mixed, with some critics dismissing it as a hatchet job in revenge for her mother leaving her and her brother out of the will. Nevertheless, it appears very likely that Joan Crawford's reputation, already badly diminished by a series of B grade films made late in her career, could be forever tarnished by this latest characterization.

Australian operatic soprano Joan Sutherland is made a Dame of the British Empire in 1978.

Rideout after the incident testified that her condition was probably consistent with a "forced act of intercourse." The arresting police officer told the court that John Rideout, when questioned about his wife's battered jaw, said, "If I'd done it right she wouldn't be here to complain."

La Stupenda Becomes Dame Commander

England, December 30: Australian opera soprano Joan Sutherland has today been appointed Dame Commander of the British Empire. A noted contributor to the *bel canto* revival of the 1950s and 1960s, Sutherland was made a Commander of the British Empire in 1961, and her further elevation today comes in recognition of her continuing services to the performing arts.

Sutherland made her European debut in 1952 as the First Lady of *The Magic Flute* at the Royal Opera House, Covent Garden. She achieved a major breakthrough in 1959, when she sang Lucia in Donizetti's *Lucia di Lammermoor* at the Royal Opera House in a production conducted by Tullio Serafin and staged

Stupenda, Sutherland has never forgotten her roots in Australia, bringing her own opera company home between 1965 and 1974, and regularly appearing with the Australian Opera in Sydney, where her husband Richard Bonynge is currently serving as music director.

Sale of Girls Outlawed in Afghanistan

Afghanistan: Workers from the ruling People's Democratic Party of Afghanistan (PDPA) are fanning out across the countryside as part of a concentrated effort to stop Afghans from selling their daughters. A communist party founded in 1965, the PDPA came to power in a coup in April this year, and is currently introducing a range of reforms dealing with a variety of issues including women's rights. As a secular regime, the PDPA is especially committed to eradicating the practices of religiously conservative Afghans who enforce traditional Islamic restrictions on women in daily life. The PDPA has declared that women deserve equal treatment, that girls are to attend school, and child marriages and feudal dowry payments are now banned.

Christina Crawford poses with her mother, Joan.

Maria de Lourdes
Pintassilgo

Iranian Women Take to the Streets

Tehran, Iran, March 8: Less than a month after the collapse of the Shah's government in Iran, at least 15,000 women took to the streets of Tehran today to protest a series of new laws and policies that restrict their freedom of action in Iranian society. Carrying placards and banners that read, "Liberty and equality are our undeniable rights" and "We will fight against compulsory veil; down with dictatorship," the demonstrators marched on Tehran University, the Ministry of Justice building, and the Office of the new Prime Minister, Mehdi Bazargan. There are reports of men, and even a number of women, attacking some of the female demonstrators as they marched through the streets. Outside the Prime Minister's office members of the Revolutionary Guard fired into the air to disperse the protesters.

"ANY WOMAN WHO UNDER-STANDS THE PROBLEMS OF RUNNING A HOME WILL BE NEARER TO UNDERSTANDING THE PROBLEMS OF RUNNING A COUNTRY."

MARGARET THATCHER
(1925–),
BRITISH PRIME
MINISTER

time out

In Egypt, 3 percent of men have more than one wife but President Sadat, under pressure from his own wife Jihan, has agreed to allow women to file for divorce should their husband take another wife.

The protests, which coincided with International Women's Day, were sparked by a series of new policies handed down by Ayatollah Ruhollah Khomeini's new regime. Women have been banned from serving as judges, and from serving in the military (female members of the Iranian armed forces were summarily dismissed). It is expected that more restrictive legislation will follow, such as forbidding women to participate in international sporting events, outlawing co-education, and closing day care centers in an effort to compel working mothers to give up their jobs and stay at home with their children.

But it is the imposition of the veil that has galvanized the protesters. Many of these women, who under the Shah enjoyed a secular, Western-style life, have baulked at the idea of being compelled by the new regime to wear a voluminous black veil that covers everything except their hands and face.

Britain's "Iron Lady" Becomes Prime Minister

London, England, May 4: The Conservative Party returned to power in Great Britain today, winning a 44-seat majority in the House of Commons. The leader of the party, Margaret Thatcher, is the new Prime Minister—and the first woman to hold the office.

Running under the slogan "Labour is not working" (the advertising giant, Saatchi and Saatchi, came up with the tagline), the Conservatives reminded voters that the Labour Government has been unable to solve high employment, widespread strikes, and deteriorating public services.

Many voters said they found Thatcher's approach to problems refreshing and reassuring; she has a reputation for

Jane Byrne, the first woman mayor of Chicago.

Margaret Thatcher is the new British Prime Minister.

confronting troubles directly, calling them by name, and taking direct action to solve them. Arguably the most famous example of her blunt style occurred during a speech she delivered in Kensington Town Hall. Speaking of the Soviet Union and Great Britain, Thatcher said, "The Russians are bent on world dominance, and they are rapidly acquiring the means to become the most powerful imperial nation the world has seen… They put guns before butter, while we put just about everything before guns." In response the Soviet Defense Ministry's newspaper derided her as "the Iron Lady," but Thatcher delighted in the nickname, and her supporters took it as a tribute to her forthright and resolute character.

As she arrived at her new home, 10 Downing Street, Thatcher took a more conciliatory note, paraphrasing a prayer popularly attributed to St Francis of

London, England, January 1: Decca releases the first digital recording.
USA, February 14: Wendy Carlos becomes the official name of pioneering synthesizer musician Walter Carlos, best known for the recording *Switched-On Bach*.
Tehran, Iran, March 8: Thousands of women march to protest the oppressive policies of Ayatollah Ruhollah Khomeini's new regime.
Kampala, Uganda, March 29: Idi Amin's murderous regime collapses as Tanzanian-backed troops invade the Ugandan capital.

Pennsylvania, USA, March 31: The Three Mile Island nuclear reactor is shut down after releasing radiation.
Los Angeles, USA, April 9: Jane Fonda wins the Best Actress Academy Award for *Coming Home*. Maggie Smith wins the Best Supporting Actress Award for *California Suite*.
Chicago, Illinois, USA, April 16: Jane Byrne takes office as the first woman mayor of Chicago.
Jerusalem, Israel, April: Gali Atari with Milk and Honey, from Israel, win the Eurovision Song Contest.

London, England, May 3: Margaret Thatcher leads the Conservative Party to victory, becoming Europe's first female prime minister.
Queensland, Australia, May 19: Jockey Pam O'Neill becomes the first Australian woman to ride against men.
France, June 10: At age 86, Louise Weiss, becomes the oldest member of the European Parliament.
North Carolina, USA, June: Debbie Shook is stripped of her Miss North Carolina crown for criticizing the sponsoring organization.

Washington DC, USA, July 2: The US Supreme Court rules in *Bellotti v. Baird* that minors don't need parental consent to obtain abortions.
Portugal, July 19: Maria de Lourdes Pintassilgo becomes the country's first woman president.
Strasbourg, France, July: French politician Simone Veil is the first woman president of the European Parliament to be elected by universal suffrage.
USSR, August 19: Soviet cosmonauts Vladimir Lyakhov and Valery Ryumin return from 175 days in space.

Juno Beach, Florida, USA, August 20: American swimmer Diana Nyad completes the longest swim in history, making the 102.5-mile (165-km) journey from the Bahamian island of Bimini to Florida.
USA, September 1: Hazel W. Johnson becomes the first African-American woman to be promoted to the rank of general in the United States army.
Paris, France, September 8: Troubled actress Jean Seberg, who made her film debut in 1957 as Joan of Arc, dies in Paris from an apparent suicide, aged 40.

Assisi, "Where there is discord, may we bring harmony. Where there is error, may we bring truth. Where there is doubt, may we bring faith. And where there is despair, may we bring hope."

Pam O'Neill Wins Three in One Day!

Queensland, Australia, May 19: Today Pam O'Neill broke down an old prejudice and set a new world's record: she is the first Australian woman jockey to ride against men; and on this day at the Gold Coast in Southport, Queensland, she won three races. No jockey, male or female, has ever won three times on their first day of racing. Furthermore, until today the Australian Jockey Club had only permitted women jockeys to compete in all-women races.

The men-only rule of horseracing was so strictly enforced that when O'Neill was 18 she was permitted to lead a horse to the gates of the Eagle Farm Racecourse in Brisbane City, but she could not step inside. She had to hand the lead-rope to a man who would bring the horse to the racetrack.

O'Neill began lobbying officials of the Queensland Turf Club to license women as jockeys with the right to ride against men. She met fierce opposition both from men within the racing establishment and racing fans, enduring a firestorm of verbal abuse that ranged from derisive to obscene.

Nonetheless, she persevered and has made it possible for other women to enter the sport.

Oldest Delegate at the European Parliament

France, June 10: When she takes her seat in the European Parliament today, Louise Weiss—at age 86—will be the oldest delegate in the assembly chamber. The horrors she witnessed in her native

Louise Weiss, oldest member of European Parliament.

France during World War I turned Weiss into a dedicated peace activist. During the 1930s she lobbied the French government to give women the vote, while trying to rally the international community against the rise of Nazi Germany and the threat of another world war. During the war she worked with the French Resistance. Since then she has made a name for herself as a writer, editor, and film director, and as an advocate for a united Europe.

New World Record for Diana Nyad

Juno Beach, Florida, USA, August 20: After two days of non-stop effort, American long-distance swimmer Diana Nyad completed the 102.5-mile (165-km) journey from the Bahamian island of Bimini to Florida, and in the process has set a new world record for the longest swim in history.

The Bimini-to-Florida swim is not Nyad's first record. In 1975, she swam around Manhattan Island in 7 hours, 57 minutes, breaking a 50-year-old record. In 1974, she swam 32 miles (51 km) across Lake Ontario, from the north to the south shore, in a record-setting 18 hours, 20 minutes. After a ten-minute rest she attempted to swim back, a decision which almost ended in tragedy: two-and-a-half hours into the return swim Nyad fell unconscious and had to be pulled from the water.

Nyad trained as a marathon swimmer with Buck Dawson of the International Swimming Hall of Fame. Beginning in 1970, she entered marathon swimming events around the world. In her first race, a 10-mile (16 km) swim in Lake Ontario, she set a woman's world record, finishing the course in 4 hours, 22 minutes. She set another record in 1974 when she swam a 22-mile (35 km) race across the Bay of Naples in Italy in 8 hours, 11 minutes.

Simone Veil

Jane Fonda wins Best Actress Academy Award for *Coming Home*.

Key Events

Rome, Italy, September 16: Sportscar racer Lella Lombardi and co-driver Giorgio Francia score their second win this year, at Vallelunga.
Northwest Territories, Canada, October 1: Nellie J. Cournoyea becomes the first native woman to lead a provincial territorial government in Canada.
USA, October 5: Bo Derek and Julie Andrews star in the film *10*.
Tehran, Iran, November 4: Followers of Ayatollah Khomeini storm the US embassy. Nearly 100 embassy staff are taken hostage.

USA, November 7: Bette Midler stars as a self-destructive rock singer in *The Rose*, released today.
Geneva, Switzerland, December 9: The World Health Organization (WHO) declares that the smallpox virus has been eradicated.
Oslo, Norway, December 10: Mother Teresa wins the Nobel Peace Prize in recognition of her work for the poor.
Zimbabwe, December 29: Robert Mugabe, Joshua Nkomo, and Bishop Abel Muzorewa sign a cease-fire agreement, bringing the seven-year civil war to an end.

Afghanistan, December 29: The build-up of Soviet troops has become an invasion, culminating in the fall of the government in Kabul.
Cambridge, England: Keynesian economist Joan Robinson becomes the first woman to be elected a fellow of King's College.
Egypt: Dr Aisha Rateb becomes the first Egyptian woman to be appointed ambassador, to Denmark.
San Francisco, USA: Feminist artist Judy Chicago's room-sized sculpture *The Dinner Party*, in the making since 1974, premieres.

England: Josephine Barnes becomes first woman president of the British Medical Association.
India: Vijaya Lakshmi Pandit, in 1953 the first woman president of the UN General Assembly, is appointed India's representative to the UN Human Rights Commission. She also publishes *The Scope of Happiness: A Personal Memoir* this year.
Pacific Ocean: American oceanographer Sylvia Earle is the first person in the world to dive to a depth of 1,250 ft (381 m), walking on the ocean floor off the Hawaiian island of Oahu.

Italy: Nilde Iotti becomes the first female president of the Italian Chamber of Deputies.
Mexico: Griselda Álvarez becomes the first female governor of a Mexican state, Colima.
Winnipeg, Canada: Rosella Bjornson becomes the first pregnant commercial air pilot. She is forced to take unpaid leave.
England: Dame Barbara Ward publishes *Progress for a Small Planet*, discussing the Earth's dwindling resources and their unequal distribution.

Lella Lombardi Wins at Vallelunga

Rome, Italy, September 16: Sportscar racer Lella Lombardi and her co-driver Giorgio Francia scored their second win this year at Vallelunga, finishing four laps ahead of the car driven by Pasquale Barberio and Enzo Coloni.

Sportscar racing is new to Lombardi. In the early 1970s she was a Formula 3 and Formula 5000 driver before debuting in 1974 as a Formula One driver. The following year at the Spanish Grand Prix, Lombardi set a record, becoming the first female Formula One driver to finish in the top six in a World Championship race.

Lombardi is an unlikely racer. Growing up in Rome, her family did not even own an automobile—their only "transportation" was a ten-speed bicycle. Lombardi discovered the joys of speed while still a schoolgirl. She had broken her nose playing handball and was waiting for a public bus to take her to the hospital when a friend zoomed up in a blue Alfa Romeo and offered to drive her there. Normally it was a half-hour trip to the hospital, but in the Alfa Romeo Lombardi and her friend covered the distance in ten minutes.

Lombardi had her boyfriend teach her drive, then met a racer who took her on as part of his pit crew—she changed the spark plugs, tended the tires, and timed the laps. Predictably, in her debut race, Lombardi drove an Alfa Romeo to victory.

Lella Lombardi

Lella Lombardi in action.

The Dinner Party is a Visual Banquet

San Francisco, California, USA: The San Francisco Museum of Modern Art is hosting feminist artist Judy Chicago's *The Dinner Party*, a massive room-size installation that has been five years in the making. Although it bears Chicago's name, the work was actually a collaborative effort of hundreds of women artists, including many skilled needleworkers who created the individual placemats/tablecloths for the 39 "guests of honor."

Judy Chicago's *The Dinner Party* premieres.

The table is an immense triangle, each side 48 ft (15 m) long. Each of the 39 place settings is unique and commemorates a woman famous in mythology or history. The design for each placemat, goblet, eating utensil, and porcelain plate is inspired by events from the individual's life and her contributions to humanity. One of the most striking visuals of *The Dinner Party* is the variety of stylized vulvas that appear in each place setting. The table stands on a vast white tile floor on which have been inscribed in gold the names of 999 important women. The size of the sculpture was intentional: Chicago wanted a work on a heroic scale, such as is typically used in monuments for men.

The first wing of the table celebrates female figures from prehistory to the Roman Empire and includes the goddesses Ishtar and Kali, warriors such as Judith and Boudica, and intellectuals such as Sappho and Hypatia.

The second wing features women from the beginning of the Christian era to the Reformation, such as the Byzantine empress Theodora, the queen and patron of the arts Eleanor of Aquitaine, and the artist Artemesia Gentileschi.

The third wing spotlights women from the American revolution to the women's revolution: Lewis and Clark's guide Sacajawea, anti-slavery activist Sojourner Truth, poet Emily Dickinson, and artist Georgia O'Keeffe.

Chicago sees an educational dimension to her work. "*The Dinner Party*," she says, "was meant to end the ongoing cycle of omission in which women were written out of the historical record."

Patti LuPone is Evita

New York City, New York, USA, September 25: Patti LuPone has her own cult following after her mesmerizing performance tonight in the title role of *Evita*.

The latest collaboration between composer Andrew Lloyd Webber and lyricist Tim Rice, *Evita* is the story of Eva Perón, the actress who became First Lady of Argentina and a political powerbroker in her own right. Since her death at age 33, Evita has been revered in Argentina as a kind of saint.

LuPone, who was among the first graduating class from Juilliard's drama program, has appeared often on Broadway, including a stand-out performance as Rosamund in *The Robber Bridegroom*. Although the character of Evita is larger than life, LuPone rises brilliantly to the challenge.

Sharing the spotlight with LuPone is a newcomer to Broadway, Mandy Patinkin, playing the role of Che, who serves as the narrator during the play.

Like Lloyd Webber and Rice's *Jesus Christ Superstar*, *Evita* was first released in 1976 as an album, with Julie Covington singing the title role. Her rendition of "Don't Cry for Me, Argentina" topped the charts in the UK. In 1977, pop singer Karen Carpenter's cover of the same song made it a hit in the United States. *Evita*

Bo Derek stars in the film *10*.

was produced as a musical in London's West End in 1978. Broadway-watchers are predicting a long run for the musical, and Tonys for the play and LuPone.

"Her Deepness" Sets a New Record

Pacific Ocean: Outfitted in a puffy atmospheric diving suit known as a JIM, American oceanographer Sylvia Earle spent two-and-a-half hours strolling along the ocean floor, 1,250 ft (381 m) below the surface. No human being has ever gone to that depth before. In fact, only submarines have ever gone that far down. Earle's record-setting solo dive took place off the coast of the Hawaiian island of Oahu.

Earle has explored the undersea world from Australia to Alaska, from the Galapagos Islands to the Indian Ocean, but it was the JIM suit that enabled her to realize her ambition of getting right down to the ocean floor.

First developed in 1969, the suit eliminates almost all of the dangers associated with deep-sea diving. It does not require a special mix of gases; no matter what the pressure may be outside, inside the suit the atmospheric pressure remains consistent; it isn't necessary for the diver to decompress; and there is no danger of suffering a case of "the bends" when returning to the surface.

First Native Woman Elected to Legislature

Northwest Territories, Canada, October 1: Nellie J. Cournoyea has won a seat in the Legislature of the Northwest Territories—the first native woman ever to be elected to office in a provincial territorial government in Canada.

Cournoyea's mother was an Inupiak from Herschel Island. Her father emigrated to Canada from Norway, and he worked as a trapper to support his family. Cournoyea grew up near the Arctic Circle, and in order to get an education enrolled in a series of correspondence courses. Since the late 1960s she has been active in winning native peoples a just settlement from the Canadian government for land claims, and ensuring that they have an equal voice in all decisions related to the use and development of the resources on tribal land.

Mother Teresa Awarded Nobel Peace Prize

Oslo, Norway, December 10: Mother Teresa of Calcutta, the 69-year-old Albanian Roman Catholic nun famed throughout the world as a humanitarian and tireless advocate for "the poorest of the poor," has won the Nobel Peace Prize. The prize Committee selected humanitarian Mother Teresa in recognition of the "work [she has] undertaken in the

Mother Teresa is honored for her tireless work for the poor of Calcutta.

struggle to overcome poverty and distress, which also constitute a threat to peace."

Mother Teresa entered the Sisters of Loreto, a missionary teaching order, in 1929. Her religious superiors assigned her to teach at the Loreto convent school in Calcutta. Although she enjoyed her work in the classroom, she found it impossible to ignore the grinding poverty that

existed just outside the convent walls. Two calamities—the famine of 1943 and the Hindu-Muslim riots of 1946—led Mother Teresa to request permission of her superiors to leave the comfort and security of her convent to live as a nun in the slums of Calcutta, working among the desperately poor, the outcast, the sick, and the dying. Granted her request, she began her mission alone in 1946; within a year or so 13 women had joined her; and in 1950 the Vatican granted its approval of her new religious order, the Missionaries of Charity.

Today the Missionaries of Charity includes thousands of nuns and brothers, as well as lay volunteers. They are found in the major cities of Europe, the United States, and Australia, and in remote villages in Asia and Africa, where they care for lepers, alcoholics, orphans, the homeless, and AIDS sufferers.

True to form, Mother Teresa has requested that the money the Nobel committee would have spent on a celebratory banquet in her honor be donated instead to the poor of Calcutta.

Bette Midler

Vijaya Lakshmi Pandit, the first woman president of the UN General Assembly, at an Assembly meeting.

Mary Decker

Born Free Author Found Dead in Northern Kenya

Kenya, Africa, January 3: Joy Adamson, conservationist and author of *Born Free: A Lioness of Two Worlds* (1960), has been found dead in suspicious circumstances on a roadside near her camp in the Shaba Nature Preserve in northern Kenya, where she had been living for the past three years.

Adamson has become a legend far beyond the confines of the African savannah. Her bestselling novel of how she raised the captive lioness Elsa and her three cubs before returning her to the wild—made into a very popular movie in 1966—made Adamson a worldwide celebrity. Anthropologist Desmond Morris cites *Born Free* as the catalyst for changing an entire generation's attitude toward animal conservation.

Joy Adamson was born Friederike Victoria Gessner in Austria on January 20, 1910. Her childhood was largely spent in Vienna where she learned the piano, typing, and photography, took singing lessons and developed an interest in psychoanalysis. In 1935 she married Victor von Klarwill, an amateur ornithologist, and together they traveled to Africa to escape the threatened annexation of Austria by the Nazis. During the voyage they met a Swiss botanist, Peter Bally, who insisted on calling the young Friederike "Joy." He soon became her second husband and they moved to Kenya in 1938. Joy met and married George Adamson in 1944, and by the end of the 1940s had painted over 700 works of Kenyan tribesmen in traditional dress, in the hope of documenting and preserving their fast-disappearing customs.

Working for Kenya's Game Department in 1956, George was charged by a lioness, which he was forced to shoot in self-defense. The lioness had three cubs,

> *"CARRY OUT A RANDOM ACT OF KINDNESS, WITH NO EXPECTATION OF REWARD, SAFE IN THE KNOWLEDGE THAT ONE DAY SOMEONE MIGHT DO THE SAME FOR YOU."*
>
> DIANA,
> PRINCESS OF WALES
> (1961–1997)

Joy Adamson pats Elsa, the subject of *Born Free*, in 1965. Adamson's ashes will be scattered over Elsa's grave.

two of which were sent to a Dutch zoo. George and Joy decided to keep and rear the third one themselves. They called the cub Elsa, and their lives changed forever. In accordance with her final wishes, Joy Adamson's ashes will be scattered over the grave of Elsa the lioness.

First Woman Elected to Académie Française

Paris, France, March 6: The French "poet historian" and novelist Marguerite Yourcenar, whose books are widely admired for their rigorous classical style and psychological subtleties, has become the first woman to be elected to the prestigious Académie Française since the learned body was founded in 1635.

In her fiction, Yourcenar tends to alter her style from novel to novel, as if in a continual quest to challenge her abilities as a writer. Her most significant works recreate past ages and historical figures and dwell on the weighty issues of power, morality, and destiny.

Born on June 8, 1903, in Brussels, Yourcenar was educated at home and began writing as a teenager. She became independently wealthy after the death of her father and led a nomadic life traveling throughout Europe before moving to the United States in 1939, where she worked as a professor of French literature at New York's Sarah Lawrence College. By this time she had accumulated an impressive portfolio of work, including *Feux* (1936), *Nouvelles Orientales* (1938), and *Le Coup de Grace* (1939). Upon acquiring American citizenship in 1947 she moved to Mt. Desert Island on the Maine coast to live with her friend and lifelong companion Grace Frick, who translated all of her works into English.

In 1951 Yourcenar published her most famous novel, *Mémoires d'Hadrien*, a fictional autobiography of the second-century Roman emperor, written as a series of letters to his nephew. She had made several unsuccessful attempts at completing this most ambitious of her novels,

time out

A court in Greece has sentenced a woman who attacked and wounded the man who raped her to three years' imprisonment. The rapist has been given a prison term of only five and a half months.

Kenya, Africa, January 3: Austrian-born wildlife conservationist Joy Adamson, author of *Born Free*, is found murdered in the Shaba Nature Preserve.
Boston, USA, January 16: Scientists synthesize Interferon—a natural virus-fighting substance—using genetic engineering.
Auckland, New Zealand, January 26: American Mary Decker is the first woman to run a mile in under four and a half minutes.

Lake Placid, New York, USA, February: Russian figure skater Irina Rodnina wins her third successive Olympic gold medal for pairs figure-skating, her second with Aleksander Zaitsev. Rodnina has also won the World Championships for ten successive years, 1969 to 1978.
Austria, February: Alpine skier Annemarie Moser-Pröll, considered to be the best female ski racer in history, retires.
Paris, France, March 6: Marguerite Yourcenar is the first woman to be elected to the Académie Française.

Iowa, USA, March 20: Former Iowa City firefighter Linda Eaton wins her sex discrimination complaint against the city of Iowa.
Canada, April 14: Jeanne Mathilde Sauvé is appointed the first woman Speaker of the House of Commons.
Los Angeles, California, USA, April 14: Sally Field wins the Best Actress Academy Award for her performance in the title role in *Norma Rae*.
The Netherlands, April 30: Queen Juliana, 71, abdicates. Her daughter Beatrix, 42, becomes queen.

Boston, USA, April: Rosie Ruiz is stripped of her Boston Marathon winner's medal after being disqualified for not running the entire race.
London, England, May 5: SAS forces storm the Iranian Embassy, killing four terrorists and releasing 19 hostages.
Iran, May 8: Farrokhrou Parsa, Iran's first woman Cabinet minister, is executed by firing squad for her feminist views.

Washington State, USA, May 19: Mt St Helens erupts, triggering an earthquake measuring 5.2 on the Richter scale and collapsing the north face of the mountain. Thousands are evacuated and at least eight people die.
Iceland, June 29: Vigdis Finnbogadottir is elected the first female president of Iceland.
Dominica, Caribbean, July 21: Eugenia Charles becomes Dominica's first female prime minister.

returning to it again and again over a period of 15 years. It went on to become an international bestseller.

Yourcenar has translated many American novels and African-American spirituals into her native French, though she mainly enjoys focusing on pivotal moments in history and unraveling the psychologies and passions of powerful men in her writing.

Right to Breastfeed Wins Court Victory in Iowa

Iowa, USA, March 20: Linda Eaton, the Iowa City firefighter who was twice suspended without pay in 1979 for insubordination—for refusing to discontinue breast-feeding her son during her work breaks—has won her case for compensation before the Iowa Civil Rights Commission.

In a precedent-setting decision, the Commission has unanimously ruled that Eaton had been the victim of discrimination by the Iowa City Fire Department. It ordered the City of Iowa to pay Eaton $26,442 in attorney's fees, $2,000 compensatory damages for emotional distress, and $145 in back pay.

Eaton was forced to resign from her job, and during the trial she cited instances of harassment prior to tendering her resignation that included malicious tampering with her firefighting equipment. Eaton, whose case has become a *cause célèbre* across the nation, is expected to pursue a civil suit against a number of city administrators.

Canada's First Female House Speaker Appointed

Canada, April 14: Jeanne Mathilde Sauvé, the Liberal Member of Parliament from Montreal and the first female French-Canadian Cabinet minister, was today appointed by Prime Minister Pierre Trudeau as the first woman Speaker of the country's House of Commons.

Annemarie Moser-Pröll, alpine skier, retires.

The woman responsible for opening the first daycare center on Parliament Hill was born on April 26, 1922, in the village of Prud'homme, Saskatchewan. She studied at the Notre Dame du Rosaire Convent in Ottawa and graduated from the University of Ottawa, where she was president of the Young Catholic Students' Group. In 1948 Jeanne Mathilde married Maurice Sauvé, an economist. Later that year, the couple moved to Europe, where she studied French civilization at the University of Paris.

Prior to her election to Parliament Sauvé was a respected journalist and radio commentator with the Canadian Broadcasting Corporation. In 1972, after her election as the Liberal member for Ahunstic, she was appointed Minister of State for Science and Technology. She gained the environment portfolio after the government's re-election in 1974 and was appointed Minister of Communications the following year.

Queen Juliana Abdicates in Favor of Princess Beatrix

The Hague, Netherlands, April 30: After reigning over the Netherlands for 32 years, Queen Juliana, aged 71, has today abdicated in favor of her eldest daughter, 42-year-old Beatrix Wilhelmina Armgard.

The investiture ceremony will take place at a specially convened session of both houses of Parliament in the New Church in Amsterdam. It will be a traditional non-religious ceremony where the new monarch will swear allegiance only to the Constitution.

Dutch monarchs are invested as heads of state and have never been crowned. The royal regalia (crown, orb, scepter, standard, sword of state) are not particularly historic pieces and were not crafted with a view to being worn.

Born on January 31, 1938, Princess Beatrix was the first child of then Princess Juliana and her husband, Prince Bernhard, and has lived with her parents in the Drakensteyn Castle in Lage Vuursche since 1963. When she was two years old, she fled with her family to Britain after German forces invaded the Netherlands in May, 1940. The royal family returned home in August, 1945, and in 1947 Beatrix's sister Christina was born.

Marguerite Yourcenar

Queen Juliana abdicates after 32 years on the throne.

Gdansk, Poland, August 30: Two months of crippling strikes in the shipyards lead the Communist regime to agree to sweeping concessions to the strikers, who are led by Lech Walesa.
Abadan, Iran, September 24: The simmering hostilities between Iraq and Iran explode into full-scale war, with Iraq attacking the oil refinery at Abadan.
Ireland, October 6: Mella Carroll becomes the first woman High Court judge in the Republic of Ireland.

El Salvador, October 7: The body of María Magdalena Henríquez, press coordinator of the Commission on Human Rights of El Salvador, is found. She was kidnapped on October 3.
Vatican, October 17: Queen Elizabeth II visits the Vatican, the first British monarch to do so.
Sri Lanka, October: Sirima Bandaranaike, the world's first female prime minister, is found guilty of misconduct.
USA, November 4: Ronald Reagan is elected president of the USA.

USA, November 21: Soap opera *Dallas* breaks viewing records as the question "Who shot JR?" is answered.
USA, November 22: Mae West, actress and sex symbol, dies at the age of 87.
Paris, France, November: UNESCO reports that one-third of the world's population is illiterate.
New York, USA, December 9: Ex-Beatle John Lennon is shot dead.
USA, December 19: The film *Nine to Five*, starring Jane Fonda, Lily Tomlin, and Dolly Parton, is released.

Iraq: Women win the right to vote and be elected to office in Iraq.
Himalayas: US mountaineer Arlene Blum leads the Indian-American Women's Expedition to the Gangotri Glacier near the India-Tibet border.
Australia: Feminist researcher and writer Dale Spender publishes *Man Made Language*.
Sweden: Princess Victoria becomes heir to the throne after reforms to the *Act of Succession* give the monarch's firstborn child of either sex the right to rule.

Atlantic Ocean: Canadian-born American artist Betty Beaumont creates a massive underwater sculpture 40 miles (64 km) from New York harbor using 500 tons of processed coal waste.
Paris, France: Senegalese author and feminist Mariama Bâ wins the inaugural Noma Prize for her novel *So Long a Letter*.
Australia: Women become eligible to be active patrolling members of the Surf Life Saving Association of Australia.

Lily Tomlin

Iranian Feminist Executed by Firing Squad

Iran, May 8: Farrokhrou Parsa, the feminist who became a member of the Iranian Parliament in 1963 and has since been a leading advocate of the modernization of school textbooks and the right of school-girls not to wear the veil, has become the first woman to be executed by firing squad under Iran's new Islamic regime.

Parsa was born while her mother, Fakhr Afagh, was under house arrest in the Iranian city of Qom. Afagh was among the first outspoken group of Iranian women who believed in equality of education for all Iranians regardless of gender, publishing two articles in the magazine *Jahan-e Zanan*. Afagh was forced to flee with her husband to Qom, where Parsa was born in 1922.

Parsa grew up accustomed to equal rights under the rule of the western-oriented Reza Shah the Great, eventually becoming a biology teacher at Tehran's Jean d'Arc High School. After her election to Parliament, Parsa initiated legislation to amend laws relating to women and family law. In 1965 she became the first woman to be appointed Deputy Minister for Education, and on August 27, 1968, the first Iranian woman to become a minister of state. Parsa used her influence to further her advocacy of modernization and equal rights, actions that brought her into conflict with the country's mullahs.

Last year's Islamic revolution has seen the veil reimposed upon Iranian women, who can be dismissed from their jobs and arrested in the street for refusing to wear traditional dress. With the execution of

"MARRIAGE IS A GREAT INSTITUTION, BUT I'M NOT READY FOR AN INSTITUTION."

MAE WEST (1893–1980), AMERICAN ACTRESS AND SEX SYMBOL

Queen Elizabeth II meets Pope John Paul II. She is the first British monarch to visit the Vatican.

one of the country's leading advocates of women's rights, it appears that the women of Iran are entering a period of prolonged struggle and hardship.

Dominica Elects First Woman Prime Minister

Dominica, Caribbean, July 21: Eugenia Charles, the Dominican lawyer who reluctantly entered politics in the late 1960s to protest the then government's proposed sedition act, and subsequently founded the Dominican Freedom Party (DFP), has today become Dominica's—and the Caribbean's—first female prime minister. The DFP defeated the interim

government of Oliver Seraphine. Charles, who is a strict constitutionalist, promises to bring to an end years of corruption and political excess.

Eugenia Charles was born in the small fishing village of Pointe Michel on the outskirts of Dominica's capital, Roseau, on May 15, 1919. She received her secondary education in convent schools and graduated from the University of Toronto, Canada, in 1946. In 1949 she returned to Dominica and set up a practice where she specialized in property law.

In 1968 the world of politics beckoned, with Charles helping to establish the DFP in response to a proposed government bill designed to stifle opposition and outlaw dissent: the so-called "shut your mouth" bill. In 1975 Charles became a Member of Parliament and leader of the opposition, an isolated woman in a male-dominated establishment. Goals for her first term in office include raising the rate of adult literacy, increasing the number of secondary schools and establishing a youth skills training program.

Sri Lankan Prime Minister Expelled from Parliament

Sri Lanka, October: The prime minister of Sri Lanka, Sirima Bandaranaike, has been expelled from Parliament and deprived of her civic rights for a period of seven years after a presidential commission found she had abused her office for personal and family gain.

The roots of her expulsion can be traced to 1977 when Bandaranaike's Sri Lankan Freedom Party (SLFP) suffered a heavy defeat at the hands of the opposition United National Party (UNP), winning a paltry eight seats compared to the

Office life gets the Hollywood treatment in the comedy *Nine to Five*, starring Lily Tomlin, Dolly Parton, and Jane Fonda.

UNP's 140. The UNP then established a commission to investigate allegations of Bandaranaike's impropriety. On February 4, 1978, Prime Minister J. R. Jayawardene (who is also leader of the UNP) became the country's first executive president by amending the constitution to read that the prime minister "should be deemed to have been elected president." This change strengthened his hold on power and enabled him to attack his opponents through the establishment of the Special Presidential Commission Law.

As early as tomorrow, Jayawardene is expected to amend the *Elections Act* and the *Presidential Elections Act* to prevent any individual who has been expelled from Parliament from contesting an election to public office during the period of disqualification, addressing election rallies, or even speaking in support of another candidate.

Bandaranaike and her SLFP supporters are claiming the commission and the proposed amendments to the elections acts are simply opportunistic grabs for power designed to remove the country's first-ever woman prime minister as a threat to the continuing rule of the UNP.

Book Claims English Language is Masculine

London, England, November: The Australian feminist researcher and writer Dale Spender has published her latest work, entitled *Man Made Language*, a comprehensive analysis of the various ways in which language is man made, with the masculine inserted into the everyday vernacular and the feminine experience made insignificant and marginalized.

Through interviews and taped conversations she has determined that it is predominantly women who play the support role in conversations between men and women. They do this by asking the right questions and providing encouragement and feedback. The moment women begin to contribute more than a third of any given conversation, they are perceived as bossy, aggressive, and dominating. The book is destined to become a classic with its pioneering look at the dynamics of language and the myriad ways in which language promotes an inherently male worldview. She argues that words that are generally acceptable and commonplace are more likely to express male experiences because men have traditionally been more visible in public life and therefore more able to get their opinions heard.

Spender was born in 1943 in Newcastle, Australia. Her feminism started early: as a child she convinced her mother not to do the housework unless her father also pitched in. She began lecturing in 1974 at James Cook University, Townsville, Queensland, before moving to London where *Man Made Language* has been published to wide acclaim.

Senegalese Author Wins Inaugural Noma Prize

Frankfurt, Germany, December: This year's inaugural Noma Prize for African writing has been awarded in Frankfurt to the Senegalese feminist and author Mariama Bâ for her novel *So Long a Letter*.

The book takes the form of letters written from a Senegalese woman to her friend, and comprises a series of reminiscences, some bitter, some wistful. The central character is Ramatoulaye, who details her emotional struggle in regaining her life after her husband chooses to take a second wife. Polygamy is permissible under strict Islamic law, but Ramatoulaye cannot see her husband's actions as anything other than a betrayal of her trust and a rejection of the life the couple once shared. Despite her own emotional

Bondi is among the Australian beaches that may now be patrolled by female lifesavers.

turmoil, Ramatoulaye reaches out to her husband's new bride—a young girl hoping to make a life for herself—fearing that the girl will suffer more than she will as time passes by.

Bâ was born into an upper-class family in Dakar, Senegal. After the death of her mother, she was raised in traditional Senegalese fashion by her grandparents. As a teenager she won an entrance exam to the École Normale de Rufisque, a teacher training college on the outskirts of Dakar, and during this time published her first book, which detailed colonial education in Senegal. In 1947 she graduated, and married Obèye Diop, a politician with whom she had nine children.

After the breakup of her marriage, she joined various women's groups, becoming a champion of women's rights.

Ocean Floor Home to New Artwork

Atlantic Ocean, December: The environmental artist Betty Beaumont has completed a unique underwater artwork entitled *Ocean Landmark*. It consists of 500 tons of processed coal waste that has been deposited on the Atlantic Ocean seabed 3 miles (5 km) off Fire Island and 40 miles (64 km) east of New York harbor.

The work has its origins in attempts by scientists to take an industrial by-product and stabilize it by placing it in water. Beaumont suggested using coal waste to create an underwater ecosystem which, it is hoped, will one day evolve into a sanctuary for marine life and eventually be listed as a "fish haven" on the coastal maps of the National Oceanographic and Atmospheric Administration (NOAA). The 17,000 coal fly-ash blocks that make up *Ocean Landmark* cannot be photographed due to poor visibility, although global positioning technology will enable the work to be located and scanned.

Betty Beaumont was born in 1946 in Toronto, Canada, and has been creating interdisciplinary artworks centering on environmental concerns for more than 30 years. Her art has been exhibited at many galleries and museums, including New York's Whitney Museum of Art. According to Beaumont, artists have an obligation to explore the potential of art for improving our environmental and economic landscapes, whether in the formation of ideas or, as with *Ocean Landmark*, the reforming of our planet's terrain.

Sally Field

Norway Elects First Female Prime Minister

Oslo, Norway, February 3: Norway has its first female prime minister. The Labor Party today elected the former Minister of the Environment, Gro Harlem Brundtland, 41, to the post, the youngest person ever to hold the office.

Brundtland was born in Oslo on April 20, 1939. Her father was a rehabilitation specialist, and Brundtland inherited both a desire to follow him into medicine, and his profound sense of social activism. She was always involved in the political debate and intellectual challenges that were an integral part of family life. At the tender age of seven she was enrolled in the children's arm of the Norwegian labor movement. She became vice-chair of the socialist schools' association in 1955, and in 1958 vice-chair of the Labor Party students' association.

Brundtland graduated in medicine from the University of Oslo in 1963, and, having won a scholarship to the Harvard School of Public Health, was awarded a Master of Public Health degree in 1965.

Shirley Williams

"CRUELTY MIGHT BE VERY HUMAN, AND IT MIGHT BE CULTURAL, BUT IT'S NOT ACCEPTABLE."

JODIE FOSTER (1962–), AMERICAN ACTOR

Returning to Oslo later that year, she took up a position at the Ministry of Health, working on children's issues.

Her strong beliefs about the link between an individual's health and the quality of the environment led her to being offered the position of Minister of the Environment in 1974, and since then her reputation in environmental and political circles has continued to grow.

Lauren Bacall Triumphs in *Woman of the Year*

New York, USA, March 29: Lauren Bacall has made a triumphant return to Broadway in the musical adaptation of the Peter Stone book, *Woman of the Year*. Based on the 1942 Spencer Tracy–Katherine Hepburn film of the same name, with lyrics by Fred Ebb and music by John Kander, it tells the story of Tess Harding, a network TV career anchorwoman who derides a comic strip on air, only to fall in love with—and marry—the cartoonist, Sam Craig, played by Harry Guardino.

Woman of the Year premieres tonight at the Palace Theater after 11 previews, with Bacall in her element as the career-driven Tess. Lauren Bacall was born Betty Joan Perske in New York on September 16, 1924, and made her motion picture debut in 1944 at the age of 19 playing opposite Humphrey Bogart in *To Have and Have Not*. Bacall married her leading man the following year.

Journalist Stripped of Pulitzer Prize

New York, USA, April 15: The writer of the Pulitzer Prize-winning account of an 8-year-old boy forced into heroin addiction by the live-in boyfriend of his own mother—

Lauren Bacall stars in the musical *Woman of the Year.*

published in the *Washington Post* newspaper last year—has been stripped of the award after it was revealed today the story was a complete fabrication.

Janet Cooke joined the *Post* in 1980 and wrote an article headed "Jimmy's World," which ran in the *Post* on September 29. Jimmy lived in one of Washington DC's low-income neighborhoods in the midst of a thriving heroin culture. According to Cooke, Jimmy was an average boy with sandy hair and brown eyes, but his thin brown arms were freckled with needle marks. When he grew up, Jimmy wanted to be a heroin dealer. A citywide search ensued after Cooke refused to provide authorities with the boy's location, claiming she needed to protect her sources. She was awarded the Pulitzer two days ago, despite doubts about the boy's existence.

But when a previous employer read the biographical notes accompanying her story, several discrepancies regarding her credentials were noted. Cooke's subsequent confession to her editors resulted in today's extraordinary press conference by the *Post*'s publisher Donald Graham, at which he promised to return the award.

Sissy Spacek wins the Best Actress Academy Award for *Coal Miner's Daughter.*

Dewsbury, England, January 5: Peter Sutcliffe, believed to be the "Yorkshire Ripper," is arrested.

Tokyo, Japan, January 17: Takeshi Hirayama, from the National Cancer Research Institute, proves that passive smoking leads to cancer.

Tehran, Iran, January 20: Fifty-two US embassy hostages are released.

London, England, January 25: The "Gang of Four" rebel MPs declare their intention to leave the Labour Party to form the Social Democratic Party. Shirley Williams is among them.

China, January 25: Jiang Qing, Mao Zedong's widow is convicted of "counter-revolutionary crimes" and sentenced to death.

Darwin, Australia, February 2: The case of Azaria Chamberlain, a baby allegedly taken by a dingo at Uluru (Ayer's Rock) is to go to a new inquest.

Oslo, Norway, February 3: Gro Brundtland becomes the first female prime minister of Norway.

London, England, February 24: The engagement of Prince Charles and Lady Diana Spencer is announced.

New York, USA, March 20: Jean Harris is found guilty of murdering Doctor Herman Tarnower, her lover and author of the *Scarsdale Diet*.

London, UK, March 27: Oxford cox Susan Brown is the first woman to take part in the annual Oxford versus Cambridge boat race.

New York USA, March 29: The musical *Woman of the Year* starring Lauren Bacall opens on Broadway.

Los Angeles, USA, March 31: Sissy Spacek wins the Best Actress Academy Award for the movie *Coal Miner's Daughter.*

Brixton, England, April 12: Racial tensions reach boiling point and explode into the largest riots in London this century.

New York, USA, April 15: Janet Cooke's story about an 8-year-old heroin addict is stripped of its Pulitzer Prize after she reveals it was completely untrue.

Miami, USA, May 11: Bob Marley, Jamaican reggae star, dies of cancer, aged 36.

Vatican, May 13: Pope John Paul II survives an assassination attempt.

Minnesota, USA, May 17: Scholar, scientist, balloonist, and explorer, Dr Jeannette Ridlon Piccard, one of the first female priests in the Episcopal Church, dies from cancer, aged 86.

Washington DC, USA, June 25: The US Supreme Court rules that excluding women from the draft is constitutional.

London, England, July 29: Lady Diana Spencer marries Prince Charles at St. Paul's Cathedral.

South Africa, July: Set in futuristic South Africa, *July's People*, a novel by Nadine Gordimer, is published.

Balloonist and Priest Jeannette Piccard Dies

Minnesota, USA, May 17: Doctor Jeannette Ridlon Piccard, the scholar, scientist, explorer, and Episcopal priest who in 1934 became the first woman to reach the stratosphere, in the balloon *Century of Progress*, has died from cancer at the age of 86.

Piccard's list of achievements exemplifies the term "over-achiever." She was the first licensed female balloonist, and the first pilot of a spherical balloon. She was co-inventor of the plastic balloon and the frost-free window.

In 1974 Piccard and ten other women—the so-called "Philadelphia 11"—were "irregularly" ordained into the all-male priesthood of the Episcopal Church. This triggered an emergency session of the House of Bishops on August 15, and resulted in an edict declaring that the ordinations were con-trary to the canon law of the Church. Undaunted, Piccard and her group cele-brated their first Episcopal service in New York. At the Church's 1976 General Con-vention, after much debate, the canon law was amended to permit ordination regardless of a person's gender.

Jeannette Piccard was born on January 5, 1895, in Chicago, Illinois. She studied psychology and philosophy at Bryn Mawr College. In 1916 she wrote an essay—a precursor of what was to come—entitled "Should Women be Admitted to the Priesthood of the Anglican Church?" She studied organic chemistry at the University of Chicago before moving to Switzerland with her husband, Swiss-born chemical engineer Jean Piccard, to teach at the University of Lausanne. Jeannette and Jean became interested in high-altitude science and began to build the *Century of Progress* for the 1933 World's Fair in Chicago. It was the largest balloon ever

time out

NO MEN ALLOWED! Is the ruling from the women who have set up a peace-camp outside a US missile base at Greenham Common in Berkshire, England. There they will form a human chain around the base, restricting entry.

constructed, with a volume of more than 600,000 cubic ft (16,990 cubic m), and measuring more than 100 ft (30.5 m) in width. It reached a height of 57,579 ft (17,550 m), and flew for eight hours over Lake Erie before landing in Ohio, with Jeannette Piccard piloting it—and herself—into the record books.

Fairy-tale Wedding in London

London, England, July 29: Lady Diana Spencer and Charles, Prince of Wales, were married today in St. Paul's Cathedral, London, before 3,500 invited guests and a global television audience estimated to be more than a billion. In the process, Lady Diana became the first Englishwoman to marry an heir to the throne since 1659, when Lady Anne Hyde married the Duke of York and Albany, who later became King James II.

Diana was resplendent in a silk taffeta dress with a 25-ft (7.6-m) train designed by David and Elizabeth Emanuel. She carried a bouquet of gardenias, golden roses, orchids, and lilies of the valley and was attended by five bridesmaics, including Princess Margaret's daughter, Lady Sarah Armstrong-Jones. The bride arrived at St. Paul's almost on time at 11.20 in a glass coach, accompanied by her father, Earl Spencer. Together they made their way to the altar where Charles was waiting in full naval officer uniform. Diana's title, Her Royal Highness, the Princess of Wales makes her the most senior royal woman after Queen Elizabeth and the Queen Mother.

The royal couple will spend their honeymoon at the Mountbatten family house in Hampshire, then board the royal yacht *Britannia* for a cruise to Egypt.

Jean Harris

Diana, Princess of Wales, and Prince Charles leave St. Paul's Cathedral as husband and wife.

Wisconsin, USA, August 16: Mary Meagher sets a new world record in the 100 m butterfly with a time of 57.93 at the US national swimming championships in Brown Deer.

New York, USA, August: IBM releases the personal computer, combining the functionality of earlier machines in a sleeker package.

Tasmania, Australia, September 2: Dame Enid Lyons, the first woman to be elected to the House of Representatives dies, aged 84.

Berkshire, England, September 5: The Welsh group "Women for Life on Earth" arrives on Greenham Common, having marched from Cardiff to protest against the decision to site cruise nuclear missiles there.

Washington DC, USA, September 25: Sandra Day O'Connor takes the oath of office as the first female justice in the US Supreme Court.

London, England, September: Baroness Young becomes the first female leader of the House of Lords.

Karachi, Pakistan, September: Asma Jahangir, a human rights activist and lawyer, founds the first all-woman law firm in Pakistan with her sister, Hina Jilani.

Miami, USA, October 1: Fidel Castro's younger sister, Juanita, joins a street protest calling for the release of Cuban political prisoners.

Washington DC, USA, October 12: Former first ladies Betty Ford and Lady Bird Johnson attend the ERA (Equal Rights Advocates) rally at the Lincoln Memorial. ERA is dedicated to equal opportunity for women.

USA, November 22: Betty Friedan publishes *The Second Stage*, which questions the ability of women to successfully juggle marriage, children, and career.

California, USA, November 29: Actress Natalie Wood drowns in a yachting accident off Catalina Island.

Virginia, USA, December 28: Elizabeth Jordan Carr, the first American test-tube baby, is born.

USA, December: Doctors have identified a new disease: Acquired Immune Deficiency Syndrome (AIDS).

Argentina: Deposed Argentine president Isabel Perón is convicted of corruption and exiled to Spain.

Paris, France: The Tokyo-based designer behind the Comme des Garcons label, Kawakubo Rei, presents her first Paris show.

Brno, Czechoslovakia: US cyclist Sheila Young wins the world sprint champ onship.

New York, USA: The Pulitzer Prize for Drama is awarded to Beth Henley for her first full-length play, *Crimes of the Heart*.

Sandra Day O'Connor

Pioneering Australian Politician Dies

Tasmania, Australia, September 2: Dame Enid Lyons, the first woman to be elected to the Australian House of Representatives—and the first to serve in the Federal Cabinet—has died at the age of 84 at her home in Devonport, Tasmania.

She was born Enid Muriel Burnell in Smithton, Tasmania, on July 9, 1897, and was educated at Hobart's teacher training college. She married Joseph Lyons in 1915 and they had 12 children, one of whom

died in childbirth. Joseph became prime minister of Australia in 1932 and died in office in 1939. In 1943 Enid won election to Federal Parliament for the division of Darwin in northwest Tasmania and served until the 1951 elections, when she retired from politics due to ill health. She spent her remaining years at Home Hill in Devonport—the house she and Joseph had built in 1916—and wrote her memoirs, *So We Take Comfort*.

"Women for Life" Start Anti-Nuclear Sit-in

Berkshire, England, September 5: Thirty-six Welsh women belonging to the protest group "Women for Life on Earth" have walked 120 miles (193 km) from Cardiff, Wales, to a NATO base at Greenham Common in Berkshire, near London, to protest the deployment of 96 Cruise Missiles there.

Upon arrival, they presented a letter to the base commander outlining their concerns about the consequences of an unchecked arms race for the future of their children. The group then established a campsite outside the airbase's fence-line, after their requests for a debate on the question of nuclear proliferation were

ignored. The women have stated they are committed to the principles of non-violent, non-aligned protest, and they seem prepared for a lengthy stay despite the absence of electricity, running water, or telephones. They issued a statement saying they are prepared to use human blockades to disrupt the convoys carrying nuclear weapons to and from the base, and are also ready to be arrested and imprisoned. For the women and their supporters, the protest brings a renewed sense of moral righteousness to the peace movement, as well as a 24-hour-a-day

Juanita Castro, sister of Fidel, takes part in a Miami protest for the release of Cuban political prisoners.

focal point for the world's media. The fact that these protesters are women has, according to some, imbued their crusade with an added moral authority.

With the US and USSR embroiled in a costly race for nuclear superiority in Europe, the women outside Greenham Common airbase wish to be seen as a rational and edifying presence. They are certain to provoke further debate about Cruise Missiles and the strategic balance its advocates claim they provide.

Situated 45 miles (72 km) to the west of London, Greenham Common was used as a base by the US army and air force during World War II, and reverted to RAF control following the Allied landings on the Normandy beaches in June, 1944. Since the beginning of the Cold War, it has been used by the US Strategic Air Command, and has been a NATO standby base since 1964.

Pakistan's First All-Woman Law Firm

Karachi, Pakistan, September: Two Pakistani sisters, Asma Jahangir and Hina Jilani, co-founders of the Women's Action Forum —a pressure group for women's rights— have, together with fellow lawyers and a

small coterie of activists, established the country's first all-female law firm. The sisters and their fellow activists represent hope for women and minority groups who are marginalized from society due to poverty and low rates of literacy, and who face repression on a daily basis—from both religious fundamentalists and a gender-biased legal system.

The sisters were born in the city of Lahore—Jahangir in 1952, and Jilani in 1953. They are no strangers to the fight for justice. Their father was imprisoned for speaking out against a succession of military dictatorships, and in 1967 the family had their lands confiscated. Today their struggle is against a discriminatory legal system, embodied in legislation such as the evidence law and the *Hadood* ordinances, both of which were introduced into Pakistan's constitution during the rule of General Zia-ul-Haq. The evidence law states that a woman's evidence in court is deemed to be only half as valid as that of a man. The *Hadood* ordinances require rape victims to prove their own innocence or face imprisonment. The laws have resulted in the imprisonment of hundreds of women.

Natalie Wood Drowns off Catalina Island

California, USA, November 29: Natalie Wood, the three-time Academy Award nominee and veteran of 45 films, has been found dead in the waters off Santa Catalina Island, 22 miles (35 km) offshore from Los Angeles and a mile (1.6 km) from where her 60-ft (18-m) yacht, *The Splendor*, was moored. She was 43.

Actress Natalie Wood drowns in a yachting accident.

Former first ladies Betty Ford and Lady Bird Johnson attend the "Call to the Nation's Conscience" rally.

"Hiroshima Chic" Blasts Paris Catwalk

Paris, France: A new phrase entered the lexicon of fashion in Paris today with the debut collection by Japanese designer Rei Kawakubo being dubbed "Hiroshima chic" by a bemused international media searching for a phrase to describe her heretical approach to fashion. Features include inside-out sweaters, ripped garments, and de-emphasized shoulders.

With her clothes' frayed, unfinished edges, extra-long sleeves, and asymmetrical designs, Kawakubo seems to be more interested in anti-fashion than any traditional notions of high fashion. "Hiroshima chic" represents an attempt by the press to capture the essence of her heavy use of black and dark grays, which give her clothes a very austere, almost deconstructed look.

Kawakubo was born in Tokyo in 1942 and studied philosophy and literature at Tokyo's Keio University. She briefly worked for a textile company, and then in 1967 became a freelance stylist. In 1973 she founded the Comme des Garçons clothing company, and two years later opened her first boutique in Tokyo.

Kawakubo received no formal training in design, or "clothesmaking" as she prefers to call it, and refuses to conform to accepted principles of silhouette and body line. Her innovative designs concentrate on the clothes' underlying structure rather than style, and aim to confront commercially conceived notions of glamor.

Betty Friedan

Born on July 20, 1938 in San Francisco, Wood was on a weekend break from filming her 46th movie, *Brainstorm*. Wood, her co-star Christopher Walken, and husband Robert Wagner sailed to Santa Catalina and anchored in one of the island's many coves. After sharing dinner and drinks at Doug's Harbor Reef restaurant, the trio returned to *The Splendor* in the yacht's dinghy, *Valiant*. According to Wagner, Wood left the main cabin around midnight and retired to her stateroom. He denied they had argued, but failed to offer a plausible explanation as to why Wood later returned to the deck dressed for bed in socks, her nightgown, and a down jacket, to untie the *Valiant*—only to fall overboard.

Wagner noticed his wife was missing at 1.30 a.m. and immediately called the harbor master, who initiated a search. At 3.26 a.m. the Coastguard was called in, and a short time later Wood's body was found floating near the empty dinghy, its lifejackets intact, its engine switched off, and its oars still stowed. The cause of her death is officially expected to be drowning from the effects of hypothermia, following a loss of consciousness. The owner of the restaurant that served the actress what was to be her final meal suggested that Wood may have been kept awake by the noise of the dinghy slapping against *The Splendor*'s hull on what was a breezy night, and that she may have fallen overboard while trying to maneuver the *Valiant* to the protected leeward side of the yacht.

Isabel Perón is Exiled to Spain

Argentina: Isabel Perón, the former president of Argentina who has been under house arrest for the past five years after being deposed by a military junta in March, 1976, has been found guilty of corruption and will be exiled to Spain.

She was born María Estela Martínez Cartas in northwestern Argentina in 1931. In the 1950s she worked under the name Isabel as a nightclub dancer, before marrying Argentinian ex-president Juan Perón in Spain on November 15, 1961. When Juan was persuaded to return to Argentina in 1973 to run again for president, he unexpectedly chose Isabel as his running mate. He won office in a landslide, but died less than a year into his first term. Isabel assumed the presidency on July 1, 1974, becoming the first female head of government in the western hemisphere. But deep divisions within the Perónist movement began to surface soon after she took office, with her personal leanings towards the right-wing Perónists sparking an increase in political violence and terrorism. With inflation running at over 300 percent, escalating unemployment, widespread strikes, and a massive foreign debt, Perón was urged to resign by military officers.

Despite a coup attempt in December, 1975, Perón stayed on as president until she was finally deposed in a bloodless coup on March 24, 1976.

Isabel Perón arrives in Spain to begin her exile.

Grace, Hollywood Princess, is Dead

Princess Grace

Monte Carlo, Monaco, September 14: Princess Grace of Monaco, beloved wife of Prince Rainier, and fairytale princess to countless moviegoers, has died as the result of head injuries she sustained in a car crash in Monte Carlo yesterday. She was 52.

Rainier and their children, Caroline, Stephanie, and Albert, were at her bedside when she died. Her death brings to a sad end the story of the daughter of an Irish bricklayer and a magazine model who captured the heart of a lonely prince through her movie roles. Grace Kelly, as she was, retired from Hollywood after making only 11 films and moved to the tiny principality to be with her prince. Though her marriage was given the fairytale treatment in much of the media, it was clearly a dynastic union made for practical reasons, as much as love.

Princess Grace is still remembered by many for her roles in the movies of Alfred Hitchcock, including the hits *Dial M for Murder*, *Rear Window*, and *To Catch a Thief*, in which she appeared opposite heart-throb Cary Grant. One scene in the movie with Grant, in which she is seen driving a sports car at speed through the hills of Monaco, is a chilling portent of the accident that took her life.

It is believed that the princess suffered a stroke while driving her 1972 Rover on a hairpin bend. The car rolled down a steep hillside and caught fire. Princess Stephanie, who was with her mother, was pulled from the burning car by a nearby resident; firemen released Princess Grace. Princess Grace never regained consciousness and died the following day.

> *"You cannot shake hands with a clenched fist."*
>
> INDIRA GANDHI, INDIAN PRIME MINISTER

Sea Gives Up the *Mary Rose*

Portsmouth, England, October 11: The *Mary Rose*, flagship of the fleet of England's King Henry VIII, was raised to the surface today after 437 years in a watery grave.

Liz Jacobs's *Salix Sepulcralis* or *Weeping Willow Tree*, painted this year.

Historians regard Henry's fleet as the forerunner of the English navy. Launched in 1510, the *Mary Rose*, named after the king's sister, was equipped with 91 guns and was one of the earliest purpose-built warships. It sank on its way to engage the French enemy fleet in July, 1545. The exact cause of the sinking is not known, but it was heavily laden and it is believed that it sank because of instability. As it went down the ship took 248 men with it.

The raising of the *Mary Rose* has been long awaited, cost £4 million, and was twice postponed because of technical problems. The ship was suspended underneath a lifting frame and today it was successfully raised in a specially crafted air-cushioned cradle. To mark the moment that it reached the surface, a cannon was fired from the ramparts of Southsea Castle.

A treasury of artefacts from the time has been found in the wreck, including navigational and medical equipment, carpentry tools, guns, longbows, cooking and eating utensils, backgammon boards, lanterns, and even a shawm, a long-lost predecessor of the oboe.

First discovered in 1836 by a fisherman's net, the wreck was rediscovered in 1965. Since 1974 it has been protected under the *Protection of Wrecks Act*. It is expected that the wreck will spend three years in dry dock where it will be constantly sprayed with chilled water to stop the remains drying out and rotting. Many of the recovered artefacts will be returned on board as they were found. The plan is to open the *Mary Rose* to the public near the place where Lord Horatio Nelson's flag-ship, *Victory*, sits in Portsmouth.

Women as Cops a TV Hit

New York City, USA, October: It began last year as a TV movie, starring Loretta Swit and Tyne Daly, about two New York City police detectives who just happen to be female. *Cagney & Lacey* is now a popular

Ada Louise Huxtable has resigned as architecture critic of the *New York Times*.

Cagney & Lacey is not just another cop show.

TV series, screening on CBS, and seems set to become a favorite among those who enjoy television detective stories.

They do everything their male counterparts do, but with a difference—they sort their problems out in the ladies' room. In the TV series, Tyne Daly continues in her role of Mary Beth Lacey, who manages to combine the demands of her job with those of being a wife and mother. Lacey's partner, Chris Cagney, who is single and career-minded, is played by Meg Foster—Loretta Swit was unavailable, having contractual obligations with another popular show, *M.A.S.H.*

Each week, these gun-toting women confront criminals and New York low life. Subplots center around Lacey's domestic life and Cagney's plans to get ahead in the New York Police Department. The show's action-packed storylines, its touches of humor, together with its unusual female focus, may be enough to make it a ratings success.

Punk Designer Shows in Paris

Paris, France, October: Vivienne Westwood, enfant terrible of Britain's fashion world, has produced her first show in the capital of fashion. Not only is this a milestone for Westwood herself, it is also significant in the history of British fashion as she is the first British designer to show in Paris since Mary Quant.

Entitled "Punkature," the range introduces the tube skirt, a style that can be worn by most women; it is expected to become a classic. The punk style began in the 1970s, when Westwood and her partner, Malcolm McLaren, dressed the Sex Pistols in bondage gear, safety pins, razor blades, chains, and dog collars from their boutique, Sex, in the King's Road, London. Westwood recently made the

outlandish recommendation to fashionistas to "take their mother's old brassiere and wear it undisguised over your school jumper and have a muddy face!" She has also been quoted as saying: "You have a much better life if you wear impressive clothes" and "Fashion is about eventually being naked."

It is expected that Westwood's fashions will continue to be a leading force and that her ideas will become part of fashion history. The Victoria and Albert Museum thinks so, having recently acquired an outfit from her earlier "Pirate" range.

Mother, Not Dingo, Killed Baby

Darwin, Australia, October 29: In a court case that has divided Australia, Lindy Chamberlain, the mother who claimed her baby had been taken by a dingo when she and her family were on a camping trip near Ayer's Rock (Uluru), in the Red Centre of the country, has been found guilty of murder. She has been sentenced to life imprisonment with hard labor.

The court decided that Chamberlain murdered her baby, Azaria, cutting her throat and disposing of the baby's body in the bush. Chamberlain's husband, Michael, has been found guilty of being an accessory after the fact, and has not yet been sentenced.

The fateful camping trip took place in August, 1980. Though baby Azaria's body has not been recovered, her bloodstained clothing has. An earlier inquest found in favor of the Chamberlains' claim that Lindy saw a dingo take the baby. But at a second inquest, a pathologist testified that marks on the baby's clothes could have been caused by cutting, implying that the baby's throat was cut. Murder charges were then laid against the Chamberlains.

There are many people, in Australia and around the world, who believe that a dingo is quite capable of taking a human baby and that the outcome of the trial is a shocking miscarriage of justice in which "trial-by-media" has played a major role. Those present at the campsite on the night that Azaria disappeared have no doubt that a dingo was responsible.

It is thought that the Chamberlains will appeal the court's decision.

30,000 Women Protest Nuclear Weapons

Berkshire, England, December 13: Snow fell as more than 30,000 women formed a ring the 9-mile (14.5 km) perimeter fence of the US Cruise Missile base at Green-ham Common, Berkshire. The women call their protest "Embrace the Base."

In the late 1970s the NATO countries agreed to approve plans to deploy nearly 600 nuclear cruise missiles in Western Europe. In 1980 the British government announced that 96 Tomahawk cruise nuclear missiles would be deployed at Greenham Common, making this one of the first places in Eruope to receive these weapons. In 1981 a group calling itself Women for Life on Earth marched from Cardiff, Wales, to Greenham Common to protest against the base; a number of women chained themselves to the perimeter fence. A peace camp was established for women and children only.

The large turnout for today's demonstration has surprised many observers, who throught that the difficult access to the site and the wintery weather would keep the masses away. At dawn, marquees and tents began to be erected at each of the eight gates to the base. Six coach-loads of women from Edinburgh had set off at 10 p.m. on the previous night and were among the first to arrive. By midday the area was packed with cars and buses. All the demonstrators were women; men had been excluded.

"We were the first peace camp," Miss Ioma Ax, a former teacher, is reported as saying in the *New York Times*, "and now there are more here, in Holland, Switzerland, Austria, and Italy. So we must be having an impact and we're determined to win in the end."

Romy Schneider

Isabelle Adjani's role in *Possession* earned her a César award.

Karen Carpenter

Slimming Disease Kills Well-known Singer

California, USA, February 4: Karen Carpenter, who with brother Richard formed the popular duo The Carpenters, has died following a long fight with anorexia nervosa. Karen had battled with the disease since she began dieting in 1975, when her doctor put her on a water diet, and at one point her weight was down to 80 pounds (36 kg). As a consequence the singer collapsed at a concert, dying from a cardiac arrest.

The Carpenters were a major force in the pop scene of the 1970s with 17 of their albums selling more than a million copies. Karen's soft rock voice was heard on such favorites as "We've Only Just Begun," "Rainy Days and Mondays," and "Close to You," which won two Grammy Awards in 1970. Carpenter's voice was considered one of the finest in popular music. She had excellent vocal control and sense of pitch and commonly recorded songs in just one take.

Born in New Haven, Connecticut, on March 2, 1950, Carpenter, with her brother and a friend, started a pop-jazz trio in 1965. Initially Karen played the drums only. Although they won a competition and were signed by RCA, the trio never made the hit parades and disbanded. Karen and Richard then worked together, combining her voice with his arrangements, and by 1975 two or three of their singles were making it to the Top 10 each year.

Karen Carpenter's illness began to affect their singing engagements, with the duo canceling a European tour in 1975. It is thought that syrup of Ipecac, an over-the-counter treatment used to induce vomiting to counteract poisoning, is a major contributor to Miss Carpenter's death. This seemingly harmless medication can have a cumulative effect on the heart and cause cardiac arrest. Though The Carpenters continued to record, Miss Carpenter's illness affected their ability to promote their records and their success waned.

Karen Carpenter was 32 years old. She is survived by her brother and parents.

Vale Ragtime Queen

Seaforth, NSW, Australia, February 28: Winifred Atwell, the first black performer to have a number one hit in the UK, died today of a heart attack at her home in Sydney, Australia.

Born in Tobago where her family owned a pharmacy, Atwell trained as a druggist. However Winnie, as she was fondly known, loved playing the piano and performed for American servicemen at the nearby air force base. Although she was classically trained, she began to play her signature boogiewoogie style for the men and wrote her first piece during this period: "Five Finger Boogie."

In 1945, at the age of 32, she moved to the USA and in 1946 gained a place at London's Royal Academy of Music, with ambitions of becoming a concert pianist. To finance her studies she worked in London clubs playing the popular piano rags, and by 1951 she had a recording contract with Decca.

Atwell's husband, Lew Levisohn, suggested she switch from a classical grand piano to a beaten-up old upright piano to play honky-tonk on stage. The old piano became known as her "other piano," and would feature in her concerts as she traveled the world.

In 1955 Atwell moved to Australia, where she has become extremely popular. She settled in Sydney and became an Australian citizen two years ago.

Three Women Gain Seats in Iceland's Parliament

Reykjavik, Iceland, March: A grassroots feminist movement that has women's

time out

The first African-American Miss America, Vanessa Williams, is crowned; however, it quickly emerges that the singer and model has posed for "indecent" photographs and the award is taken back.

The late French cabaret singer Suzy Solidor.

Winifred Atwell, the highly trained and popular pianist.

liberation as its main objective has succeeded in having three of its members win seats to Parliament in the recent elections in Iceland. The party is known as Kvennalistinn (The Women's Alliance) and was founded just this year. Membership of the party is open to any who wish to work toward women's liberation. It upholds the principles of power sharing and active democracy and so does not

Iceland's Parliament House building, in Reykjavik, was completed in 1881.

have a leader; most party decisions are made collectively.

Kvennalistinn has a number of stated objectives, including a re-evaluation of women's pay conditions, a greater say in the formation of government policy, day care for all children as soon as maternity leave ends, a shorter and more flexible working day, a minimum of nine months' maternity leave, job creation for women, improved conditions for disabled women, a radical rethinking of the environmental policy and, as well as the implementation of a prevention-oriented health policy.

There are 60 seats in total in Iceland's Parliament, called Alþing, which is the world's oldest still-operating parliament. Alþing was founded in 930 in Thingvellir, now part of the capital, Reykjavik.

Play About Suicide Wins Pulitzer

New York, USA, April: Marsha Norman's play, 'night, Mother, about an unhappy woman in her forties who announces to her mother that she intends to commit suicide that evening, has won the Pulitzer Prize for Drama. It stars Anne Bancroft, who won the Academy Award in 1962 for her role in *The Miracle Worker*, and Sissy Spacek, who also won an Oscar, in 1960, for her role in *The Coal Miner's Daughter*.

'night, Mother is Norman's fifth play. Earlier works include *Sarah and Abraham*, *Circus Valentine*, and her first play, *Getting Out* (1977), about a young woman who has been paroled after serving eight years in prison for robbery, kidnapping, and manslaughter. *Getting Out* was voted best play produced by a regional theater by the American Theatre Critics Association.

Norman was born in 1947 in Louisville, Kentucky, to a family with strict fundamentalist Methodist views. She was not allowed to play with other children or to watch television or movies, and spent her time playing the piano, reading books, and attending the theater, where she saw Tennessee Williams's *The Glass Menagerie*, a play that had a profound and lasting effect on her.

'night, Mother has been labeled pure melodrama by the *New York Times* but praised elsewhere for its emotional honesty and realistic dialogue. Marsha Norman has been reported as saying: "Success is always something that you have to recover from."

First Pulitzer Music Award for a Woman

New York, USA, April: The Pulitzer Prize for Music is awarded for a score that received its first performance in the year under consideration. This year 80 works were nominated for the award.

For the first time a woman, Ellen Taaffe Zwilich, has won the Pulitzer with her *Three Movements for Orchestra*, which the composer says is actually titled *Symphony No. l*. The work had its first performance by the American Composer Orchestra at the Alice Tully Hall on May 5, 1982. The piece lasts for 18 minutes and has been described by the *New York Times* as combining "the breadth of the older American symphonic style with a focused structural clarity characteristic of more recent American music, particularly Northeast American music."

Zwilich is a graduate of the Juilliard School and a former student of Elliott Carter and Roger Sessions. She was awarded the Guggenheim Fellowship in 1980, and prizes and grants from the Martha Baird Rockefeller Fund, among others.

Gloria Swanson

Women join the guerilla organization in El Salvador.

Space, June: Sally Ride, a 32-year-old physicist, becomes the first American woman in space.
Maine, USA, July 9: Eleven-year-old Samantha Smith of Maine visits the Soviet Union at the personal invitation of Soviet leader Andropov.
London, England, July 26: The High Court allows doctors to prescribe contraception to under-16s without parental consent.
USA, July 27: Madonna releases her self-titled debut album.

USA, September 21: Julie Walters stars in the film *Educating Rita*, about a hairdresser who signs up for a university course.
USA, September: Annie Lennox, of the band The Eurythmics, graces the cover of *Rolling Stone* magazine following the success of the single "Sweet Dreams are Made of This."
Oslo, Norway, October 11: Barbara McClintock, pioneering American scientist and one of the world's most distinguished cytogeneticists, receives the Nobel Prize for Physiology or Medicine.

Pine Gap, Australia, November 14: Police arrest over 100 militant women today when they force their way into a top-secret, joint United States-Australian military base. The group called Women for Survival organized the protest.
Canberra, Australia: The Australian Conciliation and Arbitration Commission (ACAC) acknowledges that women's work is undervalued and underpaid but claims that the economy cannot afford to commensurate women's wages.

Moscow, USSR: A commemorative one-rouble coin with the portrait of Valentina Tereshkova is issued to mark the 20th anniversary of the first space flight by a woman.
Cambridge, England: Women undergraduate students are admitted to Corpus Christi College for the first time in its 630-year history.
Europe: Rigoberta Menchu, a Guatemalan-born Mayan Indian and human rights activist, recites the narrative that forms the basis of her book *I, Rigoberta Menchu*, while working at the United Nations.

Massachusetts, USA: *The Return of Martin Guerre* by Natalie Zemon Davis is published. It is her interpretation of a true story of a man in sixteenth-century France whose identity is stolen.
Adelaide, Australia: Roma Flinders Mitchell becomes the first female Chancellor of an Australian university at the University of Adelaide.
London, England: Lady Mary Donaldson becomes the first female Lord Mayor of London.

Sally Ride

Malawi Campaigner Sentenced to Death

Malawi, May 5: Malawian political and human rights activist, Vera Chirwa, and her husband Orton, leader of the Opposition party, have been sentenced to death. Charged with plotting the overthrow of President Banda, they are scheduled to be executed in June.

Orton Chirwa was educated in Britain and is the leader of the anti-Banda Malawi Freedom Movement. He and his wife are both lawyers; Vera was the first woman in Malawi to become one. In 1973, after working for many years in the Attorney General's Department in Tanzania, Vera Chirwa went to the University of Zambia to study law.

Orton Chirwa was the founding president of the Malawi Congress Party. When Malawi became independent from British colonialists in 1964, Dr Hastings Kamuzu Banda took over the MCP presidency. The Chirwas fled into exile but were lured back and arrested.

Banda, who is the biggest stockholder in the country's largest conglomerate, runs Malawi, land-locked and poor, as a fiefdom. He has changed the country's laws to ensure he stays in power and his supremacy cannot be challenged. The country is staunchly pro-western and has strong ties with South Africa, isolating Malawi from other black African nations.

"IF I WEREN'T REASONABLY PLACID, I DON'T THINK I COULD COPE WITH THIS SORT OF LIFE. TO BE A DIVA, YOU'VE GOT TO BE ABSOLUTELY LIKE A HORSE."

DAME JOAN SUTHERLAND, AUSTRALIAN SOPRANO

American schoolgirl Samantha Smith receives flowers on her arrival in the USSR. She had written to the Soviet General Secretary Yuri Andropov regarding her concerns about the threat posed by nuclear war.

Margaret Thatcher has been returned as Prime Minister of the United Kingdom.

US Astronaut Sally Ride Returns to Earth

California, USA, June 24: Sally Ride, America's first woman in space, returned to Earth safely when *Challenger* space shuttle landed at Edwards Air Force Base. The shuttle carried five crew members instead of the usual three. Accompanying Ride on this historic flight were Robert Crippen, Rick Hauck, John Fabian, and Dr Norman Thagard. Three hours after landing, Ride and her fellow astronauts were congratulated by President Reagan.

Ride was in space for six days and was chosen to fly because of her skills, not because she was a woman, according to Flight Commander Robert Crippen. She was among 1,000 women who had applied for the training program in 1978, equipped with a master of science degree and two doctorates in physics.

As flight engineer, Sally Ride's responsibilities included monitoring the controls and ensuring smooth operations as the shuttle ascended and descended. This was the second flight for the *Challenger* and the seventh and most ambitious in NASA's space shuttle program to date. The astronauts accomplished all their major objectives including the launching of two important communications satellites.

The shuttle was expected to land at Cape Canaveral in Florida, but the weather forced it to land on the other side of the country in California. The President had planned to meet the crew of the shuttle as they landed back on Earth but the change in plan meant that this was not possible. Later, Sally Ride commented: "The thing I'll remember most about this flight was the fun, and I'm sure it's the most fun I'll ever have in my life."

Contraception Allowed for Under-16s

London, England, July 26: Victoria Gillick, mother of ten children, including five daughters, has lost her case in the High Court in which she sought to prevent

The American singer Madonna has released her first album.

Barbara McClintock

doctors prescribing contraception to girls under 16 without parental consent. Gillick burst into tears and collapsed into her husband's arms when she heard the verdict. "The judge doesn't realize there are a large number of doctors happily encouraging children to be promiscuous," the BBC reported her as saying. Gillick's husband told journalists that the case had cost £7,600, a large proportion of which has been paid by legal aid.

Mr Justice Woolf also rejected Gillick's attempt to prevent the Department of Health and Social Security from distributing a circular advising doctors they can give contraception to this age group without parental consent.

Gillick, who is a Roman Catholic, has been in dispute with the West Norfolk and Wisbech Health Authority for the last four years. She claims to have received letters from thousands of supporters and has the backing of the National Housewives Association, which has some 25,000 members.

The contention she presented to the court, that sexual behavior in individuals under the age of 16 would be restricted if they could not access contraception, is not supported by research. The House of Lords ruling established that young people under 16 are entitled to give their own consent to medical treatment provided they understand its nature and likely effects. Further, the ruling states that doctors have a duty to explore with young people the advantages of involving parents, but if this is rejected they need to be willing to advise and counsel patients independently.

Cytogeneticist Wins Nobel Prize

Oslo, Norway, October 11: Only six women had become Nobel laureates in science until Barbara McClintock received the Nobel Prize in Physiology or Medicine yesterday. McClintock was awarded the prize for her discovery that genes are not in fixed locations on chromosomes.

McClintock began her studies in 1921 at Cornell University when she began a course in genetics, which was not an accepted discipline at the time. Most of the other students in the course were interested in agriculture. She was also enrolled in a cytology course where she studied the structure of chromosomes.

McClintock continued her studies under Professor Hutchison, undertaking a postgraduate course in the new discipline of cytogenetics. When she had finished the course she was awarded her MA and PhD in botany, because women

could not major in genetics at Cornell. McClintock worked with other eminent scientists in the field of cytogenetic research including Marcus Rhoades, Charles R. Burnham, Rollins Emerson,

Twenty years ago cosmonaut Valentina Tereshkova became the first woman in space. Russia has minted a commemorative coin.

and George Beadle. She produced the first genetic map for maize, and during the 1940s and 1950s her work on transposition revealed how genes are responsible for turning physical characteristics on and off.

McClintock has been awarded a number of honorary doctorates of science, including degrees from both Harvard and Yale universities. In 1947 she was awarded the Achievement Award by the Association of University Women, in 1970 the National Science Award, and in 1981 the Wolf Prize in Medicine, among numerous other scientific awards.

Women Denied Fair Pay

Canberra, Australia: The Australian Conciliation and Arbitration Commission (ACAC) acknowledges that women's work is undervalued and underpaid but has found that the economy cannot afford to pay women the same wage as men.

Unequal pay continues to occur across all occupations in Australia, even in industries that are dominated by female workers such as the retail industry. In some sectors men earn 25 percent more than women, with the biggest pay gaps occurring in the male-dominated finance and insurance industry.

The Australian workplace continues to be dominated by a mindset that devalues the contribution of working women. Though the notion of the full-

time male breadwinner who needs to care for his family is supposed to be outdated, it strongly underpins the continued inequity. Another outdated view still commonly held is that men perform more skilled work than women and that women are better equipped for caring roles. Consequently roles that are traditionally filled by women have not been part of industrial relations campaigns.

Until 1969 legislation in Australia allowed employers to pay women a minimum rate of pay that was 25 percent less than male employees doing the same work. A decision by the Arbitration Commission in 1969 declared that women should receive 85 percent of the male wage, rising to 100 percent by 1972. However, the harsh reality is that over-award payments and other benefits awarded to men mean that women are still not paid on an equal basis. Women are more likely to be classified at a lower grade of occupation than men and, furthermore, junior workers who are paid less are more likely to be women.

French Singer Lucienne Boyer Dies

Paris, France, December 8: Remembered by many as the queen of Paris nightlife in the 1930s, Lucienne Boyer died two days ago of a stroke at the age of eighty. The epitome of the sensual French songstress, Boyer rose to fame with her song "Parlez-moi d'amour" in the late 1920s.

Boyer was born Emilienne-Henriette Boyer in 1903 in the Montparnasse quarter of Paris. By the age of 16 she was singing in the cabarets of Montparnasse and working as a part-time model. She found work in the office of a prominent Parisian theater and changed her name to Lucienne for her first singing engagements in the major Parisian music halls. Spotted by the American impresario, Lee Shubert, she was offered a contract on Broadway and moved to New York in 1927, where she spent nine months before going home to Paris, virtually unknown in America. However, she did find great success on her return to France. As World War II broke out Boyer married the cabaret singer, Jacques Pills, and their daughter, Jacqueline, was born in 1941. In 1960 Jacqueline won the Eurovision Song Contest. Boyer continued to sing throughout the war and her cabaret career flourished until shortly before she died.

Jayne Torvill

First Frozen Embryo Baby Born

Melbourne, Australia, April 10: The world's first baby conceived from a frozen embryo has been born, scientists at Monash University announced today. The baby girl, named Zoe Leyland, was delivered two weeks early, on March 28 at Queen Victoria Medical Centre in Melbourne. Victoria. Zoe weighed 5 lbs 8 oz (2.6 kg) and was born by Caesarean section. Her birth had been kept secret from the media until doctors were assured of her survival, and also to protect the family's privacy.

The embryo that produced Zoe was frozen for 11 months before it was implanted in mother Loretto Leyland's uterus. Leyland, 33, is unable to conceive naturally due to a fallopian tube blockage. Through the in-vitro fertilization (IVF) process, she produced several eggs which were fertilized with her husband's sperm in a laboratory. The embryo that produced Zoe was then frozen in a process called embryo cryopreservation, which had been developed by scientists from Monash University, the Queen Victoria Medical Centre and the Royal Women's Hospital. When it was thawed, the tiny embryo lost two cells, but retained six.

Until now, the standard IVF procedure has involved super-ovulating the mother and extracting several eggs in an abdominal surgical procedure called laparoscopy. Once the eggs are harvested, they are fertilized with sperm and incubated, with only one chance of implantation a few days later. If the egg fails to develop, the woman faces the whole process again. Embryo cryopreservation will allow women to freeze several embryos from one superovulation, thereby reducing the physical strains and cost of IVF.

> ### time out
>
> The wives of Britain's embattled coal miners form a national coalition of women's support groups in order to face the media and the consequences of strikes and mine closures around the country.

For the first time, frozen embryos result in a live birth.

> "GOOD WOMEN ALWAYS THINK IT IS THEIR FAULT WHEN SOMEONE ELSE IS BEING OFFENSIVE. BAD WOMEN NEVER TAKE THE BLAME FOR ANYTHING."
>
> ANITA BROOKNER, BRITISH WRITER, HOTEL DU LAC

First Female Governor-General Sworn in

Ottawa, Canada, May 14: Canada has its first female Governor-General after the swearing in of Jeanne Sauvé today. Her husband, Maurice Sauvé, has also created history as Canada's first male vice-regal consort. Sauvé has achieved many other "firsts" in her life. She was the first female speaker of the House of Commons, and the first female MP from Quebec to enter the cabinet. As Governor-General, her key focuses will be youth, world peace, and national unity.

Born on April 26, 1922, Sauvé was a high-profile journalist in Canada for 20 years before entering politics in 1972. As a minister, she managed the science and technology portfolio before taking on environment, then communications. She became speaker in 1980 but resigned to become Governor-General.

Australia's First Sweetheart

Sydney, Australia, February 24: A fourteen-year-old girl has become the country's youngest heart transplant recipient after a successful operation today. The four-hour surgery was performed at St Vincent's Hospital by Dr. Victor Chang, who heads the hospital's new National Heart Transplant Unit.

Fiona Coote, from Manilla in New South Wales, developed a heart condition after a bout of tonsillitis. She was airlifted to the Royal North Shore Hospital and selected for Chang's new heart transplant program at St. Vincent's. Coote is the first to receive a heart under the program, which was established last year after three years of lobbying by Chang. The nation

A grand parade marks the opening of the Canadian Parliament.

has been captivated by the plight of this shy country girl and the desperate three-day search for a donor to save her life.

Brunei, January 1: The sultanate achieves independence after 95 years of British rule.

USA, January 24: The Apple Macintosh personal computer is released at US$2,495.

London, England, January: Popular girl's toys this year include My Little Pony, Cabbage Patch Dolls, and Care Bears, while Trivial Pursuit wins Game of the Year from the British Toy Retailers' Association.

Sarajevo, Yugoslavia, February 14: Ice dancers Jayne Torvill and Christopher Dean win Olympic gold.

New York, USA, February 15: Ethel Merman, singer and actress, dies aged 76.

Sydney, Australia, February 24: The nation is captivated as 14-year-old Fiona Coote undergoes a heart transplant, performed by Dr Victor Chang at St Vincent's Hospital.

Australia, March 8: The Federal *Sex Discrimination Act* is passed. The United Nations Convention on the Elimination of All Forms of Discrimination against Women forms the basis of the Act.

Melbourne, Australia, March 28: The world's first birth resulting from a frozen embryo, a baby called Zoe, took place today.

San Marino, April 1: Gloriana Ranocchini becomes Captain Regent (Head of State) of the tiny European country of San Marino.

Los Angeles, USA, April 1: Soul singer Marvin Gaye is shot dead by his father, a priest, after a fight.

Berkshire, England, April 4: Fifty-nine women are arrested as police clear anti-nuclear protesters from their camp in Britain.

France/USA, April 23: Researchers discover a virus that leads to AIDS.

Berkshire, England, May 4: British actress and "Blonde Bombshell," Diana Dors dies, aged 52.

Canada, May 14: Jeanne Sauvé is appointed the 23rd Governor-General of Canada.

Nepal, May 23: Bachendri Pal becomes the first Indian woman and fifth woman to scale Mt Everest, the world's highest peak.

Massachusetts, USA, June 30: Writer Lillian Hellman dies.

USA, July 12: Geraldine Ferraro becomes the first female US major-party vice-presidential candidate, when Walter Mondale names her as his running mate.

USA, July 23: Vanessa Williams, the first African-American Miss America, becomes the first to resign her title, after nude photographs are published in *Penthouse* magazine.

Los Angeles, USA, August 7: US teenager Mary Lou Retton becomes the first gymnast outside Eastern Europe to win the gymnastics all-around competition.

The operation has made the headlines around the world because of the innovative procedures developed and used by Chang's team.

First Woman to Run for Vice-President

St Paul, Minnesota, USA, July 12: Democrat congresswoman Geraldine Ferraro has become the first female vice-presidential candidate for a major political party when Walter F. Mondale named her as his running mate today. Mondale and Ferraro are a long way behind Republican incumbent President Ronald Reagan and Vice-President George Bush in the election race, but Democrats are hoping Ferraro will strengthen their female vote, and that she will appeal to white and blue collar workers and ethnic voters.

Ferraro is serving her third consecutive term for New York's 9th District in Queens. She has served on powerful House committees, including Budget and Public Works, and is known for her liberal voting on social and economic issues, and her strong support for the rights of women. She led the passage of the *Economic Equity Act*, which put an end to pension discrimination for women and created more training and job opportunities for housewives.

Born in Newburgh, New York, on August 26, 1935, Ferraro attained a scholarship and arts degree at Marymount Manhattan College, and graduated from Fordham University School of Law in 1960. She married real estate businessman John Zaccaro, and had three children. She practiced as a lawyer for 13 years.

In 1974 she became Queens County Assistant District Attorney and there launched the Special Victim's Bureau, in which she prosecuted cases involving sex crimes, family violence, child abuse, and crimes against the elderly. She entered politics in 1978.

New Women's Events at Olympics

Los Angeles, USA, July 28: Women's cycling, synchronized swimming, and rhythmic gymnastics will be contested for the first time at the Olympic Games, which began today with the opening ceremony at Los Angeles Memorial Coliseum. There will be three road cycling events as well as five track cycling events.

Women's cycling, synchronized swimming, and rhythmic gymnastics are added to the Olympic calendar.

The women's-only rhythmic gymnastics will be the second gymnastics discipline showcased at the Games, along with artistic gymnastics, which is also open to men. Rhythmic gymnastics is one of only three female-only Olympic sports. The other two are softball and synchronized swimming, which was an exhibition Olympic sport from 1948 to 1968. Medals will be offered in two synchronized swimming events—solo and duet.

Retton Scores US Gymnastics Gold

Los Angeles, USA, August 4: American teenager Mary Lou Retton has become the first gymnast outside Eastern Europe to win an Olympic all-around gymnastics gold medal, and the first American woman to win an individual Olympic gymnastics medal. It was a nail-biting finish as the

16-year-old prepared for her last routine—the vault in the all-around competition against Romanian rival, Ecaterina Szabo. Retton needed a 9.95 to equal, and a 10 to win. Despite the incredible pressure, Retton gracefully achieved the perfect 10, prompting thunderous applause and celebration among the audience.

Although she faced lesser competition in the event due to the Soviet bloc—except Romania—boycott of the Games, her win was nonetheless a truly spellbinding performance. At just 4 feet 11 inches (1.5 m) tall, Retton exudes confidence and determination. Her tiny stature belies her physical strength and skill, which were fostered by her beloved coach, Romanian legend Bela Karolyi. Her big smile and tenacious spirit have impressed fellow athletes, and audiences, as well as TV viewers around the world. She will now compete in four other events.

Retton almost didn't make it to this year's Games after injuring her knee and undergoing surgery six weeks ago. She amazed doctors with her quick recovery, which was expected to take three months. Born on January 24, 1968, in West Virginia, Retton started gymnastics classes at the age of seven, and has been training for the Olympics since she was 12. In 1982, she was approached by world-renowned coaching duo, Bela and Marta Karolyi, who invited Retton to train with them in Texas. At only 14, she quit school and moved to Houston to pursue her dreams.

Geraldine Ferraro

Mary Lou Retton on the vault.

Space, July & October: Svetlana Savitskaya, Russian engineer and cosmonaut, becomes the first woman to walk in space during the *Soyuz* T-12 mission, followed on October 11 by American Kathryn Sullivan who space-walks from the space shuttle *Challenger*.
Los Angeles, USA, August 25: Author Truman Capote dies aged 59.
London, England, September 6: British author Anita Brookner's novel *Hotel du Lac* is published.

England, September 15: Alec Jeffreys stumbles upon genetic "fingerprinting"–DNA sequences unique to individuals that can be used for identification purposes.
Brighton, England, October 12: Five people die as IRA terrorists target British Prime Minister Margaret Thatcher by planting a bomb in her hotel. She escapes unharmed.
New Delhi, India, October 31: Prime Minister Indira Gandhi is assassinated by her Sikh bodyguards. Her son Rajiv takes over the leadership.

North Carolina, USA, Nov 2: Velma Barfield, who was convicted of the fatal poisoning of her boyfriend, is put to death by injection. She is the first woman executed in the USA since 1962.
Bhopal, India, December 3: Toxic gas leak from a Union Carbide chemical plant claims over 2,000 lives and affects tens of thousands of others.
UK, December 14: Britain's top pop stars record "Do They Know it's Christmas?" to raise funds for Ethiopia.

Missouri, USA: The second largest Mormon denomination, the Reorganized Church of Jesus Christ of Latter-Day Saints, authorizes the ordination of women.
USA: Billie Jean King retires from competitive tennis and becomes the first woman commissioner in professional sports as head of World Team Tennis.
London, England: The designer Katherine Hamnett is named Designer of the Year by the British Fashion Council.

Paris, France: *The Lover (L'Amant)*, an autobiographical novel by Marguerite Duras, is published. It is awarded this year's Prix Goncourt, the most prestigious prize in French literature.
London, England: Angela Carter's magic realist novel *Nights at the Circus* is published.
Vaduz, Liechtenstein: Women are granted the right to vote.
New York, USA: Fashion columnist Diana Vreeland, publishes her autobiography *D.V.*

Lillian Hellman

Women Walk in Space

USA, October 11: NASA astronaut Kathryn D. Sullivan has become the first American woman to walk in space. Her achievement follows that of Russian cosmonaut Svetlana Savitskaya, who earlier this year was the first woman to take a space walk. Sullivan performed a three-and-a-half hour Extravehicular Activity (EVA) on the sixth day of her mission aboard the space shuttle *Challenger*. The crew were sent to deploy the Earth Radiation Budget Satellite and conduct various experiments. Today's EVA was part of a satellite refueling demonstration using the new Orbital Refueling System.

Born on October 3, 1951, Sullivan holds a doctorate in oceanography, and is a scientist and researcher. She joined NASA in 1978, and was a systems engineer before becoming an astronaut in 1979. Russia's Savitskaya is a flight engineer and a highly accomplished test and sports pilot, and also the second woman in space, after Russsian Valentina Tereshkova in 1963.

Savitskaya's 11-day flight in July was her second space-flight—the first was in August 1982. She is the only woman to go into space twice. She and her team conducted scientific and technical tests, including welding tests during her space walk on July 25. Savitskaya has set many world records, including being the first female to fly at 1,667 mph (2,683 km/h), in a MiG-21 jet fighter. The daughter of an Air Force war veteran, she was an adventurous teenager who by age 17 had completed 450 parachute jumps. In 1970 she was part of the World Champion Soviet National Aerobatics Team. She studied at the Moscow Aviation Institute and is licensed to pilot over 20 different types of aircraft.

Ghandi Assassinated by Bodyguards

New Delhi, India, October 31: One of the most influential women in twentieth century politics, Indian Prime Minister Indira Gandhi, was assassinated today in her garden by two of her Sikh bodyguards. The men opened fire on Gandhi before being killed by other bodyguards. Her son, Rajiv, will succeed her as Prime Minister. Her murder was payback for an Army attack on Sikh military rebels hiding in Punjab's holy Golden Temple in June, during which many hundreds of Sikhs were killed.

Gandhi was India's first female Prime Minister, a very tough, shrewd, and ruthless politician who was privately aloof, but loyal to her family. Born Indira Priyadarshini Gandhi on November 19, 1917, in Allahabad, she was the daughter of Jawaharlal Nehru, India's first Prime Minister after British independence in 1947. Gandhi joined the National Congress Party in 1938 and married party activist Feroze Gandhi in 1942. They had two sons—Rajiv in 1944 and Sanjay in 1946. The couple later separated and she became party president in 1959. After her father's death in 1964, she entered Parliament. When her father's successor died in 1966, she became Prime Minister, and was formally elected in 1967.

Gandhi promised to modernize the country. Her control of the party led to a split, spawning her new faction, New Congress. Gandhi led India to victory in a short war with Pakistan, and her party was re-elected in 1971. Gandhi became increasingly authoritarian, and was convicted of breaching electoral laws in 1975. Despite protests and union strikes, she maintained her innocence and a national state of emergency was declared. Her conviction was overturned and she continued to rule by decree, leading a very successful 20-point plan for reform. In 1977, she called an election but was defeated by the Janata Party. She was arrested but gained public sympathy. In 1979, Janata disintegrated and the following year her party was re-elected.

Billie Jean Sets Another First for Tennis

USA: Legendary US tennis champion Billie Jean King has become the first female commissioner in professional sports history, heading up the Team Tennis organization following her recent retirement from professional

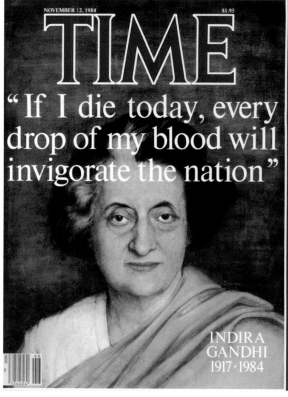

Indira Gandhi is assassinated by her bodyguards.

competition. King has brought about significant changes for women in tennis. She prompted the "open era" of professional tennis from 1968 and advocated equal prize money for females. In 1972, she won the US Open but received about US$15,000 less than the male winner. She threatened to boycott the event if the prize money was not made equal, and the following year the US Open became the first major tournament to offer equal prizes.

King launched the first professional women's tour, the Virginia Slims, and founded the Women's Tennis Association in 1973 and the Women's Sports Foundation in 1974. On court, she won 71 professional singles titles, including 12 majors; was ranked world No 1 five times, and in the Top 10 for 17 consecutive years.

In 1973 she defeated veteran men's ex-champion, Bobby Riggs, in a match dubbed "Battle of the Sexes." Riggs goaded female players into accepting his lucrative challenge match invitations, claiming that women were so inferior that he could win, even at age 55. He beat Margaret Smith Court, then faced King in front of 30,000 spectators and 50 million TV viewers. King won 6–4, 6–3, 6–3.

Svetlana Savitskaya, Russian engineer and cosmonaut, becomes the first woman to walk in space.

The site of the Brighton bomb attack on Prime Minister Thatcher.

Fashion and Politics

London, England: It has been a momentous year for British fashion designer Katharine Hamnett. Not only was she honored by the industry for her contribution to fashion, she has also firmly established herself as a political figurehead for the anti-nuclear movement. At a reception given by Prime Minister Margaret Thatcher, Hamnett arrived wearing one of her famous baggy T shirts with a large block letter statement proclaiming "58% Don't Want Pershing." The T-shirt referred to anti-nuclear sentiment among Britons regarding US Pershing ballistic missiles, which are being deployed in Europe.

In the Fashion Council inaugural Fashion Awards, the mother of two was named Designer of the Year, and the Bath Costume Museum honored her with the Menswear Designer of the Year award. As one of the world's pre-eminent designers, she also introduced us to garment dying and invented stonewashing, distressed denim, and stretch denim.

Born Katharine Eleanor Appleton on August 16, 1947, Hamnett launched her own design label using her own name, KATHARINE E HAMNETT, in 1979. She launched a menswear line in 1981 and last year received the International Institute award for Cotton Designer of the Year. Her famous T-shirts espousing political statements such as "Worldwide Nuclear Ban Now" and "Choose Life" hit the shelves last year.

Right to Vote

Vaduz, Liechtenstein, July 1: Women will have the right to vote for the first time in national elections following a narrow majority vote in Liechtenstein's third referendum on women's suffrage today. About 85 percent of the electorate voted, with 51.3 percent voting "Yes." Women were denied this right in two previous referendums, in 1971 and 1973. Since then, Liechtenstein has been the only country in Western Europe to deny women the vote. Commentators say that the country's traditionally backward thinking has contributed greatly to the delay in suffrage.

Liechtenstein is a small monarchical principality located between Austria and Switzerland, in the Alps. Its capital is Vaduz, and the country's area is just 62 square miles (160 km^2). The main religion is Catholicism, and the national language German.

Vreeland's Book Fashions Life

New York, USA: Legendary fashion guru and former columnist for *Harper's Bazaar* and *Vogue*, Diana Vreeland, has released an autobiography, titled *D.V.* The book reveals the highs and lows of Vreeland's illustrious career as a writer and editor for two of the world's pre-eminent fashion journals, and how she single-handedly changed the way fashion was reported with her witty rhetoric and practical advice.

A visionary of style, Vreeland championed new designs and trends while never losing sight of women's practical needs. Vreeland was devoted to her husband, Thomas Reed Vreeland, whom she married in 1924. The couple had two sons and lived in New York, then London.

After returning to New York in 1936, they resumed their place in high society, where Vreeland was noted for her refined European elegance. She was invited to work at *Harper's Bazaar* and her "Why Don't You?" column was an enormous success. In 1962, she joined *Vogue* and quickly became Editor-in-Chief. Her husband died in 1966. In 1971, *Vogue* fired her and in 1972 she became a consultant to the Costume Institute of the Metropolitan Museum of Art.

Katherine Hamnett

Marguerite Duras, winner of the Prix Goncourt.

Diana Vreeland, trend-setting editor of *Vogue* and *Harper's Bazaar*.

Leontyne Price

Baby Business

London, England, January 4: Britain's first surrogate mother today gave birth to a baby girl at Victoria Maternity Hospital in London. Scotland Yard, however, is investigating the mother, Kim Cotton, in the wake of reports that she is to receive £6,500 for her baby from a childless couple.

According to reports, the body responsible for organizing the Cotton surrogacy is a Surrey-based branch of an American agency operated by Barbara Manning. It is expected to earn thousands of pounds from the baby-for-cash deal. Last year, a committee investigating human fertility recommended that such agencies should be banned, but no action has yet been taken, and paying a surrogate mother for her baby is still permitted under British law.

> *"IT IS WELL THAT THE EARTH IS ROUND THAT WE DO NOT SEE TOO FAR AHEAD."*
>
> MERYL STREEP
> (1949–),
> AMERICAN ACTRESS

Tina Turner makes a comeback to the pop scene.

Amid today's furor, MPs have been subjected to renewed pressure to look into the controversial issue, and Health Minister Kenneth Clarke has declared that Parliament will move to outlaw the practice of financial compensation for surrogacy. Meanwhile, a court order imposed by the London Borough of Barnet will force Cotton to leave the still unnamed baby girl in the care of the hospital until at least next Friday, when a juvenile court will determine the child's future. A spokesman for the hospital stated: "Until we hear to the contrary the baby must remain here in a place of safety."

Honor Bound

Oxford, England, January 29: Oxford's dons have delivered a stinging snub to Prime Minister Margaret Thatcher by refusing to grant her an honorary degree. Thatcher had obtained a second-class honors degree in chemistry at Somerville College, Oxford, in 1947, and with last night's decision not to confer the honorary doctorate of civil law, she earns the dubious distinction of being the first Oxford-educated Prime Minister to be denied the honor since World War II.

The call to bestow the doctorate provoked outrage among some academics already angered by the Thatcher's cuts in funding for education, particularly in the area of scientific research, which, they say, is now at crisis level. Supporters, on the other hand, pointed to past tradition at Oxford, arguing that the award should be above politics. Despite their arguments, the vote against Thatcher at last night's ticket-only meeting was higher than anticipated, with 319 in favor of the nomination and 738 opposed. The outcome was greeted with cheers by students, who had garnered 5,000 signatures for a petition.

Professor Peter Pulzer, who led the opposition, has rejected any suggestion that the decision was ideologically motivated.

Pulzer nevertheless goes on to say: "I think we have sent a message to show our very great concern, our very great worry about the way in which educational policy and educational funding are going in this country."

Dogged to the End

Alaska, USA, March 20: Today, Libby Riddles achieved instant celebrity status when she became the first woman to win the Iditarod, Alaska's largest sporting event. Sometimes called "The Last Great Race on Earth," the Iditarod was launched in 1973 as an annual event to test the best dogsled mushers and teams over a gruel-ing route covering more than 1,000 miles (1,600 km), from Anchorage in central Alaska, through the interior and along the shore of the Bering Sea, to Nome in the state's west.

Riddles has been working towards today's victory for some time. Born in Madison, Wisconsin, she moved to Alaska before her seventeenth birthday, taking up residence outside Anchorage, and later in the small town of Nelchina. She won a

Libby Riddles is the first woman to win the grueling Iditarod in Alaska.

New York, USA, January 3: Celebrated soprano Leontyne Price bids farewell to the Metropolitan Opera in New York, singing the title role of *Aida*.

London, England, January 4: Kim Cotton becomes Britain's first surrogate mother, giving birth to a baby girl whom she is forced to leave at Victoria Maternity Hospital, after a court order is imposed.

Oxford, England, January 29: Oxford University snubs Margaret Thatcher by refusing her an honorary degree.

Melbourne, Australia, February 10: A medical research team identifies the cause of Down Syndrome.

New York, USA, February 14: After more than a decade of intense debate, the worldwide governing body of Conservative Judaism decides to admit women as rabbis. Amy Eilberg of Manhattan becomes the first female rabbi.

USA, February 26: Tina Turner makes a comeback, winning three Grammy Awards for the song "What's Love Got to Do With It?," including Best Female Pop Vocal.

Moscow, USSR, March 13: New Soviet leader Mikhail Gorbachev leads the funeral for Konstantin Chernenko, whom he replaced. At 54, Gorbachev is perceived to be a potential reformer.

Alaska, USA, March 20: Libby Riddles is the first woman to win the grueling Iditarod dogsled race across Alaska from Anchorage to Nome.

Saint-Paul, France, March 28: Marc Chagall, Jewish Belarusian painter often associated with the Surrealist movement, dies aged 97.

London, England, March: Holly Reich of Texas, USA, becomes the first conjoined twin to survive an operation to separate her from her sister Carly (who later dies.)

Tirana, Albania, April 11: Enver Hoxha, leader of the insular communist state for 40 years, dies.

Connecticut, USA, May 16: Margaret Hamilton, best known for her role as the wicked witch in *The Wizard of Oz* dies, aged 82.

Brussels, Belgium, May 29: Rioting at Heysel Stadium leaves 39 soccer fans dead.

New Jersey, USA, June 11: Karen Ann Quinlan, the comatose patient whose case prompted a historic right-to-die court decision, dies from pneumonia aged 31.

Oxford, England, July 4: Ruth Lawrence, the 13-year-old prodigy, wins a first-class degree in mathematics at Oxford University completing the course in only two years.

Wimbledon, London, England, July 6: Martina Navratilova beats Chris Lloyd in the Wimbledon women's tennis singles final.

Margaret Hamilton is best known for her role as the wicked witch in the *Wizard of Oz*.

small local dog race in 1978, then received a lead dog from long-time Iditarod racer Rick Swenson.

After finishing 18th in the 1980 Iditarod, and 20th in the 1981 event, she decided to breed her own dogs, moving to Shaktoolik, near Nome, in order to train them in Arctic conditions. Later she relocated to Teller, north-west of Nome, and teamed up with Joe Garnie, breeding and training dogs and taking turns to race them in the Iditarod.

This year, arriving first at the Shaktoolik checkpoint, Riddles tenaciously mushed her 13 dogs into a mounting blizzard that confined every other racer to the town. Unable to see from one trail marker to the next, she let the dogs lead until the marker behind was obscured, then walked ahead of them until the next marker came into sight.

Painstaking though the process was, Riddles' daring move put her in an unbeatable lead. Maintaining the lead, she reached Nome three days later, a clear winner, still well ahead of her nearest competitor.

Karen Quinlan Claims Her Right to Die

New Jersey, USA, June 11: Karen Quinlan, the comatose patient whose case once prompted the unprecedented 1976 right-to-die court decision, today succumbed to pneumonia after living for 10 years with the aid of artificial nutrition and hydration. She was 31.

Quinlan lapsed into a coma on April 15, 1975, apparently as a result of ingesting barbiturates and alcohol. After experiencing irreversible brain damage, she was placed on a respirator and fed nutrition and fluids through a gastrostomy tube. In November, 1975, her family petitioned the New Jersey Superior Court to order her removal from the respirator, but the court refused, rejecting any legal distinction between ordinary and extraordinary means to sustain life.

The family then appealed to the New Jersey Supreme Court, which in 1976 reversed the lower court decision, ruling that refusal of life-saving treatment fell under the constitutional right to privacy, and that as a result, Quinlan's privacy could be asserted by her father on his daughter's behalf.

Following the historic court ruling, the notion of substituted judgment was adopted in some other states, allowing families to withdraw life support from comatose or terminally ill patients.

The Quinlan case also stimulated very robust national debate about the complex moral and legal issues arising from the definitions of life and death, the right to die, and freedom of choice.

Many proponents of voluntary euthanasia point out that a large proportion of deaths are already hastened, by means of collaboration between the family and the doctor, who agree to increase medication in order to reduce the suffering of a loved one. It is believed that the outcome of her case may be the establishment of ethical committees.

Stars in her Eyes

Oxford, England, July 4: Child prodigy Ruth Lawrence has become the youngest graduate of Oxford University, attaining first class honors in Mathematics after completing the degree in just two years, instead of the usual three. The only student to achieve such a high grade this year, the 13-year-old has also been awarded a special commendation.

Lawrence was educated at home by her father, never attending school. She initially entered the record books when she earned a grade A for Pure Mathematics A-level at the age of nine. She claimed another record in 1981 when she became the youngest person to pass the Oxford entrance exam. Lawrence plans to remain at Oxford and undertake research.

Christa McAuliffe

Martina Navratilova serves to win at Wimbledon.

Wimbledon, London, England, July 7: German tennis star Boris Becker, 17, becomes the youngest Wimbledon singles winner.
USA, July 12: Sharon Scranage, a US Central Intelligence Agency (CIA) clerk, is accused of disclosing the names of CIA agents to representatives of the Ghanaian government when she was stationed in Ghana.
USA, July 19: Christa McAuliffe of New Hampshire is chosen to be the first schoolteacher to ride aboard the space shuttle.

California, USA, August 16: Pop star Madonna marries actor Sean Penn.
Virginia, USA, August 21: The A.H. Robins Company, producer of the Dalkon Shield birth control device, files for bankruptcy as thousands of women claim injury.
Maine, USA, August 25: Samantha Smith, the schoolgirl whose letter to Yuri Andropov resulted in an invitation to tour the USSR, is killed with her father in an airplane crash.
Cape Kennedy, USA, August 27: Australia's first telecommunications satellite AUSSAT is launched.

Atlantic Ocean, September 1: A team led by Robert Ballard locates the wreck of the liner *Titanic*.
UK, September 17: Fashion designer and home furnishing expert, Laura Ashley, dies after a fall in her home.
USA, September 14: The TV situation comedy *The Golden Girls* debuts on NBC. The show's main characters are four single older women who live together, and are sexually active and conversant with pop culture.
Antarctica, September: Scientists discover holes in the ozone layer.

Arizona, USA: Lynette Woodard, who captained the 1984 US women's basketball team, becomes the first woman to play with the Harlem Globetrotters.
New York, USA, October 15: Australian Shelley Taylor breaks the record for the fastest swim around Manhattan Island, completing the trip in just over six hours.
Republic of Ireland, November 18: Senator Mary Robinson resigns from the Irish Labour Party in protest at the lack of consultation before the Anglo-Irish Agreement (AIA).

Oklahoma, USA, December 14: Wilma Mankiller becomes the first female chief of a major Native American tribe when elected to lead the Cherokee Nation.
Republic of Rwanda, December 26: Dian Fossey, the American zoologist who studied gorillas in the wild, is found murdered in her bedroom.
London, England: Brenda Dean becomes General Secretary of SOGAT (Society of Graphical and Allied Trades), the first woman to head a major union.

Brenda Dean

A. H. Robins Seeks Shield of its Own

Virginia, USA, August 21: The A. H. Robins Company today filed for Chapter 11 bankruptcy protection amid a rising tide of lawsuits from women seeking compensatory and punitive damages for injuries caused by the Dalkon Shield, an intrauterine birth control device that was marketed by the company between 1971 and 1974. Developed by Hugh Davis, a faculty member of the Johns Hopkins Medical School, the Dalkon Shield was promoted as a technological breakthrough which would significantly lower the expulsion and infection rates of similar devices. The product was used by more than two million women in the US, and at least one million women in other parts of the world.

The defects of the Dalkon Shield, and the company's knowledge of them, did not fully emerge until the first lawsuit in 1974. Despite the company's claim that the device prevented 98.9 percent of pregnancies, the failure rate was actually 5.3 percent. Women who conceived while using the product suffered a high rate of miscarriages, premature births, and birth defects. In addition, the five fins designed to prevent the expulsion of the device, actually caused it to become embedded in the uterus in some cases, and the tail string designed to facilitate its removal became a vehicle for pelvic infections, many severe enough to warrant hospitalization and some leading to infertility, or sometimes requiring a complete hysterectomy.

Doctors and lawyers have since traced at least 18 deaths and more than 200,000 cases of serious harm linked to the use of the Dalkon Shield. Although Robins withdrew the product from the market in 1974, after pressure from the US Food and Drug Administration, it did not recall any of those devices already sold, and some doctors ignored the recommendation to remove it.

America's Youngest Ambassador Killed

Maine, USA, August 25: The nation was plunged into mourning today following news of the death of Samantha Smith, the schoolgirl whose 1982 letter to Soviet General Secretary Yuri Andropov resulted in a personal invitation to visit the USSR. She was tragically killed when the aircraft in which she was a passenger missed the runway of the Lewiston-Auburn Regional Airport and crashed, leaving no survivors among the eight on board, including her father.

Smith became an overnight celebrity when Andropov responded to her letter in 1983, and the 11-year-old's subsequent two-week visit to the Soviet Union was covered in nightly news reports on all the major US networks. Following her return home, she took on the role of political and peace activist, hosting a Disney special about politics during the 1984 presidential election campaign, and traveling to Japan, where she met with Prime Minister Yasuhiro Nakasone before attending the Children's International Symposium in Kobe.

Later she wrote a book about her visit to the USSR titled *Journey to the Soviet Union*. She then branched into acting and co-starred with Robert Wagner in the television series *Lime Street*. The crash occurred on a return flight from filming.

Samantha Smith became a young ambassador to Russia.

During her short lifetime, Smith's fame as "America's Youngest Ambassador" extended throughout the world. Her joyful countenance cheered people wherever she went, and she helped to thaw Cold War relations between the US and USSR. As President Ronald Reagan observed in his condolences to her mother: "Perhaps you can take some measure of comfort in the knowledge that millions of Americans, indeed millions of people, share the burdens of your grief."

Laura Ashley Dies

UK, September 17: Fashion and fabric designer Laura Ashley has died in hospital ten days after lapsing into a coma, following her fall down a flight of stairs while celebrating her sixtieth birthday at her daughter's Cotswolds cottage.

Born Laura Mountney in Merthyr Tydfil, South Wales, in 1925, Ashley was raised as a Baptist and educated in London. In 1948, she married Bernard Ashley and soon enjoyed her first success, selling her designs for headscarves and table linen. As sales increased, the couple opened their first factory, and launched a business which has expanded into a global empire specializing in wallpapers, furnishing fabrics, and romantic dresses featuring the distinctive Laura Ashley patterns and designs. By 1981, they had more than 5,000 outlets worldwide.

Pop star Madonna and actor Sean Penn marry after a short relationship.

Lynette Woodard

The situation comedy *The Golden Girls* debuts on NBC.

Margaret Atwood Tells a Woman's Tale

Canada: The eminent Canadian author Margaret Atwood has released her new novel *The Handmaid's Tale*, a vision of a stark totalitarian theocracy in which the female protagonist strives to break free of her enforced gender role. A prolific and varied writer, Atwood's literary repertoire includes novels, poetry, short stories, critical studies, screenplays, radio scripts, and books for children.

Atwood studied at the University of Toronto before taking her masters degree at Radcliffe College, Massachusetts, in 1962. Her poetic reputation was established in 1966 when her first publication, *The Circle Game,* won the Governor-General's Award for Poetry.

In 1977, amid continued critical success, she then received the City of Toronto Book Award and the Canadian Booksellers' Award for her third novel, *Lady Oracle,* and as her overseas readership expanded, she was awarded the 1982 Arts Council of Wales International Writers' Prize for her novel *Bodily Harm.* She has also edited numerous books, including the revised *Oxford Book of Canadian Poetry,* and published several works of feminist criticism.

A staunch human rights advocate, Atwood served as the President of the Writer's Union of Canada between 1981 and 1982, and is currently spearheading the fight against literary censorship. She is also an active member of the human rights watchdog institution, Amnesty International.

Chief Wilma Mankiller Gets Mandate

Oklahoma, USA, December 14: Wilma Mankiller today became the first woman to lead a major Native American tribe when she was elected Principal Chief of the Cherokee Nation of Oklahoma. Mankiller was also the first woman to serve as Deputy Chief of the tribe after being elected to the position in 1983.

Born in Tahlequah in 1945, Mankiller moved with her family to California in the mid-1950s as part of the Bureau of Indian Affairs relocation program. After finishing high school, she attended Skyline Junior College in San Bruno, then San Francisco State College, where she met some of the Native American activists who would later occupy and reclaim Alcatraz Island. This event steeled her resolve to devote time to the betterment of her people.

In the mid-1970s, Ms Mankiller returned to Oklahoma, where she worked with the Cherokee Nation, writing proposals for grants and also directing community projects. Impressed by her achievements, Chief Ross Swimmer, the elected leader of the Cherokee Nation, approached Mankiller to stand as his Deputy Chief in the 1983 elections, which they won, and took office on August 14 of that year.

Earlier this month, the position of Principal Chief became vacant when Swimmer was nominated to head the Bureau of Indian Affairs in Washington. In assuming the top job, Mankiller says she plans to involve the Cherokee people in their own community improvements, while continuing her predecessor's policy of industrial development.

Fossey Murdered in the Mountain Mist

Republic of Rwanda, December 26: Dian Fossey, the famous American zoologist who has spent 18 years studying the ecology and behavior of wild gorillas in the Virunga Mountains of Rwanda, was found brutally murdered at her campsite today. No arrests have yet been made, but local authorities suspect she may have been killed in retaliation for her efforts to stop the poaching of gorillas and other animals in Africa.

Fossey was born in San Francisco, California, in 1932. After graduating from San José State College in 1954 with a bachelor's degree in occupational therapy, she worked in that profession for several years. But she then turned her attention to the study of primates in Africa after meeting British anthropologist Louis Leakey, who believed that the observation of great apes could significantly improve our knowledge of human evolution. In 1967 she established the Karisoke Research Center in Rwanda and began living among the gorillas, earning their complete trust. She studied their social habits, tended to their injuries and illnesses and became a very accepted participant in the gorilla community. She returned to the USA in 1974 to receive a doctorate in zoology from Cambridge University, and in 1980 accepted a visiting associate professorship at Cornell University. It was during this time that she began work on her bestselling book *Gorillas in the Mist,* published in 1983.

The pioneering field work carried out by Fossey dispelled many myths about the aggression of mountain gorillas. She not only lived and played with them, but became particularly attached to one gorilla she named Digit, who was later beheaded by poachers. This prompted her to establish the Digit Fund, which garners international support for all primate conservation. She also housed small anti-poaching patrols at her own research center to help stop the slaying of gorillas, which are prized on the open market for their hands, heads, and feet.

Dian Fossey, the American zoologist, spent most of her life living with and studying gorillas.

Georgia O'Keeffe

One Less Option for Women as IUDs Lose Favor

USA, January: American pharmaceuticals manufacturer G.D. Searle & Company has announced that it is discontinuing the sale of its two intrauterine contraceptive devices (IUDs) in the United States. Searle's Copper-7—the most frequently prescribed IUD—and its Tatum-T are currently being used by around a million American women, and the company's decision to withdraw the products means that this type of birth control device will no longer be available in this country.

The IUD was first mass-marketed in the United States in the mid-1960s as an alternative to oral contraceptive pills that was safer, easier, and more convenient. By the mid-1970s, however, the A.H. Robins Company began receiving complaints from users of its Dalkon Shield, and in August last year filed a bankruptcy action following lawsuits from more than 14,000 women seeking damages for such injuries as pelvic infections, fertility problems, and birth defects. The publicity that ensued prompted users of other IUD brands to file similar lawsuits, and in September last year Johnson & Johnson's Ortho division was forced to withdraw its 20-year-old Lippes Loop from the market. Searle, the last major IUD manufacturer to hold out against the increasing costs of product-liability litigation and insurance, says it still believes in the safety of its products, a sentiment echoed by many doctors and family planning advocates, who have expressed disappointment at the decline of the IUD because it means the loss of a major family planning option for women.

Two Female Astronauts Die in *Challenger* Disaster

Cape Canaveral, USA, January 28: Millions of horrified television viewers today witnessed the world's worst space disaster when the American space shuttle *Challenger* exploded just 73 seconds after lift-off from the Kennedy Space Center. Among the seven astronauts killed in the tragic accident were two women— mission specialist Judith A. Resnik, and Sharon Christa McAuliffe, who was to be the first teacher ever to go into space.

Born in Ohio on April 5, 1949, Resnik graduated with a bachelor degree in electrical engineering from Carnegie-Mellon University in 1970, and a doctorate in the same subject from the University of Maryland in 1977. She was selected by NASA as an astronaut in

January 1978, the first cadre to include women, and underwent the painstaking training program for shuttle mission specialists. On August 30, 1984, she finally became the second American woman to go into orbit, as a crew member aboard the maiden flight of the space shuttle *Discovery*. During that mission, which lasted a week, she helped to deploy three satellites. It was also part of her duties to carry out biomedical research.

Unlike Resnik, McAuliffe was not a federal employee. Born on September 2, 1948, she grew up in Boston, graduating from Framingham State College in 1970 before moving to Washington, DC, where she taught history and social studies in secondary schools, while completing a master of arts degree at Bowie State University, Maryland. In 1984 she took leave of absence from teaching after being selected from 11,000 applicants to train for NASA's "teacher in space" program.

Speaking ahead of today's doomed launch McAuliffe said: "One of the things I hope to bring back into the classroom is to make that connection with the students that they too are part of history, the space program belongs to them, and to try to bring them up with the space age."

Pope Honors the Pure Heart of Mother Teresa

Calcutta, India, February 3: Pope John Paul II today paid tribute to the selfless humanitarian work of Mother Teresa when he visited the Home for the Dying, which she founded in Calcutta's worst slum. Mother Teresa has dedicated most of her life to caring for the sick, helpless, homeless, and destitute. In 1952, deeply disturbed by the poverty and misery surrounding her, she received permission from Calcutta officials to convert a section of an abandoned temple into a free

NASA considered it unnecessary to provide a launch escape system for the crew.

USA, January: Drug manufacturer Searle withdraws its two IUDs from the market after complaints of health risks associated with the contraceptive devices.

Cape Canaveral, USA, January 28: Space shuttle *Challenger* explodes one minute after take-off.

Calcutta, India, February 3: Pope John Paul II visits Mother Teresa's hospice in the slums of Calcutta.

Darwin, Australia, February 6: Lindy Chamberlain is released from prison and a new investigation into baby Azaria's disappearance announced.

Port-au-Prince, Haiti, February 7: President-for-life Jean-Claude "Baby Doc" Duvalier, who with his father "Papa Doc" ruled the country brutally for 28 years, flees to France amid widespread unrest.

Manila, Philippines, February 25: Ferdinand Marcos, president for 20 years, is marginalized by the military and the USA and is forced to resign. Political widow Maria Corazon "Cory" Aquino takes power.

Stockholm, Sweden, February 28: While walking unprotected, Swedish PM Olaf Palme is assassinated.

Canberra, Australia, March 2: Queen Elizabeth formally severs Australia's constitutional ties with the United Kingdom, signing the *Australia Act* with Prime Minister Bob Hawke.

Santa Fe, USA, March 6: Painter Georgia O'Keeffe dies, aged 98.

Hollywood, March 24: The film *Out of Africa*, based on the Isak Dinesen (Karen Blixen) novel, sweeps the Academy Awards.

Pakistan, April 10: Benazir Bhutto returns from exile in London to bury her brother.

Paris, France, April 14: Simone de Beauvoir dies, aged 78.

Tripoli, Libya, April 15: US and British aircraft strike terrorist targets, killing dozens of civilians.

Swaziland, April 25: Ntombi Thwala becomes Queen Mother of Swaziland.

Windsor, England, April 29: Wallis Simpson, the Duchess of Windsor, dies, aged 90.

Ukraine, USSR, April 30: The Chernobyl nuclear reactor melts down, releasing massive amounts of deadly radiation.

Norway, May 9: Gro Harlem Brundtland is elected prime minister for the second time.

Yugoslavia, May 15: Milka Planinc finishes her term as Prime Minister.

Vienna, Austria, June 8: Former United Nations Secretary-General Kurt Waldheim is elected UN President, amid accusations of his involvement in Nazi war crimes.

Washington DC, USA, June 25: Nicaraguan Contras are paid by US Congress to overthrow the Sandinista government.

Farewell Georgia O'Keeffe

Santa Fe, USA, March 6: Artist Georgia O'Keeffe, renowned for her stunning New Mexico landscapes, and sensuous representations of flowers, passed away today, aged 98. Recipient of the Medal of Freedom in 1976, and the Medal of the Arts last year, O'Keeffe was one of the most important and successful figures in the US art world.

Born in Sun Prairie, Wisconsin, in 1887, O'Keeffe studied at the Art Institute of Chicago and the Art Students' League, New York, between 1905 and 1908. Her work was well received, but she found the pervasive painterly tradition of imitative realism stifling and soon abandoned artistic life. Her interest was rekindled in 1915 by the innovative ideas of Arthur Dow, and a year later, ten of her charcoal abstractions were exhibited at Alfred Stieglitz's 291 Gallery in New York.

Stieglitz and O'Keeffe subsequently worked and lived together in New York, marrying in 1924, and it was during this period that she produced some of her most famous paintings. From 1929, much of her work was inspired by the landscape of New Mexico. She worked there for part of each year, and when Stieglitz died in 1946 took up permanent residence.

Benazir Bhutto

The work of Mother Teresa's hospice is recognized and honored by a visit from Pope John Paul II.

hospice for the terminally ill, which she named Nirmal Hriday, meaning "Pure Heart." Since then, she and her fellow nuns have gathered thousands of dying people from the streets and brought them to the Home, granting them a peaceful and dignified end in an environment of kindness and compassion.

In an address marking the occasion the Pontiff said: "I am grateful to God that my first stop in Calcutta has been at Nirmal Hriday Ashram, a place that bears witness to the primacy of love."

Chamberlain Dingo Case Reopened in Darwin

Australia, February 6: The Northern Territory Government has ordered the immediate release of convicted murderer Lindy Chamberlain, and reopened the investigation into the disappearance of her nine-week-old baby daughter Azaria from a camping ground near Uluru (Ayer's Rock) on the evening of August 17, 1980. Today's dramatic development follows the chance discovery of the baby's

matinee jacket, a hitherto missing piece of evidence, in a scrubby area full of dingo lairs at the base of the giant rock.

Chamberlain, who has previously lost two appeals against her life sentence for murder, has always staunchly maintained her innocence, insisting that Azaria was taken from the family tent by a dingo. This theory was supported by the initial coroner's inquest, but police and prosecutors remained unconvinced, and, following a second inquest, Lindy and her husband Michael were charged with the baby's murder and taken into custody.

During the subsequent trial, public and media opinion was mostly against them, partly because they were Seventh-day Adventists and partly because Lindy Chamberlain displayed little emotion during the proceedings.

The jury likewise rejected the defense case, and on October 29, 1982, Lindy Chamberlain was convicted of murder and sentenced to life imprisonment with hard labor. Michael was found guilty as an accessory to the murder and given a suspended 18-month sentence.

Maria Corazon "Cory" Aquino takes power in the Philippines.

Key Events

USA, July 1, 1986: Nancy Perkins, in collaboration with Charles Dushek and Roy Hennen, invents the battery container.

New Zealand, July 11: Consensual adult same-sex relationships are legalized by the *Homosexual Law Reform Act*.

London, England, July 23: Prince Andrew marries Sarah Ferguson at Westminster Abbey.

K2, Himalayas, August 9: Mountaineer Julie Tullis dies after climbing the world's second highest mountain.

Karachi, Pakistan, August 14: Benazir Bhutto is arrested while leading demonstrations against the government of President Zia al-Huq.

Australia, August 26: Senator Janine Haines is elected leader of the Australian Democrats.

Cameroon, August 25: Toxic gas is released from a volcanic lake, resulting in 1,700 deaths.

USA, September 8: *The Oprah Winfrey Show* debuts on TV.

Canberra, Australia, October 1: The *Affirmative Action Act* is passed by Federal Parliament.

New York, USA, October 29: An abortion clinic is bombed, one of several attacks in the US this year by pro-life campaigners.

Basel, Switzerland, November 10: A fire at a chemical plant dumps more than 1,000 tons of toxic chemicals into the Rhine River.

Washington DC, USA, November 25: The "Irangate" affair comes to light when President Ronald Reagan admits to secret arms deals with Nicaraguan Contras. Lieutenant-Colonel Oliver North and Vice-Admiral John Poindexter resign.

Stockholm, Sweden, December 10: Italian-born neurologist Rita Levi-Montalcini co-wins the Nobel Prize in Physiology or Medicine with Stanley Cohen, for their discoveries of nerve growth factors.

Shanghai, China, December 21: Fifty thousand students hold demonstrations urging democratic reforms, including freedom of the media.

California, USA, December 23: *Voyager*, a sleek plane piloted by Dick Rutan and Jeana Yaeger, encircles the world in nine days on one tank of fuel.

Dallas, USA, December 26: American Airlines Flight 412 arrives at Dallas / Fort Worth airport, the first commercial jetliner flight with an all-women crew.

USA, December: Golfer Pat Bradley becomes the first woman to top $2 million in career earnings.

Canada: Margaret Atwood publishes *The Handmaid's Tale*.

USA: Karleen Koen publishes *Through a Glass Darkly*.

USA: Judy Blume publishes *Letters to Judy: What Kids Wish They Could Tell You*.

Simone de Beauvoir Says Au Revoir

Milka Planinc

Paris, France, April 14: Simone de Beauvoir, famous French feminist, philosopher, novelist, and essayist, died today, aged 78. Beauvoir will be remembered as a seminal figure in the struggle for women's rights, as well as an eminent writer and thinker and lifelong companion of existentialist philosopher Jean-Paul Sartre.

After meeting Sartre while she was studying philosophy at the Sorbonne University in Paris in 1928, Beauvoir began what she described as a "moral" phase of life, the culmination of which was her philosophical work *The Ethics of Ambiguity,* published in 1948. The following year she released her famous two-volume feminist treatise *The Second Sex,* acknowledged as an important work today, but considered an affront to decency by many at the time.

Her literary major breakthrough came in 1954 with the publication of her novel *The Mandarins,* for which she received the Prix Goncourt, France's most prestigious literary award. Best known for this and other metaphysical novels, she also wrote monographs on philosophy, politics, and social issues, essays, biographies, and in later life, while still championing women's issues, a four-volume autobiography. She explored the many

> *"FROM THE HOUR YOU'RE BORN YOU BEGIN TO DIE. BUT BETWEEN BIRTH AND DEATH THERE'S LIFE."*
>
> SIMONE DE BEAUVOIR (1908–1986), FRENCH WRITER AND FEMINIST

Simone de Beauvoir in Paris, 1971.

problems of ageing in such books as *A Very Easy Death* (1964). One of her last works, *Adieux: A Farewell to Sartre* (1981), recorded the events leading up to her lifelong friend's demise, and anticipated her own: "My death will not bring us together again. This is how things are. It is in itself splendid that we were able to live our lives in harmony for so long."

Wallis Simpson nicknamed the Queen "Shirley" as a young girl; she called the Queen Mother "Mrs Temple."

A Duchess Joins Her Duke

Windsor, England, April 29: The Duchess of Windsor, Wallis Simpson, was today laid to rest alongside her late husband, the abdicated King Edward VIII, under a spreading plane tree at Frogmore. Her English oak coffin was marked with a silver plate inscribed "Wallis, Duchess of Windsor, 1896–1986."

Earlier in the day, over 100 guests, including prominent members of the Royal Family, the government, and the opposition, attended a simple funeral service at St George's Chapel. Although flags were flown at half-mast, there were few flowers and no funeral address. In accordance with the Duchess's wishes, her status within the Royal Family was mentioned only in the final blessing, given by the Archbishop of Canterbury, Doctor Robert Runcie.

Mountain Claims Woman

K2, Himalayas, August 9: British mountaineer Julie Tullis has perished just days after becoming the third woman ever to reach the summit of K2, the world's second highest peak. Tragically, Tullis is the second woman to lose her life on the slopes of the infamous "Savage Mountain" within the space of a few weeks.

Legendary Polish mountaineer Wanda Rutkiewicz, the first European woman to reach the summit of Mount Everest, made history again on June 23 this year when she became the first woman to complete the ascent of K2. Later that day she was joined on the summit by French team members Michael Parmentier, Maurice Barrard, and his wife Liliane Barrard, who became the second woman to accomplish the feat. Due to the lateness of the hour, the team members decided not to return to Camp III at 25,900 feet (7,900 m) but

to spend the night in bivouac tents at 27,230 feet (8,300 m). The next morning, as the team descended, both the Barrards disappeared in swirling snow. Rutkiewicz finally made her way back to base camp, but on July 19 Liliane was found dead, having fallen several thousand feet.

Undeterred by the Barrards' fate, Tullis, along with pioneering Himalayan mountaineer Kurt Diemberger, became the third woman to conquer the formidable peak, on August 4. Although she seemed to have recovered from a fall near the summit on the descent, the pair failed to reach the high camp on the shoulder until the following day, by which time a ferocious storm was already battering the mountain. Trapped for days at high altitude with dwindling supplies of food, gas, water, and oxygen, Tullis eventually succumbed to exposure and exhaustion. Of the six climbers from several expeditions trapped with her on K2, only two survived, including Diemberger.

Janine Haines to Lead Australian Democrats

Australia, August 26: Senator Janine Haines was today elected leader of the Australian Democrats, becoming the first woman to head a political party in Australia. Haines succeeds retiring leader Don Chipp, who founded the party in 1977 after he was approached by members of the Australia Party and the New Liberal Movement.

Chipp held a series of nationwide public meetings to garner support for the formation of a new political party, one in which ordinary people could have input, and Haines was one of those ordinary people. Born in the South Australian Barossa Valley town of Tanunda in 1945, she spent a decade working as a schoolteacher in Adelaide. After the launch of the Australian Democrats, she was thrust into the public eye as the first member of the new party to enter the Federal Parliament, filling a casual vacancy created by the resignation of Senator Steele Hall in December that year. At the time, there were only seven other women senators—

with a degree in French from New York's Mount Saint Vincent College in 1953, she returned to the Philippines to study law, but soon married Benigno "Ninoy" Aquino, Jr., one of the country's rising political stars. When President Marcos

Geraldine Page (right, with Rebecca de Mornay) wins the Oscar for Best Actress in *The Trip to Bountiful*.

and no women among the 177 members of the House of Representatives. From the outset, Haines used her role in public life to represent and articulate the interests of women and other disempowered groups. In 1978 she lost her Senate seat when the term of the casual vacancy expired, but her dedication, intelligence, and political skills saw her returned to the Upper House at the 1980 elections.

Cory Counters Plotters in Cabinet Reshuffle

Manila, Philippines, November: President Corazon "Cory" Aquino has reshuffled her Cabinet, dropping some leftists in a tactical move designed to appease the military and head off another rightist coup. The dramatic reshuffle comes just months after coup plotters failed to establish a rival government. They had planned to install Arturo Tolentino as acting president. In the election held earlier this year, Tolentino was the unsuccessful running mate of the deposed ex-President Ferdinand Marcos.

For most of her life Aquino neither sought nor expected to gain political power. Born into the wealthy Cojuangco family on January 25, 1933, she was educated at an exclusive Catholic school for girls in Manila before traveling to the United States to attend Philadelphia's Raven Hill Academy. After graduating

declared martial law in 1972, Benigno— then a senator and an outspoken critic of the Marcos regime—was arrested and held in prison for seven years. On his release the Aquinos traveled to the United States.

In August 1983, anti-Marcos factions persuaded them to return to the Philippines, but Benigno was gunned down within seconds of his arrival at Manila airport.

The assassination of her husband was a turning point in Aquino's life. As his widow, she suddenly became a unifying figure for opposition factions, and when Marcos called a snap election for February 1986, she agreed to run for president as their common candidate. Though both sides declared victory in this seriously flawed election, mass protests soon forced Marcos to flee the country, leaving Aquino to assume the office of president. She has been attempting to restore social harmony to the Philippines after more than two decades of autocratic rule.

Two-Million-Dollar Woman Voted Player of the Year

USA, December: American golfer Pat Bradley has been named Ladies' Professional Golfing Association (LPGA) Player of the Year, capping a sensational 1986 season which saw her claim the money title after winning six tournaments.

Born in Westford, Massachusetts in 1951, Bradley started playing golf at the age of 11, winning the New Hampshire Amateur title in 1967 and 1969, and the New England Amateur title in 1972 and 1973. After joining the LPGA in 1974, she scored her first professional win at the 1976 Girl Talk Classic, a victory that prompted her mother to clang a cowbell on the back porch—a celebratory ritual she has continued to perform after each of her daughter's successes.

There have been many. Bradley's first victory in a major tournament came at the 1980 Peter Jackson Classic, followed by the 1981 US Women's Open, and the 1985 du Maurier Classic (formerly the Peter Jackson). This year, however, has been her best so far, with six titles to her credit, including three of the four LPGA majors—the du Maurier, the Nabisco Dinah Shore, and the LPGA Championship. In addition to Player of the Year, she has won the Vare Trophy for the lowest average strokes per round, set a single season record by winning $492,021, and become the first woman golfer to surpass $2 million in career earnings.

Oprah Winfrey

Prince Andrew marries Sarah Ferguson at Westminster Abbey.

Aretha Franklin

Aretha Now in Hall of Fame

New York, USA, January 21: The world-renowned American soul singer, Aretha Franklin, has become the first woman to be inducted into the Rock and Roll Hall of Fame. Franklin received this honor during the Hall of Fame's second annual induction dinner at the Waldorf-Astoria Hotel in Manhattan.

The Hall of Fame Foundation was founded four years ago. Its annual awards recognize those who have made a significant contribution to rock and roll music. Among the inaugural inductees last year were Chuck Berry, James Brown, Ray Charles, and Elvis Presley.

Born on March 25, 1942, in Memphis, Tennessee, Aretha Louise Franklin grew up in Detroit where her father was a Baptist minister. She began singing in church at a young age and recorded her first album when she was 14 years old.

Dubbed the "Queen of Soul," Franklin was heavily influenced by blues, jazz, and gospel music. Despite her incredible vocal talent and musical abilities, she was not immediately successful and spent six lackluster years with Columbia Records before switching to Atlantic in 1966.

"I'VE ALWAYS FELT ROCK AND ROLL WAS VERY, VERY WHOLESOME MUSIC."

ARETHA FRANKLIN
(1942–), AMERICAN
SOULD SINGER

Martina Navratilova wins the Flo Hyman Award.

Her first Atlantic single, and album, was "I Never Loved a Man (the Way I Loved You)." Also on the album was the song for which she is best known, "Respect," which topped both pop and R&B charts, and led to her first Grammy Award. Aretha Franklin made 19 albums with Atlantic. She later joined Arista Records and in 1985 returned to the Top 10 with "Freeway of Love."

Maltese Leader Retires

Valletta, Malta, February 15: The Republic of Malta's first female leader, Agatha Barbara, finishes her five-year presidency today, concluding 40 years of political service during which time she has fundamentally changed the lives of the population.

Elected to parliament representing the Labour Party in 1947, she never lost her seat. In her first year as the Minister for Education in 1955, Barbara introduced free and compulsory education for children aged 5 to 14 and built or expanded 44 schools. She recruited hundreds of teachers; textbooks and transport were free; and in 1956 the country's first schools for disabled children were established.

A fierce advocate for Malta's independence, Barbara was sentenced to 43 days' hard labor in 1958 for participating in protests against the British occupation.

In 1971, when the Labour Party was returned to power, Barbara again served as the Minister for Education. In 1974, she was given a new portfolio—Labor, Social Services, and Culture—and she soon introduced equal pay for women; paid pregnancy leave; the 40-hour week; unemployment benefits; and good pensions. Industrial harmony ensued and unemployment dropped to two percent.

Agatha Barbara set up several national museums and headed up major domestic and international charities. She established many international friendships on behalf of Malta. She will now retire in Zabbar, where she was born 64 years ago.

Archbishop Robert Runcie ordains the first women deacons.

Maria's Music Silenced

Vermont, USA, March 28: Maria von Trapp, the woman whose life inspired the classic musical, *The Sound of Music*, has died following a short illness, aged 82.

Maria Augusta Kutschera was born on January 26, 1905 in Vienna, Austria, and was raised as a socialist and atheist until a chance meeting with a Jesuit priest influenced her beliefs, prompting her to enter a convent as a novitiate. Before she could take orders, however, she was sent in 1926 to the home of the retired naval captain, Georg Ritter von Trapp, in Salzburg, to tutor his youngest daughter Maria, who was too sick after scarlet fever to attend lessons at school. His wife, Agathe, had died in 1922.

Kutschera and von Trapp were married on November 26, 1927. In 1929, their first

USA, January 21: Aretha Franklin is the first woman inducted into the Rock and Roll Hall of Fame.
USA, January: The Directors Guild nominates a woman for best director of a film for the first time: Randa Haines for *Children of a Lesser God*.
USA, February 7: The first National Women and Girls in Sports Day is celebrated, with the inaugural Flo Hyman award going to Martina Navratilova.
Malta, February 15: Agatha Barbara finishes her term as president of the country.

Beirut, Lebanon, February 22: At the request of Lebanese leaders, 7,000 Syrian troops enter West Beirut in an attempt to end fighting between Muslims and Christians.
England, February 26: A majority of the Anglican General Synod votes in favor of ordaining women as priests.
Rome, Italy, March 1: Bettino Craxi's socialist government, the longest serving since World War II, resigns.

Vatican City, March 10: Pope John Paul II condemns all forms of artificial fertilization in his "Instruction on respect for human life in its origin and on the dignity of procreation."
USA, March 23: Daytime soap *The Bold and the Beautiful* premieres.
Vermont, USA, March 28: Maria von Trapp, the woman whose life was the inspiration for the musical, *The Sound of Music*, dies, aged 82.
Washington DC, USA, April 7: The National Museum of Women in the Arts is opened.

USA, April 7, 1987: Nancy Perkins invents the canister vacuum.
USA, April 16: Rita Dove wins the Pulitzer Prize for poetry for *Thomas and Beulah*.
Iceland, April 25: The feminist party, the Women's Alliance of Iceland, wins 10 percent of the popular vote in the general elections.
Germany, May 1: Sister Edith Stein, a victim of the holocaust, is beatified by Pope John Paul II.

Suva, Fiji, May 14: Lieutenant-Colonel Sitiveni Rabuka enters parliament and arrests the prime minister and 27 members of the Indian-dominated government.
New York, USA, May 14: Actress Rita Hayworth dies, aged 68.
Washington DC, USA, June 6: Dr. Mae Jemison is named the first black woman astronaut.
UK, June 11: Margaret Thatcher's Conservative Party is re-elected for a third term.

Maria von Trapp and her family at a reunion gathering near her home.

child together, Rosmarie, was born. She was followed by Eleonore in 1931 and Johannes in 1939.

Georg von Trapp lost his money in 1935, so the family turned its favorite pastime of singing and playing musical instruments into a career, and became a popular touring act called The Trapp Family Singers. After the Nazi annexation of Austria in 1938, the large family escaped to Italy, and from there, emigrated to the USA in 1939.

In 1942, they purchased a big farm in Stowe, Vermont, which became the Trapp Family Lodge. Maria von Trapp founded a music camp at the lodge in 1944.

Georg von Trapp died of lung cancer in 1947, but the Trapp Family Singers continued performing until 1957, after which Maria and three of the children became missionaries in the South Pacific. She later returned to Vermont and spent the rest of her life managing the lodge.

Maria's 1949 book, *The Story of the Trapp Family,* was a bestseller and was first adapted by a German film company in 1956. In 1959, the Rogers & Hammerstein musical, *The Sound of Music,* opened on Broadway. Hollywood followed with

its 1965 hit motion picture starring Julie Andrews as Maria and Christopher Plummer as von Trapp.

Women Artists on Show

Washington DC, USA, April 7: The world's first museum dedicated to recognizing the achievements of women in the arts opened today. Its first exhibition, "American Women Artists 1830–1930," will be curated by revered US feminist art historian, Dr. Eleanor Tufts.

The National Museum of Women in the Arts was founded by art collectors Wilhelmina Cole Holladay and her husband, Wallace, six years ago.

Collectors since the 1960s, the couple had noticed the lack of representation of women in exhibitions and books, and started their nonprofit museum with docent-led tours of their collection at home. Seeking to educate the public, they displayed works by artists from many different eras and countries, including Artemisia Gentileschi, Angelica Kauffmann, Judith

Leyster, Lavinia Fontana, and Sofonisba Anguissola. In 1983, they purchased a dilapidated former temple, and meticulously renovated it. This is now the permanent home of the museum.

Love Goddess Rita is No More

New York, USA, May 14: American actress and sex symbol of the 1940s, Rita Hayworth, has died from complications related to Alzheimer's disease, aged 68.

Rita Hayworth rose to stardom in the 1930s and 1940s with a string of hit movies, including *Blood and Sand* (1941) and *Cover Girl* (1944). With her glamorous red hair and enviable figure, she was a World War II pin-up, and starred opposite Hollywood's most dashing actors, including Fred Astaire and Gene Kelly.

Born Margarita Carmen Dolores Cansino in Brooklyn on October 17, 1918, Hayworth began performing at 6 years of age with her family's troupe, The Dancing Cansinos. She was signed by Fox Studios in 1935 and made a few movies before marrying Edward Judson, who became her manager, in 1937. She dyed her hair red, changed her name, and in 1939 starred in her first major motion picture, *Only Angels Have Wings.*

Rita was nicknamed the "love goddess," following her appearance in a magazine in a sexy nightgown and her legendary striptease in the 1946 movie, *Gilda.*

Rita Hayworth divorced Judson in 1943 and married four more times. She had two daughters by two different husbands—Rebecca with actor-director Orson Welles, and Yasmin from her marriage to Prince Ali Khan. Around 1960, Rita Hayworth suffered early onset Alzheimer's disease, but despite her illness, she continued to work. She made her last film in 1972.

Rita Hayworth

time out

Tammy Faye Bakker, the fake-eyelashed host of the evangelist program *PTL (People That Pray) Club* on US television, is out of a job, as her husband has been charged with embezzlement and other crimes.

Seoul, South Korea, June 20: Massive protests throughout South Korea over ten days climax with widespread riots in the capital. Rioters demand democratic reform.

Mt. Fuji, Japan, July 24: American mountaineer Hulda Crooks is the oldest woman, at 91, to climb Mt. Fuji.

Colombo, Sri Lanka, July 29: India and Sri Lanka sign a peace accord.

Mecca, Saudi Arabia, July 30: Saudi police shoot 400 pilgrims, mostly Iranians, during the annual hajj.

London, England, July: Artists Helen Chadwick and Terese Oulton are the first women nominated for the Turner Art Prize.

San Antonio, Texas, USA, August 1: Pola Negri, Polish star of silent films, dies, aged 92.

Guatemala City, Guatemala, August 7: The presidents of Costa Rica, Nicaragua, Honduras, Guatemala, and El Salvador sign a peace agreement.

Soviet Union, August 7: American Lynne Cox swims the Bering Strait in 2 hours and 6 minutes.

Manila, Philippines, August 29: The fifth coup attempt against President Corazon Aquino's government fails, 40 people are dead and hundreds have been injured.

Ethiopia, September 10: A new civilian constitution is drafted, ending 13 years of military rule. Colonel Megistu Haile Mariam is elected president.

Washington DC, USA, October 9: Writer and politician Clare Boothe Luce dies, aged 84.

UK, October 16: Hurricane force winds batter the British Isles, leaving a £300 million damage bill.

England, October 19: Acclaimed cellist Jacqueline du Pré dies of multiple sclerosis, aged 42.

Worldwide, October 19: Stock markets slump dramatically following the lead of Wall Street.

England, October: Queen Elizabeth II changes the statutes of the Most Noble Orders of the Garter and Thistle to allow women citizens to be admitted.

England, October: Penelope Lively wins the Booker Prize for her novel *Moon Tiger.*

Washington DC, USA, October: A march for gay and lesbian rights attracts around half a million demonstrators.

Washington DC, USA, December 18: Presidents Ronald Reagan and Mikhail Gorbachev sign a treaty to diminish the size of their country's nuclear arsenals.

Germany: Leni Riefenstahl publishes her autobiography.

Randa Haines

Jemison Joins Astronaut Trainees

Washington DC, USA, June 5: The National Aeronautics and Space Administration (NASA) has today announced the first selection of an African-American woman for its astronaut training program.

Dr. Mae C. Jemison, a general practitioner from Los Angeles, California, has a background in chemical engineering and medical research, and has also served with the US Peace Corps.

Born in Decatur, Alabama, on October 17, 1956, Jemison was raised in Chicago, Illinois. She was an exceptional student, and always interested in science. At just 16, she entered Stanford University on a National Achievement Scholarship and graduated with a Bachelor of Science in Chemical Engineering in 1977. She then began her medical doctorate degree at Cornell University, during which time she worked in Cuba and Kenya in 1979, as well as in Thailand at a Cambodian refugee camp in 1980.

After graduating from Cornell in 1981, Jemison completed her internship at a Los Angeles medical center and began working as a general practitioner.

In 1982 she joined the US Peace Corps and spent 2½ years serving as the Area Peace Corps Medical Officer in the West African countries of Sierra Leone and Liberia, where she was responsible for the health of corps and embassy personnel.

After returning to the US in 1985, Dr. Jemison resumed general practice and decided to pursue her long-held dream of joining the space program. She is among just 15 people who have been selected from a field of almost 2,000 applicants. She will begin a one-year training program at the Johnson Space Center in Houston, Texas, on August 17.

Nonagenarian on Mt Fuji

Mt Fuji, Japan, July 24: Today, 91-year-old American has become the oldest woman to climb to the top of Japan's highest mountain, Mt Fuji.

Margaret Thatcher has won the British elections.

Californian Hulda Crooks, of Loma Linda, completed the three-day ascent of the 12,388-foot (3,776 m) dormant volcano with a group of employees from the Dentsu Inc. advertising company. They had invited Crooks to climb with them to celebrate their sixth annual trek.

Crooks's mountaineering hobby began when she was 66, in 1962, when she climbed the 14,505-foot (4,421 m) Mt Whitney, the highest peak in the continental USA. She has climbed it every year since then, and is widely known as "Grandma Whitney" to her legions of fans.

Hulda Crooks has now climbed more than 90 mountains and competed in senior Olympic marathons and road races. She has a collection of world records and is considered an inspiration in the field of health. A series of medical test last year found that Hulda's level of fitness was equivalent to that of an average woman aged 30 years younger. But it hasn't always been this way—good health came late in life. Born on May 19, 1896, in Canada, Hulda was raised on a farm, with a diet of meat, potatoes, milk, and butter. By age 16, she weighed 160 pounds (72 kg) and was just 5 feet 2 inches (1.57 m) tall. Two years later, Crooks joined the Seventh-Day Adventist Church and became a lacto-ovo-vegetarian. Her beliefs allowed her to eat milk and eggs, but no meat.

Hulda studied nutrition and dietetics at Loma Linda University, but did not complete her degree in nutrition until after her marriage to Dr. Samuel Crooks in the 1940s. She also learned the value of a positive outlook and how the mind dictates what the body does. She then combined her need for exercise with her love of nature and took up hiking, which ultimately led to her amazing feats.

Silent Star Fades Away

San Antonio, Texas, August 1: Pola Negri, the Polish silent film vamp of the early 1920s and 1930s, died today at Northeast Baptist Hospital of pneumonia.

Born Barbara Apolonia Chałupiec on December 31, 1894, Pola was raised in poverty, but won a place to train as a ballerina with the St Petersburg Imperial Ballet. Her promising dancing career was cut short after she contracted tuberculosis, after which she joined the Warsaw Imperial Academy of Dramatic Arts and worked on films in Warsaw and Germany.

Her first film, *Die Bestie*, was made in 1915. In 1918 she starred in *Slave of Sin*, and later received worldwide attention with *Madame du Barry*, which was renamed *Passion* for its US release. She moved to Hollywood and starred in *Bella Donna*, *The Cheat*, *Forbidden Paradise*, and *Hotel Imperial*. Her exotic, glamorous looks and strong, passionate characters made her one of Hollywood's most celebrated femme fatales. Pola Negri married and divorced twice, and her romances with Charlie Chaplin and Rudolph Valentino created quite a stir among her audiences.

Her career began to fade with the advent of talking pictures, as her heavy Polish accent was not attractive to US audiences. In addition, the 1930 Hays Code, which limited "scenes of passion," significantly curtailed her career. Pola Negri made several films in Germany which revived her career, and on return to the USA she became a naturalized US citizen in 1951. Her last film, in 1964, was Walt Disney's *The Moon-Spinners*.

Bering Strait Swim

Big Diomede Island, Soviet Union, August 8: Long-distance open-water American swimmer, Lynne Cox, has become the

Bangladeshi Opposition leader, Khaleda Zia, is arrested at a strike.

Lynne Cox braved the icy waters of the Bering Strait to gain herself a place in history.

Riefenstahl Tells All

Leni Riefenstahl

Germany: Controversial German filmmaker Leni Riefenstahl, who made films for the Nazis, has published a 669-page autobiography titled *Leni Riefenstahl: A Memoir,* documenting her life as a dancer, actress, filmmaker, and photographer.

Riefenstahl has received both acclaim for her artistic talent, and condemnation for her work with the Nazis during World War II. Although she denies supporting the Nazis, she produced one of Hitler's most powerful propaganda films, *Triumph of the Will.* Banned in the USA, the film won prestigious awards in Europe for its masterful visuals created through innovations including cameras on cranes and tracking rails, and the use of telephoto lenses for facial close-ups.

Born Berta Helene Amalie Riefenstahl on August 22, 1902 in Berlin, she was a stage dancer, then an actress. She eventually set up her own production company and produced, directed, and starred in *The Blue Light* in 1932. That same year, Riefenstahl saw Hitler speak at a rally and was spellbound. She arranged a meeting and he asked her to film rallies in 1933 and 1934, the latter resulting in *Triumph of the Will.* In 1936, the Nazis asked her to film the Berlin Olympics, resulting in another famous work, *Olympia.*

After the war, Leni Riefenstahl spent four years in a detention camp and was investigated, but never convicted, of being a Nazi propagandist. Riefenstahl maintains that her work with the Nazis was artistic, not political. She describes her films as documentaries, not propaganda.

In the 1960s she produced two photographic books on the Sudanese Nuba tribe. She has more recently taken up underwater photography. It remains to be seen whether her autobiography will settle the controversy over her relationship with the Nazi regime.

first person to swim across the Bering Strait between Alaska and the Soviet Union. Her historic swim today took 2 hours and 6 minutes.

Lynne completed the 5-mile (8-km) swim from Little Diomede Island to Big Diomede Island. She swam through 39°F (4°C) waters wearing just a swimsuit, cap, and goggles. She was met by a crowd of American and Russian well-wishers, who celebrated together. This was symbolically important to Cox, who had spent years negotiating permission for the swim, believing it could help unite the nuclear superpowers after decades of tension.

Born in 1957, Cox was a childhood prodigy who by age 15 had broken the men's and women's world records for swimming the English Channel.

Du Pré Succumbs to MS

London, England, October 19: The classical music world lost one of its greatest stars today with the tragic death of 42-year-old British cellist Jacqueline du Pré, after a 14-year battle with multiple sclerosis.

Born on January 26, 1945, in Oxford, Jacqueline du Pré began playing the cello when she was 5 years of age. Among her famous tutors was William Pleeth. She began performing BBC concerts in London when she was 12 years old. In 1960, Jacqueline graduated from the Guildhall School of Music and won its Gold Medal.

In 1961, the 16-year-old made her formal debut at London's Wigmore Hall,

playing Elgar's *Cello Concerto.* She began recording with EMI in 1962, and in 1965 achieved world fame when, with the London Symphony Orchestra, she recorded the Elgar concerto. That same year she made her US debut with the BBC Symphony Orchestra at Carnegie Hall.

Du Pré performed with the world's top orchestras, including the Berlin, London, New York, Israel, and Los Angeles Philharmonics. In 1966 she met pianist and conductor Daniel Barenboim and they wed a year later. They produced many exquisite musical pieces together.

In 1971, Jacqueline du Pré began losing the feeling in her fingers, and by 1973 her physical pain had a significant impact on her performances. The cellist retired from public performances and was diagnosed with multiple sclerosis. Despite her illness she managed to continue teaching. In 1976, du Pré became an Officer of the Order of the British Empire.

Jacqueline du Pré was a giant of classical music. Her virtuosity lives on in her recordings.

First Woman Appointed to British Court of Appeal

London, England, January 11: Elizabeth Butler-Sloss has been made a Justice of the Court of Appeal following her chairing of the Cleveland child abuse inquiry in 1987, becoming the first female law lord in British history.

Born Anne Elizabeth Oldfield Havers, she is daughter to judges Sir Cecil Havers, sister to Lord Chancellor Havers, and aunt to his son, actor Nigel Havers. Her stellar legal career began in 1955 in London. She was first appointed a registrar at the principal registry of the family division in 1970, and in 1979 became the first woman to be made a high court judge. Butler-Sloss has been widely acknowledged for her commitment to opening up the judicial system to women, and is known for her fair and decisive handling of sensitive matters in the family court, such as custody rulings, divorce, and child abuse. This has made her a target for men's rights groups.

Christina Onassis

"Sisters Are Doin' It For Themselves."

ARETHA FRANKLIN
SONG TITLE
PERFORMED WITH
ANNIE LENNOX

Successful Cord Blood Transplant

France, February: Dr. Elaine Gluckman has become the first person to perform a successful umbilical cord blood transplant, giving a six-year-old boy, Matthew Farrow, a second chance at life. Matthew suffered from the very rare genetic blood disease Fanconi's anemia, which prevents the body from producing healthy blood cells, and his life expectancy was just 12 years. Doctors proposed a radically new—but untried—procedure, a cord blood stem cell transplant, hoping it could replace the painful and intrusive bone marrow transplant which, until now, was the only known treatment. The umbilical cord is a rich source of stem cells known as CD34 cells—much richer than adult blood or bone marrow. The CD34 is a primitive cell which can renew itself and produce mature blood cells. Earlier this month umbilical cord blood was collected from Matthew's newborn sister and carefully stored. As US law doesn't allow for such a transplant, the family traveled to Paris, home of renowned bone marrow transplant specialist Dr. Gluckman. Matthew underwent chemotherapy and irradiation to kill off his diseased blood system, then received a transfusion of the cord blood.

For 28 days Dr Gluckman, the transplant team, and the boy's parents waited and watched. Their patience was well rewarded and excitement set in when Matthew's blood counts rose faster than anyone had ever expected or hoped. It is hoped that this successful procedure marks a new chapter in medical history, saving children particularly from other painful treatments.

time out

Margaret Thatcher is now Britain's longest serving Prime Minister, taking office in 1979. Thatcher also has the longest continuous period in office since Lord Liverpool in the early nineteenth century.

Toni Morrison Wins Pulitzer for *Beloved*

New York, USA, March 31: African-American writer Toni Morrison has won the Pulitzer Prize for fiction for her novel *Beloved*. This success follows the publication of an open letter in the *New York Times Book Review* in January of this year, signed by 48 prominent black reviewers, protesting against the book's failure to win the National Book Award last year.

Born Chloe Anthony Wofford in Ohio, USA—where her parents had fled to escape southern racism—Morrison grew up reading voraciously. In 1949 she enrolled at Howard University in Washington DC and went on to Cornell University, completing a masters degree thesis about suicide in the works of William Faulkner and Virginia Woolf. Morrison explores the social implications of being a black woman in contemporary America, and her complex and multi-layered narratives are intensely imaginative responses to experiences in a racist and male-dominated society.

African-American writer Toni Morrison has won the Pulitzer Prize for her book *Beloved*.

London, England, January 11: Elizabeth Butler-Sloss is appointed to the Court of Appeals, the first female law lord in British history.
East Jerusalem, Israel, January 15: Israeli police open fire on Muslim protestors at the Dome of the Rock mosque, one of Islam's holiest sites.
United Kingdom, February 3: Nurses right across the UK strike for better pay and conditions.
Sri Lanka, February 16: Vijaya Kumaratunga–movie star, politician, and husband of Chandrika Kumaratunga–is assassinated.

France, February: Dr. Elaine Gluckman is the first person to perform a cord blood transplant to cure a case of Franconi's anemia.
Calgary, Canada, February: The Winter Olympics end with Dutch speed skater Yvonne Van Gennip winning three gold medals and breaking two world records. Christa Rothenburger wins gold in the 1,000 meter speed skating.
New York, USA, March 31: Toni Morrison wins the Pulitzer Prize for her novel *Beloved*.

Islamabad, Pakistan, April 10: The Ojhri ammunition depot explodes, killing 100 and injuring over 1,000. Afghani agents are suspected.
New York, USA, April 17: Sculptor Louise Nevelson dies, aged 88.
North Pole, April 20: Helen Thayer–along with her husky, Charlie–becomes the first person to complete a solo trek to the north magnetic pole.
Afghanistan, May 16: Soviet troops begin to withdraw, after over eight years bogged down against US-backed Islamic militants.

Cambodia, June 4: Vietnamese forces, who have occupied Cambodia for ten years, begin to withdraw 50,000 troops.
Sydney Harbour, Australia, June 5: Australian Kay Cottee becomes the first woman to sail non-stop solo around the world.
New Jersey, USA, June 13: The cigarette company Liggett Group is found liable in the death by lung cancer of Rose Cipollone.
Ohio, USA, June 25: Mildred Gillars, known as "Axis Sally," dies, aged 87.

Arabian Gulf, July 3: US Navy warship *Vincennes* mistakenly shoots down an Iranian passenger plane, killing 290 people.
Managua, Nicaragua, July 14: Woman and children from the organization Mothers of Heroes and Martyrs, holding crosses, demonstrate in front of the office of Archbishop Obando y Bravo, asking him to stop the civil war.
Tehran, Iran, July 20: Ayatollah Khomeini declares an end to the eight-year holy war with Iraq, accepting the UN cease-fire conditions.

Nurses across the United Kingdom protest during a strike for better pay and conditions.

Inspired by the true story of African-American slave Margaret Garner, the novel *Beloved* is an intricate and harrowing story, with supernatural elements, about an escaped slave who was driven to kill her child to save it from slavery.

The book made an immediate and powerful impact. It sold by the million and book rights were optioned by Oprah Winfrey, who has thrown her considerable resources behind the production of a major film based on the book.

Kiwi Trekker and Trusty Husky Reach North Pole

North Pole, April 27: New Zealander Helen Thayer today became the first person to travel solo to the magnetic north pole, accompanied only by her dog, Charlie. An active and athletic woman, Thayer had a career as an international discus thrower, representing three countries before winning the US national luge championship in 1975. She was a cross-country ski racer and instructor, kayak racer, high altitude mountain climber, and instructor. She has climbed the highest mountains in New Zealand, North America and the Soviet Union.

Thayer's journey to the pole was conceived as an educational project. At the age of 50, she decided to walk there alone without the aid of aircraft, dog teams, or snowmobiles, and pulling her own 160 lb (72 kg) sled filled with supplies. She aims to draw support for the conservation of one of the world's harshest and least-spoiled environments. Particularly fascinated with polar bears, Thayer chose the home of one of the world's largest polar bear populations for her expedition. Her only companion on this epic undertaking was Charlie, a black husky. Charlie protected her from bears and other beasts, and saved her life at least once.

The magnetic north pole is constantly in motion, and its location is charted annually by a Canadian geological survey. Thayer criss-crossed the polar area—traveling most of the journey across cracking sea ice—photographing and taking notes as she went, and braving frostbite, sub-zero temperatures, and wild Arctic storms.

She took a roughly triangular trail, covering as much ground as possible in order to document the barren islands, hardy plant life, and animals and birds of this fascinating environment for the educational program she plans to develop using the research.

Kay Cottee Sails into Record Book

Sydney Harbour, Australia, June 5, 1988: Kay Cottee, the first woman to sail solo, unassisted, and non-stop around the world, today cruised into Sydney Harbour in her 35 foot (11 m) yacht *First Lady*, after 189 days at sea. She was met by tens of thousands of well-wishers.

Cottee faced dangers such as icebergs, whales, and breaking seas, and took just six months to sail over 22,000 nautical miles. Her life hung in the balance in the Southern Ocean when her boat turned upside down and she was washed overboard. She was saved by the safety lines which harnessed her to the deck.

The historic voyage was the culmination of a childhood dream. Cottee was born into a yachting family, taking her first voyage when only a few weeks old. Fascinated with sailing, she helped her father build a 34 ft (10 m) sloop in the backyard, and went on to build *First Lady*.

Yvonne Van Gennip

Woman and children from the organization Mothers of Heroes and Martyrs stand vigil in Managua, in front of the office of Archbishop Obando y Bravo, asking him to stop the civil war in Nicaragua.

Rangoon, Burma, July 23: Rioting students destroy police stations in the worst violence seen in the past quarter century. Premier Bo Ne Win is ousted from office after 26 years.

Vatican City, August 15: Pope John Paul outlines two "particular dimensions of the fulfilment of the female personality" as virginity or motherhood, in an apostolic letter.

London, England, August 23: The newest member of the British royal family is born. Beatrice Elizabeth Mary is daughter to the Duke and Duchess of York.

Burma, September 19: The recent flirtation with freedom of speech is short-lived. The Army takes control of the civilian government, banning all public demonstrations.

Burma, September 24: Aung Sun Suu Kyi forms a new political party, the National League for Democracy.

USA, September: Barbara Harris is elected first woman bishop of the Episcopal church.

France, September: The nation approves the use of the abortion pill RU-486—the first western nation to do so.

Seoul, Korea, October 2: The closing ceremony of the games of the XXIV Olympiad is held. Highlights of these games included Steffi Graf completing her grand slam-winning year with Olympic gold in tennis; US sprinter Florence Griffith Joyner winning three gold medals and a silver on the track; German speed-skater and cyclist Christa Luding-Rothenburger making Olympic history by winning gold medals in both the summer and winter games, and women winning all three dressage medals for the first time.

Penzance, England, October 12: Children's author Ruth Manning-Sayers dies, aged 93.

USA, October 18: TV sitcom *Roseanne,* starring Roseanne Barr, premieres.

New York, USA, October 22: Ferdinand and Imelda Marcos are indicted on charges of fraud and racketeering.

Buenos Aires, Argentina, November 20: Greek shipping magnate Christina Onassis dies of a heart attack, aged 37.

Leicester, England, November 30: Artist and naturalist Margaret Mee is killed in a car accident.

Pakistan, December 3: Benazir Bhutto is elected Prime Minister.

Stockholm, Sweden, December 10: Gertrude B. Elion co-wins the Nobel Prize in Physiology or Medicine with Sir James Black and George Hitchings for "their discoveries of important principles for drug treatment."

England: Doris Lessing publishes her novel, *The Fifth Child.*

USA: Shirley Temple Black publishes her autobiography, *Child Star.*

Christa Rothenburger

Papal Pronouncement Slams Feminism

Vatican City, August 15: Pope John Paul II today published an apostolic letter in nine chapters—in which he addresses the challenge presented to the church by contemporary feminism—with a theological reflection on the true meaning of womanhood, motherhood and consecrated virginity.

In the letter titled *Mulieris Dignitatem (On the Dignity and Vocation of Women)*,—the Pope calls on women to value their

The newest member of the British royal family, daughter to the Duke and Duchess of York, is named Beatrice Elizabeth Mary.

"feminine genius" as mothers and care-givers, and promotes such feminine qualities as empathy, interpersonal skills, emotional capacity, communication, and their intuition. The letter reflects his belief that men and women are formed as complementary beings whose strengths, weaknesses, and purpose in life are expressed in their physical bodies. He restricts the acceptable vocations of a woman to the categories of mother or virgin, as embodied by Mary, mother of Christ.

Magic Bullet for Fertility Control

France, September: France has become the first western nation to approve the use of the controversial abortion pill RU-486, also known as mifepristone. It is a synthetic steroid compound that is used as an abortifact in the first two months of pregnancy, and in smaller doses as an emergency contraceptive. The steroid compound was discovered by researchers at the Roussel Uclaf (RU) chemical company in France in 1980, with clinical testing beginning in 1982.

The release of the drug has been greeted with both euphoria and outrage. The prospect of an apparently safe and simple alternative to surgical abortion

delights many women and pro-choice advocates who are hailing RU-486 as a miracle drug, a remarkable scientific achievement, and the "magic bullet" of the decade. The drug has not, of course, been welcomed by right-to-life groups. After licensing approval, but before the market release, intense pressure was brought to bear on Roussel Uclaf by pro life groups. Their threat of a boycott induced the company to announce that it would abandon dis-tribution of the drug.

But the French government—a part-owner of Roussel Uclaf—has stepped in to defend the moral right of French women to access the most up-to-date abortion technology, and production and the distribution of RU-486 has resumed. Some observers are sounding a note of caution, however, pointing out that no large-scale testing of the drug has yet been carried out.

Christina Onassis Dies

Buenos Aires, Argentina, November 19: Christina Onassis, daughter of billionaire shipping magnate Aristotle Onassis and Athina Livanos, has died of a heart attack at the age of 37.

New York-born Onassis had a wealthy but disrupted childhood, marked by her parents' bitter divorce in the mid-1960s, extensive media coverage, and years of lonely education in New York and then in Switzerland. In 1968, after a highly publicized courtship, her father Aristotle married Jacqueline Kennedy, the widow of assassinated president John F. Kennedy, thus triggering an increase in the media interest in the Onassis family. In an effort to escape the scrutiny—and a reportedly stormy relationship with her stepmother—Onassis moved to London and enrolled in Queen's College to study fashion. Her formal education ended a few months

later when she dropped out, aged 19. She then began working at her father's headquarters in Monaco, where she proved herself an intelligent, competent business-woman—managing millions of dollars, acquiring ships, and brokering lucrative deals. She was considered a "natural" in the business world, and had evidently inherited her father's good judgment and social skills.

But despite her professional success, Onassis's personal life was troubled. She married four times, each marriage ending in divorce. Her fourth marriage, to Thierry Roussel, produced her only child, a daughter Athina, whom she doted on. Within a period of two years in the early 1970s, Onassis lost her entire immediate family. In 1973, her brother Alexander was killed in a plane crash. The following year her mother died, and her beloved father died in March, 1975. Onassis was plagued with a poor self-image, and used a variety of drugs to control her weight, resulting in struggles with addiction, and dramatic fluctuations in weight which may have contributed to her early death. Athina is now the sole heir to the Onassis fortune.

Tragic Death of Famous Botanist

Leicester, England, November 30: The well-known botanical artist and naturalist Margaret Mee has been killed in a car accident in her native England. Although 79 years old, Mee was still extremely active in her field. She leaves behind

Florence Joyner takes gold at the Olympics.

Gertrude B. Elion co-wins the Nobel Prize in Physiology or Medicine with Sir James Black and George Hitchings for "their discoveries of important principles for drug treatment."

Doris Lessing

400 folios of stunning gouache illustrations, 40 sketchbooks, and 15 diaries, and will be always be remembered for her significant contributions to the field of botanical illustration.

Born in 1909 in Chesham, Buckinghamshire, Margaret Ursula Mee studied art in London at St. Martin's School of Art; Centre School of Art, and Camberwell School of Art. She received a national diploma in painting and design in 1950. In 1952, she and her second husband, Greville, moved to Brazil to teach art, and she began working as a botanical artist at the Instituto de Botânica in São Paulo. In 1958 Margaret Mee made the first of many explorations of the Brazilian jungles, before concentrating her attention on the Amazon River and its tributaries from 1964 to 1988. She explored the river by boat, accompanied only by a local pilot, attempting to create a record of the rare and exotic species of flowers of the Amazon basin before they disappeared as a result of environmental destruction. The best-known publications of these exquisite paintings are *Flowers of the Brazilian Forests* (1968), *Flowers of the Amazon* (1980), and *In Search of Flowers of the Amazon Forest*, which was released in 1988.

Benazir Bhutto Elected Pakistan PM

Pakistan, December 2: Benazir Bhutto has been sworn in as the Prime Minister of Pakistan, making her the first woman—and at 35 the youngest person—to lead a post-colonial Islamic state. Charismatic and glamorous, she is a symbol of modernity and democracy, and a refreshing contrast to mostly male-dominated political establishments in the Islamic world.

Born on June 21, 1953, into an old Pakistani political dynasty, Bhutto is the oldest child of Prime Minister Zulfikar Ali Bhutto and Begum Nusrat Bhutto. Her paternal grandfather was Sir Shah Nawaz Bhutto, a key figure in Pakistan's independence movement. A brilliant student, Bhutto enrolled at Harvard at the age of 16, graduating with a degree in political science in 1973. She went on to take a degree in politics, philosophy, and economics at Oxford University, where she was president of the Oxford Union. In 1977, her father was imprisoned and later executed. During this time Bhutto was imprisoned in Pakistan and spent almost five years in solitary confinement.

Allowed to return to Britain in 1984, she became leader-in-exile of her father's party, the Pakistan People's Party, but was unable to make her political presence felt in Pakistan until the death of General Muhammad Zia-ul-Haq.

The November 16 elections were the first open elections in Pakistan for over a decade. An outspoken advocate for the rights of women, Bhutto has pledged that her new government will improve social, health, and economic conditions for women, and will also repeal the *Hudood* and *Zina* laws which curtail women's rights. Bhutto has also promised to set up women's police stations, courts, and development banks.

It remains to be seen whether these efforts will be successful, as Bhutto's government faces intense opposition from the right-wing religious and political establishment.

"Curly Top" Shirley Tells Her Story

USA: Former child star and Academy Award winner Shirley Temple Black has published her first book, *Child Star: An Autobiography.* This candid memoir chronicles her famous career as a child star of the 1930s and 40s, but completely omits her later career in politics.

Born on April 23, 1928, Shirley Jane Temple enrolled in dance classes at Meglin's dance school in Hollywood at the age of three. She was discovered by a visiting casting director in spite of her attempts to hide behind a piano. Temple began her career in "Baby Burlesks"—short films which spoofed popular movies by remaking them with children—but made her name starring in light-hearted and charming films which offered optimism and escapism at the height of the Depression, and which showcased her talents for singing and tap dancing. Known as "Curly Top" for her blonde ringlets, her appealing lisp and cute songs led to her being adored by millions. Temple earned more than any other actor in Hollywood and her movies restored the Fox studio's waning fortunes.

In 1950 she married Charles Black and in 1967 ran for Congress as a Republican on a platform that strongly supported US involvement in the Vietnam war. She was unsuccessful in the election but went on to hold several diplomatic posts. She was appointed Ambassador to Ghana in 1974, and to Czechoslovakia in 1989, where she witnessed the "velvet revolution." Black has said of her ambassadorship: "That was the best job I ever had!"

Cher wins an Academy Award for *Moonstruck.*

Lucille Ball

Madonna Sells Out, but Pepsi Sells Less

Worldwide, March 2: For a fee of $5 million, pop singer Madonna has released a version of her new hit single, "Like A Prayer," as a commercial for Pepsi-Cola. In the meantime, MTV debuted a second video version of the song that features scenes of burning crosses, and the suggestion of an erotic relationship between Madonna and the Catholic saint, Martin de Porres.

Many consumers have condemned the video as blasphemous, and have mounted a campaign for a worldwide Pepsi boycott. The company has tried to distance itself from the MTV video, but since the music and imagery in both versions are virtually identical, the public is not buying Pepsi's

> *"IF YOU WANT ANYTHING SAID, ASK A MAN. IF YOU WANT ANYTHING DONE, ASK A WOMAN."*
>
> MARGARET THATCHER, BRITISH PRIME MINISTER

Madonna's new song has polarized listeners.

arguments—or its soft drinks. Pepsi is expected to pull the commercial.

Daphne du Maurier Dies

Cornwall, England, April 19: The first lady of modern Gothic fiction, Dame Daphne du Maurier DBE, has died at her home near Fowey in Cornwall. She was 81 years old. Dame Daphne will remembered for her

best-selling novels *Rebecca, Jamaica Inn, Frenchman's Creek,* and the chilling short story *The Birds*—all of which were made into successful motion pictures.

Early in her writing career, Daphne du Maurier discovered that a large segment of the reading public still yearned for "old fashioned" stories that featured love and adventure, a touch of danger, a hint of sexual tension, and perhaps an encounter with the paranormal. Her assessment was apparently correct, because all her novels and short stories proved highly popular with critics and readers alike.

Rebecca will no doubt remain Dame Daphne's undisputed masterpiece. First published in 1938, this vivid tale of suspense, told in the Gothic style, has been a bestseller for nearly 70 years. The film version, directed by Alfred Hitchcock and starring Laurence Olivier, Joan Fontaine, and Dame Judith Anderson as the witchy Mrs. Danvers, is one of the few motion picture versions of her stories that Dame Daphne actually liked.

We Loved Lucy

Hollywood, USA, April 26: America's "Queen of Comedy," the talented Lucille Ball, died early this morning of a ruptured aorta. She was 77 years old.

From 1951 through to 1974 Ball was an almost constant presence on network television, bringing her unique brand of screwball comedy to three different programs: *I Love Lucy* (1951–1957), *The Lucy Show* (1962–1968), and *Here's Lucy* (1968–1974). It was *I Love Lucy* that elevated her to star status, and also had the greatest impact on various aspects of television production. With her husband, Desi Arnaz, Lucille Ball founded Desilu Studios, which was a pioneer in television production during the 1950s and 1960s. For *I Love Lucy*, Ball and Arnaz insisted on using movie-quality film to improve the visual excellence of the show. They hired Karl Freund, the eminent Euro-

Barbara Clementine Harris is now a bishop.

pean-trained cameraman, and he developed the three-camera set-up for long shots, medium shots, and close-ups that has since become the standard for all television sitcoms. In its six-year run, *I Love Lucy* won five Emmys.

Even after her shows ceased production, Ball continued to make a fortune from the re-run rights. It has been said that there has never been a day when an episode from one of Ball's TV sitcoms was not playing somewhere in the world.

In its obituary, the *New York Times* praised Ball for her "impeccable timing, deft pantomime and an endearing talent for making the outrageous believable."

Burmese Dissident Suu Kyi Under House Arrest

Rangoon, Burma (Myanmar), July 20: Today Burma's military dictatorship attempted to silence one of its most vocal critics, by placing Aung Sun Suu Kyi under house arrest. Suu Kyi's detention began just one day after the 42nd anniversary of the assassination of her father, General Aung Sun, the man who negotiated Burma's

USA, January 3: Television evangelists Jim and Tammy-Faye Bakker broadcast for the first time in two years.

Tokyo, Japan, January 7: Emperor Hirohito dies, aged 82.

Washington DC, USA, January 20: Republican George H. W. Bush is inaugurated as the 41st president.

Asuncion, Paraguay, February 3: Alfredo Stroessner, Paraguay's president for 35 years, is overthrown in a military coup.

Connecticut, USA, February 6: Historian Barbara Tuchman dies, aged 77.

Boston, USA, February 11: Barbara Clementine Harris is consecrated as a bishop in the episcopal church.

World, March 2: Madonna's new song "Like a Prayer" premieres on a worldwide Pepsi-Cola commercial.

Prince William Sound, Alaska, USA, March 24: The *Exxon Valdez* oil tanker runs aground, spilling over 11 million gallons (42 million liters) of oil. The captain is alleged to have been intoxicated.

USSR, March 26: The first democratic elections take place to elect the congress of people's deputies. Boris Yeltsin comes out ahead, largely because of his criticism of Mikhail Gorbachev.

New York, USA, March 30: Pulitzer Prizes are awarded to Wendy Wasserstein, for her play *The Heidi Chronicles*, and to Ann Tyler, for her novel *Breathing Lessons*.

Sheffield, England, April 15: The UK's worst sporting disaster occurs when supporters of Liverpool Football Club rush onto an already overcrowded stand. Ninety-four people are killed and 170 injured.

Cornwall, England, April 19: Author Daphne du Maurier dies, aged 81.

Seoul, Korea, April 23: Princess Dok Hye of Korea dies, aged 77.

Hollywood, USA, April 26: Comedian Lucille Ball dies, aged 76.

USA, May 15: The tele-movie *Roe vs Wade*, based on the famous abortion trial, airs on NBC TV.

Los Angeles, USA, May 20: Comedian Gilda Radner dies of ovarian cancer, aged 42.

Poland, June 5: Voters deliver a resounding mandate to the Solidarity party, led by Lech Walesa, in the first free elections.

Tehran, Iran, June 6: Hysterical mourning greets the death of spiritual leader, Ayatollah Seyyed Ruhollah Khomeini, aged 86.

independence from the British. Even after her father's murder, Suu Kyi's family continued to move in the highest levels of Burmese politics. In 1960 her mother, Daw Khin Kyi, was appointed Burma's ambassador to India. Suu Kyi, however, was not particularly political. In 1972 she married Michael Aris, a student of Tibetan civilization. For the next 27 years Aung Sun Suu Kyi lived in India, writing books about the kingdoms of the Himalayas and caring for her husband, and sons Alexander and Kim, but her quiet life ended last year.

In March, Suu Kyi returned home to Rangoon to look after her mother who had suffered a severe stroke. Then, in July, General Ne Win, the dictator of Burma since 1962, stepped down. His rule saw prosperous Burma, which was once well-known as "the rice-bowl of Asia," become an economic basket-case as his army brutally suppressed all forms of dissent, and enslaved, raped, and murdered his opponents in large numbers. The local currency, the *kyat*, is now unrecognized anywhere in the world, and is banned from all foreign currency trading markets. There is a thriving black market which sees the kyat trade at 10 times its official value, and which is based on

> ### time out
> "Only the little people pay taxes." So said New York socialite and hotelier Leona Helmsley when she was sentenced to four years in prison, convicted on over 30 charges of tax evasion and also fined $7.1 million.

smuggled luxury imports, mostly from nearby Thailand and India. Tourist books currently advise travelers that a carton of cigarettes (preferably "555" brand) and a bottle of Johnnie Walker whisky, bought duty-free and then sold on the black market, will be sufficient to fund a seven-day sojourn in the country (one week being the maximum visa limit for most overseas visitors).

With pro-democracy demonstrations breaking out all over Burma, the military has responded with force, and killed thousands of protesters. The violent crackdown inspired Suu Kyi to publish an open letter to the government which called for free elections. Some days later, she delivered her first major address to hundreds of thousands of supporters at the Shwedagon pagoda, calling for democracy in Burma.

As the military responded with more arrests and killings of pro-democracy activists, Suu Kyi founded the National League for Democracy (NLD), establishing a Gandhi-style policy of non-violence and civil disobedience. Today it is obvious that Suu Kyi's NLD party has overwhelming support among voters in Burma. With the national election due in ten months, it is apparent that the arrest of Suu Kyi is

a military ploy designed to intimidate her supporters and to quash dissent.

The "Ice Maiden" of Tennis Quits

Queens, New York, USA, September: At the completion of this year's US Open tennis tournament, Chris Evert—the six-time winner of the event and former world Number 1—announced her retirement. During her 20 years in the sport, Evert has won $8,896,195 in prize money and

Princess Anne

Tennis champion Chris Evert with Zena Garrison.

racked up a record 157 professional singles titles. The statistics for her career are an unprecedented 1,309 wins and 146 losses, a winning average of 0.8966, the highest in the history of professional women's tennis. Evert brought a calm, quiet, steely determination to her game, earning her the nickname "Ice Maiden." She was a powerhouse on all court surfaces, but excelled on clay courts—from August 1973 to May 12, 1979, she won a record 125 consecutive matches on clay. Chris Evert won the Wimbledon championship three times, and did not lose one singles match in the Wightman Cup competition from 1971 to 1982.

Jane Foster and Deanna Brasseur are now qualified CF-18 jet fighter pilots.

Gro Harlem Brundtland

First Lady of Film is Dead

Neuilly-sur-Seine, France, October 6: Screen doyenne Bette Davis has succumbed to breast cancer at the American Hospital in Neuilly-sur-Seine, aged 81.

By turns glamorous and combative, tough and seductive, Bette Davis's career on stage and screen spanned some 66 years, and she became one of the world's most admired, dreaded, and mimicked actresses. Nominated for 11 Academy Awards, she won two—as best actress for *Jezebel* (1938) and *Dangerous* (1935). In a candid conversation with Hollywood producer Jack Warner during the 1940s, Davis confessed that audiences always responded best to her "bitch" perform-ances. And she was right—among her most memorable roles are the scheming Regina in *The Little Foxes* (1941) and the temperamental Margot Channing in *All About Eve* (1950). But she also moved audiences with her performances in *Dark Victory* (1939) and *Now, Voyager* (1942).

In 1981 Davis found an entirely new audience among teenagers, thanks the publicity arising from pop singer Kim Carnes's worldwide hit *Bette Davis Eyes*.

The 1980s were difficult—she suffered a stroke, was diagnosed with breast can-cer, and saw her daughter, B.D. Hyman, publish a scandal-mongering account of her life. In response, the star published a rebuke of her daughter, then disinherited her. Bette Davis composed her own epi-taph: "She did it the hard way."

> *"EVERYBODY HAS A HEART. EXCEPT SOME PEOPLE."*
>
> BETTE DAVIS,
> AMERICAN ACTRESS

Prime Minister Brundtland Steps Down

Oslo, Norway, October 16: Dr. Gro Harlem Brundtland, now 51, has completed her second term as prime minister of Norway. She commenced her first term in 1981, when she was 41 years old—making her the first woman and the youngest prime minister in the history of Norway. During her term of office Dr Brundtland brought eight women into her cabinet as ministers.

Dr Brundtland trained as a physician at the University of Oslo, then went on to earn a masters degree in public health at Harvard University. In 1983, as a result of her interest in the link between public health issues and the environment, she was invited to help establish the World Commission on Environment and De-velopment for the United Nations.

"Guildford Four" Freed: Police Perjury Exposed

London, England, October 19: Today Carole Richarson, Gerard Conlon, Patrick Armstrong, and Paul Hill, popularly known as the "Guildford Four," returned to the courtroom at the Old Bailey in London where 15 years earlier they were convicted of killing five people and injur-ing 65 in a series of pub bombings in Guildford and Woolwich. As Geoffrey Dawson Lane, the Lord Chief Justice, reviewed the false confessions and false evidence produced by the police, Carole Richardson—who was only 17 years old at the time of her conviction—began to weep uncontrollably.

In the aftermath of the 1975 bombings, the police arrested Richardson and her boyfriend, Patrick Armstrong. The two were petty criminals who had been living in a "squat," or abandoned house. At their trial they strongly protested their inno-cence, saying that they were not members of the Provisional Irish Republican Army, which claimed credit for the bombings, and that they had signed their confessions only after they had been tortured by the police. Nevertheless, the pair was found guilty of murder and given a sentence of life imprisonment. The judge said that he regretted they had not been found guilty of treason, which would have enabled him to impose the death sentence. A number of appeals to higher courts and authorities followed over the next 15 years, but it was not until earlier this year that a detective who was examining Pat-rick Armstrong's file discovered that the police had rewritten substantial portions of the notes taken during Armstrong's interrogation, which suggested that the police had deliberately manufactured evidence against the four.

As he ordered the release of Carole Richardson and the others, Dawson declared, "If [the police] were prepared to tell these sort of lies, then the whole of their evidence must be suspect."

Romanian "Perfect 10" Gymnast Defects to USA

New York, New York, USA, December 1: The gymnast Nadia Comaneci, who at the age of 14 at the 1976 Montreal Olympics won three gold medals and achieved the first-

Nadia Comaneci demonstrates her gymnastic skills.

ever perfect score of 10 in an Olympic gymnastics event, has joined the tens of thousands of eastern Europeans who have been flooding into the west since the Berlin Wall fell on November 9. Traveling from her home in Romania via Hungary and Austria, Comaneci has defected to the United States of America.

At Montreal, Nadia Comaneci won everybody's hearts, and their admiration, with perfect scores in the uneven parallel bars, beam, vault, and all-around floor disciplines, winning the gold medal for the latter three. She quickly became a media favorite. Comaneci also retained her beam and floor gold medals in the 1980 Olympics in Moscow.

Bette Davis, the queen of the silver screen.

Were it not for the revolutions that are toppling Communist governments across eastern Europe, Nadia Comaneci would still be a virtual prisoner in her own country. Her troubles with the Romanian Communist government began in 1981 when she traveled to the US on a gymnastics exhibition tour. During the tour Nadia's two coaches, Béla and Marta Károlyi, and the Romanian gymnastics team's choreographer, Geza Pozar, defected. Following this, her movements were closely monitored by government agents and she was forbidden to leave the country. In 1984 she was permitted to attend the Olympic Games in Los Angeles, but again, government agents followed her everywhere she went. In recent times, Comaneci has been an international judge, and coach of the Romanian national gymnastics team.

It is not known where Comaneci will settle in the US, but rumors are circulating that she has been in contact with her fellow gymnast and Olympic gold medalist, Bart Conner. There are whispers that the diminutive star may be planning to launch a modeling career.

Romanian Rebels Execute Tyrants

Bucharest, Romania, December 25: The couple who ruled Romania with a brutal ferocity—Elena and Nicolae Ceausescu—were executed by firing squad today at the Tirgoviste military base. Their downfall came very quickly—just seven days ago, as Nicolae was leaving the country to visit Iran, he instructed Elena to crush an uprising among the workers at the industrial town of Timisoara. Elena called out the military, and tried to turn the strikers against one another by spreading rumors that they had been duped by agitators. However, her strategy failed. Within just 48 hours a full-blown revolution against Communism in general—and the Ceausescus in particular—was sweeping across Romania. This sudden turn of affairs stunned Nicolae and enraged Elena.

For decades, sycophants have referred to Elena Ceausescu as "the best mother Romania could have," but in real life she was as far from being maternal as it is possible to be. During the 1970s and 1980s, she banned any form of artifical birth control, leading to thousands of unwanted infants and children living in deplorable conditions in state-run orphanages. As head of the state health

Elena and Nicolae Ceausescu's brutal reign ends with their execution.

ministry she refused to permit AIDS prevention education or even treatments for the disease, insisting that AIDS did not exist in Romania. In the 1980s, Elena herself ruthlessly ordered the destruction of the villages of ethnic minorities, razed churches and other sacred sites, and then instituted a system of food rationing that brought large segments of Romanian society to the very brink of starvation.

On December 22, as many hundreds of thousands of citizens of Bucharest took over the capital, the Ceausescus hurriedly escaped from the city by helicopter—or so they thought. Their pilot was not a sympathizer, and landed the helicopter near the town of Tirgoviste, forcing the couple out. They were then picked up by waiting local police and taken to a nearby military base. After a very quick trial, the Ceausescus were charged and convicted of genocide, and sentenced to death. Nicolae was 71, Elena 73. There are few in Romania, or indeed the rest of the world, who will mourn their deaths.

Hanan al-Shaykh's New Novel Released

Mary McCarthy

Beirut, Lebanon: Hanan al-Shaykh, a Lebanese novelist and journalist living in London, has just published her fifth novel, *Misk al-Ghazal (Women of Sand and Myrrh.)* Al-Shaykh has set her story in an unnamed Middle Eastern country where four women are trying to gain some degree of control over their lives. Nur resents being hemmed in by Arab cultural traditions, Tamr struggles to make her beauty shop a success, Suha misses the independence she enjoyed when she lived in Lebanon, and the only American among the four, Suzanne, compensates for her unhappy marriage with a series of extramarital affairs.

For this novel Hanan Al-Shaykh drew upon her own experiences. She grew up in a conservative Shi'ite family in Beirut, where her father and brother attempted to limit her freedom and force her into the subservient role that they believed was a woman's destiny.

Al-Shaykh sold her first essays to a newspaper when she was only 16 years old. After studying at the American College for Girls in Cairo, she returned to Beirut to take a job in television, then became a journalist for two magazines, *Al-Hasna* and *Al-Nahar.* She published her first novel, *Intihar Rajul Mayyit (Suicide of a Dead Man)* in 1967. It is the story of a middle-aged man obsessed with a young girl, and it set the stage for themes that Al-Shaykh has returned to again and again in her fiction—sex and male power in the Islamic world.

The funeral procession for Korea's Princess Dok Hye, the last princess of the Yi Dynasty.

Carole Gist

> "MAYBE THE
> MOST THAT
> YOU CAN
> EXPECT FROM A
> RELATIONSHIP
> THAT GOES BAD
> IS TO COME OUT
> OF IT WITH A
> FEW GOOD
> SONGS."
>
> MARIANNE FAITHFULL
> BRITISH SINGER

Women to Serve on Royal Navy Ships

Scotland, January: A memorandum from Admiral Sir Brian Brown, the Second Sea Lord, has stated that in response to an estimated 300 manpower "gaps" at sea—that include shortages in every officer and ranking category—the Royal Navy will permit women in the Women's Royal Navy Service (WRNS) to serve at sea for the first time.

The decision is a controversial one. Concerns have been aired that placing women on combat ships may harm a warship's operational effectiveness, and some say that women should be able to serve at sea during times of peace, but withdrawn if a ship is ordered into battle. However, others believe that such an arrangement would damage the credibility of the WRNS, whose members could be viewed merely as "fair weather sailors."

Chamorro Defeats Ortega in Election Shock

Managua, Nicaragua, February 25: In a shock election victory today, Violeta Barrios de Chamorro, the former editor of her family's newspaper *La Prensa*—which she transformed into a platform for

Mourners at the graveside of actress Ava Gardner.

Violeta Chamorro defeats Sandinista's Daniel Ortega.

Nicaragua's opposition—has led the National Opposition Union to victory over Daniel Ortega's Sandinista National Liberation Front. The victory makes Chamorro Central America's first female head of government.

After Ortega's Sandinista regime bowed to international pressure and announced free elections, Chamorro began to cobble together her loose coalition of 14 opposition parties into the National Opposition Union. Its disparate membership ranges from right-wing businessmen and ranchers to the Communist Party, united by the singular aim of removing the Sandinistas from power.

Chamorro was born in 1930, one of seven children in a wealthy ranching family in the southern Nicaraguan town of Rivas. Her family sent her to the United States where she received her education at a Catholic girls' school in San Antonio, Texas, and was attending college in Virginia until she returned home in 1948 after her father

suffered a heart attack. The following year she met the dynamic Pedro Chamorro whose family were vocal critics of the dictatorial regime of Antonio Somoza, and who owned the anti-government newspaper *La Prensa*. After the death of her husband, Chamorro became a member of the Sandinista junta that replaced Somoza, but resigned shortly afterwards, angry at the level of Sandinista influence in the new government.

Chamorro plans to reduce the size of the military, end compulsory military service, and bring peace to a nation wracked by ten years of civil war.

Veteran Tandy wins Best Actress Oscar

Hollywood, USA, March 26: Jessica Tandy, 80, became the oldest recipient of a best actress Oscar today when she won the award for her performance as an independent, eccentric, southern US Jewish woman in the touching Bruce Beresford-directed film *Driving Miss Daisy*.

Beresford's simple, sentimental adaptation of Alfred Uhry's Pulitzer Prize-winning play about the complex 25-year relationship between an African-American chauffeur (Morgan Freeman) and a feisty widowed grandmother (Tandy), is a multi-layered film about friendship, ageing, and racial inequality—and a deft portrayal of decades of social change in the southern US.

Tandy was born in London on July 7, 1909, and studied drama at the Ben Greet Academy of Acting. She debuted on stage in London at the age of 16 and took her first bows on Broadway at 21. Primarily a stage actor, she has been married to the Canadian actor Hume Cronyn since 1942. Tandy received great acclaim for her performance as Blanche DuBois in the

time out

Politician and porn star Anna Ilona Staller ("Cicciolina") engaged in a political stunt to rival Lady Godiva by riding through Italian streets topless, declaring she would make love to Saddam Hussein to achieve peace in the Middle East.

Western Europe, January 25: Forty-seven die in the UK and up to three million trees are uprooted as hurricane-force winds cause havoc.

London, England, January 25: Film star Ava Gardner dies, aged 67.

Scotland, January: Women in the Royal Navy are allowed to serve at sea for the first time.

Cape Town, South Africa, February 11: Nelson Mandela is released from jail after 27 years.

Managua, Nicaragua, February 25: Violeta Chamorro defeats Sandinista leader Daniel Ortega in the first free elections since 1979.

Canberra, Australia, February 28: Deirdre O'Connor is instated as Australia's first female federal court judge.

Witchita, Kansas, USA, March 2: Carole Gist is crowned Miss USA, the first African-American woman to win the pageant.

Washington DC, USA, March 9: Antonia Novello is sworn in as the first woman US surgeon-general.

Vilnius, Lithuania, March 11: The tiny Baltic republic declares itself independent after half a century of Soviet rule.

Haiti, March 13: Dame Ertha Pascal-Trouillot is sworn in as interim president.

Australia, March 26: The Labor government of Bob Hawke wins a record fourth term.

Hollywood, USA, March 26: At the age of 80 years and 252 days, Jessica Tandy becomes the oldest person to win the Best Actress Oscar.

Hollywood, USA, March 26: *Driving Miss Daisy*, starring Morgan Freeman and Jessica Tandy, wins four Oscars.

San Marino, April 1: Gloriana Ranocchini ends her tenure as co-Captain-Regent.

German Democratic Republic, April 5: Sabine Bergmann-Pohl begins her tenure as chairman of the Volkskammer.

Kathmandu, Nepal, April 8: King Birendra lifts a 30-year ban on political parties and agrees to end the country's feudal-style rule.

New York, USA, April 15: Actress Greta Garbo dies, aged 84.

Moscow, Russia, May 29: "Radical" Boris Yeltsin is elected president of the Russian republic, successfully challenging Mikhail Gorbachev.

Portland, Oregon, USA, June 4: Fifty-four-year-old Alzheimer's sufferer Janet Adkins ends her life using a suicide machine.

Iran, June 22: A massive earthquake in the northwest of the country leaves 40,000 dead and 100,000 injured.

Jessica Tandy wins Best Actress Academy Award for *Driving Miss Daisy*.

stage version of Tennessee Williams's *A Streetcar Named Desire* in 1947, and as Amanda Wingfield in Williams's *The Glass Menagerie*—though she refutes the claim that she seems to be typecast in the role of a southern belle. "I have just had some very good southern parts."

East Germany Elects Female President

German Democratic Republic, April 5: In the wake of the German Democratic Republic's first democratic parliamentary elections on March 18, the conservative politician Sabine Bergmann-Pohl was today elected president of the Volkskammer, the people's chamber of parliament. Her election makes her the first woman in the short history of the Soviet satellite state to hold the post.

Bergmann-Pohl leads the Volkskammer into a new era where the democratic push for change has led some commentators to predict reunification with West Germany

by the end of this year. If so, her tenure is likely to be a short one. Until last month's election, the Volkskammer existed only to rubber-stamp the decisions made by the council of ministers, the council of state, or specific departments within the central committee of the Socialist Unity Party, all of which have been abolished by today's vote. Bergmann-Pohl is expected to quickly offer an apology to Jews and to the people of the Soviet Union for Nazi atrocities during World War II, and to acknowledge the complicity of East Germany in the 1968 invasion of Czechoslovakia.

Born on April 20, 1946 in Eisenach, East Germany, Bergmann-Pohl studied medicine and specialized in pneumology. She became a member of the Christian Democratic Party in 1981, which in turn became the largest party in the Volkskammer after last month's vote.

Suicide By Machine For Alzheimer's Patient

Portland, Oregon, USA, June 4: Janet Adkins, a 54-year-old Portland resident recently diagnosed with the neurodegenerative Alzheimer's disease, has ended her life with the assistance of a so-called "suicide machine" developed by the Michigan-based pathologist Dr Jack Kevorkian. Adkins was mentally competent and resolute in her decision, being in the early stages of the illness. Married with three sons, Adkins taught piano, trekked in the Nepalese Himalayas, climbed Oregon's Mt Hood, enjoyed hang gliding, and

wanted to die before the disease robbed her of her memory and competence.

Despite the objections of her own sons as well as various doctors, and still having a life expectancy of some ten years, Adkins contacted Dr Kevorkian and arranged a meeting. Last night, in Detroit, Michigan, Adkins went to dinner with her family, friends, and Dr Kevorkian, with whom she rhapsodized about the music of Bach. She also composed a suicide note, stating that her decision was fully considered and that she was in full control of her faculties.

This morning in a Detroit park, an intravenous line was inserted into a vein, electrodes were attached to her wrists and ankles, and a syringe was inserted into her arm. Adkins then pulled down on a lever protruding from a wooden, three-sided box designed by Kevorkian that cut off the supply of saline, and opened an adjoining line to a bottle of pentothal, which put her to sleep.

After one minute, a timing device introduced a mix of potassium chloride and succinylcholine. Six minutes later an EEG showed that Adkins's heart had stopped. Dr Kevorkian immediately reported her death to police, and it is expected that the state of Michigan will soon bring murder charges against the former pathologist.

Antonia Novello

Sabine Bergmann-Pohl, chairwoman of the Volkskammer.

Otago, New Zealand, June 29: Penny Jamieson is consecrated Bishop of Dunedin.

Mecca, Saudi Arabia, July 2: Fourteen hundred pilgrims are crushed to death in a tunnel leading to Islam's holiest site.

London, England, July 7: Martina Navratilova wins the Wimbledon singles title for a record-breaking ninth time.

Kuwait, August 2: Iraqi troops invade, meeting with little resistance.

Pakistan, August 6: President Ghulam Ishaq Kahn dismisses Premier Benazir Bhutto amid corruption allegations.

South Africa, August 24: Following two weeks of violence that has left 500 dead, a state of emergency is imposed on 27 townships.

Guatemala City, Guatemala, September 11: Sociologist Myrna Mack Chang is stabbed to death.

Germany, October 3: East and West Germany reunify.

New Zealand, November 2: Ruth Richardson becomes the first female Minister of Finance.

Oslo, Norway, November 3: Gro Harlem Brundtland commences her third term as prime minister.

Riyadh, Saudi Arabia, November 6: Around 50 Saudi women dismiss their drivers and drive their own vehicles in a convoy, in a rebellion against the law which precludes women from driving. Their protest ends after police stop them.

Dublin, Ireland, November 8: Mary Robinson is elected president.

Paris, France, November 19: The Cold War officially ends with 22 heads of state agreeing to dismantle their arsenals.

London, England, November 27: John Major becomes leader of the Conservative Party following Margaret Thatcher's resignation.

New Zealand, December 1: Dr Elizabeth Morgan is granted custody of her daughter, after spending nearly two years in prison for refusing to reveal the girl's whereabouts. She alleged that her ex-husband was abusing the child.

Poland, December 9: Lech Walesa, the founder of the Solidarity Union, is elected President.

New Zealand, December 12: Catherine Tizard is appointed Governor-General.

Missouri, USA, December 26: Nancy Cruzan dies 12 days after a judge agreed to allow her family to remove the feeding tube which was keeping her alive.

Anthropologist Murdered in Guatemala

Guatemala City, Guatemala, September 11: Myrna Mack Chang, the 40-year-old anthropologist who produced pioneering studies into the destructive effects of armed conflict on rural populations, was brutally murdered in Guatemala City tonight by two assailants as she was leaving her office to return home. The attack was particularly vicious, with 27 stab wounds inflicted upon Chang's neck, thorax, and abdomen. Her assailants fled the scene, stealing her purse, a plastic bag, and Chang's personal portfolio.

Her death comes just two days after the publication of a report for which she was a principal advisor. Titled "Assistance and Control: Policies towards Internally Displaced Populations in Guatemala," and published by the Georgetown University Press, it detailed the murder of as many as 200,000 Mayan civilians at the hands of government forces and military death squads during the 30-year period of Guatemala's civil unrest.

Chang was a founding member of the Guatemalan research group AVANCSO, for which she published the ground-breaking paper last year. It detailed how the government's counter-insurgency policies caused enormous suffering, and bemoaned the displacement of Guatemala's indigenous communities in Ixil in Quichi Guatemala, describing their legal marginalization since they returned to Guatemala from exile in Mexico. Chang's

work led her to confront the full horror of her government's repression as she traveled to rural communities, and listened to the testimony of villagers forced to abandon their ancestral homes. In the reporting of these testimonies and the resultant exposure of the barbaric policies of the Guatemalan regime, Chang became an enemy of the state.

Chang was born in 1949 in the town of Barrio San Nicholas to a mixed Mayan/Chinese family, and studied anthropology in the UK at Durham University and the University of Manchester.

Female Finance Minister for New Zealand

New Zealand, November 2: After bringing an end to six years of Labour rule on October 27 with the largest landslide in New Zealand political history, the National Party leader and new prime minister Jim Bolger announced the appointment of Ruth Richardson as Finance Minister.

New Zealand's first female finance minister has inherited an economy in deep recession, with a ballooning budget deficit and a recently devalued credit rating. She has indicated that she will take up the reformist baton of England's Margaret Thatcher and initiate steep cuts in welfare programs, and shake up New Zealand's labor laws in the hope of slashing the deficit and stimulating growth. A staunch free-market reformer, Richardson was born in southern Taranaki on December 13, 1950. She

Benazir Bhutto

UK Prime Minister Margaret Thatcher resigns.

earned a law degree from the University of Canterbury and was elected to parliament in 1981.

Saudi Women Flout Driving Ban

Riyadh, Saudi Arabia, November 6: In open defiance of a long-held Saudi law that prohibits women from driving cars, a group of 50 Saudi women have dismissed their drivers and driven their own vehicles in a convoy—until they were stopped by police. Their passports have been confiscated and they will be spending one day in jail.

Saudi Arabia is the only country in the world where it is illegal for a woman to drive. Saudi lawmakers feel that if women are allowed to drive, they may be tempted to leave home by themselves without a male escort, thus risking encounters with men outside of their own families that could lead them into temptation and improper conduct. When a member of the Saudi Arabia consultative council recently suggested that perhaps it was time to look at the possibility of allowing women over the age of 35 or 40 to drive cars within city limits, but not on highways, there were calls for his resignation and the confiscation of his passport.

The issue resurfaced recently when it was announced a woman had taken control of her car and driven to a nearby

South African anti-apartheid activists protest against two weeks of township violence between rival factions.

Screen legend Greta Garbo dies in New York.

hospital after her husband suffered a heart attack at the wheel. The government announced that it will not press charges against her.

Mary Robinson Elected Irish President

Dublin, Ireland, November 8: In Ireland's first contested presidential election for 17 years, human rights lawyer and activist Mary Robinson—who has fought the Irish government's positions on divorce, contraception, and homosexuality—was today elected the seventh president of the Irish Republic. Robinson, a nominee of both the Socialist Workers' Party and the Labour Party, entered the contest as a 100/1 outsider, but won with 52.8 percent of the vote, defeating the former deputy prime minister and defense minister Brian Leniham, of the governing Fianna Fáil party.

Born in Ballina, Ireland, on May 21, 1944, Robinson is the first woman to hold the largely ceremonial role. She was educated at Trinity College, where she then held the post of Reid Professor of constitutional, criminal, and European law. In 1970 the then Mary Bourke married Nicholas Robinson, and in 1988 they co-founded the Irish Centre for European Law. In 1969 she was elected to the Irish senate where she served until 1989 when, to the surprise of many, she chose not to seek re-election.

Robinson will be inaugurated on December 3. Her election represents a shift in the traditional values and social norms of Irish society, and Robinson seems certain to apply her liberal leanings to the office.

Epic International Custody Battle Resolved

New Zealand, December 1: Dr Elizabeth Morgan, the plastic surgeon who spent 25 months in jail for refusing to reveal the whereabouts of her daughter Hilary—who she believed had been sexually abused by her father, Dr Morgan's ex-husband Dr Eric Foretich—has been granted custody of her daughter by a New Zealand court.

Dr Morgan sent her daughter to live with her grandparents in New Zealand rather than allow Foretich the access visits ordered by a District of Columbia superior court, and was imprisoned for contempt of court in 1987. In 1989 Morgan's lawyers argued that her incarceration violated her constitutional rights. She was released on September 25, 1989, after the Congress passed a bill limiting to 12 months the amount of time a person can serve in prison on civil contempt charges. It was a bill tailored to free her from jail, but not before she had endured the longest period of imprisonment for contempt of court in American history.

Morgan emerged from prison a heroine to women's groups across the country. In response to her claims that he had molested Hilary almost since infancy, Dr Foretich has steadfastly maintained his innocence. In 1985 Foretich was granted unsupervised visits with Hilary during vacations and on alternate weekends, after evidence on the question of abuse proved inconclusive. Dr Morgan's reaction to this finding was to send her daughter into hiding.

Coma Victim's Family Pulls the Plug

Missouri, USA, December 26: In Jasper County, Missouri, on the night of January 11, 1983, Nancy Cruzan lost control of

her car, and was found by paramedics face down in a ditch with no apparent respiratory or cardiac function. It was later estimated that her brain had been deprived of oxygen for almost 14 minutes. Revived at the scene, she was transported to a nearby hospital where she was diagnosed with severe cerebral contusions compounded by a lack of oxygen. With the permission of her husband, surgeons implanted feeding and hydration tubes into Cruzan, who remained in a coma for three weeks before regressing to a vegetative state.

The battle by Cruzan's family to allow Nancy to die with dignity has been a long and complex one. Five years after the accident, with Cruzan's condition unchanged, her parents went before a Missouri circuit court judge who ruled that they could, on their daughter's behalf, have the feeding tubes removed. This decision was successfully appealed to the Missouri supreme court by the state attorney-general, the court ruling that the state's interest in keeping Nancy Cruzan alive outweighed her right to refuse treatment. After having been kept alive in a persistent vegetative state for seven years, Nancy Cruzan died peacefully today at the age of 33 in a Missouri nursing home, twelve days after the state of Missouri withdrew its objections to the removal of feeding tubes. Cruzan's family produced evidence that she no longer wished to go on living, and would not have wanted to be kept alive by artificial means.

The case has sparked an intense national debate over the right to die, as well as the circumstances under which families can choose to withdraw medical treatment. The American Hospital Association estimates that some 70 percent of hospital deaths are in part pre-determined by consultation between families and attending doctors.

Dr Elizabeth Morgan

Nancy Cruzan's parents discuss the right-to-die case of their daughter, who is being kept alive by artificial means.

Susan Faludi

Ogata Made Commissioner for Refugees

United Nations, January 1: The Japanese academic Sadako Ogata today began her three-year tenure as the United Nations High Commissioner for Refugees, after being elected to the post by the UN General Assembly in December.

Ogata was born in 1927 to a prominent Tokyo family, and developed a keen interest in foreign affairs from an early age. She has proved a popular choice and brings with her an intimate understanding of the UN's bureaucratic processes. From 1982–85 she was Japan's representative on the UN Commission on Human Rights (UNCHR), and in 1990 was an independent expert of the UNCHR in Myanmar (Burma). Her past appointments include dean of the faculty of

time out

Édith Cresson is the first woman French prime minister. Appointed by President François Mitterrand on May 15 , her views are considered by many as conservative and racist.

foreign studies at Sophia University in Tokyo, and associate professor in diplomatic history and international relations at the International Christian University, also in Tokyo. She has been awarded 13 honorary degrees from universities around the world as well as earning a masters degree in international relations from Georgetown University in Washington DC, and a doctorate in political science from the University of California at Berkeley in 1963.

Ogata takes up her post at a pivotal time for a UN still embroiled in the aftermath of the Gulf War. Four hundred thousand Kurds remain trapped in northern Iraq, but are not technically refugees, which means that they fall outside the mandate of the UNCHR. She also faces refugee crises in Rwanda, Afghanistan, Burundi, Bosnia, and Mozambique.

Ogata believes that all refugee crises are political in nature, and that they begin when governments act aggressively towards their own citizens, and also when basic rights are denied. She is acutely aware that the welfare of every refugee—in every corner of the world— is now her responsibility.

> "IT IS NOT POWER THAT CORRUPTS, BUT FEAR. FEAR OF LOSING POWER CORRUPTS."
>
> AUNG SAN SUU KYI, NOBEL PEACE PRIZE WINNER AND PRO-DEMOCRACY ACTIVIST

Sadako Ogata, UN High Commissioner for Refugees.

Cancer Beats Dame Margot Fonteyn

Panama, February 21: Dame Margot Fonteyn, who devoted her entire career to Britain's Royal Ballet and was known as the greatest ballerina of her generation, has died of cancer at the age of 71. Fonteyn had a tumor in her left leg, but refused to have an amputation. She passed away today with instructions that her ashes be placed at the foot of her husband Roberto Aria's tomb in a small cemetery on the outskirts of Panama City, rather than in Westminster Abbey.

The legendary Dame Margot Fonteyn dies.

Her dancing was the personification of grace and lyricism. When she first danced with the Russian dancer Rudolph Nureyev in 1962 in a performance of *Giselle*, the Russian dropped to his knees during the curtain calls and kissed her hands. Her collaboration with Nureyev will long be remembered as one of ballet's greatest and most stimulating partnerships. At their peak they were regarded as being without peer in the dancing world. They remained friends, with Nureyev often visiting her at her ranch in Panama, and paying many of the prima ballerina's medical bills in her final years.

Faludi Denies Feminist Struggle Has Been Won

New York, USA, March: Author Susan Faludi has become a spokeswoman for a growing popular movement against "excessive" feminism. She has also won the National Book Critic's Circle Award for her latest

Kuwait, January 16: A US-led coalition launches an offensive to liberate Kuwait following Iraq's failure to comply with UN deadline for withdrawal.

Mogadishu, Somalia, January 27: General Mohamed Siad Barre flees the capital after 21 years of brutal rule over the East African country.

Haiti, February 7: Ertha Pascal-Trouillot completes her term as interim prime minister.

Panama, February 21: Dame Margot Fonteyn dies, aged 71.

Bangkok, Thailand, February 23: With King Bhumibol's support, the military overthrows the government. Martial law is declared.

Kuwait, February 28: US president George Bush announces the end of the war to liberate Kuwait.

New York, USA, March: The National Book Critics Circle Award goes to *Backlash: The Undeclared War on American Women*, by Susan Faludi.

Los Angeles, USA, March 15: Four police officers are indicted for the beating of Rodney King. The event was captured on video.

Bangladesh, March 20: Khaleda Zia becomes the country's first woman prime minister.

World, April: Japanese academic Sadako Ogata is elected United Nations High Commissioner for Refugees.

Tbilisi, Georgia, April 9: After 70 years of Soviet rule, independence from Moscow is declared. Ninety percent of voters support change.

Cannes, France, May: Women's buddy film *Thelma and Louise* premieres.

South Africa, May 14: Winnie Mandela is given a six-year jail term for kidnapping.

Paris, France, May 15: Édith Cresson is appointed Prime Minister.

Washington DC, USA, May 16: Queen Elizabeth II is the first British monarch to address the US Congress.

Space, May 18: Helen Sharman becomes the first Briton in space.

India, May 21: Former PM Rajiv Gandhi is assassinated. Tamil separatists are suspected.

India, May 22: Rajiv Gandhi's widow, Sonia, is designated to lead the her husband's party through the elections, but she declines the position.

Ethiopia, May 25: After Stalinist dictator Mengitsu Haile Mariam flees, Israeli forces airlift 15,000 black Jews, known as *flashas*, out of the country in 21 hours.

London, England, June 14: Actress Dame Peggy Ashcroft dies, aged 83.

South Africa, June 17: The apartheid law classifying citizens by race is repealed.

work, titled *Backlash: The Undeclared War on American Women.*

Faludi's investigative work examines myths that women's social and economic status are improving, and has turned the author into something of a feminist icon. It is an exhaustively documented and researched book that challenges many of the conventional assumptions surrounding the women's movement in America, and the supposed corporate and social advances that have been claimed. She also challenges a prevailing assumption that the feminist movement is largely responsible for the unhappiness of American women—rather that the reason for any despondency, perceived or real, is that the struggle is far from over.

Faludi was born into a Jewish family in 1959 in Queens, New York. Her father, a survivor of the Nazi holocaust, was a photographer, her mother a journalist.

Road movie *Thelma and Louise* premieres at Cannes.

She graduated in history and literature from Harvard University in 1981, having served as managing editor of the university's magazine *The Crimson*. She also writes for the *Miami Herald*, *Wall Street Journal*, and *New York Times*.

Bangladesh Elects First Woman Prime Minister

Bangladesh, March 20: Khaleda Zia ur-Rahman has today been sworn in as the first female Prime Minister of Bangladesh after leading her Bangladesh Nationalist Party (BNP) to a thumping victory in last month's parliamentary elections.

Zia was born in 1945, the third of five children, in the Dinajpur district of India, and attended the Dinajpur missionary school. She was thrust into the mainstream of Bangladeshi politics after her husband, the leader of the opposition, was brutally assassinated on May 30, 1981. Zia was determined to continue with her husband's vision of a free and democratic Bangladesh, and agreed to become leader of the BNP. During her time in opposition Zia was instrumental in forming a seven-party alliance which last month saw the defeat of the autocratic government of general Hossain Mohamad Ershad.

Her path to victory has been long and tortuous; she was arrested eight times in nine years, and has endured continual harassment and repression at the hands of the Ershad regime. Responding to the wishes of the people, Zia has promised to introduce an historic constitutional amendment guaranteeing the transformation of the executive branch of government from a presidential model into a parliamentary democracy, similar to the Westminster system.

Among other social reforms, she has promised to introduce free and compulsory primary education for all children, and free education for girls up to 16 years of age.

Winnie Mandela to Appeal Kidnapping Charge

South Africa, May 14: Winnie Mandela, the wife of anti-apartheid campaigner Nelson Mandela, today received a six-year jail term for kidnapping and assault. The African National Congress has reacted with dismay, and Mandela emerged from court claiming that she and her two co-accused had been found guilty in a trumped-up "trial by media." She will appeal the decision.

Khaleda Zia ur-Rahman

The severity of the sentence came as a shock to many, largely because Mandela had already been found guilty on the lesser charge of conspiring to kidnap, for which she was sentenced to five years imprisonment, with an additional 12 months for being an accessory after the fact to assault. Justice Stegman ruled, however, that her position of leadership served to compound her culpability. Mrs Mandela was implicated in the kidnapping of four youths from the township of Soweto. They were taken to a room next door to Mrs Mandela's house and beaten, and one of them, 14-year-old Stompie Moeketsi, later died of his injuries.

Winnie Mandela is sentenced to a six-year jail term.

Key Events

London, England, June 28: Margaret Thatcher announces her retirement from the House of Commons at the general election.
England, July 23: Australian Susie Maroney completes the fastest return crossing of the English Channel, in 17 hours and 13 minutes.
Tokyo, Japan, August 31: Algerian Hassiba Boulmerka wins gold in the 1,500 meters at the World Track and Field Championship, the first time a woman from an Arab nation has won an event in the history of these championships.

Poland, September: The Polish government discontinues its subsidy of birth-control medication, resulting in a threefold price increase.
USA, September: Patty Wagstaff becomes the first woman to win the National Aerobatics Championship.
USSR, September 5: The Congress of People's Deputies votes for the dissolution of the Union of Soviet Socialist Republics.
Austria, September 19: German hikers Erika and Helmut Simon find the remains of a 4,000-year-old Bronze Age hunter.

Stockholm, Sweden, October: South African Nadine Gordimer is awarded the Nobel Prize for Literature.
San Marino, October 1: Edda Ceccoli is elected co-Captain-Regent.
Madrid, Spain, October 4: The Madrid Protocol governing Antarctica comes into effect, designating the continent as a natural reserve, devoted to peace and science.
Phnom Penh, Cambodia, November 14: Prince Norodom Sihanouk returns after 13 years in exile.

London, England, November 30: Embryologist Dr Anne McLaren becomes foreign secretary of the prestigious natural sciences body, the Royal Society.
Oslo, Norway, December 10: Burmese dissident Aung Sun Suu Kyi is awarded the Nobel Peace Prize.
Moscow, Russia, December 25: Mikhail Gorbachev resigns the presidency of the USSR.
New York, USA: TV celebrity Oprah Winfrey begins a campaign to introduce a national register of convicted child abusers.

London, England: Patricia Scotland becomes the first black woman to be appointed to a Queen's Counsel position.
England: Gail Rebuck becomes chief executive of Random House UK.
USA: Diane Ackerman publishes *The Moon by Whale Light*.
USA: Katharine Hepburn publishes her autobiography *Me: Stories of My Life*.
England: Catherine Cookson publishes *The Wingless Bird*.

Algeria's Track and Field World Champion

Tokyo, August 31: Algerian middle-distance athlete Hassiba Boulmerka today scored a stunning upset at the Tokyo World Track and Field Championships, sprinting ahead in the home straight of the 1,500 meters to win gold, and become the first woman from an Arabic nation to win a world track championship. Born in the north-eastern Algerian town of Constantine in 1968, Boulmerka began running as a young girl—in a nation that once considered banning women competing in athletic events. Today, some see Boulmerka as a pioneer and heroine; others condemn her for running barelegged, and insist that she should have been covered in traditional Muslim dress. In response, Boulmerka has told reporters that Islamic dress would only serve to slow her down and make her uncompetitive.

At the presentation ceremony, unable to disguise her joy at winning, Algeria's new world champion screamed proudly for her country and—she said—for every Algerian woman.

Édith Cresson

"TRUTH ISN'T ALWAYS BEAUTY, BUT THE HUNGER FOR IT IS."

NADINE GORDIMER, SOUTH AFRICAN AUTHOR

Algerian Hassiba Boulmerka wins gold.

Female Aerobat Flies to the Top

USA, September: Patty Wagstaff, an aerobatics pilot from St. Louis, Missouri, who took her first flying lesson in a C-185 flying boat off Alaska in 1979, has become the first woman to win the US national aerobatics championship. Her achievement in a discipline traditionally dominated by men has even surprised female pilots. She has smashed gender barriers, and opened doors for other women, who will no doubt be inspired to follow her example. She achieved it in one extraordinary day of competition.

Born in Missouri in 1951, Patty moved to Japan at the age of nine with her father, a commercial pilot with Japan Airlines who flew US B-25 Flying Fortress bombers during World War II. She piloted her first plane when she was only 10, her father allowing her to circle Mt Fuji in a DC-6. Flying ran in the blood of Robert and Rosalie Combs' two daughters. Patty's sister Toni began training as a pilot for Continental Airlines while Patty spent her 20s traveling through Asia, Europe and Australia.

In 1979 she moved to Alaska with her family and worked as an economic development planner, a job that took her into wilderness areas accessible only by plane. Wagstaff taught herself how to fly, racing through her ratings to become an instructor in bush and tailwind flying.

It wasn't until she turned 30 that she started training in aerobatics, after attending her first air show at Abbotsford in 1983. Two years later, and only five years since gaining her pilot license, Wagstaff had earned a spot on the US aerobatic team.

Her virtuosity has thrilled audiences around the world. She invented the multiple vertical snap roll, and routinely executes low-level displays of precision and complexity. Her schedule sees her train up to three times a day, and she has set new standards for aerobatic pilots the world over.

Her victory was not without incident. A floorboard beneath her rudder pedals broke, and a Cessna airplane strayed into the aerobatics area during her routine. Nevertheless she finished the day with 28 perfect "10s" to her nearest competitor's score of 17, and went on to win a gold medal in each of her three competition flights.

British author Catherine Cookson publishes *The Wingless Bird*.

Gordimer Wins Nobel Prize for Literature

Stockholm, Sweden, October: South African novelist, short-story writer, political activist, and critic Nadine Gordimer has today been awarded the Nobel Prize for Literature at a ceremony in Stockholm.

Born November 20, 1923, in the segregated East Rand gold-mining township of Springs in Transvaal, Gordimer began writing at the age of nine. Her first work, a short story entitled *Come Again Tomorrow*, was published in 1937 in the Johannesburg magazine *The Forum* when she was only fourteen. She was educated at a convent school and attended Witwaterstrand University.

Despite being born an English-speaking Jew in South Africa, Gordimer resisted the pressure to conform to supremacist principles, instead becoming a political activistand a champion of the disenfranchised. Gordimer secretly attended meetingsof the African National Congress, eventually becoming a member of the then outlawed organization.

One of the founding members of the Congress of South African Writers, Gordimer's works invariably focus on the complexities and moral tensions that arise from living in a divided nation. She has been praised for her authentic portrayals of black African traditions and culture and, even at the height of apartheid, never considered living abroad.

Her later works highlight what Gordimer perceives as a progressively deteriorating society, and her own increasing sense of isolation from the oppressive, white ruling class which she so effectively holds to account.

South African Nadine Gordimer is awarded the Nobel Prize for Literature.

Oprah Winfrey

Royal Society's First Female Foreign Secretary

London, England, November 30: The post of foreign secretary of the Royal Society, one of the scientific community's most prestigious honorary positions, was taken up today by eminent developmental biologist Dr Anne McLaren. Last year she received the society's Royal Medal, and has now become the first female foreign secretary in the society's illustrious 330-year history.

McLaren was appointed a fellow of the Royal Society in 1975 for her work on reproductive physiology in mammals, which shed light on processes such as egg transfer, placental and foetal growth, and various interactions between the embryo and the uterus during implantation. Her life's work has involved many and varied aspects of life; how it develops, and how it is transmitted from one being to another. With John Biggers at University College, London, in 1958, she created the procedure which led to the first successful birth of mice grown outside of the mother's body, and paved the way for advancements in the greater understanding of reproductive processes that led to today's IVF infertility treatments.

Born in 1927, McLaren completed undergraduate and postgraduate degrees in zoology at Oxford University. She worked for 15 years at Edinburgh's Institute of Animal Genetics, followed by 18 years as director of the Medical Research Council's mammalian development unit in London.

Burmese Democracy Activist Wins Peace Prize

Oslo, Norway, December 10: The children of the leader of Burma's pro-democracy movement, Aung San Suu Kyi, today accepted the Nobel Peace Prize on her behalf, because their mother is still under house arrest in the nation's capital, Rangoon. They have rejected—on her behalf—the army's offer to free her if she

Activist Aung Sun Suu Kyi wins the Nobel Peace Prize.

agrees to leave Burma and withdraw completely from political life.

In 1988 Suu Kyi returned to Rangoon from London, where she had been studying at the London School of Oriental and African Studies, to care for her mother, who had suffered a severe stroke. Nationwide protests were sparked after General Ne Win, military ruler since 1962, resigned in July, 1988. A military crackdown on August 8 killed hundreds, and a week later Suu Kyi, in her first demonstration of political activism, sent an open letter to the government requesting the formation of an independent committee to prepare the framework for multi-party elections.

On August 26, she gave a speech before a crowd of hundreds of thousands outside the Shwedagon pagoda, calling for the establishment of a democratic government. The ruling junta then promised to hold parliamentary elections in May, 1990. September 1988 saw the formation of the National League for Democracy (NLD), and Suu Kyi was elected general-secretary. Suu Kyi campaigned amid intense personal harassment, and the arrest and killing of many of her supporters. In July, 1989, she was placed under house arrest, without charge or trial.

The parliamentary elections of May, 1990, saw the NLD win a staggering 82 percent of the vote, but the regime refused to acknowledge the party's validity. In a travesty of justice, the winner of the 1990 Rafto Human Rights Prize, last year's Sakharov Human Rights Prize, and now the Nobel Peace Prize, remains in detention at her home on the shoreline of Rangoon's Inya Lake, with no end to her house arrest in sight.

Hollywood Great Publishes Candid Autobiography

USA: Screen legend and American icon Katharine Hepburn has published her autobiography *Me: Stories of my Life*. It is a chatty and compelling account of her childhood misadventures in Connecticut, her early life in the theater and in film, the highlights and otherwise of her stellar career, and the men she loved. She recounts the details of her remarkable life in a conversational tone, and with great candor. The book is an instant bestseller.

Hepburn is the recipient of a record 12 Academy Award nominations and a four-time winner. She became a best-selling author in 1977 at the age of 70 with her first book with the long-winded title, *The Making of The African Queen: or, How I Went to Africa with Bogart, Bacall and Huston and Almost Lost My Mind.*

Ruth P. Jhabvala

Canadian Woman Blasts into Space

Space, January 22: At 9:52:33 a.m. today at Florida's Kennedy Space Center, the photographer, physician, scientist, and now astronaut Dr Roberta Lynn Bondar became the first Canadian woman in space when the space shuttle *Discovery* lifted off on its fourteenth mission

Bondar was born in Ontario, Canada, and attended elementary and secondary school in her hometown of Sault Ste. Marie. Her accreditations include a bachelor degree in zoology and agriculture from the University of Guelph in 1968, and a doctorate in neurobiology from the University of Toronto in 1974. She was admitted as a fellow of the Royal College of Physicians and Surgeons of Canada in 1981, as a specialist neurologist. In 1983 Bondar was made assistant professor of neurology at the McMaster medical center in Hamilton when she was accepted into the Canadian space program.

Her expertise in the human nervous system, in particular the inner ear balancing system and its relationship to the functioning of the eye, made her the ideal candidate to perform the series of experiments that are scheduled to be carried out on this mission. During her eight days in space, Bondar will engage in the series of experiments in life and material sciences on behalf of 14 countries.

Marlene Dietrich dies alone in her beloved city of Paris.

> *"A SHIP IN PORT IS SAFE, BUT THAT IS NOT WHAT SHIPS ARE FOR. SAIL OUT TO SEA AND DO NEW THINGS."*
>
> REAR ADMIRAL DR. GRACE HOPPER, THE COMPUTER SCIENTIST WHO INVENTED COBOL (1906-1992)

Lgubov Egorova wins the women's cross country relay.

House of Commons Elects Female Speaker

London, England, April 27: A woman has today been elected to the position of speaker in the House of Commons for the first time in its 700-year history. After an historic 134-vote majority, the 62-year-old Labour MP Betty Boothroyd has promised to stand up for the rights of backbenchers against cabinet ministers and members of the executive, and has also vowed that she will not wear the traditional speaker's wig.

Boothroyd is no stranger to the House of Commons, having worked there in the 1950s as a secretary and also as political assistant to various MPs including Barbara Castle. After she unsuccessfully contested two parliamentary seats in the late 50s she traveled to the US and worked as a legislative assistant from 1960–1962. Returning to London, she again contested the seats of Nelson and Colne (1968) and Rossendale (1970) before finally gaining her seat of West Bromwich—later named West Bromwich West—in 1973.

A succession of government posts were to follow, including assistant government whip in 1974, and chair of the select committee on foreign affairs in 1979.

She was elected deputy-speaker of the House of Commons in 1987, and today the new speaker—a one-time headmistress, nanny, and publican—instructed her assembled MPs to "Call me Madam."

Marlene Dietrich Dies Alone in Paris

Paris, France, May 6: The luminous screen legend Marlene Dietrich, who has spent the last 12 years bedridden in her Paris apartment, died today of kidney failure, aged 90. At the height of her film career in the 1930s she was the highest-paid actress in the world, a cultivated, beguiling woman who epitomized glamor and sensuality.

Dietrich was born Marie Magdalene Dietrich in Berlin-Schöneberg on December 27, 1901. She made her film debut in 1923 in *Der Kleine Napoleon (The Young Napoleon)*, but it was Josef von Sternberg's *The Blue Angel* (1930) that brought her international fame and stardom. Her

Japan, January 13: Japan acknowledges that Korean women were used as sex slaves by Japanese soldiers during World War I.

Europe, January 15: The European Commission recognizes Croatia and Slovenia as independent states.

Space, January 22: Neurologist Roberta Bondar is the first Canadian woman in space.

USA, February 4: Nan Robertson publishes *The Girls on the Balcony*, about the Elizabeth Boylan sex discrimination lawsuit.

London, England, February 16: Writer Angela Carter dies.

South Africa, March 17: White voters give a resounding "yes" to constitutional reforms giving equality to their black and colored countrymen.

London, England, March 19: Sarah Ferguson and Prince Andrew officially separate.

Hollywood, USA, March 29: Ruth Prawer Jhabvala wins the Oscar for Best Screenplay Based on Materials Previously Produced or Published, for her adaptation of *Howard's End*.

Paris, France, April 2: Prime Minister Édith Cresson is forced to resign.

Miami, USA, April 9: Former Panamanian dictator Manuel Noriega is found guilty of drug trafficking.

Fukuoka, Japan, April 16: Fukuoka local court finds a woman was forced to resign after a male employee harassed her in the first successful lawsuit against sexual harassment in the workplace.

London, England, April 27: Betty Boothroyd is appointed first woman speaker in the House of Commons.

England, April: Barbara Mills becomes Director of Public Prosecutions.

Los Angeles, USA, May 2: A jury decision to acquit four police indicted in the beating of Rodney King leads to days of rioting, looting, and arson, and 52 deaths.

Paris, France, May 6: Acting legend Marlene Dietrich dies, aged 90.

Himalayas, May 13: Wanda Rutkiewicz, hailed as the world's greatest female climber, dies while scaling her ninth "eight thousander."

Rio de Janeiro, Brazil, June 3-14: Treaties to avert climate change are signed at the UN earth summit.

England, June 16: Andrew Morton publishes a controversial new biography of Princess Diana.

London, England, June 30: Margaret Thatcher takes a seat in the House of Lords.

Sarajevo, Bosnia, July 2: UN peacekeeping forces move into position around the airport so that humanitarian aid can commence. Heavy resistance is encountered from Serbian troops.

first Hollywood movie was *Morocco* (1930), followed by *Shanghai Express* (1932.) Dietrich became an American citizen in 1937, and continually refused Adolf Hitler's persistent requests that she return to Germany. On the contrary, she spent much time entertaining Allied troops during the war.

Dietrich continued her highly successful cabaret act after the war but, as the years passed, she seemed to become trapped in her own image of glamor and sophistication, to the point where she concealed her ageing body from the world. She finally retired from performing in 1975 after breaking her leg in a stage fall. She then moved to Paris where she spent the remainder of her life alone and in virtual seclusion.

Wanda Rutkiewicz dies while scaling the Himalayas.

Greatest Female Climber Lost on Nepalese Peak

Himalayas, May 20: Wanda Rutkiewicz, the famed pioneering mountaineer and environmentalist who has been climbing the world's highest peaks for more than a quarter of a century, is feared to have died last week while climbing the south-west face of the peak Kanchenjunga in Nepal, during her ninth ascent of the 26,247 ft

(8,000 m) peak. Rutkiewicz was born in 1943, in the small town of Plungiany in present-day Lithuania. She was the third woman to reach the summit of Mt. Everest, and first to reach the summit of the harsh Kanchenjunga, the world's third highest peak. She was generally thought to be the finest female mountain climber in the world. Rutkiewicz was last seen on the evening of May 12 establishing a bivouac less than 1,000 feet (300 m) from the summit of Kanchenjunga, which because of its position, claims records in two countries. It is the second highest peak in Nepal and the highest mountain in India.

Japan Acknowledges "Comfort Stations"

Japan, July: The Japanese government has released a report entitled "Results of Investigation into the Question of Military Comfort Women Originating from the Korean Peninsula," in which it admits for the first time that a World War II network of so-called "comfort stations" did, in fact, exist, despite previous denials.

The term "comfort stations" is a euphemism for the brothels which were staffed by approximately 200,000 women—some as young as 12—from Indochina, Korea, and China, who were taken prisoner and forced by the Japanese army to live in confinement as virtual sex slaves for the duration of the war. The Japanese government has been under intense pressure to establish an investigation since last January, when history professor, Yoshimi Yoshiaki, went public with several documents he had obtained from the library of the National Institute for Defense. Last year an open letter was sent to the heads of govern-

ment in Japan by the Korean Women's Association, demanding an apology, a memorial, and a thorough enquiry into the matter. The government, still in denial on the issue, said that there was no evidence of any forced draft of Korean women. Then in August, Kim Hak-soon testified that she was taken as a "comfort woman" by the Japanese military. Four months later she and others filed a damages suit in the Tokyo district court. Japan is still struggling to come to terms with its wartime atrocities. Until recently the government has defended its actions by claiming that, prior to 1945, rape was not classified as a war crime, and that the invasion and colonization of neighboring countries was necessary to protect the home islands from western expansionism.

Sarah Ferguson

Jodie Foster wins Academy Award for *Silence of the Lambs*.

Poland, July 8: Hanna Suchocka becomes Prime Minister of Poland.
Barcelona, Spain, July 25: The Olympic Games opening ceremony takes place. At this Olympics, women's judo and badminton are introduced.
Palermo, Sicily, July: The Association of Women Against the Mafia stages a hunger strike against the unpunished murders of judges, lawyers, police, and civilians.
Bosnia, August 15: Images of emaciated Bosnians in concentration camps are shown to the world.

London, England, August 20: London's *Daily Mirror* publishes photographs of the Duchess of York, Sarah Ferguson, topless with her financial advisor, John Bryan.
Space, September 12: Dr. Mae Jemison launches into space to spend a week orbiting Earth.
Vietnam, September 23: As the only candidate, General Le Duc Anh is elected president.
New York, USA, September: Tina Brown becomes editor of the *New Yorker* magazine.

Salisbury Cathedral, England, October: An all-girl choir performs here for the first time.
USA, October 3: Irish singer Sinéad O'Connor rips up a picture of the Pope on comedy show *Saturday Night Live*.
USA, October: Mona Van Duyn becomes the country's first female poet laureate.
USA, November 4: Bill Clinton is elected President. Carol Moseley Braun is the first African-American woman elected to the senate.

London, England, November 24: Queen Elizabeth II refers to 1992 as an *annus horribilis*. Bad luck has plagued the royals this year, with scandals, income tax demands, divorce, and a fire at Windsor Castle.
Ireland, November 25: Referendum declares that it is legal for a woman to obtain information about abortion, and travel to the UK for an abortion, but abortion is still illegal in Ireland.
Japan, November: Professor Orie Endo researches the art of *nushu*, a form of ancient writing carried out by women in Hunan, China.

London, England, December 9: The Prince and Princess of Wales announce their legal separation.
Oslo, Norway, December 10: Rigoberta Menchú Tum is awarded the Nobel Peace Prize.
Spain, December: Cuban poet Dulce María Loynaz wins the Cervantes Award.
USA: The movie *A League of Their Own*, directed by Penny Marshall, is released.
USA: Terry McMillan publishes the novel *Waiting to Exhale*.

Mae Jemison

Sicilian Women Protest Mafia Murders

Palermo, Sicily, July: The recent assassinations of Sicilian judicial figures at the hands of the Italian mafia has resulted in today's demonstration through the streets of Palermo, staged by the Association of Women Against the Mafia. The murder of anti-mafia judges Giovanni Falcone and Paolo Borsellino has led Sicily's women to act, staging a hunger strike in the center of Palermo in the hope of shaming the authorities into taking action to reclaim their communities and bring Sicily's vicious cycle of death and violence to an end.

The Association of Women Against the Mafia was formed 10 years ago by numerous widows of lawyers, judges, and police who were murdered in the line of duty.

New Image for *New Yorker* as Tina Brown Takes Over

New York, USA, September: The editor-in-chief of *Vanity Fair*, Tina Brown—who turned the ailing magazine's fortunes around with a mix of hard-nosed news, high-gloss fashion, and vacuous celebrity pieces—has today been appointed editor of the *New Yorker* magazine. Brown has made her intentions as editor abundantly clear. She aims to increase circulation by at least 30 percent by shortening some of its occasionally self-absorbed articles, reducing deadline times, and pursuing topical stories designed to grab the public's eye. Photographs will feature more prominently, and it is rumored

she intends to continue the practice she began at *Vanity Fair* of commissioning more articles than can fit in one issue, and discarding those that she dislikes.

Born in 1953, Brown was appointed editor of her first magazine, the 270-year-old social gossip periodical *The Tatler*, when she was just 25 years old. She then joined *Vanity Fair* as an editorial advisor, and, a mere six weeks later, was promoted to editor-in-chief. Brown also intends to host her fair share of parties in the coming months. After all, as she says: "You don't make friends, you make contacts."

First US Female Poet Laureate Announced

USA, October: Mona Van Duyn, whose poems about the everyday pleasures and drudgeries of middle-Americans have made her one of the nation's best-loved poets, has become the first woman to be named US poet laureate. Writing with the unique insights of a small-town Midwesterner, her works are renowned for optimistically linking the frustrations and various disappointments and of life with a higher sense of purpose and the light-hearted. Her deceptively simplistic phrasing and descriptions of common images manage to combine the thoughts, humor, and humanity of ordinary people, in works of elegance laced with subtle insights into the many areas of human concern.

Born in the north-east Iowa town of Waterloo in 1921, Van Duyn spent her childhood in Eldora, where she was able to indulge her love of reading while working as a cleaner in the local library. She graduated from the University of Northern Iowa in 1942, and the following year married Jarvis A. Thurston, together founding the literary magazine *Perspective: A Quarterly of Literature*. Her first novel, *Valentines to the Wide World*, was published in 1959, and in 1971 her second work, *To See, To Take*, won the National Book Award for poetry. Van Duyn also won the 1970 Bollingen Prize, and Cornell College's Carl Sandburg Prize in 1982. She is also a member of the American Academy and Institute of Arts and Letters.

The title of poet laureate is bestowed annually by the Library of Congress, and honors an American poet's lifetime achievements in literature.

Annus horribilis: Queen Elizabeth's Dreadful Year

London, England, November 24: In a speech at Guildhall to mark the 40th anniversary of her accession to the throne, Queen Elizabeth II has referred to 1992 as an *annus horribilis* for Britain's royal family.

The troubles began in March when Buckingham Palace announced that the Duke and Duchess of York would separate. April saw the Queen's only daughter, Princess Anne, the Princess Royal, divorce her husband Captain Mark Philips. In August, pictures of John Bryan sucking the toes of a topless Sarah Ferguson, Duchess of York, were published in the tabloid newspaper *The Daily Mirror*. Just when the Queen must have been thinking things couldn't possibly get worse, a fire broke out in a private chapel on the first floor of Windsor Castle, the Queen's weekend

A fire at Windsor Castle destroys valuable tapestries.

residence. The blaze moved swiftly through St. George's Hall before badly damaging the state apartments, affecting more than 100 rooms. Over 250 firefighters took more than 15 hours and millions of gallons of water to bring the fire under control, and a debate has since been raging over who should pay the estimated £40 million damage bill, as the castle is owned by the British Government, not the royal family. Investigators believe that the fire was started by a spotlight shining on a curtain.

The term *annus horribilis* is derived from the Latin phrase *annus mirabilis*, ("year of wonders"), used by poet John Dryden in his master epic: *Annus Mirabilis: The Year of Wonders* (1666), which commemorates the defeat of the Dutch Navy at the hands of the English fleet, and also the Great Fire of London.

Tina Brown becomes editor of the *New Yorker*.

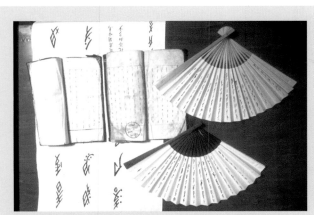
Chinese fans and books inscribed with ancient *nushu* ideograms.

Ireland Referendum to Clarify Abortion Laws

Ireland, November 25: Ireland will vote today in three referendums on abortion, designed to clarify the nation's laws and form a consensus between the country's diametrically opposing points of view on the issue. The first question centers on a woman's right to choose, and pro-choice advocates admit this is the referendum least likely to be adopted. Ireland is a conservative country in which the Roman Catholic church, despite losing some of its all-pervasive influence in recent times, is still a dominant force.

The second referendum concerns a woman's right to travel abroad to procure an abortion. When a 14-year-old rape victim was prevented from flying to England for an abortion in February, street protests erupted across the country, forcing the government to act to clarify the country's abortion laws despite the Supreme Court later overturning the decision. It is estimated that over 5,000 Irish women per year travel to England for terminations, and this figure is not likely to alter drastically if this referendum is defeated.

The third referendum—on the availability of information for women who may be considering an abortion—seems certain to pass. The Supreme Court ruling that allows abortion in certain exceptional cases has made it virtually impossible for the Irish government to maintain its argument against the provision of factual information. Currently the laws regarding access to information within Ireland are so draconian that it is illegal even to publish the telephone number of an overseas abortion clinic. Earlier this year 2,000 copies of the English newspaper *The Guardian* were withdrawn from newsstands because it contained the phone numbers and addresses of abortion clinics in England.

Prime Minister Albert Reynolds has stated that if the referendum on the "substantive" issue of abortion fails, he will seek to enact legislation that will allow for the Supreme Court ruling to become the "default" law. The Catholic Church, however, continues to oppose abortion except where the termination of a fetus is the direct result of treating the mother for a life-threatening illness. The concept of the illegality of abortion is implicit within the Irish constitution and was reaffirmed in a 1983 referendum. Ireland is the only country in the EU where abortion is illegal.

Guatemalan Activist Wins Nobel Peace Prize

Oslo, Norway, December 10: Rigoberta Menchú Tum, the indomitable advocate of Guatemala's Mayan Indians—and of indigenous peoples around the world—today became the youngest recipient of the Nobel Prize for Peace in recognition of her work in the pursuit of social justice and ethno-cultural reconciliation.

Born into an impoverished family in Guatemala's western highlands in 1959, Menchú grew up in an era of civil war where the massacre of civilians and of suspected "subversives" by the army and government-sanctioned "death squads" was commonplace. In 1978 the civil war began to escalate when military strongman General Fernando Romeo Lucas Garcia became President. Garcia was overthrown in a military coup in 1982 that saw Brigadier-General Rios Montt assume power, annul the constitution, dissolve parliament, and outlaw all political parties.

What followed was the bloodiest 14 months in the country's history, as torture became a widespread instrument of government repression. More than 400 Mayan villages were razed to the ground, and thousands of girls and women raped. Menchú assisted the formation of an opposition group, the United Representation of the Guatemalan Opposition. During a trip to Paris in 1982 she told her life story to a French journalist over a four-day period, and the recording became the basis of her autobiography *I, Rigoberta Menchú: An Indian Woman in Guatemala*. The book highlights the plight of Guatemala's Mayans; it has been translated into 12 languages and received widespread acclaim.

Sinead O'Connor

Spanish Language Poet Wins Cervantes Prize

Havana, Cuba, December: The "grande dame of Cuban letters", 90-year-old Dulce Maria Loynaz, has been awarded Spain's equivalent of the Nobel Prize for Literature, the Cervantes Prize, for a lifetime of letters and poetry.

Born in Havana in 1902, Loynaz was the eldest of four children, all educated at home, and all aspiring poets. Her most fruitful period was from the late 1940s through to the early 1950s, when she published her most accomplished works, including her classic work of magical realism, *Jardin (Garden)*. Her last 38 years have been spent in virtual seclusion at her home in Havana. She is almost unrecognized in her own country.

The Penny Marshall movie *A League of Their Own* opens in cinemas across the USA.

Hillary Rodham Clinton

Malawi Lawyer Released After 11 Years in Prison

Malawi, January 24: Malawi activist and prisoner of conscience, Vera Chirwa, was released from prison today after being convicted in 1981—along with her husband, Orton—of high treason by a "traditional court." These courts were a parallel quasi-judicial system established by the Malawi government, where procedural matters and rules of evidence were entirely at the discretion of the court. The first female lawyer in the history of Malawi, Vera, with her husband Orton, was an influential figure in the country's 1964 campaign for independence, but the couple was eventually forced into exile in Tanzania.

They were kidnapped by Malawi security forces in Zambia in 1981 and convicted after a staged two-month trial, in which they defended themselves in surroundings more akin to an inquisition than a trial. Pressure on the Malawi

"I AM NOT A POLITICAL FIGURE, NOR DO I WANT TO BE ONE; BUT I COME WITH MY HEART."

PRINCESS DIANA
1961–1997

government by Amnesty International for their release saw a delegation of British legal experts visit Vera and Orton in the autumn of 1992. It was the first time the two had seen each other for eight years. When Orton died in his cell three weeks later Vera was refused permission to attend his funeral.

Upon her release today, Chirwa made it clear that she would continue to fight for human rights in Malawi, and in particular for an end to the death penalty, the use of which has widespread support among Malawians.

Screen Star Audrey Hepburn Dies

Switzerland, January 20: Audrey Hepburn, the screen legend whose grace, style, and child-like innocence wrapped in a waif-life fragility endeared her to a generation of movie-goers—and placed her in the pantheon of Hollywood royalty—has died of colon cancer at her home in Switzerland, aged 63. Her on-screen persona was the product of a shared and intimate lifelong friendship with the French designer Hubert de Givenchy. In an age of voluptuous large-breasted film starlets, Hepburn and Givenchy showed women that they could achieve a dignified and stunningly elegant look without having to sacrifice intelligence or sophistication.

Blueblood Hepburn was born Edda van Heemstra Hepburn-Ruston in Brussels, Belgium in 1929. Her father was a banker, her mother a Dutch baroness. She studied ballet at the Arnhem Conservatory of Music in Amsterdam, Holland, and was holidaying with her family in Arnhem when the Germans invaded on May 10, 1940. During the occupation her family endured many hardships,

Emma Thompson wins an Oscar for *Howard's End.*

eating dog biscuits when there was nothing else, and bread that was green because the only available flour came from ground peas.

After the war Hepburn moved to London, making her stage debut in the chorus of *High Button Shoes* in 1949. She became an international star following her first on-screen performance in *Roman Holiday* (1953), playing a bored, sheltered princess who escapes her guardians only to fall in love with a visiting newspaperman. The film was a huge hit and won Hepburn the Academy Award for Best Actress. Her most sophisticated and acclaimed roles were as Holly Golightly in *Breakfast At Tiffany's* (1961) and as the naïve Cockney flower girl Eliza Doolittle in the film version of *My Fair Lady* (1964). In the late 1960s she retired from full-time acting to live in Switzerland, occasionally returning to the screen in films such as *Robin and Marian*

Screen legend and beauty Audrey Hepburn dies.

Czech Republic and Slovakia, January 1: In direct contrast to the strife and conflict in the former Yugoslavia, Czechoslovakia splits into two separate entities in a "velvet divorce."

Switzerland, January 20: Stylish screen legend Audrey Hepburn dies, aged 63.

Washington DC, USA, January 26: First Lady Hillary Rodham Clinton is appointed head of a committee to prepare legislation to overhaul the country's healthcare system.

Malawi, January 24: Activist Vera Chirwa is released from prison.

New York, USA, February 26: A bomb blast in the garage under the World Trade Center leaves five dead and hundreds injured.

USA, March 29: Emma Thompson receives the Best Actress Oscar for her 1992 role in *Howard's End.*

Bombay, India, March 12: Car bomb blasts kill 300 people.

USA, March: Janet Reno becomes the country's first female Attorney-General.

San Marino, April 1: Patricia Busignani is made co-Captain-Regent of the country.

Waco, Texas, USA, April 19: Fires lit by Branch Davidian cult members rage through their compound.

USA, April 28: The country participates in the first Take Our Daughters to Work Day.

London, England, April 29: Queen Elizabeth II opens the doors of Buckingham Palace to the public for the first time.

Hamburg, Germany, April 30: US tennis star Monica Seles is stabbed in the back by a deranged fan during a match.

Agrigento, Sicily, May 9: Following the recent spate of mafia-linked murders of judicial officials, the Pope calls for an end to violence.

Paris, France, May 15: Teacher Laurence Dreyfus will receive a bravery award after keeping her kindergarten students calm and alive during a two-day siege with an armed man who had dynamite strapped to his body.

Mount Everest, Himalayas, May 17: Rebecca Stephens becomes the first British woman to reach the summit of the world's highest peak.

New York, USA, June 5: Julie Krone is the first woman to win a Triple Crown event, riding Colonial Affair to victory in the Belmont Stakes.

Tokyo, Japan, June 9: Crown Prince Naruhito marries Masako Owada, who becomes the first commoner to join the Imperial Dynasty.

Turkey, June 14: Tansu Çiller is elected the country's first female Prime Minister.

(1976) in which she played Maid Marian to Sean Connery's Robin Hood.

In 1988 Hepburn became a goodwill ambassador for the United Nations Children's Fund (UNICEF), visiting many field missions and publicizing the plight of children forced to live in the world's war-torn and drought-ridden regions.

Deranged Spectator Stabs Tennis Star Seles

Hamburg, Germany, April 30: A 38-year-old man has stabbed the world's No. 1 tennis player, Monica Seles, in the back during a rest break in the Citizen Cup in Hamburg today. Seles was leading 6-4, 4-3 in a quarter-final match against Bulgarian Magdalena Maleeva in front of a crowd of 6,000 people when a man leaned over a nearby barrier and plunged a 10 inch (25 cm) knife into her upper back. Seles screamed, fell to the court and was immediately rushed to hospital.

The wound is not believed to be serious, and appears to have missed her spinal cord and lungs. One of the first

Monica Seles is ranked No. 1 in the tennis world.

officials to reach the stricken athlete was Lisa Grattan, a Women's Tennis Association tour director, who advised her to take steady breaths, and held a towel to her back to minimize the loss of blood.

Teacher Hailed a Heroine in Paris

Paris, France, May 15: Laurence Dreyfus, the teacher at the center of the Neuilly-sur-Seine hostage drama, is being hailed a heroine today for keeping her six female students safe and composed during the two-day siege.

This morning masked police commandos burst into the classroom while the hostage-taker was sleeping, shooting him three times in the head. At the same time a second team placed mattresses in front of each of the children so that they could not witness the shooting.

All the children appeared to be remarkably unaffected by their ordeal when reunited with their parents within minutes of their release. Dreyfus is being praised for her presence of mind, as she told her class that the man was merely out "hunting wolves" to explain the weapons in his possession, which included several sticks of dynamite strapped to his body. Occasionally Dreyfus was permitted to leave the class-room to bring back food and water. She was given a video camera by police, which was then used by the commandos to plan their assault on the gunman.

When the hostage-taker burst into the classroom on Thursday morning there were 21 three- and four-year-old children present. In subsequent negotiations with police, they were intermit-tently released in small groups selected by Dreyfus. Although the negotiators initially agreed to a ransom demand of US$18.5 million, they decided to intervene after the man told them that he intended to take one

time out

The female condom is now available throughout most of Europe and the UK. However, it will not be available in the USA until final tests are completed and it is approved for sale to the general public.

child with him, to use as a human shield in his escape. Dreyfus will be awarded France's highest civilian award, the Legion of Honor, by Interior Minister Charles Pasqua.

Female Jockey Victorious

New York, USA, June 5: Julie Krone has become the first woman to win a prestigious Triple Crown race after riding 13-1 chance Colonial Affair to victory in the Belmont Stakes. She was born in 1963 in Benton Harbor, Michigan, USA, and, after deciding at the age of 13 that she wanted to be the greatest jockey in the world, Krone entered the world of thoroughbred racing—first as a groom, and finally as a jockey.

She won her first race in 1981 at Tampa Bay Downs riding Lord Farkle. On March 6, 1988, at Aqueduct racecourse, Krone became the most successful female jockey in US history with her 1,205th winner. At various times she has led the jockey standings at the Monmouth Park, Meadowlands, Gulfstream Park, and Atlantic City tracks.

Julie Krone

Julie Krone wins the prestigious Belmont Stakes.

Canada, June 14: Kim Campbell is elected the country's first female Prime Minister.

Canada, June: Nunavut Inuit and the Canadian government sign a land claim for 135,000 square miles (350,000 km²) of the Arctic Region. Inuit are granted title.

Georgia, July 6: Georgian Prime Minister and former Soviet foreign minister, Eduard Shevardnadze, is given sweeping powers to deal with Abkhazi rebels, who are seeking their own state.

Burundi, July 10: Sylvie Kinigi becomes Prime Minister.

London, England, July 16: Stella Rimington is the first Director-General of Britain's secret service, MI5, to have her name and photograph released to the public.

Rwanda, July 18: Agathe Uwilingiyimana is made Prime Minister.

Washington DC, USA, September 13: Palestinians gain a modicum of self-rule in the occupied territory, with the signing of an accord brokered by President Bill Clinton.

Phnom Penh, Cambodia, September 24: Prince Sihanouk is returned to power after a 30-year exile.

Manila, Philippines, September 24: Imelda Marcos, wife of the disgraced former dictator Ferdinand, is sentenced to 18 years' imprisonment for corruption.

Islamabad, Pakistan, October 20: Benazir Bhutto is reinstalled as Prime Minister three years after being ousted.

New York, USA, October: Rita Dove is awarded the Pulitzer Prize for Poetry.

Maastricht, Netherlands, November 1: A treaty signed by the members of the European Community comes into force.

New York, USA, November 17: E. Annie Proulx wins the National Book Award for *The Shipping News.*

Wellington, New Zealand, December 1: Helen Clark becomes leader of the Labour Party.

Stockholm, Sweden, December 10: Toni Morrison is awarded the Nobel Prize for Literature.

USA, December 18: Myrna Loy, the glamorous actress, dies aged 88.

Canberra, Australia, December 22: The *Native Title Act* passes through Parliament, granting Aboriginals the right to claim land lost since European colonization.

Pretoria, South Africa: Parliament votes for the first all-race election, to take place next year. It will inevitably lead to black majority rule.

USA: Sister Helen Prejean publishes *Dead Man Walking,* about her relationship with a man on death row.

Commoner Marries into Japanese Imperial Family

Toni Morrison

Tokyo, Japan, June 9: Masako Owada, 29-year-old Harvard University graduate and daughter of senior diplomat Hisashi Owada, became the first career woman to marry into Japan's imperial family when she married Crown Prince Naruhito at the Imperial Palace's Kashikodokoro shrine today.

Owada was born on December 9, 1963 and—for a Japanese woman—experienced an unusually cosmopolitan upbringing. She attended kindergarten in Moscow before her father's job took the family to New York, where she attended primary school. After receiving an economics degree from Harvard in 1985, she returned to study law at Tokyo University, joining the Japanese foreign ministry in 1987 as a translator.

Owada is only the second commoner to marry into the imperial family, and on crossing the moat separating the royal palace from the rest of Japan has entered a world few people could ever imagine. The new princess will learn an archaic imperial language that is barely used outside the palace's forbidding stone ramparts. She will have to learn how to bow at precisely 60° when she greets the Emperor, and submit to ceremonies such as having her body rubbed with rice bran to ensure her fertility. The Japanese imperial household agency and its staff of over 1,100 will determine what she says and does—from whom she is permitted to meet, to every public word she utters.

Owada's preparations for today's ceremony have included many crash courses in Shinto religious rituals and traditional poetry. This morning began with a traditional purifying bath, after which the soon-to-be princess began the donning of the first of a dozen layers of her silk bridal kimono, which weighs 30 lbs (14 kg) and is worth an estimated US$100,000.

> *"PEOPLE, EVEN MORE THAN THINGS, HAVE TO BE RE-STORED, RENEWED, REVIVED, RECLAIMED, AND REDEEMED; NEVER THROW OUT ANYONE."*
>
> AUDREY HEPBURN
> (1929–1993),
> AMERICAN ACTRESS

England's Top Spook Revealed

London, England, July 16: English tabloids are calling her the "housewife superspy" after the name and the photograph of Britain's first female director-general of the MI5 counter-intelligence agency, Stella Rimington, was published today in an agency report.

Born in South London in 1935, Ms Rimington traveled to India when her civil servant husband was posted there, dutifully filling the role of a diplomatic wife until she was approached by the head of MI5 in Delhi to become a part-time office assistant. Upon her return to England with her husband in 1969, she decided to apply for full-time employment with the agency. She was appointed to a junior assistant officer position at MI5 headquarters in Leconfield House, London, and rose very quickly through the ranks of the male-dominated agency, gaining promotion as an officer in 1973. She was later trans-ferred to an agent-running section, where she mounted a series of senior operations against Soviet agents and double-agents within the UK, before being promoted to director of counter-espionage in 1986.

Rimington was made deputy-director-general in early 1990, and was advised later on that year that she was being groomed for the director-general position. Until today MI5 had not revealed any identification details about its head.

Five Nations Elect First Female Leaders

World: The second half of 1993 has seen five nations elect female prime ministers—Turkey, Canada, Burundi, Rwanda and Pakistan.

In Turkey on June 14, in a political ascendancy that was nothing short of meteoric, Tansu Çiller was named Turkey's first female Prime Minister. Çiller was born in 1946, in Istanbul, and received an economics degree at the University of the Bosphorus before traveling to the United States, where she earned a doctorate from the University of Connecticut, then completed her postdoctoral studies at Yale. She joined Turkey's True Path Party in November 1990 and was elected to parliament as deputy of Istanbul in 1991. As a member

Tansu Ciller, the first female Prime Minister of Turkey.

of the government of Süleyman Demirel she served as Minister of State in charge of economics. She is described in the European press as the new symbol of modern Turkey.

In Canada, also on June 14—in the aftermath of Prime Minister Brian Mulroney's retirement from politics and the leadership of the Conservative Party—the Minister of National Defense, Kim Campbell, was elected as the country's first female Prime Minister after defeat-ing her only challenger for the post, Jean Charest, at the party's national convention earlier this month. She faces almost insurmountable odds to rebuild her party's fortunes in time for the

Japanese Crown Prince Naruhito and Princess Masako.

Kim Campbell is elected Prime Minister of Canada.

Myrna Loy, in *Love Me Tonight* (1932). The glamorous and funny star died this year, aged 88.

Shipping News Wins Book Award

New York, USA, November 17: Connecticut-born author E. Annie Proulx, who began her writing career at the age of 56, has won the National Book Award for her novel *The Shipping News*, a very moving account of a widowed father's attempts to create a new home for himself in an isolated and desolate Newfoundland community in Canada.

Proulx is an entrenched New Englander—her ancestors have worked in the region as farmers, mill workers, and artists for over 350 years. As a child she learned how to tell stories by listening to her mother, who would spin stories of adventure and magic out of everyday events. Born in Norwich in 1935, Proulx's debut novel *Postcards* (1992) saw her become the first woman to win the prestigious PEN/Faulkner Book Award.

Imelda Marcos

Death Penalty Opponent Nominated for Pulitzer

USA: One of America's leading advocates for the abolition of the death penalty, Sister Helen Prejean, has published *Dead Man Walking: An Eyewitness Account of the Death Penalty in the United States*, detailing her role as spiritual adviser to convicted murderer Patrick Sonnier.

Born in Baton Rouge, Louisiana, Prejean joined the Sisters of St Joseph of Medaille in 1957. Her prison ministry began in 1981, and she began to correspond with Sonnier, who was incarcerated in Louisiana's Angola State Prison and sentenced to death by electric chair for the murder of two teenagers. *Dead Man Walking* has been nominated for the 1993 Pulitzer Prize and is racing its way up the *New York Times* bestseller list.

probable October election, with public dissatisfaction rising over free trade, consumption taxes, economic recession, and previous constitutional fiascos.

In Burundi on July 10, Sylvie Kinigi, a member of the Tutsi tribe, was elected Prime Minister. It is hoped that her election will bring unity to the two warring ethnic groups in the country, and counterbalance the election earlier this month of Melchior Ndadaye—a Hutu—as President. Kinigi was born in 1952 and studied economic management at Burundi University before joining the civil service as an economic advisor in the office of the prime minister. Her primary goal as prime minister is to assist reconciliation between the Hutu and Tutsi tribes.

In Rwanda on July 18, the former Minister for Small and Medium-sized Businesses and Minister for Education, Agathe Uwilingiyimana, was elected the first female Prime Minister of Rwanda, replacing Dismas Nsengiyaremye. Her immediate challenge is to successfully complete talks with the Rwandan Patriotic Front—the very powerful Tutsi-dominated guerilla movement—and move towards the signing of a peace accord. Uwilingiyimana was born in 1953 in a village south of Kigali, the Rwandan capital, and taught school science for 10 years after earning a master's degree in chemistry. As the Minister for Education, Uwilingiyimana abandoned the despised ethnic quota program, and introduced scholarships and new public school positions based on merit.

In Pakistan on October 19, Benazir Bhutto was returned to power for the second time, being sworn in as Prime Minister after elections which saw her

Pakistan People's Party win 86 seats in the country's 217-seat National Assembly. Failing to gain an absolute majority, Bhutto has since built a strong alliance of independent and regional members that will enable her to govern with a total of 121 seats as the head of a coalition gov-ernment. The elections were described as the fairest in Pakistan's history—although participation was low, with an estimated voter turnout of just 40 percent.

New Zealand Appoints First Female Party Leader

Wellington, New Zealand, December 1: Helen Clark, the former New Zealand deputy prime minister, was today elected leader of the Labour Party over Mike Moore. This makes the new leader of the opposition the first woman to head a political party in New Zealand.

Clark joined the Labour Party in 1971 and was elected to parliament in 1981. Her role on the Foreign Affairs and Defence Select Committee (1984–87) saw her play a pivotal role in her government's development of its anti-nuclear policy. During the 1987 Labour Government she held several cabinet posts including housing, conservation, and labor, as well as the health portfolio.

Born in 1950 in the town of Hamilton, New Zealand, the eldest of four daughters, Clark's mother was a school teacher and her father a farmer. Clark went on to attend the University of Auckland where she gained a masters degree in political science in 1974. Clark enjoys a reputation as a very skillful negotiator and persuasive spokeswoman for public health and nuclear disarmament.

After being ousted in 1990, Benazir Bhutto is re-elected Prime Minister of Pakistan.

Duchess Converts to Catholicism

Nancy Kerrigan

London, England, January 14: The Duchess of Kent today became the first member of the British Royal Family to convert to Catholicism in more than 300 years. The Duchess was received into the Church in a private service conducted by Cardinal Basil Hume, the Archbishop of Westminster and spiritual leader of the Roman Catholic Church in England and Wales.

The Duchess was born Katharine Lucy Mary Worsley on February 22, 1933. In 1961, she married Prince Edward, Duke of Kent, cousin of Queen Elizabeth II and the eighteenth in line to the British throne. The *Act of Settlement*, passed in 1701, banned heirs to the throne from being Catholic or marrying a person of that faith, but the Duke's place in the line of succession will not be affected by his wife's conversion because she was an Anglican at the time of their marriage.

A spokesman for the Duchess stressed that her conversion was a very personal decision and was unrelated to current issues facing the Church of England, such as the controversial decision to allow the ordination of women priests.

> *"Be faithful in small things because it is in them that your strength lies."*
>
> MOTHER TERESA (1910–1997), HUMANITARIAN AND NOBEL PEACE PRIZE WINNER

The Duchess herself has offered her own explanation for her action: "I do love guidelines and the Catholic Church offers you guidelines. I like to know what's expected of me."

Lorena Bobbit Acquitted

Manassas, Virginia, USA, January 21: After six hours of deliberation, a jury of seven women and five men today found Lorena Bobbit not guilty of malicious wounding. They concluded that she was temporarily insane and acting under an irresistible impulse last year when she cut off her husband's penis with a kitchen knife. As mandated by state law, the trial judge did not free the 24-year-old manicurist, but instead ordered that she spend 45 days in a psychiatric hospital to undergo evaluation as to whether she poses a present danger to herself and others.

During the seven-day court hearing, the jury heard extensive evidence of the couple's strained relationship, with a series of witnesses testifying that John Bobbit repeatedly raped and abused his wife in the years following their 1989 marriage. According to Lorena Bobbit, matters came to a head on June 23 last year when the 26-year-old ex-Marine raped her after arriving home from a night of partying. She told the court that she was so traumatized by the experience that she had absolutely no memory of severing her sleeping husband's penis later that evening, and that she only realized what she had done as she drove away from their apartment clutching the organ in her hand. Horrified, she said she tossed it from the car before finally recovering her senses and calling the emergency services.

Lorena Bobbit is found not guilty of malicious wounding due to insanity.

Initially, physicians told John Bobbit that he would probably never be able to have sex again. After an intensive search, however, police located the severed penis and rushed it to the hospital, where it was surgically reattached in an operation lasting more than nine hours. A few months later, John Bobbit stood trial on charges of marital sexual abuse stemming from the events of June 23. Unlike his wife's trial, which has attracted massive media attention at home and abroad, the proceedings and his ultimate acquittal received little press coverage.

Aung San Suu Kyi Remains Resolute

Yangon, Myanmar, February 14: Aung San Suu Kyi, the detained leader of Myanmar's opposition party, National League for Democracy, today received a visit from United States Congressman Bill Richardson and the *New York Times* reporter Philip Shenon. Although the pro-democracy campaigner has been held under house arrest since July 1989, she again rejected suggestions that she leave the country and join her family in Britain, instead repeating her call for dialog with Myanmar's military junta.

The Duchess of Kent has converted to Catholicism.

Detroit, USA, January 6: Figure-skater Nancy Kerrigan withdraws from competition after an attack with a crowbar on her leg by an unknown assailant.

London, England, January 14: The Duchess of Kent converts to Catholicism. She is the first British royal to do so in over 300 years.

Manassas, Virginia, USA, January 21: Lorena Bobbit, who severed her husband's penis, is found not guilty of malicious wounding, due to insanity.

Los Angeles, USA, February 2: Archeologist, Marija Alseika-Gimbutas, dies, aged 73.

Japan, February 8: Justice Hisako Takahashi is appointed to the country's Supreme Court. She is the first woman to hold the post.

Yangon, Myanmar, February 14: Pro-democracy activist, Aung San Suu Kyi, refuses to leave the country.

Arlington, Virginia, USA, February 23: CIA spy, Aldrich Ames, and his wife, Rosario, are arrested on charges of treason.

France, February 25: Member of Parliament for the Riviera, Yann Piat, a strong opponent of organized crime, is shot and killed in her car. There is speculation it is a contract killing.

Bosnia, February 28: Four Bosnian Serb warplanes are shot down over the UN no-fly zone by NATO forces. This is the first offensive action by NATO in its 45-year history.

Bristol, England, March 13: Thirty-two women are ordained priests in the Church of England, at Bristol Cathedral.

Somalia, March 20: Italian journalist Ilaria Alpi, and her cameraman, Miran Hrovatin, are shot and killed. They had been collecting evidence of brutality by Italian soldiers against Somalis.

Hollywood, USA, March 24: Jane Campion wins an Oscar for Best Original Screenplay, Holly Hunter wins Best Actress, and Anna Paquin wins Best Supporting Actress for *The Piano*.

Rwanda, April 7: A rocket brings down the plane of Prime Minister Agathe Uwilingiyimana, who is killed.

New York, USA, April 12: E. Annie Proulx wins the Pulitzer Prize for her novel, *The Shipping News*.

Boston, USA, April 18: Disabled athlete Jean Driscoll sets a record in the women's wheelchair section of the Boston Marathon, of 1 hour, 34 minutes, 22 seconds.

Rwanda, April 21: The Red Cross estimates 100,000 people have been killed in two weeks of bloodshed since the Prime Minister's death.

USA, April: Scientist Polly Matzinger challenges concepts of immunity and proposes a new "danger" theory.

Born in Yangon (Rangoon) in 1945, Aung San Suu Kyi was educated in Myanmar, India, and then Britain, where she studied philosophy, politics, and economics at Oxford University. In 1972, she married British scholar Dr Michael Aris, with whom she had two sons. After returning to Myanmar in 1988 to nurse her dying mother, she was propelled into leading a burgeoning pro-democracy movement, which soon then became the National League for Democracy party. Despite her subsequent detention, the party proceeded to win a landslide victory in the 1990 elections, but the military refused to surrender power to the party.

Recognized as a prisoner of conscience by Amnesty International, Aung San Suu Kyi has received a number of awards for her long non-violent struggle against oppression. When she won the Nobel Peace Prize in 1991, she selflessly used her US$1.3 million prizemoney to establish a health and education trust in support of the people of Myanmar.

Women Ordained as Anglican Priests

Bristol, England, March 13: In a dramatic break with tradition, the Church of England today ordained 32 women as priests during a ceremony conducted by Bishop Barry Rogerson at Bristol Cathedral. Until now, women have only been allowed to serve as deacons, performing baptisms, marriages, and burials, but they have not been allowed to give communion or administer any of the other sacraments.

The issue of women priests has divided the Church of England since it was first debated almost 20 years ago. In November 1992, supporters finally celebrated

Thirty-two women are ordained priests in the Church of England.

the very narrowest of victories when the General Synod approved the necessary legislation by just two votes. At the time, however, opponents warned of continuing division, saying the controversial move would undoubtedly "pit diocese against diocese, parish against parish, and parishioner against parishioner."

Italian Journalist Murdered

Mogadishu, Somalia, March 20: The Italian investigative journalist Ilaria Alpi, and her cameraman, Miran Hrovatin, have been shot and killed by gunmen in the capital of Somali, Mogadishu. Alpi was on her fifth trip to Somalia, assigned by the Italian state broadcaster, RAI, to cover the withdrawal of Italian troops deployed in 1992 as peacekeepers in the now-defunct multinational task force code-named Operation Restore Hope.

Somalia has been in anarchy since its dictator of two decades, Mohamed Siad Barre, was ousted by rebel armies in 1991. With the capital reduced to rubble and all the nation's grain-producing areas overrun by militias, the international community responded and Operation

time out

Jacqueline Lee Bouvier Kennedy Onassis dies at home with her children at her side. The woman who became a devotee to literature through work as an editor was a symbol of feminine style and grace throughout her life.

Aung San Suu Kyi

Restore Hope was launched. In December 1992, United States marines landed on the beaches of Mogadishu, only to be withdrawn after an incident on October 3, 1993, when 18 Americans were killed and one of their bodies dragged through the streets of the capital.

Meanwhile, crime flourished as Somalia became a center for smuggling, kidnapping, hijacking, arms trafficking, and toxic waste dumping, some of it linked to foreign countries. There have also been allegations of abuses committed by peacekeeping forces, including Italian soldiers. It is believed that Alpi was gathering evidence about some of these matters, thus questions inevitably remain concerning the circumstances behind her death which, according to the eyewitness reports, was not a random act of violence but a targeted killing. Ilaria Alpi was part of the press group who came to Somalia at the end of Restore Hope, the mission to end famine. Though the job was unfinished, Western peacekeeping forces were leaving the job to soldiers from Malaysia, India and Pakistan.

Aldrich and Rosario Ames are tried for treason.

New York City, USA, May 19: Former first lady, Jacqueline Onassis, dies of cancer, aged 64.

London, England, May 30: Dr Carole Jordan is elected the first woman president of the prestigious Royal Astronomical Society.

Algiers, Algeria, June 29: Fifteen thousand Algerians peacefully demonstrate against violence.

Colorado Springs, USA, June 30: Olympic skater Tonya Harding is banned from the sport for life, following her involvement in the attack on skater Nancy Kerrigan.

Gaza, Israel, July 1: Yasser Arafat returns after 27 years in exile.

Pyongyang, North Korea, July 8: Kim Il Sung, dictator since World War II, dies, aged 82.

Northern Ireland, August 31: After a quarter-century of heavy armed resistance, the IRA at last announces a "complete cessation of military operations."

USA, August: Barbra Streisand's first concerts in 30 years sell out despite the exorbitant price tag.

Connecticut, USA, September 11: Jessica Tandy dies, aged 85.

Washington DC, USA, September 31: President Clinton signs the *Violence Against Women Act*.

Haiti, September 19: US troops invade the Caribbean island. Bloodshed is spared after eleventh-hour negotiations ensure the removal of the military junta.

Baltic Sea, September 28: An Estonian passenger ferry sinks rapidly in heavy weather off the Finnish coast; 912 people lose their lives in the freezing waters.

Utah, USA, October 7: A team of researchers led by Dr Mark Skolnick identify the breast cancer gene.

Iraq, October 13: Saddam Hussein pulls back 60,000 troops and 700 tanks from the Kuwaiti border after the USA rushes troops back.

Bulgaria, October 17: Reneta Indzhova becomes interim Prime Minister.

China, October 27: The *Maternal Infant Health Care Law* is passed.

Sri Lanka, November 10: Chandrika Kumaratunga is swept to power in a landslide election result.

Tennessee, USA, November 12: Track and field legend Wilma Rudolph dies of a brain tumor.

USA, November 16: Martina Navratilova retires from singles tennis.

Chechnya, December 11: After two weeks of bombing the breakaway republic, Russia sends tanks across the border in an attempt to "re-establish constitutional order."

Malaysia: After years of campaigning, Malaysia passes a *Domestic Violence Act*.

Martina Navratilova

Jane Campion Triumphs

Hollywood, USA, March 24: New Zealand writer/director Jane Campion has won the Academy Award for Best Original Screenplay for her acclaimed 1993 film *The Piano*, which last year earned her the coveted Palme d'Or at the Cannes Festival and Best Director award from the Australian Film Institute.

Campion brings a range of talents to her work. Born in Wellington, New Zealand in 1954, she studied anthropology at Wellington's Victoria University, graduating in 1975. At the age of 21, she left New Zealand for Australia, obtaining a painting major from Sydney College of the Arts in 1979 before crafting her writing and directing skills at the Australian Film, Television, and Radio School.

Success for Campion was relatively swift, with her first short film, *Peel* (1982), receiving the Palme d'Or at the 1986 Cannes Film Festival. Further recognition followed when her first feature film, *Sweetie* (1989), won the prestigious 1990 Los Angeles Film Critics' New Generation Award as well as several other awards for the best foreign film.

That same year, she was awarded the Silver Lion at the Venice Film Festival for her second feature film, *An Angel At My Table*, which was based on the autobiographical writings of the New Zealand poet Janet Frame.

"I HAVE A LITTLE BIT OF PENIS ENVY. YEAH THEY'RE RIDICULOUS, BUT THEY'RE COOL."

K. D. LANG, CANADIAN SINGER

The Piano, however, is considered Campion's masterpiece. The story is focused on Ada, a mute British woman forced into an arranged marriage with a New Zealand landowner, her treasured piano her sole means of expression.

The temporal setting is Victorian, but the landscape is rich in symbolism, with the forest, like the piano, playing an intensely emotional role in the story. In preparation for the filming, Campion recorded in her production notes for the movie and cast: "I feel a kinship between the kind of romance that Emily Bronte portrayed in *Wuthering Heights* and this film. Hers is not the notion of romance that we've come to use; it's very harsh and extreme, a Gothic exploration of the romantic impulse."

Agathe Uwilingiyimana Assassinated

Rwanda, April 7: Prime Minister Agathe Uwilingiyimana has been shot dead by members of the Rwandan presidential guard. The assassination of the Prime Minister comes a day after President Juvenal Habyarimana was killed when a rocket brought down the plane in which he was traveling as it approached the airport in the capital, Kigali.

An ethnic Tutsi, Uwilingiyimana taught high school mathematics and science before entering politics in 1992 as a member of the opposition Republican and Democratic Movement. The following year, on July 17, 1993, she became Rwanda's first woman Prime Minister. Although she was officially dismissed less than 30 days after her appointment to the office, she stayed on in a caretaker capacity pending the formation of a new government under a power-sharing agreement between President Habyarimana's Hutu-dominated administration, the five opposition parties, and the Tutsi-dominated Rwandan Patriotic Front.

In an interview with Radio France last night, Uwilingiyimana promised an immediate investigation into the circumstances of President Habyarimana's assassination earlier that day. In what would be her last recorded words, she also went on to warn of wider bloodshed: "…there is shooting, people are being terrorized, people are inside their homes lying on the floor. We are suffering the consequences of the death of the head of state, I believe. We, the civilians, are in no way responsible for the death of our head of state." At the time of her death, she had just reached agreement for a new government to be sworn in the next day.

Former First Lady Buried

Virginia, USA, May 24: Jacqueline Kennedy Onassis was today laid to rest next to her assassinated first husband, President John F. Kennedy, and their two infant children in Arlington National Cemetery, Virginia. The former First Lady passed away in her New York City apartment on May 19 after a short battle with lymphoma, a form of cancer. She was 64 years of age.

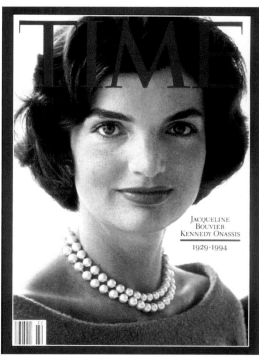

Former First Lady Jacqueline Onassis dies of cancer.

Born Jacqueline Lee Bouvier on July 28, 1929 in Southampton, New York, Onassis met Kennedy in 1952 while working as a photographer for a Washington newspaper. The couple married in 1953, and after her husband won the presidency in 1960, she set about restoring the White House to its original glory, a project brutally cut short in 1963 when Kennedy was assassinated in Dallas. In 1968, she married Greek shipping magnate Aristotle Onassis, but became a widow for a second time following his death in 1975.

Since her passing last week, historians, politicians, and most commentators have unanimously praised Jackie Onassis for her elegance, taste, courage in the face of tragedy, and devotion to her children, as well as the charm she used to deal with politicians from the many countries to which she traveled with the President. Images of her stoic presence with her two young children at the state funeral of John Kennedy remain part of America's legacy. At her graveside today, President Bill Clinton's words were no less glowing: "God gave her very great gifts and imposed upon her great burdens. She bore them all with dignity and grace and uncommon common sense."

Holly Hunter and Anna Paquin in *The Piano*.

Track and field legend Wilma Rudolph, "The Tennessee Tornado," dies of a brain tumor at the age of 54.

Chandrika Kumaratunga

Harding's Denial Cuts No Ice with Officialdom

Colorado Springs, USA, June 30: The United States Figure Skating Association today stripped Tonya Harding of her 1994 national championship and banned her from the organization for life. The USFSA move comes nearly six months after Harding's rival, national champion figure skater Nancy Kerrigan, was clubbed on the leg by a male assailant after a practice session at the US Olympic trials

Tonya Harding is banned from skating for life.

in Detroit. In reaching its decision, the USFSA says it concluded that Tonya Harding "had prior knowledge and was involved prior to the incident," and that her actions as they related to the assault against Kerrigan evidenced "a clear disregard for fairness, good sportsmanship, and ethical behavior." Harding's exhusband, Jeff Gillooly, her bodyguard,

and two other men were implicated in the attack on Kerrigan from the start. On February 2, Gillooly pleaded guilty to one count of racketeering for helping plan the assault, and was sentenced to two years in prison and a fine of $100,000. Gillooly, however, insisted that Harding was also deeply involved in the scheme to disable Kerrigan and that she approved a final plan, an accusation she has steadfastly denied, citing her ex-husband's "continued practice of abusive conduct."

On March 17, Harding pleaded guilty to a lesser charge of obstructing the course of the investigation into the attack on Ms. Kerrigan. Although she avoided a prison term under a plea agreement with prosecutors, she was obliged to surrender membership of the USFSA and resign from the team to compete at the upcoming figure skating world championships in Japan. She was also ordered to pay a $100,000 fine, establish a $50,000 fund to benefit Special Olympics, reimburse the prosecutor's office for $10,000 in costs, and to perform 500 hours of community service work, as well as participate in any psychiatric treatment ordered by the court.

Farewell to Jessica Tandy

Connecticut, USA, September 11: Stage and screen actress Jessica Tandy today succumbed to ovarian cancer at the age of 85. Tandy's distinguished acting career spanned more than six decades, during which time she earned numerous awards and also enjoyed a remarkable film renaissance in the latter years of her life.

Born in London, England, in 1909, Tandy studied drama at the Ben Greet Academy of Acting. She made her professional stage debut at the age of 16 and appeared in her first film, *The Indiscretions of Eve*, in 1932.

Following her marriage to actor Hume Cronyn in 1942, she moved to the USA, where she achieved great success on the stage, winning the coveted Tony award in 1947 for her portrayal of Blanche Dubois in the first production of the Tennessee Williams play, *A Streetcar Named Desire*. She won a second Tony for her appearance in *The Gin Game* (1978), and a third for her work in *Foxfire* (1983), also collecting an Emmy in 1987 for the same role in the televised version.

Initially sporadic, Tandy's Hollywood film career was renewed by her appearances in *The World According to Garp* (1982), and *Cocoon* (1985). In 1989, at the age of 80, she achieved a major career milestone when she was presented with an Oscar for her exceptional performance as a feisty Southern widow in *Driving Miss Daisy*.

Chandrika Kumaratunga Wins Presidency

Sri Lanka, November 10: People's Alliance candidate, Chandrika Kumaratunga, was elected President of Sri Lanka with a record 62 percent of votes cast. Last month, Kumaratunga was appointed Prime Minister after her party secured an overwhelming election victory.

Kumaratunga brings impeccable family credentials to her new post, with both her parents having served as prime ministers in the past. She also brings more than her fair share of personal tragedy, as her father was assassinated when she was 14 years old and her husband, Wijaya Kumaratunga, was gunned down by political opponents in 1988. She nevertheless says that politics is in her blood, and that one of her priorities will be to accelerate the process of economic liberalization in Sri Lanka.

Actress Jessica Tandy won many awards for her work.

Queen Elizabeth II

Six Women Enter the Rock and Roll Hall of Fame

New York, USA, January 12: Six women are the latest inductees into the Rock and Roll Hall of Fame. The legendary visceral-voiced Janis Joplin and the chart-topping Martha and the Vandellas were among the nine outstanding individuals and groups honored at tonight's 10th annual awards ceremony at the Waldorf-Astoria Hotel. Other inductees include Al Green, the Allman Brothers Band, Led Zeppelin, Neil Young, and Frank Zappa. These talented musicians all meet the Hall's eligibility requirement of having released their first recording at least 25 years ago.

Janis Joplin, who died from a heroin overdose in 1970 at the age of 27, has been described as both brash and vulnerable, with a passionate voice that was a high-energy mix of blues, soul, and psychedelic rock. One of the most influential singers of the 1960s, her music reflected the conflicted yearnings of an entire generation of women who strove for sexual equality without sacrificing the feminine, and who longed to experience transcendent love without being enslaved by it.

Her fellow female inductees, Martha and the Vandellas, who disbanded in 1972, recorded an impressive run of hit singles and danceable blockbusters in the mid-sixties, including "Dancing in the Street." The group comprises vocalists Martha Reeves, Rosalyn Ashford, Betty Kelly, Lois Reeves, and Annette Sterling. These passionate women's lives and careers will now be honored in permanent exhibits at the Museum's Hall of Fame.

Daydreams of Flying Go Stratospheric

Space, February 6: A woman whose family was too poor to send her to college, and whose childhood hobby was visiting the airport and dreaming of flying, has made history. Today, space shuttle pilot Lt Col Eileen Marie Collins successfully guided the space shuttle *Discovery* within 37 feet (11 m) of the Russian space station *Mir*, completing its mission rendezvous.

Lt Col Collins is the first woman ever to pilot a space shuttle and her involvement in the new joint Russian-American Space Program is causing excitement around the world. Further tasks on this

Space shuttle *Discovery*, piloted by Eileen Marie Collins.

historic mission include the deployment and retrieval of an astronomy satellite, and a space walk.

Collins was born on November 19, 1956, in Elmira, New York and had her heart set on flying from an early age, joining the Air Force ROTC while still attending Syracuse University. There is no doubt that determination and hard work, as well as talent, have contributed to the success of this remarkable woman. She holds an impressive list of credentials, including an associate in science degree in mathematics/science from Corning Community College, a BA in mathematics and economics from Syracuse University, an MSc in operations research from Stanford University, and an MA in space systems management from Webster University. Collins has also been the recipient of an array of honors and decorations, testament to a pioneering woman on course to change the world.

Feminist Assassinated

Tizi Ouzou, Algeria, February 15: Feminists and human rights groups around the world have expressed outrage at today's assassination of an Algerian feminist. Witnesses report that Nabila Djahnine, an architect and author in her mid-thirties, was gunned down by two men in a car as she walked to work. No single

> "THE MYTH THAT MEN ARE THE ECONOMIC PROVIDERS AND WOMEN, MAINLY, ARE MOTHERS AND CARE GIVERS IN THE FAMILY HAS NOW BEEN THOROUGHLY REFUTED. THIS FAMILY PATTERN HAS NEVER BEEN THE NORM, EXCEPT IN A NARROW MIDDLE-CLASS SEGMENT."
>
> GRO HARLEM BRUNDTLAND, PRIME MINISTER OF NORWAY, 1995

Martha and the Vandellas become the second girl group after the Supremes to be inducted into the Hall of Fame.

New York, USA, January 12: At a ceremony at the Waldorf Astoria Hotel, Janis Joplin and Martha and the Vandellas are among inductees into the Rock and Roll Hall of Fame.
Kobe, Japan, January 17: Over 6,000 people die in Japan's largest quake in nearly 50 years.
Bulgaria, January 25: Reneta Indzhova completes her term as interim Prime Minister.
Space, February 6: The US space shuttle *Discovery* completes its rendezvous with the Russian *Mir* space station.

Tizi Ouzou, Algeria, February 15: Feminist and author Nabila Diahnine (also Djahnine) is shot and killed by Islamic extremists.
Frankfurt, Germany, March 2: Trader Nick Leeson, 28, responsible for a $1.4 billion loss to Barings Bank, is arrested.
Belfast, Northern Ireland, March 9: Queen Elizabeth II makes a symbolic visit to Belfast, her first since the ceasefire came into effect last year.
Seville, Spain, March 18: Spain's Princess Elena marries Jaime de Marichalar y Saenz de Tejada.

Tokyo, Japan, March 20: Sarin, a deadly nerve gas, is released into the subway system, killing eight and affecting 4,000. The Aum Supreme Truth religious sect appears to be linked to the attacks.
Iraq, March 20: Thirty-five thousand Turkish troops cross into northern Iraq to crush the PII, Kurdish separatist rebels waging a guerrilla war that has claimed 15,000 lives.
Vatican City, March 25: Pope John Paul II publishes *Evangelium Vitae*, reaffirming the Catholic Church's position against abortion.

New York, USA, April 18: Carol Shields wins the Pulitzer Prize for *The Stone Diaries*.
Oklahoma City, USA, April 19: A massive car bomb explodes in front of a federal building, killing 168 and injuring over eight hundred. Prime suspect Timothy McVeigh is arrested less than one hour after the blast.
Kibeho, Rwanda, April 22: Government troops massacre Hutu refugees.
California, USA, April 25: Ginger Rogers dies, aged eighty-three.

USA, May 1: Charges of attempted murder against Qubilah Shabazz, the daughter of Malcolm X, are dropped.
Zaire, Congo, May 28: The deadly Ebola hemorrhagic fever kills 256 of the 315 people infected in the second largest outbreak recorded.
Bosnia, May 28: Bosnian Serbs capture more than 350 UN peacekeepers from the "safe haven" of Gorazde, and use them as human shields against NATO attacks.
Dominica, June 14: Mary Eugenia Charles finishes her term as Prime Minister.

group has claimed responsibility, but it is believed the men were part of a growing number of Islamist militant extremists opposed to the political goals of the women's rights movement.

Human rights in Algeria have deteriorated dramatically since parliamentary elections were canceled in 1992, and the continuation of fighting between Algerian government forces and the armed Islamist opposition has resulted in escalating attacks on activists, intellectuals, and women who do not comply with the strict Islamic codes of dress and behavior. It is estimated that around 30,000 people have died in the three years since the start of the rebellion, and it is clear that the extremism exhibited by the fundamentalists has forced the more liberal and peaceful elements of Islam into a defensive posture.

Ms Djahnine, who led an organization called the Cry of Women, was a courageous and committed activist and an outspoken advocate of women's rights. Cry of Women has lobbied for changes to Algeria's family code, including the elimination of outdated provisions governing divorce, marriage, inheritance, and child custody. Female activists in Algeria claim that the current family code is unjust, discriminatory and denies them their rights. However, the emancipation

time out

The abduction and rape of a twelve-year-old Japanese schoolgirl by three American servicemen raises questions about the US presence in Okinawa, which has been significant and ongoing since the end of WWII.

of women poses a serious threat to forces wishing to establish Algeria as a strict Islamist state. Driving women back into their homes is one of the primary aims of the Muslim fundamentalists, and unveiled women—symbols of opposition to fundamentalist oppression—have become regular military targets.

Ms Djahnine, who will be greatly missed, will be remembered for her dedication and for her outstanding contribution toward the emancipation of Islamic women.

Queen's Historic Irish Visit

Belfast, Northern Ireland, March: Queen Elizabeth's visit to Northern Ireland today is an historic occasion. Not only is it her first visit to the country since last year's IRA ceasefire came into effect on August 31, but it is also the first time since the Reformation that a British monarch and a Catholic primate of Ireland have met. Her meeting with Cardinal Daly and his Anglican counterpart, Archbishop Robin Eames, is seen as a symbol of hope for a more peaceful future.

When she visited Belfast, the Queen met the city's lord mayor and shook hands with Democratic Unionist MP, Peter Robinson, as well as SDLP party MP, Joe Hendron. In her address to the people of Northern Ireland, she praised them for their extraordinary courage and compassion.

Ginger Takes a Last Bow

California, USA, April 25: The story of a little girl who was once described as being able to dance before she could walk, and who grew up to become the other half of the world's greatest dance partnership, has ended. Ginger Rogers, who was 83, died today of congestive heart failure in

Cry of Women is seen as a threat by Islamic extremists.

her home in Rancho Mirage, California. In her recently published autobiography, she laments the fact that she is more famous for her partnership with Fred Astaire than for her many independent acting achievements, but admits to being pleased that she will be remembered for being young and beautiful.

The elegant and versatile Rogers was born on July 16, 1911 in Independence, Missouri, and made her performing debut at age 14, arriving in Hollywood in 1931. Both a gifted actress and accomplished dancer, she had a film career spanning over 50 years and made 73 films. Her most memorable performances include *Top Hat* and *Swing*, the classic 1930s musicals she made with Astaire.

In 1940, she earned the Best Actress Oscar for her dramatic performance in *Kitty Foyle*, and was considered RKO's hottest property in the years that followed. A woman of diverse talents, Rogers was also an accomplished artist, and for 50 years ran a dairy farm in Oregon. She was a keen golfer, swimmer, and tennis player. Though she married and divorced five times, her mother, Lela Rogers (1891–1977), a reporter, scriptwriter, and movie producer, lived with her for much of her life. Rogers will be cremated and her ashes interred in Oakwood Memorial Park Cemetery in Chatsworth.

Ginger Rogers

Oscar winner Jessica Lange in *Blue Sky*.

Iris Murdoch

Charges against Malcolm X's Daughter Dropped

USA, May 1: Attempted murder charges against Malcolm X's daughter, Qubilah Shabazz, were dropped today. Shabazz, who has repeatedly maintained her innocence, was implicated earlier this year in a murder-for-hire scheme. She was charged with traveling interstate and using a telephone to arrange the contract murder of the leader of the Nation of Islam, Minister Louis Farrakhan.

The case, which has given rise to much speculation and considerable debate, was dropped in a plea bargain agreement that will see the 34-year-old Shabazz begin treatment for alcohol abuse and psychiatric problems.

This affair is exceptional both for its historical context and for the identities of the defendant and alleged target. The most bizarre twist has come from Louis Farrakhan himself, who has claimed that the entire case was an FBI construct devised to undermine the relationship between the Nation of Islam and the forces of Afro-American Unity. There are also claims that Michael Fitzpatrick, a former high school classmate of Shabazz and long-time FBI informer, set her up.

This case, which has been described as one that should never have been brought to court, comes 30 years after Shabazz saw her father assassinated in Manhattan's Audubon Ballroom. One thing is clear through all the debate and finger pointing: this is not the end of the story of the family of Malcolm X.

> *"When I was in high school, I never thought I would be an astronaut. We didn't have women astronauts then. Let me tell you, dreams can come true!"*
>
> LT. COL. EILEEN MARIE COLLINS

A relieved Qubilah Shabazz and her mother.

Mountaineering Mother Dies in Himalayan Storm

Himalayas, August 13: The worldwide climbing community has been rocked by the tragic death today of 33-year-old British mountaineer and mother of two, Alison Hargreaves. Early reports indicate that the climber and her teammates were caught in a sudden storm shortly after reaching the summit of the 28,251-foot (8,610 meters) peak of Pakistan's K2. Although climbers are always prepared for fickle weather patterns at these high altitudes, survivors reported that this storm was particularly ferocious.

There is speculation that high winds may have knocked some of the climbers, including Hargreaves, off the mountain, or that they were struck by an avalanche. Other team members who also perished on the ill-fated expedition were Rob Slater of the USA, Bruce Grant of New Zealand, and three Spanish climbers: Javier Escartin, Lorenzo Ortiz Monson, and Javier Olivar. Another climber, Jeff Lakes from Canada, died that night after abandoning the summit bid and fighting his way back down to a lower camp.

Hargreave's K2 climb was part of a personal challenge she had set herself to scale the world's three highest mountains—Mount Everest, K2 and Kanchenjunga—unaided. In May of this year, she completed a successful climb of Mount Everest, reaching the summit without bottled oxygen and without the aid of Sherpas, becoming the first woman ever to climb Everest unassisted. She also notched up a soloing first by climbing all the great north faces of the Alps, including the notoriously difficult north face of the Eiger, in a single season, when she was in her second term of pregnancy.

This season has been one of the worst on record on one of the world's most dangerous mountains. The tenacious and talented Hargreaves was considered one of the best mountaineers in the world. She will be missed by both her family and the climbers she inspired.

Conference Celebrates the Fight for Women's Rights

Beijing, China, September 4-15: Although we are doing well, we still have a long way to go. This is the message coming out of the fourth United Nations World Conference on Women: Action for Equality, Development and Peace, which is currently being held in Beijing.

The aim of the conference is to place the improvement of women's status high on the global agenda and to address the deeply entrenched attitudes and practices that affect opportunities for women all around the world.

Attended by 189 government representatives and over 5,000 representatives from 2,100 non-governmental organizations, the conference will touch on a wide range of themes, but its focus will be on issues directly affecting women's rights. It is also being used as an occasion to celebrate the contributions women make on both a domestic and global level.

Lori Berenson arrested for treason in Peru.

Confessions of a Princess

England, November 20: Over 200 million people sat glued to their televisions tonight as the steamy truths behind a real life soap opera unfolded in their living rooms. It had all the ingredients of a popular television drama: infidelity, wealth, fame, a beautiful princess, and an assortment of dashing, royal men.

Television journalist Martin Bashir's *Panorama* interview with Princess Diana was irresistible, mesmerizing viewing—a magnificent piece of public relations choreography. The interview, which was taped without Buckingham Palace or Prince Charles's knowledge, is widely seen as Diana's response to the Prince's own 1994 interview, in which he admitted to adultery.

The Princess talked frankly about what she sees as Buckingham Palace's fear and resentment of her popularity with the British public, and gave calm and open responses to Bashir's questions, many of which focused on rumors and reports that have been circulating over the past few years. She spoke with great candor about the pressures and hectic schedule of royal life, her troubled relationship with Prince Charles, and subsequent infidelities and betrayals. She also talked about James Hewitt, publicly admitted her relationship with him, and revealed how hurt she had been when he attempted to capitalize on their love affair.

A fair portion of the interview focused on the relationship between Charles and Camilla, which is widely regarded as the catalyst for the eventual breakdown of Charles and Diana's marriage. "There were three of us in this marriage," said the Princess, "so it was a bit crowded." She also admitted to lingering insecurities from an unhappy childhood, to "postnatal depression, which no one ever discusses," to bulimia, and to finding the demands

Cup Shaken and Stirred by Female Yachties

Newport, USA April 17: A team of women has claimed the seas, rattling the traditional chains of yachting's oldest and most prestigious race—the male-dominated America's Cup.

For 150 years, the America's Cup has all but excluded women, but today, in a magnificent performance by the first boat ever to be sailed by an all-female crew, *Mighty Mary USA 43* staged a unique win against *Stars and Stripes USA 34* in the sixth race of the 32nd America's Cup defenders' final trials.

There has been much anticipation surrounding this race, in which Dennis Connor, the world's most experienced skipper, locked horns with skipper, Leslie Egnot, and her 14 female teammates. Egnot, one of New Zealand's top sailors, explained afterwards that they felt hunted by *Stars and Stripes* in the exhilarating neck-and-neck race and that they had pushed Connor to the end.

The American-born Egnot grew up in New Zealand and was the first woman to win the New Zealand national title in the P Class, the Tanner Cup. In 1988, she won the women's 470 New Zealand championship and in 1989 she took second place at the 470 women's world championship in Japan. She also participated in the 1992 Olympics in Barcelona, where she added a silver medal to her to her trophies.

There seems little doubt that Egnot's latest win will make a lasting impression on the world of sailing.

Rosemary West

BBC television broadcasts an interview with Princess Diana in which she talks frankly about her life.

of royal life at times overwhelming. "I've never encouraged the media," she said. "There was a relationship which worked before, but now I can't tolerate it because it's become abusive and it's harassment."

This story of a young woman abruptly catapulted from her life as a shy schoolteacher to another life completely as one of the most famous, most photographed women in the world made compelling viewing. Princess Diana, once described as Mother Teresa and *Vogue* magazine rolled into one, will no doubt continue to capture the public's imagination, and for as long as she does that, she will attract media attention.

Fruit Fly Enthusiast Wins Nobel Prize for Physiology

Oslo, Norway, December 10: A woman who loves flies and admits they often appear in her dreams is a co-winner of this year's Nobel Prize for Physiology or Medicine. Christiane Nüsslein-Volhard shares the prestigious prize with Edward B. Lewis and Eric F. Wieschaus, "for their discoveries concerning the genetic control of early embryonic development."

The three developmental biologists used the fruit fly—an organism frequently used in the study of genetics—to identify and classify key genes determining body plan and the formation of body segments. Nüsslein-Volhard, who finished her basic scientific training at the end of the 1970s, was offered her first independent research position at the European Molecular Biology Laboratory (EMBL) in Heidelberg along with Eric Wieschaus. Deciding to work as a team was a brave step for these two young scientists at the beginning of their careers, but their cooperation paid

off when they published the results of their findings in *Nature Magazine* in 1980. The article, which outlined their unique approach to gene classification, encouraged developmental biologists to search for similar genes in other species.

Nüsslein-Volhard has been Director of the Max Planck Institute for Developmental Biology in Tübingen since 1985. She also leads its Genetics Department. Last year, she established the Christiane Nüsslein-Volhard Foundation to assist promising German female scientists with children balance family obligations with professional commitments.

Leslie Egnot skippers *Mighty Mary*, the first boat in the history of the America's Cup to boast an all-woman crew.

American Jailed in Peru for "Marxist Plot"

Marguerite Duras

Lima, Peru, January 11: American Lori Berenson was today sentenced by a Peruvian military tribunal to life in prison for terrorism-related offenses. The court found that the 26-year-old had "plotted with Marxist rebels to attack the Peruvian Congress." Neither Berenson—who vehemently denies the charge—nor her lawyer were allowed to attend the trial or given any opportunity to mount a defense.

New York-born Berenson, a journalist with a keen sense of social activism, has traveled widely through Central and South America. On November 30, 1995, she went to the Congress building to research two articles for American magazines. Boarding a bus in central Lima afterwards, she was arrested by anti-terrorism police and interrogated for nine days.

The exact nature of the charges was never properly articulated, but it appears Berenson was accused of leading the Marxist insurgency group MRTA. Following the "trial," presided over by a hooded judge who found her guilty of "treason against the fatherland," Berenson is destined to spend years languishing in Peru's notoriously harsh maximum-security prison system. She is determined to fight to establish her innocence, however, and has said she would never condone terrorist acts and was certainly never a member of, or involved with, MRTA.

> *"GAY ICONS USUALLY HAVE SOME TRAGEDY IN THEIR LIVES, BUT I'VE ONLY HAD TRAGIC HAIRCUTS AND OUTFITS."*
>
> KYLIE MINOGUE, AUSTRALIAN POP SINGER

Human Rights Activist Arrested for "False News"

Kuala Lumpur, Malaysia, March 18: Irene Fernandez, founder of human rights group Tenaganita, was today arrested for "maliciously spreading false news." Police arrested Fernandez at her home, citing a breach of the *Printing Presses and Publications Act* of 1984.

time out

Monica Lewinsky quickly becomes a household name after phone tapes suggest that the blue dress she wore to one liaison with President Clinton has never been dry cleaned and is now potential evidence.

In 1995, Tenaganita released a report titled "Abuse, Torture and Dehumanised Treatment of Migrant Workers at the Detention Camps." It was based on a series of interviews with 300 former detainees who provided detailed allegations of mistreatment, stating that as well as enduring physical abuse, they had been denied access to legal representation and medical assistance, and in some cases starved, sexually assaulted and forced to witness

American activist Lori Berenson has been sentenced to life in prison.

Christy Martin is the first woman pro boxer.

the death of other detainees. Tenaganita representatives had been visiting Malaysia's migrant detention centers to gather information on HIV/AIDS and the health of those in the camps. When it became apparent that the problems were far more serious than they could have imagined, the nature of their investigation altered.

The report claimed that the Malaysian authorities responsible for running the camps were contravening Article 5 of the Universal Declaration of Human Rights, which states that "no-one shall be subjected to torture or to cruel, inhuman or degrading treatment or punishment." Tenaganita called for the camps to be opened for public inspection and an inquiry into the alleged human rights abuses to be set up.

Tenaganita's findings sparked an international outcry but the Malaysian government swiftly denied any wrongdoing and held Fernandez responsible for "errors" in the report. Tenaganita—which can be translated as "Women's Force"—was set up by Fernandez in the 1990s after she found herself appalled by the plight of migrant workers. The maximum penalty for the offense she has been charged with is three years in jail, a 20,000 ringgit fine, or both.

Key Events

Bosnia, January 2: US combat troops enter northern Bosnia to keep the peace between Bosnian Serbs and Muslims following the Dayton Peace Agreement signed last month.

Paris, France, January 8: François Mitterrand, socialist prime minister for 14 years, dies, aged 79.

Lima, Peru, January 11: American activist Lori Berenson is imprisoned for terrorism-related offenses.

Colombo, Sri Lanka, January 31: A truck laden with explosives crashes into the Central Bank, killing 57 people and injuring over 1,000.

London, England, February 9: An explosion in the Docklands marks the end of a 17-month cease-fire by the IRA.

London, England, February 14: One of the last survivors of the *Titanic* sinking, Eva Hart, dies aged 90.

USA, February: Christy Martin is the first woman boxer to have her match televised.

Kuala Lumpur, Malaysia, March 18: Irene Fernandez, founder of human rights group Tenaganita, is arrested.

Paris, France, March 3: Iconic writer Marguerite Duras dies, aged 81.

Dunblane, Scotland, March 13: Gunman Thomas Hamilton goes on a shooting spree in the local primary school, killing 16 students and a teacher before taking his own life.

London, England, March 15: Controversial artist Helen Chadwick dies of heart failure, aged 43.

England, March 18: Archeologist, writer, and wife of J.B. Priestley, Jacquetta Hawkes, dies, aged 85.

Hollywood, USA, March 25: Emma Thompson wins the Oscar for Best Adapted Screenplay.

Hollywood, USA, March 25: Susan Sarandon receives the Oscar for Best Actress for her performance as Sister Helen Prejean in the 1995 film *Dead Man Walking*.

Boston, USA, April 15: German Uta Pippig is the first woman to win the Boston Marathon three years in a row.

Cairo, Egypt, April 18: Islamic militants open fire outside a Cairo hotel, killing 17 Greek tourists.

London, England, April 23: Australian-born author of *Mary Poppins*, Pamela Lyndon Travers, dies, aged 96.

Tasmania, Australia, April 28: Martin Bryant shoots and kills 35 people at Port Arthur.

Iraq, May 20: Iraq and the United Nations agree on the oil-for-food program, allowing Iraq to sell oil for humanitarian necessities.

Belfast, Northern Ireland, May 30: Two delegates from the newly formed Northern Ireland Women's Coalition are elected to the Northern Ireland Assembly.

London, England, May: Helen Dunmore wins the inaugural Orange Prize for Fiction for *A Spell of Winter*.

Dead Man walking won Susan Sarandon an Oscar.

Controversial British Artist Dies in Her Prime

London, England, March 15: Controversial artist Helen Chadwick, 43, died today of heart failure. Lauded as one of the most important British installation artists of the 1980s and early 1990s, Chadwick's work often included a feminist subtext. Her 1987 work *Of Mutability*—nominated for the Turner Prize, making her one of the first women to be shortlisted for this award—consisted of two parts: *Carcass*, featuring a glass tower of rotting vegetation, and *The Oval Court*, a large collage of photocopied images of the naked artist in various emotionally charged poses arranged to form a "pool." Chadwick once said of this work: "I want to catch the physical sensations passing across the body—sensations of gasping, yearning, breathing, fullness."

Her art was provocative, popular and deeply personal, and often included images of her own body. Her best-known works include *Piss Flowers*, a series of bronze sculptures cast in holes left in the snow where she and her partner had urinated, and *Cacao*, which featured a slowly bubbling fountain of chocolate. These pieces attracted a great deal of media attention and saw Chadwick become something of a celebrity.

Given the prematurity of her death, it is ironic that one of Chadwick's last collections, *Stilled Lives*, centered on a series of photographs of dead human embryos. In the series *Viral Landscapes* (1988), she investigated viruses and how they relate to the natural landscape. Rather poignantly, it was a virus that weakened the muscles of Chadwick's heart and caused her death.

Passing of a Pioneer

England, March 18: Eminent archeologist and writer Jacquetta Hawkes has died at the age of 85. She will be remembered not only for her outstanding archeological discoveries, but for sharing them with others by presenting her findings in an accessible and exciting manner.

Hawkes, daughter of Nobel Prize-winning scientist Sir Frederick Gowland Hopkins, was married to fellow archeologist Christopher Hawkes, then later to broadcaster and writer J.B. Priestley.

Hawkes was a prolific writer, producing everything from newspaper columns on archeology to children's books, academic papers and plays. Her best-known work is probably *A Land*, a book in which she combines archeology with geology and history to produce the story of Britain. In 1968's *Dawn of the Gods* she explored the possibility of ancient Minoan society being ruled by women. Later in life she was a campaigner for nuclear disarmament and worked for UNESCO.

Third Time Still Lucky

Boston, USA, April 15: German athlete Uta Pippig has become the first woman to win the Boston Marathon three years in a row. She completed the race in two hours, 25 minutes, 11 seconds—a remarkable feat for someone suffering reversible colitis, which causes inflammation of the bowel.

Pippig was born in Leipzig, East Germany, and her athletic ability was spotted at a young age. In 1983 she joined a top sporting club and soon became one of the country's best long-distance runners. Aware that her potential for continued growth was limited by the political situation in the East, Pippig and her coach crossed into West Germany shortly after the fall of the Berlin Wall. Among her proudest achievements was winning the Unification Marathon in Berlin in 1990.

In this symbolically charged race, she and 25,000 other runners passed through the city's Brandenburg Gate to enter the former East Germany. She said afterwards: "It's a moment that I will cherish for as long as I live."

In 1993, Pippig became the only German to have won a New York marathon. In 1994 and 1995 she was ranked the number one marathon and half-marathon runner in the world. Her win in today's Boston Marathon marks the centenary of the event.

Jacquetta Hawkes

Uta Pippig wins the Boston Marathon yet again.

K e y   E v e n t s

Lagos, Nigeria, June 4: Kudirat Abiola is killed by gunmen.
Dhaka, Bangladesh, June 23: Sheikh Hasina Wajed becomes Prime Minister.
Bosnia, July 19: Bosnian Serb President Radovan Karadzic resigns from office and withdraws from public life after being indicted for war crimes.
Atlanta, USA, July 19: The opening ceremony of the Olympic Games takes place. At these Olympics, women's soccer will be played for the first time.

Atlanta, USA, July 27: A bomb explodes at a concert during the Olympic Games, injuring 200 people and killing two.
Atlanta, USA, July: Australian swimmer Susie O'Neill wins gold, silver, and bronze medals.
Reykjavik, Iceland, August 1: Vigdis Finnbogadottir bows out of office after four terms as president.
Chechnya, Russia, August: After two years of fierce fighting between separatist rebels and the Russian Army, a peace accord is signed allowing for limited autonomy.

Monrovia, Liberia, September 3: Ruth Perry acts as Chairman of the Council of State of the republic.
Cape Canaveral, Florida, USA, September 26: Shannon Lucid returns from her mission at the *Mir* space station, having spent the longest time in space of any US citizen thus far.
Kabul, Afghanistan, September 27: Taliban militia take the capital, their aim to establish the "purest" Islamic regime in the world.

New York, USA, October 3: Controversial feminist play *The Vagina Monologues*, written and performed by Eve Ensler, premieres off Broadway.
UK, November 4: The Spice Girls' debut album *Spice* hits number one.
USA, November 6: Andrea Barret wins the National Book Award for *Ship Fever and Other Stories*.
Canada, November: Margaret Atwood wins the Giller Prize for Canadian Fiction for her novel *Alias Grace*.

Nairobi, Kenya, December 9: Archeologist and paleontologist Mary Leakey dies, aged 83.
Stockholm, Sweden, December 10: Polish poet Wislawa Szymborska is awarded the Nobel Prize for Literature.
UK, December: The government culls 100,000 cows in a bid to stop the spread of Mad Cow Disease.
Japan: This year teen idol Namie Amuro sold 3 million copies of her debut solo album, *Sweet 19 Blues*.

Mary Poppins Author Dies

Susie O'Neill

London, England, April 23: Pamela Lyndon Travers, best known for her Mary Poppins books, died today at the age of 96. In 1934 she published the first of her eight stories about the magical no-nonsense nanny who has captured the hearts and minds of young readers ever since.

In the original book, Mary Poppins is blown by a strong wind into the London home of the Banks family, where she takes up the task of caring for and enchanting the four young children. Mary Poppins's tale has since been made into a hit movie starring Julie Andrews.

Travers was born Helen Lyndon Goff in Queensland, Australia, and after achieving some success as an actress and dancer moved to England, where she started writing—first news articles, then drama, poetry, and fiction. After *Mary Poppins* became a bestseller, she traveled around the world seeking inspiration for her stories. She took up several writer-in-residence positions and later in her life published a series of travel books. She said: "As a writer, you can feel awfully imprisoned, because people, having had so much of one thing, want you always to go on doing more of the same."

A view of Russia's *Mir* space station from the flight deck of the US space shuttle *Atlantis*.

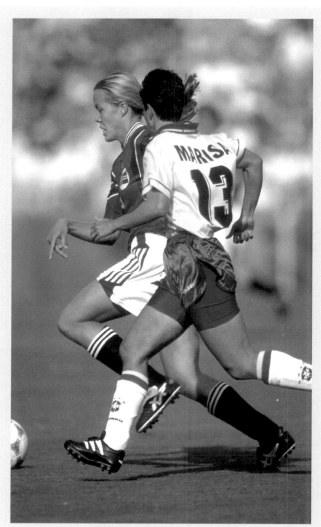

Women's soccer at the Atlanta Olympics.

Women MPs Get the Nod in Northern Ireland

Belfast, Northern Ireland, May 30: Monica McWilliams and Pearl Sagar were today elected to the Northern Ireland Assembly. They represent the Northern Ireland Women's Coalition (NIWC)—a political party formed in response to frustrations felt by women that their voices are not being heard as negotiations for a peace process get underway.

Significantly, the group has members from both the unionist and nationalist sides of the Northern Ireland divide. Initially established to lobby the major political parties to include women as candidates, the NIWC decided to stand candidates of its own after its calls were effectively ignored. With few resources behind it, the party has relied on donations and word-of-mouth support.

The NIWC was successful in winning one percent of the vote in the elections for the Northern Ireland Assembly, securing it the two seats now taken up by McWilliams and Sagar.

Nigerian Opposition Leader's Wife Murdered

Lagos, Nigeria, June 4: Kudirat Abiola, one of the many wives of Nigeria's imprisoned opposition leader Moshood Abiola, has been shot as she traveled along a Lagos street. According to witness reports, three gunmen in a car fired on Abiola, killing her and her driver.

After the attack, 44-year-old Abiola lost consciousness and was taken to Lagos's Eko Hospital, where surgeons were unable to save her life. The incident is being treated as an assassination and already there have been calls by activists for an inquiry into the killing.

Abiola was an outspoken supporter of the movement to free her husband from prison, where he has been serving a sentence for treason since June 1994. Moshood Abiola, representing the Social Democratic Party, won Nigeria's lawfully conducted presidential elections in 1993 with a 60 percent majority. Shortly afterwards however, the ruling junta became concerned at his popularity and annulled the results, claiming power themselves.

After he spoke out about the unfairness of not being able to assume the presidential role he had won legitimately, he found himself facing treason charges. Likewise, Kudirat Abiola had been very vocal in her criticism of the Nigerian government, organizing pro-democracy rallies and publicizing her husband's plight in the international press. In an interview last year with *The News* magazine, she called on foreign governments to become involved by doing more to ensure that human rights were not ignored in Nigeria. She said: "Although they have done very well, I still expect them to go beyond talking. I expect concrete actions because, the way things are going, this regime is becoming more vicious and it takes only powerful international countries' intervention before such a rampaging dictatorship is curtailed."

Just a month before her murder, Abiola had been detained overnight by police and charged with false publication. Initial reports suggest that her death was politically motivated.

Liberia Gives Africa its First Female Leader

Monrovia, Liberia, September 3: After being formally sworn in today as Chairman of the Council of State of the National Transitional Government of Liberia, Ruth Perry is Liberia's head of state—and Africa's first female government leader.

Perry, a former senator, has been handed the unenviable task of managing the strife-torn nation's government until next year, when a general election can be held. She was appointed to the role by representatives of the Economic Community of West African States, who are hoping that she will be able to help calm the civil unrest that has plagued Liberia for about six years. Perry has described the country's civil war to UN representatives as a "man-made disaster." Before taking on the role, Perry was involved with the National Democratic Party of Liberia and had held the position of supervisor with the Chase Manhattan Bank of Liberia. During her time in government, the widow and mother of seven has lobbied hard to protect the rights of women and children.

One of her first priorities in quelling the unrest in Liberia to is disarm the many children who have been forced to fight in the six-year conflict.

Afghan Women Oppressed under Taliban Regime

Kabul, Afghanistan, September 27: Taliban militia have taken control of the national capital, stating that their aim is to establish the "purest" Islamic regime in the world. On entering the city they met with little resistance from the war-wearied government forces, and President Burhanuddin Rabbani has fled for his life.

The Taliban have swiftly made it clear that under their regime the women of Afghanistan will have their freedoms severely restricted. They have issued an edict that forbids women and girls to go to work or school. Afghan women are also prohibited from leaving their homes without the accompaniment of a male family member. It is no longer acceptable for a woman to speak in public to a man who is not a close relative, nor can she attend any form of public gathering.

Dress restrictions apply, too, with all women instructed to wear the *burqa*, a garment which covers them from head to toe. Prior to the Taliban taking power, the *burqa* was only seen occasionally on the streets of Kabul. Women now face the prospect of being beaten for showing so much as a flash of ankle. A woman seen in public with painted fingernails could have her fingers cut off.

International observers are concerned that the restrictions will compromise the

Women must now wear the traditional *burqa* in Afghanistan.

general health of the nation's women as 40 percent of doctors in Kabul are women. Now they are only permitted to work in a small number of women-only hospitals, leaving the bulk of the female population to go without medical care, as they are not allowed to be seen by a male doctor.

The strictures imposed by the Taliban carry very heavy penalties. If women are caught not wearing the correct attire, for example, they can be whipped. If accused of infidelity or prostitution, they face being hung or stoned to death.

Spice Girls' Album Debuts at No. 1

UK, November 4: The pop group Spice Girls today have what they really, really want: a debut album that has entered the charts at No. 1. Britain is in the grip of Spice Girls fever, endowing its five singers with superstar status virtually overnight.

Each of the Spice Girls has her own onstage persona and name. Geri Halliwell becomes Ginger Spice because of her reddish hair; Melanie Chisholm is Sporty Spice for her athletic attire; the cool demeanor of Victoria Adams has earned her the name Posh Spice; Melanie Brown's piercings and "tough girl" attitude make her Scary Spice; and Emma Bunton is Baby Spice, thanks to her youthful looks and penchant for baby-doll dresses. These personae are clever marketing devices, in keeping with the band's roots. In

1994, an advertisement in *The Stage* magazine called for expressions of interest from "streetwise" female singers aged 18 to 23 in forming a manufactured all-girl group. Halliwell, Chisholm, Brown and Adams all sailed through the auditions; Bunton was selected later to join them. Their debut album, *Spice*, features "Wannabe," the catchy single that propelled the group into the public spotlight. Almost as soon as "Wannabe" was released on July 8, the British media became obsessed with the group and the "girl power" ethos they purported to represent. Now a new term, "Spicemania," has been used to describe the increasing public interest in the group. There is much discussion about whether or not the Spice Girls' "we can do whatever we want" credo represents a contemporary take on feminism that young women can identify with and embrace.

Margaret Atwood

The Spice Girls' debut album has raced to No. 1.

Susie Maroney

Twenty Women Team Up to Take on Polar Challenge

The Arctic, March 14: After two long years of planing and preparation, adventurer and businesswoman Caroline Hamilton's dream of an all-women relay team walking to the North Pole is set to become a reality. Today, the first of the McVities Penguin Polar Relay teams set out from Canada's Ward Hunt Island.

The relay of five teams of women, who come from all walks of life, will haul sleds of up to 150 lbs (68 kilos) across 500 miles (800 km) of shifting pack ice in temperatures as low as –40°F(–40°C). Team Echo comprises Hamilton (the leader), Zoe Hudson, Pom Oliver, and Lucy Roberts.

They will be on the ice from May 9 to 27. The final team hopes to reach the North Pole in late May. Hamilton, who studied history and philosophy of science at Cambridge, says that as a child she loved reading stories of the Arctic and Antarctic. Her ambitions to excel were sparked by her brother, who teased her as a child, calling her a sissy and a weakling.

Hamilton's concept of a supported relay walk to the North Pole is entirely original, enabling participants to take part in an epic adventure safely and economically. Many have been wondering what the enterprising Williams's next challenge will be. There is speculation that she may tackle the South Pole, and become the first woman to conquer both poles.

Arundhati Roy wins the Booker Prize.

Martina Hingis, youngest Wimbledon singles champion.

Intelligence Officer Brutally Murdered

Lima, Peru, March 25: The dismembered remains of a young woman were found in plastic bags on a roadside north of Lima early this morning. Her head and hands had been cut off, apparently to frustrate any attempt to identify her.

It is suspected that the remains belong to former Army Intelligence Service officer and agent, Mariela Barreto, who was last seen alive by her family members early on the morning of March 22, 1997. At that time, she was leaving her home in Lima, and was on her way to arrange a blood type certificate for her newborn daughter.

The body had multiple lesions in the neck area, along both sides of the abdomen and on one of the legs, indicating torture. The perpetrators are suspected to be fellow members of the Army Intelligence Service. There is speculation Barreto was murdered because she gave journalists information about the La Cantuta Massacre, in which a professor

time out

Food giant McDonald's wins a libel action taken out by UK environmentalists Helen Steel and Dave Morris ("the McLibel pair," as they became known), but will not be collecting the £40K the company was awarded in costs.

and nine students from Lima's La Cantuta University were abducted and subsequently executed by military agents. She also revealed information about the location of the victims' bodies. Sources indicate Barreto had also been filtering information to the press about secret intelligence plans to intimidate journalists and members of the opposition.

Authorities are refusing to speculate, saying only that proper legal procedures must be followed in order to investigate, prosecute, and punish any wrongdoers. But there are concerns that the country's judiciary, whose independence has been seriously compromised by President Alberto Fujimori, will not be impartial in this investigation. Massive human rights violations, rigged elections and wholesale corruption have characterized President Fujimori's tenure, and there are concerns that this case will remain unresolved.

is also three-time winner of the Manhattan Island swim race in the years 1991, 1992, and 1994.

Boy Wizard Charms World

London, England, July: An orphaned boy wizard has cast a spell over British and American schoolchildren. J.K. Rowling's *Harry Potter and the Philosopher's Stone* (renamed *Harry Potter and the Sorcerer's Stone* in the US) tells the story of Harry Potter and his adventures at the Hogwarts School of Witchcraft and Wizardry.

Gifted storyteller and first-time novelist, Joanne Rowling, was asked to use her initials in her nom de plume as her British publisher, Bloomsbury, feared that boys might not want to read a book written by a woman. The publisher also told her not to expect huge sales.

In fact, the book has been a huge success, with both boys and girls. This spring, Scholastic Books won an auction for the American rights to the planned seven-book series, giving Rowling an advance of over $100,000, a record for a foreign children's book. The skillfully crafted story has captured imaginations around the world, and looks set to be quite a phenomenon.

Iran Appoints First Female Vice President

Tehran, Iran, August 23: The appointment of Massoumeh Ebtekar today as Iran's first female Vice President and Head of the Environment Protection Organization of Iran heralds a political breakthrough for Iranian women. Dr Ebtekar is an adviser to President Khatami, whose newly elected reformist party, Islamic Iran Participation Front, defeated the conservative establishment candidate earlier this year. Born in 1960 in Tehran, Dr Ebtekar went to school in the United States. She was a first-year student at Tehran's Polytechnic Institute during the 1979 Iranian hostage crisis and, at age 19, played a key role in negotiations. Dubbed "Mary" by the US press (because of her head scarf), she was selected because of her good command of English as spokeswoman for the students who took 52 diplomats hostage during the American Embassy siege.

In 1981, Dr Ebtekar was appointed editor-in-chief of the English-language newspaper, *Kayhan International*, by Khatami, who was head of the Kayhan publishing house at the time. Since 1993, she has been managing editor of *Farzaneh*, a bilingual quarterly devoted to the advancement of women's studies. In 1995 Dr Ebtekar earned a doctorate in immunology from Tarbiat Modares University.

Dr Ebtekar has told the *Hamshahri* newspaper that if women are promoted on merit, many of Iran's problems will eventually be solved.

Juliette Binoche

Children's author J. K. Rowling.

Australian Swimmer Conquers Florida Straits

Florida, USA, May 12: Australian marathon swimmer, 22-year-old Susie Maroney, wearily stepped ashore at Key West, Florida, this afternoon, the first person to swim the 112-mile (180-km) Florida Straits from Cuba to the United States. Maroney, who failed in an attempt to make the same swim last June, completed the crossing in 26 hours and 22 minutes.

After diving into the water in Havana, Cuba, strong overnight winds and rain nearly forced her to abandon this crossing as well, but as dawn broke she found extra strength to continue and looked happy and relieved as she was eventually helped from the surf at Key West.

In 1990, Maroney broke the speed record for swimming the English Channel, and also became the youngest Australian to swim the Channel, at age 16. A year later, in 1991, she went on to complete the fastest double English Channel crossing (there and back). This remarkable athlete

Frances McDormand wins an Oscar for *Fargo*.

**Diana,
Princess of Wales**

Mother Teresa Is No More

Calcutta, India, September 5: The world lost a legend today with the passing of 87-year-old Mother Teresa. She died at 9.30 p.m., reportedly of cardiac arrest, at her religious order's headquarters in eastern India. An example of true self-sacrifice, Mother Teresa spent her life taking care of those she lovingly called "the poorest of the poor." She regularly visited the victims of major disasters, praying for their recovery and helping to raise money for their care. Her Missionaries of Charity grew from her 12 original followers to thousands of sisters working in 450 centers around the world.

Mother Teresa was born Agnes Gonxha Bojaxhiu to Albanian parents on August 27, 1910 in Macedonia. She was 18 years old when she went to Dublin, Ireland, to take her vows and become a nun of Loreto, a teaching order that ran convent schools in India. She took the name Sister Teresa after Saint Teresa of Lisieux, the patroness of missionaries. Then in 1946 she experienced "the call," as she described it, "to leave the convent and help the poor while living among them."

Mother Teresa's efforts on behalf of world peace brought her several important humanitarian awards, including the Nobel Peace Prize in 1979. The diminutive nun worked tirelessly to the very end of her life, and demonstrated to the world the stunning power of humility.

Mother Teresa's message of love and of hope reached millions. It is a message she prayed would still be heard long after her time on earth was over.

Floral and written tributes to Diana crowded the gates of Kensington Palace.

Diana Mourned by Rich and Poor Alike

Westminster, England September 6: London came to a standstill today as over a million people crowded the city's streets to bid farewell to Diana, Princess of Wales. An estimated 2.5 billion people around the world watched her funeral on television.

This morning, mourners wept openly as the princess's coffin was carried from Kensington Palace to Buckingham Palace, past St James Palace and on to Westminster Abbey. The coffin was draped with the Windsor family flag, and covered with a floral arrangement. A single card sitting in the midst of the flowers had one word written on it: "Mummy." Prince William, Prince Harry, Prince Charles, Diana's brother, Lord Spencer, and the Queen's husband, Prince Philip, walked behind the coffin for the last mile, and 500 people from the charities the princess supported followed behind the main mourners.

Diana's very public life and humanitarian efforts were reflected in the diverse range of people who came to pay their last respects. In addition to the royal family, celebrities, dignitaries, the rich and the poor attended the service, which lasted just over an hour.

Huge television screens were installed in Hyde Park where thousands of people gathered. Before her casket was carried out of the Abbey, the nation paused for a minute's silence.

Princess Diana's body has now been taken to the Spencer family home where she will be buried on an island in the grounds of Althorp Park.

The princess was killed when the car in which she was traveling crashed in a Paris tunnel as the chauffeur attempted to evade paparazzi. Her companion, Dodi Al Fayed, was killed instantly, and Diana died later in hospital.

The loss felt by those witnessing her funeral is best summed up in the words of Elton John's song "Candle in the Wind:" "Your candle's burned out long before your legend ever will."

Mother Teresa was made famous by Malcolm Muggeridge's 1969 documentary *Something Beautiful for God.*

Between 300,000 and one million African-American women joined the Million Woman March.

Jenny Shipley

Million Woman March Held in Philadelphia

Philadelphia, USA, October 25: Thousands of women gathered in a light rain early today for the Million Woman March. The march began at the Liberty Bell, followed a two-mile route up Benjamin Franklin Parkway, and ended outside the Philadelphia Museum of Art.

At the height of the march, an estimated 300,000 to one million mostly African-American women jammed the streets of Philadelphia to show solidarity and to spotlight issues they feel are being ignored by many mainstream women's groups. Among them are human rights abuses against blacks, the founding of independent black schools, and recent allegations of CIA involvement in the crack trade in black neighborhoods.

The day-long program of prayer, music and inspirational speeches was designed to help bring about positive change, especially in black communities.

Peacemaker Honored

Oslo, Norway, December 10: Organizer, activist, teacher, and writer Jody Williams has today become the tenth woman in the almost 100-year history of the Nobel Peace Prize to receive the honor, sharing today's prize with the campaign she led, the

International Campaign to Ban Landmines (ICBL). The high-powered Williams has been chief strategist and spokesperson for the campaign, pioneering the use of people power by lobbying organizations initially via fax and later via email. Through her unprecedented cooperative effort with governments, UN bodies and the International Committee of the Red Cross, the ICBL this year achieved its goal of an international treaty banning antipersonnel landmines—the Ottawa Treaty—from which the USA, China, Russia, and others refrained.

Born on October 9, 1950 in Vermont, Williams trained as a teacher of English as a second language, receiving a BA from the University of Vermont in 1972, before going on to earn further degrees in ESL, Spanish, and international relations. Her first appointment in aid work came in 1984, when she became coordinator of the Nicaragua-Honduras Education Project for two years. She was then deputy director of a Los Angeles-based charity, Medical Aid for El Salvador, until 1992. In the same year, she took up her position with the newly formed ICBL and has overseen its growth to more than 1,000 NGOs in more than 60 countries.

Williams is internationally recognized as an eloquent and inspirational speaker on the power of individuals to bring about dramatic change in the world.

Shipley Faces Challenge

Wellington, New Zealand, December 8: Jenny Shipley, New Zealand's first female prime minister, was sworn in today. Shipley (nicknamed "The Perfumed Steamroller") takes over as Prime Minister and Leader of the National Party from Jim Bolger and has thus gained leadership of an unstable Coalition Government.

Born Jennifer Mary Robson in the South Island town of Gore, Shipley developed an interest in politics at

community and local government level in the 1970s and joined the National Party (NP). She was elected to national parliament in 1987, representing the electorate of Ashburton, and until the 1990 general election served as Spokesperson on Social Welfare. Since then she has held portfolios in Women's Affairs, Health and State Services, Transport and State Owned Enterprises.

Shipley has a tough job ahead. The National Party now governs in coalition with New Zealand First, an inexperienced centrist party led by Deputy Prime Minister and Treasurer Winston Peters. Since last year's general election, NZF and the coalition government have plummeted in opinion polls, though support for National has remained at around 33 percent.

Shipley's main tasks will be to distinguish National from its partner without upsetting coalition relations and to ensure that her government lasts its full three-year term, due to end in late 1999.

Guyana's New President an American Woman

Georgetown, Guyana, December 19: Guyana's new president, Janet Jagan, is the South American nation's first US-born, white woman leader. Sworn in today, she becomes the second female president in the history of South America (after Isabel Perón of Argentina) and the first to be democratically elected.

Wife of the late, left-leaning President Cheddi Jagan, Mrs Jagan was a communist political activist in her youth. Originally Janet Rosenberg from Chicago, she first met Dr Jagan in 1943, when she went to Guyana to work in his dental office. She became involved almost immediately in the Guyanan labor movement, and in 1946 helped found the Women's Political and Economic Organization and the Political Affairs Committee, editing the PAC bulletin. In 1950, she and her husband founded the People's Progressive Party (PPP), an organization instrumental in attaining Guyana's independence from British rule.

While her husband gained prominence in the PPP, Jagan continued as a leader in the struggle for workers' rights. In 1970, she was elected president of the Union of Guyanese Journalists, and from 1973 to 1997 edited the *Mirror*, a national newspaper. Very much involved in the literary and cultural life of Guyana, she is the author of several children's books.

Through this appointment, the sharp and determined Jagan is fulfilling the final spoken wish of her husband of 54 years, that she carry on his work. His presidency saw a renewed commitment to union power, education, and infrastructure.

Jody Williams and ICBL win the Nobel Peace Prize.

Oprah Winfrey

Artist Who Did it Her Way Dies at 105

Ojai, California, USA, March 12: The "Mama of Dada," ceramic artist Beatrice Wood, known for her exquisite, pioneering luster glazes and works of social commentary, has died at her home in Ojai, California, aged 105, just days after she presented *Titanic* director, James Cameron, with the annual Beatrice Wood Film Award.

Wood was born into a wealthy family in San Francisco on March 3, 1893, but felt no affinity with the conventional life her parents wanted for her. While living in France she left home, rented an apartment, and spent all her time painting. In 1933 she enrolled in a ceramics course at Hollywood High School in Los Angeles and studied glaze chemistry. Within a few years Beatrice had opened her first shop on Sunset Boulevard.

Wood's techniques and approach to glazing were learned under the watchful eyes of Gertrud and Otto Natzler, world-class potters renowned for their highly refined pieces and technical prowess. The

"My idea of a perfect world is one in which we really appreciate each other's differences: Short, tall; Democrat, Republican; black, white; gay, straight. A world in which all of us are equal, but definitely not the same."

BARBRA STREISAND,
AMERICAN SINGER
AND ACTRESS

relationship soured when Wood's own career took off and the Natzlers asked her to leave amid claims she was using their glazes and copying their designs.

Beatrice Wood built her home in Ojai in 1947, where she met the philosopher Krishnamurti, and began to develop her Dadaist sense of humor and a romantic view of life. She was in her late eighties when she wrote her first book, *The Angel Who Wore Black Tights.* Her autobiography, *I Shock Myself*, was published in 1985, reflecting the charm and spirit of a woman who defied propriety to eventually become a true national treasure.

A New Gandhi Steps Up to the Plate

New Delhi, India, March 15: Sonia Gandhi, the wife of assassinated former Indian prime minister, Rajiv Gandhi, has been elected to lead the Congress Party. The

Party aims to return the concept of secularism to government and to offer a real alternative to the right-wing policies of the nationalist Bharatiya Janata Party. The Gandhi family has been linked with the Congress Party for generations.

Born in Ovassanjo, Italy, on December 9, 1946, Sonia was raised a Roman Catholic and studied at Cambridge University in England. During her studies she met Rajiv Gandhi, the grandson of India's first prime minister, Jawaharlal Nehru. They were married in 1968 and soon returned to India to live.

When Rajiv's brother Sanjay died in a plane crash in 1980, Rajiv chose to enter politics as a mark of respect to his brother, and despite Sonia's intense dislike of politics, she assumed the role as wife of an Indian political figure.

Pleas for her to assume the leadership of the Congress Party began to emerge almost immediately after Rajiv Gandhi was murdered on May 21, 1991, but she refused, choosing instead to live in virtual seclusion with her children.

With the passing of Indira Gandhi, Sonia's brother-in-law Sanjay, and her husband Rajiv, Sonia Gandhi was the only living adult bearing the name that has supplied India with its prime ministers for 37 of the past 47 years. Sonia and her children are the only remaining members of the Nehru–Gandhi dynasty.

Pioneer in Congress Bows Out

New York, USA, March 31: The Democratic Congresswoman from New York, Bella Abzug, the first woman to be elected to Congress on a platform of women's rights, who campaigned for comprehensive child care, who railed against US involvement in Vietnam, and who supported gay rights, died yesterday from

Sonia Gandhi listens to the people's concerns during the election campaign.

Rostaq, Afghanistan, February 4: An earthquake in the mountainous north of the country leaves 4,000 dead and 15,000 homeless. Fighting between the Taliban and the Northern Alliance continues.

Texas, USA, February 26: Oprah Winfrey is found not guilty of defamation against Texan cattlemen after making negative comments about meat during a program about Mad Cow Disease two years ago.

London, England, February: Rosie Boycott becomes the editor of *The Independent*.

Pristina, Kosovo, March 8: Thousands of Albanian women march to demand autonomy from the Serbs.

Ojav, California, USA, March 12: Ceramic artist Beatrice Wood dies, aged 105.

New Delhi, India, March 15: Sonia Gandhi, widow of assassinated prime minister Rajiv Gandhi, is elected to lead the Congress Party.

New York, USA, March 31: Former Congresswoman Bella Abzug dies, aged 77.

Belgrade, Serbia, March: Women in Black, a group of activists, issue a statement condemning the war in Kosovo.

Belfast, Northern Ireland, April 10: The "Good Friday" agreement for peace is signed by the British and Irish governments and endorsed by most of Northern Ireland's political parties.

Cambodia, April 15: Former Khmer Rouge leader, Pol Pot, dies, aged 72.

Santa Barbara, California, USA, April 17: Linda McCartney dies of breast cancer, aged 56.

USA, May 18: Twenty US states and the Department of Justice submit that Microsoft has abused its monopoly.

Pakistan, May 28: In response to Indian nuclear tests two weeks ago, Pakistan explodes five warheads underground.

Sudan, June 11: Up to one million people are at risk of starvation from a famine affecting the south of the country.

USA, May: Actress Helen Hunt wins Golden Globe, an Oscar, and an Emmy Award.

Newcastle, England, June 11: Novelist Dame Catherine Cookson dies, aged 91.

Dublin, Ireland, June 13: German writer Herta Muller wins the IMPAC Dublin Literary Award for *The Land of Green Plums*.

Orlando, Florida, USA, June 16: The first live internet broadcast of a human birth takes place.

Ankara, Turkey, June 24: The country's Constitutional Court rules that adultery is no longer a crime for women.

Bella Abzug spent her life fighting for justice.

Women in Black Call for End to Ethnic Cleansing

Belgrade, Serbia, March 18: Women in Black Belgrade, a feminist group opposed to the fascist regime of Slobodan Milosovic and his wars in the Balkans, have just issued a statement condemning the war in Kosovo.

Women in Black are calling for an end to all military operations, as well an end to the torture and terrorizing of civilian populations. They have demanded the disarming of various paramilitary forces, and the unconditional retreat of all the special Serbian police forces in Kosovo.

Women in Black was formed in 1991 and began calling attention to Serbian war crimes long before they came to the attention of the international community. In 1992, they called for the naming of war crimes and for the arrest and prosecution of those responsible for them.

Beatle's Soul Mate Loses Struggle with Cancer

Tucson, Arizona, USA, April 17: The wife of former Beatle Sir Paul McCartney, Linda McCartney, died today, aged 56, at the family ranch in Tucson, Arizona, after a long struggle with breast cancer. Linda McCartney was first diagnosed with cancer in December 1995, and a malignant tumor was successfully removed. Just last month, it was found that the cancer had spread to her liver.

The daughter of two Russian immigrants who first met on New York's Ellis Island, Linda Louise Eastman was born on September 24, 1941. She grew up in Westchester County and graduated from Scarsdale High School in 1959. While working for *Town and Country* magazine in New York in the early 1960s she photographed the Rolling Stones on a yacht sailing up the Hudson River, and soon this self-taught photographer was taking portraits of stars such as Aretha Franklin, Jimmy Hendrix, and The Who.

In 1962 she married the geophysicist John Melvin See, Jr, and together they had a daughter, Heather Louise, born in December 31, 1962. It was a short marriage, the couple divorcing in June 1965.

Linda first met Paul McCartney at a Georgie Fame concert on May 15, 1967, and then four days later at a launch party for the Beatles' new album, *Sgt. Pepper's Lonely Hearts Club Band*. The two began living together in October 1968 and were married on March 12, 1969.

In 1971 Paul, Linda, and the guitarist Denny Lane formed the band Wings. The popular group had two phenomenally successful world tours in 1989–1990 and 1993, playing to an estimated audience of over five million people.

Linda's reputation as a vegetarian and animal lover was such that her guide to vegetarian cooking, *Linda McCartney's Home Cooking*, sold 350,000 copies and became one of the bestselling vegetarian cookbooks in the world.

Linda McCartney is survived by her husband, Paul, and four children.

Helen Hunt

complications following heart surgery at Manhattan's Columbia-Presbyterian Medical Center. She was 77 years of age.

Bella Savitsky Abzug was born in the Bronx, New York, on July 24, 1920, to Russian-Jewish immigrant parents. From the age of 11, she wanted to be a lawyer, and while she was collecting money for a Zionist Youth Program she gave her first public speech, in a subway station.

One of the first to call for the impeachment of President Richard Nixon, Abzug was a tireless coalition-builder, establishing Women Strike for Peace and the National Women's Political Caucus. Hers was a lifetime spent pushing for change, through community PTA meetings all the way up to the United Nations. She was elected to Congress in 1970 and worked for the Equal Rights Amendment. She also became chair of the House subcommittee on government information and individual rights. Despite a prolonged battle with breast cancer in recent years, Bella Abzug remained a tireless and dedicated campaigner to the end.

Linda McCartney has succumbed to breast cancer.

Key Events

London, England, June: Carol Shields is awarded the Orange Prize for fiction for her novel, *Larry's Party*.

Lagos, Nigeria, July 11: Four days of rioting, sparked by the death of opposition figure, Chief Abiola, leave 60 dead.

London, England, July: J. K. Rowling's *Harry Potter and the Chamber of Secrets* is published.

Dar es Salaam, Tanzania and Nairobi, Kenya, August 7: Bombs explode at two US embassies.

Central China, August 13: The Yangtze River, which has risen to its highest level since 1954, threatens the city of Wuhan. The death toll is 2,500; millions are left homeless.

Washington DC, USA, August 17: After denying a sexual relationship with White House intern Monica Lewinsky in January, President Clinton publicly admits his deceit.

Iran, August: Faezeh Hashemi founds the daily *Zan*, a magazine dedicated to women's issues.

Halifax, Canada, September 3: A Swissair DC-11 crashes, killing all 229 people on board.

Kosovo, September 22: Serbian forces bombard the breakaway region in an attempt to rush the Kosovo Liberation Army (KLA).

London, England, September: The Marylebone Cricket Club allows women to become members.

Australia, October 3: Pauline Hanson's right-wing political party, One Nation, fails to win a seat in the House of Representatives in the country's federal election.

Vatican City, October 11: Edith Stein is canonized by Pope John Paul II.

USA, October 13: Britney Spears's debut single, "Hit Me Baby One More Time," goes straight to No. 1 on the US charts.

South Africa, October 29: The Truth and Reconciliation Commission hands down its findings on political crimes conducted under the apartheid regime.

Zurich, Switzerland, October: Tennis player Venus Williams records a 127 mph (204 km/h) serve at the Swisscom Challenge.

Toronto, Canada, November 3: Alice Munro wins the Giller Prize for her collection of stories, *The Love of a Good Woman*.

Kuala Lumpur, Malaysia, November 15: The US Secretary of State, Madeleine Albright, has a meeting with Azizah Ismail, wife of the imprisoned former deputy prime minister, Anwar Ibrahim.

Iraq, November 15: Saddam Hussein's regime readmits UN weapons inspectors at the eleventh hour, thus averting US and British air strikes.

Madeleine Albright

> "THE PAST
> HAS BROUGHT
> US BOTH
> ASHES AND
> DIAMONDS.
> IN THE
> PRESENT WE
> FIND THE
> FLOWERS OF
> WHAT WE'VE
> PLANTED AND
> THE SEEDS OF
> WHAT WE ARE
> BECOMING."
>
> JULIA CAMERON,
> AMERICAN WRITER
> AND ARTIST,
> *BLESSINGS: PRAYERS
> AND DECLARATIONS
> FOR A HEARTFUL LIFE*
> 1998

Queen of Romance Dies at Home

Newcastle, England, June 11: One of the most admired romantic novelists in the world, Dame Catherine Cookson, has died, aged 91, at her home near Jesmond Dene, Newcastle upon Tyne. She was a highly popular writer—over 100 million copies of Dame Catherine's books have sold in more than 30 countries.

Cookson often said that she had been a storyteller from the time she was able to talk, always seeking an audience, and often passing the time by spinning tales of living in beautiful houses with sweeping staircases and grand furniture.

The illegitimate daughter of a poverty-stricken single mother in South Shields, an industrial region in England's north-east, Catherine Cookson was born in 1906. She wrote her first story, "The Wild Irish Girl," when she was just 11 years old, sending it to the *South Shields Gazette*, who returned it to her three days later.

Cookson left home at 13 and worked as a housemaid in wealthy households, where she began to gain insights into the privileged lives of the elite, and the realities of class division in England.

She met her husband, Tom Cookson, in 1940 when she was 34. After several miscarriages, she immersed herself in writing, and wrote her first book, the semi-autobiographical *Kate Hannigan* in 1950. That was followed by *Colour Blind* (1953), an account of the social tensions and prejudices inherent in English society, as experienced by a white woman who chooses to marry a black man.

Her books are thoroughly researched accounts that trace events in the life of an individual or family, often set in the nineteenth century against a background of shipyards, coalmines, or farms, the sentiments often born from her own experiences and recollections.

Her first 16 books were written in longhand with her husband playing the role of her personal assistant, helping with spelling and punctuation. Almost 100 novels later, Cookson, who also wrote under the pseudonym Catherine Marchant, has become the most-borrowed author from UK libraries and has had her works translated into over 20 languages. Catherine Cookson was awarded an OBE in 1985 and became a Dame Commander of the Order of the British Empire in 1993.

Newspaper for Women a Force for Change

Tehran, Iran, August: Faezeh Hashemi, a member of parliament and daughter of the former Iranian president, Rafsanjani, has this month launched *Zan (Woman)*, the first Iranian newspaper solely devoted to women to be published in the country for over 100 years.

The magazine is representative of a vibrant and varied women's movement in the Islamic republic where women are slowly increasing their public role, from being merely observers of societal trends to beginning to actively influence the political process and the struggle toward their stated goals of full citizenship and the desegregation of the sexes in public places.

Faezeh Hashemi hopes that *Zan,* and other such publications, will help bring about many much needed changes in education, family planning, divorce law, and the return of female judges to Iran's judiciary, as well as being a broad forum for modern interpretations of Islamic law and its implications for women's rights and gender equality.

Exclusion of Women Just Not Cricket

London, England, September: The members of the all-male Marylebone Cricket Club (MCC) voted today to allow women to join the 211-year-old gentlemen's stronghold, after Sports Minister Tony Banks threatened to withhold National Lottery cash from the club until the ban on women was lifted. The first woman to apply for membership, former England women's cricket captain, Rachel Heyhoe-Flint, pointed out that the 18-year waiting list will mean many older women who have waited years just for the opportunity to put their names down for membership will be dead by the time they are eligible.

Requiring a two-thirds majority to effect change, almost 70 percent of the

Monica Lewinsky and President Clinton–a cautionary tale.

MCC's 13,482 members, with an average age of 57, voted in favor of the amendment. Until this month, the club's patron, Her Majesty Queen Elizabeth II, has been the only female permitted to enter the Pavilion during play.

After a failed ballot last February that returned a yes vote of 57 percent, pressure on the MCC executive from Westminster and Downing Street has been intense, and there has been a growing realization that a continuation of the ban posed a serious threat to the club's future.

Women have been playing cricket in England since 1745. Over 3,600 women are members of a cricket club in the UK today. The game is played by over 374,000 girls in primary schools and more than 80,000 at secondary level.

One Nation Party Fails to Gain a Foothold

Australia, October 3: Australia's right-wing political party, One Nation, has failed to win a single House of Representatives seat in today's federal election, despite polling over 8 percent of the national vote and outperforming the combined vote of the two other significant minor parties, the Australian Democrats and the Greens.

The increasing prominence of minor Australian political parties is reflective of an electorate that feels that its views on issues such as social justice and multiculturalism are not being listened to by John Howard's Liberal–National Coalition

Trudy Todd, Australian women's surfing champion.

Synchronized divers, Ca Yuyan and Sang Xue, show why China won the gold medal at the Goodwill Games.

Britney Spears

won the writer her first Governor-General's Literary Award for fiction.

In 1992 Munro was made an honorary foreign member of the American Academy of Arts and Letters and last year she became the first Canadian author ever to win the PEN Malamud Award for Excellence in Short Fiction.

In *The Love of a Good Woman*, the three-time winner of the Governor-General's Award and nominee for the 1977 Booker Prize offers a collection of eight short stories on the themes of passion, the vagaries of love, the often comic wants of the human heart, and the inherent chaos that lurks just below the surface of our otherwise structured lives.

Alice Munro writes about girls and women: their schooling, their transition to adulthood, their loves, and their varied experiences as wives and mothers. Where men are present in her stories, they are seen through the eyes of the author's female characters. Munro, however, stops short of being categorized as a feminist writer—her stories possess a somewhat androgynous quality, completely unencumbered by the weighty issues of gender equality or women's rights.

government. A decision by the Liberals and the opposition Labor Party not to direct their preferences to One Nation also contributed to the party's founder, Pauline Hanson, failing in her bid to win the Queensland seat of Blair, despite the fact that her primary vote exceeded that of the successful Liberal candidate.

One Nation grew out of the disaffection of rural and regional voters, as well as a deep mistrust within the community toward political leaders, coupled with a perceived lack of national leadership.

Pope John Paul II Canonizes Carmelite Nun

Rome, October 11: In a moving ceremony today at St Peter's Basilica in Rome, Pope John Paul II canonized Blessed Teresa Benedicta of the Cross, Edith Stein, the Carmelite nun and scholar who, in 1917, converted from Judaism only to perish in the gas chambers of the Nazi concentration camp, Auschwitz, in August of 1942.

Born in Breslau, Germany, on October 12, 1891, Edith Stein was the youngest of 11 children. Her father died when she was two, and before long, the young Edith lost all faith in God, and made a conscious decision to give up prayer.

In 1913 Edith studied philosophy at Gottingen University under Edmund Husserl, where she met the philosopher Max Scheler, who encouraged her to study Catholicism. Stein read the New Testament as well as works by existential writers such as Soren Kierkegaard, and the founder of the Jesuit order, St. Ignatius Loyola. In 1921 she read the autobiography of St. Theresa of Avila, was converted, and baptized on January 1, 1922 on the Feast of the Circumcision of Jesus.

Edith joined the Carmelite Convent of Cologne on October 14, 1934, where her only vocation was simply to love. A writer, her final book was a study of John of the Cross, written in 1942 on the 400th anniversary of his birth.

The Gestapo arrested Edith Stein in August 1942, in an act of retaliation against a letter of protest from Catholic bishops criticizing the Nazi deportation of Jews. On August 7 she was transported to Auschwitz where she was murdered, a witness to God's love in a world where God seemed absent.

Giller Prize Awarded to Alice Munro

Toronto, Canada, November 3: One of Canada's most successful and awarded authors, Alice Munro, has won the prestigious Giller Prize, which carries prize money of $25,000, for her collection of stories, *The Love of a Good Woman*, an absorbing account of the unexpected turns ordinary lives can take.

Alice Ann Munro was born on July 10, 1931 in the small farming town of Wingham, Ontario, and from 1949–1951 she attended the University of Western Ontario. She began writing in her teens, and her first short story, "The Dimensions of a Shadow," was published in 1951. Munro's first collection of short stories, *Dance of the Happy Shades*, was published in 1968 and

Venus Williams plays a mighty backhand in the Grand Slam Cup.

Iris Murdoch

Madame President

Switzerland, January 1: Ruth Dreifuss today became the first woman president of the Swiss Confederation. A member of the Swiss Socialist Party since 1964, and a member of the Bern legislative council from 1989 to 1992, Dreifuss was elected a federal councilor by the Federal Assembly in March 1993, and has served as head of the Federal Department of the Interior since April that year.

Prior to entering politics, Dreifuss enjoyed a varied professional career. She worked as a hotel secretary, as editor of the weekly journal *Cooperation*, and then as an assistant at the Geneva University Psychosocial Center. After graduating with a degree in economics in 1970, she was employed as an assistant at the Geneva University Faculty of Economics and Social Sciences. In 1981, she was appointed Secretary of the Swiss Trade Union Federation.

"FASHION IS VERY IMPOR-TANT. IT IS LIFE-ENHANCING AND, LIKE EVERYTHING THAT GIVES PLEASURE, IT IS WORTH DOING WELL."

VIVIENNE WESTWOOD, FASHION DESIGNER

Ruth Dreifuss is President of the Swiss Confederation.

Iris Murdoch Dies

Oxford, England, February 8: Irish-born writer Iris Murdoch has passed away at age 79. Murdoch was best known as the author of 26 novels, in which fantasy and gothic elements were often employed to explore everyday ethical or moral issues.

Born in Dublin on July 15, 1919, Murdoch grew up in London, attending progressive schools before going on to read classics, ancient history, and philosophy at Somerville College, Oxford. She later took up a postgraduate studentship in philosophy under Ludwig Wittgenstein at Newnham College, Cambridge, and in 1948 was elected a fellow of St. Anne's College, Oxford, where she worked as a tutor until 1963.

Murdoch's first published work was the critical study *Sartre, Romantic Rationalist* (1953). She made her debut as a novelist with *Under the Net* (1954), followed by *The Flight from the Enchanter* (1956), and *The Sandcastle* (1957). One of her most successful novels, *The Bell* (1958), was adapted for television. Her 1961 novel *A Severed Head* was dramatized by J. B. Priestley and later turned into a film starring Richard Attenborough, Claire Bloom, and Lee Remick. In 1978, she was awarded the Booker Prize for what is now considered to be her major work, *The Sea, the Sea*, a novel dealing with the power of love and loss.

In recognition of her contribution to literature, Murdoch was made a Dame Commander of the British Empire in 1987. She wrote her last novel, *Jackson's Dilemma* (1995), while suffering from Alzheimer's disease.

Indigenous Women Win Goldman Prize

Washington DC, USA, April 19: Two indigenous Australian women, Jacqui Katona and Yvonne Margarula, have been named as recipients of the United States-based

Louise Sauvage wins at Boston Marathon.

Goldman Environment Prize. The two women have been honored for leading a passionate campaign against a proposed uranium mine at a site called Jabiluka, located at the heart of the Kakadu World Heritage Area in Australia's Northern Territory. Approval for mining at the site, the world's richest undeveloped uranium deposit, was granted by the Australian government despite a prohibition on mining within the Kakadu World Heritage Area and despite opposition from the indigenous people whose ancestors have lived there for more than 40,000 years.

Katona, a member of the Djok Aboriginal clan, is executive officer of the Gundjehmi Aboriginal Corporation, a non-profit organization established, managed, and controlled by the Mirrar people, the spiritual guardians and legal owners of part of Kakadu National Park. Margarula, the chairperson of the organization, is also the Senior Traditional

Shakespeare in Love wins three Oscars.

Owner of the Mirrar people charged with protecting traditional lands and preserving them for future generations. The two women regard their struggle as not only a fight for the right of Aborigines to determine their own destinies, but also a fight to keep Northern Australia nuclear free.

Thus far, their campaign has involved forms of protest including legal action, education, and mobilization of national and international support. In March last year, the two women led the Mirrar people in a blockade of the mine site, which over a period of several months attracted some 5,000 additional protesters from across the nation and overseas. Many protesters were arrested for trespassing, including Katona and Margarula. As a result of their efforts, however, the World Heritage Committee sent an inspection team to the site late last year to assess possible threats to the protected area from mining.

Golden Girl Gunned Down

London, England, April 26: A devastated nation remains in shock today following the slaying of BBC television presenter Jill Dando on the doorstep of her home in Fulham, west London. The 37-year-old presenter suffered a brain injury as a result of a single gunshot wound to the head and was pronounced dead on her arrival by ambulance at nearby Charing Cross Hospital.

Described as the "golden girl of television," Dando began her career as a newspaper reporter in her home town of Weston-super-Mare. Five years later, she entered the broadcasting industry with a move to BBC Radio Devon, and then in 1986 she progressed to television as presenter of the evening regional news magazine program at BBC Television South West. Her big break came in 1988 when she relocated to the BBC's London operation to present *Breakfast News*. In the early 1990s, Dando was elevated to peak time television as the presenter of the BBC's *Holiday* series, and in 1995 she became co-host on the popular *Crimewatch* program. This week, she was featured on the cover of *Radio Times* magazine promoting her new Sunday evening show, *The Antiques Inspectors*.

A household name, Dando was hugely popular with viewers, and the BBC News Online has already received thousands of tributes. Meanwhile, police have launched a murder inquiry and are appealing for anyone with information to come forward.

Rosa Parks Honored

Washington DC, USA, June 15: Rosa Parks, "mother of the modern day civil rights movement" in America, has been awarded the Congressional Gold Medal of Honor. Parks is one of only 250 individuals to receive the medal, which is the highest honor awarded to a civilian citizen in the United States.

Parks was an unknown seamstress when, on December 1, 1955, she was arrested and charged with disorderly conduct for refusing to yield her seat to a white passenger on a Montgomery, Alabama city bus. The incident sparked a boycott of the city-owned bus company that lasted 382 days and reverberated throughout the United States, triggering

time out

One of the world's prostitution capitals, The Netherlands, this year legalizes its brothels. The legislation comes after polls suggest that 78 percent of citizens think prostitution is a job like any other.

equal-rights protests and ultimately leading to the end of legal segregation. Two years after her historic act of defiance, Parks moved to Detroit, becoming a deaconess in the African Methodist Episcopal Church in 1964. From 1965 to 1988, she worked on the staff of Congressman John Conyers, and following the death of her husband in 1977 she established the Rosa and Raymond Parks Institute for Self-Development, an organization aimed at motivating and directing youth. In 1996, President Bill Clinton presented her with the Presidential Medal of Freedom.

In 1997, she became the first living person to be honored with a holiday when the state of Michigan designated the first Monday following February 4 as Mrs Rosa Parks' Day.

Jill Dando

Rosa Parks receiving the Congressional award.

Palo Alto, California, USA, July 15: Carleton S. Fiorina becomes CEO of Hewlett Packard.
Cape Canaveral, USA, July 23: The shuttle STS-93 *Columbia* is launched, commanded by a woman for the first time: Eileen Collins.
Georgetown, Guyana, August 8: The country's first woman Prime Minister, Janet Jagan, resigns due to ill health.
Izmit, Turkey, August 17: A massive earthquake measuring 7.4 kills thousands and injures more.

Panama City, Panama, September 1: Mireya Moscoso becomes Prime Minister.
Berlin, Germany, September 26: Kenyan Tegla Loroupe sets a new record in the Berlin Marathon.
Brussels, Belgium, September 28: President of the European Commission, Romano Prodi, announces that he has made a more representative executive. Of the 120 posts in the commissioner's staff, 45 have so far gone to women.

San Marino, October 1: Rosa Zafferani finishes her term as co Captain Regent.
Islamabad, Pakistan, October 12: General Pervez Musharraf ousts Prime Minister Nawaz Sharif in a bloodless coup.
North Carolina, USA, October 23: Elizabeth Dole withdraws from the Republican Presidential campaign.
Orissa, India, October 29: A huge tidal surge caused by a cyclone with 155 mph (250 km/h) winds hits eastern India, killing 10,000 and leaving 1.5 million homeless.

London, England, October: The London Eye, designed by David Marks and Julia Barfield, is erected over the River Thames.
Toronto, Canada, November 3: Bonnie Burnard wins the Giller Prize for Fiction for her novel *A Good House*.
Vilnius, Lithuania, November 3: Irena Degutien finishes her second period acting as interim Prime Minister.
Wellington, New Zealand, November 27: Helen Clark is elected Prime Minister of New Zealand.

Guadalupe, December 3: Tori Murden arrives from the Canary Islands, becoming the first woman to row solo across the Atlantic Ocean.
London, England, December 15: New parental leave law is passed, allowing 13 weeks' parental leave per year for children under five.
England: Expat Australian Germaine Greer writes a follow-up to *The Female Eunuch*, titled *The Whole Woman*.

Latvia's First Woman President

Riga, Latvia, July 8: Parliament has elected Vaira Vike-Freiberga as the nation's first woman president. Vike-Frieberga's election comes under a year of her return to Latvia after almost five decades in exile.

Vike-Freiberga was just seven when her family fled the Soviet invasion in the closing days of World War II, living in several countries before finally settling in Canada, where she later became a professor of psychology at Montreal University. It was 1998 before she returned to the land of her birth after being invited to head the Latvian Institute, an organization devoted to raising the profile of Latvia around the world.

While she has no political experience, Vike-Freiberga brings a range of other qualifications to the presidency. Over the years, she has served in senior positions in a long list of prestigious organizations, including the Canadian Psychological Association, the Social Science Federation of Canada, and the Association for the Advancement of Baltic Studies. She is fluent in English, French, German, and Spanish, as well as Latvian. In addition, she is committed to promoting women's issues in what is still a heavily male-dominated society. Citing her own election as evidence of Latvia's willingness to embrace gender equality, Vike-Freiberga says: "Men here are saying to me they're delighted they will now have a role model for their daughters, to show them that there are no doors closed to them."

> "WE LIVE IN A FANTASY WORLD, A WORLD OF ILLUSION. THE GREAT TALK IN LIFE IS TO FIND REALITY."
>
> IRIS MURDOCH, BRITISH WRITER

Eileen Collins

Space shuttle *Columbia* ready for lift-off.

Eileen Collins in Command

Cape Canaveral, USA, July 23: Eileen Collins today became the world's first woman commander of a space shuttle when *Columbia* lifted off from Cape Canaveral, Florida, on a mission to deploy the Chandra X-Ray Observatory. It is the third flight for Collins, who made history in 1995 as the first woman pilot of a space shuttle, receiving the Harmon Trophy in recognition of her achievement.

Born in Elmira, New York, Collins attended Corning Community College, earning an associate degree in mathematics/science in 1976. After receiving a degree in mathematics and economics from Syracuse University in 1978, she completed a master of science degree in operations research at Stanford University in 1986, and then a master of arts degree in space systems management from the Webster University in 1989.

Collins was selected for NASA's astronaut training program while she was attending an Air Force Test Pilot School in 1990. She made her first historic space flight as pilot aboard the shuttle *Discovery* in February 1995.

The mission highlights were a rendezvous with the Russian Space Station *Mir* and a space walk. In May 1997, Collins embarked upon her second space shuttle mission aboard *Atlantis*, again docking with the *Mir* space station to transfer tons of supplies and equipment for the astronauts living there.

Queen of the Road

Sydney, Australia, October: Australian Paralympian Louise Sauvage has been named International Female Wheelchair Athlete of the Year for 1999, a year which saw her claim her third straight victory in the Boston Marathon, one of the world's most prestigious road races.

Originally from Western Australia, Sauvage now lives and trains in Sydney. She has dominated wheelchair racing since the Barcelona Paralympic Games in 1992, when she won gold in the 100, 200, and 400 meters, and silver in the 800 meters. At the Atlanta Olympic Games in 1996, she received a gold medal for winning the 800 meter wheelchair demonstration event, before going on to overcome her competitors in the 400, 800, 1500, and 5000 meters Paralympic events.

It was after her success at Barcelona in 1992 that Sauvage made the decision to expand her training in preparation for long distance wheelchair road racing. She has since recorded numerous wins in the Los Angeles, Berlin, Honolulu, and Boston marathons.

In recognition of her outstanding achievements, she was voted Australian Paralympian of the Year in 1994, 1996, 1997, and 1998. She was also named Australian Institute of Sport Athlete of the Year in 1997, the same year that the Australian Olympic Committee presented her with the International Olympic Committee Trophy "Sport For All" within Australia. Last year, she was honored with the National Sports Award as part of the Young Australian of the Year Awards.

Bonnie Burnard Wins Giller Prize

Toronto, Canada, November 3: This year's Giller Prize, Canada's most prestigious literary award, has gone to the author Bonnie Burnard for her novel *A Good House*. A bestseller in Canada throughout the past few months, the novel follows the life of one family and its ever expanding circle over a period of about 50 years.

Burnard is no stranger to literary awards. In 1989, she won the Commonwealth Best Book Award for *Women of Influence*, her first collection of short stories. Her second collection, *Casino and Other Stories*, was equally well received, attracting the Saskatchewan Book of the Year Award and the Periodical Publishers Award in 1994.

The following year, Burnard was the recipient of the Marian Engel Award, which is presented in honor of a woman writer in mid-career.

Vaira Vike-Freiberga is elected President of Latvia.

Helen Clark is elected Prime Minister of New Zealand.

Lady of the House

Wellington, New Zealand, November 27:
Helen Clark has been elected Prime Minister of New Zealand, the culmination of almost 30 years of involvement with the Labour Party that has seen her hold a range of parliamentary positions and cabinet portfolios.

Born in Hamilton in 1950, Clark attended Epsom Girls' Grammar School in Auckland before entering the University of Auckland to study politics. She joined the Labour Party in 1971 and 10 years later was elected as member of parliament for Mt Albert. Between 1984 and 1987, at a time when New Zealand declared itself nuclear free, she was chairperson of the Foreign Affairs and Defence Select Committee, earning the 1986 Peace Prize of the Danish Peace Foundation for her efforts in promoting international peace and disarmament. She also represented the Labour Party at congresses of the Socialist International and the Socialist International Women in 1976, 1978, 1983, and 1986, and was a government delegate to the 1985 World Conference in Nairobi to mark the end of the United Nations Decade for Women.

Clark was promoted to cabinet following the Labour Party's re-election in 1987, holding the posts of Minister of Conservation, Minister of Housing, and Minister of Health before becoming Minister of Labour and Deputy Prime Minister in 1989. During this time, she also chaired the Cabinet Social Equity Committee. When the Labour Party lost office in 1990, she served as the Deputy Leader of the Opposition until her election as Leader of the Opposition on

December 1, 1993. When not engaged in politics, Clark enjoys attending concerts and the opera, and is also a keen supporter of the arts in general. She likes to keep fit with regular visits to the gym, and by indulging her passion for hiking and cross-country skiing. Earlier this year, she climbed Mt Kilimanjaro, Africa's highest peak, a prophetic milestone for a woman about to reach the pinnacle of her career.

Tori Murden Rows into history

Guadalupe, December 3: Tori Murden today became the first woman and the first American to row solo across the Atlantic Ocean when she entered Bas du Fort Harbor in Guadeloupe after traveling 3,330 miles (5,328 km) in 81 days, 7 hours, and 31 minutes. The 36-year-old rower began her historic east-to-west journey on September 13, setting out from the Canary Islands in the craft *American Pearl*, a 23-foot (7 m) self-righting rowboat that she designed and built herself.

Murden first attempted an Atlantic crossing in 1997, teaming with Louise

Graff as the only American and only all-female entry in the Port St Charles Atlantic Rowing Race. After only two days, however, an electrical system failure forced them to abandon their quest. Her second attempt was launched on June 14 last year when she left from Nags Head, North Carolina, intending to row solo across the North Atlantic from west to east. On Day 85, just 950 miles (1,530 m) short of her destination in France, she was hit by Hurricane Danielle and its 50-foot (15 m) waves. Her boat capsized 15 times and she was finally picked up suffering from a dislocated shoulder and concussion. On her third and successful attempt this year, Murden was battered by the elements when Tropical Storm Lenny cap-sized her boat and sent it on a violent roller-coaster ride that lasted for hours. This time she managed to weather the ordeal and was rewarded with the return of favor-able winds within a couple of days.

In previous years, Murden's adventurous spirit has led her to conquer other challenges, including expeditions of ice-climbing on Alaska's Brooks and Muldrow Glacier. In 1988, she became the first woman and the first American to reach the summit of Lewis Nunatuk in the Antarctic. The following year, she became the first woman and the first American to complete a skiing expedition to the geographic south pole.

Janet Jagan

Julie Inkster wins the LPGA Championship at DuPont Country Club in Wilmington, USA.

Christina Aguilera

Women at the South Pole

Antarctica, January: This month records have been tumbling in Antarctica. On January 4, Catherine Hartley and Fiona Thornewill were the first British women to make the walk overland to the South Pole. They were members of a nine-person team which included Thornewill's husband, Mike. The Thornewills are the first married couple to complete the polar trek. The adventurers walked around 700 miles (1,125 km) in 60 days over glaciers and mountains to reach their goal. Temperatures were as low as –58°F (–50°C). To train for the grueling expedition the women pulled tractor tires instead of sleds, and spent time sitting in freezers.

On January 24, another five-woman British team, led by Caroline Hamilton, also arrived at the South Pole. This makes Hamilton the first woman to complete expeditions to both Poles.

"I'M THINKING BALLS ARE TO MEN, WHAT PURSES ARE TO WOMEN. IT'S JUST A LITTLE BAG BUT WE'D FEEL NAKED IN PUBLIC WITHOUT IT."

CARRIE IN *SEX AND THE CITY* (CANDICE BUSHNELL)

Rosie Stancer cheers her Chile to South Pole walk.

Kuwaiti Women Writers Jailed

Kuwait, January 25: Two female Kuwaiti writers have been handed two-month suspended prison sentences. Leila Al-

Hillary Swank in her award-winning role in *Boys Don't Cry*.

Othman has been found guilty of using indecent language in her new novel, *The Departure*, and philosophy professor Alia Shuaib of ridiculing religion in her book of poetry, *Spiders Bemoan a Wound*.

Fundamentalist Muslim clerics have brought the cases against the women to raise moral standards, they said. Although the books had been passed for publication by Kuwait's censorship body, those prosecuting the case said: "We are ready to raise similar lawsuits against anyone who tries to go against morals…when we find the authorities are unable to stop them." The women's attorneys say the only thing that could be construed as obscene in *The Departure* is a description of the sea's waves as "lustful," and that the only line referring to religion in *Spiders Bemoan a Wound* is "I dream of passing, even for one moment, through God's secret map."

The women may really have been targeted because they support women's rights, and write honestly about women's experiences. In a statement to the press Al-Othman said: "Through my writing I disturbed the calm waters…by having the will to uphold the dignity of all women living under oppression and subjugation." Shuaib has postponed the publication of two more books. The women have appealed their convictions.

Egyptian Women File "No Fault" Divorce

Cairo, Egypt, January 27: Today, Egyptian president Hosni Mubarak signed a law that permits women to file for divorce on grounds of incompatibility. Until now, Egyptian men have been able to divorce without giving a reason, or appearing in court, or even informing their wives. Women, on the other hand, have had to provide a reason such as their husband's impotence, abusive behavior, drug addiction, or unwillingness to provide financially for the family. They have also had to provide documents or witnesses to prove allegations. Their cases are heard in a virtually all-male legal system, and the husband can appeal again and again, leading to expensive legal battles that sometimes take up to 10 years to resolve.

For 15 years there has been a push for family law reforms to give women something like the same rights as men. Now a woman can apply for a "no fault" divorce, known as *khula*, but if she chooses this path she must forfeit all financial rights, forgo alimony, and pay back her dowry. However, she will still be able to claim adequate financial support for her children.

Opponents of the new law claim that women are by nature flighty, and will divorce their husbands on a mere whim. They say men will be undermined as the rulers of their home.

Those pushing for reform were able to win public approval partly because they had the backing of moderate Muslim clerics, who say the new law has a precedent in Sharia law, noting that in the *Koran*, Mohammed permitted a woman to leave her husband, as long as she returned the garden that her husband had given her.

Moscow, Russian Federation, January 1: After Boris Yeltsin's resignation, Prime Minister Vladimir Putin is named acting president until elections are held in 90 days.
Bern, Switzerland, January 1: Ruth Dreifuss ends her term as President.
Antarctica, January 4: Catherine Hartley, and a team of women and men, reach the South Pole after walking across Antarctica.
Ottawa, Canada, January 7: Beverley McLachlin is named Chief Justice of Canada's Supreme Court.

United Kingdom, January 12: The British government allows openly homosexual men and women to serve in the armed forces.
Antarctica, January 23: Rosie Stancer is one of five women who complete a 1200 km walk from Chile to the South Pole.
Kuwait, January 25: Writers Laila al-Othman and Alia Shuaib receive prison sentences for "blasphemy."
Egypt, January 27: Egyptian women are allowed divorce on the grounds of incompatibility, but must repay dowry and forfeit financial rights.

Baia Mare, Romania, January 30: A leak from a mine tailings dump pollutes the Sassar and Danube rivers with cyanide.
Osaka, Japan, February 6: Ota Fusae is elected governor of Osaka.
Los Angeles, USA, February 23: Grammy award winners are Shania Twain (best female country artist); Christina Aguilera (best new artist).
Los Angeles, USA, March 26: Hilary Swank wins the best actress Oscar for her performance in last year's film *Boys Don't Cry*.

Helsinki, Finland, March 1: Tarja Halonen becomes the country's first female President.
Morocco, March 12: King Mohammed IV announces controversial new plans to expand women's rights.
San Marino, April 1: Maria Domenica Michelotti starts her term as co-Captain-Regent.
New York, USA, April 3: A federal judge rules that Microsoft violated antitrust laws, using its monopoly power in the computer market to stifle competition.

Zimbabwe, April 15: President Mugabe commences an agricultural land reform program by killing white farmer David Stevens.
Taipei, Taiwan, May 19: Chen Shui-bian is inaugurated President after the first democratic elections.
Israel, May 22: The Supreme Court rules that women may pray aloud from the Torah at the Wailing Wall.
Brussels, Belgium, June 7: The European Union proposes to outlaw sexual harassment in the workplace throughout the Union.

Tarja Halonen acknowledges her win as President.

50 percent, another round of voting was held. This time 51.6 percent voted for her.

Born in 1943, Halonen completed her masters degree in law at Helsinki University in 1968, and was general secretary of the National Union of Students. In 1970 she became a lawyer with the Central Organization of Finnish Trade Unions. In 1971 she joined the Social Democratic Party and became parliamentary secretary in 1974. She was elected to the Helsinki city council in 1975, holding the position until 1996. Meanwhile, she had a daughter in 1978 and was elected to parliament in 1979. A number of committee and ministerial posts followed, including that of Minister of Foreign Affairs.

Throughout her career Halonen has championed equal rights for all people, and has been an outspoken supporter of gay and lesbian rights. In her inaugural speech, she pledged to "…do my best to make sure that in six years' time we Finns will be able to feel that we are living in a country of greater equality."

Morocco to Boost Women's Rights

Morocco, March 12: In 1999, on the death of his repressive father, King Mohammed VI inherited the throne of Morocco. The kingdom is beset by extreme poverty and illiteracy, and the new king soon announced his intent to reform and modernize the nation, giving reassurances that as Commander of the Faithful he would do this within an Islamic framework.

The plight of Moroccan women has also drawn the attention of the king. With a recent report outlining their dire situation. While 48 percent of adults are illiterate, the figure for women is 62 percent, and in rural areas the rate soars to over 80 percent.

time out

Janet Reno, the first US woman Attorney-General, rules that seven-year-old Elián González must be returned to his father in Cuba. This custody battle has caused conflict among the people of both nations.

Many women are unemployed, and few who work are professionals. Rates of domestic violence are extremely high.

In light of these findings, the king has announced that the law covering family matters, *murdwana*, will be reviewed. At present it decrees that women must obey their nearest male relative. They can also be ordered to marry against their will. However, a man may take a second wife without consulting his first, and men can divorce a wife at will. Reforming such laws will go at least some some way toward giving women a say in their own lives.

Today, approximately 200,000 supporters of the proposed *murdwana* reforms marched in the capital of Morocco, Rabat, while at the same time, an almost equal number of conservative Muslims took part in a march against them in the city of Casablanca.

The rallies and controversy surrounding the issue means it could take some considerable time for the king's reforms to be implemented.

Shania Twain

Supporters of women's rights laws march in Morocco.

While Egyptian women's rights have apparently made a great step forward with this reform, in reality only those with the financial ability to support themselves—or who are desperate enough—will take advantage of it.

Finland's First Woman President

Helsinki, Finland, March 1: Tarja Halonen has officially taken up her position as president of Finland. She is the nation's eleventh—and its first female—president.

She began her campaign in 1999, and in the first round of voting gained just over 40 percent, with her nearest opponent gaining 34 percent. With none of the candidates reaching the requisite

Pyongyang, North Korea, June 14: President Kim Jong-il hosts South Korean President Kim Dae-jung for the first summit between the two countries.
Cuba, June 28: Elián Gonzalez, the Cuban child found floating on an inner-tube off Florida in November last year—and the focus of an international tug-of-war—returns to Cuba with his father.
England and USA, July 8: J. K. Rowling's book *Harry Potter and the Goblet of Fire* is released. It breaks all pre-publishing sales records.

Kabul, Afghanistan, July 9: Mary MacMakin is arrested for employing women, and ordered to leave.
Gonesse, France, July 25: An Air France Concorde airliner crashes, killing all 109 people on board and four people on the ground.
UK, August 4: Throughout the UK celebrations are held to commemorate the 100th birthday of the Queen Mother.
St Augustine, Florida, September: Judy Rankin, Juli Inkster, and Beth Daniel inducted into golf's International Hall of Fame.

Sydney, Australia, October 1: The closing ceremony of the Games of the XXVIIIth Olympiad takes place. At these games, Cathy Freeman won the 400 m sprint for the home country.
Colombo, Sri Lanka, October 10: Former Prime Minister Sirimavo Bandaranaike dies, aged 84, just hours after casting her vote in the general elections.
Aden, Yemen, October 12: US Navy destroyer *USS Cole* is attacked by two suicide bombers, killing 17 and injuring more than 40.

New York, USA, November 7: Democrat Hillary Rodham Clinton is elected to the US senate.
London, England, November 7: Canadian Margaret Atwood is awarded the Booker Prize for her novel *The Blind Assassin*.
Israel, November 12: Leah Rabin, widow of assassinated Israeli Prime Minister Yitzhak Rabin, dies at 72.
USA, December 13: George W. Bush becomes the 43rd US president, with Democrat Al Gore conceding defeat. The vote in Florida was decided in the Supreme Court.

Cairo, Egypt: A meeting which includes Queen Rania of Jordan, and First Ladies Suha Arafat, Fatima Bashir, and Ándrée Lahoud is held in Cairo to discuss improved status for women in Arabic countries.
Skibo, Scotland, December 22: Rock star Madonna marries film director Guy Ritchie in a ceremony at Skibo Castle.
USA: Australian golfer Karrie Webb is named women's golf player of the year by the LPGA.

Cathy Freeman

> "ALL CREATIVE
> PEOPLE WANT
> TO DO THE
> UNEXPECTED."
>
> HEDI LAMARR
> (1913–2000),
> AMERICAN ACTRESS

Women's Right to Pray at Wall Challenged

Jerusalem, Israel, May 31: On December 1, 1988, a group of women held a prayer meeting at the western wall, praying aloud from the Torah and wearing the *tallit*, the sacred shawl usually worn only by men. They were jeered and harassed by orthodox men—and women—and were then attacked with bottles and various other missiles.

Orthodox Jews believe that only men should read aloud from the Torah, especially at this most sacred of Jewish sites, the retaining wall of the second temple which was destroyed by Romans in 70 CE. They also say that the women are not motivated by a desire to pray, but rather wish to challenge orthodox beliefs. The women formed a campaign group named Women of the Wall. They believe that God wishes to hear the voices of all Jews—not just those of men. The women rejected a compromise that they be allowed to pray in an area set aside for them nearby, instead making an appeal to Israel's Supreme Court. On May 22, the court gave them the right to pray aloud from the Torah, and wear the *tallit* at the wall. The government, fearful of a conservative backlash and more riots, hasn't acted on the court's order, and many fear that it may never be enacted.

Today, right-wing members of Parliament proposed an act which would ban women from praying or wearing inappropriate garments, with a seven-year jail sentence for offenders. It seems the women and their supporters are in for a long fight, and there is absolutely no guarantee that they will eventually succeed in their cause.

Afghanistan Aid Worker Arrested, Deported

Kabul, July 9: Mary MacMakin is a 71-year-old physical therapist and aid worker, who has worked on and off in Afghanistan since the early 1960s. For almost 10 years she has run the aid agency Physiotherapy and Rehabilitation Support for Afghanistan, or PARSA.

After two decades of war, the plight of Afghani widows and their children is desperate. When the fundamentalist Taliban forces took power in 1996, they declared an Islamic state based on a highly restrictive interpretation of the Koran, and made it illegal for a woman to leave home without a male relative, receive an education, or work—among many other restrictions. Thousands of widows must rely on aid agency handouts or beg to feed their families.

MacMakin founded PARSA to help the widows help themselves. She purchased sewing supplies, and invited groups of widows to gather in her living room to make handcrafts, which were sold from the house. PARSA also began to distribute food and medicine, run home-schooling programs for girls, supply more women with the means to start their own cottage industries, and provide young male household heads with employment training.

Until July, the Taliban allowed a few women to work in the health area. But when a foreign aid group advertised for female employees, they were outraged, and demanded that aid agencies sack all their female staff. Because of some critical statements about the Taliban in some of its newsletters, PARSA was a prime target.

On July 9 MacMakin, eight of her male and seven of her female staff were arrested. The men were soon released but the UN officials had to intervene in order that the women were freed. MacMakin, accused of employing women and dubbed a "spy," was ordered to leave the country within 24 hours. Speaking from Pakistan, Mac-Makin says she will continue her work from there "…because things must get better for Afghan women, for everybody."

A fragile Queen Mother celebrates her 100th birthday.

British Queen Mother Turns 100

United Kingdom, August 4: The main celebrations for the Queen Mother's 100th birthday took place today. Like all British and Commonwealth centenarians, she received a congratulatory telegram from the Queen.

At Clarendon House, the Queen Mother walked to the main gate with her grandson, the Prince of Wales, to receive a salute. They were then driven by open carriage to Buckingham Palace, where thousands of well-wishers, many of whom had camped out to gain good positions, waved and cheered as the royal party passed by.

At Buckingham Palace the Queen Mother waved from the balcony with Queen Elizabeth II, Princess Margaret, and her grandchildren and great-grandchildren. She then lunched with her

Women praying aloud from the Torah at the Wailing Wall.

family, and that evening attended the ballet at the Royal Opera House with her daughters.

The Queen Mother was born Elizabeth Bowes-Lyon, the ninth child of an earl. Wary of public life, she initially refused the proposal of the King's second son, Albert, but finally married him in 1923. When King Edward VIII abdicated in 1936, she supported her shy husband in his unexpected role as King George VII, and soon established herself as a popular consort. At no time was her dedication to duty more apparent than during World War II. During the blitz of 1941, the royal family stayed in Buckingham Palace, the Queen stating that: "The children will not leave unless I do. I shall not leave unless their father does, and the King will not leave the country in any circumstances whatever." The King and Queen also made many public visits to bombed-out areas of London.

After her husband's death in 1952, she took the title Queen Mother. She remains one of the most popular members of the royal family and her 100th birthday has given the public an opportunity to express their affection for her.

Hillary Rodham Clinton is elected a US Senator.

Hillary Clinton Elected to US Senate

New York, USA, November 7: Hillary Rodham Clinton has been elected New York's first female senator. She is also the first First Lady to be elected to public office.

Clinton's high-profile campaign successfully painted her as "the people's candidate." She made many informal public appearances, met many constituents face to face, and continually returned to the themes of job creation, education, childcare, and the environment. Her opponent, republican Rick Lazio, made much of the fact that Clinton did

Fan proudly displaying her copy of *Goblet of Fire*.

not buy a house in New York until she decided to run for the Senate, but exit polling showed that most voters considered this unimportant.

Clinton's experience as a politically active First Lady seems to have outweighed, in the public eye, the damage caused by the numerous high-publicity scandals that beset her husband Bill's presidency. Clinton gained 56 percent of the vote, with strong support from women, Hispanics, African-Americans, and voters in New York City.

Arab Women's Summit in Cairo

Cairo, Egypt, November 20: A major three-day assembly has been held to discuss the status of women and girls throughout the Arab world, and make recommendations about the challenges they face.

More than 400 women from 19 Arab League nations attended. Among them were nine First Ladies, including Queen Rania of Jordan, Lebanon's Ándrée Lahoud, and Suha Arafat—wife of Palestinian leader Yasser Arafat. Egypt's Suzanne Mubarak chaired the conference and delivered the opening address. The attendees included many scientists, academics, parliamentarians, political activists, and aid workers. Only Saudi Arabia, Qatar, and Algeria did not send delegates. The successes of Arab women, and the setbacks they have experienced in recent years were discussed, and many speakers noted that women in different nations can have very different experiences. For instance, in Tunisia polygamy is banned and women have a large degree of control over their lives, and in Libya female bodyguards protect Colonel Gaddafi. But in Saudi Arabia and several other countries, women are not allowed to drive—or even leave their homes—

without being accompanied by a male relative. Delegates discussed the dire poverty and health of women in the region, their lack of economic power, and their high levels of illiteracy. The stereotyping of Arab women by the world media as submissive and weak was refuted. On the last day of the conference the Cairo Declaration was drawn up. The statement supports women's access to political decision-making, and their right to work and care for their families. It supports the principle of equal opportunities for women and men, especially in relation to education, training, and access to health services. The delegates made a commitment to promote a positive view of Arab women, to create a fund to help Arab women living in poverty and to meet again every two years. They then declared 2001 the Year of Arab Women.

Queen Rania

Madonna Christens Son, Marries Guy Ritchie

Skibo Castle, Scotland, December 22: After yesterday christening their infant son, Rocco, at Dornoch Cathedral, today pop star Madonna Ciccone married director Guy Ritchie in a private ceremony at nearby Skibo Castle.

Madonna has always sought the limelight, attracting much attention for her controversial songs, videos and statements, but her second wedding was a strictly private affair. Skibo Castle is surrounded by dense pine trees, and has the finest security money can buy. The only glimpse the media caught of such celebrity guests as Sting and wife Trudie—who introduced the newlyweds in 1998—was through the windows of limousines as they arrived. Madonna is reported to have worn a Gothic-style gown with a tartan sash of the same fabric as her husband's kilt. The couple are said to have written their own vows, with the guests being served salmon.

Skibo Castle was chosen for Madonna's wedding.

Maria Gloria Arroyo

Hillary Takes Oath as New York Senator

New York, USA, January 1: Hillary Rodham Clinton today became the first First Lady to be elected to national office when she was sworn in as the junior senator from New York, and will have the unique privilege of holding both titles for the next 20 days, until her husband's term as President expires on January 20.

Clinton redefined the role of First Lady from the moment she assumed the title, and was the first First Lady to have an office in the west wing of the White House. Just five days into her tenure, on January 20, 1993, President Clinton appointed her to head the President's task force on health care reform. She is refusing to comment on media speculation that today is actually the first step in a long campaign to become the first female US president.

Arroyo Replaces Corrupt Estrada in Philippines

Manila, Philippines, January 20: In the wake of the sudden resignation of former leader Joseph Estrada on Saturday over corruption charges, Maria Gloria Arroyo was today sworn in as the new Philippines president in front of a massive gathering of jubilant supporters. With a final salute to his guards and staff, Estrada and his family departed the royal palace by river barge shortly after Arroyo's swearing in ceremony, having lost the moral authority to govern the nation. Despite being sworn in by Chief Justice Hilario Davide Jr, after the Supreme Court declared the position of the president vacant, it is expected that the opposition will question Arroyo's legitimacy to govern, and that Estrada will personally challenge the ruling and pursue his reinstatement as leader.

Arroyo, the daughter of the late president Diosdado Macapagal, hopes to unite the Philippine people and then restore faith in their country's democratic institutions. Her stated aims are to increase the strength of the bureaucracy, improve the nation's gross domestic product, lower crime rates, and reduce tax evasion. Arroyo was born on April 5, 1947, and moved into Malacañang Palace in Manila at 14 when her father was elected president. She graduated valedictorian from Manila's Assumption convent in 1964, then studied in the United States for two years at Georgetown University's Walsh School of Foreign Service.

Elected to the Senate in 1992 and re-elected in 1995, Arroyo was twice named the country's outstanding senator, and sponsored 55 laws on economic and social reform during her tenure.

Julia Roberts as Erin Brockovich, with Albert Finney.

Condoleezza Rice is New NSA Boss

Washington DC, USA, January 22: Stanford-educated Dr Condoleezza Rice has been appointed the assistant to the President for national security affairs, and is the first woman to occupy the post.

Easily the most academically-inclined of President

Condoleezza Rice–president's national security advisor.

George W. Bush's foreign affairs team, Rice has enjoyed a strong working relationship with the President ever since his campaign, and her influence over the new administration's foreign policy is expected to be quite considerable.

Rice was born in Birmingham, Alabama, on November 14, 1954. She gained a bachelor's degree in political science from the University of Denver (1974), earned her masters at the University of Notre Dame (1975), and a doctorate from the Graduate School of International Studies at the University of Denver (1981). She has also received several honorary doctorates and is a member of the American Academy of Arts and Sciences.

An expert on US–Soviet relations, Rice speaks fluent Russian and begins each day reading *Pravda*, the Soviet daily newspaper. In presenting Ms Rice to Mikhail Gorbachev during an official visit in 1989, president George Bush Sr was quoted as saying that everything he knew about the USSR, he had learned from her. Upon taking office as the nation's 43rd President,

"AMERICA'S MILITARY POWER MUST BE SECURE BECAUSE THE UNITED STATES IS THE ONLY GUARANTOR OF GLOBAL PEACE AND STABILITY."

CONDOLEEZZA RICE, AMERICAN SECRETARY OF STATE

New York, USA, January 3: Hillary Rodham Clinton is sworn in as senator of New York, the first former First Lady to win elected national office.
Manila, Philippines, January 20: After President Estrada resigns amid corruption allegations, Maria Gloria Arroyo becomes President.
England, January 22: The UK government declares that the combined measles, mumps, and rubella vaccine is safe. There have been concerns that it was linked to incidents of autism in some children.

London, England, January 24: Clara Furse becomes the first female CEO of the London stock exchange.
Iran, January 24: The Iranian guardian council vetoes a proposal that would allow Iranian women to study abroad.
Washington DC, USA, January: Condoleezza Rice becomes the first female national security advisor to the President.
New Orleans, USA, January: Karen E. Smith and Sijue Wu are awarded the Ruth Lyttle Satter Prize in Mathematics.

Vermont, USA, February 2: Anne Morrow Lindbergh, writer and wife of aviator Charles Lindbergh, dies, aged 94.
Israel, February 6: Ariel Sharon, leader of the right-wing Likud party, becomes Prime Minister in a decisive election result.
London, England, February 22: UK judge Dame Elizabeth Butler-Sloss rules that a woman who is paralyzed from the neck down has the right to end her life by refusing treatment.
Dakar, Senegal, March 3: Mame Madior Boye is made Prime Minister.

Paris, France, March 7: The FIA international court of appeal confirms that Jutta Kleinschmidt was indeed the first female winner of this year's Paris-Dakar road rally, after dismissing a competitor's challenge.
World, March 8: International Women's Day is marked by celebrations, holidays, and protests around the world. Director-general of the World Health Organization, Gro Harlem Brundtland, says: "There isn't a single country or institution in the world where men and women enjoy equal opportunity."

Amsterdam, Netherlands, April 1: Four couples wed in the world's first same-sex marriages after the Dutch government legislation earlier today.
Hawaii, USA, April 12: Twenty-one men and 2 women–the crew of a US spy plane–touch down on American soil after an uncertain week of detainment in China.
Palawan, Philippines, May 27: Muslim terrorist group Abu Sayaf seizes 20 people from a tourist resort.
England, May: A foot-and-mouth disease outbreak shuts down large parts of the countryside.

George W. Bush told reporters that Rice was the only person he knew capable of explaining to him the complex world of foreign policy.

Men Protest but Jutta Wins Paris-Dakar Rally

Paris, France, March 7: Germany's Jutta Kleinschmidt has been confirmed as the winner of this year's Paris-Dakar rally in a statement released by the FIA international court of appeal. After 11 attempts, Kleinschmidt has become the first female winner of the very grueling 6,670 mile (10,740 km) event.

The race results were thrown into doubt when it was announced that the Frenchman Jean-Louis Schlesser, the pre-race favorite, would appeal against the decision of race stewards to penalize the Monaco-based buggy driver one hour for failing to respect the starting order when he set off on the penultimate stage of the rally ahead of the then leader Hiroshi Masuoka.

The court of appeal heard arguments from the Automobile Club of Monaco, acting on behalf of Schlesser, the Deutscher Motor Sport Bund representing Kleinschmidt, and the Japanese Automobile Federation acting for Masuoka,

Jutta Kleinschmidt, winner of Paris-Dakar road rally.

before confirming the original decision and awarding the race to Kleinschmidt.

Masuoka eventually finished just 2 minutes 39 seconds behind Kleinschmidt. Both were driving a Mitsubishi Pajero/Montero. Kleinschmidt was born in 1962 in Cologne, Germany. She grew up in the state of Bavaria and studied physics there at the Bavaria Polytechnic. In 1987 she took part in her first desert rally, riding a motorbike in the Pharaoh's Rally in Egypt.

International Women's Day Sparks Controversy

Worldwide, March 8: Women and men across the world are today celebrating International Women's Day, a global recognition of the crucial importance women play in the well-being of our communities, and of their contribution to economic growth of their countries as well as the standard of living.

The first International Women's Day was held on March 19, 1911, and its genesis can be traced to the first US National Women's Day in February 1908. In 1910 a conference of socialist women in Copenhagen convened to discuss the possibility of holding an annual International Women's Day, when the treatment of women was becoming a very controversial socialist ideological battleground. Clara Zetkin, a member of the German Socialist Party, led the assemblage of over 100 women from over 17 countries to formally adopt the proposal.

International Women's Day is more than simply an annual event. It is also a reminder that the elimination of discrimination against women and the creation of conditions that allow for their full and equal participation in society is a daily struggle.

time ou

Julia Roberts wins an Academy Award for playing Erin Brokovich, the single mom who took on a Californian power company that had poisoned the local water supply, and won compensation for those affected.

Of the poorest 1.3 billion people in the world, 70 percent are women, and women represent two-thirds of the world's 900 million illiterate people.

International Women's Day re-focuses our efforts at reducing the discrimination that permits those in power—whether male-dominated governments, or village elders, or traditional healers—to prevent women from achieving their potential and exercising their basic human rights.

For over 80 years International Women's Day, rooted in the suffragette movement that emerged in Europe and the US at the close of the nineteenth century, has been a day for reflection, action, and celebration. The day is marked as a non-working day in many countries where the repression of woman has been most severe. It is often marked by men giving gifts to women.

Mame Madior Boye

Gro Harlem Brundtland, Director-General of WHO.

Key Events

Katmandu, Nepal, June 1: Crown Prince Dipendra shoots dead nine members of the royal family before shooting himself.
Wilmington, Delaware, USA, June 24: Twenty-six-year-old Australian golfer Karrie Webb wins the LPGA Championship, becoming the youngest player to win a major.
Canberra, Australia, June 25: Judith Wright, one of the country's greatest poets dies, aged 85. She campaigned for Aboriginal and conservation issues.

Idaho, USA, July 17: Publishing magnate Katharine Graham dies.
Jakarta, Indonesia, July 23: The Indonesian legislature removes President Wahid, and installs Megawati Sukarnoputri.
New Delhi, India, July 25: Phoolan Devi, India's "bandit queen" turned politician, is murdered by a masked gunmen.
Los Angeles, USA, August 8: Nicole Kidman and Tom Cruise divorce after separating in February. All attention now turns to the terms of the divorce settlement.

Tehran, Iran, August 26: Filmmaker Tahmineh Milani is arrested on counter-revolutionary charges, as authorities crack down on her films.
England, August: Irene Zubaida Khan becomes Secretary-General of rights watchdog Amnesty International.
New York and Washington DC, USA, September 11: The World Trade Center in New York is destroyed when two hijacked aircraft smash into the twin towers. A third plane hits the Pentagon. The death toll is estimated at 3,000.

Afghanistan, October 7: The US launches a retaliatory campaign for the September 11 attacks. The Taliban regime and al-Qaeda are the targets of the operation, which began with 50 cruise missiles being launched at Kandahar and Kabul.
Chicago, USA, October 8: At the Chicago marathon, Catherine Ndereba breaks the record set by Japan's Nakao Takahashi at the Berlin marathon last week.
Bangladesh, October 10: Khaleda Zia becomes Prime Minister for the third time.

Washington DC, USA, October 10: Nancy Pelosi is elected house Democratic Whip, the highest post a woman has ever held in the House.
USA, September 18–November: Twenty-two people have been infected with anthrax, resulting in five deaths from exposure to the deadly disease.
South Korea, December 26: Park Geun-hye, daughter of the ex-president of Korea, announces she will run for president.

Katharine Graham

Karrie Webb Wins Career Grand Slam

Wilmington, Delaware, USA, June 24: Twenty-six-year-old Australian golfer Karrie Webb today won the LPGA Championship at the DuPont Country Club in Delaware to become the youngest player to win a career grand slam. Webb had a three-shot lead going into the final round, but learned this morning that her grandfather had had a stroke, and was not expected to survive. She wanted to withdraw but her parents urged her to continue. In an emotional final round she fought back tears to win the tournament by three strokes. Webb described her victory as overwhelming, but her thoughts were clearly focused back home in Australia where her grandfather remains in a critical condition. Webb will be flying home immediately to be by his side.

Comparisons with Tiger Woods are beginning to emerge. Woods completed his own career grand slam—winning each of the four majors but in different years—when he was just 24 years old, but it took him 15 major tournaments to amass four wins, while Webb has managed it in only eight. She has now won five of the last eight majors in a period of dominance not matched since the great Mickey Wright won five out of six in the early 1960s. She now joins Wright, Louise Suggs, Pat Bradley, and Juli Inkster as the only women to have completed the career grand slam, and her coach Kelvin Haller has told reporters that there is no telling just how far she can go from here.

Karrie Anne Webb was born in 1974 in Ayr, Queensland, Australia, and began her professional career in 1994, finishing second at the Australian Ladies' Open. She won her first LPGA tournament in 1996, and in the same year became the first LPGA player to win more than US$1 million in a single season.

Poet and Activist Judith Wright Dies

Canberra, Australia, June 25: Poet, conservationist, and Aboriginal rights campaigner Judith Arundell Wright, has died of a heart attack in a Canberra hospital, aged 85.

Wright was born in the New England region of New South Wales, Australia, in 1915, into a family of wealthy pioneering pastoralists, and started writing poetry at the age of six. She was taken in by one of her aunts when her mother died, and was 14 when her father remarried and sent her to boarding school in New England. She moved to Sydney in 1934 and studied philosophy, history, and English at Sydney University, without taking a degree. Her first poems emerged in the late 1930s in various literary journals and were inspired by her surroundings.

A commitment to conservation slowly began to appear in her work as she came to a realization that art and culture must relate us not only to society, but also to the land that we inhabit. She challenged herself to find words that provide a bridge between our human experiences and the natural world. Wright also took on a very public role championing the cause of indigenous people—as recently as last month she attended a reconciliation rally in Canberra. Wright published over 56 volumes of poetry and short stories and was the recipient of many awards, including the prestigious Grace Leven prize (1950), the Robert Frost Memorial Award (1974), and the Queen's Medal for poetry (1992).

Sukarnoputri Succeeds as Indonesian President

Jakarta, Indonesia, July 23: President Abdurrahman Wahid, the leader of the incumbent Democratic Party of Struggle (PDI-P), and former head of the 40 million-strong Muslim organization Nahdlatul Ulama, has been removed from office by Indonesia's parliament. The PDI-P's vice-president, 54-year-old Megawati Sukarnoputri, has been installed as the new leader.

Megawati Sukarnoputri, President of Indonesia.

Sukarnoputri inherits a country beset by economic hardship and sectarian violence exacerbated by Wahid's erratic and autocratic style, which alienated the PDI-P from the various minor parties whose support he needed to govern effectively. Confidence in Wahid, Indonesia's first democratically-elected president, plunged when he was implicated in the pocketing of $2 million in aid money from the sultan of Brunei, and the theft of $4.1 million from the state commodities regulator. These accusations led to today's dumping of the accident-prone leader. In a measure of his political irrelevance, Wahid's announcement this morning that he would dissolve parliament and call fresh elections has simply been ignored by the armed forces and the political establishment.

Despite her overwhelming popularity, it is unknown whether Sukarnoputri's rise to power is as a result of her own devices, or the political savvy of others who may intend to rule through her. She is an intensely private person who rarely grants interviews, and has never spoken publicly about the policies she would pursue as president.

Megawati Sukarnoputri was born in January 1947 into one of Indonesia's most powerful political families. She is the daughter of President Sukarno, who led Indonesia to independence from the Dutch in 1964. She has been married three times and has three children. She is preparing to move back into Jakarta's Merdeka Palace, where she lived as a child and where she used to dance for visiting dignitaries.

Karrie Webb wins a career Grand Slam.

Heroine to India's Oppressed Murdered

New Delhi, India, July 25: Phoolan Devi, the so-called "bandit queen" of India, victim of caste oppression and gender exploitation turned politician and champion of the downtrodden, has been murdered in broad daylight in New Delhi by a group of masked gunmen.

Devi had just returned from a parliamentary session and was standing in her front yard when the gunmen fired six bullets into her from point-blank range, escaping in a car that was later found abandoned nearby. The murder took place in the high-security area of the capital just about half a mile (1 km) from Parliament House and the Parliament Street police station.

Devi was born on August 10, 1963, into a low caste family in the state of Uttar Pradesh. She was given away in marriage at the age of 11 for a dowry of a single cow. Her husband, three times her age, continually beat and raped her until Devi did the unthinkable—in India—and deserted him. In the late 1970s Devi was kidnapped by a group of wealthy landowners. After further beatings and humiliations, which included being led from village to village at the end of a rope, she ran away and became the mistress of a bandit leader. She was sent to prison without trial in 1983 for the alleged murder of over 70 people. Released in 1994 and already a hero to millions of downtrodden women—and a militant proponent and symbol of women's rights—Devi joined the Samajwadi Party of Uttar Pradesh. She was elected to parliament with a staggering 50,000 majority. But Devi was to prove ineffective as a member of parliament, although her popularity among India's lower castes continued unabated. She lost her bid for re-election in 1998—the same year that a group of British MPs nominated her for the Nobel Peace Prize.

Khaleda Zia again becomes Prime Minister of Bangladesh.

Nicole Kidman and Tom Cruise have divorced.

Kidman and Cruise Untie Knot

Los Angeles, USA, August 8: Nicole Kidman and Tom Cruise are officially divorced today, the decree coming through just hours before the two stars were due to separately attend the premiere of their new film *The Others*.

The superstars announced their separation last February, citing the difficulties inherent in maintaining two independently successful careers. Cruise was the first to file for divorce, which reportedly left Kidman devastated. Late in March her publicist announced that she had suffered a miscarriage. Over the past six years Kidman has made a name for herself as a consummate actress of great depth. Her portrayal of a homicidal weather girl in Gus Van Sant's *To Die For* (1995) was her breakthrough role, showcasing an impressive range and deadly comic timing. Her first American film was *Dead Calm* (1989) and a year later, she met Tom Cruise for the first time on the set of their movie *Days of Thunder* (1990.)

Nicole Kidman was born in Honolulu, Hawaii, USA, on June 20, 1967, and moved with her family to the Sydney suburb of Longueville when she was four.

Kenyan Catherine Runs Marathon Record

Chicago, USA, October 8: When the Japanese distance runner Naoko Takahashi set a world record time of 2:19:46 on September 30 in the Berlin marathon, she could have been forgiven for thinking that her record would stand a little longer than a mere eight days. Today in Chicago, however, Kenyan runner Catherine Ndereba ran a new world record time of 2:18:47 to win the Chicago marathon and stun the world of women's distance running.

Ndereba was born on July 31, 1972, and lives in Nyeri, Kenya with her husband Anthony Maina and daughter Jane. In 1999 she ran the world's fastest times in the 5 km, 12 km, 15 km, and 10 miles, and further cemented her place in the pantheon of distance runners by winning both the Boston and Chicago marathons last year. In 1998, she was named Road Racer of the Year by the leading magazine *Running Times,* an award she won also the following year after winning eight events. Her brother Samuel is also a marathon runner.

Nancy Pelosi

Catherine Ndereba's winning time on display.

Astrid Lindgren

> "*I HAVE A
> BRAIN AND A
> UTERUS, AND
> I USE BOTH.*"
>
> PATRICIA SCHROEDER,
> AMERICAN LAWYER
> AND POLITICIAN

Pippi Longstocking is Lindgren's Legacy

Stockholm, Sweden, January 28: One of Sweden's best-known authors and most-loved citizens, Astrid Lindgren, has died, aged 94. Lindgren was born in 1907, the second of four children, and grew up on a farm in Vimmerby, Sweden. She loved nothing more than to spend hours and hours reading books, and her parents encouraged their children's experience of literature with storytelling nights where they indulged in the world of imagination and fantastic adventure.

She became pregnant in 1925 at the age of 18 and left home. Her son was placed in a foster home and eventually cared for by Lindgren's parents. In 1944 she published her first book, *Britt-Mari Opens her Heart*. This was followed, in 1945, by the publication of a book about an unconventional, independent, and untidy child that would bring Lindgren everlasting fame and praise—*Pippi*

Longstocking. Pippi had no parents, which led to some criticism about the character's "permissive" upbringing. Of course, what this meant for child readers was the creation of a world free of parental restraints and boundaries, with no one to tell you to stop bouncing on the bed, or to brush your teeth, or to stay away from sweets before dinner.

Lindgren challenged the established views of children and wanted to create a world in which they were treated as ordinary human beings. In *Pippi Goes on Board* (1946) and *Pippi in the South Seas* (1948), the reader sees a physically and mentally mature nine-year-old who asks philosophical questions about courage, friendship, and the pursuit of knowledge. Astrid Lindgren published over 100 books that sold tens of millions of copies worldwide and brought immeasurable happiness into the hearts of children everywhere.

Woman Wins Prestigious Maths Prize

Cambridge, England, February 26: The world's most prestigious award for mathematics, Cambridge University's Adams Prize, has been awarded to 29-year-old Dr Susan Howson—a young UK-based mathematician and researcher—for her insightful work in the abstract field of elliptic curves and number theory. She is the first woman to win the award in its 120-year history. Elliptic curves are one of the oldest branches in mathematics and have important applications in the field of cryptology.

Born in Oxford in 1972, Dr Howson is a lecturer at Nottingham University and a Royal Society Dorothy Hodgkin research fellow. With women comprising only 40 percent of undergraduates in the

Cartoon still of the character Pippy Longstocking.

UK, Dr Howson feels there are no impediments to women progressing in mathematics—though she concedes the innate competitiveness and single-

Versatile opera singer Eileen Farrell dies, aged 82.

minded aspects of higher mathematics may be reasons why women tend to keep out of its way.

Multitalented Soprano Loved Jazz and Blues

New York City, USA, March 23: Eileen Farrell, the great American soprano famous for her operatic repertoire but equally at home with jazz and blues ballads, has died in a nursing home in Park Ridge, New Jersey, aged 82.

Considering her immense talent, Farrell entered the world of opera scandalously late in life. Born in Connecticut in 1920, she made her operatic debut at the age of 36 in Tampa, Florida. Her New York debut at the Metropolitan Opera in December 1960, singing the title role in Gluck's *Alcestis*, began a glory-filled period at "The Met," which culminated in Farrell's opening its 1962 season with

Europe, January 1: The common currency of the European Union, the Euro, is legal tender in 12 countries.
Stockholm, Sweden, January 28: Children's author and creator of *Pippi Longstocking*, Astrid Lindgren, dies aged 94.
Washington DC, USA, January 29: George W. Bush delivers his first State of the Union address to Congress, labeling North Korea, Iran, and Iraq an "axis of evil."
Zabbar, Malta, February 4: Agatha Barbara, first female president of Malta, dies, aged 79.

The Hague, Netherlands, February 12: Slobodan Milosevic's war crime trial begins, with the former Yugoslav president representing himself in a fiery rebuttal of the legitimacy of the tribunal.
Cambridge, England, February 26: The 120-year-old mathematical Adams Prize has been awarded to a woman for the first time. Susan Howson wins it for her work on elliptical curves.
Godhra, India, February 27: A train fire kills 57 Hindu pilgrims, sparking days of rioting in Gujarat state.

Zimbabwe, March 9: Robert Mugabe returns to power in an election characterized by violence and intimidation.
New York City, USA, March 23: Opera star Eileen Farrell dies, aged 82.
Hollywood, USA, March 24: At the Academy Awards, Halle Berry in *Monster's Ball* becomes the first African-American woman to win the Best Actress Award, and Australian Catherine Martin wins Art Direction and Costume Design for the Baz Luhrmann production *Moulin Rouge*.

Nigeria, March 25: Safiya Husaini's life is spared after a court overturns her sentence of death by stoning.
Windsor, England, March 30: The Queen Mother dies, aged 101.
Afghanistan, March: UN forces mount Operation Anaconda, a massive push to round up Taliban and al-Qaeda south of Gardez.
Ramallah, Israel, April 1: After a suicide bombing left over 100 Israelis dead, Israel launches a massive military operation in which Yasser Arafat's compound is besieged and battles rage in Jenin refugee camp.

New York City, USA, April 8: Suzan-Lori Parks wins the Pulitzer Prize for drama, becoming the first African-American woman to win the drama award.
East Timor, May 20: East Timor achieves independence.
Sydney, Australia, May 31: Cherry Hood wins Australia's Archibald Prize for portraiture with her portrait of pianist Simon Tedeschi.
London, England, June 3: Queen Elizabeth II celebrates 50 years on the throne with a rock concert in the grounds of Buckingham Palace.

Giordano's *Andrea Chénier*. Farrell held the positions of Distinguished Professor of Music at Indiana University at Bloomington from 1971–80, and at the University of Maine at Orono from 1983–1985. Her autobiography *Can't Help Singing* was released in 1999.

Halle Berry Wins Oscar for *Monster's Ball*

Hollywood, USA, March 24: Actress Halle Berry has become the first African-American in the 74-year history of the Academy Awards to win the Oscar for best actress for her role in the dark romantic drama *Monster's Ball*. Berry has received wide critical acclaim for her role as a woman who becomes romantically involved with a racist ex-prison guard who witnessed the execution of her husband, played by Sean Combs.

Berry was born in Ohio to an African-American father and a white mother on August 14, 1968. As a teenager she contested various beauty pageants and appeared in episodes of the TV series *Living Dolls* and *Knots Landing* before winning her first movie role in Spike Lee's *Jungle Fever* (1991). In 1999 she won a Golden Globe and an Emmy for her title role in the biopic *Introducing*

Monster's Ball brings Halle Berry an Academy Award.

Dorothy Dandridge, a gritty depiction of the actress's struggle to succeed in racially-biased 1950s Hollywood. In her acceptance speech, Berry said she hoped her win would open doors for struggling African-American women hoping to succeed in the entertainment industry.

The Oscars for best art direction and best costume design went to Australian Catherine Martin for her work in Baz Luhrmann's *Moulin Rouge*. Martin and Luhrmann have been working together since 1987 on operas such as *La Bohème* and the films *Strictly Ballroom* and *Romeo & Juliet*. Martin was born on January 26, 1965 in the Sydney suburb of Lindfield.

Beloved Stalwart Queen Mother Dies

Windsor, England, March 30: Queen Elizabeth, the Queen Mother, passed away in her sleep at 3.15 p.m. today at the Royal Lodge, Windsor, with her daughter, the Queen, at her bedside. She was 101 years old. Prince Charles is said to be devastated, while Prime Minister Tony Blair called her a symbol of Britain's dignity and courage. Her funeral will be held on Tuesday, April 9 at Westminster Abbey.

On Friday, her coffin will be taken in a ceremonial procession to Westminster Hall where it will lie in state overnight before being taken to St George's Chapel at Windsor, where she will at last be reunited with her late husband King George VI, who died of cancer 50 years ago. Books of Condolence have been started at Glamis Castle in Angus, the Castle of Mey in Caithness, and Holyrood Palace in Edinburgh.

The young Lady Elizabeth Bowes-Lyons initially had reservations about becoming part of the protocol-driven house of Windsor. It took the future king of England three proposals of marriage before she acquiesced. Elizabeth married Prince Albert in 1923, and in 1926 the couple celebrated the birth of their first

daughter, Elizabeth. When King George V died in 1936, succession passed to Albert's older brother Edward, who in turn abdicated in 1937 to marry American divorcée Wallis Simpson. Albert was crowned King George VI, and the woman who once had reservations about life as a royal found herself consort to the monarch. During World War II the Queen became a rallying point for the beleaguered nation, choosing to stay in London and endure nightly bombing raids from the German Luftwaffe even after Buckingham Palace was hit in September 1940. Today the Union Jack is at half-mast over the palace, while a grieving populace lays hundreds of flowers at the gates of Buckingham Palace and other royal residences.

Suzan-Lori Parks

The Queen Mother was an enduring symbol of royalty.

Key Events

Wilmington, Delaware, USA, June 9: Korean golfer Se Ri Pak becomes the youngest woman to win all four major championships when she wins the LPGA Championship.
New York City, USA, June 9: Boxing promoter Aileen Eaton is posthumously inducted into the International Boxing Hall of Fame. She is the first woman inductee.
Kabul, Afghanistan, June 19: Hamid Karzai is endorsed as president at the *loya jirga*, or grand assembly. The process took over a week, with intense factional lobbying.

Beverly Hills, California, USA, June 29: Singer Rosemary Clooney dies, aged 74.
Seoul, South Korea, August 1: The National Assembly rejects the newly appointed Prime Minister, Chang Sang, and she steps down from the position after just one month.
Tehran, Iran, August 25: Iran's parliament votes in favor of granting women the right to sue for divorce.
England, September 5: Former head of MI5, Stella Rimington, publishes her autobiography *Open Secret*.

New York, USA, September 12: Mary Robinson finishes her term as UN High Commissioner for Human Rights.
Kuta, Bali, October 12: Bombs explode in two tourist bars, killing more than 180 people. Australia suffers the biggest brunt, with 88 citizens killed.
Bahrain, October 24: Women vote in general elections for the first time.
Moscow, Russian Federation, October 26: Russian forces storm theater where Chechen separatists have been holding over 800 hostages.

New York, USA, November 8: The UN Security Council adopts resolution 1441, requiring Iraq to submit to weapons inspections.
Nigeria, November 23: The Miss World pageant is forced to relocate to London after riots by Muslims opposed to the pageant leave more than 100 dead.
Madrid, Spain, December 17: Soccer player Mia Hamm wins the FIFA International Woman Player of the Year award for the second consecutive year. The award is based on scores from the previous season.

England: Popular Japanese writer Yu Miri has her novel *Goldrush* translated and published in England.
Washington DC, USA: The National Building Museum's Vincent Scully prize is awarded to Robert Venturi and Denise Scott-Brown.
Worldwide: This year the following books are published: *The Lovely Bones* by Alice Sebold, *Unless* by Carol Shields, *The Little Friend* by Donna Tartt, and *Fingersmith* by Sarah Waters.

Queen's 50th Year Celebration Rocks

Chang Sang

London, England, June 3: Over a million people are gathering in London's Mall and the parklands surrounding Buckingham Palace today for a rock concert in the palace grounds, in celebration of Queen Elizabeth's 50 years as monarch of Great Britain and Northern Ireland. An estimated worldwide audience of 200 million will tune in to the greatest collection of musical talent since Live Aid. Paul McCartney, Elton John, Mick Jagger, Rod Stewart, Eric Clapton, and Tom Jones—to name but a few—will honor Her Majesty and cele-brate the 50 years of peace, stability and prosperity that must have seemed very unlikely to the post-World War II generation who witnessed the coronation of the young queen.

The concert will start at 3 p.m. with the Queen and Duke of Edinburgh due to arrive at 10 p.m. for their official welcome to the event by cross-dressing hyperstar Dame Edna Everage. The royals will then make their way along the Mall to light the national beacon on the Queen Victoria Memorial, escorted by about 300 lantern-carrying children. A spectacular fireworks display is scheduled and a light show will be played out upon the façade of Buckingham Palace. After 50 years, the Queen remains unblemished and her reputation undiminished, despite the scandals and tragedies that have befallen many of those around her. This year's Golden Jubilee celebrations again demonstrate the enduring favor and timeless appeal the house of Windsor enjoys in the hearts of the British public.

"I DON'T MIND DYING, I'LL GLADLY DO THAT, BUT NOT RIGHT NOW, I NEED TO CLEAN THE HOUSE FIRST."

ASTRID LINDGREN (1907–2002), SWEDISH WRITER

Queen Elizabeth II enjoys celebrations with Prince Charles.

Woman in Boxing Hall of Fame

New York City, USA, June 9: Aileen Eaton, one of boxing's most successful promoters—whose influence throughout the west coast boxing scene has spanned more than five decades—has become the first woman to be inducted into the boxing Hall of Fame, albeit posthumously. Nicknamed "The Redhead," Eaton handled some of the sport's biggest names, including Floyd Patterson, Joe Frazier, George Foreman, and Sugar Ray Robinson, and possessed a reputation for toughness and honesty.

Born in Vancouver, Canada in 1909, Eaton was half of a dynamic promoting team with husband Col Eaton. After his death in 1966, she went on to promote over 2,500 fight cards and more than 10,000 contests. Eaton died back in 1987 but her induction today is being hailed as a victory for female athletes and feminists alike.

Crooner Clooney Dies

Beverly Hills, California, USA, June 29: Legendary singer Rosemary Clooney, one of America's most beloved singers and entertainers, has died of complications relating to lung cancer at her Beverly Hills home surrounded by family and friends. She was 74.

Born in Maysville, Kentucky on May 23, 1928, Rosemary Clooney's career had humble beginnings, singing duets with her younger sister on Cincinnati radio in 1945 for $20 a week.

The following year band leader Tony Pastor heard them singing on the radio while he was traveling through Ohio, and offered the sisters a position with his orchestra. Within three years, Rosemary's simple, exquisite singing style saw her travel to New York while sister Betty returned to Cincinnati. Clooney's career took off with a bang in 1950, with her single "Beautiful Brown Eyes" selling over half a million copies. In 1953 Rosemary's

Tahrain women at last vote in general elections.

face was on the cover of *Time* magazine, and in 1954 she starred opposite Bing Crosby in the smash hit motion picture *White Christmas*. Clooney suffered a series of personal traumas in the late 1960s. She divorced her husband Jose Ferrer, then became addicted to prescription medicines, and was present at the Ambassador Hotel when her friend Senator Robert Kennedy was assassinated.

After years of struggling with depression, she rebuilt her career, singing in small clubs before an invitation to join her previous co-star Bing Crosby on his farewell tour cemented her comeback to the industry.

In 1991 she recorded a series of autobiographical songs that offered intimate glimpses into her personal life. In 1995 she won the ASCAP Pied Piper award, and then in 2002 she received a Grammy award for lifetime achievement in music and entertainment.

Rosemary Clooney starred in *White Christmas*.

Top Spook's Memoir Doesn't Tell All

England, September 5: Stella Rimington, the former head of Britain's counter-intelligence service MI5, has put a human face to the nation's security network with the publication of her autobiography *Open Secret*.

But the book is already being criticized as a vague—and at times evasive—account of her time at the top. It possesses a pervasive "chip-on-your-shoulder feminism" viewpoint in which Rimington seems to see herself as singlehandedly transforming an elitist men's club into an organization promoting equality and political correctness. But several former colleagues—female and male—have disputed this, claiming that Rimington is concerned only with her own advancement, and has no real interest in fighting gender discrimination.

Open Secret fails to illuminate the shadowy world of MI5 and runs the risk of increasing public distrust, and fueling the perception that its author is simply cashing in on the celebrity of being a former spy. Her failure to provide insights into key events leads the reader to suspect that her allegiance to the establishment outweighs any moral inclination toward honesty to the public. She fails to mention whether MI5 has done anything to address the culture of *laissez-faire* and heavy drinking that has led to embarrassing disappearances of briefcases, sensitive documents, and computers. There is also no attempt to explain or justify why files on mainstream "dissidents" such as Patricia Hewitt and Jack Straw existed, when MI5 claimed that it never officially concerned itself with political activists.

Open Secret seems to have been written by someone determined to preserve her reputation. Her accounts parrot long-held government positions, even on pivotal events such as the SAS's Gibraltar operation, the Pan-Am bombing over Lockerbie, or the demise of the west's traditional foes in Eastern Europe. The book's plodding pace conveys nothing of the difficult moral and ethical decisions that surely must have gone hand in hand with her position, and its humdrum, chronological account of her progress from clerk to director-general fails to engage the reader in any way.

Former MI5 head, Stella Rimington gets a book panning.

"Miss World" Riots Kill Hundreds in Nigeria

Nigeria, November 23: The Miss World pageant has been forced to relocate to London after hundreds of people were killed in the predominantly Muslim town of Kaduna, 375 miles northwest of Lagos, in the wake of a newspaper article that suggested the prophet Mohammed would gladly take one of the contestants as a wife. Angry mobs have been rampaging through the city's streets, bludgeoning and stabbing bystanders to death.

Churches have been burned to the ground and more than 500 people have been admitted to Kaduna's hospitals, many with horrific injuries.

Cars have been torched and shops looted. Representatives of the Kaduna-based aid agency Alsa Care have told of people being burned alive after being dragged from their cars by mobs shouting "God is Great."

Residents have sheltered in their homes, and despite the arrival of the military, sporadic gunshots could still be heard into the evening as palls of smoke hung over the city skyline.

Nigeria won the right to host this year's event when Agbani Darego became the first black woman from an African nation to win the title in 2001. Darego's "Black is beautiful" comment in her acceptance speech made pageant history. Protests began almost as soon as it was announced that Nigeria would host the event. Human rights groups called for a boycott to protest the treatment of women under the country's Islamic Sharia law, while many Nigerian Muslims have condemned the event as an indecent spectacle. Some countries' delegates have already refused to attend, focusing their attention on the case of a Nigerian woman, Amina Lawal, who was ordered by an Islamic court to be buried up to her neck, then stoned to death for committing adultery. Lawal is currently in hiding, and Miss World officials have been pleading with the Nigerian government to reconsider the verdict.

Pageant president Julia Morley has meanwhile boarded a plane and is returning to London with 90 contestants. Controversy is set to further dog this year's contest, with most British television stations so far refusing to televise the pageant.

Hamm is Soccer's Woman Player of the Year...Again

Madrid, Spain, December 17: American soccer player Mia Hamm tonight remains the only woman to win FIFA's Woman Player of the Year award, when she repeated last year's inaugural success, receiving this year's prize at a star-studded gala event in Madrid, Spain.

Born on March 17, 1972 in Selma, Alabama, Hamm was the youngest person to play in the US national team when she debuted in 1987 at the age of 15. In 1994, she graduated with a degree in political science from the University of North Carolina, and in 1997 was named the Women's Sports Foundation Athlete of the Year. She was a member of the US gold medal-winning team at the Atlanta Olympic Games in 1996, and in 1999 helped the US team to victory in the Women's World Cup. She won US Soccer's Female Athlete of the Year award every year from 1994 to 2000.

Sarah Waters

Mia Hamm wins the FIFA International Woman Player of the Year award.

Martha Burk

Astronauts Perish in Shuttle Disaster

Texas, USA, February 1: Just 16 minutes before its scheduled landing at Florida's Kennedy Space Center, the space shuttle *Columbia* has disintegrated over northern Texas, killing all seven astronauts. Traveling at 12,500 mph (20,110 kmh) at a height of 200,000 feet (60,950 m), it was the second loss of a shuttle in the program's history, and the first to be lost on landing. The dead astronauts were Rick Husband, commander; William McCool, pilot; Michael Anderson, payload commander; David Brown, mission specialist 1; Ilan Ramon, payload specialist 1; and two women—Laurel Clark, mission specialist 4; and Kalpana Chawla, mission specialist 2.

Laurel Clark was born in Iowa on March 10, 1962, and graduated from William Horlick High School in Racine, Wisconsin, before earning a bachelor's degree in science and zoology from the University of Wisconsin-Madison in

"I BELIEVE THE CHOICE TO BE EXCELLENT BEGINS WITH ALIGNING YOUR THOUGHTS AND WORDS WITH THE INTENTION TO REQUIRE MORE FROM YOURSELF."

OPRAH WINFREY,
US TALK SHOW HOST

Kalpana Chawla and Laurel Clark die on *Columbia*.

1987. She joined the Navy and became an undersea medical officer and later a flight surgeon. She was selected by NASA for astronaut training in April, 1996.

Kalpana Chawla was the first Indian-American to fly a shuttle mission when she made her first flight on *Columbia* flight STS-87 on November 19, 1997, as a mission special-ist. Born in Karnal, India on July 1, 1961, Chawla moved to the United States in 1982 where she earned a master's degree and doctorate in aerospace engineering. She was chosen by NASA in 1988 and began work at the Ames Research center in California, before being selected for astronaut training in December, 1994.

Afghan Women Make Radio Waves

Kabul, Afghanistan, March 8: To help celebrate International Women's Day today, the Voice of Afghan Women—Afghanistan's only radio station dedicated solely to promoting women's issues—has begun broadcasting from the ANIA media center in the nation's capital, Kabul. The station is broadcast-ing on a frequency of 91.6 FM, with a 600-watt transmitter that can reach hundreds of thousands of Afghani women in the capital and surrounding provinces.

Station director Jamileh Mujahed was one of the first broadcasters to appear on television to announce the demise of the hated Taliban regime in 2001, and is known for her outspokenness on women's rights in a country where many women are not permitted to leave their homes unaccompanied by a male. A mother of five, Jamileh Mujahed will focus on programs designed to enlighten and emanci-

pate Afghani women. The Voice of Afghan Women has been established with financial and administrative assistance from UNESCO, which has provided the training workshops and funding. When the Taliban came to power in 1995 they seized control of all print media, as well as radio and television stations. It was then illegal to own a television or a satellite dish, leaving radio as the dominant form of media with 85 percent of all Afghans now owning a radio. But many Afghani women experience difficulty in accessing radios in a culture where listening to broadcasts is still a male-dominated activity.

Jazz Diva Nina Dies

Southern France, April 21: Nina Simone—diva of jazz, composer of over 500 songs, and a performer whose every appearance became the stuff of legend—has died in her sleep of natural causes after a long illness at her home in the south of France.

Simone was born Eunice Waymon in Tryon, North Carolina on February 21, 1933. At the age of four, she began to play

US chart-topping country group The Dixie Chicks.

time out

It is estimated that over 30 million women throughout Africa have been subjected to genital mutilation. While not prescribed in any particular religious texts it has continued as a dangerous and unnecessary ritual.

Paris, France, January 14: France mourns the country's first minister for women's affairs, Françoise Giroud, who has died, aged 86.

Canberra, Australia, January 26: The Australian of the Year Award goes to Professor Fiona Stanley.

Texas, USA, February 1: Two female astronauts, Kalpana Chawla and Laurel Clark, are among the seven crew members who die when the space shuttle *Columbia* disintegrates.

World, February 15: As the threat of war in Iraq grows, hundreds of thousands protest around the world.

Texas, USA, February: Dentist Clara Harris is sentenced to 20 years for killing her husband, David Harris, after she discovers he is having an affair with his receptionist.

Mexico, February: Seventeen-year-old Jessica Santillan dies, after a second lung and heart transplant.

Kabul, Afghanistan, March 8: A radio station run by women and programed with women's content starts broadcasting today.

Iraq, March 20: Coalition troops enter Iraq the day after the first American bombs hit Baghdad.

London, England, March: Album sales plummet for US chart-topping country group Dixie Chicks, as they experience backlash from a statement criticizing US President George W. Bush and the Iraq invasion.

Utah, USA, March: Nine months after being abducted from her bedroom by 49-year-old Brian Mitchell, Utah teenager Elizabeth Smart is reunited with her parents.

California, USA: Nicole Kidman wins an Academy Award for her outstanding role in last year's movie, *The Hours*.

Southern France, April 21: Singer Nina Simone dies, aged 70.

Georgia, USA, April: Martha Burk, head of the National Council of Women's Organizations, campaigns against the exclusion of women at Augusta National Golf Club where the US Masters tournament is held.

Iraq, April: American prisoner of war Jessica Lynch is rescued from a hospital in Nasiriya. She was one of 12 troops captured by Iraqi soldiers.

Fort Worth, Texas, USA, May: Annika Sorenstam competes in the men's PGA Open golf tournament.

USA, May: Chinese-American businesswoman Katrina Leung is indicted on espionage charges. The FBI believes that she was passing on highly sensitive documents to Beijing while working as an FBI informant.

Cannes, France, May: Iranian filmmaker Samira Makhmalbaf's *Five in the Afternoon* premieres at the Cannes Film Festival.

USA, June 4: Domestic icon Martha Stewart is indicted on charges of insider trading.

Classically-trained pianist Nina Simone dies, aged 70.

Annika Sorenstam

the piano, and dreamt of becoming the first African-American concert pianist. She attended the prestigeous Juilliard School of Music in New York City, but hope turned to disappointment when she was refused entry into Philadelphia's prestigious Curtis Institute of Music—a failure which she attributed to color discrimination. Eunice Waymon then turned to jazz, becoming a singer/pianist in Atlantic City, New Jersey. She changed her name to Nina Simone, signed a recording contract, and in 1959 had a hit single with "I Loves You Porgy" from the hit musical *Porgy and Bess*. Her first major concert was at Town Hall in Manhattan on September 12, 1959 where she immediately fell foul of the media, who insisted on labeling her a jazz singer.

Preferring to be known as someone who played black classical music, Simone felt that the term "jazz singer" was used merely to categorize her as "black," and

was therefore derogatory and irrelevant. She viewed attempts to compare her with Billie Holliday as simply highlighting America's inability to deal with the complexities and multiple forms of black music.

Lynch Busted from Iraq Hospital

Iraq, Thursday, April 3: Private First Class Jessica Lynch, held captive by Iraqi forces since she and other members of her unit were captured on March 23, was rescued on Tuesday by special operations forces and returned to a coalition-controlled area. Green-cast night-scope video footage of the rescue shows a relieved Lynch, draped in an American flag, being stretchered onto a waiting Black Hawk helicopter. *Associated Press* reported that Lynch suffered two broken legs, a broken arm, and gunshot wounds.

Lynch, 19, of Palestine, West Virginia, was on patrol with 11 other members of the 507th maintenance company in the town of Nasiriya when they took a wrong turn and drove into an ambush. Lynch was caught up in a fierce gunfight, receiving several wounds and continuing to fire until she was out of ammunition. Having watched as several soldiers in her unit were killed, she was then stabbed as Iraqi forces overran her position. Coalition forces then infiltrated Iraqi lines, and fought their way into Nasiriya's Saddam hospital to retrieve Lynch under cover of darkness—in a classic joint operation involving air force pilots, Navy SEALs, Army rangers, and marines. Seven members of the 507th are still missing.

Although there was a firefight on the way into—and out of—the hospital, there are no reports of any further coalition casualties. Ammunition, maps, mortars, and a terrain model were found inside the hospital, making it clear that it was secretly being used as a military command post. A prominent Iraqi lawyer,

Mohammed Odeh al-Rehaief, provided the information that made Lynch's rescue possible from the hospital.

Annika Putts with the Boys

Fort Worth, Texas, USA, May 22: The world's leading female golfer, Annika Sorenstam, made history today by becoming the first woman to play in a men's PGA tour event since Babe Zaharias in 1945, when she teed off at the Colonial Country Club in Fort Worth, Texas.

The frenzy surrounding her appearance befitted a Hollywood celebrity. On Monday over 200 reporters were on hand to see her practice, and what golfer has ever faced greater scrutiny than when she walked out to the 10th hole to a deafening roar from a packed gallery and very crowded clubhouse balcony, and chose a 4-wood for that first swing down the fairway? At the close of play today, she had putted for birdie on every hole and shot a 71. But the question on everyone is contemplating tonight is "Will she make the cut tomorrow?"

Nicole Kidman's remarkable role in *The Hours*.

USA, June 5: Tammy Wynette's 1968 hit *Stand by your Man* tops a poll as the best song in country music history.

Thailand, June 5: Thai women are no longer required by law to assume their husband's name after marriage.

Helsinki, Finland, June 24: Following allegations of improper conduct, Anneli Jäätteenmäki steps down as Prime Minister barely two months after being elected.

New York, USA, June 29: Screen legend Katharine Hepburn dies at the age of 96.

Victoria, Canada, July 16: Novelist Carol Shields dies, aged 68.

Wimbledon, England, July 5: Serena Williams wins her first Wimbledon tournament, beating older sister Venus 7-6, 6-3.

San Antonio, USA, August 16: Veteran cowgirl Connie Reeves, aged 101, dies after being thrown from her horse.

New York, USA, August 20: Kathy Boudin is granted parole. She served 22 years for a 1981 armed robbery which resulted in the deaths of three people.

London, England, September 16: At Buckingham Palace, Professor Julia Polak is awarded the DBE for her services to medicine.

Nigeria, September 25: Thirty-year-old Muslim woman Amina Lawal has her "death by stoning" sentence repealed by the Sharia court of appeal. She had been found guilty of adultery.

New York, USA, October 23: Madame Chiang Kai-shek (Soong Mai-ling), wife of president Chiang Kai-shek, dies, aged 105.

Stockholm, Sweden, September 11: Foreign Minister Anna Lindh dies in hospital after being stabbed while shopping in a department store.

New Jersey, USA, November 30: Gertrude Ederle, the first woman to swim the English Channel, at 98.

England, November: *The Sunday Times* publishes a list which reveals that J.K. Rowling earned £124 million this year, making her the world's best-paid author.

Oslo, Norway, December 10: Iranian human rights activist Shirin Ebadi receives Nobel Peace Prize.

Tikrit, Iraq, December 14: A disheveled Saddam Hussein is captured after being found in a tiny underground bunker, south of his home town of Tikrit.

Northern Territory, Australia, December 15: Marion Scrymgour is appointed Australia's first female Aboriginal government minister.

Hong Kong, December 30: Pop queen Anita Mui dies of cervical cancer, aged 40.

Japan: Natsuo Kirino's *Grotesque* wins the Izumi Kyoka literary award.

Screen Doyenne Katharine Hepburn Dies

Samira Makhmalbaf

New York, USA, June 29: One of the great luminaries of Hollywood, screen legend Katharine Hepburn—whose strong character roles and independent life made her a role model for millions of women the world over—has died at her home in the seaside town of Old Saybrook, Connecticut. A statement released by the executor of her estate, Cynthia McFadden, said that Ms Hepburn died peacefully at 2.50 p.m. after enduring declining health over the past several years.

Throughout a glittering career Hepburn played witty, sophisticated characters with such aplomb that there seemed to be only a very thin line between her private and screen lives. Her comedic and dramatic talents were prodigious, allowing her to play in comedies like the screwball classic *Bringing Up Baby*, through to capturing the essence of the great historic figure Eleanor of Aquitaine in *The Lion In Winter*. Hepburn won the best actress Oscar four times—for *Morning Glory* (1933), *Guess Who's Coming To Dinner* (1967), *The Lion in Winter* (1968), and *On Golden Pond* (1981). She held a record 12 Oscar nominations, a mark that stood until this year when it was finally surpassed by Meryl Streep. Her career

"DEATH WILL BE A GREAT RELEASE. NO MORE INTERVIEWS."

KATHARINE HEPBURN (1907–2003), AMERICAN ACTRESS

her role from a wheelchair. Katharine Hepburn was born May 12, 1907, in Hartford, Connecticut.

Bucking Bronco Beats Connie, 101

San Antonio, Texas, USA, August 16: The oldest living honoree of the National Cowgirl Hall of Fame, Connie Reeves, has died of a heart attack after being thrown from the saddle of her favorite horse, Dr Pepper. She was 101 years old, and had been riding horses for 95 years. It is estimated Reeves taught more than 30,000 young girls how to ride over 67 summers at Camp Waldemar in Texas hill country—with the maxim: "Always saddle your own horse!"

Constance Douglas was born in the town of Eagle Pass on the Mexican border in 1901 and was one of the first women to study law at the University of Texas at Austin. She later married retired rodeo star Jack Reeves in 1942, and barely a day passed thereafter when she wasn't on horseback.

Plastic Surgeon Fiona Wood Awarded AM

Canberra, Australia, October 17: Western Australia's only female plastic surgeon, director of Royal Perth Hospital's burns unit, and mother of six, Dr Fiona Wood, has been awarded the Order of Australia medal for her services to medicine.

The daughter of a Yorkshire coal miner, Wood graduated from St Thomas's Hospital Medical School in London before meeting her Australian-born husband Tony Keirath and emigrating to Australia in 1987. In 1993 Wood teamed up with medical scientist Marie Stoner to establish a skin culture laboratory. In 1998, it became Clinical Cell Culture, a private company dedicated to skin cell and burns research. Initially using cultured skin technology from the United States, Wood and Stoner moved on to growing skin sheets, and finally to the spraying-on of skin cells. These techniques have earned the duo a worldwide reputation as pioneers in their field.

Wood was catapulted to national prominence last year when 28 survivors of the terrorist bombings in Bali were flown to Royal Perth Hospital for treatment. Wood led a team of 60 doctors and nurses who worked continually

Pop queen Anita Mui dies of cervical cancer at 40.

over a five-day period to save the lives of all 28 patients. The victims suffered burns covering up to 92 percent of their bodies, along with life-threatening infections and delayed shock. Wood received widespread praise for her spray-on skin treatment, which reduces the period required for skin culturing to produce enough cells to heal a major burn from 21 days to just five. Wood discovered that scarring is greatly reduced if cultured skin grafts can be applied within the first 10 days.

The cell-spray system is an aerosol that applies cultured skin cells evenly over large wounds—reducing scarring,

American prisoner of war Jessica Lynch is rescued.

and personal life were dominated by her love affair with Spencer Tracy, with whom she made such classic films as *Adam's Rib* and *Pat and Mike*.

Hepburn was also tireless in her devotion to the stage. Undaunted when she broke her ankle during a run of *A Matter of Gravity* in 1976, she played

Serena Williams defeats her sister at Wimbledon tournament.

the victim's recovery period, and the risk of secondary infections, and bringing closer to reality Wood's oft-stated dream of one day achieving "scarless healing."

Shreesha Karki's Death Sparks Angry March

Kathmandu, Nepal, October 27: The suicide earlier this month of the popular Nepali actress Shreesha Karki—three days after the tabloid *Jana Aastha* published a nude photograph of her—has provoked a heated demonstration by more than 1,000 members of Nepal's entertainment industry, protesting the harassment that has apparently led to her death.

The angry protesters, along with members of Karki's family who led the way, marched through central Kathmandu to the Hanuman Dhoka station in the city's historic heart to vent their frustration and grief upon the Chief of Police, Topendra Hamal. They then moved on to offices of *Jana Aastha*, burning copies of the newspaper as they went, and chanting "Death to yellow journalism, death to *Jana Aastha*." Meanwhile the journalist responsible for the damning photograph, Uddhav Bhandari, is being sought by police for questioning. Members of the government from the Prime Minister down say that once arrested, he will be severely dealt with.

Bandhari claimed in the story that Karki, one of the country's most-loved actresses, was also a prostitute with a list of clients that included the Crown Prince as well as senior politicians and members of the military.

Harry Potter Puts Rowling on Top Shelf

England, November: This year, the creator of the *Harry Potter* books, J. K. Rowling, has earned £124 million, to come in at number 122 in the *Sunday Times* annual Rich List—eleven places ahead of Queen Elizabeth II. This makes her the world's highest paid author—according to the newspaper's definitive guide to Britain and Ireland's 1,000 wealthiest individuals. Rowling's wealth is now estimated to be £280 million, a far cry from her income as a single mother some 10 years ago, struggling to survive on £70 a week in a two-bedroom Edinburgh flat, and writing *Harry Potter and the Philosopher's Stone* in a local café. Her fortune has quadrupled in the past two years.

Rowling's fourth book, *Harry Potter and the Goblet of Fire,* became the fastest selling book in British publishing history with a total of over 370,000 hardback copies sold in the UK alone on its first weekend on sale.

J. K. Rowling is the world's highest paid author.

Joanne K. Rowling was born in the town of Chipping Sodbury, England, on July 31, 1965. Her four books about a young boy who discovers he is a wizard have turned her into an international superstar and made her one of the world's best-known authors. The *Harry Potter* novels are a global phenomenon, having been translated into more than 40 languages—including ancient Greek—and amassing sales in excess of 200 million copies worldwide.

Rowling conceived Harry Potter while on a train journey from London to Manchester in 1990. Not having a pen and too shy to ask for one, she waited, and scribbled down her thoughts upon arrival in Manchester.

When she completed the manuscript in 1995, her agent spent a year looking for a publisher. Bloomsbury finally gave her an advance of £1,500 because the editor's eight-year-old daughter, who had read the first chapter, thought it showed promise.

However, the publishers were careful to caution Rowling not to use her first name, fearing that boys would shy away from any adventure story that was written by a woman.

Iranian Activist Wins Nobel Peace Prize

Oslo, Norway, December 10: Shirin Ebadi, the Iranian lawyer, judge, and representative of a reformed Islam that honors gender equality, religious freedom, and democracy, has become the first Muslim woman to be awarded the Nobel Prize for Peace. The 56-year-old was en route to Tehran from Paris when the Nobel committee advised her.

Ebadi is the founder of the Association for the Support of Children's Rights in Iran and has authored many books on human rights, including *The Rights of the Child* (1994) and *History and Documentation of Human Rights in Iran* (2000). In 2001 she received Norway's Rafto Prize recognizing her unrelenting fight against oppression in Iran.

Born in 1947, Shirin Ebadi received a law degree from the University of Tehran and soon went on to become one of her country's handful of female judges. She has served as president of the city court of Tehran from 1975–79 until forced to resign the position upon the rise to power of Ayatollah Khomeini.

She has often said her fight is not with Islam, but rather with the outdated and militant interpretations of Islamic law by reactionary clerics pushing their own political and personal agendas.

Anna Lindh

Iranian lawyer Shirin Ebadi receives the Nobel Peace Prize.

Justine Henin-Hardenne

"An infant prodigy is nothing more than a rug-rat with unbelievably ambitious parents."

CATHY LETTE
(1958–),
AUSTRALIAN AUTHOR

Author Dies after Cosmetic Surgery

New York, January 15: Olivia Goldsmith, the American novelist whose first book, *The First Wives Club*, was a bestseller and was later made into a smash hit movie, died today following complications during plastic surgery.

Goldsmith, 54, had been in a coma since January 7 when she underwent general anesthetic for a chin-tuck at the Manhattan Eye, Ear, and Throat Hospital. Within minutes, she slipped into a coma and could not be revived. She was transferred to Lenox Hill Hospital where friends kept a vigil.

Born Randy Goldfield in New Jersey in 1949, Goldsmith wrote several novels with feminist themes such as women's empowerment and revenge against philandering husbands. She combined humor with serious undertones, and delighted millions of women and men around the world with her witty, insightful plotlines. Goldsmith once said she wrote *The First Wives Club* "in true indignation" after she went through an acrimonious divorce with John T. Reid.

The 1992 novel was made into a movie starring Bette Midler, Goldie Hawn, and Diane Keaton in 1996. Known for her charm, wit, and unpredictability, Goldfield had tumultuous relationships—with friends and lovers—and was extremely generous. Before turning to writing, she was a very successful management consultant and ran her own company, the Omni Group.

Novelist Janet Frame (center) suffered a tragic youth in mental institutions.

NZ Loses Literary Treasure

Dunedin, New Zealand, January 29: New Zealand's most famous modern writer, Janet Frame, died today at Dunedin Hospital after a short battle with cancer. She was 79. Her death has prompted great mourning in literary circles as fellow writers lament her quiet reclusive existence, tragic youth, and her brilliant mind.

Born Janet Paterson Frame on August 28, 1924, she grew up in poverty with four siblings, two of whom died young in separate drowning incidents. She began a teaching career, but after experiencing a panic attack in class was committed to a mental hospital and erroneously diagnosed with schizophrenia. She suffered dreadfully, but continued writing and in 1951 published her first collection of stories, *The Lagoon and Other Stories*, which won a prestigious literary prize. This prompted her doctors to cancel a planned lobotomy. Later she penned her first novel, *Owls Do Cry*. She moved to London in 1956, where she was pronounced sane, and wrote *Faces in The Water*, a fictional story based on her experiences in mental institutions.

She returned to New Zealand in 1964 as an internationally-acclaimed writer. She wrote 11 novels, five short story collections, a volume of poetry, a children's book and a three-part autobiography. Revered film director Jane Campion adapted the trilogy into the 1990 film *An Angel at my Table*. Frame chose to live a reclusive life, even changing her name by deed poll to Nene Janet Paterson Clutha in 1958 to further her anonymity. She was intensely shy, quiet, and private, with a sharp wit, superior intelligence, and pleasant nature. Frame was made a Commander of the Order of the British Empire (CBE) for services to literature in 1983, and a member of the Order of New Zealand (ONZ)—the country's highest civil honor—in 1990. In 1999 she set up the Janet Frame charitable literary trust, with the royalties to be used for financial grants to New Zealand writers.

Mother of Boiled Son Freed

Tashkent, Uzbekistan, February 24: An elderly woman jailed after drawing international attention to the murder of her son—who was boiled to death

A scene from *The First Wives Club*.

in prison—has been released just hours before US Secretary of Defense, Donald Rumsfeld, arrives for talks on the two countries' military alliance. In a closed trial on February 12, Fatima Mukhadirova, 62, received the maximum six-year sentence in a high security jail for possessing unsanctioned religious literature, being a member of a banned religious group, and undermining the Constitution.

Citing age and gender, the court today reduced her punishment to a $250 fine. The decision follows international demands for Uzbekistan to clean up its human rights record, with Rumsfeld expected to raise the case during his visit. Mukhadirova's son, Muzafar Avazov, 35, who was jailed for belonging to an illegal Islamic organization, was murdered in prison in 2002. A forensic report showed that he was beaten, had his fingernails removed, and was immersed in boiling water. The Uzbek government says he died after a fight with inmates who threw hot tea at him. His mother was arrested after she called for an investigation and sent the photos of his corpse to the British Embassy. After the September 11 terrorist attacks, the US has allied itself with Uzbekistan, where it has a support base for NATO soldiers serving in nearby Afghanistan.

Hadid Wins Highest Architecture Honor

England, March 21: Iraqi-born architect Zaha Hadid has become the first woman awarded the prestigious Pritzker Prize, the world's highest architectural honor. It recognizes contributions to humanity and built-up environment.

The 53-year-old British citizen was chosen for her very convention-defying, modernist, inventive works. Known for her energy, passion and talent, Hadid has received many honors during her 25-year

Zaha Hadid wins the prestigious Pritzker Prize.

career, including the Kenzo Tange chair at Harvard University's graduate school of design. She is a fellow of the American Institute of Architecture and is also a Commander of the Order of the British Empire (CBE). Her best-known projects include a fire station in Germany, the "mind zone" in England, a tram station and car park in France, as well as the Contemporary Arts Center in Cincinnati, USA.

time out

Martha Stewart, USA's favorite homemaker, is given a five-month jail term and a fine of $30,000. She was charged with lying to investigators about the sale of stock, and has been given the most lenient sentence possible.

Bashed Saudi Wife Creates Legacy of Hope

Saudi Arabia, June: Former television presenter and young Saudi beauty Rania al-Baz, bashed almost to death by her husband in April, can now begin a new life. Her husband is in jail and she has been granted a divorce, and full custody of their two sons.

Al-Baz caused an international outcry when she agreed to have photographs of

herself—severely bruised and in a coma—published. Al-Baz said she felt an obligation to speak out to show Saudi women that Sharia law does protect them and that women do not have to suffer in silence. Her husband, Yunus al-Fallatta, was sentenced to six months jail and 300 lashings for the April 12 incident, in which he bashed al-Baz's head against their home's marble floor, causing about 13 fractures and horrendous bruising which required extensive surgery. Al-Fallatta initially thought he had killed his wife and panicked when she regained consciousness. He took her to hospital, claiming she had been in a car crash, and then left immediately.

After the photos were published, al Fallatta came out of hiding and was charged with attempted murder. A six-week trial in the all-male Sharia court led to his conviction. Al-Baz then sued for divorce and also received custody of their two sons—both rare achievements for a Saudi woman. Although a talented and very popular TV personality, al-Baz is now without a job—a tangible reminder that although she is admired by many all over the world, many in her homeland perceive her as a dangerous dissident.

Sofia Coppola

Charlize Theron is unrecognizable in *Monster*.

Saudi Arabia, June: Rania al-Baz, a popular TV host whose husband was convicted this month of beating her, says she publicized the case so that Saudi women would know that they have recourse under Sharia law if they are victims of any form of domestic violence.
Mexico City, Mexico, July 25: Mexico's 1997 Woman of the Year, Dr Carmen Gutierrez, is found dead. She was kidnapped several days ago.
Liverpool, England, July 27: Politician Margaret Simey dies, aged 98.

Vatican City, July 31: The Pope issues a document condemning feminism, worried that it will erode women's prescribed maternal and subservient roles.
Philippines, July: President Gloria Macapagal-Arroyo is condemned for giving in to demands of Iraqi insurgents who kidnapped a Filipino truck driver.
Wimbledon, London, England: Maria Sharapova is the first Russian and the youngest woman to win the singles championships.

Greece, August 13-29: The games of the XXVIIIth Olympiad are held in Athens. Udomporn Polsak is the first Thai woman to win an Olympic gold medal, in the 53 kg weightlifting division. Carly Patterson becomes the second US woman to win gold in the all-around gymnastics.
Beslan, Russia, September 3: Over 300 adults and children die when a school siege ends tragically.
Georgia, USA, September 25: Laila Ali, daughter of Mohammed Ali, wins International Women's Boxing Federation light-heavyweight title.

West Virginia, USA, September: Homemaker tycoon Martha Stewart is imprisoned for perjury and insider share trading.
USA, October 3: *Psycho* star Janet Leigh dies, aged 77.
Baghdad, Iraq, October 19: British aid worker Margaret Hassan is kidnapped by an armed gang.
Paris, France, October 20: Two female students are expelled from school after flouting the new mandate banning the wearing of headscarves in school.

Oslo, Norway, December 10: Kenyan Wangari Maathai wins the Nobel Peace Prize for her contribution to sustainable development. She is the first African woman to win the prize.
Stockholm, Sweden, December 10: Austrian playwright Elfriede Jelinek is awarded Nobel Prize for Literature. Americans Richard Axel and Linda Buck are awarded Nobel Prize in Physiology or Medicine for work on the olfactory system.
Indian Ocean, December 26: A tsunami devastates coastal communities, killing more than 150,000.

Thai Woman Lifts Gold Medal

Athens, Greece, August 15: Udomporn Polsak today became the first Thai woman to win an Olympic gold medal, taking out the 53 kg weightlifting. The 22-year-old lifted 97.5 kg in the snatch and 125 kg in the clean and jerk for a total of 222.5 kg. Polsak missed only once during six lifts. Indonesia's Raema Lisa Rumbewas took silver with 210.5 kg and Columbian Mabel Mosquera won bronze with 197.5 kg.

It is the crowning glory of Polsak's 14-year career. Last year, she won two gold medals at the world weightlifting championships in Vancouver, Canada. Her gold medal is the third ever for Thailand, the first two awarded to boxers Wijan Ponlid in 2000 and Somluck Kamsing in 1996. Polsak visited several Buddhist temples and spent time with Thai monks as part of her training. She said this unconventional training technique helped her develop stronger concentration and confidence.

In another female Olympic first, women's freestyle wrestling will be contested. Four events will take place over two days, with the preliminary eliminations beginning on August 22. Fifty wrestlers from around the world will compete in the new Olympic discipline, which will be held at Ano Liossia Olympic Hall.

Elfriede Jlinek

"I DON'T CARE IF PEOPLE THINK I'M EXPLOITING MY CHILD, SHE'S THE ONLY SUCCESSFUL THING I'VE DONE IN MY LIFE."

COURTNEY LOVE (1964–), AMERICAN ROCK SINGER

Disgraced Kitchen Tycoon Martha Stewart Jailed

Alderson, West Virginia, USA, October 8: At 6.15 a.m. today, notorious homemaking mogul Martha Stewart arrived at the minimum security Federal prison camp to begin her five-month sentence. The author and television personality was convicted in March and sentenced in July for conspiracy, obstruction of justice, and lying to federal investigators

Wangari Maathai is awarded the Nobel Peace Prize for her contribution to sustainable development.

about why she sold shares in a pharmaceutical company just before its price plunged in 2001.

Authorities began investigating Stewart in 2002 and indicted her on charges of obstructing justice and securities fraud in June, 2003. The fraud charge was later dismissed. She will be released in March on a two-year supervised release, including five months of home confinement. Although free on bond pending her appeal, Stewart last month asked the court to begin her sentence as soon as possible. Her lawyers have up until October 20 to file her appeal.

Born on August 3, 1941, Martha Helen Kostyra grew up in New Jersey, USA, with five siblings. Her mother taught her how to cook and sew and her father introduced her to gardening. She studied history and architectural history at Barnard College and worked as a model. She married Andy Stewart and they had a daughter, Alexis, in 1965. Stewart was a successful Wall Street stockbroker but left the profession when the family moved to Connecticut in 1972. She then started a catering business in her basement in 1976, emphasizing food presentation and sophisticated recipes. A chance meeting with a publisher led to her first best-selling cookbook, *Entertaining*, in 1982. She wrote more books and newspaper and magazine columns, and appeared on television. In 1987, she and Andy separated, and later divorced. In 1990 she launched the very successful

Martha Stewart Living magazine, and adapted it into a long-running television program in 1993. In 1997, she consolidated all her television, print, and merchandising interests under Martha Stewart Living Omnimedia, which listed on the New York Stock Exchange in 1999.

Muslim Schoolgirls Expelled for Headscarves

Paris, France, October 20: Two young Muslim girls have become the first students to be expelled from school, for wearing traditional headscarves in defiance of a new law banning conspicuous religious symbols in public schools. The new law, passed in March, but in effect from the start of the school term on September 2, is designed to uphold France's constitutional secularism. It targets Muslim headscarves but also includes Jewish caps, Christian crosses, and Sikh turbans.

The girls, aged 12 and 13, have the right to appeal to their local school board, or continue their education at a private school or by correspondence until they turn 16, the legal school-leaving age. More than five million Muslims and five thousand Sikhs live in France.

Nobel Trio of Women

Scandinavian Peninsula, December 10: Three pioneering women from different corners of the world received their Nobel Prizes

Queen Juliana of the Netherlands has died, aged 94.

today in twin ceremonies in Oslo, Norway, and Stockholm, Sweden. Kenyan Wangari Maathai won the Nobel Peace Prize, American Linda Buck won the Prize for Physiology or Medicine with Richard Axel, and Austrian playwright Elfriede Jelinek took out the Literature Prize.

In 1977 Professor Maathai founded the Green Belt movement, which encourages and funds Kenyan women to plant trees—over 20 million so far. She joined the National Council of Women of Kenya in 1976 and chaired it from 1981–1987. She co-chaired the Jubilee 2000 Africa Campaign, advocating debt cancellation for poor nations, and has campaigned to reduce the inequitable acquisition of land and forests by developers. She has represented women's interests at the United Nations and was elected to Kenya's parliament in 2002 with a 98 percent majority. She is currently assistant minister for environment and natural resources.

American professors Linda Buck and Richard Axel received their prize for identifying odorant receptors and clarifying how the body's olfactory system enables us to recognize and remember the over 10,000 odors that exist. Using rats, they discovered a large family of unique but related odorant receptors, encoded by a multi-gene family of unprecedented size and diversity. These findings explained at last how it was possible for mammals (including humans) to identify such a vast array of distinct odors. The duo had their findings published in 1991.

Mohammed Ali's daughter Laila (left) wins the International Women's Boxing Federation light-heavyweight title.

Carly Patterson wins Olympic gold in gymnastics.

Michelle Kwan

Elfriede Jelinek's early writings were social critiques of popular culture. She has also produced many novels along the themes of social class, gender inequality, and sexual violence. She began writing plays for radio in 1974, then expanded her repertoire to embrace the theater. She has also written many successful film and opera scripts.

Laila Ali Takes Title

Atlanta, Georgia, USA, September 24: Laila Ali, daughter of boxing legend Muhammad Ali, won the International Women's Boxing Federation light-heavyweight championship today. She beat Guyana's Gwen O'Neil with a third round knockout at the Philips Arena.

Born on December 30, 1977, in Miami Beach, Florida, she is the second daughter of Muhammad Ali and his third wife, Veronica Porsche Ali, and the best-known of his nine children. Her parents divorced when she was eight, and she grew up in Malibu, California. Ali took business management in college and owned a Californian manicure salon before being inspired to start boxing after watching a women's boxing match on television. A year later she sold her business, started training, and made her professional boxing debut in New York on October 8, 1999. The 21-year-old knocked out her opponent, April Fowler, just 31 seconds into the first round. She went on to win many more bouts, including her first world title—the IBA super middleweight championship—in Las Vegas, Nevada in August, 2002. The same year she was named the Women's Boxing Archive Network (WBAN) fighter of the year. Commentators have praised her power, mobility, and natural talent. Her striking good looks have landed her on the covers of the world's most glamorous sports and women's magazines. Last year she published a book titled *Reach!*, which encourages young women to overcome adversity.

Ex-Prostitute Wins Businessman Award

California, USA: A former prostitute and brothel madam has been named California's Businessman of the Year by the National Republican Congressional Committee. Marlene Baldwin, a grandmother who has run a successful direct-mail advertising company from her San Rafael home for 20 years, previously spent 15 years running a high society brothel in San Francisco. The committee was caught off-guard when Baldwin's past was revealed. The award program rewards businesspeople who run companies that are based on Republican values and ideas—as well as those who contribute financially to its candidates' coffers.

Born in Idaho in 1940, Baldwin married straight after high school. She fell pregnant and had an abortion, and the couple later split. She remarried and had a daughter, but the difficult labor resulted in a large medical bill. She began working as a prostitute to pay off the debt. Eventually she started her own brothel, targeting high society clients who taught her the ins and outs of business. Shortly afterwards, a Hollywood producer persuaded her to make a biographical film. The television movie *Dixie: Changing Habits* aired in 1983.

After serving jail time for her fourth pandering conviction, Baldwin changed direction and began her direct-mail advertising business from home in 1984.

Aussie Opera Diva June Bronhill Dies

Yuliya Tymoshenko

Sydney, Australia, January 24: Australian-born opera diva June Bronhill, whose diction and impeccable, lyrical, color-atura soprano voice made her one of Australia's greatest talents, has died in Sydney at the age of 75.

Bronhill was born June Gough in the outback New South Wales town of Broken Hill on June 26, 1929. After coming third in a newspaper singing competition called the *Sun* Aria, she traveled to England to study singing, with the financial assistance of Broken Hill residents. In London she became one of the most popular light repertory sopranos in Britain in the 1950s and 60s, delighting audiences as the star of a series of operettas staged by the Sadler's Wells Opera Company, including over 200 performances in the lead role of Hanna Glawari in their London production of *The Merry Widow*. In 1960 she trium-phantly returned to Broken Hill to crowds as large as those that had gathered for the visit of Queen Elizabeth in 1954.

In Australia, she played the lead role in a production of *The Sound of Music* before she returned to London in 1964 for a revival of *The Gypsy Baron* by Strauss. Bron-hill returned to Australia in 1977 to be awarded an OBE for her services to the performing arts. After being diagnosed with breast cancer in 1987 and later with Alzheimer's disease, she retired in 1993.

> *"I THINK IT'S A LAME EXCUSE FOR A LOT OF THESE RAPPERS TO SAY THEY ONLY CALL GIRLS BITCHES OR HO'S BECAUSE THEY ACT LIKE THAT. IT DOESN'T MAKE THEM RIGHT."*
>
> QUEEN LATIFAH (1970–), US RAPPER AND ACTRESS

Rice is New US Secretary of State

Washington DC, USA, January 26: In a small ceremony in the formal dining room of the State Department tonight, Con-doleezza Rice, the former national

Condoleezza Rice is sworn in as US Secretary of State.

security advisor and confidant of President George W. Bush, was sworn in as the nation's 66th Secretary of State. The oath was administered by Su-preme Court Justice Ruth Bader Ginsburg, and follows a vote held earlier today on the floor of the US Senate in which Rice's nomination was overwhelmingly confirmed by a vote of 85 to 13.

Condoleezza Rice is the first female African-American Secretary of State. Her appointment sees her become one of the world's most powerful women, places her fourth in line to the presidency, and confers upon her the honor of being the United States' senior diplomat. Despite a long-held convention that Presi-dents have a right to have their nominations for cabinet posts rubber-stamped without extensive debate, the Senate gave Rice some uncomfortable moments during its

time out

Mike Leigh's film *Vera Drake*, starring Imelda Staunton, is nominated for three Oscars. The film magnificently illustrates the grim story of an English abortionist working in the 1950s and "helping girls out."

nine-hour debate on her confirmation, and the 13 "nays" represent the largest "no" vote for a Secretary of State since 1825. Democrat senators John Kerry and Edward Kennedy from Massachusetts, and Barbara Boxer from California, led the charge against her nomination, accusing her of misleading statements. They cited her involvement in helping to develop a phony rationale for going to war in Iraq, and the subsequent failure to locate the weapons of mass destruction that Rice insisted existed.

Rice was born in Birmingham, Alabama on November 14, 1954, and received a doctorate in political science from the Graduate School of Interna-tional Studies at the University of Denver in 1981, and is a fellow of the American Academy of Arts and Sciences. She was also director, then senior director, of Soviet and East European affairs at the National Security Council during the first Bush administration.

Million Dollar Baby Swank Wins Another Oscar

Hollywood, California, USA, February 27: Hilary Swank, the girl from Lincoln, Nebraska, who grew up in a Washington trailer park and first appeared on stage

Artist Aurélie Nemours dies, aged 94.

Washington DC, USA, January 12: Chief investigator Charles Duelfer confirms that the US has stopped searching for weapons of mass destruction (WMD) in Iraq. One of the chief justifications for the war, the existence of WMDs, has been doubted since May 2003.
Ukraine, January 24: Yuliya Tymoshenko becomes the Prime Minister.
Paris, France, January 27: Artist Aurélie Nemours dies, aged 94.

Washington DC, USA, January 26: Condoleezza Rice is sworn in as US Secretary of State, making her one of the most powerful women in the world.
Riyadh, Saudi Arabia, February 10: Men vote in local elections for the first time. However, women are not permitted to vote.
Beirut, Lebanon, February 14: Former Prime Minister Rafik Hariri dies when a car bomb explodes near his motorcade. Syria, which has great influence in the country, is thought to be involved.

Turkey, February 23: The government announces an amnesty, allowing expelled students to return to university. This includes women who had been expelled for wearing Islamic scarves–but the scarf ban still applies.
Hollywood, California, USA, February 27: Hilary Swank wins the best actress Oscar for her role in *Million Dollar Baby*.
West Virginia, USA, March 4: Homemaking mogul and perjurer Martha Stewart is released after being jailed for insider trading.

Istanbul, Turkey, March 8: Women marking International Women's Day with a protest are beaten and kicked by riot police for their unauthorized demonstration.
Menton, France, March 28: Concert pianist Moura Lympany dies, at 88.
Kabul, Afghanistan, March 30: US first lady Laura Bush visits the country. The focus of her talks is women's rights and education in post-Taliban Afghanistan.
Windsor, England, April 9: Prince Charles and Camilla Parker Bowles wed in a civil ceremony.

The Vatican, April 19: German Cardinal Joseph Ratzinger becomes the new pontiff, Benedict XVI.
Central African Republic, April 26: Former Prime Minister Elisabeth Domitien dies.
England, April: Ellen MacArthur, the youngest person to sail solo around the world, is now the youngest person to receive a damehood.
Kuwait, May 17: Parliament announces that women will be granted full suffrage, to take effect in the 2007 elections.

with insiders considering it crucial to the party's future that she be re-elected unopposed. Immediately after her election was announced by Congress's central election authority chief Oscar Fernandes, Gandhi was garlanded by cheering party workers and friends. Her election is set to be formally ratified at a party plenary session in a few months' time.

June Bronhill performing in *The Merry Widow*.

Kuwaiti Government Swears in Female Minister

Kuwait, June 20: US-educated Kuwaiti activist, Dr. Massouma al-Mubarak, was sworn in as the country's Minister for Planning and Administrative Development today, despite the opposition of Islamic fundamentalists and tribal representatives. She becomes the first female to be elected to a cabinet post, an appointment made possible by the government's decision on May 16 to give women the right to vote and to stand for election. Kuwaiti women will exercise this right en masse when Kuwait goes to the polls in parliamentary elections that are scheduled for next year.

Many opposed her appointment, claiming that she was not eligible for the post because she was not a registered voter. But constitutional scholars ruled that voter registration is not a requirement— a view accepted by the Prime Minister, Sheik Sabah al-Ahmed al-Sabah.

Political rights for women vary widely throughout the Gulf. Qatar gave women the right to vote in municipal elections in 1999, while Bahrain granted women the vote in a referendum on a new constitution in 2001 that led to the establishment of a bicameral parliament.

In recent times, Kuwaiti women have risen to positions of prominence in the diplomatic corps, and the oil and education industries. They were previously barred from any participation in the political process by a 43-year-old law.

Sorenstam's Japan Streak Reaches Five

Japan, November 6: Annika Sorenstam, the Swedish golfing champion, today became the first woman in LPGA history to win the same tournament five consecutive times when she shot a superb final round 8-under-par 64 to win the Mizuno Classic in Otsu, Japan. She obviously delights in playing on this course, hitting 95 under par over 15 rounds there since 2001, and along the way breaking Laura Davies's record of four straight wins at the Standard Register Ping from 1994–97.

Sorenstam's victory was built upon her two opening rounds of 64 and 67, ending in a 21-under-par total of 195 with just a single bogey. The win brings her tournament victories this year to nine from 19 starts for a total of 65 LPGA career wins. Her fourth straight win here last year saw her move to equal fifth place on LPGA's all-time winners list alongside Betsy Rawls, with 55 wins.

Sorenstam was born on October 9, 1970, in Stockholm, Sweden. She dominated women's golf in the late 1990s and early 2000s, winning her first title at the 1995 US Open, and successfully defending her title the following year. Between 1995 and 2002 she was named Player of the Year five times, and became the first woman since Babe Didrikson Zaharias in 1945 to play in a men's PGA event when she entered The Colonial in May 2003.

Liberia Elects Africa's First Female Leader

Liberia, November 23: The national elections commission of Liberia has confirmed that the head of the victorious Unity Party, Ellen Johnson-Sirleaf, will be installed as the country's president-elect after defeating George Weah by a convincing 20 percent margin in November's crucial run-off vote. Johnson-Sirleaf, Liberia's so-called "Iron Lady," will become Africa's first elected head of state—and only the world's second elected black female head of state.

After gaining a diploma in economics from the University of Colorado in 1970, Johnson-Sirleaf began her political life as Minister of Finance in 1972 in the government of President Tolbert. When the government was overthrown by forces loyal to Samuel Doe in a military coup in

1980, she fled to exile in Kenya before returning to Liberia in 1985 to campaign against Doe in that year's general elections. After speaking out against the many excesses of Doe's military regime she was imprisoned for a short time before being released and once again forced into exile. Returning to Kenya she worked for Citibank and later became the vice-president of Citibank's African regional office.

When Charles Taylor's National Patriotic Front of Liberia murdered Doe in September, 1990, the country was plunged into a civil war that saw a succession of un-elected officials run a series of interim governments until fresh elections were held in 1997. She again returned from exile to contest the elections, securing 10 percent of the popular vote in comparison to Taylor's 75 percent. Civil war returned in 1999, and in 2003 Taylor eventually handed over power to his chosen successor, Moses Zeh Blah, before a UN-backed transitional government was established. Johnson-Sirleaf played a pivotal role in the transitional government, eventually taking over leadership of the Unity Party and leading it to victory.

Born in Liberia's capital Monrovia on October 29, 1938, Johnson-Sirleaf faces a monumental task to rebuild her war-ravaged nation. With the country's electrical grid in ruins, candles light Monrovia's doorways at night. Only 55 percent of Liberia's population of three million people can read, and only 15 percent of the population is employed.

Angela Merkel

Ellen Johnson-Sirleaf, President of Liberia.

Major Coup for Chinese Tennis Duo

Wendy Wasserstein

Melbourne, Australia, January 31: China's Zheng Jie and Yan Zi have made tennis history today, becoming the first Chinese players to win a major tournament with their 2-6, 7-6 (9-7), 6-3 win over top seeds Lisa Raymond of the United States and Australia's Samantha Stosur in the women's final of the Australian Open in Melbourne. The victory caps off a remarkable 12 months for the two long-time friends and playing partners that has seen them claim two doubles titles—in Hobart and Hyderabad—as well as reaching the quarter-finals of the US Open. Last season saw Zheng and Yan each win career-first singles titles.

Seeded twelfth in Melbourne, they displayed tenacity and a fighting spirit which saw them claw their way back from a set down only to weather two match points in the pivotal second set, before using a back-court strategy of

"I'M NOT HERE FOR YOUR ENTERTAIN-MENT / YOU DON'T REALLY WANT TO MESS WITH ME TONIGHT."

PINK, AMERICAN SINGER

Jie Zheng and Zi Yan win China's first grand slam.

passing shots and lobs to neutralize the serve-volley tactics of their more fancied rivals in a match lasting just on 2 hours and 15 minutes.

Although compatriots Li Ting and Sun Tiantian created history by winning the gold medal in women's doubles at the 2004 Athens Olympics, this is the first time a Chinese player has even reached the final of a major tournament.

Chile Turns Left, Elects Woman

Santiago, Chile, March 11: Chile took a dramatic turn to the political left today with the swearing in of Michelle Bachelet as President in a ceremony at the national congress in Valparaiso. The 54-year-old pediatrician, single mother, and self-proclaimed agnostic defeated billionaire Sebastián Piñera in run-off elections in January, winning 53.51 percent of the vote to become the country's first woman president—and the first popularly-elected female leader in Latin America whose political rise occurred independently of her spouse.

The Chilean right failed in the end to distance itself from the atrocities committed during the 17-year rule of Augusto Pinochet. Piñera tried in vain to portray himself as a "Christian human-ist," but was unable to gain the confidence of the poor and the working class whose votes swept Bachelet and her Coalition for Democracy to an emphatic victory.

Bachelet was born in Santiago on September 29, 1951, the daughter of an Air Force general who was tortured to death in 1974 by the Pinochet regime for his close association with the former Allende government. Bachelet was herself imprisoned and tortured before spending five years in exile in Australia and East Germany. Returning to Chile in 1979, she worked as a doctor treating the children of families suffering political repression. In the late 1990s she served on the Socialist

Michelle Bachelet is sworn in as Chile's president.

Party's commission on military affairs, and went on to hold the health and defense portfolios in the government of President Ricardo Lagos before being approached late last year to become her party's presidential candidate.

Iraqi Captors Free Kidnapped Journalist

Baghdad, Iraq, March 30: Jill Carroll, the freelance journalist kidnapped 82 days ago by an obscure group known as the Brigades of Vengeance, has walked into the offices of the Iraqi Islamic Party today after being released by her captors.

On January 7 Carroll, her driver, and interpreter Allan Enwiya were on their way to interview the Sunni leader Adnan al-Dulaimi in a western Baghdad suburb when gunmen seized her, killing her interpreter. The driver managed to escape unharmed. Her release was a high priority for the Bush administration, with Secretary of State Condoleezza Rice expressing her relief and delight at Carroll's release at a press conference in Berlin today. In Iraq on assignment for the *Christian Science Monitor*, Carroll said that she was permitted to watch television, interact with Iraqi women and children, and also read newspapers during her captivity. But frosted windows in her room made it impossible to determine where she was being held. At no point was she threatened with violence.

Support for Carroll, who was in Iraq as part of a humanitarian aid mission, came from some unlikely sources. The militant group Hamas lobbied for her release, describing Carroll as a person sympathetic to the needs of the Iraqi people, who observed and was sensitive to Arab and Islamic traditions.

Scottish Literary Titan Muriel Spark Dies

Florence, Italy, April 13: The most acclaimed Scottish novelist of the modern era, Dame Muriel Spark, died today in a Florence hospital, aged 88. Spark was a true literary giant, often spoken of in the same breath as Beckett or Joyce. She wrote 24 novels as well as many short stories and three biographies, and is best remembered for her masterful 1962 account of a narcissistic Scottish teacher, *The Prime of Miss Jean Brodie*. Muriel Spark was, however, far more than just Jean Brodie.

Born on February 1, 1918, as Muriel Sarah Camberg, she was educated at Edinburgh's James Gillespie's High School for Girls where, at the age of 12, she won the first of many literary awards. She married in 1937 and traveled to South Africa, only to divorce in 1944

The Prime of Miss Jean Brodie by Muriel Spark was filmed in 1969, starring Maggie Smith.

and return to a battle-scarred, war-weary London where she wrote anti-Nazi propaganda for the British foreign office. Spark burst onto the literary scene in 1951 when her story *The Seraph and the Zambezi* won the *Observer* newspaper's short story competition. A conversion to Catholicism in 1954 brought her into contact with some of Britain's most high-profile Catholic authors such as Evelyn Waugh and Graham Greene. In 1957 she found critical acclaim and some measure of financial independence with her novel *The Comforters*.

She moved to Italy in 1967 and lived in a converted thirteenth-century church in the nondescript Tuscan village of Civitella della Chiana. Spark was twice nominated for the Booker Prize, and her final novel *The Finishing School* was published in 2004.

time out

Almost 10 years after the death of Pricess Diana comes Stephen Frears' film *The Queen*, starring Helen Mirren. With a script seeming to defy legal restrictions, the private and public ordeal of Diana's death is explored with candor.

Men Barred from Rio Train Carriages

Rio de Janeiro, Brazil, April 24: Recent legislation to curb sexual harassment on Rio de Janeiro's metro and suburban train routes came into effect today, with one railway carriage on each of Rio's 33 trains bearing a pink stripe painted across its doors and windows signifying the carriage is for women only. Supervia, the company responsible for running carriages, has also installed symbols similar to those for female restrooms.

State legislators were forced to act in the face of mounting complaints from female passengers about sexual harassment on carriages during crowded peak hour services. But some Brazilian women's groups have called the move a giant leap backwards in the fight for equal rights, whilst men have reportedly complained of discrimination after being forcibly removed from carriages.

Diana Ossana

Reese Witherspoon wins Oscar for *Walk the Line*.

Cornwall, England, May 18: Dee Caffari becomes the first woman to sail solo and nonstop around the world the "wrong way," or east to west.

New York, USA, June 8: The 61st session of the UN General Assembly elects Bahraini Sheikha Haya Rashed al-Khalifa President.

Baghdad, June 8: Al-Qa'eda's leader in Iraq, Abu Musab al-Zarqawi, is killed in a US air raid.

Mumbai, India, July 11: Two hundred people die when a terrorist bomb explodes on a train.

Southern Lebanon, July 12: Israel invades Lebanon in response to the kidnapping and killing of two Israeli soldiers by Hezbollah.

Turkey, July 30: Best-selling author Duygu Asena dies of a brain tumor.

Chile, July 31: Fidel Castro appoints his brother, Raoul, as caretaker president while he recovers from a stomach operation.

Prague, Czech Republic, August 24: The International Astronomical Union votes to rescind Pluto's status as a planet. It becomes a dwarf planet.

Tokyo, Japan, September 6: The royal family announces that Princess Kiko gave birth to a boy today.

Thailand, September 19: Prime Minister Thaksin Shinawatra is overthrown in a bloodless coup by the military while he is at UN headquarters in New York.

Space, September 28: Iranian-born US citizen Anousheh Ansari becomes the first woman space tourist when she blasts off for the International Space Station for an eight-day stay.

Moscow, Russia, October 15: Journalist Anna Politkovskaya is found dead in her apartment building, shot in the head. She had been a vocal critic of the Russian government.

Turkey, November 6: Academic Muazzez Ilmiye Cig, aged 92, is acquitted of inciting religious hatred by making sexual references to the Islamic headscarf in her classroom.

Paris, France, November 17: Ségolène Royal is elected leader of the Socialist Party before next year's general election.

Pakistan, November 24: The Protection of Women Bill is passed, enabling adultery and sexual assault cases to be tried under civil law, rather than Islamic law.

Milan, Italy, December: In an attempt to combat eating disorders, organizers of Fashion Week state that at next year's event, models must have a Body Mass Index of at least 18.5.

Baghdad, Iraq, December 30: Former dictator Saddam Hussein is executed. His final moments are broadcast on public television.

Margaret Beckett

Emma Brown Author Dies

Dublin, Ireland, May 16: Irish-born award-winning novelist and journalist Clare Boylan, famous for her evocative and erudite prose, has died of ovarian cancer in Dublin, aged 58. She is best remembered for her brilliant completion of a 20-page unfinished manuscript by Charlotte Bronte.

Boylan's completion of the novel *Emma Brown* brought her worldwide recognition. Despite failing to emulate the deep theological and moral themes so common to Bronte's writing, Boylan nevertheless merged her famous co-author's voice seamlessly into her own in a convincing, daring, and plausible expansion of Bronte's work. Boylan was born in Dublin in 1948. Her novels included *Holy Pictures* (1983), *That Bad Woman* (1995), and *Beloved Stranger* (1999), in which she examined the depression, jealousy, and madness inherent in her parents' marriage.

"HATE IS TOO GREAT A BURDEN TO BEAR. IT INJURES THE HATER MORE THAN IT INJURES THE HATED."

CORETTA SCOTT KING (1927–2006), HUMAN RIGHTS ADVOCATE AND WIDOW OF MARTIN LUTHER KING

Dee Caffari Completes Historic Circumnavigation

Cornwall, England, May 18: Yachtswoman and former schoolteacher Dee Caffari became the first woman to complete a solo circumnavigation of the globe against the prevailing currents and winds when she crossed the finish line off Cornwall's Lizard lighthouse after a journey lasting 178 days, 3 hours, 5 minutes, and 34 seconds. Caffari, 33, completed her marathon 29,100 mile

Dee Caffari ends her "impossible voyage."

(49,000 km) journey in her yacht *Aviva*, a 72 ft (22 m) vessel designed to be sailed by a crew of 18. Upon arrival in Cornwall she was greeted by crowds of cheering supporters including Sir Chay Blyth—the first yachtsman to complete the "backwards" voyage in 1971—the Princess Royal, and Caffari's mother.

Circumnavigating from east to west involves a straight-line course of about 24,500 miles (41,000 km), to which she was forced to add a further 4,600 miles (7,700 km) as the merciless Southern Ocean storms forced continual course changes that put her yacht under considerable strain and danger.

Other obstacles included having to navigate iceberg fields in the dead of night, overcome equipment failures, climb up her mast after a lightning strike to repair damaged wind instruments, and simply cope with the mental challenges created by exhaustion, isolation, and lack of sleep.

Caffari was born in Hertfordshire, England in 1973, and sailed with her father as a child before becoming a dinghy instructor. She attended Leeds Metropolitan University in Yorkshire where she gained a bachelor degree in human movement studies.

After watching the 2000–2001 BT Global Challenge race, her thoughts turned to ocean racing. She joined a yacht charter company and entered the 2004–2005 Global Challenge as the only female skipper in the field. It was at the halfway point of that race, deep in the Southern Ocean, that Caffari first determined to sail her own solo voyage from east to west around the world.

The Japanese royal family presents the new prince to the waiting media. He is third in line to the imperial throne.

Princess Kiko's New Son may Spark Baby Boom

Tokyo, Japan, September 6: After more than four decades of waiting patiently for an imperial heir, Japan was rejoicing and breathing a sigh of relief today at the news that Princess Kiko has given birth to a 5 lb 10 oz (2.6 kg) boy, thus ending the intense succession crisis that has been plaguing the oldest hereditary monarchy in the world.

Women's advocates are ruing the fact that the birth of Princess Kiko's third child—and only son—will probably put an end to the debate as to whether a woman should be allowed to become emperor. With no direct male heir, government legislation was being framed to end a 1947 ban on female succession, but this is now likely to be put aside.

The last female to take the royal throne was in 1762. Japan has had eight reigning empresses over the centuries, but many conservatives are quick to point out that they served in interim capacities only until a suitable male ruler could be found. The new prince was born this morning at 8.27 a.m. local time at Aiiku Hospital in Tokyo's Minato Ward, and both mother and baby are reported to be in good health. The child is third in line to the throne after Crown Prince Naruhito and Prince Akishino.

A naming day will be held in a week and the child's name will be inscribed upon the Imperial family member list. Share prices in baby-goods companies have been rising in recent weeks in anticipation that the royal birth will lift the nation's stagnant birth rate.

Last Frontier Has First Tourist

Space, September 18: Anousheh Ansari, an Iranian-born US citizen and entrepreneur, has become the world's first female space tourist, blasting into orbit aboard a Russian Soyuz TMA-9 rocket launched from the Baikonur cosmodrome in Kazakhstan today. She will spend eight days aboard the International Space Station (ISS), performing experiments for the European Space Agency that will include measuring the effects of space radiation on crew members and

Anousheh Ansari, the first woman space tourist.

the various species of microbial life that call the ISS home. Her fellow expedition astronauts include the veteran shuttle astronaut Michael Lopez-Alegria and the Russian cosmonaut Mikhail Tyurin. They will be only the second three-person team to visit the space station since the 2003 *Columbia* space shuttle disaster. Originally training as a backup for Japanese business executive Daisuke Enomoto, Ansari was promoted to the primary crew when Enomoto was disqualified on medical grounds.

Born in the religious center of Mashhad in northeastern Iran on September 12, 1966, Ansari was a first-hand witness to the Iranian revolution in 1979 that saw the rise to power of the Ayatollah Khomeini and establishment of Iran's Islamic theocracy.

Ansari moved to the United States with her parents in 1984, gaining a bachelor degree in electronics and computer engineering from Virginia's George Mason University and a master's degree in electrical engineering from George Washington University. She will return to Earth on September 29 with US astronaut Jeff Williams and Russian cosmonaut Pavel Vinogradov.

Ségolène Royal Wins French Socialist Candidacy

Paris, France, November 17: Ségolène Royal, a political outsider and mother of four, has won an extraordinary victory over her two Socialist party rivals to become the party's candidate in next April's presidential elections.

Initially dismissed as a lightweight contender and maligned by critics who continually asked: "Who would mind the children?," Royal romped home with a staggering 60 percent of the vote—three times that of her nearest rival. Her undeniable beauty and chic taste in clothes leave her conservative male contemporaries in the shade and make her the most photogenic politician in recent French history. Her socialist rivals Dominique Strauss-Kahn and Laurent Fabius have declared their support for Royal, recognizing the recent polls that clearly indicate she is the only one of the three capable of defeating the center-right's likely candidate, Nicolas Sarkozy.

Royal was born in Dakar, Senegal in 1953 and studied politics at the Institute of Political Studies in Paris. She has served as a magistrate to the administrative court and was an adviser to President Francois Mitterrand. She has also held a succession of government posts including environment minister and vice-minister for family and childhood. Her quest to occupy the Elysée Palace will bring Royal face to face with centuries of ingrained sexism in a country where women could not vote until 1944, and where only 71 of the country's 577 MPs are women.

Matchstick Models Banned from Milan Catwalk

Milan, Italy, December: In Milan—the capital of Italian fashion—organizers have bowed to international pressure and are promoting a healthier image by prohibiting models under the age of 16, and any model with a body mass index (BMI) lower than 18.5, from participating in next February's fashion week. The ban follows a move by the Spanish government earlier this month to ban models with a BMI lower than 18. Brazil also supports the ban—in an industry that has seen the death of at least three anorexic models over the past year alone.

Models in Milan will be compelled to carry medical certificates, and young models will have to be accompanied by a guardian or tutor, indicating that the officials are no longer prepared to tolerate the exploitation of vulnerable and naïve teenagers intent on pursuing a modeling career at any cost. The BMI formula represents the ratio of weight to the square of height. It achieved prominence in the 1980s as a tool for measuring obesity rates. A healthy BMI reading is considered to be anywhere from 18.5 through to 24.9, although its ability to determine precise levels of body fat can be distorted by variables such as bone structure, muscle mass, and a person's general level of fitness.

Milan's influence as one of the world's premier fashion centers is set to put enormous pressure on venues such as Paris and New York to follow suit. But some models have complained that banning someone from doing their job because of their weight is discriminatory, and likely to make the model—rather than the clothes—the center of attention.

The move by Milan is also likely to dramatically cull the number of models available for the Milan show and possibly others. Only 68 models tried out for Madrid's Pasarela Cibeles show last month, down from the 300 originally expected to apply.

Muazzez Ilmiye Cig

Models must have a Body Mass Index of 18.5 or higher.

Dublin, Ireland, March–April 1900: Revolutionary and actress Maude Gonne founds the nationalist organization, Inghinidhe na hEireann, the Daughters of Ireland.

New York, USA, May 15, 1900: Florence Parpart and Hiram Layman invent the street cleaning machine.

Tokyo, Japan, 1900: Dr Yoshioka Yayoi establishes the Tokyo Joigakko, the Tokyo Women's Medical School, the first training college in Japan for women doctors.

New York, USA, 1900: Activist and feminist Carrie Chapman Catt succeeds Susan B. Anthony as president of the National American Woman's Suffrage Association.

Cowes, England, January 2, 1901: After a 64-year reign, Queen Victoria dies, aged 82.

China, September 7, 1901: The end of the Boxer Rebellion is negotiated.

UK and Canada, December 12, 1901: Italian Guglielmo Marconi transmits wireless telegraphic signals from Cornwall to Newfoundland, a distance of 2,232 miles (3,593 km).

Broadway, New York, USA, 1901: Actress Ethel Barrymore appears on Broadway in *Captain Jinks of the Horse Marines*, her first starring role.

Australia, 1901: Miles Franklin (Stella Maria Sarah Miles Franklin) publishes *My Brilliant Career*.

Gournia, Crete, 1901: American archeologist Harriet Boyd begins excavating Minoan ruins at Gournia.

Massachusetts, USA, May 12, 1902: Dr Marie Zakrzewska, co-founder of the New York Infirmary and the New England Hospital for Women and Children, dies aged 72.

Australia, June 12, 1902: Revised electoral laws give Australian women the right to vote and to stand as candidates in elections.

New York City, USA, October 26, 1902: Women's rights activist Elizabeth Cady Stanton dies, aged 86.

Victoria, Australia, December, 1902: Journalist and women's rights activist, Vida Goldstein becomes the first female candidate for the Australian parliament. Earlier this year, she founded the journal *The Australian Woman's Sphere*.

London, England, 1902: Physicist Hertha Marks Ayrton publishes *The Electric Arc*, and is the first woman nominated a Fellow of the Royal Society of London, a distinction denied her because she is married.

England, 1902: Beatrix Potter publishes *The Tale of Peter Rabbit*.

Hamburg, Germany, 1902: The Union for Women's Suffrage is founded by a group of women including Lida Heymann and Anita Augsburg.

St Petersburg, Russia, January 22, 1905: One hundred thousand workers march to the Tsar's Winter Palace to present a petition. Cossack troops open fire, killing 100.

London, England, July 8, 1905: May Sutton (USA) becomes the first non-Briton to win at Wimbledon.

Dublin, Ireland, November 28, 1905: Sinn Fein, a group of nationalists aiming to unite Ireland, is formed.

Massachusetts, USA, 1905: Nettie Stevens publishes her finding that gender is determined by a particular chromosome.

Stockholm, Sweden, 1905: Writer and pacifist, Bertha von Suttner, is the first woman to win the Nobel Peace Prize.

Berlin, Germany, January 4, 1906: American dancer, Isadora Duncan, is forbidden to dance when police label her work obscene.

London, England, January 31, 1906: Suffragette leader Emmeline Pankhurst warns that women are impatient with waiting for the right to vote and are ready to take radical action to advance their cause.

Tahiti, February 8, 1906: A fierce typhoon inundates the Pacific kingdom, killing 10,000 people.

Rochester, New York, USA, March 13, 1906: Suffragette and civil rights campaigner, Susan B. Anthony, dies, aged 86.

San Francisco, USA, April 19, 1906: More than 1,000 people are killed and the city is devastated in the aftermath of an earthquake.

Dunedin, New Zealand, August 26, 1906: Educator Learmonth White Dalrymple, campaigner for women's education, dies, aged 79.

Russia, November 2, 1906: Bolshevik Leon Trotsky is exiled to Siberia for revolutionary activities. Anti-tsarist feelings run high after Nicholas II suspends the Duma.

Paris, France, 1906: Marie Curie is appointed Professor of General Physics in the faculty of sciences at the Sorbonne, the first woman to hold the post.

St Petersburg, Russia, 1906: Anna Pavlova is named prima ballerina at the Maryinsky Theater.

England, 1906: Economist Beatrice Potter Webb and her husband Sidney Webb publish the first volume of their nine-volume work, *English Local Government*.

Rome, Italy, January 1907: Educator and doctor, Maria Montessori, opens her first school, using her own teaching techniques.

London, England, February 13, 1907: Police repel suffragettes attempting to storm Westminster.

Helsinki, Finland, March 15, 1907: Finland is the first European country to give women the right to vote.

Egypt, February 21, 1910: Prime Minister Boutros-Ghali is assassinated.

Worldwide, May 20, 1910: Halley's Comet passes within 13 million miles (21 million km) of Earth. In France and Russia, the comet's passing is thought to be responsible for the poor weather this year.

Sussex, England, May 31, 1910: Dr Elizabeth Blackwell, the first woman to graduate from an American medical school, dies, aged 89. Her sister, Dr Emily Blackwell, dies in September at 33.

South Africa, May 31, 1910: The Union of South Africa comes into being as a British dominion. Boer War hero Louis Botha is Prime Minister, but is already challenged by many Boers for being too pro-British.

London, England, August 13, 1910: Nurse Florence Nightingale dies, aged 90.

Skopje, Eastern Europe, August 26, 1910: Agnes Gonxha Bojaxhiu (Mother Teresa of Calcutta) is born.

Greece, October 18, 1910: Eleftherios Venizelos becomes Prime Minister of Greece.

Boston, Massachusetts, USA, May 21, 1911: Scottish-born astronomer, Williamina Paton Stevens Fleming, who found 10 novae, 52 nebulae, and hundreds of variable stars, dies at 54.

Kansas, USA, June 9, 1911: Carry Nation, famous axe-wielding temperance activist dies, aged 64.

Paris, France, June 13, 1911: Tamara Karsavina dances in *Petrushka*.

Peru, July 16, 1911: American mountaineer, Annie Smith Peck, aged 61, climbs to the top of Mt Coropuna, where she is said to have planted a banner declaring "Votes for Women."

Machu Picchu, Peru, July 24, 1911: American explorer Hiram Bingham rediscovers the ancient Inca city.

Stockholm, Sweden, December 10, 1911: Marie Curie is the recipient of an unprecedented second Nobel Prize, this time for chemistry due to her work on radium.

South Pole, December 14, 1911: Norwegian Roald Amundsen, reaches the South Pole. Both poles have been conquered in just three years.

Nanking, China, December 29, 1911: Leader of the revolutionary forces, Sun Yat-sen, is elected president of a provisional government.

France, 1911: Feminist, anthropologist, and cross-dresser, Madeleine Pelletier, publishes *L'Emancipation sexuelle de la femme (The Sexual Emancipation of Women)*.

USA, 1911: Writer Edith Wharton publishes her novel, *Ethan Frome*.

Japan, 1911: The writer and feminist known as Raicho founds the all-women's journal *Seito*.

North Sea, February 4, 1915: Germany declares blockade; U-boats attack Allied and neutral shipping. Britain retaliates with the seizure of all goods bound for Germany.

Gallipoli Peninsula, Turkey, February 19, 1915: Churchill orders a bombardment of Turkish positions to divert the Turks from Caucasian objectives.

UK, March 18, 1915: The government appeals for women to take up jobs in industry, as men depart for war.

Atlantic Ocean, May 7, 1915: German U-boats torpedo the *Lusitania*.

Italy, May 22, 1915: Italy joins the Allies, having quit the Triple Alliance.

Warsaw, Poland, August 4, 1915: The Polish capital falls to Germany.

Brussels, Belgium, October 12, 1915: Found guilty of assisting Allied prisoners to escape custody, British nurse Edith Cavell is executed by a German firing squad.

Berlin, Germany, November 25, 1915: Einstein's General Theory of Relativity is published.

The Hague, Netherlands, 1915: International Women's Congress for Peace discusses ways to end the Great War.

California, USA, 1915: Appointed one of America's first sworn policewomen in 1910, Alice Stebbins Wells founds the International Policewomen's Association.

England, 1915: *The Voyage Out* by Virginia Woolf is published.

Dublin, Ireland, May 1, 1916: The Easter Uprising of republicans is put down by British forces. An Irish Republic is declared. Constance Markiewicz, Irish patriot, fights against the British, is arrested, and charged with treason.

The Somme, France, July 1, 1916: The first day of the new Western Front offensive claims over 58,000 casualties, one-third fatalities.

Montana, USA, November 6, 1916: Jeannette Pickering Rankin is the first woman elected to Congress.

Petrograd, Russia, December 30, 1916: "Mad monk" Rasputin is murdered.

Alberta, Canada, 1916: Feminist and social activist Emily Ferguson Murphy becomes the first female magistrate of a court in the British Empire.

Manitoba, Canada, 1916: Women in the Prairie Provinces win provincial voting rights.

Puerto Rico, March 2, 1917: Puerto Rico becomes a US protectorate, with all citizens awarded American citizenship.

Ohio, USA, March 13, 1917: Lizzie Dickelman is issued a patent for her invention of the grain storehouse.

Washington DC, USA, April 6, 1917: The USA declares war on Germany. The discovery of the "Zimmerman Note," outlining German designs on the Americas, was a deciding factor.

Massachusetts, USA, January 6, 1903: Margaret Knight receives a patent for her improvements to the rotary engine.

Kishinev, Russia, April 16, 1903: Officials under Tsar Nicholas II stoke peasants' anti-Semitic feelings and a bloody pogrom results in the deaths of hundreds of Jews.

Toronto, Canada, April 30, 1903: Dr Emily Howard Jennings Stowe, suffragette and the first woman to practice as a doctor in Canada, dies, aged 72.

Bancroft, Omaha, USA, May 26, 1903: Susette La Flèsche Tibbles, also known as "Bright Eyes," dies, aged 49. The daughter of the last Omaha chief, she was one of the first women to promote the rights of Native Americans.

Deadwood, South Dakota, USA, August 1, 1903: Frontierswoman and star of Buffalo Bill's Wild West Show, Calamity Jane (Martha Jane Cannary Burke), dies, aged 51.

Alabama, USA, November 10, 1903: Mary Anderson invents the windshield wiper.

Manchester, England, October 1903: Suffragettes Emmeline and Christabel Pankhurst found the Women's Social and Political Union.

Stockholm, Sweden, December 10, 1903: Marie and Pierre Curie share the Nobel Prize in Physics with Henri Becquerel for their work on radioactivity.

Chicago, Illinois, USA, 1903: Factory worker Agnes Nestor is elected president of the International Glove Workers Union of America.

Havana, Cuba, February 5, 1904: US troops withdraw from Cuba.

Aceh, Dutch East Indies, April 3, 1904: Dutch colonial forces kill over 500 Achenese in 30-year Aceh War.

Ireland, April 5, 1904: Frances Power Cobbe, Irish writer on theology and ethics, and social reformer, dies, aged 81.

Edinburgh, Scotland, October 7, 1904: Travel writer Isabella Bird Bishop dies, aged 72.

Ain Sefra, Algeria, October 21, 1904: Swiss-born explorer Isabella Eberhardt dies, aged 27. She had traveled extensively through Africa dressed as a man.

Washington DC, USA, December 6, 1904: Theodore Roosevelt's Corollary to the Monroe Doctrine, invoked to force the Dominican Republic to pays its debts, sees the USA take on the role of international policeman.

Dublin, Ireland, 1904: Dramatist Lady Augusta Gregory becomes a director of the Abbey Theatre, which she co-founded with poet W. B. Yeats.

Massachusetts, USA, 1904: Helen Keller becomes the first deaf and blind person to graduate from a college when she completes her studies at Radcliffe.

Transvaal, March 22, 1907: Mohandas Gandhi vows a campaign of passive resistance if restrictive racial legislation is introduced.

Stuttgart, Germany, August, 1907: Indian nationalist Madame Bhikaji Cama unveils her design for the Indian flag.

China, September 8, 1907: Sun Yat-sen founds the Kuomintang Party.

Brussels, Belgium, 1907: British nurse Edith Cavell is appointed Head of Nursing at the Birkendael Institute.

Massachusetts, USA, February 21, 1908: American sculptor, Harriet Goodhue Hosmer, dies, aged 77.

New York, USA, March 8, 1908: Thousands of women march to demand suffrage, better pay, and an International Women's Day.

Detroit, USA, August 12, 1908: Model T Ford production begins.

Mt Huascarán, Peru, September 2, 1908: American Annie Smith Peck is the first person to climb the highest peak in the Peruvian Andes.

London, England, October 31, 1908: The Olympic Games end; more than 2,000 athletes participated, including about 35 women.

Peking, China, December 2, 1908: Three-year-old Pu Yi is crowned Emperor of China.

Dresden, Germany, December, 1908: Having devised coffee filter papers, Melitta and Hugo Bentz found the Melitta Bentz Company.

Oregon, USA, 1908: In the case of Muller v. Oregon, the US Supreme Court upholds state restrictions of women's working hours.

Antarctica, January 9, 1909: Ernest Shackleton's party is forced to turn back 97 miles (156 km) from the South Pole, as food supplies run low.

New York, USA, January 29, 1909: The world's tallest building, the 50-story Metropolitan Life Insurance building in Manhattan, is completed.

Constantinople. Turkey, April 26, 1909: Sultan Abdul Hamid II is deposed.

Boston, Massachusetts, USA, October 22, 1909: Harvard Law School excludes Inez Mulholland.

Stockholm, Sweden, 1909: Swedish writer Selma Lagerlöf is the first woman to be awarded the Nobel Prize for Literature.

Buenos Aires, Argentina, 1909: Peruvian writer and campaigner for Indian rights, Clorinda Matto de Turner, dies, aged about 57.

New York, USA, 1909: Canadian-born Florence Nightingale Graham changes her name to Elizabeth Arden and opens her first beauty salon on New York's Fifth Avenue.

Savannah, Georgia, USA, March 12, 1912: Juliette Gordon Low starts the American Girl Guides.

Atlantic Ocean, off Newfoundland, April 14, 1912: The liner *Titanic*, on its maiden voyage, strikes an iceberg and sinks. About 1,500 people perish.

Stockholm, Sweden, July 15, 1912: Australian swimmer, Sarah "Fanny" Durack, wins the 100 meter (109-yard) freestyle, the only individual swimming event for women at the Olympic Games.

India, 1912: Poet and feminist, Sarojini Naidu, publishes *The Bird of Time*.

Istanbul, Turkey, January 23, 1913: Young Turks overthrow the Ottoman government in a coup.

Tuskegee, Alabama, USA, February 4, 1913: Civil rights pioneer Rosa Parks is born.

Auburn, New York, USA, March 10, 1913: Harriet Tubman dies, aged around 93. She led more than 300 slaves to freedom from the South on the "Underground Railroad" during the 1860s.

Canberra, Australia, March 12, 1913: The foundation stone for the new Australian capital is laid.

Epsom, England, June 4, 1913: Emily Davison is struck by a horse when she runs onto the Derby track in order to gain publicity for the suffragette cause.

Finland, December 24, 1913: Women's rights advocate Alexandra Grippenberg dies, aged 56.

Norway, 1913: Norwegian women are granted the right to vote.

USA, March 31, 1914: Actress Pearl White stars in the first of the film serials, *The Perils of Pauline*.

New York, USA, March, 1914: Margaret Sanger publishes *The Woman Rebel*, a journal promoting contraception.

USA, May 9, 1914: The first Mother's Day is announced by President Woodrow Wilson, to recognize the contribution to society made by mothers.

Montevideo, Uruguay, July 6, 1914: Delmira Agustini, Uruguayan poet, is murdered.

Sarajevo, Bosnia, June 28, 1914: The heir to the Austrian throne, Archduke Franz Ferdinand, is assassinated.

Europe, August 2, 1914: Germany, having declared war on Russia on August 1, invades Luxembourg.

London, England, August 4, 1914: Britain declares war on Germany as German troops invade Belgium.

Turkey, November 5, 1914: France and Britain declare war on Turkey.

Russia, 1914: Princess Eugenie Shakhovskaya becomes one of Russia's women military pilots.

Washington DC, USA, May 19, 1917: Belva Ann Lockwood, who in 1879 became the first woman admitted to practice before the US Supreme Court, dies, aged 86.

Vincennes, France, October 15, 1917: Dutch dancer and double agent, Mata Hari, is executed by the French.

Egypt, December 15, 1917: Arabic scholar, traveler, and horsewoman, Lady Anne Blunt, daughter of Ada Lovelace, dies, aged 80.

Los Angeles, USA, December 25, 1917: Ida Forbes invents the electric hot water heater.

Hollywood, USA, 1917: Theda Bara stars in the the film *Cleopatra*.

Ireland, May 17, 1918: Eamon de Valera, leader of Sinn Féin, and 500 nationalists are imprisoned on grounds of colluding with Germany.

Canada, May 24, 1918: Female citizens over 21 are allowed to vote.

Victoria, Australia, June 17, 1918: Feminist and women's rights leader, Henrietta Dugdale, dies, aged 91.

Ekaterinberg, Russia, July 16, 1918: The Romanov dynasty ends with the execution of Tsar Nicholas and his family by Bolsheviks.

Japan, November 1918: Deguchi Nao, founder of the Omoto religion, dies, aged 81.

Worldwide, November 11, 1918: The Great War comes to an end.

Berlin, Germany, 1918: Austrian physicist Lise Meitner, working with Otto Hahn, isolates the element protactinium.

Austria, Canada, Estonia, Germany, Hungary, Latvia, Poland, Russia, and the United Kingdom, 1918: Women are granted the right to vote.

Paris, France, February 14, 1919: At the Paris Peace Conference, 27 nations vote for the establishment of a League of Nations.

Moscow, Russia, March 4, 1919: Lenin convenes the *Third International*, with the goal of international Communist revolution.

Hollywood, USA, April 17, 1919: Mary Pickford, Douglas Fairbanks, D. W. Griffith, and Charlie Chaplin found United Artists to produce their own motion pictures.

London, England, July, 1919: Wimbledon resumes after the war. Frenchwoman Suzanne Lenglen wins the women's title.

Rawalpindi, India, August 8, 1919: The end of the third Anglo-Afghan War is negotiated.

London, England, November 28, 1919: US-born Lady Nancy Astor becomes the first woman Member of Parliament.

Chicago, USA, December 21, 1919: Lithuanian-born American anarchist, Emma Goldman, is deported from the United States to Russia.

USA, January 16, 1920: The 18th Amendment officially bans beer, wine, and liquor.

San Remo, Italy, April 25, 1920: The League of Nations gives Britain a mandate over Mesopotamia and Palestine.

Geneva, Switzerland, June 13, 1920: The first International Feminist Conference opens.

Chelmsford, England, June 15, 1920: Australian soprano Nellie Melba makes the first advertised radio broadcast at Marconi headquarters.

USA, August 26, 1920: American women gain the right to vote.

Ireland, December 14, 1920: The British government partitions Ireland into two separate territories, following Bloody Sunday (November 21), when 26 people were killed.

Japan, 1920: The New Women's Association is established, calling for equal rights for Japanese women.

Mongolia, March 13, 1921: Mongolia expels the Chinese after 200 years.

London, England, March 17, 1921: Author and women's rights advocate, Marie Stopes, opens Britain's first family planning clinic.

Panama, April 20, 1921: The Colombian Treaty grants Colombia free access to the Panama Canal and $25 million in exchange for US possession of the strategic waterway.

Paris, France, May 1921: Gabrielle "Coco" Chanel unveils Chanel No. 5.

Russia, August 4, 1921: Lenin appeals for Western aid to combat a famine that is sweeping the country.

San Francisco, USA, September 9, 1921: Actress Virginia Rappe dies from a ruptured bladder after allegedly being raped by silent film star Roscoe "Fatty" Arbuckle.

USA, September, 1921: Bessie Coleman returns to America, the first African-American woman to be licensed as a pilot, having learned to fly in France.

Ireland, December 6, 1921: Southern Ireland becomes a free state under the dominion of Britain. The eight counties in the north forming Ulster remain part of the UK.

Fontainebleau, France, 1921: French composer, conductor, and teacher Nadia Boulanger is appointed to the staff of the American Conservatory.

Hollywood, USA, 1921: Sisters Lillian and Dorothy Gish star in D. W. Griffith's film *Orphans of the Storm*.

New York, USA, 1921: Margaret Sanger establishes the National Birth Control League.

USA, 1921: Edith Wharton's novel *The Age of Innocence*, published last year, wins the 1921 Pulitzer Prize for fiction.

New York, USA, January 9: English-born pianist and composer Ethel Leginska makes her conducting debut at Carnegie Hall, when she conducts the New York Symphony Orchestra.

Peking, China, March 12: Sun Yat-sen, the "father of the republic," dies, aged 58. His political philosophy, the Three Principles of the People, is highly influential.

Tennessee, USA, March 23: The teaching in schools of Charles Darwin's theory of evolution is banned in favor of creationism.

Indiana, USA, April 14: Twenty-eight-year-old Madge Oberholtzer dies of complications following her abduction, rape, and torture by the leader of the Ku Klux Klan. Klan membership numbers drop as a result.

Chicago, USA, April 18-25: The Women's World's Fair is held, showcasing women's achievements and ideas in science, industry, and the arts. Over 160,000 people visit the fair.

Sydney, Australia, April 20: Australian feminist and suffragist Rose Scott dies, aged 77.

England, April 22: Lucy Caroline Lyttelton Cavendish, advocate for women's education, dies, aged 83. She was the first woman to be awarded an honorary degree by Leeds University.

Germany, April 25: Field Marshal von Hindenburg is elected president.

Chicago, USA, April 25: The official closing by Vice President Charles G. Dawes of the Women's World's Fair.

Massachusetts, USA, May 12: Poet Amy Lowell dies, aged 51.

The Vatican, May 17: St Thérèse of Lisieux, who died in 1897, is canonized by Pope Pius XI.

South Africa, June 29: The parliament legislates to prohibit non-whites from working in skilled and semi-skilled jobs.

Olyphant, Pennsylvania, USA, August 6: Loretta Perfectus Walsh dies, aged 29. She was the first woman to serve in the US armed forces in a capacity other than nurse, and saw active duty in the Great War.

Auckland, New Zealand, August 19: Feminist and trade unionist Harriet Morison dies, aged 63. In 1888, she established New Zealand's first trade union for women.

Locarno, Switzerland, October 16: Germany and France sign a peace treaty, seven years after hostilities ended, recognizing a demilitarized zone along the Rhine.

Paris, France, October 17: Nineteen-year-old African-American dancer Josephine Baker is the toast of Paris due to her erotic dancing in *La Revue Nègre*.

Mecca, Hejaz, January 8: Abdel-Aziz ibn Saud takes the title of King of the Hejaz, stating his intention to rename his kingdom Saudi Arabia.

London, England, January 27: John Logie Baird demonstrates his invention, "television," to the Royal Institute.

Berlin, Germany, January: Austrian singer and actress Lotte Lenya marries composer Kurt Weill.

Canada, January: Canada joins the Commonwealth of Nations.

Turkey, February 17: Under the modernizing influence of Kemal Ataturk, new civil, criminal, and law codes based on European systems are adopted by Turkey.

Hollywood, USA, February 21: *The Torrent*, with Swedish actress Greta Garbo in her first starring Hollywood role, is released.

Rome, Italy, April 7: Irishwoman Violet Albina Gibson attempts to assassinate Mussolini, but the Italian leader suffers only an injured nose.

London, England, April 21: A daughter, the Princess Elizabeth, is born to the Duke and Duchess of York.

Sweden, April 25: Swedish feminist and educator Ellen Key dies, aged 77.

Calcutta, India, April: Sectarian riots between Muslims and Hindus erupt, injuring hundreds.

Broadway, New York, USA, April: Actress Mae West is arrested for obscenity when *Sex*, the play she wrote, directed, and stars in, opens on Broadway.

England, May 12: Paralyzing general strike, precipitated by the walkout of coal miners, ends.

Barcelona, Spain, June 9: Architect Antoni Gaudi dies, aged, 74, after being run over by a tram.

Paris, France, June 14: American painter Mary Cassatt dies, aged 82.

Arizona, USA, June: Having disappeared, presumed drowned, in May, evangelist Aimee Semple McPherson reappears, claiming to have been kidnapped and drugged. Although the evidence does not support her claim, she gains worldwide publicity for her evangelical tours.

Kingsdown, England, August 6: US swimmer Gertrude Ederle becomes the first woman to swim the English Channel and sets a new record of 14.5 hours.

Savannah, Georgia, USA, January 17: Founder of the American Girl Scouts, Juliette Gordon Low, dies, aged 66.

Poona, India, January: Suffragette Margaret Cousins and a group of activist women found the All India Women's Conference.

Meise, Belgium, January 19: Charlotte of Belgium, Empress of Mexico, dies, aged 86.

Canada, January: The *Indian Act* prohibits "First Nations" from raising money or hiring a lawyer for the purpose of pursuing land claims.

Hollywood, USA, February 15: Release of the motion picture *It*, starring Clara Bow, who is dubbed the "It Girl."

Lisbon, Portugal, February 9: A revolt against the dictatorship of General Carmona is crushed. Since becoming a republic in 1910, Portugal has been wracked with instability.

Pendine Sands, Wales, February 4: Malcolm Campbell, driving the automobile *Bluebird*, sets a new land speed record of 174.88 mph (279.81 km/h).

The Hague, Netherlands, April 30: Princess Juliana, who turns 18 today, comes of age. She is next in line to the Dutch throne.

Berlin, Germany, May 1: The German government lifts its ban on the Nazi Party; Adolf Hitler addresses a rally.

Massachusetts, USA, June 1: Lizzie Borden, acquitted of the murders of her father and stepmother in 1892, dies, aged 66.

West Midlands, England, June 9: American suffragette and 1872 US presidential candidate, Victoria Woodhull, dies, aged 88.

Dublin, Ireland, July 15: Constance Gore-Booth Markiewicz, Irish freedom fighter and politician, dies, aged 59.

Solo, Central Java, Indonesia, August 31: Scientists believe that *Pithecanthropus erectus*, "Java man," may be the earliest human forebear.

Geneva, Switzerland, August-September: The first World Population Conference takes place, organized by American birth control campaigner Margaret Sanger.

Massachusetts, USA, September 12: Physicist, astronomer, and educator, Sarah Frances Whiting, dies, aged 80.

Nice, France, September 14: American dancer Isadora Duncan dies in a car accident, aged 49.

Ahmedabad, India, March 18, 1922: Mahatma Gandhi is sentenced to six years in prison for civil disobedience.
India, April 5, 1922: Writer, women's rights advocate, and social reformer Pandita Ramabai dies, aged 64.
Northern Iraq, June 18, 1922: Led by Sheikh Mahmud, Iraqi Kurds revolt, demanding independence or autonomy from Baghdad.
Valley of the Kings, Egypt, November 26, 1922: Lord Carnarvon and Howard Carter open the tomb of Tutankhamen.

Moscow, USSR, December 30, 1922: The Union of Soviet Socialist Republics is proclaimed, tying together Russia, White Russia, Ukraine, and Transcaucasia.
USA, 1922: Emily Post publishes *Etiquette in Society, in Business, in Politics and at Home.*
Fontainebleau, France, January 9, 1923: New Zealand-born writer Katherine Mansfield dies, aged 34.
Paris, France, March 26, 1923: After 50 years in the theater, *la divine* Sarah Bernhardt dies, aged 79.

London, England, April 26, 1923: Lady Elizabeth Bowes-Lyon marries Albert, Duke of York.
London, England, July 7, 1923: Frenchwoman Suzanne Lenglen wins her fifth consecutive Wimbledon singles championship.
Lausanne, Switzerland, July 24, 1923: The Near East Treaty establishes peace between Greece and Turkey.
New York, USA, August, 1923: Bessie Smith's recording of "Downhearted Blues" sells over 750,000 copies in six months.

Angora (Ankara), Turkey, October 29, 1923: Leader of the nationalist movement that brought an end to the Ottoman Empire, Mustafa Kemal has been elected president of the new Turkish republic.
New York, USA, November 6, 1923: El Dorado Jones is issued a patent for her invention of the engine muffler, which is designed to cut car engine noise.
Cairo, Egypt, 1923: Pioneering feminist Huda Sh'arawi founds the Egyptian Feminist Union.

England, 1923: Mystery writer Dorothy L. Sayers publishes *Whose Body?*, featuring Lord Peter Wimsey.
USA, 1923: Bacteriologists Gladys Dick and her husband George Dick publish their findings that scarlet fever is caused by the streptococcus bacteria.
USA, 1923: Poet Edna St Vincent Millay is the first woman to win the Pulitzer Prize for Poetry.
Denmark, 1924: Politician Nina Bang is appointed Minister for Education. She is the world's first woman cabinet minister.

Hollywood, USA, October 18: Mary Pickford stars as a 12-year-old slum girl in *Little Annie Rooney.*
Egypt, November 13: Egyptologists unwrap the mummy of King Tutankhamen; the king was only a youth, dying at the age of 15.
Paris, France, November 13: The first exhibition of Surrealist art opens with works by Ernst, Klee, de Chirico, Miro, and Picasso.
Persia, December 13: After deposing the self-exiled Shah, Reza Khan is crowned the new Shah of Persia. He initiates a new reform policy.

England: Dora Black Russell, wife of philosopher Bertrand Russell, publishes *Hypatia: Women and Knowledge*, espousing sexual freedom for women.
Kanpur, India: Poet and social reformer Sarojini Naidu becomes the first woman president of the Indian National Congress.
Berlin, Germany: German physicist Ida Tacke and her husband Walter Noddack discover element 75, which they name rhenium.

Vienna: Psychoanalyst Anna Freud is appointed secretary of the Vienna Psychoanalytic Institute, where she gives lectures on the psychological analysis of children.
Alabama, USA: Margaret Murray Washington, founder of the Tuskegee Woman's Club, dies, aged 60. Between 1912 and 1916, she was president of the National Association of Colored Women.
England: Novelist Virginia Woolf publishes *Mrs Dalloway.*

Cambridge, Massachusetts, USA: Astronomer Cecilia Payne is awarded Harvard's first ever PhD in astronomy.
Kenya: Anthropologists Osa and Martin Johnson continue their research in Africa.
England: British botanist and philosopher Agnes Arber publishes her work, *Monocotyledons: a Morphological Study.*
USA: Artist Georgia O'Keeffe paints *Petunias.*

Paris, France: Polish harpsichordist Wanda Landowska founds the Ecole de Musique Ancienne.
San Francisco, USA: Florence Prag Hahn is elected to the House of Representatives, the first Jewish woman to serve in the US Congress.
England: British novelist Ivy Compton-Burnett publishes *Pastors and Masters.*
Sweden: Author Selma Lagerlöf, winner of the 1909 Nobel Prize for Literature, publishes the first part of her trilogy, *Löwensköldska ringen (The Ring of the Löwenskölds).*

Transvaal, South Africa, August 22: The discovery of massive reserves of diamonds brings 50,000 people to the region.
Hankou, China, September 6: Nationalist Kuomintang troops, led by General Chiang Kai-shek, capture the strategic treaty port of Hankou. The northern troops have retreated and there is fear that Peking will fall.
New Zealand, September 9: The *Maori Arts and Crafts Act* revives traditional Maori skills.

Greenville, Ohio, November 3: Sharpshooter and former member of Buffalo Bill's Wild West Show, Annie Oakley, dies, aged 66.
Japan, December 25: Hirohito becomes Emperor following his father Yoshihito's death, ending the Taisho period.
London, England: Turkish novelist and feminist Halide Adivar Edib publishes her English-language autobiography, *Memoirs*, which describes recent Turkish history, her pacifism, and the struggle for women's emancipation.

Yorkshire, England: After disappearing for several days, British crime writer Agatha Christie is found in a hotel, claiming to have suffered amnesia.
Berlin, Germany: Austrian physicist Lise Meitner is appointed professor of physics at the University of Berlin, the first woman in Germany to attain this position.
Boston, Massachusetts, USA: Mathematician and logician Christine Ladd-Franklin receives her PhD in mathematics from Harvard University.

New York, USA: The Lucy Stone League successfully fights for the right of married women to be granted copyright in their own names.
New York, USA: Dancer and choreographer Martha Graham founds her own dance company.
Paris, France: Fashion designer Coco Chanel creates the little black dress.
Stockholm, Sweden: Italian novelist Grazia Deledda wins the Nobel Prize for Literature.
New York, USA: Poet, critic, and wit Dorothy Parker publishes her collection of poetry, *Enough Rope.*

Tamil Nadu, India: Social reformer E. V. Ramasany Naicker founds the Self-Respect Movement. One of his aims is for women to be more independent.
Paris, France: "Esthetic surgeon" Dr Suzanne Noel publishes *La Chirurgie Esthétique, Son Rôle Social*, which describes the importance of cosmetic surgery.
London, England: Ballerina Ninette de Valois founds the Academy of Choreographic Art.

USA, October 6: *The Jazz Singer*, starring Al Jolson, is the first "talkie" to gain widespread success.
USA, October 28: Pan American Airlines launches the world's first commercial international flight.
New York, USA, October: Civil rights campaigner and writer Mary White Ovington publishes *Portraits in Color*, a biography of a number of leading African-Americans.
Canton, China, December 19: General Chiang Kai-shek crushes a Communist uprising and expels all Russian citizens.

New York, USA, December 27: Adapted from Edna Ferber's novel, *Show Boat*, a spectacular musical by Oscar Hammerstein and Jerome Kern, opens to large audiences.
New York/London, December 31: The first transatlantic telephone service is operational.
Paris, France: Polish-born artist Tamara de Lempicka paints *Kizette in Pink*, a portrait of her daughter.

Lima, Peru: The Lima Geographical Society names the north peak of Mount Huascaran after American mountaineer Anna Smith Peck. It is now known as Cumbre Ana Peck.
Helsinki, Finland: Miina Sillanpää becomes Finland's first female government minister, serving as Minister for Social Affairs.
USA: Novelist Willa Cather publishes *Death Comes for the Archbishop.*

Fremont, Michigan, USA: Dorothy Gerber, who has been straining food for her baby, asks her husband, cannery owner Daniel Gerber to produce a line of strained baby food.
Turkmenistan: Women gain the right to vote and to stand for election.
Paris, France: Fashion designer Jeanne Lanvin releases her new perfume, Arpège.
USA: Engineer Elsie Eaves is the first woman admitted to the American Society of Civil Engineers and the American Association of Cost Engineers.

West Sussex, England: Dora Russell and her husband Bertrand Russell establish Beacon Hill School, the aim of which is to provide children with a liberal education, rather than a strictly academic one.
Memphis, Tennessee, USA: Pilot Phoebe Fairgrave Omlie becomes the first woman to gain an aircraft mechanic's license.

1928

UK, January 5: The British government introduces the aged pension of 10 shillings per week for people over 65 on a low income.
Dorchester, England, January 11: Author Thomas Hardy dies, aged 87. His ashes are to be interred in Westminster Abbey.
New York, USA, January 12: Found guilty of murdering her husband, Ruth Snyder is executed.
Oakland, California, USA, January 28: Astronomer Dorothea Klumpke Roberts is the first member of the Eastbay Astronomical Society.

Darwin, Australia, February 22: Aviator Bert Hinkler completes the first solo flight from England.
St Moritz, Switzerland, February 19: Norwegian figure skater Sonja Henie wins her first Olympic gold medal at the Winter Olympic Games.
Denmark, March 26: Nina Bang, Danish politician and the world's first female government minister, dies, aged 61.
Turkey, April 29: Premier Mustafa Kemal introduces the Latin alphabet in preference to the Arabic.

Oxford, England, April: The final volume of the *Oxford English Dictionary* is published. The project was initiated in 1879.
USA, May 11: The first commercial television broadcasts begin with three 90-minute sessions per week.
Amsterdam, Netherlands, May 17-August 12: The IX Olympic Games introduces women's athletics and gymnastics.
London, England, June 14: Suffragette Emmeline Pankhurst dies, aged 69, weeks before British women finally gain the right to vote.

Carmarthenshire, Wales, June 18: Aviatrix Amelia Earhart crosses the Atlantic from Newfoundland in 21 hours.
UK, July 3: Women are granted the right to vote in Great Britain.
London, England, July 21: Acclaimed British stage actress Ellen Terry dies, aged 80.
Lucknow, India, August 30: Dissatisfied with the adoption of the Nehru Plan, the Independence of India League is established under the leadership of Jawaharlal Nehru, son of the author of the plan.

London, England, September 15: Bacteriologist Alexander Fleming makes a discovery while studying *Staphylococcus* bacteria; *Penicillium notatum*, a mold growing on some specimens, has killed the bacteria.
Dresden, Germany, September 16: German women's rights leader Marie Stritt dies, aged 72.
Illinois, USA, September: Blues singer Ma Rainey (Gertrude Pridgett) makes a hit recording, "Leaving this Morning."

1929

Los Angeles, USA, January 2: Twenty-two-year-old pilot Evelyn "Bobbi" Trout sets a new women's solo endurance record when she flies non-stop for 12 hours and 11 minutes.
Yugoslavia, January 6: Alexander I takes direct control of the Kingdom of the Serbs, Croats, and Slovenes, renaming it Yugoslavia.
Calcutta, India, January 6: Nineteen-year-old Sister (later Mother) Teresa goes to India with the Sisters of Loreto, where she becomes a teacher at St Mary's High School.

Belgium and USA, January: Two comic strip characters make their debut: Hergé's *Tintin*, and *Popeye*, drawn by Elzie Segar.
Rome, Italy, February 11: Mussolini and the Papacy sign the Lateran Treaty, creating the Vatican and re-establishing the sovereignty of the Pope after 60 years of tension.
Monte Carlo, Monaco, February 12: British stage actress Lillie Langtry, who gained notoriety through her affair with the Prince of Wales, dies aged 75.

Hollywood, USA, March 30: The film *Coquette* is released, starring Mary Pickford in her first "talkie."
New York, USA, April 17: Actress Claire Hodgson marries baseball star Babe Ruth.
Picardy, France, April 24: Journalist and feminist Caroline Rémy de Gueghard, known as Séverine, dies, three days before her 74th birthday.
Brussels, Belgium, May 4: Screen actress Audrey Hepburn is born.

Los Angeles, USA, May 16: The first Academy Awards ceremony is held at the Roosevelt Hotel in Hollywood.
Berlin, Germany, May 17: Soprano Lilli Lehmann, known for her performances of Wagner's operas, dies aged 80.
London, England, June 10: Margaret Bondfield becomes Britain's first female Cabinet minister, in the new Labour government of Prime Minister Ramsay MacDonald.
Frankfurt, Germany, June 12: World War II diarist Annelies Marie Frank, known as Anne Frank, is born.

Southampton, New York, USA, July 28: Jacqueline Bouvier (Kennedy Onassis) is born.
London, England, August 5: Death of Dame Millicent Fawcett, feminist and suffragist.
Baarn, Netherlands, August 10: Women's rights activist, campaigner for birth control, and the first Dutch woman to qualify as a physician, Dr Aletta Jacobs, dies aged 75.
Jerusalem, Palestine, August 31: Jewish access to the Wailing Wall causes a violent Arab uprising, leaving 500 dead.

1930

England, January: Engineer Frank Whittle submits a patent for the first turbojet engine.
New York, USA, February 25: *The International Review*, starring Gertrude Lawrence, premieres.
London, England, March 14: Plans to build a tunnel from England to France are approved by the Channel Tunnel Committee.

USSR, March 16: Joseph Stalin begins a terror campaign to eradicate wealthy farmers.
Turkey, March 28: The name of the city of Constantinople is officially changed to Istanbul.
Bayreuth, Germany, April 1: Cosima Liszt, daughter of composer Franz Liszt and wife of composer Richard Wagner, dies aged 92.

Dandi, India, April 6: After completing his 100-mile (161-km) Salt March, Mahatma Gandhi defies the British salt tax laws by evaporating sea water to make his own salt.
China, April 23: Nationalists and Soviet Communists challenge General Chiang Kai-shek's efforts to control China.
Berlin, Germany, May 13: Educator and women's rights campaigner Helene Lange dies, aged 82.

California, USA, May 15: Nurse Ellen Church is hired as the first airline stewardess, flying the route between San Francisco and Chicago.
Johannesburg, South Africa, May 19: White women in South Africa now have the right to vote.
Darwin, Australia, May 24: British aviatrix Amy Johnson arrives in Darwin 19 days after commencing her solo flight from London.

Cincinnati, USA, June: Sarah E. Dickson is ordained as the first female Presbyterian elder in the country.
Lambeth, England, August 14: The Church of England reluctantly accepts the use of contraception.
New York, USA, October 14: Singer Ethel Merman appears in her first starring role, in *Girl Crazy*, by George and Ira Gershwin.
Ithaca, New York, USA, August 24: Natural historian, conservationist, and illustrator Anna Botsford Comstock dies, aged 75.

1931

Iraq, January 6: Archeologists unearth a 550 BCE royal palace at the ancient city of Ur.
The Hague, Netherlands, January 23: Anna Pavlova, famous ballerina, dies, aged 49.
Noank, Connecticut, USA, February 7: Aviator Amelia Earhart marries publisher George Palmer Putnam.
Sydney, Australia, February 23: Australian soprano Dame Nellie Melba, dies, aged 69.

Washington DC, USA, March 3: President Hoover signs an act declaring that the national anthem will be "The Star-Spangled Banner."
Washington DC, USA, March 14: Ida Harper, journalist, suffragist, and biographer of Susan B. Anthony, dies, aged 80.
India, March 25: Racial riots in Cawnpore kill hundreds in a throat-slitting bloodbath.

Chicago, USA, March 25: Feminist, journalist, and anti-lynching campaigner Ida Wells-Barnett dies, aged 68.
Madrid, Spain, April 14: King Alfonso XIII abdicates the throne and flees the country, and the Republic of Spain is proclaimed. Niceto Alcalá Zamora takes over the presidency under a provisional government.
Eretz, Israel, April 16: Hebrew poet Rachel Bluwstein, known simply as Rachel the Poet, dies, aged 41.

London, England, April 30: Editor, feminist, and physician Harriet Clisby dies, aged 100.
Morristown, New Jersey, USA, August: The Seeing Eye, a school for training guide dogs for the visually impaired, founded by Dorothy Harrison Eustis, moves from Nashville to New Jersey.
London, England, September 7: King George V takes a £50,000-a-year pay cut to help deal with the economic crisis.

Manchuria, September 18: Japan invades Manchuria in a surprise attack, thus violating the Kellogg-Briand pact.
Phoenix, Arizona, USA, October: Winnie Ruth Judd allegedly shoots Agnes Anne LeRoi and Hedvig Samuelson, cuts up their bodies, and sends them in her baggage to Los Angeles where they are discovered a few days later.

1928

Moscow, USSR, October 1: The beginning of Stalin's first five-year plan. Farms are made collectives and heavy industry is expanded.

Addis Ababa, Ethiopia, October 7: Ras Tafari is crowned King. For the last 10 years, he has shared power with his aunt, Empress Zauditu.

Boston, USA, October 12: The iron lung, a machine enabling a person to breathe, is used for the first time on a child with infantile paralysis.

USA, November 18: Walt Disney's short cartoon film *Steamboat Willie* introduces Mickey Mouse.

Illinois, USA, November 27: Marjorie Joyner invents the permanent hair wave machine.

Nanking, China, November: The Kuomintang government headed by Chiang Kai-shek gains international legitimacy, signing treaties with 12 countries.

Rhodesia, December: British archeologist Gertrude Caton-Thompson begins her excavations of the ruins of Great Zimbabwe.

London, England, December: An appeal against the banning of Marguerite Radclyffe-Hall's *The Well of Loneliness* fails.

Sydney, Australia: Feminist Adela Pankhurst Walsh, daughter of Emmeline Pankhurst, founds the Australian Women's Guild of Empire, which assists working-class women.

China: Xiang Jingyu, feminist and head of the Communist Party's Women's Bureau, is executed.

England: Novelist Virginia Woolf publishes *Orlando*, an examination of the meaning of gender.

Europe, 1928-29: Dancer and choreographer Bronislava Nijinska creates the ballets *Nocturne, Bolero, Le Baiser de la Fée* and *La Valse*, all for ballerina Ida Rubinstein.

Jerusalem, Palestine: Golda Myerson is elected secretary of the Histadrut Women's Labor Council.

Puerto Rico: Women are granted the right to vote.

Hollywood, USA: Gloria Swanson stars in *Sadie Thompson*, a film adaptation of W. Somerset Maugham's story "Rain."

USA: Bacteriologist Alice Evans becomes the first woman to be elected president of the Society of American Bacteriologists.

USA: Psychologist Leta Hollingworth, who works with women and children, publishes *The Psychology of the Adolescent*.

USA: Anthropologist Margaret Mead publishes *Coming of Age in Samoa*.

USA: Artist Georgia O'Keeffe paints *White Calla Lilies with Red Anemone* and *Black Petunias*.

1929

London, England, October 18: Canadian magistrate and women's right campaigner, Emily Ferguson Murphy, and four other women, bring the "Persons Case" to the Privy Council in Britain, which rules that the word "person" covers both men and women.

New York, USA, October 24: The "Black Thursday" stock market crash wipes millions off the value of shares.

Valley Stream, New York, USA, November 2: Female aviators found an association of women pilots. Its first secretary is Louise Thaden.

New York, USA, November 7: The Museum of Modern Art opens, confirming the significance of avant-garde artists this century.

Philadelphia, USA, November 12, 1929: Film actress and later Her Serene Highness of Monaco, Grace Kelly, is born.

Montlhéry, France, December 18: Racing car driver Hélène Delangle, known as Hellé Nice, breaks the land speed record for women.

Lahore, India, December: Violence between Hindus and Muslims leads to the All India Congress calling for independence from Britain.

Paris, France: Twenty-one-year-old Simone de Beauvoir is the youngest person to qualify as a philosophy teacher in France. This year she also meets Jean-Paul Sartre, a fellow philosopher.

Macau, South China Seas: Female pirate Lai Choi San, who commands 12 ships, begins her pirating career.

Ecuador and Romania: Women in Ecuador and Romania are granted the right to vote.

Dakar, Senegal: Writer and feminist Mariama Bâ is born.

India: The government passes the *Child Marriage Restraint Act*, proposed by Harbilas Sarda at the urging of Mahatma Gandhi, which raises the minimum age of marriage for girls to 14.

London, England: Novelist Virginia Woolf publishes the feminist essay *A Room of One's Own*, which originated from lectures she gave the year before at Cambridge University.

USA: Social reformer Katharine Bement Davis, a former head of New York City's Department of Correction, and the first woman to head a municipal agency, publishes *Factors in the Sex Life of Twenty-Two Hundred Women*, the culmination of nine years' survey work.

1930

New York, USA, November 16: Greta Garbo's first talkie, *Anna Christie*, is released. Garbo's first screen words are: "Gimme a vhisky ..."

New York, USA, December 31: The collapse of the Bank of the United States, which has 60 branches in New York alone, leads to a run on banks throughout the country.

The Vatican, December 31: The papal encyclical *Casti Connubii* reaffirms the Catholic Church's ban on contraception, apart from the natural rhythm method.

USA: Mildred Wirt Benson, under the pen name Carolyn Keene, publishes *The Secret of the Old Clock*, the first of her mystery books for children featuring Nancy Drew.

England: The National Birth Control Council is founded by Helena Wright, providing information to married women about contraception.

Georgia, USA: Feminist and anti-racism campaigner Jessie Daniel Ames founds the Association of Southern Women for the Prevention of Lynching.

Shanxi, China: Englishwoman Gladys Aylward and another female European missionary open an inn, with the idea of converting travelers to Christianity.

USA: Aviatrix Anne Morrow Lindbergh, wife of Charles Lindbergh, is the first woman to be granted a glider pilot's license.

Russia: The Zhenotdel (Women's Department), set up by Communist Alexandra Kollontai to look after the "needs of women," including child care, housing, and employment, is closed down.

London, England: Polish-born dancer and ballet producer, Marie Rambert, establishes the Ballet Club at the Mercury Theatre. Within a decade, it becomes known as Ballet Rambert.

South America: Uruguayan poet Juana de Ibarbourou publishes *La rosa de los vientos*.

USA: Anthropologist Margaret Mead publishes *Growing up in New Guinea*.

Western Desert, Egypt: British archeologist Gertrude Caton-Thompson begins her survey and excavations of Kharga Oasis.

England: Crime writer Agatha Christie publishes *Murder at the Vicarage*, which introduces her amateur detective Miss Jane Marple.

China: The Kuomintang government passes legislation intended to promote gender equality.

1931

Spain, October 16: Divorce is legalized in Spain.

Oslo, Norway, December 10: American pacifist social worker Jane Addams receives the Nobel Peace Prize.

New York, USA: Archeologist Ann Axtell Morris publishes *Digging in the Yucatán*, an account of digs carried out at Chichén Itzá in Mexico and Yucatán in Mexico State.

USA: Florence Merriam Bailey, the first female member of the American Ornithologists' Union, is awarded their Brewster Medal.

London, England: Ninette de Valois establishes the Vic-Wells Ballet Company.

Los Angeles, USA: Painter and playwright Alice Pike Barney dies, aged 74.

Paris, France: Italian-born fashion designer Elsa Schiaparelli introduces shoulder pads into her women's tailored suits.

California, USA: Mexican actress Lupe Velez pursues her career in Hollywood.

USA/UK: Educator and writer Vida Dutton Scudder, who in 1911 founded the Episcopal Church Socialist League, publishes *The Franciscan Adventure: A Study in the First Hundred Years of the Order of St Francis of Assisi*.

Göttingen, Germany: Engineer and mathematician Irmgard Lotz publishes the Lotz method, dealing with the distribution of "lift" in aeroplane wings.

New York, USA: Gertrude Vanderbilt Whitney establishes the Whitney Museum of American Art.

England: The controversial British writer and gardener, Vita Sackville-West, publishes her novel *All Passion Spent*.

Spain, Portugal, Chile, and Ceylon: Women are granted the right to vote.

Hollywood, USA: Canadian actress Marie Dressler wins Best Actress at this year's Academy Awards.

England: Suffragist and writer Sylvia Pankhurst publishes *The Suffrage Movement*.

Germany: Writer and poet Ricarda Huch is the first woman admitted to the Prussian Academy of Literature.

USA: Writer Pearl S. Buck publishes *The Good Earth*.

USA: Irene Dunne stars in several movies, including *Cimarron* and *Consolation Marriage*.

1932

India, January 4: Mahatma Gandhi is arrested at 3 a.m. after the Indian National Congress is declared illegal.
Arkansas, USA, January 12: Hattie Wyatt Caraway is the first woman elected to the US Senate.
El Salvador, January 22: Socialist Augustín Farabundo Martí leads a peasant uprising against the government. Government retaliation is to massacre of 15,000 to 30,000 people.

New York, USA, February 15: Actress and theater director, Minnie Maddern Fiske, usually known as Mrs Fiske, dies, aged 67.
Sydney, Australia, March 19: The Sydney Harbour Bridge opens, providing road access between the city's north and south.
USA, April 28: A yellow fever vaccine is in development.

Tokyo, Japan, May 15: Prime Minister Tsuyoshi Inukai is assassinated by radical young naval officers. The original plan includes killing Charlie Chaplin, presently in Japan.
Newfoundland, Canada, May 20: Aviator Amelia Earhart sets off across the Atlantic Ocean, the first woman to fly solo across this distance.

Galway, Ireland, May 22: Playwright Augusta Gregory, known as Lady Gregory, founder of Dublin's Abbey Theatre, dies, aged 80.
Siam, June 24: The military seizes power, which leads to Siam becoming a constitutional monarchy.
Los Angeles, USA, August: Athlete Mildred "Babe" Didrikson wins Olympic gold medals in javelin and hurdles, and a silver medal in high jump.

Los Angeles, USA, September 18: Actress Peg Entwistle commits suicide by jumping from the letter "H" of the Hollywoodland sign.
Saudi Arabia, September 18: King Ibn Saud unites the Kingdom of the Hejaz and the Sultanate of Nejd as the Kingdom of Saudi Arabia.
Gorham, New Hampshire, USA, September 19: Octogenarian mountaineer Annie Smith Peck reaches the top of Mount Crescent.

1933

Rochester, New York, USA, January 9: Engineer and business-woman Kate Gleason dies, aged 67. She was the first female member of the Society of Mechanical Engineers.
Berlin, Germany, January 30: Recha Freier founds Support for Jewish Youth, an organization to help young Jews find employment, and provide for refugee children.

USA, February 17: Blondie Boopadoop marries Dagwood Bumstead in the popular comic strip *Blondie*.
Hollywood, USA, March 2: Actress Fay Wray appears with a giant gorilla in the motion picture hit *King Kong*.
Germany, March 22: The first Nazi concentration camp at Dachau, near Munich, begins operation.

Germany, March 23: Adolf Hitler becomes dictator of Germany after the Reichstag grants him full powers, less than two months after he was appointed Chancellor of Germany.
Germany, April 11: The Nazis decree "non-Aryans" to include anyone descended from non-Aryan, particularly Jewish, parents or grandparents.
Scotland, May 2: A bizarre creature is reportedly seen in Loch Ness.

Washington DC, USA, May 3: President Roosevelt appoints Nellie Tayloe Ross the first female director of the US Mint.
Paraguay, May 10: Paraguay declares war on Bolivia.
Moscow, Russia, June 20: German-born politician and women's rights activist Clara Eissner Zetkin dies, aged 75.
Providence, Rhode Island, USA, June 24: African-American soprano Sissieretta Joyner Jones, dies at 64 years of age.

Tervete, Latvia, June 25: Writer Anna Brigadere dies, aged 71.
UK, July 7: Doctors announce that they have been able to isolate the influenza virus.
Poona, India, August 23: An emaciated Mahatma Gandhi is released from hospital, five days into a fast protesting his exclusion from working with untouchables while in prison. Earlier in the year he had been on a three-week hunger strike to protest the poor treatment of lower castes.

1934

Berlin, Germany, January 1: Nazi law forcing people with genetic defects to be sterilized comes into effect.
New York, USA, February: *It Happened One Night,* starring Claudette Colbert and Clark Gable, is released.
World, February 11: Friendship treaties are signed between Saudi Arabia and Britain, and between Britain, India, and Yemen.

New York, USA, February 25: Botanist Elizabeth Britton, who specialized in the study of mosses, dies, aged 76.
Hsinking, Manchukuo (China), March 1: Henry Pu-yi becomes emperor of Manchukuo, but is a puppet ruler under Japan.
Bienville Parish, Louisiana, USA, March 23: Murderers and robbers Bonnie Parker and Clyde Barrow are shot dead by law enforcement officers.

Darwin, Australia, May 23: New Zealand aviatrix Jean Batten arrives in Darwin in record time, after flying solo from England.
Callender, Ontario, Canada, May 28: Identical quintuplets, the Dionne sisters, are born.
Savoy, France, July 4: Discoverer of radium and Nobel Prize winner, Marie Curie, dies, aged 66.
Christchurch, New Zealand, July 13: Kate Malcolm Sheppard, who played a critical role in New Zealand becoming the world's first country to grant women the vote, dies, aged 87.

Germany, August 2: Adolf Hitler proclaims himself Führer of Germany, making him both head of state and chancellor.
Istres, France, August 11: French aviatrix and stunt pilot Hélène Boucher is officially the fastest woman in the world after flying at 276 miles per hour (444 km/h).
Nuremburg, Germany, September 4: Adolf Hitler asks film-maker Leni Riefenstahl to direct a propaganda film about a Nazi Party rally in Nuremburg. It will be called *Triumph des willens (Triumph of the Will).*

Prague, Czechoslovakia, September 12: Russian revolutionary Catherine Breshkovsky, known as *Babushka* ("Little Grandmother"), dies at 90.
Hollywood, USA, September 14: German-born actress Marlene Dietrich stars as Catherine the Great in the film *The Scarlet Empress.*

1935

Libya, Africa, January 1: The Italian colonies of Kyrenaika and Tripoli are joined as Libya.
Florida, USA, January 16: Members of the notorious Barker gang, led by Ma Barker, are killed by FBI agents during a shootout at Lake Weir.
The Pacific, January: Aviator Amelia Earhart flies solo from Hawaii to California, becoming the first person to fly solo over the Pacific. Later this year, she flies solo from Mexico City to Newark.

Hollywood, USA, February 27: Six-year-old actress Shirley Temple is presented with a special Academy Award for her performance in 1934's *Bright Eyes.*
Berlin, Germany, March 16: Germany denounces the disarmament clauses of the Versailles Treaty, resuming military conscription.
Bryn Mawr, Pennsylvania, USA, April 14: German-born mathematician Emmy Noether, whose work in algebra has been much admired, dies, aged 53.

USA, April 22: Elsa Lanchester stars in *The Bride of Frankenstein*, released today.
Middlesex, England, April: An aircraft-locating device, "radar," is patented by Scottish physicist Robert Watson-Watt.
Philadelphia, Pennsylvania, USA, May 3: Children's book illustrator Jessie Willcox Smith dies, aged 71.
Chicago, USA, May 21: Jane Addams, social worker and Nobel Peace Prize winner, dies, aged 74.

Moscow, USSR, August 20: The Seventh World Congress of the Communist International calls for the USSR and all communists to unite with democracies against their common enemy, the fascist dictatorships.
Washington DC, USA, August 31: As tensions mount in Europe, Congress passes the first of its Neutrality Acts designed to keep the USA out of foreign conflict.

Venice, Italy, August: The movie adaptation of Leo Tolstoy's *Anna Karenina,* starring Swedish actress Greta Garbo, is the highlight of the Venice Film Festival.
Srinigar, Kashmir, August: Swiss-born journalist, photographer, and adventurer Ella Maillart arrives in Srinigar after a seven-month journey from Peking via the Silk Road, her mission to have explored Chinese Turkestan.
Nuremberg, Germany, September 15: The Nuremberg decree legalizes the Nazi persecution of Jews.

1932

Hollywood, USA, September 30: Stage actress Katharine Hepburn makes her film debut in *A Bill of Divorcement*, directed by George Cukor and starring John Barrymore.
Zurich, Switzerland, September: German mathematician Emmy Noether is the first woman to present a lecture at the International Mathematical Congress.
Iraq, October 3: Iraq gains independence from its British-imposed rule under a treaty granting the UK certain privileges.

USA, October 21: Shirley Temple, aged four, makes her film debut in *The Red-Haired Alibi*.
USSR, November 9: Nadezhda "Nadya" Alliluyeva, the wife of Joseph Stalin, dies, aged 30.
London, England, December 8: Garden designer Gertrude Jekyll dies, aged 89.
Pretoria, South Africa, December 30: Suspected of poisoning two husbands in order to collect their life insurance, and found guilty of poisoning her son for reasons not clear, Daisy de Melker is hanged.

USA: Laura Ingalls Wilder publishes *Little House in the Big Woods*, the first in her series of *Little House* books, describing her childhood in the Midwestern frontier.
England: British composer Elisabeth Lutyens writes the music for the ballet *The Birthday of the Infanta*.
Germany: Film-maker Leni Riefenstahl co-writes, directs, and appears in *Das Blaue Licht* (*The Blue Light*), which brings her to the attention of Adolf Hitler.

London, England: Lilian Wyles becomes the first woman Chief Inspector of the Metropolitan Criminal Investigation Department.
Japan: Feminist, birth control campaigner, and politician Kato Shidzue founds the Women's Birth Control League of Japan.
Brazil, Uruguay, and Thailand: Women are granted the right to vote.

India: Independence fighter Rani Gaidinliu is arrested by the British colonial government and sentenced to life imprisonment.
Lake Placid, USA: Norwegian-born figure skater Sonja Henie wins the European skating championship in Paris, the world title in Montreal, as well as another Olympic gold medal at Lake Placid.
Hollywood, USA: Helen Hayes wins Best Actress for her debut sound film, *The Sin of Madelon Claudet*, at the Academy Awards.

1933

New Zealand, September 13: Elizabeth McCombs becomes New Zealand's first female Member of Parliament.
Adyar, India, September 20: The British-born social reformer and theosophist Annie Wood Besant dies, aged 85.
Turin, Italy, September 24: A crowd of 25,000 people flocks to see the Turin Shroud.

County Meath, Ireland, October 2: British artist Elizabeth Thompson Butler, known for her depictions of British military battles, dies at 86.
Tujunga, California, USA, October 5: French-born film actress Renée Adorée dies of tuberculosis at 35 years of age.
Edmonton, Alberta, Canada, October 17: Lawyer, suffragist, social activist, and member of Canada's "Famous Five," Emily Ferguson Murphy, dies, aged 65.

New York, USA, November 27: Jazz singer Billie Holiday makes her first studio recording with band leader Benny Goodman.
Washington DC, USA, December 5: The prohibition against intoxicating liquor ends. The repeal of the law goes into effect after Utah becomes the 36th state to ratify it.
France: American writer Gertrude Stein publishes *The Autobiography of Alice B. Toklas*, which is, in fact, her own autobiography.

New York, USA: Journalist Clare Boothe is appointed editor of *Vanity Fair*.
Germany: Gertrud Scholtz-Klink is appointed Reich women's leader and head of the Nazi Women's League. She urges all Aryan women to bear more children for Germany.
Portugal: Portugal's new constitution declares that everybody is equal, "except for women, the differences resulting from their nature and for the good of the family."

Washington DC, USA: Frances Perkins is appointed Secretary of Labor by President Roosevelt, becoming the first female US Cabinet member.
USA: Senator Hattie Caraway is the first woman to chair a senate committee, the Committee on Enrolled Bills.

1934

Marseilles, France, October 9: Croatian and Macedonian extremists assassinate King Alexander of Yugoslavia and French foreign minister Louis Barthou.
China, October: The communist Red Army commences a great northward march, retreating from southeastern China after being encircled by General Chiang Kai-shek's nationalist forces and suffering heavy losses.
England, November 11: Evangeline Booth is elected.

New York, USA, November 26: The Supreme Court deems "Little Gloria" Vanderbilt's mother an unfit parent, and the child is placed in the custody of her aunt, Gertrude Vanderbilt Whitney.
France, November 30: French aviatrix Hélène Boucher, 26 years of age, is killed when her plane crashes during a training flight.
Turkey, December 5: Turkish women are granted the right to vote and stand for election.

Hollywood, USA: Constance Cummings plays opposite Spencer Tracy in the film *Looking for Trouble*.
Ohio, Michigan, Kentucky, Tennessee, USA: Florence Ellinwood Allen is the first female judge appointed to the sixth circuit court of appeal.
USA: Danish writer Karen Blixen publishes *Seven Gothic Tales*, under the pen name Isak Dinesen.
Cuba, Brazil, Portugal: Women are granted the right to vote, although some restrictions are still in place in Portugal.

India: Indian lawyer and writer Cornelia Sorabji publishes her memoir *India Calling*.
Hollywood, USA: Oscar-winning actress Katharine Hepburn surprises her fans by playing a tomboy faith healer called Trigger Hicks in the film *Spitfire*.
England: British sculptor Barbara Hepworth sculpts *Mother and Child*.

Paris, France: Irène Curie, daughter of Marie and Pierre, and her husband Frédéric Joliot publish their findings on the synthesis of new radioactive elements. They are nominated for the Nobel Prize for Chemistry.
USA: Birth control campaigner Margaret Sanger publishes *Code to Stop the Overproduction of Children*.
Berlin, Germany: Painter and pacifist Käthe Kollwitz, whose work focuses on social injustice, paints *Death and the Woman*.

1935

Baden, Germany, September: Chemist and physicist Ida Tacke Noddack publishes a paper proposing that atoms are split into large fragments, a theory denigrated by the scientific community.
Yenan, China, October 20: Mao Tse-tung concludes the Red Army's Long March.
Weimar, Germany, November 8: Elisabeth Förster-Nietzsche, sister and literary executor of Friedrich Nietzsche, dies, aged 89.

New York, USA, November 23: Former managing editor of *Vanity Fair*, Clare Boothe, marries the founder and publisher of *TIME* magazine, Henry Robinson Luce.
Chicago, USA, November: Katharine Kuh opens her art gallery, which showcases modern American and European art.
Greensburg, Pennsylvania, USA, November: Helen Richey, hired as the first woman airplane pilot, resigns her position after months of ostracism by her male colleagues.

New York, USA, December 5: Mary McLeod Bethune founds the National Council of Negro Women.
Pennsylvania, USA: African-American writer and anthropologist Zora Neale Hurston publishes *Mules and Men*, a study of the African-American people of the southern American states.
USA: Aviator Anne Morrow Lindbergh publishes *North to the Orient*, describing her flights across Alaska, Canada, China, and Japan with her husband Charles Lindbergh.

Myanmar (Burma): Women are granted the right to vote.
England: The British novelist Ivy Compton-Burnett publishes *A House and its Head*.
New York, USA: American anthropologist Margaret Mead publishes *Sex and Temperament in Three Primitive Societies*, which challenges long-held assumptions about gender.
Paris, France: Edith Piaf, who becomes known as the "Little Sparrow," makes her singing debut.

USA: Laura Ingalls Wilder's *Little House on the Prairie*, a children's novel based on her pioneering family's experiences, is published.
Persia: Persia officially changes its name to Iran to gain favor with Germany; "Iran" is derived from the word "Aryan."
UK: Dame Lilian Barker is appointed Assistant Commissioner of Prisons, with special responsibility for female prisoners, and begins working toward reforming the women's prison system in the United Kingdom.

1936

Paris, France, January 6: American-born journalist and feminist Louise Bryant dies, aged 50.

Hollywood, USA, January 10: Screen legend Mary Pickford divorces Douglas Fairbanks.

Lima, Peru, January: Chilean-born *torera* (female bullfighter) Conchita Cintrón has her first public bullfight.

Madrid, Spain, February 16: Dolores Ibárruri, Communist Party politician, is elected to the Cortes (parliament).

Germany, March 7: France decides a large military force will be needed after German troops reoccupy the Rhineland.

France, March 16: Journalist, actress, and founder of the feminist journal *La Fronde,* Marguerite Durand, dies, aged 72.

Berne, Switxerland, March 19: Actress Ursula Andress is born.

Birmingham, England, April 16: Nurse Dorothea Waddington, convicted of murdering two patients with morphine, is hanged.

Vienna, Austria, May 5: Marianne Hainisch, founder of the Austrian women's rights movement, dies, aged 97.

Abyssinia, May 5: Abyssinia is taken by Italy, crumbling under the weight of the massive offensive.

USA, May 14: The film *Show Boat* is released, starring Irene Dunne and Allan Jones.

Tokyo, Japan, May 21: Sada Abe, a former prostitute, is arrested after wandering the streets of Tokyo for three days with her dead lover's penis and scrotum in her hand.

Vienna, Austria, May 28: Bertha Pappenheim dies, aged 77. Known as "Anna O," she was a patient of Sigmund Freud and Doctor Josef Breuer, and a subject in their book *Studies on Hysteria.*

Berlin, Germany, August 1: The Games of the XIth Olympiad open. Hitler temporarily abstains from his actions against Jews.

Athens, Greece, August 4: Prime Minister General John Metaxas leads a military coup and establishes a dictatorship.

Rome, Italy, August 15: Writer and Nobel Prize winner Grazia Deledda dies, aged 64.

London, England, August 31: Elizabeth Cowell is the first female announcer on the new BBC television service.

London/North America, September 4-5: British-Kenyan aviator Beryl Markham flies solo across the Atlantic Ocean from east to west.

London, England, September 21: J. R. R. Tolkien's book *The Hobbit* is published.

1937

Moscow, USSR, January 23: The trial begins of 17 leading Communists accused of participating in Leon Trotsky's plot to overthrow Joseph Stalin's regime and assassinate its leaders.

Göttingen, Germany, February 5: Russian-born writer and psychoanalyst Lou Andreas Salomé dies, a few days before turning 76.

India, April 1: The British Parliament's *Government of India Act,* aimed at transforming India's governmental system, comes into effect, giving provincial governments greater authority.

Hollywood, USA, April 27: Janet Gaynor and Fredric March star in *A Star is Born.*

New York, USA, May 3: Author Margaret Mitchell wins a Pulitzer Prize for her debut novel *Gone With the Wind.*

New Jersey, USA, May 6: The German airship *Hindenburg* bursts into flame while mooring, killing 36 people.

London, England, May 12: The coronation of King George VI and Queen Elizabeth takes place at Westminster Abbey.

USSR, May 13: Ekaterina Geladze, the mother of Joseph Stalin, dies, aged 79.

South America, May 26: The Chaco War between Bolivia and Paraguay comes to an end.

Vienna, Austria, June 2: Soprano Nuri Hadzic stars in the première of the opera *Lulu,* written by Austrian composer Alban Berg.

Los Angeles, USA, June 7: Actress Jean Harlow dies, aged 26.

Washington DC, USA, June 25: The *National Fair Labor Standards Act* rules in favor of a minimum wage law for both women and men.

South Pacific Ocean, July 2: Aviator Amelia Earhart disappears between New Guinea and Howland Island near the end of a round-the-world flight.

Peking, China, July 28: Japanese forces complete their occupation of the city following an initial strike on July 7 at Lukochiao.

USA, July: The American Medical Association now teaches students about birth control and the various forms of contraception.

Saint-Brice-sous-Forêt, France, August 11: American-born novelist Edith Wharton dies, aged 75.

1938

London, England, January 3: The government plans to provide all schoolchildren with gas masks.

Vienna, Austria, January 19: Women's rights campaigner and writer, Rosa Mayreder, dies, aged 79. She was a former head of the International Women's League for Peace and Liberty.

Washington, USA, January 25: Gertrude Simmons Bonnin, also known as Zitkala-Sa (Red Bird), writer and campaigner for Native American rights, dies, aged 61.

London, England, January: Art collector, Peggy Guggenheim, opens the Guggenheim-Jeune art gallery. Her first exhibition shows works by Cocteau.

Oxford, England, February: The drug, diethylstilbestrol (DES), is synthesized.

Saudi Arabia, March 3: Oil is discovered in Saudi Arabia.

Hollywood, USA, March 10: Luise Rainer wins the Best Actress Academy Award for her performance in *The Good Earth,* based on the novel by Pearl S. Buck.

Nanking, China, March: Japanese troops slaughter up to 300,000 civilians and prisoners of war in a massacre.

Paris, France, April 7: Suzanne Valadon, artist and model for Degas, Renoir, and Toulouse-Lautrec, among others, dies, aged 73.

Toronto, Canada, May 26: Soprano Teresa Stratas is born.

Berlin, Germany, June 20: Communist resistance activist, Liselotte Hermann, convicted of treason, is beheaded, a few days before her twenty-ninth birthday.

USA, June: The *Helen Keller Journals* are published, in which Keller recalls four decades with her teacher and friend Anne Sullivan Macy.

Doncaster, England, July 20: Film and television actress, Diana Rigg, is born.

Miami, Florida, USA, July 21: Janet Reno, the first female Attorney-General of the USA, is born.

Rome, Italy, August 3: Mussolini introduces his anti-Semitic laws into Italy, following the lead of his German allies.

Hollywood, USA, August 26: Norma Shearer plays the title role in *Marie Antoinette* opposite Tyrone Power and John Barrymore.

Zagreb, Croatia, September 21: Writer Ivana Brlic-Mazuranic, twice nominated for the Nobel Prize for Literature, commits suicide, aged 64.

Czechoslovakia, October 5: Hitler's army marches into Czechoslovakia.

Hollywood, USA, November 1: Margaret Lockwood and Michael Redgrave star in Alfred Hitchcock's movie, the suspense thriller *The Lady Vanishes.*

1939

Paris, France, January 12: Romanian-born soprano Hariclea Darclée dies, aged 78.

Melbourne, Australia, January 29: Writer, scholar, and feminist Germaine Greer is born.

Washington DC, USA, January: The Daughters of the American Revolution refuse to let African-American singer Marian Anderson perform at Constitution Hall.

New York, USA, February 15: Lillian Hellman's new play *The Little Foxes* opens on Broadway with Tallulah Bankhead in the lead role.

Hollywood, USA, February 23: Bette Davis wins the Academy Award for Best Actress in the 1938 film *Jezebel,* co-starring Henry Fonda.

Czechoslovakia, March 16: The German army occupies Prague, and Czechoslovakia becomes a Nazi protectorate.

Spain, April 1: Franco declares the end of the Civil War.

New York, USA, April 18: Polish-born actress Bertha Kalich, a star of the city's Yiddish theater scene, dies, aged 64.

Oslo, Norway, April 20: Gro Harland Brundtland, later prime minister of Norway and director of the World Health Organization, is born.

New York, USA, April: Jazz singer Billie Holiday records "Strange Fruit," an anti-lynching song written by Lewis Allan (Abel Meeropol).

Cambridge, England, May 6: Dorothy Garrod is appointed the Disney Professor of Archeology at Cambridge University, the university's first woman professor.

Rome, Italy, May 22: Mussolini signs a military pact with Hitler, obligating Italy to fight alongside Germany.

Florida, USA, June 4: The USA denies entry to the *St Louis,* a ship carrying 907 Jewish refugees, after it is turned away by Cuba.

Sheffield, England, June 5: British novelist Margaret Drabble is born.

Britain, July: The Women's Land Army is re-formed after disbanding at the end of the Great War.

New York, USA, July 22: Jane M. Bolin is the first African-American woman to be appointed as a judge.

Europe, September 3: Britain and France declare war on Germany in accord with treaty obligations to Poland, followed by Australia, New Zealand, and India.

Fukushima Prefecture, Japan, September 22: Mountaineer Junko Tabei, the first woman to reach the top of Mt Everest, is born.

Poland, September 29: The Nazis and Soviets divide up Poland. More than 2 million Jews reside in Nazi-controlled areas, and 1.3 million in the Soviet area. Warsaw surrenders.

1936

Spain, October 1: General Franco is appointed commander-in-chief of the rebel forces in the civil war after capturing Toledo.
New York, USA, October 20: Annie Sullivan Macy, the teacher best known for her work with deaf and blind girl Helen Keller, dies, aged 70.
London, England, November 16: Edward VIII announces his intention of marrying Mrs Wallis Simpson.
Hollywood, USA, November 17: Austrian-American contralto Ernestine Schumann-Heink dies, aged 75.

UK, November 20: New *Matrimonial Causes Act* permits divorce, but only on grounds of drunkenness, incurable insanity, cruelty, desertion, or imprisonment on death row.
London, England, December 12: Prince Albert is proclaimed King George VI after his brother Edward VIII abdicates the British throne.
China, December 12-25: Nationalist general Chiang Kai-shek is kidnapped in an attempt to force him to negotiate with the Communists against their enemy, Japan.

Washington DC, USA, December 30: First Lady Eleanor Roosevelt's daily syndicated newspaper column called "My Day" has been running for one year. She uses the column to express her opinions on a range of topics, including the plight of the poor.
Spain: Dancer Antonia Mercé, whose stage name is La Argentina, after the country of her birth, dies at 48 years of age. She is often referred to as the "Flamenco Pavlova."

Denver, USA: The first Tampax tampons are sold in the US. Tampons had been patented by Dr Earle Haas in 1929.
Belfast, Ireland: Social reformer, writer, and promoter of birth control and sex education in the United Kingdom, Dr Marie C. Stopes, opens the Mother's Clinic, the first family planning clinic in Ireland.
London, England: Writer and painter Phyllis Pearsall creates and publishes *A to Z: The Atlas and Guide to London and Suburbs*.

England/USA: Russian-American novelist Ayn Rand publishes *We, the Living*, which describes life in Russia under Soviet rule. Other important novels released this year include *The House of Incest* by Anaïs Nin, *Jamaica Inn* by Daphne du Maurier, and *Nightwood* by Djuna Barnes.
London, England: Laura Knight is the first woman to be admitted into the Royal Academy of Arts.

1937

Clarksdale, Mississippi, USA, September 26: Bessie Smith, considered the greatest blues singer of all time, dies, aged about 42.
China, September 29: General Chiang Kai-shek unites forces with his rival, Communist Mao Tse-tung, against the Japanese.
Baku, Azerbaijan, October 15: Actress Pamphylia Tanailidi, accused of being a spy, is executed.

New York, USA, December 27: Mae West is banned from radio broadcasts by NBC on the grounds of indecency.
Ireland, December 29: The new Irish Constitution comes into force and the Irish Free State officially becomes Eire.
New York, USA, December: *Ruth Wakefield's Toll House Tried and True Recipes*, which includes her famous Toll House cookies, is published.

Vienna, Austria: Anna Freud, the daughter of Sigmund Freud, publishes *The Ego and the Mechanisms of Defence*.
China: Song Qingling, widow of Sun Yat-sen, organizes the China Defence League, providing medical care to rural Chinese.
Denmark and England: Danish writer Isak Dinesen (Karen Blixen-Finecke) publishes *Out of Africa*.
Cambridge, England: British chemist Dorothy Crowfoot Hodgkin is awarded a doctorate from Cambridge University.

Paris, France: Acclaimed choreographer Bronislava Nijinska creates one of her most famous ballets, *Chopin Concerto*.
Uttar Pradesh, India: Vijaya Lakshmi Pandit is the first woman to be given a government portfolio.
Paris, France: Nobel Prize winner Irène Joliot-Curie is appointed professor of science at the Sorbonne.
Manchuria: The Japanese invade. Thousands of girls and young women are abducted and forced into having sex with Japanese soldiers.

The Philippines: Women are granted the right to vote.
Edinburgh, Scotland: Jessie Chrystal MacMillan, the first woman to graduate in science from the University of Edinburgh, lawyer, and suffragette, dies, aged 55.
New York, USA: German-born American psychoanalyst Karen Horney publishes *The Neurotic Personality of Our Time*.

1938

Pennsylvania, USA, November 8: Crystal Bird Fauset is the first African-American woman elected to a state legislature.
Berlin, Germany, November 9: Jewish shops, homes, and synagogues are looted and destroyed as Hitler puts into practice throughout Germany his anti-Jewish policies.
Stockholm, Sweden, December 10: American author, Pearl S. Buck, wins the Nobel Prize in Literature for her novel, *The Good Earth*.

East London, South Africa, December 22: Naturalist Marjorie Courtenay-Latimer identifies a coelacanth, a fish thought to be extinct, when it is hauled up in a fishing trawler.
London, England, December: Gracie Fields stars in the musical comedy film, *Keep Smiling*.
New York, USA: Doctor Dorothy Hansine Andersen discovers that cystic fibrosis is a distinctive disease, and begins working on a means of diagnosis.

Buenos Aires, Argentina: Chilean-born poet and feminist, Gabriela Mistral (Lucila Godoy y Alcayaga), publishes *Tala*, dealing with themes of motherhood and childhood.
Bolivia and Uzbekistan: Women are granted the right to vote.
China: Former actress and later notorious political figure, Jiang Qing, marries Mao Tse-tung.
England: Physician, feminist, and politician Edith Summerskill establishes the Married Women's Association, which is aimed at achieving equality in marriage.

Harlem, New York, USA: Jazz singer Ella Fitzgerald records "A-Tisket, A-Tasket," a huge hit.
Dublin, Ireland: Revolutionary, actress, and feminist, Maude Gonne, publishes a memoir, *A Servant of the Queen*.
Shanxi Province, China: When Japanese forces invade the region, British missionary Gladys Aylward leads nearly 100 children to safety on a 27-day trek.
Hollywood, USA: Fashion designer Edith Head is the first woman chief designer in a major movie studio.

Bamburgh, Scotland: One hundred years after Grace Darling heroically rescued shipwrecked passengers off the Scottish coast, the Grace Darling National Memorial Museum opens to commemorate her bravery.
Norway: Women are permitted to join the military services.
California, USA: American tennis champion Helen Wills-Moody, who won this year's women's singles title at Wimbledon, announces her retirement from the sport.

1939

South Africa and Canada, September: South Africa (September 6) and Canada (September 10) declare war on Germany.
Germany, October: The Nazis begin a program to euthanaze the sick and disabled in Germany.
Ottawa, Canada, November 18: Canadian writer and literary critic Margaret Atwood is born.
Finland, November 30: The USSR attacks Finland after strategic negotiations of November 12 fail.

Atlanta, Georgia, USA, December 15: *Gone With the Wind* premières. African-American co-star Hattie McDaniel and other African-American cast members are prevented from attending.
Georgia, USA, December 22: Blues singer Ma Rainey (Gertrude Pridgett), known as "Mother of the Blues," dies, aged 57.
Buenos Aires, Argentina: Actress Eva Duarte is given a starring role in a radio program.
El Salvador: Women are granted the right to vote.

London, England: South African-born composer Priaulx Rainier writes her *First String Quartet*.
England: Actress Anna Neagle stars in a film version of the life of nurse and war heroine Edith Cavell.
Paris, France: Chemist Marguerite Perey discovers the element francium.
London, England: The record-setting Irish aviatrix Lady Sophie Mary Heath dies, aged 43.
Paris, France: French-born writer Anaïs Nin, now an American citizen, publishes *The Winter of Artifice*.

Mexico City, Mexico: Artist Frida Kahlo paints *The Two Fridas*, a double self-portrait conveying her anguish over her divorce from artist Diego Rivera.
Hollywood, USA: This year was an exceptional one for quality motion pictures. Some notable women's roles include Judy Garland in *The Wizard of Oz*, Vivien Leigh in *Gone With the Wind*, Merle Oberon in *Wuthering Heights*, and Bette Davis in *Dark Victory*.

Michigan, USA: Doctors Pearl Kendrick and Grace Eldering publish the results of their trials with a vaccine against pertussis (whooping cough).
New York, USA: German-born psychoanalyst Karen Horney publishes *New Ways in Psychoanalysis*, suggesting that environmental factors have an influence on personality.
New York, USA: Marjorie Kinnan Rawlings is awarded the Pulitzer Prize for her bestselling 1938 novel *The Yearling*.

1940

London, England, January 8: Food rationing is introduced to the UK. Butter, sugar, meat, and other essentials may only be purchased with government-issued coupons.
Europe, February 20: Hitler orders his U-boat captains to attack all shipping, Allied vessels and neutral ships alike.
Hollywood, USA, February 29: *Gone With the Wind* wins eight Academy Awards, including Best Actress for British-born Vivien Leigh, and Best Supporting Actress for Hattie McDaniel.

Moscow, USSR, March 13: Russia defeats Finland following its 200,000-strong invasion on January 2; a peace treaty is signed in which Finland loses territory.
Sweden, March 16: Writer Selma Lagerlöf, who won the 1909 Nobel Prize for Literature, dies, aged 81.
Nyeri, Kenya, April 1: Politician and environmentalist Wangari Maathai is born. She becomes the first African-American woman to win a Nobel Prize.

Aquitaine, France, April 9: Acclaimed British stage actress Mrs Patrick Campbell (Beatrice Stella Tanner) dies, aged 75.
Hollywood, USA, April 12: *Rebecca*, the film adaptation of Daphne du Maurier's novel, is released starring Joan Fontaine and Laurence Olivier.
Canada, April 25: The women of Quebec are the final non-indigenous group in Canada to receive voting rights. Indigenous women still cannot vote.

Europe, May 10: After invading Norway and Denmark on April 9, Germany invades Luxembourg, Belgium, the Netherlands, and France.
Netherlands, May 13: The Netherlands surrenders to Germany; Queen Wilhelmina escapes to England.
Toronto, Canada, May 14: American women's rights campaigner and anarchist "Red Emma" Goldman dies, aged 70.
Stockholm, Sweden, May 25: Danish painter Marie Krøyer dies, aged 72.

Dalkey, Ireland, May 28: Novelist and journalist Maeve Binchy is born.
Rome, Italy, June 10: Under an agreement made with Germany on May 30, Italy declares war on Britain and France.
Clarksville, Tennessee, USA, June 23: Wilma Rudolph, the first African-American to win three gold medals in a single Olympic Games, is born.
Chicago, USA, June 30: Dale Messick, creator of the comic strip *Brenda Starr, Reporter,* becomes the first female comic strip artist to be syndicated.

1941

London, England, January 5: Aviator Amy Johnson is believed drowned after her airplane goes down in the Thames Estuary.
California, USA, March 8: Princess Stephanie Hohenlohe, a Jewish member of German royalty and Nazi spy, is arrested.
Sussex, England, March 28: Novelist Virginia Woolf commits suicide, aged 59.
New York, USA, April 1: *Watch on the Rhine,* by playwright Lillian Hellman, opens on Broadway.

Cambridge, Massachusetts, USA, April 13: American astronomer Annie Jump Cannon dies, aged 77.
London, England, May 10: A mass bombing is carried out by Germany in the city's worst air raid.
Scotland, May 10: Rudolf Hess, Hitler's deputy, is detained in the United Kingdom.
Hollywood, USA, May 11: Actress Peggy Shannon dies, aged 31.
North Atlantic Ocean, May 27: Germany's battleship *Bismarck* is destroyed by British forces.

New York, USA, May: Hannah Arendt, a German Jewish essayist, arrives in New York City from Germany via occupied France.
USSR, June 22: Germany invades the USSR, thus breaking the Nazi-Soviet pact.
New Zealand, June 26: After a decree from the prime minister's office, all women's volunteer units, which have sprung up since the beginning of the war, are merged into the New Zealand Women's War Auxiliary Service.

Syria, June 28: Allied troops take Damascus.
French Indochina, July 27: Japanese troops take Saigon.
Canada, August 13: The Canadian Women's Army Corps is formed.
Elabuga, USSR, August 31: Russian poet and author Marina Ivanovna Tsvetaieva commits suicide.
Oryol, USSR, September 11: Russian revolutionary personality Maria Spiridovna dies, aged 57.
Chicago, USA, October 9: Helen Morgan, American singer and actress, dies, aged 41.

Cannes, France, October 27: French soprano and author, Georgette Leblanc, dies, aged 66.
New York, USA October 31: Biologist Rachel Carson publishes *Under the Sea-Wind.*
USSR, October: Women are recruited for all-female pilot regiments.
Pittsburgh, Pennsylvania, USA, November 12: Mary Cardwell Dawson founds the National Negro Opera Company, the first African-American opera company in the country.

1942

Washington DC, USA January 1: The Declaration of United Nations to pledge support for the Atlantic Charter is signed by 25 countries.
Mexico City, Mexico, January 5: Tina Modotti, actress, photographer, and radical, dies of heart failure, although the exact cause of her death is disputed, many believing she was murdered for her political beliefs and actions.
Mount Potosi, Nevada, USA, January 17: Actress Carole Lombard is confirmed among 22 dead found in the wreckage of a TWA flight.

Berlin, Germany, January 20: Nazi leaders at the Wannsee Conference structure the "final solution of the Jewish question," with an aim to exterminate over 11 million European Jews.
Darwin, Australia, February 19: Australia's northernmost city becomes a ghost town following Japanese air strikes.
London, February 23: BBC announcer, Una Marson (1905-1965), broadcasts to British troops in the West Indies from London studio.

Canada, February 25: Men of Japanese descent living in Canada are removed from their homes and interned in camps.
Germany, March 28: Allied forces drop thousands of bombs on Lubeck, near Berlin.
USA, May 15: US Congress creates the Women's Army Auxiliary Corps.
Illinois, USA, May 18: Gertrude Scharff Goldhaber discovers that neutrons are emitted in spontaneous fission; her findings are classified by the US government and will not be published until 1946.

Sydney, Australia, May 31: Three midget Japanese submarines enter Sydney Harbour; one manages to fire two torpedoes and sink the barracks ship *Kuttabul.*
Midway Atoll, USA, June 7: Following an attack by US naval forces, the Japanese Navy withdraws from the Pacific atoll.
Amsterdam, Netherlands, June 12: Anne Frank receives a diary for her 13th birthday; a month later she and her family go into hiding and she will diarize the experience.

Siam, June: Japan begins forcing 60,000 Allied POWs to construct a crucial 260-mile (418 km) rail link between Burma and Siam.
London, England, July 1: BBC announces the deaths of 700,000 Jews in Hitler's gas chambers.
USA, July 30: US Congress creates Women Accepted for Volunteer Service (WAVES), the US Navy's arm for female volunteers.
New Zealand, July: The New Zealand Government creates the NZ Women's Army Auxiliary Corps, paying servicewomen.

1943

Tripoli, Libya, January 23: British forces capture Tripoli.
Stalingrad, USSR, February 2: Axis troops surrender to the Red Army.
Germany, February 16: Member of the Red Orchestra resistance group, Mildred Harnack, is executed for treason.
London, February 16: The British government accepts the principle, long championed by Member of Parliament Eleanor Rathbone, of paying a child allowance to parents.

Rosenstrasse, Berlin, Germany, February 27-March 6: In the only protest of German people against the Nazis, women campaign against the imprisonment of their Jewish husbands. The group of 1,700 men is released.
Texas, USA, March 21: Cornelia Fort crashes her plane and becomes the first American woman to die flying a military aircraft.
Kentucky, USA, March 26: Elsie Ott is the first American woman to receive an Air Medal for her services as an army nurse.

Austria, March 30: Sister Restituta Kafka is beheaded by the Nazis for putting up crucifixes in a hospital.
Izieu, France, April: Sabina Zlatin opens a farmhouse to hide Jewish children from Nazi capture.
England, April 30: Writer and social reformer Beatrice Potter Webb dies, aged 85.
USA, May 29: Norman Rockwell's painting "Rosie the Riveter" appears on the cover of the *Saturday Evening Post.*

USA, May 30: Play commences in the newly formed All-American Girls Professional Baseball League, founded by Chicago Cubs owner Philip K. Wrigley.
Italy, July 25: Premier Benito Mussolini is ousted. A new Italian government under Marshal Pietro Badoglio places him under arrest.
Kharkov, USSR, August 1: Renowned Soviet fighter pilot Lilya Litvyak is shot down by German planes over Kharkov.

USA, August 5: Jacqueline Cochran is appointed to direct the newly formed Women Airforce Service Pilots (WASP), a merger of the Women's Auxiliary Flying Squadron and the Women's Flying Training Detachment.
Italy, August 17: Allied forces occupy Sicily. With North Africa already under occupation, the Allies now control the Mediterranean Sea.
Canberra, Australia, August 21: Dame Enid Lyons and Dorothy Tangney are the first women elected to the Australian Federal Parliament.

1940

Paris, France, June: Following the German occupation of France, scientists Irène Joliot-Curie and her husband Frédéric Joliot send their heavy water to England for safekeeping, and hide their stockpile of uranium. They also apply for patents for the utilization of atomic energy, and win the Barnard College Gold Medal for meritorious service to science.

USA, June: The 23-year-old writer Carson McCullers causes a stir in the literary world when she publishes *The Heart is a Lonely Hunter*.

London, England, June: Princess Juliana of the Netherlands is sent to Canada to establish a government-in-exile.

Hollywood, USA, July 26: The movie *Pride and Prejudice*, based on Jane Austen's novel, opens. It stars Greer Garson, Laurence Olivier, and Maureen O'Sullivan.

Coyoacán, Mexico, August 21: Soviet leader Leon Trotsky is assassinated with an ice-pick.

Lascaux, France, September 12: Four schoolboys discover Paleolithic paintings in a cave.

Berlin, Germany, September 27: Japan, Germany, and Italy sign a 10-year pact.

London, England, September: Buckingham Palace is bombed several times with the royal family in residence.

London, England, November 7: The Women's Corps, which reports to the Free French Forces, is established.

UK, November 30: Germany mass-bombs regional cities Glasgow, Birmingham, Coventry, Manchester, and Sheffield.

Hollywood, USA, December 1: *The Philadelphia Story*, starring Katharine Hepburn, Cary Grant, and James Stewart, is released.

England, December 17: Amateur mathematician Alicia Boole Stott dies, aged 80.

Hollywood, USA: Photographer Ruth Harriet Louise, MGM studio's official photographer and the only female portrait photographer working in Hollywood, dies of complications in childbirth, aged 37.

New York, USA: Founding member of the American Civil Liberties Union, Elizabeth Gurley Flynn, is expelled for being a Communist.

USA: The Equal Rights Amendment to the constitution, proposed in 1925, is endorsed by the Republican Party.

Greece: Journalist and women's rights campaigner Kalliroe Parren dies, aged about 79.

USA: American anthropologist Ruth Benedict publishes *Race: Science and Politics*, in which she attacks racism and other forms of bigotry.

1941

Petrishchevo, USSR, November 29: Zoya Anatolyevna Kosmodemyanskaya, a Russian partisan volunteer, is captured and killed by Nazi troops.

London, England, November: Vera Lynn's radio show makes her the sweetheart of the British troops.

Minnesota, USA, December 5: Australian nurse Sister Elizabeth Kenny's new treatment for infantile paralysis is approved.

Honolulu, Hawaii, December 7: Japanese planes make a surprise attack on the US fleet at Pearl Harbor.

Europe, December 8: Hungary and Romania declare war on Britain. Britain reciprocates.

Washington DC, USA, December 8: The USA, Britain, Australia, and New Zealand declare war on Japan. Congresswoman and pacifist Jeanette Rankin casts the only vote against US involvement in World War II.

Central America, December 11: Cuba, Costa Rica, Nicaragua, and the Dominican Republic declare war on Germany and Italy.

USA, December 11: The USA reciprocates Germany's and Italy's declarations of war.

Europe, December 12: Hungary, Romania, and Bulgaria declare war on the USA.

London, England, December 18: The *National Service Act* is passed, conscripting all women aged between 20 and 40 to register for war work.

Hong Kong, December 25: Japan seizes Hong Kong.

St Petersburg (Leningrad), USSR, December 25: Over 3,000 people have starved to death since the German siege on the city began in September.

USA, December: Wonder Woman first appears in *All Star Comics #8*.

France: French photographer Dora Maar models for her lover, Pablo Picasso. The painting *Dora Maar au Chat* is considered a masterpiece.

Ethiopia: Emperor Haile Selassie and Empress Menon return from exile.

France: An independent women's volunteer corps is created within the French Air Force.

Panama: Women win the right to vote.

South Africa: Elizabeth Tshatshu of the AmaNtinde line becomes acting paramount chief of the Xhosa Tribe.

USA: Marlene Dietrich stars in *The Flame of New Orleans*.

1942

Auschwitz, Poland, August 9: Carmelite nun, Edith Stein, is executed by Nazis.

USA, August 11: Actress Hedy Lamarr and composer George Antheill patent a shield for wireless radio communications.

Dieppe, France, August 19: A nine-day Allied offensive takes out key German infrastructure.

Auschwitz, Poland, August 19: French-Jewish author Irène Némirovsky dies in a camp, leaving a novel, *Suite Francaise*, about a village occupied by Nazi forces.

Boisrenard, France, September 24: Andrée Borrel and Lise de Baissac are parachuted into occupied France, the first female Special Operations Executive (SOE) agents to do so.

USA, September: Nancy Love is appointed to direct the new Women's Auxiliary Ferrying Squadron (WAFS).

Volgograd (Stalingrad), USSR, October: German aerial attacks kill thousands of civilians and destroy 80 percent of the city area.

Theresienstadt, Europe, October 9: Elise Richter, Austrian professor, is deported to a concentration camp.

Papua New Guinea, November 2: Australian troops take Kokoda after surviving horrific conditions of steep inclines, mud, and malaria, while fighting on the Kokoda Track.

UK, November 6: Women are allowed into church without hats.

Morroco and Algeria, North Africa, November 8: A major Allied invasion of North Africa, Operation Torch, is launched.

USA, November 23: The US Coast Guard Women's Auxiliary is formed.

Minnesota, USA, December 17: The Sister Kenny Institute for trainee nurses and physiotherapists opens.

USA, December: Superintendent of the Army Nurses Corps, Julia Flikke, becomes the first woman colonel in the US Army.

USA: Black author Margaret Walker Alexander writes her famous poem, "For My People."

USA: Aviator Beryl Markham publishes her memoirs, *West With the Night*, although many speculate it was written by her husband, journalist Raoul Schumacher.

USA: Mary McCarthy publishes her first novel, *The Company She Keeps*.

New York, USA: Dawn Powell publishes her novel *A Time to be Born*.

USA: J. Howard Miller paints an image of a factory worker for Westinghouse, with the slogan "We can do it!"—an image commonly dubbed *Rosie the Riveter*.

Dominican Republic: Women win the right to vote.

Warsaw, Poland: Irena Sendler poses as a nurse and persuades women that children will be safer if smuggled out of the Warsaw Ghetto.

1943

Italy, September 12: Italy surrenders unconditionally to Allied forces.

China, September 13: General Chiang Kai-shek is elected president of the Republic of China.

USA, September 30: The Women's Army Corps is formed, affording women the same status as other army services, and replacing the Women's Auxiliary Army Corps.

Paris, France, September: After months of listening and flirting with German officers, spy Jeannie Rousseau has enough information to send a detailed report on V-2 rockets to England.

Italy, October 13: Marshal Badoglio declares war on Germany.

Italy, October 14: Allied forces take control of southern Italy.

Lyon, France, October 21: Lucie Aubrac, together with others in her French Resistance group, frees her husband Raymond Aubrac from Nazi imprisonment.

Paris, France, October 22: Actress Catherine Deneuve is born.

Lebanon, November 22: France grants Lebanon independence.

Auschwitz, Poland, November 30: Diarist and letter writer Etty Hillesum dies.

Cairo, Egypt, December 1–4: The USA. Britain, and China sign the Cairo Declaration, a joint plan to force Japan to surrender.

Lancashire, England, December 22: Author and artist Beatrix Potter dies, aged 77. She is best known for *The Tale of Peter Rabbit*.

USSR, December 31: Soviet troops force the Axis powers to retreat from the central area of the Eastern Front in Belarus (White Russia).

Boston, USA: Doctor, chemist, and social reformer Alice Hamilton publishes her autobiography, *Exploring the Dangerous Trades*, which outlines her work studying industrial and occupational diseases.

USA, December: More than 486,000 women are employed in the aircraft industry.

New York, USA: Betty Smith's coming-of-age novel, *A Tree Grows in Brooklyn*, is published, and becomes a bestseller.

USA: Physicist Elda Emma Anderson is recruited to help further develop the atomic bomb at Los Alamos.

USA: George Papanicolaou and Herbert Traut publish "Diagnosis of Uterine Cancer by the Vaginal Smear," which paves the way for Pap smears to become a routine way to detect cervical cancer.

Paris, France: Artist Françoise Gilot meets Pablo Picasso.

France: The Rochambelles Corps is created. It consists of nurses and first-aid personnel, and through it female staff will take part in campaigns in Tunisia, France, Italy, and Germany.

1944

Argentina, January 22: Juan Perón meets Eva Duarte at a charity event.
Porstmouth, England, January 19: Helen Duncan is arrested after holding a séance in Portsmouth. Her accurate pronouncement on the sinking of a British warship had aroused suspicion.
Berlin, Germany, January 21: Allied bombing leaves the city in ruins.
Birmingham, Alabama, USA, January 26: Radical and writer Angela Davis is born.

January 27: The siege of Leningrad is lifted; over 640,000 people died during the 900 days of the siege.
Truk Island, The Carolines, February 18: Japanese soldiers massacre a hundred women (mostly girls forced into prostitution) in a dugout behind the naval base on Truk Island.
USSR, February 1: A new USSR constitution allows Soviet republics to conduct their own armies and negotiations.
Eatonton, Georgia, USA, February 9: Writer Alice Walker is born.

Hungary, March 23: A German puppet government is created in Hungary after German occupation on March 22.
Izieu, France, April 6: Sabina Zlatin's children's home, where Jewish children found refuge, is raided by Klaus Barbie's Lyon Gestapo.
Broadway, New York, USA, April 12: Lillian Hellman's play, The Searching Wind, has its first performance.
France, April 21: The Comité Français de Libérations National pronounces the ordinance which grants women the right to vote.

Rome, June 4: Rome is liberated by Allied forces.
Japan, June 15: The USA begins heavy bombing of Kyushu, Japan.
Iceland, June 17: Iceland breaks free of Danish rule, becoming a republic.
Natzweiler, Germany, July 6: SOE spies Vera Leigh, Sonia Olschanezky, Andrée Borrel, and Diana Rowden, are executed by the Nazis.
Rastenburg, East Prussia, July 20: Count von Stauffenberg, German officer, plants a bomb in an attempt to assassinate Hitler. The bomb explodes, but Hitler survives.

India, August 11: An advance by Allied troops forces the Japanese to retreat to Burma.
Paris, France, August 23: Citizens and the French Resistance assist Allied forces in taking Paris.
Buchenwald, Germany, August 27: Princess Mafalda of Savoy dies after being seriously wounded during an American bombing raid on a munitions factory in Buchenwald concentration camp.

1945

Poland, January 27: Soviet forces seize the Auschwitz concentration camp to find thousands of starving prisoners near death; most prisoners had already been herded out of the camp by the SS.
USSR, February 4-11: At a conference in Yalta, President Roosevelt, Prime Minister Churchill, and Marshal Stalin finalize their plans for the defeat of Germany.
Palestine, February 13: Henrietta Szold, US Zionist, feminist, and founder of Hadassah, dies at age 85.

Germany, February 14: The city of Dresden lies in ruins after massive bombing by Allied forces.
Bergen-Belsen, Netherlands, March: Diarist Anne Frank dies of typhus.
Netherlands, March: Queen Wilhelmina returns to her home country briefly.
Georgia, USA, March 5: African-American Lena Baker is denied clemency by the State of Georgia, and executed for the murder of her former white employer. She was tried and sentenced in one day by an all-male, all-white jury.

Los Angeles, USA, March 7: Ingrid Bergman wins the Best Actress Academy Award for her performance in Gaslight.
USA, March 8: The first African-American nurse to serve in World War II, Phyllis Mae Daley, receives her commission in the US Navy Nurse Corps.
Warm Springs, Georgia, USA, April 12: President Franklin D. Roosevelt dies. Harold S. Truman is sworn in as US president.

Netherlands, April 17: Dutch resistance fighter Hannie Schaft (known as "The Girl with the Red Hair") is executed by the Nazis.
San Francisco, USA, April 25: Heads of government meet to establish the United Nations, the organization that is to replace the League of Nations. It will officially come into existence on October 24.
Milan, Italy, April 28: Mussolini and his mistress, Clara Petacci, are strung up for public display after being shot dead by partisans.

Germany, April: Allied forces liberate Nazi concentration camps, finding starved, critically ill captives and grounds piled with rotting corpses.
Berlin, Germany April 30: German test pilot Hanna Reitsch flies a Luftwaffe general into Berlin to meet with Hitler, dodging Soviet anti-aircraft fire.
Berlin, Germany, April 30: As Soviet forces move to take Berlin, Hitler commits suicide in his bunker by shooting himself. His newly wed wife, Eva Braun, poisons herself and dies.

1946

Southampton, England, January 26: The first official boatload of GI brides sails on the SS Argentina.
London, England, January 30: The first meeting of the United Nations General Assembly is held.
Fulton, Missouri, USA, March 5: Winston Churchill makes a speech, "Sinews of Peace," in which he warns the western powers of the dangers of Soviet expansion and refers to an "iron curtain" descending across Europe.

Paris, France, March 6: France recognizes Vietnam as a free state within the Indochina Federation.
New York, USA, March: Doctor Mamie Clark founds the Northside Center for the assessment of child development.
Los Angeles, USA, March 7: Joan Crawford takes the Oscar for Best Actress in the title role of Mildred Pierce. Muriel Box, with her husband, Sydney Box, wins the Oscar for the Best Original Screenplay for The Seventh Veil.

Australia, April 11: The War Crimes Commission reports that Japan routinely committed acts of torture on Australian prisoners of war.
Geneva, Switzerland, April 18: The League of Nations is dissolved.
USA, May 1: Emma Clarissa Clement is named Mother of the Year. She is the first black woman to be given the honor.
San Francisco, USA, May 2-4: Nine guards are taken hostage by inmates at Alcatraz prison; five people are killed.

New York, May 15: Georgia O'Keeffe gives the first solo exhibition by a female artist at New York's Museum of Modern Art.
New York, USA, May 16: Irving Berlin's musical, Annie Get Your Gun, opens on Broadway. Ethel Merman stars as Annie Oakley. The song "There's No Business Like Show Business" is a hit.
USA, May 25: Patty Smith Hill, credited with writing "Happy Birthday to You," dies at age 78.

London, England, May 30: The organic farming charity, the Soil Association, is founded. It is inspired by Lady Eve Balfour's 1943 book The Living Soil.
Italy, June 3: Italy abolishes its monarchy after a referendum and becomes a republic.
Argentina, June 4: Juan Perón is inaugurated as Argentina's first president. His wife, Eva, is fondly known as Evita by the people of Argentina.

1947

London, England, February 6: Trade unionist and politician "Red" Ellen Wilkinson dies of an overdose of barbiturates, aged 65.
Paris, France, February 10: Peace treaties for Italy, Finland, Hungary, Romania, and Bulgaria are signed.
Germany, February 20: The state of Prussia is abolished and becomes part of the newly formed Federal Republic of Germany and German Democratic Republic.
New York, USA, March 9: Carrie Lane Chapman Catt, feminist and political activist, dies, aged 88.

Los Angeles, USA, March 13: Olivia de Havilland wins the Best Actress Academy Award for her performance in To Each His Own.
Los Angeles, USA, March 21: Premiere of the movie The Egg and I, a romantic comedy starring Claudette Colbert, Fred MacMurray, and Marjorie Main.
Washington DC, USA, April 16: The Army-Navy Nurse Act is passed by US Congress, granting permanent commissions and officer status to female military nurses.

New York, USA, April 24: Writer Willa Cather dies, aged 73.
Connecticut, USA, April: Six doctors are sacked from three Catholic hospitals for supporting a bill which would allow them to provide birth control information to a patient whose life might be endangered by pregnancy.
Tokyo, Japan, May 3: Japan's new constitution guarantees women's equality.
London, England, May 9: The first laundrette in Britain opens in Queensway for a six-month trial.

London, England, May 23: Britain agrees to the plan proposed by Lord Mountbatten, the Viceroy of India, to divide India into two states—one for Muslims and one for Hindus.
Jerusalem, Palestine, March-May: A Bedouin shepherd finds mysterious religious scrolls in Qumran on the Dead Sea.
Paris, France, March-May: Christian Dior launches the "New Look." The British government requests women boycott the trend for long skirts to avoid wasting material.

Amsterdam, Netherlands, June: The diary of a young Dutch Jewish girl, Anne Frank, is published.
China, July 1: General Chiang Kai-shek mobilizes his troops across the country to fight the Communists.
New Zealand, July 10: The government decrees that in official correspondence the word "native" will be replaced by the word "Maori."
Paris, France, July 11-13: Europe's foreign ministers meet to draw up a plan for European post-war recovery.

1944

Bucharest, Romania, August 31: Soviet forces occupy Bucharest, six days after Romania declares war against Germany and takes control of German oil supplies.
France, September: Charles de Gaulle becomes president of the French provisional government.
Oakland, California, USA, September 7: Evangelist Aimee Semple McPherson dies, aged 53.
London, England, September 9: The city is again under German attack, this time from the new, silent V-2 bombs.

Dachau, Germany, September 11: SOE spies Yolande Beekman, Madeleine Damerment, Eliane Plewman, and Noor Inayat Khan, are executed by the Nazis.
Greece, October 14: British forces retake Athens, freeing it after four years of German occupation.
Budapest, Hungary, November 7: Poet Hannah Senesh is executed by the Nazis.
Leyte Gulf, Philippines, October 20: Allied forces tackle Japanese forces occupying the Philippines.

Belgium, December 16: German forces make a surprise attack in the Ardennes region in an attempt to penetrate the Allied front in Belgium.
USA, December 20: The US Women Airforce Service Pilots (WASP) is deactivated.
Hungary, December 27: Sister Sara Salkahazi is killed by the Hungarian pro-Nazi Arrow Cross Party for hiding Jews in a Budapest hospital.

USA, December 28: The Distinguished Flying Cross is posthumously awarded to Lt Aleda E. Lutz, the first woman in the US military to die in a combat zone during the war.
Boston, USA: Grace Hopper is a member of the Harvard Navy team working on Mark I, the world's first programmable calculator.
Oswego, New York: Ruth Gruber continues her fight to have the 1,000 Jewish refugees she accompanied to the US granted USA citizenship.

USA: Marty Mann co-founds the National Council on Alcoholism and Drug Dependence (NCADD).
Michigan, USA: Anna and the King of Siam, by Margaret Landon, is published.
Jamaica and Bulgaria: Women are granted the right to vote.
USA: Helen Gahagan Douglas, actress, singer, and wife of Hollywood star Melvyn Douglas, is elected to the US House of Representatives.

1945

Netherlands, May 2: Queen Wilhelmina returns to a liberated area of her country. She is known as the "Mother of the Resistance."
Reims, France, May 7: Germany signs an unconditional surrender after the foreign minister gives notice in a radio broadcast.
London, England, May 8: Crowds of spectators jam London's streets to hear Churchill's broadcast announcing the war in Europe will end at midnight. Around 50,000 gleeful revellers take to the streets—singing, dancing, and embracing.

Japan, June 21: American troops take Okinawa after two months of intense fighting.
New Mexico, USA, July 16: The first atomic bomb is successfully tested in the desert near Alamogordo.
London, England, July 26: Winston Churchill loses the British general election to Clement Attlee, leader of the Labour Party, who wins a landslide victory.

Japan, August 6: The United States drops an atomic bomb on the city of Hiroshima. On August 9, another atomic bomb is dropped on the city of Nagasaki.
Japan, September 2: Japan signs an unconditional surrender to the Allied powers.
Yokohama, September 5: Iva Toguri d'Aquino, who some have identified as "Tokyo Rose," is arrested for broadcasting pro-Japanese wartime propaganda.

Boston, USA, September 26: Harvard Medical School's first class of women is enrolled in the university.
Nuremberg, Germany, November 20: Hitler's collaborators, including Hermann Goering and Rudolf Hess, stand trial for war crimes.
USA, December: President Truman appoints Eleanor Roosevelt as a delegate to the General Assembly of the newly created United Nations.

Stockholm, Sweden, December: Chilean poet Gabriela Mistral wins the Nobel Prize for Literature. She is the first Latin American to win this prestigious prize.
San Francisco, USA: Artist Georgia O'Keeffe paints Pelvis Series Red with Yellow.
USA: The Pulitzer Prize for Drama goes to Mary Coyle Chase for the play Harvey.
Italy, Japan, and the Dutch East Indies (Indonesia): Women win the right to vote.

1946

USA, June 20: The motion picture Anna and the King of Siam, starring Irene Dunne and Rex Harrison, premieres.
New York, June: Mary Lou Williams's Zodiac Suite is performed by the New York Philharmonic Orchestra at Carnegie Hall.
Germany, June–September: One hundred thousand Jews have left Poland for displaced peoples' camps in Germany.
Marshall Islands, July 1: The USA tests a 20,000-ton atomic bomb at Bikini Atoll.

Philippines, July 4: The nation gains independence from the USA, and becomes known as the Republic of the Philippines.
Paris, France, July 5: The bikini debuts at a fashion show.
Vatican City, July 7: The first American saint is canonized: Mother Frances Xavier Cabrini.
USA, July 14: Doctor Benjamin Spock's book on how to raise children, The Commonsense Book of Baby and Child Care, is published.

Paris, France, July 27: Author and poet Gertrude Stein dies at age 72.
India, August 19: Up to 4,000 Muslims and Hindus die during days of religious riots in Calcutta.
Nuremburg, Germany, October 1: The International Military Tribunal finds 22 Nazi leaders guilty of war crimes.
USA, October 19: Wartime economy on skirt length ends. Order L85 now allows dressmakers to increase the length of women's skirts and dresses.

England, October: The Royal Commission on Equal Pay recommends men and women civil servants receive equal pay for equal work.
Siessen, Germany, November 6: Sister Maria Innocentia Hummel, whose artwork inspired the famous Hummel figurines, dies at age 37.
Oslo, Norway, December 10: Emily Greene Balch, founder of the Women's International Committee for Permanent Peace, co-wins the Nobel Peace Prize.

Indochina, December 19: Communist leader Ho Chi Minh attacks the French in Hanoi, prompting the beginning of a new war.
Liberia and Yugoslavia: Women win the right to vote.
USA: The winner of the Houghton Mifflin prize for poetry, North and South, by newcomer Elizabeth Bishop, is published.
Paris, France: Prostitutes are forced on to the streets as "La Loi Marthe Richard" dictates the closure of brothels.

1947

Haifa, Palestine, July 18: The Exodus, a ship loaded with nearly 4,500 Jewish Holocaust survivors, is refused refugee status by the UK.
Verona, Italy, August 2: Maria Callas makes her operatic debut in Amilcare Ponchielli's La Gioconda.
Dutch East Indies, August 3: A UN-brokered ceasefire comes into effect between Indonesian and Dutch military forces.
Egypt, August 12: Women's rights activist and nationalist Huda Shaarawi dies, aged 68.

India, August 15: The newly formed countries of Pakistan and India gain independence after 163 years under British rule.
New Zealand, August 23: The first post-war assisted migrants arrive on New Zealand shores.
Sydney, Australia, August: Soprano Joan Sutherland debuts as Dido in Purcell's Dido and Aeneas.
Hungary, September 1: The Communists win the election.

Amritsar, India, September 24: Violence explodes in India when 1,200 Muslim refugees heading for Pakistan by train are slaughtered by Sikh troops and civilians.
Argentina, September: Women win the right to vote.
India, October 22: Tribal forces in Pakistan invade the Indian border state of Kashmir.
London, England, November 12: Baroness Emmuska Orczy, author of The Scarlet Pimpernel, dies aged 82.

London, England, November 20: Princess Elizabeth, daughter of King George VI, and Lieutenant Philip Mountbatten marry.
New York, USA, December 3: Premiere of Tennessee Williams's play, A Streetcar Named Desire, starring Jessica Tandy as Blanche DuBois and Marlon Brando as Stanley Kowalski.
Stockholm, Sweden, December: Gerty Cori and her husband Carl Ferdinand Cori win the Nobel Prize in Physiology or Medicine.

Florida, USA: The Everglades, River of Grass, by Marjory Stoneman Douglas, is published.
1946-47: American golfer Babe Didrikson wins 17 straight golf tournaments around the world.
USA: The book Goodnight Moon, by Margaret Wise Brown, is published.
China: China's new constitution comes into effect, giving women the right to vote.
London, England: Rebecca West publishes The Meaning of Treason, an account of the Nazi war crimes trials in Nuremberg.

1948

Burma, January 4: At 4.20 a.m. Burma is granted independence by Britain. Astrologers choose this auspicious timing.
Indonesia, January 17: The Renville Truce Agreement is signed by UN representatives, proposing a truce between the Netherlands and the Republic of Indonesia along the Van Mook Line.
New Delhi, India, January 30: Mahatma Gandhi is assassinated by Nathuram Godse, a fanatical Hindu.
Ceylon (Sri Lanka), February 4: Ceylon is granted independence.

USA, February 12: Nancy Leftenant becomes the first African-American to enter the Army Nursing Corps.
Prague, Czechoslovakia, February 27: The Communist Party of Czechoslovakia seizes full power in a coup; democratic politicians are taken prisoner.
Los Angeles, USA, March 20: Loretta Young takes out the Oscar for Best Actress for her role in the 1947 movie The Farmer's Daughter. Celeste Holm receives the Best Supporting Actress award for her role in Gentlemen's Agreement.

New Zealand, April: The New Zealand Women's Army Corps is incorporated into the New Zealand regular army.
Seattle, USA, April-September: Activist Clara Fraser organizes a strike against Boeing, and pressures the Machinists Union to represent women and minorities.
Tel Aviv, Israel, May 14: The state of Israel is proclaimed.
South Africa, May 26: The Afrikaner National Party, with its apartheid manifesto, wins the election.

London, England, June 10: A surgeon at Guy's Hospital performs the first open-heart operation.
Washington, DC, USA, June 12: With the introduction of the Women's Armed Services Integration Act, women are granted permanent status in the nation's armed forces.
Toronto, Canada, June 24: The Toronto School Board grants female teachers pay equal to that of males.
London, England, June 24: Dame Lillian Penson is named vice-chancellor of the University of London.

Cambridge, England, July 4: Cambridge University admits women to full degrees for the first time.
USA, July 5: The first episode of the radio show My Favorite Husband, with Lucille Ball, is aired on CBS.
London, England, July 5: The government introduces the National Health Service, which gives free health care to all.
USA, July 7: Six female reservists are sworn in to the regular US Navy, the first women to do so since the introduction of the Women's Armed Services Integration Act.

1949

Dartford, England, January 31: Margaret Roberts (Margaret Thatcher) becomes Dartford's Conservative candidate.
Great Britain, February 1: The Woman's Royal Army Corps (WRAC) replaces the Auxiliary Territorial Service (ATS) in Great Britain.
Rhodes, Greece, February 24: Israel finally signs an armistice with Egypt after many weeks of difficult talks.
Uttar Pradesh, India, March 2: Poet, political activist, and provincial governor Sarojini Naidu dies.

Texas, USA, March 12: Lillian Barber dies of smallpox in Elsa.
Washington DC, USA, April 4: The North Atlantic Treaty is signed by 12 nations to forge a military alliance, the North Atlantic Treaty Organization, designed to deter aggressors.
Ireland, April 18: The Republic of Ireland Bill officially comes into force, making Eire a republic.
Paris, France, April 19: Paloma Picasso is born to Françoise Gilot and artist Pablo Picasso.

Israel, April 20: Golda Myerson (Golda Meir) is named Minister of Labor by Prime Minister Ben-Gurion.
Philippines, April 28: The nation is shocked by the assassination of Aurora Aragón de Quezon.
Israel, May 11: Israel becomes the 59th member of the United Nations.
West Berlin, Germany, May 12: The blockade has ended after successful United Nations negotiations; cars, cheered on by large crowds, are making their way into the city.

Germany, May 23: The western part of Germany has been formally established as the Federal Republic of Germany. The eastern zone remains occupied by the Soviets.
Canberra, Australia, July 5: Dame Enid Lyons, the first Australian woman to hold cabinet rank, becomes Vice-President of the Executive Council.
USA, July 8: Vietta M. Bates becomes the first enlisted woman to be sworn into the regular US Army.

Argentina, July 26: Eva Perón founds the Peronista Feminist Party.
Ecuador, August 5: An earthquake measuring 6.75 on the Richter Scale kills more than 6,000 people and destroys at least 50 towns.
Atlanta, Georgia, USA, August 16: Author Margaret Mitchell dies, aged 48, after being hit by a car.
USSR, August 29: The Soviets successfully test their first atomic bomb at Semipalantinsk.

1950

Israel, January 23: A resolution proclaiming Jerusalem the capital of Israel is approved by the Israeli Knesset.
India, January 26: India becomes a republic no longer under British dominion. Doctor Rajendra Prasad, the new president, is sworn in.
USA, January 31: President Harry Truman puts through an order to rapidly develop the hydrogen bomb.
USSR, March 8: The Soviets announce they have developed their own atomic bomb.

USA, March 20: President Truman denounces Senator Joseph McCarthy as sabotaging US foreign policy.
Jordan, April 24: King Abdullah of Jordan annexes the West Bank, offering citizenship to Palestinians.
South Africa, April 27: The Group Areas Act comes into effect, formally segregating blacks from whites.
New York, USA, May 1: Gwendolyn Brooks is the first African-American to be awarded the Pulitzer Prize, for her poetry collection Annie Allen.

China, May 1: New marriage laws legalizing divorce and banning bride sales and concubinage come into effect in China.
USA, May 6: Actress Elizabeth Taylor marries hotel magnate Conrad "Nicky" Hilton Jr.
Oxford, England, May 6: Controversial journalist Agnes Smedley dies.
New York, USA, May 13: Lillian Ross's innovative and talk-provoking profile of Ernest Hemingway appears in The New Yorker.

Washington DC, USA, June 1: In her "Declaration of Conscience" speech, Senator Margaret Chase Smith denounces Senator McCarthy's tactics for eliminating Communism.
Korea, June 25: War breaks out after North Korean communists invade South Korea.
USA, June 30: President Truman calls up reserve units to aid South Korea in their fight against the North.
New York, USA, July 17: Evangeline Booth, fourth General of the Salvation Army, dies aged 85.

London, England, July 26: The United Kingdom announces it is sending troops into Korea. Other US allies, Australia and New Zealand, announce that they will do likewise.
Boston, USA, August 1: Harvard Law School admits women to degrees.
Rochester, New York, USA, August 3: Martha Matilda Harper, inventor of beauty salons and the franchise system, dies at the age of 93.
Los Angeles, USA, August 4: Premiere of Sunset Boulevard, starring William Holden, and Gloria Swanson as Norma Desmond.

1951

West Germany, January 15: War criminal Ilse Koch is sentenced to life imprisonment.
USA, January 29: Actress Elizabeth Taylor divorces her husband, Conrad "Nicky" Hilton Jr.
London, England, February 10: An article in The Lancet describes Munchausen's Syndrome, a psychiatric condition in which people feign illnesses to attract medical attention.
USA, February 17: J. Edgar Hoover begins an unauthorized program to flush out FBI employees suspected of having communist interests.

Melbourne, Australia, February 19: Jean Lee and her two male companions are hanged for the murder of 73-year-old dwelling-house landlord and bookmaker, William "Pop" Kent.
Hollywood, USA, March 29: Judy Holliday wins the Oscar for Best Actress for her role in Born Yesterday. All About Eve wins Best Picture.
New York, USA, March: Hannah Arendt publishes The Origins of Totalitarianism.

New York, USA, April 5: Julius and Ethel Rosenberg are found guilty of espionage and sentenced to death.
London, England, April 9: Judy Garland performs in London.
Zurich, Switzerland, April 10: Nora Barnacle, wife of eccentric Irish author James Joyce, dies.
Australia, April: The Women's Royal Australian Army Corps (WRAAC) is established.

Hollywood, California, USA, May 29: Singer and actress Fanny Brice dies at the age of 59.
London, England, May: Freda Lingstrom, creator of the children's classic Andy Pandy, becomes Head of BBC Children's Television.
London, England, May: Crazy People premieres on BBC Radio. It stars Peter Sellers, Spike Milligan, Harry Secombe, and Michael Bentine.
Philadelphia, USA, June 15: Doctor John Mauchly and J. Presper Eckert Jr demonstrate UNIVAC, the first commercial computer.

South Africa, June 18: Black people and those of mixed racial heritage are denied the right to vote.
Geneva, Switzerland, June 29: Items proposed at the Equal Remuneration Convention, concerning equal pay for men and women workers for work of equal value, are adopted by the International Labour Organization.
London, England, June: Althea Gibson becomes the first black player to compete at Wimbledon.

1948

London, England, July 29: King George VI opens the first Olympic Games since 1936.
Pennsylvania, USA, August 8: Feminist and journalist Rheta Childe Dorr dies, aged 80.
Korea, August 15: The Independent Republic of Korea is proclaimed.
London, England, August: Dutch-woman Fanny Blankers-Koen wins four Olympic gold medals. Alice Coachman becomes the first African-American woman to win a gold medal.

Netherlands, September 4: Queen Wilhelmina abdicates in favor of her daughter, Princess Juliana.
North Korea, September 9: Kim Il-sung proclaims North Korea a republic, and becomes its first president. As head of the Korean Communist Party, Kim Il-sung has close ties with the Soviets, who helped him into power after he led the resistance against the Japanese.
Washington, DC, USA, September 10: Mildred Gillars, aka "Axis Sally," is indicted on treason charges.

New York, USA, September: The movie *Hamlet* has its US premiere. It stars Laurence Olivier in the lead role, with Jean Simmons as his leading lady.
USA, September: Margaret Chase Smith is the first woman to be elected to the US Senate.
Massachusetts, USA, October: Harlem Renaissance member Dorothy West publishes her first novel, *The Living is Easy*.

London, England, November 14: Princess Elizabeth, heir to the throne of Britain, gives birth to a son and heir, Charles Philip Arthur George.
England, November: Edith Sitwell's book of poetry, *Song of the Cold*, is published.
Paris, France, December 10: The Universal Declaration of Human Rights is adopted by the UN General Assembly. Eleanor Roosevelt was the driving force behind it.

Tokyo, Japan, December 23: The Japanese prime minister, General Tojo Hideki, nicknamed "The Razor," is hanged after being found guilty of war crimes on November 12. Six other Japanese wartime leaders are also executed.
Bayreuth, Germany, December: Winifred Wagner, daughter-in-law of the late Richard Wagner and close friend of Hitler, is tried for her role in the Nazi regime.
Belgium: Women win full suffrage.
Israel and South Korea: Women win the right to vote.

1949

London, England, September 18: The pound sterling is devalued by a massive 30 percent.
San Francisco, USA, October 6: Iva Toguri d'Aquino, AKA "Tokyo Rose," is sentenced to 10 years' imprisonment and fined $10,000 for treason.
Germany, October 7: The eastern part of Germany becomes the German Democratic Republic under Soviet rule.

USA, October 12: Eugenie Anderson is named ambassador to Denmark. She is America's first woman ambassador.
Greece, October 16: Communist troops surrender and the civil war comes to an end.
Washington DC, USA, October 21: President Truman creates a recess appointment for Burnita Shelton Matthews as a Federal District Court judge.

New Zealand, November 29: Iriaka Ratana is elected; she is the first female Maori member of parliament.
Korea, December 15: A typhoon strikes the coast, leaving several thousand dead.
Indonesia, December 27: Indonesia becomes a united country after settling its conflict with the Dutch.
Paris, France: Simone de Beauvoir publishes *The Second Sex (Le deuxième sexe)*.
USA: Gwendolyn Brooks publishes her book of poetry, *Annie Allen*.

USA: Margaret Mead's *Male and Female: A Study of the Sexes in a Changing World* is published.
Jaén, Spain: Popular South American female bullfighter Conchita Cintrón causes a stir when, during a bullfight in Spain, she dismounts from her horse in the bullring. Spanish law forbids women to fight on foot, and she is arrested as she leaves the arena. However, the huge public support following her excellence in the bullring sees Cintrón released.

England: Elizabeth Bowen's *The Heat of the Day* is published.
South Africa: Marriage between whites and people of other races is forbidden under the new *Prohibition of Mixed Marriages Act No. 55*.
Haiti: Black civil rights leader Mary McLeod Bethune receives the Haitian Medal of Honor and Merit, the highest honor Haiti can bestow.
World: In this year, suffrage is granted to women in Bosnia and Herzegovina, Chile, China, Costa Rica, and Syria.

1950

Dover, England, August 8: Florence Chadwick sets a new women's record for swimming the English Channel.
London, England, August 15: Princess Elizabeth gives birth to her second child, a girl.
USA, August 24: Judge Edith Sampson becomes the first African-American to be named a delegate to the United Nations.
Calcutta, India, October 7: A nun known as Mother Teresa establishes the Missionaries of Charity.
New York, USA, October 13: Premiere of *All About Eve*.

Austerlitz, New York, USA, October 19: Poet Edna St Vincent Millay dies at the age of 58.
Canberra, Australia, October 24: The Commonwealth Court of Conciliation and Arbitration determines a basic female wage, which is set at 75 percent of the basic male wage.
North Korea, November 28: China joins forces with the North Koreans in the Korean War.

USA, November 30: President Truman says the United States is giving "active consideration" to the use of atomic bombs in Korea.
Tibet, December 19: The Dalai Lama flees Chinese-occupied Tibet after the invasion of his country on October 21.
England: Catherine Cookson publishes her first book, the autobiographical *Kate Hannigan*.
England: Elizabeth David inspires British housewives with her *Book of Mediterranean Food*.

Boston, USA: Felicia Kaplan publishes her first book, *Mink on Weekdays*.
USA: Judith Merril publishes the sci-fi nuclear war thriller, *Shadow on the Hearth*.
England: Elizabeth Jane Howard publishes her diaristic novel, *The Beautiful Visit*.
New York, USA: South African author Doris Lessing's first novel, *The Grass is Singing*, is published in the United States.
Thailand: King Phumiphon Aduldet is formally crowned Rama IX.

USA: Babe Didrikson is named Female Athlete of the Half-century by Associated Press.
London, England: At King's College, Maurice Wilkins and Rosalind Franklin produce the first pictures of DNA.
England: Grace Robertson makes an exclusive freelance arrangement with *Picture Post* to document daily life in Britain with her camera.
India: Women are granted the right to vote.
Haiti: Women are granted the right to vote.

1951

London, England, August 15: The first Miss World competition, initially called the Festival Bikini Contest, is won by Miss Sweden.
San Francisco, USA, September 8: Forty-nine nations sign a peace treaty with Japan.
Dover, England, September 11: Florence Chadwick swims the English Channel in both directions.
Wellington, New Zealand, September 24: The Maori Women's Welfare League holds its first conference.

Mexico City, Mexico, October 15: Doctor Carl Djerassi develops a synthetic oral contraceptive.
USA, October 15: The first episode of *I Love Lucy* goes to air.
California, USA, October 24: Doctor Albert Bellamy, Head of Radiological Services, assures residents that test explosions of a hydrogen bomb near Las Vegas will cause no ill effects.
London, England, October 25: Winston Churchill becomes Prime Minister again after winning the election against the Labour Party.

Vatican, October 29: Pope Pius XII cautiously sanctions the use of the rhythm method as a natural form of birth control.
New York, USA, November 13: Ballerina Janet Collins becomes the first black artist to perform at the Metropolitan Opera House.
USA, November: Deborah Kerr and Robert Taylor star in the movie epic, *Quo Vadis*.
Los Angeles, USA, December 23: Premiere of the film *The African Queen*, starring Katharine Hepburn and Humphrey Bogart.

Connecticut, USA: Marion Donovan patents the "Boater," a precursor to the first fully disposable diaper.
Jerusalem, Israel: The *Women's Equal Rights Law*, which prohibits gender discrimination, is passed.
Florida, USA: Brownie Wise is appointed Vice-President of the Tupperware Plastics Co.
England: The BBC broadcasts a very successful serial adaptation of Edith Nesbit's *The Railway Children* for Children's Hour, produced by Dorothea Brooking.

England: The British comic *Girl* is published, the first to be aimed specifically at the female market.
England: Frida Lingstrom, creator of children's classics Andy Pandy, Looby Lou, and Teddy, becomes Head of BBC Children's Television.
Geneva, Switzerland: The World Health Organization publishes *Maternal Care and Mental Health*.
New York, USA: American photographer Eve Arnold becomes the first woman to work for the celebrated Magnum agency.

527

1952

New York, USA, January 8: Antonia Maury, American astronomer, dies. Maury's system for classifying stars plays a vital role in the discovery of giant and dwarf stars.

USA, January: Backyard nuclear fallout shelters are proliferating all around the country.

Greece, February 1: *Gynaika*, the first Greek women's magazine, is published.

Sandringham, England, February 6: King George VI dies. His 25-year-old daughter, on safari in Kenya, accedes to the throne as Elizabeth II.

California, USA, March 4: Film stars Ronald Reagan and Nancy Davis are married in the San Fernando Valley.

Moscow, USSR, March 9: Russian revolutionary and socialist feminist Alexandra Kollontai dies.

Washington DC, USA, April 3: Queen Juliana of the Netherlands becomes only the second woman to address a joint session of Congress; the first was her mother, Queen Wilhelmina, in 1942.

Vietnam, April 26: France seeks UN aid in Vietnam if China gets involved in its conflict against the Viet Minh.

Noordwijk aan Zee, Netherlands, May 6: Maria Montessori, physician, scientist, and educator, dies.

Cambridge, England, May: Rosalind Franklin, working alone at King's College, makes a clear X-ray photograph of the wet form of DNA. Her revolutionary photograph demonstrates that the structure of the DNA molecule is a helix, but Franklin keeps the photo in a drawer.

East Germany, June 1: East Germany closes access to West Germany from midnight. Now, only permit holders may enter.

London, England, June 2: Edith Evans stars as Lady Bracknell in the film adaptation of Oscar Wilde's play, *The Importance of Being Earnest*.

USA, June 5: Doris Day records the hit single "When I Fall in Love."

USA, July 16: *The Diary of a Young Girl* by Anne Frank, who died during the war, is published in English.

Argentina, July 26: Eva "Evita" Perón, dies, aged 33.

Cairo, Egypt, July 26: King Farouk I abdicates following a military coup by General Gamal Abdel Nasser's Free Officers, a nationalist group.

New York, USA, September 6: British actress Gertrude Lawrence dies while starring on Broadway in *The King and I*. She was 54.

USA, October 3: *Our Miss Brooks*, formerly a radio show, premieres on television, starring Eve Arden.

Australia, October 3: The British atomic bomb is tested in the remote Monte Bello Islands off the northwest coast of Western Australia.

California, USA, October 11: Researchers announce the discovery of a polio vaccine that is suitable for large-scale manufacture.

1953

Washington DC, USA, January 3: Frances Bolton and her son, Oliver, from Ohio, become the first mother-son combination to serve at the same time in the US Congress.

New York, USA, January 5: Eleanor Roosevelt argues that the United Nations should encourage equal political rights for women.

Vix, France, January: The tomb of a Gaulish princess, discovered near Vix by local archeologist René Joffroy, reveals jewelry and artifacts of Greek origin dating back to the sixth century BCE.

USA, March: Playwright and journalist Clare Boothe Luce is appointed Ambassador to Italy—the first woman to represent the USA in a major diplomatic office.

Washington DC, USA, April 11: Oveta Culp Hobby is appointed the first Secretary of the newly created Department of Health, Education, and Welfare—the only woman in the cabinet.

Mexico City, Mexico, April 13: Internationally acclaimed artist Frida Kahlo is finally invited to exhibit in her own country.

Vevey, Switzerland, April 17: Charlie Chaplin vows never to return to the USA after being banned last year on suspicion of Communism.

Cambridge, UK, April 25: James Watson and Francis Crick solve the mystery of reproduction in their findings of the molecular model of DNA.

California, USA, May 18: American aviator Jacqueline Cochran becomes the first woman to pilot a plane faster than the speed of sound, flying an F-86 Sabre over Rogers Dry Lake at Edwards Air Force Base.

London, England, June 2: The coronation of Queen Elizabeth II is one of the first television broadcasts to be intentionally recorded for posterity. Sales of TV sets rose sharply in the preceding weeks.

East Berlin, June 17: Tanks are brought in to quell an uprising against Communism.

Cairo, Egypt, June 18: Egypt becomes a military-ruled republic, led by General Muhammad Neguib.

Moncada, Cuba, July 26: The leader of a Communist rebel group, Fidel Castro, is jailed.

Panmunjeom, North Korea, July 27: An armistice signed by the United Nations, Korea, and China ends three years of war.

Miami, USA, August 12: Ann Davidson, the first woman to sail solo across the Atlantic Ocean, arrives in port.

Wales, August: Dilys Cadwaladr is the first woman to win the Welsh Bardic Crown.

Geneva, Switzerland, September 12: Melinda Maclean, wife of missing British diplomat Donald Maclean, disappears with her three children.

1954

Groton, USA, January 21: USS *Nautilus*, the first atomic submarine, is launched today by First Lady Mamie Eisenhower.

Sydney, Australia, February 3: Over one million well-wishers turn out to greet Queen Elizabeth II as she sails into the harbor on her first royal trip to the country.

UK, February 12: A report by the British Standing Committee on cancer says cigarette smoking is directly linked to lung cancer.

USA, March 6: Doris Day reaches Number 1 on the Cash Box charts with her song "Secret Love."

Hollywood, USA, March 25: From *Here to Eternity* wins eight Academy Awards.

Johannesburg, South Africa, April 17: Rachel (Ray) Simons forms the Federation of South African Women with others such as Helen Joseph, Lillian Ngoyi, and Amina Cachalia. This is the first attempt to establish a broad-based women's organization in this country.

Darwin, Australia, April 20: Evdokia Petrov, Soviet Union spy, elects to defect with her husband, Vladimir Petrov.

New York, USA, May 13: Broadway musical *The Pajama Game* premieres today. Actress and dancer Carol Haney shoots to instant fame for her role as Gladys Hotchkiss.

Paris, France, May 25: Eighteen-year-old author Françoise Sagan wins the Prix des Critiques for her first, somewhat scandalous novel *Bonjour Tristesse*.

London, England, May: Irish-born British philosopher and author, Iris Murdoch, publishes her first novel, *Under the Net*.

New Guinea, June 10: A hitherto unknown tribe of 100,000 people is found.

Ohio, USA, July 4: Marilyn Sheppard, aged 31 and pregnant, is found brutally beaten to death at her home near Cleveland. Amid extensive publicity, her husband Dr Sam Sheppard is accused, tried, and jailed for the murder.

UK, July 4: Food rationing ends, with meat finally removed from the list nearly nine years after the end of World War II.

Ulanbataar, Mongolia, July 7: Sühbaataryn Yanjmaa ends nine months as acting President of Mongolia. She is the first modern woman to take the role of head of state of a country.

Mexico City, Mexico, July 13: Artist Frida Kahlo dies. Her final painting is an incomplete portrait of Joseph Stalin.

1955

London, England, January 31: The government agrees to give women in the civil service equal pay to men.

Johannesburg, South Africa, February 9: Police forcibly evict 65,000 black Africans, razing their homes and forcibly resettling them in new black townships.

Alabama, USA, March 2: Sixteen-year-old African American Claudette Colvin is arrested for refusing to give up her seat on a bus to a white passenger.

Pennsylvania, USA, March 3: Mother Katharine Drexel, a Philadelphia heiress turned Catholic nun, dies. She gave away most of her considerable fortune in her work with Native and African Americans.

New York, USA, March 7: The Broadway musical version of *Peter Pan*, starring Mary Martin, is televised for the first time by NBC to the largest audience to date.

Los Angeles, USA, April 7: Theda Bara (Theodosia Goodman), silent screen sex symbol, dies.

Michigan, USA, April 12: The results of the field trials of Jonas Salk's polio vaccine reveal that the vaccine is effective.

USA, April 16: The McGuire Sisters' single "Sincerely" enjoys its tenth week at No. 1.

West Germany, May 5: West Germany reverts to its pre-war sovereign state.

Warsaw, Poland, May 14: The Warsaw Pact, a mutual defense agreement between Eastern European nations, is signed.

Daytona Beach, USA, May 18: Mary McLeod Bethune, educator and civil rights leader, dies at 79 years of age.

London, England, July 13: Ruth Ellis is hanged after she is found guilty of shooting her lover, racing driver David Blakeley.

California, USA, July 17: Walt Disney opens Disneyland, an amazing 243 acre (98 ha) amusement park.

California, USA, July 20: The body of missing schoolgirl Stephanie Bryan is found in a shallow grave. The 14-year-old had been missing since April 28.

New Zealand, August 2: Publications containing sex or violence are burned by publishers following raids.

California, USA, August 5: Carmen Miranda, Portuguese/Brazilian singer and actress, dies.

New York, USA, August 13: Soprano Florence Easton dies.

Argentina, September 19: President Juan Perón is ousted and hides out in a gunboat in Buenos Aires harbor.

San Francisco, USA, September 21: The Daughters of Bilitis is formed to improve the status of lesbians and to provide a social alternative to bars.

Ontario, Canada, October: Project Magnet, which was set up to investigate Canada's UFO sightings, reports that there is a "substantial probability of the real existence of extra-terrestrial vehicles."
Eniwetok Island, Pacific Ocean, November 6: The USA explodes its first hydrogen bomb on a Pacific island, blasting it apart.
Kenya, November 8: Prominent Kenyan nationalist leader, Jomo Kenyatta, is among hundreds of people rounded up as suspects in the Mau Mau terrorist uprising.

Nice, France, November 13: Margaret Wise Brown, American author of the classic children's story, *Goodnight Moon*, dies.
London, England, November 25: Agatha Christie's whodunit *The Mousetrap* premieres in the West End, starring Richard Attenborough and Sheila Sims.
Denmark, December 1: Revealed: Former GI George William Jorgensen Jr has undergone a sex change, and is now Christina Jorgensen.

Denver, Colorado, USA, December 2: The delivery by caesarean section of Gordon Campbell Kerr becomes the first ever publicly televised birth. His mother, Lillian Kerr, receives a $100 defence bond for her efforts, broadcast on a 49-station NBC network.
New York, USA: Chilean Ana Figueroa becomes the first woman appointed to the United Nations Security Council.
South Korea: Louise Yim (Yim Yong-shin), the county's first female MP, becomes the Founding Chairperson of the Women's Party.

Tokyo, Japan: Kinuyo Tanaka stars in director Kenji Mizoguchi's newly released film, *The Life of Oharu*.
UK: *Excellent Women*, a novel by Barbara Pym, is published.
Philadelphia, Pennsylvania, USA: Rear Admiral Grace Murray Hopper, US naval officer and mathematician, is part of the team that invents the first computer compiler.
New York, USA: Nineteen-year-old puppeteer Shari Lewis wins the Arthur Godfrey television talent scout show on CBS.

Mexico City, Mexico: Amalia Hernández founds the Ballet Folklórico de México. Her aim is to preserve the country's colorful dance traditions.
USA: Maureen Connolly is named Associated Press Female Athlete of the Year, after winning both the US Open and Wimbledon tennis championships.
Paris, France: Jacqueline du Bief wins the gold medal at the World Figure Skating Championships.
England: Mary Norton wins the Carnegie Medal in Literature for her children's book *The Borrowers*.

Philadelphia, USA, September 14: Alfred C. Kinsey's controversial report *Sexual Behavior in the Human Female* is published.
New York, USA, September 18: Vijaya Lakshmi Pandit becomes the first woman president of the United Nations General Assembly.
USA, September 20: *The Loretta Young Show* ("A Letter to Loretta") premieres on NBC TV.
New York, USA, November 9: Acclaimed Welsh poet Dylan Thomas dies in hospital, aged 39.

England, November 21: "Piltdown Man," the skull found by Charles Dawson in Sussex in 1912, and believed ancient, is proved a hoax.
Iowa, USA, December 3: Announced: frozen sperm first used to successfully impregnate a woman.
New Zealand, December 23: Elizabeth II is the first reigning British monarch to visit New Zealand.
USA, December 28: Folk artist Grandma Moses graces the cover of *Time* magazine, having achieved global fame for her paintings. Her real name is Anna Mary Robertson.

Chicago, USA, December: Marilyn Monroe is the first cover girl and nude centerfold in the first issue of Hugh Hefner's *Playboy* magazine.
UK and USA: *The Second Sex*, by French writer Simone de Beauvoir, is published in the US and Britain. In this book, the phrase "women's liberation" appears for the first time.
Washington DC, USA: Helenor Foerster is named "Woman of the Year for Science" by the Women's National Press Club for her work on the link between the parasite *Toxoplasma gondii* and blindness.

USA: Meta Neumann, American neuropathologist, establishes that Alzheimer's disease is a metabolic disorder rather than a function of old age.
Long Island, USA: Abstract expressionist artist Lee Krasner creates *City Verticals*, a work in oil paint and collage on board.
USA: Patti Page's recording of "How Much is That Doggy in the Window?" is Number One on both Billboard and Cash Box charts.

UK: British sculptor Barbara Hepworth creates her work *Hieroglyph* in Ancaster stone.
New York, USA: Botanist Katherine Esau publishes *Plant Anatomy*, a new text on plant structure.
USA: Maureen Connolly becomes the first woman to win a Grand Slam—all four major tennis championships.

Geneva, Switzerland, July 20: War in Indochina ends with the signing of the Geneva Accords.
Paris, France, August 3: Sidonie-Gabrielle Colette, French actress, librettist, novelist (the *Claudine* series), and critic, dies. Her body is interred in Le Père Lachaise Cemetery in Paris.
Christchurch, New Zealand, August 28: Two teenage girls, Juliet Hulme and Pauline Parker, are found guilty of murdering Juliet's mother in a brutal bashing.

Ontario, Canada, September 8: Sixteen-year-old Marilyn Bell is the first person to swim across Lake Ontario.
USA, September 13: Alicia Patterson, founder and editor of *Newsday*, appears on the cover of *Time* magazine after the tabloid wins its first Pulitzer Prize.
Drummoyne, NSW, Australia, September 19: Author (*My Brilliant Career*) and feminist Miles Franklin dies, leaving provision for an award for Australian literature.

Hollywood, USA, September 29: Judy Garland stars in the movie musical *A Star is Born*.
New York, USA, October 7: Marian Anderson is the first black soloist to be hired by the Metropolitan Opera.
USA, October 7: Marilyn Monroe and Joe Di Maggio are divorced, just nine months after their marriage.
Egypt, October 19: Egypt and Britain agree to terms over the Suez Canal.
Alabama, USA, November 30 A woman is struck by an 8 lb 8 oz (4 kg) meteorite as she sleeps on her sofa, suffering only bad bruising.

USA, December: Swanson and Sons' new TV dinner—a ready-to-heat meal of turkey and vegetables—costs 98 cents.
USA: Babe Zaharias wins the US Women's Open Golf Tournament, and is also named Associated Press Female Athlete of the Year.
New Delhi, India: Aruna Asaf Ali helps to establish the National Federation of Indian Women (NFIW), the women's wing of the Communist Party of India. The NFIW is intended to be a radical alternative to existing women's organizations.

Bogota, Colombia: Women are granted the right to vote.
Paris, France: Couturier Coco Chanel reopens her design house, which was closed in 1939 with the onset of the war.
New Mexico, USA: Georgia O'Keeffe paints *My Last Door*, an abstract image of a patio door that has fascinated the artist for a number of years and inspired many variations.

London, England, September 23: Barbara Mandell is the first female newsreader on British television.
UK, September 26: Birdseye frozen fish fingers appear in stores.
USA, October 3: A new children's television program, *The Mickey Mouse Club*, starts on ABC TV.
New York, USA, October 5: A stage adaptation of *The Diary of Anne Frank* opens at the Cort Theater.
USA, October 6: The drug LSD is made illegal.

London, England, October 31: Princess Margaret announces she will not marry Captain Peter Townsend because he is divorced.
Chelsea, England, October 31: Fashion designer Mary Quant opens a clothes shop called Bazaar.
New York, USA, October: Kay Thompson's book *Eloise*, about a mischievous six-year-old who lives at the Plaza Hotel, is published.
Alabama, USA, December 1: Rosa Parks is arrested in Montgomery for refusing a bus driver's order to give up her seat to a white man.

New York, USA, December 6: After seven weeks on the program, psychologist Doctor Joyce Brothers becomes the second person and only woman to win the top prize on the CBS game show *The $64,000 Question*.
USA, December 29: The 13-year-old singer Barbra Streisand makes her first recording, "You'll Never Know."
Cannes, France: American actress Grace Kelly meets Prince Rainier of Monaco at the Cannes Film Festival in May. Their engagement is announced in December.

London, England: Dame Evelyn Sharp becomes the first woman permanent secretary in the civil service as Head of the Housing Ministry.
Canada: The Canadian Army and Navy begin to recruit women for regular service, not just reserves.
London, England: The Women of the Year Lunch and Assembly at the Savoy Hotel is founded by Tony (Antonella) Lothian, Odette Hallowes, and Georgina Coleridge.

New York, USA: Anne Morrow Lindbergh's *Gift from the Sea*, a meditation on women's lives in the twentieth century, is published.
Toronto, Canada: With no leagues for girls, 8-year-old Abigail "Abby" Hoffman cuts her hair and joins an ice hockey team disguised as a boy, "Ab" Hoffman. The ploy is discovered when she is required to submit her birth certificate in order to compete in a major game.
Norway: The "Ice Woman," explorer Louise Arner Boyd, is the first woman to fly over the Arctic Circle.

1956

San Francisco, California, USA, January 9: Abigail Van Buren begins her career as advice columnist Dear Abby on the *San Francisco Chronicle*.
Cyprus, January 12: British troops are sent to quell the rising tension between Greeks and Turks.
UK, January 26: Heroin imports and exports are made illegal.
West Virginia, USA, January 28: Iva Toguri D'Aquino, the woman most identified as "Tokyo Rose," is released from prison by the US Federal Prison Bureau after serving over six years for treason.

Melbourne, Australia, February 21: Dawn Fraser wins a gold medal in the 100 meter freestyle at the Olympic Games in Melbourne.
Cairo, Egypt, February 27: Women are granted the right to vote and the right to nominate themselves for membership of the National Assembly.
Paris, France, March 17: Irène Joliot-Curie, French scientist, and daughter of Marie and Pierre Curie, dies. Jointly with her husband, Irène was awarded the Nobel Prize for Chemistry in 1935.

Rome, Italy, March 25: The Treaty of Rome is signed, which removes tariff barriers and establishes the European Common Market. Signatories to the Treaty are France, West Germany, Belgium, the Netherlands, Luxembourg, and Italy.
San Francisco, USA, March: Comedian Phyllis Diller's popularity at the Purple Onion continues.
New York, USA, April 2: The soap operas *As the World Turns* and *The Edge of Night* premiere on CBS.
Monaco, April 19: Grace Kelly marries Prince Rainier III.

Washington DC, USA, June 1: Doris Day signs a $1 million recording contract with Columbia Records.
New York, USA, June 29: Marilyn Monroe and playwright Arthur Miller are married.
USA, June 29: Deborah Kerr and Yul Brynner star in *The King And I*.
Israel, June: Golda Meir becomes Israeli foreign minister.
Paris, France, June: Tennis player Althea Gibson becomes the first African American to win a Grand Slam singles title.

London, England, July 5: The Clean Air Bill is passed today in a bid to remove the threat of the city's toxic "pea soup" smogs.
Pretoria, South Africa, August 9: Over 20,000 women march to petition the Prime Minister against the introduction of Pass Laws.
USA, August 31: Marilyn Monroe teams with Don Murray in the movie *Bus Stop*.
London, England, August: *This is Tomorrow*, an art exhibition featuring the new "Pop Art" style, is put on at the Whitechapel Gallery.

1957

London, England, January 10: Prime Minister Anthony Eden resigns due to ill health. His deputy Harold Macmillan takes his place.
Nevada, USA, January 12: Actress Jean Peters marries billionaire industrialist Howard Hughes.
Missouri, USA, February 10: Laura Ingalls Wilder, author of the *Little House on the Prairie* books, dies.
England, February 16: The "Toddlers' Truce" (an arrangement whereby no TV broadcasts were made between 6 pm and 7 pm, to allow parents to put their children to bed) is abolished.

London, England, February 28: Cancer experts express health concerns about Australians exposed to radiation from British atomic tests.
USA, February: *Annie Oakley*, a Western television series that fictionalized the life of the famous sharpshooter, ends a three-year run.
West Africa, March 6: The Gold Coast and Togoland become Ghana, gaining independence from Britain.
London, England, April 1: A spoof on the BBC's *Panorama* fools the public into believing that spaghetti is grown on trees in Switzerland.

Egypt, April 10: The Suez Canal re-opens to all shipping.
Chicago, USA, April 15: Ray Kroc's McDonald's franchise celebrates its second anniversary.
Jordan, April 25: King Hussein declares martial law in the aftermath of a failed coup earlier this month.
Amsterdam, Netherlands, May 3: Otto Frank establishes the Anne Frank Foundation.
US, May 6: "The Ricardos Dedicate a Statue"–the last episode of the sixth and final season of the *I Love Lucy* television show–was aired today.

London, England, July 6: Althea Gibson becomes the first black tennis player to win a Wimbledon singles title, defeating fellow American Darlene Hard 6–3, 6–2.
Alabama, USA, July 16: Anti-segregationist Juliette Hampton Morgan dies by her own hand.
Tunisia, July 25: Tunisia abolishes its monarchy, becomes a republic.
London, England, June 26: The Medical Research Council releases a report highlighting the link between smoking and lung cancer.

Philadelphia, USA, August 5: Dick Clark hosts the first episode of *American Bandstand* on ABC TV.
Juarez, Mexico, September 17: 22-year-old actress Sophia Loren and producer Carlo Ponti wed by proxy as two male attorneys stand in for the couple.
California, USA, September: Oceanographers Roger Revelle and Hans Seuss reveal that the oceans cannot absorb all the carbon dioxide being released and that this will lead to global warming.

1958

Antarctica, January 3: Edmund Hillary reaches the South Pole.
USA, January 10: Jerry Lee Lewis's "Great Balls of Fire" hits number one.
New York, USA, January 15: Over 11,000 scientists from 49 countries petition to ban nuclear testing.
Las Vegas, USA, January 29: Actors Paul Newman and Joanne Woodward are married.
London, England, January 30: A bill passed by the House of Lords allows women admission to the chamber.
Middle East, February 1: Syria and Egypt form the United Arab Republic.

New York, USA, February 11: Hired by Mohawk Airlines, Ruth Carol Taylor becomes the first African-American flight attendant in the United States.
California, USA, February 13: English suffragette, Dame Christabel Pankhurst, dies in Los Angeles.
Yemen, March 2: Yemen announces it will join the United Arab Republic.
USA, March 19: Richard Rodgers and Oscar Hammerstein's *South Pacific* sees Mitzi Gaynor and Rossano Brazzi in lead roles.

USA, March 27: CBS Laboratories announce the development of stereophonic records, which require two loudspeakers but give better sound.
New York, USA, April: Connie Francis's new single "Who's Sorry Now," reaches No. 4 in the USA, and is top of the UK chart.
Beverly Hills, California, USA, April 4: Cheryl Crane, daughter of actress Lana Turner, is suspected of murder.
Tehran, Iran, April 6: Soraya Esfandiary Bakhtiari divorces the Shah of Iran, Mohammad Reza Pahlavi.

London, England, April 16: Scientist Rosalind Franklin dies, aged 37.
Ottawa, Canada, May 12: Ellen Louks Fairclough, who last year became the first woman in the Canadian federal cabinet, becomes Minister of Citizenship and Immigration.
Switzerland, May 13: Velcro is trademarked by Georges de Mestral.
New York, USA, May: Leslie Caron plays Gigi opposite Maurice Chevalier.
Monte Carlo, Monaco, May 18: Maria-Teresa de Filippis of Italy, driving for Maserati, is the first woman to compete in a European Grand Prix.

Transkei, South Africa, June 19: Nomzamo Winifred (Winnie) Madikizela marries Nelson Mandela.
Alaska, USA, July 10: A tsunami caused by an earthquake rises 1,600 feet (500 m) up a mountain.
London, England, July 10: Parking meters first appear in Mayfair.
USA, September: Elizabeth Taylor and Paul Newman star in the film version of *Cat on a Hot Tin Roof*.
USA, September: Sarah Vaughan divorces trumpeter George Treadwell after 12 years of marriage and weds Clyde "C.B." Atkins.

1959

Cuba, January 2: Revolutionary leader Fidel Castro has seized power as president. Incumbent General Fulgencio Batiswta resigns.
Alaska, USA, January 3: Alaska is admitted as the 49th state of the USA, with Juneau as its capital.
Barcelona, Spain, January 6: Writer Ana María Matute wins the country's prestigious Nadal Prize.
Nepal, February 18: Nepal's first national parliamentary election is held. Nepali women are allowed to vote, but are segregated from men.

Cyprus, February 19: Cyprus gains independence in an agreement signed by Britain, Turkey, and Greece.
California, USA, February 26: Gabrielle Renard, artist's model to French painter Pierre-August Renoir, and nanny and mentor to his son, film-maker Jean Renoir, dies at her home in Beverley Hills.
Zimbabwe (Rhodesia), February 27: A state of emergency is declared as violent outbreaks are feared.
New York, USA, March 9: The Barbie doll is unveiled at the American Toy Fair by the Mattel toy company.

New York, USA, March 11: *Raisin in the Sun*, the first Broadway play by a black woman, Lorraine Hansberry, opens at Ethel Barrymore Theater.
USA, March 29: Premiere of the movie *Some Like it Hot*, starring Marilyn Monroe and Jack Lemmon.
Arizona, USA, April 9: Acclaimed architect Frank Lloyd Wright dies at the age of 91.

Tokyo, Japan, April 10: Prince Akihito marries a commoner, Michiko Shoda.
New York, USA, April 22: British ballerina Dame Margot Fonteyn arrives in New York after spending 24 hours in a Panamanian prison.
West Germany, May 1: The five-day working week is introduced.
Toronto, Canada, May 8: The use of the strap as punishment in Canadian schools is banned.
New York, USA, May 21: The musical *Gypsy*, based on the memoirs of burlesque artist Gypsy Rose Lee, opens at the Broadway Theater.

Havana, Cuba, May 23: Ofelia Miriam Ortega becomes the first Hispanic woman ordained in the Presbyterian Church.
London, England, May 28: Johnson and Bart's musical *Lock Up Your Daughters* premieres in London at the Mermaid Theatre.
London, England, June 11: Unveiling of the hovercraft–a new vehicle that goes on both land and sea.
New York, USA, June 18: *The Nun's Story*, starring Audrey Hepburn, Peter Finch, and Edith Evans, premieres.

1956

USA, September 25: The first transatlantic telephone cable commences functioning.

Texas, USA, September 27: Mildred (Babe) Didrikson Zaharias, famed athlete, dies of cancer, aged 42.

Illinois, USA, October 17: As breastfeeding rates in the US drop, the first meeting of La Leche League, an organization which promotes breastfeeding, is convened with seven founding members.

USA, October 18: Ruth Alice Kistler gives birth to a daughter. At 57, she is the oldest woman to bear a child.

Budapest, Hungary, October 25: The Soviets open fire with machine guns on men, women, and children, with estimates of up to 3,000 killed.

Egypt, October 29: Israel invades Egypt, entering via the Sinai Peninsula toward the Suez Canal.

Cairo, Egypt, October 31: French and British forces bomb military airfields after a 12-hour ultimatum to Egypt and Israel to withdraw troops is ignored.

Egypt, November 8: The UN imposes a cease-fire in the Suez Canal that will take effect at midnight.

UK, December: Electric trains replace steam trains between London, Liverpool, and Manchester.

Montgomery, Alabama, USA, December: The bus boycott begun by the arrest of Rosa Parks is ended.

Texas, USA: Bette Nesmith Graham introduces the best-selling correction fluid, Mistake Out.

New York, USA: Grace Metalious writes *Peyton Place*.

New York, USA: Physicist Chien-Shiung Wu disproves the law of conservation of parity.

California, USA: Phyllis Lyon and Del Martin publish *The Ladder*, the first national lesbian periodical.

Ottawa, Canada: The Canadian government passes a law granting women equal pay for "identical or substantially identical" work as men.

London, England: In Britain, legal reforms say that women teachers and civil servants should receive equal pay to men.

Minnesota, USA: Scotchgard, the fabric protector invented by Patsy Sherman, appears in stores.

Wales, UK: Jan Morris, Welsh essayist and travel writer, authors her book *Coast to Coast* based on traveling around America.

New York, USA: Maria Callas, US-born Greek soprano, makes her debut at the Metropolitan Opera House in New York City.

France: Brigitte Bardot stars in *And God Created Woman*, directed by her husband Roger Vadim. The role earns her the title of "sex kitten."

England: Dodie Smith writes the children's novel *101 Dalmatians*.

1957

USSR, October 4: The space age begins as the USSR launches the first satellite to orbit Earth, *Sputnik I*.

Montecatini, Italy, October 24: Fashion designer Christian Dior dies of a heart attack after choking on a fishbone and is succeeded by his assistant, Yves Saint Laurent.

New York, USA, October: Ayn Rand publishes *Atlas Shrugged* to negative reviews and good sales figures.

New York, USA, November 27: Jacqueline Kennedy, wife of John F. Kennedy, gives birth to their daughter Caroline Bouvier Kennedy.

Essex, England, December 17: Writer Dorothy Sayers dies.

Las Vegas, USA, December 29: Singers Steve Lawrence and Eydie Gormé marry.

USA, December: *The Cat in the Hat* by Theodor Seuss Geisel (Dr Seuss) is published.

Cambridge, England, October: Astrophysicists show that all of the elements except the very lightest are produced in stellar interiors.

Illinois, USA: Margaret Hillis founds the Chicago Symphony Chorus.

USA: Dorothy Parker, American writer and poet best known for her caustic wit, wisecracks, and sharp eye for twentieth century urban foibles, begins writing book reviews for *Esquire* magazine.

California, USA: Adaline Kent, surrealist sculptor, dies in an automobile accident and bequeaths $10,000 for an annual award to a promising California artist.

New York, USA: *Memories of a Catholic Girlhood* by Mary McCarthy is published.

USA: A pill developed for treating menstrual problems is approved by the FDA in America.

Berlin, East Germany: Ruth Werner, who had channeled atomic bomb secrets to the Soviets under the code name Sonya during World War II, publishes *An Unusual Girl*.

London, England: *Voltaire in Love*, by Nancy Mitford, is published.

Illinois, USA: The newly established breastfeeding organization La Leche League brings Dr. Grantly-Dick Read, childbirth expert, to speak to a packed house at a local high school.

Manchester, England: Mary Stott sets up the *Guardian's* women's page and becomes its first editor.

Japan: The first Japanese women's weekly magazine, *Shukan Josei*, is published.

New York, USA: Gypsy Rose Lee publishes an autobiography, *Gypsy*.

California, USA: Stripper Annie Banks, after legally changing her name to Tempest Storm, signs a $100,000 contract in San Francisco to tour the burlesque circuit.

1958

New York, USA, September 20: The lesbian group Daughters of Bilitis forms a New York chapter with Barbara Gittings as president.

London, England, October 21: The *Life Peerages Act* entitles women to sit in the House of Lords for the first time. Baroness Swanborough, Lady Reading, and Baroness Barbara Wooton take their seats.

USSR, October 31: Boris Pasternak, the author of *Dr Zhivago*, refuses his Nobel Prize in Literature because he is angry about his expulsion from the Union of Soviet Writers.

USA, November 18: Susan Hayward stars in *I Want to Live!*, the true story of a prisoner facing execution.

California, USA, November 22: Actors Janet Leigh and Tony Curtis become the proud parents of a baby daughter, Jamie Lee Curtis.

New York, USA, December 26: Mezzo-soprano Eva Gauthier dies.

UK, December: The ban on portraying homosexuality in the theater is lifted.

USA, December: Popular toys with children this year include hula hoops and the new Lego bricks.

London, England: Claudia Jones founds *The West Indian Gazette*, the first black newspaper in Britain.

London, England: Hilda Harding becomes the first woman bank manager, taking charge of Barclays in Hanover Street.

England: Ultrasound becomes available to examine unborn babies.

Reims, France: Cyclist Elsy Jacobs from Luxembourg wins the Elite Women's World Road Championships and Balina Ermolaeva becomes the first women's World Sprint Champion.

Ottawa, Canada: Blanche Margaret Meagher becomes the first woman to be appointed as a Canadian ambassador. She is posted to Israel.

New York, USA: Ketti Frings's adaptation of the Thomas Wolfe novel *Look Homeward, Angel* wins the Pulitzer Prize for Drama and Frings is named "Woman of the Year" by the *Los Angeles Times*.

Kobe, Japan: *Shufu no Mise Daisei*, a Japanese supermarket, opens in Sanbomiya, and is soon imitated.

London, England: Publication of Mary Renault's *The King Must Die*.

Japan: Sue Sumii publishes *The River With No Bridge*.

Illinois, USA: *The Womanly Art of Breastfeeding* is published as a loose-leaf booklet by La Leche League. Founders had planned to distribute separate chapters by mail, but soon realized that most mothers needed all the information at once.

USA: There are 320 registered women architects in the USA, equal to 1 percent of the total number of registered architects in the country.

Australia: Nancy Cato's *All the Rivers Run* is published.

1959

Brussels, Belgium, July 2: Prince Albert marries Italian princess Paola Ruffo di Calabria at the Royal Palace.

New York, USA, July 15: Jazz singer Billie Holiday dies from cirrhosis of the liver.

Olduvai Gorge, Tanzania, July 17: Doctor Mary Leakey discovers the oldest known hominid skull, dubbed "Nutcracker Man."

USA, September 25: The 37-year-old advertizing executive Helen Gurley marries film producer David Brown (aged 43).

Colombo, Sri Lanka (Ceylon), September 26: Prime Minister Solomon Bandaranaike dies in hospital after being shot by a Buddhist monk, Talduwe Somarama.

South Africa, October 17: De Beers announces the manufacture of synthetic diamonds.

New York, USA, November 16: Rodgers and Hammerstein's musical *The Sound of Music* opens.

Tehran, Iran, December 21: Farah Diba marries the recently divorced Shah of Iran, becoming his third wife, and Empress of Iran.

Washington DC, USA: The Newbery Medal is won by Elizabeth George Speare for her historical novel *The Witch of Blackbird Pond*.

Rome, Italy: After working as a design assistant at Guy Laroche in Paris, Valentino Garavani, better know as Valentino, returns home to open his own studio.

New York, USA: Abstract expressionist artist Lee Krasner paints *Cool White*. It is a difficult year for the artist: Her mother dies and there are problems with her late husband Jackson Pollock's estate.

Kathmandu, Nepal: The Family Planning Association of Nepal (FPAN) is founded to increase support for sexual health and rights.

Virginia, USA: The Du Pont Company develops a new fabric, Lycra®, at its Waynesboro plant.

New York, USA: Anna Balakian writes *Surrealism: The Road to the Absolute*, an exposition of surrealist literature and art.

New York, USA: Joyce Ballantine Brand, commercial artist, creates the Coppertone Girl for Coppertone suntan lotion.

North Carolina, USA: Pantyhose, which give the appearance of stockings without garters, garter-belts, or corsets, are introduced by Glen Raven Mills.

Ontario, Canada: Betty Oliphant and Celia Franca found the National Ballet School of Canada in Toronto.

Maine, USA: Landscape architect Beatrix Farrand dies, aged 87.

Brasilia, Brazil: Clairvoyant Tia Neiva founds Valley of the Dawn, a sect of 2000 mediums that incorporates Egyptian, Inca, Aztec, Catholic, and Afro-Brazilian rituals.

Florida, USA, January 28: Writer, folklorist, and anthropologist Zora Neale Hurston, best known for her novel *Their Eyes Were Watching God*, dies, aged 69.

Algiers, Algeria, January 29: France teeters on the brink of civil war as the European inhabitants of Algiers protest the French government's self-determination policy for the North African colony.

USA, February: African-Americans stage sit-ins at restaurants across the southern states in a bid to end racial segregation.

Agadir, Morocco, February 29: Twelve thousand people die as an earthquake hits the seaside town.

California, USA, March 4: The day after taping the last of her television shows, Lucille Ball files for divorce from Desi Arnaz.

Sharpeville Township, South Africa, March 1: Police open fire on a peaceful demonstration, killing 69 unarmed women, children, and men, and wounding hundreds of others. The demonstration was organized by the Pan African Congress against hated Pass Laws.

Brasília, Brazil, April 21: The new capital city is inaugurated, and the country's administration moves there from Rio de Janeiro.

Uppsala, Sweden, April: On Palm Sunday, the church of Sweden announces the ordination of three women priests.

London, England, May 6: Princess Margaret marries Anthony Armstrong-Jones in the first televised royal wedding.

USA, May 9: The US Food and Drug Administration approves the pill, Enovid, as safe for birth control use.

USA, May 16: Eileen Fulton debuts as television's first bad girl, Lisa Miller, in *As the World Turns*.

Bucharest, Romania, June 14: Ana Pauker, former Romanian communist leader, dies.

USA, June 19: Country singer Loretta Lynn records her first hit, "I'm a Honky Tonk Girl."

Gombe Reserve, Tanzania, July 4: Zoologist Jane Goodall begins her study of chimpanzees.

London, England, July 10: Lionel Bart's musical *Oliver!* is a hit from the day it opens in London.

Colombo, Ceylon, July 21: Sirimavo Bandaranaike becomes the world's first female prime minister.

Rome, Italy, August 25: The Games of the XVII Olympiad begin.

Rome, Italy, August-September: Wilma Rudolph becomes the first African-American to win three gold medals in a single Olympiad.

Rome, Italy, August-September: Ukrainian Larissa Latynina wins a bronze, two silver, and three gold medals for gymnastics while three months pregnant.

USA, January 9: Nobel Peace Prize recipient Emily Greene Balch dies.

Detroit, USA, January 15: A female singing group The Primettes, are asked to change their name to something else when they sign with Motown Records. They choose to be known as The Supremes.

Katanga, Congo, January 18: After less than a year as prime minister in the newly independent nation, Patrice Lumumba is brutally murdered, and several western countries are implicated in his death.

London, England, January 31: The contraceptive pill goes on sale.

California, USA, February 2: Film actress Anna May Wong dies.

Belgium, February 15: A Boeing 707 crashes, killing 73 people, including 18 figure skaters from the USA.

Canberra, Australia, February: A new *Matrimonial Causes Act* establishing "no fault" divorce comes into effect.

London, England, March 2: Yesterday, cellist Jacqueline du Pré made her debut to critical acclaim.

USSR, March 10: Boris Pasternak's lover, Olga Ivinskaya, appeals to the authorities to repeal her detention in a Soviet gulag.

Nice, France, March 13: At the age of 79, Pablo Picasso marries 37-year-old Jacqueline Rocque.

USA, March 13: Mattel's popular Barbie doll gets a boyfriend, Ken.

Charleston, England, April 7: Vanessa Bell, artist, interior designer, and sister of novelist Virginia Woolf, dies, aged 81.

South Vietnam, April 10: Staunch anti-Communist President Ngo Dinh Diem is re-elected. His Catholic faith, nepotism, and authoritarian rule have made him unpopular with the mostly Buddhist population.

Cuba, April 20: Yesterday 1,400 US-backed Cuban exiles landed at the Bay of Pigs hoping to overthrow the government of Fidel Castro. The invasion was repelled with over 200 killed, sparking a major diplomatic incident with the USA.

Havana, Cuba, May 1: Fidel Castro proclaims Cuba a socialist country.

Columbia University, New York, USA, May 1: Harper Lee wins the Pulitzer Prize for fiction for her novel, *To Kill a Mockingbird*.

New York, USA, May 8: Former editor of *Harper's Bazaar*, Carmel Snow, dies aged 74.

Dominican Republic, May 30: After a 31-year rule, ruthless dictator General Trujillo is assassinated with the assistance of the CIA.

Ranrahirca, Peru, January 11: Whole villages are destroyed and 4,000 people perish in a massive landslide of rocks and ice.

Paris, France, January 21: Director Nadine Marquand and actor Jean-Louis Trintignant announce the birth of their daughter, Marie Trintignant.

Woodville, South Australia, February 4: Activist, educationist, and trade union official Adelaide Laetitia Miethke dies.

USA, February 14: Jacqueline Kennedy leads a televised tour of the White House.

Argentina, February 25: Sister Maria Ludovica de Angelis, of the Buenos Aires Children's Hospital, dies, aged 81.

Garden City, Michigan, USA, March 1: A new discount department store called Kmart opens.

Algiers, Algeria, April 20: Head of the OAS, General Raoul Salan, is captured, ending the anti-colonial uprising in Algeria and France.

USA, April 29: In a paper for the American Medical Association, Dr Helen Glaser draws attention to the problem of adolescent glue-sniffing.

Athens, Greece, May 14: Princess Sophia of Greece weds Prince Don Juan Carlos of Spain.

Laos, May: US troops are deployed to fight the communist group Pathet Lao, which captured Nam Tha.

Kent, England, June 2: Poet and novelist Vita Sackville-West dies at the age of 70.

USA, June 13: The controversial movie, *Lolita*, is released in cinemas. Directed by Stanley Kubrick, the film stars James Mason and Sue Lyon in the lead roles.

New York, USA, June: Rachel Carson's *Silent Spring* is serialized in *The New Yorker*.

Algeria, July 3: Two days after the Algerian people vote in a referendum on independence, France's President de Gaulle severs 132 years of colonial ties.

Hollywood, USA, August 5: Marilyn Monroe is found dead, aged 36.

Jamaica, August 6: Jamaica becomes independent within the British Commonwealth; Alexander Bustamente of the Jamaica Labour Party is the first prime minister.

USA, August 7: The US Food and Drug Commissioner warns doctors that women may risk blood clots when taking the oral contraceptive, Searle's Enovid. In the past year, 28 women are known to have developed clots, and six of them have died.

New York, USA, August 15: The Netherlands signs the *New York Agreement*, ceding West New Guinea to Indonesia.

Congo, January 15: Secessionist leader of breakaway Katanga province, Moise Tshombe, is forced to reunite with the Congo under intense pressure from the UN and other African states.

Paris, France, January 29: President de Gaulle vetoes Britain's entry into the European Economic Community and is supported by Germany's Chancellor Adenauer.

London, England, February 11: Writer Sylvia Plath commits suicide, aged 30

Paris, France, February 15: A plot is uncovered to assassinate President de Gaulle, one of numerous attempts on his life in the past year.

Tennessee, USA, March 5: An airplane crash claims the life of country music singer Patsy Cline.

Atlantic Ocean, April 10: The nuclear-powered submarine, USS *Thresher*, is lost off Cape Cod with 129 men on board.

New York, USA, May 6: Barbara Tuchman receives a Pulitzer Prize for *Guns of August*.

Jakarta, Indonesia, May 18: Sukarno, hero of the struggle against the Dutch in the 1940s, declares himself president for life.

USA, May 20: *Newsweek* magazine hails Chinese-American Chien-Shiung Wu as "Queen of Physics."

Washington DC, USA, May 31: Author Edith Hamilton dies, aged ninety-six.

London, England, June 3: Christine Keeler's affair with Secretary of State for War, John Profumo, leads to his resignation after he admits misleading Parliament.

Washington, DC, USA, June 10: The *Equal Pay Act* is passed by Congress.

USSR, June 16: Valentina Tereshkova becomes the first woman in space.

USA, June 17: The Supreme Court rules that the Lord's Prayer and bible recitation should be banned from public schools, after a challenge by Madelyn Murray.

Berlin, Germany, June 26: West Berliners gather to hear US President Kennedy's speech denouncing Communism. "Ich bin ein Berliner," he states.

London, England, July 8: Australian Margaret Smith, 21, wins the Wimbledon singles title.

London, England, July 31: The *Peerage Act* permits female and Scottish peers to sit in the House of Lords.

Washington, DC, USA, August: Following her husband's suicide, Katharine Graham assumes presidency of the *Washington Post*.

Mexico: Madre Lupita, co-founder of the congregation of the Servants of St Margaret Mary and the Poor, dies, aged 85.

1960

New York, USA, September 25: Mrs. Emily Post, for many years a leading authority on all matters of etiquette, dies at the age of 86.
Addis Ababa, Ethiopia, September 27: Sylvia Pankhurst, social activist and prominent British suffragette, dies at the age of 78.
New York USA, October 4: Angela Lansbury and Joan Plowright star in A Taste of Honey by Shelagh Delaney. Written when the author was still a teenager, the play focuses on a working-class girl who rejects her ordinary surroundings.

London, England, October: Poet Sylvia Plath publishes her first book of poems, The Colossus.
USA, November 9: John F. Kennedy is elected president of the USA, narrowly defeating Richard Nixon.
UK, November 10: Penguin Books sells out of D. H. Lawrence's 1928 novel Lady Chatterley's Lover on its first day of release.
New Orleans, Louisiana, November 14: Six year-old Ruby Bridges is the first African-American child to attend a whites only school in Louisiana.

Toronto, Canada, November 24: Grand Duchess Olga Alexandrovna, the last surviving sister of Tsar Nicholas II, dies, aged 78.
England, December 7: Granada Television broadcasts the first episode of "Coronation Street."
Sweden, December 10: US Chemist Willard F. Libby is awarded the Nobel Prize in Chemistry for developing carbon dating techniques.
California, USA: The Daughters of Bilitis hold the first National Lesbian Conference in San Francisco.

Sydney, Australia: Painter Judy Cassab wins the Archibald Prize for her portrait of Stanislaus Rapotec.
England: British sculptor Barbara Hepworth casts the hollow bronzes Figure for Landscape and Archaeon.
Jonquiere, Quebec, Canada: The breastfeeding association, La Leche League, establishes its first group outside the USA.
Wirral, England: Maureen Nichol establishes the National Housewives' Register, for "housebound wives with liberal interests and a desire to remain individuals."

USA: American teen Brenda Lee hits number one with her song I'm Sorry.
Brisbane, Australia: Madam Chao Feng from the National Women's Federation of China, and Madame Roesijati R. Sukardi from the Indonesian Women's Organization, attend meetings of International Women's Day committees.
Copenhagen, Denmark: This year marks the 50th anniversary of International Women's Day, and delegates from 73 countries attend a conference to mark the occasion.

1961

Montgomery, Alabama, USA, May: White pro-segregation residents attack the "Freedom Riders," a multiracial group touring the southern states.
Stüttgart, Germany, July 19: African-American Wilma Rudolph sets a new world record for the 100-meter dash.
Berlin, Germany, August 13: East German troops begin erecting a wall to divide East from West Berlin.

Ndola, Rhodesia, September 18: UN Secretary-General Dag Hammerskjold dies in a plane crash in suspicious circumstances.
Zurich, Switzerland, September 27: US poet H.D., aka Hilda Doolittle, dies, aged 75.
New York, USA, October 14: The Prime of Miss Jean Brodie, by Muriel Spark, appears in The New Yorker magazine.

New York, USA, October 16: Mastering the Art of French Cooking, by Julia Child, Simone Beck, and Louisette Bertholle, is published.
Novaya Zemlya, USSR, October 30: Russia explodes the world's largest nuclear bomb, provoking worldwide condemnation. At 58 megatons, it is 4,000 times more powerful than the bomb dropped on Hiroshima in 1945.
USA, November 1: An estimated 50,000 women across the USA stage a strike for peace, imploring governments to "End the arms race, not the human race."

Saigon, South Vietnam, December 11: Following President Kennedy's pledge to increase military aid to South Vietnam, 400 US troops land in Saigon.
USA, December 13: US folk artist Grandma Moses dies, aged 101.
USA, December 14: President Kennedy establishes the President's Commission on the Status of Women.
Albuquerque, New Mexico, USA: Thirteen women pass the same rigorous tests as the "Mercury 7" men passed to become astronauts.

USA: Academic Women by Professor Jessie Barnard published.
New Zealand: Faces in the Water by Janet Frame published.
USA: New Mathematical Library, a series edited by Anneli Cahn Lax, commences.
New York, USA: Shadows on the Grass, a memoir by Isak Dinesen, is published by Random House.
USA: Witch Doctor's Apprentice by Nicole Hughes Maxwell, an account of the author's time in the Amazon jungle studying medicinal plants, is published.

1962

Berlin, Germany, August 17: Eighteen-year-old East German Peter Fechter is the first person to be shot and killed while attempting to cross the Berlin Wall to the West.
Phoenix, Arizona, USA, August 26: Sherri Finkbine's Swedish abortion ignites a storm of controversy.
Rungstedlund, Denmark, September 7: Writer Isak Dinesen dies, aged 77.
Könnersreuth, Germany, September 18: Mystic Therese Neumann dies.

Oxford, Mississippi, USA, October 1: Three die and 50 are injured as riots beak out at the University of Mississippi after the first African-American is admitted as a student.
Vatican City, October 11: Pope John XXIII convenes the first session of the second Vatican Council.
India, October 26: Indian and Chinese troops engage in heavy fighting over the disputed border region of Arunachal Pradesh.

Cuba, October 28: Seven days of escalating tension bring the world to the brink of nuclear confrontation before the USA and USSR reach a compromise.
New York City, USA, November 7: Former first lady and United Nations delegate Eleanor Roosevelt dies, aged 78.
Netherlands, November 28: Former Queen of the Netherlands, Wilhelmina, dies, aged 82.

Massawa, Eritrea (Ethiopia), December 19: A group of police desert the Ethiopian force to join the Eritrean Liberation Front, formed in 1961 in response to Ethiopia's UN-sanctioned annexation of the strategically important nation.
England: The Pre-school Playgroups Association is founded.
California, USA: Dolores Huerta helps to unionize the state's farm workers, reputedly among the most exploited in the United States.

New York City, USA: The first international conference on intra-uterine devices is held.
Strasbourg, France: Marguerite Perey is admitted to the Académie des Sciences.
London, England: The Golden Notebook, an experimental feminist novel by Doris Lessing, is published.
USA: Sex and the Single Girl by Helen Gurley Brown is published.
USA: Capitalism and Freedom by Milton Friedman, a landmark book on economic thinking, is published.

1963

Cheddington, England, August 8: Approximately £2.6 million in cash and jewelry is seized in a daring train robbery.
Washington, DC, USA, August 28: Martin Luther King delivers his "I have a dream..." speech.
Neuilly, France, September 11: Painter Suzanne Duchamp dies, aged 74.
Aberdeen, San Diego, USA, September 14: The US's first surviving quintuplets are born to Mary Ann Fischer.

Birmingham, Alabama, USA, September 15: A bomb explodes in the Sixteenth Street Baptist Church, killing four black schoolgirls: Addie Collins, Denise McNair, Carol Robertson, and Cynthia Wesley.
Malaysia, September 16: Malaysia is formed by unifying Singapore, Malaya, North Borneo, and Sarawak.
Hollywood, USA, October 1: The extremely costly epic, Cleopatra, starring Richard Burton and Elizabeth Taylor, is a box-office dud, with audiences dismissing it as dull and overblown.

Paris, France, October 11: "The Little Sparrow," Edith Piaf, dies of cancer, aged 47.
Australia, November 1: Indigenous men and women are granted the right to vote in Australian elections.
Dallas, USA, November 22: President Kennedy is assassinated; Lyndon B. Johnson is sworn in as President less than two hours after the tragedy.
New York USA: Barbara Epstein and Robert Silver found the New York Review of Books.

South Vietnam, November: Madame Nhu, sister-in-law and spokeswoman for assassinated despotic leader, Ngo Dinh Diem, is refused the right to return to the country by the new military government.
Stockholm, Sweden, December 10: Maria Goeppert-Mayer wins the Nobel Prize for Physics jointly with Hans D. Jensen for "their discoveries concerning nuclear shell structure."
Boston, USA: Julia Childs' The French Chef airs for the first time on American television.

Detroit, Michigan, USA, December 14: The "Queen of Harlem Blues," Dinah Washington, dies, aged 39.
South Africa, December, 1963: Journalist and activist, Ruth First, departs for exile in England after 117 days in solitary confinement.
USA: Betty Friedan publishes The Feminine Mystique.
USA: Hannah Arendt's Eichmann in Jerusalem: A Report on the Banality of Evil is published.
Leeds, England: Pianist, Fanny Waterman, founds the Leeds International Pianoforte Competition.

1964

Calcutta, India, January 13: Over 100 people are killed in rioting between Hincus and Muslims.
California, USA, February 5: Pilot Mathilde Moisant dies, aged 84.
New York City, USA, February 7: Beatlemania hits the USA when the band arrives in New York City.
Tasman Sea, Australia, February 10: HMAS *Melbourne* collides with HMAS *Voyager*, killing 82.
Boston, USA February 25: Author Grace Metalious dies of cirrhosis of the liver.

London, England, March 10: Queen Elizabeth gives birth to Prince Edward, her fourth child.
Chattanooga, Tennessee, USA, March 12: Jimmy Hoffa, president of the powerful Teamsters Union, is sentenced to eight years in jail for jury tampering.
Montreal, Canada, March 15: Film stars Elizabeth Taylor and Richard Burton wed.
Columbus, Ohio, USA, March 19: Geraldine "Jerrie" Mock finishes the first solo flight around the world by a woman.

London, England, March 25: The *Married Women's Property Act* is passed into law.
Cleveland, Ohio, USA, March 30: Singer Tracy Chapman is born.
St. Augustine, Florida, USA, April 2: Seventy-two-year-old mother of the governor of Massachusetts, Mrs Malcolm Peabody, is released from jail on $450 bail after taking part in an anti-segregation demonstration.
Rhodesia, April 13: Ian Smith is elected Prime Minister, vowing to keep the black majority from participating in elections.

Maryland, USA, April 14: Author of the environmentally prophetic book *Silent Spring*, Rachel Carson, dies, aged 57.
Lincolnshire, England, May 2: Politician Nancy Langhorne Astor, dies, aged 85.
USA, May 4: Jacqueline Cochran sets the world speed record for women of 1,428 mph (2,298 kmh) in a Lockheed F-104G Starfighter jet.
Lima, Peru, May 24: A riot at a soccer match between Peru and Argentina leaves 318 people dead and 500 injured.

Jerusalem, Israel, June 2: The Palestine Liberation Organization (PLO) is founded, after the first Arab League summit laid the groundwork.
Port Moresby, Papua New Guinea, June 8: The first House of Assembly opens. It is a major constitutional step—the country has been administered by Australia since the 1920s.
Pretoria, South Africa, June 12: Nelson Mandela and seven other African National Congress activists are given life sentences for sabotage.

1965

Canberra, Australia, January 15: Champion swimmer, Dawn Fraser, is named Australian of the Year.
London, England, January 30: A state funeral is held for wartime leader, Sir Winston Churchill, who died six days ago, aged 91.
Canada, February 15: The red and white maple leaf flag is adopted.
New York, USA, February 21: Firebrand black nationalist leader, Malcolm X, is assassinated by two members of his former organization, the Nation of Islam.

New York City, March 2: The movie version of Rodgers & Hammerstein's Broadway hit, *The Sound of Music*, starring Julie Andrews, premieres at the Rivoli Theater.
USA, March 11: A collection of reviews by Pauline Kael, *I Lost It at the Movies*, is published by Little, Brown & Co.
New York, USA, March 25: The opera *Lizzie Borden* premieres.
Sri Lanka, March 27: The world's first elected woman prime minister, Sirimavo Bandaranaike, is voted out in favor of Dudley Senanayake.

Danang, South Vietnam, March 31: The first US troops are sent to Vietnam to protect the US air base at Danang. In February, American bombers began to pound Vietcong positions in the north.
New York, USA, April 1: Cosmetics manufacturer and entrepreneur, Helena Rubinstein, dies in her 90s.
Hollywood, USA, April 6: Julie Andrews wins the Best Actress Oscar for *Mary Poppins*.
Glenville, Illinois, USA, April 10: Actress Linda Darnell dies in a house fire, aged 47.

Canberra, Australia, April 29: Prime Minister Menzies commits 1,000 Australian troops to fight in South Vietnam.
New York City, USA, May 14: Politician Frances Perkins dies, aged 83.
Dominican Republic, May: The USA sends 14,000 troops to the Caribbean island after civil war breaks out in April following a coup.
USA, June 7: Use of contraceptives by married couples is finally legal in the state of Connecticut, after a landmark Supreme Court decision.

New York, USA, June 7: Film star Judy Holliday dies of breast cancer, aged 43.
Algeria, June 19: Independence hero and Prime Minister, Ahmed Ben Bella, is deposed in a bloodless coup led by Colonel Boumedienne.
Tokyo, Japan, June 22: Japan and South Korea sign a treaty of basic relations, normalizing relations for the first time since Japan annexed the Korean peninsula in 1910. Japan agrees to pay $800 million in compensation.

1966

New Delhi, India, January 19: Indira Gandhi, daughter of former prime minister Pandit Jawaharlal Nehru, is elected Prime Minister.
Afghanistan, January: Kubra Noorzai is appointed Minister of Public Health. She is the first woman ever to be appointed to the cabinet.
Hollywood, USA, February 1: Gossip columnist Hedda Hopper dies at the age of 80.
New York City, USA, February 9: Russian-American singer Sophie Tucker dies, aged 79.

Accra, Ghana, February 24: An army coup deposes Prime Minister and self-styled redeemer of Ghana, Kwame Nkrumah, while he is on an official visit to China.
Los Angeles, USA, March 3: Actress Alice Pearce dies from cancer. She was aged 49.
Leningrad, USSR, March 5: Poet Anna Akhmatov, dies, aged 78.
Amsterdam, Netherlands, March 10: Crown Princess Beatrix of the Netherlands marries German-born Claus von Amsberg amid public demonstrations.

Jakarta, Indonesia, March 11: General Soeharto receives a letter of instruction from President Sukarno, transferring state power to the army, amid chaos following an abortive coup in September last year.
Rome, Italy, March 27: Pope Paul VI meets Dr Ramsey, Archbishop of Canterbury—the first meeting for 400 years between the heads of the two Churches.
Sydney, Australia, April 19: Violent scenes erupt in Sydney as Australia's first National Service conscripts fly out for Vietnam.

Boston, USA, April 19: Roberta Gibb is the first woman to complete the Boston Marathon. She hid herself in the bushes at the race's start, and finished ahead of two-thirds of the male competitors.
Indiana, USA, May 16: Pop singer Janet Jackson is born.
London, England, May 26: Murderers Ian Brady and Myra Hindley are sentenced to life imprisonment.
Wimbledon, England, June: Powerful hitter Billie Jean King wins her first Wimbledon title.

Memphis, USA, June 7: James Meredith, in 1962 the first African-American to attend the University of Mississippi, is shot and wounded in a civil rights march. Martin Luther King takes over as march leader.
London, England, June 12: Sheila Scott returns to Heathrow after flying solo around the world. She has set a new speed record of 189 hours.
Mururoa Atoll, French Polynesia, July 2: France explodes a nuclear device in the Pacific.
USA, July 19: Frank Sinatra weds Mia Farrow, 30 years his junior.

1967

Sacramento, USA, January 2: Former film actor, Ronald Reagan, is sworn in as Governor of California.
Scotland, January 3: Scottish opera legend Mary Garden dies, aged ninety-two.
Cape Kennedy, USA, January 27: Astronauts Virgil "Gus" Grissom, Ed White, and Roger Chaffee, die in *Apollo* spacecraft fire.
New York City, USA, February 22: Barbara Garson's satirical play, *MacBird*, premieres.

India, March 9: Josef Stalin's daughter, Svetlana Alliluyeva, seeks political asylum at the US embassy.
Connecticut, USA, March 11: Soprano Geraldine Farrar dies, aged eighty-five.
Aachen, Germany, March 14: Executives of Chemie Grünenthal are charged over Thalidomide drug, which caused deformities in babies.
Cornwall, England, March 29: Armed forces bomb stricken oil tanker, *Torrey Canyon*, which ran aground, spreading oil on beaches in France and the UK.

Athens, Greece, April 21: Right-wing army officers under Colonel George Papadopoulos seize power, deposing George Papandreou.
Las Vegas, USA, May 1: Elvis Presley marries Priscilla Beaulieu.
Canberra, Australia, May 27: Australians vote for a proposal to count Aboriginal people in the national census.
Wimbledon, England, June: Billie Jean King wins all three possible titles at Wimbledon: women's singles, women's doubles, and mixed doubles.

London, England, June 7: Queen Elizabeth meets the Duchess of Windsor, healing the 30-year rift caused by Edward VII's abdication.
New York City, USA, June 7: Critic and author Dorothy Parker dies, aged seventy-three.
California, USA, June 15: Governor Reagan signs the *Therapeutic Abortion Act*, legalizing abortion in certain circumstances in California.
Middle East, June 10: The six-day war against Syria and Egypt comes to an end as Israel finally observes a UN ceasefire.

Virginia, USA, June 12: The US Supreme Court rules that Virginia's ban on interracial marriage is unconstitutional in its ruling of the *Loving vs. Virginia* case.
Hawaii, USA, June 20: Actress, Nicole Kidman is born.
New Orleans, USA, June 29: Film actress Jayne Mansfield is killed in a car accident; her three children survive in the back seat.
London, England, July 8: Vivien Leigh, the screen beauty who immortalized Scarlett O'Hara in *Gone with the Wind*, dies at fifty-three.

1964

New Delhi, India, June 13: One and a half million people line the route of the funeral of Prime Minister and independence hero, Jawaharlal Nehru. He has led the country since independence from Britain in 1947.

Washington DC, USA, July 2: President Lyndon Johnson continues Kennedy's reforming mandate, signing the new *Civil Rights Act* prohibiting racial or sexual discrimination.

Malawi, July 6: After significant campaigning from Vera and Orton Chirwa, Malawi gains independence.

Georgia, July 16: Future president Nino Burdzhanadze is born.

Atlantic City, New Jersey, USA, August 22: Fannie Lou Hamer addresses the Democratic Party National Convention on behalf of the Mississippi Freedom Democratic Party, asking, on national television, "Is this America, the land of the free and the brave, where we are threatened daily because we want to live as decent human beings?"

Hollywood, USA, August 27: The well-loved comedian Gracie Allen dies, at age 71.

USA, August 29: The Disney film version of Pamela Lyndon Travers's beloved series, *Mary Poppins*, starring Julie Andrews, is released.

Labis, Malaysia, September 3: Indonesian paratroopers land in Labis, after two years of conflict between Indonesia and the new Federation of Malaysia. New Zealand, Britain, and Australia have all pledged assistance to the Malaysians.

Moscow, USSR, October 15: Premier Nikita Khrushchev resigns, to be replaced by Leonid Brezhnev.

Tokyo, October 24: The closing ceremony of the Tokyo Olympics takes place. At these Olympics, Mary Rand became the first British woman to win a gold medal, and Australian swimmer Dawn Fraser won her third successive gold medal for the 100-meter freestyle.

Kenya, November 10: Kenya becomes a republic under the leadership of Jomo Kenyatta.

Luxembourg, November 12: Charlotte, Grand Duchess of Luxembourg, abdicates in favor of her son, Jean.

England, December 9: Poet, Dame Edith Sitwell, dies.

Stockholm, Sweden, December 10: Dorothy Crowfoot Hodgkin wins the Nobel Prize for Chemistry.

USA: Mary Steichen Calderone establishes the Sexuality Information and Education Council of the US.

USA: Helen Frankenthaler paints *Interior Landscape*.

USA: The controversial novel for young people, *Harriet the Spy*, by Louise Fitzhugh, is published.

1965

Auckland, New Zealand, July 25: Shirley Ann Lawson gives birth to the world's first set of quintuplets as a result of fertility treatment.

Washington DC, USA, July 30: US Congress amends the *Social Security Act*, establishing Medicaid, which funds various family programs.

USA, July: The first edition of *Cosmopolitan*–edited by Helen Gurley Brown, author of *Sex and the Single Girl*–hits the stands.

Vermont, USA, August 8: Horror fiction author, Shirley Jackson, dies.

Singapore, August 9: Serious racial tensions between Malays and Chinese force Singapore to declare independence from Malaysia.

Los Angeles, USA, August 15: Six days of rioting leaves 34 people dead and over 1,000 injured. The trouble began when a black motorist was arrested in the Watts area.

Kashmir, September 6: The Indian army invades West Pakistan in response to earlier incursions by Pakistani soldiers.

Hollywood, California, USA, September 8: Actress Dorothy Dandridge dies of an antidepressant drug overdose, aged 41. She was the first African-American nominated for the Best Actress Oscar for her role in *Carmen Jones*.

London, England, September 19: Dusty Springfield, the "white lady of soul," is voted best female singer in Britain.

USA, September 27: Silent film star Clara Bow dies of a heart attack, aged 60.

New York City, USA, October 15: Thousands attend the latest anti-war protest as movement gains favor.

Melbourne, Australia, October 30: British model Jean Shrimpton shocks the world and sets a new trend by wearing a mini-skirt and no gloves to a Melbourne horse race meeting.

USA, October: Patricia Harris becomes the first African-American ambassador when she takes a post in Belgium.

USA, November 8: Soap opera, *Days of Our Lives*, premieres on TV.

Rhodesia, November 11: World-wide condemnation greets Prime Minister Ian Smith's decision to sever links with Britain and maintain white-minority rule.

London, England, December 10: As Maria Callas gives her last performance in *Tosca* at the Royal Opera, Australian Joan Sutherland takes the mantle as supreme diva.

Tonga, December 15: Salote Tupou, former Queen of Tonga, dies, aged 65.

London, England December 23: Barbara Castle becomes England's first female Secretary of State.

1966

Kuala Lumpur, Malaysia, August 11: Three years of guerrilla warfare between Indonesia and Malaysia come to an end.

Beijing, China, August 13: Mao Tse-tung's Cultural Revolution targets professionals and intellectuals for re-education to Communism.

Vung Tau, South Vietnam, August 18: At Long Tan, Australian troops fight a pitched battle against Vietcong about four times their number.

London, England, August 27: Model Twiggy appears on the cover of *Woman's Mirror*.

Pretoria, South Africa, September 6: Prime Minister Hendrik Verwoerd, the "Father of Apartheid," is stabbed to death by Demetrio Tsafendas.

Arizona, USA, September 6: Family planning advocate Margaret Sanger dies, aged 86.

New York City, USA, September 14: Actress Gertrude Berg dies at the age of 66.

Colorado, USA, September 29: Poet Mina Loy dies, aged 84.

New York, USA, October 19: Cosmetics manufacturer Elizabeth Arden dies.

Aberfan, Wales, October 21: A sliding slagheap of mine tailings buries a school, killing 116 children and 28 adults.

USA, October 29: The National Organization for Women (NOW), formed in June, holds its first national conference.

Moscow, USSR, November 27: The Soviet Communist Party denounces Chinese leadership as the Cultural Revolution gathers speed.

Australia: The ban on married women entering the federal public service is lifted.

Salisbury, Rhodesia, December 6: The leader of the rebel regime, Ian Smith, rejects proposals by Britain, including bringing black politicians into his cabinet, to end a 13-month dispute initiated by Smith's declaration of independence.

Stockholm, Sweden, December 10: German-born Nelly Sachs co-wins the Nobel Prize for Literature.

England: The Jockey Club allows women to hold training licences.

USA: *The Valley of the Dolls*, by Jacqueline Sussan, is published.

USA: *Jubilee*, by Margaret Walker Alexander, is published.

USA: Dusty Springfield records "You Don't Have to Say You Love Me."

Cornwall, England: Caribbean writer Jean Rhys publishes *The Wide Sargasso Sea*.

Nigeria: The first Nigerian woman to be published is Flora Nwapa, with her book, *Efuru*.

Canada: Jean Sutherland Boggs becomes Director of the National Gallery of Canada. She is the first woman in the world to be appointed director of a national art gallery.

1967

Port Harcourt, Nigeria, July 16: The Igbo (Ibo) people of Nigeria set up the separate state of Biafra in the oil-rich south-east of Nigeria, initiating civil war between Nigerian forces and the rebels.

New York City, USA, July 31: Feminist author Elizabeth Wurtzel is born.

Beijing, China, August 30: Red Guards set fire to the British Mission in Beijing and bar all members from leaving without permission.

Bolivia, August 31: Argentinean-born guerrilla and disciple of Che Guevera, Haydee Tamara Bunke Bider, is killed by Bolivian soldiers in an ambush.

Cambridge, England, September: Astronomical research student Jocelyn Bell discovers pulsars.

USA, September 11: *The Carol Burnett Show* premieres on American television.

Villa Grande, Bolivia, October 10: The body of Ernesto "Che" Guevera is put on display after he is shot by troops in Bolivia.

Oakland, California, USA, October 20: The fifth day of anti-Vietnam War protests sees 4,000 demonstrators battling police. Four days ago folk singer Joan Baez was arrested at a sit-in at a military induction center in Oakland.

England, October 27: In England, Scotland and Wales, under medical supervision and in certain circumstances, abortion is legalized.

South Vietnam, November: General Westmoreland is heavily fortifying Khe Sanh in preparation for attacks on the Ho Chi Minh Trail.

Portsea, Australia, December 22: Australian Prime Minister Harold Holt drowns while swimming in rough seas off Cheviot Beach.

New York City, USA, December 28: Muriel Siebert wins a seat on the New York Stock Exchange, the first woman to do so.

New Zealand: The National Council on the Employment of Women is established.

USA: Diane Arbus takes her famous *Identical Twins* photograph.

London, England: Dame Cicely Saunders establishes St. Christopher's Hospice, revolutionizing the way the medical profession deals with the dying.

USA: Denise Levertov publishes *The Sorrow Dance*, a book of poetry about the Vietnam War and the death of her sister.

San Francisco, USA: Marjorie Fiske Lowenthal's *Aging and Mental Disorder* is published by Jossey-Bass Inc.

1968

Sydney, Australia, January 14: Dorothea Mackellar, renowned poet, dies, aged 82.

South Vietnam, January 31: North Vietnamese and the Vietcong launch the Tet offensive.

UK, February 4: Kenyan Asians start to arrive in the UK, fleeing the repressive laws that have prevented them from making a living since independence in Kenya.

Memphis, USA, February 4: The first child of Elvis and Priscilla Presley, Lisa Marie, is born.

Grenoble, France, February 6-18: Gender tests on women are carried out for the first time in international sports at the Winter Olympic Games.

Kentucky, USA, March 1: Country singers Johnny Cash and June Carter marry.

My Lai, South Vietnam, March 16: US troops massacre hundreds of unarmed civilians.

Mahwah, New Jersey, March 24: Alice Guy-Blaché, the first woman film director, as well as the first person to direct a narrative movie, dies, aged 94.

Iowa, USA, April 5: Jane Elliot, a grade-three teacher, uses an exercise in which she segregates blue-eyed children to demonstrate the nature of racism to her students.

Atlanta, USA, April 9: The funeral of Martin Luther King, who was assassinated in Memphis on April 4, is attended by 150,000 people.

Wellington, New Zealand, April 10: The ferry *Wahine* capsizes in Wellington Harbour in a severe storm. Of the 734 passengers and crew on board, 51 lose their lives.

New York, April 16: Edna Ferber, author of *Showboat*, dies, aged 82.

New York, USA, May 9: Writer and costume designer Mercedes de Acosta dies, aged 75.

Paris, France, May 10: The Paris Peace talks commence. The Vietnamese delegation is led by a woman, Nguyen Thi Binh.

Washington DC, USA, May 12: A protest against poverty by approximately 5,000 "welfare mothers" is led by Ethel Kennedy and Coretta Scott King.

Maryland, USA, May 17: Nine protesters—including two women, Mary Moylan and Marjorie Melville—burn stolen draft cards and recite the Lord's Prayer, before arrest.

France, May: Ten million workers strike in solidarity with students after leftist student riots earlier this month were brutally suppressed by the police. President de Gaulle issues an ultimatum for the country to back his reforms or sack him.

Connecticut, USA, June 1: Deaf and blind academic, and advocate of the disabled, Helen Keller, dies, aged 87.

1969

Chicago, USA, January 14-16: The National Association for the Repeal of Abortion Laws (NARAL) is set up at a conference on abortion.

Paris, France, January 18: The Paris peace talks open between the USA, South Vietnam, North Vietnam, and the Vietcong.

USA, January: Elisabeth Kübler-Ross publishes *On Death and Dying*.

Florida, USA, February 7: Amid boos and cheers, 20-year-old Diane Crump enters the Hialeah Racetrack and becomes the first woman to ride in a pari-mutuel race in the country.

Cambridge, England, February 13: At Cambridge Physiological Laboratory, human eggs taken from female volunteers are fertilized outside the body (in test tubes) for the first time.

London, England, March 12: Beatle Paul McCartney weds Linda Eastman in a civil ceremony.

Tel Aviv, Israel, March 17: Golda Meir is Israel's first woman prime minister.

The Netherlands, March 25: Five days after their wedding, John Lennon and Yoko Ono stage a "bed-in" in the Hilton Hotel in Amsterdam, protesting against the Vietnam War.

Louisiana, USA, March 26: Writer John Kennedy Toole commits suicide. His mother Thelma Ducoing Toole promises to get his only novel, *A Confederacy of Dunces*, published.

Franklin, Victoria, Australia, April 6: Annie Moriah Sage, military nurse and women's advocate, dies at 73.

Belfast, Northern Ireland, UK, April 17: Bernadette Devlin becomes the country's youngest ever woman MP.

USA, May 2: *Time* magazine reports in "The Pros and Cons of the Pill" that seven million American women are using the contraceptive pill.

Ottawa, Canada, May 14: Abortion is legalized in Canada.

Midway Island, USA, Pacific Ocean, June 8: US President Nixon meets with South Vietnamese leader Nguyen Van Thieu to discuss the "Vietnamization" of the Vietnam War. Around 25,000 US troops are projected to withdraw by September.

Canberra, Australia, June 19: The Commonwealth Court of Arbitrations rules that equal pay for equal work be phased in by 1972.

Dallas, Texas, USA, June 21: Maureen Catherine Connolly ("Little Mo") dies of cancer, aged 34. In 1953 she became the first woman to win the four major tennis titles in a year.

New York, USA, June 28-July 3: After a raid on the Stonewall Hotel, hundreds of gays and lesbians riot against police.

Nigeria, June 30: The Nigerian government bans Red Cross night flights from distributing food aid in the disputed state of Biafra, jeopardizing the survival of four million people.

1970

Las Vegas, USA, January 14: Diana Ross and the Supremes perform their last concert together at the Frontier Hotel.

Tripoli, Libya, January 16: Colonel Muammar Gaddafi becomes premier of Libya, promoting an Arab nationalist ideology.

London, England, January 23: The first Jumbo jet lands at Heathrow. The airport's infrastructure is overloaded by 362 passengers, twice as many as a Boeing 707 carries.

Paris, France, January 25: Opera star Jane Bathori dies, aged 92.

New York City, USA, February/March: Judith Heumann founds Disabled in Action, after her application for a teaching license is denied because she uses a wheelchair.

Tuscon, Arizona, February 20: Playwright Sophie Treadwell dies, aged 85.

London, England, February: Anna Ford becomes the first woman newscaster on ITN when she appears on *News at Ten*.

Geneva, Switzerland, March 5: The Nuclear Non-Proliferation Treaty is ratified by 43 nations.

New York City, USA, March 6: Diana Oughton, Ted Gold, and Terry Robbins—members of the student activist group the Weathermen—are killed when a bomb is unintentionally detonated while being manufactured at a student residence.

Africa, April 24: Gambia becomes a republic. Seven weeks earlier, Rhodesia was also declared a republic by Prime Minister Ian Smith.

Los Angeles, USA, April 26: Former actress and burlesque performer Gypsy Rose Lee dies of lung cancer, aged in her late 50s.

New York, USA, May 1: Lesbians in the National Organization for Women protest homophobia at the national conference.

Kentucky, USA, May 2: Jockey Diane Crump is the first woman to race in the Kentucky Derby.

USA, May 4: Six students in anti-war protests at Ohio and Mississippi university campuses are shot dead.

United Kingdom, May 19: Baroness Betty Lockwood is instrumental in the passage of the *Equal Pay Act*.

New York City, USA, May 29: Eva Hesse dies of a brain tumor, aged 34.

USA, June 11: Anna Mae McCabe Hays becomes the first woman general in the US Army.

Indonesia, June 21: Sukarno, the first president of Indonesia, dies of kidney disease, aged 69.

Londonderry (Derry), Northern Ireland, June 26: Riots break out as news of MP Bernadette Devlin's arrest for her part in the Bogside riots spreads.

Sydney, Australia, July 2: Suffragette Jessie Mary Grey Street dies, aged 81.

1971

Paris, France, January 10: French fashion designer Gabrielle (Coco) Chanel dies, aged 87.

Berlin, Germany, January 31: Telephone services between East and West Berlin are re-established after 19 years.

Geneva, Switzerland, February 7: Switzerland gives women the right to vote in federal elections.

USA, February 13: The six-part TV miniseries *Elizabeth*, Glenda Jackson's tour-de-force as the fiercely independent Elizabeth I of England, debuts.

London, England, February 15: The decimal system of currency is introduced. The previous system was in place for 1,200 years.

Liechtenstein, February 28: The tiny country's male electorate refuses the vote to women.

London, UK March 6 : 4,000 women protesters march from Hyde Park to Downing Street in the UK's biggest women's liberation demonstration.

USA, March: Janis Joplin's hit song "Me and Bobby McGee" is released posthumously.

USA, March: Ike and Tina Turner's "Proud Mary" peaks at No. 4 on the popular music charts.

Dubin, Ireland, April 3: Severine, representing Monaco, wins the Eurovision Song Contest with the song "Un banc, un arbre, une rue."

France, April 5: The *Manifeste des 343* is published, in which 343 French women, including some celebrities, risk arrest for declaring publicly that they have undergone abortions.

North Pole, April 5: Canadian Fran Phipps becomes the first woman to reach the North Pole.

Hollywood, USA, April 15: Glenda Jackson wins the Academy Award for Best Actress for her performance in *Women in Love*.

Saigon, South Vietnam, May: Buddhist Nguyen Thi Co immolates herself to protest the Vietnam War.

London, UK June 8: Members of the Women's Institute convene for the 50th AGM of the National Federation of Women's Institutes.

California, USA, June: Computer "floppy disks" are developed by IBM to store data.

Wimbledon, England, July 2: Nineteen-year-old Evonne Goolagong wins Wimbledon title, beating fellow Australian Margaret Court 6-4, 6-1.

New York, USA, July 10: Gloria Steinem addresses the first meeting of the National Women's Political Caucus, formed by US feminists Steinem, Betty Friedan, Fannie Lou Hamer, Congresswoman Bella Abzug, and others.

1968

New York, USA, June 3: Andy Warhol is shot by the founder of the Society for Cutting Up Men (SCUM), Valerie Solanis.

Los Angeles, USA, June 6: Presidential candidate Robert Kennedy is assassinated by Palestinian militant, Sirhan Sirhan.

Dagenham, Essex, England, June 7: Eight hundred and fifty female machinists at a Ford car plant strike to protest against unfair pay. They are asking to be paid as class "C" machinists like their male counterparts who do the same job.

World, July 1: The Nuclear Non-Proliferation Treaty is signed by 62 nations, including the USA, the USSR, and the UK.

Vatican City, Italy, July 29: Pope Paul VI confirms the ban on the use of contraceptives by Catholics, despite calls for change, with the release of *Humanae Vitae*.

Toronto, Canada, August 9: Dr Norma Ford Walker, renowned geneticist and researcher of childhood diseases, dies, aged 74.

Prague, Czechoslovakia, August 21: The "Prague Spring" program of liberalization initiated by Alexander Dubcek comes to an abrupt end when Warsaw Pact countries send in tanks to reinstate hard-line communist policy. Czechoslovaks take to the streets to show their support for the reforms.

Moscow, USSR, August 25: Larisa Bogoraz and Natalya Gorbanecskaya are among seven protesters arrested in Red Square after coming out in support of the Prague Spring.

New York, USA, August: Janice Joplin and Big Brother and the Holding Company record the album *Cheap Thrills*.

USA, August: For the first time, a black model appears on the cover of a national woman's magazine, *Glamour*, edited by Ruth Whitney.

Atlantic City, New Jersey, USA, September 7: The Miss America pageant is disrupted by feminists protesting the demeaning of women.

Birmingham, England, October 2: Sheila Thorns gives birth to sextuplets—four boys and two girls.

Mexico City, Mexico, October 12: The Summer Olympics begin with the lighting of the Olympic flame by Norma Enriqueta Basilio Satelo, the first woman to be awarded the honor.

Scorpios, Greece, October 20: Widow of John F. Kennedy, Jacqueline Kennedy, marries shipping magnate Aristotle Onassis.

New York, USA, December 12: Actress Tallulah Bankhead dies, aged 65.

USA: Shirley Chisholm becomes first African-American woman elected to Congress.

1969

USA, July 18: President Nixon calls for increased federal funding for family planning facilities.

The Moon, July 21: Neil Armstrong walks on the Moon.

San Diego, California, USA, July 26: Sharon Sites Adams is the first woman to sail solo across the Pacific.

Los Angeles, California, USA, August 9: Charles Manson and his "family" kill Sharon Tate and four others.

California, USA, September 4: The state adopts the country's first "no fault" divorce law.

Washington DC, USA, September 4: A report declares birth control pills safe, despite the slight risk of fatal blood-clotting.

Digne, France, September 8: Alexandra David-Néel, adventurer, author, and translator, dies, aged 100.

Chicago, USA, September 26: The Seventh Circuit Court of Appeals, in the case of *Bowe v. Colgate-Palmolive Company*, rules that women meeting the physical requirements of a position should be allowed to work in such positions previously open to men only.

Greenmount, Western Australia, Australia, October 2: Writer Katharine Susannah Prichard dies, aged 85.

Oslo, Norway, October 12: Champion Norwegian figure skater Sonja Henie dies of leukemia, aged 57.

Chicago, USA, October 31: The Chicago Women's Liberation Union is founded. This is the US's first women's union, and the organization behind the underground abortion clinic, Jane.

South Africa, October: Political activist Winnie Mandela and 21 other South Africans are charged under the *Securities Act* with supporting the African National Congress (ANC).

Washington DC, USA, November 15: A group of around 250,000 people marches to the US capitol to demand an end to the Vietnam War.

Okinawa, Japan, November, 21: A joint US-Japanese communiqué announces that Okinawa and the other Ryukyu Islands are to be handed back to the Japanese.

Antarctica, November: Lois Jones, Kay Lindsay, Jean Pearson, Eileen McSaveney, Terry Ticknill, and Pam Young are the first women to visit the South Pole.

Sweden: Norwegian actress Liv Ullman has again teamed with director Ingmar Bergman, this time on the film *The Passion of Anna*.

Canada: Margaret Atwood publishes her first book, *The Edible Woman*.

China: Madame Mao (Jiang Qing) becomes a member of the Politburo, thereby strengthening her position in Chinese politics.

1970

Munich, Germany, July 14: Chi Cheng of Formosa sets a new world record in the women's 200 meters and equals the record of 12.8 seconds in the 100 meters hurdle.

Egypt, July 21: The Aswan High Dam is completed at a cost of $800 million, regulating the flow of the Nile and relieving the threat of flooding downstream.

Lisbon, Portugal, August 18: Horror movie actress Soledad Miranda (also known as Susan Korda) is killed in a car accident, aged 27.

New York City, August 26: Betty Freidan leads a march as part of Women's Strike for Equality.

Jordan, September: After the hijacking of several planes by Palestinian terrorists, the PLO is ejected from its Jordanian stronghold. King Hussein orders his army to attack Palestinians who threaten his leadership.

Atlantic City, USA, September: Cheryl Brown is the first black woman to make the finals of the Miss America pageant.

New York, USA, September 13: Margaret Smith Court wins the US Open women's final, beating Rosie Casals in three sets, and becoming the second woman in tennis history to win a grand slam.

USA, September 19: Television sitcom, *The Mary Tyler Moore Show*, premieres.

London, England, September 30: Popular Front for the Liberation of Palestine member Leila Khaled, the notorious hijacker, is released by Prime Minister Edward Heath in exchange for 56 western hostages.

Los Angeles, October 4: Blues and rock singer Janis Joplin dies of an accidental drug overdose, aged 27.

Rome, Italy, October 9: The Italian Senate passes a bill which will legalize divorce.

Pakistan, November 12-13: Cyclonic winds, an earthquake, and tidal waves kill over 150,000 people.

England: *The Female Eunuch*, by Australian feminist Germaine Greer, is published.

Washington DC, USA, December 24: Congress passes Title X of the Family Planning Act, allowing public funding for family planning services.

Boston, USA: The Boston Women's Health Book Collective publish Our Bodies, Ourselves.

England: *The Female Eunuch*, by Australian feminist Germaine Greer, is published.

USA: Susan Lyndon writes the article "The Politics of Orgasm" for *Ramparts Magazine*.

1971

UK, July 16: Terry Clark, who has passed the Football Association's referee's exam, becomes one of a handful of women referees.

South Africa, July 25: Christiaan Barnard performs the first combined heart–lung transplant.

Newport, USA, July 26: British sailor Nicolette Milnes-Walker is the first woman to sail solo across the Atlantic, from Wales to Newport, Rhode Island, in 45 days.

The Moon, July 30: *Apollo 15* lands a four-wheeled "moon buggy" and astronauts drive 17 miles (27 km).

USA, August 1: The *Sonny and Cher Comedy Hour* premieres on TV.

Paris, France, August 1: French swimmer Christine Caron wins the 100m backstroke event at the Nautic Stadium Georges Vallerey in Paris

London, England, August 4: Sheila Scott lands at Heathrow after making the first solo light-aircraft flight around the world, equator to equator over the North Pole.

Australia and New Zealand, August 18: Australia and New Zealand announce they will pull troops out of Vietnam by December.

Chicago, USA, August 27: Jazz musician Lil Hardin Armstrong, ex-wife of Louis Armstrong, dies onstage while playing "St Louis Blues" at a televised memorial concert for Armstrong, just seven weeks after his death.

Vatican City, October 20: Barbara Ward is the first woman to address the Vatican Council.

Belfast, Ireland, November 10: Two Belfast women are tarred for dating British soldiers, and a Catholic girl in Londonderry is also tarred for her intention to marry a British soldier.

London, UK November 10: Women's libbers demonstrate outside the Royal Albert Hall, London, during the Miss World contest.

Alberta, Canada, November 12: Canadian flight attendant Mary Dohey saves the lives of passengers and crew when her Air Canada flight is hijacked.

California, USA, November 15: Intel produces the first micro-processor.

Hong Kong, November 28: Jane Hwang Hsien Yuen and Joyce Bennett are the first women to be ordained as Anglican priests.

London, England: Erin Pizzey sets up the Chiswick's Women's Aid, a pioneering shelter for battered women.

France, December 20: A group of doctors form Médecins Sans Frontières to assist the people of the Biafra region of Nigeria. They form the group in frustration at the neutrality of the Red Cross.

France: Exiled Greek actress and singer, Melina Mercouri ,publishes her autobiography, *I Was Born Greek*.

Vatican City: Barbara Ward is first woman to address Vatican Council.

1972

Copenhagen, Denmark, January 15: Margrethe II is crowned Queen of Denmark—the first Danish queen to succeed directly to the throne under the new Act of Succession.
New York, USA, January 25: Shirley Chisholm announces her Democratic candidacy for president, becoming the second African-American woman to run for the US presidency.
Washington DC, USA, March 22: The Equal Rights Amendment is sent to the states for ratification after passing both Houses of Congress.

USA, March 24: Francis Ford Coppola's cinematic masterpiece about a Mafia family, *The Godfather*, opens.
Madrid, Spain, March: Maria del Carmen Martinez-Bordiu y Franco, grand-daughter of General Franco, marries Don Alfonso, Duke of Anjou and Cadiz.
World, March: The El Niño weather pattern is seen to reverse trade winds on the equator.

Hayman Island, Australia, April 22: Sylvia Cook becomes the first woman to row across any ocean in her Pacific crossing with John Fairfax. They left San Francisco, USA, on April 26, 1971.
New York, USA, April 30: Seven nuns are arrested at St. Patrick's Cathedral for disrupting a Mass in an anti-war protest.
New York, USA, May: Barbara Tuchman wins her second Pulitzer Prize for non-fiction for *Stilwell and the American Experience in China*, published in 1971.

San Jose, California, USA, June 4: Angela Davis is acquitted on charges that she supplied guns for a shooting at Marin County Courthouse in 1970.
Washington, D.C., USA, June 17: Five men are arrested breaking into the Democratic National Committee offices in the Watergate Hotel.
Geneva, New York, USA, June 24: Bernice Gera becomes the first woman to umpire a professional baseball game.
USA, July: *Ms.* magazine goes monthly. The first issue hit the newsstands in January.

New York, USA, August: Juanita Morris Kreps becomes the first woman on the board of directors of the New York Stock Exchange.
North Vietnam, August 22: Jane Fonda, actress and anti-war protester, makes an address to American servicemen in Vietnam.
New York, USA, August 30: Yoko Ono performs with John Lennon in the "One to One" charity concert at Madison Square Garden.
Munich, Germany, September 6: Palestinian terrorists kill 11 members of the Israeli Olympic team.

1973

Washington DC, USA, January 22: In the historic *Roe v. Wade* decision, the US Supreme Court overturns state laws prohibiting abortion.
Paris, France, January 27: The US and Vietnamese combatants in the Vietnam War sign a peace accord.
Pakistan, February: Begum Rana Liaquat Ali Khan is appointed as the first female Governor of Sindh Province.
Denver, Colorado, USA, February: Pilot Emily Howell Warner becomes the first woman to join the flight crew of a US airline.

USA, March 4: Roberta Flack wins the Record of the Year Grammy Award for "Killing Me Softly."
London, England, March 26: Ten women brokers are admitted to the London Stock Exchange.
Los Angeles, California, USA, March 27: Liza Minnelli wins Best Actress award for her role in *Cabaret*.
New York, USA, April 4: The two 110-story towers of the World Trade Center are completed.

Luxembourg, April 7: Anne Marie David, representing Luxembourg, wins the Eurovision Song Contest with her song *"Tu te reconnaitras"* ("Wonderful Dream").
Taft, Oklahoma, USA, April 16: Leila Foley becomes the first black woman mayor of an American city.
Mandal, Uttar Pradesh, India, April: The Chipko Movement is born when a group of village women prevent the logging of their local forest by throwing their arms around the trees and refusing to move.

Florida, USA, May 14: NASA launches its first crewed space station, *Skylab*.
Cannes, France, May: Italian director Lina Wertmuller's film is nominated for a Golden Palm award at the Cannes Film Festival.
USA, June 1: Jeanne Holm becomes the first female major general in the US Air Force.
London, England, June 21: The first board meeting of Virago Press, "the first mass-market publisher for 52 percent of the population—women," conceived the previous year by Carmen Callil, takes place.

Santa Monica, California, USA, July 2: American actress Betty Grable, whose legs had been insured for $1 million each, dies.
Moscow, USSR, August 16: The US children's TV series "Sesame Street" is denounced as "veiled neocolonialism" by the Kremlin.
London, England, August 17: The first use of a "CAT" scan heralds a breakthrough in medical imaging.
Santiago, Chile, September 11: A bloody military coup led by General Pinochet results in the death of Marxist president Salvador Allende.

1974

Vatican City, January 27: Nineteenth-century Spanish nun Teresa Ibars is canonized by Pope Paul VI.
Moscow, USSR, February 13: Nobel Prize-winning author Aleksandr Solzhenitsyn is expelled from the USSR after being arrested. He is offered asylum in Switzerland.
Detroit, USA, March: Olga Madar forms the Coalition of Labor Union Women, and is elected its first national president.
Tel Aviv, Israel, April 10: Golda Meir resigns as Israel's Prime Minister.

Lisbon, Portugal, April 25: Military leaders seize control. Civil liberties are reinstated after 40 years of dictatorship under Antonio Salazar.
France, May 5: Union activist Arlette Laguiller wins 2.3 percent of the votes in her campaign for the French presidency.
West Germany, May 6: Chancellor Willy Brandt resigns after an East German spy is found working as a top aide in his office.
Italy, May 13: Italians agree to retain the three-year-old law allowing divorce.

Rajasthan, India, May 18: India becomes the sixth nation to detonate a nuclear device.
England, May 20: Pat Arrowsmith is jailed for 18 months for leafleting soldiers about Northern Ireland.
Portugal, May: Charges are dropped against "The Three Marias," whose book was denounced by the now-deposed Salazar regime as obscene.
Ohio, USA, June 26: The world's first barcode is scanned on a pack of Wrigley's chewing gum.

Toronto, Canada, June 30: Soviet Bolshoi Ballet star Mikhail Baryshnikov, described by one dance critic as "the most perfect dancer I have ever seen," defects to the west.
Argentina, July 1: Isabel Perón becomes president on the death of her husband, Juan.
London, England, July 29: "Mama" Cass Elliot, US pop singer, dies of a heart attack in her hotel room.
Leningrad, USSR, July: Kirov Ballet stars Galina and Valery Panov are granted permission to emigrate to Israel.

Washington, DC, USA, August 8: US president Richard Milhous Nixon resigns in the aftermath of the Watergate scandal.
Spain, August: Angela "Angelita" Hernández wins her three-year battle to allow women to fight in the bullfight ring.
Washington DC, USA, August: Former child star Shirley Temple Black is appointed ambassador to Ghana.
Addis Ababa, Ethiopia, September 12: Emperor Haile Selassie is overthrown in a military coup.

1975

United Nations, January 1: The United Nations proclaims the International Year of the Woman.
France, January 17: Minister of Health Simone Veil achieves the legalization of abortion.
England, February 11: Margaret Thatcher becomes Tory leader and the first woman to lead a major British political party.
USA, March 1: Barbra Streisand's "The Way We Were," from the movie of the same name in which she starred, wins Song of the Year at this year's Grammy Awards.

USA, March 1: Spanish pianist Alicia de Larrocha wins her second Grammy Award, for Best Classical Performance for Soloist with Orchestra. Her first was in 1974 for Best Classical Performance for Soloist without Orchestra.
Beverly Hills, Los Angeles, USA, March 14: Oscar-winning actress Susan Hayward dies of cancer.
Stockholm, Sweden, March 22: Austrian vocalist Getty Kaspers and the group Teach-In, representing the Netherlands, win the Eurovision Song Contest with the song "Ding-a-Dong."

Riyadh, Saudi Arabia, March 25: King Faysal is assassinated in the palace by his nephew, who has a history of mental illness.
USA, April: *Jaws*, a terrifying film about a man-eating shark by Steven Spielberg, opens.
New York, USA, April 7: Soprano Beverly Sills makes her Metropolitan Opera debut in Rossini's *The Siege of Corinth*.
Los Angeles, USA, April 8: Ellen Burstyn wins Academy Award for Best Actress for the 1974 movie, *Alice Doesn't Live Here Anymore*.

Paris, France, April 12: American-born singer and dancer Josephine Baker, who became a major European star in cabaret, musical theater, and film, dies.
Saigon, Vietnam, April 30: Saigon falls to the North Vietnamese, ending 30 years of war and uniting North and South Vietnam.
The Himalayas, May 16: Deputy leader of an all-woman Japanese expedition, Junko Tabei, 35, is the first woman to climb Mt Everest and with her Sherpa guide, is the 36th person to reach the summit.

New York, USA, May 20: The First Women's Bank is chartered in New York City.
New Delhi, India, June: Prime Minister Indira Gandhi declares a state of emergency to retain power after a High Court conviction for election fraud.
Lyons, France, June 2: Some 150 French prostitutes occupy a church to protest against violence and police repression.
USA: Betty Friedan is named Humanist of the Year by the American Humanist Association.

1972

Munich, Germany, September 11: Tiny Soviet gymnast, Olga Korbut, takes home one silver and three gold medals from the Munich Olympics.

New York: Playwright Cynthia Buchanan publishes her novel *Maiden*.

USA, October: Helen Reddy's "I Am Woman," reaches number one on the popular music charts.

Nashville, USA, October: Loretta Lynn becomes the first woman to win the Country Music Association's Entertainer of the Year award.

United Nations, November 15: Jeanne-Martin Cissé of Guinea is elected the first woman president of the United Nations Security Council.

Bolivia, November 16: Lydia Gueiler Tejada becomes Bolivia's first woman president—in a caretaker role.

West Germany, December 13: Annemarie Renger becomes the first female president of the West German Bundestag.

Austria: Hertha Firnberg is elected the first Austrian minister for science and research (SPO - social democrat).

Greenwich, England: British astronomer, Margaret Burbidge, becomes the first woman director of the Royal Observatory at Greenwich, although without the traditional honorary title of Astronomer Royal.

USA: Health food guru, Adele Davis, publishes *Let's Have Healthy Children*.

Sweden: Harriet Andersson, Ingrid Thulin, and Liv Ullmann star in Ingmar Bergman's film *Viskningar och rop* (*Cries and Whispers*).

Ahmedabad, India: Ela Bhatt forms the Self-Employed Women's Association, to help lower class female workers.

United Kingdom: Ann Oakley's classic survey of women's social position—*Sex, Gender and Society*—is published.

Washington DC, USA: Dr. Barbara Sizemore is elected superintendent of schools for the District of Columbia public school system, making her the first African-American woman to head the public school system of a major city.

New York, USA: Finland's Helvi Linnea Sipila becomes the highest-ranking woman in the UN Secretariat as Assistant Secretary General for Social Development and Humanitarian Affairs.

Cape Town, South Africa: Yvonne Bryceland, with her husband Brian Astbury, founds the Space Theatre, the country's first racially integrated theater.

1973

Houston, Texas, USA, September 20: Billie Jean King beats Bobby Riggs in the "Battle of the Sexes," 6-4, 6-3, 6-3, in front of 40 million television viewers.

Sydney, Australia, October 20: Queen Elizabeth II opens the Sydney Opera House, declaring it "one of the wonders of the world." It cost 14 times the original estimate.

Philippines, October 29: Cecilia Muñoz-Palma becomes the first woman justice appointed to the Supreme Court.

England, October: Renowned English cellist Jacqueline du Pré is diagnosed with multiple sclerosis.

USA, November 6: Computer whiz Patricia Wiener patents one of the first memory systems to be contained on a single silicon computer chip.

New Jersey, USA, November 7: Sylvia Pressler, hearing examiner for the New Jersey Civil Rights Division, rules that Little League Baseball must admit girls into its programs.

London, England, November 14: Princess Anne marries Captain Mark Phillips.

Melbourne, Australia, November 25: State Supreme Court judge Justice Marilyn Warren is appointed Victoria's Chief Justice, the first woman to fill the position in Australia.

USA, November: Erica Jong's *Fear of Flying* is published.

New York, USA, December 10: Mexican lawyer and politician Maria Lavalle Urbina is awarded a United Nations Human Rights Prize.

Vancouver, Canada: Canada's first rape crisis center opens.

San Francisco, USA: Margo St James founds the sex workers' rights group, COYOTE (Call Off Your Old Tired Ethics).

Israel: Shulamit Aloni establishes the Ratz Party (Movement for Citizens' Rights and Peace).

England: Cricketer Rachael Heyhoe-Flint becomes television's first woman sports commentator.

France: Lebanese poet Nadia Tuéni is awarded the Prix de l'Académie Française.

England: Alicia Markova, sometimes called "the miniature Pavlova," is named a governor of the Royal Ballet. She was born in England as Lilian Alicia Marks, but Serge Diaghilev changed her name during her time with the Ballets Russes.

Los Angeles, California, USA: Canadian-born pathologist Elizabeth Stern Shankman links prolonged oral contraceptive use with cervical cancer.

USA: Danielle Steel publishes her first novel, *Going Home*.

1974

Ottawa, Canada, September 16: Renaude Lapointe becomes the first woman speaker of the Senate.

Saskatchewan, Canada, September 18: The first women recruits for the Royal Canadian Mounted Police arrive for training.

Melbourne, Australia, September: Australia's first rape crisis center opens in Collingwood.

Boston, USA, October 4: Poet Anne Sexton commits suicide, aged 45.

Oklahoma, USA, November 13: Nuclear plant worker Karen Silkwood is killed in a car crash.

Hadar, Ethiopia, November 24: The "Lucy" hominid skeleton, believed to be three million years old, is found.

Germany, November 29: Terrorist Ulrike Meinhof is sentenced to eight years in prison.

Darwin, Australia, December 24-25: Sixty-six people die and thousands are injured as Cyclone Tracy devastates the Northern Territory.

Central African Republic, December: Elizabeth Domitien becomes the country's first woman prime minister.

Antarctica, Winter: Biologists Mary Alice McWhinnie and Sister Mary Odile Cahoon are the first women to spend a winter on the frozen continent.

France: Philosopher and feminist Simone de Beauvoir becomes president of the French League for Women's Rights.

USA: Lithuanian-born archeologist and feminist Marija Gimbutas publishes *Goddesses and Gods of Old Europe*, a book that challenges the traditional concepts of the origins of western civilization.

Jordan: Women get the right to vote and be elected to office.

London, England: Nadine Gordimer wins the Booker Prize for *The Conservationist*.

USA: Marabel Morgan's bestselling book *Total Woman* advises housewives to pamper and submit to their husbands.

Norway: Politician Eva Kolstad becomes the first woman leader of a Norwegian political party, Venstre.

Los Angeles, USA: Glenda Jackson wins her second Academy Award for Best Actress in *A Touch of Class*.

Houston, USA: Anita Martini becomes the first female journalist to report from a professional sportsmen's locker room.

France: Author and journalist Françoise Giroud becomes secretary of state for the status of women.

New York, USA: Billie Jean King establishes the Women's Sports Foundation.

New York, USA: New Zealand lyric soprano Kiri Te Kanawa makes a widely acclaimed debut at New York's Metropolitan Opera as Desdemona in Verdi's *Otello*.

1975

Shaanxi Province, China, July 11: Archeologists find 6,000 life-size terracotta statues of warriors, together with horses, chariots, and weapons, dating from 221-206 BCE.

Mauritania, August 22: Toure Aissata Kane is the first woman to attain cabinet rank, as Minister for the Protection of the Family and for Social Affairs.

Sacramento, California, USA: "Manson family" member Lynette Alice "Squeaky" Fromme attempts to assassinate President Gerald Ford and is arrested.

Forrest Hills, New York, USA, September 6: Czech tennis player Martina Navratilova, aged 18, asks for asylum in the US.

The Vatican, September 14: Mother Elizabeth Ann Seton (1774-1821) becomes the first native-born American to be canonized by the Roman Catholic Church.

UK, October: Rock group Queen release their innovative song "Bohemian Rhapsody."

Rome, Italy: Women demonstrate for reform on behalf of the Italian Women's Movement.

Iceland, October 24: Around 25,000 housewives, 90 percent of the nation's women, strike for the day to call attention to the low value placed on women's work.

Tanzania, October 30: British paleontologist Mary Leakey announces her discovery of 3.75-million-year-old human remains.

USA, November: Bill Gates and Paul Allen form a business partnership called "Micro-Soft."

Madrid, Spain, November 22: Juan Carlos de Borbón is proclaimed King of Spain following Franco's death.

Ethiopia: Youdith Imre is appointed the country's first female ambassador, to Denmark, Sweden, Finland, Norway, and Iceland.

Tehran, Iran: Shirin Ebadi, who was the first woman judge in Iran, becomes president of the Tehran City Court.

England: Agatha Christie kills off her famous detective Hercule Poirot in the book *Curtain*.

USA: Ariel and Will Durant publish the eleventh book, *The Age of Napoleon*, in their Story of Civilization series.

Mozambique: Women win the right to vote and be elected to office.

Ireland: Bernadette Devlin McAliskey serves on the national executive of the Irish Republican Socialist Party, which she co-founded last year.

Toulon, France: French-born filmmaker Babette Mangolte wins the Prix de la Lumière at the Toulon film festival for *What Maisie Knew*.

Barbados: Barbadian public health official Nita Barrow is named medical commissioner of the Pan American Health Organization.

1976

Wallingford, England, January 12: Agatha Christie, mystery writer, dies, aged 85.

New York, USA, January 13: Sarah Caldwell becomes the first woman conductor at the Metropolitan Opera.

London and Paris, January 21: Two Concorde jets take off on their first commercial flights.

Innsbruck, Austria, February: West German Rosi Mittermaier turns in the greatest Olympic performance by a female alpine skier at the Winter Olympic Games.

Australia, February 6: Patricia O'Shane becomes Australia's first Aboriginal barrister.

Croydon, England, February 7: Joan Bazeley is the first woman to referee an all-male football match.

USA, February 8: Jodie Foster stars as a teenage prostitute opposite Robert De Niro in Martin Scorsese's film *Taxi Driver*, released today.

Cambridge, Massachusetts, USA, February 21: Susan Estrich becomes first woman president of the prestigious *Harvard Law Review*.

San Francisco, USA, March 20: Patty Hearst, heiress and former hostage, is found guilty of armed robbery, after being kidnapped.

California, USA: Louise Fletcher wins Academy Award for *One Flew Over the Cuckoo's Nest*.

March 24: President Isabel Perón, who succeeded her late husband Juan in 1974, is overthrown by a military junta. She is to be charged with corruption.

Brighton, England, March 26: British cosmetics entrepreneur Anita Roddick opens The Body Shop.

California, USA, April 1: Two college dropouts, Stephen Wozniak and Steven Jobs, form the Apple Computer Company.

San Francisco, USA, April 7: Genentech, the first commercial company engaged in genetic engineering, is established.

New York, USA, May: Poet and author Gwendolyn Brooks is the first woman and first African-American elected to the 250-member National Institute of Arts and Letters.

USA: Shere Hite publishes *The Hite Report*, analyzing women's sexuality.

Montreal, Canada, July: Romanian Nadia Comaneci is the first gymnast to earn a perfect score of 10, at the Summer Olympic Games. She goes on to receive seven perfect scores during the competition.

Entebbe, Uganda, July 4: Israeli commandos storm the airport to free 105 hostages being held by terrorists. Three hostages were killed, as was Israeli commander, Colonel Y. Netanyahu.

Canberra, Australia, July 8: Senator Margaret Guilfoyle becomes the first woman Federal Cabinet minister.

1977

New York, USA, January 7: Australian Rupert Murdoch purchases the *New York Post*.

Los Angeles, USA, January 14: Anais Nin, novelist and diarist, dies, aged 73.

Saudi Arabia, January: Princess Misha is executed for eloping and marrying a man of her own choice rather than one of her father's.

Washington DC, USA, January 19: Iva Toguri d'Aquino, who was found guilty of treason in 1949 as "Tokyo Rose," is pardoned by President Gerald Ford.

Washington DC, USA, January: Patricia Harris becomes the first African-American woman to serve in a Cabinet post.

Los Angeles, USA, February 19: Ella Fitzgerald wins her first Grammy Award since 1962, for Best Jazz Vocal Performance

USA, March 2: Bette Davis is the first woman to be given the Life Achievement Award by the American Film Institute.

New Delhi, India, March 22: Indira Gandhi quits politics following a crushing defeat in the elections.

Los Angeles, USA, March 29: Lina Wertmuller is the first woman to be nominated for an Oscar as Best Director, for *Seven Beauties*.

Liverpool, England, April 2: 21-year-old Charlotte Brew is the first woman to ride in the Grand National steeplechase.

Buenos Aires, Argentina, April 30: Mothers of children who have disappeared hold a rally at the Plaza de Mayo.

Indianapolis, Indiana, USA, May: Driver Janet Guthrie is first woman to qualify for the Indianapolis 500.

Switzerland, May 2: Dr. Elisabeth Blunschy becomes the first woman president of the National Council of Switzerland.

USA, May 25: Carrie Fisher stars in the spectacular film *Star Wars*, which is released today.

Spain, June: Communist leader Dolores Ibárruri, exiled for 38 years during Spanish dictator Franco's regime, is re-elected to Parliament.

UK, June 7: Week-long celebrations commemorating Queen Elizabeth's 25 years on the throne commence.

London, England, July 7: Marie Myriam, representing France, wins the Eurovision Song Contest with the song "L'oiseau et l'enfant."

Santo Domingo, Dominican Republic, July 16: Janelle Penny Commissiong, representing Trinidad-Tobago, is the first black woman to win the Miss Universe title.

Northamptonshire, England, August: British parasitologist and world expert on fleas Miriam Rothschild hosts the first international flea conference. More than 100 flea experts attend.

1978

USA, January: Physician Anna L. Fisher and Sally Ride are among six women selected as the first female astronaut trainees by NASA.

Ethiopia, February 24: Mary Leakey finds footprints dated at 3.5 million years old. They are thought to belong to a bipedal hominid.

California, USA: Diane Keaton stars in the Woody Allen movie *Annie Hall*, loosely based on herself.

New York, USA, April 7: The *Gutenberg Bible* is sold at auction for US$2 million. It is the most expensive book on record.

Canary Islands, April 21: Krystyna Chojnowska-Liskiewicz of Poland completes her circumnavigation of the world, making her the first woman to sail solo around the world.

England, May 1: Writer Sylvia Townsend Warner dies, aged 84.

USA, May 11: Margaret A. Brewer is made brigadier general, the first female general in the US Marine Corps.

New York, USA, May 20: Mavis Hutchinson arrives in New York from Los Angeles, the first woman to run across the USA.

USA, June 16: The rock 'n' roll film, *Grease*, starring Olivia Newton-John and John Travolta, opens.

East Berlin, East Germany, July 3-4: East Germany's Andrea Pollack breaks the women's 100m and 200m butterfly world records on consecutive days.

Manchester, England, July 25: Louise Brown, the first baby fertilized in vitro, is born.

Kentucky, USA, August 30: Marla Pitchford, aged 22, the first woman tried for self-induced abortion, is found not guilty because of insanity.

USA: *The Life of the Mind*, an unfinished trilogy by Hannah Arendt, is published posthumously.

Canada, September 21: Marguerite d'Youville (1701-1771), founder of the Grey Nuns, is honored by the Canadian Post Office with a commemorative stamp.

Sweden, October 8: Ingrid Bergman and Liv Ullman star in Ingmar Bergman's film *Autumn Sonata*, released today.

Himalayas, October 16: Wanda Rutklewicz is the first European woman to climb Mt Everest.

Salem, Oregon, USA, October: Greta Rideout accuses her husband John of raping her, making him the first man in the USA to be indicted for marital rape while living together.

Jonestown, Guyana, November 18: People's Temple cult leader, Reverend Jim Jones, orders his followers to drink poisoned soft drink. A total of 913 people die.

San Francisco, USA, November 19: The first Take Back the Night march is held in the USA. The first Reclaim the Night march was held in Belgium in 1976.

1979

London, England, January 1: Decca releases the first digital recording.

USA, February 14: Wendy Carlos becomes the official name of pioneering synthesizer musician Walter Carlos, best known for the recording *Switched-On Bach*.

Tehran, Iran, March 8: Thousands of women march to protest the oppressive policies of Ayatollah Ruhollah Khomeini's new regime.

Kampala, Uganda, March 29: Idi Amin's murderous regime collapses as Tanzanian-backed troops invade the Ugandan capital.

Pennsylvania, USA, March 31: The Three Mile Island nuclear reactor is shut down after releasing radiation.

Los Angeles, USA, April 9: Jane Fonda wins the Best Actress Academy Award for *Coming Home*. Maggie Smith wins the Best Supporting Actress Award for *California Suite*.

Chicago, Illinois, USA, April 16: Jane Byrne takes office as the first woman mayor of Chicago.

Jerusalem, Israel, April: Gali Atari with Milk and Honey, from Israel, win the Eurovision Song Contest.

London, England, May 3: Margaret Thatcher leads the Conservative Party to victory, becoming Europe's first female prime minister.

Queensland, Australia, May 19: Jockey Pam O'Neill becomes the first Australian woman to ride against men.

France, June 10: At age 86, Louise Weiss, becomes the oldest member of the European Parliament.

North Carolina, USA, June: Debbie Shook is stripped of her Miss North Carolina crown for criticizing the sponsoring organization.

Washington DC, USA, July 2: The US Supreme Court rules in *Bellotti v. Baird* that minors don't need parental consent to obtain abortions.

Portugal, July 19: Maria de Lourdes Pintassilgo becomes the country's first woman president.

Strasbourg, France, July: French politician Simone Veil is the first woman president of the European Parliament to be elected by universal suffrage.

USSR, August 19: Soviet cosmonauts Vladimir Lyakhov and Valery Ryumin return from 175 days in space.

Juno Beach, Florida, USA, August 20: American swimmer Diana Nyad completes the longest swim in history, making the 102.5-mile (165-km) journey from the Bahamian island of Bimini to Florida.

USA, September 1: Hazel W. Johnson becomes the first African-American woman to be promoted to the rank of general in the United States army.

Paris, France, September 8: Troubled actress Jean Seberg, who made her film debut in 1957 as Joan of Arc, dies in Paris from an apparent suicide, aged 40.

1976

New York, USA, July 12: Barbara Jordan becomes the first woman and the first African-American to address a political convention, the Democratic National Convention.
Italy, July 30: Tina Anselmi becomes the first woman in the Italian Cabinet, as Labor Minister.
Brisbane, Australia, August: Australian squash player Heather McKay wins the inaugural Women's World Open Championship.
East Sussex, England, August 21: Mary Joy Langdon becomes the first female firefighter in Britain.

Forrest Hills, New York, USA, August 21: Transsexual Renée Richards (formerly Richard Raskind) is barred from competing in the US Tennis Open.
Beijing, China, September 9: Mao Zedong, father of the Chinese revolution, dies, aged 82.
USA, September 22: The television series *Charlie's Angels* premieres.
China, October 6: Jiang Qing, widow of Mao Zedong, and the rest of the Gang of Four, are arrested in China for reportedly plotting a coup.

New York, USA, October 6: Barbara Walters appears as the first woman co-anchor on an American network evening news program, on ABC, partnered with Harry Reasoner. Her contract is for $1 million a year over the next five years.
USA, November 3: Sissy Spacek and Piper Laurie star in Brian DePalma's film *Carrie*, released today.
London, England, December 1: The punk band Sex Pistols cause a furor by swearing on live TV.
Sweden: Karin Söder is the first female Minister for Foreign Affairs.

World: Thailand's Princess Prem Purachatra is elected president of the International Council of Women.
England: Islamic scholar and writer Charis Waddy publishes *The Muslim Mind*, giving insight into Muslim beliefs, family life, and women's rights. She was the first woman graduate of Oriental Languages at Oxford University.
Paris, France: Historian Hélène Ahrweiler is elected the first woman president in the 700-year history of the Sorbonne.

Jaipur, India: Indian politician Gayatri Devi, born Princess Gayatri Devi of Cooch Behar and until 1970 the Maharani of Jaipur, publishes her memoir, *A Princess Remembers*.
Los Angeles, USA: Paige Rense, editor-in-chief of *Architectural Digest*, is named Woman of the Year by the *Los Angeles Times* for her dynamic editorial policies.
Colombia: María Elena Jimenéz de Crovo, the first woman to serve as Colombia's Minister of Labor and Social Security, is named Ambassador to Mexico.

1977

English Channel, September: Canadian swimmer Cindy Nicholas is the first woman to complete a round-trip, non-stop solo swim across the English Channel.
Paris, France, September 16: Maria Callas "La Divina", the American-born Greek opera star whose life was as dramatic as her stage roles, dies.
New York, USA, September 29: Eva Shain becomes the first woman to referee a world heavyweight fight, between Muhammad Ali and Ernie Shavers at Madison Square Garden.

Washington DC, USA, October 11: Carolyn R. Payton becomes the first woman and first African-American to serve as director of the Peace Corps.
Washington DC, December 3: Karen Farmer becomes the first African-American to be admitted into the Daughters of the American Revolution.
Stockholm, Sweden, December 10: American nuclear physicist Rosalyn Yalow wins the Nobel Prize for medicine for her work in the 1950s in developing radioimmunoassay of peptide hormones.

Oslo, Norway, December 10: Mairead Corrigan and Betty Williams share the postponed 1976 Nobel Peace Prize.
New York, December 16: The General Assembly of the United nations adopts a resolution calling for a day to be observed by member states as International Women's Day.
California, USA: Jane Goodall and Genevieve, Princess di San Faustino, co-found the Jane Goodall Institute for Wildlife Research, Education, and Conservation.

Baltimore, USA: Oprah Winfrey becomes co-host of the morning TV talk show *People Are Talking*.
Ireland: Mary Harney, aged 24, becomes the youngest member of the Irish Senate.
Australia: Colleen McCullough publishes *The Thorn Birds*.
USA: Conservative anti-feminist Phyllis Schlafly publishes *The Power of the Positive Woman*.
Paris, France: Leading international dancer Violette Verdy (born Nelly Guillerm) becomes the first woman director of the Paris Opera Ballet.

Beijing, China: Conductor Zheng Xiaoying, China's first woman orchestra conductor, becomes head conductor at Beijing's Central Opera Theatre.
Israel: Miriam Ben Porat becomes the country's first female Supreme Court judge.
Canada: Sandra Lovelace, an Aboriginal woman from Tobique Reserve in New Brunswick, appeals to the UN Human Rights Commission against the *Canadian Indian Act*, which gives native status through the male head of the household.

1978

United Nations, New York, USA, December 10: South African anti-apartheid campaigner Helen Suzman wins the United Nations Human Rights Award.
Salem, Oregon, USA, December 27: Women's rights are dealt a blow when John Rideout, the first American man to be charged with marital rape, is acquitted. He did admit to beating his wife, Greta.
England, December 30: Australia's beloved operatic soprano Joan Sutherland is made a Dame of the British Empire.

England: Iris Murdoch wins the Booker Prize for her novel, *The Sea, The Sea*.
New York, USA: Jacqueline Kennedy Onassis becomes an editor at Doubleday publishers.
Angola: Maria de Jesus Haller is appointed the country's first female ambassador, to Sweden.
USA: Julia Child begins a new television series, *Julia Child and Company*, and publishes a book by the same title.

London, England: The Women's Press, a feminist publishing house, is founded.
Afghanistan: The sale of girls is outlawed.
Europe: The use of diethylstilbestrol (DES) for pregnant women is banned throughout Europe. It was banned in the USA in 1971. DES was commonly used to prevent miscarriages and other complications of pregnancy.
London, England: American Episcopal priest Mary Michael Simpson is the first woman to preach at Westminster Abbey.

London, England: American journalist Bonnie Angelo becomes bureau chief of *Time* magazine's London bureau, the first woman to head a foreign bureau for the magazine.
Rhodesia (Zimbabwe): Women gain the right to be elected to office.
London, England: The musical *Evita* opens at the Prince Edward Theatre in London's West End.
USA: Swimmer Tracy Caulkins, aged 15, becomes the youngest recipient of the Amateur Athletic Union's James E. Sullivan Award.

New Zealand: Barbara Angus becomes the nation's first female ambassador, to the Philippines.
USA: Christina Crawford publishes *Mommie Dearest*, a scathing memoir about her childhood as an adopted daughter of actress Joan Crawford. *The Far Pavilions* by M. M. (Mary Margaret) Kaye is published. Academy Award for Best Actress goes to Jane Fonda (*Coming Home*). Academy Award for Best Supporting Actress goes to Maggie Smith (*California Suite*). US Women's Open (tennis): Chris Evert

1979

Rome, Italy, September 16: Sportscar racer Lella Lombardi and co-driver Giorgio Francia score their second win this year, at Vallelunga.
Northwest Territories, Canada, October 1: Nellie J. Cournoyea becomes the first native woman to lead a provincial territorial government in Canada.
USA, October 5: Bo Derek and Julie Andrews star in the film *10*.
Tehran, Iran, November 4: Followers of Ayatollah Khomeini storm the US embassy. Nearly 100 embassy staff are taken hostage.

USA, November 7: Bette Midler stars as a self-destructive rock singer in *The Rose*, released today.
Geneva, Switzerland, December 9: The World Health Organization (WHO) declares that the smallpox virus has been eradicated.
Oslo, Norway, December 10: Mother Teresa wins the Nobel Peace Prize in recognition of her work for the poor.
Zimbabwe, December 29: Robert Mugabe, Joshua Nkomo, and Bishop Abel Muzorewa sign a cease-fire agreement, bringing the seven-year civil war to an end.

Afghanistan, December 29: The build-up of Soviet troops has become an invasion, culminating in the fall of the government in Kabul.
Cambridge, England: Keynesian economist Joan Robinson becomes the first woman to be elected a fellow of King's College.
Egypt: Dr Aisha Rateb becomes the first Egyptian woman to be appointed ambassador, to Denmark.
San Francisco, USA: Feminist artist Judy Chicago's room-sized sculpture *The Dinner Party*, in the making since 1974, premieres.

England: Josephine Barnes becomes first woman president of the British Medical Association.
India: Vijaya Lakshmi Pandit, in 1953 the first woman president of the UN General Assembly, is appointed India's representative to the UN Human Rights Commission. She also publishes *The Scope of Happiness: A Personal Memoir* this year.
Pacific Ocean: American oceanographer Sylvia Earle is the first person in the world to dive to a depth of 1,250 ft (381 m), walking on the ocean floor off the Hawaiian island of Oahu.

Italy: Nilde Iotti becomes the first female president of the Italian Chamber of Deputies.
Mexico: Griselda Álvarez becomes the first female governor of a Mexican state, Colima.
Winnipeg, Canada: Rosella Bjornson becomes the first pregnant commercial air pilot. She is forced to take unpaid leave.
England: Dame Barbara Ward publishes *Progress for a Small Planet*, discussing the Earth's dwindling resources and their unequal distribution.

Kenya, Africa, January 3: Austrian-born wildlife conservationist Joy Adamson, author of *Born Free*, is found murdered in the Shaba Nature Preserve.

Boston, USA, January 16: Scientists synthesize Interferon–a natural virus-fighting substance–using genetic engineering.

Auckland, New Zealand, January 26: American Mary Decker is the first woman to run a mile in under four and a half minutes.

Lake Placid, New York, USA, February: Russian figure skater Irina Rodnina wins her third successive Olympic gold medal for pairs figure-skating, her second with Aleksander Zaitsev. Rodnina has also won the World Championships for ten successive years, 1969 to 1978.

Austria, February: Alpine skier Annemarie Moser-Pröll, considered to be the best female ski racer in history, retires.

Paris, France, March 6: Marguerite Yourcenar is the first woman to be elected to the Académie Française.

Iowa, USA, March 20: Former Iowa City firefighter Linda Eaton wins her sex discrimination complaint against the city of Iowa.

Canada, April 14: Jeanne Mathilde Sauvé is appointed the first woman Speaker of the House of Commons.

Los Angeles, California, USA, April 14: Sally Field wins the Best Actress Academy Award for her performance in the title role in *Norma Rae*.

The Netherlands, April 30: Queen Juliana, 71, abdicates. Her daughter Beatrix, 42, becomes queen.

Boston, USA, April: Rosie Ruiz is stripped of her Boston Marathon winner's medal after being disqualified for not running the entire race.

London, England, May 5: SAS forces storm the Iranian Embassy, killing four terrorists and releasing 19 hostages.

Iran, May 8: Farrokhrou Parsa, Iran's first woman Cabinet minister, is executed by firing squad for her feminist views.

Washington State, USA, May 19: Mt St Helens erupts, triggering an earthquake measuring 5.2 on the Richter scale and collapsing the north face of the mountain. Thousands are evacuated and at least eight people die.

Iceland, June 29: Vigdis Finnboga-dottir is elected the first female president of Iceland.

Dominica, Caribbean, July 21: Eugenia Charles becomes Dominica's first female prime minister.

Dewsbury, England, January 5: Peter Sutcliffe, believed to be the "Yorkshire Ripper," is arrested.

Tokyo, Japan, January 17: Takeshi Hirayama, from the National Cancer Research Institute, proves that passive smoking leads to cancer.

Tehran, Iran, January 20: Fifty-two US embassy hostages are released.

London, England, January 25: The "Gang of Four" rebel MPs declare their intention to leave the Labour Party to form the Social Democratic Party. Shirley Williams is among them.

China, January 25: Jiang Qing, Mao Zedong's widow is convicted of "counter-revolutionary crimes" and sentenced to death.

Darwin, Australia, February 2: The case of Azaria Chamberlain, a baby allegedly taken by a dingo at Uluru (Ayer's Rock) is to go to a new inquest.

Oslo, Norway, February 3: Gro Brundtland becomes the first female prime minister of Norway.

London, England, February 24: The engagement of Prince Charles and Lady Diana Spencer is announced.

New York, USA, March 20: Jean Harris is found guilty of murdering Doctor Herman Tarnower, her lover and author of the *Scarsdale Diet*.

London, UK, March 27: Oxford cox Susan Brown is the first woman to take part in the annual Oxford versus Cambridge boat race.

New York USA, March 29: The musical *Woman of the Year* starring Lauren Bacall opens on Broadway.

Los Angeles, USA, March 31: Sissy Spacek wins the Best Actress Academy Award for the movie *Coal Miner's Daughter*.

Brixton, England, April 12: Racial tensions reach boiling point and explode into the largest riots in London this century.

New York, USA, April 15: Janet Cooke's story about an 8-year-old heroin addict is stripped of its Pulitzer Prize after she reveals it was completely untrue.

Miami, USA, May 11: Bob Marley, Jamaican reggae star, dies of cancer, aged 36.

Vatican, May 13: Pope John Paul II survives an assassination attempt.

Minnesota, USA, May 17: Scholar, scientist, balloonist, and explorer, Dr Jeannette Ridlon Piccard, one of the first female priests in the Episcopal Church, dies from cancer, aged 86.

Washington DC, USA, June 25: The US Supreme Court rules that excluding women from the draft is constitutional.

London, England, July 29: Lady Diana Spencer marries Prince Charles at St. Paul's Cathedral.

South Africa, July: Set in futuristic South Africa, *July's People*, a novel by Nadine Gordimer, is published.

Valletta, Malta, February 16: Agatha Barbara is appointed the third president of Malta. She is the first woman to hold this post.

Christchurch, New Zealand, February 18: Ngaio Marsh, New Zealand detective writer and theater director, dies at the age of 87.

London, England, March 18: Morals campaigner Mary Whitehouse drops her case against National Theatre director Michael Bogdanov over the play *Romans in Britain*, which features a male rape scene.

Brighton, England, March 24-25: The International Whaling Commission passes a resolution banning all commercial whaling (to take effect in 1986).

Yugoslavia, May 17: The Yugoslav Parliament elects Milka Planinc as prime minister, the first time the position has been held by a woman.

Caserta, Italy, May 19: Sophia Loren begins serving a jail term for tax evasion.

Paris, France, May 29: Austrian-German actress Romy Schneider dies at the age of 43.

New York, USA, June 12: More than 800,000 people demonstrate against nuclear proliferation.

Falkland Islands, June 14: The British rout Argentine forces.

London, England, June 21: Diana, Princess of Wales, gives birth to her first child, Prince William, at St. Mary's Hospital. The boy is second in line to the throne.

USA, June: The novel *The Color Purple*, by Alice Walker, is published.

London, England, July 7: Michael Fagan, 30, is found on the Queen's bed drinking a bottle of wine taken from the royal cellars.

Maputo, Mozambique, August 17: Ruth First, exiled South African anti-apartheid activist, is killed by a letter bomb sent to her university.

London, England, August 29: Swedish-born Hollywood film star Ingrid Bergman dies on her 67th birthday of breast cancer.

London, England, September 1: Caryl Churchill's feminist play *Top Girls* is first performed at London's Royal Court Theatre.

Monte Carlo, Monaco, September 14: Princess Grace of Monaco dies after her car plunges off a mountain road.

Japan, October 1: Sony releases the compact disk and compact disk player, with 112 music titles.

Portsmouth, England, October 11: The Tudor warship the *Mary Rose* is raised after 437 years, and is found to be remarkably intact.

Missouri, USA, October 18: Widow of President Harry S. Truman, Elizabeth Virginia Wallace Truman, known as Bess, dies at the age of 97. She was the longest-lived First Lady of the United States.

USA, January: American zoologist, Dian Fossey, publishes *Gorillas in the Mist*, a book about her work observing gorillas in the forests of Rwanda.

USA, January: Marion Zimmer Bradley publishes *The Mists of Avalon*, a woman's perspective on the King Arthur legend.

California, USA, February 4: Karen Carpenter, American singer and drummer with the band The Carpenters, suffers a heart attack and dies after a protracted battle with anorexia nervosa.

Washington DC, USA, February 7: Elizabeth H. Dole joins Ronald Reagan's cabinet as the first female Secretary of Transportation.

Arizona, USA, February 8: Giovanni Vigliotto, who has married 105 women, is found guilty of polygamy.

Seaforth, NSW, Australia, February 28: Winifred Atwell, popular entertainer, pianist, and the first black performer to have a No. 1 hit in the UK, dies.

USA, March 23: The "Star Wars" missile defense program is announced.

Sydney, Australia, March 31: Novelist Christina Stead dies.

Cagnes sur Mer, France, March 31: Suzy Solidor, French cabaret singer and nightclub owner, who was painted by some of the best-known artists of her day, including Braque and Picasso, dies.

Canberra, Australia, March: Senator Susan Ryan becomes the first Labor woman Federal minister, as the Minister Assisting the Prime Minister on the Status of Women.

Reykjavik, Iceland, March: Kvennalistinn (The Women's Alliance) gains three seats out of 60 in the Icelandic Parliament.

New York, USA, April 4: Gloria Swanson, American actress and legend of the silent screen, dies.

Managua, Nicaragua, April 6: Ana Maria, a leader with the El Salvadorian guerrilla organization Farabundo Martí National Liberation Front (FMLN), is murdered.

New York, USA, April: The Pulitzer Prize for Drama is awarded to Marsha Norman for *'night Mother*.

New York, USA, April: Ellen Taaffe Zwilich becomes the first woman to win the Pulitzer Prize for Music.

Malawi, May 5: Malawian lawyer, human rights campaigner, and political prisoner, Vera Chirwa, is sentenced to death for treason.

London, England, May: The Format Photography Agency, a unique all-women agency dedicated to documenting the world from a different perspective, is established.

UK, June 9: The Conservative government of Margaret Thatcher is returned for a second term.

1980

Gdansk, Poland, August 30: Two months of crippling strikes in the shipyards lead the Communist regime to agree to sweeping concessions to the strikers, who are led by Lech Walesa.

Abadan, Iran, September 24: The simmering hostilities between Iraq and Iran explode into full-scale war, with Iraq attacking the oil refinery at Abadan.

Ireland, October 6: Mella Carroll becomes the first woman High Court judge in the Republic of Ireland.

El Salvador, October 7: The body of María Magdalena Henríquez, press coordinator of the Commission on Human Rights of El Salvador, is found. She was kidnapped on October 3.

Vatican, October 17: Queen Elizabeth II visits the Vatican, the first British monarch to do so.

Sri Lanka, October: Sirima Bandaranaike, the world's first female prime minister, is found guilty of misconduct.

USA, November 4: Ronald Reagan is elected president of the USA.

USA, November 21: Soap opera *Dallas* breaks viewing records as the question "Who shot JR?" is answered.

USA, November 22: Mae West, actress and sex symbol, dies at the age of 87.

Paris, France, November: UNESCO reports that one-third of the world's population is illiterate.

New York, USA, December 9: Ex-Beatle John Lennon is shot dead.

USA, December 19: The film *Nine to Five*, starring Jane Fonda, Lily Tomlin, and Dolly Parton, is released.

Iraq: Women win the right to vote and be elected to office in Iraq.

Himalayas: US mountaineer Arlene Blum leads the Indian-American Women's Expedition to the Gangotri Glacier near the India-Tibet border.

Australia: Feminist researcher and writer Dale Spender publishes *Man Made Language*.

Sweden: Princess Victoria becomes heir to the throne after reforms to the *Act of Succession* give the monarch's firstborn child of either sex the right to rule.

Atlantic Ocean: Canadian-born American artist Betty Beaumont creates a massive underwater sculpture 40 miles (64 km) from New York harbor using 500 tons of processed coal waste.

Paris, France: Senegalese author and feminist Mariama Bâ wins the inaugural Noma Prize for her novel *So Long a Letter*.

Australia: Women become eligible to be active patrolling members of the Surf Life Saving Association of Australia.

1981

Wisconsin, USA, August 16: Mary Meagher sets a new world record in the 100 m butterfly with a time of 57.93 at the US national swimming championships in Brown Deer.

New York, USA, August: IBM releases the personal computer, combining the functionality of earlier machines in a sleeker package.

Tasmania, Australia, September 2: Dame Enid Lyons, the first woman to be elected to the House of Representatives dies, aged 84.

Berkshire, England, September 5: The Welsh group "Women for Life on Earth" arrives on Greenham Common, having marched from Cardiff to protest against the decision to site cruise nuclear missiles there.

Washington DC, USA, September 25: Sandra Day O'Connor takes the oath of office as the first female justice in the US Supreme Court.

London, England, September: Baroness Young becomes the first female leader of the House of Lords.

Karachi, Pakistan, September: Asma Jahangir, a human rights activist and lawyer, founds the first all-woman law firm in Pakistan with her sister, Hina Jilani.

Miami, USA, October 1: Fidel Castro's younger sister, Juanita, joins a street protest calling for the release of Cuban political prisoners.

Washington DC, USA, October 12: Former first ladies Betty Ford and Lady Bird Johnson attend the ERA (Equal Rights Advocates) rally at the Lincoln Memorial. ERA is dedicated to equal opportunity for women.

USA, November 22: Betty Friedan publishes *The Second Stage*, which questions the ability of women to successfully juggle marriage, children, and career.

California, USA, November 29: Actress Natalie Wood drowns in a yachting accident off Catalina Island.

Virginia, USA, December 28: Elizabeth Jordan Carr, the first American test-tube baby, is born.

USA, December: Doctors have identified a new disease: Acquired Immune Deficiency Syndrome (AIDS).

Argentina: Deposed Argentine president Isabel Perón is convicted of corruption and exiled to Spain.

Paris, France: The Tokyo-based designer behind the Comme des Garcons label, Kawakubo Rei, presents her first Paris show.

Brno, Czechoslovakia: US cyclist Sheila Young wins the world sprint championship.

New York, USA: The Pulitzer Prize for Drama is awarded to Beth Henley for her first full-length play, *Crimes of the Heart*.

1982

Darwin, Australia, October 29: Lindy Chamberlain is found guilty of the murder of her baby daughter, Azaria. Michael Chamberlain is found guilty of being an accessory after the fact.

California, USA, October: Betty Ford, former First Lady, co-founds the Betty Ford Center for drug treatment.

USA, October: *Cagney & Lacey* premieres on CBS.

Poland, November 12: Lech Walesa, leader of the Solidarity trade union, is released from detention.

Salt Lake City, USA, December 1: Barney Clark, 61, is the first recipient of an artificial heart.

Sweden, December 10: Colombian author Gabriel Garcia Márquez receives the Nobel Prize for Literature.

Berkshire, England, December 12: More than 30,000 women surround the Greenham Common airbase in a protest known as "Embrace the Base."

Australia: Fay Zwicky, Australian poet and academic, wins this year's Kenneth Slessor Prize for Poetry.

Spain: *The House of the Spirits*—the debut novel of Isabel Allende—is published.

Chicago, USA: The Midway Manufacturing Company introduces *Ms. Pac-Man*, a more challenging version of the successful *Pac-Man* game.

London, England: Debbie Moore, becomes the first female director to walk the floor of the London Stock Exchange as her company goes public.

New York, USA: Ada Louise Huxtable, pioneer of contemporary architectural journalism and architecture critic for the *New York Times* since 1963, leaves the newspaper to become an independent architectural consultant and critic.

New York, USA: Sylvia Plath, American poet, novelist, short story writer, and essayist, becomes the first poet to win a Pulitzer Prize posthumously (for *The Collected Poems*). Plath died in 1963.

France: Actress Isabelle Adjani receives a César award for Best Actress for her role in the horror movie *Possession*.

Fife, Scotland: British journalist Katharine Whitehorn is elected the first female rector of the University of St. Andrews, Scotland's oldest university.

York, England: Writer Jung Chang receives her PhD in linguistics from York University, becoming the first person from the People's Republic of China to be awarded a doctorate from a British university.

1983

Space, June: Sally Ride, a 32-year-old physicist, becomes the first American woman in space.

Maine, USA, July 9: Eleven-year-old Samantha Smith of Maine visits the Soviet Union at the personal invitation of Soviet leader Andropov.

London, England, July 26: The High Court allows doctors to prescribe contraception to under-16s without parental consent.

USA, July 27: Madonna releases her self-titled debut album.

USA, September 21: Julie Walters stars in the film *Educating Rita*, about a hairdresser who signs up for a university course.

USA, September: Annie Lennox, of the band The Eurythmics, graces the cover of *Rolling Stone* magazine following the success of the single "Sweet Dreams are Made of This."

Oslo, Norway, October 11: Barbara McClintock, pioneering American scientist and one of the world's most distinguished cytogeneticists, receives the Nobel Prize for Physiology or Medicine.

Pine Gap, Australia, November 14: Police arrest over 100 militant women today when they force their way into a top-secret, joint United States-Australian military base. The group called Women for Survival organized the protest.

Canberra, Australia: The Australian Conciliation and Arbitration Commission (ACAC) acknowledges that women's work is undervalued and underpaid but claims that the economy cannot afford to commensurate women's wages.

Moscow, USSR: A commemorative one-rouble coin with the portrait of Valentina Tereshkova is issued to mark the 20th anniversary of the first space flight by a woman.

Cambridge, England: Women undergraduate students are admitted to Corpus Christi College for the first time in its 630-year history.

Europe: Rigoberta Menchu, a Guatemalan-born Mayan Indian and human rights activist, recites the narrative that forms the basis of her book *I, Rigoberta Menchú*, while working at the United Nations.

Massachusetts, USA: *The Return of Martin Guerre* by Natalie Zemon Davis is published. It is her interpretation of a true story of a man in sixteenth-century France whose identity is stolen.

Adelaide, Australia: Roma Flinders Mitchell becomes the first female Chancellor of an Australian university at the University of Adelaide.

London, England: Lady Mary Donaldson becomes the first female Lord Mayor of London.

1984

Brunei, January 1: The sultanate achieves independence after 95 years of British rule.

USA, January 24: The Apple Macintosh personal computer is released at US$2,495.

London, England, January: Popular girl's toys this year include My Little Pony, Cabbage Patch Dolls, and Care Bears, while Trivial Pursuit wins Game of the Year from the British Toy Retailers' Association.

Sarajevo, Yugoslavia, February 14: Ice dancers Jayne Torvill and Christopher Dean win Olympic gold.

New York, USA, February 15: Ethel Merman, singer and actress, dies aged 76.

Sydney, Australia, February 24: The nation is captivated as 14-year-old Fiona Coote undergoes a heart transplant, performed by Dr Victor Chang at St Vincent's Hospital.

Australia, March 8: The Federal *Sex Discrimination Act* is passed. The United Nations Convention on the Elimination of All Forms of Discrimination against Women forms the basis of the Act.

Melbourne, Australia, March 28: The world's first birth resulting from a frozen embryo, a baby called Zoe, took place today.

San Marino, April 1: Gloriana Ranocchini becomes Captain Regent (Head of State) of the tiny European country of San Marino.

Los Angeles, USA, April 1: Soul singer Marvin Gaye is shot dead by his father, a priest, after a fight.

Berkshire, England, April 4: Fifty-nine women are arrested as police clear anti-nuclear protesters from their camp in Britain.

France/USA, April 23: Researchers discover a virus that leads to AIDS.

Berkshire, England, May 4: British actress and "Blonde Bombshell," Diana Dors dies, aged 52.

Canada, May 14: Jeanne Sauvé is appointed the 23rd Governor-General of Canada.

Nepal, May 23: Bachendri Pal becomes the first Indian woman and fifth woman to scale Mt Everest, the world's highest peak.

Massachusetts, USA, June 30: Writer Lillian Hellman dies.

USA, July 12: Geraldine Ferraro becomes the first female US major-party vice-presidential candidate, when Walter Mondale names her as his running mate.

USA, July 23: Vanessa Williams, the first African-American Miss America, becomes the first to resign her title, after nude photographs are published in *Penthouse* magazine.

Los Angeles, USA, August 7: US teenager Mary Lou Retton becomes the first gymnast outside Eastern Europe to win the gymnastics all-around competition.

1985

New York, USA, January 3: Celebrated soprano Leontyne Price bids farewell to the Metropolitan Opera in New York, singing the title role of *Aida*.

London, England, January 4: Kim Cotton becomes Britain's first surrogate mother, giving birth to a baby girl whom she is forced to leave at Victoria Maternity Hospital, after a court order is imposed.

Oxford, England, January 29: Oxford University snubs Margaret Thatcher by refusing her an honorary degree.

Melbourne, Australia, February 10: A medical research team identifies the cause of Down Syndrome.

New York, USA, February 14: After more than a decade of intense debate, the worldwide governing body of Conservative Judaism decides to admit women as rabbis. Amy Eilberg of Manhattan becomes the first female rabbi.

USA, February 26: Tina Turner makes a comeback, winning three Grammy Awards for the song "What's Love Got to Do With It?," including Best Female Pop Vocal.

Moscow, USSR, March 13: New Soviet leader Mikhail Gorbachev leads the funeral for Konstantin Chernenko, whom he replaced. At 54, Gorbachev is perceived to be a potential reformer.

Alaska, USA, March 20: Libby Riddles is the first woman to win the grueling Iditarod dogsled race across Alaska from Anchorage to Nome.

Saint-Paul, France, March 28: Marc Chagall, Jewish Belarusian painter often associated with the Surrealist movement, dies aged 97.

London, England, March: Holly Reich of Texas, USA, becomes the first conjoined twin to survive an operation to separate her from her sister Carly (who later dies.)

Tirana, Albania, April 11: Enver Hoxha, leader of the insular communist state for 40 years, dies.

Connecticut, USA, May 16: Margaret Hamilton, best known for her role as the wicked witch in *The Wizard of Oz* dies, aged 82.

Brussels, Belgium, May 29: Rioting at Heysel Stadium leaves 39 soccer fans dead.

New Jersey, USA, June 11: Karen Ann Quinlan, the comatose patient whose case prompted a historic right-to-die court decision, dies from pneumonia aged 31.

Oxford, England, July 4: Ruth Lawrence, the 13-year-old prodigy, wins a first-class degree in mathematics at Oxford University completing the course in only two years.

Wimbledon, London, England, July 6: Martina Navratilova beats Chris Lloyd in the Wimbledon women's tennis singles final.

1986

USA, January: Drug manufacturer Searle withdraws its two IUDs from the market after complaints of health risks associated with the contraceptive devices.

Cape Canaveral, USA, January 28: Space shuttle *Challenger* explodes one minute after take-off.

Calcutta, India, February 3: Pope John Paul II visits Mother Teresa's hospice in the slums of Calcutta.

Darwin, Australia, February 6: Lindy Chamberlain is released from prison and a new investigation into baby Azaria's disappearance announced.

Port-au-Prince, Haiti, February 7: President-for-life Jean-Claude "Baby Doc" Duvalier, who with his father "Papa Doc" ruled the country brutally for 28 years, flees to France amid widespread unrest.

Manila, Philippines, February 25: Ferdinand Marcos, president for 20 years, is marginalized by the military and the USA and is forced to resign. Political widow Maria Corazon "Cory" Aquino takes power.

Stockholm, Sweden, February 28: While walking unprotected, Swedish PM Olaf Palme is assassinated.

Canberra, Australia, March 2: Queen Elizabeth formally severs Australia's constitutional ties with the United Kingdom, signing the *Australia Act* with Prime Minister Bob Hawke.

Santa Fe, USA, March 6: Painter Georgia O'Keeffe dies, aged 98.

Hollywood, March 24: The film *Out of Africa,* based on the Isak Dinesen (Karen Blixen) novel, sweeps the Academy Awards.

Pakistan, April 10: Benazir Bhutto returns from exile in London to bury her brother.

Paris, France, April 14: Simone de Beauvoir dies, aged 78.

Tripoli, Libya, April 15: US and British aircraft strike terrorist targets, killing dozens of civilians.

Swaziland, April 25: Ntombi Thwala becomes Queen Mother of Swaziland.

Windsor, England, April 29: Wallis Simpson, the Duchess of Windsor, dies, aged 90.

Ukraine, USSR, April 30: The Chernobyl nuclear reactor melts down, releasing massive amounts of deadly radiation.

Norway, May 9: Gro Harlem Brundtland is elected prime minister for the second time.

Yugoslavia, May 15: Milka Planinc finishes her term as Prime Minister.

Vienna, Austria, June 8: Former United Nations Secretary-General Kurt Waldheim is elected UN President, amid accusations of his involvement in Nazi war crimes.

Washington DC, USA, June 25: Nicaraguan Contras are paid by US Congress to overthrow the Sandinista government.

1987

USA, January 21: Aretha Franklin is the first woman inducted into the Rock and Roll Hall of Fame.

USA, January: The Directors Guild nominates a woman for best director of a film for the first time: Randa Haines for *Children of a Lesser God.*

USA, February 7: The first National Women and Girls in Sports Day is celebrated, with the inaugural Flo Hyman award going to Martina Navratilova.

Malta, February 15: Agatha Barbara finishes her term as president of the country.

Beirut, Lebanon, February 22: At the request of Lebanese leaders, 7,000 Syrian troops enter West Beirut in an attempt to end fighting between Muslims and Christians.

England, February 26: A majority of the Anglican General Synod votes in favor of ordaining women as priests.

Rome, Italy, March 1: Bettino Craxi's socialist government, the longest serving since World War II, resigns.

Vatican City, March 10: Pope John Paul II condemns all forms of artificial fertilization in his "Instruction on respect for human life in its origin and on the dignity of procreation."

USA, March 23: Daytime soap *The Bold and the Beautiful* premieres.

Vermont, USA, March 28: Maria von Trapp, the woman whose life was the inspiration for the musical, *The Sound of Music,* dies, aged 82.

Washington DC, USA, April 7: The National Museum of Women in the Arts is opened.

USA, April 7, 1987: Nancy Perkins invents the canister vacuum.

USA, April 16: Rita Dove wins the Pulitzer Prize for poetry for *Thomas and Beulah.*

Iceland, April 25: The feminist party, the Women's Alliance of Iceland, wins 10 percent of the popular vote in the general elections.

Germany, May 1: Sister Edith Stein, a victim of the holocaust, is beatified by Pope John Paul II.

Suva, Fiji, May 14: Lieutenant-Colonel Sitiveni Rabuka enters parliament and arrests the prime minister and 27 members of the Indian-dominated government.

New York, USA, May 14: Actress Rita Hayworth dies, aged 68.

Washington DC, USA, June 6: Dr. Mae Jemison is named the first black woman astronaut.

UK, June 11: Margaret Thatcher's Conservative Party is re-elected for a third term.

1984

Space, July & October: Svetlana Savitskaya, Russian engineer and cosmonaut, becomes the first woman to walk in space during the *Soyuz* T-12 mission, followed on October 11 by American Kathryn Sullivan who space-walks from the space shuttle *Challenger*.
Los Angeles, USA, August 25: Author Truman Capote dies aged 59.
London, England, September 6: British author Anita Brookner's novel *Hotel du Lac* is published.

England, September 15: Alec Jeffreys stumbles upon genetic "fingerprinting"–DNA sequences unique to individuals that can be used for identification purposes.
Brighton, England, October 12: Five people die as IRA terrorists target British Prime Minister Margaret Thatcher by planting a bomb in her hotel. She escapes unharmed.
New Delhi, India, October 31: Prime Minister Indira Gandhi is assassinated by her Sikh bodyguards. Her son Rajiv takes over the leadership.

North Carolina, USA, Nov 2: Velma Barfield, who was convicted of the fatal poisoning of her boyfriend, is put to death by injection. She is the first woman executed in the USA since 1962.
Bhopal, India, December 3: Toxic gas leak from a Union Carbide chemical plant claims over 2,000 lives and affects tens of thousands of others.
UK, December 14: Britain's top pop stars record "Do They Know it's Christmas?" to raise funds for Ethiopia.

Missouri, USA: The second largest Mormon denomination, the Reorganized Church of Jesus Christ of Latter-Day Saints, authorizes the ordination of women.
USA: Billie Jean King retires from competitive tennis and becomes the first woman commissioner in professional sports as head of World Team Tennis.
London, England: The designer Katherine Hamnett is named Designer of the Year by the British Fashion Council.

Paris, France: *The Lover (L'Amant)*, an autobiographical novel by Marguerite Duras, is published. It is awarded this year's Prix Goncourt, the most prestigious prize in French literature.
London, England: Angela Carter's magic realist novel *Nights at the Circus* is published.
Vaduz, Liechtenstein: Women are granted the right to vote.
New York, USA: Fashion columnist Diana Vreeland, publishes her autobiography *D.V.*

1985

Wimbledon, London, England, July 7: German tennis star Boris Becker, 17, becomes the youngest Wimbledon singles winner.
USA, July 12: Sharon Scranage, a US Central Intelligence Agency (CIA) clerk, is accused of disclosing the names of CIA agents to representatives of the Ghanaian government when she was stationed in Ghana.
USA, July 19: Christa McAuliffe of New Hampshire is chosen to be the first schoolteacher to ride aboard the space shuttle.

California, USA, August 16: Pop star Madonna marries actor Sean Penn.
Virginia, USA, August 21: The A.H. Robins Company, producer of the Dalkon Shield birth control device, files for bankruptcy as thousands of women claim injury.
Maine, USA, August 25: Samantha Smith, the schoolgirl whose letter to Yuri Andropov resulted in an invitation to tour the USSR, is killed with her father in an airplane crash.
Cape Kennedy, USA, August 27: Australia's first telecommunications satellite AUSSAT is launched.

Atlantic Ocean, September 1: A team led by Robert Ballard locates the wreck of the liner *Titanic*.
UK, September 17: Fashion designer and home furnishing expert, Laura Ashley, dies after a fall in her home.
USA, September 14: The TV situation comedy *The Golden Girls* debuts on NBC. The show's main characters are four single older women who live together, and are sexually active and conversant with pop culture.
Antarctica, September: Scientists discover holes in the ozone layer.

Arizona, USA: Lynette Woodard, who captained the 1984 US women's basketball team, becomes the first woman to play with the Harlem Globetrotters.
New York, USA, October 15: Australian Shelley Taylor breaks the record for the fastest swim around Manhattan Island, completing the trip in just over six hours.
Republic of Ireland, November 18: Senator Mary Robinson resigns from the Irish Labour Party in protest at the lack of consultation before the Anglo-Irish Agreement (AIA).

Oklahoma, USA, December 14: Wilma Mankiller becomes the first female chief of a major Native American tribe when elected to lead the Cherokee Nation.
Republic of Rwanda, December 26: Dian Fossey, the American zoologist who studied gorillas in the wild, is found murdered in her bedroom.
London, England: Brenda Dean becomes General Secretary of SCGAT (Society of Graphical and Allied Trades), the first woman to head a major union.

1986

USA, July 1, 1986: Nancy Perkins, in collaboration with Charles Dushek and Roy Hennen, invents the battery container.
New Zealand, July 11: Consensual adult same-sex relationships are legalized by the *Homosexual Law Reform Act*.
London, England, July 23: Prince Andrew marries Sarah Ferguson at Westminster Abbey.
K2, Himalayas, August 9: Mountaineer Julie Tullis dies after climbing the world's second highest mountain.

Karachi, Pakistan, August 14: Benazir Bhutto is arrested while leading demonstrations against the government of President Zia al-Huq.
Australia, August 26: Senator Janine Haines is elected leader of the Australian Democrats.
Cameroon, August 25: Toxic gas is released from a volcanic lake, resulting in 1,700 deaths.
USA, September 8: *The Oprah Winfrey Show* debuts on TV.
Canberra, Australia, October 1: The *Affirmative Action Act* is passed by Federal Parliament.

New York, USA, October 29: An abortion clinic is bombed, one of several attacks in the US this year by pro-life campaigners.
Basel, Switzerland, November 10: A fire at a chemical plant dumps more than 1,000 tons of toxic chemicals into the Rhine River.
Washington DC, USA, November 25: The "Irangate" affair comes to light when President Ronald Reagan admits to secret arms deals with Nicaraguan Contras. Lieutenant-Colonel Oliver North and Vice-Admiral John Poindexter resign.

Stockholm, Sweden, December 10: Italian-born neurologist Rita Levi-Montalcini co-wins the Nobel Prize in Physiology or Medicine with Stanley Cohen, for their discoveries of nerve growth factors.
Shanghai, China, December 21: Fifty thousand students hold demonstrations urging democratic reforms, including freedom of the media.
California, USA, December 23: *Voyager*, a sleek plane piloted by Dick Rutan and Jeana Yaeger, encircles the world in nine days on one tank of fuel.

Dallas, USA, December 26: American Airlines Flight 412 arrives at Dallas / Fort Worth airport, the first commercial jetliner flight with an all-women crew.
USA, December: Golfer Pat Bradley becomes the first woman to top $2 million in career earnings.
Canada: Margaret Atwood publishes *The Handmaid's Tale*.
USA: Karleen Koen publishes *Through a Glass Darkly*.
USA: Judy Blume publishes *Letters to Judy: What Kids Wish They Could Tell You*.

1987

Seoul, South Korea, June 20: Massive protests throughout South Korea over ten days climax with widespread riots in the capital. Rioters demand democratic reform.
Mt. Fuji, Japan, July 24: American mountaineer Hulda Crooks is the oldest woman, at 91, to climb Mt. Fuji.
Colombo, Sri Lanka, July 29: India and Sri Lanka sign a peace accord.
Mecca, Saudi Arabia, July 30: Saudi police shoot 400 pilgrims, mostly Iranians, during the annual hajj.

London, England, July: Artists Helen Chadwick and Terese Oulton are the first women nominated for the Turner Art Prize.
San Antonio, Texas, USA, August 1: Pola Negri, Polish star of silent films, dies, aged 92.
Guatemala City, Guatemala, August 7: The presidents of Costa Rica, Nicaragua, Honduras, Guatemala, and El Salvador sign a peace agreement.
Soviet Union, August 7: American Lynne Cox swims the Bering Strait in 2 hours and 6 minutes.

Manila, Philippines, August 29: The fifth coup attempt against President Corazon Aquino's government fails, 40 people are dead and hundreds have been injured.
Ethiopia, September 10: A new civilian constitution is drafted, ending 13 years of military rule. Colonel Megistu Haile Mariam is elected president.
Washington DC, USA, October 9: Writer and politician Clare Boothe Luce dies, aged 84.

UK, October 16: Hurricane force winds batter the British Isles, leaving a £300 million damage bill.
England, October 19: Acclaimed cellist Jacqueline du Pré dies of multiple sclerosis, aged 42.
Worldwide, October 19: Stock markets slump dramatically following the lead of Wall Street.
England, October: Queen Elizabeth II changes the statutes of the Most Noble Orders of the Garter and Thistle to allow women citizens to be admitted.

England, October: Penelope Lively wins the Booker Prize for her novel *Moon Tiger*.
Washington DC, USA, October: A march for gay and lesbian rights attracts around half a million demonstrators.
Washington DC, USA, December 18: Presidents Ronald Reagan and Mikhail Gorbachev sign a treaty to diminish the size of their country's nuclear arsenals.
Germany: Leni Riefenstahl publishes her autobiography.

1988

London, England, January 11: Elizabeth Butler-Sloss is appointed to the Court of Appeals, the first female law lord in British history.
East Jerusalem, Israel, January 15: Israeli police open fire on Muslim protestors at the Dome of the Rock mosque, one of Islam's holiest sites.
United Kingdom, February 3: Nurses right across the UK strike for better pay and conditions.
Sri Lanka, February 16: Vijaya Kumaratunga—movie star, politician, and husband of Chandrika Kumaratunga—is assassinated.

France, February: Dr. Elaine Gluckman is the first person to perform a cord blood transplant to cure a case of Franconi's anemia.
Calgary, Canada, February: The Winter Olympics end with Dutch speed skater Yvonne Van Gennip winning three gold medals and breaking two world records. Christa Rothenburger wins gold in the 1,000 meter speed skating.
New York, USA, March 31: Toni Morrison wins the Pulitzer Prize for her novel *Beloved*.

Islamabad, Pakistan, April 10: The Ojhri ammunition depot explodes, killing 100 and injuring over 1,000. Afghani agents are suspected.
New York, USA, April 17: Sculptor Louise Nevelson dies, aged 88.
North Pole, April 20: Helen Thayer—along with her husky, Charlie—becomes the first person to complete a solo trek to the north magnetic pole.
Afghanistan, May 16: Soviet troops begin to withdraw, after over eight years bogged down against US-backed Islamic militants.

Cambodia, June 4: Vietnamese forces, who have occupied Cambodia for ten years, begin to withdraw 50,000 troops.
Sydney Harbour, Australia, June 5: Australian Kay Cottee becomes the first woman to sail non-stop solo around the world.
New Jersey, USA, June 13: The cigarette company Liggett Group is found liable in the death by lung cancer of Rose Cipollone.
Ohio, USA, June 25: Mildred Gillars, known as "Axis Sally," dies, aged 87.

Arabian Gulf, July 3: US Navy warship *Vincennes* mistakenly shoots down an Iranian passenger plane, killing 290 people.
Managua, Nicaragua, July 14: Woman and children from the organization Mothers of Heroes and Martyrs, holding crosses, demonstrate in front of the office of Archbishop Obando y Bravo, asking him to stop the civil war.
Tehran, Iran, July 20: Ayatollah Khomeini declares an end to the eight-year holy war with Iraq, accepting the UN cease-fire conditions.

1989

USA, January 3: Television evangelists Jim and Tammy-Faye Bakker broadcast for the first time in two years.
Tokyo, Japan, January 7: Emperor Hirohito dies, aged 82.
Washington DC, USA, January 20: Republican George H. W. Bush is inaugurated as the 41st president.
Asuncion, Paraguay, February 3: Alfredo Stroessner, Paraguay's president for 35 years, is overthrown in a military coup.

Connecticut, USA, February 6: Historian Barbara Tuchman dies, aged 77.
Boston, USA, February 11: Barbara Clementine Harris is consecrated as a bishop in the episcopal church.
World, March 2: Madonna's new song "Like a Prayer" premieres on a worldwide Pepsi-Cola commercial.
Prince William Sound, Alaska, USA, March 24: The *Exxon Valdez* oil tanker runs aground, spilling over 11 million gallons (42 million liters) of oil. The captain is alleged to have been intoxicated.

USSR, March 26: The first democratic elections take place to elect the congress of people's deputies. Boris Yeltsin comes out ahead, largely because of his criticism of Mikhail Gorbachev.
New York, USA, March 30: Pulitzer Prizes are awarded to Wendy Wasserstein, for her play *The Heidi Chronicles*, and to Ann Tyler, for her novel *Breathing Lessons*.

Sheffield, England, April 15: The UK's worst sporting disaster occurs when supporters of Liverpool Football Club rush onto an already overcrowded stand. Ninety-four people are killed and 170 injured.
Cornwall, England, April 19: Author Daphne du Maurier dies, aged 81.
Seoul, Korea, April 23: Princess Dok Hye of Korea dies, aged 77.
Hollywood, USA, April 26: Comedian Lucille Ball dies, aged 76.
USA, May 15: The tele-movie *Roe vs Wade*, based on the famous abortion trial, airs on NBC TV.

Los Angeles, USA, May 20: Comedian Gilda Radner dies of ovarian cancer, aged 42.
Poland, June 5: Voters deliver a resounding mandate to the Solidarity party, led by Lech Walesa, in the first free elections.
Tehran, Iran, June 6: Hysterical mourning greets the death of spiritual leader, Ayatollah Seyyed Ruhollah Khomeini, aged 86.

1990

Western Europe, January 25: Forty-seven die in the UK and up to three million trees are uprooted as hurricane-force winds cause havoc.
London, England, January 25: Film star Ava Gardner dies, aged 67.
Scotland, January: Women in the Royal Navy are allowed to serve at sea for the first time.
Cape Town, South Africa, February 11: Nelson Mandela is released from jail after 27 years.

Managua, Nicaragua, February 25: Violeta Chamorro defeats Sandinista leader Daniel Ortega in the first free elections since 1979.
Canberra, Australia, February 28: Deirdre O'Connor is instated as Australia's first female federal court judge.
Witchita, Kansas, USA, March 2: Carole Gist is crowned Miss USA, the first African-American woman to win the pageant.
Washington DC, USA, March 9: Antonia Novello is sworn in as the first woman US surgeon-general.

Vilnius, Lithuania, March 11: The tiny Baltic republic declares itself independent after half a century of Soviet rule.
Haiti, March 13: Dame Ertha Pascal-Trouillot is sworn in as interim president.
Australia, March 26: The Labor government of Bob Hawke wins a record fourth term.
Hollywood, USA, March 26: At the age of 80 years and 252 days, Jessica Tandy becomes the oldest person to win the Best Actress Oscar.

Hollywood, USA, March 26: *Driving Miss Daisy*, starring Morgan Freeman and Jessica Tandy, wins four Oscars.
San Marino, April 1: Gloriana Ranocchini ends her tenure as co-Captain-Regent.
German Democratic Republic, April 5: Sabine Bergmann-Pohl begins her tenure as chairman of the Volkskammer.
Kathmandu, Nepal, April 8: King Birendra lifts a 30-year ban on political parties and agrees to end the country's feudal-style rule.

New York, USA, April 15: Actress Greta Garbo dies, aged 84.
Moscow, Russia, May 29: "Radical" Boris Yeltsin is elected president of the Russian republic, successfully challenging Mikhail Gorbachev.
Portland, Oregon, USA, June 4: Fifty-four-year-old Alzheimer's sufferer Janet Adkins ends her life using a suicide machine.
Iran, June 22: A massive earthquake in the northwest of the country leaves 40,000 dead and 100,000 injured.

1991

Kuwait, January 16: A US-led coalition launches an offensive to liberate Kuwait following Iraq's failure to comply with UN deadline for withdrawal.
Mogadishu, Somalia, January 27: General Mohamed Siad Barre flees the capital after 21 years of brutal rule over the East African country.
Haiti, February 7: Ertha Pascal-Trouillot completes her term as interim prime minister.
Panama, February 21: Dame Margot Fonteyn dies, aged 71.

Bangkok, Thailand, February 23: With King Bhumibol's support, the military overthrows the government. Martial law is declared.
Kuwait, February 28: US president George Bush announces the end of the war to liberate Kuwait.
New York, USA, March: The National Book Critics Circle Award goes to *Backlash: The Undeclared War on American Women*, by Susan Faludi.
Los Angeles, USA, March 15: Four police officers are indicted for the beating of Rodney King. The event was captured on video.

Bangladesh, March 20: Khaleda Zia becomes the country's first woman prime minister.
World, April: Japanese academic Sadako Ogata is elected United Nations High Commissioner for Refugees.
Tbilisi, Georgia, April 9: After 70 years of Soviet rule, independence from Moscow is declared. Ninety percent of voters support the change.
Cannes, France, May: Women's buddy film *Thelma and Louise* premieres.

South Africa, May 14: Winnie Mandela is given a six-year jail term for kidnapping.
Paris, France, May 15: Édith Cresson is appointed Prime Minister.
Washington DC, USA, May 16: Queen Elizabeth II is the first British monarch to address the US Congress.
Space, May 18: Helen Sharman becomes the first Briton in space.
India, May 21: Former PM Rajiv Gandhi is assassinated. Tamil separatists are suspected.

India, May 22: Rajiv Gandhi's widow, Sonia, is designated to lead the her husband's party through the elections, but she declines the position.
Ethiopia, May 25: After Stalinist dictator Mengitsu Haile Mariam flees, Israeli forces airlift 15,000 black Jews, known as *flashas*, out of the country in 21 hours.
London, England, June 14: Actress Dame Peggy Ashcroft dies, aged 83.
South Africa, June 17: The apartheid law classifying citizens by race is repealed.

1988

Rangoon, Burma, July 23: Rioting students destroy police stations in the worst violence seen in the past quarter century. Premier Bo Ne Win is ousted from office after 26 years.

Vatican City, August 15: Pope John Paul outlines two "particular dimensions of the fulfilment of the female personality" as virginity or motherhood, in an apostolic letter.

London, England, August 23: The newest member of the British royal family is born. Beatrice Elizabeth Mary is daughter to the Duke and Duchess of York.

Burma, September 19: The recent flirtation with freedom of speech is short-lived. The Army takes control of the civilian government, banning all public demonstrations.

Burma, September 24: Aung Sun Suu Kyi forms a new political party, the National League for Democracy.

USA, September: Barbara Harris is elected first woman bishop of the Episcopal church.

France, September: The nation approves the use of the abortion pill RU-486—the first western nation to do so.

Seoul, Korea, October 2: The closing ceremony of the games of the XXIV Olympiad is held. Highlights of these games included Steffi Graf completing her grand slam-winning year with Olympic gold in tennis; US sprinter Florence Griffith Joyner winning three gold medals and a silver on the track; German speed-skater and cyclist Christa Luding-Rothenburger making Olympic history by winning gold medals in both the summer and winter games, and women winning all three dressage medals for the first time.

Penzance, England, October 12: Children's author Ruth Manning-Sayers dies, aged 93.

USA, October 18: TV sitcom *Roseanne*, starring Roseanne Barr, premieres.

New York, USA, October 22: Ferdinand and Imelda Marcos are indicted on charges of fraud and racketeering.

Buenos Aires, Argentina, November 20: Greek shipping magnate Christina Onassis dies of a heart attack, aged 37.

Leicester, England, November 30: Artist and naturalist Margaret Mee is killed in a car accident.

Pakistan, December 3: Benazir Bhutto is elected Prime Minister.

Stockholm, Sweden, December 10: Gertrude B. Elion co-wins the Nobel Prize in Physiology or Medicine with Sir James Black and George Hitchings for "their discoveries of important principles for drug treatment."

England: Doris Lessing publishes her novel, *The Fifth Child*.

USA: Shirley Temple Black publishes her autobiography, *Child Star*.

1989

Germany, June 9: Ingrid Strobl is convicted of being a member of the terrorist group Red Zora, and imprisoned for five years.

Canada, June 9: Deanna Brasseur and Jane Foster graduate from the CF18 jet fighter training program.

Burma, July 21: One day after she cancels a rally to commemorate her father's assassination, the opposition leader Aung Sun Suu Kyi is placed under house arrest by the Burmese government.

Japan, July 23: Prime Minister Sousuke Uno's party loses the election. He lost favor with Japanese women after it was revealed he paid a geisha for sex.

London, England, July 25: Princess Diana opens the Landmark Aids Centre.

London, England, August 30: Princess Anne and her husband Mark Phillips announce their separation.

USA, September: Tennis star Chris Evert announces that she will retire after the US Open.

Neuilly, France, October 6: Acting legend Bette Davis dies, aged 81.

Norway, October 16: Gro Harlem Brundtland finishes her second term as prime minister.

London, England, October 19: The "Guildford Four" are released from prison following revelations of police perjury.

San Francisco, USA, October 21: A massive earthquake rocks the Bay area, measuring 6.9 on the Richter Scale. Eighty-three deaths are reported and damage is widespread.

New York, USA, October 25: Writer Mary McCarthy dies, aged 77.

Berlin, West/East Germany, November 10: The Berlin Wall is opened after 28 years.

Darwin, Australia, November: Gaby Kennard returns home after flying solo around the world.

New York, USA, December 1: Champion gymnast Nadia Comaneci defects to the USA from her home country of Romania, via Hungary.

Panama, December 20: US troops invade. General Manual Noriega flees and is replaced by Guillermo Endara.

Bucharest, Romania, December 25: Following two weeks of social and political turmoil, brutal dictator Nicolae Ceausescu and his wife Elena are executed.

USA: Amy Tan publishes *The Joy Luck Club*.

USA: Bharati Mukherjee publishes *Jasmine*.

Lebanon: Hanan al-Shaykh publishes *Misk al-Ghazal (Women of Sand and Myrrh)*.

1990

Otago, New Zealand, June 29: Penny Jamieson is consecrated Bishop of Dunedin.

Mecca, Saudi Arabia, July 2: Fourteen hundred pilgrims are crushed to death in a tunnel leading to Islam's holiest site.

London, England, July 7: Martina Navratilova wins the Wimbledon singles title for a record-breaking ninth time.

Kuwait, August 2: Iraqi troops invade, meeting with little resistance.

Pakistan, August 6: President Ghulam Ishaq Kahn dismisses Premier Benazir Bhutto amid corruption allegations.

South Africa, August 24: Following two weeks of violence that has left 500 dead, a state of emergency is imposed on 27 townships.

Guatemala City, Guatemala, September 11: Sociologist Myrna Mack Chang is stabbed to death.

Germany, October 3: East and West Germany reunify.

New Zealand, November 2: Ruth Richardson becomes the first female Minister of Finance.

Oslo, Norway, November 3: Gro Harlem Brundtland commences her third term as prime minister.

Riyadh, Saudi Arabia, November 6: Around 50 Saudi women dismiss their drivers and drive their own vehicles in a convoy, in a rebellion against the law which precludes women from driving. Their protest ends after police stop them.

Dublin, Ireland, November 8: Mary Robinson is elected president.

Paris, France, November 19: The Cold War officially ends with 22 heads of state agreeing to dismantle their arsenals.

London, England, November 27: John Major becomes leader of the Conservative Party following Margaret Thatcher's resignation.

New Zealand, December 1: Dr Elizabeth Morgan is granted custody of her daughter, after spending nearly two years in prison for refusing to reveal the girl's whereabouts. She alleged that her ex-husband was abusing the child.

Poland, December 9: Lech Walesa, the founder of the Solidarity Union, is elected President.

New Zealand, December 12: Catherine Tizard is appointed Governor-General.

Missouri, USA, December 26: Nancy Cruzan dies 12 days after a judge agreed to allow her family to remove the feeding tube which was keeping her alive.

1991

London, England, June 28: Margaret Thatcher announces her retirement from the House of Commons at the general election.

England, July 23: Australian Susie Maroney completes the fastest return crossing of the English Channel, in 17 hours and 13 minutes.

Tokyo, Japan, August 31: Algerian Hassiba Boulmerka wins gold in the 1,500 meters at the World Track and Field Championship, the first time a woman from an Arab nation has won an event in the history of these championships.

Poland, September: The Polish government discontinues its subsidy of birth-control medication, resulting in a threefold price increase.

USA, September: Patty Wagstaff becomes the first woman to win the National Aerobatics Championship.

USSR, September 5: The Congress of People's Deputies votes for the dissolution of the Union of Soviet Socialist Republics.

Austria, September 19: German hikers Erika and Helmut Simon find the remains of a 4,000-year-old Bronze Age hunter.

Stockholm, Sweden, October: South African Nadine Gordimer is awarded the Nobel Prize for Literature.

San Marino, October 1: Edda Ceccoli is elected co-Captain-Regent.

Madrid, Spain, October 4: The Madrid Protocol governing Antarctica comes into effect, designating the continent as a natural reserve, devoted to peace and science.

Phnom Penh, Cambodia, November 14: Prince Norodom Sihanouk returns after 13 years in exile.

London, England, November 30: Embryologist Dr Anne McLaren becomes foreign secretary of the prestigious natural sciences body, the Royal Society.

Oslo, Norway, December 10: Burmese dissident Aung Sun Suu Kyi is awarded the Nobel Peace Prize.

Moscow, Russia, December 25: Mikhail Gorbachev resigns the presidency of the USSR.

New York, USA: TV celebrity Oprah Winfrey begins a campaign to introduce a national register of convicted child abusers.

London, England: Patricia Scotland becomes the first black woman to be appointed to a Queen's Counsel position.

England: Gail Rebuck becomes chief executive of Random House UK.

USA: Diane Ackerman publishes *The Moon by Whale Light*.

USA: Katharine Hepburn publishes her autobiography *Me: Stories of My Life*.

England: Catherine Cookson publishes *The Wingless Bird*.

Japan, January 13: Japan acknowledges that Korean women were used as sex slaves by Japanese soldiers during World War II.

Europe, January 15: The European Commission recognizes Croatia and Slovenia as independent states.

Space, January 22: Neurologist Roberta Bondar is the first Canadian woman in space.

USA, February 4: Nan Robertson publishes *The Girls on the Balcony*, about the Elizabeth Boylan sex discrimination lawsuit.

London, England, February 16: Writer Angela Carter dies.

South Africa, March 17: White voters give a resounding "yes" to constitutional reforms giving equality to their black and colored countrymen.

London, England, March 19: Sarah Ferguson and Prince Andrew officially separate.

Hollywood, USA, March 29: Ruth Prawer Jhabvala wins the Oscar for Best Screenplay Based on Materials Previously Produced or Published, for her adaptation of *Howard's End*.

Paris, France, April 2: Prime Minister Édith Cresson is forced to resign.

Miami, USA, April 9: Former Panamanian dictator Manuel Noriega is found guilty of drug trafficking.

Fukuoka, Japan, April 16: Fukuoka local court finds a woman was forced to resign after a male employee harassed her in the first successful lawsuit against sexual harassment in the workplace.

London, England, April 27: Betty Boothroyd is appointed first woman speaker in the House of Commons.

England, April: Barbara Mills becomes Director of Public Prosecutions.

Los Angeles, USA, May 2: A jury decision to acquit four police indicted in the beating of Rodney King leads to days of rioting, looting, and arson, and 52 deaths.

Paris, France, May 6: Acting legend Marlene Dietrich dies, aged 90.

Himalayas, May 13: Wanda Rutkiewicz, hailed as the world's greatest female climber, dies while scaling her ninth "eight thousander."

Rio de Janeiro, Brazil, June 3-14: Treaties to avert climate change are signed at the UN earth summit.

England, June 16: Andrew Morton publishes a controversial new biography of Princess Diana.

London, England, June 30: Margaret Thatcher takes a seat in the House of Lords.

Sarajevo, Bosnia, July 2: UN peacekeeping forces move into position around the airport so that humanitarian aid can commence. Heavy resistance is encountered from Serbian troops.

Czech Republic and Slovakia, January 1: In direct contrast to the strife and conflict in the former Yugoslavia, Czechoslovakia splits into two separate entities in a "velvet divorce."

Switzerland, January 20: Stylish screen legend Audrey Hepburn dies, aged 63.

Washington DC, USA, January 26: First Lady Hillary Rodham Clinton is appointed head of a committee to prepare legislation to overhaul the country's healthcare system.

Malawi, January 24: Activist Vera Chirwa is released from prison.

New York, USA, February 26: A bomb blast in the garage under the World Trade Center leaves five dead and hundreds injured.

USA, March 29: Emma Thompson receives the Best Actress Oscar for her 1992 role in *Howard's End*.

Bombay, India, March 12: Car bomb blasts kill 300 people.

USA, March: Janet Reno becomes the country's first female Attorney-General.

San Marino, April 1: Patricia Busignani is made co-Captain-Regent of the country.

Waco, Texas, USA, April 19: Fires lit by Branch Davidian cult members rage through their compound.

USA, April 28: The country participates in the first Take Our Daughters to Work Day.

London, England, April 29: Queen Elizabeth II opens the doors of Buckingham Palace to the public for the first time.

Hamburg, Germany, April 30: US tennis star Monica Seles is stabbed in the back by a deranged fan during a match.

Agrigento, Sicily, May 9: Following the recent spate of mafia-linked murders of judicial officials, the Pope calls for an end to violence.

Paris, France, May 15: Teacher Laurence Dreyfus will receive a bravery award after keeping her kindergarten students calm and alive during a two-day siege with an armed man who had dynamite strapped to his body.

Mount Everest, Himalayas, May 17: Rebecca Stephens becomes the first British woman to reach the summit of the world's highest peak.

New York, USA, June 5: Julie Krone is the first woman to win a Triple Crown event, riding Colonial Affair to victory in the Belmont Stakes.

Tokyo, Japan, June 9: Crown Prince Naruhito marries Masako Owada, who becomes the first commoner to join the Imperial Dynasty.

Turkey, June 14: Tansu Çiller is elected the country's first female Prime Minister.

Detroit, USA, January 6: Figure-skater Nancy Kerrigan withdraws from competition after an attack with a crowbar on her leg by an unknown assailant.

London, England, January 14: The Duchess of Kent converts to Catholicism. She is the first British royal to do so in over 300 years.

Manassas, Virginia, USA, January 21: Lorena Bobbit, who severed her husband's penis, is found not guilty of malicious wounding, due to insanity.

Los Angeles, USA, February 2: Archeologist, Marija Alseika-Gimbutas, dies, aged 73.

Japan, February 8: Justice Hisako Takahashi is appointed to the country's Supreme Court. She is the first woman to hold the post.

Yangon, Myanmar, February 14: Pro-democracy activist, Aung San Suu Kyi, refuses to leave the country.

Arlington, Virginia, USA, February 23: CIA spy, Aldrich Ames, and his wife, Rosario, are arrested on charges of treason.

France, February 25: Member of Parliament for the Riviera, Yann Piat, a strong opponent of organized crime, is shot and killed in her car. There is speculation it is a contract killing.

Bosnia, February 28: Four Bosnian Serb warplanes are shot down over the UN no-fly zone by NATO forces. This is the first offensive action by NATO in its 45-year history.

Bristol, England, March 13: Thirty-two women are ordained priests in the Church of England, at Bristol Cathedral.

Somalia, March 20: Italian journalist Ilaria Alpi, and her cameraman, Miran Hrovatin, are shot and killed. They had been collecting evidence of brutality by Italian soldiers against Somalis.

Hollywood, USA, March 24: Jane Campion wins an Oscar for Best Original Screenplay, Holly Hunter wins Best Actress, and Anna Paquin wins Best Supporting Actress for *The Piano*.

Rwanda, April 7: A rocket brings down the plane of Prime Minister Agathe Uwilingiyimana, who is killed.

New York, USA, April 12: E. Annie Proulx wins the Pulitzer Prize for her novel, *The Shipping News*.

Boston, USA, April 18: Disabled athlete Jean Driscoll sets a record in the women's wheelchair section of the Boston Marathon, of 1 hour, 34 minutes, 22 seconds.

Rwanda, April 21: The Red Cross estimates 100,000 people have been killed in two weeks of bloodshed since the Prime Minister's death.

USA, April: Scientist Polly Matzinger challenges concepts of immunity and proposes a new "danger" theory.

New York, USA, January 12: At a ceremony at the Waldorf Astoria Hotel, Janis Joplin and Martha and the Vandellas are among inductees into the Rock and Roll Hall of Fame.

Kobe, Japan, January 17: Over 6,000 people die in Japan's largest quake in nearly 50 years.

Bulgaria, January 25: Reneta Indzhova completes her term as interim Prime Minister.

Space, February 6: The US space shuttle *Discovery* completes its rendezvous with the Russian *Mir* space station.

Tizi Ouzou, Algeria, February 15: Feminist and author Nabila Diahnine (also Djahnine) is shot and killed by Islamic extremists.

Frankfurt, Germany, March 2: Trader Nick Leeson, 28, responsible for a $1.4 billion loss to Barings Bank, is arrested.

Belfast, Northern Ireland, March 9: Queen Elizabeth II makes a symbolic visit to Belfast, her first since the ceasefire came into effect last year.

Seville, Spain, March 18: Spain's Princess Elena marries Jaime de Marichalar y Saenz de Tejada.

Tokyo, Japan, March 20: Sarin, a deadly nerve gas, is released into the subway system, killing eight and affecting 4,000. The Aum Supreme Truth religious sect appears to be linked to the attacks.

Iraq, March 20: Thirty-five thousand Turkish troops cross into northern Iraq to crush the PII, Kurdish separatist rebels waging a guerrilla war that has claimed 15,000 lives.

Vatican City, March 25: Pope John Paul II publishes *Evangelium Vitae*, reaffirming the Catholic Church's position against abortion.

New York, USA, April 18: Carol Shields wins the Pulitzer Prize for *The Stone Diaries*.

Oklahoma City, USA, April 19: A massive car bomb explodes in front of a federal building, killing 168 and injuring over eight hundred. Prime suspect Timothy McVeigh is arrested less than one hour after the blast.

Kibeho, Rwanda, April 22: Government troops massacre Hutu refugees.

California, USA, April 25: Ginger Rogers dies, aged eighty-three.

USA, May 1: Charges of attempted murder against Qubilah Shabazz, the daughter of Malcolm X, are dropped.

Zaire, Congo, May 28: The deadly Ebola hemorrhagic fever kills 256 of the 315 people infected in the second largest outbreak recorded.

Bosnia, May 28: Bosnian Serbs capture more than 350 UN peacekeepers from the "safe haven" of Gorazde, and use them as human shields against NATO attacks.

Dominica, June 14: Mary Eugenia Charles finishes her term as Prime Minister.

1992

Poland, July 8: Hanna Suchocka becomes Prime Minister of Poland.

Barcelona, Spain, July 25: The Olympic Games opening ceremony takes place. At this Olympics, women's judo and badminton are introduced.

Palermo, Sicily, July: The Association of Women Against the Mafia stages a hunger strike against the unpunished murders of judges, lawyers, police, and civilians.

Bosnia, August 15: Images of emaciated Bosnians in concentration camps are shown to the world.

London, England, August 20: London's *Daily Mirror* publishes photographs of the Duchess of York, Sarah Ferguson, topless with her financial advisor, John Bryan.

Space, September 12: Dr. Mae Jemison launches into space to spend a week orbiting Earth.

Vietnam, September 23: As the only candidate, General Le Duc Anh is elected president.

New York, USA, September: Tina Brown becomes editor of the *New Yorker* magazine.

Salisbury Cathedral, England, October: An all-girl choir performs here for the first time.

USA, October 3: Irish singer Sinéad O'Connor rips up a picture of the Pope on comedy show *Saturday Night Live*.

USA, October: Mona Van Duyn becomes the country's first female poet laureate.

USA, November 4: Bill Clinton is elected President. Carol Moseley Braun is the first African-American woman elected to the senate.

London, England, November 24: Queen Elizabeth II refers to 1992 as an *annus horribilis*. Bad luck has plagued the royals this year, with scandals, income tax demands, divorce, and a fire at Windsor Castle.

Ireland, November 25: Referendum declares that it is legal for a woman to obtain information about abortion, and travel to the UK for an abortion, but abortion is still illegal in Ireland.

Japan, November: Professor Orie Endo researches the art of *nushu*, a form of ancient writing carried out by women in Hunan, China.

London, England, December 9: The Prince and Princess of Wales announce their legal separation.

Oslo, Norway, December 10: Rigoberta Menchú Tum is awarded the Nobel Peace Prize.

Spain, December: Cuban poet Dulce María Loynaz wins the Cervantes Award.

USA: The movie *A League of Their Own*, directed by Penny Marshall, is released.

USA: Terry McMillan publishes the novel *Waiting to Exhale*.

1993

Canada, June 14: Kim Campbell is elected the country's first female Prime Minister.

Canada, June: Nunavut Inuit and the Canadian government sign a land claim for 135,000 square miles (350,000 km²) of the Arctic Region. Inuit are granted title.

Georgia, July 6: Georgian Prime Minister and former Soviet foreign minister, Eduard Shevardnadze, is given sweeping powers to deal with Abkhazi rebels, who are seeking their own state.

Burundi, July 10: Sylvie Kinigi becomes Prime Minister.

London, England, July 16: Stella Rimington is the first Director-General of Britain's secret service, MI5, to have her name and photograph released to the public.

Rwanda, July 18: Agathe Uwilingiyimana is made Prime Minister.

Washington DC, USA, September 13: Palestinians gain a modicum of self-rule in the occupied territory, with the signing of an accord brokered by President Bill Clinton.

Phnom Penh, Cambodia, September 24: Prince Sihanouk is returned to power after a 30-year exile.

Manila, Philippines, September 24: Imelda Marcos, wife of the disgraced former dictator Ferdinand, is sentenced to 18 years' imprisonment for corruption.

Islamabad, Pakistan, October 20: Benazir Bhutto is reinstalled as Prime Minister three years after being ousted.

New York, USA, October: Rita Dove is awarded the Pulitzer Prize for Poetry.

Maastricht, Netherlands, November 1: A treaty signed by the members of the European Community comes into force.

New York, USA, November 17: E. Annie Proulx wins the National Book Award for *The Shipping News*.

Wellington, New Zealand, December 1: Helen Clark becomes leader of the Labour Party.

Stockholm, Sweden, December 10: Toni Morrison is awarded the Nobel Prize for Literature.

USA, December 18: Myrna Loy, the glamorous actress, dies aged 88.

Canberra, Australia, December 22: The *Native Title Act* passes through Parliament, granting Aboriginals the right to claim land lost since European colonization.

Pretoria, South Africa: Parliament votes for the first all-race election, to take place next year. It will inevitably lead to black majority rule.

USA: Sister Helen Prejean publishes *Dead Man Walking*, about her relationship with a man on death row.

1994

New York City, USA, May 19: Former first lady, Jacqueline Onassis, dies of cancer, aged 64.

London, England, May 30: Dr Carole Jordan is elected the first woman president of the prestigious Royal Astronomical Society.

Algiers, Algeria, June 29: Fifteen thousand Algerians peacefully demonstrate against violence.

Colorado Springs, USA, June 30: Olympic skater Tonya Harding is banned from the sport for life, following her involvement in the attack on skater Nancy Kerrigan.

Gaza, Israel, July 1: Yasser Arafat returns after 27 years in exile.

Pyongyang, North Korea, July 8: Kim Il Sung, dictator since World War II, dies, aged 82.

Northern Ireland, August 31: After a quarter-century of heavy armed resistance, the IRA at last announces a "complete cessation of military operations."

USA, August: Barbra Streisand's first concerts in 30 years sell out despite the exorbitant price tag.

Connecticut, USA, September 11: Jessica Tandy dies, aged 85.

Washington DC, USA, September 31: President Clinton signs the *Violence Against Women Act*.

Haiti, September 19: US troops invade the Caribbean island. Bloodshed is spared after eleventh-hour negotiations ensure the removal of the military junta.

Baltic Sea, September 28: An Estonian passenger ferry sinks rapidly in heavy weather off the Finnish coast; 912 people lose their lives in the freezing waters.

Utah, USA, October 7: A team of researchers led by Dr Mark Skolnick identify the breast cancer gene.

Iraq, October 13: Saddam Hussein pulls back 60,000 troops and 700 tanks from the Kuwaiti border after the USA rushes troops back.

Bulgaria, October 17: Reneta Indzhova becomes interim Prime Minister.

China, October 27: The *Maternal Infant Health Care Law* is passed.

Sri Lanka, November 10: Chandrika Kumaratunga is swept to power in a landslide election result.

Tennessee, USA, November 12: Track and field legend Wilma Rudolph dies of a brain tumor.

USA, November 16: Martina Navratilova retires from singles tennis.

Chechnya, December 11: After two weeks of bombing the breakaway republic, Russia sends tanks across the border in an attempt to "re-establish constitutional order."

Malaysia: After years of campaigning, Malaysia passes a *Domestic Violence Act*.

1995

Burma, July 10: Aung San Suu Kyi is released from house arrest.

Srebrenica, Bosnia, July 15: Poorly armed Dutch peacekeepers are unable to prevent up to 40,000 Muslims being rounded up by Serbian forces in the largest incident of "ethnic cleansing" since WWII.

Himalayas, August 13: English mountaineer Alison Hargreaves is killed in a storm on K2.

Washington DC, USA, September 28: The PLO and the Israelis sign a deal handing over control of the West Bank to the Palestinians.

Beijing, China, September: The United Nations World Conference on Women takes place, attended by representatives from 185 countries.

Haiti, October 24: President Jean Bertrand Aristide announces that Claudette Werleigh is to become Prime Minister of Haiti.

Tel Aviv, Israel, November 4: Prime Minister Yitzhak Rabin is assassinated by a right-wing Jewish extremist at a peace rally.

London, England, November 8: The Booker Prize is awarded to Pat Barker for *The Ghost Road*.

England, November 20: BBC television broadcasts an interview with Princess Diana, in which she talks of her depression, frustrations, and marital infidelities.

London, England, November 22: Serial killer Rosemary West is sentenced to life imprisonment.

New York, USA, December 5: *The New York Times* reports that American Lori Berenson has been arrested on charges of treason for aiding the terrorist group Tupac Amaru Revolutionary Movement (MRTA) in Peru.

Oslo, Norway, December 10: Christiane Nusslein-Volhard co-wins, with Edward B. Lewis and Eric F. Wieschaus, the Nobel Prize for Physiology or Medicine, "for their discoveries concerning the genetic control of early embryonic development."

Paris, France, December 14: Croatian, Bosnian, and Serbian leaders sign a peace accord ending three years of bloody conflict.

England, December 18: In letters to each of them, Queen Elizabeth II asks Prince Charles and Princess Diana to divorce.

Turkey, December 26: After failing to win the parliamentary elections, Prime Minister Tansu Ciller resigns.

England: Iris Murdoch publishes *Jackson's Dilemma*.

Newport, USA: Leslie Egnot skippers the first all-women crew to compete in the America's Cup on *Mighty Mary*.

1996

Bosnia, January 2: US combat troops enter northern Bosnia to keep the peace between Bosnian Serbs and Muslims following the Dayton Peace Agreement signed last month.

Paris, France, January 8: François Mitterrand, socialist prime minister for 14 years, dies, aged 79.

Lima, Peru, January 11: American activist Lori Berenson is imprisoned for terrorism-related offenses.

Colombo, Sri Lanka, January 31: A truck laden with explosives crashes into the Central Bank, killing 57 people and injuring over 1,000.

London, England, February 9: An explosion in the Docklands marks the end of a 17-month cease-fire by the IRA.

London, England, February 14: One of the last survivors of the *Titanic* sinking, Eva Hart, dies aged 90.

USA, February: Christy Martin is the first woman boxer to have her match televised.

Kuala Lumpur, Malaysia, March 18: Irene Fernandez, founder of human rights group Tenaganita, is arrested.

Paris, France, March 3: Iconic writer Marguerite Duras dies, aged 81.

Dunblane, Scotland, March 13: Gunman Thomas Hamilton goes on a shooting spree in the local primary school, killing 16 students and a teacher before taking his own life.

London, England, March 15: Controversial artist Helen Chadwick dies of heart failure, aged 43.

England, March 18: Archeologist, writer, and wife of J.B. Priestley, Jacquetta Hawkes, dies, aged 85.

Hollywood, USA, March 25: Emma Thompson wins the Oscar for Best Adapted Screenplay.

Hollywood, USA, March 25: Susan Sarandon receives the Oscar for Best Actress for her performance as Sister Helen Prejean in the 1995 film *Dead Man Walking*.

Boston, USA, April 15: German Uta Pippig is the first woman to win the Boston Marathon three years in a row.

Cairo, Egypt, April 18: Islamic militants open fire outside a Cairo hotel, killing 17 Greek tourists.

London, England, April 23: Australian-born author of *Mary Poppins*, Pamela Lyndon Travers, dies, aged 96.

Tasmania, Australia, April 28: Martin Bryant shoots and kills 35 people at Port Arthur.

Iraq, May 20: Iraq and the United Nations agree on the oil-for-food program, allowing Iraq to sell oil for humanitarian necessities.

Belfast, Northern Ireland, May 30: Two delegates from the newly formed Northern Ireland Women's Coalition are elected to the Northern Ireland Assembly.

London, England, May: Helen Dunmore wins the inaugural Orange Prize for Fiction for *A Spell of Winter*.

1997

Angola, January 15: Princess Diana condemns anti-personnel landmines.

Hebron, West Bank, Israel, January 19: 60,000 Palestinians greet Yasser Arafat in Hebron after 30 years of Israeli occupation of the area.

Washington DC, USA, January 23: The US Senate confirms Madeleine Albright as secretary of state.

London, England, January: Marjorie Scardino becomes CEO of the Pearson Group, the first woman to head up a FTSE 100 company.

Beijing, China, February 19: Paramount leader Deng Xiaoping dies, aged 92.

The Arctic, March 14: Caroline Hamilton leads a women-only expedition to the North Pole.

Los Angeles, USA, March 24: Frances McDormand wins the Oscar for Best Actress for her performance in *Fargo*. Juliette Binoche is awarded an Oscar for her supporting role in *The English Patient*.

Lima, Peru, March: A dismembered body is found, presumed to be that of intelligence officer Mariela Barreto.

Sarajevo, Bosnia, April 12: A plot to assassinate the Pope is unearthed, involving 20 anti-tank mines under a bridge on the pontiff's route.

UK, May 1: The Labour Party, led by Tony Blair, wins the general election after 18 years in opposition.

Florida, USA, May 12: Susie Maroney swims to Florida from Cuba, the first person to do so.

Kinshasa, Congo, May 20: One day after President Mobutu Sese Seko flees, Laurent Kabila's troops enter the capital, ending the civil war.

London, England, May 26: A record 120 women are returned as MPs in the general election as a result of women-only shortlists.

Paris, France, June 1: Women win 63 seats in the French elections.

Japan, June 16: Novelist Sumii Sue dies, aged ninety-five.

Kuala Lumpur, Malaysia, June: Three Muslim beauty pageant contestants arrested for "indecent dressing" face a $200 fine, six months' imprisonment, or both.

Hong Kong, July 1: The former British colony is handed back to China.

London, England, July 5: At age 16, Swiss tennis player Martina Hingis becomes the youngest Wimbledon singles champion this century.

London, England, July 19: Two activists are found partially liable in a libel case against McDonald's.

Monrovia, Liberia, July 19: Ellen Johnson-Sirleaf unsuccessfully challenges Charles Taylor at the presidential election.

1998

Rostaq, Afghanistan, February 4: An earthquake in the mountainous north of the country leaves 4,000 dead and 15,000 homeless. Fighting between the Taliban and the Northern Alliance continues.

Texas, USA, February 26: Oprah Winfrey is found not guilty of defamation against Texan cattlemen after making negative comments about meat during a program about Mad Cow Disease two years ago.

London, England, February: Rosie Boycott becomes the editor of *The Independent*.

Pristina, Kosovo, March 8: Thousands of Albanian women march to demand autonomy from the Serbs.

Ojav, California, USA, March 12: Ceramic artist Beatrice Wood dies, aged 105.

New Delhi, India, March 15: Sonia Gandhi, widow of assassinated prime minister Rajiv Gandhi, is elected to lead the Congress Party.

New York, USA, March 31: Former Congresswoman Bella Abzug dies, aged 77.

Belgrade, Serbia, March: Women in Black, a group of activists, issue a statement condemning the war in Kosovo.

Belfast, Northern Ireland, April 10: The "Good Friday" agreement for peace is signed by the British and Irish governments and endorsed by most of Northern Ireland's political parties.

Cambodia, April 15: Former Khmer Rouge leader, Pol Pot, dies, aged 72.

Santa Barbara, California, USA, April 17: Linda McCartney dies of breast cancer, aged 56.

USA, May 18: Twenty US states and the Department of Justice submit that Microsoft has abused its monopoly.

Pakistan, May 28: In response to Indian nuclear tests two weeks ago, Pakistan explodes five warheads underground.

Sudan, June 11: Up to one million people are at risk of starvation from a famine affecting the south of the country.

USA, May: Actress Helen Hunt wins Golden Globe, an Oscar, and an Emmy Award.

Newcastle, England, June 11: Novelist Dame Catherine Cookson dies, aged 91.

Dublin, Ireland, June 13: German writer Herta Muller wins the IMPAC Dublin Literary Award for *The Land of Green Plums*.

Orlando, Florida, USA, June 16: The first live internet broadcast of a human birth takes place.

Ankara, Turkey, June 24: The country's Constitutional Court rules that adultery is no longer a crime for women.

1999

Switzerland, January 1: Ruth Dreifuss becomes president of the Confederation.

London, England, January 1: Merlyn Lowther is appointed Chief Cashier of the Bank of England.

Colombia, January 25: An earthquake measuring 6 on the Richter scale leaves 1,000 dead and many more homeless.

Oxford, England, February 8: Writer Iris Murdoch dies, aged 79.

Nigeria, February 27: Former military ruler Olusegun Obasanjo wins first free elections in 15 years.

Los Angeles, USA, March 21: At the Academy Awards, Gwyneth Paltrow wins Best Actress and Judi Dench Best Supporting Actress for their roles in the 1998 release, *Shakespeare in Love*, which also received the Oscar for best film.

Canada, April 1: The new territory of Nunavut is established, with its capital located at Iqaluit.

Scotland, April 5: The UN lifts sanctions against Libya as the two key suspects in the 1988 Lockerbie bombing of Pan-Am flight 102 are handed over to Scottish authorities.

Boston, USA, April 19: Australian Louise Sauvage wins the wheelchair section of the Boston Marathon for the third time.

Washington DC, USA, April 19: Jacqui Katona and Yvonne Margarula are among this year's recipients of the Goldman Environmental Prize.

London, England, April 26: Journalist Jill Dando is murdered outside her home. She was the host of a television crime-fighting program television.

Baghdad, Iraq, April: The *Zan* newspaper—a daily publication focusing on women's issues—is ordered to close down, after publishing controversial material.

Belgrade, Yugoslavia, May 7: NATO bombers mistakenly target the Chinese embassy in a bombing raid in response to atrocities occurring in Kosovo. Four die and massive demonstrations follow.

Kashmir, India/Pakistan, May 26: India launches air strikes in the disputed region following incursions by Pakistani forces.

Kosovo, Yugoslavia, June 10: NATO forces call off bombing raids as Serbian forces begin to withdraw from the disputed province.

Washington DC, USA, June 15: The original freedom rider, Rosa Parks, is awarded the Congressional Medal of Honor.

Edinburgh, Scotland, July 1: The rock band Garbage, headed up by Shirley Manson, plays at the opening of the new Scottish Parliament.

Riga, Latvia, July 8: Vaira Vike-Freiberga is elected president.

1996

Lagos, Nigeria, June 4: Kudirat Abiola is killed by gunmen.

Dhaka, Bangladesh, June 23: Sheikh Hasina Wajed becomes Prime Minister.

Bosnia, July 19: Bosnian Serb President Radovan Karadzic resigns from office and withdraws from public life after being indicted for war crimes.

Atlanta, USA, July 19: The opening ceremony of the Olympic Games takes place. At these Olympics, women's soccer will be played for the first time.

Atlanta, USA, July 27: A bomb explodes at a concert during the Olympic Games, injuring 200 people and killing two.

Atlanta, USA, July: Australian swimmer Susie O'Neill wins gold, silver, and bronze medals.

Reykjavik, Iceland, August 1: Vigdis Finnbogadottir bows out of office after four terms as president.

Chechnya, Russia, August: After two years of fierce fighting between separatist rebels and the Russian Army, a peace accord is signed allowing for limited autonomy.

Monrovia, Liberia, September 3: Ruth Perry acts as Chairman of the Council of State of the republic.

Cape Canaveral, Florida, USA, September 26: Shannon Lucid returns from her mission at the *Mir* space station, having spent the longest time in space of any US citizen thus far.

Kabul, Afghanistan, September 27: Taliban militia take the capital, their aim to establish the "purest" Islamic regime in the world.

New York, USA, October 3: Controversial feminist play *The Vagina Monologues*, written and performed by Eve Ensler, premieres off Broadway.

UK, November 4: The Spice Girls' debut album *Spice* hits number one.

USA, November 6: Andrea Barret wins the National Book Award for *Ship Fever and Other Stories*.

Canada, November: Margaret Atwood wins the Giller Prize for Canadian Fiction for her novel *Alias Grace*.

Nairobi, Kenya, December 9: Archeologist and paleontologist Mary Leakey dies, aged 83.

Stockholm, Sweden, December 10: Polish poet Wislawa Szymborska is awarded the Nobel Prize for Literature.

UK, December: The government culls 100,000 cows in a bid to stop the spread of Mad Cow Disease.

Japan: This year teen idol Namie Amuro sold 3 million copies of her debut solo album, *Sweet 19 Blues*.

1997

London, England, July: Children's author J. K. Rowling publishes her first novel of a boy wizard, *Harry Potter and the Philosopher's Stone*.

Tehran, Iran, August 23: President Khatami appoints a woman, Massoumeh Ebtekar, to high office.

Houston, Texas, August 25: Dow Corning Corporation offers $2.4 billion to the 300,000 women who claim that silicone breast implants made by the company have made them unwell.

Paris, France, August 31: Diana, Princess of Wales, dies in a car crash.

Jerusalem, Israel, September 4: Three Palestinian suicide bombers kill seven and injure 170 in a crowded pedestrian area.

Calcutta, India, September 5: Mother Teresa dies, aged 87.

San Francisco, USA, September 6: The USS *Hopper*, named after the pioneering naval computer programmer Grace Murray Hopper, is commissioned.

Westminster, England September 6: Princess Diana is laid to rest.

Dublin, Ireland, September 12: Former president, Mary Robinson, is appointed United Nations High Commissioner for human rights.

Assisi, Italy, September 26: Two earthquakes in central Italy kill 10 and severely damage priceless works of art, including frescos.

London, England, October 15: Arundhati Roy's *The God of Small Things* wins the Booker Prize.

Philadelphia, USA, October 25: Between 300,000 and one million African-American women rally at the Million Woman March.

Vancouver, B.C., Canada, October 31: Violet Palmer and Denise Kantner are the first women to referee an NBA game, Vancouver Grizzlies versus Dallas Mavericks.

Dublin, Ireland, November 11: Mary McAleese is elected President of Ireland, following Mary Robinson.

Luxor, Egypt, November 17: Sixty-two tourists are slain at the Deir al-Bahri temple complex.

Oslo, Norway, December 10: Jody Williams and the International Campaign to Ban Landmines win the Nobel Peace Prize.

Wellington, New Zealand, December 8: Jenny Shipley becomes the first woman prime minister of New Zealand.

Georgetown, Guyana, December 19: Janet Jagan is sworn in as President.

Relizane, Algeria, December 30: About 350 people are massacred by Islamic extremists on the first day of Ramadan. The countryside descends into anarchy; thousands die.

London, England, December: Gillian Wearing wins the Turner Art Prize.

1998

London, England, June: Carol Shields is awarded the Orange Prize for fiction for her novel, *Larry's Party*.

Lagos, Nigeria, July 11: Four days of rioting, sparked by the death of opposition figure, Chief Abiola, leave 60 dead.

London, England, July: J. K. Rowling's *Harry Potter and the Chamber of Secrets* is published.

Dar es Salaam, Tanzania and Nairobi, Kenya, August 7: Bombs explode at two US embassies.

Central China, August 13: The Yangtze River, which has risen to its highest level since 1954, threatens the city of Wuhan. The death toll is 2,500; millions are left homeless.

Washington DC, USA, August 17: After denying a sexual relationship with White House intern Monica Lewinsky in January, President Clinton publicly admits his deceit.

Iran, August: Faezeh Hashemi founds the daily *Zan*, a magazine dedicated to women's issues.

Halifax, Canada, September 3: A Swissair DC-11 crashes, killing all 229 people on board.

Kosovo, September 22: Serbian forces bombard the breakaway region in an attempt to rush the Kosovo Liberation Army (KLA).

London, England, September: The Marylebone Cricket Club allows women to become members.

Australia, October 3: Pauline Hanson's right-wing political party, One Nation, fails to win a seat in the House of Representatives in the country's federal election.

Vatican City, October 11: Edith Stein is canonized by Pope John Paul II.

USA, October 13: Britney Spears's debut single, "Hit Me Baby One More Time," goes straight to No. 1 on the US charts.

South Africa, October 29: The Truth and Reconciliation Commission hands down its findings on political crimes conducted under the apartheid regime.

Zurich, Switzerland, October: Tennis player Venus Williams records a 127 mph (204 km/h) serve at the Swisscom Challenge.

Toronto, Canada, November 3: Alice Munro wins the Giller Prize for her collection of stories, *The Love of a Good Woman*.

Kuala Lumpur, Malaysia, November 15: The US Secretary of State, Madeleine Albright, has a meeting with Azizah Ismail, wife of the imprisoned former deputy prime minister, Anwar Ibrahim.

Iraq, November 15: Saddam Hussein's regime readmits UN weapons inspectors at the eleventh hour, thus averting US and British air strikes.

1999

Palo Alto, California, USA, July 15: Carleton S. Fiorina becomes CEO of Hewlett Packard.

Cape Canaveral, USA, July 23: The shuttle STS-93 *Columbia* is launched, commanded by a woman for the first time: Eileen Collins.

Georgetown, Guyana, August 8: The country's first woman Prime Minister, Janet Jagan, resigns due to ill health.

Izmit, Turkey, August 17: A massive earthquake measuring 7.4 kills thousands and injures more.

Panama City, Panama, September 1: Mireya Moscoso becomes Prime Minister.

Berlin, Germany, September 26: Kenyan Tegla Loroupe sets a new record in the Berlin Marathon.

Brussels, Belgium, September 28: President of the European Commission, Romano Prodi, announces that he has made a more representative executive. Of the 120 posts in the commissioner's staff, 45 have so far gone to women.

San Marino, October 1: Rosa Zafferani finishes her term as co Captain Regent.

Islamabad, Pakistan, October 12: General Pervez Musharraf ousts Prime Minister Nawaz Sharif in a bloodless coup.

North Carolina, USA, October 23: Elizabeth Dole withdraws from the Republican Presidential campaign.

Orissa, India, October 29: A huge tidal surge caused by a cyclone with 155 mph (250 km/h) winds hits eastern India, killing 10,000 and leaving 1.5 million homeless.

London, England, October: The London Eye, designed by David Marks and Julia Barfield, is erected over the River Thames.

Toronto, Canada, November 3: Bonnie Burnard wins the Giller Prize for Fiction for her novel *A Good House*.

Vilnius, Lithuania, November 3: Irena Degutien finishes her second period acting as interim Prime Minister.

Wellington, New Zealand, November 27: Helen Clark is elected Prime Minister of New Zealand.

Guadalupe, December 3: Tori Murden arrives from the Canary Islands, becoming the first woman to row solo across the Atlantic Ocean.

London, England, December 15: New parental leave law is passed, allowing 13 weeks' parental leave per year for children under five.

England: Expat Australian Germaine Greer writes a follow-up to *The Female Eunuch*, titled *The Whole Woman*.

2000

Moscow, Russian Federation, January 1: After Boris Yeltsin's resignation, Prime Minister Vladimir Putin is named acting president until elections are held in 90 days.

Bern, Switzerland, January 1: Ruth Dreifuss ends her term as President.

Antarctica, January 4: Catherine Hartley, and a team of women and men, reach the South Pole after walking across Antarctica.

Ottawa, Canada, January 7: Beverley McLachlin is named Chief Justice of Canada's Supreme Court.

United Kingdom, January 12: The British government allows openly homosexual men and women to serve in the armed forces.

Antarctica, January 23: Rosie Stancer is one of five women who complete a 1200 km walk from Chile to the South Pole.

Kuwait, January 25: Writers Laila al-Othman and Alia Shuaib receive prison sentences for "blasphemy."

Egypt, January 27: Egyptian women are allowed divorce on the grounds of incompatibility, but must repay dowry and forfeit financial rights.

Baia Mare, Romania, January 30: A leak from a mine tailings dump pollutes the Sassar and Danube rivers with cyanide.

Osaka, Japan, February 6: Ota Fusae is elected governor of Osaka.

Los Angeles, USA, February 23: Grammy award winners are Shania Twain (best female country artist); Christina Aguilera (best new artist).

Los Angeles, USA, March 26: Hilary Swank wins the best actress Oscar for her performance in last year's film *Boys Don't Cry*.

Helsinki, Finland, March 1: Tarja Halonen becomes the country's first female President.

Morocco, March 12: King Mohammed IV announces controversial new plans to expand women's rights.

San Marino, April 1: Maria Domenica Michelotti starts her term as co-Captain-Regent.

New York, USA, April 3: A federal judge rules that Microsoft violated antitrust laws, using its monopoly power in the computer market to stifle competition.

Zimbabwe, April 15: President Mugabe commences an agricultural land reform program by killing white farmer David Stevens.

Taipei, Taiwan, May 19: Chen Shui-bian is inaugurated President after the first democratic elections.

Israel, May 22: The Supreme Court rules that women may pray aloud from the Torah at the Wailing Wall.

Brussels, Belgium, June 7: The European Union proposes to outlaw sexual harassment in the workplace throughout the Union.

2001

New York, USA, January 3: Hillary Rodham Clinton is sworn in as senator of New York, the first former First Lady to win elected national office.

Manila, Philippines, January 20: After President Estrada resigns amid corruption allegations, Maria Gloria Arroyo becomes President.

England, January 22: The UK government declares that the combined measles, mumps, and rubella vaccine is safe. There have been concerns that it was linked to incidents of autism in some children.

London, England, January 24: Clara Furse becomes the first female CEO of the London stock exchange.

Iran, January 24: The Iranian guardian council vetoes a proposal that would allow Iranian women to study abroad.

Washington DC, USA, January: Condoleezza Rice becomes the first female national security advisor to the President.

New Orleans, USA, January: Karen E. Smith and Sijue Wu are awarded the Ruth Lyttle Satter Prize in Mathematics.

Vermont, USA, February 2: Anne Morrow Lindbergh, writer and wife of aviator Charles Lindbergh, dies, aged 94.

Israel, February 6: Ariel Sharon, leader of the right-wing Likud party, becomes Prime Minister in a decisive election result.

London, England, February 22: UK judge Dame Elizabeth Butler-Sloss rules that a woman who is paralyzed from the neck down has the right to end her life by refusing treatment.

Dakar, Senegal, March 3: Mame Madior Boye is made Prime Minister.

Paris, France, March 7: The FIA international court of appeal confirms that Jutta Kleinschmidt was indeed the first female winner of this year's Paris-Dakar road rally, after dismissing a competitor's challenge.

World, March 8: International Women's Day is marked by celebrations, holidays, and protests around the world. Director-general of the World Health Organization, Gro Harlem Brundtland, says: "There isn't a single country or institution in the world where men and women enjoy equal opportunity."

Amsterdam, Netherlands, April 1: Four couples wed in the world's first same-sex marriages after the Dutch government legislation earlier today.

Hawaii, USA, April 12: Twenty-one men and 2 women—the crew of a US spy plane—touch down on American soil after an uncertain week of detainment in China.

Palawan, Philippines, May 27: Muslim terrorist group Abu Sayaf seizes 20 people from a tourist resort.

England, May: A foot-and-mouth disease outbreak shuts down large parts of the countryside.

2002

Europe, January 1: The common currency of the European Union, the Euro, is legal tender in 12 countries.

Stockholm, Sweden, January 28: Children's author and creator of *Pippi Longstocking*, Astrid Lindgren, dies aged 94.

Washington DC, USA, January 29: George W. Bush delivers his first State of the Union address to Congress, labeling North Korea, Iran, and Iraq an "axis of evil."

Zabbar, Malta, February 4: Agatha Barbara, first female president of Malta, dies, aged 79.

The Hague, Netherlands, February 12: Slobodan Milosevic's war crime trial begins, with the former Yugoslav president representing himself in a fiery rebuttal of the legitimacy of the tribunal.

Cambridge, England, February 26: The 120-year-old mathematical Adams Prize has been awarded to a woman for the first time. Susan Howson wins it for her work on elliptical curves.

Godhra, India, February 27: A train fire kills 57 Hindu pilgrims, sparking days of rioting in Gujarat state.

Zimbabwe, March 9: Robert Mugabe returns to power in an election characterized by violence and intimidation.

New York City, USA, March 23: Opera star Eileen Farrell dies, aged 82.

Hollywood, USA, March 24: At the Academy Awards, Halle Berry in *Monster's Ball* becomes the first African-American woman to win the Best Actress Award, and Australian Catherine Martin wins Art Direction and Costume Design for the Baz Luhrmann production *Moulin Rouge*.

Nigeria, March 25: Safiya Husaini's life is spared after a court overturns her sentence of death by stoning.

Windsor, England, March 30: The Queen Mother dies, aged 101.

Afghanistan, March: UN forces mount Operation Anaconda, a massive push to round up Taliban and al-Qaeda south of Gardez.

Ramallah, Israel, April 1: After a suicide bombing left over 100 Israelis dead, Israel launches a massive military operation in which Yasser Arafat's compound is besieged and battles rage in Jenin refugee camp.

New York City, USA, April 8: Suzan-Lori Parks wins the Pulitzer Prize for drama, becoming the first African-American woman to win the drama award.

East Timor, May 20: East Timor achieves independence.

Sydney, Australia, May 31: Cherry Hood wins Australia's Archibald Prize for portraiture with her portrait of pianist Simon Tedeschi.

London, England, June 3: Queen Elizabeth II celebrates 50 years on the throne with a rock concert in the grounds of Buckingham Palace.

2003

Paris, France, January 14: France mourns the country's first minister for women's affairs, Françoise Giroud, who has died, aged 86.

Canberra, Australia, January 26: The Australian of the Year Award goes to Professor Fiona Stanley.

Texas, USA, February 1: Two female astronauts, Kalpana Chawla and Laurel Clark, are among the seven crew members who die when the space shuttle *Columbia* disintegrates.

World, February 15: As the threat of war in Iraq grows, hundreds of thousands protest around the world.

Texas, USA, February: Dentist Clara Harris is sentenced to 20 years for killing her husband, David Harris, after she discovers he is having an affair with his receptionist.

Mexico, February: Seventeen-year-old Jessica Santillan dies, after a second lung and heart transplant.

Kabul, Afghanistan, March 8: A radio station run by women and programed with women's content starts broadcasting today.

Iraq, March 20: Coalition troops enter Iraq the day after the first American bombs hit Baghdad.

London, England, March: Album sales plummet for US chart-topping country group Dixie Chicks, as they experience backlash from a statement criticizing US President George W. Bush and the Iraq invasion.

Utah, USA, March: Nine months after being abducted from her bedroom by 49-year-old Brian Mitchell, Utah teenager Elizabeth Smart is reunited with her parents.

California, USA: Nicole Kidman wins an Academy Award for her outstanding role in last year's movie, *The Hours*.

Southern France, April 21: Singer Nina Simone dies, aged 70.

Georgia, USA, April: Martha Burk, head of the National Council of Women's Organizations, campaigns against the exclusion of women at Augusta National Golf Club where the US Masters tournament is held.

Iraq, April: American prisoner of war Jessica Lynch is rescued from a hospital in Nasiriya. She was one of 12 troops captured by Iraqi soldiers.

Fort Worth, Texas, USA, May: Annika Sorenstam competes in the men's PGA Open golf tournament.

USA, May: Chinese-American businesswoman Katrina Leung is indicted on espionage charges. The FBI believes that she was passing on highly sensitive documents to Beijing while working as an FBI informant.

Cannes, France, May: Iranian filmmaker Samira Makhmalbaf's *Five in the Afternoon* premieres at the Cannes Film Festival.

USA, June 4: Domestic icon Martha Stewart is indicted on charges of insider trading.

2000

Pyongyang, North Korea, June 14: President Kim Jong-il hosts South Korean President Kim Dae-jung for the first summit between the two countries.

Cuba, June 28: Elián Gonzalez, the Cuban child found floating on an inner-tube off Florida in November last year—and the focus of an international tug-of-war—returns to Cuba with his father.

England and USA, July 8: J. K. Rowling's book *Harry Potter and the Goblet of Fire* is released. It breaks all pre-publishing sales records.

Kabul, Afghanistan, July 9: Mary MacMakin is arrested for employing women, and ordered to leave.

Gonesse, France, July 25: An Air France Concorde airliner crashes, killing all 109 people on board and four people on the ground.

UK, August 4: Throughout the UK celebrations are held to commemorate the 100th birthday of the Queen Mother.

St Augustine, Florida, September: Judy Rankin, Juli Inkster, and Beth Daniel inducted into golf's International Hall of Fame.

Sydney, Australia, October 1: The closing ceremony of the Games of the XXVIIIth Olympiad takes place. At these games, Cathy Freeman won the 400 m sprint for the home country.

Colombo, Sri Lanka, October 10: Former Prime Minister Sirimavo Bandaranaike dies, aged 84, just hours after casting her vote in the general elections.

Aden, Yemen, October 12: US Navy destroyer *USS Cole* is attacked by two suicide bombers, killing 17 and injuring more than 40.

New York, USA, November 7: Democrat Hillary Rodham Clinton is elected to the US senate.

London, England, November 7: Canadian Margaret Atwood is awarded the Booker Prize for her novel *The Blind Assassin*.

Israel, November 12: Leah Rabin, widow of assassinated Israeli Prime Minister Yitzhak Rabin, dies at 72.

USA, December 13: George W. Bush becomes the 43rd US president, with Democrat Al Gore conceding defeat. The vote in Florida was decided in the Supreme Court.

Cairo, Egypt: A meeting which includes Queen Rania of Jordan, and First Ladies Suha Arafat, Fatima Bashir, and Ándrée Lahoud is held in Cairo to discuss improved status for women in Arabic countries.

Skibo, Scotland, December 22: Rock star Madonna marries film director Guy Ritchie in a ceremony at Skibo Castle.

USA: Australian golfer Karrie Webb is named women's golf player of the year by the LPGA.

2001

Katmandu, Nepal, June 1: Crown Prince Dipendra shoots dead nine members of the royal family before shooting himself.

Wilmington, Delaware, USA, June 24: Twenty-six-year-old Australian golfer Karrie Webb wins the LPGA Championship, becoming the youngest player to win a major.

Canberra, Australia, June 25: Judith Wright, one of the country's greatest poets dies, aged 85. She campaigned for Aboriginal and conservation issues.

Idaho, USA, July 17: Publishing magnate Katharine Graham dies.

Jakarta, Indonesia, July 23: The Indonesian legislature removes President Wahid, and installs Megawati Sukarnoputri.

New Delhi, India, July 25: Phoolan Devi, India's "bandit queen" turned politician, is murdered by a masked gunmen.

Los Angeles, USA, August 8: Nicole Kidman and Tom Cruise divorce after separating in February. All attention now turns to the terms of the divorce settlement.

Tehran, Iran, August 26: Filmmaker Tahmineh Milani is arrested on counter-revolutionary charges, as authorities crack down on her films.

England, August: Irene Zubaida Khan becomes Secretary-General of rights watchdog Amnesty International.

New York and Washington DC, USA, September 11: The World Trade Center in New York is destroyed when two hijacked aircraft smash into the twin towers. A third plane hits the Pentagon. The death toll is estimated at 3,000.

Afghanistan, October 7: The US launches a retaliatory campaign for the September 11 attacks. The Taliban regime and al-Qaeda are the targets of the operation, which began with 50 cruise missiles being launched at Kandahar and Kabul.

Chicago, USA, October 8: At the Chicago marathon, Catherine Ndereba breaks the record set by Japan's Nakao Takahashi at the Berlin marathon last week.

Bangladesh, October 10: Khaleda Zia becomes Prime Minister for the third time.

Washington DC, USA, October 10: Nancy Pelosi is elected house Democratic Whip, the highest post a woman has ever held in the House.

USA, September 18-November: Twenty-two people have been infected with anthrax, resulting in five deaths from exposure to the deadly disease.

South Korea, December 26: Park Geun-hye, daughter of the ex-president of Korea, announces she will run for president.

2002

Wilmington, Delaware, USA, June 9: Korean golfer Se Ri Pak becomes the youngest woman to win all four major championships when she wins the LPGA Championship.

New York City, USA, June 9: Boxing promoter Aileen Eaton is posthumously inducted into the International Boxing Hall of Fame. She is the first woman inductee.

Kabul, Afghanistan, June 19: Hamid Karzai is endorsed as president at the *loya jirga*, or grand assembly. The process took over a week, with intense factional lobbying.

Beverly Hills, California, USA, June 29: Singer Rosemary Clooney dies, aged 74.

Seoul, South Korea, August 1: The National Assembly rejects the newly appointed Prime Minister, Chang Sang, and she steps down from the position after just one month.

Tehran, Iran, August 25: Iran's parliament votes in favor of granting women the right to sue for divorce.

England, September 5: Former head of MI5, Stella Rimington, publishes her autobiography *Open Secret*.

New York, USA, September 12: Mary Robinson finishes her term as UN High Commissioner for Human Rights.

Kuta, Bali, October 12: Bombs explode in two tourist bars, killing more than 180 people. Australia suffers the biggest brunt, with 88 citizens killed.

Bahrain, October 24: Women vote in general elections for the first time.

Moscow, Russian Federation, October 26: Russian forces storm theater where Chechen separatists have been holding over 800 hostages.

New York, USA, November 8: The UN Security Council adopts resolution 1441, requiring Iraq to submit to weapons inspections.

Nigeria, November 23: The Miss World pageant is forced to relocate to London after riots by Muslims opposed to the pageant leave more than 100 dead.

Madrid, Spain, December 17: Soccer player Mia Hamm wins the FIFA International Woman Player of the Year award for the second consecutive year. The award is based on scores from the previous season.

England: Popular Japanese writer Yu Miri has her novel *Goldrush* translated and published in England.

Washington DC, USA: The National Building Museum's Vincent Scully prize is awarded to Robert Venturi and Denise Scott-Brown.

Worldwide: This year the following books are published: *The Lovely Bones* by Alice Sebold, *Unless* by Carol Shields, *The Little Friend* by Donna Tartt, and *Fingersmith* by Sarah Waters.

2003

USA, June 5: Tammy Wynette's 1968 hit *Stand by your Man* tops a poll as the best song in country music history.

Thailand, June 5: Thai women are no longer required by law to assume their husband's name after marriage.

Helsinki, Finland, June 24: Following allegations of improper conduct, Anneli Jäätteenmäki steps down as Prime Minister barely two months after being elected.

New York, USA, June 29: Screen legend Katharine Hepburn dies at the age of 96.

Victoria, Canada, July 16: Novelist Carol Shields dies, aged 68.

Wimbledon, England, July 5: Serena Williams wins her first Wimbledon tournament, beating older sister Venus 7-6, 6-3.

San Antonio, USA, August 16: Veteran cowgirl Connie Reeves, aged 101, dies after being thrown from her horse.

New York, USA, August 20: Kathy Boudin is granted parole. She served 22 years for a 1981 armed robbery which resulted in the deaths of three people.

London, England, September 16: At Buckingham Palace, Professor Julia Polak is awarded the DBE for her services to medicine.

Nigeria, September 25: Thirty-year-old Muslim woman Amina Lawal has her "death by stoning" sentence repealed by the Sharia court of appeal. She had been found guilty of adultery.

New York, USA, October 23: Madame Chiang Kai-shek (Soong Mai-ling), wife of president Chiang Kai-shek, dies, aged 105.

Stockholm, Sweden, September 11: Foreign Minister Anna Lindh dies in hospital after being stabbed while shopping in a department store.

New Jersey, USA, November 30: Gertrude Ederle, the first woman to swim the English Channel, at 98.

England, November: *The Sunday Times* publishes a list which reveals that J.K. Rowling earned £124 million this year, making her the world's best-paid author.

Oslo, Norway, December 10: Iranian human rights activist Shirin Ebadi receives Nobel Peace Prize.

Tikrit, Iraq, December 14: A disheveled Saddam Hussein is captured after being found in a tiny underground bunker, south of his home town of Tikrit.

Northern Territory, Australia, December 15: Marion Scrymgour is appointed Australia's first female Aboriginal government minister.

Hong Kong, December 30: Pop queen Anita Mui dies of cervical cancer, aged 40.

Japan: Natsuo Kirino's *Grotesque* wins the Izumi Kyoka literary award.

2004

Morocco, January: Parliament passes laws giving women more rights in marriage and divorce.

New York, USA, January 15: Novelist Olivia Goldsmith dies after complications following plastic surgery at age 54.

Dunedin, New Zealand, January 29: NZ novelist Janet Frame dies.

Melbourne, Australia, January 31: Belgian Justine Henin-Hardenne wins the Australian Open; she now holds three of the four major singles titles in the world.

Georgia, USA, January: Michelle Kwan wins her seventh straight national title (and her eighth overall) at the US Figure-skating Championships in Atlanta.

New York, USA, February 3: Austrian doctor Andrea Mayr wins the women's section of the annual Empire State Building stair race, in a time of 12 minutes 8 seconds.

Campinas, Brazil, February 4: Novelist Hilda Hilst dies.

London, England, February 5: Writer and last surviving member of the Bloomsbury group, Frances Partridge, dies.

Maputo, Mozambique, February 17: Luisa Dias Diogo becomes Prime Minister.

Uzbekistan, February 24: After much international pressure, an Uzbek court orders the release of Fatima Mukhadirova, convicted of anti-constitutional activity after she publicized her son's torture and death in prison.

Hollywood, USA, February 27: Sofia Coppola is nominated for the best director Academy Award. She is only the third woman to receive the nomination in award's history.

Port-au-Prince, Haiti, February 29: Beleaguered President Jean-Bertrand Aristide flees the country.

California, USA: Charlize Theron takes the Academy Award for best actress for her amazing performance in last year's movie *Monster*.

Madrid, Spain, March 11: Bomb blasts tear through three train stations, killing hundreds.

Baarn, Netherlands, March 20: Princess Juliana, former Queen of Netherlands dies, aged 94.

England, March 21: Iraqi-born Zaha Hadid is the first woman to win the Pritzker Prize in architecture.

Salisbury Cathedral, England, May 1: June Osborne becomes the most senior woman in the Church of England after she is made Dean of Salisbury Cathedral.

Lisbon, Portugal: Former Prime Minister Maria de Lourdes Pintasilgo dies, aged 74.

2005

Washington DC, USA, January 12: Chief investigator Charles Duelfer confirms that the US has stopped searching for weapons of mass destruction (WMD) in Iraq. One of the chief justifications for the war, the existence of WMDs, has been doubted since May 2003.

Ukraine, January 24: Yuliya Tymoshenko becomes the Prime Minister.

Paris, France, January 27: Artist Aurélie Nemours dies, aged 94.

Washington DC, USA, January 26: Condoleezza Rice is sworn in as US Secretary of State, making her one of the most powerful women in the world.

Riyadh, Saudi Arabia, February 10: Men vote in local elections for the first time. However, women are not permitted to vote.

Beirut, Lebanon, February 14: Former Prime Minister Rafik Hariri dies when a car bomb explodes near his motorcade. Syria, which has great influence in the country, is thought to be involved.

Turkey, February 23: The government announces an amnesty, allowing expelled students to return to university. This includes women who had been expelled for wearing Islamic scarves—but the scarf ban still applies.

Hollywood, California, USA, February 27: Hilary Swank wins the best actress Oscar for her role in *Million Dollar Baby*.

West Virginia, USA, March 4: Homemaking mogul and perjurer Martha Stewart is released after being jailed for insider trading.

Istanbul, Turkey, March 8: Women marking International Women's Day with a protest are beaten and kicked by riot police for their unauthorized demonstration.

Menton, France, March 28: Concert pianist Moura Lympany dies, at 88.

Kabul, Afghanistan, March 30: US first lady Laura Bush visits the country. The focus of her talks is women's rights and education in post-Taliban Afghanistan.

Windsor, England, April 9: Prince Charles and Camilla Parker Bowles wed in a civil ceremony.

The Vatican, April 19: German Cardinal Joseph Ratzinger becomes the new pontiff, Benedict XVI.

Central African Republic, April 26: Former Prime Minister Elisabeth Domitien dies.

England, April: Ellen MacArthur, the youngest person to sail solo around the world, is now the youngest person to receive a damehood.

Kuwait, May 17: Parliament announces that women will be granted full suffrage, to take effect in the 2007 elections.

2006

Monrovia, Liberia, January 6: Ellen Johnson-Sirleaf is inaugurated as President.

Ramallah, January 25: Celebrations erupt after radical group Hamas wins the Palestinian elections.

Finland, January 29: Tarja Kaarina Halonen is re-elected President.

New York City, USA, January 30: Playwright and feminist Wendy Wasserstein dies, aged 55.

Melbourne, Australia, January 31: Zheng Jie and Yan Zi win China's first major tennis tournament in women's doubles at the Australian Open.

Washington DC, USA, February 4: Feminist and author Betty Friedan dies, aged 85.

London, England, February 17: German-born novelist and non-fiction writer Sybille Bedford dies, aged 94.

Worldwide, February 18: The Muslim world reacts with anger to a cartoon in a Danish newspaper ridiculing the prophet Mohammed.

Germany, February 22: Poet Hilde Domin dies, aged 96.

Santiago, Chile, March 11: Michelle Bachelet is sworn in as Chile's first female president.

Hollywood, California, March 11: *Brokeback Mountain* is awarded Oscar for best adapted screenplay. The screenplay, based on a story by E. Annie Proulx, was written by Larry McMurtry and Diana Ossana. Reese Witherspoon wins Best Actress for her role in *Walk the Line*.

Israel, March 28: Ehud Olmert's Kadima Party wins the elections.

Jamaica, March 30: Portia Simpson-Miller is elected Prime Minister.

India, March 30: A doctor is jailed for two years for disclosing the sex of a fetus to a couple and offering to terminate the pregnancy. It is the first prosecution of its kind since the implementation of legislation to stop the abortions of unwanted females.

Baghdad, Iraq, March 30: American reporter Jill Carroll is released after being kidnapped and held for over two months.

Israel, April 12: PM Ariel Sharon is declared inept, as he has not regained consciousness since his January stroke.

Florence, Italy, April 13: Scottish writer Muriel Spark dies, aged 88.

Seoul, South Korea, April 19: Han Myung-sook becomes Prime Minister.

Rio de Janeiro, Brazil, April 24: Women-only train carriages are introduced to curb sexual harassment and assault.

London, England, May 6: Margaret Beckett is appointed Foreign Secretary.

Dublin, Ireland, May 16: Novelist Clare Boylan dies, aged 58.

2 0 0 4

Saudi Arabia, June: Rania al-Baz, a popular TV host whose husband was convicted this month of beating her, says she publicized the case so that Saudi women would know that they have recourse under Sharia law if they are victims of any form of domestic violence.

Mexico City, Mexico, July 25: Mexico's 1997 Woman of the Year, Dr Carmen Gutierrez, is found dead. She was kidnapped several days ago.

Liverpool, England, July 27: Politician Margaret Simey dies, aged 98.

Vatican City, July 31: The Pope issues a document condemning feminism, worried that it will erode women's prescribed maternal and subservient roles.

Philippines, July: President Gloria Macapagal-Arroyo is condemned for giving in to demands of Iraqi insurgents who kidnapped a Filipino truck driver.

Wimbledon, London, England: Maria Sharapova is the first Russian and the youngest woman to win the singles championships.

Greece, August 13-29: The games of the XXVIIIth Olympiad are held in Athens. Udomporn Polsak is the first Thai woman to win an Olympic gold medal, in the 53 kg weightlifting division. Carly Patterson becomes the second US woman to win gold in the all-around gymnastics.

Beslan, Russia, September 3: Over 300 adults and children die when a school siege ends tragically.

Georgia, USA, September 25: Laila Ali, daughter of Mohammed Ali, wins International Women's Boxing Federation light-heavyweight title.

West Virginia, USA, September: Homemaker tycoon Martha Stewart is imprisoned for perjury and insider share trading.

USA, October 3: *Psycho* star Janet Leigh dies, aged 77.

Baghdad, Iraq, October 19: British aid worker Margaret Hassan is kidnapped by an armed gang.

Paris, France, October 20: Two female students are expelled from school after flouting the new mandate banning the wearing of headscarves in school.

Oslo, Norway, December 10: Kenyan Wangari Maathai wins the Nobel Peace Prize for her contribution to sustainable development. She is the first African woman to win the prize.

Stockholm, Sweden, December 10: Austrian playwright Elfriede Jelinek is awarded Nobel Prize for Literature. Americans Richard Axel and Linda Buck are awarded Nobel Prize in Physiology or Medicine for work on the olfactory system.

Indian Ocean, December 26: A tsunami devastates coastal communities, killing more than 150,000.

2 0 0 5

India, May 28: Sonia Gandhi is elected President of the Indian National Congress.

Iraq, May: Insurgent attacks have escalated since the formation of the new government in April; over 800 Iraqis and 80 foreigners are killed in one month.

Rome, Italy, June 20: Italian aid worker Clementina Cantoni returns home after her kidnapping ordeal in Kabul.

Kuwait, June 20: Kuwait's first woman cabinet member, Massouma al-Mubarak, takes office.

Iran, June 24: Hard-line mayor of Tehran, Mahmoud Ahmadinejad, wins the run-off (second-round) poll for President by a resounding margin.

Sydney, Australia, June 25: Opera singer June Bronhill dies.

London, England, July 7: Four coordinated terrorist attacks on the underground and bus systems during the morning rush hour kill 72 people and injure 700, bringing chaos to the capital.

China, August 28: Parliament amends law on Protection of Women, making sexual harassment illegal.

Martinique, September 6: Former Prime Minister of Dominica Mary Eugenia Charles dies, aged 86.

New Orleans, USA, September: In the aftermath of hurricane Katrina, anarchy descends after levees fail and the city is flooded. Thousands die in the disaster.

London, England, October 4: Andrew Levy's book *Small Island* is chosen as the best Orange Prize winner in the prize's ten-year history.

Paris, France, October 27-November 8: After two teenagers are electrocuted as they hide from police, widespread rioting grips Paris and the government declares a state of emergency.

Tokyo, Japan, November 6: Singer Minako Honda dies of leukemia, at 38.

Brussels, Belgium, November 10: European Commission President José Manuel Barroso appoints Catherine Day as Secretary-General.

Germany, November 22: Angela Merkel, leader of the Christian Democrats, becomes Chancellor.

Liberia, November 23: Ellen Johnson-Sirleaf is elected President of Liberia. She is Africa's first elected female leader.

Jeddah, Saudi Arabia, November 27: Two women, Lama al-Sulaiman and Nashwa Taher, are elected to the Jeddah chamber of commerce—women are largely excluded from public office.

Sweden, December 25: Soprano Birgit Nilsson dies, aged 87.

USA: Svetlana Jitomirskaya wins the Ruth Lyttle Satter Prize in mathematics.

2 0 0 6

Cornwall, England, May 18: Dee Caffari becomes the first woman to sail solo and nonstop around the world the "wrong way," or east to west.

New York, USA, June 8: The 61st session of the UN General Assembly elects Bahraini Sheikha Haya Rashed al-Khalifa President.

Baghdad, June 8: Al-Qa'eda's leader in Iraq, Abu Musab al-Zarqawi, is killed in a US air raid.

Mumbai, India, July 11: Two hundred people die when a terrorist bomb explodes on a train.

Southern Lebanon, July 12: Israel invades Lebanon in response to the kidnapping and killing of two Israeli soldiers by Hezbollah.

Turkey, July 30: Best-selling author Duygu Asena dies of a brain tumor.

Chile, July 31: Fidel Castro appoints his brother, Raoul, as caretaker president while he recovers from a stomach operation.

Prague, Czech Republic, August 24: The International Astronomical Union votes to rescind Pluto's status as a planet. It becomes a dwarf planet.

Tokyo, Japan, September 6: The royal family announces that Princess Kiko gave birth to a boy today.

Thailand, September 19: Prime Minister Thaksin Shinawatra is overthrown in a bloodless coup by the military while he is at UN headquarters in New York.

Space, September 28: Iranian-born US citizen Anousheh Ansari becomes the first woman space tourist when she blasts off for the International Space Station for an eight-day stay.

Moscow, Russia, October 15: Journalist Anna Politkovskaya is found dead in her apartment building, shot in the head. She had been a vocal critic of the Russian government.

Turkey, November 6: Academic Muazzez Ilmiye Cig, aged 92, is acquitted of inciting religious hatred by making sexual references to the Islamic headscarf in her classroom.

Paris, France, November 17: Ségolène Royal is elected leader of the Socialist Party before next year's general election.

Pakistan, November 24: *The Protection of Women Bill* is passed, enabling adultery and sexual assault cases to be tried under civil law, rather than Islamic law.

Milan, Italy, December: In an attempt to combat eating disorders, organizers of Fashion Week state that at next year's event, models must have a Body Mass Index of at least 18.5.

Baghdad, Iraq, December 30: Former dictator Saddam Hussein is executed. His final moments are broadcast on public television.

Key: (t) top of page; (b) bottom of page;
(l) left side of page; (r) right side of page;
(c) center of page.

Getty Images:

1(c), 2(l), 2(c), 2(r), 3(l), 3(c), 3(r), 5(c), 6–7, 10(c),
12(c), 15(r), 15(b), 16(t), 16(l), 16–17(b), 17(t),
17(b), 18(l), 18(t), 18(b), 19(r), 20(c), 22(c), 23(b),
25(tr), 26(l), 26(c), 26(b), 27(l), 27(r), 30(c), 34(l),
35(l), 35 (r), 36(l), 36(b), 37(r), 37(b), 38(l), 39(r),
40(l), 40(t), 41(r), 42(b), 42(l), 46(l), 47(r), 48(l),
50(l), 51(r), 51(b), 54(l), 55(r), 55(b), 57(t), 59(r),
60(b), 61(r), 61(b), 62(l), 63(r), 63(l), 64(l), 65(l),
65(r), 65(b), 70(b), 70(c), 71(r), 73(l), 73(b), 74(l),
76(r), 77(b), 77(r), 78(r), 78(b), 79(t), 79(b), 82(l),
82(b), 84(l), 84(r), 85(r), 86(r), 86(b), 87(b), 88(l),
88(r), 90(l), 90(r), 91(r), 91(b), 92(l), 92(b), 93(r),
94(l), 95(r), 95(b), 69(r), 96(b), 97(b), 98(l), 98(b),
99(b), 100(l), 100(c), 100(r), 101(t), 101(r), 101(b),
102(l), 102(b), 103(t), 104(r), 105(r), 105(t),
105(b), 106(b), 107(r), 108(l), 108(b), 109(r),
111(r), 114(l), 115(r), 115(t), 115(c), 116(l), 116(r),
117(b), 118(l), 119(r), 119(b), 120(l), 121(t),
122(b), 123(r), 123(b), 124(l), 124(r), 125(l),
125(r), 126(l), 126(c), 126(b), 127(l), 127(r), 128(l),
128(r), 129(r), 130(b), 131(l), 131(r), 132(l),
133(r), 133(c), 133(b), 134(l), 134(b), 135(t),
136(b), 137(r), 137(b), 138(l), 138(t), 140(l), 141(l),
141(r0, 141(b), 142(l), 142(r), 143(b), 144(b),
145(b), 146(l), 146(b), 147(l), 147(r), 147(b),
151(t), 151(r), 152(l), 152(r), 153(r), 153(b), 154(l),
155(r), 155(b), 156(l), 156(r), 157(r), 158(l),
158(t), 159(t), 160(l), 161(r), 161(l), 161(b), 162(l),
162(b), 163(r), 163(b), 164(l), 164(b), 165(r),
165(c), 165(b), 166(l), 166(r), 166(c), 167(r),
167(c), 167(b), 168(l), 168(r), 168(b), 169(t),
169(b), 170(l), 170(b), 172(l), 173(t), 173(r),
174(r), 174(b), 175(l), 175(r), 175(b), 176(l),
177(r), 178(r), 179(l), 179(r), 179(b), 180(c),
180(b), 181(l), 183(l), 183(r), 184(b), 186(l),
186(b), 187(r), 187(c), 188(l), 189(r), 190(l),
190(b), 191(c), 192(l), 192(b), 193(r), 194(l),
194(b), 195(r), 196(l), 196(b), 197(t), 197(r),
198(l), 198(r), 198(b), 200(l), 200(t), 201(t), 201(r),
201(b), 202(l), 203(r), 203(b), 204(r), 204(b),
205(r), 205(l), 206(l), 207(l), 207(b), 209(r),
210(b), 210(r), 211(b), 211(r), 212(l), 212(b),
213(l), 213(b), 214(l), 215(r), 215(r), 215(l), 215(b),
216(l), 216(t), 217(r), 217(l), 218(l), 218(c), 218(r),
219(t), 219(r), 219(b), 220(l), 220(r), 220(b),
221(l), 221(b), 222(l), 222(r), 222(b), 223(b),
224(l), 224(r), 224(b), 225(r), 225(l), 225(b),
226(l), 226(r), 226(b), 227(c), 227(r), 228(l),
228(r), 228(b), 229(l), 229(r), 229(b), 230(t),
230(c), 230(l), 230(b), 231(r), 232(l), 232(b),
233(b), 234(l), 234(t), 234(b), 235(r), 235(b),
236(l), 236(b), 237(r), 237(b), 237(l), 238(l),
238(r), 238(b), 239(l), 239(r), 239(c), 239(b),
240(l), 240(t), 241(t), 241(r), 241(b), , 242(b),
42(t), 243(t), 243(r), 243(b), 244(l), 244(b),
45(t), 245(b), 246(l), 246(l), 246(b), 247(l),
47(b), 248(l), 248(r), 248(b), 249(r), 249(c),
9(b), 250(l), 251(l), 251(r), 251(l), 251(b), 253(l),
3(r), 253(c), 254(l), 254(b), 255(l), 255(r),
(b), 256(l), 256(r), 257(l), 257(r), 258(l), 258(t),
b), 259(l), 259(b), 258(b), 260(l), 260(r),
b), 261(r), 262(l), 262(t), 262(b), 262(r),

263(l), 263(r), 263(b), 264(l), 264(c), 265(r),
265(c), 266(l), 266(t), 266(c), 267(t), 268(l),
268(b), 269(r), 269(b), 270(l), 270(c), 270(b),
271(r), 271(b), 272(l), 273(t), 273(b), 274(l),
274(b), 275(t), 275(r), 275(c), 276(l), 276(b),
276(r), 277(t), 277(b), 278(l), 278(t), 278(b),
279(t), 279(r), 279(b), 280(l), 280(r), 281(r),
281(b), 282(l), 282(t), 282(b), 283(r), 284(l),
284(b), 285(r), 285(c), 286(l), 286(b), 287(t),
287(r), 288(l), 288(t), 288(b), 289(r), 290(l), 290(t),
290(c), 291(c), 291(b), 292(l), 292(b), 293(l),
293(r), 293(b), 294(l), 295(r), 296(l), 296(b),
297(t), 297(r), 297(b), 298(l), 298(t), 298(c),
299(c), 299(r), 300(b), 301(r), 301(b), 302(l),
302(b), 303(t), 303(r), 303(b), 304(l), 304(b),
305(r), 305(t), 305(b), 306(l), 306(t), 306(c), 307(l)
307(r), 307(b), 308(l), 308(r), 308(c), 309(r),
309(b),310(l), 310(t), 310(c), 310(b), 311(t) 311(r);
311(b); 312(l), 312(c), 312(b), 313(t), 313(r),
313(b), 314(l), 314(b), 314(r), 315(l), 315(r),
315(b), 316(l), 316(t), 317(l), 317(r), 317(c), 318(l),
318(t), 318(b), 319(l), 319(r), 319(b), 320(l),
321(r), 321(l), 321(b), 322(l), 322(b), 323(t),
323(r), 323(b), 324(l), 325(t), 325(r), 325(c),
326(l), 326(t), 326(b), 327(l), 327(r), 327(b), 328(l),
328(t), 328(b), 329(r), 329(l), 330(l), 330(t),
330(b), 331(l), 331(r), 331(c), 331(b), 332(l),
332(t), 333(r), 333(c), 333(l), 334(l), 334(t), 334(b),
335(t), 335(r), 335(l), 335(b), 336(l), 336(t),
336(b), 337(r), 337(b), 338(l), 338(t), 339(t),
339(r), 339(b) 340(l), 340(t), 340(b), 341(t), 341(r),
342(l), 342(r), 342(b), 343(t), 343(r), 343(b),
343(l), 343(t), 343(b), 345(l), 346(l), 346(b), 347(t),
347(r), 347(b), 348(l), 348(b), 349(r), 349(l),
349(b), 350(l), 350(r), 3050(b), 351(t), 351(r),
351(b), 352(l), 352(r), 353(r), 353(b), 354(r),
354(b), 355(l), 355(r), 355(b), 356(l), 356(t),
356(b), 357(t), 357(r), 358(l), 358(t), 358(b),
359(t), 359(r), 359(b), 360(l), 360(r), 360(b),
361(r), 361(l), 362(l), 362(b), 363(l), 363(b), 364(l),
364(b), 365(l), 365(r), 365(b), 366(l), 366(t),
367(t), 367(c), 367(r), 369(l), 369(r), 369(b),
370(t), 370(r), 370(c), 371(l), 371(r), 371(c),
372(l), 372(c), 372(r), 373(l), 373(c), 373(b),
374(l), 374(r), 374(b), 375(l), 375(t), 375(c),
376(t), 376(r), 377(r), 377(b), 378(l), 378(r),
378(c), 379(t), 379(r), 379(b), 380(l), 380(t),
380(b), 381(r), 381(l), 382(l), 382(r), 382(c),
383(r), 383(b), 384(l), 384(r), 385(r), 385(b),
386)l, 386(t), 386(b), 387(t), 387(r), 387(b),
388(l), 389(l), 389(r), 389(b), 390(l), 390(t), 390(b),
391(r), 391(l), 391(b), 392(c), 392(b), 393(r),
394(l), 394(t), 394(b), 395(t), 395(r), 395(c), 396(l),
397(l), 397(b), 398(l), 398(t), 398(b), 399(r), 399(l),
399(b), 400(l), 400(r), 400(b), 401(t), 401(r) ,
402(l), 402(t), 402(c), 403(t), 403(b), 404(l), 404(t),
405(t), 405(r), 405(b), 406(l), 406(t), 407(r), 408(l),
408(r), 409(r), 409(b), 410(l), 410(c), 410(b),
411(t), 411(r), 411(b), 412(l), 413(t), 413(r),
413(b), 414(l), 414(b), 415(r), 415(b), 416(l),
416(r), 416(b), 417(l), 417(b), 418(l), 418(t),
418(c), 418(b), 419(c), 419(r), 420(l), 420(r),
420(b), 421(r), 421(c), 421(b), 422(l), 422(r),
422(b), 423(t), 423(r), 423(c), 423(b), 424(l),
424(c), 424(b), 425(l), 425(r), 425(b), 426(l),
426(r), 426(b), 427(l), 427(r0, 427(c), 428(l),
428(b), 429(l), 429(r), 429(b), 430(l), 430(t), 430c),

431(r), 431(b), 432(l), 432(r), 432(b), 433(t),
433(r), 434(c), 434(b), 435(t), 435(r), 435(b),
436(l), 436(b), 437(l), 437(r), 437(b), 438(l),
438(c), 438(b), 439(l), 439(r), 439(b), 440(l),
440(t), 440(c), 441(r), 441(c), 441(b), 442(l),
442(b), 442(r), 443(t), 443(r), 443(b), 444(l),
444(t), 444(b), 445(r), 445(b), 446(l), 446(r),
446(b), 447(r), 447(b), 448(l), 448(r), 448(b),
449(r), 449(l), 449(b), 450(l), 450(t), 450(b),
451(t), 451(r), 451(b), 452(l), 452(r), 452(b),
453(r), 453(l), 453(b), 454(l), 454(l), 454(b), 455(t),
455(r), 456(l), 456(r), 456(b), 457(t), 457(l),
457(b), 458(l), 458(t), 458(b), 458(r), 459(r),
459(b), 460(l), 460(t), 460(b), 461(t), 461(r),
461(b), 462(l), 462(r), 463(t), 463(r), 463(c),
463(b), 464(l), 464(r), 464(b), 465(r), 465(l),
466(l), 466(r), 466(c), 467(l), 467(r), 467(b), 468(l),
468(r), 468(b), 469(r), 469(l), 469(b), 470(l),
470(t), 470(b), 471(t), 471(r), 471(b), 472(l),
472(t), 472(b), 473(t), 473(r), 473(b), 474(l),
474(t), 475(t), 475(r), 475(b), 476(l), 476(b),
477(l), 477(r), 477(b), 478(l), 478(r), 478(b),
479(t), 479(r), 479(b), 480(l), 480(r), 480(b),
481(l), 481(r), 481(b), 482(l), 482(c), 482(b),
483(l), 483(r), 483(b), 484(l), 484(c), 485(l), 485(r),
485(b), 486(l), 486(r), 486(b), 487(t), 487(r),
487(l), 487(b), 488(l), 488(r), 489(r), 489(l),
489(b), 490(l), 490(r), 490(b), 491(t), 491(r),
491(l), 491(b), 492(l), 492(r), 492(b), 493(r),
493(b), 494(l), 494(t), 494(r), 494(b), 495(r),
495(l), 495(b), 496(l), 496(b), 496(r), 497(l),
497(r), 497(b), 498(l), 498(r), 498(c), 498(b),
499(t), 499(r), 499(b), 500(l), 500(b), 501(t),
501(r), 502(l), 502(t), 502(b), 503(t), 503(r),
503(b), 504(l), 504(t), 504(b), 505(l), 505(r),
505(b), 506(l), 506(t), 506(b), 506(r), 507(l),
507(r), 507(b), 508(l), 508(t), 508(b), 509(r),
510(l), 510(t), 510(b), 511(l), 511(r), 511(b)

Millennium House:

176(r), 217(b), 250(b), 214(r), 280(b), 285(t).

The Picture Desk:

The Art Archive: 24(b), 27(t), 28(r), 32(l);
46(b), 70(l), 85(b), 112(b), 118(c), 178(b) 208(b);
The Art Archive / Musée Thomas Dobrée Nantes /
Gianni Dagli Orti: 8(c); The Art Archive / Palace of
Chihil Soutoun Isfahan / Gianni Dagli Orti: 9(c);
The Art Archive / Musée Carnavalet Paris / Gianni
Dagli Orti: 14(b); The Art Archive / Museo del
Prado Madrid / Gianni Dagli Orti: 15(l), 29(b);
The Art Archive / Musée des Beaux Arts Nantes /
Gianni Dagli Orti: 19(b); The Art Archive /
National Anthropological Museum Mexico /
Gianni Dagli Orti: 22(tl); The Art Archive / Musée
des Antiquités St Germain en Laye / Gianni Dagli
Orti: 22(bl); The Art Archive / National Museum
La Valletta Malta / Alfredo Dagli Orti: 22(br); The
Art Archive / Museo Civico Vicenza / Gianni Dagli
Orti: 23(c); The Art Archive / Christies / Eileen
Tweedy: 23(r); The Art Archive / Egyptian Museum
Cairo / Alfredo Dagli Orti: 24(t); The Art Archive /
Museum of Anatolian Civilisations Ankara /
Gianni Dagli Orti: 24(r); The Art Archive /
Heraklion Museum / Gianni Dagli Orti: 25(l),
25(br); The Art Archive / Nicolas Sapieha; 28(l);
The Art Archive / Musée Archéologique Naples /